THE UNHEALTHY BRAIN

Scientists have identified clear brain abnormalities only for some severe mental disorders. A *stroke* is caused by a loss of blood supply to a region of the brain, and it kills off nearby cells (see Chapter 14). Cells die rapidly near the center of the damaged tissue, the umbra. Cells die less rapidly in the periphery, the penumbra, and may be saved by future medical advances. *Alzheimer's disease* is a severe cognitive disorder associated with aging (see Chapter 14) that is characterized by atrophied brain tissue, "senile plaques" (caused by clumps of beta amyloid protein), and tangles of diseased or dead neurons. *Schizophrenia* is a very serious psychotic illness (see Chapter 13) that remains a mystery as a brain disorder, despite some promising leads. For example, among people with schizophrenia the ventricles often are enlarged, and asymmetries in the planum temporale may be reversed.

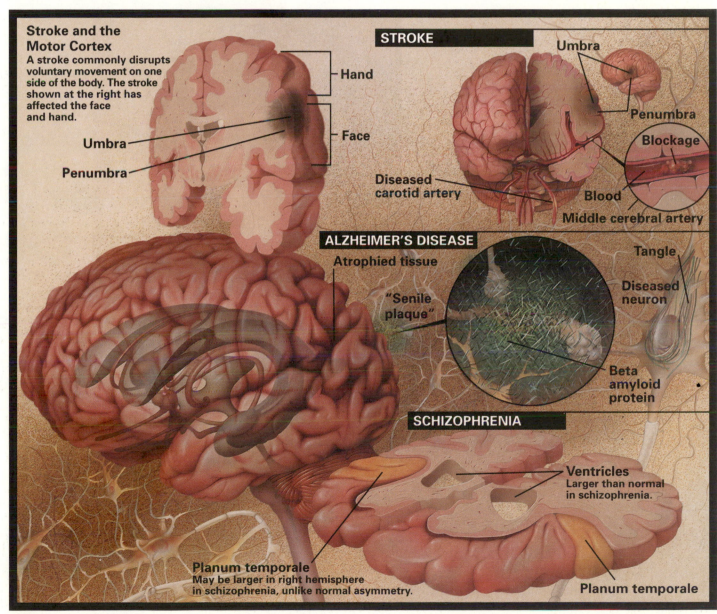

Stroke and the Motor Cortex
A stroke commonly disrupts voluntary movement on one side of the body. The stroke shown at the right has affected the face and hand.

- Hand
- Face
- Umbra
- Penumbra

STROKE
- Umbra
- Penumbra
- Blockage
- Diseased carotid artery
- Blood
- Middle cerebral artery

ALZHEIMER'S DISEASE
- Atrophied tissue
- "Senile plaque"
- Tangle
- Diseased neuron
- Beta amyloid protein

SCHIZOPHRENIA
- Ventricles
Larger than normal in schizophrenia.
- Planum temporale
May be larger in right hemisphere in schizophrenia, unlike normal asymmetry.
- Planum temporale

Source: Keith Kasnot, Copyright National Geographic Image Collection.

Abnormal Psychology Second Edition

Thomas F. Oltmanns
University of Virginia

Robert E. Emery
University of Virginia

PRENTICE HALL
Upper Saddle River
New Jersey 07458

Library of Congress Cataloging-in-Publication Data

Oltmanns, Thomas F.
   Abnormal psychology / Thomas F. Oltmanns, Robert E. Emery.—2nd
ed.
     p. cm.
   Includes bibliographical references and index.
   ISBN 0-13-728197-8 (case)
   1. Psychology, Pathological.   2. Mental illness.   I. Emery,
Robert E. II. Title.
RC454.044 1998
616.89–dc21
                                  97-14478
                                  CIP

Editor-in-Chief: Nancy Roberts
Acquisitions Editor: Bill Webber
Development Editor-in-Chief: Susanna Lesan
Development Editor: Robert Weiss
Editorial Assistant: Emsal Hasan
Director of Production and Manufacturing: Barbara Kittle
Senior Production Manager: Bonnie Biller
Production Editor: Joan E. Foley
Copyeditor: Mary Louise Byrd
Manufacturing Manager: Nick Sklitsis
Prepress and Manufacturing Buyer: Lynn Pearlman
Marketing Director: Gina Sluss
Marketing Manager: Michael Alread
Creative Design Director: Leslie Osher
Art Director: Carole Anson
Interior and Cover Design: Carbone Smolan Associates
Cover and Chapter Opening Art: Zita Asbaghi
Portraits: Van Howell
Line Art Supervisor: Michele Giusti
Illustrator: ElectraGraphics, Inc.
Photo Researcher: Eloise Donnelly

To Gail, Sara, and Josh

TFO

**To Kimberly, Maggie,
Jacey, Robert, and Lucy**

REE

This book was set in 10/12½ Joanna by The Clarinda Company
and was printed and bound by Von Hoffman Press, Inc.
The cover was printed by The Lehigh Press, Inc.

© 1998 by Prentice-Hall, Inc.
Simon & Schuster / A Viacom Company
Upper Saddle River, New Jersey 07458

For permission to use copyrighted material, grateful
acknowledgment is made to the copyright holders listed
on pages 727-29, which are considered an extension of this
copyright page.

Printed in the United States of America

10   9   8   7   6   5   4   3   2   1

ISBN 0-13-728197-8

Prentice-Hall International (UK) Limited, *London*
Prentice-Hall of Australia Pty. Limited, *Sydney*
Prentice-Hall Canada Inc., *Toronto*
Prentice-Hall Hispanoamerica, S.A., *Mexico*
Prentice-Hall of India Private Limited, *New Delhi*
Prentice-Hall of Japan, Inc., *Tokyo*
Simon & Schuster Asia Pte. Ltd., *Singapore*
Editora Prentice-Hall do Brasil, Ltda., *Rio de Janeiro*

Brief Contents

Contents

2

Causes of Abnormal Behavior: From Paradigms to Systems 30

Treatment of Psychological Disorders 70

4 Classification and Assessment 110

5 Mood Disorders 150

Anxiety Disorders 198

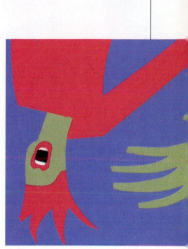

7 Acute and Posttraumatic Stress Disorders, Dissociative Disorders, and Somatoform Disorders 238

8 Stress and Physical Health 282

Personality Disorders 314

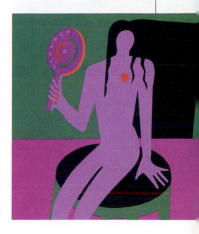

10

Eating Disorders 354

11

Substance Use Disorders 384

Sexual and Gender Identity Disorders 424

Schizophrenic Disorders 458

14

Dementia, Delirium, and Amnestic Disorders 500

Mental Retardation and Pervasive Developmental Disorders 530

15

Psychological Disorders of Childhood 570

16

17 Adjustment Disorders and Difficult Life Events: Life-Cycle Transitions 608

Mental Health and the Law 640

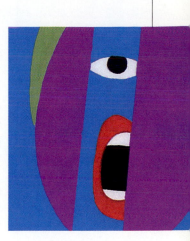

Preface

From the time we sat down to write the first edition of *Abnormal Psychology* we've had an ambitious goal: to anticipate the future of abnormal psychology and to write a text that would help shape the discipline itself. To accomplish this we abandoned the paradigms approach—the time-worn notion that psychologists have a hammer (medical, behavioral, or psychoanalytic) so they therefore see the world as a nail (biological, learning, or unconscious). Thus *Abnormal Psychology* became the first text in this field to embrace systems theory, the integrative conceptual framework that has revolutionized scientific disciplines ranging from computer science to biology. The systems approach integrates research on biological, psychological, and social factors in understanding the etiology of abnormal behavior. This second edition has allowed us to integrate evidence on multiple risk factors more fully, to point to multiple pathways (equifinality) in the development of mental disorders, and to highlight both unique and common factors across approaches to psychotherapy.

Abnormal Psychology, Second Edition, continues to be innovative not only in its systems approach but also in its pedagogical features. These features include substantial case studies that open each chapter, a similar organization across chapters, and our unique approach to teaching research methods through special instructional inserts that are found in every chapter. The staff at Prentice Hall has once again given the book a distinctive design that students have called "fun," "young," and "engaging." As an example of what's new in the text design, we call your attention to the beautiful two-page figures illustrating the healthy and unhealthy brain in Chapter 2 and on the back endpapers of the text.

Let us tell you what is new and exciting in our second edition before describing our "old" innovations in a little more detail.

Abnormal Psychology has a new chapter on eating disorders, one of the most important and prevalent psychological problems of our time (and a separate diagnostic category for the first time in DSM-IV). Because eating disorders are particularly common among college students, this chapter is an especially relevant addition.

We discuss posttraumatic stress disorder (PTSD) in the same chapter that considers dissociative and somatoform disorders (Chapter 7). By placing the discussion in this chapter we call attention both to the importance of PTSD and to controversies about whether PTSD is best viewed as an anxiety disorder, a dissociative disorder, or its own distinct category of psychopathology.

The second edition offers either new or expanded coverage of a number of important and timely topics, including a brief introduction to the history of abnormal psychology (Chapter 1); a discussion of the new *Consumer Reports* study of psychotherapy (Chapter 3); a far more extensive overview of suicide (Chapter 5); a review of the role of stress in AIDS, cancer, and pain management (Chapter 8); a new discussion of dependent personality disorder (Chapter 9); expanded coverage of substance abuse (Chapter 11); detailed consideration of a major new study of normal sexuality as well as more information on paraphilias (Chapter 12); a discussion of mental retardation and autism through the eyes of people suffering from these developmental disorders (Chapter 15); and an expanded overview of aging and the transition to later life (Chapter 17).

In addition the second edition of *Abnormal Psychology* calls even more attention to multicultural issues in abnormal psychology. For example, Chapter 3 has a new Further Thoughts discussion of psychotherapy with ethnic minorities, and Chapter 9 has a new Research Methods discussion of cross-cultural studies.

Finally, *Abnormal Psychology* continues to offer students easy access to challenging material. The pedagogical elements and engaging tone of the text are magnified by an outstanding illustration program that contains almost twice as many figures as the first edition.

INTEGRATIVE SYSTEMS APPROACH

Some of the major innovations introduced in the first edition of *Abnormal Psychology* also deserve elaboration. The book follows a systems approach that integrates evidence on diverse risk factors that contribute to abnormal behavior. The systems perspective not only highlights integration beyond a single diathesis and a single stressor, but it also points out that biological, psychological, and social theories can be complementary explanations of psychopathology. Furthermore, our systems approach calls attention to the essential fact that different psychological disorders have different causes; no single paradigm can accurately explain all psychological disturbances. In fact, because current diagnostic groupings represent heterogeneous categories, the same psychological disorder may have different causes in different cases. Thus the most productive scientific research focuses on the specific etiology of a single disorder.

In addition to etiology, we extend the systems approach to cover treatment in an integrated fashion. We introduce biological, psychological, and social treatments for psychological disorders early in the text (Chapter 3). This discussion emphasizes research on psychotherapy process and outcome. Our early placement of the treatment chapter and our empirical focus on psychotherapy allow us in later chapters to highlight only the most promising, empirically based approaches to psychotherapy, medication, and other forms of intervention.

CASE STUDIES AND CONSISTENT ORGANIZATION

In our own classes we note that students pay special attention to case studies during lectures, and they often plead for more cases in evaluations at the end of the semester. Therefore we have included detailed case studies throughout the text. Our goals in presenting case studies in the book are the same as in lecture: (1) to illustrate the symptoms and phenomenology of different psychological problems; (2) to raise questions about etiology and treatment; and (3) to "hook" students—to motivate them to master the scientific material that forms the core of abnormal psychology.

Every chapter opens with a memorable case from our own clinical experience or, occasionally, from the literature. We refer back to the case throughout the chapter to make our scientific points more concrete and to emphasize that science is indeed relevant to practice. Most chapters also contain two or three additional brief cases to make key points or to describe the different forms of a disorder.

Every chapter on a major diagnostic category follows a consistent organization, including major sections on typical symptoms and associated features, classification, epidemiology, etiology, and treatment. This gives students a framework for understanding and assimilating new material. It also allows students to appreciate the systematic manner in which clinical psychologists approach their work.

RESEARCH METHODS

As we previously mentioned, *Abnormal Psychology, Second Edition*, adopts a unique approach to teaching research methods. Rather than covering everything at once in a chapter that students typically describe as "boring" and "irrelevant," our book integrates methodology into the substance of abnormal psychology throughout the text. Every chapter includes featured discussions titled "Research Methods" that introduce a new topic in scientific methodology. Students are introduced to our general approach to research methods in the first chapter, in which all 18 Research Methods inserts are listed. For example, Research Methods in Chapter 1 highlights the issues of skepticism and the burden of proof in science. Research Methods in Chapter 2 covers the correlational method; the discussion in Chapter 3 focuses on the experiment. In subsequent chapters Research Methods addresses more specialized topics, for example, longitudinal designs, alternative comparison groups, the heritability ratio, and the influence of base rates on prediction.

In addition to Research Methods, every chapter contains another featured discussion called Research Close-Up, which is a detailed review of a single study. The Research Close-Up and Research Methods are often coordinated to enhance their value to students. For example, Research Methods in Chapter 10 (Eating Disorders) addresses the use of placebo control groups in psychotherapy outcome research. It discusses the impossibility of conducting double-blind, placebo-controlled studies of psychotherapy, and it considers the allegiance effect, in which investigators often find that their favored treatment proves to be the most effective treatment in psychotherapy outcome research. In turn, the Research Close-Up in Chapter 10 presents a study in which interpersonal psychotherapy was included as a placebo therapy for bulimia nervosa, but the placebo proved to be an effective treatment over the long run. We suggest that such outcome results that overcome the positive expectations behind the allegiance effect merit special scrutiny. Positive expectations are an essential part of the placebo effect and of effective psychotherapy; thus a treatment that is effective despite negative or modest expectations deserves special attention.

ADDITIONAL FEATURES

We have retained and enhanced a number of additional distinguishing features in the second edition of *Abnormal Psychology*. We continue to include a developmental psychopathology perspective as exemplified by our inclusion of attachment theory; detailed coverage of childhood disorders (two chapters); a focus on the course of abnormal behavior; a life-span orientation; and detailed consideration of aging, dementia, and family issues (including coverage of family law). We include a brief historical perspective in every chapter as a way of introducing contemporary concepts and controversies. And we offer a unique, separate chapter (17) on adjustment disorders and difficult transitions during the course of adult life.

SUPPLEMENTS

An extensive and useful array of instructor and student supplements are available with this book:

The Instructor's Manual, written by Gordon Atlas of Alfred University, contains detailed lecture outlines and teaching suggestions for each chapter, as well as a compendium of handouts and transparency masters and a coordinated list of video segments by chapter.

The Study Guide, written by Shelly Martin of Wesleyan College, provides a chapter review, learning objectives, key concepts and terms (with definitions), self-tests, and activities for each chapter of the text.

The Test Item File, written by Joseph Palladino of the University of Southern Indiana, contains over 2000 test items.

Prentice Hall Test Manager 2.0 testing software for PC's and Macintoshes allows users to select or edit existing test items or to insert additional questions, and it provides a wide range of printing and scrambling options.

Instructional Videos Two distinct types of video, providing more than 400 minutes of video material, accompany our text:

ABC News/Prentice Hall Video Libraries I and II provide more than 30 relevant segments from award-winning ABC News programs, including "Nightline," "20/20," "Prime Time Live," and "American Agenda." A summary of each segment and suggestions on how to incorporate the video into the classroom are included in the Instructor's Manual.

Video Cases in Abnormal Psychology: The Patients as Educators, James H. Scully, Jr., MD, and Alan M. Dahms, Ph.D., Colorado State University. This exclusive video contains a series of ten patient interviews illustrating a range of disorders. Each interview is preceded by a brief history of the patient and a synopsis of some major symptoms of the disorder and ends with a summary and a brief analysis.

Prentice Hall Color Transparencies for Abnormal Psychology

The New York Times Abnormal Psychology Supplement. The *New York Times* and Prentice Hall are sponsoring Themes of The Times, a program designed to enhance access to current information of relevance in the classroom.

Through this program, the core subject matter provided in the text is supplemented by a collection of time-sensitive articles from one of the world's most distinguished newspapers, *The New York Times*. These articles demonstrate the vital, ongoing connection between what is learned in the classroom and what is happening in the world.

To help you enjoy the wealth of information of *The New York Times* daily, a reduced subscription rate is available. For information, call toll-free: 1-800-631-1222.

Prentice Hall and *The New York Times* are proud to cosponsor Themes of The Times. We hope it will make the reading of both textbooks and newspapers a more dynamic, involving process.

Asking the Right Questions About Abnormal Psychology, Stuart M. Keeley, Bowling Green State University. Keeley presents a basic critical thinking methodology and then asks students to apply this method to a variety of classic research studies in psychopathology.

World Wide Web. In keeping with recent advances in technology, Prentice Hall has established a web site. *Abnormal Psychology, Second Edition,* now has its own site on the World Wide Web. Please visit this site at http://prenhall.com/oltmanns.

ACKNOWLEDGMENTS

Years of effort have gone into writing and revising this book, and we are grateful to a number of people who assisted us in this arduous but fruitful task. We would like to start by expressing our appreciation to the following colleagues who reviewed all or parts of the manuscript for the second edition: Gail Bruce-Sanford, University of Montana; Ann Calhoun-Seals, Belmont Abbey College; Laurie Chassin, Arizona State University; Lee H. Coleman, Miami

University of Ohio; Juris G. Draguns, Pennsylvania State University; Marjorie L. Hatch, Southern Methodist University; Jennifer A. Haythornwaite, Johns Hopkins University; Debra L. Hollister, Valencia Community College; Richard D. McAnulty, University of North Carolina–Charlotte; Tracy L. Morris, West Virginia University; William O'Donohue, University of Nevada–Reno; Joseph J. Palladino, University of Southern Indiana; Paul Rasmussen, Furman University; Danny Shaw, University of Pittsburgh; Heather Shaw, American Institutes of Research; Eric Stice, Stanford University; Michael Wierzbicki, Marquette University.

In addition we would like to acknowledge once again the reviewers for the first edition: Gordon Atlas, Alfred University; Deanna Barch, University of Pittsburgh; Caryn L. Carlson, University of Texas at Austin; William Edmonston, Jr., Colgate University; Ronald Evans, Washburn University; John Foust, Parkland College; Alan Glaros, University of Missouri, Kansas City; Ian H. Gotlib, Stanford University; Irving Gottesman, University of Virginia; Mort Harmatz, University of Massachusetts; Jennifer Jenkins, University of Toronto; Stuart Keeley, Bowling Green State University; Carolin Keutzer, University of Oregon; Roger Loeb, University of Michigan, Dearborn; Carol Manning, University of Virginia; Richard McFall, Indiana University; John Monahan, University of Virginia School of Law; Demetrios Papageorgis, University of British Columbia; Patricia H. Rosenberger, Colorado State University; Forrest Scogin, University of Alabama; Janet Simons, Central Iowa Psychological Services; Cheryl Spinweber, University of California, San Diego; Bonnie Spring, The Chicago Medical School; Milton E. Strauss, Case Western Reserve University; J. Kevin Thompson, University of South Florida; Robert H. Tipton, Virginia Commonwealth University; Douglas Whitman, Wayne State University; Michael Wierzbicki, Marquette University; Robert D. Zettle, Wichita State University.

We have been fortunate to work in a stimulating academic environment that has fostered our interests in studying psychopathology and in teaching undergraduate students. We are particularly grateful to our current colleagues Irving Gottesman, Eric Turkheimer, Mavis Hetherington, John Monahan, Joseph Allen, Dan Wegner, and Mary Ainsworth for extended (and ongoing) discussions of the issues that are considered in this book. Close friends and colleagues at Indiana University have also served in this role, especially Richard McFall and Alexander Buchwald. Many undergraduate and graduate students who have taken our courses have helped to shape the viewpoints that are expressed in this book. They are too numerous to identify individually, but we are grateful for the intellectual challenges and excitement that they have provided over the past several years.

Many other people have contributed to the book in various important ways. Kimberly Carpenter Emery did extensive legal research and helped organize Chapter 18; Carol Manning and Charles Vandenberg provided consultation on case study materials; and Linda Christian, Debbie Snow, and Nina Pierce have provided important secretarial support.

We would also like to express our sincere appreciation to several people at Prentice Hall who made major contributions to this effort. First, we thank Robert Weiss for his detailed and extremely helpful developmental editing of the manuscript. He has been with us through both editions of this book, and he has made enormous contributions to its success. We also thank our editors, Bill Webber, Heidi Freund, Pete Janzow, and Nancy Roberts for their constant encouragement and support, and the division president, Phil Miller, for the special attention he has offered to us. We are grateful to Joan Foley for her skillful handling of the production of our text, and to Emsal Hasan for his numerous contributions. The visual appeal of the text reflects the efforts of Carole Anson and Leslie Osher, who contributed to the attractive design. Eloise Donnelly has once again done an outstanding job on photo research. We are also grateful to Mike Alread for directing marketing efforts.

Finally, we once again acknowledge our profound gratitude to our families: Gail, Sara, and Josh Oltmanns; and Kimberly, Maggie, Jacey, "Bubba," and Lucy Emery. You remain the loving sources of our inspiration and our motivation.

TOM OLTMANNS

BOB EMERY

1

Examples and Definitions of Abnormal Behavior

Mental disorders touch every realm of human experience. They can disrupt the way people think, the way they feel, and the way they behave. Ultimately, they affect relationships with other people. It would be surprising if you hadn't already heard about most of the problems that will be addressed in this book, such as depression, alcoholism, and schizophrenia. In fact, you are likely to know someone—a friend or family member—who has struggled with one of these disorders. One national study begun by the President's Commission on Mental Health found that, during a specific 12-month period, 1 out of every 5 Americans exhibited active symptoms of at least one mental disorder. Almost 1 in 3 of the 20,000 men and women who were interviewed had experienced at least one kind of mental disorder at some point during their lives (Robins, Locke, & Regier, 1991). The purpose of this book is to help you become familiar with the nature of these disorders and the various ways in which psychologists are advancing knowledge of their causes and treatment.

Abnormal Psychology: An Overview

The study of mental disorders is often called abnormal psychology. **Psychology** is the scientific study of behavior, cognition, and emotion. Since the late nineteenth century, psychologists have generated an extensive body of knowledge that is concerned with perception, motivation, learning, memory, problem solving, attitudes, emotions, and language—to name only a few of the most general issues that have been studied. Psychologists have also conducted research on brain mechanisms and the physiological underpinnings of these phenomena, as well as on the societal and environmental factors that influence each realm of behavior. Developmental psychologists have traced the growth of factors such as cognitive abilities, emotional responses, and personality traits from infancy to old age. Comparative psychologists have examined the same, or analogous, phenomena in other species, placing human behavior in evolutionary perspective. Taken collectively, this body of knowledge—including the research tools by which knowledge has been generated and the concepts that have guided the search—is referred to as *psychological science*. That base of knowledge sheds crucial light on the problems that fall under the general heading of mental disorders. **Abnormal psychology** is the application of psychological science to the study of mental disorders.

Clinical Science

Psychologists who treat people with mental disorders are often trained according to the **scientist-practitioner model,** which emphasizes the integration of science and practice (Belar & Perry, 1992). Scientist-practitioners operate simultaneously as behavioral scientists and practicing clinicians. These are two aspects of the same professional role, regardless of whether the person happens to be doing applied clinical work—assessment and therapy with a client—or research on abnormal behavior (McFall, 1991, 1995).

The way in which psychologists collect information about a clinical problem is guided by scientific principles. Hypotheses about the causes of the problem, even at the level of the individual client, are based on psychological science, and they are formulated in a testable fashion. In fact, the treatment process parallels the scientific process. Assessment leads to the formulation of a hypothesis, interventions are implemented based on that hypothesis, and the validity of the hypothesis is tested by the success or failure of the treatment. Moreover, most of the important scientific advances in abnormal psychology have been made by researchers who work directly with clinical problems—that is, by people who are familiar with the signs and symptoms of psychopathology and who simultaneously bring to bear the attitudes and methods of scientific inquiry.

We believe that the scientist-practitioner model of training should be applied to the study of abnormal psychology. Descriptions of real clinical problems must be integrated with discussions of more abstract issues. Students should be introduced to the study of abnormal psychology by learning about specific cases—people whose efforts to grapple with various behavioral, emotional, and mental difficulties bring the issues of the field to life. In this way, we hope to convey to our readers our own enthusiasm for this fascinating field.

The Uses and Limitations of Case Studies

Before we present our first case, we should consider the ways in which case studies can be helpful in the study of psychopathology, as well as some of their limitations. A **case study** presents a description of the problems experienced by one particular person. Detailed case studies can provide an exhaustive catalog of the symptoms that the person displayed, the manner in which these symptoms emerged, the developmental and family history that preceded the onset of the disorder, and whatever response the person may have shown to treatment efforts. Descriptions of this sort are especially important for conditions that have not received much attention in the literature and for problems that are relatively unusual. Multiple personality disorder and transsexualism are examples of conditions that are so infrequent that it is difficult to find groups of patients for the purpose of research studies. Much of what we know about these conditions is based on descriptions of individual patients.

Case studies can also be used to generate *hypotheses*—highly specific and testable predictions about cause and effect. For example, Freud developed his psychoanalytic theory on the basis of extended case studies (see Chapter 2). His compelling descriptions and insightful analyses of the circumstances under which his patients' problems developed helped make his ideas enormously popular during the first half of the twentieth century.

Case studies also have several drawbacks. The most obvious limitation of case studies is that they can be viewed from many different perspectives. Any case can be interpreted in several ways, and competing explanations may be equally plausible. Consider, for example, Abraham Lincoln, who suffered through periods of profound depression throughout his adult life. Some historians have argued that Lincoln's mood disorder can be traced to the sudden death of his mother when he was 9 years old (Burlingame, 1994). The impact of this tragic experience was later intensified by several other losses, including the deaths of two of his four sons. Heredity may also have played a role in the origins of Lincoln's depression. Some of Lincoln's cousins were apparently also depressed, and neighbors recalled that Lincoln's father "often got the blues." Speculation of this sort is intriguing, particularly in the case of a man who played such an important role in the history of the United States. But we must remember that case studies are not conclusive. Lincoln's experience does not indicate conclusively whether the loss of a parent can increase a person's vulnerability to depression, and it does not prove that genetic factors are involved in the transmission of this disorder. These questions must be resolved through scientific investigation.

▼ **Many Americans, both past and present, have experienced some type of mental disorder. For example, Abraham Lincoln suffered episodes of severe depression. Awareness of the prevalence of emotional problems can help reduce the stigma associated with mental illness.**

The other main limitation of case studies is that it is risky to draw general conclusions about a disorder from a single example. How can we know that this individual is representative of the disorder as a whole? Are his or her experiences typical for people with this disorder? Again, hypotheses generated on the basis of the single case must be tested in research with larger, more representative samples of patients.

What Is Abnormal Behavior?

The cases in this chapter describe the experiences of people whose behavior would be considered abnormal by mental health professionals. Their difficulties illustrate two specific forms of abnormal behavior: schizophrenia and eating disorders. These problems are examples of **psychopathology,** which, literally translated, means "pathology of the mind" and is a term that is generally used to describe abnormal behavior. A *psychopathologist* is a person who studies psychopathology. This term can apply to people with various types of professional training, including psychologists, psychiatrists, and social workers. We use the cases in this chapter to introduce several fundamental concepts and controversies that are addressed later in this book. The cases allow us to consider definitions of abnormal behavior, processes by which abnormal behaviors are classified, and ways in which psychopathologists think about factors that cause these disorders.

Our first case raises fundamental questions about the definition of abnormal behavior. What is the basis for the distinction between normal and abnormal behavior? What kinds of problems are associated with abnormal behavior, and in what ways do they affect a person's life?

CASE STUDY

Schizophrenia

Kevin and Joyce Warner (not their real names[†]) had been married for 8 years when they sought help from a psychologist for their marital problems. Joyce was 34 years old, worked full time as a pediatric nurse, and was 6 months pregnant with her first child. Kevin, who was 35 years old, was finishing his third year working as a librarian at a local university. Joyce was extremely worried about what would happen if Kevin lost his job, especially in light of the baby's imminent arrival.

Although the Warners had come for couples therapy, the psychologist soon became concerned about certain eccentric aspects of Kevin's behavior. In the first session, Joyce described one recent event that had precipitated a major argument. One day, after eating lunch at work, Kevin had experienced sharp pains in his chest and difficulty breathing. Fearful, he rushed to the emergency room at the hospital where Joyce worked. The physician who saw Kevin found nothing wrong with him, even after extensive testing. She gave Kevin a few tranquilizers and sent him home to rest. When Joyce arrived home that evening, Kevin told her that he suspected that he had been poisoned at work by his supervisor. He still held this belief.

Kevin's belief about the alleged poisoning raised serious concern in the psychologist's mind about Kevin's mental health. He decided to interview Joyce alone so that he could ask more extensive questions about Kevin's behavior. Joyce realized that the poisoning idea was "crazy." She was not willing, however, to see it as evidence that Kevin had a mental disorder. Joyce had known Kevin for 15 years. As far as she knew, he had never held any strange beliefs before this time, and he had never taken hallucinogenic drugs or smoked marijuana. Joyce said

---

[†] Throughout this text we use fictitious names to protect the identities of the people involved.

that Kevin had always been "a thoughtful and unusually sensitive guy." She did not attach a great deal of significance to Kevin's unusual belief. She was more preoccupied with the couple's present financial concerns and insisted that it was time for Kevin to "face reality."

Kevin's condition deteriorated noticeably over the next few weeks. He became extremely withdrawn, frequently sitting alone in a darkened room after dinner. On several occasions, he told her that he felt as if he had "lost pieces of his thinking." It wasn't that his memory was failing, but rather he felt as though parts of his brain were shut off.

Kevin's problems at work also grew worse. His supervisor informed Kevin that his contract would definitely not be renewed. Joyce exploded when Kevin indifferently told her the bad news. His apparent lack of concern was especially annoying. She called Kevin's supervisor, who confirmed the news. He told her that Kevin was physically present at the library, but he was only completing a few hours of work each day. Kevin sometimes spent long periods of time just sitting at his desk and staring off into space and was sometimes heard mumbling softly to himself.

Kevin's speech was quite odd during the next therapy session. He would sometimes start to speak, drift off into silence, then reestablish eye contact with a bewildered smile and a shrug of his shoulders. He had apparently lost his train of thought completely. His answers to questions were often off the point, and when he did string together several sentences, their meaning was sometimes obscure. For example, at one point during the session, the psychologist asked Kevin if he planned to appeal his supervisor's decision. Kevin said:

> I'm feeling pressured, like I'm lost and can't quite get here. But I need more time to explore the deeper side. Like in art. What you see on the surface is much richer when you look closely. I'm like that. An intuitive person. I can't relate in a linear way, and when people expect that from me, I get confused.

Kevin's strange belief about poisoning continued to expand. The Warners received a letter from Kevin's mother, who lived in another city 200 miles away. She had become ill after going out for dinner one night and mentioned that she must have eaten something that made her sick. After reading the letter, Kevin became convinced that his supervisor had tried to poison his mother too.

When questioned about this new incident, Kevin launched into a long, rambling story. He said that his supervisor was a Vietnam veteran, but he had refused to talk with Kevin about his years in the service. Kevin suspected that this was because the supervisor had been a member of army intelligence. Perhaps he still was a member of some secret organization. Kevin suggested that an agent from this organization had been sent by his supervisor to poison his mother. Kevin thought that he and Joyce also were in danger. He was particularly wary around men who were about his supervisor's age, because they too might be Vietnam veterans. Kevin also had some concerns about Asians, but he would not specify these worries in more detail. He said that he knew many more things about "what was really going on," but he was not ready to share them.

Kevin's bizarre beliefs and his disorganized behavior convinced the psychologist that he needed to be hospitalized. Joyce reluctantly agreed that this was the most appropriate course of action. She had run out of alternatives. Arrangements were made to have Kevin admitted to a private psychiatric facility, where the psychiatrist prescribed haloperidol (Haldol), a type of antipsychotic medication. Kevin seemed to respond positively to the drug, because he soon stopped talking about plots and poisoning—but he remained withdrawn and uncommunicative. After 3 weeks of treatment, Kevin's psychiatrist thought that he had improved significantly. Kevin was discharged from the hospital in time for the birth of their baby girl. Unfortunately, when the couple returned to consult with the psychologist, Kevin's adjustment was still a major concern. He did not talk with Joyce about the poisonings, but she noticed that he remained withdrawn and showed few emotions, even toward the baby.

When the psychologist questioned Kevin in detail, he admitted reluctantly that he still believed that he had been poisoned. Slowly, he revealed more of the plot. Immediately after admission to the hospital, Kevin had decided that his psychiatrist, who happened to be from Korea, could not be trusted. Kevin was sure that he too was working for army intelligence or perhaps for a counterintelligence operation. Kevin believed that he was being interrogated by this clever psychiatrist, so he had "played dumb." He did not discuss the suspected poisonings or the secret organization that had planned them. Whenever he could get away with it, Kevin simply pretended to take his medication. He thought that it was either poison or truth serum.

Kevin was admitted to a different psychiatric hospital soon after it became apparent that his paranoid beliefs had expanded. This time, he was given intramuscular injections of antipsychotic medication in order to be sure that the medicine was actually taken. Kevin improved considerably after several weeks in the hospital. He acknowledged that he had experienced paranoid thoughts. Although he still felt suspicious from time to time, wondering whether the plot had actually been real, he recognized that it could not really have happened, and he spent less and less time thinking about it. ■

Descriptive Psychopathology

Schizophrenia is a form of **psychosis,** a general term that refers to several types of severe mental disorder in which the person is considered to be out of contact with reality. Kevin exhibited several psychotic symptoms. For example, his belief about being poisoned by his supervisor would be called a delusion. A **delusion** is an idiosyncratic belief—one not shared by other members of the society—that is rigidly held in spite of its preposterous nature. In addition, Kevin's speech at times was odd and difficult to understand. This symptom is called *disorganized speech* or *formal thought disorder*. Judgments regarding the presence of disorganized speech depend on the listener's sense that a person's speech is exceedingly vague or difficult to understand. In other words, it involves the form of the person's speech—the way in which a thought is expressed—rather than the content of the speech.

You may also be familiar with other words that are commonly used in describing abnormal behavior. One term is *insanity*, which does not refer to any specific type of psychopathology. In current practice, insanity is actually a legal term that refers to judgments about whether a person should be held responsible for criminal behavior if he or she is also mentally disturbed (see Chapter 18). If Kevin had murdered his Korean psychiatrist, for example, based on the delusional belief that the psychiatrist was trying to harm him, a court of law might consider whether Kevin should be held to be *not guilty by reason of insanity*.

Another old-fashioned term that you may have heard is *nervous breakdown*. If we said that Kevin had "suffered a nervous breakdown," we would be indicating in very general terms that he had developed some sort of incapacitating but otherwise unspecified type of mental disorder. This expression no longer conveys any specific information about the nature of the person's problems. Some people might also say that Kevin was acting *crazy*. This is an informal, pejorative term that does not convey specific information and carries with it many unfortunate, unfounded, and negative implications. Mental health professionals refer to psychopathological conditions as mental disorders or abnormal behaviors. We will define these terms in the pages that follow.

Kevin's situation raises several fundamental questions about abnormal behavior. One of the most difficult issues in the field centers on the processes by which mental disorders are identified. Once Kevin's problems came to the attention of a mental health professional, could he have been tested in some way to confirm the presence or absence of a mental disorder?

At the present time, psychopathology is defined in terms of signs and symptoms—such as delusions and disorganized speech—rather than inferred causes. This approach is sometimes called *descriptive psychopathology*. Psychologists and psychiatrists do not have laboratory tests that can be used to confirm definitively the presence of psychopathology because the processes that are responsible for mental disorders have not yet been discovered. Unlike specialists in other areas of medicine where many specific disease mechanisms have been discovered by advances in the biological sciences, psychologists and psychiatrists cannot test for the presence of a viral infection or a brain lesion or a genetic defect to confirm a diagnosis of mental disorder. Clinical psychologists must still depend on their observations of the person's behavior and descriptions of personal experience.

Is it possible to move beyond our current dependence on descriptive definitions of psychopathology? Will we someday have valid tests that can be used to establish independently the presence of a mental disorder? If we do, what form might these tests take? The answers to these questions are being sought in many kinds of research studies that will be discussed throughout this book.

Mental disorders are typically defined by a set of characteristic features. A group of symptoms that appear together and are assumed to represent a specific type of disorder is referred to as a **syndrome.** One problematic behavior is seldom necessary or sufficient to establish a diagnosis. The primary consideration in Kevin's case was his paranoid delusion. Additional problems included his peculiar and occasionally difficult to understand patterns of speech and his flat emotional responses. These are all symptoms of the disorder known as *schizophrenia*. Each symptom is taken to be a fallible, or imperfect, indicator of the presence of the disorder. The significance of any specific feature depends on whether the person also exhibits additional behaviors that are characteristic of a particular disorder. A person must usually exhibit more than one symptom to be diagnosed as having a particular disorder.

The duration of a person's symptoms is also important. Mental disorders are defined in terms of persistent maladaptive behaviors. Many unusual behaviors and inexplicable experiences are short-lived; if we ignore them, they go away. Unfortunately, some forms of problematic behavior are not transient, and they eventually interfere with the person's social and occupational functioning. In Kevin's case, he had become completely preoccupied with his suspicions about poison. Joyce tried for several weeks to ignore certain aspects of Kevin's behavior, especially his delusional beliefs. She didn't want to think about the possibility that his behavior was abnormal, and instead chose to explain his problems in terms of lack of maturity or lack of motivation. But as the problems accumulated, she finally decided to seek professional help. The magnitude of Kevin's problem was measured, in large part, by its persistence and by the cumulative disruption it caused at work and in the family.

Defining Abnormal Behavior

Why do we consider Kevin's behavior to be abnormal? By what criteria do we decide whether a particular set of behaviors or emotional reactions should be viewed as a mental disorder? These are important questions because they determine, in many ways, how other people will respond to the person, as well as who will be responsible for providing help (if help is required). Many attempts have been made to define abnormal behavior, but none is entirely satisfactory. No one has been able to provide a consistent definition that easily accounts for all situations in which the concept is invoked (Frances, First, & Pincus, 1995; Gorenstein, 1992).

One approach to the definition of abnormal behavior places principal emphasis on the individual's experience of personal distress. We might say that abnormal behavior is defined in terms of subjective discomfort that leads the person to seek help from a mental health professional. This definition is fraught with problems, however. Kevin's case illustrates one of the major reasons that this approach does not work. Before his second hospitalization, Kevin was unable or unwilling to appreciate the extent of his problem or the impact his behavior had on other people. A psychologist would say that he did not have *insight* regarding his disorder (Markova & Berrios, 1992). The discomfort was primarily experienced by Joyce, and she had attempted for many weeks to deny the nature of the problem. It would be useless to adopt a definition that considered Kevin's behavior to be abnormal only after he had been successfully treated.

Another approach is to define abnormal behavior in terms of statistical norms—the relative frequency of a specific condition in the general population. By this definition, people with unusually high levels of anxiety or depression would be considered abnormal because their experience deviates from the expected norm. Kevin's paranoid beliefs would be defined as pathological because they are idiosyncratic.

▼ In the movie *The Fisher King,* actor Robin Williams played a man with schizophrenia. To be diagnosed with a disorder such as schizophrenia, an individual must exhibit a set of symptoms, which are referred to as a *syndrome.*

Mental disorders are, in fact, defined in terms of experiences that most people do not have.

This approach, however, does not specify *how* unusual the behavior must be before it is considered abnormal. Some conditions that are typically considered to be forms of psychopathology are extremely rare. For example, gender identity disorder, the belief that one is a member of the opposite sex trapped in the wrong body, affects less than 1 person out of every 30,000. In contrast, other disorders are much more common. In the United States, major depression affects 1 out of every 20 women, and alcoholism affects at least 1 out of every 10 men (Robins, Locke, & Regier, 1991).

Another weakness of the statistical approach is that it does not distinguish between deviations that are harmful and those that are not. Many rare behaviors are not pathological. Some "abnormal" qualities have relatively little impact on a person's adjustment. Examples are being extremely pragmatic or unusually talkative. Other abnormal characteristics, such as exceptional intellectual, artistic, or athletic ability, may actually confer an advantage on the individual. For these reasons, the simple fact that a behavior is statistically rare cannot be used to define psychopathology.

HARMFUL DYSFUNCTION

One useful approach to the definition of mental disorder has been proposed by Jerome Wakefield of Columbia University (Wakefield, 1992a, 1992b). According to Wakefield, a condition should be considered to be a mental disorder if, and only if, it meets two criteria:

1. The condition causes some harm to the person as judged by the standards of the person's culture.
2. The condition results from the inability of some mental mechanism to perform its natural function.

A mental disorder therefore is defined in terms of **harmful dysfunction.** This definition incorporates one element that is based as much as possible on an objective evaluation of performance—dysfunction. The dysfunctions in mental disorders represent disruptions of cognitive, perceptual, emotional, linguistic, and motivational mechanisms.

In Kevin's case, the most apparent dysfunctions involved failures of cognitive, perceptual, and linguistic mechanisms. Disruption of these systems was presumably responsible for

his delusional beliefs and his disorganized speech. The *natural function* of cognitive and perceptual processes is to allow the person to perceive the world in ways that are shared with other people and to engage in rational thought and problem solving. The natural function of linguistic mechanisms is to allow the person to communicate clearly with other people. Kevin's abnormal behavior can be viewed as a pervasive dysfunction cutting across several mental mechanisms.

There is, of course, room for argument about the specific nature of these mental mechanisms and the ways in which they are supposed to function naturally. At present, dysfunction is largely inferred on the basis of impaired performance. Some of the confusion and controversy about what is, and what is not, a mental disorder can be traced to our ignorance about the natural functions of cognitive, behavioral, and emotional systems. The connections between these systems and psychopathological symptoms are also unresolved. More precise descriptions of basic mental mechanisms presumably will be provided by scientific research in the psychological and biological sciences.

Wakefield's definition of mental disorder also recognizes that every type of dysfunction does not lead to a disorder. Only dysfunctions that result in significant *harm* to the person are considered to be disorders. This is the second element of his definition. There are, for example, many types of physical dysfunction, such as albinism, reversal of heart position, and fused toes, that clearly represent a significant departure from the way that some biological process ordinarily functions. These conditions are not considered to be disorders, however, because they are not necessarily harmful to the person.

Kevin's dysfunctions were, in fact, harmful to his adjustment. These problems were evident in both his family relationships—his marriage to Joyce and his ability to function as a parent—and his performance at work. His social and occupational performances were clearly impaired. There are, of course, other types of harm that are also associated with mental disorders. These include subjective distress, such as high levels of anxiety or depression, as well as more tangible outcomes, such as suicide.

DSM-IV DEFINITION

The definition of abnormal behavior presented in the official *Diagnostic and Statistical Manual of Mental Disorders,* published by the American Psychiatric Association and currently in its fourth edition—DSM-IV (APA, 1994)—incorporates many of the factors that we have already discussed.

Each of the mental disorders is conceptualized as a clinically significant behavioral or psychological syndrome or pattern that occurs in an individual and that is associated with present distress (e.g., a painful symptom) or disability (i.e., impairment in one or more important areas of functioning) or with a significantly increased risk of suffering death, pain, disability, or an important loss of freedom. Whatever its original cause, it must currently be considered a manifestation of a behavioral, psychological, or biological dysfunction in the individual. (pp. xxi–xxii)

This definition is summarized in Table 1–1, along with a number of conditions that are specifically excluded from the DSM-IV definition of mental disorders. The DSM-IV definition places primary emphasis on the consequences of certain behavioral syndromes. Accordingly, mental disorders are defined by clusters of persistent, maladaptive behaviors that are associated with personal distress, such as anxiety or depression, or with an impairment in social functioning, such as job performance or personal relationships. The official definition therefore recognizes the concept of dysfunction, and it spells out ways in which the

CALVIN AND HOBBES © Watterson. Dist. by UNIVERSAL PRESS SYNDICATE. Reprinted with permission. All rights reserved.

harmful consequences of the disorder might be identified.

In an attempt to avoid becoming a vehicle for social regulation, the DSM-IV definition excludes voluntary behaviors, as well as beliefs and actions that are shared by religious, political, or sexual minority groups. In the 1930s, for example, participants in the Dada movement in the arts deliberately performed bizarre acts that were designed to provoke other members of society. In the 1960s, members of the Yippie Party intentionally engaged in disruptive behaviors, such as throwing money off the balcony at a stock exchange. Their purpose was to challenge traditional values. These were, in some ways, maladaptive behaviors that could have resulted in social impairment if those involved had been legally prosecuted. But they were *not* dysfunctions. They were intentional artistic and political gestures.

In actual practice, abnormal behavior is defined in terms of an official diagnostic system.

TABLE 1–1

Summary of the DSM-IV Definition of Mental Disorders

Defining Characteristics

A behavioral or psychological syndrome (groups of associated features) that is associated with:
1. Present distress (painful symptoms), or
2. Disability (impairment in one or more important areas of functioning), or with
3. A significantly increased risk of suffering death, pain, disability, or an important loss of freedom

Conditions Excluded from Consideration

This syndrome or pattern must not be merely:
1. An expectable and culturally sanctioned response to a particular event (such as the death of a loved one)
2. Deviant behavior (such as the actions of political, religious, or sexual minorities)
3. Conflicts that are between the individual and society (such as voluntary efforts to express individuality)

▲ **Abnormal behavior is not defined simply in terms of nonconforming behavior or appearance. A "punk" appearance is an example of social deviance flouting social norms—not a form of abnormal behavior.**

Mental health, like medicine, is an applied rather than a theoretical field. It draws on knowledge from research in the psychological and biological sciences in an effort to help people whose behavior is disordered. Mental disorders are, in some respects, those problems with which mental health professionals attempt to deal. As their activities and explanatory concepts expand, so does the list of abnormal behaviors. The practical boundaries of abnormal behavior are defined by the list of disorders that are included in the official *Diagnostic and Statistical Manual of Mental Disorders*. The categories in that manual are listed on the inside of the front cover of this book. The DSM-IV thus provides another simplistic, though practical, answer to our question as to why Kevin's behavior would be considered abnormal: He would be considered to be exhibiting abnormal behavior because his experiences fit the description of schizophrenia, which is one of the officially recognized forms of mental disorder.

SOCIAL AND POLITICAL CONSIDERATIONS

The process by which the *Diagnostic and Statistical Manual* is constructed and revised is necessarily influenced by social and political considerations. The impact of particular behaviors and experiences on an individual's adjustment will, of course, depend on the culture in which the person lives. To use Jerome Wakefield's (1992a) terms, "only dysfunctions that are socially disvalued are disorders" (p. 384). For example, a woman who grew up in a society that discouraged female sexuality might not be distressed or impaired by the absence of orgasmic responses. According to DSM-IV, she would not be considered to have a sexual problem. Therefore this definition of abnormal behavior is not culturally universal and might lead us to consider a particular pattern of behavior to be abnormal in one society and not in another.

There have been many instances in which groups that represent particular political or social values have brought pressure to bear on decisions shaping the diagnostic manual (see Further Thoughts). For example, feminist organizations (both within and outside the mental health professions) expressed legitimate concern over the possible inclusion of premenstrual dysphoric disorder in DSM-IV, because they are concerned about the implications of labeling women who have these problems as mentally ill (Caplan, 1995). In a compromise struck by APA's committee on DSM-IV, premenstrual dysphoric disorder appears in an appendix for disorders recommended for further study. These deliberations are a reflection of the practical nature of the manual and of the health-related professions. Value judgments are an inherent part of any attempt to define "disorder" (Sedgwick, 1981).

FURTHER THOUGHTS

Homosexuality: Culture, Politics, and Diagnosis

The influence of political groups on psychiatric classification is perhaps nowhere better illustrated than in the case of homosexuality. The psychiatric community had maintained in the first and second editions of the DSM that homosexuality was, by definition, a form of mental disorder. This position reflected, in large part, the views of psychodynamic therapists and was adopted in spite of the attitudes expressed by scientists such as Alfred Kinsey, who argued that homosexual behavior was not abnormal (see Chapter 12). Toward the end of the 1960s, as the gay and lesbian rights movement became more forceful and outspoken, some of its leaders began to challenge the assumption that homosexuality was pathological. They opposed the inclusion of homosexuality in the official nomenclature.

Between 1970 and 1974, a dramatic series of events led to important changes in the American Psychiatric Association's classification of sexual disorders, especially homosexuality (see Bayer, 1981, for a detailed description of these events). The first incident took place at an APA meeting in 1970, where gay activists disrupted presentations concerned with psychodynamic theories of sexual deviation. Among the demands presented by gay leaders was a call for the removal of homosexuality from the DSM-II.

Direct discussions between members of the gay community and members of the American Psychiatric Association began in 1972 and continued throughout the following year. A compromise position was eventually presented to the board of trustees of APA at the end of 1973. The trustees voted unanimously to remove homosexuality from DSM-II. In the spring of 1974, the entire membership of the organization participated in a referendum on the board's decision. Approximately 60 percent of the 10,000 votes were cast in favor of the board's decision, thus affirming the removal of homosexuality as a form of mental illness. This sequence of events illustrates quite clearly the ways in which social and political events can influence the classification of mental disorders.

One important consequence of this debate was a shift in the focus on how sexual disorders are classified. The authors of DSM-III came to believe that the classification system should be concerned primarily with subjective distress. They were impressed by the numerous indications, in both personal appeals as well as the research literature, that homosexuality, per se, was not invariably associated with impaired functioning. They decided that, in order to be considered a form of mental disorder, a condition ought to be associated with subjective distress or seriously impaired social or occupational functioning. This emphasis opened the door to a more detailed consideration of problems that centered around impaired sexual performance, such as inability to reach orgasm. Relatively less concern was directed toward the choice of sexual partners or preferred sexual activities, as long as the participants were mutually consenting adults.

Political forces triggered the removal of homosexuality from the diagnostic manual, but the stage was set for these events by gradual shifts in society's attitudes toward several aspects of sexual behavior (Bullough, 1976). For example, more and more people came to believe that reproduction was not the main purpose of sexual behavior. Along with this view came increased tolerance for greater variety in human sexuality. The revision of the DSM's system for describing sexual disorders was therefore the product of several forces, cultural as well as political. ■

Boundaries of Abnormal Behavior

Having introduced many of the issues that are involved in the definition of abnormal behavior, we now turn to another clinical example. The woman in our second case study, Mary Childress, suffered from a serious eating disorder known as *bulimia nervosa*. Her problems raise additional questions about the definition of abnormal behavior.

Consider the defining characteristics of mental disorders listed in Table 1–1. As you are reading the case, ask yourself about the impact of Mary's eating disorder on her subjective experience and social adjustment. In what ways are these consequences similar to those seen in Kevin Warner's case? How are they different? This case also introduces another important concept associated with the way that we think about abnormal behavior: How can we identify the *boundary* between normal and abnormal behavior? Is there an obvious distinction between eating patterns that are considered to be part of a mental disorder and those that are not? Or is there a gradual progression from one end of a continuum to the other, with each step fading gradually into the next?

CASE STUDY

Eating Disorder

Mary Childress was, in most respects, a typical 18-year-old sophomore at a large state university. She was popular with other students and a good student, in spite of the fact that she spent little time studying. She and her boyfriend had been dating for about 2 years. They got along well, cared about each other very much, and planned to get married after they finished college. Everything about Mary's life was relatively normal—except for her bingeing and purging.

Mary's eating patterns were wildly erratic. She preferred to skip breakfast entirely, and often missed lunch as well. By the middle of the afternoon, she could no longer ignore the hunger pangs. At that point, on 2 or 3 days out of the week, Mary would drive her car to the drive-in window of a fast-food restaurant. Her typical order included three or four double cheeseburgers, several orders of french fries, and a large milk shake (or maybe two). Then she binged, devouring all the food as she drove around town by herself. Later she would go to a private bathroom, where she wouldn't be seen by anyone, and purge the food from her stomach by vomiting. Afterward, she returned to her room, feeling angry, frustrated, and ashamed.

Mary was 5'5" tall and weighed 110 pounds. She was neither fat nor thin, but she believed that her body was unattractive, especially her thighs and hips. She was extremely critical of herself and had worried about her weight for many years. Her weight fluctuated quite a bit, from a low of 97 pounds when she was a senior in high school to a high of 125 during her first year at the university. Her mother was a "full-figured" woman and bought most of her clothes at a special store. Mary swore to herself at an early age that she would never let herself gain as much weight as her mother had.

Purging had originally seemed like an ideal solution to the problem of weight control. You could eat whatever you wanted and quickly get rid of it so you wouldn't get fat. Unfortunately, the vomiting became a vicious trap. Disgusted by her own behavior, Mary often promised herself that she would never binge and purge again, but she couldn't stop the cycle.

For the past year Mary had been vomiting at least once almost every day and occasionally as many as three or four times a day. The impulse to purge was very strong. Mary felt bloated after having only a bowl of cereal and a glass of orange juice. If she ate a sandwich and drank a diet soda, she began to ruminate about what she had eaten, thinking "I've got to get rid of that!" Before long, she usually found a bathroom and threw up. Her excessive binges were less frequent than the vomiting. Four or five times a week she experienced an overwhelming urge to eat forbidden foods, especially fast food. Her initial reaction was usually a short-lived attempt to resist the impulse. Then she would space out or "go into a zone," becoming only vaguely aware of what she was doing and feeling. In the midst of a serious binge, Mary felt completely helpless and unable to control herself. When she first started to binge and purge, Mary had to stick her fingers down her throat to make herself vomit. Now, 3 years after she began experimenting with this pattern of eating, she could vomit without using her fingers.

There weren't any obvious physical signs that would alert someone to Mary's eating problems, but the vomiting had begun to wreak havoc with her body, especially her digestive system. She had suffered severe throat infections and frequent, intense stomach pains. Her dentist had noticed problems beginning to develop with her teeth and gums, undoubtedly a consequence of constant exposure to strong stomach acids.

Mary's attitudes toward nutrition and health were irrational. Although she sometimes ate 10 or 12 double cheeseburgers a day, Mary insisted that she hated junk food, and she considered herself to be a vegetarian. The meat that she ate didn't count, she reasoned, because she seldom kept it down. For someone who could be described as totally preoccupied with food, she gave little thought to its consumption, never planning her meals. Mary was extremely concerned about the health consequences of obesity. She could cite detailed statistics regarding the increased risk for heart disease that are associated with every additional 5 pounds that a person gains over her ideal body weight. Of course, the physical consequences of repeated bingeing and purging are infinitely more severe than those associated with modest weight gain, but this irony was lost on Mary.

Her eating problem started to develop when Mary was 15. She had been seriously involved in gymnastics for several years but eventually developed a knee condition that forced her to give up the sport. She gained a few pounds in the next month or two and decided to lose weight by dieting. Buoyed by unrealistic expectations about the immediate, positive benefits of a diet that she had seen advertised on television, Mary initially adhered rigidly to its recommended regimen. Six months later, after three of these fad diets had failed, she started throwing up as a way to control her intake of food.

Then her father got sick. He was diagnosed with bone cancer when she was a junior in high school (only a couple of months after she had starting purging), and he died the next year. Everyone in the family was devastated. Mary's mother became seriously depressed. Her brother dropped out of high school after his sophomore year and continued living at home. Mary's eating problems multiplied. Her grades suffered, but she managed to maintain an adequate record through the remainder of her senior year and to graduate, gaining admission to the state university.

Mary looked forward to leaving home and starting over again at the university, but her problem followed her. She felt guilty and ashamed about her eating problems. She was much too embarrassed to let anyone know what she was doing and would never eat more than a few mouthfuls of food in a public place like the dorm cafeteria. Her roommate, Julie, was from a small town on the other side of the state. They got along reasonably well, but Mary managed to conceal her bingeing and purging, thanks in large part to the fact that she was able to bring her own car to campus. The car allowed her to drive away from campus several times a week so that she could binge.

Mary's boyfriend, Tim, was a freshman at a community college in her hometown. They saw each other one or two weekends each month, usually when she went home. Tim was completely unaware of Mary's eating problems, and she would do anything to keep him from finding out. Mary and Tim had been sexually active since shortly after they met, but they had only had intercourse five times, mostly because Mary had a difficult time enjoying sex. She was frightened by her sexual impulses, which often seemed difficult to control, and she worried about what might happen if she ever let herself go completely. Sexual experiences were a source of great conflict to her. She didn't like her own body, but it made her feel good to know that Tim found her desirable. ■

Mary's case illustrates many of the characteristic features of bulimia nervosa. As in Kevin's case, her behavior could be considered abnormal not only because it fit the criteria for one of the categories in DSM-IV but also because she suffered from a dysfunction (in this case, of the mechanisms that regulate appetite) that was obviously harmful. The impact of the disorder was greatest in terms of her physical health: Eating disorders can be fatal if they are not properly treated because they affect so many vital organs of the body, including the heart and kidneys. Mary's social functioning and her academic performance were not yet seriously impaired. There are many different ways in which to measure the harmful effects of abnormal behavior.

Mary's case also illustrates the subjective pain that is associated with many types of abnormal behavior. In contrast to the situation described in Kevin's case, Mary was acutely aware of her disorder. She was frustrated and unhappy. In an attempt to relieve this emotional distress, she entered psychological treatment. Unfortunately, painful emotions associated with mental disorders can also interfere with, or delay, the decision to look for professional help. Guilt, shame, and embarrassment often accompany psychological problems and sometimes make it difficult to confide in another person.

Dimensions versus Categories

If we accept the argument that Mary's behavior is abnormal, how can we identify the boundaries of this condition? Should we expect to find clear-cut boundaries? It is relatively easy to

▲ **This young dancer suffers from an eating disorder. Some experts maintain that the differences between abnormal and normal behavior are essentially differences in degree; that is, quantitative differences.**

describe an obvious or typical case of bulimia, where there is no question that the behavior is causing serious problems. There are many borderline cases, however, and borderline cases may outnumber typical cases. What if Mary purged only once a month instead of several times each week? What if she binged but didn't purge, and when she binged she didn't eat such large quantities of food?

If we assume that there is an eating disorder that Mary either has or does not have, we have adopted a **categorical approach to classification.** But it might be more useful to assume that there is a continuous distribution of uncontrolled eating, with the best description of Mary's behavior lying somewhere along that continuum from normal behavior to complete loss of control. This is known as a **dimensional approach to classification.** The distinction between these approaches is one of the central issues involved in the way we think about abnormal behavior. It is always difficult to identify a clear boundary between normal patterns of behavior and psychopathology.

The dimensional and categorical approaches can be combined in the form of a **threshold model** (Gottesman, 1991). According to this approach, the various features of a disorder may be distributed as continuous dimensions. People can presumably exhibit these characteristics in different numbers and combinations and in varying levels of severity without experiencing any adverse impact on their adjustment until they pass a *critical threshold*. Beyond that level, there is presumably a dramatic increase in the number of problems that they encounter. A diagnosis would be assigned only above the threshold, even though the features themselves are continuously distributed.

The DSM-IV follows the categorical approach to classification. Each disorder is defined in terms of specific diagnostic criteria, and the dividing line between normal and abnormal is clearly identified. The clinician's job, in assigning a diagnosis, is to make a *dichotomous decision*—to determine whether a particular individual fits the category, not to determine how much or to what degree the person possesses a particular characteristic. In establishing their diagnostic cutoff points, the committees that wrote DSM-IV obviously made somewhat arbitrary decisions. We discuss the relative merits of the categorical and dimensional approaches to classification in Chapter 4.

Epidemiology

Many important decisions about mental disorders are based on data regarding the frequency with which these disorders occur. With regard to bulimia nervosa, data obtained in surveys and community-based interview studies indicate that perhaps as many as 40 percent of normal-weight college women consider themselves to be fat. Approximately 80 percent report eating episodes that seem beyond their control, and 75 percent have tried dieting. At least 24 percent have engaged in binge eating, and 16 percent have purged (Strober, 1991). Four percent would meet the full set of diagnostic criteria for the syndrome of bulimia nervosa (see Chapter 10). These data are the source of considerable concern, especially among those who are responsible for health services on college campuses.

Epidemiology is the scientific study of the frequency and distribution of disorders within a population. Epidemiologists are concerned with questions such as whether the frequency of a disorder has increased or decreased during a particular period of time, whether it is more common in one geographic area than in another, and whether certain types of people—based on factors such as gender, race, and socioeconomic status—are at greater risk than other types for the development of the disorder. Health administrators often use such information to make decisions about the allocation of resources for professional training programs, treatment facilities, and research projects.

Two terms are particularly important in epidemiological research (Zahner, Hsieh, & Fleming, 1995). **Incidence** refers to the number of *new* cases of a disorder that appear in a population during a specific period of time. **Prevalence** refers to the total number of active cases, both old and new, that are present in a population during a specific period of time. The *lifetime prevalence* of a disorder is the total proportion of people in a given population who have been affected by the disorder at some point during their lives.

How prevalent are the disorders listed in DSM-IV? One large-scale study, known as the Epidemiologic Catchment Area (ECA) study, was conducted in the 1980s (Robins & Regier, 1991). Approximately 20,000 people were interviewed in five large metropolitan areas in the United States. Questions were asked pertaining to 30 of the major disorders listed in the DSM. Table 1–2 lists some results from this study. Notice that gender differences are found in many types of mental disorder: Anxiety disorders (phobias and panic) and depression are more common among women; alcoholism and antisocial personality are more common among men. Other conditions, like schizophrenia and mania, appear with equal frequency in both women and men. Patterns of this sort raise interesting questions about possible causal mechanisms. What conditions would make women more vulnerable to one kind of disorder and men more vulnerable to another? There are many possibilities, including factors such as hormones, patterns of learning, and social pressures.

Comparisons between 1-year prevalence rates—the number of people with active symptoms during the 12 months prior to the interview—and lifetime prevalence rates are also interesting. In most cases, the lifetime rates are much higher. This discrepancy reflects the fact that mental disorders are not always chronic conditions. Most people experience periods of remission, in which their symptoms improve, in between active episodes of disorder. Many people recover completely. Therefore, although the relatively high lifetime prevalence rates in Table 1–2 are a source of serious concern, the contrast with 1-year prevalence rates is also an indication that mental disorders are not always enduring.

Culture and Psychopathology

One important aspect of epidemiological studies involves comparison of the frequency of mental disorders in different cultures. Is abnormal behavior more common in certain societies than in others? Is it possible that the social values or living circumstances of some societies are particularly likely to lead to psychopathology? The

	TABLE 1–2
Prevalence Rates for Various Mental Disorders (ECA data)	

	Women (%)		Men (%)	
	1-year	Lifetime	1-year	Lifetime
Phobic disorder	12.9	17.8	6.3	10.4
Alcohol abuse/dependence	2.2	4.6	11.9	23.8
Major depression	4.0	7.0	1.4	2.6
Antisocial personality	0.4	0.8	2.1	4.5
Obsessive–compulsive disorder	1.9	3.2	1.4	2.0
Panic disorder	1.2	2.1	0.6	1.0
Schizophrenia	1.1	1.7	0.9	1.2
Bipolar mood disorder	0.8	0.9	0.6	0.7

Source: Adapted from L. N. Robins, B. Z. Locke, and D. A. Regier, 1991, An overview of psychiatric disorders in America. In L. N. Robins and D. A. Regier (Eds.), *Psychiatric Disorders in America: The Epidemiological Catchment Area Study,* pp. 328–366. New York: Free Press.

literature suggests that some disorders, like schizophrenia, show important consistencies in cross-cultural comparisons (see Research Close-Up). Others, like bulimia, are more specifically associated with certain demographic, cultural, and socioeconomic conditions.

There are, for example, dramatic differences between women and men in the frequency of eating disorders. Almost 90 percent of bulimic patients are women (Woodside & Kennedy, 1995). The incidence of bulimia is 5 times higher among university women than among working women, and it is more common among younger women than among older women. Bulimia is relatively rare among African-American women, although it may be increasing among more affluent African Americans who have adopted the attitudes of the dominant culture toward slimness (Dolan, 1991; Hsu, 1989). This pattern suggests that holding particular sets of values related to eating and to women's appearance is an important ingredient in establishing risk for development of an eating disorder.

The strength and nature of the relationship between culture and psychopathology vary from one disorder to the next. Several general conclusions can be drawn from cross-cultural studies of psychopathology (Draguns, 1980, 1994), including the following points:

1. All mental disorders are shaped, to some extent, by cultural factors.

▲ Lee Robins, professor of sociology in psychiatry at Washington University, was the principal investigator in the ECA Study, which is one extensive base of information regarding the prevalence of mental disorders in the United States.

Cross-Cultural Study of Abnormal Behavior

Some severe forms of psychopathology have been found in virtually every culture that social scientists have studied. One classic paper that supports this conclusion was written by Jane Murphy (1976), an anthropologist at Harvard University. Murphy studied two groups of non-Western people: the Inuit (or Eskimos) of northwest Alaska and the Yoruba of rural, tropical Nigeria in West Africa. Murphy lived with each group for several months, talking with them about their lives and observing their everyday behaviors. She became intimately acquainted with their languages and the ways in which they think about problem behaviors. A key informant described for Murphy the life experiences of all 500 people in the Inuit village. Among the Yoruba, most of the data were provided by three native healers.

Murphy discovered that both cultures recognize certain forms of behavior as "being crazy." These behaviors center around aberrant beliefs, feelings, and actions: hearing voices when no one is talking; laughing when there is nothing to laugh at; believing things that are so strange that other people cannot imagine them to be true; talking in strange ways that do not make sense to other people; and behaving in erratic or unpredictable ways. These syndromes bear a striking resemblance to the disorder called schizophrenia in DSM-IV. The specific content of hallucinations and delusions varies from one culture to the next, but the underlying processes appear to be the same. Perhaps most important was the observation that the words that the Inuit and Yoruba use to describe "losing one's mind" refer to a set of problematic behaviors rather than to a single problem.

Murphy also noted that members of both groups viewed "crazy behavior" as being quite different from the behaviors associated with being a shaman or spiritual healer. At certain times, the shaman also behaved in unusual ways, such as responding to voices that other people could not hear or speaking in ways that other people did not understand. This distinction is apparently based primarily on the extent to which these behaviors are controlled (turned on and off voluntarily by the person) and utilized for a socially approved purpose, such as attempting to heal a sick person. One Yoruba villager explained, "When the shaman is healing, he is out of his mind, but he is not crazy." Murphy was able to identify 18 Inuit villagers who had served the group as shaman at some point during their lives. They appeared to be a random sample from the entire group of 500 people. None of them was considered to be mentally disturbed by their fellow villagers.

The Inuit and Yoruba have their own hypotheses concerning the origins of mental disorders, which often involve magic. They also have developed special treatment procedures, or native healing rituals, that they use to help people with these disorders. The prevailing attitudes in both groups appeared to be neither entirely positive nor entirely negative. These observations indicate that the ways in which societies respond to psychopathology can vary greatly, even if the basic forms of abnormal behavior with which they are confronted are quite similar.

Murphy's conclusions have been supported by a large-scale epidemiological study of schizophrenia, sponsored by the World Health Organization (WHO) (Jablensky et al., 1992). This study included 1,200 patients who were admitted to psychiatric hospitals in nine countries: Colombia, Czechoslovakia, Denmark, India, Nigeria, Taiwan, Russia, England, and the United States. In each setting, the investigators found patients who exhibited symptoms of schizophrenia. The frequency of this disorder was approximately the same in each location, in spite of obvious cultural contrasts between sites in developing (India, Nigeria) and developed (Denmark, England) countries. As in Murphy's report, the WHO study found some cross-cultural variations with regard to the specific subtypes of schizophrenic symptoms and with regard to the outcome of the disorder 5 years after treatment. Nevertheless, the data support the conclusion that severe forms of mental illness are not limited to Western cultures or developed countries. ■

2. No mental disorders can be traced entirely to cultural or social factors.
3. Psychotic disorders are less influenced by culture than are nonpsychotic disorders.
4. The *symptoms* of certain disorders are more likely to vary across cultures than

are the disorders themselves (when viewed at the level of a *syndrome*).

We will return to these points as we discuss specific disorders, such as depression, phobias, and alcoholism, throughout the rest of this book.

Causes of Abnormal Behavior

The cases of Kevin Warner and Mary Childress illustrate why it is difficult to define abnormal behavior. They also raise questions about the causes of mental illness. Some people may be born with a predisposition to disorder that will emerge later in their lives. Was Kevin genetically vulnerable to schizophrenia? Did Mary possess a genetic makeup that tended toward obesity? Could it have increased the probability that she would develop an eating disorder?

Traumatic experiences may set the stage for emotional problems. Did the stress of Kevin's job or Joyce's pregnancy cause Kevin's condition to deteriorate? Was the death of Mary's father responsible for a serious escalation of her eating problems? Finally, what is the role of society in creating psychological problems? Would Mary have begun her frantic efforts to control her weight if our culture didn't place such a high value on thin female figures? These are all questions about the **etiology,** or causes, of psychopathology.

Once a disorder has been carefully described, the next step for the scientist is to attempt to uncover its cause. Case studies of the sort that you have read in this chapter do not provide definitive answers. We can ponder questions about the cause of Kevin's delusional beliefs and Mary's eating disorder informally, but the scientist must shape each of these queries into a formal hypothesis.

The etiology of most forms of abnormal behavior is poorly understood. This is true both at the level of the individual and at the level of the disorder as a whole. This textbook cannot provide many unequivocal answers about the causes of abnormal behavior. We hope that you will become intrigued rather than frustrated by this uncertainty. The origins of psychopathology represent a compelling mystery that motivates the search for knowledge.

Nature and Nurture

Of all of the questions about the cause of abnormal behavior, the **nature–nurture controversy** is perhaps the most long-standing. This debate pits genetic and biological factors against life experiences as causes of abnormal behavior. Those who argue for nature believe that psychopathology is caused by genes, by infectious diseases, by physical injuries, or by malfunctions of the brain or other parts of the nervous system. The abnormality presumably resides in the person's physical makeup. Life experiences may shape the development of psychological disorders, but their ultimate cause is biological (McGuffin et al., 1994).

The nurture side of the controversy makes the opposite assumption: Experience is the central cause of abnormal behavior. Proponents of this view often focus on different types of life experiences at different times in development. Some proponents of this perspective emphasize how well or how poorly parents care for children during the first years of life. They suggest that these early experiences mold each individual's personality. Others point to the role of learning throughout life in shaping and maintaining abnormal behavior. Some argue that dysfunctional relationships and societal demands cause people to behave in abnormal ways.

Many scientists have come to believe that the nature–nurture controversy is based on a false distinction between the physical and psychological worlds. We agree with this conclusion. Nature and nurture are not as different as they may seem at first glance (Eisenberg, 1995; Plomin, 1990a). The mind cannot be separated from the body. The dominant perspective on the cause of psychological disorders views abnormal behavior as resulting from a combination of nature and nurture. We discuss these issues in more depth in Chapter 2.

Systems of Influence

The consideration of different levels or systems of influence is another way in which we focus on nature *and* nurture, not nature *or* nurture, in this textbook. Abnormal behavior can be studied on many different levels. Psychobiologists and neuroscientists sometimes study abnormal behavior in terms of the various chemicals in the brain. Clinical psychologists frequently focus on characteristics of the individual, such as the tendency to blame oneself or others for life's problems. Other clinical psychologists emphasize social contributions to psychopathology, such as the role of social support or community resources in protecting people against the stresses of everyday life.

The study of biological, psychological, and social systems each offers a valuable perspective on understanding abnormal behavior. Mary Childress provides a good example of the contributions of these different levels of conceptualization.

Several biological considerations might be important. Genetic factors may have predisposed Mary toward problems with her weight. Brain mechanisms that are responsible for the regulation of appetite could also be involved. From a psychological point of view, Mary's disturbed pattern of eating could be viewed as one part of a struggle for control—control of her own weight, her feelings, and her relationships with other people. From a social perspective, she had undoubtedly absorbed unrealistic expectations about the ideal female figure from the media and from prevailing community attitudes. These expectations can be especially harmful when coupled with our culture's undue emphasis on the importance of physical appearance, especially for women. Thus Mary's bingeing and purging cannot be explained by a single biological, psychological, or social factor. Her eating disorder probably developed and was maintained through some combination of all three systems of influence.

In our view, too much time has been spent arguing about which approach to psychopathology is most valuable. Are most disorders psychological in nature? Are they ultimately biological? We believe that the task for scientists and for practitioners is not to decide whether mental disorders are caused by biological or psychological or societal influences. Rather, their task is to uncover how these different levels of influence interact to cause emotional suffering and psychological disorders. The analytic approach that combines these various levels of influence is called the **biopsychosocial model.**

▲ **The Nobel Prize–winning author Ernest Hemingway was a chronic alcohol abuser who ended his own life with a shotgun. Uncovering the causes of behavior such as substance abuse is one of the major challenges facing mental health professionals.**

Treatment of Abnormal Behavior

The case of Kevin Warner allowed us to introduce one of the most common forms of treatment for psychopathology: *psychopharmacology* (medication). Various types of medication are used in the treatment of schizophrenia, depression, anxiety disorders, and other forms of abnormal behavior. *Psychotherapy* is another popular form of treatment, which involves the use of psychological procedures in the context of a special, helping relationship. There are many different approaches to psychotherapy (see Chapter 3). In cognitive therapy, for example, therapists help their patients identify and correct patterns of illogical thinking and maladaptive

assumptions about themselves and their environments. Cognitive therapists emphasize replacing self-defeating thoughts with more rational self-statements. In actual practice, it is not unusual for patients to receive medication at the same time that they are engaged in psychotherapy.

Unfortunately, we cannot assume that everyone who needs treatment gets it. At the beginning of this chapter, we noted that 1 out of every 5 Americans exhibited active symptoms of at least one mental disorder during a particular year (Robins, Locke, & Regier, 1991). That same study also found that only about 1 out of 5 people with an active disorder had received treatment for their condition within the past few months. Similar findings have been reported in a more recent survey of 8,000 nationally representative young and middle-aged adults across the United States (Kessler et al., 1994). Many factors may account for this result. Some people who qualified for a formal diagnosis may not have been impaired to such an extent that they were willing to seek treatment. Others may not have recognized their disorder. In some cases, treatment may not have been available, the person may not have had the time or resources to obtain treatment, or the person may have tried treatments in the past that failed. For whatever reason, many people who experience mental disorders do not receive proper treatment.

Much of what we know about psychopathology has been learned in the attempt to help people who are suffering from mental disorders. The connection between etiological speculation and treatment procedures is a two-way street. Theories sometimes spawn new therapies, and successful therapies often spawn new theories. One classic example of the latter case comes from Freud's experience at the turn of the century with the use of hypnosis and, later, free association to treat patients with a variety of physical and emotional complaints. Some of the patients showed remarkable improvement in their condition. To explain the success of this therapy, Freud developed what is now known as *psychoanalytic theory*. Another example comes from medication. The first antipsychotic drugs were discovered accidentally around 1950. Their dramatic success in relieving symptoms of schizophrenia led quickly to speculation about the neurochemical basis of psychotic disorders.

The success of a treatment does not prove the cause of a problem. After reading Kevin Warner's case, for example, it might be tempting to conclude that Kevin's delusional beliefs were caused by a biochemical imbalance in his brain.

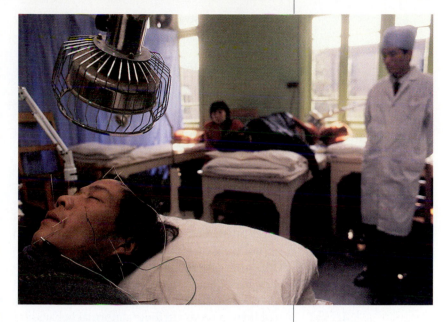

His positive response to antipsychotic drugs does not prove, however, that biochemical factors caused his psychotic symptoms in the first place. They may have been caused by a combination of other factors. By itself, the solution to a problem does not prove the problem's cause.

Assuming the presence of a cause based on response to treatment represents an error in logic. Consider two analogies. Aspirin may cure headaches, but this does not mean that headaches are caused by a lack of aspirin. A filling is used to restore a cavity, but this does not mean that cavities are caused by a lack of fillings. The errors in reasoning are obvious in these examples, but logical fallacies are far less apparent when the cause of a disorder is unknown. When a psychological treatment solves a problem, we often assume that the disorder must have a psychological cause. Similarly, when biological treatments are successful, we often assume that this proves that the cause is biological. Even experienced scientists can fall victim to such errors in reasoning.

▲ **The success of a treatment does not necessarily enlighten us as to the cause of the disorder. In China, for example, acupuncture has been used to treat depression. Regardless of how effective this procedure might be, it is not certain that the results of this therapeutic procedure can teach us much about the origins of depression.**

Psychopathology in Historical Context

In most countries, mental disorders are widely recognized health problems. Their etiology is viewed largely in scientific terms, even though cultural, economic, and political considerations still influence the ways in which they are defined and treated. Society accepts responsibility for

the care of people who have these disorders. State and local governments have established various types of treatment facilities, such as mental health centers and psychiatric hospitals, where patients can be treated. Federal governments in countries such as the United States and Canada provide extensive support for the pursuit of new knowledge regarding their causes and treatments.

You should not assume, however, that contemporary approaches to psychopathology are a simple reflection or extension of earlier views. Throughout history, many other societies have held quite different views of the problems that we consider to be mental disorders. Before leaving this introductory chapter, we must begin to place contemporary approaches to psychopathology in historical perspective.

The search for explanations of the causes of abnormal behavior dates to ancient times, as do conflicting opinions about the etiology of emotional disorders. References to abnormal behavior have been found in ancient accounts from Chinese, Hebrew, and Egyptian societies. Many of these records attribute abnormal behavior to the disfavor of the gods or the mischief of demons. In fact, abnormal behavior continues to be attributed to demons in some preliterate societies today.

The Greek Tradition in Medicine

More earthly and less supernatural accounts of the etiology of psychopathology can be traced to the Greek physician Hippocrates (460–377 B.C.), who ridiculed demonological accounts of illness and insanity. Instead, Hippocrates hypothesized that abnormal behavior, like other forms of disease, had natural causes. Health depended on maintaining a natural balance within the body, specifically a balance of four body fluids (which were also known as the four *humors*): blood, phlegm, black bile, and yellow bile. Hippocrates argued that various types of disorder, including psychopathology, resulted from either an excess or a deficiency of one of these four fluids. The specifics of Hippocrates' theories obviously have little value today, but his systematic attempt to uncover natural, biological explanations for all types of illness represented an enormously important departure from previous ways of thinking.

The Hippocratic perspective dominated medical thought in Western countries until the middle of the nineteenth century (Golub, 1994). People trained in the Hippocratic tradition viewed "disease" as a unitary concept. In other words, physicians (and others who were given responsibility for healing people who were disturbed or suffering) did not distinguish between mental disorders and other types of illness. All problems were considered to be the result of an imbalance of body fluids, and treatment procedures were designed in an attempt to restore the ideal balance. These were often called "heroic" treatments because they were drastic (and frequently painful) attempts to quickly reverse the course of an illness. They involved bloodletting (intentionally cutting the person to reduce the amount of blood in the body) and purging (the induction of vomiting), as well as the use of heat and cold. These practices continued to be part of standard medical treatments well into the nineteenth century (Starr, 1982).

The Creation of the Asylum

In Europe during the Middle Ages, "lunatics" and "idiots," as the mentally ill and mentally retarded were commonly called, aroused little interest and were given marginal care. Most people lived in rural settings and made their living through agricultural activities. Disturbed behavior was considered to be the responsibility of the family rather than the community or the state. Many people were kept at home by their families, and others roamed freely as beggars. Mentally disturbed people who were violent or appeared dangerous often were imprisoned with criminals. Those who could not subsist on their own were placed in almshouses for the poor.

In the 1600s and 1700s, "insane asylums" were established to house the mentally disturbed. Several factors changed the way that society viewed people with mental disorders and reinforced the relatively new belief that the community as a whole should be responsible for their care (Grob, 1994). Perhaps most important was a change in economic, demographic, and social conditions. Consider, for example, the situation in the United States at the beginning of the nineteenth century. The period between 1790 and 1850 saw rapid population growth and the rise of large cities. The increased urbanization of the American population was accompanied by a shift from an agricultural to an industrial economy. Lunatic asylums—the original mental hospitals—were created to serve heavily populated cities and to assume responsibilities that had previously been performed by individual families.

Early asylums were little more than human warehouses, but as the nineteenth century began, the *moral treatment* movement led to improved conditions in at least some mental hospitals. Founded on a basic respect for human dignity and the belief that humanistic care would help to relieve mental illness, moral treatment reform efforts were instituted by leading mental health professionals of the day, such as Benjamin Rush in the United States, Phillipe Pinel in France, and William Tuke in England. Rather than simply confining mental patients, moral treatment offered support, care, and a degree of freedom. Belief in the importance of reason and the potential benefits of science played an important role in the moral treatment movement. In contrast to the fatalistic, supernatural explanations that had prevailed during the Middle Ages, these reformers touted an optimistic view, arguing that mental disorders could be treated successfully.

Many of the large mental institutions in the United States were built in the nineteenth century as a result of the philosophy of moral treatment. In the middle of the 1800s, mental health advocate Dorothea Dix gave particular impetus to this trend. Dix argued that treating the mentally ill in hospitals was both more humane and more economical than caring for them haphazardly in their communities, and she urged that special facilities be built to house mental patients. Dix and like-minded reformers were successful in their efforts. In 1830, there were only four public mental hospitals in the United States that housed a combined total of less than 200 patients. By 1880, there were 75 public mental hospitals, with a total population of more than 35,000 residents (Torrey, 1988).

The creation of large institutions for the treatment of mental patients led to the development of a new profession—psychiatry. By the middle of the 1800s, superintendents of asylums for the insane were almost always physicians who had experience caring for people with severe mental disorders. The Association of Medical Superintendents of American Institutions for the Insane (AMSAII), which later became the American Psychiatric Association (APA), was founded in 1844. The large patient populations within these institutions provided an opportunity for these men to observe various types of psychopathology over an extended period of time. They soon began to publish their ideas regarding the causes of these conditions, and

they also experimented with new treatment methods (Grob, 1994).

Worcester Lunatic Hospital: A Model Institution

In 1833, the state of Massachusetts opened a publicly supported lunatic asylum in Worcester. Samuel Woodward, the asylum's first superintendent, also became the first president of the Association for Medical Superintendents of American Institutions for the Insane, when that organization was founded in 1844. Woodward became extremely well known throughout the United States and Europe because of his claims that mental disorders could be cured just like other types of disease. We will describe this institution and its superintendent briefly because, in many ways, it became a model for psychiatric care on which other nineteenth-century hospitals were built.

Woodward's ideas about the causes of disorder represented a combination of physical and moral considerations. Moral factors focused on the person's lifestyle. Violations of "natural" or conventional behavior could presumably cause mental disorders. Judgments regarding the nature of these violations were based on the prevailing middle-class, Protestant standards that were held by Woodward and his peers, who were almost invariably well-educated, white males. After treating several hundred patients during his first 10 years at the Worcester asylum, Woodward argued that at least half of the cases could be traced to immoral behavior, improper living conditions, and exposure to unnatural stresses. Specific examples included intemperance (heavy drinking), masturbation, overwork, domestic difficulties, excessive ambitions, faulty

▲ **Dorothea Dix (1802–1887) was an early advocate for the humane treatment of the mentally ill. Many mental institutions were built during the late 1800s due in large part to Dix's efforts.**

▼ **The Massachusetts Lunatic Asylum (as it appeared in 1835) was the first large state mental institution in the United States.**

education, personal disappointment, marital problems, excessive religious enthusiasm, jealousy, and pride (Grob, 1994). The remaining cases were attributed to physical causes, such as poor health or a blow to the head.

Treatment at the Worcester Lunatic Hospital included a blend of physical and moral procedures. If mental disorders were often caused by improper behavior and difficult life circumstances, presumably they could be cured by moving the person to a more appropriate and therapeutic environment, the asylum. Moral treatment focused on efforts to reeducate the patient, fostering the development of self-control that would allow the person to return to a "healthy" lifestyle. Procedures included occupational therapy, religious exercises, and recreation. Mechanical restraints were employed only when considered necessary.

Moral treatments were combined with a mixture of physical procedures. These included standard heroic interventions, such as bleeding and purging, which the asylum superintendents had learned as part of their medical training. For example, some symptoms were thought to be produced by inflammation of the brain, and it was believed that bleeding would restore the natural balance of fluids. Woodward and his colleagues also employed various kinds of drugs. Patients who were excited, agitated, or violent were often treated with opium or morphine. Depressed patients were given laxatives.

Woodward claimed that "no disease, of equal severity, can be treated with greater success than insanity, if the remedies are applied sufficiently early." He reported that the recovery rates at the Worcester Hospital varied from 82 percent to 91 percent between 1833 and 1845. His reports were embraced and endorsed by other members of the young psychiatric profession. They fueled enthusiasm for establishing more large public hospitals, thus aiding the efforts of Dorothea Dix and other advocates for public support of mental health treatment.

Lessons from the History of Psychopathology

The opinions and procedures that prevailed in psychiatry during the middle of the nineteenth century are, in some very general ways, obvious forerunners of contemporary views. Our etiological theories still focus on a blend of environmental and biological factors, though the specific elements of these theories are now much different. Today's treatment procedures still include the use of medication, as well as efforts to foster personal insight and teach new skills.

The invention and expansion of public mental hospitals set in motion a process of systematic observation and scientific inquiry that led directly to our current system of mental health care. The creation of psychiatry as a professional group, committed to treating and understanding psychopathology, laid the foundation for expanded public concern and financial resources for solving the problems of mental disorders.

There are, of course, many aspects of nineteenth-century psychiatry that, in retrospect, seem to have been naive or misguided. To take only one example, it now seems silly to have thought that masturbation would cause mental disorders. In fact, masturbation is now taught and encouraged as part of treatment for certain types of sexual dysfunction (see Chapter 12). The obvious cultural biases that influenced the etiological hypotheses of Woodward and his colleagues seem quite unreasonable today.

Our own cultural values continue to influence the ways in which we define, think about, and treat mental disorders. Thomas Szasz (1970), who is perhaps the most eloquent and influential critic of contemporary psychiatric views, has noted that social values still play an important role in our system for classifying mental disorders. Paula Caplan (1995) has drawn attention to the potential influence of gender bias in shaping DSM-IV. One lesson therefore is that the cultural context will determine, in part, which problems are selected for consideration and how they are defined. Learning about the history of psychiatry can make these biases more obvious. We must not let it lull us into thinking, however, that we have outgrown or progressed beyond these difficulties. It seems unlikely that mental disorders can be defined in a cultural vacuum or in a completely objective fashion. The best we can do is to be aware of the problem and include a variety of cultural and social perspectives in thinking about and defining the issues (Manson, 1994).

The other lesson that we can learn from history involves the importance of scientific research. Viewed from the perspective of contemporary care, we can easily be skeptical of Samuel Woodward's claims regarding the phenomenal success of treatment at the Worcester Hospital. No one today believes that 90 percent of seriously disturbed, psychotic patients are cured by currently available forms of treatment. Therefore it is preposterous to assume that such astounding success might have been achieved at the Worcester Lunatic Hospital. During the nineteenth century, physicians were not trained in scientific research methods. Their optimistic statements about treatment outcome were accepted, in large part, on the basis of their professional authority. Clearly, Woodward's enthusiastic assertions should have been evaluated with more stringent, scientific methods.

Unfortunately, the type of naive acceptance that met Woodward's idealistic claims has become a regrettable tradition. For the past 150 years, mental health professionals and the public alike have repeatedly embraced new treatment procedures that have been hailed as cures for mental disorders. Perhaps most notorious was a group of somatic treatment procedures that was introduced during the 1920s and 1930s (Valenstein, 1986). They included fever therapy, insulin coma, and lobotomy (see Table 1–3). These dramatic procedures, which have subsequently proved to be ineffective, were accepted with the same enthusiasm that greeted the invention of large public institutions in nineteenth-century America. Thousands of patients were subjected to these procedures, which remained widespread until the early 1950s, when more effective pharmacological treatments were discovered. The history of psychopathology

teaches us that people who claim that a new form of treatment is effective should be expected to prove it scientifically (see Research Methods).

TABLE 1-3

Somatic Treatments Introduced and Widely Employed in the 1920s and 1930s

Name	Procedure	Original Rationale
Fever therapy	Blood from people with malaria was injected into psychiatric patients so that they would develop a fever.	Observation that symptoms sometimes disappeared in patients who became ill with typhoid fever.
Insulin coma therapy	Insulin was injected into psychiatric patients to lower the sugar content of the blood and induce a hypoglycemic state and deep coma.	Observed mental changes among some diabetic drug addicts who were treated with insulin.
Lobotomy	A sharp knife was inserted through a hole that was bored in the patient's skull, severing nerve fibers connecting the frontal lobes to the rest of the brain.	Observation that the same surgical procedure with chimpanzees led to a reduction in the display of negative emotion during stress.

Note: Lack of critical evaluation of these procedures is reflected in the unusual notoriety bestowed upon their inventors. Julius Wagner-Jauregg, an Austrian psychiatrist, was awarded a Nobel Prize in 1927 for his work in developing fever therapy. Egaz Moniz, a Portugese psychiatrist, was awarded a Nobel Prize in 1946 for introduction of the lobotomy.

RESEARCH METHODS

The Null Hypothesis and the Burden of Proof

Scientists have established a basic and extremely important rule for making and testing any new hypothesis: The scientist who makes a new prediction must prove it to be true. Scientists are not obligated to disprove other researchers' assertions. Until a hypothesis is supported by empirical evidence, the community of scientists assumes that the new prediction is false.

The concepts of the experimental hypothesis and the null hypothesis are central to understanding this essential rule of science. An **experimental hypothesis** is any new prediction made by an investigator. Researchers must adopt and state their exper-

imental hypothesis in both correlational studies and experiments (see Research Methods in Chapters 2 and 3). In all scientific research, the **null hypothesis** is the alternative to the experimental hypothesis. The null hypothesis always predicts that the experimental hypothesis is not true. The rules of science dictate that scientists must assume that the null hypothesis holds until research contradicts it. That is, the burden of proof falls on the scientist who makes a new prediction—who offers an experimental hypothesis.

These rules of science are analogous to rules about the burden of proof that have been adopted in trial courts. In U.S. courtrooms, the law assumes that a defendant is innocent until proven guilty. Defendants do not need to prove their innocence; rather, prosecutors need to prove the defendants' guilt. Thus the null hypothesis is analogous to the assumption of innocence, and the burden of proof in science falls on any scientist who challenges the null hypothesis, just as it falls on the prosecutor in a court trial.

These rules in science and in law serve important purposes. Both are conservative principles designed to protect the field from false assertions. Our legal philosophy is that "it is better to let ten guilty people go free than to punish one innocent person." Scientists adopt a similar philosophy—that false "scientific evidence" is more dangerous than undetected knowledge. Because of these safeguards, we can be reasonably confident when an experimental hypothesis is supported or when a defendant is found guilty.

We can easily apply these concepts and rules to claims that were made for the effectiveness of treatment methods such as lobotomy. In this example, the experimental hypothesis is that severing the nerve fibers that connect the frontal lobes to other areas of the brain will result in a significant decrease in psychotic symptoms. The null hypothesis is that this treatment is not any more effective than having no treatment at all. According to the rules of science, a clinician who claims to have discovered a new treatment must prove that it is true. Scientists are not obligated to prove that the assertion is false, because *the null hypothesis holds until it is rejected.*

The value of this conservative approach is obvious when we consider the needless suffering and permanent, neurological dysfunction that was ultimately inflicted upon thousands of patients who were given lobotomies or subjected to fevers and comas during the 1940s (Valenstein, 1986). Similar conclusions can be drawn about less invasive procedures, such as institutionalization, medication, and psychotherapy. These treatments are also associated with costs, which range from financial considerations, which are certainly important in today's health care environment, to the disappointment brought about by false hopes. In all these cases, clinicians who provide mental health services should be required to demonstrate scientifically that their treatment procedures are effective (Dawes, 1994; Wilson, 1995).

There is one more similarity between the rules of science and the rules of the courtroom. Courtroom verdicts do not lead to a judgment that the defendant is "innocent," but only to a decision that she or he is "not guilty." In theory, the possibility remains that a defendant who is found "not guilty" did indeed commit a crime. Similarly, scientific research does not lead to the conclusion that the null hypothesis is true. Scientists never prove the null hypothesis; they only fail to reject it. The reason for this position is that the philosophy of knowledge, *epistemology,* tells us that it is impossible ever to prove that an experimental hypothesis is false in every circumstance. ∎

We close this section of our introductory chapter with one final note about history. A brief discussion of historical material is included in each chapter of this book. Our knowledge of mental disorders—ways in which they are classified, our ideas about their etiology, and the procedures that are used to treat people with abnormal behavior—is still in a state of flux. In order to understand the process that is currently unfolding, you will have to know something about where we have been in the recent past. Therefore, before talking about current etiological hypotheses, we will explain briefly the ways in which clinicians viewed these problems in the past. Our discussion of contemporary treatment will be based on a brief overview of prior methods. And our description of the current classification system for various disorders will begin with a brief consideration of earlier definitions.

The Mental Health Professions

Many forms of training prepare people to provide professional assistance to those who suffer from mental disorders. The two professional groups that are mentioned in the cases in this chapter are psychiatrists and clinical psychologists.

Psychiatry is the branch of medicine that is concerned with the study and treatment of mental disorders. Psychiatrists complete the normal sequence of coursework and internship training in a medical school (usually 4 years) before going on to receive specialized residency training (another 4 years) that is focused on abnormal behavior. By virtue of their medical training, psychiatrists are licensed to practice medicine and therefore are able to prescribe medication. Most psychiatrists are also trained in the use of psychosocial intervention.

Clinical psychology is concerned with the application of psychological science to the assessment and treatment of mental disorders (APA, 1991). A clinical psychologist typically completes 5 years of graduate study in a department of psychology, as well as a 1-year internship, before receiving a doctoral degree. Clinical psychologists are trained in the use of psychological assessment procedures and in the use of psychotherapy.

Within clinical psychology, there are two primary types of clinical training programs. One course of study, which leads to the Ph.D. degree (doctor of philosophy), involves a traditional sequence of graduate training with a serious emphasis on research methods. The other approach, which culminates in a Psy.D. degree (doctor of psychology), places greater emphasis on practical skills of assessment and treatment and does not require an independent research project for the dissertation.

Social work is a third major profession that is concerned with helping people achieve an effective level of psychosocial functioning (Hopps & Pinderhughes, 1987). Most practicing social workers have a master's degree in social work. In contrast to psychology and psychiatry, social work is based less on a body of scientific knowledge than on a commitment to action. The practice of social work encompasses a wide range of settings, from courts and prisons to schools and hospitals, as well as other social service agencies. The emphasis tends to be on social and cultural factors, such as the effects of poverty on the availability of educational and health services, rather than individual differences in personality or psychopathology. Psychiatric social workers receive training that is specialized in treatment of mental health problems.

A profession is largely defined in terms of what its members do. In that sense, the mental health professions are similar to one another, and it is not surprising that they are often confused by the public. Clinical psychologists, psychiatrists, and social workers can all be trained

to conduct psychotherapy. Some members of all three professions are actively involved in research; others become administrators in hospitals and clinics. All are licensed in their own specialties by state boards of examiners. Table 1–4 gives estimated numbers of mental health professionals currently practicing in the United States.

▲ **Clinical psychologists perform many roles. Some provide direct clinical services. Many are involved in research, teaching, and various administrative activities.**

The distinctions among clinical psychology, psychiatry, and social work have developed gradually over the past 100 years, and it is likely that they will continue to do so in the future. Boundaries between professions change as a function of technological advancement (such as the discovery of antipsychotic drugs), economic pressures (such as decisions by insurance companies regarding which procedures and professions will be reimbursed), legislative action, and courtroom decisions. This has been particularly true in the field of mental health, where enormous changes have taken place over the past few decades (Reisman, 1991). Two landmark court decisions in the early 1970s, *Blue Shield of Virginia v. McCready* and *Wyatt v. Stickney*, held that licensed clinical psychologists and social workers should be able to treat patients without

TABLE 1–4	
Estimated Number of Professionals Providing Mental Health Services in the United States, 1996	
Profession	**Number**
Specialty Providers	
Psychiatrists	33,200
Psychologists	42,000
Social workers	45,000
Other Providers	
Family therapists	28,000
Psychiatric nurses	3,000
Primary care physicians	116,600

Source: K. I. Howard, T. A. Cornille, J. S. Lyons, J. T. Vessey, R. J. Lueger, and S. M. Saunders, 1996, Patterns of mental health service utilization, *Archives of General Psychiatry, 53,* 696–703.

the supervision of a psychiatrist. Perhaps most importantly, they ruled that these professionals were entitled to receive payments for their services from insurance companies. This ruling essentially established the legal right of patients to freedom of choice in selecting their own practitioners.

At present, many clinical psychologists are pursuing the right to prescribe medication (DeLeon, Sammons, & Sexton, 1995; cf. Klein, 1995). Decisions regarding this issue and related questions will have a dramatic impact on the boundaries that separate the mental health professions. The ongoing conflict over the containment of health care costs suggests that debates over the rights and privileges of patients and their therapists will intensify in the coming years. Therefore it is difficult to say with certainty what the mental health professions will be like in the future.

Goals of This Book

The terms and concepts introduced in this chapter provide a springboard to more detailed discussions of mental disorders. Most of the issues that we have raised are unresolved; many continue to be the focal points of heated controversies that will be considered later in this book. Before we leave this chapter, we want to highlight some additional questions that might be raised with regard to the cases that we have described.

The process of studying a mental disorder inevitably leads to careful consideration of the signs and symptoms by which it is defined. Were any of the symptoms that Kevin exhibited more useful than others in establishing his diagnosis? Definitions of all mental disorders are still being debated. Most clinical psychologists and psychiatrists agree that schizophrenia is a meaningful syndrome, but not everyone agrees on the most useful definition of the disorder. Delusions and disorganized speech are included in almost all definitions of schizophrenia. There has been disagreement, however, regarding symptoms such as diminished emotional responsiveness and lack of insight. The boundaries of specific mental disorders have not been firmly established.

A syndrome such as schizophrenia must be evaluated using scientific evidence. Does the syndrome have any systematic meaning or importance? Does one diagnosis call for a different type of treatment than another diagnosis? Is it more useful for Kevin's psychiatrist to think in terms of treating the cluster of symptoms rather than treating each symptom separately? These are extremely important and difficult questions. Research in the field of abnormal behavior is concerned with providing answers.

This book will provide you with an introduction to the study of psychopathology, viewed from the perspective of psychological science. The application of science to questions regarding abnormal behavior carries with it the implicit assumption that these problems can be studied objectively. We believe that order can be found in the frequently chaotic and puzzling world of mental disorders. This order will eventually allow us to understand the processes by which abnormal behaviors are created and maintained.

Clinical scientists adopt an attitude of open-minded skepticism, tempered by an appreciation for the research methods that are used to collect empirical data. They formulate specific hypotheses, test them, and then refine them based on the results of these tests. This book is, for the most part, an attempt to explain that process. In order to get the most from it, you may have to set aside—at least temporarily—personal beliefs that you have already acquired about mental disorders. Try to adopt an objective, skeptical attitude. We hope to pique your curiosity and share with you the satisfaction, as well as perhaps some of the frustration, of searching for answers to questions about complex behavior problems.

This book has several goals that focus on developing your familiarity with specialized topics within the field of abnormal psychology. The most important are highlighted with headings and features that are consistent from chapter to chapter. We list these goals here:

1. To describe the experiences of a number of individuals who suffer from various types of psychopathology (case studies)

2. To specify more objectively the clinical problems that are associated with mental disorders (typical symptoms)

3. To explain the system that is used to classify these disorders, emphasizing how it has evolved and the criteria by which it is evaluated (classification)

4. To outline current knowledge regarding the frequency and distribution of these problems (epidemiology)

5. To highlight contemporary hypotheses regarding the causes of abnormal behaviors, focusing in particular on complementary relations among psychological, biological, and environmental systems (etiology)

6. To provide selected examples of ways in which clinical scientists collect data to test these hypotheses (research close-ups)

7. To discuss psychological and biological interventions that are used to help people who experience various types of mental disorder (treatment)

We will consider these topics as they apply to each of the major categories of mental disorder. Each chapter will include a summary of current knowledge regarding psychopathology. Keep in mind, however, the preliminary nature of our knowledge. Very little is actually known about the etiology of these problems. Therefore we believe that it is more important for you to understand the principles that guide our ongoing search for knowledge than to digest whatever information is currently available.

The importance of the search for new information has inspired us to build a special feature into this textbook. Each chapter includes a Research Methods feature that explains one particular issue in some detail. The Research Methods feature in this chapter, for example, is concerned with the null hypothesis and the burden of proof. A list of the issues addressed in Research Methods throughout this textbook appears in Table 1–5. They are arranged to progress from some of the more basic issues, such as correlational and experimental designs, toward more complex issues, such as genetic linkage analysis and heritability.

We decided to discuss methodological issues in small sections throughout the book, for two primary reasons. First, the problems raised by research methods are often complex and challenging. Some students find it difficult to digest and comprehend an entire chapter on research methods in one chunk, especially at the beginning of a book. Thus we have broken it down into more manageable bites. Second, and perhaps more important, the problems involved in designing and evaluating research studies are best understood in the context of a particular practical problem. You have to know *what* is being studied before you can become truly interested in *how* it is being studied. Our discussions of research methods are, therefore, introduced while we are explaining contemporary views of particular clinical problems.

Methodological issues are very important. The fact that someone has managed to collect and present data on a particular topic does not mean that the data are useful. We want you to learn about the problems of designing and interpreting research studies so that you will become a more critical consumer of scientific evidence. If you do not have a background in research design or quantitative methods, the Research Methods features will familiarize you with the procedures that psychologists use to test their hypotheses. If you have already had an introductory course in methodology, they will show you how these problems are handled in research on abnormal behavior.

TABLE 1-5

List of Research Methods Features in This Book

Chapter	Topic
1	The Null Hypothesis and the Burden of Proof
2	The Correlational Study
3	The Experiment
4	Diagnostic Reliability
5	Analogue Studies of Psychopathology
6	Statistical Significance and Clinical Importance
7	Retrospective Reports
8	Longitudinal Research Designs
9	Cross-Cultural Comparisons
10	Credible Placebo Control Groups
11	Risk, Risk Factors, and Studies of People at Risk
12	Hypothetical Constructs and Construct Validity
13	Meaningful Comparison Groups
14	Genetic Linkage Analysis
15	Central Tendency, Variability, and Standard Scores
16	Samples and Sampling
17	The Concept of Heritability
18	Base Rates and Predictions

Summary

One of our goals in this chapter is to make you more familiar with certain symptoms of **psychopathology.** We have described two relatively common forms of mental disorder: schizophrenia and bulimia nervosa. Schizophrenia is a form of **psychosis.** The symptoms of this disorder include **delusions** and disorganized speech. Bulimia nervosa is an eating disorder that involves recurrent episodes in which the person cannot control what (or how much) he or she eats. These episodes of binge eating are followed by efforts to prevent weight gain, such as self-induced vomiting. These and many other types of mental disorder are described in greater detail in the subsequent chapters of this book.

KEY TERMS

- abnormal psychology
- biopsychosocial model
- case study
- categorical approach
- clinical psychology
- delusion
- dimensional approach
- epidemiology
- etiology
- experimental hypothesis
- harmful dysfunction
- incidence
- nature–nurture controversy
- null hypothesis
- prevalence
- psychiatry
- psychology
- psychopathology
- psychosis
- scientist-practitioner model
- social work
- syndrome
- threshold model

Mental disorders are defined in terms of typical signs and symptoms rather than identifiable causal factors. A group of symptoms that appear together and are assumed to represent a specific type of disorder is called a **syndrome.** There are no definitive psychological or biological tests that can be used to confirm the presence of psychopathology. At present, the diagnosis of mental disorders depends on observations of the person's behavior and descriptions of personal experience.

No one has been able to provide a universally accepted definition of abnormal behavior. Statistical infrequency and subjective distress cannot be used for this purpose because not all infrequent behaviors are pathological and because some people who exhibit abnormal behaviors do not have insight into their conditions. One useful approach defines mental disorders in terms of **harmful dysfunction.** The official classification system, DSM-IV, defines mental disorders as a group of persistent maladaptive behaviors that result in personal distress or impaired functioning.

Various forms of voluntary social deviance and efforts to express individuality are excluded from the DSM-IV definition of mental disorders. Political and religious actions, and the beliefs on which they are based, are not considered to be forms of abnormal behavior, even when they seem unusual to many other people. We must recognize, however, that the process of defining psychopathology is still influenced by cultural and political values. The categories described in DSM-IV have been appropriately subjected to public debate and criticism.

The boundaries of mental disorders are often difficult to define. They can be classified using either **dimensional** or **categorical** concepts. A **threshold model** incorporates elements of both approaches. DSM-IV has adopted a categorical approach to classification, but we do not have enough information to determine which is the more appropriate.

The scientific study of the frequency and distribution of disorders within a population is known as **epidemiology.** Some severe forms of abnormal behavior, such as schizophrenia, have been observed in virtually every society that has been studied by social scientists. There are also forms of psychopathology—including eating disorders—for which substantial cross-cultural differences have been found. These epidemiological patterns may provide important clues that will help identify factors that influence the etiology of mental disorders.

Some of the best information that is currently available on the epidemiology of mental disorders in the United States was collected in the Epidemiologic Catchment Area (ECA) study. According to this study, the 12-month **prevalence** rate for at least one form of mental disorder was 20 percent. Lifetime prevalence was higher, with 32 percent of adults reporting at least one mental disorder at some point in their lives. The ECA study found significant gender differences for several types of mental disorder, including anxiety disorders, mood disorders, and alcoholism.

Abnormal psychology represents the application of psychological science—its concepts and research tools—to the study of mental disorders. Various forms of professional training prepare people to work with those who suffer from mental disorders. These professions include **clinical psychology, psychiatry,** and **social work.** People who study and treat mental disorders are best trained as scientist-practitioners. We want to introduce you to both sides of this process: learning more about the phenomenology of the disorders as well as the methodologies that are used to study them.

The **etiology** of mental disorders is not well understood. It is undoubtedly the product of an interaction among biological, psychological, and social factors. These are complementary systems. The interactive nature of these systems can be described as a **biopsychosocial model** of psychopathology. The resolution of the **nature–nurture controversy** hinges on the recognition that the artificial distinction between biological causes and environmental causes is not helpful in our search for knowledge about mental disorders.

Several types of psychopharmacology and psychotherapy have been shown to be effective in the treatment of mental disorders. Many important hypotheses about the origins of mental disorders have been derived from efforts to treat these conditions. These hypotheses must then be tested in the context of carefully planned research programs. An individual **case study** does not provide definitive evidence for or against any hypothesis.

Critical Thinking

1. What does it mean for a behavior to be classified as "abnormal"? Why is it so difficult to produce an abstract definition of abnormal behavior? Some people argue that psychopathology is nothing more than the list of disorders presented in the *Diagnostic and Statistical Manual.* Do you agree? Can you provide a better definition?

2. Do you think it is possible to eliminate social values from a definition of abnormal behavior? How would you accomplish this goal? Is there any way of defining mental disorders that would avoid value judgments about which behaviors are adaptive and which are not?

3. Case studies provide interesting descriptions of problems, but they don't help us choose among etiological theories. What kinds of limitations do you see with case studies? Why should we be careful about drawing general conclusions from them?

4. Why is it useful for clinical psychologists to be experts in understanding and conducting research? Does the scientist-practitioner model have any advantages for the training of clinical psychologists?

2

Causes of Abnormal Behavior: From Paradigms to Systems

You have probably heard or read a great deal of conflicting information about the causes of abnormal behavior. Magazine articles explain that depression is caused by a chemical imbalance in the brain, a problem that can be corrected with medication. Television advertisements tell us that alcoholism is a genetic disease that is best treated in a hospital. Books and films often portray emotional disturbances as going back to traumatic childhood experiences that are relived in psychotherapy. Many manuals on parenting tell us that mothers and fathers cause psychological problems when they love their children too little—or too much. Finally, television shows and newspaper headlines blame violence in our cities on everything from the breakdown of families to the breakdown of schools to the breakdown of society.

Overview

Like the popular media, scientists also may offer different—and often conflicting—explanations concerning the causes or *etiology* of psychopathology. Conflicting scientific explanations sometimes confuse the public, but such disagreements may actually be of benefit to science. Scientists pit theories against one another in a competition of research, and the "winner" is the most accurate explanation of psychopathology.

We favor the competition of theories in scientific enterprises. The rivalry encourages skepticism and challenges theorists to test their hypotheses. Unfortunately, the broad theories that have been proposed to explain psychopathology have many problems. One difficulty is that the traditional biological, psychoanalytic, behavioral, and humanistic approaches are more than alternative theories. They also are alternative *paradigms*. In other words, they conflict not only in their theories of abnormal behavior but also in what they view as acceptable scientific methods, as we discuss shortly.

The more substantial problem, however, is that most forms of psychopathology do not have a single cause or set of causes. Rather, abnormal behavior appears to be determined by **multifactorial causes,** the combination of a variety of different biological, psychological, and social factors. Thus, for example, the persistent

nature–nurture debate is wrong in suggesting that psychopathology is caused either solely by nature or solely by nurture. In fact, abnormal behavior is caused by nature *and* nurture. Similarly, early childhood experience *and* current life events are important to abnormal behavior, as are individual personality characteristics *and* conflict in close relationships, or inner psychological turmoil *and* societal expectations about gender or ethnicity.

The challenge for science, therefore, is not to identify a single theory that explains the causes of all forms of abnormal behavior. Rather, the challenge is to integrate evidence on the etiologies of different disorders into a coherent whole, a system of contributing factors (Rutter & Rutter, 1993). In this chapter—and throughout the text—we adopt such a systems approach to understanding the etiology of psychopathology. Rather than arguing for or against one theoretical perspective, the systems approach integrates evidence across and among different biological, psychological, and social domains of behavior. Thus the systems approach often is referred to as a *biopsychosocial* perspective. Biological contributions to abnormal behavior range from specific biochemical processes in the brain to broad genetic liabilities passed across generations. Psychological contributions range from unconscious cognitive processes to reinforcement for abnormal behavior. Social and cultural contributions range from conflict in relationships with family members to the broad influences of television and other popular media.

In adopting an integrative systems approach, we must be clear about three issues. First, we do not mean to imply that all theories of the etiology of abnormal behavior are equally valid. Unlike the Dodo bird from *Alice in Wonderland*, we are *not* arguing that "everyone has won, and all must have prizes" (Luborsky, Singer, & Luborsky, 1975). The systems approach highlights biopsychosocial contributions to psychopathology, but clear hypotheses still must be supported by empirical evidence. Second, we recognize that different types of abnormal behavior have very different causes, just as different physical diseases are caused by various underlying conditions. In fact, two people may have the same disorder for very different reasons. Third, we must acknowledge that scientists currently do not know what causes most forms of abnormal behavior. Scientific evidence provides insight into the origins of various psychological disorders, but you should be suspicious of people who claim to know the cause of psychopathology—they are almost certainly wrong.

In this chapter we explain the systems approach as a general method for understanding abnormal behavior. We also introduce a number of biological, psychological, and social concepts relevant to the etiology of psychopathology. In later chapters we return to these basic concepts when critically reviewing evidence on the multifactorial contributions to the etiology of particular psychological disorders.

Each chapter in this text includes a case study. The case study illustrates key topics from the practitioner side of the scientist-practitioner model. Most cases, including the following one, come from our own therapy files.

CASE STUDY

Possible Causes of Behavioral Problems

At the age of 14, Meghan B. attempted to end her life by taking approximately 20 Tylenol capsules. Meghan took the pills after an explosive fight with her mother over Meghan's grades and over a boy she was dating. Meghan was in her room when she impulsively took the pills, but shortly afterward she told her mother what she had done. Her parents rushed Meghan to the emergency room, where her vital signs were closely monitored. As the crisis was coming to an end, Meghan's parents agreed that she should be hospitalized to make sure that she was safe and to begin to treat her problems.

Meghan talked freely about many of her problems during the 30 days she spent on the adolescent unit of a private psychiatric hospital. Most of her complaints focused on her mother. Meghan insisted that her mother was always "in her face," telling her what to do and when and how to do it. Her father was "great," but he was too busy with his job as a chemical engineer to spend much time with her.

Meghan also said she had long-standing problems in school. She barely maintained a C average despite considerable efforts to do better. Meghan said she didn't care about school, and her mother's insistence that she could do much better was a major source of conflict between them. Meghan also complained that she had few friends, either in school or outside of school. She described her classmates as "preppy" and "straight," and said she had no interest in them. Meghan was obviously angry as she described her family, school, and friends, but she also showed sadness on a few occasions. She denounced herself as being "stupid" one time, and she cried about being a "reject" when discussing why no friends, including her boyfriend, contacted her while she was in the hospital.

Mrs. B. provided details on the history of Meghan's problems. When Meghan was 2 years old, she had been adopted by Mr. and Mrs. B., who could not have children of their own. According to the adoption agency, Meghan's birth mother was 16 years old when she had the baby. Meghan's biological mother was a drug user, and she haphazardly left the baby in the care of friends and relatives for weeks at a time. Little was known about Meghan's biological father except that he had had some trouble with the law, and Meghan's mother had known him only briefly. When Meghan was 14 months old, her pediatrician reported her mother to a child abuse agency after noting bruises on Meghan's thighs and hips. After a 6-month legal investigation, Meghan's mother decided to give her up for adoption. Meghan came to live with Mr. and Mrs. B. shortly thereafter.

Mrs. B. was eager to give Meghan all the love they both had missed in their lives to that point, and she happily doted on her daughter. Mr. B. also was very loving with Meghan, although Mrs. B., like Meghan, noted that he was rarely at home. Everything seemed fine with Meghan until first grade, when teachers began to complain about her. She disrupted the classroom with her restlessness, and she did not complete her schoolwork. In second grade, Meghan was diagnosed by a school psychologist as a "hyperactive" child who also had a learning disability, and her pediatrician recommended medication as a treatment. Mrs. B. was horrified by the thought of medication or of sending Meghan to a "resource room" for part of the school day. Instead, she decided to redouble her efforts at parenting.

According to Mrs. B., she and Meghan succeeded in getting Meghan through elementary school in reasonably good shape. Meghan's grades and classroom behavior remained acceptable as long as Mrs. B. consulted repeatedly with the school. Mrs. B. noted with bitterness, however, that the one problem that she could not solve was Meghan's relationships with other girls. The daughters of Mrs. B.'s friends and neighbors were well behaved and were excellent students. Meghan did not fit in with them. They were polite when they saw her, but Meghan never got invited to play with the other girls.

Mrs. B. was obviously sad when discussing Meghan's past, but she became agitated and angry when discussing the present. She was very concerned about Meghan, but she wondered out loud if the suicide attempt had been manipulative. Mrs. B. said that she had had major conflicts with Meghan ever since Meghan started middle school at the age of 12. Meghan would no longer work regularly with her mother on her homework for the usual 2 hours each night. In addition, her mother said that Meghan fought with her about everything from picking up her room to her boyfriend, an 18-year-old whom Mrs. B. abhorred. Mrs. B. complained that she did not understand what had happened to her daughter. She clearly stated, however, that whatever it was, she would fix it. ■

What was causing Meghan's problems? Her case study suggests many plausible alternatives. Some of her troubles seem to be a reaction to a mother whose attentiveness at age 8 seems more like intrusiveness at age 14. Maybe Mrs. B. became more concerned with her own needs for love than with Meghan's changing needs for parenting. Meghan's problems seem bigger than this, however. We could trace some of her troubles to anger over her failures in school or to rejection by her peers. We also can speculate about the effects of Meghan's early childhood experiences. Surely she was affected adversely by the physical abuse, inconsistent love, and chaotic living arrangements during the first, critical years of her life. Finally, we can wonder about possible biological contributions to Meghan's problems. Did Meghan's mother take drugs during pregnancy that affected the developing baby? Was Meghan a healthy, full-term newborn? Given her biological parents' history of troubled behavior, could Meghan's problems be caused by genetic factors?

These searching questions defy a ready answer. Abnormal psychology does not now have objective tools for pinpointing the specific cause of most types of abnormal behavior. Still, psychological theory and research does offer some good leads about etiology. We introduce current psychological approaches to understanding the causes of psychopathology by first considering them in historical perspective.

Brief Historical Perspective on Approaches to Etiology

As we saw in Chapter 1, the search for explanations of the causes of abnormal behavior dates to ancient times. Unfortunately, many of the traditions begun by Hippocrates died away after the fall of the Roman Empire. Although systematic, naturalistic accounts of mental illness were kept alive in Arab cultures (Grob, 1994), the emphasis on objectivity and careful observation faded in Europe. In fact, some scholars have concluded that, during the Middle Ages, mental illness came to be blamed on witchcraft. Historical accounts indicate that fear of witches abounded during this period, and witch hunts were conducted with fervor under the formal sanctions of the Roman Catholic Church. However, witchcraft was not the dominant explanation of mental illness. In examining records from British mental incompetency trials dating back to the thirteenth century, Neugebauer (1979) uncovered only one case where officials judged that insanity was caused by witches. Explanations in the medieval records that seem reasonable even today were much more frequent. Records directly attributed "lunacy" (a medieval synonym for mental illness) in various cases to "a blow received on the head," "a long and incurable infirmity," "her husband's death," and "fear of his father" (Neugebauer, 1979). Thus medieval notions about the causes of abnormal behavior were not as far-fetched as suggested by some accounts of demonology and witchcraft.

The rudiments of the scientific method were rediscovered during the Renaissance (approximately 1300 to 1600), but the scientific method was not applied to the study of abnormal behavior until much later. In fact, advances in the scientific understanding of the etiology of psychopathology were not made until the nineteenth and early twentieth centuries, when three major events occurred. One was the discovery of the cause of general paresis, a severe mental disorder that has a deteriorating course and eventually ends in death. The second was the writing of Sigmund Freud, a thinker who has had a profound influence not only on the field of abnormal psychology but also on Western society as a whole. The third was the creation of a new academic discipline called psychology.

General Paresis and the Biomedical Approach

The **biomedical approach** to abnormal psychology can be traced to the study of the condition we now know as *general paresis* (general paralysis). Prior to 1800, general paresis was not recognized as a distinct disorder and therefore attracted no special attention. In 1798, John Haslam distinguished general paresis from

other forms of "lunacy" based on its symptoms, which include delusions of grandeur, cognitive impairment (dementia), and progressive paralysis, all of which have an unremitting course that ends in death after many years. The diagnosis inspired a search for the cause of the new disorder. Many different etiological hypotheses were considered and evaluated, and most correctly focused on biological explanations. Still, it took more than 100 years of investigation before the search was successful.

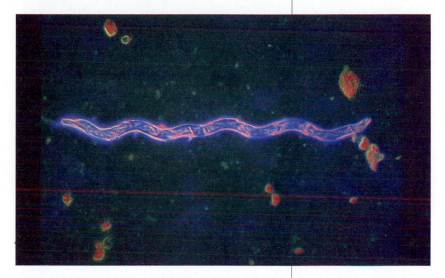

▲ A microscopic image of the spirochete that causes syphilis and eventually causes general paresis if the syphilis goes untreated.

The etiological breakthrough began with the observation that people with general paresis had contracted the sexually transmitted disease *syphilis* earlier in their lives. However, recognition of this essential correlation was not without missteps. One study conducted by Fournier in 1894, for example, concluded that only 65 percent of paretic patients reported having a history of syphilis. Thus questions were raised about whether syphilis alone caused general paresis. Research conducted in 1897 by Kraft-Ebbing demonstrated that Fournier's statistic was wrong. Kraft-Ebbing attempted to inoculate paretic patients against syphilis, but none of them became infected when exposed to a mild form of the disease. There could be only one explanation for their body's failure to respond to the inoculation: All of the patients—not 65 percent of them—had been infected with syphilis previously.

After the turn of the twentieth century, the spirochete that causes syphilis was discovered. Postmortem examination of the brains of paretic patients proved that the infection had invaded and destroyed parts of the central

▲ **Sigmund Freud (1856–1939) developed psychoanalytic theory. Freud's approach has been criticized as being unscientific, but the influence of his ideas is unquestionable.**

nervous system. In 1910, Paul Ehrlich, a German microbiologist, developed arsphenamine, an arsenic-containing chemical that destroyed the spirochete and prevented general paresis. Unfortunately, the drug worked only if the patient was treated in the early stages of infection. Later, it was learned that syphilis could be cured by a new discovery, penicillin—the first antibiotic. As a result, general paresis was virtually eliminated when antibiotics became widely available after the end of World War II.

The slow but dramatic discoveries about general paresis gave great impetus to the search for biological causes for other mental disorders. For some problems, a purely biomedical approach has been successful in establishing etiology. This is most notable for the cognitive disorders (see Chapter 14) and for many forms of mental retardation (see Chapter 15). Unfortunately, the causes of most forms of mental illness do not appear to be as straightforward as for general paresis. Like heart disease and cancer, most mental disorders appear to be "lifestyle diseases," problems that have multifactorial causes, including biological, psychological, and social contributions. These disorders may defy straightforward etiological explanations and dramatic, "magic bullet" treatments (as Ehrlich's treatment was called in a 1940 film about his discovery).

Freud and Psychoanalytic Theory

Unlike the biomedical approach, which has been influenced by many notable people, **psychoanalytic theory** owes its origins primarily to the writings of a single individual, Sigmund Freud (1856–1939). Freud introduced many influential ideas, but perhaps his most basic contribution was to provide a counterpoint to the growing biomedical approach. Although he was trained as a neurologist and remained interested in biological influences throughout his lifetime, Freud argued that early childhood experiences played a central role in the development of mental illness, even in illnesses that had physical manifestations (see Further Thoughts).

Freud was trained in Paris by Jean Charcot (1825–1893), a neurologist who successfully used hypnosis to treat what used to be called *hysteria*. One type of hysteria is characterized by the conversion of psychological conflicts into physical symptoms. It is now called *conversion disorder* (see Chapter 7). "Hysterical blindness," for example, is the inability to see. This dramatic symptom is not caused by a known organic impairment, and the afflicted individual sometimes recovers functioning after resolving an emotional problem.

FURTHER THOUGHTS

An Outline of Freudian Theory

Freud's direct influence on psychology is diminishing, but his ideas continue to have a tremendous influence on the intellectual culture of Western society. As one example of this, many of the terms he coined have become a part of everyday language. If for no other reason, Freud's influence on our culture is sufficient justification for introducing some of his basic concepts.

Freud divided the mind into three parts: the id, the ego, and the superego. He suggested that the **id** is present at birth and is the source of basic drives and motivations. The id houses biological drives, such as hunger, as well as two key psychological drives: sex and aggression. (Freud's term *libido* can

be viewed as a synonym for sexual or life energy.) In Freudian theory, the id operates according to the *pleasure principle*—the impulses of the id seek immediate gratification and create discomfort or unrest until they are satisfied. Thus, in Freud's view, sexual or aggressive urges are akin to biological urges, like hunger.

The **ego** is the part of the personality that must deal with the realities of the world as it attempts to fulfill id impulses as well as perform other functions. Thus the ego operates on the *reality principle*. The ego begins to develop in the first year of life, and it continues to evolve, particularly during the preschool years. Unlike id impulses, which are primarily unconscious, much of the ego resides in conscious awareness.

The third part of the personality is the **superego,** which is roughly equivalent to the *conscience.* The superego contains societal standards of behavior, particularly rules that children learn from trying to be like their parents in their later preschool years. In Freud's view, societal rules are attempts to govern id impulses. For the individual, this means that the three parts of the personality are often in conflict with one another. The ego must constantly mediate between the demands of the id and the prescriptions of the superego. According to Freud, conflict between the superego and the ego produces *moral anxiety,* whereas conflict between the id and the ego produces *neurotic anxiety.*

Freud suggested that the ego protects itself by utilizing various **defense mechanisms,** unconscious processes that reduce conscious anxiety by distorting anxiety-producing memories, emotions, and impulses. For example, the defense of *projection* turns the tables psychologically. When you use projection, you project your own feelings on to someone else: "I'm not mad at you. You're mad at me!" According to Freud, projection and other defense mechanisms protect the ego from the conflict and anxiety produced by unacceptable id impulses. A list of some of the more important and familiar defenses can be found in Table 2–1. One index of Freud's continuing influence is the fact that all these defense mechanisms, and several additional ones, appear in an appendix in DSM-IV on issues requiring further study.

Freud also formulated a stage theory of child development, as we discuss briefly toward the end of this chapter (see Table 2–4). Freud highlighted sexual conflicts in his theory of *psychosexual development.* The most important psychosexual conflict is the **Oedipal conflict.** Freud reasoned that boys harbor forbidden sexual desires for their mothers. Because these impulses are both overwhelming and impossible to fulfill, boys typically resolve the dilemma between the ages of 4 and 6 by *identifying* with their fathers. In a sense, they fulfill their desire for their mother by adopting the actions and values of her spouse. In Freud's view, girls face a similar dilemma that he termed the **Electra complex.** Freud hypothesized that girls, unlike boys, do not desire their opposite-gender parent sexually as much as they yearn for something their fathers have and they are "missing"—a penis. This is the Freudian notion of "penis envy," which has been roundly criticized for being blatantly sexist.

It is not difficult to criticize other Freudian concepts as well. Many of these criticisms call the theory to task for being too vague, broad, and untestable. We certainly agree with these objections. We also recognize, however, that Freud offered a host of innovative and sometimes penetrating ideas. Some followers of psychoanalytic theory insist on interpreting Freud literally. We believe, however, that Freud would have criticized a literal interpretation of his theories, since he revised them often during the course of his life. In this spirit, we prefer to view Freud's ideas as broad metaphors. Freudian theory has few answers, but it offers many challenging concepts, some of which are worthy of attempts at careful definition and research. ■

Patients neither fake conversion symptoms, nor do they consciously associate them with emotional distress. Thus it would seem that psychological conflicts are somehow "converted" into physical symptoms outside conscious awareness. The peculiar problem of hysteria led Freud to emphasize the importance of **the unconscious** in the etiology of emotional disorders. Freud argued that many memories, motivations, and protective psychological processes reside in the unconscious mind, which explains how problems like hysteria might be produced outside conscious awareness.

Freud was derided by many of his contemporaries who favored biological explanations of abnormal behavior, but he proved to have an immense influence on psychiatry and psychology. He can be credited with calling attention to unconscious processes, formulating a stage theory of child development, creating the metaphorical division of the personality into the id, ego, and superego, and identifying numerous intrapsychic defenses (see Further Thoughts). However, Freud built his elaborate theory of the development of normal and abnormal behavior on introspection about himself and his past, as well as on several key case histories. His failure to offer more specific hypotheses—and to test them empirically—has been the source of many legitimate criticisms of Freudian theory, as we discuss at various points throughout the text.

TABLE 2–1

Examples of Some Common Defense Mechanisms

Denial	Insistence that an experience, memory, or internal need did not occur or does not exist. For example, you completely block a painful experience from memory as if it never occurred.
Displacement	Feelings or actions are transferred from one person or object to another that is less threatening. For example, you kick your dog when you are upset with your boss.
Projection	Attributing one's own feelings or thoughts to other people. For example, a husband argues that his wife is angry at him when, in fact, he is angry at her.
Rationalization	Intellectually justifying a feeling or especially a disappointment. For example, after not getting the offer, you decide that a job you applied for was not the one you really wanted.
Reaction formation	Converting a painful or unacceptable feeling into its opposite. For example, you "hate" a former lover, but underneath it all you still really love that person.
Repression	Suppressing threatening material from consciousness, although you do not deny the memory when reminded of it. For example, you "forget" about an embarrassing experience.
Sublimation	Diverting id impulses into constructive and acceptable outlets. For example, you study hard to get good grades rather than giving in to desires for immediate pleasure.

Experimental Psychology and Behaviorism

The nineteenth century witnessed another critical development in approaches to understanding abnormal behavior: the beginning of the science of psychology, in 1879, at the University of Leipzig in the laboratory of Wilhelm Wundt (1842–1920). Wundt's ambitious goal was to understand the nature of human consciousness. He attempted to achieve this end by using a technique called *introspection*, in which his subjects reported systematically and in detail about their inner experiences. Wundt's introspective method proved to be inadequate, and he failed in his attempt to detail the components of human consciousness. Still, Wundt made a profound and lasting contribution by scientifically studying psychological phenomena.

▲ Psychologist B. F. Skinner (1904–1990) outlined the principles of operant conditioning. Skinner's determination to make psychology a science profoundly influenced the discipline in the twentieth century.

The development of a scientific understanding of learning was a central goal for Wundt and other early psychologists. The two most prominent contributors to early learning theory and research were the Russian physiologist Ivan Pavlov (1849–1936) and the U.S. psychologist B. F. Skinner (1904–1990). These psychological scientists articulated, respectively, the principles of classical conditioning and operant conditioning—concepts that continue to be central to contemporary learning theory.

In his famous experiments, Pavlov (1928) rang a bell every time he fed meat powder to dogs. After repeated trials, the salivation that was produced by the sight of food came to be elicited by the sound of the bell alone. Pavlov developed his theory of **classical conditioning** based on these and related experiments. He defined an **unconditioned stimulus** (the meat powder) as a stimulus that automatically produces a reaction, that is, an **unconditioned response** (salivation). A **conditioned stimulus** (the bell) is a neutral stimulus that, when repeatedly paired with an unconditioned stimulus, comes to produce a **conditioned response** (salivation).[†] Finally, **extinction** occurs once a conditioned stimulus no longer is presented together with an unconditioned stimulus. Eventually, the conditioned stimulus no longer elicits the conditioned response.

Skinner's (1953) principle of **operant conditioning** asserts that behavior is a function of its consequences. Specifically, behavior increases if it is rewarded, and it decreases if it is punished. In his numerous studies of rats and pigeons in the famous "Skinner box," Skinner identified four different, crucial consequences of behavior. **Positive reinforcement** occurs when the onset of a stimulus increases the frequency of behavior (for example, you get paid for your work). **Negative reinforcement** occurs when the cessation of a stimulus increases the frequency of behavior (when you give in to a nagging friend, thereby stopping the nagging). **Punishment** occurs when the introduction of a stimulus decreases the frequency of behavior (you spend less money after your parents scold you), and **response cost** is when the removal of a stimulus decreases the frequency of behavior (you no longer stay out late after your

---

[†] Note that the unconditioned response and the conditioned response are very similar (both involve salivation in this example). One difference, though, is that conditioned responses generally are somewhat weaker than unconditioned responses.

parents take away use of the car).[†] *Extinction* results from ending the contingency or association between a behavior and its consequences, similar to the concept of extinction in classical conditioning.

The person most responsible for applying learning theory to the study of abnormal behavior was the U.S. psychologist John B. Watson (1878–1958). Watson wanted to promote psychology as a science, and he founded the approach called **behaviorism,** arguing that observable behavior was the only appropriate subject matter for the science of psychology. Watson believed that thoughts and emotions could not be measured objectively; thus he rejected the study of these "internal events." In contrast to Freud, Watson did not offer an elaborate theory of the etiology of abnormal behavior. He did make the very important assumption that abnormal behavior was learned in much the same manner as normal behavior. In his well-known experiment with Little Albert, Watson and Rosalie Rayner (1920) used classical conditioning to induce the fear of a rat in an 11-month-old boy. They paired the sight of the rat with a loud noise, thus demonstrating that fears could be learned through classical conditioning. Although this was his most famous experiment, Watson and his followers were less concerned with etiology—how people learn abnormal behavior—than with treatment—how people learn new, more adaptive ways of coping with their difficulties.

Free Will and Humanistic Psychology

Abraham Maslow (1908–1970), Fritz Perls (1893–1970), and Carl Rogers (1902–1987) were the major advocates of **humanistic psychology,** a fourth major approach to conceptualizing abnormal behavior that did not emerge until the middle of the twentieth century. In many respects, humanistic psychology was a reaction against biomedical, psychoanalytic, and behavioral theories of abnormal behavior. Humanistic psychologists objected to the *determinism* of these approaches—the assumption that human behavior is caused by predictable and potentially knowable internal and/or external events. To humanistic psychologists, the very essence of humanity is *free will*, the idea that human behavior is *not* determined but is a product of how people choose to act. Humanistic psychology also is distinguished by its explicitly positive view of human behavior. Human nature is assumed to be inherently good, and humanistic psychologists, therefore, blame dysfunctional, abnormal, or aggressive behavior on society instead of on the individual. (See Table 2–2, where the assumptions of the four major approaches are compared.)

The assumption of free will makes it impossible to conduct research on the causes of normal or abnormal behavior, because free will, by definition, is not predictably determined. For this reason, humanistic psychology perhaps

---

[†] People frequently use the terms *negative reinforcement* and *punishment* interchangeably, but the two are quite different. With negative reinforcement, behavior becomes more frequent after an aversive stimulus is removed. With punishment, behavior becomes less frequent after an aversive stimulus is introduced.

TABLE 2-2

Some Comparisons among the Biomedical, Psychoanalytic, Behavioral, and Humanistic Paradigms

Topic	Biomedical	Psychoanalytic	Behavioral	Humanistic
Inborn human nature	Competitive, but some altruism	Aggressive, sexual	Neutral—a blank slate	Basic goodness
Cause of abnormality	Genes, neurochemistry, physical damage	Early childhood experiences	Social learning	Frustrations of society
Type of treatment	Medication, other somatic therapies	Psychodynamic therapy	Cognitive behavior therapy	Nondirective therapy
Paradigmatic focus	Bodily functions and structures	Unconscious mind	Observable behavior	Free will

is best considered an alternative philosophy of human behavior, not an alternative psychological theory. In this regard, we note that the term *humanistic* must be considered carefully. All attempts to understand the etiology of psychopathology are humanistic in the sense that the ultimate goal is to improve the human condition.

Paradigms and the Causes of Abnormal Behavior

As we have noted, the biomedical, psychoanalytic, behavioral, and humanistic approaches are more than alternative theories of abnormal behavior (see Table 2–2). They are also alternative paradigms. A **paradigm** includes both the substance of a theory and a set of assumptions about how scientists should collect data and test theoretical propositions. The term *paradigm* was applied to the progress of science by Thomas Kuhn (1962), an influential historian and philosopher who argued that paradigms can both direct and misdirect scientists. Paradigms tell the researcher or clinician where and how to look for answers to questions, but sometimes the apparent guidance can be a hindrance. The idea that a paradigm can be either enlightening or blinding can be illustrated by a brain teaser. Try to solve the following enigma, written by Lord Byron, before looking ahead for the answer:

> I'm not in earth, nor the sun,
>   nor the moon.
> You may search all the sky—
>   I'm not there.
> In the morning and evening—
>   though not at noon,
> You may plainly perceive me,
>   for like a balloon,
> I am suspended in air.
> Though disease may possess me,
>   and sickness and pain,
> I am never in sorrow nor gloom;
> Though in wit and wisdom
>   I equally reign
> I am the heart of all sin and have
>   long lived in vain;
> Yet I ne'er shall be found in the tomb.

What is this poem about? The topic of this rhyme is not the soul or ghosts. It is not life or shadows, or a dozen other possibilities that may have occurred to you. Rather, the topic is the letter i. (Suspended in air. The heart of all sin.) Why

is the puzzle so difficult to solve? Because most people approach it with the assumption that the solution lies in the *content* of the poem, not in its *form*. The misdirection of this brain teaser illustrates one of Kuhn's central points about paradigms. The assumptions made by a paradigm can act as blinders; they can lead an investigator to overlook what otherwise might be obvious. At the same time, however, sometimes paradigms open up new perspectives and avenues for research. For example, now that you have been able to adopt a new "paradigm"—to focus on the form, not the content of words—you can easily solve the following puzzle:

> The beginning of eternity, the end of
>   time and space,
> The beginning of every end, the end of
>   every place.

It is obvious that the answer is the letter e.

The four traditional paradigms of psychopathology make assumptions about the appropriate focus of abnormal psychology that, like your initial approach to the brain teaser, sometimes are too narrow. The biomedical paradigm can be criticized for overemphasizing the *medical model*, the analogy between physical and psychological illnesses, and for consistently locating emotional problems "within the skin" of the individual. Objections to the psychoanalytic paradigm highlight its unyielding focus on the unconscious, even in the face of current life difficulties. As noted, the approach also is criticized for failing to offer testable hypotheses and for relying on case histories instead of systematic research. The behavioral paradigm often is critiqued for being too literal in focusing on observable events, as well as for considering too little biological or social context specific to the development of human behavior. Finally, the humanistic approach is chided for being unscientific, for reasons we have already discussed.

We agree that each of these approaches has weaknesses—and strengths. The clash of paradigms has dominated abnormal psychology for half a century, but our concern is not to determine which approach is "right." Rather, our goal is to highlight the scientific understanding of the multifactorial causes of specific emotional disorders. In attempting to understand psychological disorders, we find promise in elements of each of the four traditional paradigms. As with the word puzzles, the trick is knowing when to use which strategy.

Systems Theory

Unlike the traditional paradigms, our approach to etiology begins with **systems theory,** an innovation in understanding and conducting science, not just psychology. The Austrian biologist and philosopher of science Ludwig von Bertalanffy (1901–1972), who taught in universities in Austria, England, Canada, and the United States, has been called the "father of systems theory" (Davidson, 1982). Systems theory, however, has multiple origins; its roots lie not only in psychology but also in engineering, computer science, biology, and philosophy. Systems theory has revolutionized scientific approaches within each of these disciplines and in other scientific fields as well (Davidson, 1982; Ford & Lerner, 1992; Gleick, 1987; Hinde, 1992; von Bertalanffy, 1968).

Holism

The central principle of systems theory is **holism,** the idea that the whole is more than the sum of its parts. This common statement can be illustrated with numerous familiar examples across many disciplines. A water molecule (H_2O) is much more than the sum of two hydrogen atoms and one oxygen atom. A human being is much more than the sum of a nervous system, an organ system, a circulatory system, and so on. Similarly, psychopathology is more than the sum of inborn temperament, early childhood experiences, and learning history. Psychopathology is more than the sum of nature and nurture.

REDUCTIONISM

We can better appreciate the importance of the principle of holism when we consider its scientific counterpoint, **reductionism.** According to reductionist views, the whole *is* the sum of its parts, and the task for scientists is to divide the world into its smallest components. To give a very general example, a reductionistic approach to understanding abnormal behavior might explain dysfunctional families in terms of disordered individuals, disordered individuals in terms of specific psychological disturbances, psychological disturbances in terms of disrupted brain functions, and disrupted brain functions in terms of specific chemical deviations. According to the principle of reductionism, ultimate explanations are found when problems are reduced to their smallest possible components.

The influence of reductionism is pervasive in everyday thinking about the causes of abnormal behavior (Cacioppo & Bernston, 1992). For example, when scientists discover that the depletion of certain chemicals in the brain accompanies depression, the public assumes that brain chemistry is *the* cause of depression. However, it is entirely possible that experiences such as a negative view of the world or living in a prejudiced society cause the changes in brain chemistry that accompany depression (see Chapter 5). That is, the "chemical imbalance in the brain" may be merely a consequence of adverse life experiences. Unfortunately, the public, and many scientists, seem to overlook this possibility, because reductionism assumes that truth comes in smaller and smaller packages.

Subsystems and Levels of Analysis

The principle of holism asserts that it is a mistake to view the smallest cause as *the* cause of something. Rather, smaller units are better conceived as *subsystems* within a larger system. The human circulatory system is an example of a subsystem of the human body, which is also made up of the skeletal, muscular, nervous, digestive, respiratory, and reproductive subsystems.

A far-out example can illustrate some implications of the concept of subsystems for reasoning about causality. Assume for a moment that three Martian scientists are sent to Earth to discover what causes those metallic vehicles to speed, sometimes recklessly and sometimes slowly, across the planet's landmass. One Martian, an ecologist by training, reports back that the vehicles (called "automobiles," the scientist discovers) move at different speeds based on the width of the black paths on which they are set, whether the paths are straight or curved, and the presence of some unexplained phenomenon known as "radar traps." A second Martian, a psychologist, disagrees. This scientist notes that the speed of automobiles is determined by the age, gender, and mood of the individual who sits inside them. Together these factors cause automobiles to move at different speeds. The third scientist, a physicist, derides the other two for their

The Biopsychosocial Model

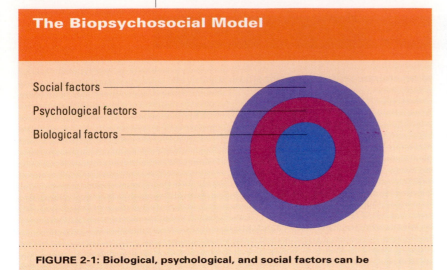

Social factors
Psychological factors
Biological factors

FIGURE 2-1: Biological, psychological, and social factors can be conceptualized as different subsystems or levels of analysis within the biopsychosocial model.

simplistic thinking. This Martian notes that the speed of automobiles is caused by a chemical process that occurs inside an antiquated machine called an internal combustion engine. The process involves oxygen, fuel, and heat and results in mechanical energy.

In this example, it is obvious that the most reductionistic, or *molecular*, explanation is no more (or less) accurate than the most general, or *molar*, one. Reductionist traditions in science often lead us to believe that the most molecular account (biological or biochemical) is the

ultimate explanation of causality (Alessi, 1992; Rachlin, 1992). The Martian example, however, demonstrates the potential fallacy of blind reductionism.

The Martian example also suggests an important way of integrating information about multiple influences on the development of psychopathology. Various subsystems can be conceptualized as different *levels of analysis* for conceptualizing causal factors (Hinde, 1992). As illustrated in Figure 2–1, the biological, psychological, and social approaches to psychopathology are potentially compatible explanations at different levels of analysis. Each approach uses a different lens to analyze the subject; one is a microscope, another a magnifying glass, and the third a telescope. In fact, the various academic disciplines also can be ordered according to levels of analysis (Schwartz, 1982; see Table 2–3). The use of a different "lens" by different academic disciplines does not make one approach right and the others wrong.

Causality: Multiple Factors and Multiple Pathways

We want you to recognize that the biological, psychological, and social levels of analysis simply can be different ways of conceptualizing the same problem. It is also true, however, that a specific abnormality might occur within any one of these subsystems. In the Martian example, an engine might break down, a driver might be reckless, or a road could be washed out. Similarly, the cause of any one type of abnormal behavior might be located primarily within biological, psychological, or social functioning. Scientists hope to identify such specific causes at one or another level of analysis for at least some psychological problems. Our caution, however, is that, with current technology, scientists can only rarely attribute *differences* in biological, psychological, or social functioning to *disturbances* or abnormalities within the same level of analysis. When scientists identify a chemical imbalance in the brain that is associated with depression, for example, we cannot yet determine whether the imbalance is an inborn abnormality that causes depression, or whether the imbalance was reaction to a stressful life event (see Research Methods). The same cautions about interpretation apply to molar life experiences. For example, genetically determined personality traits may make some people more likely to experience difficult life events (McGue & Lykken, 1992).

TABLE 2-3

An Ordering of Traditional Academic Disciplines According to Level of Analysis

Level of Analysis	Academic Discipline
Beyond Earth	Astronomy
Supranational	Ecology, economics
National	Government, political science
Organizations	Organizational science
Groups	Sociology
Organisms	Psychology, ethology, zoology
Organs	Cardiology, neurology
Cells	Cellular biology
Biochemicals	Biochemistry
Chemicals	Chemistry, physical chemistry
Atoms	Physics
Subatomic particles	Subatomic physics
Abstract systems	Mathematics, philosophy

Source: Based on G. E. Schwartz, 1982, Testing the biopsychosocial model: The ultimate challenge facing behavioral medicine, *Journal of Consulting and Clinical Psychology, 50,* 1040–1053.

The Correlational Study

Scientists have developed sophisticated methods for conducting research. The most basic scientific tools are the correlational study and the *experiment* (see Research Methods in Chapter 3.) In a **correlational study,** the relation between two factors (their co-relation) is studied in a systematic fashion. For example, you might hypothesize that psychology majors on your campus learn more about research methods than biology majors learn. To support this hypothesis, you might simply argue your point, or you could rely on case studies—"I know more about research than my roommate, and she's a biology major!"

If you were to conduct a correlational study on the question, you would collect a large sample of both psychology and biology majors and compare them on an objective measure of knowledge of research methods. You would then use statistics to test whether research knowledge is *correlated* with academic major. (As we discuss in Research Methods in Chapters 9 and 16, the findings of correlational studies—and all scientific research—are influenced greatly by the sample that is recruited and the quality of measurement; for now, we will skip over these important issues.)

An important statistic for measuring how strongly two factors are related is the **correlation coefficient**. The correlation coefficient is a number that always ranges between -1.00 and $+1.00$. If all psychology majors got 100 percent correct on your test of research methods and all biology majors got 0 percent correct, the correlation between academic major and research knowledge would be 1.00. If all psychology and biology majors got 50 percent of the items correct, the correlation between major and knowledge would be zero.

Positive correlations (from 0.01 to 1.00) indicate that, as one factor goes up, the other factor also goes up. For example, height and weight are positively correlated, as are years of education and employment income. Taller people weigh more; educated people earn more money. *Negative correlations* (from -1.00 to -0.01) indicate that, as one number gets bigger, the other number gets smaller. For example, population and open space are negatively correlated. As more people move into an area, the amount of open land diminishes. Two factors are more strongly correlated when a correlation coefficient has a higher absolute value, regardless of whether it is positive or negative.

In this chapter, we note a number of putatively causal factors that are correlated with psychological problems. The levels of neurotransmitters in the brain are positively correlated with some emotional problems (they are elevated in comparison to normal), and they are negatively correlated with other types of emotional problems (they are depleted in comparison to normal). Self-esteem is negatively correlated with emotional problems. The higher your self-esteem, the fewer problems you have. However, a correlation between two factors must be interpreted cautiously. In particular, you should constantly remember that *correlation does not mean causation.*

In interpreting any correlation, there are always two alternative explanations to making a causal conclusion: reverse causality and third-variable alternative interpretations. We might want to conclude that *X* causes *Y*—that depleted neurotransmitters cause depression. However, the concept of **reverse causality** indicates that causation could be operating in the opposite direction: *Y* could be causing *X*. Depression could be causing the depletion of neurotransmitters.

The **third-variable** possibility offers yet another alternative to causal interpretations. A correlation between any two variables could be explained by their joint relation with some unmeasured factor—a third variable. For example, stress might cause both depression *and* the depletion of neurotransmitters.

Let us return to your study of psychology and biology majors to illustrate these issues further. Assume that you did find that psychology majors know more about research methods. Based on this correlational finding, could you conclude that studying psychology *causes* students to learn more about research? No, you could not. A reverse causality interpretation of the correlation might suggest that people who know more about research methods decide to become psychology majors. Knowledge about research causes them to choose this major, not vice versa. A third-variable interpretation of the correlation might suggest that more intelligent people choose to major in psychology, and more intelligent people also know more about the methods of scientific research. According to this interpretation, the correlation between academic major and research knowledge is *spurious,* an artifact of the relation of both of these variables with the third variable of intelligence.

As we discuss in Research Methods in Chapter 3, another method of research, the experiment, *does* allow scientists to determine cause and effect relations. However, it often is impractical or unethical to conduct experiments on psychological problems, whereas correlational studies can be conducted with far fewer practical or ethical concerns. Thus the correlational method has the weakness that correlation does not mean causation; it also has the strength that it can be used to conduct research in many real-life circumstances. ■

Our point is this: It is not enough to focus on one subsystem or level of analysis. Ultimately, we must understand the relations among biological, psychological, and social functioning. In fact, many emotional problems apparently are caused by a *combination* of biological, psychological, and social risk factors.

THE DIATHESIS-STRESS MODEL

The **diathesis-stress model** is a useful way of conceptualizing how multiple risk factors may interact to produce a mental disorder. A **diathesis** is a predisposition toward developing a disorder, for example, an inherited tendency toward depression. A **stress** is a difficult life experience, for example, the loss of a loved one through an unexpected death (see Chapter 8). The diathesis-stress model indicates that mental disorders develop only when a stress is added on top of a predisposition; neither the diathesis nor the stress alone is sufficient to cause the disorder.

We commonly think that a diathesis must be a biological risk factor, such as a genetic predisposition. However, a psychological characteristic such as an aggressive personality style can also be a diathesis for a particular disorder. Similarly, a stress need not be a psychological factor. A stress could be a biological experience, such as an injury or an infection.

Although it is a very useful concept, one limitation of the diathesis-stress model is the implication that disorders are caused by the combination of two risk factors. As we have noted, however, some mental disorders may be produced by the combination of several biological, psychological, and/or social risk factors. It also is true, moreover, that a disorder may have

several different causes. In some circumstances, many risk factors may be involved in the disorder's etiology. In other cases, a diathesis—or a stress—may be so powerful that the single risk factor produces the disorder.

EQUIFINALITY OR MULTIPLE PATHWAYS

Systems theory articulates the principle of **equifinality,** the idea that the *same* psychological disorder may have *different* causes. That is, there may be many routes to the same destination (or disorder). For this reason, we also refer to the principle of equifinality in terms of *multiple pathways*.

To help you appreciate the principle of equifinality, let us pose a simple question: What is the cause of automobile accidents? Of course, automobile accidents have many different causes. A car accident may be caused by a single defect, such as faulty brakes or a drunk driver. Or a car accident may be caused by a combination of risk factors, such as excessive speed, a wet road, and worn tires. It would be fruitless to search for *the* cause of automobile accidents, because car accidents have many causes, not one. Similarly, there may be many different causes for the same psychological disorder. In some cases, depression may be caused primarily by abnormal brain chemistry. In other cases, depression may be caused by a pessimistic style of interpretation. In still other circumstances, a serious personal loss may cause an episode of depression.

The media—and scientists—often talk about discovering *the* cause of mental (and physical) disorders. Much like the discovery of the cause of general paresis, we anticipate that scientists will discover specific causes for some disorders, especially as experts recognize and identify truly unique subcategories of any given mental disorder. However, we believe that, much like cancer or heart disease (see Chapter 8), there are multiple pathways to most mental disorders, and multiple risk factors involved in many of these alternative pathways. Thus, like controlling heart disease or cancer, our best strategy for lowering the risk for mental disorders is to recognize and reduce the factors that increase the risk.

Reciprocal Causality and Control Processes

The concepts of holism, multiple levels of analysis, and equifinality are three major contributions of systems theory. A fourth is the idea that the same or very similar *control processes* operate within biological, psychological, and social systems (von Bertalanffy, 1968).

Reciprocal causality, the idea that causality is bidirectional, is one of the most important of processes identified by systems theory. Reciprocal causality is most easily understood when contrasted with *linear causality*, a scientific corollary of reductionism. According to linear assumptions, causation operates in one direction only: Parents cause their children to behave in a certain way, for example. Both formal reviews of the literature and informal observations by millions of parents indicate, however, that children also change their parents' behavior (Bell, 1968; Maccoby, 1992). Such mutual influences define reciprocal causality, a process that occurs in all types of natural interaction. Even the traditional operant conditioning experiment must be conceptualized in terms of reciprocal causality (Skinner, 1956). Psychologists cause rats to press the bar in a Skinner box, but rats also cause scientists to feed them, as the cartoon on this page illustrates.

Cybernetics, another critical control process, uses *feedback loops* to adjust progress toward a goal. The operation of a thermostat is a good example of a simple cybernetic process. Air temperature is monitored continuously to maintain room temperature within a constant range by either turning on or shutting off a heat source.

The concept of cybernetics is essential to understanding **homeostasis**—the tendency to maintain a steady state. The systems concept of homeostasis is familiar in biology, but it is also widely applicable in psychology. For example, people attempt to maintain a balance between too little stimulation and too much stress or anxiety. Some people are thrill seekers. They find that challenging activities like skydiving provide the right balance between the push of boredom and the pull of excitement. Other people are timid, and they find an equilibrium between the need for novelty and fear of the unknown in a limited and carefully controlled world. The setpoints for optimal levels of stimulation differ like the hotter and cooler settings on a thermostat, but all people engage in the homeostatic process of finding an individualized balance between too little and too much stimulation.

"Boy, have I got this guy conditioned! Every time I press the bar down he drops a piece of food."

Development

Homeostasis maintains equilibrium, but change is also essential in systems. *Development* is the most basic source of change. Over time, people follow a fairly predictable trajectory of change. Children learn to crawl, walk, and run in an established sequence, and their cognitive skills also unfold in a predictable manner. Development, though, is not limited to children or to the physical and intellectual domains. Development continues throughout adult life, and predictable changes occur in both psychological and social experiences. In fact, we devote an entire chapter of the text (Chapter 17) to a discussion of the normal but psychologically trying changes that result from developmental transitions during adult life.

Because people develop and change over time, knowledge of normal development is essential to understanding psychopathology. **Developmental psychopathology** is a new approach to abnormal psychology that emphasizes the importance of *developmental norms*—age-graded averages—to determining what constitutes abnormal behavior (Cicchetti & Cohen, 1995; Rutter & Garmezy, 1983). Developmental norms tell us that a full-blown temper tantrum is normal at 2 years of age, for example, but that kicking and screaming to get one's own way is abnormal at the age of 22. Similarly, we need to understand the developmental progression of a difficult psychological experience like normal grief in order to recognize when mourning should be considered pathological (too intense) or unresolved (too long-lasting).

For these reasons, we frequently consider questions about normal development in this textbook on abnormal psychology. We also discuss the development of abnormal behavior itself. Many psychological disorders follow unique developmental patterns. Sometimes there is a characteristic **premorbid history,** a pattern of behavior that precedes the onset of the disorder. People with schizophrenia, for example, often are withdrawn and awkward before the onset of their psychosis.

A disorder may also have a predictable course, or **prognosis,** for the future. When schizophrenia is untreated, the condition often deteriorates—psychotic symptoms may improve, but day-to-day coping becomes less adequate (see Chapter 13). By discussing the premorbid adjustment and the course of different psychological disorders, we hope to present abnormal behavior as a moving picture of development and not just as a diagnostic snapshot.

The remainder of this chapter is divided into sections on biological, psychological, and social factors in the development of psychopathology. In each of these sections we focus most of our discussion on normal development. This material forms a basis for our critical consideration of the causes of abnormal behavior in subsequent chapters on specific psychological disorders.

Biological Factors

We begin our discussion of biological factors by considering the smallest anatomic unit within the nervous system, the neuron or nerve cell. Next, we present an overview of the major brain structures and current knowledge of their primary behavioral functions. We then turn to a discussion of psychophysiology, the effect of psychological experience on the functioning of various body systems. Finally, we consider the broadest of all biological influences, the effect of genes on behavior.

In considering biological influences, it is helpful to note the distinction between the study of biological structures and of biological functions. The field of *anatomy* is concerned with the study of biological structures, and the field of *physiology* investigates biological functions. *Neuroanatomy* and *neurophysiology* are subspecialties within these broader fields that focus specifically on brain structures and brain functions.

The Neuron and Neurotransmitters

Billions of tiny nerve cells—**neurons**—form the basic building blocks of the brain. Each neuron has four major anatomic components: the soma or cell body, the dendrites, the axon, and the terminal buttons (see Figure 2–2). The **soma**—the cell body and largest part of the neuron—is where most of the neuron's metabolism and maintenance are controlled and performed. The **dendrites** branch out from the soma; they serve the primary function of receiving messages from other cells. The **axon** is the trunk of the neuron. Messages are transmitted down the axon toward other cells with which a given neuron

The Neuron

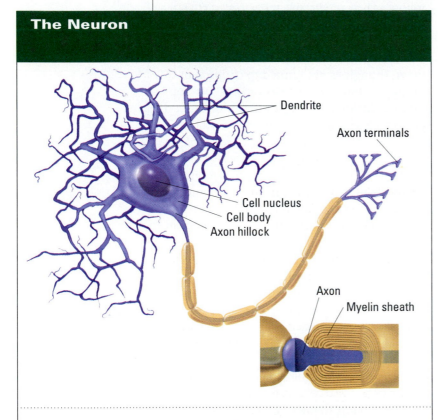

FIGURE 2-2: The anatomic structure of the neuron, or nerve cell.

Source: Adapted from *Fundamentals of Human Neuropsychology,* 2nd ed., by Brian Kolb and Ian Q. Whislaw. Copyright © 1980, 1985, by W.H. Freeman and Company. Reprinted with permission.

communicates. Finally, the **terminal buttons** are "buds" found on the small branches at the end of the axon where messages are sent out to other neurons (Barondes, 1993).

Scientists have made great strides in deciphering the neurophysiological processes involved in communication within and among neurons. Within each neuron, information is transmitted as a change in electrical potential that moves from the dendrites and cell body, along the axon, toward the terminal buttons. The terminal buttons are separated from other cells by a **synapse,** a small gap filled with fluid. Neurons typically have synapses with thousands of other cells (see Figure 2–3).

Unlike the electrical communication within a neuron, information is transmitted chemically across a synapse to other neurons. The terminal buttons release chemical substances called **neurotransmitters** into the synapse, which are received at the **receptors** on the dendrites or soma of another neuron. Dozens of different chemical compounds serve as neurotransmitters in the brain, and the functions of particular neurotransmitters vary. Moreover, different receptor sites are more or less responsive to particular neurotransmitters.

Not all neurotransmitters cross the synapse and reach the receptors on another neuron. The process of **reuptake** captures some neurotransmitters in the synapse and returns the chemical substances to the terminal button. The neurotransmitter then is reused in subsequent neural transmission.

In addition to the neurotransmitters, a second type of chemical affects communication in the brain. **Neuromodulators** are chemicals that may be released from neurons or from endocrine glands (which we will discuss shortly). Neuromodulators can influence communication among many neurons by affecting the functioning of neurotransmitters, although neuromodulators are not thought to act directly as neurotransmitters (Ciaranello et al., 1995). Neuromodulators often affect regions of the brain that are quite distant from where they were released. The most familiar neuromodulators are the *endorphins*—chemicals that have a structure similar to that of the drug opium (see Chapter 11). Thus they are often referred to as *opioids*. The endorphins were discovered in the 1970s, but active research is still being conducted on their possible role in a number of emotional disorders (Barondes, 1993; Nemeroff & Bissette, 1986).

Synaptic Transmission

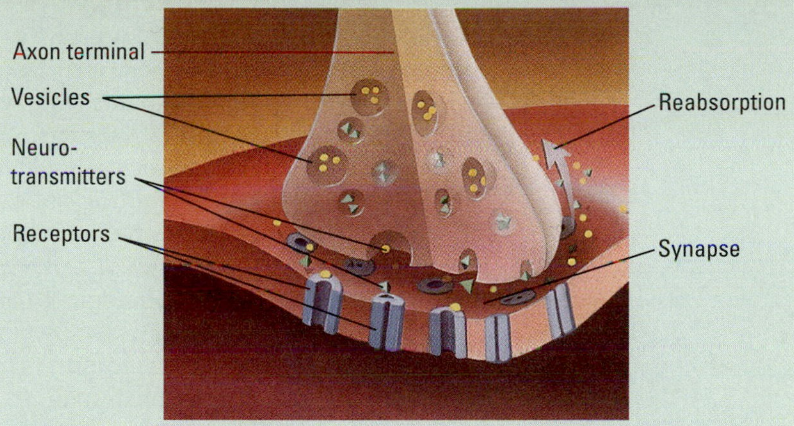

FIGURE 2-3: When an electrical nerve impulse reaches the end of a neuron, synaptic vesicles release neurotransmitters into the synapse. The chemical transmission between cells is complete when neurotransmitters travel to receptor sites on another neuron.

Source: Keith Kasnot, Copyright National Geographic Image Collection.

NEUROTRANSMITTERS AND THE ETIOLOGY OF PSYCHOPATHOLOGY

Scientists have found that disrupted communication among neurons, particularly disruptions in the functioning of various neurotransmitters, plays a role in the etiology of several types of abnormal behavior. An oversupply of certain neurotransmitters is found in some mental disorders, an undersupply in other cases, and disturbances in reuptake in other psychological problems. In addition, the density and/or sensitivity of postsynaptic receptors has been implicated as playing a role in some forms of abnormal behavior.

Much research linking mental disorders with neurotransmitters has investigated how drugs affect the symptoms of a disorder and how they alter brain chemistry. For example, medications that alleviate some of the symptoms of schizophrenia are known to affect the availability of the neurotransmitter *dopamine* in the brains of animals (see Chapter 13). (Scientists cannot currently measure neurotransmitters in the living human brain, so neurotransmitter levels must be inferred either from animal studies or from indirect measures in humans.) These and related findings suggest that abnormalities in the dopamine system in the brain may be involved in the development of schizophrenia. Other evidence links disruptions in the functioning of various neurotransmitters with different forms of abnormal behavior, as we discuss throughout the text.

MIND-BODY DUALISM

Investigations of neurophysiology have produced exciting findings, and several medications have been developed that have remarkable benefits in treating certain mental disorders. Still, the technical and practical advances should not cloud reasoning about the etiology of psychopathology. In particular, we must not equate a neurophysiological *explanation* of a psychological disorder with the identification of a biological *abnormality*. We have already discussed our concerns about biological reductionism in this regard. Another potential problem stems from **dualism,** the philosophical view that the mind and body are somehow separable.

Dualism dates to the writings of the French philosopher René Descartes (1596–1650), who attempted to balance the dominant religious views of his times with emerging scientific reasoning. Descartes recognized the importance of studying human biology, but he wished to elevate human spirituality beyond that of other animals. In so doing, he argued that many human functions have biological explanations, but some human experiences have no somatic representation. Thus he argued for a distinction—a *dualism*—between mind and body.

Similar attempts to separate the psyche and the soma have clouded thinking for centuries. One contemporary dualism is that biological explanations may account for psychological abnormalities, but normal psychological experience is somehow independent of biology. (For example, see the discussion of free will and determinism in Chapter 18.) Because of this persistent notion of dualism, biological explanations of psychological experience sometimes are erroneously equated with the identification of an abnormality. However, no aspect of the psychological world exists apart from the physical world. Just as a computer software program has an invisible electronic representation in the hardware of microchips, all psychological experience has an underlying representation in the brain. Even love must have a biochemical explanation, a fact that Calvin ponders in the accompanying cartoon. Love will still be love (we hope) even after scientists identify the "chemical imbalance in the brain" that explains it. The same logic applies to biochemical explanations of psychopathology, which cannot be automatically equated with biochemical abnormalities.

Major Brain Structures

Neuroanatomists divide the brain into three subdivisions: the hindbrain, the midbrain, and the forebrain (see Figure 2–4 on pp. 50–51). Basic bodily functions are regulated by the structures of the *hindbrain*, which include the medulla, pons, and cerebellum. The *medulla* controls various bodily functions involved in sustaining life, including heart rate, blood pressure, and respiration. The *pons* serves functions in regulating stages of sleep. The **cerebellum** serves as a control center in helping to coordinate physical movements. The cerebellum receives information on body movements and integrates this feedback with directives from higher brain structures about desired actions. Few forms of abnormal behavior are identified with disturbances in the hindbrain, because the hindbrain's primary role is limited to supervising these basic physical functions (Matthysse & Pope, 1986).

The *midbrain* also is involved in the control of some motor activities, especially those related to fighting and sex. Much of the **reticular activating system** is located in the midbrain, although it extends into the pons and medulla as well. The reticular activating system regulates sleeping and waking. Damage to areas of the midbrain can cause extreme disturbances in sexual behavior, aggressiveness, and sleep, but such abnormalities typically result from specific and unusual brain traumas or tumors (Matthysse & Pope, 1986).

Most of the human brain consists of the *forebrain*. The forebrain evolved more recently than the hindbrain and midbrain and therefore is the location of most sensory, emotional, and cognitive processes. These higher mental processes of the forebrain are linked with the midbrain and hindbrain by the limbic system. The *limbic system* is made up of a variety of different brain structures that are central to the regulation of emotion and basic learning processes. Two of

the most important components of the limbic system are the thalamus and the hypothalamus. The **thalamus** is involved in receiving and integrating sensory information both from the sense organs and from higher brain structures. The **hypothalamus** also plays a role in sensation, but its more important functions are behavioral ones. The hypothalamus controls basic biological urges, such as eating, drinking, and sexual activity. Much of the functioning of the autonomic nervous system (which we will discuss shortly) also is directed by the hypothalamus.

CEREBRAL HEMISPHERES

Most of the forebrain is composed of the two **cerebral hemispheres** (see Figure 2–4). Many brain functions are **lateralized,** so that one hemisphere serves a specialized role as the site of specific cognitive and emotional activities. In general, the *left cerebral hemisphere* is involved in language and related functions, and the *right cerebral hemisphere* is involved in spatial organization and analysis. The lateralization and localization of certain brain functions often make it possible to pinpoint brain damage based solely on behavioral difficulties.

The two cerebral hemispheres are connected by the *corpus callosum,* which is involved in coordinating the different functions that are performed by the left and the right hemispheres of the brain. When we view a cross section of the forebrain, four connected chambers, or **ventricles,** become apparent. The ventricles are filled with cerebrospinal fluid, and they become enlarged in some psychological and neurological disorders.

The **cerebral cortex** is the uneven surface area of the brain that lies just underneath the skull. It is the site of the control and integration of sophisticated memory, sensory, and motor functions. The cerebral cortex is divided into four lobes (see Figure 2–4). The **frontal lobe,** located just behind the forehead, is involved in controlling a number of complex functions, including reasoning, planning, emotion, speech, and movement. The **parietal lobe,** located at the top and back of the head, receives and integrates sensory information and also plays a role in spatial reasoning. The **temporal lobe,** located beneath much of the frontal and parietal lobes, processes sound and smell, regulates emotions, and is involved in some aspects of learning, memory, and language. Finally, the **occipital lobe,** located behind the temporal lobe, receives and interprets visual information.

MAJOR BRAIN STRUCTURES AND THE ETIOLOGY OF PSYCHOPATHOLOGY

The brain is incredibly complex, and scientists are only beginning to understand the relations among various anatomic structures and functions. Because of the rudimentary knowledge we have about the brain, only obvious brain injuries and infections and the most severe mental disorders have clearly been linked with abnormalities in neuroanatomy. In most of these cases, brain damage is extensive. For example, during a *stroke,* blood vessels in the brain rupture, cutting off the supply of oxygen to parts of the brain and thereby killing surrounding brain tissue. This in turn disrupts the functioning of nearby healthy neurons because the brain cannot remove the dead tissue (see Figure 2–4). Tangles of neurons are found in patients with *Alzheimer's disease,* but the damage can be identified only during postmortem autopsies (see Figure 2–4 and Chapter 14). In patients with schizophrenia, the ventricles of the brain are enlarged, and asymmetries are also found in other brain structures (see Figure 2–4 and Chapter 13).

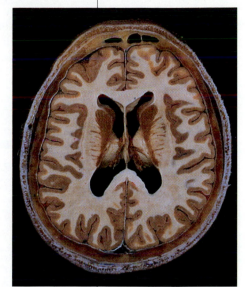

▲ **This cross-sectional image of the brain shows the ventricles, four connected chambers that are filled with cerebrospinal fluid.**

Still, research on the brain holds great promise. Scientists have made breakthroughs in observing the anatomic structure of the living brain and in recording some of its global physiological processes. These various imaging procedures are now being used to study psychological disorders ranging from schizophrenia to learning disabilities; they are discussed in Chapter 4, along with several methods of psychological assessment.

At present, the new brain imaging measures are more exciting technically than practically in terms of their contributions to furthering our understanding of the etiology of psychopathology. Scientific advances frequently follow the development of new measures, however, and there is every reason to hope that advances in brain imaging will lead to improvements in understanding abnormalities in brain structure and function.

Psychophysiology

Psychophysiology is the study of changes in the functioning of the body that result from

THE HEALTHY BRAIN

Scientists are only beginning to discover how the healthy brain performs its complex functions. Despite the continuing mysteries, increasingly sophisticated tools have allowed researchers to identify more and more of the functions performed by different areas of the brain. For example, the four lobes of the brain's cortex play very different roles in thought, emotion, sensation, and motor movement (see top right of figure). Still, our incomplete knowledge of the healthy brain limits our understanding of brain abnormalities.

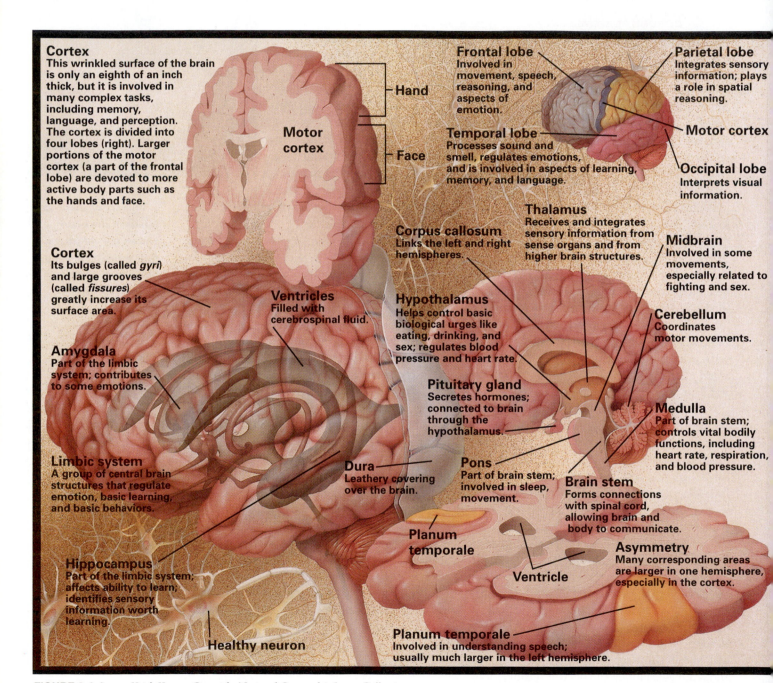

Cortex
This wrinkled surface of the brain is only an eighth of an inch thick, but it is involved in many complex tasks, including memory, language, and perception. The cortex is divided into four lobes (right). Larger portions of the motor cortex (a part of the frontal lobe) are devoted to more active body parts such as the hands and face.

Cortex
Its bulges (called *gyri*) and large grooves (called *fissures*) greatly increase its surface area.

Amygdala
Part of the limbic system; contributes to some emotions.

Limbic system
A group of central brain structures that regulate emotion, basic learning, and basic behaviors.

Hippocampus
Part of the limbic system; affects ability to learn; identifies sensory information worth learning.

Healthy neuron

Motor cortex

Hand

Face

Ventricles
Filled with cerebrospinal fluid.

Corpus callosum
Links the left and right hemispheres.

Hypothalamus
Helps control basic biological urges like eating, drinking, and sex; regulates blood pressure and heart rate.

Pituitary gland
Secretes hormones; connected to brain through the hypothalamus.

Dura
Leathery covering over the brain.

Pons
Part of brain stem; involved in sleep, movement.

Planum temporale

Ventricle

Planum temporale
Involved in understanding speech; usually much larger in the left hemisphere.

Frontal lobe
Involved in movement, speech, reasoning, and aspects of emotion.

Temporal lobe
Processes sound and smell, regulates emotions, and is involved in aspects of learning, memory, and language.

Parietal lobe
Integrates sensory information; plays a role in spatial reasoning.

Motor cortex

Occipital lobe
Interprets visual information.

Thalamus
Receives and integrates sensory information from sense organs and from higher brain structures.

Midbrain
Involved in some movements, especially related to fighting and sex.

Cerebellum
Coordinates motor movements.

Medulla
Part of brain stem; controls vital bodily functions, including heart rate, respiration, and blood pressure.

Brain stem
Forms connections with spinal cord, allowing brain and body to communicate.

Asymmetry
Many corresponding areas are larger in one hemisphere, especially in the cortex.

FIGURE 2-4 *Source:* Keith Kasnot, Copyright National Geographic Image Collection.

THE UNHEALTHY BRAIN

Scientists have identified clear brain abnormalities only for some severe mental disorders. A *stroke* is caused by a loss of blood supply to a region of the brain, and it kills off nearby cells (see Chapter 14). Cells die rapidly near the center of the damaged tissue, the umbra. Cells die less rapidly in the periphery, the penumbra, and may be saved by future medical advances. *Alzheimer's disease* is a severe cognitive disorder associated with aging (see Chapter 14) that is characterized by atrophied brain tissue, "senile plaques" (caused by clumps of beta amyloid protein), and tangles of diseased or dead neurons. *Schizophrenia* is a very serious psychotic illness (see Chapter 13) that remains a mystery as a brain disorder, despite some promising leads. For example, among people with schizophrenia the ventricles often are enlarged, and asymmetries in the planum temporale may be reversed.

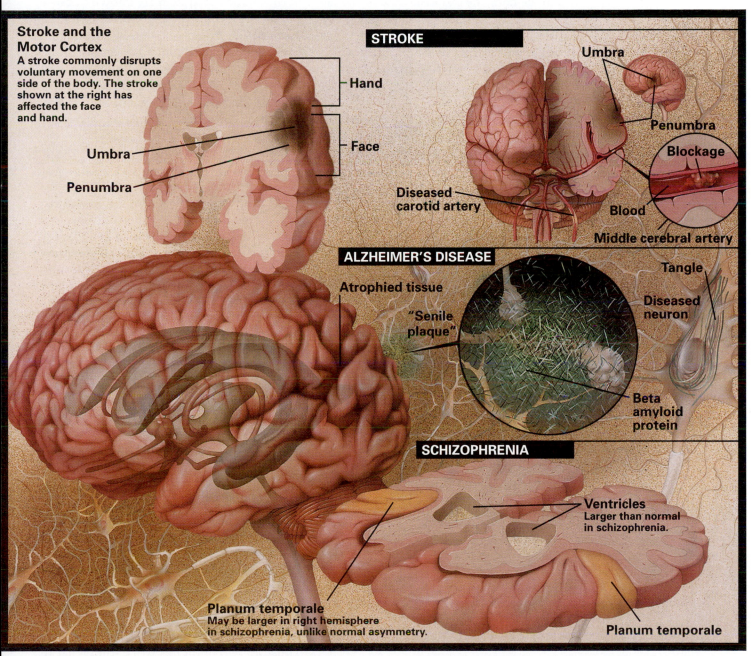

Stroke and the Motor Cortex
A stroke commonly disrupts voluntary movement on one side of the body. The stroke shown at the right has affected the face and hand.

Umbra
Penumbra
Hand
Face

STROKE
Umbra
Penumbra
Blockage
Diseased carotid artery
Blood
Middle cerebral artery

ALZHEIMER'S DISEASE
Atrophied tissue
"Senile plaque"
Tangle
Diseased neuron
Beta amyloid protein

SCHIZOPHRENIA
Ventricles
Larger than normal in schizophrenia.
Planum temporale
May be larger in right hemisphere in schizophrenia, unlike normal asymmetry.
Planum temporale

psychological experiences. Some of these physical reactions to environmental provocations are familiar. A pounding heart, a flushed face, tears, sexual excitement, and numerous other reactions are psychophysiological responses. These and other psychophysiological responses reflect a person's psychological state, particularly the degree and perhaps the type of the individual's emotional arousal.

ENDOCRINE SYSTEM

Psychophysiological arousal results from the activity of two different communication systems within the body, the endocrine system and the nervous system. The **endocrine system** is a collection of glands found at various locations throughout the body. Its major components include the ovaries or testes and the pituitary, thyroid, and adrenal glands (see Figure 2–5).

Endocrine glands produce psychophysiological responses by releasing **hormones** into the bloodstream—chemical substances that affect the functioning of distant body systems and sometimes act as neuromodulators. The endocrine system regulates some aspects of normal development, particularly physical growth and sexual development. Parts of the endocrine system, particularly the adrenal glands, also are activated by stress and help prepare the body to respond to an emergency (see Chapter 8).

Certain abnormalities in the functioning of the endocrine system are known to cause psychological symptoms. For example, in *hyperthyroidism*, or *Graves' disease*, the thyroid gland secretes too much of the hormone thyroxin, causing restlessness, agitation, and anxiety. Recent research on depression also suggests that endocrine functioning sometimes may be involved in the etiology of this disorder (see Chapter 5).

AUTONOMIC NERVOUS SYSTEM

The more familiar and basic system of communication within the body is the *nervous system*. The human nervous system is divided into the *central nervous system*, which includes the brain and the spinal cord, and the *peripheral nervous system*. The peripheral nervous system includes all connections that stem out from the central nervous system and innervate the body's muscles, sensory systems, and organs.

The peripheral nervous system itself has two subdivisions. The *voluntary*, or *somatic nervous*, *system* governs muscular control, and the *involuntary*, or **autonomic nervous, system** regulates the functions of various body organs, such as the heart and stomach. The somatic nervous system controls intentional or voluntary actions like scratching your nose. The autonomic nervous system is responsible for psychophysiological reactions—responses that occur with little or no conscious control.

The autonomic nervous system can be further divided into two branches, the sympathetic and parasympathetic nervous systems. In general, the **sympathetic nervous system** controls activities associated with increased arousal and energy expenditure, and the **parasympathetic nervous system** controls the slowing of arousal and energy conservation. Thus the two branches work somewhat in opposition to each other as a means of maintaining homeostasis.

The Endocrine System

Pineal body
Pituitary gland
Parathyroid gland
Thyroid gland
Thymus gland
(Stomach)
Adrenal glands
Pancreas
Kidney
Ovary (In female)

Testis
(In male)

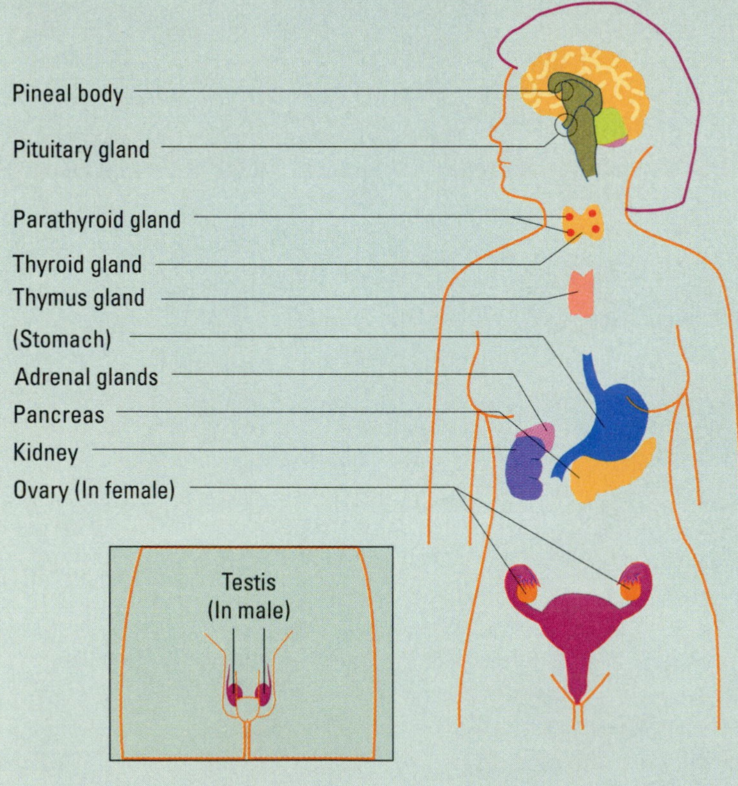

FIGURE 2-5: The glands that comprise the endocrine system, which affects physical and psychophysiological responses through the release of hormones into the bloodstream.

Source: John G. Seamon and Douglas T. Kenrick, 1994, *Psychology* (2nd ed.), p.67. Upper Saddle River, NJ: Prentice Hall.

Both psychophysiological overarousal and under-arousal have been implicated in various theories of the causes of abnormal behavior. For example, autonomic overactivity is hypothesized to be responsible for excessive anxiety (see Chapter 6). In contrast, some theories suggest that chronic autonomic underarousal is responsible for the indifference to social rules and the failure to learn from punishment that characterize antisocial personality disorder (see Chapter 9).

Other theories of psychophysiology and abnormal behavior do not focus on dysfunctions in the autonomic nervous system. Instead, they emphasize psychophysiological assessment as a way of objectively measuring atypical reactions to psychological events. Scientists have developed numerous methods of measuring psychophysiological activity, ranging from assessments of sexual response to indices of muscle tension. We examine some of these psychophysiological measures in Chapter 4.

Behavior Genetics

The study of genetics is both the most molecular and the most molar approach to examining biological influences on behavior. **Genes** are ultramicroscopic units of DNA that carry information about heredity. Genes are located on **chromosomes,** chainlike structures found in the nucleus of cells. Humans normally have 23 pairs of chromosomes. The field of *genetics* identifies specific genes and their hereditary functions, often by literally focusing at the level of molecules. Geneticists typically have training in biochemistry, not psychology.

Behavior genetics is a much more molar approach that studies genetic influences on the evolution and development of normal and abnormal behavior (Goldsmith, 1988; McGuffin et al., 1994; Plomin, DeFries, & McClearn, 1990; Scarr, 1992). Behavior geneticists study various human characteristics in an attempt to demonstrate that the behavior has a more or less genetic origin. Behavior geneticists seldom posit specific genetic causes of a disorder, however, and they rarely study individual genes.

SOME BASIC PRINCIPLES OF GENETICS

One of the most important principles of genetics is the distinction between genotype and phenotype. A **genotype** is an individual's actual genetic structure. Advances in biochemistry have allowed scientists to determine more and more aspects of genetic structure, but it is still impossible to observe much of an individual's genotype directly. Instead, what we observe is the **phenotype,** the expression of a given genotype. There is no one-to-one correspondence between phenotypes and genotypes. Different genotypes can produce similar phenotypes. And phenotypes, but not genotypes, are influenced by environmental experience. This means that it usually is impossible to infer a precise genotype from a given phenotype.

Differences between genotypes and phenotypes are evident in the simple mode of dominant/recessive inheritance that was discovered by the Austrian monk Gregor Mendel (1822–1884) in his famous studies of garden peas. Mendel discovered that certain traits are dominant over other traits; for example, in peas, yellow color is dominant over green color. Today we know that inherited traits are controlled by genes, which have alternative forms known as *alleles*. Dominant/recessive inheritance occurs when a trait is caused by a gene that has only two alleles (for example, A and a) and only one *locus*, a specific location on a chromosome. In dominant/recessive inheritance, the phenotypic trait is either present or absent. In the case of Mendel's peas, for example, the gene for color has only two alleles, A (yellow, dominant) and a (green, recessive). Through cross-breeding, three genotypes are possible: AA, aA (or Aa), and aa. Because A is dominant over a, however, both AA and aA plants will have yellow color. Thus, although three genotypes are possible, only two phenotypes are observed: yellow and green. The top panel in Figure 2–6 illustrates this concept.

Dominant/recessive inheritance causes some forms of mental retardation (Plomin, DeFries, & McClearn, 1990; Thapar et al., 1994; see Chapter 15), but most forms of abnormal behavior

Single Gene and Polygenic Inheritance

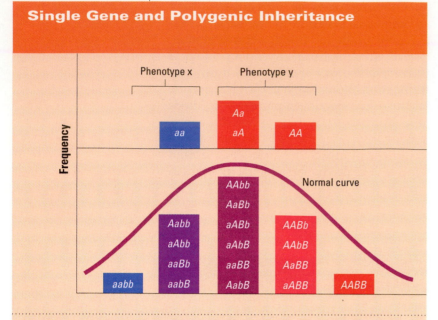

FIGURE 2-6: Single genes produce phenotypes that differ qualitatively, as illustrated in the top panel. Multiple genes produce phenotypes that differ quantitatively. As more genes are involved, the distribution of traits approximates the normal curve, as illustrated in the bottom panel.

are not caused by a single gene—if they have genetic causes at all. Instead, they are **polygenic,** that is, they are caused by more than one gene (Gottesman, 1991). Polygenic inheritance has an important effect on the distribution of traits. In contrast to the categorical phenotypes produced by a single gene, polygenic inheritance produces dimensional characteristics. In fact, the distribution of a phenotype in the population begins to resemble the normal distribution as more genes are involved in determining the trait (see the bottom panel in Figure 2–6). Thus, when behavior geneticists find that a given mental disorder is "genetic," we must be cautious about interpreting the meaning of this finding. Such a findings does *not* mean that the disorder is caused by the presence or absence of one or two genes. Rather, behavior genetic findings typically imply that genes, probably many genes, contribute to a disorder that we can conceptualize as lying on a continuum with normal behavior, because of the nature of polygenic inheritance.

Behavior geneticists have developed innovative methods for studying broad, genetic contributions to behavior. The most important behavior genetic methods are twin studies, adoption studies, and family incidence studies.

TWIN STUDIES

Identical, or **monozygotic (MZ),** twins are produced from a single fertilized egg. One egg is fertilized by one sperm; thus MZ twins have identical genotypes. *Fraternal,* or **dizygotic (DZ),** twins are produced from separate fertilized eggs. There are two eggs and two sperm. Thus, like all siblings, DZ twins share an average of 50 percent of their genes, whereas MZ twins share 100 percent of their genes. Of course, most MZ and DZ twin pairs are raised in the same family. Thus the two types of twins differ in their degree of genetic similarity, but they are alike in their environmental experiences.

Comparisons between MZ and DZ twin pairs, therefore, can shed light on the genetic and environmental contributions to a disorder. The key comparison involves determining whether MZ twins are more alike than DZ twins are alike. In the case of psychological disorders, the measure of interest is the degree of **concordance** between the twin pairs. A twin pair is concordant when both twins either have the same disorder or are free from the disorder. The twin pair is discordant when one twin has the disorder but the other does not.

If we assume that the environmental effects on a disorder are the same for DZ twin pairs as they are for MZ twin pairs, then any differences between the concordance rates for MZ and DZ twins must be caused by genetics. If a disorder is purely genetic, for example, scientists should find a concordance rate of 100 percent for MZ twins (who are genetically identical) and 50 percent for DZ twins (who share half of the same genes on average).

In contrast, similar concordance rates for MZ and DZ twins rule out genetic contributions and instead implicate environmental causes of a disorder. Environmental causes are implicated regardless of whether the concordance rates for MZ and DZ twins are both 0 percent, both 100 percent, or both anywhere in between. However, the level of concordance does provide information about the nature of the environmental contribution. Higher concordance rates for both MZ and DZ twins point to the etiological role of the **shared environment,** for example, the experience of a parental divorce or growing up in poverty. Because both MZ and DZ pairs have similarly high concordance rates, we know that genes do not explain the high concordance. Instead, the common cause must be found in the environment shared by the twins.

In contrast, similar but low concordance rates for both MZ and DZ pairs point to the influence of the **nonshared environment,** for example, being the favored child. In this case, genetic causes are again ruled out, and the importance of unique experiences is indicated by the fact that only one twin has a psychological disorder (Goldsmith, 1988; Plomin, 1994).

All of this reasoning depends on the assumption that the environment affects DZ twins in the same way that it influences MZ twins. A number of critics have questioned this assumption. One important question is whether MZ twins, because of their striking physical resemblance, are treated more similarly than DZ twins. If so, then higher concordance rates for MZ twins might result from more similar environmental experiences and not from more similar genetic endowments. To address this criticism, many scientists have used another method of behavior genetic research, namely, adoption studies.

ADOPTION STUDIES

Adoption studies also provide evidence on the genetic versus the environmental contributions to the development of a disorder. In this research design, people who have been adopted as infants are compared with their biological versus their adoptive relatives (usually their parents) in terms of concordance for a disorder. If concordance is higher for biological than for adoptive relatives, then genetic factors are involved, because adopted children share their biological relatives' genes but not their environment. On the other hand, if children are more similar to their adoptive than to their biological relatives, then environment must influence the characteristic, because adopted children share their adoptive relatives' environment but not their genes. Adoption studies also have some potential problems, for example, the fact that adoption placement is selective. Still, you can be confident in the findings of behavior genetic research when adoption and twin studies produce similar results (Goldsmith, 1988; Plomin, 1994).

FAMILY INCIDENCE STUDIES

The family incidence study deserves brief mention, if only because findings from these studies are often misinterpreted. Family incidence studies ask whether diseases "run in families." Investigators identify normal and ill **probands,** or index cases, and tabulate the frequency with which other members of their families suffer from the same disorder. If a higher prevalence of illness is found in families where there is an ill proband, this is consistent with genetic causation. The finding also is consistent with environmental causation, however, because families share environments as well as genes. For this reason, no firm conclusions about the relative role of genes or the environment can be reached from family incidence studies alone.

MISINTERPRETING BEHAVIOR GENETICS FINDINGS

The methods of behavior genetics research are powerful, and mounting evidence indicates that genes contribute to a wide variety of psychological disorders. Unfortunately, people often misinterpret findings from behavior genetic research.

One serious misinterpretation is that, if it has a genetic component, the emergence of a psychological disorder is inevitable, even predestined. This conclusion is wrong, in part, because of polygenic inheritance. The probabilities of alternative outcomes are easily identified for simple dominant/recessive inheritance, but predicting the likelihood of a disorder is far more difficult for polygenic transmission. Moreover, genetics alone does not cause the vast majority of emotional disorders. Behavior genetics studies of mental illnesses typically find concordance rates for MZ twins that are well below 100 percent. Thus genes may predispose someone toward developing a psychological problem, but the disorder emerges only when the predisposition is combined with environmental stressors.

It also is wrong to think that genetic characteristics cannot be modified or controlled. For example, even in cases where mental

▼ **Monozygotic (MZ) twins are identical; they develop from a single fertilized egg. Dizygotic (DZ) twins are fraternal; they develop from two different fertilized eggs.**

retardation has a known genetic cause, certain environmental experiences such as diet or early stimulation have been demonstrated to lead to substantial increases—or decreases—in IQ (Turkheimer, 1991; see Chapter 15). The conclusion "It's genetic" does not provide an excuse for accepting the status quo. With rare exceptions, society remains responsible for helping people to maximize their genetic potential, and individuals remain personally responsible for their actions.

Finally, it is not clear what mechanism, or *mediating process*, may explain the genetic contribution to a disorder. For example, researchers have found genetic contributions to adult criminality, but there obviously are no genes that predetermine assault, armed robbery, and so on. The critical question is: What partially inherited mediating process accounts for the behavior genetics finding? In the case of criminal behavior, one possible mediating process is the inheritance of a chronically underaroused autonomic nervous system. Thus some people may be more likely to engage in criminal acts because they are less

fearful and less likely to learn from experience (see Chapter 9).

GENETICS AND THE ETIOLOGY OF PSYCHOPATHOLOGY

There can be no doubt that genes have very broad effects on abnormal behavior, despite our cautions about interpreting behavior genetics research. Most influences appear to be polygenic; thus psychologists continue to be vexed by the question of where to draw the line between normal and abnormal behavior. Still, a relatively small number of genes may contribute to certain disorders, and the identification of specific genes could lead to breakthroughs in diagnosis and treatment.

Genes partially determine *individual differences*, or why people are different from one another. Genes also are basic to determining *species-typical characteristics*—characteristics that people have in common as a part of all human nature. We consider species-typical characteristics—basic human nature—as part of our next topic, psychological factors in abnormal behavior.

Psychological Factors

Psychology has not reached a consensus about its core contents and processes—the psychological equivalents of neuroanatomy and neurophysiology. In fact, proponents of the psychoanalytic, behavioral, and humanistic paradigms have clashed in theorizing about the etiology of psychopathology. Psychologists are struggling to define common ground, however, and common themes can be found across all approaches. We highlight four such topics in our discussion of psychological factors and the causes of abnormal behavior: basic human motivation, emotion, and temperament; learning and cognition; the sense of self; and stages of psychological development.

Motivation, Emotion, and Temperament

The foundation of any psychological theory is formed in its species-typical assumptions about human nature. In fact, we have already compared the traditional paradigms in terms of

this essential starting assumption (see Table 2–2). What are our basic psychological motivations—motivations that we may or may not share with other animals?

HIERARCHY OF NEEDS

One influential ordering of human motivations is the *hierarchy of needs* developed by humanistic psychologist Abraham Maslow (1954). Maslow classified human needs according to more and less pressing priorities, giving precedence to biological needs over psychological ones (see Figure 2–7). According to Maslow, physical survival is the most basic human need, and it requires obtaining food, water, warmth, oxygen, and other necessities for human life. Safety needs come next, but these are of somewhat lesser priority. Humans will risk physical safety in order to maintain survival; for example, starving people will confront danger in order to obtain food.

In Maslow's theory the most basic psychological need is the need to belong to some social unit. The next psychological need is to be esteemed or valued by others. Just as psychological needs are sacrificed when biological needs are pressing, the need for esteem will be forsaken in order to meet the need to be a part of relationships. Finally, what distinguishes Maslow's theory as a humanistic approach is his identification of self-actualization as a basic human need. Maslow believed that the need to fulfill one's human potential, to self-actualize, was an innate characteristic. The need for self-actualization clearly is a unique aspect of his theory, but when examined carefully, Maslow's hierarchy of human needs shares many broad assumptions with other approaches.

ATTACHMENT THEORY

The most basic psychological need in Maslow's hierarchy, the need to form close relationships, was the focus of detailed theorizing by the influential British psychiatrist John Bowlby (1907–1990). Bowlby was trained in psychoanalysis, but he explicitly rejected Freudian theory by placing the need to form close relationships at the core of his view of development (Bowlby, 1969, 1982). The heart of Bowlby's theory is the observation that infants form **attachments** early in life—that is, they develop special and selective bonds with their caregivers. We discuss his approach, known as *attachment theory*, at various points throughout the text. Bowlby's Canadian-American counterpart, psychologist Mary Ainsworth, can be credited with conducting and stimulating widespread empirical research on attachment theory, which we also discuss throughout the text (Bretherton, 1992).

Bowlby based attachment theory on findings from *ethology*, the study of animal behavior. Ethologists have documented that close relationships develop between infants and caregivers in many species of animals. In some species, selective relationships develop in the first hours or days of life, a process called *imprinting*. Imprinting is best understood as a product of evolution, and Bowlby theorized that evolution also explains why humans form selective attachments during the first year of life. Attachments are far more flexible than imprinting, but like other animals, human infants become distressed when separated from their caregivers. Their displays of distress—long and loud cries—keep caregivers in proximity. Proximity between infants and their caregivers has

FIGURE 2-7: Maslow's five basic human needs. Needs located at the bottom of the hierarchy are more basic. For example, unmet biological needs (in red) will supersede psychological ones (in blue).

Source: Adapted from A.H. Maslow, 1954, *Motivation and Personality*. New York: Harper & Row.

survival value; thus Bowlby theorized that attachment behavior developed as a result of natural selection.

DOMINANCE RELATIONS

The development of attachments, or more generally of *affiliation*, is only one of two basic social behaviors studied by ethologists. The second is the development of **dominance,** the hierarchical ordering of a social group into more and less powerful members (Sloman, Gardner, & Price, 1989). Dominance hierarchies are easily observed in human as well as animal social groups; thus it would seem that we also share this pattern of behavior with other animals. Note that the development of dominance relations in humans is not inconsistent with Maslow's theory that people need to be esteemed or valued by others.

Thus we conclude that, in addition to more basic biological needs, humans have at least two, sometimes competing, psychological motivations: to form attachments and to compete for dominance. Our conclusion is consistent with the theories of U.S. psychiatrist Harry Stack Sullivan (1892–1949). As we discuss in Chapter 3, Sullivan developed an interpersonal theory of personality based on these two dimensions. In fact, some contemporary psychoanalytic theorists view the Freudian drives for sex and aggression not as literal instincts but as broad metaphors, much like the contemporary social motivations of affiliation and dominance (Cameron & Rychlak, 1985).

EMOTIONS AND EMOTIONAL SYSTEMS

To this point, we have discussed basic psychological motivations at the level of social behavior—but how are they represented within the individual? Many contemporary theorists assert that key social interactions are motivated by **emotions,** internal feeling states, much like searching for food is motivated by hunger. For example, attachment behavior is motivated both by the fear experienced during separations and by the security felt by infant and caretaker during close contact.

We have hundreds of words for different emotions in the English language, but researchers have used statistical analysis to reduce the list to six basic emotions (National Advisory Mental Health Council, 1995):

- Love
- Joy
- Surprise
- Anger
- Sadness
- Fear

This list can be grouped into the even smaller classifications of *positive emotion* and *negative emotion*. Of course, negative emotions are most relevant to abnormal psychology, and we have separate chapters that focus primarily on sadness (Chapter 5) and fear (Chapter 6); anger is considered in relation to a number of different disorders.

Negative emotions tend to occur together, but somewhat surprisingly, negative emotions also tend to occur together with positive emotions. Apparently, different brain systems process positive and negative emotions. More generally, it is useful to think of emotions in terms of *emotional systems* instead of discrete feelings. That is, experiences may not activate a single isolated feeling, but instead different events may elicit a group of emotions related to a particular social motivation (Panksepp, 1988). For example, fear and security are complementary emotions, not separate feelings, in the attachment system. Together these feelings motivate infants and caretakers to maintain proximity. Other emotional systems may include the rage–fear emotional system associated with fight or flight (see Chapter 8) and the security–anger–sadness emotional constellation linked with grief (see Chapter 17).

The concept of emotional systems is consistent with evolutionary theory and with the biological realities of the brain (Panksepp, 1988). The focus on systems of emotion also holds important implications for understanding human feelings. The same feeling may have a different meaning and a different opposing emotion, depending on its social function or motivation. For example, anger in reaction to a physical threat clearly is different from anger in reaction to loss. In the first case, fear is the emotion opposing anger, but in the second case anger has two opposing emotions: security and sadness.

A final point to note is that emotion may be more "primitive" than cognition (which we consider shortly). Emotions often come to us without intention, effort, or desire, whereas we typically can direct our thoughts. Similarly, we may try to control our feelings with our thoughts, but it often seems difficult to do so. In fact, research indicates that emotions are controlled primarily by subcortical brain structures, whereas more abstract cognitive abilities are localized in the cerebral cortex, a more recent product of evolution. Cognition can shape or modify emotion, but feelings are more "basic": They are not wholly created or controlled by our intellectual interpretations of psychophysiological arousal (Panksepp, 1988).

TEMPERAMENT

Basic motivations and emotions are species-typical characteristics, but there are wide individual differences in how people relate to the social and physical worlds. An important approach to research on individual differences is the study of **temperament,** characteristic styles of relating to the world. Some theorists assert that temperament is the expression of inborn characteristics (Goldsmith, 1988), whereas other psychologists equate temperament with the broader construct of personality (Zuckerman, 1991). In all cases, however, research on temperament focuses on the "how" of behavior, not the "what."

For decades, psychologists have debated which elements comprise the basic

▼ Emotion is a distinctively human quality as characters from "Star Trek: The Next Generation" illustrated. The android, Data (on the left), had superb cognitive capacities but lacked emotion. Troi came from a race with extrahuman empathic abilities.

temperamental styles, but recently researchers have reached a consensus at least about the dimensions of adult temperament (Goldberg, 1993; Zuckerman, 1991). Based on extensive analysis of subjects' responses to structured questionnaires, researchers have identified five bipolar dimensions of personality, sometimes called "the big five." These are (1) *neuroticism*—nervous and moody versus calm and pleasant; (2) *extraversion*—active and talkative versus passive and reserved; (3) *openness to experience*—imaginative and curious versus shallow and imperceptive; (4) *agreeableness*—trusting and kind versus hostile and selfish; and (5) *conscientiousness*—organized and reliable versus careless and negligent.

Individual differences in temperamental styles have been hypothesized to play a role in the development of a number of psychological disorders. Not surprisingly, these basic dimensions of personality have particularly influenced thinking about the development of personality disorders, as we discuss in Chapter 9. Temperament also holds a special place in research on the etiology of behavior problems among children, a topic we take up in Chapter 16.

MOTIVATION, EMOTION, TEMPERAMENT, AND THE ETIOLOGY OF PSYCHOPATHOLOGY

Attachment theorists assert that the origins of psychopathology can be traced to the failure to meet a child's basic need to form a secure attachment. Of particular concern are the effects of *insecure* or *anxious attachments*—uncertain or ambivalent parent–child relationships that are a consequence of inconsistent and unresponsive parenting, particularly during the first year of life (Ainsworth et al., 1978). Anxious attachments are hypothesized to cause children to be mistrustful, dependent, and/or rejecting when approaching subsequent relationships, a pattern that may continue into adult life. Attachment theorists also assert that similar uncertainties about relationships are created by parental separation and loss during childhood (Bowlby, 1973, 1980). Critics argue that early attachment difficulties are more easily overcome than attachment theory asserts, but they agree that close, supportive relationships promote mental health throughout the life span (Rutter & Rutter, 1993).

Little research has been conducted on the consequences of unfulfilled needs for social dominance or esteem. Much evidence does indicate, however, that children need to be "dominated"—"disciplined" is a much better word—if they are to learn to conform their behavior to social norms. It is worth noting, moreover, that according to a leading developmental theory, the most effective parents are those who are able to meet (or control) their children's needs in both of the two basic areas that we have highlighted. Specifically, children whose parents are loving *and* firm in their discipline are better adjusted in comparison to children whose parents are inadequate on one or both of these dimensions (Maccoby & Martin, 1983).

Finally, the role of temperament in the development of psychopathology generally is viewed in terms of the diathesis-stress model. Specifically, researchers have focused on the *goodness of fit* between children's temperament and their environment. A "difficult" temperament may increase the risk for the subsequent development of abnormal behavior, but experience determines whether problems emerge (Chess & Thomas, 1984).

Learning and Cognition

Emotions, motivations, and temperamental styles can be modified, at least to some degree, by the higher processes of learning and cognition. In our historical review, we have already discussed two critical learning processes: classical and operant conditioning. These modes of learning are essential to normal development. As you will see in later chapters, classical and operant conditioning also play an important role in the etiology or maintenance of several psychological disorders.

MODELING

A third method of learning, known as modeling, was originally identified by U.S. psychologist Albert Bandura of Stanford University (Bandura & Walters, 1963). The concept of **modeling** suggests that people learn much of their behavior by imitating others, a process that you surely have observed many times.

A similar but more complex concept is the process of learning through identification. The concept of **identification** was introduced by Freud (1940/1969), who asserted that children identify strongly with one adult, normally the same-gender parent. The process of identification suggests that children not only imitate an adult's behavior but also adopt his or her values. Freud's emphasis on the need to

▲ **Stanford University psychologist Albert Bandura extensively studied modeling, the process of learning through imitation.**

identify with the parent of the same gender has been roundly criticized. However, the basic idea of identification—that children not only *act* like certain adults but want to *be* like them—suggests that modeling may involve more than mere imitation.

SOCIAL COGNITION

Cognitive psychologists commonly draw analogies between human thinking and the operation of computers in discussing additional, more complex processes of learning. Thus the field highlights concepts such as information processing, memory systems, and retrieval processes. Social psychologists, in turn, have developed the parallel field of *social cognition*—the study of how humans process information about themselves and others.

The important concept of attribution illustrates the social cognition approach. **Attributions** are perceived causes—people's beliefs about cause–effect relations. In evaluating a friend's hostility toward you, for example, you rarely examine it scientifically. Instead, you attribute his or her actions to some reasonable cause, perhaps a tendency to overreact. Attribution theorists suggest that humans are "intuitive scientists" who routinely draw such conclusions about causality. We use shorthand calculations instead of more detailed methods in attributing causes because the quick assessments are efficient—they require little cognitive processing. Attributions can be inaccurate, however, in part because they are made intuitively rather than scientifically (Nisbett & Wilson, 1977). Moreover, errors in making attributions, and other cognitive biases, have increasingly been suggested to play a role in the development of abnormal behavior (Peterson & Seligman, 1984).

LEARNING, DISTORTED COGNITION, AND THE ETIOLOGY OF PSYCHOPATHOLOGY

At least some abnormal behavior apparently is learned. Fears can be classically conditioned, antisocial behavior often is rewarded, and some children imitate or identify with an alcoholic parent, to cite a few examples. Abnormal behavior also may be learned through more complex cognitive processes, particularly as a result of systematic errors or distortions in information processing.

Learned helplessness theory, for example, suggests that depression is caused by wrongly attributing negative events to internal, global, and stable causes (Peterson & Seligman, 1984; see Chapter 5). According to this theory, you are at risk for depression if you conclude that the reason for your bad grade on a calculus exam is: "I'm stupid." The "stupid" attribution blames the grade on internal, global, and stable causes, a cognition that makes you feel more helpless and ultimately more depressed. According to learned helplessness theory, healthier attributions are "the teacher was unfair," "I'm lousy at math," or "I didn't work hard enough," because each attribution is, respectively, external, specific, and unstable in quality.

Another theory suggests that depression is caused by automatic and distorted perceptions of reality, particularly negative *cognitive errors* (Beck, Rush, Shaw, & Emery, 1979). For example, people prone to depression may draw inaccurate, negative generalizations in processing information about themselves. For instance, they conclude that they are inadequate based on a single unpleasant experience. It is interesting to note that a treatment based on this theory encourages depressed people to be more scientific and less intuitive in evaluating their conclusions (see Chapter 5).

The Sense of Self

We share emotions and motivations with other animals, and we share some information-processing strategies with computers. Still, our sense of self seems to be a uniquely human quality. The exact definition of our sense of self is elusive. This often is true personally, and the definition of self clearly is elusive in its numerous psychological conceptualizations.

One important and influential conceptualization is Erik Erikson's (1968) concept of **identity.** Erikson viewed identity as the product of the adolescent's struggle to answer the question "Who am I?" In his view, the conflict caused by this persistent question eventually produces an enduring identity, an integrated sense of individuality, wholeness, and continuity.

Some theorists have countered that identity is not a unitary construct. Instead, they argue that there are many "selves." Psychologist George Kelly (1905–1966), for example, emphasized the many different roles that people play in life. These include such obvious roles as being a daughter, a student, and a friend, and they also include less obvious roles, like being a "caretaker," a "jock," or "the quiet one." Thus, rather than having a single identity, Kelly argued, people develop many different *role identities*, various senses of oneself that correspond with actual life roles.

Even more specific views on the individual's sense of self are found in cognitive conceptualizations that discuss specific *self-schema*—cognitions about oneself. Albert Ellis (1970), the most prominent advocate of rational emotive therapy (see Chapter 3), provides one example of this approach. He points to people's irrational beliefs as the source of much of their psychological distress. *Irrational beliefs* are impossible, absolute standards, such as "Everyone must love me all of the time." According to Ellis, failure and psychological distress are the inevitable consequences of irrational beliefs, because nobody can live up to such impossible standards.

SELF SYSTEMS AND THE ETIOLOGY OF PSYCHOPATHOLOGY

There is no commonly accepted definition of self in psychology. Still, two ideas—self-control and self-esteem—are frequently found in theorizing and research on psychopathology.

The idea that children and adults must develop **self-control**—internal rules for guiding appropriate behavior—is commonly accepted in research on abnormal behavior. Self-control is learned through the process of *socialization*, wherein parents, teachers, and peers use discipline, praise, and their own example to teach children prosocial behavior and set limits on their antisocial behavior. Over time, these standards are *internalized*—that is, the external rules become internal regulations. The result is self-control (Maccoby, 1992).

A sense of self-worth is a different aspect of the self. Various discussions of the importance of high self-esteem have been emphasized by psychoanalytic, behavioral, and humanistic theorists. Sigmund Freud (1940/1969) discussed the importance of a healthy ego, a strong and confident inner reserve (see Further Thoughts earlier in this chapter). Carl Rogers (1961) highlighted a healthy *self-concept*—feeling worthy and capable—as the core structure of personality in his humanistic approach. Finally, social learning theorist Albert Bandura (1977) argued for the primacy of **self-efficacy,** the belief that one can achieve desired goals.

Each theorist highlights the importance of the individual's sense of self-worth for mental health. You should consider, however, that low self-esteem could be a *result* rather than a cause of abnormal behavior. High self-esteem grows from success and fulfillment, whereas anxiety and depression—and low self-esteem—result from failure, loss, conflict, and rejection. In short, low self-esteem may only be an index of emotional problems, not a cause of them.

Stages of Development

Developmental change is especially relevant to psychological factors in the etiology of psychopathology. Of particular importance are periods of very rapid developmental change, or what we can consider to be qualitative, as opposed to quantitative, shifts in development. Such shifts mark the end of one **developmental stage,** a period of continuous and slow change, and the beginning of a new one.

As an illustration of the idea of stages of development, consider the schools you have attended. You have experienced at least four important "developmental stages" in your schooling: elementary school, middle school, high school, and college. The shift from one "stage" to another (for example, going to college) required you to make rapid and perhaps challenging changes in your life. Moreover, once you entered a new "stage" you had to learn to master new tasks and perform according to a new set of expectations.

Stages of psychological development similarly challenge routine functioning and force the individual to learn new ways of thinking, feeling, and acting. Normal distress in response to such difficult transitions sometimes can be confused with abnormal behavior. On the other hand, the stress associated with a developmental transition may precipitate a mental disorder if there is a predisposing diathesis.

Two prominent stage theories are especially relevant to abnormal psychology: Freud's theory of psycho*sexual* development and Erikson's theory of psycho*social* development. As is evident in the name given to his theory, Freud highlighted the child's internal struggles with sexuality as marking the various stages of development. In contrast, Erikson emphasized social tasks and the conflicts involved in meeting the demands of the external world. Importantly, Erikson also suggested that development does not end with adolescence; rather, he proposed that qualitative

TABLE 2-4

Comparison of Freud's and Erikson's Stage Theories of Development

Age[1]	0–1½	1–3	2–6	5–12	11–20	18–30	25–70	65 on
Freud	**Oral** Oral gratification through breastfeeding. Meeting one's own needs.	**Anal** Learning control over environment and inner needs through toilet training.	**Phallic** Recognition of sexuality and rivalry with opposite-gender parent. Oedipal conflicts, penis envy.	**Latency** Not a stage, as psychosexual development is dormant during these ages.	**Genital** Mature sexuality and formation of mutual heterosexual relationships.			
Erikson	**Basic Trust vs. Basic Mistrust** Developing basic trust in self and others through feeding and care taking.	**Autonomy vs. Shame and Doubt** Gaining a sense of competence and independence through success in toileting and mastering environment.	**Initiative vs. Guilt** Gaining parental approval for initiative rather than guilt over rivalry and inadequacy.	**Industry vs. Inferiority** Curiosity and eagerness to learn leads to a sense of competence or inadequacy.	**Identify vs. Role Confusion** Identity crisis is a struggle to answer question, "Who am I?"	**Intimacy vs. Self-absorption** Sense of aloneness of young adult resolved by forming close friendships and a lasting intimate relationship.	**Generativity vs. Stagnation** Success in work but especially in raising the next generation or failure to be productive (even if children are born).	**Integrity vs. Despair** A sense of satisfaction with the life one lived rather than despair over lost opportunities.

[1]Ages are approximate as indicated by overlap in age ranges.

developmental stages continue throughout the life span.

The key tasks, age ranges, and defining events of these two stage theories are summarized in Table 2–4. In considering differences between the theories, also note an interesting similarity. Both theorists use similar ages to denote the beginning and end of their developmental stages of childhood. Others also have suggested that key developmental transitions occur around the ages of 1½, 6, and 12. Included among this group is the noted Swiss psychologist Jean Piaget, who theorized about cognitive development. Irrespective of substantive focus, these ages seem to be key times of transition for children.

DEVELOPMENT AND THE ETIOLOGY OF PSYCHOPATHOLOGY

The idea of developmental stages suggests some new concepts for understanding the etiology of psychopathology. One key concept is the notion of a *developmental transition*, the idea that stressful and important changes occur during times of rapid biological, psychological, or social development. People often are stressed by normal developmental transitions and frequently seek the help of a mental health professional as a result. Chapter 17 is devoted exclusively to a discussion of difficult developmental transitions throughout the adult life span.

Two other concepts relevant to stage theories are the ideas of fixation and regression. *Fixation* occurs when psychological development is arrested at a particular stage. The person continues to grow physically but stops growing emotionally. *Regression* is characterized by the return to an earlier stage or style of coping or behaving. These concepts may be less useful as explanations of the etiology of psychopathology than they are as descriptions of the symptoms of some psychological disorders, as we discuss in later chapters.

Social Factors

The broadest perspective for understanding the causes of abnormal behavior is at the level of the social system. There are an almost endless number of potential social influences on behavior, including many aspects of interpersonal relationships, social institutions, and cultural values. Therefore we must be selective in reviewing social contributions to psychopathology. In this section we begin with a focus on relationships and then move on to a consideration of gender roles, ethnicity, poverty, and broad societal values.

These social perspectives all emphasize that the definition and development of psychopathology are a product of people's *social roles*, styles of behaving according to the expectations of the social situation. Much the way an actor assumes a role in a play, people play roles in their families and in social relationships. Prescribed social roles also stem from the very broad expectations associated with gender, race, social class, and culture in the United States. In fact, *labeling theory* views emotional disorders themselves in terms of role theory (Rosenhan, 1973). According to labeling theory, abnormal behavior is created by social expectations; it is only what a given group or society deems to be abnormal (see Chapter 4). Labeling theory also suggests that people's actions conform to the expectations created by the label, a process that has been termed the *self-fulfilling prophesy* (Rosenthal, 1966). For example, when an elementary school boy is labeled as "a troublemaker," both he and his teachers may act in ways that make the label come true.

There is little doubt that expectations affect behavior. Still, labeling alone cannot somehow cause the severe hallucinations, delusions, and life disruptions that characterize severe disorders like schizophrenia, for example. The roles people play in life help to shape who they become, but psychopathology is much more than the expectancies a label creates.

Relationships and Psychopathology

Much evidence links abnormal behavior with distressed or conflicted relationships. Obvious difficulties like anger and conflict in relationships are linked with a number of emotional disorders ranging from schizophrenia to conduct problems among children (Emery, 1982; Fontana, 1966). Still, often it is impossible to determine if troubled relationships actually *cause* abnormal behavior. In many cases, it seems equally or more likely that relationship distress is the *effect* of individual problems (see Research Methods on p. 43).

MARITAL STATUS AND PSYCHOPATHOLOGY

The relationship between marital status and psychopathology is a good example of the cause–effect dilemma we have just discussed. The demographics of the U.S. family have changed greatly over the last few decades. Cohabitation before marriage is frequent, many children are born outside of marriage, and half of all marriages end in divorce (Cherlin, 1992). In part because of the uncertainty created by these rapid changes, researchers have frequently examined the psychological consequences of alternative family structures for children and for adults (Amato & Keith, 1991a, 1991b; Emery, 1988, 1994; Gotlib & McCabe, 1990).

The findings of this large body of research must be interpreted with caution and care. On the one hand, marital status and psychological problems clearly are *correlated*. Somewhat more emotional problems are found among children and adults from divorced or never-married families than among people living in always-married families (see Chapter 18). On the other hand, despite common assumptions to the contrary, it is not clear that marital status is a direct *cause* of the emotional problems. Alternative explanations of the correlation include suggestions that common genetic factors cause both emotional disorders and marital disruption (McGue & Lykken, 1992), as well as the likelihood that marital status can be a consequence, not a cause, of some psychological problems among adults (Gotlib & McCabe, 1990). Thus marital status may cause psychopathology, but abnormal behavior also can create dysfunctional families (see Research Close-Up).

Marriage and Mental Health

Psychologists and social policy makers often raise concerns about a factor that is commonly found to be correlated with psychological well-being: marital status. We discuss the consequences of divorce for children in some detail in Chapters 16 and 18. Here we consider the correlation between adults' mental health and their marital status.

Valuable data on the relation between marriage and mental health are available from the Epidemiologic Catchment Area (ECA) study (Robins & Regier, 1991). Thousands of people were interviewed in this study in order to obtain state-of-the-art measurements of their mental health. The researchers also examined various life circumstances that were correlated with mental illness, including marital status.

The investigators found consistent correlations between marriage and mental health. As one example, 1.5 percent of people still in their first marriage were diagnosed with depression in the past year. For people who had never married, the 1-year prevalence of depression was 2.4 percent. Among those who had been divorced once, 4.1 percent had experienced depression in the past year. Finally, 5.8 percent of the people who had been divorced more than once had experienced an episode of depression in the previous 12 months. Thus, in comparison to people still in their first marriage, the never-married were about 1.5 times as likely to be depressed; people who had been divorced once were almost 3 times as likely to be depressed; and people divorced more than once were nearly 4 times as likely to be assigned the diagnosis.

Alcoholism also was found to be correlated with marital status. Among people in their first marriage, 8.9 percent met the diagnostic criteria for alcoholism at some time *in their life* (not the past year, which was the time frame for depression). For the never-married, the lifetime prevalence was 15 percent. Comparable figures were 16.2 percent for people divorced once and 24.2 percent for people divorced two or more times.

Marital status also was strongly related to a diagnosis of schizophrenia. The lifetime prevalence of schizophrenia was 1.0 percent among the married, 2.1 percent among the never-married, and 2.9 percent among those who had ever separated or divorced. In fact, marital status was related to virtually every psychological disorder that was diagnosed in this study.

How do we interpret the correlation between marriage and mental illness? The usual causal interpretation is that not being married causes emotional problems. According to this reasoning, the absence of a supportive mate makes unmarried people more susceptible to psychological problems, as do divorce and the conflict and loss of support that accompany it.

As we discussed in Research Methods in this chapter, however, reverse causality needs to be considered as an alternative explanation. Specifically, emotional problems may be the cause of marital status. Psychologically disturbed people may have more trouble dating and forming permanent relationships. If they do get married, their emotional struggles may make them or their spouses more unhappy with their marriages and more prone to divorce. Third-variable interpretations offer yet another possibility. Any number of third variables could create a spurious correlation between marital status and abnormal behavior. We know, for example, that poverty is correlated with an increased risk for remaining single or getting divorced, and we also know that poverty is correlated with an increased risk for developing psychological disorders. Perhaps poverty is a third variable that creates an artificial relation between marriage and mental health.

These alternative explanations or *models* of the relation between marriage and mental health hold vastly different implications for the treatment of psychological disorders and for social policy. If marital troubles are the cause of mental illness, our interventions should focus on improving or promoting marriage. For example, rather than treating individuals in therapy, psychologists may be more effective if they treat troubled marriages or family relationships. If mental illness causes marital troubles, however, psychologists still may want to treat couples or families (in addition to individual patients), but the therapy might focus on helping family members to cope with the trying stressor of mental illness. Finally, if the correlation between marital status and psychopathology is caused by a third variable like poverty, our interventions should focus on the third variable. If this is the case, eradicating poverty should both improve marriage and lower rates of mental illness.

We have discussed marriage and mental health from a theoretical/methodological perspective, but you may be wondering what psychologists have concluded about the correlation between marriage and mental health. First, the correlation between marriage and mental health may be partly explained by third variables like poverty, but much of it is "real." The correlation is still found even when we exclude the effects of poverty and related "third variables" (Gove, Hughes, & Styles, 1983). Second, for severe psychological disorders like schizophrenia, it seems clear that being single or getting divorced is a

reaction to, not a cause of, the emotional problem. Severe mental illness causes social difficulties that interfere with getting and staying married. Third, it does appear that being single, getting divorced, or having an unhappy marriage can cause some other, more common psychological problems, such as depression (Beach, Sandeen, & O'Leary, 1990; Gotlib & McCabe, 1990). This conclusion is consistent with what many people say about their emotional struggles with divorce or with being single when "everyone else" is married.

These differing conclusions remind us of one reason why we follow the systems approach to etiology in this text rather than adopting a paradigms approach. The same life event can play a different role in the etiology of different psychological disorders. Our theory about the relation between marriage and mental illness must be adapted for different psychological disorders. ■

SOCIAL RELATIONSHIPS

In addition to relationships within the family, key relationships outside the family can also affect mental health. For example, research indicates that a good relationship with an adult outside the family can buffer children from the effects of troubled family circumstances (National Advisory Mental Health Council, 1995; Werner & Smith, 1992; Werner & Smith, 1982). Close relationships also provide protection against the development of psychopathology (Cohen & Wills, 1985).

Research suggests that a few things are critical about **social support**—the emotional and practical assistance received from others. Significantly, one close relationship can provide as much support as being involved in many relationships. The greatest risk comes from having no social support. In addition, it is much worse to be actively rejected than to be neglected (Coie & Kupersmidt, 1983). Especially among children, it is far worse to be "liked least" than not to be "liked most" by your peers.

The association between abnormal behavior and the lack of supportive peer relationships may have several different causes. In some circumstances, peer rejection may be the cause of emotional difficulties. Being made an outcast surely can cause much distress. In other cases, the lack of a close relationship may be a

consequence of psychopathology, as when a disturbed individual is extremely awkward in social relationships. Finally, social support may help people to cope more successfully with emotional problems. The presence or absence of a close relationship might not cause a psychological problem, but once the problem emerges, social support may be the difference between successful and failed coping.

▼ Social isolation and especially active rejection by peers are linked with an increased prevalence of psychological disorders.

Gender and Gender Roles

Gender and **gender roles** can dramatically affect social relationships and social interaction. Boys and girls, men and women, are different. One common distinction argues that women are more *relational,* or oriented toward others, whereas men are more *instrumental,* or oriented toward action and achievement (Gilligan, 1982). Whether such differences really exist—and, if they do, what causes them—is open to debate. There is no doubt that some gender differences are determined by genetics and hormones, but there also is little doubt that socially prescribed gender roles exert a strong influence on our behavior (Maccoby, 1991).

Gender roles may influence the development, expression, or consequences of psychopathology. Some theorists have suggested, for example, that women's traditional roles foster dependency and helplessness, which accounts for the considerably higher rates of depression among women (Nolen-Hoeksema, 1990; see Chapter 5). Others have suggested that gender roles are not responsible for the etiology of abnormal behavior, but they do influence how psychopathology is expressed. According to this view, each gender may experience helplessness, but women are allowed to be depressed, whereas men's gender roles dictate that they "carry on" as if nothing were wrong. Instead of becoming depressed, men may express their inner turmoil as a psychosomatic disorder (see Chapter 7). In other cases, gender roles may shape the course and consequences of abnormal behavior. For example, women's but not men's gender roles may allow them to avoid feared circumstances following a panic attack, and this avoidance may help determine whether the difficulty develops into the generalized problem of agoraphobia (see Chapter 6).

Gender and gender roles are controversial and politically charged topics. To a lesser extent, so is the idea of *androgyny*—the possession of both "female" and "male" gender-role characteristics. Many people believe that androgyny is the answer to the problems associated with being either overly "feminine" or overly "masculine." Others reject this perspective and believe that traditional gender roles should be embraced, not criticized. We do not attempt to address such conflicting values in this text. We do, however, repeatedly consider evidence on epidemiological differences between men and women in the prevalence of psychological disorders. When appropriate, we interpret this evidence in terms of the roles played by men and women in U.S. society.

Race and Poverty

Race and poverty are broad social influences on psychological well-being in the United States today. We consider these two factors together because they are so commonly linked in American life. In 1993, 13 percent of white children were living below the poverty level, compared with 46 percent of black children and 40 percent of Latino children. Race and poverty also are closely linked to marital status. Among African-American children who lived with married parents, 15 percent lived in poverty, in comparison to 57 percent of children who lived with a single mother. Comparable figures among whites were 8 percent and 39 percent (Zill & Nord, 1994).

Evidence indicates that various psychological disorders are related to race and poverty (National Advisory Mental Health Council, 1995). In examining this evidence, one task is to disentangle the separate consequences of race and poverty. Poverty potentially may play several roles in the development of psychopathology. Children from poor inner-city neighborhoods witness and are victims of an incredible amount of violence in their communities. For example, one researcher found that 12 percent of school-aged children living in a Washington, D.C., neighborhood reported having seen a dead body in the streets outside their homes (Richters, 1993). Poverty also increases exposure to chemical toxins, such as to the lead found in old, chipping paint and automotive exhaust fumes. When ingested at toxic levels, lead can cause damage to the central nervous system.

The conditions of poverty are more likely to affect blacks, because more blacks live in poverty. However, the experiences of American blacks and whites differ in many more ways than socioeconomic status. African Americans have endured a history of slavery and discrimination, and broad racial prejudices can undermine social opportunities and self-image. Moreover, distinctive

▼ **Children's mental health can be undermined by extreme poverty and poor living conditions.**

aspects of African-American culture have too readily been labeled as deficits instead of differences. For example, the maternal grandmother often fulfills the role of a supportive second parent among African-American single-mother families, but these families are sometimes viewed by psychologists and policy makers as flawed nevertheless (Wilson, 1989). Some differences among ethnic groups are adaptive, some are maladaptive, and some are merely differences.

Broad Societal Values

Broad social values also may influence the nature and development of abnormal behavior. For example, humanistic psychologists have questioned the conflict between the requirements for healthy psychological development and societal demands in our frenzied and competitive culture of materialism (Szasz, 1961). Other people, however, find great value in the material, technological, and scientific gains that accompany industrialization. From this perspective, concerns about society's frustration of personal growth are, in fact, luxuries of the very success that commentators deride. Higher needs for belongingness and for self-actualization can only be satisfied once the more basic needs for survival and safety are met (see Figure 2–7).

We do not attempt to address the "mental health" of American culture in this textbook. However, we do recognize the broad influences of society and culture on abnormal behavior. Our personal lives, our education, and even our science are deeply embedded within contemporary U.S. culture. The broad practices, beliefs, and values of our society play a role in the definition and development of abnormal behavior and in shaping the scientific enterprise that attempts to uncover the roots of psychopathology.

Summary

The **biomedical, psychoanalytic, behavioral,** and **humanistic** approaches to understanding the causes of abnormal behavior are alternative **paradigms,** and not just alternative theories. Biological approaches emphasize causes that occur "within the skin." Psychoanalytic theory highlights unconscious processes and detailed case histories. Behavioral viewpoints focus on observable, learned behavior. Finally, humanistic psychology argues that behavior is not determined but, instead, is a product of free will. In short, these approaches conflict not only in their explanations of abnormal behavior but also in what they view as acceptable scientific methods.

Although science benefits from competition, the conflict between these broad paradigms has outlived its usefulness, because none of these approaches offers the "right" explanation. Rather, abnormal behavior is determined by **multifactorial causes,** the combination of different biological, psychological, and social factors. The current challenge for scientists is to integrate evidence on the etiology of different psychological disorders into a coherent whole, a system of contributing factors.

Systems theory is an innovation in understanding and conducting science that offers assistance in this integration. Its central principle is **holism,** the idea that the whole is more than the sum of its parts—a scientific counterpoint to **reductionism.** In systems theory, smaller units are not "ultimate" causes but subsystems of the larger whole. Other important systems principles include **reciprocal causality**—the idea that causality is bidirectional—and **cybernetic** processes—the use of feedback loops to adjust

KEY TERMS

- attachment
- attribution
- autonomic nervous system
- axon
- behavioral approach
- behavior genetics
- behaviorism
- biomedical approach
- cerebellum
- cerebral cortex
- cerebral hemispheres
- chromosomes
- classical conditioning
- concordance
- conditioned response
- conditioned stimulus
- correlational study
- correlation coefficient
- cybernetics
- defense mechanism
- dendrites
- developmental psychopathology
- developmental stage
- diathesis

progress toward a goal. Systems theory also emphasizes **equifinality,** the idea that there are multiple pathways to the development of any one disorder.

Biological factors relevant to abnormal behavior begin with the smallest anatomic unit within the nervous system, the **neuron** or nerve cell. Each neuron has four major anatomic components: the **soma** or cell body, the **dendrites,** the **axon,** and the **terminal buttons.** Communication between neurons occurs when the terminal buttons release chemical substances called **neurotransmitters** into the **synapse** between nerve cells. Disrupted communication among neurons, particularly disruptions in the functioning of various neurotransmitters, is implicated in the etiology of several types of abnormal behavior. We must not equate a neurophysiological explanation of a psychological disorder with a biological abnormality, however, since such a conclusion raises concerns about biological reductionism and mind–body **dualism.**

Neuroanatomists commonly divide the brain into three subdivisions: the hindbrain, the midbrain, and the forebrain. Basic bodily functions are regulated by the structures of the hindbrain, which is rarely implicated in abnormal behavior. The midbrain controls some motor activities, especially those related to fighting and sex. Damage to the midbrain can cause extreme disturbances, but such abnormalities typically result from specific and unusual brain traumas or tumors. The forebrain is the location of most sensory, emotional, and cognitive processes. Most of the forebrain is composed of the two **cerebral hemispheres,** and many brain functions are **lateralized,** so that each hemisphere is the site of specific cognitive and emotional activities. Finally, the **cerebral cortex** is the uneven surface area of the brain that lies just underneath the skull. It is the site of the control and integration of sophisticated memory, sensory, and motor functions. Because of the rudimentary state of our knowledge about the brain, only the most severe mental disorders have been clearly linked with abnormalities in neuroanatomy. In most of these cases, brain damage is extensive and obvious.

Psychophysiology is the study of changes in the functioning of the body that result from psychological experiences. Psychophysiological arousal is caused by two different communication systems within the body; the **endocrine system** and the nervous system. Endocrine glands release **hormones** into the bloodstream, thus regulating some aspects of normal development as well as some responses to stress. The **autonomic nervous system** is the part of the central nervous system that is responsible for psychophysiological reactions. It has two branches, the **sympathetic** and the **parasympathetic nervous systems.** In general, the sympathetic nervous system controls arousal, and the parasympathetic nervous system controls energy conservation. Psychophysiological overarousal and underarousal both have been implicated in theories of the causes of abnormal behavior.

Behavior genetics is the study of genetic influences on the development of behavior. Most forms of abnormal behavior are **polygenic;** they are caused by more than one **gene.** Polygenic inheritance makes the study of genetic contributions to behavior difficult but not impossible. Comparisons of **monozygotic (MZ)** and **dizygotic (DZ) twins** can yield information about polygenic contributions, as can adoption studies. It is important to understand that the fact that a psychological disorder has a polygenic component does not mean that the disorder will inevitably appear, and that genetically influenced behavior is influenced by the environment. Moreover, it is not clear what mechanism may account for behavior genetic findings. Few single genes directly affect abnormal behavior; thus genetic effects probably occur at some more basic level—for example, by affecting psychophysiological arousal.

Psychology has not reached a consensus about its core constructs, but certain commonalities found across theories include issues of motivation and temperament, learning and cognition, a sense of self, and stages of psychological development. In addition to biological needs, humans apparently have at least two basic psychological motivations: to form **attachments** and to compete for **dominance. Emotion** drives these basic motivations, and recent observations suggest that organized systems of emotion may be activated by certain social needs or challenges. **Temperament** is the individual's characteristic style of relating to the world. Researchers recently have agreed on consistencies in temperamental styles—the "how" of behavior.

Learning mechanisms include **classical conditioning, operant conditioning, modeling,** and information processing. At least some abnormal behavior is learned, and in the last two decades researchers have highlighted systematic cognitive biases that relate to some psychological disorders.

The sense of self is a uniquely human quality that would seem to play a role in causing emotional problems. It is possible, however, that self-esteem merely is another index of mental health. Finally, the idea of **developmental stages** not only charts the course of normal development, against which abnormal behavior must be compared, but it also highlights the important issue of developmental transitions.

Social roles influence the definition and development of psychopathology. Evidence links abnormal behavior with distressed or conflicted family relationships, and **social support** from people other than family members can be an important buffer against stress. **Gender roles** may influence the development, expression, or consequences of psychopathology. Some theorists suggest, for example, that women's traditional roles foster dependency and helplessness. Race and poverty, which are often related, also are broad social influences on psychological well-being in the United States today. Finally, humanistic psychologists have pointed out that there may be conflict between the demands of our competitive society and the requirements for healthy psychological development.

- reverse causality
- self-control
- self-efficacy
- shared environment
- social support
- soma
- stress
- superego
- sympathetic nervous system
- synapse
- systems theory
- temperament
- temporal lobe
- terminal buttons
- thalamus
- third variable
- unconditioned response
- unconditioned stimulus
- the unconscious
- ventricles

Critical Thinking

1. What are your beliefs about the causes of abnormal behavior? Do you adhere to one of the paradigms described here? Are your reasons for preferring a particular approach personal or scientific? Has the information in this chapter changed your thinking?

2. Think about your social groups—your family, friends, clubs or organizations, or the people you live with. Consider the relationships between people in these groups, and try to understand them better by using concepts from systems theory—for example, reciprocal causality, cybernetics, homeostasis, subsystems.

3. Some people believe that we blame too many social and personal problems on biology. What are your thoughts? Do you think biological abnormalities cause (most) mental disorders? If so, what are the implications for personal responsibility for change? What are our societal responsibilities to people with emotional problems?

4. In what ways do social roles contribute to your behavior (e.g., your gender, ethnicity, or more subtle roles like being the "smart one" or the "responsible one" in your family)? What roles do you see friends and family playing? Do any of these roles encourage maladaptive or abnormal behavior?

Treatment of Psychological Disorders

How are psychological disorders treated? Pause to consider some stereotypes you may harbor. Perhaps you imagine someone lying on a couch, talking at length about childhood memories. Suddenly, he remembers a long-forgotten trauma, and the memory frees him from his pain. Then, again, perhaps you find such an approach silly—instead, you may envision a doctor sitting behind a desk and writing a prescription. The patient is relieved to learn that she has a biological problem that can be treated with medication. Perhaps you view the treatment of some mental disorders as inhumane—you may think of some unfortunate individual locked up and forgotten inside a dreary mental hospital. Or maybe you conceive of a therapist as a kind and wise elder—someone who listens, who cares, and who knows just the right things to say.

Overview

One reason for these conflicting images is our ambivalence about the treatment of psychological disorders. Emotional problems are widely misunderstood, as are the professions of clinical psychology, psychiatry, and social

"He's in an H.M.O. Get some of the King's horses and a few of the King's men."

Courtesy *The New Yorker*

work (see Chapter 1). Less than 30 percent of people with a diagnosable mental disorder receive treatment, including many people with severe disturbances (Howard et al., 1996; see Figure 3–1). At the same time, many people seek psychotherapy for personal growth or as a means of coping with life distress. Policy debates about health insurance coverage reflect the controversy about whether psychological treatments are used too little or too much. On the one hand, mental health advocates are fighting for parity in the coverage of mental and physical disorders. On the other hand, managed care organizations often drop or restrict mental health coverage, for example, by limiting reimbursed visits to 10 or even fewer therapy sessions.

Another reason for our conflicting stereotypes about psychological treatment is the wide variety of approaches to therapy. According to one review, there are more than 400 different "schools" of psychotherapy for adults and 200 for children (Kazdin, 1994). The number of different therapies creates practical as well as intellectual quandaries. How do you choose a good therapist? How do you know whether you are receiving the most effective treatment? Someone who picks a therapist out of the Yellow Pages will get very different treatment depending on which name he or she chooses.

We can greatly simplify the overwhelming array of psychological treatments by grouping them according to the four paradigms: the biomedical, psychoanalytic, behavioral, and humanistic approaches (see Chapter 2). Advocates of each paradigm have developed very different treatments. In fact, mental health professionals often ask one another, "What is your theoretical orientation?" and the answer to the question is supposed to be "biological," "psychoanalytic," "behavioral," or "humanistic."

As we explained in Chapters 1 and 2, we reject the paradigms approach. Rather, our focus on scientific evidence emphasizes the need to use different treatments for different disorders. Nevertheless, the first section of this chapter elaborates on the contrasting biomedical, psychoanalytic, behavioral, and humanistic treatments of psychological disorders. We focus on the paradigms because each theory has had an important historical influence on contemporary treatments. You need to be familiar with the general approach so you can better understand the specific treatments for specific disorders that we discuss in subsequent chapters. We also highlight differences among paradigms, because researchers have not yet identified the most promising treatment for many psychological disorders. Thus clinicians often must rely on a more general theory for guidance in planning treatments.

In the second section of the chapter, we emphasize the similarities rather than the differences across the four paradigms. One basic similarity is that three of the paradigms—the psychoanalytic, behavioral, and humanistic approaches—are forms of **psychotherapy:** Each of these three approaches uses psychological techniques to produce change in the context of a special, helping relationship. We highlight this basic similarity in reviewing research on psychotherapy outcome and on psychotherapy process. *Psychotherapy outcome research* compares the effectiveness of alternative forms of treatment. One major finding from outcome research is that all three major schools of psychotherapy produce significantly more benefit than does no treatment at all. This finding suggests that there may be more similarities among alternative treatments in practice than is apparent in theory. *Psychotherapy process research* investigates similarities in practice by studying aspects of the therapist–client relationship. For example, psychotherapy process research indicates that all

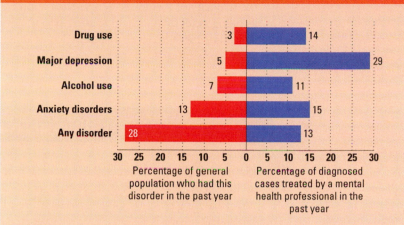

The Prevalence and Treatment of Some Psychological Disorders

FIGURE 3-1: **Many people with emotional problems do not receive treatment. These data from the Epidemiologic Catchment Area Study indicate the percentage of people in the general population who met diagnostic criteria for various mental disorders during the past year (bar graph on the left). The percentage of diagnosed cases that received treatment by a mental health professional in the past year appears on the right side of the figure.**

Source: K.I. Howard, T.A. Cornille, J.S. Lyons, J.T. Vessey, R.J. Lueger, and S.M. Saunders, 1996, Patterns of service utilization, *Archives of General Psychiatry, 53,* 696–703.

treatments are more effective when there is a positive relationship between therapist and client. Psychotherapy has a very human side irrespective of the therapist's theoretical orientation.

Although we discuss research and theory on traditional paradigms, the chapter also follows the biopsychosocial model. Our overview of biological treatments early in the chapter highlights efforts to produce psychological change through physiological means. The detailed discussion of psychotherapy process and outcome research highlights intervention at the psychological level. Toward the end of the chapter, we discuss treatments that focus on social relationships and societal institutions. Research increasingly supports the effectiveness of couples therapy, family therapy, and group therapy. Wider attempts at changing social institutions also have been advocated as promoting mental health and preventing mental illness.

At the end of the chapter we highlight the most important finding about the treatment of psychological disorders: Different therapies vary in their effectiveness for treating different problems. The most promising advances have come from the development and evaluation of specific treatments for specific disorders. In fact, the majority of therapists identify their approach as being **eclectic** (Garfield & Kurtz, 1976; Zook & Walton, 1989). Eclectic therapists do not adhere to any one paradigm; rather, they tailor their treatment for individual disorders and clients. In subsequent chapters we are eclectic in discussing alternative treatments. We focus only on specific treatments that, based on research evidence, hold particular promise for specific psychological disorders.

Traditional Treatment Paradigms

Biomedical (biological) therapies approach mental illness by drawing an analogy to physical illness. Changing psychological experience through biological means is the goal of these treatments. Medication is by far the most common biomedical treatment for psychological disorders. Other biological techniques include convulsive therapy and psychosurgery.

Freudian psychoanalysis has spawned a number of related treatments that generally are referred to as *psychodynamic psychotherapy*. Like psychoanalysis, psychodynamic psychotherapy begins with an exploration of the client's past, unconscious motivations, and defense mechanisms. Psychodynamic therapy also shares the psychoanalytic goal of promoting insight, the heightened awareness of unconscious conflicts and motivations. According to the psychodynamic tradition, conscious awareness of what was formerly unconscious—insight—is sufficient for a cure.

Behavior therapy emphasizes the application of basic psychological research to the treatment of psychological disorders. Behavior therapists believe that both normal and abnormal behavior are learned, and therapy is seen as a form of education. Promoting change, and not insight, is the major goal of behavior therapy, although the target for change may be behavior, cognition, or emotion. In fact, many behavior therapists prefer to call themselves "cognitive behavior therapists" or simply "cognitive therapists." These terms underscore the increasing importance of cognition in psychological science and in therapy.

Unlike other approaches, humanistic psychotherapists do *not* act as experts who diagnose and solve problems. Instead, humanistic therapy tries to help people to make their own life choices. In order to help clients make choices, humanistic therapists encourage their clients to become more aware of their emotions. In exploring emotions, humanistic therapists focus on present feelings, not past experiences, and they urge clients to take responsibility for their feelings and ultimately for their actions.

The following case history and discussion illustrate some of the contrasting ways in which biological, psychodynamic, behavioral, and humanistic therapists conceptualize treatment.

CASE STUDY

Depression as Seen from the Four Paradigms

Frances was a 23-year-old woman who sought psychotherapy for depression. Frances reported having been depressed for almost 3 years, with intermittent periods of relative happiness or deeper despair. When she came into therapy, her depression was quite severe. She had little appetite and had lost 10 pounds over the previous 6 weeks, and her erratic sleeping patterns were worse than usual. She awoke around 2 or 3 A.M. every night, tossed in bed for several hours, and finally fell asleep again near dawn.

Frances reported feeling profoundly depressed about herself, her new marriage, and life in general. She freely admitted to frequent thoughts of suicide. She once sat in her bathroom holding a razor blade for over an hour, contemplating whether to slash her wrists. But she decided she could never commit the act. Now, she often wished she was dead, but she felt that she "lacked the courage" to take her own life.

Frances also noted that she found herself without motivation. She withdrew from her husband and the few friends she had, and she frequently called in sick at work when she felt blue. Frances's reports of depression were underscored by her careless dress, frequent bouts of crying, and slowed speech and body movements.

Frances reported that she had experienced a happy childhood. She had not known depression until the current episode began in her senior year in college. At first, she convinced herself that she was only suffering from "senior year syndrome." She wasn't sure what to do with her life. Secretly, she longed to move to New York and finally break out and do something exciting. But when she told her parents about her plans, her mother begged Frances to return home. She insisted the two of them needed to have fun together again after 4 long years with Frances away at college. After graduation, Frances returned home to live with her parents.

It was shortly after moving home that Frances realized that her difficulties were much more serious than she had thought. She found herself intermittently screaming at her anxious and doting mother and being "super-nice" to her after feeling guilty about losing her temper. Frances described her mother as "a saint." Frances thought that her erratic behavior toward her mother was all her fault. Her mother apparently agreed. In Frances's mind, she was a failure as a daughter.

Frances described both her mother and her father as loving and giving, but some of her comments about them were far from glowing. She said she was her mother's best friend. When asked if her mother was her best friend, Frances began to cry. She felt like her mother's infant, her parent, or even her husband, but not her friend and certainly not like her grown daughter. Frances had little to say about her father. She pictured him drinking beer, eating meals, and falling asleep in front of the television.

Throughout the time she lived at home, Frances's depression only seemed to deepen. After a year of living with her parents, she married her high school sweetheart. Frances felt pressured to get married. Both her future husband and her mother insisted that it was time for her to settle down and start a family. At the time, she had hoped that marriage would be the solution to her problems. The excitement of the wedding added to this hope. But after the marriage, Frances said that things were worse—if that were possible. Still, she insisted that her marriage problems were all her fault.

Frances's husband was a young accountant who she said reminded her more and more of her father. He didn't drink, but he spent most of his brief time at home working or reading in his study. She said they had little communication, and she felt no warmth in her marriage. Her husband often was angry and sullen, but Frances said she couldn't blame him for feeling that way. His problem was being married to her. She wanted to love him, but she never had. She was a failure as a wife. She was a failure in life.

The theme of self-blame pervaded Frances's descriptions of her family. She repeatedly noted that, despite their flaws, her parents and her husband were good and loving people. She was the one with the problem. She had everything that she could hope for, yet she was unhappy. One reason she wanted to die was to ease the burden on them. How could they be happy when they had to put up with her foul moods? When she talked about these things, however, Frances's tone of voice often made her sound more angry than depressed. ■

Biological, psychodynamic, behavioral, and humanistic therapists all would note Frances's depressed mood, her self-blame, and her troubled close relationships. However, therapists working within these different theoretical frameworks would approach treatment with Frances in very different ways (see Table 3–1 on p. 76).

A biologically oriented psychiatrist or psychologist would focus first on making a diagnosis of Frances's problems. This would not be difficult in Frances's case, because her symptoms paint a clear picture of depression. The therapist surely would take note of Frances's description of her father, who seems chronically depressed. Perhaps a genetic predisposition toward depression runs in her family.

A biologically oriented therapist would sympathize with Frances's interpersonal problems, but the therapist would not blame either Frances or her family for their troubles. Rather, he or she would blame a problem that neither Frances nor her family members could control: depression.

TABLE 3-1

Some Comparisons among Biomedical, Psychodynamic, Behavioral, and Humanistic Treatments

Topic	Biomedical	Psychodynamic	Behavioral	Humanistic
Goal of treatment	Alter biology to relieve psychological distress	Gain insight into defenses/ unconscious motivations	Learn more adaptive behaviors/cognitions	Increase emotional awareness and make life choices
Primary treatment methods	Diagnosis, medications	Discussion and interpretation of defenses	Instruction, guided, learning, homework	Empathy, support, exploring emotions
Role of therapist	Active, directive, diagnostician	Passive, nondirective, interpreter (may be aloof)	Active, directive, nonjudgmental, teacher	Passive, nondirective, but warm, accepting, supporter
Length of treatment	Very brief initially, occasional visits to manage medication	Usually long term; some new short-term treatments	Mostly short term; may include later "booster" sessions	Varies; length not typically structured

It is exhausting to deal with someone who is constantly agitated and depressed. In the end, the therapist probably would explain that depression can be caused by a chemical imbalance in the brain. Medication would be recommended, and follow-up appointments would be scheduled to monitor the effects of the medication on Frances's mood and on her life.

In contrast, a psychodynamic therapist would take note of Frances's *defensive style*. For example, the therapist would see Frances's justification of her parents' and husband's behavior as a form of *rationalization*. Perhaps the therapist would also see a pattern of *denial* in Frances's refusal to acknowledge the imperfections of her loved ones and their failure to fulfill her needs. In Frances's seeing herself as a burden on her family, the therapist also might wonder if she was *projecting* onto them her own sense of feeling burdened by her mother's demands and her husband's indifference. Some psychodynamic theorists view depression as "anger turned inward" (see Chapter 5). Thus, getting Frances to express her anger directly toward her family rather than continually castigating herself might be a goal in overcoming her defenses.

Although a psychodynamic therapist would note her unexpressed anger, he or she would not challenge Frances's defenses early in therapy. Instead, the first part of treatment would be more exploratory, focusing largely on Frances's past and her hopes, feelings, and frustrations. The exploration would be directed minimally by the therapist, who would encourage Frances to talk about issues she wanted to discuss. The goal of the unstructured discussions would be to illuminate Frances's unconscious motivations,

intrapsychic conflicts, and defenses to the therapist and, over time, to Frances herself. To facilitate therapy, the psychodynamic therapist gradually would confront Frances's defenses in order to help her gain insight into her hidden resentment toward her mother, longing for a relationship with her father, and unfulfilled fantasies about marriage.

A cognitive behavior therapist would note many of the same issues in Frances's life but would approach therapy quite differently. Rather than focusing on defense mechanisms, a behavior therapist would note Frances's cognitive and behavioral patterns. Frances's self-blame—her pattern of attributing all of her interpersonal difficulties to herself—would be seen as a cognitive error. Her withdrawal from pleasing activities and her apparent unassertiveness also would be seen as contributing to her depression. In comparison to a psychodynamic therapist, a behavior therapist would be far more directive in discussing these topics. For example, he or she likely would tell Frances that her thinking was distorted and her cognitive errors were contributing to her depression.

Learning new ways of thinking and acting in the present would be the focus of behavior therapy. For example, the therapist probably would encourage Frances to appropriately blame others, not just herself, for her relationship problems, and the psychologist or psychiatrist might urge her to try out new ways of relating to her mother, father, and husband. The behavior therapist would want Frances to play an active role in this learning process by completing *homework*—activities designed to continue her treatment outside the therapy session.

Homework might include careful monitoring of specific conflicts with her family in an attempt to help Frances understand that she is not the cause of *all* family disputes. A behavior therapist also might teach Frances how to assert herself more with family members. The therapist would expect Frances's depressed mood to begin to lift once she learned to assert her rights and no longer blamed herself for everything that went wrong in her life.

A humanistic therapist also would note Frances's depression, her self-blame, and her unsatisfactory relationships with loved ones. A more prominent focus, however, would be her lack of emotional *genuineness*—her inability to "be herself" with other people and within herself. Frances's tendencies to bury her true feelings would be explored as they related to the emotions she expressed in the therapy session. The humanistic therapist would want Frances to recognize her inner feelings and would encourage her to make life choices based on her heightened emotional awareness.

In conducting therapy, the humanistic therapist probably would be nondirective in terms of specific topics for discussion but would continually focus therapy on emotional issues. Initially, the therapist might simply empathize with Frances's feelings of sadness, loneliness, and isolation. Over time, he or she likely would suggest that Frances had other feelings that she did not express. These might include frustration and guilt over her mother's controlling yet dependent style, and anger at her husband's and her father's self-centeredness. The humanistic therapist would tell Frances that her feelings were legitimate and might encourage Frances to "own" her feelings. The humanistic therapist would not directly encourage Frances to act differently, but Frances would be expected to make some changes in her life as a result of her increased emotional awareness.

These approaches to treating Frances are very different, but they may not be as different as they seem. All three approaches to psychotherapy focus on Frances's distorted thoughts and feelings, and each hones in on her self-blame for her troubled close relationships. Even a biologically oriented therapist might recommend psychotherapy in addition to medication, in order to help Frances cope with some aspects of her depression and family troubles. We discuss such integrated approaches to treatment in more detail later in this chapter. First, we elaborate further on the differences among the four approaches. The contrasts among them can best be understood by examining the treatments from a historical perspective.

Brief Historical Perspective

If we use a broad definition of "treatment," practices that date back to ancient times must be included in a history of the treatment of psychological disorders. In searching back through time, we can trace the roots of psychotherapy to two broad traditions of healing: the spiritual/religious tradition and the naturalistic/scientific tradition (Frank, 1973).

The spiritual/religious tradition attributes both physical and mental ailments to supernatural forces. This tradition dates back through ancient times, and it continues today both inside and outside formal religions. An ancient practice called *trephining* is one of the earliest examples of the spiritual/religious tradition. From skulls unearthed by archaeologists, researchers have concluded that tribal healers performed a primitive form of surgery as a treatment for mental disorders. Trephining involved chipping a hole through the unfortunate sufferer's skull with a crude stone tool. Presumably, the purpose of trephining was to allow evil spirits to escape.

There are numerous other examples throughout history and across cultures in which demons have been viewed as the cause of abnormal behavior and exorcism has been used as the treatment. Until the seventeenth century, some cases of mental disturbance in Europe and in the American colonies were attributed to witchcraft (Neugebauer, 1979). Those suspected of being witches were put through painful tests that they often could not pass. One examination was to dunk the suspected witch under water. The only way to pass the test—to be found not to be a witch—was to drown!

The spiritual/religious tradition certainly has produced bizarre explanations for and treatments of abnormal behavior. Still, the influence of spiritual beliefs and rituals cannot be ignored. Believing is a powerful part of healing. Spiritual beliefs influence how people cope with all

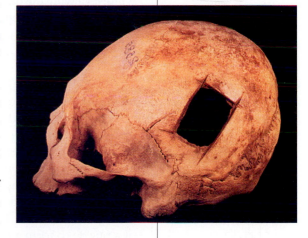

▼ Trephining was a primitive attempt to treat psychological problems by cracking a hole in the skull of the sufferer. Presumably, evil spirits could escape through the hole, thereby curing the problem.

sorts of life difficulties in contemporary society, and ministers, priests, rabbis, and other religious figures provide both spiritual guidance and practical counseling to millions of people.

Naturalistic/scientific approaches to helping the mentally disturbed also have ancient roots. Hippocrates recommended treatments such as rest, exercise, and a healthy diet (see Chapter 1). Witch hunting did occur during the Middle Ages, but naturalistic approaches similar to those outlined by Hippocrates were far more common during those times (Neugebauer, 1979). Later, "insane asylums" were developed as a new treatment for the mentally ill. One rationale for these institutions was to remove disturbed individuals from society, but another was the hope that rest and isolation would alleviate their bizarre behavior. Unfortunately, asylums for the mentally ill too often were little more than human warehouses (see Chapters 1 and 18).

Although their beginnings can be traced to ancient times, contemporary biological, psychodynamic, behavioral, and humanistic treatments are tied much more directly to developments in the nineteenth and twentieth centuries. Some innovation has been due to improvements in theory; others are the result of the development of scientific research methods, particularly the experimental method. We discuss these historically more recent developments while reviewing the different approaches to the treatment of psychological disorders.

Biological Treatments

The scientific beginnings of biological treatments can be traced to the nineteenth century and the discovery of the diagnosis, cause, and cure for general paresis (see Chapter 2). This remarkable achievement paralleled other medical advances in its course of discovery. As the first step, an increasingly refined and accurate diagnosis is developed. Next, information pertaining to causal factors is put together like pieces of a puzzle to form a complete picture of the specific etiology of the disease. Finally, scientists develop treatments by experimenting with various methods for preventing or curing the disorder. These are far from simple tasks, of course, as is evident in the span of over a century between the diagnosis of general paresis, the discovery of syphilis as its cause, and the development of antibiotics as a treatment for the disease.

A similar success story cannot be told about the development of biological treatments for many other mental disorders. Uncovering specific etiologies has proved to be a vexing task. As a result, many efforts to develop biological treatments have attempted to skip the middle step in the process of discovery; that is, they experiment with alternative treatments before discovering a specific etiology. These treatments focus on *symptom alleviation*, reducing the dysfunctional symptoms of a disorder but not eliminating its root cause.

Experimentation has produced mixed results in the biological treatment of emotional problems. Bleeding, forced hot baths, the use of various physical restraints, and the surgical removal of sexual organs are some of the unhappy experimental treatments that were used in the not-so-distant past. In contrast, the second half of the twentieth century has witnessed the discovery of numerous medications, many of which are remarkable in their effectiveness at symptom alleviation. Before presenting an overview of these new drugs, we briefly consider two controversial biological treatments: electroconvulsive therapy and psychosurgery.

ELECTROCONVULSIVE THERAPY

Electroconvulsive therapy (ECT) involves the deliberate induction of a seizure by passing electricity through the brain. The technique was developed in 1938 by Ugo Cerletti and Lucio Bini, two Italian physicians who were seeking a treatment for schizophrenia (see Chapter 13). At the time, schizophrenia was erroneously thought to be rare among people who had epilepsy. This led to speculation that epileptic seizures somehow prevented the disorder. Cerletti and Bini discovered their means of inducing seizures when visiting a slaughterhouse. There they observed electric current being passed through the brains of animals, which produced a convulsion and unconsciousness. Shortly thereafter, the two physicians began to use a modified electroconvulsive technique as an experimental treatment for schizophrenia.

Approximately 100 volts of electric current was passed through the patients' brains in what is now termed *bilateral ECT*. Electrodes are placed on the left and right temples, and the current passes through both brain hemispheres. In *unilateral ECT,* the electric current is passed through only one side of the brain, the nondominant hemisphere. Both procedures induce brief unconsciousness and seizures, but unilateral ECT apparently produces less memory loss—a common side effect of ECT (Squire & Slater, 1978). Unfortunately, unilateral ECT may not be as effective as bilateral ECT. Thus some experts now recommend unilateral ECT only when bilateral ECT leads to severe memory impairments (Weiner & Krystal, 1994). In any case, the dangerous, jerking body movements that occur during a convulsion—and often resulted in broken bones and other physical injuries— are now controlled by restraints and the administration of a muscle relaxant. Typically, ECT involves a series of 6 to 12 sessions scheduled over the course of a few weeks (Weiner & Krystal, 1994).

As you are probably aware, ECT is a controversial technique. It certainly was ineffective in achieving its original objective of curing schizophrenia. Moreover, as illustrated in popular movies like *One Flew Over the Cuckoo's Nest,* there is no doubt that ECT has been overused and abused. In addition, the side effects linked with ECT can be severe. These include long-term memory loss, bone fractures, and death in about 1 to 2 of every 10,000 patients (NIMH, 1985; Weiner & Krystal, 1994). Still, evidence indicates that ECT is quite effective in treating severe depressions that do not respond to other treatments (see Chapter 5). Because of its potential side effects, however, ECT must be used cautiously even when other treatments fail (NIMH, 1985). Nevertheless, estimates indicate that about 36,000 courses of ECT are administered in the United States each year, and interest in ECT— and possibly the frequency of using it—have increased in recent years (Weiner & Krystal, 1994).

PSYCHOSURGERY

Psychosurgery is an even more controversial biological treatment, as it involves the surgical destruction of specific regions of the brain. Psychosurgery was introduced in 1935 by Egas Moniz (1874–1953), a Portuguese neurologist. **Prefrontal lobotomy** was the technique refined by Moniz—a procedure in which the frontal lobes of the brain are surgically and irrevocably severed. The technique was widely adopted throughout the world, and thousands of prefrontal lobotomies were performed throughout the middle of this century—between 10,000 and 20,000 in the United States alone. In fact, Moniz won a Nobel Prize in 1949 for his discovery of this treatment.

Prefrontal lobotomy was subsequently discredited because of its limited effectiveness and its frequent and severe side effects, which included a 25 percent mortality rate, excessive tranquillity, and the absence of emotional responsiveness. Ironically, Moniz himself was shot and paralyzed by one of his lobotomized patients, a sad testament to the unpredictable outcome of the procedure (Snaith, 1994; Swayze, 1995).

Although prefrontal lobotomies are no longer performed, some forms of highly circumscribed psychosurgery are used today to treat severe disorders. For example, a form of limited psychosurgery called *cingulotomy* may be effective in treating some very severe cases of obsessive–compulsive disorder when all other treatments have failed (Baer, Rauch, Ballantine et al., 1995; Mindus & Jenike, 1992; see Chapter 6). Contemporary psychosurgery techniques like cingulotomy are highly refined, and only small, precisely pinpointed regions of the brain are selectively destroyed. Still, the complexity of the brain, our limited knowledge of its functions, and the irreversibility of brain damage combine to make psychosurgery a procedure that is used very rarely today for clear practical and ethical reasons (see Further Thoughts).

FURTHER THOUGHTS

Some Ethical Concerns in Psychological Treatment Research

Scientists often need to ask important ethical questions when conducting treatment research; for example, does a particular treatment poses a serious risk to the participants? Moniz's experiments with prefrontal lobotomy are an extreme illustration of a seeming disregard for human life in the name of "science." Such a dangerous experimental treatment could not take place in the United States today. Experimental procedures can be used only after extensive institutional review. In fact, every research institution in the United States has a specially designated panel that must review the ethics of proposed research with human subjects. These *human subjects committees* often must consider controversial issues.

Research on psychotherapy often raises questions about the ethics of experimentation and risks for human subjects. One set of ethical concerns involves coercive psychological treatments, particularly the use of punishment. You may be familiar with the book and film *A Clockwork Orange,* which raises this concern in a dramatized manner. In this fictional portrayal, a violent young man is conditioned to find violence repulsive by having pain inflicted on him while he watches or imagines violent scenes. These are *not* the kinds of treatments that are taking place in clinics and hospitals, but the story perhaps reflects the public's fear of coercion. The use of punishment is controversial even when it is an effective treatment and involves relatively minor consequences. For example, many people oppose the use of mild punishment as a treatment for the extreme self-injury found in the severe disorder autism, even though this treatment has proved effective in many cases (see Chapter 15).

Some psychologists also believe that it is unethical to offer psychological treatments in the absence of evidence supporting their effectiveness. The treatment of sexual offenders is an example. Although some specialized treatments may have modest benefits (Hall, 1995; Marshall, Jones, Ward, et al., 1991), little evidence supports the general effectiveness of psychotherapy for sex offenders. Nevertheless, courts routinely refer sex offenders to mental health professionals—and mental health professionals routinely accept them into psychotherapy. The ethics of this practice can be questioned on several grounds, including the costs to the public, the consequences of perpetuating the myth that therapy works, and questions about the intellectual honesty of practitioners who fail to acknowledge the limits of psychological treatments (McFall, 1991).

The opposite concern has also been raised in psychological research: Sometimes it may be unethical to withhold a treatment (O'Leary & Borkovec, 1978). Experimental treatments are commonly withheld when clients are randomly assigned to a no-treatment control group so that the outcome of a new treatment can be compared with the outcome of no treatment. One question that arises in this research is whether it is ethical to withhold a potentially effective treatment. Many researchers would respond that we do not know if a treatment is effective until it has been studied.

In addition to institutional review, ethical concerns are addressed in psychological research by the requirement that every human subject be able to give **informed consent** to participate in research. Participants in treatment research must be (1) informed about the potential risks and benefits of a study, (2) competent to understand them, and (3) able to agree to participate voluntarily (Carroll, Schneider, & Wesley, 1985). The first condition includes a detailed presentation of information, and it typically is made in writing. The second condition excludes both people whose understanding is impaired and minors, whose parents must give consent for their children. The third condition protects research subjects against excessive coercion. Coercion to participate in research is a particular worry in institutional settings like mental hospitals and prisons, where potential subjects may feel pressured into participating in order to gain privileges.

Scientific investigators must constantly balance their ethical commitment to protect individuals from harm against their ethical obligation to increase knowledge and thereby better the human condition. The potential to create new knowledge that may benefit many people is, in fact, the ultimate justification for conducting research that may hold some risk or discomfort for the participants in a study. We revisit tricky ethical issues periodically throughout the text, and we discuss mental health, ethics, and the law in some detail in Chapter 18. ■

PSYCHOPHARMACOLOGY

Psychopharmacology—the study of the use of medications to treat psychological disturbances—has been the most promising avenue of biological treatment. In recent years, scientists have developed new medications that have increasingly refined effects on emotional states and mental disorders (see Table 3–2).

You may be familiar with the effects of some **psychoactive drugs,** chemical substances that affect psychological state. Alcohol, for example, produces rapid and notable changes in thinking, mood, and behavior. Some psychoactive medications produce similarly obvious changes. Many antianxiety agents, such as Xanax or Librium, have effects that become apparent soon

TABLE 3-2

Major Medications Used in Treating Psychological Disorders

Therapeutic Use	Chemical Structure or Psychopharmacologic Action	Generic Name	Trade Name
Antipsychotics (also called major tranquilizers or neuroleptics)	Phenothiazines		
	Aliphatic	Chlorpromazine	Thorazine
	Piperidine	Thioradazine	Mellaril
	Piperazine	Triflouperazine	Stelazine
	Thioxanthenes		
	Aliphatic	Chlorprothixene	Taractan
	Piperazine	Thiothixene	Navane
	Butyrophenones	Haloperidol	Haldol
	Dibenzoxazepines	Loxapine	Loxitane
	Dihydroindolines	Molindone	Moban
	Rauwolfia alkaloids	Reserpine	Sandril
	Benzoquinolines	Tetrabenazine	
	Atypical neuroleptics	Clozapine	Clozaril
Antidepressants	Tricyclic antidepressants (TCAs)		
	Tertiary amines	Amitriptyline	Elavil
		Imipramine	Tofranil
		Doxepin	Sinequan
	Secondary amines	Desipramine	Norpramin
		Nortriptyline	Pamelor
		Protriptyline	Vivactil
	Monoamine oxidase inhibitors (MAOIs)	Phenelzine	Nardil
		Tranylcypromine	Parnate
		Pargyline	Eutonyl
		Isocarboxazid	Marplan
	Atypical antidepressants	Trazodone	Desyrel
		Amoxapine	Asendin
	Selective serotonin reuptake inhibitor (SSRI)	Bupropion	Wellbutrin
		Fluoxetine	Prozac
Psychomotor stimulants	Amphetamines	Amphetamine	Benzedrine
		Dextroamphetamine	Dexedrine
	Other	Methylphenidate	Ritalin
		Pemolline	Cylert
Antimanic		Lithium	Eskalith
		Carbamazepine	Tegretol
		Valproic acid	Depakene
Anxiolytic (also called antianxiety or minor tranquilizers)	Benzodiazepines	Chlordiazepoxide	Librium
		Diazepam	Valium
		Chlorazepate	Tranxene
		Oxazepam	Serax
		Lorazepam	Activan
	Triazolobenzodiazepine	Alprazolam	Xanax
	Propanediol carbamates	Meprobamate	Miltown
Sedative hypnotic	Barbiturates	Phenobarbital	
	Benzodiazepines	Triazolam	Halcion
Antipanic	Benzodiazepines	Alprazolam	Xanax
	MAOIs	Phenelzine	Nardil
	TCAs	Imipramine	Tofranil
Antiobsessional	TCA	Clomipramine	Anafranil
	SSRI	Fluoxetine	Prozac

Source: G. L. Klerman, M. M. Weissman, J. C. Markowitz, I. Glick, P. J. Wilner, B. Mason, and M. K. Shear 1994. Medication and psychotherapy. In A. E. Bergin and S. L. Garfield (Eds.), *Handbook of Psychotherapy and Behavior Change,* 4th ed., pp. 734–782. New York: Wiley.

after the medication is taken (see Chapter 6). Others have more subtle influences that build up gradually over time. The antidepressant medications are an example of this type of effect (see Chapter 5). Other psychoactive drugs affect people with mental disorders very differently from the way they affect someone who is functioning normally. Antipsychotic medications help to eliminate delusions and hallucinations among people suffering from schizophrenia (see Chapter 13), but the same medications would disorient most people and send them into a long, groggy sleep.

The success of psychopharmacology is evident in the proliferating discovery and use of psychoactive medications in recent years. For example, in the 1990s the antidepressant medication Prozac has outsold *every* prescription medication, including any medications used to treat physical ailments. (In the 1970s, the antianxiety medication Valium held this distinction.) In fact, more than $2 billion worth of Prozac was sold in 1995, and the drug has been prescribed to an estimated 21 million people around the world (*Wall Street Journal*, January 31, 1996). A listing of the major categories of psychoactive medications and their chemical, generic, and common trade names is found in Table 3–2. We review each of these categories of medication in more detail in later chapters.

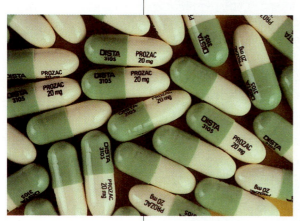

▲ Prozac is an effective antidepressant that is the best-selling medication for treating psychological problems. More than $2 billion of Prozac was sold in 1995.

There are a few general points that you should note about psychopharmacology. First, much evidence indicates that various medications are effective and safe treatments for particular mental disorders. Psychopharmacology lies well within the realm of modern medicine. A second point, however, is that psychoactive medications typically offer symptom relief, not a cure of underlying pathology. Symptom alleviation is extremely important. Where would we be without aspirin, another drug that treats symptoms but not causes? Still, some commentators worry that medication is given too readily to address psychological or social problems (Breggin, 1994). Third, all medications have side effects, some of which are very unpleasant. Partly as a result of unpleasant side effects, many patients do not take their medication as prescribed, and they often

experience a relapse as a result. Finally, many psychoactive drugs must be taken for long periods of time. Because the medications alleviate symptoms but do not produce a cure, it may be necessary to keep taking the drug—for months, years, or sometimes for a lifetime (Klerman et al., 1994).

Psychodynamic Psychotherapies

Psychodynamic approaches to treatment were first developed during the nineteenth and early twentieth centuries. Joseph Breuer's (1842–1925) pioneering technique known as the "cathartic method" was one of the earliest influences. Breuer used hypnosis to induce his troubled patients to talk freely about problems in their lives. Upon awakening from the hypnotic trance, many patients reported relief from their symptoms, although they were unable to recall what they had said while hypnotized. Breuer used the principle of **catharsis** to explain the benefits of his hypnotic method. The concept suggests that psychological problems are caused by pent-up emotions and that the release of previously unexpressed feelings—catharsis—reduces psychic strain. The sudden release of steam through the whistle of a boiling teapot is an appropriate visual metaphor for catharsis.

FREUDIAN PSYCHOANALYSIS
Breuer's contemporary and collaborator, Sigmund Freud (1856–1939), adopted the cathartic method for a time, but he soon concluded that hypnosis was not necessary to encourage open expression. Instead, Freud simply told his patients to speak freely about whatever thoughts crossed their mind. This method, called **free association,** became a cornerstone of Freud's famous treatment, **psychoanalysis.**

Unlike Breuer, Freud did not see catharsis as an end in itself. The true benefit of free association, in Freud's view, was that it revealed aspects of the unconscious mind. Freud found clues to his patients' intrapsychic lives in their unedited speech. Freud also believed that dreams (during which intrapsychic defenses presumably are weaker) and slips of the tongue (known commonly as "Freudian slips") provided especially revealing information about the unconscious. Thus, according to Freud, free association, dreams, and slips of the tongue are valuable, because they serve as "windows into the unconscious."

According to Freud, the psychoanalyst's task is to uncover the unconscious conflicts and motivations that cause psychological difficulties. However, this discovery is only the first step in treatment. In order to overcome their dysfunctions, patients must come to share the psychoanalyst's understanding of their intrapsychic life. The ultimate goal of psychoanalysis is to bring formerly unconscious material into conscious awareness. This is what Freud called **insight.** Freud asserted that insight is sufficient for curing psychological disorders.

The analyst's main tool for promoting insight is **interpretation.** In offering an interpretation, the analyst suggests hidden meanings to patients' accounts of their past and present life. Typically, interpretations relate to past experiences, especially experiences with loved ones. Recall from Chapter 2, however, that according to Freudian theory, the ego defense mechanisms keep intrapsychic conflicts from conscious awareness. Thus psychoanalysts must overcome defenses like denial and projection as patients resist their interpretations. Timing is everything in overcoming *resistance.* The patient must be on the verge of discovering the hidden meaning himself or herself; otherwise, the interpretation will be rejected. For example, return to the case history and consider the dilemma of convincing Frances that deep resentment lies beneath her professed, unwavering love for her mother. Given her long history of subjugating her own needs to those of her mother, Frances would be unlikely to accept such an interpretation if it were made too early in her treatment.

One essential element in probing the unconscious mind and offering interpretations is *therapeutic neutrality.* Psychoanalysts maintain a distant and uninvolved stance toward their patients in order to minimize their influence on free association. The classical psychoanalyst "sits behind the patient where the patient cannot see him, and avoids either telling the patient about his own private affairs or having social contacts with him. He tries to create, as far as possible, a controlled laboratory situation in which the individual peculiarities of the analyst shall play as little role as possible in stimulating the patient's reactions" (Alexander & French, 1947, p. 83).

The analyst's distant stance is thought to encourage **transference,** the process whereby patients transfer the feelings about some key figure in their life onto the shadowy figure of the analyst. For psychoanalysis to succeed, the analyst must not respond to transference in a manner that the patient views as critical or threatening.

Psychoanalysts particularly must guard against *countertransference*, or letting their own feelings influence their responses to their patients. Analysts also must avoid reacting to their patients in the same way as the transference figure had reacted. Otherwise, the past will be repeated, and patients' fears will be confirmed. Instead, the analyst's job is to interpret the patient's actions and motivations in order to promote insight about the transference.

Insight into the transference relationship presumably helps patients understand how and why they are relating to the analyst in the same dysfunctional manner in which they related to a loved one. This awareness thus creates a new understanding both of past relationships and of unconscious motivations in present relationships. For example, consider a transference that might develop between Frances and a psychoanalyst. Frances might have difficulty accepting a therapeutic relationship in which she was receiving care instead of giving it. She might therefore try to get the analyst to reveal personal problems, or perhaps she would bring gifts to her therapist. The therapist's polite refusal of the gifts and of Frances's attempts at caretaking might cause Frances to feel hurt, rejected, and, eventually, angry. As therapy proceeded, these actions could be interpreted as reflecting Frances's style of relating to her mother and her tendency to deny her own needs.

A common misconception about psychoanalysis is that the ultimate goal of insight is to rid the patient of all defenses. This is not the case. According to Freud, defenses are essential for the functioning of a healthy personality. Thus, rather than ridding the patient of defenses, one goal of psychoanalysis is to replace them. Defenses such as denial and projection are confronted because they distort reality dramatically, whereas "healthier" defenses, such as rationalization and sublimation, are left unchallenged. A second goal of psychoanalysis is to help patients become more aware of their basic needs or drives so that they may find socially and psychologically appropriate outlets for them (Maddi, 1980). A goal for Frances, for example, would be to admit that anger is a legitimate and acceptable part of her personality.

CURRENT STATUS OF FREUDIAN PSYCHOANALYSIS

Patients meet with psychoanalysts for an hour several times each week, and psychoanalysis often lasts for years. Because psychoanalysis requires substantial time, expense, and self-exploration, it is accessible only to people who are relatively well functioning, introspective, and financially secure. In many respects, psychoanalysis now is construed more as a process of self-understanding than as a treatment for specific emotional disorders. This view is bolstered by the fact that very little therapy outcome research has been conducted on classical psychoanalysis. Freud believed that not every patient would benefit from the treatment—a belief shared by many contemporary practitioners. Those suffering from psychotic and personality disorders are thought to be especially unlikely to benefit, whereas people suffering from "neurotic" disorders, especially excessive anxiety, have been thought to benefit most.

Although it is still practiced, the expense and time involved, and the limited amount of data available on outcome, have made Freudian psychoanalysis less popular. However, variations on Freudian theory have led to the development of new forms of insight-oriented therapy. These revisionist approaches are termed **psychodynamic** rather than psychoanalytic. Psychodynamic psychotherapists often are more engaged and directive in therapy, and treatment may be relatively brief in comparison to psychoanalysis.

EGO ANALYSTS AND PSYCHODYNAMIC PSYCHOTHERAPY

The development of **ego analysis** is the most important innovation in Freudian theory and therapy. Ego analysis originated in the work of a number of therapists who were trained in Freudian psychoanalysis but who independently developed innovations in theory and technique. Whereas Freud emphasized the paramount role of the id in personality and psychopathology, these new theorists focused much more on the ego. The major function of the ego, according to Freudian theory, is to mediate between the conflicting impulses of the id and the superego (see Chapter 2). Of equal importance to ego analysts, however, is the ego's role in dealing with reality (Hartmann, Kris, & Loewenstein, 1947). Ego analysts therefore are concerned with unconscious motivations, but they also consider the patient's dealings with the external world. They attend to the role of society and culture in producing emotional disturbance, as well to the effects of current life circumstances and the patient's reactions to them.

Of greatest importance in ego analysis are the patient's past and present interpersonal relationships. Ego analyst Harry Stack Sullivan (1892–1949) was extremely influential in highlighting this paramount role of relationships. He suggested that many characteristics of the personality could be conceptualized in interpersonal rather than intrapsychic terms. Like many interpersonal theorists, Sullivan saw two basic dimensions of interpersonal relationships. One dimension reflects interpersonal power, ranging from dominance to submission. A second dimension concerns interpersonal closeness, with affiliation on one end of the continuum and hostility at the opposite pole. Sullivan's followers, in fact, have developed a classification of personality based on these two dimensions (Leary, 1957).

Other especially influential ego analysts include Erik Erikson (1902–1994) and Karen Horney (1885–1952). Horney's (1939) most lasting contribution has been her suggestion that people have conflicting ego needs to move toward, against, and away from others. Essentially, Horney argued that there are competing human (ego) needs for closeness, for dominance, and for autonomy. She viewed people with interpersonal or intrapsychic conflicts as being too rigid in fulfilling only one of these needs. In her view, the key to a healthy personality is finding a balance among the three styles of relating to others. Pause for a moment to reconsider the case of Frances to help you understand Horney's ideas. Frances's characteristic style and her conflicting needs should not be too difficult to discern.

We introduced Erikson's stage theory of development in Chapter 2. As with other ego analysts, Erikson's critical departure from Freud focused on the interpersonal context. This can be seen in his emphasis on the externally oriented psycho*social* stages of development rather than the internally oriented psycho*sexual* stages. Erikson also introduced the argument that an individual's personality is not fixed by early experience but continues to develop as a result of predictable psychosocial conflicts throughout the life span (see Chapter 17). In contrast, Freud viewed personality patterns as being fixed by intrapsychic conflicts that occurred primarily during the first few years of life. He assumed that personality is difficult to change thereafter.

John Bowlby's (1907–1991) attachment theory (see Chapter 2) perhaps has had the greatest effect on contemporary thought about interpersonal influences on personality and psychopathology. Freud viewed closeness in

▲ Harry Stack Sullivan (1892–1949) was a U.S. psychiatrist and ego analyst. Sullivan suggested that personality could be conceptualized in interpersonal terms and not just in intrapsychic ones.

relationships as merely an outgrowth of the reduction of primary drives, such as hunger and sex. In contrast, Bowlby elevated the need for close relationships from a secondary to a primary human characteristic. From an attachment theory perspective, close relationships—including the patient–therapist relationship—are of paramount importance to healthy functioning.

SHORT-TERM PSYCHODYNAMIC PSYCHOTHERAPY

Many different approaches to psychotherapy have been developed based on the writings of Sullivan, Horney, Erikson, Bowlby, and other theorists who have been influenced by Freud. As with psychoanalysis, all these approaches emphasize insight, but psychodynamic psychotherapists are much more actively involved with their patients. They are more ready to direct the patient's recollections, to focus on current life circumstances, and to offer interpretations quickly and directly. Most psychodynamic psychotherapists are also much more "human" in conducting therapy. They may be distant and reflective at times, but they also are willing to offer appropriate emotional support (Garfield, 1989).

Short-term psychodynamic psychotherapy is a form of treatment that uses many psychoanalytic techniques. Therapeutic neutrality is typically maintained, and transference remains a central issue, but the short-term psychodynamic therapist actively focuses on a particular emotional issue rather than relying on free association (Garfield, 1989; Sifneos, 1988). The short-term approach is gaining increased attention because it typically is limited to 25 sessions or less and therefore is less expensive and more amenable to research (Garfield, 1989; Luborsky, 1984; Luborsky, Barber, & Beutler, 1993). Current research on psychodynamic psychotherapy generally supports Freud's observation that psychodynamic therapy is ineffective in treating more severe disorders, although it may be effective in treating milder anxiety (Luborsky et al., 1993). There still is a pressing need for further evidence on the technique, however.

Behavior Therapy

Behavior therapy focuses on behavior change in the present, not on insight about the past. The approach includes a diverse array of techniques, many of which were developed on the basis of psychological research findings. Despite the many approaches, all behavior therapists adhere to the truism, "Actions speak louder than words."

The beginnings of behavior therapy can be traced to John B. Watson's (1878–1958) writings in the early part of the twentieth century. Watson was the key figure in developing **behaviorism** in American psychology—the belief that observable behaviors, not unobservable cognitive or emotional states, are the appropriate focus of psychological study. Watson maintained that abnormal behavior was learned and could be unlearned, just like normal behavior. He viewed the behavior therapist's job as analogous to that of a teacher. The therapeutic goal is to provide new, more appropriate learning experiences. In developing treatments, Watson and his followers relied heavily on the findings of animal learning researchers, particularly Pavlov's theories of classical conditioning and Skinner's theories of operant conditioning (see Chapter 2). More recently, behavior therapy has been extensively influenced by the findings of cognitive psychologists (Mahoney, 1991).

Watson and his followers articulated some basic and continuing themes in behavior therapy. Unlike psychoanalysis, behavior therapy does not offer a substantive theoretical core concerning the composition of the human personality. Rather, it is an outcome-oriented approach. Perhaps the most important theme of behavior therapy is its reliance on empirical evaluation. This empirical emphasis is evident in the behavior therapist's application of psychological science to clinical problems and in the hundreds of treatment outcome experiments that have been conducted on behavior therapy (see Research Methods). We will raise and examine some questions about research on behavior therapy later in this chapter and throughout the book. Regardless of how the evidence is interpreted, however, behavior therapists clearly have contributed greatly by constantly emphasizing the empirical evaluation of psychotherapy.

The behavior therapist's focus on present behavior, learning processes, and empirical evaluation can be seen in the diverse treatment techniques that are part of the approach. In the following sections we consider some of the most common techniques: classical conditioning, operant conditioning, and cognitive behavior therapy techniques.

The Experiment

Two basic methods are used in conducting empirical research on psychological disorders. We introduced the *correlational method* in Research Methods in Chapter 2. The second basic method of scientific investigation is the **experiment**. The experiment is the most powerful of all scientific methods in one extremely important way: Researchers who use experimental methods can determine cause and effect relationships.

The experiment has four essential features. It begins with a **hypothesis**—the experimenter's specific prediction about cause and effect. For example, a researcher might predict that in comparison to no treatment at all, a particular type of medication will reduce certain symptoms of a given emotional disorder. The experimenter might further hypothesize that psychotherapy also will alleviate symptoms more than no treatment, but psychotherapy will cause no more and no less symptom change than will medication.

The second feature of an experiment is the manipulation of an **independent variable**. Independent variables are controlled and deliberately manipulated by the experimenter. The independent variable in the hypothesis just outlined is whether the patients receive medication, psychotherapy, or no treatment. The experimenter controls the independent variable by deciding what specific type of medication or psychotherapy will be made available to the patients in the experiment and by determining who will receive one of these treatments and who will receive no treatment at all. People who receive an active treatment belong to the **experimental group**. Those who receive no treatment or merely a placebo belong to the **control group**. On average, members of the experimental group are hypothesized to improve more than members of the control group.

The third feature of the experiment is **random assignment,** ensuring that each subject has a statistically equal chance of receiving different levels of the independent variable. In the present example, picking the number 1, 2, or 3 out of a hat is one of many possible ways of ensuring random assignment to medication, psychotherapy, or no treatment. Random assignment is essential, because it ensures that any differences among groups are caused by the independent variable and not by biased selection into groups.

The fourth feature of the experiment is the measurement of the **dependent variable.** The dependent variable is the outcome that is hypothesized to vary according to manipulations in the independent variable. The outcome *depends* on the experimental manipulation—thus the term "dependent variable." In the present example, the various symptoms of the disorder make up the dependent variables of the study. The symptoms are expected to change depending on whether the patients receive medication, psychotherapy, or no treatment at all.

Statistical tests typically are conducted to establish whether the independent variable has changed the dependent variable in a predictable manner, or whether the outcome is a result of chance. According to current conventions, a finding is considered to be *statistically significant* if it would occur by chance in less than 1 out of every 20 experiments. That is, the probability of a chance outcome is less than 5 percent, a specification that is often written as $p < .05$. As we discuss in Research Methods in Chapter 6, however, a statistically significant result is not the same as a clinically significant finding. A treatment may produce a reliable change in symptoms, for example, but the change may be too small to produce a meaningful difference in the patient's life.

We can conclude that an independent variable *causes* changes in a dependent variable when the experimental method is used correctly and it produces statistically significant results. The ability to establish causation is a powerful strength of the experiment in comparison to the correlational study. The experimental method is limited, however, because many theoretically interesting independent variables cannot be manipulated practically or ethically in real life. We may hypothesize that abusive parenting causes psychological problems, for example, but we obviously cannot randomly assign children to grow up in abusive and nonabusive homes. In fact, practical and ethical limitations make it impossible to use the experiment to test most hypotheses about the causes of abnormal behavior. Thus, when studying the etiology of abnormal behavior, we often must rely on correlational studies or analogue studies (see Research Methods in Chapter 5).

The effectiveness of various psychological treatments often can be studied using an experiment, because researchers can control whether someone receives a particular medication or form of psychotherapy. Still, it is not easy to completely control the independent variable in treatment outcome research. Some people may drop out of treatment, and others may seek additional help. Clinicians might not conduct psychotherapy according to the design of the experiment, or patients might not take their medication as prescribed.

These examples are only a few of the many ways in which the independent variable can be *confounded* with other factors in psychological research. Each of these examples is a threat to the **internal validity** of the experiment. An experiment has internal validity if changes in the dependent variable can be accurately attributed to changes in the independent variable. As we have noted, however, the independent variable can be manipulated poorly, or it can be confounded with other variables. For example, in our hypothetical study it obviously would be wrong to conclude that medication was ineffective if the patients failed to take it, or it would be difficult to draw conclusions about psychotherapy if many of the patients dropped out of the study.

In contrast to internal validity, **external validity** refers to whether the findings of an experiment generalize to other circumstances. A number of questions typically can be raised about an experiment's external validity, because some artificiality needs to be introduced to give the experimenter control over the independent variable. In our hypothetical study, perhaps only a very narrow group of patients would be treated. Thus the findings might not generalize to other people with other problems. Or perhaps psychotherapy might last for exactly 10 sessions in the experiment in order to ensure control of the independent variable. Although this would help the study's internal validity, it might compromise the experiment's external validity. The findings might not apply in the real world, where the length of treatment is tailored to the individual client's needs.

There is no finite list of questions that can be raised about the internal and external validity of experiments. A common trade-off, however, is that the experimenter often must sacrifice one for the other. Recognizing this compromise is essential to conducting and evaluating science. We therefore raise questions throughout this book about the strengths and limitations of the experiment—and of correlational research.

You now have a basic, abstract knowledge of these methods. In the pages that follow, we will help you apply these concepts to specific research findings. ■

CLASSICAL CONDITIONING TECHNIQUES

A number of behavior therapy techniques have been developed from Pavlov's theory of classical conditioning (see Chapter 2). All classical conditioning techniques use *counterconditioning* procedures. Counterconditioning involves altering existing responses by pairing new responses with old stimuli.

Joseph Wolpe developed the most influential counterconditioning technique. Wolpe is a South African psychiatrist who has concentrated his research and therapy efforts on eliminating phobias. Wolpe (1958) assumed that at least

some phobias were learned through classical conditioning. He reasoned that if fears could be learned, they could be unlearned. The key was to break the association between stimulus and response. The technique he developed to do so is called **systematic desensitization.**

Systematic Desensitization   Systematic desensitization has three key elements. The first is relaxation training. Wolpe believed that in order to replace anxiety as a response to a feared stimulus, the new conditioned response, relaxation, must be easily elicited. He focused on the technique of *progressive muscle relaxation*, a method

▲ **Joseph Wolpe is a leading behavior therapist. Wolpe developed systematic desensitization, a pioneering technique that uses classical conditioning to eliminate fears.**

of inducing a calm state through the contraction and subsequent relaxation of all of the major muscle groups. The second component of systematic desensitization is the construction of a *hierarchy of fears* ranging from very mild to very frightening stimuli. Because anxiety initially is a stronger response to the feared stimulus than is relaxation, Wolpe thought that exposure to fears must be gradual, or the relaxation would be overwhelmed by the anxiety. The third part of systematic desensitization is the *learning process*, namely, the pairing of the feared stimulus with the relaxation response. Wolpe had his clients carry out this pairing in their imagination. Thus systematic desensitization involves imagining increasingly fearful events while simultaneously maintaining a state of relaxation.

Systematic desensitization has been the subject of volumes of research. In fact, the development of the technique can be credited with spurring psychotherapy outcome research in general. Overall, evidence supports the effectiveness of systematic desensitization as a treatment for fears and phobias (O'Leary & Wilson, 1987; Wolpe, 1990). It is not clear, however, that counterconditioning accounts for the change. Alternative interpretations suggest that the true mechanisms for change are the removal of reinforcement for avoidance, the extinction of the fear, an increased sense of self-efficacy that comes from confronting one's fears, or even the formation of a supportive therapeutic relationship (Kazdin & Wilcoxin, 1976; O'Leary & Wilson, 1987).

In Vivo Desensitization   Although it is not clear exactly why systematic desensitization is an effective treatment, research has helped to pinpoint the crucial elements of the procedure. Most investigators agree that *exposure* is the key to fear reduction. This observation has led to the development of variations on desensitization techniques, the most notable of which is **in vivo desensitization.** In vivo desensitization involves gradually being exposed to the feared stimulus in real life while simultaneously maintaining a state of relaxation. Research on in vivo desensitization indicates that the way to overcome fears is to confront them. Thus behavior therapists follow another truism: If you fall off a horse, the best way to conquer the fear of riding is to get back in the saddle.

Flooding   Another exposure technique is **flooding.** Unlike desensitization, exposure to the feared stimulus is not gradual in flooding, and there is no attempt to calm initial anxiety. Rather, flooding involves exposure at full intensity. The goal is to eliminate anxiety through extinction by repeatedly presenting the conditioned stimulus until it no longer produces the unconditioned response (see Chapter 2). Someone who was afraid of heights might be brought to the top of the CN Tower in Toronto (the world's tallest structure). The intense anxiety initially produced by this experience gradually should be extinguished as the individual spends more time at the top of the building. The key to this treatment, and to flooding in general, is to prevent avoidance. Clients must not be allowed to retreat from the stimulus in fear, because the resulting reduction in anxiety would be negatively reinforcing (O'Leary & Wilson, 1987; Wolpe, 1990).

Aversion Therapy   The counterconditioning in **aversion therapy** differs from that in systematic desensitization and flooding. The goal in aversion therapy is to create rather than eliminate an unpleasant response. As such, aversion therapy is used primarily in the treatment of substance use disorders such as alcoholism and cigarette smoking. Aversion therapy for these problems involves pairing an unpleasant response with the stimuli that elicit substance use. In working with alcoholism, for example, the typical procedure is to pair the sight, smell, and taste of alcohol with severe nausea produced artificially by a drug.

Aversion therapies have the goal of reducing substance use by associating it with unpleasant consequences. Such treatments are controversial, however, precisely because of their aversive nature. Moreover, data on the effectiveness of aversion therapies are ambiguous (O'Leary & Wilson, 1987). Although these treatments often achieve short-term success, relapse rates are high. Everyday life offers the substance abuser the opportunity, and perhaps the motivation, to desensitize himself or herself to the classically conditioned responses learned in aversion therapy.

OPERANT CONDITIONING TECHNIQUES

A second set of behavior therapy techniques is based on Skinner's work on operant conditioning (see Chapter 2). The major assumption of these approaches is straightforward: Behaviors that are reinforced will increase, and those that are punished will diminish.

Contingency Management   One form of operant behavior therapy, **contingency**

management, focuses on directly changing the rewards and punishments for various behaviors. A *contingency* is the relationship between a behavior and its consequences; thus, contingency management involves changing this relationship. The goal of contingency management is to reward desirable behavior systematically and to extinguish or punish undesirable behavior. In order to achieve this goal, the therapist must control relevant rewards and punishments. Thus contingency management is used primarily in circumstances where the therapist has considerable direct or indirect control over the client's environment, such as in institutional settings or when children are brought for treatment by their parents.

The **token economy** is an example of contingency management that has been adopted in many institutional settings. In a token economy, desired and undesired behaviors are clearly identified, contingencies are defined, behavior is carefully monitored, and rewards or punishments are given according to the rules of the token economy. For example, in a group home for juvenile offenders, a token economy may specify that residents earn tokens for completing schoolwork and household chores, while they lose tokens for arguing or fighting. Each resident's behavior is monitored and recorded, and tokens are "paid" accordingly. The key to the success of the program is that tokens can be exchanged for rewards desired by the residents—for example, going out unescorted on a Saturday night.

Research shows that contingency management successfully changes behavior for diverse problems such as institutionalized clients with schizophrenia (Paul & Lentz, 1977) and juvenile offenders living in group homes (Phillips, Phillips, Wolf, & Fixsen, 1973). The evidence for success must be interpreted carefully, however. Improvements that occur in the setting where the operant program is in place often do not generalize to real-life situations (Emery & Marholin, 1977). Rewards and punishments in controlled settings often differ from those in the natural environment. A psychologist can set up clear and consistent contingencies for a juvenile living in a group home, but it may be impossible to alter the rewards and punishments the teenager encounters when he or she returns to live with a chaotic family or delinquent peers. In the real world, undesirable behavior often is rewarded, and punishments for inappropriate behavior—and rewards for appropriate behavior—often are inconsistent or delayed.

Thus contingency management programs work in controlled environments, but generalization to other settings is limited.

Social Skills Training Another behavior therapy technique based on operant conditioning principles is **social skills training.** The goal of social skills training is to teach clients new ways of behaving that are both desirable and likely to be rewarded in the everyday world (McFall, 1982). Two commonly taught skills are assertiveness (Lange & Jakubowski, 1976) and social problem solving (D'Zurrilla & Goldfried, 1971; Spivack & Shure, 1974).

The goal of *assertiveness training* is to teach clients to be direct about their feelings and wishes. The training may involve a variety of levels of detail in social skills, from learning to make eye contact to asking a boss for a raise. In teaching assertiveness, therapists frequently use **role playing,** an improvisational acting technique that allows clients to rehearse new social skills. Clients try out new ways of acting, while the therapist assumes the role of some person in their life. Later, the therapist offers feedback and suggests different approaches to the client. In addition to teaching new social skills, assertiveness training seeks to produce cognitive change, such as learning to recognize personal "rights." Returning to the case history, for example, a behavior therapist might teach Frances that she has a right to express her feelings. She does not necessarily have the right to get everything that she wants, however. Thus assertiveness would be defined in terms of her actions, not in terms of her success in changing her mother.

Social problem solving is a multistep process that has been used to teach children and adults ways to go about solving a variety of life's problems (D'Zurrilla & Goldfried, 1971; Spivack & Shure, 1974). The first step in social problem solving involves assessing and defining the problem in detail. This step is important, as we often see problems as being more manageable when they are defined specifically. "Brainstorming" is the second step in social problem solving. In order to encourage creativity, therapists ask clients to come up with as many alternative solutions as they can imagine—even wild and crazy options—without evaluating these alternatives. The third step in social problem solving involves carefully evaluating each of the options that has been generated. Finally, one alternative is chosen and implemented, and its success in solving the problem is evaluated objectively. If the solution is unsuccessful, the entire process can be repeated until an effective solution is found.

It is difficult to draw general conclusions about the effectiveness of social skills training because the technique has been applied to many specific problems with varying degrees of success. Clients can learn new social skills in therapy, but it is less clear whether these skills are used effectively in real life (Wilson & O'Leary, 1987). We consider the effectiveness of social skills training in treating specific problems in subsequent chapters.

Cognitive Behavior Therapy

Many practitioners have expanded the scope of behavior therapy into the cognitive realm, a broader approach called **cognitive behavior therapy.** Cognitive behavior therapy departs from Watson's exclusive focus on observable behavior and recognizes that many unobservable cognitive processes are central to human learning. Some cognitive therapy treatments have been developed in working with clinical populations. Other cognitive behavior therapy techniques involve direct attempts to apply basic research from cognitive psychology to clinical issues. Two examples of this latter approach are attribution retraining and self-instruction training.

ATTRIBUTION RETRAINING

Attribution retraining is based on research on social cognition that defines humans as "intuitive scientists" who are constantly ascribing causes to various events in their lives. These perceived causes, which may or may not be objectively accurate, are called *attributions*. Attribution retraining involves trying to change attributions, often by asking clients to abandon intuitive strategies. Instead, clients are instructed in more scientific methods, such as objectively testing hypotheses about themselves and others (Wilson & Linville, 1982).

Altering attributions may be especially relevant to the treatment of depression. Depressed people often attribute failures to themselves and attribute successes to other people (Peterson & Seligman, 1984; see Chapter 5). Frances's self-blame can be viewed as an example of this depressive attributional style, as she wrongly blamed herself for all her family's problems. In order to change these erroneous attributions, a cognitive behavior therapist might ask Frances to be more objective in evaluating her life. In so doing, she could learn about her own biased attributions as well as about the problems of others in her family. Attribution retraining also has been used to treat other problems. Examples are helping new students realize that struggling in the first year of college is not a personal failure but a common problem (Wilson & Linville, 1982), and helping unhappily married partners change the tendency to attribute negative interactions to a spouse's flawed personality (Fincham & Bradbury, 1990).

SELF-INSTRUCTION TRAINING

Self-instruction training draws on principles articulated by Luria (1961) and others about how children come to internalize rules over the course of their development. Meichenbaum (1977) has applied these theories in developing cognitive therapies for impulsive children. In Meichenbaum's self-instruction training, the adult first models an appropriate behavior while saying the self-instruction aloud. Next, the child is asked to repeat the action and also to say the self-instruction aloud. Following this, the child repeats the task while whispering the self-instructions. Finally, the child does the task while repeating the instructions silently. This procedure is designed to offer a structured way of helping children learn the internal controls that typically are acquired during the course of normal development.

COGNITIVE THERAPY

In addition to specific applications of research from cognitive psychology, cognitive behavior therapy has been strongly influenced by the clinical work of Aaron Beck (1976). Beck's **cognitive therapy** was developed specifically as a treatment for depression (Beck et al., 1979; see Chapter 5). Beck suggested that depression is caused by errors in thinking. These hypothesized distortions lead depressed people to draw incorrect, negative conclusions about themselves, thus creating and maintaining the depression. Simply put, Beck hypothesized that depressed people see the world through gray-colored glasses (as opposed to the rose-colored variety). According to Beck's analysis, this negative filter makes the world appear much bleaker than it really is.

Beck's cognitive therapy involves challenging these negative distortions through a technique he calls *collaborative empiricism*. Cognitive therapists gently confront their clients' cognitive fallacies in therapy, but they ask clients to decide for themselves whether their thinking is distorted based on their analysis of their own life (Beck et al., 1979). For example, a cognitive therapist might ask Frances to keep a record of her various family conflicts, including a brief description of the disputes and of the circumstances that preceded and followed each episode. Together with Frances, the cognitive therapist would use this information to challenge Frances's tendency to blame herself for the troubled relationships, a tendency that presumably results from a cognitive distortion rather than an accurate appraisal of her interactions.

RATIONAL–EMOTIVE THERAPY

Albert Ellis's (1973) **rational–emotive therapy (RET)** is also designed to challenge cognitive distortions. According to Ellis (1962), emotional disorders are caused by *irrational beliefs*. Irrational beliefs are absolute, unrealistic views of the world, such as "Everyone must love me all the time." The rational–emotive therapist searches for a client's irrational beliefs, points out the impossibility of fulfilling them, and uses any and every technique to persuade the client to adopt more realistic beliefs. Rational–emotive therapy shares concepts and techniques in common with Beck's approach. A major difference, however, is that rational–emotive therapists directly challenge the client's beliefs during therapy (Dryden & DiGuisseppe, 1990; Ellis, 1962).

INTEGRATION: THE EVOLUTION OF COGNITIVE BEHAVIOR THERAPY

Clearly, cognitive behavior therapy comprises diverse treatments. What unites cognitive behavior therapists is a commitment to empiricism, not to a particular form of treatment. Cognitive behavior therapists want treatments that work, and they have been vigorous in conducting psychotherapy outcome research. Research indicates that cognitive behavior therapies are not the only effective treatments, but this finding does not distress empirically oriented cognitive behavior therapists. Rather, it challenges them to identify alternative approaches and to incorporate them into the ever-expanding realm of cognitive behavior therapy. In fact, we envision a blurring of the lines between behavior therapy, cognitive behavior therapy, and other paradigms in the not-so-distant future, as empirical evidence and an integrated systems approach identify diverse but effective treatments for different disorders.

Humanistic Therapies

Humanistic psychotherapy originally was promoted as a "third force" to counteract what were seen as the overly mechanistic and deterministic views of both the psychodynamic and behavioral approaches to psychotherapy (see Table 3–3). Humanists argue that psychodynamic, behavioral, and biomedical therapists overlook the most essential of all human qualities: The individual's ability to make choices and freely determine his or her future.

Humanistic therapists believe that emotional distress results from the frustrations of human existence, particularly from alienation from the self and others. They also argue that each individual has the responsibility for finding meaning in her or his own life. Unlike the behavior therapist, the humanistic therapist does not believe that treatment can solve problems. Rather, treatment is seen only as a way to help individuals make their own life choices and resolve their own dilemmas (Rogers, 1961).

To help clients make choices, humanistic therapists strive to increase *emotional awareness*. They encourage clients to recognize and experience their true feelings. Like psychodynamic approaches, this involves "uncovering" hidden emotions, and some psychologists therefore classify the two treatments together as insight therapies (London, 1964). However, humanistic therapists are more concerned with how their clients are feeling than with why they are feeling that way. They focus on experiencing life, not on the structure of the personality. Thus, like behavior therapy, humanistic therapy is much more oriented to the present than is psychodynamic treatment.

One unique aspect of humanistic psychotherapy is the paramount importance placed on the therapist–client relationship. Humanistic therapists view a genuine and reciprocal relationship between therapist and client as the central means of producing therapeutic change. Therapists from other schools also place importance on the therapist–client relationship, but the relationship is viewed primarily as a means of delivering the treatment. In humanistic therapy, the relationship *is* the treatment.

CLIENT-CENTERED THERAPY

Carl Rogers (1902–1987) and his **client-centered therapy** provide the clearest example of the humanistic focus on the therapeutic relationship. Rogers (1951) wrote extensively

▲ **Carl Rogers (1902–1987) was a U.S. psychologist who developed client-centered therapy. Rogers asserted that therapeutic warmth, empathy, and genuineness were the necessary and sufficient conditions for successful psychotherapy.**

Some Treatment Variations within the Major Paradigms of Psychotherapy

Paradigm or Variation	Distinguishing Features
Psychoanalytic/Psychodynamic Therapy	
Psychoanalysis	Freud's classic treatment focuses on childhood memories and unconscious conflicts; techniques include free association, dream analysis, transference, and interpretation; several meetings a week for several years; therapist aloof.
Ego analysis	Psychodynamic treatments developed by Sullivan, Horney, Erikson, and other followers of Freud; insight is goal but the present, the conscious mind, and social relationships (the ego) considered by more active, warm therapist. Long-term but shorter than psychoanalysis.
Psychodynamic psychotherapy	Many variations of this short-term, insight-oriented treatment; therapist is more directive or confrontational in interpreting defenses; treatment focuses on single issue or theme.
Behavior Therapy	
Radical behaviorism	Adheres to Watson's and Skinner's focus on behavior and eschews consideration of "internal events"; many treatments offered but therapies focus on operant and classical conditioning; short-term treatment.
Cognitive behavior therapy	Recognizes or emphasizes cognition in human learning; many techniques in addition to operant and classical conditioning, including cognitive therapy, rational–emotive therapy, self-instruction training, and attribution retraining; short-term treatment.
Humanistic Therapy	
Client-centered therapy	Rogers' nondirective therapy emphasizes warmth, genuineness, and empathy as necessary and sufficient conditions for treatment success. Length not typically structured.
Gestalt therapy	Perls's confrontational therapy focusing on the "here and now" of genuine emotional expression and experience; may be short term, especially experiential groups designed for personal growth.

about the process of fostering a warm and genuine relationship between therapist and client. He particularly noted the importance of **empathy,** or emotional understanding. Empathy involves "putting yourself in someone else's shoes" as a way of understanding the other person's unique feelings and perspectives. In order to demonstrate empathy, the therapist must communicate this emotional understanding. Empathy is conveyed by reflecting the client's feelings and, at a deeper level, by sharing an understanding of emotions that remain unexpressed.

In forming an empathic relationship, the client-centered therapist does not act as an "expert" who knows more about the client than the client knows about himself or herself. Rather, the humanistic therapist endeavors to share in another human's experience. In fact, Rogers encouraged *self-disclosure* on the part of the therapist. In contrast to the psychoanalyst's distance, client-centered therapists may intentionally reveal aspects of their own feelings and experiences to their clients. The ability to share another's perspective can come from many life experiences, not just from professional training. For this reason, Rogers felt that client-centered therapists did not need to be professionals. Rather, they could be ordinary people who had faced life difficulties similar to those of their clients.

Rogers also felt that client-centered therapists must be able to demonstrate *unconditional positive regard* for their clients. This involves valuing the clients for who they are and refraining from judging them. Because of this basic respect for the client's humanity, client-centered therapists avoid directing the therapeutic process. According to Rogers, if clients are successful in experiencing and accepting themselves, they will achieve their own resolution to their difficulties. Thus client-centered therapy is *nondirective*.

GESTALT THERAPY

Frederich (Fritz) Perls's (1893–1970) **Gestalt therapy** is another variation of the humanistic approach.[†] Perls (1969) shared many of Rogers' therapeutic goals, particularly the goal of helping clients recognize and accept their emotional experiences. Perls especially underscored the importance of experiencing the moment—what he called living in the "here and now." He urged people to be genuine, and he accused many of being phony instead.

Gestalt techniques for increasing emotional awareness differ greatly from client-centered approaches. Rather than being supportive, the Gestalt therapist confronts phoniness, hoping that the client's frustration will provoke genuine emotion. As long as the client is phony, the Gestalt therapist is confrontational. When genuine emotion is expressed, however, the therapist's confrontation switches to support and shared experience. The here and now is critical to this distinction. Talking about emotions is phony. Feeling them is genuine. To a Gestalt therapist, an engaged "I hate you!" is much more genuine than a detached "I'm feeling very angry with you right now."

Gestalt therapists also differ from Rogerians in that they are very directive. In fact, Perls developed a number of specific exercises designed to provoke emotion and thereby heighten awareness. One of the better known strategies is the *empty chair technique*, in which the client has a dialogue with another part of himself or herself who is imagined to be sitting in an empty chair. For example, a Gestalt therapist might tell Frances (from the case history) to talk about her loving feelings toward her mother—directing the argument to "herself" in an empty chair. Later, the therapist would ask Frances to switch seats and vent her angry feelings about her mother. As with other Gestalt techniques, the goal of the empty chair exercise would be to heighten Frances's emotional awareness, including awareness of her conflicting emotions, and thereby increase her genuineness.

HUMANISTIC PSYCHOTHERAPY: A MEANS, NOT AN END?

Little research supports the effectiveness of client-centered or Gestalt therapy in treating abnormal behavior (Greenberg, Elliott, & Lietaer, 1994). One problem in evaluating effectiveness is that clients who seek humanistic treatments often are functioning rather well in their lives. They view therapy as a growth experience, not as a treatment for an emotional problem. Another problem is that few investigators have conducted psychotherapy outcome research on humanistic therapy.

We should note, however, that Rogers and his colleagues were strongly committed to psychotherapy *process* research. In fact, process research may be the lasting legacy of humanistic psychotherapy. As we discuss in more detail shortly, research on psychotherapy processes indicates that therapists who are humanistic in style are more effective when using virtually any treatment technique. Empathy and other relationship factors have been empirically documented to predict successful outcome across different approaches to psychotherapy (Rogers, 1957; Truax & Carkhuff, 1967). The major task for psychotherapy research is to identify the most effective treatments for specific disorders, but psychologists must not lose sight of the fact that caring, concern, and respect for the individual are essential components of all processes of treating emotional disorders.

"So, while extortion, racketeering, and murder may be bad acts, they don't make you a bad person."

Courtesy *The New Yorker*

[†] A *Gestalt* is an organized whole. Gestalt psychology emphasizes wholeness, whether at the level of perception or the level of life experience.

Research on Psychotherapy

Now that we have an introduction to the major treatments for psychological disorders, we can begin to ask some basic and important questions about psychotherapy. Does psychotherapy work? Many people claim not to "believe" in psychotherapy. Is their skepticism founded? And if therapy is helpful, what approach to psychotherapy works best? Which is more effective, psychotherapy or medication? These questions are straightforward, but psychotherapy research does not offer simple answers. Psychological researchers often disagree, sometimes vehemently, about whether therapy works, and, if so, which treatments work better than others.

Based on our own evaluation of the extensive research on psychotherapy, we have reached three major conclusions about psychotherapy. First, psychotherapy *does work*—for many people and for many problems. Second, the major approaches to psychotherapy share basic similarities that are often overlooked (e.g., the therapist–client relationship), and these "common factors" contribute to the success of therapy in important ways. Third, different treatments, including medication, are more or less effective for different disorders. We discuss evidence pertaining to the first conclusion in reviewing psychotherapy *outcome* research. We address the second conclusion when we consider psychotherapy *process* research. We focus on the third conclusion throughout subsequent chapters of the text where we discuss specific biological, psychological, and social interventions that are most effective in preventing or treating specific disorders.

Psychotherapy Outcome Research

Psychotherapy outcome research examines the outcome, or result, of psychotherapy—that is, its effectiveness for relieving symptoms, eliminating disorders, and/or improving life functioning. Hundreds of studies have compared the outcome of psychotherapy with the results of alternative treatments or with the effect of receiving no treatment at all. In fact, psychologists have developed a new method for combining results across studies, called meta-analysis, in order to summarize findings across the huge number of psychotherapy studies.

META-ANALYSIS

Meta-analysis is a statistical technique that allows the results from different studies to be combined in a standardized way. The results of a meta-analysis are expressed in standard deviation units, a measure of deviation from the mean (see Research Methods in Chapter 15).[†]

In evaluating hundreds of studies of psychotherapy outcome, meta-analysis indicates that the average change produced by psychotherapy is .85 standard deviations units (Smith, Glass, & Miller, 1980; see Figure 3–2). This means that the average client who receives therapy is better off than 80 percent of untreated persons. As another way of evaluating this finding, consider that 9 months of reading instruction leads to a .67 standard deviation unit increase in reading achievement among elementary school children (Lambert, Shapiro, & Bergin, 1986). And many well-accepted medical treatments have

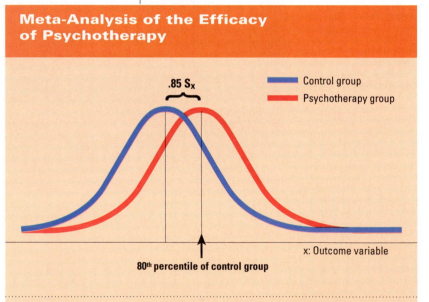

Meta-Analysis of the Efficacy of Psychotherapy

.85 S$_x$

Control group
Psychotherapy group

x: Outcome variable

80th percentile of control group

FIGURE 3-2: Average effect of psychotherapy (in standard deviation units) based on a meta-analysis of 475 controlled studies.

Source: M.L. Smith, G.V. Glass, and T.I. Miller, 1980, *The Benefits of Psychotherapy.* Baltimore: Johns Hopkins University Press.

[†] The formula for computing the standard deviation is $S = \sqrt{\dfrac{\Sigma (X_i - M)^2}{N}}$.

considerably smaller effect sizes. For example, chemotherapy has about a .10 effect size in reducing mortality following breast cancer (Lipsey & Wilson, 1993).

Meta-analysis is a useful way of summarizing information from a large number of studies, but you may have trouble grasping the meaning of a standard deviation unit. Fortunately, we can convert the figure into a simple improvement rate. A .85 standard deviation change indicates that two-thirds of clients who undergo psychotherapy improve significantly, whereas about one-third of people who receive no treatment improve over time (Rosenthal, 1983).

IMPROVEMENT WITHOUT TREATMENT

Treatment outcome researchers widely accept that about two-thirds of clients improve as a result of psychotherapy. Some skeptics have suggested, however, that far more than one-third of untreated emotional disorders have a *spontaneous remission*. That is, many people with psychological problems may improve without any treatment at all. In fact, British psychologist Hans Eysenck—who wrote one of the earliest and most famous criticisms of psychotherapy—concluded that treatment was totally ineffective for this very reason. In reviewing early evidence on psychotherapy, Eysenck (1952/1992) agreed that about 2 out of 3 people were helped by therapy. However, he asserted that *two*-thirds, not one-third, of people with emotional problems improve without treatment. Thus he concluded that psychotherapy offered little in the way of extra help.

NO TREATMENT CONTROL GROUPS

Who is right? How many people improve without treatment? This is a complicated question to answer, because most people in distress seek help informally if they cannot get professional treatment. For example, if they cannot see a mental health professional, emotionally distraught people are like to seek counseling and advice from family members, friends, or religious leaders. Thus "treatment" can be difficult to define, and researchers face numerous practical and ethical problems trying to ensure that clients assigned to "no treatment" control groups actually do not receive treatment (see Further Thoughts on p. 79 and Research Methods on p. 86).

Informal counseling often is helpful, as you surely know from your own life experiences. Thus some experts argue that "no treatment" controls actually receive some form of "treatment." If so, at least some people in "no treatment" control groups improve as a result of the support they receive and not because of a spontaneous remission. Other people argue that informal help is *not* psychotherapy. In fact, researchers have found that as many as one-half of people seeking psychotherapy improve as a result of simply having unstructured conversations with a professional—which is not considered a form of psychotherapy (Lambert, Shapiro, & Bergin, 1986).

Is the estimate that one-third of people improve without treatment too high or too low? We think it is about right. We believe that social support *is* an important element of psychotherapy, but, in any case, improvement rates following psychotherapy exceed improvement rates following unstructured meetings with a therapist (e.g., Borkovec & Costello, 1993; see Research Close-Up on p. 107). Thus we conclude that psychotherapy does, indeed, work for many people with many problems (Lambert, Shapiro, & Bergin, 1986).

EFFICACY AND EFFECTIVENESS: THE *CONSUMER REPORTS* STUDY

We have been discussing the most basic type of psychotherapy outcome research, that is, the *efficacy study*, in which researchers conduct experiments in which they randomly assign patients to alternative treatments or to no treatment at all. The best efficacy studies are tightly controlled. Not only do efficacy studies assign patients to treatments at random, but they also select patients with clearly defined problems and offer carefully controlled treatments (Seligman, 1995). For example, an efficacy study may treat only clients who are clinically depressed but suffer from no other disorder. Therapy may be restricted to 12 sessions of Beck's cognitive therapy, and therapists may not be allowed to depart from restrictions about what should and should not be discussed in treatment—typically as spelled out in a lengthy "treatment manual."

Efficacy studies tell us if psychotherapy *can* work under prescribed circumstances, but efficacy studies do not tell us whether psychotherapy *does* work as it is actually practiced. That is, efficacy studies have strong *internal validity* but uncertain *external validity* (see Research Methods on p. 86). In everyday psychotherapy, most clients have multiple problems and choose therapists with care, not at random. Moreover, most therapists are eclectic and tailor the type and length of treatment to the perceived needs of individual clients (Seligman, 1995). How does psychotherapy fare under these circumstances? This question is examined by a second type of psychotherapy outcome research, the *effectiveness study*.

Effectiveness studies do not use random assignment; thus they are correlational studies that cannot inform us about cause and effect (see Research Methods in Chapter 2). Correlational studies can provide valuable descriptive information, however. In fact, the magazine *Consumer Reports* (1995, November) recently conducted an effectiveness study of psychotherapy by surveying readers who had seen a mental health professional in the past 3 years. The nearly 3000 respondents generally rated their experiences in psychotherapy highly. Among the major findings of the *Consumer Reports* study were the following (1995, November; Seligman, 1995):

- Therapy helped. Of the 426 people who were feeling "very poor" at the beginning of treatment, 87 percent reported feeling "very good," "good," or at least "so-so" when they were surveyed.

- The major mental health professionals were equally effective. The clients of psychologists, psychiatrists, and social workers reported no differences in treatment outcome, but all three professions were *more* effective than marriage counselors.

- Medication added little to psychotherapy. People who received psychotherapy alone improved no more or less than people who received psychotherapy plus medication.

Because the *Consumer Reports* study was a correlational study, you can and should question the interpretation of these findings. It is possible, for example, that people who had good experiences in psychotherapy were more likely to respond to the survey than were people who had bad experiences. Nevertheless, the findings of this survey bolster our conclusion that psychotherapy works for many people and many problems, because they are broadly consistent with the results of numerous carefully controlled efficacy studies.

TWO PREDICTORS OF TREATMENT OUTCOME: TREATMENT LENGTH AND THE YAVIS CLIENT

A number of factors predict when psychotherapy is likely to be more or less effective. As we discuss in later chapters, the most important predictor is the nature of a client's problems—the diagnosis. Here, we consider two more general predictors of treatment outcome: the length of treatment and the client's background characteristics.

Research indicates that if therapy is going to be effective, it usually will be effective rather quickly. As Figure 3–3 indicates, most people who improve in psychotherapy do so in the first several months of treatment. Improvement continues with longer-term therapy but at a notably slower rate (Howard et al., 1986). The *Consumer Reports* study revealed a similar pattern, although the rate of improvement did not slow as dramatically after 6 months of treatment (Seligman, 1995). Other evidence suggests that 1 year, and not 6 months, may be a more realistic trial period for clients who do not respond earlier in treatment (Kopta, Howard, Lowry, & Beutler, 1994). In any event, these findings buttress the trend toward providing short-term psychotherapy. Improvement usually occurs early in therapy, and as a rule, therapy, therefore, should be brief. As always, rules have exceptions, and longer-term psychotherapy may be warranted under certain circumstances—circumstances that psychologists must identify and justify in future research.

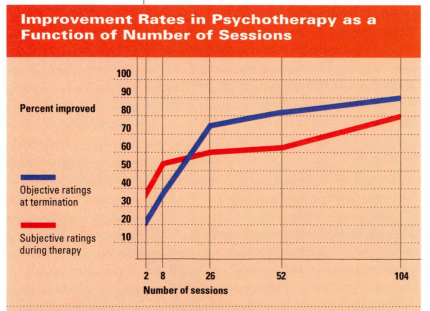

Improvement Rates in Psychotherapy as a Function of Number of Sessions

Percent improved

— Objective ratings at termination

— Subjective ratings during therapy

Number of sessions

FIGURE 3-3: Relation between number of psychotherapy sessions and percentage of clients improved.

Source: K.I. Howard, S.M. Kopta, M.S. Krause, and D.E. Orlinsky, 1986, The dose–effect relationship in psychotherapy, *American Psychologist*, 41, 159–164.

Significantly, clients' background characteristics also predict outcome in psychotherapy. The acronym *YAVIS* was coined to indicate that clients improve more in psychotherapy when they are "young, attractive, verbal, intelligent, and successful." This finding has caused considerable concern, for it seems to indicate that psychotherapy works best for the most advantaged members of our society (Lorion & Felner, 1986). We are particularly concerned that psychotherapy must be sensitive to the unique issues facing members of different ethnic groups in our multicultural society (Casas, 1995; Sue, Zane, & Young, 1994; see Further Thoughts).

FURTHER THOUGHTS

Psychotherapy with Ethnic Minorities

More than 25 percent of people living in the United States today are members of ethnic minority groups, and demographers predict that during the twenty-first century the number of ethnic minorities will surpass the number of white Americans of European descent. Among the dozens of ethnic minority groups in the United States, the most numerous are African Americans, Latinos, Asian Americans, and Native Americans. Treating people from such diverse backgrounds represents a major challenge to the psychology profession. Indeed, critics have questioned the sensitivity, appropriateness, and effectiveness of mainstream psychotherapy in meeting the mental health needs of ethnic groups (Casas, 1995; Sue et al., 1994).

One basic concern is that mental health professionals recognize the unique cultural values and societal experiences of members of different ethnic minority groups. Psychotherapists must be aware of both commonalities and diversity in experience. Minority groups share experiences, such as the historical and ongoing racism faced by African Americans, but members of minority groups also are heterogenous in terms of their societal, political, and cultural backgrounds. For example, the experience of Asian Americans, who have come to the United States voluntarily, is very different from the experience of Native Americans, who were driven from their homeland and confined to reservations. Wide individual differences in experience are also found *within* minority groups. For example, peoples designated as "Latino" are actually a diverse group with origins in Mexico, the Caribbean, and Central and South America. Similarly, the experiences of African Americans differ widely based on socioeconomic status, religion, and region of upbringing.

A second basic concern is that mental health professionals recognize that many of the emotional and adjustment problems faced by ethnic minorities stem from social and cultural experiences and not from individual psychological problems. A general challenge faced by all ethnic minorities is *acculturation,* the process of learning or adopting the cultural patterns of the majority group (Casas, 1995; Sue et al., 1994). The acculturation of diverse ethnic groups into the mainstream is a political goal of the American "melting pot." However, the process of acculturation taxes individual coping resources, as people's prior beliefs and actions may not be supported by the dominant culture. In fact, ethnic values and social customs may be undermined or even derided by the majority culture, and acculturation pressures often disrupt adaptive ethnic traditions and relationships. Yet another problem is that our society makes acculturation more difficult for the members of some ethnic minority groups who are not readily accepted by members of the dominant culture unless—or even if—the individual minority member wholly adopts the majority culture. In particular, African Americans and Native Americans have faced tremendous challenges in acculturation. Unlike immigrants, the members of these ethnic groups did not choose to become Americans, and historically both groups have faced discrimination in mainstream society and repeated attempts to obliterate their cultural heritage.

Acculturation and other social forces often challenge and change *ethnic identity,* the ethnic minority members' understanding of self in terms of their own culture. Atkinson, Morten, and Sue (1993) have proposed a five-stage model of the development of ethnic identity. The stages include (1) *conformity,* a time of self-depreciation and discrimination; (2) *dissonance,* a period of conflict between self-depreciation and appreciation of one's ethnicity; (3) *resistance and immersion,* a stage of self-appreciation and ethnocentrism, accompanied by depreciation of the majority group; (4) *introspection,* a phase of questioning the basis of self-appreciation, as well as the basis for depreciation of the majority group; and (5) *synergetic articulation and awareness,* including both self-appreciation and appreciation of the basis for majority group values. The model of ethnic identity development can be viewed as analogous to how the group process of acculturation proceeds at the level of the individual. Although researchers have only begun to study this model of ethnic identity development, recognition of the influence of acculturation pressures on the development of individual identity is essential both to assessing individual well-being and to

establishing a strong therapeutic relationship (Casas, 1995).

Research on psychotherapy with ethnic minorities is limited in scope. A recent review of the literature concluded that there is not enough evidence to decide whether psychotherapy is effective or ineffective for minority group members (Sue et al., 1994). Some evidence suggests that psychotherapy is more effective when client and therapist share a similar cultural background and when the treatment is tailored to the specific culture. Therapy also may be more effective when therapists are trained to be sensitive to minority issues (Sue et al., 1994). Clearly, there is a need for much more research on the various issues involved in treating ethnic minorities, who soon will make up the majority of the population in the United States. ∎

OUTCOME RESEARCH ON DIFFERENT PARADIGMS FOR PSYCHOTHERAPY

Are psychodynamic, behavioral, or humanistic treatments more or less effective when compared with one another? Meta-analysis generally reveals few sizable differences among approaches (Smith, Glass, & Miller, 1980), although behavior therapies may be somewhat more effective, especially in the treatment of anxiety (Shapiro & Shapiro, 1982). A major study of medication and two forms of psychotherapy in the treatment of depression—perhaps the largest psychotherapy study ever conducted—also found similar rates of improvement for the different treatments (Elkin et al., 1989; see Chapter 5). But the general conclusion that different therapies often produce similar results masks important issues in comparing treatment approaches. We illustrate some of these issues by examining an exemplary investigation in some detail.

Sloane and his colleagues (1975) conducted what remains a classic comparison of contrasting forms of psychotherapy. These investigators compared the effectiveness of behavior therapy and psychodynamic psychotherapy in treating outpatients who were suffering from mild to moderate anxiety, depression, personality disorders, and similar problems. We will briefly summarize the investigators' procedures, because they highlight some of the key considerations in efficacy studies of psychotherapy outcome research.

Clients with problems that were very mild (for example, job problems) or very severe (for example, suicide risk, serious substance abuse) were excluded from the study, and the remaining 90 patients were assigned at random to receive either psychodynamic psychotherapy, behavior therapy, or no treatment. The different therapies were delivered by three psychodynamic and three behavior therapists, all of whom were highly experienced in their preferred form of treatment. Both treatments lasted for an average of 14 sessions. To ensure that the treatments were offered as planned, the differences between the two therapies were clearly defined (see Table 3–4), and tape recordings of the fifth therapy sessions were made and coded so that the actual treatments could be compared. Finally, an independent team of evaluators made detailed, objective assessments of the clients' functioning. Assessments were made before treatment, 4 months into therapy, and at 1 and 2 years after the original assessment. Assessments included ratings of symptom severity made by the evaluators; self-reports on objective measures including the MMPI, an objective measure of psychopathology (see Chapter 4); client and therapist ratings of therapeutic success and attainment of therapy goals; and ratings from a friend or relative who knew the client.

All three groups, including the no-treatment group, improved over time, but the treated groups improved significantly more than the untreated groups. In general, behavior therapy and psychodynamic psychotherapy were equally effective. A few differences did favor behavior therapy. For example, the assessors found significantly more improvement in target symptoms for behavior therapy clients at 1-year follow-up. On most measures, however, there were no differences between the two treatment groups. The alternative treatments were similar in their effectiveness and superior to no treatment at all.

How can this be? Behavior therapy and psychodynamic psychotherapy clearly differ (see Table 3–4). In fact, the investigators found that behavior therapists talked about as often as their clients talked, gave specific advice, and directed much of the course of therapy. In contrast, psychodynamic therapists talked only one-third as often as their clients, refused to answer specific questions, and followed their clients' lead during the session. Psychodynamic therapists also were more likely to focus on feelings, their underlying causes, and techniques such as free association, whereas behavior therapists focused on specific behaviors, ways of changing them, and techniques such as systematic desensitization.

What did the very different treatments have in common? Perhaps more than is readily apparent. Surprisingly, behavior therapists and psychodynamic therapists offered the same number of interpretations. Most importantly, the clients' ratings of therapist warmth, empathy, and genuineness predicted successful outcome in both treatment groups. Clients also rated their personal relationship with their therapists as the single most important aspect of both behavior therapy and psychoanalytic psychotherapy (Sloane et al., 1975). Perhaps an important part of the healing process might simply be engaging in psychotherapy of any form.

This suggestion may seem outlandish at first, but it is not an unfamiliar one. By way of analogy, consider children's sports. Baseball and soccer surely differ greatly, but they also share similarities at a higher level of abstraction. For children, participating in some sport, any sport, may be more important to their development than whether they play basketball or lacrosse. Similarly, the fact of holding some belief in a higher power is an essential commonality across religions despite dramatic differences in dogma. Perhaps different approaches to psychotherapy also share important similarities at a higher level of abstraction. This is an issue examined in psychotherapy process research.

	TABLE 3-4

Working Definitions of Psychotherapy and Behavior Therapy in Sloane Study

Technique	Psychotherapy	Behavior Therapy
Specific advice	Given infrequently	Given frequently
Transference interpretation	May be given	Avoided
Resistance interpretation	Used	Not used
Dreams	Interested and encouraged	Disinterested
Level of anxiety	Maintained when possible	Diminished when possible
Relaxation training	Only indirect	Directly undertaken
Desensitization	Only indirect	Directly undertaken
Assertion training	Indirectly encouraged	Directly encouraged
Report of symptoms	Discouraged	Encouraged
Childhood memories	Explored	Historical interest only

Source: Differences in technique in behavior therapy and psychotherapy, as adapted from R. B. Sloane, F. R. Staples, A. H. Cristo, N. J. Yorkston, and K. Whipple, 1975, *Psychotherapy versus Behavior Therapy,* pp. 237–240. Cambridge, MA: Harvard University Press.

Psychotherapy Process Research: Toward the Integration of Psychotherapies

Psychotherapy process research studies qualities of the therapist–client relationship that predict successful outcome irrespective of the theoretical orientation of the therapist. This approach to research investigates whether different psychotherapies contain "common factors" that are responsible for therapeutic success. If common factors explain similarities in the effectiveness of different treatment paradigms, as many investigators suspect, then it may be possible to integrate diverse treatments into an eclectic but coherent approach to psychotherapy (Goldfried, 1982). Much interest in common factors and psychotherapy integration was prompted by Jerome Frank, especially his incisive book on psychotherapy, *Persuasion and Healing* (1961, 1973; Frank & Frank, 1991). Frank is an American trained both in psychology and psychiatry and has spent most of his career at the Johns Hopkins Medical School. Frank's analysis begins with his very broad definition of psychotherapy as involving

(1) a trained, socially sanctioned healer, whose healing powers are accepted by

▲ **Jerome Frank is a U.S. psychologist and psychiatrist. Frank has analyzed psychotherapy as a process of persuasion and healing, drawing broad analogies between therapy and healing rituals in both industrialized and nonindustrialized cultures.**

the sufferer and by his social group or an important segment of it

(2) a sufferer who seeks relief from the healer

(3) a circumscribed, more-or-less structured series of contacts between the healer and the sufferer, through which the healer, often with the aid of a group, tries to produce certain changes in the sufferer's emotional state, attitudes, and behavior. All concerned believe these changes will help him. Although physical and chemical adjuncts may be used, the healing influence is primarily exercised by words, acts, and rituals in which sufferer, healer and—if there is one—group, participate jointly." (Frank, 1973, pp. 2–3)

Frank goes on to point out, "These three features are common not only to all forms of psychotherapy as the term is generally used, but also to methods of primitive healing" (p. 3).

It is easy to misunderstand Frank's argument. Is he saying that psychotherapy is little more than voodoo? No, Frank's point is just the opposite. He argues that psychotherapists should attempt to harness the powerful psychological tools used intuitively by both primitive and modern healers. He notes that rituals performed by healers in different cultures often provoke strong emotions that have been demonstrated to have powerful effects on health. He cites the "taboo death" as one dramatic example. In some primitive cultures, actual deaths have been documented to result from elaborate death curses, even when no physical harm is inflicted (Frank, 1973).

Frank (1961, 1973) notes that, like primitive healers, psychotherapists and other helping professionals are imbued with powers that stem from culturally sanctioned roles. The power comes from the mystery of the unconscious mind, incomprehensible medical treatments, or even from science itself. In the United States today, we strongly believe in the effectiveness of science, and we often treat science as if it were a mystical force. In short, even in modern societies part of the professional helper's healing power comes from the belief that doctors can heal.

THE PLACEBO EFFECT

The **placebo effect** is one important and dramatic illustration of the healing power of beliefs in medicine and in psychotherapy. In medicine, *placebos* are pills that are pharmacologically inert; that is, they have no medicinal value. More broadly, placebos are any type of treatment that contains no known "active ingredients" for treating the condition being evaluated. But the absence of active ingredients does not prevent placebos from healing. Placebos have powerful influences on both physical and psychological ailments. In medicine, potent placebo effects have been demonstrated in dentistry, optometry, cancer treatment, and even surgery (Shapiro & Morris, 1978). Some psychiatric outpatients who are given placebo medications report greatly improved comfort that lasts over an extended period of time (Frank, 1973). The power of placebos also lies behind the common wisdom to "use new treatments quickly before they lose their power to heal." All helping professionals know that the latest treatment owes part of its effectiveness to its being the latest treatment (Shapiro & Morris, 1978).

The ultimate goal of treatment research is to identify therapies that produce change above and beyond placebo effects, that is, to find interventions that contain one or more active ingredients for treating a particular disorder. Thus many investigations in medicine and psychotherapy include **placebo control groups**—groups of patients who are given treatments that are intentionally designed to have no active ingredients.

Placebos apparently work because they create an *expectation* of change. They work because the patient expects them to work. Placebos also work because the healer expects them to work, thus making double-blind placebo control studies necessary. In a **double-blind study,** neither the physician nor the patient knows whether the prescribed pill is the real medication or a placebo. These double precautions are necessary because the expectations of both the patient and the physician repeatedly have been found to influence the success of all kinds of biomedical treatments (Rosenthal & Rosnow, 1969).

Unfortunately, it is impossible to conduct double-blind studies of psychotherapy because

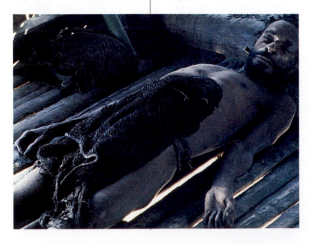

▼ **Biami tribesman willing himself to death. Such "taboo deaths" illustrate the power of belief and ritual.**

researchers cannot disguise from therapists whether a particular psychological intervention is a placebo. Thus it is important to be aware of **allegiance effects** in psychotherapy research. That is, psychotherapy researchers typically find that their favorite treatment—the one to which they hold an allegiance—is the most effective treatment. Allegiance effects tell us that, as with other treatments, the therapist's expectations influence the effectiveness of different forms of psychotherapy.

Some people view placebo effects as nuisances or even as hoaxes. This opinion is understandable, because a goal of research is to isolate the "active ingredients" in a treatment beyond placebo effects. But we can also view placebo effects as treatments—treatments that heal through psychological mechanisms. Of course, psychological healing is also the goal of psychotherapy. Thus, for the purposes of understanding and improving psychotherapy, placebo effects should be embraced and not dismissed (Critelli & Neumann, 1984; Frank & Frank, 1991). Ironically, psychotherapy researchers need to identify the "active ingredients" in placebos.

In fact, health care providers attempt to maximize expectancies in many subtle ways. Consider your physician's office. An exclusive address, expensive furniture, and diplomas on the wall all help to heighten the expectancy that this is a powerful healer. (You might not be as hopeful if the office was in some beat-up basement and there were no signs indicating the physician is a licensed professional.) Much more important to expectancies is the sense of confidence and competence that a helper instills. People seek professional help when they have been unable to solve their own problems, and they will not accept assistance if the helper fails to instill some hope or reassurance (Frank & Frank, 1991). The helper also must be able to fulfill or reshape a client's expectations about particular forms of treatment. Someone who wants direct advice is unlikely to return to a therapist who offers nothing but reflection (Eisenthal, Emery, Lazare, & Udin, 1979).

Heightened expectations for change are created by different approaches to psychotherapy; thus they are one common factor in psychotherapy. There are many more important common factors in therapy, however, most of which involve aspects of the therapist–client relationship (Mahoney, 1991; see Table 3–5). Different schools of therapy construe the therapist–client relationship in various ways,

but they all recognize its importance (Strupp, 1986). We consider some essential components of this unique relationship—basic issues if diverse approaches to psychotherapy are to be integrated—in the two brief sections that follow.

PSYCHOTHERAPY AS SOCIAL SUPPORT

All major schools of psychotherapy emphasize the importance of warmth in the therapist–client relationship. Rogers (1961) argued that warmth, empathy, and genuineness formed the center, and not the periphery, of the healing process. Freud (1912) also suggested that a client's positive feelings toward the psychoanalyst added to the success of the treatment, even though he clearly viewed this influence as secondary. Similarly, behavior therapists have emphasized warmth in the therapeutic relationship in practice even if it plays a minor role in theory. For example, consider Wolpe's (1958) comments about systematic desensitization: "All that the patient says is accepted without question or criticism. He is given the feeling that the therapist is unreservedly on his side. This happens not because the therapist is expressly trying to appear sympathetic, but as a natural outcome of a completely nonmoralizing objective approach to the behavior of human organisms" (p. 106).

Research on psychotherapy process indicates that a therapist's supportiveness is related to positive outcomes across approaches to treatment (Parloff, Waskow, & Wolfe, 1978). Significantly, objective indicators of a therapist's

---

TABLE 3-5

Common Characteristics of Effective Brief Psychotherapies

1. Treatment is offered soon after the problem is identified.
2. Assessment of the problem is rapid and occurs early in treatment.
3. A therapeutic alliance is established quickly, and it is used to encourage change in the client.
4. Therapy is designed to be time-limited, and the therapist uses this to encourage rapid progress.
5. The goals of therapy are limited to a few specified areas.
6. The therapist is directive in managing the treatment sessions.
7. Therapy is focused on a specific theme.
8. The client is encouraged to express strong emotions or troubling experiences.
9. A flexible approach is taken in the choice of treatment techniques.

Source: Adapted from M. P. Koss and J. M. Butcher, 1986. Research on brief psychotherapy. In S. L. Garfield and A. E. Bergin (Eds.), *Handbook of Psychotherapy and Behavior Change*, 3rd ed., pp. 627–670. New York: Wiley.

▲ **Warmth is a vital aspect of relationships with family and friends. Social support also is instrumental to the therapy relationship.**

support are less potent predictors of successful outcome than are a client's rating of the therapist. A supportive relationship is not defined simply by a therapist's behavior, but by a therapist's behavior in relation to a particular client. Some, perhaps most, people feel that they are understood by a therapist who makes empathic statements, but others may be more comfortable with a therapist who is somewhat detached (Beutler, Crago, & Arizmendi, 1986). Thus clients may perceive different therapeutic stances as supportive, depending on the particular types of relationships with which they are most comfortable.

A supportive therapeutic relationship is important, but is therapy more than this? Rogers (1957) argued that warmth, empathy, and genuineness were *necessary and sufficient* conditions for therapeutic success. He clearly stated that a therapist must be warm, empathetic, and genuine in order to be successful, and further, that this supportiveness was all that was needed for therapy to be effective. However, research indicates that therapist supportiveness is neither necessary nor sufficient for therapeutic success, despite the fact that supportiveness predicts a more successful outcome (Beutler, Crago, & Arizmendi, 1986). Many other factors influence treatment effectiveness.

PSYCHOTHERAPY AS SOCIAL INFLUENCE

Psychotherapy is a process of social influence as well as one of social support. The three major schools of therapy clearly differ in terms of the degree to which therapists directly attempt to influence clients. Beyond their explicit theoretical stance, however, all therapists influence clients in ways that are both obvious and subtle, intentional and unintentional.

One social influence is the nonjudgmental attitude found in all major approaches to psychotherapy. People often fear that their secret fears and failures will be met with criticism or ridicule, and the therapist's acceptance can come as a welcome relief. Whether construed as catharsis, extinction, or a corrective emotional experience, a common change process found in all psychotherapies is the provision of a safe forum for secret revelations (Pennebaker, 1990; Strong, 1978).

All therapists also influence their clients by pointing out discrepancies to them, that is, by offering interpretations. For example, a therapist may note inconsistencies between Frances's professed beliefs and her actions: "You talk about being sad, but you sound angry." Such an interpretation can create *dissonance* or internal conflict for Frances. As a way of resolving dissonance, we all alter our beliefs to be more consistent. Thus Frances may be forced to grapple with the inconsistency between her avowed sadness and her angry tone. For example, she might decide that she *is* angry—justifiably so—or perhaps she may instead recognize that she is uncomfortable showing genuine sadness. Of course, a therapist must be a credible source if interpretations are to be effective (Strong, 1978). If a therapist is not credible, a client can resolve dissonance not by challenging personal beliefs but by discounting the therapist's perspective.

Process research clearly demonstrates the social influence of psychotherapy. For example, researchers have found that clients tend to adopt beliefs similar to those of their therapists. In fact, treatment is more effective when, over time, clients' beliefs become more similar to those of their therapists (Beutler, Crago, & Arizmendi, 1986; Kelly, 1990). Positive outcomes are more likely when the changed beliefs relate directly to psychotherapy—for example, the importance of expressing emotions—than when they reflect broad social and religious values (Beutler, Machado, & Neufeldt, 1994).

Nevertheless, recognition of social influence raises questions about values in psychotherapy. Psychotherapy is not value-free. There are values inherent in the nature of therapy itself—for example, the belief that expressing emotions is good. Moreover, the values of individual therapists about such topics as love, marriage, work, and family necessarily influence clients. Like the rest of the human race, psychotherapists cannot transcend their own beliefs and values. All we can do is to recognize our biases and inform our clients about them. Because psychotherapy is a process of social influence, values invariably enter into therapy.

Changing Social Systems: Couples, Family, and Group Therapy

Biomedical approaches and psychotherapy are not the only treatments for individual psychological problems. Systems theory recognizes reciprocal influences across biological, psychological, and social functioning. Returning to the case of Frances, we realize that her family relationships should improve if we successfully treat her depression with medication or psychotherapy. Conversely, therapy with her parents and/or husband also might alleviate Frances's depression. More broadly, some theorists would argue that Frances would be less depressed if women were encouraged to assume more independent roles in society.

In fact, social interventions for psychological disorders include treatments for couples and entire families, group therapy, and even broader efforts at preventing emotional disorders through improving society. As is true of individual psychotherapy, there are different "schools" of couples, family, and group therapy, and the goals of alternative social interventions vary widely. For these reasons, we must be selective in our overview of social approaches to treatment. Still, our survey encompasses approaches aimed at eliminating social causes of abnormal behavior and less ambitious interventions designed to help family and friends cope more effectively with loved ones whose psychopathology clearly is caused by biological or psychological abnormalities.

Couples Therapy

Couples therapy involves seeing intimate partners together in psychotherapy. This approach is sometimes called *marital therapy* or *marriage counseling,* but the reference to couples captures the range of partners who may seek treatment together. Dating pairs, prospective mates, live-in partners, and gay and lesbian couples also may seek couples therapy.

The goal of couples therapy typically is to improve the relationship, and not to treat the individual. However, couples treatment also may be used to help both partners function more adequately when one member suffers from a psychological problem. In treating relationships, all couples therapists focus on resolving conflicts and promoting mutual satisfaction. Couples therapists do not tell their clients what compromises they should accept or how they should change their relationship. Instead, they typically help partners to improve their *communication* and *negotiation* skills (Baruth & Huber, 1984; Fincham & Bradbury, 1990; Margolin, 1987).

The goal of improving communication is best illustrated with an example. A couples therapist might suggest to Frances that she had a problem with "mind reading" in her marriage. Frances may be hoping (or expecting) that her husband would know what she wanted without telling him directly. She might want more attention, for example, but perhaps she never told her husband that lack of attention was a problem. She may want him to "figure it out for himself." Couples therapists point out that it is impossible to read another person's mind, and they encourage partners in close relationships to communicate their wishes directly (Gottman et al., 1976). This may sound simple, but learning to be direct can be tricky for many people. Frances may have felt selfish when making requests, for example, or perhaps she wanted to be "surprised" with her husband's attention. She may have thought that his attention would be less meaningful if she asked for it.

Another component of most couples therapies is negotiation or *conflict resolution* (Heitler, 1992). Negotiation is the imprecise art of give and take. Most approaches to negotiation emphasize the importance of clearly defining problems, considering a wide range of solutions, uncovering "hidden agendas" (unstated issues), and experimenting with alternative solutions. These strategies are similar to the social problem-solving model discussed earlier, and this approach has been effectively applied to work with couples (Emery, 1994). Polite communication also is an essential component of negotiation, and setting ground rules can be essential to encouraging polite communication. Examples of ground rules include not raising your voice, not interrupting the other person, and speaking about your own feelings—that is, not telling your partner how he or she feels (Gottman et al., 1976).

Research has documented that couples therapy can improve satisfaction in marriages (Baucom & Epstein, 1990; Holtzworth-Munroe & Jacobson, 1991). However, questions remain about the long-term effectiveness of couples therapy, the relative efficacy of alternative approaches to couples therapy, and the role of couples therapy in the broader societal context (Alexander, Holtzworth-Munroe, & Jameson, 1994). Some people view marital problems as stemming from broader social forces, such as financial pressures or the roles assumed by men and women. In contrast, others view many societal problems as a result of the breakdown of marriage in the United States today. From the former perspective, couples therapy faces many obstacles and may help preserve a problematic status quo. From the latter perspective, couples therapy holds the promise of improving marital happiness and promoting marriage.

Couples therapy also has been used in the treatment of specific disorders, including depression, anxiety, substance abuse, and child behavior problems. This typically is done either as a supplement or an alternative to individual therapy. When couples therapy is used in conjunction with individual treatment, the combined approach often is more effective than individual therapy alone, as we discuss in subsequent chapters on specific disorders (Barlow, O'Brien, & Last, 1984; Beach, Sandeen, & O'Leary, 1990; Dadds, Schwartz, & Sanders, 1987; Jacobson, Holtzworth-Monroe, & Schmaling, 1989).

Family Therapy

Family therapy might include two, three, or more family members in the psychotherapy

▼ **Family therapy includes at least two and perhaps many or all family members in treatment. Family therapists strive to improve mental health by altering family relationships.**

sessions. Family therapy shares many features in common with couples therapy, for example, improving communication and negotiation. Including children in family therapy can add complexity to this treatment approach, however, as does the obvious fact that relationships and treatments get more complicated when more people are involved.

Like couples therapy, family therapy has the general goal of improving satisfaction with relationships. Some forms of family therapy also are designed to resolve specific conflicts, such as disputes between adolescents and their parents (Robin, Koepke, & Nayar, 1986). *Parent management training* is an approach that teaches parents new skills for rearing troubled children (Patterson, 1982; Forehand & McMahon, 1981; see Chapter 16). Moreover, some important forms of family therapy are designed to educate families about how best to cope with the serious psychopathology of one family member (Falloon, 1985; see Chapter 13).

As with individual and couples therapy, there are many different theoretical approaches to family therapy (Gurman & Kniskern, 1991). Many approaches to family therapy differ from other treatments, however, in their long-standing emphasis on the application of systems theory. In applying systems theory, family therapists emphasize interdependence among family members and the paramount importance of the family within the larger social system. For example, family systems therapists often call attention to the pattern of *alliances* or strategic loyalties among family members (P. Minuchin, 1985). In well-functioning families, the primary alliance is between the two parents, even when the parents do not live together. In contrast, dysfunctional families often have alliances that cross generations—that is, "teams" that include one parent and some or all of the children opposing the other parent or another child. Like a poorly organized business, families function inadequately when their leaders fail to cooperate. Thus a common goal in systems approaches to family therapy is to strengthen the alliance between the parents, to get parents to work together and not against each other (S. Minuchin, 1974).

Early family therapists overemphasized the role of the family in causing individual psychopathology, particularly severe psychological disorders. Many contemporary approaches to family therapy have a much broader view of etiology. Irrespective of etiology, however, troubled relationships often intensify individual psychopathology, and individual psychopathology commonly strains relationships. It is not surprising therefore that family therapy may serve as an effective alternative or adjunct to individual treatment (Alexander, Holtzworth-Munroe, & Jameson, 1994).

Group Therapy

Like couples therapy and family therapy, **group therapy** involves the treatment of more than one person at one time. Therapy groups may be as small as 3 or 4 people or as large as 20 or more. Group therapy has numerous variations in terms of paradigmatic approaches and targets for treatment (Yalom, 1985). These variations are far too numerous to discuss here, so we highlight only a few facets of the group approach.

Psychoeducational groups are designed to teach group members specific information or skills relevant to psychological well-being. The term *psychoeducational* aptly conveys the goals of this type of group. Teaching is the primary mode of treatment, but the content of the "course" focuses on psychological issues. For example, assertiveness might be taught in a group format. Other psychoeducational groups focus on teaching systematic desensitization or cognitive therapy. In still other circumstances, a common disorder such as an eating disorder, not a common treatment, is the reason for group membership (see Chapter 10). In fact, psychoeducational groups have been developed for virtually every disorder discussed in this textbook.

There are at least two basic reasons for offering therapy in a psychoeducational group instead of in individual psychotherapy. Lower expense is one obvious justification. A second rationale is the support, encouragement, and practice that group members can offer to one another. Many people who have psychological problems feel isolated, alone, and sometimes "weird." Thus the simple act of coming to a group can be part of the therapeutic process (Bloch & Crouch, 1987). Learning that you are not alone with your problems can be a powerful experience that is one of the unique "active ingredients" in group therapy.

In contrast to psychoeducational groups, in *experiential group therapy* the relationships among group members form the primary, not a secondary, component of treatment. The experience of interacting with others in a unique setting is the rationale for experiential groups. Group members might be encouraged to look beyond one another's "facades," to reveal secrets about themselves, or otherwise to break down the barriers that we all erect in relationships (Bloch & Crouch, 1987; Yalom, 1985). Group members, in turn, can offer one another feedback and support. In an *encounter group*, for example, group members may question self-disclosure when it is "phony" but support more honest appraisals of oneself.

Experiential group leaders typically adhere to a humanistic approach to therapy, and the members often are well-functioning people who view the group as an opportunity for personal growth. Little research has been conducted on the effectiveness of this type of group.

The *self-help group* has grown tremendously in popularity. Self-help groups bring together people who share a common problem. Self-help group members share information and experiences in an attempt to help themselves and one another. There are thousands of topics that bring people together, and you are no doubt familiar with at least a few self-help groups.

Technically, self-help groups are not therapy groups, and typically are not led by a professional. If there is a leader, it may be someone who already has faced the particular problem, perhaps a former group member. The popularity of self-help groups attests to their perceived benefits. Moreover, available evidence suggests that self-help groups and other treatments can be quite effective even when they are delivered by *paraprofessionals*—people who do have limited professional training but who have personal experience with the problem (Christensen & Jacobson, 1994). However, the lack of research on process and outcome is a notable shortcoming for self-help groups and for group therapy in general (Kaul & Bednar, 1986).

Community Psychology and Prevention

Social influences on psychopathology extend far beyond interpersonal relationships. Social

▼ **Group therapy gives clients the opportunity to meet with and learn from other people who have similar problems.**

institutions such as child-care centers, schools, and work environments are important contributors to mental health, as are such broad societal concerns as poverty, racism, and sexism. Of course, the goal of improving society is hardly the exclusive domain of psychologists. Still, **community psychology** is one approach within clinical psychology that attempts to improve individual well-being by promoting social change.

The concept of prevention is an important consideration in promoting social change. Community psychologists often distinguish among three levels of prevention (Kaplan, 1964). **Primary prevention** tries to improve the environment in order to prevent new cases of a mental disorder from developing. The goal of primary prevention is to promote health, not just treat illness. Efforts at primary prevention range from offering prenatal care to impoverished pregnant women to teaching schoolchildren about the dangers of drug abuse.

Secondary prevention focuses on the early detection of emotional problems in the hope of preventing them from becoming more serious and difficult to treat. The screening of "at-risk" schoolchildren is one example of an effort at secondary prevention. Crisis centers and hot lines are other examples of efforts to detect and treat problems before they become more serious.

Finally, **tertiary prevention** may involve any of the treatments discussed in this chapter, because the intervention occurs after the illness has been identified. In addition to providing treatment, however, tertiary prevention also attempts to address some of the adverse, indirect consequences of mental illness. Helping the chronically mentally ill to find adequate housing and employment is an example of a tertiary prevention effort.

No one can doubt the importance of prevention, whether directed toward biological, psychological, or social causes of abnormal behavior. Unfortunately, many prevention efforts face an insurmountable obstacle: We simply do not know the specific cause of most psychological disorders. Prevention efforts directed at broader social change face another obstacle that also seems insurmountable at times. Poverty, racism, and sexism defy easy remedies. We do not wish to blame the victim of social injustice, but blaming the system can be equally problematic. Each individual must take personal responsibility for changing his or her own life, even as we collectively work to shape a world that promotes mental health.

Specific Treatments for Specific Disorders

The field of psychotherapy began with the development of treatments based solely in theory and case histories. It progressed as researchers documented the superiority of some form of psychotherapy over no treatment at all. Contemporary psychotherapy researchers are advancing knowledge by recognizing and studying factors common to all therapies and by using these common factors to predict successful outcome across different approaches to therapy.

These efforts are important, and scientists can point with increasing pride to research on psychotherapy, which has grown both in volume and in quality. The ultimate goal of treatment research, however, is to discover more than the common factors across paradigmatic approaches to psychotherapy. Researchers must continue to work to identify different therapies that have specific ingredients for treating specific disorders (see Research Close-Up). Consistent with this goal, in subsequent chapters we discuss only treatments that either are promising or have proved to be effective for alleviating the symptoms of specific disorders.

We strongly believe that the client's problems, not the therapist's theoretical orientation, should determine the choice of treatment. For many emotional problems, sufficient scientific evidence exists to identify the treatment of choice or at least to rule out some less effective forms of therapy (Chambless et al., 1996). In these cases, we feel very strongly that mental health professionals must inform their clients about research evidence and treatment alternatives. If a therapist is not skilled in offering the most effective approach, he or she should offer to refer the client to someone with specialized training in that approach.

For other emotional problems, researchers have not yet identified a clear treatment of choice, but this does not mean that "anything goes" in treating these problems. Rather, more

Identifying Common Factors and Isolating Specific Treatments

A recent study by Thomas Borkovec and Ellen Costello (1993) illustrates how psychotherapy outcome research can account for some common factors across treatments while also isolating specific effects. These psychologists at Pennsylvania State University wanted to identify the effectiveness of different approaches to behavior therapy in treating generalized anxiety disorder, an emotional problem characterized by excessive anxiety that is experienced in a variety of circumstances (see Chapter 6).

Borkovec and Costello compared two types of behavior therapy. *Applied relaxation (AR)* involved training clients in the use of relaxation techniques to cope with thoughts, feelings, or situations that provoked anxiety. Most of the 12-session treatment involved discussions of how to anticipate and deal with stressful events, including practice at using relaxation techniques. *Cognitive behavior therapy (CBT)* began with the same types of discussions and relaxation training as AR did. Most of the sessions, however, involved elements of Beck's cognitive therapy as well as other cognitive techniques designed to alter anxiety-producing thoughts. Finally, a third group of clients received *nondirective therapy (ND)* in order to test and control for the contributions of common factors to treatment outcome. The 12 sessions of nondirective therapy consisted of offering support and empathy in response to issues the clients chose to explore in therapy.

Borkovec and Costello randomly assigned 55 clients carefully diagnosed as suffering from generalized anxiety disorder to one of the three treatments. All treatments were offered by the same therapists, thus ensuring that differences in outcome would not be due to differences in therapists. This raised a new problem, however. The therapists generally held a cognitive behavioral orientation, and their low expectations about ND might have affected the success of the treatment. To help control for

this possibility, an expert nondirective therapist helped to supervise the ND cases. Finally, audiotapes of a portion of the sessions were coded to ensure that what was supposed to happen during the therapy sessions actually occurred.

A number of measures of the clients' anxiety were administered prior to treatment, immediately after treatment, and 6 months and 1 year after treatment. No differences were found among groups prior to treatment, but statistically significant differences were found immediately after treatment. The AR and CBT groups both were functioning significantly better than the ND clients at this time, but they were not significantly different from each other. Both the AR and CBT groups also improved significantly from the beginning to the end of treatment. The anxiety of the ND group did not change during this time. Finally, evidence indicated that differences among groups were clinically significant—and they favored CBT. A year after treatment, 58 percent of the CBT group was functioning within a normal range, in comparison with 37 percent of the AR clients and 28 percent of ND participants.

These findings indicate that specific treatment effects can be obtained beyond the influence of common factors. In the treatment of generalized anxiety disorders, cognitive behavior therapy has specific benefits both in the short term and in the long run, and these benefits exceed the general improvement associated with seeking psychotherapy. Still, the study also demonstrated the importance of common factors despite the "active ingredients" in cognitive behavior therapy. The best predictor of a successful outcome across all three groups was the clients' expectations for success, which were measured after the first therapy appointment. It is not clear what aspects of treatment raised or lowered expectations, but the finding underscores that nonspecific factors like increasing expectancies are an important part of the process of psychotherapy. ■

experimental therapies must be acknowledged as experimental, and the rationale for the approach must be clear to both the therapist and the client. In considering more experimental treatments in subsequent chapters, we examine a range of approaches to psychopharmacology, psychotherapy, and couples, family, and group therapies. Our coverage of alternative treatments is selective, however, and based on current knowledge about the particular disorder.

The identification of specific, effective treatments for specific disorders is necessary if clinical psychology is to fulfill its scientific promise. Still, we must not overlook the importance of establishing a human, helping relationship in psychotherapy. Individual people, not diagnostic categories, seek treatment for psychological disorders. The challenge for the mental health professional is to approach treatment both as a scientist and as a practitioner. Awareness of diagnostic categories is essential for applying scientific knowledge, but sensitivity to the individual is also essential to maximizing the effectiveness of clinical practice.

Summary

A tremendous number of different treatments have been developed for psychological disorders, but the various forms of **psychotherapy** can be roughly classified into four broad groups. Biomedical approaches alter the functioning of the body in an attempt to improve psychological well-being, primarily by using **psychopharmacology** or medication that has psychoactive effects. **Psychodynamic psychotherapies** encourage the exploration of the past in order to obtain insight into unconscious motivations. **Cognitive behavior therapy** focuses on present experience in helping their clients overcome maladaptive behaviors and learn adaptive ones. **Humanistic psychotherapy** offers clients warmth, empathy, and unconditional positive regard in helping them to heighten emotional awareness and make life choices.

Psychotherapy "works" in that research indicates that approximately two-thirds of outpatient clients benefit from treatment, whereas about one-third of the same population improves without treatment. However, psychotherapy outcome researchers have documented only small differences in the effectiveness of the alternative paradigmatic approaches to treatment. **Behavior therapy** is somewhat more effective in treating some disorders, but there is a clear need to establish the effectiveness of different treatments for different disorders. The rates of "spontaneous remission" of different psychological problems also need to be clearly identified.

A renewed interest in psychotherapy process research and the integration of diverse approaches is one consequence of evidence that different psychotherapies produce similar outcomes (Goldfried & Castonguay, 1993). Dimensions of the therapist–client relationship that are related to improved outcome include increasing the client's expectations of help, forming a warm therapist–client relationship, encouraging the experience of emotions in therapy, offering new learning experiences, and persuading clients to accept new, more adaptive explanations for their problems.

Another area of innovation in psychotherapy is the development of effective treatments

KEY TERMS

- allegiance effect
- aversion therapy
- behaviorism
- behavior therapy
- catharsis
- client-centered therapy
- cognitive behavior therapy
- cognitive therapy
- community psychology
- contingency management
- control group
- couples therapy
- dependent variable
- double-blind study
- eclectic
- ego analysis
- electroconvulsive therapy (ECT)
- empathy
- experiment
- experimental group
- external validity
- family therapy
- flooding
- free association
- Gestalt therapy
- group therapy
- humanistic psychotherapy
- hypothesis
- independent variable

that extend into the social system. These interventions include **couples therapy, family therapy,** and **group therapy.** They also include efforts to change dysfunctional aspects of the broader society. Thus consistent with the systems approach, intervention for psychological problems may be directed toward biological, psychological, or social systems.

The future of psychotherapy outcome research involves developing therapies that have effectiveness beyond the "common factors" found across different approaches to psychotherapy. The task is to identify specific therapies for specific disorders. In subsequent chapters of this text, we review progress toward this goal, as we highlight those treatments that have demonstrated success or promise in alleviating the symptoms of a particular disorder.

Critical Thinking

1. What are your personal beliefs about the treatment of psychological disorders? Were your beliefs changed by the ideas or evidence presented in this chapter? Why or why not? What research evidence would convince you that treatments for psychological disorders do (or do not) "work"?

2. Do you prefer one of the major paradigms discussed in this chapter? If you were looking for a therapist for yourself, would you pick one based on her or his "theoretical orientation"? We argue that mental health professionals should offer treatments based on proven effectiveness rather than on theoretical orientation. Do you agree?

3. Some critics have argued that psychotherapy is "the purchase of friendship." What do you think? How are "common factors" found across different schools of psychotherapy similar to, and different from, friendship?

4. What is the appropriate level for intervention with psychological disorders? Do you favor medication, psychotherapy, family treatment, or social change? In what ways do your views about the nature and causes of abnormal behavior influence your thoughts about treatment?

- informed consent
- insight
- internal validity
- interpretation
- in vivo desensitization
- placebo control group
- placebo effect
- prefrontral lobotomy
- primary prevention
- psychoactive drugs
- psychoanalysis
- psychodynamic psychotherapy
- psychopharmacology
- psychosurgery
- psychotherapy
- random assignment
- rational–emotive therapy
- role playing
- secondary prevention
- self-instruction training
- social skills training
- systematic desensitization
- tertiary prevention
- token economy
- transference

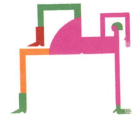

4

Classification and Assessment

Mental disorders are seldom easy to understand. Psychologists need extensive information before they can make decisions about the nature of a person's problems and formulate plans for treatment. They need to examine various aspects of the person, as well as the social context in which the problem has appeared. The process of gathering this information is called **assessment.** Psychologists use many different assessment tools to generate information about their clients. Interviews, observations, questionnaires, and psychological tests are among the most frequently used procedures. These measures are often supplemented by information from other sources, including formal records from schools and clinics, as well as informal reports from people who are well acquainted with the person. Psychologists must organize and integrate this information before it can be useful. Therefore the assessment process also involves judgments and decisions.

Overview

One important part of the assessment process is making a diagnostic decision based on the official classification system—the set of categories in DSM-IV that describe mental disorders. **Diagnosis** refers to the identification or recognition of a disorder on the basis of its characteristic symptoms. In psychopathology, a clinician assigns a diagnosis if the person's behavior meets the specific criteria for a particular type of disorder, such as schizophrenia or major depressive disorder. This decision is important because it tells the clinician that the person's problems are similar to those that have been experienced by some other people. The diagnosis enables the clinician to refer to the base of knowledge that has accumulated with regard to the disorder. For example, it will provide clues about associated symptoms and treatments that are most likely to be effective. To formulate a comprehensive treatment plan, the clinician utilizes the person's diagnosis plus many other types of information that we will discuss in this chapter.

There is another way to interpret the meaning of the word "diagnosis." In some fields,

diagnosis refers to *causal* analysis. If your car doesn't start, you expect that your mechanic's "diagnosis" will explain the origins of the problem. Has the battery lost its charge? Is the fuel line blocked? Is the ignition switch dead? In this situation, the "diagnosis" leads directly to the problem's solution. In the field of psychopathology, assigning a diagnosis does *not* mean that we understand the etiology of the person's problem (see Chapter 2). Specific etiologies have not been identified for mental disorders. Psychologists can't "look under the hood" in the same way that a mechanic can examine your car. In the case of a mental disorder, assigning a diagnostic label simply identifies the nature of the problem without implying exactly how the problem came into existence.

Our consideration of the assessment enterprise and diagnostic issues will begin with an example from our own clinical experience. In the following pages we will describe one person's problems and the social context in which they appeared. This case study illustrates the kinds of decisions that psychologists have to make about ways to collect and interpret information.

Obsessions, Compulsions, and Other Unusual Behaviors

Michael was an only child who lived with his mother and father. He was 16 years old, a little younger than most of the other boys in the 11th grade, and he looked even younger. From an academic point of view, Michael was an average student, but he was not a typical teenager in terms of social behavior. He felt completely alienated from other boys, and he was extremely anxious when he talked to girls. He hated being at school; he despised everything about school. His life at home was not much more pleasant than his experience at school. Michael and his parents argued frequently. His relationship with his father was especially volatile.

One awful incident seemed to sum up Michael's bitter feelings about school. As a sophomore, he decided to join the track team. Michael was awkward and somewhat clumsy, hardly an athlete; when he worked out with the other long-distance runners at practice, he soon became the brunt of their jokes. One day, a belligerent teammate forced Michael to take off his clothes and run naked from the bushes to a shelter in the park. When he got there, Michael found an old pair of shorts, which he put on and wore back to the locker room. The experience was humiliating. Later that night, Michael started to worry about those shorts. Who had left them in the park? Were they dirty? Had he been exposed to some horrible disease? Michael quit the track team the next day, but he couldn't put the experience out of his mind. Every time he saw the other boys in school, he became enraged.

Although he knew it was irrational, Michael began to fear that he would catch AIDS from those shorts. He couldn't get the thought out of his mind. He read everything he could find regarding early symptoms of the disease. These fears progressed to the point where every time he coughed, he thought he was getting a respiratory infection. If he lost his balance, he thought he had a neurological complication. The list of "symptoms" went on and on.

In the following year, Michael became more and more consumed by anxiety. He was constantly obsessed about "contamination," which he imagined to be spreading from his books and school clothes to the furniture and other objects in his house.

When the clothes that he had worn to school rubbed against a chair or a wall at home, he felt as though that spot had become contaminated. He didn't believe this was literally true; it was more like a reminder by association. When he touched something that he had used at school, he was more likely to think of school. That triggered unpleasant thoughts and the negative emotions with which they were associated (anger, fear, sadness).

Michael tried in various ways to minimize the spread of contamination. For example, he took a shower and changed his clothes every evening at 6 o'clock immediately after he finished his homework. After this "cleansing ritual" he was careful to avoid touching his books or dirty clothes as well as anything that they had touched. If he bumped into one of these contaminated objects by accident, he would go into the bathroom and wash his hands. Michael washed his hands 10 or 15 times in a typical evening. He also paced back and forth watching television without sitting down so that he would not touch contaminated furniture.

Whenever he was not in school, Michael preferred to be alone at home. Being with other people made him very uncomfortable. If he spent more than a few minutes with other people, he felt drained, and he had to recuperate by withdrawing to his room to play games on his computer. He did not enjoy sports, music, or outdoor activities. The only literature that interested him was fantasy and science fiction. Dungeons and Dragons was the only game that held his attention. It had, in fact, become an important escape for Michael. He read extensively about the magical powers of fantastic characters and spent hours dreaming up new variations on themes described in books about this imaginary realm. When Michael talked about the Dungeons and Dragons characters and their adventures, his speech would sometimes become vague and difficult to follow. He would begin to speak more rapidly and his thoughts would jump from one topic to the next in an excited and confused manner. Although other students at Michael's school shared his interest in Dungeons and Dragons, he didn't want to play the game with them. Michael said he was different from the other students. He expressed disdain and contempt for other teenagers, as well as for the city in which he lived and for his own neighborhood.

Michael and his parents had been working with a family therapist for more than 2 years. Although the level of interpersonal conflict in the family had been reduced, Michael's anxiety seemed to be getting worse. He had become even more isolated from other boys his own age, and was actually quite suspicious about their motives. He said that he sometimes felt that they were talking about him, and that they were planning to do something else to him in order to humiliate him again.

His worries about contamination had become almost unbearable to his parents, who were deeply confused and frustrated by his behavior. They could obviously see that he had become socially isolated and extremely unhappy. They believed that he would never be able to resume a more normal pattern of development until he gave up these "silly" ideas. Michael's fears also disrupted his parents' own activities in several ways. They weren't allowed to touch him or his things after being in certain rooms of the house. His peculiar movements and persistent washing were troublesome to them. Michael's father usually worked at home, and he and Michael frequently ended up quarreling with each other, especially when Michael ran water in the bathroom

next to his father's study. The conflict became so severe that Michael's father once asked his wife to make a choice: "Is it me or Michael? One of us has to go!"

Michael and his mother had always been very close. In fact, he was quite dependent on her, and she was devoted to him. They spent a lot of time together while his father was working. Although they still supported each other, his mother had begun to find it difficult to be close to Michael. He shunned physical contact. When she touched him, he sometimes cringed and withdrew. Once in a while he would shriek, reminding her that she was contaminated by her contact with chairs and other objects like his laundry. Recently, Michael had also become aloof intellectually. His mother felt that he was shutting her out as he seemed to withdraw further into his world of Dungeons and Dragons fantasy and obsessional thoughts about contamination.

Michael's parents eventually decided to seek individual treatment for him. They talked with their family therapist and asked her whether anything could be done to help Michael deal with his fear of contamination. Could he stop his repeated washing? Would he be able to develop normal friendships? ■

Levels of Analysis

Michael's situation raises several fundamental issues with regard to assessment and classification. The first is the level of analysis at which a psychologist should think about the problem. Is this primarily Michael's problem, or should we consider this problem in terms of all members of the family? One possibility is that Michael has a psychological disorder that is disrupting the life of his family. It may be the other way around, however: Perhaps the family system as a whole is dysfunctional, and Michael's problems are only one symptom of this dysfunction.

Another set of choices involves the type of data that a psychologist will employ to describe Michael's behavior. What kinds of information should be collected? We can consider several sources of data. One is Michael's own report. Another is the report of his parents. A psychologist may also decide to employ psychological tests. Although biological tests have

not achieved definitive status in psychopathology, there are some intriguing suggestions that biochemical tests and images of the brain may shed important light on the distinctions among different forms of abnormal behavior.

In conducting an assessment and arriving at a diagnosis, one question we must face is whether Michael's abnormal behavior is similar to problems that have been exhibited by other people. Given the information that the psychologist has obtained, the two most likely diagnostic alternatives are obsessive–compulsive disorder (OCD) and schizotypal personality disorder (see Chapters 6 and 9). These conditions can be difficult to tell apart. Because they respond to different forms of treatment, the distinctions are extremely important. The process of making an individual diagnosis for Michael is guided by the general system of classification. In the next section we will review the development and modification of classification systems for abnormal behavior.

Basic Issues in Classification

A **classification system** is used to subdivide or organize a set of objects. The objects of classification can be inanimate things, such as rocks or books; living organisms, such as plants, insects, or primates; or abstract concepts, such as numbers, religions, or historical periods. Formal classification systems are essential for the collection and communication of knowledge in all sciences and professions. For example, biologists depend on the classification system for living organisms that was introduced in 1758 by Carolus Linnaeus, who is typically considered the father of taxonomy (taxonomy is the theory of classification procedures and systems).

There are many ways to subdivide any given class of objects. Classification systems can be based on different principles. Some systems are based on descriptive similarities. For example, both a diamond and a ruby may be considered jewels because they are valuable stones. Other systems are based on less obvious characteristics, such as structural similarities. A diamond and a piece of coal, for example, may belong together because they are both made of carbon. They don't look or feel similar to each other, but they are created in similar ways. Other examples can be taken from the classification of living organisms. From a descriptive point of view, dolphins may appear to be more similar to sharks than to zebras. But dolphins and zebras breathe oxygen through their lungs, they are warm-blooded, and they share many other functional and structural similarities that serve to distinguish them (and other mammals) from fish.

The point is simple. Classification systems can be based on various principles, and their value will depend primarily on the purpose for which they were developed (Clementz & Iacono, 1993). Different classification systems are not necessarily right or wrong; they are simply more or less useful. In the following section we will consider several fundamental principles that affect all attempts to develop a useful classification or typology of human behavior.

Categories versus Dimensions

Classification is often based on "yes or no" decisions (Hempel, 1961). After a category has been defined, any object is either a member of the category or it is not. A **categorical approach to classification** assumes that distinctions between members of different categories are qualitative. In other words, the differences reflect a difference in kind (quality) rather than a difference in amount (quantity). In the classification of living organisms, for example, we usually consider species to be qualitatively distinct; they are different kinds of living organisms. Human beings are different from other primates; an organism is either human or it is not. Many medical conditions are categorical. Pregnancy is one clear example. A woman is either pregnant or she is not. It doesn't make sense to talk about "how pregnant" a woman might be.

Although categorically based classification systems are often useful, they are not the only kind of system that can be used to organize information systematically. As an alternative, scientists often employ a **dimensional approach to classification**—that is, one that describes the objects of classification in terms of continuous dimensions. Rather than assuming that an object either has, or does not have, a particular property, it may be useful to focus on a specific characteristic and determine how much of that characteristic the object exhibits. This kind of system is based on an ordered sequence or on quantitative measurements rather than on qualitative judgments.

For example, in the case of intellectual ability, psychologists have developed sophisticated measurement procedures. Rather than asking whether or not a particular person is intelligent (a "yes or no" judgment), the psychologist sets out to determine *how much* intelligence the person exhibits on a particular set of tasks. This process offers some advantages over categorical distinctions. It allows scientists to record subtle distinctions that would be lost if they were forced to make all-or-none

▼ **Primates are classified, in part, on the basis of skeletal factors: the size and shape of their skulls and whether they are able to walk erect on their hind legs. These skeletons came from three types of primates: a human, a gorilla, and an orangutan.**

decisions. It also provides for more powerful quantitative measurements.

Monothetic versus Polythetic Classes

Some classification systems define categories in terms of a small number of singly necessary and jointly sufficient characteristics. Any object that possesses these characteristics is considered a member of the category, and objects that fail to possess exactly these characteristics are not members of the category. For example, within geometry, the category "square" is defined by four features: the number of sides (four), the number of angles (four), the length of the sides (equal), and the size of the angles (equal). Each feature is necessary, and taken together they are sufficient to identify a geometric figure as a square. This is an example of a **monothetic class.**

An alternative approach to classification involves the use of polythetic categories (Corning, 1986). A **polythetic class** is defined in terms of a set of criteria that are neither necessary nor sufficient. Each member of the category must possess a certain minimal number of the defining features, but none of the features has to be found in each member of the category. The category "mammals" is an example of a polythetic class; each member of the class possesses a significant number of the defining features, but there are mammals that do not possess certain features. For example, some mammals lay eggs, and some are not warm-blooded.

There are some important differences between monothetic and polythetic classification systems. In polythetic classes, not all members of a particular category are identical, even with regard to the defining features of the category. There is no central characteristic that they all share. Furthermore, some members of the class possess more of the defining features than other members of the class do. This fact results in the observation that certain members are good examples of the category, whereas others are marginal. Scientists must determine at which point to establish a cutoff for group membership. How many criteria should an object possess before it is considered a member of the class? The number is determined by utility: Which definition allows scientists and clinicians to make the most useful predictions about members of the group?

From Description to Theory

The development of scientific classification systems typically proceeds in an orderly fashion from the initial stages, which involve simple descriptions or observations, to more advanced theoretical stages. At the latter point, greater emphasis is placed on scientific concepts that explain causal relationships among objects. In the study of many medical disorders, this progression begins with an emphasis on the description of specific symptoms that cluster together and follow a predictable course over time. The systematic collection of further information regarding this syndrome may then lead to the discovery of etiological factors.

An example may help to illustrate the progression from descriptive to theoretically based classification. One form of mental retardation can be produced by an inherited metabolic disorder known as phenylketonuria (PKU). People with PKU are missing a liver enzyme that is required to break down a common amino acid, phenylalanine, that is present in protein foods (Pollitt, 1987) (see Chapter 15). If a child with PKU is allowed to eat a normal diet containing protein foods, incompletely metabolized products of phenylalanine will accumulate in the blood, cause damage to the developing central nervous system, and eventually lead to mental retardation.

The etiology of PKU was discovered in 1934 when a woman in Norway brought her two young sons, who were both mentally retarded, to a physician. The woman reported that the boys often gave off a peculiar, musty odor. Using ordinary laboratory tests, the physician found high concentrations of phenylalanine in the children's blood and urine. Using the descriptive features of mental retardation and urinary tests to isolate further cases of the disorder, clinical scientists were able to identify the specific nature of the metabolic defect and establish that it is caused by a recessive gene (Bickel, 1980). Methods of early detection of PKU, using blood tests that are employed soon after birth, were developed in the 1950s. Treatment methods were introduced shortly thereafter. Infants who test

▼ Although a person's height clearly lies on a continuous dimension, it is sometimes convenient and useful to describe people in categorical terms. Basketball players are often described as inside players (like Manute Bol, who at 7'7" is one of the tallest players ever to play in the National Basketball Association) and perimeter players (like Mugsy Bogues, who at 5'3" is one of the shortest players ever to play in the NBA).

positive are placed on a special diet that is very low in phenylalanine, preventing the development of severe mental retardation.

The classification of phenylketonuria illustrates the progression from descriptive to theoretical systems. The disorder was originally identified on the basis of observable symptoms—intellectual deficiencies and a peculiar odor. Now PKU is classified in terms of a specifically identified etiological pathway involving a recessive gene and a known metabolic defect. Clinical scientists hope that similar progress will be made in the field of psychopathology. Mental disorders are currently classified on the basis of descriptive features because specific causal mechanisms have not yet been discovered. Research studies that employ our current classification system may eventually provide the foundation for a more sophisticated, theoretically based understanding of certain disorders. This does not necessarily mean, of course, that the etiological mechanisms will turn out to be solely biological in nature (as in the case of PKU). In fact, the most likely explanations for mental disorders involve complex interactions of psychological, biological, and social systems (see Chapter 2).

Classification of Abnormal Behavior

We need a classification system for abnormal behavior for two primary reasons. First, the system will be used in making management and treatment decisions. A classification system is useful to clinicians who must match their clients' problems with the form of intervention that is most likely to be effective. Second, a classification system must be used in the search for new knowledge. The history of medicine is filled with examples of problems that were recognized long before they could be treated successfully. The definition of a specific set of symptoms has often laid the foundation for research that eventually identified a cure or a way of preventing the disorder.

Brief Historical Perspective

There have been many attempts to classify personality and psychopathology throughout history. The oldest written descriptions can be traced to the Egyptians, Greeks, and Romans, but these bear little resemblance to contemporary perspectives. Progress toward the adoption of a single, internationally accepted system began during the nineteenth century, when cities in Europe and the United States established large asylums for people with major mental disorders. The physicians who presided over these institutions had an unprecedented opportunity to observe the behavior of many patients over an extended period of time. Many different classification systems were introduced during the ensuing years. In some areas, each hospital or university clinic developed and used its own unique system (Kendell, 1975a).

Emil Kraepelin (1856–1926), a German psychiatrist, is generally regarded as the father of the categorical classification system that currently prevails in psychopathology. He believed that mental illness could be understood in terms of a finite number of specific disorders. Each disorder was presumed to have an identifiable set of symptoms and a unique course and was the product of a yet to be determined form of cerebral pathology (Berrios & Hauser, 1988). Kraepelin identified two primary forms of psychosis: *dementia praecox* (which we now call schizophrenia) and *manic–depressive psychosis* (which we now call bipolar mood disorder). His views were widely influential, but they did not lead directly to a formal, universally adopted classification system.

Currently, two diagnostic systems for mental disorders are widely recognized. One—the *Diagnostic and Statistical Manual* (DSM)—is published by the American Psychiatric Association. The other—the *International Classification of Diseases* (ICD)—is published by the World Health Organization. Both systems were developed shortly after World War II, and both have been revised several times. Because the American diagnostic manual is now in its fourth edition, it is called DSM-IV. The World Health Organization's manual is in its tenth edition and is therefore known as ICD-10.

During the 1950s and 1960s, psychiatric classification systems were widely criticized. One major criticism focused on the lack of consistency in diagnostic decisions (Spitzer & Fleiss, 1974). Independent clinicians frequently disagreed with one another about the use of

▲ **Robert Spitzer, professor of psychiatry at Columbia University, chaired the committee that produced DSM-III. Spitzer's vision and forceful leadership helped the committee to accomplish one of the most important changes in psychiatric classification of the twentieth century.**

diagnostic categories as they were listed in the first two editions of the American classification system, DSM-I and DSM-II. Objections were also raised from philosophical, sociological, and political points of view. Some critics charged that diagnostic categories in psychiatry would be more appropriately viewed as "problems in living" than as medical disorders (Szasz, 1960). Others were concerned about *self-fulfilling prophesies*. In other words, once a psychiatric label had been assigned, the person so labeled might be motivated to continue behaving in ways that were expected from someone who is mentally disturbed (see Further Thoughts). For all of these reasons, many mental health professionals paid less and less attention to the formal process of diagnosis during these years.

Renewed interest in the value of psychiatric classification grew steadily during the 1970s, culminating in the publication of the third edition of the DSM in 1980. This version of the manual represented a dramatic departure from previous systems. It was clearly a major turning point in the history of psychiatric classification (Kendell, 1991; Sabshin, 1990). The committee that was responsible for

developing DSM-III was chaired by Robert Spitzer, a psychiatrist at the New York State Psychiatric Institute. Spitzer and his colleagues made several bold changes in the manual. One broad consideration was their commitment to the production of a classification system that was based on clinical description rather than on theories of psychopathology that had not been empirically validated. This principle led to the elimination of some terms and categories that had been based on psychoanalytic concepts, like neurosis and hysteria (see Chapters 6 and 8). Other major changes included the introduction of a multiaxial system and the production of specific, detailed criterion sets for each disorder.

All these changes have been retained in both DSM-IV and ICD-10. These features will be described in the following section. The two manuals are very similar in most respects. Deliberate attempts were made to coordinate the production of DSM-IV and ICD-10. Most of the categories listed in the manuals are identical, and the criteria for specific disorders are usually similar.[†]

[†] There are some interesting differences between DSM-IV and ICD-10. There are, for example, differences in the ways in which they subdivide mood disorders and personality disorders. The U.S. system also devotes more attention to eating disorders and sexual disorders, which appear to be less prevalent in other cultures (Kendell, 1991).

FURTHER THOUGHTS

Labeling Theory

L **abeling theory** is a perspective on mental disorders that is primarily concerned with the social context in which abnormal behavior occurs and the ways in which other people respond to this behavior. It assigns relatively little importance to specific behaviors as symptoms of a disorder that resides within the person. Labeling theory is more interested in social factors that determine whether a person will be given a psychiatric diagnosis than in psychological or biological reasons for the abnormal behaviors (Levine & Perkins, 1987). In other words, it is concerned with events that take place after a person has behaved in an unusual way rather

than with factors that might explain the original appearance of the behavior itself.

Thomas Scheff, a sociologist at the University of California at Santa Barbara, is one of the leading figures in labeling theory. According to Scheff (1966, 1984), it is useful to think of mental disorders as maladaptive social roles, with the process of diagnostic labeling being the most important factor in establishing that role for a particular person. Scheff's theory is concerned with the violation of residual rules, which are implicit social expectations that are usually taken for granted. Scheff suggests that the symptoms of mental disorders are best viewed as violations of residual rules: showing too much emotion; not showing enough emotion; or talking too much or in strange ways. These behaviors create situations in which a person might be labeled as mentally disturbed.

Scheff maintains that people break residual rules frequently and for many different reasons. These behaviors are usually ignored or dismissed as unimportant. Scheff assumes that in such cases the behaviors will be relatively brief. Persistent abnormal behaviors develop only after someone has been brought to the attention of the mental health system and assigned an official diagnostic label. That process sets in motion a number of other events that ensure that the person will accept the social role associated with the diagnosis and will continue to exhibit abnormal behaviors that are expected from people in that role. We all presumably learn the role of "mental patient" through cultural stereotypes, such as the negative images of people with mental disorders that are repeatedly displayed in the media (Signorielli, 1989). After a diagnosis has been assigned, patients are rewarded for accepting the role—behaving as if they were "crazy"—and punished if they attempt to return to normal social and occupational roles.

According to labeling theory, the probability that a person will receive a diagnosis is determined by several factors. These include the extent of the rule breaking and its visibility, as well as the tolerance level of the community. The most important considerations are the social status of the person who breaks the rules and the social distance between that person and mental health professionals. People from disadvantaged groups, such as racial and sexual minorities and women, are presumably more likely to be labeled than are white males.

The merits and limitations of labeling theory have been hotly debated since the mid-1960s. The theory has inspired research on a number of important questions. Some studies have found that people from lower-status groups are indeed more likely to be assigned severe diagnoses (Holman & Caston, 1987). On the other hand, it would also be a great exaggeration to say that the social status of the patient is the most important factor influencing the diagnostic process. In fact, clinicians' diagnostic decisions are determined primarily by the form and severity of the patient's symptoms rather than by such factors as gender, race, and social class (Farmer & Griffiths, 1992; Gove, 1990).

Another focus of the debate regarding labeling theory is the issue of stigma. Is a diagnosis of mental disorder a sign of disgrace or discredit? Do people avoid those who have mental disorders? Labeling theory assumes that negative attitudes toward mental disorders prevent patients from obtaining jobs, finding housing, and forming new relationships. Negative attitudes are undoubtedly associated with many types of mental disorder, such as alcoholism, schizophrenia, and sexual disorders (Fabrega, 1991; Fink & Tasman, 1992).

Research studies have also found, however, that stigma is a complicated issue. Critics of labeling theory have argued that the effects of stigma are generally short-lived (Gove, 1970, 1990). Furthermore, some patients maintain positive attitudes about their own difficulties and about the mental health systems in which they are treated (Weinstein, 1983). The impact of stigma on a person's self-esteem is difficult to predict (Major & Crocker, 1993).

Although labeling theory has drawn needed attention to a number of important problems associated with the classification of mental disorders, it does not provide an adequate explanation for abnormal behavior. It is clearly an exaggeration to think of mental disorders as nothing more than social roles. Many factors other than the reactions of other people contribute to the development and maintenance of abnormal behavior. Furthermore, a diagnosis of mental illness can have positive consequences, such as encouraging access to proper treatment. Many patients and their family members are relieved to learn that their problems are similar to those experienced by other people and that help may be available. The effects of diagnostic labeling are not always harmful.

In addition to these reservations, several other questions about the theory should be mentioned. The analogy between residual rule breaking and symptoms of mental disorders is strained at best. Many symptoms of psychopathology, such as anxiety and depression, are subjective. People who endure these experiences often define themselves as suffering, regardless of the reactions of other people. Furthermore, there is no evidence to support the contention that abnormal behaviors will disappear if they are ignored. In fact, data from the Epidemiologic Catchment Area Study and National Comorbidity Survey indicate that many problems are long-lasting, even if they have not been treated (Robins & Regier, 1991; Kessler et al., 1994). ■

The DSM-IV System

The DSM-IV employs a **multiaxial classification system;** that is, the person is rated on five separate axes. Each axis is concerned with a different domain of information. Two are concerned with diagnostic categories, and the other three provide for the collection of additional relevant data. The rationale for this approach is that to manage individual cases, the clinician must consider several important factors besides specific symptoms. These supplementary factors include the environment in which the patient is living, aspects of the person's health that might affect psychological functions, and fluctuations in the overall level of the patient's adjustment. Table 4–1 lists the five specific axes from DSM-IV.

DIAGNOSTIC AXES

The first two axes are concerned with clinical disorders that are defined largely in terms of symptomatic behaviors. Most diagnoses appear on Axis I, which includes conditions such as schizophrenia and mood disorders that are the topics of most chapters in this text. Many of the diagnoses that are described on Axis I are characterized by episodic periods of psychological turmoil. Axis II is concerned with more stable, long-standing problems, such as personality disorders and mental retardation. The separation of disorders on Axis I and Axis II is designed to draw attention to conditions that might be overlooked in the presence of a more dramatic symptomatic picture, such as the hallucinations and delusions frequently found in schizophrenia. Clinicians are encouraged to list both types of problems when they are present. A person can be assigned more than one diagnosis on either Axis I or Axis II (or on both axes) if he or she meets criteria for more than one disorder.

More than 200 specific diagnostic categories are described in DSM-IV. These are arranged under 18 primary headings. A complete list appears inside the front cover of this book. Disorders that present similar kinds of symptoms are grouped together. For example, conditions that include a prominent display of anxiety are listed under "Anxiety Disorders," and conditions that involve a depressed mood are listed under "Mood Disorders."

The manual lists specific criteria for each diagnostic category. Most of the categories are based on the polythetic approach to classification. We can illustrate the ways in which these criteria are used by examining the diagnostic decisions that would be considered in Michael's case. The criteria for obsessive-compulsive disorder (OCD), which is an Axis I disorder, and schizotypal personality disorder, which is an Axis II disorder, are listed in Table 4–2.

First, let's consider obsessive–compulsive disorder. Michael would meet all of the criteria in "A" for both obsessions and compulsions. His repetitive hand-washing rituals were performed in response to obsessive thoughts regarding contamination. He also meets criterion "C" in that these rituals were time-consuming and interfered with his family's routine. His relationships with friends were severely limited because he refused to invite them to his house, fearing that they would spread contamination.

On Axis II, Michael would also be coded as meeting criteria for schizotypal personality disorder. He exhibited five of the nine symptoms listed under criterion "A": odd speech, suspiciousness, eccentric behavior, no close friends, and excessive social anxiety. This pattern illustrates an important feature of DSM-IV. For many disorders, a patient must exhibit a certain number of symptoms, but the specific pattern is not determined. Michael exhibited symptoms 4, 5, 7, 8, and 9. Another person who happened to exhibit a different combination could also be classified as having schizotypal personality disorder. The specific items are not weighted in terms of their importance for making the diagnosis. These are, of course, somewhat arbitrary diagnostic standards. Little evidence suggests that five symptoms is a better cutoff point than four or six.

In addition to the **inclusion criteria,** symptoms that must be present, many disorders are

TABLE 4–1

Major Axes in DSM-IV

Axis I	Clinical Syndromes
Axis II	Personality Disorders and Mental Retardation
Axis III	General Medical Conditions
Axis IV	Psychosocial and Environmental Problems
Axis V	Global Assessment of Functioning

TABLE 4-2

DSM-IV Criteria for Obsessive–Compulsive Disorder

A. Either obsessions or compulsions:
Obsessions as defined by (1), (2), (3), and (4):

1. Recurrent and persistent thoughts, impulses, or images that are experienced, at some time during the disturbance, as intrusive and inappropriate, and that cause marked anxiety or distress

2. The thoughts, impulses, or images are not simply excessive worries about real-life problems

3. The person attempts to ignore or suppress thoughts, impulses, or images or to neutralize them with some other thought or action

4. The person recognizes that the obsessional thoughts, impulses, or images are a product of his or her own mind (not imposed from without as in thought insertion)

Compulsions as defined by (1) and (2):

1. Repetitive behaviors (such as hand washing, ordering, checking) or mental acts (such as praying, counting, repeating words silently) that the person feels driven to perform in response to an obsession, or according to rules that must be applied rigidly

2. The behaviors or mental acts are aimed at preventing or reducing distress or preventing some dreaded event or situation; however, these behaviors or mental acts either are not connected in a realistic way with what they are designed to neutralize or prevent, or are clearly excessive

B. At some point during the course of the disorder, the person has recognized that the obsessions or compulsions are excessive or unreasonable.

C. The obsessions or compulsions cause marked distress; are time-consuming (take more than one hour a day); or significantly interfere with the person's normal routine, occupational (or academic) functioning, or usual social activities or relationships with others.

D. If another Axis I disorder is present, the content of the obsessions or compulsions is not restricted to it (for example, preoccupation with food in the presence of an Eating Disorder; preoccupation with drugs in the presence of a Substance Use Disorder; or guilty ruminations in the presence of Major Depressive Disorder).

continued

also defined in terms of certain **exclusion criteria.** In other words, the diagnosis can be ruled out if certain conditions prevail. For example, in the case of schizotypal personality disorder, the diagnosis would not be made if the symptoms occurred only during the course of a schizophrenic disorder (criterion B).

You should also note that, in certain instances, the duration of a problem is considered as well as the clinical picture. Criterion "C" for obsessive–compulsive disorder specifies that the patient's compulsive rituals must take more than 1 hour each day to perform.

OTHER DOMAINS FOR ASSESSMENT

Axis III is concerned with general medical conditions that are outside the realm of psychopathology but may be relevant to either the etiology of the patient's abnormal behavior or the patient's treatment program. Examples include thyroid conditions, which may lead to symptoms of psychosis, and diabetes in children, which is sometimes associated with conduct disorders. In Michael's case, there were no known physical disorders that were relevant to his psychological problems.

TABLE 4-2 CONTINUED

DSM-IV Criteria for Schizotypal Personality Disorder

A. **A pervasive pattern of social and interpersonal deficits marked by acute discomfort with, and reduced capacity for, close relationships as well as by cognitive or perceptual distortions and eccentricities of behavior, beginning by early adulthood and present in a variety of contexts, as indicated by five (or more) of the following:**

1. Ideas of reference (excluding delusions of reference)

2. Odd beliefs or magical thinking that influence behavior and are inconsistent with subcultural norms—for example superstitiousness, belief in clairvoyance, telepathy, or "sixth sense"

3. Unusual perceptual experiences, including bodily illusions

4. Odd thinking and speech (for example, vague, circumstantial, metaphorical, overelaborate, or stereotyped)

5. Suspiciousness or paranoid ideation

6. Inappropriate or constricted affect

7. Behavior or appearance that is odd, eccentric, or peculiar

8. Lack of close friends or confidants other than first-degree relatives

9. Excessive social anxiety that does not diminish with familiarity and tends to be associated with paranoid fears rather than negative judgments about self

B. **Does not occur exclusively during the course of Schizophrenia, a Mood Disorder with Psychotic Features, another Psychotic Disorder, or a Pervasive Developmental Disorder.**

Axis IV is concerned with psychosocial and environmental problems that may affect the diagnosis or treatment of a mental disorder. The clinician is asked to indicate specific factors that are present in the person's life (see Chapter 8 for a more complete discussion of stressful life events and their measurement). The clinician is asked to record those problems that were present during the year prior to the current assessment. Problems that occurred prior to the previous year may be noted if the clinician is convinced that they made a significant contribution to the development of the person's current problems or if they have become a focus of treatment.

Michael's therapist noted the presence of three psychosocial problems: frequent arguments within the family, social isolation, and discord with classmates at school. Note that stressful circumstances may be the products as well as the causes of mental disorders. In Michael's case, for example, many of the family's arguments were precipitated by his hand-washing rituals. In deciding whether to list social stresses on Axis IV, psychologists need not determine whether the stresses primarily arose from or contributed to the condition. They are all listed if they are relevant to treatment planning, and these were all important considerations in Michael's case.

Finally, Axis V provides for a global rating of adaptive functioning (Goldman, Skodol, & Lave, 1992). This rating is made on a scale that ranges from 1 to 100, with higher numbers representing better levels of adjustment. The scale applies to psychological, social, and occupational functioning. Ratings are typically made for the person's current level of functioning. In some circumstances, the clinician might also consider the person's highest level of functioning during the past year. This information is considered useful because it draws attention to recent changes in the patient's condition and because it provides a balanced view of the patient's strengths as well as his or her weaknesses.

Michael's psychologist assigned a rating of 50 for his current level of functioning. Michael was performing at an adequate level academically, but his social life was clearly impaired as a consequence of his rituals.

Evaluation of Classification Systems

The Diagnostic and Statistical Manual is an evolving document. An enormous effort was devoted to the revision process that resulted in the publication of DSM-IV in 1994. The work extended over a period of more than 5 years. Final decisions about the manual were made by the Task Force on DSM-IV, which was composed of 30 distinguished mental health professionals (26 psychiatrists and 4 psychologists) and chaired by Allen Frances, a psychiatrist at Duke University. Work groups were appointed to examine each of the major diagnostic categories, such as anxiety disorders, mood disorders, and so on. Each work group included experienced clinicians who were widely recognized experts in studying and treating the disorders with which their group was concerned. The work groups made recommendations to the task force on the basis of reviews of the existing literature on the problem, new analyses performed on already-collected sets of data, and large-scale, issue-focused field trials. Thomas Widiger, a clinical psychologist at the University of Kentucky, served as the research coordinator for the DSM-IV Task Force. Many documents that served as the core of this empirical review process have been published in a series of five edited books (see Widiger, 1994).

How can we evaluate a system like DSM-IV? Is it a useful classification system? Utility can be measured in terms of two principal criteria: reliability and validity.

Reliability

Reliability refers to the consistency of measurements, including diagnostic decisions. If a diagnostic category is to be useful, it will have to be used consistently. One important form of reliability, known as *inter-rater reliability*, refers to agreement among clinicians. Suppose, for example, that two psychologists interview the same patient and that each psychologist independently assigns a diagnosis using DSM-IV. If both psychologists decide that the patient fits the criteria for a major depressive disorder, they have used the definition of that category consistently. Of course, one or two cases would not provide a sufficient test of the reliability of a diagnostic category. The real question is whether the clinicians would agree with each other over a large series of patients. The process of collecting and interpreting information regarding the reliability of diagnosing mental disorders is discussed in Research Methods.

Validity

The ultimate issue in the evaluation of a diagnostic category is whether it is useful. By knowing that a person fits into a particular group or class, do we learn anything *meaningful* about that person? For example, if a person fits the diagnostic criteria for schizophrenia, is that person likely to improve when he or she is given antipsychotic medication? Or is that person likely to have a less satisfactory level of social adjustment in 5 years than a person who meets diagnostic criteria for bipolar mood disorder? Does the diagnosis tell us anything about the factors or circumstances that might have contributed to the onset of this problem? These questions are concerned with the validity of the diagnostic category. The term **validity** refers to the meaning or importance of a measurement—in this case, a diagnostic decision (Hempel, 1961; Kendell,

▼ A lawyer presenting a case to a court of appeals. Just as judges sometimes disagree in their assessment of evidence presented during trial, psychologists and psychiatrists do not always agree on how various disorders should be diagnosed and classified. Of course, both judges and mental health professionals attempt to be reliable, that is, consistent.

Diagnostic Reliability

Several formal procedures have been developed to evaluate diagnostic reliability. Most studies of psychiatric diagnosis in the past 20 years have employed a measure known as **kappa**. Instead of measuring the simple proportion of agreement between clinicians, kappa indicates the proportion of agreement that occurred *above and beyond that which would have occurred by chance.* Negative values of kappa indicate that the rate of agreement was less than that which would have been expected by chance in this particular sample of people. Thus kappa of zero indicates chance agreement, and a kappa of +1.0 indicates perfect agreement between raters.

How should we interpret the kappa statistic? There is no easy answer to this question (Grove et al., 1981; Kirk & Kutchins, 1992). It would be unrealistic to expect perfect consistency, especially in view of the relatively modest reliability of other diagnostic decisions that are made in medical practice (Cameron & McGoogan, 1981; Koran, 1975). On the other hand, it isn't very encouraging simply to find that the level of agreement among clinicians is somewhat better than chance. We expect more than that from a diagnostic system, especially when it is used as a basis for treatment decisions. One convention suggests that kappa values of .70 or higher indicate relatively good agreement (Matarazzo, 1983; Spitzer, Foreman, & Nee, 1979). Values of kappa below .40 are often interpreted as indicating poor agreement.

The reliability of many diagnostic categories has improved since the publication of DSM-III. Increased reliability can be attributed, in part, to the use of more detailed diagnostic criteria for specific disorders. Still, most studies also indicate that there is considerable room for improvement. The reliability of some diagnostic categories remains well below acceptable standards. Consider, for example, evidence from field trials that were conducted by the World Health Organization when ICD-10 was being prepared (Sartorius et al., 1993). Data were collected at more than 100 clinical centers in 39 countries around the world. Assessment interviews were conducted with 2,460 psychiatric patients by more than 700 clinicians. Each person was interviewed separately by two clinicians who independently

arrived at a diagnosis. Kappa values for several of the diagnostic categories are presented in Table 4–3.

The reliability data in Table 4–3 are organized according to major headings (such as anxiety disorders), which are then subdivided into more specific forms (such as obsessive–compulsive disorder). Note that kappa values for major headings are, in most cases, higher than those for specific subtypes. This pattern indicates that clinicians are more likely to agree on the general category into which an individual's problems fall than they are on the specific nature of those problems. To understand this process, imagine that you and a friend try to identify types of automobiles as they pass on the street. You might find it relatively easy to agree that a particular vehicle is a minivan, but you might have

---

TABLE 4–3

Reliability for Diagnoses of Several Types of Mental Disorder

Disorder	kappa
Schizophrenic Disorders	**.82**
Paranoid schizophrenia	.73
Catatonic schizophrenia	.39
Hebephrenic schizophrenia	.43
Anxiety Disorders	**.74**
Phobic disorder	.63
Obsessive–compulsive disorder	.81
Generalized anxiety disorder	.48
Mood Disorders	**.77**
Manic episode	.69
Depressive episode	.66
Bipolar mood disorder	.81
Personality Disorders	**.47**
Schizotypal*	.37
Histrionic	.12
Dependent	.33
Substance Use Disorders	**.80**
Alcohol dependence	.70
Opioid dependence	.77

*In ICD-10, schizotypal disorder is grouped with Schizophrenic Disorders rather than with Personality Disorders. We list it here for consistency with DSM-IV.
Source: Based on the World Health Organization's field trial for ICD-10 (see Sartorius et al., 1993).

more trouble deciding whether it is the specific type of minivan made by Chrysler, Ford, or Toyota.

Using the standard of .70 or higher, good agreement was found for many specific categories, especially obsessive–compulsive disorder, bipolar mood disorder, and paranoid schizophrenia. For some other categories, such as phobic disorder and depressive episode, diagnostic reliability was acceptable while clearly leaving room for improvement. Reliability for generalized anxiety disorder was only fair, and the reliability for diagnosing personality disorders was very low. In the case of schizotypal personality disorder, for example, the kappa coefficient was only .37, a poor level of agreement.

You should note that the data presented in Table 4–3 may represent a "best-case scenario" with regard to reliability of diagnostic decisions. These figures are estimates of reliability based on a study that was designed to be a hallmark in the field of psychiatric research. The clinicians who made the diagnostic decisions were leading mental health professionals in their own countries. They were carefully tutored in the use of the new diagnostic criteria, and they knew that their rates of agreement were being carefully monitored. If we expect agreement in any particular setting, it would seem most likely among those clinicians who are intimately familiar with the diagnostic system and especially careful in the application of diagnostic procedures. The reliability of diagnostic systems may be lower among clinicians who do not have time to employ standardized interview procedures and who may not scrutinize carefully the list of specific diagnostic criteria each time they make diagnoses. Therefore we should not accept uncritically the assumption that DSM-IV and ICD-10 are always used reliably (Kirk & Kutchins, 1992). ■

1989). Importance is not an all-or-none phenomenon; it is a quantitative issue. Diagnostic categories are more or less useful, and their validity (or utility) can be determined in several ways.

Validity is, in a sense, an index of the success that has been achieved in understanding the nature of a disorder. Have important facts been discovered? Systematic studies aimed at establishing the validity of a disorder often proceed in a sequence of phases (Robins & Guze, 1989), which are listed in Table 4–4. The field trials that were conducted during preparation of DSM-IV are examples of studies aimed at clinical description (see Research Close-Up). After a clinical description has been established, these phases may occur in any order. Diagnostic categories are refined and validated through this process of scientific exploration.

The types of information generated by the research studies listed in Table 4–4 are associated with specific types of validity. It may be helpful to think of these types of validity in terms of their relationship in time with the appearance of symptoms of the disorder. *Etiological validity* is concerned with factors that contribute to the onset of the disorder. These are things that have happened in the past. Was the disorder regularly triggered by a specific set of events or circumstances? Did it run in families? The ultimate question with regard to etiological validity is whether there are any specific causal factors that are regularly, and perhaps uniquely, associated with this disorder. If we know that a person exhibits the symptoms of the disorder, do we in turn learn anything about the circumstances that originally led to the onset of the problem?

Concurrent validity is concerned with the present time and with correlations between the disorder and other symptoms, circumstances, and test procedures. Is the disorder currently associated with any other types of behavior, such as performance on psychological tests? Do precise measures of biological variables, such as

TABLE 4-4
Types of Studies Used to Validate Clinical Syndromes
Identification and description of the syndrome, either by clinical intuition or by statistical analyses.
Demonstration of boundaries or "points of rarity" between related syndromes.
Follow-up studies establishing a distinctive course or outcome.
Therapeutic trials establishing a distinctive treatment response.
Family studies establishing that the syndrome "breeds true."
Demonstration of association with some more fundamental abnormality—psychological, biochemical, or molecular.

Source: Adapted from R. E. Kendell, (1989), Clinical validity, *Psychological Medicine, 19*, 47.

brain structure and function, distinguish reliably between people who have the disorder and those who do not? Clinical studies that are aimed at developing a more precise description of a disorder also fall into this type of validity. For example, the data generated in the various DSM-IV field trials contribute to the concurrent validity of the diagnostic categories with which they were concerned.

Predictive validity is concerned with the future and with the stability of the problem over time. Will it be persistent? If it is short-lived, how long will an episode last? Will the disorder have a predictable outcome? Do people with this problem typically improve if they are given a specific type of medication or a particular form of psychotherapy? The overall utility or validity of a diagnostic category depends on the body of evidence that accumulates as scientists seek answers to these questions.

You should not assume that every diagnostic category in DSM-IV will eventually be found to be useful. Many thorny problems are involved in the process of validating a disorder. Important questions remain to be answered for all forms of mental disorder. The list of categories included in DSM-IV is based heavily on conventional clinical wisdom. Each time the manual is revised, new categories are added and old categories are dropped, presumably because they are not sufficiently useful. Up to the present time, clinicians have been more willing to include new categories than to drop old ones. It is difficult to know when we would decide that a particular diagnostic category is not valid. At what point in the accumulation of knowledge are clinical scientists willing to conclude that a category is of no use and to recommend that the search for more information should be abandoned? This is a difficult question that the authors of

DSM-IV have confronted, and it will become increasingly important in the production of future revisions.

Unresolved Questions

Several important issues will have to be addressed as more systematic information is collected about the diagnostic categories in DSM-IV. One set of questions is centered on the polythetic criteria that are employed for many disorders. In the current system, cutoff points for establishing a diagnosis were chosen with little empirical justification. Future research should be able to determine optimal thresholds for each disorder. For example, in the case of schizotypal personality disorder, the present cutoff point is five out of nine features. Perhaps one of the features is unnecessary or redundant with another. In that case, the list could be shortened to eight criteria. Should one or more of the features be given special weight? Are they all equally important? These questions will have to be answered by investigators who explore the validity of each individual category.

Another set of questions is concerned with the use of specific time periods in the definition of various disorders. To what extent will the pattern of onset and the duration of symptoms be considered diagnostically important? The course of a disorder is often considered to be diagnostically important in medical disorders, and there are places in DSM-IV in which the course of the disorder is used to define that disorder. For example, in the case of schizophrenia, DSM-IV requires that the person exhibit symptoms for a period of at least 6 months. Again, the utility of these aspects of the diagnostic criteria is an important topic for future empirical studies.

RESEARCH CLOSE-UP

The DSM-IV Field Trial for Obsessive–Compulsive Disorders

The validation of a diagnostic category proceeds in several steps. One important part of this process involves careful clinical studies that identify the symptoms of the disorder. As research progresses, these descriptions become more detailed and refined. Field trials that were conducted during the development of DSM-IV illustrate this process. Consider, for example, the field trial for obsessive–compulsive disorders (OCD) (Foa & Kozak, 1995). This study focused on two major issues:

1. Do people with OCD view their symptoms as being unreasonable or excessive? The previous version of the manual (DSM-III-R) had required that the person recognize his or her obsessions as being senseless in order to meet the criteria for OCD.
2. Can compulsions take the form of mental events? DSM-III-R had defined compulsions only in terms of observable behaviors, such as hand-washing or checking doors to be sure that they are locked.

The investigators collected information regarding these questions by interviewing more than 450 people who were seeking treatment for OCD. Each person was interviewed by an experienced clinician who followed the questions listed in the Structured Clinical Interview for DSM (SCID) and also filled out the Yale-Brown Obsessive-Compulsive Scale (Y-BOCS; see Table 4–6 on p. 135). These standard assessment instruments were supplemented with a number of questions regarding such factors as whether the person recognized that his or her obsessive–compulsive beliefs were unreasonable. Inter-rater reliability was estimated using audiotapes of 50 randomly selected interviews. Each of the tapes was rated again by a second clinician who did not know what ratings had been assigned by the original interviewer. Kappa coefficients for agreement regarding the presence of various types of obsessions and compulsions were moderate to high, ranging between .55 and .88.

In order to address the first major issue, the investigators considered responses from 250 people whose obsessions involved fear of some harmful consequence if they did not engage in a compulsive ritual, such as washing or checking. Forty percent of these people said they were certain (or mostly certain) that their feared consequence would *not* occur, even if they did not perform their rituals. The symptoms of these people conformed to the traditional notion—reflected in the DSM-III-R criteria for OCD—that obsessions must be experienced as being senseless. On the other hand, 30 percent of the OCD patients indicated that they were uncertain whether the feared consequence would occur, and the remaining 30 percent indicated that they were mostly (or in a few cases completely) certain

that it would occur. These people obviously did not experience their obsessions as being senseless.

On the basis of this evidence, the authors of the field trial recommended that DSM-IV should include an indication that some OCD patients have poor insight regarding their obsessions. The manual does hold that, *at some point during the course of the disorder,* the person must recognize that the obsessions or compulsions are excessive or unreasonable. In order to meet diagnostic criteria for OCD, however, the person does not always have to view his or her intrusive thoughts as being senseless. This change reduces the chance that a person with OCD and poor insight might be misdiagnosed as suffering from a psychotic disorder and inappropriately treated with antipsychotic medication, which can have serious side effects and is seldom effective for patients with OCD.

Data regarding the second issue indicated that 8 percent of the patients reported experiencing both mental and behavioral compulsions. Mental compulsions are apparently an important symptom of OCD. Their function is similar to that of behavioral compulsions; patients said that the vast majority of both behavioral and mental rituals were intended either to prevent harm or to reduce discomfort. Based on these results, the authors of DSM-IV distinguished more clearly between obsessions—mental events that increase anxiety or distress—and compulsions—either behavioral or mental rituals that decrease anxiety or distress. By clearly stating that rituals can be mental as well as behavioral, the DSM-IV should help reduce diagnostic confusion between OCD and disorders in which other types of mental rumination play an important role, such as generalized anxiety disorder.

The questions asked in this field trial and the data that were collected to answer them illustrate that in the production of DSM-IV the authors demanded solid empirical evidence when considering changes in criterion sets. Efforts to refine diagnostic categories will undoubtedly continue, even though the next official version of the DSM will not be produced for several years. Careful descriptive research can always make a useful contribution to our knowledge of mental disorders such as OCD. ∎

Finally, we should also mention the continuing discussion of ancillary axes. The three that have been included in DSM-IV could have been supplemented (or replaced) by other important considerations. In addition to psychosocial problems and a global assessment of functioning, it might be useful to record information regarding factors such as premorbid history, quality of interpersonal relationships, work functioning, family functioning, and/or response to

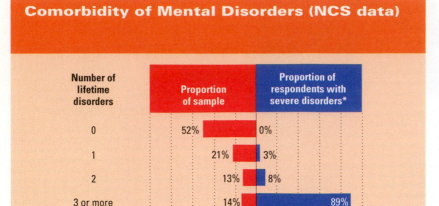

Comorbidity of Mental Disorders (NCS data)

Number of lifetime disorders	Proportion of sample	Proportion of respondents with severe disorders*
0	52%	0%
1	21%	3%
2	13%	8%
3 or more	14%	89%

100 80 60 40 20 0 20 40 60 80 100

FIGURE 4-1: Most severe mental disorders are concentrated in a group of people (about one sixth of the population) who qualify for at least three lifetime disorders.

*"Severe disorders" were defined to include active mania, nonaffective psychosis, or active disorders of other types that either required hospitalization or created severe role impairment.

Source: R.C. Kessler et al., 1994, Lifetime and 12-month prevalence of DSM-III-R psychiatric disorders in the United States: Results from the National Comorbidity Survey, *Archives of General Psychiatry, 51,* 13.

treatment. Although each of these factors might provide useful information, classification systems can become too unwieldy and complicated. In fact, many practicing clinicians limit their DSM diagnoses to Axis I and Axis II.

Problems and Limitations of the DSM-IV System

Although DSM-IV represents a clear improvement over the early versions of APA's classification system, it is also hampered by a number of problems (Clark, Watson, & Reynolds, 1995). One of the most thorny issues involves **comorbidity,** which is defined as the simultaneous appearance of two or more disorders in the same person. Comorbidity rates are very high for mental disorders as they are defined in the DSM system. For example, in the National Comorbidity Survey, among those people who qualified for at least one diagnosis at some point during their lifetime, 56 percent met the criteria for two or

more disorders (Kessler, 1995; Kessler et al., 1994). A small subgroup, 14 percent of the sample, actually met the diagnostic criteria for *three or more* lifetime disorders. That group of people accounted for almost 90 percent of the severe disorders in the study in Figure 4–1.

There are several ways to interpret comorbidity. Some people may independently develop two separate conditions. In other cases, the presence of one disorder may lead to the onset of another. Unsuccessful attempts to struggle with prolonged alcohol dependence, for example, might lead a person to become depressed. Neither of these alternatives creates conceptual problems for DSM-IV. Unfortunately, the very high rate of comorbidity suggests that these explanations account for a small proportion.

The real problem associated with comorbidity arises when a person with a mixed pattern of symptoms, usually of a severe nature, simultaneously meets the criteria for more than one disorder. Consider, for example, a client who was treated by one of the authors of this text. This man experienced a large number of diffuse problems associated with anxiety, depression, and interpersonal difficulties. According to the DSM-IV system, he would have met the criteria for major depressive disorder, generalized anxiety disorder, and obsessive–compulsive disorder, as well as three types of personality disorder listed on Axis II. It might be said therefore that he suffered from at least six types of mental disorder. But is that really helpful? Is it the best way to think about his problems? Would it be more accurate to say that he had a complicated set of interrelated problems that were associated with worrying, rumination, and the regulation of high levels of negative emotion, and that these problems constituted one complex and severe type of disorder?

Such questions must be faced by clinicians when they use the DSM-IV system, and are another reason why we can expect the classification system to continue to be revised. As before, these changes will be driven by the interaction of clinical experience and empirical evidence.

Basic Issues in Assessment

Up to this point, we have discussed the development and use of classification systems. But we haven't talked about the way in which a

psychologist might collect the information that is necessary to arrive at a diagnostic decision. Furthermore, we have looked at the problem only in relatively general terms. The diagnostic decision is one useful piece of information. It is not, however, a systematic picture of the specific person's situation. It is only a starting point. In the following section we extend our discussion to consider methods of collecting information. In so doing, we discuss a broad range of data that may be useful in understanding psychopathological behavior.

The Purposes of Clinical Assessment

To appreciate the importance and complexity of assessment procedures, let's go back to the example of Michael. When Michael and his parents initially approached the psychologist, they were clearly upset. But the nature of the problem, in terms of Michael's behavior and the family as a whole, was not clearly defined. Before he could attempt to help this family, the psychologist had to collect more information. He needed to know more about the range and frequency of Michael's obsessions and compulsions, including when they began, how often he experienced these problems, and the factors that made them better or worse. He also needed to know whether there were other problems, such as depression or psychotic thought processes, that might either explain these responses or interfere with their treatment. In addition, he had to learn how Michael got along with classmates, how he was doing in school, and how his parents responded when he behaved strangely. Was his behavior, at least in part, a response to environmental circumstances? How would the family support (or interfere with) the therapist's attempts to help him change? The psychologist needed to address Michael's current situation in terms of several different facets of his behavior and at both the broad and specific levels of abstraction.

Psychological assessment is the process of collecting and interpreting information that will be used to understand another person. Numerous data-gathering techniques can be used in this process. Several of these procedures are described in the following pages. We must remember, however, not to confuse the process of assessment with this list of techniques. Assessment procedures are tools that can be used in many ways. They cannot be used in an intellectual vacuum. Interviews can be used to collect all sorts of information for all sorts of reasons. Psychological tests can be interpreted in many different ways. The value of assessment procedures

can be determined only in the context of a specific purpose (McFall & McDonel, 1986).

Three primary goals guide most assessment procedures: making predictions, planning interventions, and evaluating interventions. The practical importance of predictions should be obvious: Many crucial decisions are based on psychologists' attempts to determine the probability of future events. Will a person engage in violent behavior? Can a person make rational decisions? Is a parent able to care for his or her children? Assessment is also commonly used to evaluate the likelihood that a particular form of treatment will be helpful for a specific patient and to provide guideposts by which the effectiveness of treatment programs can be measured (Hayes, Nelson, & Jarrett, 1987). Different assessment procedures are likely to be employed for different purposes. Those that are useful in one situation may not be helpful in another.

Assumptions about Behavior

Assessment is governed by several important concepts and assumptions regarding the nature of human behavior and the ability of psychological science to measure and explain these events (Goldfried & Kent, 1972; McFall & McDonel, 1986). We will examine a number of these, beginning with assumptions concerning the consistency of human behavior.

CONSISTENCY OF BEHAVIOR

Assessment involves the collection of specific samples of a person's behavior. These samples may include things that the person says during an interview, responses that the person makes on a psychological test, or things that the person does while being observed. None of these would be important if we assumed that they were isolated events. They are useful to the extent that they represent examples of the ways in which the person will feel or behave in other situations. Psychologists therefore must be concerned about the consistency of behavior across time and situations. They want to know if they can *generalize*, or draw inferences about the person's behavior in the natural environment on the basis of the samples of behavior that are obtained in their assessment. If the client is depressed at this moment, how did she feel 1 week ago, and how will she feel tomorrow? In other words, is this a persistent phenomenon, or is it a temporary state? If a child is anxious and unable to pay attention in the psychologist's office, will he also exhibit these problems in his classroom? And how will he behave on the playground?

Psychologists typically employ more than one source of information when conducting a formal assessment. Because we are trying to compose a broad, integrated picture of the person's adjustment, we must collect information from several sources and then attempt to integrate these data. Each piece of information may be considered to be one sample of the person's behavior. One way of evaluating the possible meaning or importance of this information is to consider the consistency across sources. Do the conclusions drawn on the basis of a diagnostic interview agree with those that are suggested by a psychological test? Do the psychologist's observations of the client's behavior and the client's self-report agree with observations that are reported by parents or teachers?

LEVELS OF ANALYSIS

The kind of information that is collected will depend on the way in which the clinician views the problem. Mental disorders are embedded in multiple, interacting systems that involve biological, psychological, and social factors (see Chapter 2). Assessment instruments can be aimed at any of these levels. Some of the factors that might be considered at each level are illustrated in Figure 4–2. At one level, the clinician must decide whether to concentrate on the individual client or to focus more broadly on social systems. For example, a depressed married person might be treated as an individual or as part of a couple. In Michael's case, his problem might be viewed in terms of the family system, which also involves his parents. Michael's relatively poor relationships with his peers could also be considered relevant to understanding his problems.

At another level, the clinician has to decide whether to concentrate on psychological variables or biological factors that might also influence the etiology of the problem. In all cases, the clinician's choice of the level of analysis will determine in large part the sorts of instruments that will be employed in the assessment process. Because assessment is a finite process, the decision to use one set of procedures will inevitably lead to the omission of others.

Suppose we decide to focus primarily on psychological variables, as we have done in our description of Michael's case. We must then make decisions regarding the level of analysis within the psychological system. One relatively broad conceptual scheme involves the consideration of diagnostic categories. Does Michael meet the DSM-IV criteria for obsessive–compulsive disorder? If he does, then the clinician is likely to employ particular forms of intervention. But we also know that not all obsessive–compulsive clients are exactly the same. Their fears and worries may involve many different kinds of things, and the ways in which they attempt to cope with, or neutralize, these fears may also vary tremendously. Response to treatment will also be influenced by additional considerations, such as personality traits, cognitive abilities, social skills, and the presence or absence of comorbid conditions, such as a seriously depressed mood. Therefore the clinician will require a great deal of additional information in order to formulate a treatment plan.

Evaluating the Utility of Assessment Procedures

The same criteria that are used to evaluate diagnostic categories are used to evaluate the utility of assessment procedures: reliability and validity. We have already discussed inter-rater reliability with regard to diagnostic decisions. In the case of assessment procedures, reliability can refer to various types of consistency. For example, the consistency of measurements over time is known as *test–retest reliability*. Will a person

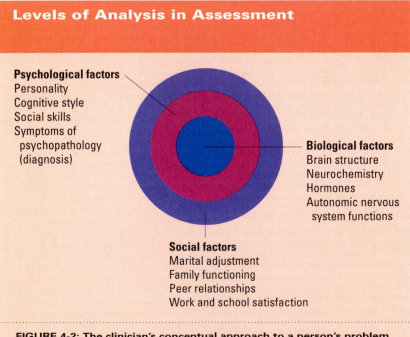

Levels of Analysis in Assessment

Psychological factors
Personality
Cognitive style
Social skills
Symptoms of
 psychopathology
 (diagnosis)

Biological factors
Brain structure
Neurochemistry
Hormones
Autonomic nervous
 system functions

Social factors
Marital adjustment
Family functioning
Peer relationships
Work and school satisfaction

FIGURE 4-2: The clinician's conceptual approach to a person's problem will determine the selection of assessment instruments. This figure lists examples of variables that might be considered within each broad conceptual level.

receive the same score if an assessment procedure is repeated at two different points in time? The internal consistency of items within a test is known as *split-half reliability*. If a test with many items measures a specific trait or ability, and if the items are divided in half, will the person's scores on the two halves agree with each other? Assessment procedures must be reliable if they are to be useful in either clinical practice or research.

The validity of an assessment procedure refers to its meaning or importance (Foster & Cone, 1995). Is the person's score on this test or procedure actually a reflection of the trait or ability that the test was designed to measure? And does the score tell us anything useful about the person's behavior in other situations? Knowing that the person has achieved a particular score on this evaluation, can we make meaningful predictions about the person's responses to other tests, or about the person's behavior in future situations? These are all questions about the validity of an assessment procedure. In general, the more consistent the information provided by different assessment procedures, the more valid each procedure is considered to be.

Assessment Procedures

The most useful assessment procedures are likely to vary from one problem to the next. Assessment procedures that are useful in evaluating the effectiveness of a drug treatment program for hospitalized depressed patients may be quite different from those used to predict the need for medication among hyperactive schoolchildren. Our purpose in the rest of this chapter is to outline a range of assessment procedures. This is a selective sampling of measures rather than an exhaustive review of assessment procedures.

An enormous array of assessment tools is available to clinicians who are interested in treating or studying abnormal behavior. Many of these procedures are commonly employed in clinical practice, and they are also used in the process of research. We consider several prominent alternatives in the following section, which is organized in accordance with our emphasis on systems that influence mental disorders. We begin our discussion with measures that are typically concerned with psychological variables—characteristic traits and behaviors that are associated with abnormal behavior. From there, we move to a consideration of the assessment of social systems, such as families and institutional environments (schools and hospitals). The last section of this chapter will be concerned with measures used in biological systems—the neurological and biochemical underpinnings of mental disorders. In many cases, the assessment of psychopathology is based on the combined use of measures that cover selective aspects of all of these systems.

At the end of each section, we have provided a quick summary of the advantages and limitations of each type of procedure. These are intended only as general guides and not as definitive critiques. Please keep in mind our earlier comment: Each procedure is a tool that can be used for different purposes. The true value of the tool can be determined only in light of the specific purpose for which it is used.

Assessment of Psychological Systems

"Person variables" are typically the first thing that comes to mind when we think about the assessment of psychopathology. What did the person do or say? How does the person feel about his or her current situation? What skills and abilities does the person possess, and are there any important cognitive or social deficits that should be taken into consideration? These questions about the individual person can be addressed through a number of procedures, including interviews, observations, and various types of self-report instruments and psychological tests.

INTERVIEWS

Often, the best way to find out about someone is to talk with that person directly. The clinical interview, which has been described as "a conversation with a purpose" (Bingham & Moore, 1924), is the most commonly used procedure in psychological assessment. Most of the categories that are defined in DSM-IV are based on information that can be collected in an interview. These data are typically supplemented by information that is obtained from official records (previous hospital admissions, school reports, court files) and interviews with other informants (for example, family members), but the clients' own direct descriptions of their problems are the primary basis for diagnostic decisions. Except for mental retardation, none of the diagnostic categories in DSM-IV is defined in terms of psychological or biological tests.

Interviews provide an opportunity to ask people for their own descriptions of their problems. Many of the symptoms of psychopathology are subjective, and an interview can provide a detailed analysis of these problems. Consider, for example, Michael's problems with anxiety. The unrelenting fear and revulsion that he experienced at school was the central feature of his problem. His obsessive thoughts of contamination were private events that could only be known to the psychologist on the basis of Michael's self-report, which was quite compelling. His family could observe Michael's peculiar habits with regard to arranging his schoolbooks, changing his clothes, and washing his hands, but the significance of these behaviors to Michael was not immediately apparent without the knowledge that they were based on an attempt to control or neutralize his anxiety-provoking images of taunting classmates.

Interviews also allow clinicians to observe important features of a person's appearance and nonverbal behavior. In Michael's case, the psychologist noticed during their initial interview that the skin on Michael's hands and lower arms was red and chafed from excessive scrubbing. He was neatly dressed but seemed especially self-conscious about his hair and glasses, which he adjusted repeatedly. Michael was reluctant to make eye contact, and his speech was soft and hesitant. His obvious discomfort in this social situation was consistent with his own descriptions of the anxiety that he felt during interactions with peers. It was also interesting to note that Michael became visibly agitated when discussing particular subjects, such as the incident with his track team. At these points in the interview, he would fidget restlessly in his seat and clasp his arms closely around his sides. His speech became more rapid, and he began to stutter a bit. On one occasion, he found it impossible to sit still, and he began to pace quickly back and forth across the psychologist's office. These nonverbal aspects of Michael's behavior provided useful information about the nature of his distress.

The psychologist asked Michael to describe the sequence of events in a typical day. How did he spend his time when he was at school?

What were his interests outside of school? How did his rituals and obsessive thoughts interfere with these activities? Taken together, this information provides a broader context in which the specific symptoms can be understood. The relationship that was established between Michael and his psychologist became an essential factor in the subsequent efforts they made toward changing Michael's behavior.

Structured Interviews Assessment interviews vary with regard to the amount of structure that is imposed by the clinician. Some are relatively open-ended, or nondirective. In this type of interview, the clinician follows the train of thought supplied by the client. One goal of nondirective interviews is to help people clarify their subjective feelings and to provide general empathic support for whatever they may decide to do about their problems. In contrast to this open-ended style, some interviews follow a more specific question-and-answer format. Structured interviews, in which the clinician must ask each patient a specific list of detailed questions, are frequently employed for collecting information that will be used to make diagnostic decisions and to rate the extent to which a person is impaired by psychopathology.

Several different structured interviews have been developed for the purpose of making psychiatric diagnoses in large-scale epidemiological and cross-national studies. Investigators reasoned that the reliability of their diagnostic decisions would improve if they could ensure that clinicians always made a consistent effort to ask the same questions when they interviewed patients. One currently popular example of this procedure is the Structured Clinical Interview for DSM (SCID), which was written by Robert Spitzer and his colleagues at the New York State Psychiatric Institute. The SCID includes modules that are designed to address all of the different disorders that are represented in DSM-IV. Other forms of structured diagnostic interviews have been designed for use in the diagnosis of specific types of problems, such as personality disorders, anxiety disorders, dissociative disorders, and the behavior problems of children.

Structured interviews list a series of specific questions that lead to a detailed description of the person's behavior and experiences. As an example, consider the Structured Interview for DSM-IV Personality Disorders (SIDP-IV; Pfohl,

Blum, & Zimmerman, 1995), which could have been used as part of the assessment process in Michael's situation. The SIDP is a widely adopted semistructured interview that covers all of the DSM-IV personality disorder categories. The interview contains approximately 160 questions that are organized into several topical areas, such as "interests and activities," "close relationships," "emotions," "self-perception," and "perceptions of others." In addition to recording the person's answers to the questions, the interviewer is also asked to make a number of observations regarding the person's appearance and behavior during the interview. Selected questions from the SIDP-IV are presented in Table 4–5. We have included in this table several of the questions that are specifically relevant to a diagnosis of schizotypal personality disorder.

Structured interview schedules provide a systematic framework for the collection of important diagnostic information, but they don't eliminate the need for an experienced clinician. If the interviewer is not able to establish a comfortable rapport with the client, then the interview might not elicit useful information. Furthermore, it is difficult to specify in advance all the questions that should be asked in a diagnostic interview. The client's responses to questions may require clarification. The interviewer must determine when it is necessary to probe further and in what ways to probe. Having lists of specific questions and clear definitions of diagnostic criteria will make the clinician's job easier, but clinical judgment remains an important ingredient in the diagnostic interview.

Advantages The clinical interview is the primary tool employed by clinical psychologists in the assessment of psychopathology. Several features of interviews account for this popularity, including the following issues:

1. The interviewer can control the interaction and can probe further when necessary.
2. By observing the patient's nonverbal behavior, the interviewer can detect areas of resistance. In that sense, the validity of the information may be enhanced.
3. An interview can provide a lot of information in a short period of time. It can cover past events and many different settings.

TABLE 4-5

Sample Items from the Structured Interview for DSM-IV Personality (SIDP-IV)

Scoring Guidelines:
0 = not present or limited to rare isolated examples.
1 = subthreshold—some evidence of the trait but it is not sufficiently pervasive or severe to consider the criterion present.
2 = present—criterion is clearly present for most of the last 5 years (i.e., present at least 50% of the time during the last 5 years).
3 = strongly present—criterion is associated with subjective distress or some impairment in social or occupational functioning, or intimate relationships.

Close Relationships

This part of the interview asks about your relationships with friends and family. Remember that I'm interested in the way you are when you are your usual self.

1. Neither desires nor enjoys close relationships, including being part of a family   0 1 2 3

Do you have close relationships with friends or family?
    (IF YES): What do you enjoy about these relationships?
    (IF NO): Do you wish you had some close relationships?

2. Lacks close friends or confidants other than first-degree relatives   0 1 2 3

Not counting your immediate family, do you have close friends you can confide in?

Perception of Others

The questions in this section ask about experiences you may have had with other people. Remember that I'm interested in knowing how you feel about these situations when you are your usual self, not during an episode of illness or hospitalization.

1. Suspects, without sufficient basis, that others are exploiting, harming, or deceiving him or her   0 1 2 3

Have you had experiences where people who pretended to be your friends took advantage of you?
    (IF YES): What happened?
           How often has this happened?
Are you good at spotting someone who is trying to deceive or con you?
    (IF YES): Examples?

2. Ideas of reference (excluding delusions of reference)   0 1 2 3

Have you ever found that people around you seem to be talking in general, but then you realize their comments are really meant for you?
    (IF YES): How do you know they're talking about you?
Have you felt like someone in charge changed the rules specifically because of you, but they wouldn't admit it?
Do you sometimes feel like strangers on the street are looking at you and talking about you?
    (IF YES): Why do you think they notice you in particular?

Source: Bruce Pfohl and Nancee Blum, Department of Psychiatry, University of Iowa, Iowa City.

Limitations   Several limitations in the use of clinical interviews as part of the assessment process must be kept in mind. These include the following considerations:

1. Some patients may be unable or unwilling to provide a rational account of their problems. This may be particularly true of young children, who have not developed verbal skills, as well as some psychotic and demented patients who are unable to speak coherently.

2. People may be reluctant to admit experiences that are embarrassing or frightening. They may feel that they should report to the interviewer only those feelings and behaviors that are socially desirable.

3. Subjective factors play an important role in the interpretation of information provided in an interview. The person's responses to questions are not scored objectively, and there is always some variation in the format. The situation is not entirely structured and depends heavily on the training and experience of the interviewer.

4. Information provided by the client is necessarily filtered through the client's eyes. It is a subjective account and may be influenced or distorted by errors in memory and by selective perception.

5. The interviewer may, in some circumstances, suggest symptoms and problems to the client. Interviewers can influence their clients' accounts by the ways in which they phrase their questions and respond to the clients' responses.

OBSERVATIONAL PROCEDURES

In addition to the information that we gain from what people are willing to tell us during interviews, we can also learn a lot by watching their behavior. Observational skills play an important part in most assessment procedures. Sometimes the things that we observe confirm the person's self-report, and at other times the person's overt behavior appears to be at odds with what he or she says. A juvenile delinquent might express in words his regret at having injured a classmate, but his smile and the twinkle in his eye may raise doubts about the sincerity of this statement. In situations such as this, we must reconcile information that is obtained from different sources. The picture that emerges of another person's adjustment is greatly enriched when data collected from interviews are supplemented by observations of the person's behavior.

Observational procedures may be either informal or formal. *Informal observations* are primarily qualitative. The clinician observes the person's behavior and the environment in which it occurs without attempting to record the frequency or intensity of specific responses. Michael's case illustrates the value of informal observations in the natural environment. When the therapist visited Michael and his parents at their home, he learned that his ritualistic behaviors were more extreme than Michael had originally described. This was useful but not particularly surprising, as patients with OCD are often reluctant to describe in an interview the full extent of their compulsive behavior. The therapist also learned that the parents themselves were quite concerned with rules and order. Everything in their home was highly polished and in its place. This observation helped the therapist understand the extent to which Michael's parents might contribute to, or reinforce, his rigid adherence to a strict set of rules.

Although observations are often conducted in the natural environment, there are times when it is useful to observe the person's behavior in a situation that the psychologist can arrange and control. Sometimes it isn't possible to observe the person's behavior in the natural environment because the behavior in question occurs infrequently or at times when an observer cannot be present; at other times the environment is inaccessible; and sometimes the behavior that is of

▼ Direct observations can provide one of the most useful sources of information about a person's behavior. In this case, the children and their teacher are being observed from behind a one-way mirror in order to minimize reactivity, the effect that the observer's presence might have on their behavior.

interest is inherently a private act. In these cases, the psychologist may arrange to observe the person's behavior in a situation that in some ways approximates the real environment. These artificial situations may also allow for more careful measurements of the person's problem than could be accomplished in a more complex situation.

In the case of obsessive–compulsive behavior, this approach might involve asking the person deliberately to touch an object that would ordinarily trigger ritualistic behaviors. The therapist might collect a set of objects that Michael would not want to touch, such as a schoolbook, a pair of old track shorts, and the knob of a door leading to the laundry room. It would be useful to know specifically which objects he would touch, the degree of discomfort that he experienced when touching them, and the length of time that he was able to wait before washing his hands after touching these objects. This information could also be used as an index of change as treatment progressed.

Rating Scales Various types of procedures can be used to provide quantitative assessments of a person's behavior that are based on observations. One alternative is to use a **rating scale** in which the observer is asked to make judgments that place the person somewhere along a dimension. For example, a clinician might observe a person's behavior for an extended period of time and then complete a set of ratings that are concerned with dimensions such as the extent to which the person exhibits compulsive ritualistic behaviors.

Ratings can also be made on the basis of information collected during an interview. The Yale-Brown Obsessive Compulsive Scale (Y-BOCS; Goodman et al., 1989; Woody, Steketee, & Chambless, 1995) is an example of an interview-based rating scale that is used extensively in the evaluation of people with problems like Michael's. Examples of items from the Y-BOCS are presented in Table 4–6. For each topic or set of questions, the interviewer is required to make a rating from 0 to 4, indicating the person's level of distress or impairment. The composite rating—the total across all the items in the scale—can be used as an index of the severity of the disorder.

Rating scales provide abstract descriptions of a person's behavior rather than a specific record of exactly what the person has done. They require social judgments on the part of the observer, who must compare this person's behavior with

an ideal view of other people (Cairns & Green, 1979). How does this person compare to someone who has never experienced any difficulties in this particular area? How does the person compare to the most severely disturbed patients? Consider the fourth Y-BOCS item in Table 4–6. The interviewer must determine whether the person's attempts to ignore or resist the repetitive thoughts are excessive or unreasonable. In many cases, that is a difficult judgment. The value of these judgments will depend, in large part, on the experience of the person who makes the

TABLE 4–6

Sample Items from the Yale-Brown Obsessive–Compulsive Scale

Time Occupied by Obsessive Thoughts
How much of your time is occupied by obsessive thoughts?
0 = None
1 = Mild, less than 1 hour per day
2 = Moderate, 1 to 3 hours per day
3 = Severe, greater than 3 and up to 8 hours per day
4 = Extreme, greater than 8 hours per day

Interference Due to Obsessive Thoughts
How much do your obsessive thoughts interfere with your social or work (or role) functioning? Is there anything that you don't do because of them?
0 = None
1 = Mild, slight interference, but overall performance not impaired
2 = Moderate, definite interference, but still manageable
3 = Severe, causes substantial impairment
4 = Extreme, incapacitating

Distress Associated with Obsessive Thoughts
How much distress do your obsessive thoughts cause you?
0 = None
1 = Mild, not too disturbing
2 = Moderate, disturbing, but still manageable
3 = Severe, very disturbing
4 = Extreme, near constant and disabling distress

Resistance Against Obsessions
How much of an effort do you make to resist the obsessive thoughts? How often do you try to disregard or turn your attention away from these thoughts as they enter your mind?
0 = None
1 = Mild, not too disturbing
2 = Moderate, disturbing, but still manageable
3 = Severe, very disturbing
4 = Extreme, near constant and disabling distress

Degree of Control Over Obsessive Thoughts
How much control do you have over your obsessive thoughts? How successful are you in stopping or diverting your obsessive thinking? Can you dismiss them?
0 = None
1 = Mild, not too disturbing
2 = Moderate, disturbing, but still manageable
3 = Severe, very disturbing
4 = Extreme, near constant and disabling distress

ratings. They are useful to the extent that the observer is able to synthesize accurately the information that has been collected and then rate the frequency or severity of the problem relative to the behavior of other people.

Behavioral Coding Systems Another approach to quantifying observational data depends on recording the person's actual activities. Rather than making judgments about where the person falls on a particular dimension, **behavioral coding systems**—also known as *formal observation schedules*—focus on the frequency of specific behavioral events (Foster & Cone, 1986). This type of observation therefore requires fewer inferences on the part of the observer. Coding systems can be used with observations that are made in the person's natural environment as well as with those that are performed in artificial, or contrived, situations that are specifically designed to elicit the problem behavior under circumstances in which it can be observed precisely. In some cases, the observations are made directly by a therapist, and at other times the information is provided by people who have a better opportunity to see the person's behavior in the natural environment, including teachers, parents, spouses, and peers.

Systematic observations are intended to provide a detailed record of the frequency of particular behaviors. This information is based on selective observations that are made during a given time interval. The formal record includes only those specific behaviors that have been identified as relevant. Efforts are also made to describe, as specifically as possible, the situation in which the behaviors are observed. These descriptions may include information regarding other people who are present and any events that happened just prior to or following the target behaviors.

Some approaches to systematic observation can be relatively simple. Consider, once again, the case of Michael. After the psychologist had conducted several interviews with Michael and his family, he asked Michael's mother to participate in the assessment process by making detailed observations of his hand-washing over a period of several nights. The mother was given a set of forms—one for each day—that could be used to record each incident, the time at which it occurred, and the circumstances that preceded the washing. The day was divided into 30-minute intervals starting at 6:30 A.M., when Michael got out of bed, and ending at 10:30, when he usually went to sleep. On each line (one for each

time interval), his mother indicated whether he had washed his hands, what had been going on just prior to washing, and how anxious (on a scale from 1 to 100) Michael felt at the time that he washed.

Some adult clients are able to complete this kind of record by keeping track of their own behavior—a procedure known as *self-monitoring*. In this case, Michael's mother was asked to help because she was considered a more accurate observer and because Michael did not want to touch the form that would be used to record these observations. He believed that it was contaminated because it had touched his school clothes, which he wore to the therapy session.

Two weeks of observations were examined prior to the start of Michael's treatment. They indicated several things, including the times of the day when Michael was most active with his washing rituals (between 6 and 9 o'clock at night) and those specific objects and areas in the house that were most likely to trigger a washing incident. This information helped the therapist to plan the treatment procedure, which would depend on approaching his problem at the level that could most easily be handled and moving toward those situations that were the most difficult for him. The observations provided by Michael's mother were also used to mark his progress after treatment began.

Advantages Observational measures, including rating scales and more detailed behavioral coding systems, can provide an extremely useful supplement to information that is typically collected in an interview format. Their advantage lies primarily in the fact that they can provide a more direct source of information than interviews can, because clinicians observe behavior directly rather than relying on patients' self-reports (Foster & Cone, 1986; Gottman, 1985). Specific types of observational measures have distinct advantages:

1. Rating scales are primarily useful as an overall index of symptom severity or functional impairment.
2. Behavioral coding systems provide detailed information about the person's behavior in a particular situation.

Limitations Observations are sometimes considered to be similar to photographs: They provide a more direct or realistic view of behavior than do people's recollections of their actions and feelings. But just as the quality of a photograph is influenced by the quality of the camera, the film, and the process that is used to develop it, the value of observational data depends on the procedures that are used to collect them (Nietzel, Bernstein, & Milich, 1994).

1. Observational procedures can be time-consuming and therefore expensive. Raters usually require extensive training before they can use a detailed behavioral coding system.
2. Observers can make errors. Their perception may be biased, just as the inferences of an interviewer may be biased. The reliability of ratings as well as behavioral coding must be monitored.
3. People may alter their behavior, either intentionally or unintentionally, when they know that they are being observed. This phenomenon is known as **reactivity.** In other words, the way in which the person reacts to the presence of an observer may cause a change such that the observation is not a meaningful sample of the person's behavior in the absence of an observer. For example, a person who is asked to count the number of times that he washes his hands may wash less frequently than he does when he is not keeping track.
4. Observational measures tell us only about the particular situation that was selected to be observed. We don't know if the person will behave in a similar way elsewhere or at a different time, unless we extend the scope of our observations.
5. There are some aspects of psychopathology that cannot be observed by anyone other than the person who has the problem (Jacobson, 1985). This is especially true for subjective experiences, such as guilt or low self-esteem.

PERSONALITY TESTS AND SELF-REPORT INVENTORIES

Personality tests are another important source of information about an individual's adjustment. Tests provide an opportunity to collect samples of a person's behavior in a standardized situation. These samples of behavior presumably reflect underlying abilities or personality traits. In any psychological test, the person who is being tested is presented with some kind of standard stimuli. The stimuli may be specific questions that

can be answered "true" or "false." They might be problems that require solutions, or they can be completely ambiguous inkblots. Exactly the same stimuli are used every time that the test is given. In that way, the clinician can be sure that differences in performance can be interpreted as differences in abilities or traits rather than differences in the testing situation.

The psychologist observes people's responses in the test situation and draws inferences or makes predictions about how they will behave in other situations. For example, achievement tests present students with a series of mathematical and verbal problems. Performance on these standardized problems is taken as a reflection of the amount the student has learned and is also used to predict how well he or she will do in future academic situations.

Personality Inventories Because of their structure, **personality inventories** are sometimes referred to as "objective tests." They consist of a series of straightforward statements; the person being tested is typically required to indicate whether each statement is true or false in relation to himself or herself. Several types of personality inventories are widely used. Some are designed to identify personality traits in a normal population, and others focus more specifically on psychopathological problems. We have chosen to focus on the most extensively used personality inventory—the Minnesota Multiphasic Personality Inventory (MMPI)—to illustrate the characteristics of these tests as assessment devices.

The original version of the MMPI was developed in the 1940s at the University of Minnesota by Starke Hathaway (1903–1984) and his colleagues. For the past 30 or 40 years, it has been the most widely used psychological test. Thousands of research articles have been published on the MMPI (Archer, 1992). A revised version of the MMPI, known as the MMPI-2, has also been developed (Graham, 1990; Greene, 1991). Some psychologists still prefer to use the original version of the MMPI because the extensive body of research evidence that has accumulated over the past 50 years is based on that version. It may take several years before people are able to untangle all the similarities and differences between the two versions (Butcher, Graham, & Ben-Porath, 1995; Helmes & Reddon, 1993).

The MMPI and the MMPI-2 are based on a series of more than 500 statements that cover topics ranging from physical complaints and

▲ **Starke Hathaway, professor of psychology at the University of Minnesota, created the Minnesota Multiphasic Personality Inventory (MMPI), which has become the most widely employed objective test of personality.**

psychological states to occupational preferences and social attitudes. Examples are statements such as "I sometimes keep on at a thing until others lose their patience with me"; "My feelings are easily hurt"; and "There are persons who are trying to steal my thoughts and ideas." After reading each statement, the person is instructed to indicate whether it is true or false. Scoring of the MMPI is objective. After totaling the responses to all questions, the person receives a numerical score on each of 10 clinical scales as well as 4 validity scales.

Before considering the possible clinical significance of a person's MMPI profile, the psychologist will examine a number of *validity scales*, which reflect the patient's attitude toward the test and the openness and consistency with which the questions were answered. The L (Lie) Scale is sensitive to unsophisticated attempts to avoid answering in a frank and honest manner. For example, one statement on this scale says, "At times I feel like swearing." Although this is perhaps not an admirable trait, virtually all normal subjects indicate that the item is true. Subjects who indicate that the item is false (does not apply to them) receive one point on the L scale. Several responses of this sort would result in an elevated score on the scale and would indicate that the person's overall test results should not be interpreted as a true reflection of his or her feelings. Other validity scales reflect tendencies to exaggerate problems, carelessness in completing the questions, and unusual defensiveness.

If the profile is considered valid, the process of interpretation will be directed toward the 10 clinical scales, which are described in Table 4–7. Some of these scales carry rather obvious meaning, whereas others are associated with a more general or mixed pattern of symptoms. For example, Scale 2 (Depression) is a relatively straightforward index of degree of depression. Scale 7 (Psychasthenia), in contrast, is more complex and is based on items that measure anxiety, insecurity, and excessive doubt. There are many different ways to obtain an elevated score on any of the clinical scales, because each scale is composed of many items. The schizophrenia scale, for example, is based on 78 items, and a person who endorses any 20 of these statements in a deviant direction will receive an elevated score. Therefore even the more obvious scales can indicate several different types of problems, and the pattern of scale scores is more important than the elevation of any particular scale.

Rather than depending only on their own experience and clinical judgment, which may be subject to various sorts of bias and inconsistency, many clinicians analyze the results of a specific test on the basis of an explicit set of rules that are derived from empirical research. This is known as an **actuarial interpretation.** We can illustrate this process using Michael's profile. The profile is first described in terms of the pattern of scale scores, beginning with the highest and proceeding to the lowest. Those that are elevated above a scale score of 70 are most important, and interpretations are sometimes based on the "high-point pair." Following this procedure, Michael's profile could be coded as a 2-0; that is, his highest scores were on Scales 2 and 0. The clinician then looks up this specific configuration of scores in a kind of MMPI

TABLE 4-7

Clinical Scales for the MMPI

Scale Number	Scale Name	Interpretation of High Scores
1	Hypochondriasis	Excessive bodily concern; somatic symptoms
2	Depression	Depressed; pessimistic; irritable; demanding
3	Hysteria	Physical symptoms of functional origin; self-centered; demands attention
4	Psychopathic Deviate	Asocial or antisocial; rebellious; impulsive, poor judgment
5	Masculinity–Femininity	Male: aesthetic interests Female: assertive; competitive; self-confident
6	Paranoia	Suspicious, sensitive; resentful; rigid; may be frankly psychotic
7	Psychasthenia	Anxious; worried; obsessive; lacks self-confidence; problems in decision making
8	Schizophrenia	May have thinking disturbance, withdrawn; feels alienated and unaccepted
9	Hypomania	Excessive activity; lacks direction; low frustration tolerance; friendly
0	Social Introversion	Socially introverted; shy; sensitive; overcontrolled; conforming

"cookbook" to see what sort of descriptive characteristics apply. One cookbook offers the following statement about adolescents (mostly 14 and 15 years old) who fit the 2-0/0-2 code type:

> Eighty-seven percent of the 2-0/0-2s express feelings of inferiority to their therapists. They say that they are not good-looking, that they are afraid to speak up in class, and that they feel awkward when they meet people or try to make a date (91 percent of high 2-0/0-2s). Their therapists see the 2-0/0-2s as anxious, fearful, timid, withdrawn, and inhibited. They are depressed, and very vulnerable to threat. The 2-0/0-2 adolescents are overcontrolled; they cannot let go, even when it would be appropriate for them to do so. They are afraid of emotional involvement with others and, in fact, seem to have little need for such affiliation. These adolescents are viewed by their psychotherapists as schizoid; they think and associate in unusual ways and spend a good deal of time in personal fantasy and daydreaming. They are serious young people who tend to anticipate problems and difficulties. Indeed, they are prone toward obsessional thinking and are compulsively meticulous. (Marks, Seeman, & Haller, 1974, p. 201)

Several comments must be made about this statement. First, nothing is certain. Actuarial descriptions are probability statements. They indicate that a certain proportion of the people who produce this pattern of scores will be associated with a certain characteristic or behavior. If 87 percent of the adolescents who produce this code type express feelings of inferiority, 13 percent do not. Many aspects of this description apply to Michael's current adjustment, but they don't all fit. Second, the 2-0/0-2 code type represents only one aspect of the test results. In Michael's case, the elevation on Scales 8 and 5 was also prominent. Unfortunately, cookbooks often don't include code types that are that detailed, and the clinician must attempt to piece together descriptions from close approximations. Third, any profile can be interpreted in several ways (Greene, 1991).

The MMPI must be used in conjunction with other assessment procedures. The accuracy of actuarial statements can be verified through interviews with the person or through direct observations of his or her behavior.

Advantages The MMPI has several advantages in comparison to interviews and observational procedures. In clinical practice, it is seldom used by itself, but, for the following reasons, it can serve as a useful supplement to other methods of collecting information.

1. The MMPI provides information about the person's test-taking attitude, which alerts the clinician to the possibility that clients are careless, defensive, or exaggerating their problems.
2. The MMPI covers a wide range of problems in a direct and efficient manner. It would take a clinician several hours to go over all of these topics using an interview format.
3. Because the MMPI is scored objectively, the initial description of the person's adjustment is not influenced by the clinician's subjective impression of the client.
4. The MMPI can be interpreted in an actuarial fashion, using extensive banks of information regarding people who respond to items in a particular way.

Limitations The MMPI also has a number of limitations. Some of its problems derive from the fact that it has been used for many years. When the MMPI-2 was developed in the late 1980s, its authors decided to maintain the same clinical scales (see Table 4–7). New standardization data were obtained, and some old-fashioned items were replaced, but the underlying structure of the MMPI-2 is still based on diagnostic concepts and dimensions of psychopathology that were used 40 years ago (Helmes & Reddon, 1993). More specific limitations of the MMPI are listed below.

1. The test is not particularly sensitive to certain forms of psychopathology, especially those that have been added with the publication of DSM-III and DSM-IV. These include certain types of anxiety disorders, personality disorders, and subtypes of mood disorders.
2. The test depends on the person's ability to read and respond to written statements. Some people cannot complete the rather extensive list of questions. These include many people who are acutely psychotic, intellectually impaired, or poorly educated.

3. Specific data are not always available for a particular profile. Many patients' test results do not meet criteria for a particular code type with which extensive data are associated. Therefore, actuarial interpretation is not really possible for these profiles.

4. Some studies have found that profile types are not stable over time. It is not clear whether this instability should be interpreted as lack of reliability or as sensitivity to change in the person's level of adjustment.

Other Self-Report Inventories Sophisticated personality inventories like the MMPI are not the only approach to the measurement of subjective psychological states. Many other questionnaires and checklists have been developed to collect information about adjustment problems including subjective mood states such as depression and anxiety; patterns of obsessive thinking; and attitudes about drinking alcohol, eating, and sexual behavior. One example is the Beck Depression Inventory (BDI), which is used extensively in both clinical and research settings as an index of severity of depression. Sample items from the BDI are presented in Table 4–8.

The format of most *self-report inventories* is similar to that employed with objective personality tests like the MMPI. The primary difference is the range of topics covered by the instrument. Tests like the MMPI are designed to measure several dimensions that are related to abnormal behavior, whereas a self-report inventory is aimed more specifically at a focal topic or at one aspect of the person's adjustment. Self-report inventories usually don't include validity scales, and they may be based on less extensive research evidence. In other words, they may not be standardized on large samples of normal subjects prior to their use in a clinical setting.

Self-report inventories offer many advantages as supplements to information that is collected during clinical interviews. They are an extremely efficient way to gather specific data regarding a wide range of topics. They can also be scored objectively and therefore provide a specific index that is frequently useful in measuring change from one period of time to the next—for example, before and after treatment.

Despite their many advantages, self-report inventories can lead to serious problems if they are used carelessly. The BDI, for example, was designed as an index of change. Unfortunately, many investigators and clinicians have erroneously used it for diagnostic purposes. It is a serious mistake to assume that anyone who appears to be depressed on the basis of a self-report inventory would necessarily be diagnosed as being depressed after a clinical interview (Myers & Weissman, 1980; Oliver & Simmons, 1984). Self-report scales sometimes fail to identify patients who are considered depressed on the basis of a clinical interview. One reason for this discrepancy is the fact that some depressed patients consider themselves to be less depressed than they appear to a clinician when they are interviewed (Sayer et al., 1993).

PROJECTIVE PERSONALITY TESTS

In **projective tests,** the person is presented with a series of ambiguous stimuli. The best-known projective test, introduced in 1921 by Hermann Rorschach (1884–1922), a Swiss psychiatrist, is based on the use of inkblots. The *Rorschach test* consists of a series of 10 inkblots. Five contain various shades of gray on a white background, and five contain elements of color. The person is asked to look at each card and indicate what it looks like or what it appears to be. There are, of course, no correct answers. The instructions

---

TABLE 4-8

Sample Items from the Beck Depression Inventory

A. Sadness
0   I do not feel sad
1   I feel sad
2   I am sad all the time and I can't snap out of it
3   I am so sad or unhappy that I can't stand it

B. Pessimism
0   I am not particularly discouraged about the future
1   I feel discouraged about the future
2   I feel I have nothing to look forward to
3   I feel that the future is hopeless and that things cannot improve

C. Sense of Failure
0   I do not feel like a failure
1   I feel I have failed more than the average person
2   As I look back on my life, all I can see is a lot of failures
3   I feel I am a complete failure as a person

D. Dissatisfaction
0   I get as much satisfaction out of things as I used to
1   I don't enjoy things the way I used to
2   I don't get real satisfaction out of anything any more
3   I am dissatisfied or bored with everything

are intentionally vague in order to avoid influencing the person's responses through subtle suggestions.

Projective techniques such as the Rorschach test were originally based on psychodynamic assumptions about the nature of personality and psychopathology. Considerable emphasis was placed on the importance of unconscious motivations—conflicts and impulses of which the person is largely unaware. In other words, people being tested presumably *project* hidden desires and conflicts when they try to describe or explain the cards. In so doing, they may reveal things about themselves of which they are not consciously aware or that they might not be willing to admit if they were asked directly. The cards are not designed or chosen to be realistic or representational; they presumably look like whatever the person wants them to look like.

Michael did not actually complete any projective personality tests. We can illustrate the way in which these tests might have been used in his case, however, by considering a man who had been given a diagnosis of obsessive–compulsive disorder on Axis I, as well as showing evidence of two types of personality disorder, dependent and schizotypal features. This patient was 22 years old, unemployed, and living with his mother. His father had died in an accident 4 years earlier. Like Michael, this man was bothered by intrusive thoughts of contamination, and he frequently engaged in compulsive washing (Hurt, Reznikoff, & Clarkin, 1991). His responses to the cards on the Rorschach frequently mentioned emotional distress ("a man screaming"), interpersonal conflict ("two women fighting over something"), and war ("two mushrooms of a nuclear bomb cloud"). He did not incorporate color into any of his responses to the cards.

The original procedures for scoring the Rorschach were largely impressionistic and placed considerable emphasis on the content of the person's response. Responses given in the example above might be taken to suggest a number of important themes. Aggression and violence are obvious possibilities. Perhaps the man was repressing feelings of hostility, as indicated by his frequent references to war and conflict. These themes were coupled with a guarded approach to emotional reactions, which is presumably reflected by his avoidance of color. The psychologist might have wondered whether the man felt guilty about something, such as his father's death. This kind of interpretation, which depends heavily on symbolism and

clinical inference, provides intriguing material for the clinician to puzzle over. Unfortunately, the reliability and validity of this intuitive type of scoring procedure are very low (Shontz & Green, 1992).

When we ponder the utility of these interpretations, we should also keep in mind the relative efficiency of projective testing procedures. Did the test tell us anything that we didn't already know or that we couldn't have learned in a more straightforward manner? Consider the following story, told by Robyn Dawes, a psychologist at Carnegie Mellon University:

> I once tested a very depressed man who responded to the first blot that "it looks like a bat that has been squashed on the pavement under the heel of a giant's boot." Wow! A confabulated response indicative of extreme depression and feelings of being overwhelmed and crushed by forces beyond one's control. What response could possibly have been more "one-down"? The fact that the man was obviously depressed led me to believe in the validity of the Rorschach at that point. I realized only later that I already knew that he was depressed and hence that the response provided me with no new information whatsoever." (Dawes, 1994, p. 149)

In this young man's case, the clinician might have become aware of his feelings of anger or guilt through clinical interviews, which would be a more direct and efficient way of collecting information.

More recent approaches to the use of projective tests view the person's descriptions of the cards as a sample of his or her perceptual and cognitive styles. Psychologist John Exner has developed an objective scoring procedure for the Rorschach that is based primarily on the form rather than the content of the subject's responses (Exner, 1986; Kleiger, 1992). According to Exner's system, interpretation of the test depends on the way in which the descriptions take into account the shapes and colors on the cards. Does the person see movement in the card? Does she focus on tiny details, or does she base her descriptions on global impressions of the entire form of the inkblot? These and many

▼ **Projective tests require a person to respond to ambiguous stimuli. Here, a woman is taking the Thematic Apperception Test (TAT), in which she will be asked to make up a story about a series of drawings of people.**

other considerations contribute to the overall interpretation of the Rorschach test. The reliability of this scoring system is better than would be achieved by informal, impressionistic procedures. The validity of the scores, however, remains open to question (Davis, 1978; Shontz & Green, 1992).

There are many different types of projective tests. Some employ stimuli that are somewhat less ambiguous than the inkblots in the Rorschach. The Thematic Apperception Test (TAT), for example, consists of a series of drawings that depict human figures in various ambiguous situations. Most of the cards portray more than one person. The figures and their poses tend to elicit stories with themes of sadness and violence. The person is asked to describe the identities of the people in the cards and to make up a story about what is happening. These stories presumably reflect the person's own ways of perceiving reality.

To illustrate the way in which the TAT is used, consider once again the man whose Rorschach responses were described above. His TAT stories reflected a preoccupation with death as well as the disruptive consequences for those who tried, usually unsuccessfully, to cope with such a loss. For example, the following was his response to a picture in which a young man is seen standing next to an older woman who appears to be looking out of a window.

> A mother and son are really, really close, especially since her husband died. His father. And he lives right near her now that he's grown up, and takes care of her. And one day he finds out that because of his job he has to move away. He decides—and when he tells her here, he's really saddened, and she's shocked and depressed and confused, and doesn't know what she's gonna do. He finally moves away and she seems to adjust, but he doesn't like being away from his home and he really misses his mother. So eventually he moves back to home—quits his job, and moves back home. And even though he can't make as much money and things like that, he's a lot happier being home. (Hurt, Reznikoff, & Clarkin, 1991, p. 293)

The clinicians inferred from this and his other responses to the TAT, as well as from the results of the Rorschach, that this man was afraid that he would not be able to cope with the difficulties associated with moving out of his mother's home. They recommended that treatment would need to address the considerable anger that he felt toward his parents. Again, it seems reasonable to ask whether this conclusion might also have been reached on the basis of interviews with the man and his mother, without the use of projective tests.

Advantages The advantages of projective tests center on the fact that the tests are interesting to give and interpret and they sometimes provide a way to talk to people who are otherwise reluctant or unable to discuss their problems. Projective tests are more appealing to psychologists who adopt a psychodynamic view of personality and psychopathology. Some specific advantages are listed below.

1. Some people may feel more comfortable talking in an unstructured situation than they would if they were required to participate in a structured interview or to complete the lengthy MMPI.
2. Projective tests can provide an interesting source of information regarding the person's unique view of the world.
3. To whatever extent a person's relationships with other people are governed by unconscious cognitive and emotional events, projective tests may provide information that cannot be obtained through direct interviewing methods or observational procedures (Stricker & Healey, 1990).

Limitations There are many serious problems with the use of projective tests. The popularity of projective tests has declined considerably since the 1970s, even in clinical settings, primarily because research studies have found little evidence to support their reliability and validity (Wierzbicki, 1993; Wood, Nezworski, & Stejskal, 1996).

1. Lack of standardization in administration and scoring is a serious problem, even though Exner's system for the Rorschach has made some improvements in that regard.
2. Little information is available to use as norms for either adults or children.
3. Some projective procedures, such as the Rorschach, can be very time-consuming, particularly if the person's

responses are scored with a standardized procedure such as Exner's system.

4. The reliability of scoring and interpretation tends to be low.

5. Information regarding the validity of projective tests is primarily negative.

Assessment of Social Systems

The same range of procedures that we have discussed for the assessment of person variables (psychological systems) can also be used to examine situation variables (social systems). For example, clinical interviews can be used to describe the client's family and social environment, both past and present. These are obviously important considerations in planning a treatment program.

In Michael's case, the psychologist was interested in Michael's social relationships with classmates as well as his interactions with his parents. His father indicated that he was quite concerned about Michael's problems and that he was willing to help as they planned a treatment procedure that would allow Michael to learn to cope more effectively with his obsessive thoughts about contamination. Michael's mother also told the psychologist that arguments between Michael and his father often seemed to trigger an increase in the frequency of his compulsive washing rituals. This information convinced the psychologist that Michael's treatment should focus on improving his relationship with his father and not just on his compulsive washing. He made this decision knowing that family conflict and negative family attitudes have a negative impact on the results of treatment for obsessive–compulsive disorder (Leonard et al., 1993; Steketee, 1993).

Clinicians have developed structured as well as informal interviews to assess the social and emotional climate within families. One example is the Camberwell Family Interview (CFI), a measure of expressed emotion, or EE, that has been used extensively in studying families in which one of the members has a serious mental disorder, especially schizophrenia or depression (Hooley, 1986; see Chapter 13 for a discussion of this concept in relation to schizophrenia). Questions in the CFI are designed to elicit comments from the patient's parents or spouse that reflect their own attitudes and feelings about the patient's behavior. It is therefore an index of the emotional climate of the

home that is based primarily on whether the person expresses a significant level of criticism or hostility toward the patient. Patients who return to high-EE homes after being discharged from a psychiatric hospital are much more likely to experience another episode of disorder within the next few months than are patients who live in a more tolerant family environment. The parents of adolescents with obsessive–compulsive disorder are likely to be rated as high in EE (Hibbs et al., 1993). Family conflict and negative family attitudes are often produced by the need to change personal and family routines in an effort to accommodate compulsive rituals, such as Michael's decontamination rituals and his insistence that he not be touched (Calvocoressi et al., 1995).

Many self-report inventories, rating scales, and behavioral coding systems have been designed for the assessment of marital relationships and family systems. One popular self-report inventory is the Family Environment Scale (FES), which is composed of 90 true–false items and was designed to measure the social characteristics of families (Moos, 1974, 1981). The scale is composed of 10 subscales that are aimed at three dimensions of the family: *relationships* (cohesion, expressiveness, and conflicts); *personal growth* (independence, achievement orientation, intellectual-cultural orientation, active-recreational orientation, and moral-religious emphasis); and *system maintenance* (organization and control). Extensive testing with large numbers of families has been used to establish norms on the FES for distressed and nondistressed families. The FES has been used widely in clinical settings and in research studies. Unfortunately, evidence regarding test–retest reliability and the validity of the subscales is not impressive (L'Abate & Bagarozzi, 1993).

Direct observations can also be used to assess the social climate within a family. The Family Interaction Coding System (FICS) was developed by Gerald Patterson and John Reid, clinical psychologists at the Oregon Research Institute, to observe interactions between parents and children in their homes (Jones,

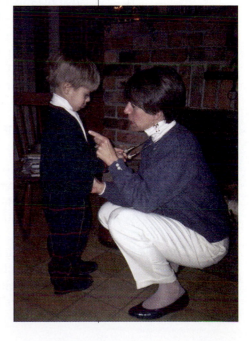

▼ In this interaction, a behavioral coding system could be used to record specific features of the mother's behavior, such as whether she spoke to her son, whether she touched him, and whether or not she approved or disapproved of his behavior.

Reid, & Patterson, 1975; Reid, 1978). A trained observer visits the family's home and collects information for at least 70 minutes just prior to lunch or dinner. Everyone in the family must be present during this time period, and they must stay in a two-room area. For each 5-minute block of time, the observer focuses on two members of the family and describes their behavior, using the coding system. The observer rotates his or her attention from one "target" to the next throughout the observation period.

The FICS code includes 29 non-mutually-exclusive categories that are used to describe a single interaction between two members of the family. These include behaviors such as approval; attention; command; compliance; cry; disapproval; destructiveness; humiliate; ignore; laugh; play; physical negative; physical positive; talk; tease; touch; whine; and yell. Standards have been published for normal boys and girls as well as for children who have been treated for conduct disorders and aggression.

Trained raters can achieve high levels of reliability with the FICS. In addition, a number of research studies have demonstrated that it is a valid measure of aggressive behaviors in children, as well as a useful way to assess the family context in which these behaviors occur. It can distinguish between the families of children with antisocial behavior or conduct disorders and nondisturbed families. The FICS is also a useful clinical tool that is sensitive to changes that occur during the course of family treatment (Grotevant & Carlson, 1989). The main disadvantages of this coding system are that the process of training observers is expensive and the collection of data is time-consuming. Remember also that a number of other limitations, such as reactivity and generalizability, are generally associated with direct observational measures.

Assessment of Biological Systems

In addition to psychological and social factors, biological factors affect human behavior. Clinicians have developed a number of techniques for measuring the behavioral effects of biological systems. These techniques are seldom used in clinical practice (at least for the diagnosis of psychopathology), but they have been employed extensively in research settings, and it seems possible that they will one day become an important source of information on individual patients.

PSYCHOPHYSIOLOGICAL ASSESSMENT

Changes in physiological response systems, such as heart rate, respiration rate, and skin conductance, are another important source of information regarding a person's psychological adjustment. The basic components of the human nervous system (reviewed in Chapter 2) include the central nervous system (CNS) and the peripheral nervous system (PNS). The PNS is divided into two parts: the somatic nervous system and the autonomic nervous system. The *somatic nervous system* is responsible for communication between the brain and external sense receptors, as well as regulation of voluntary muscle movements. The *autonomic nervous system* is responsible for body processes that occur without conscious awareness, such as heart rate. It maintains equilibrium in the internal environment.

The autonomic nervous system is highly reactive to environmental events and can provide useful information about a person's internal states, such as emotion (Miller & Kozak, 1993). Recording procedures have been developed to measure variables such as respiration rate, heart rate, and skin conductance. Table 4–9 summarizes some of the most important psychophysiological responses. As the person becomes aroused, the activity of these systems changes. Psychophysiological measures can therefore provide sensitive indices of the person's internal state.

It must be emphasized, however, that all of these measures do not act together. The concept of general arousal was abandoned many years ago (for example, see Lacey, 1967). If several physiological responses are measured at the same time, they may not all demonstrate the same strength, or even direction, of response. Moreover, physiological measures frequently disagree with the person's own subjective report. Therefore, as with other assessment procedures, physiological recordings should be used in conjunction with other measures. They represent supplements to, rather than substitutes for, the other types of measures that we have already considered (Iacono, 1991).

Anxiety disorders are one type of problem in which psychophysiological measurements have been used (Turpin, 1991). Consider Michael's case. He was afraid to touch contaminated objects in his house. If he had been forced to do so, it is

TABLE 4-9

Characteristics of Biological Response Systems and Psychophysiological Measurement Procedures

Response System	Psychophysiological Response	Basis of Response
Cardiovascular	Electrocardiogram (EKG)	Action potential of cardiac muscle during contraction
	Blood pressure (BP)	Systolic: Force of blood leaving the heart Diastolic: Residual pressure in the vascular system
Electrodermal	Skin resistance level (SRL) and response (SRR); skin conductance level (SCL) and response (SCR)	Source of signal is uncertain; current theories favor sweat gland activity
Central Nervous System	Electroencephalogram (EEG)	Electrical activity of cortical neurons
	Average evoked response (AER) and event-related potential (ERP)	Same as EEG in response to specific stimulus
	Contingent negative variation (CNV)	Same as EEG, appears during preparatory responses
Specialized Responses	Sexual (plethysmograph)	Engorgement of genital tissue with blood
	Respiration rate	Inhalation and exhalation of air
	Rapid eye movement (REM) sleep latency	Latency to onset of pattern associated with dreaming
	Smooth-pursuit eye movement (SPEM)	Visual tracking of an oscillating, pendulum-like stimulus

Kallman, W. M., and Feuerstein, M. J. , 1986, Psychophysiological procedures. In A. R. Ciminero, K. S. Calhoun, and H. E. Adams (Eds), *Handbook of behavioral assessment* (2nd edition). New York: Wiley-Interscience. Pp. 325–350.

likely that his heart rate would have increased dramatically. Psychophysiological events of this sort can be monitored precisely. To the extent that the clinician might be in need of information that would confirm data from other sources (observation, self-report) or that could be used to measure changes in the person's response to particular stimuli in the environment, physiological measurements may be very useful.

Physiological measurements have been employed extensively in the study of sexual arousal and in the treatment of sexual disorders (Freund & Watson, 1991; see Chapter 12). In both men and women, sexual arousal is associated with the engorgement of genital tissue with blood, which causes erection in the male and lubrication in the female. Scientists have developed electronic recording devices that can measure these responses precisely. The *penile plethysmograph*, an index of male sexual arousal, is used to measure changes in the circumference of the penis. A thin rubber tube filled with mercury is placed over the penis and connected to an electronic device known as a polygraph. As the man becomes sexually aroused, the tube stretches and the electrical resistance inside the tube changes. A similar device, known as the *vaginal photometer*, is used to measure sexual arousal in women. This device, which is shaped like a tampon, is inserted into the vagina and records changes in blood flow using a tiny photocell.

Physiological assessments have also been used in studies of patterns of marital interaction and divorce (see Chapter 17). These measures provide an interesting perspective on the emotional responses of both marital partners. Husbands and wives who are dissatisfied with

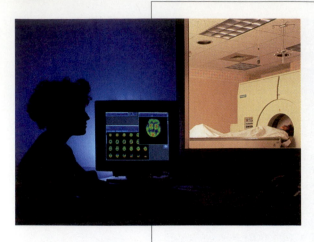

▲ **Positron emission topography (PET scan) can provide useful images of dynamic brain functions. Areas that appear red or yellow indicate areas of the brain that are active (consuming the labeled glucose molecules), whereas those that are blue or green are relatively inactive. Different areas of the brain become active depending on whether the person is at rest or engaged in particular activities when the image is created.**

their marriages experience higher levels of negative emotion. In assessments conducted during interactions that are contrived in the laboratory, husbands often exhibit physiological responses, such as changes in heart rate and skin conductance, that indicate intense arousal, but these feelings are not expressed in their verbal behavior. Men who show this response are more likely to be dissatisfied with their marriages, and their relationships are more likely to end in divorce (Gottman & Levenson, 1986, 1992). These data suggest that psychophysiological measures represent an important addition to the assessment of marital interactions.

Advantages Physiological procedures are not used frequently in clinical settings, but they are used extensively in research on psychopathology. One clinical situation in which they are employed is in the assessment of sexual arousal, which is difficult or awkward to measure using direct observations and in which self-report measures are often questionable. These tools have several advantages in comparison to other assessment procedures.

1. Psychophysiological recording procedures do not depend on self-report and therefore may be less subject to voluntary control. People may be less able to make the assessment show what they want it to show.
2. Some of these measures can be obtained while the subject is sleeping or while the subject is actively engaged in some other activity.

Limitations In addition to the fact that they require relatively sophisticated equipment and a technician who is trained in their use, physiological measures have a number of drawbacks.

1. The recording equipment and electrodes may be frightening or intimidating to some people.

2. There are generally low correlations between different autonomic response systems. It is not wise to select arbitrarily one specific physiological measure, such as heart rate, and assume that it is a direct index of arousal.
3. Physiological reactivity and the stability of physiological response systems vary from person to person. The measures may be informative for some people but not for others.
4. Physiological responses can be influenced by many other factors. Some are person variables, such as age and medication, as well as psychological factors, such as being self-conscious or fearing loss of control (Anderson & McNeilly, 1991). Other important considerations are situational variables, such as extraneous noise and electrical activity.

BRAIN IMAGING TECHNIQUES

The past several decades have seen a tremendous explosion of information and technology in the neurosciences. We now understand in considerable detail how neurons in the central nervous system communicate with one another, and scientists have invented sophisticated methods to create images of the living human brain (Daniel, Zigun, & Weinberger, 1994; Posner, 1993). Some of these procedures provide static pictures of various brain structures at rest, just as an X-ray provides a photographic image of a bone or some other organ of the body. Other methods can be used to create dynamic images of brain functions—reflecting the rate of activity in various parts of the brain—while a person is performing different tasks.

Static Brain Imaging Many investigations of brain structure in people with various forms of psychopathology have employed an imaging technique called *computerized tomographic (CT) scanning* (Coffman, 1989). In CT scanning, X-ray beams are passed through the brain to a series of detectors that measure the density of the tissues through which the beams have passed. A series of two-dimensional images are created at sequential slices or planes of the brain by rotating the scanner around the body for the full 360 degrees.

A much more precise measure of brain structure can be obtained with *magnetic resonance imaging (MRI)*. In MRI, images are generated using electromagnetic phenomena rather than X-rays (Andreasen, 1989). Both CT scanning and MRI provide a static image of specific brain structures. MRI provides better images than CT scans and is able to identify smaller parts of the brain. For this reason, and because it lends itself more easily to the creation of three-dimensional pictures of the brain, MRI is replacing CT scanning where it is available.

Dynamic Brain Imaging In addition to CT scanning and MRI, which provide a static view of brain structures, advances in the neurosciences have also produced techniques that create images of brain functions (Raichle, 1994a, 1994b). Unlike CT scanning, which is available at most hospitals, the dynamic imaging procedures are very expensive, and they are currently available only to a few investigators.

Positron emission tomography (PET) is one scanning technique that can be used to create dynamic brain images (Holcomb, Links, Smith, & Wong, 1989). This procedure is much more expensive than the other imaging techniques because it requires a nuclear cyclotron to produce special radioactive elements. PET scans are capable of providing relatively detailed images of the brain. In addition, they can reflect changes in brain activity as the person responds to the demands of various tasks.

A second functional imaging procedure is *single photon emission computed tomography*, or *SPECT* (Devous, 1989). SPECT is more widely available than PET because single-photon-emitting compounds have relatively long physical half-lives. Therefore they can be manufactured in one location and transported to another, distant location where the imaging procedure is being conducted. On the other hand, the resolution of SPECT images is not as good as that obtained using PET.

Dynamic brain imaging procedures have been used extensively to study possible neurological underpinnings of various types of mental disorder. For example, in the case of obsessive–compulsive disorder (OCD), considerable research has focused on the *basal ganglia*, a complex set of nuclei connecting structures in the cerebral cortex with the thalamus (Insel, 1992; see Figure 14–3, which illustrates the location of these structures in the brain). Studies using SPECT (Edmonstone et al., 1994) and PET (Perani et al., 1995) have suggested that increased metabolic rates in the basal ganglia

may be correlated with the presence of obsessions and compulsions. The photograph on this page shows a set of functional images (PET scans) obtained from a patient with OCD.

These results are intriguing because they suggest that this circuit in the brain may somehow be associated with the presence of obsessive–compulsive symptoms. We must emphasize, however, that the results of such imaging procedure are not useful diagnostically with regard to an individual person. In other words, some people with OCD do not exhibit increased metabolism rates in the basal ganglia, and some people who do not have OCD do show increased levels of activity in their basal ganglia.

Advantages Brain imaging techniques provide detailed information regarding the structure of brain areas and activity levels in the brain that are associated with the performance of particular tasks. They have important uses, primarily as research tools:

1. In clinical practice, imaging techniques can be used to rule out various neurological conditions that might explain behavioral or cognitive deficits. These include such conditions as brain tumors and vascular disease.

2. Procedures such as MRI and PET can help research investigators explore the relation between brain functions and specific mental disorders. This type of

▼ **These PET scan images of an OCD patient's brain show areas in which activity increases as symptoms get stronger. The brain is sectioned axially (left), sagittally (center), and coronally (right).**

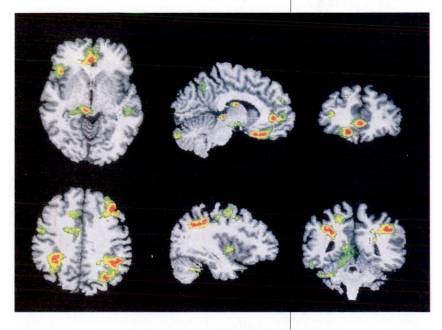

information will be considered in several chapters later in this book.

Limitations   Brain imaging procedures are used extensively in the study and treatment of neurological disorders. In the field of psychopathology, they are currently research tools and have little clinical importance outside the assessment and treatment of disorders such as Alzheimer's disease (see Chapter 14). Some of the major limitations are listed below.

1. Norms have not been established for any of these measures. It is not possible to use brain imaging procedures for diagnostic purposes.
2. These procedures are relatively expensive—especially PET scans—and some procedures must be used cautiously because the patient may be exposed to radioactive substances.

Summary

Formal **classification systems** for mental disorders have been developed in order to facilitate communication, research, and treatment planning. The current official system published by the American Psychiatric Association is the fourth edition of the *Diagnostic and Statistical Manual of Mental Disorders,* or DSM-IV. It is based on a **categorical approach to classification** and typically employs **polythetic** criterion sets to define specific types of disorder. The categories that are defined in DSM-IV are based primarily on descriptive principles rather than on theoretical knowledge regarding the etiology of the disorders. Five axes are included in this system. Axes I and II are employed for describing mental disorders (personality disorders and mental retardation on Axis II). The remaining three axes are concerned with supplementary information that may also be useful in treatment planning.

The utility of a classification system depends on several criteria, especially **reliability** and **validity.** The reliability of many categories in DSM seems to have improved with the introduction of specific **inclusion criteria** and **exclusion criteria.** Nevertheless, serious questions remain about this issue. The reliability of some categories, such as the personality disorders, is still marginal in many studies. Reliability is also likely to be diminished in clinical settings where clinicians are not experts in a particular disorder and reliability is not being monitored. The **validity,** or systematic meaning, of most categories is still under active investigation.

The general process of collecting and interpreting information is called **assessment.** Many different assessment tools can be used to generate information systematically. Interviews, observations, and tests are among the most frequently used procedures. Assessments can be directed toward biological, psychological, and social systems. In many cases, information is collected and integrated across more than one system, but it is never possible to learn everything about a particular person. Choices have to be made, and some information must be excluded from the analysis.

Psychological systems are typically assessed using interviews, observations, or self-report inventories. Structured diagnostic interviews are used extensively in conjunction with the DSM-IV classification system. They can also form the basis for ratings of the person's adjustment on a number of dimensions. Interviews can be used to collect additional information that is relevant to planning treatment. Their main advantage is their flexibility. Their primary limitation lies in the inability or unwillingness of some clients to provide a rational description of their own problems, as well as the subjective factors that influence the clinician's interpretation of data collected in an interview.

Psychological tests are also used in the assessment of psychological systems. **Personality inventories,** like the MMPI, offer several advantages as supplements to interviews and observations. They can be scored objectively, they often contain validity scales that reflect the person's attitude and test-taking set, and they can be interpreted in reference to well-established standards for people with and without specific types of adjustment problems. Some psychologists use projective personality tests, like the Rorschach, to acquire information that might not be obtained from direct interviews or observations. Unfortunately, research studies have found little evidence to support the reliability and validity of projective tests. The continued use of these tests is therefore controversial.

Social systems, including marital relationships and families, can also be evaluated using interviews, observations, and self-report inventories. Although the instruments that are used for this purpose have not been developed as extensively as those that address psychological systems, they represent an important consideration in thinking about mental disorders and their treatment.

Many different tools are available for assessing biological systems related to mental disorders. These include psychophysiological recording procedures as well as brain imaging techniques, such as MRI and PET scans. Biological assessment procedures are used extensively in research studies. They do not have diagnostic value in clinical situations, except for the purpose of ruling out certain conditions, such as brain tumors and vascular disease.

Critical Thinking

1. Do we need a classification system in the field of psychopathology? If so, how should it be evaluated? What are the characteristics of a useful classification system? Should we expect that such a system will be based solely on scientific considerations?

2. What are some of the inherent limitations of a classification system? What are the advantages and disadvantages associated with the process of psychiatric diagnosis? If there are problems, how can they be resolved, or at least minimized?

3. How will your choice of an assessment procedure be influenced by the conceptual frame of reference that you adopt in thinking about a clinical problem? How will it be influenced by the nature of the specific problem that you are trying to address? Why isn't it possible to have a universal assessment battery that could be used consistently for all clinical problems?

5
Mood Disorders

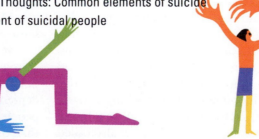

S ome of the simplest emotions require little description. We all know how it feels to be angry or sad. Most of our feelings are momentary—like the apprehension that grips us when we are watching a frightening movie, or the amusement we experience when listening to a comedian. Others can be relatively enduring, like the grief we may suffer when a close friend moves away. Most emotional fluctuations, including many that are unpleasant, represent part of normal experience. Unfortunately, some people experience extreme fluctuations in emotion that become persistent and severely debilitating. In this chapter we will consider emotional disorders that involve prolonged periods of severe depression.

Overview

Psychopathologists use several terms to describe problems that are associated with emotional response systems. This language can become confusing because most of us already use these words in our everyday vocabulary. We must define these terms as they are used in psychopathology so that our discussion will be clear. **Emotion** refers to a state of arousal that is defined by subjective states of feeling, such as sadness, anger, and disgust. Emotions are often accompanied by physiological changes, such as changes in heart rate and respiration rate. **Affect** refers to the pattern of observable behaviors that are associated with these subjective feelings. People express affect through changes in their facial expressions, the pitch of their voices, and their hand and body movements. **Mood** refers to a pervasive and sustained emotional response that, in its extreme form, can color the person's perception of the world (APA, 1994). The disorders that are discussed in this chapter are primarily associated with two specific moods: depression and elation.

Depression can refer either to a mood or to a clinical syndrome—a combination of emotional, cognitive, and behavioral symptoms. The feelings associated with a *depressed mood* often include disappointment and despair. Although sadness is a universal experience, profound depression is not. People who are in a severely depressed mood describe the feeling as overwhelming, suffocating, or numbing. In the syndrome of depression, which is also called

clinical depression, a depressed mood is accompanied by several other symptoms, such as fatigue, loss of energy, difficulty in sleeping, and changes in appetite. Clinical depression also involves a variety of changes in thinking and overt behavior. The person may experience cognitive symptoms, such as extreme guilt, feelings of worthlessness, concentration problems, and thoughts of suicide. Behavioral symptoms may range from constant pacing and fidgeting to extreme inactivity. Throughout the rest of this chapter, we will use the term *depression* to refer to the clinical syndrome rather than the mood.

Mania, the flip side of depression, also involves a disturbance in mood that is accompanied by additional symptoms. Euphoria or elated mood is the opposite emotional state from a depressed mood: It is characterized by an exaggerated feeling of physical and emotional well-being (APA, 1994). Manic symptoms that frequently accompany an elated mood include inflated self-esteem, decreased need for sleep, distractibility, pressure to keep talking, and the subjective feeling of thoughts racing through the person's head faster than they can be spoken. Mania is therefore a syndrome in the same sense that clinical depression is a syndrome.

Mood disorders are defined in terms of episodes—discrete periods of time in which the person's behavior is dominated by either a depressed or manic mood. Unfortunately, most people with a mood disorder experience more than one episode. The following case studies illustrate the way that numerous symptoms combine to form syndromes that are used to define mood disorders. They also provide examples of the two primary types of mood disorders: (1) those in which the person experiences only episodes of depression, known as **unipolar mood disorder,** and (2) those in which the person experiences episodes of mania as well as depression, known as **bipolar mood disor-** **der.** A small number of patients have only manic episodes with no evidence of depression; they are included in the bipolar category. Years ago, bipolar mood disorder was known as *manic–depressive disorder*. Although this term has been replaced in the official diagnostic manual, some clinicians still prefer to use it because it offers a more direct description of the patient's experience (Jamison, 1995).

Unipolar Mood Disorder: Major Depressive Episode

Cathy was a 31-year-old attorney who had been promoted to the rank of partner the previous year and was considered one of the brightest, most promising young members of her firm. In spite of her apparent success, she was plagued by doubts about her own abilities and was convinced that she was unworthy of her promotion. Cathy decided to seek treatment because she was profoundly miserable. Beyond being depressed, she felt numb. She had been feeling unusually fatigued and irritable for a period of several months, but her mood took a serious swing for the worse after one of the firm's clients, for whom Cathy was primarily responsible, decided to switch to another firm. Although the decision was clearly based on factors that were beyond her control, Cathy blamed herself. She interpreted this event as a reflection of her professional incompetence, in spite of the fact that virtually all of her other clients had praised her work and the senior partners in her firm had given her consistently positive reviews.

Cathy had always looked forward to going to the office, and she truly enjoyed her work. After she lost this client, however, going to work had seemed like an overwhelming burden. She found it impossible to concentrate and instead brooded about her own incompetence. Soon she started calling in sick.

She began to spend her time sitting in bed staring at the television screen, without paying attention to any program, and she never left her apartment. She felt lethargic all the time, but she wasn't sleeping well. Her appetite disappeared. Her best friend tried repeatedly to get in touch with her, but Cathy wouldn't return her calls. She listened passively as her friend left messages on the answering machine. She just didn't feel like doing anything or talking to anyone.

Cathy considered her social life to be a disaster, and it didn't seem to be getting any better. She had been separated from her husband for 5 years, and her most recent boyfriend had started dating another woman. She had tried desperately for several weeks to force herself to be active, but eventually she stopped caring. The situation seemed completely hopeless. Although she had often gone to parties with other members of her law firm, she usually felt as though she didn't fit in. Everyone else seemed to be part of a couple, and Cathy was usually on her own. Other people didn't appreciate the depth of her loneliness. Sometimes it seemed to Cathy that she would be better off dead. She spent a good deal of time brooding about suicide, but she feared that if she tried to harm herself she might make things worse than they already were. ■

Cathy's problems would be classified as a unipolar mood disorder because she had experienced at least one episode of major depression and she had never had a manic episode. Our next case illustrates the symptoms of mania, which often appear after a person has already experienced at least one episode of depression. People who experience episodes of both depression and mania are given a diagnosis of bipolar mood disorder. The symptoms of a full-blown manic episode are not subtle. People who are manic typically have terrible judgment and may get into considerable trouble as a result of their disorder. The central feature of mania is a persistently elevated or irritable mood that lasts for at least 1 week.

Bipolar Mood Disorder: Manic Episode

Debbie, a 21-year-old single woman, was admitted to a psychiatric hospital in the midst of a manic episode. She had been in psychotherapy for depression for a period of several months while she was in high school but had not received any type of treatment since that time. After she completed two semesters at a community college, Debbie found a well-paying job in the advertising office of a local newspaper, where she had been working for 2 years.

Debbie's manic episode could be traced to experiences that began 3 or 4 months prior to her admission to the hospital. Debbie had been feeling unusually good for several weeks. At first she didn't think anything was wrong. In fact, her impression was quite the opposite. Everything seemed to be going right for her. Her energy level was up, and she felt a renewed confidence in herself and her relationships with other people, especially with her boyfriend, who had recently moved to a distant city. Debbie initially welcomed these feelings, especially because she had been so lethargic and also tended to be reserved interpersonally.

One day when she was feeling particularly exhilarated, Debbie impulsively quit her job and went to visit her boyfriend. Giving up her job without careful consideration and with no prospect for alternative employment was the first indication that Debbie's judgment was becoming impaired. Although she left home with only enough money to pay for her airplane ticket, she stayed for several weeks, mostly engaged in leisure activities. It was during this time that she started having trouble sleeping. The quality of her mood also began to change. It was less often cheerful and frequently irritable. She was extremely impatient and would become furious if her boyfriend disagreed with her. On one occasion, they had a loud and heated argument in the parking lot of his apartment complex. She took off her blouse and angrily refused to put it on again in spite of his demands and the presence of several interested bystanders. Shortly after the fight, she packed her clothes and hitchhiked back home.

After returning to her parents' home, Debbie argued with them almost continuously for several days. Her moods shifted constantly. One moment she would be bubbling with enthusiasm, gleefully throwing herself into new and exciting activities. If her plans were thwarted, she would fly into a rage. She phoned an exclusive tennis club to arrange for private lessons, which she obviously could not afford, especially now that she was unemployed. Her mother interrupted the call and canceled the lessons. Debbie left the house in a fury and set off to hitch a ride to the tennis club. She was picked up by two unknown men, who persuaded her to accompany them to a party rather than go to the club. By the time they arrived at the party, her mood was once again euphoric. She stayed at the party all night and had intercourse with three men whom she had never met before.

The following day, Debbie borrowed money from a friend and took a train home. Another argument ensued when she arrived at home. Debbie struck her father and took the family car. Angry and frightened by her apparently irrational behavior, her parents phoned the police, who found her and brought her home. When another argument broke out, even more hostile than the first, the police took Debbie to their precinct office, where she was interviewed by a psychiatrist. Her attitude was flippant, and her language was abusive and obscene. On the basis of her clearly irrational and violent mood as well as her marked impairment in judgment, the psychiatrist arranged for her to be committed to a psychiatric hospital.

Debbie's behavior on the ward was belligerent, provocative, and demanding. Although she hadn't slept a total of more than 4 hours in the previous 3 days, she claimed to be bursting with energy. Her affect vacillated quickly and frequently. The slightest provocation could change an elated, expansive mood into a furious burst of anger. She behaved seductively toward some of the male patients, sitting on their laps, kissing them, and occasionally

Typical Symptoms and Associated Features

The cases of Cathy and Debbie illustrate many of the most important symptoms and signs of mood disorders, which can be divided into four general areas: emotional symptoms, cognitive symptoms, somatic symptoms, and behavioral symptoms. Each area is typically involved in episodes of major depression and mania.

Emotional Symptoms

Depressed, or **dysphoric** (unpleasant), mood is the most common and obvious symptom of depression. Most people who are depressed describe themselves as feeling utterly gloomy, dejected, or despondent. There is no clear-cut line dividing normal sadness from the depressed mood that is associated with clinical depression. Clinicians use several features to help guide this diagnostic distinction, including the severity, the quality, and the pervasive impact of the depressed mood.

The severity of a depressed mood can reach painful and overwhelming proportions. William Styron, a Pulitzer Prize–winning author, has described the feeling as "despair beyond despair." Styron's account of his own experience with profound depression, which took him to the brink of suicide, provides a compelling description of the disorder. He says that the sensation most closely resembled drowning or suffocation. Styron pointed out that the word *depression*, which can also be used to describe an economic decline or a rut in the ground, is somehow inadequate to describe the catastrophic depths to which a person's mood can descend. He argued that clinicians should employ a more dramatic term to describe this dreadful experience:

As one who has suffered from the malady in extremis yet returned to tell the tale, I would lobby for a truly arresting designation. "Brainstorm," for instance, has unfortunately been preempted to describe, somewhat jocularly, intellectual inspiration. But something along these lines is needed. Told that someone's mood disorder has evolved into a storm—a veritable howling tempest in the brain, which is indeed what a clinical depression resembles like nothing else—even the uninformed layman might display sympathy rather than the standard reaction that "depression" evokes, something akin to "So what?" or "You'll pull out of it" or "We all have bad days." (1990, pp. 37–38)

The suffocating gloom and despair associated with clinical depression often has a somewhat different character than normal sadness. Styron also wrote about the unique quality of his depressed mood:

What I had begun to discover is that, mysteriously and in ways that are totally remote from normal experience, the gray drizzle of horror induced by depression takes on the quality of

▼ The quality of a depressed mood is often different from the sadness that might arise from an event such as the loss of a loved one. Some depressed people say that they feel like they are drowning or suffocating.

physical pain. But it is not an immediately identifiable pain, like that of a broken limb. It may be more accurate to say that despair, owing to some evil trick played upon the sick brain by the inhabiting psyche, comes to resemble the diabolical discomfort of being imprisoned in a fiercely overheated room. And because no breeze stirs this caldron, because there is no escape from this smothering confinement, it is entirely natural that the victim begins to think ceaselessly of oblivion. (p. 50)

In contrast to the unpleasant feelings associated with clinical depression, manic patients like Debbie experience periods of inexplicable and unbounded joy known as **euphoria.** Debbie felt extremely optimistic and cheerful—"on top of the world"—in spite of the fact that her inappropriate behavior had made a shambles of her current life circumstances. Bursting with energy, she exhibited boundless enthusiasm, even after she was admitted to the psychiatric hospital. In bipolar mood disorders, periods of elated mood tend to alternate with phases of depression. The duration of each episode and the frequency of the cycle vary from one patient to the next.

Kay Jamison, professor of psychiatry at Johns Hopkins University School of Medicine, has written an eloquent and moving description of her own experiences with mania and depression. The symptoms of mania are initially quite pleasant. The person may experience periods of increased energy that are accompanied by feelings of enhanced productivity and creativity.

My manias, at least in their early and mild forms, were absolutely intoxicating states that gave rise to great personal pleasure, an incomparable flow of thoughts, and a ceaseless energy that allowed the translation of new ideas into papers and projects. (1995, pp. 5–6)

Unfortunately, as these feelings become more intense and prolonged, they may become ruinous. It may not be clear when the person's experience crosses the unmarked boundary between being productive and energetic to being out of control and self-destructive. Jamison described this subtle transition in the following way:

There is a particular kind of pain, elation, loneliness, and terror involved in this kind of madness. When you're high it's tremendous. The ideas and feelings are fast and frequent like shooting stars, and you follow them until you find better and brighter ones. Shyness goes, the right words and gestures are suddenly there, the power to captivate others a felt certainty. There are interests found in uninteresting people. Sensuality is pervasive, and the desire to seduce and be seduced irresistible. Feelings of ease, intensity, power, well-being, financial omnipotence, and euphoria pervade one's marrow. But, somewhere, this changes. The fast ideas are far too fast, and there are far too many; overwhelming confusion replaces clarity. Memory goes. Humor and absorption on friends' faces are replaced by fear and concern. Everything previously moving with the grain is now against—you are irritable, angry, frightened, uncontrollable, and enmeshed totally in the blackest caves of the mind. You never knew those caves were there. It will never end, for madness carves its own reality. (p. 67)

Many depressed and manic patients are irritable. Their anger can be directed either at themselves or at others, and frequently at both. Even when they are cheerful, people in a manic episode, like Debbie, are easily provoked to anger. Debbie became extremely argumentative and abusive, particularly when people challenged her grandiose statements about herself and her inappropriate judgment.

Anxiety is also common among people with mood disorders, just as depression is a common feature of some anxiety disorders (see Chapter 6). Two out of every 3 depressed patients also report feeling anxious (Kendall & Watson, 1989). People who are depressed are sometimes apprehensive, fearing that matters will become even worse than they already are or that others will discover their inadequacy. They sometimes report that they are chronically tense and unable to relax.

Cognitive Symptoms

In addition to changes in the way people feel, mood disorders also involve changes in the way people think about themselves and their surroundings. People who are clinically depressed frequently note that their thinking is slowed down, that they have trouble concentrating, and that they are easily distracted. Cathy's ability to concentrate was so disturbed that she became unable to work. She had extreme difficulty making even the simplest decisions. After she started staying home, she sat in front of the television set but was unable to pay attention to the content of even the simplest programs. Her thought processes were almost completely shut down.

Guilt and worthlessness are common preoccupations. Depressed patients blame themselves for things that have gone wrong, regardless of whether they are in fact responsible. They focus considerable attention on the most negative features of themselves, their environments, and the future—a combination that A. T. Beck (1967) has labeled the "depressive triad." Cathy exhibited this pattern. She saw herself as an incompetent person, both professionally and personally. She viewed her occupational and social worlds as being lonely and overwhelming. Her future looked gloomy and threatening.

In contrast to the cognitive slowness associated with depression, manic patients commonly report that their thoughts are speeded up. Ideas flash through their minds faster than they can articulate their thoughts. Manic patients can also be easily distracted, responding to seemingly random stimuli in a completely uninterpretable and incoherent fashion. Grandiosity and inflated self-esteem are also characteristic features of mania.

SUICIDAL IDEAS

Many people experience self-destructive ideas and impulses when they are depressed. Interest in suicide usually develops gradually and may begin with the vague sense that life is not worth living (Hamilton, 1982). Such feelings may follow directly from the overwhelming fatigue and loss of pleasure that typically accompany a seriously depressed mood. In addition, feelings of guilt and failure can lead depressed people to consider killing themselves. Over a period of time, depressed people may come to believe that they would be better off dead or that their family would function more successfully and happily without them. Preoccupation with such thoughts then leads to specific plans and may culminate in a suicide attempt.

Somatic Symptoms

The **somatic symptoms** of mood disorders are related to basic physiological or bodily functions. They include fatigue, aches and pains, and serious changes in appetite and sleep patterns. People, like Cathy, who are clinically depressed often report feeling tired all the time. The simplest tasks, which she had previously taken for granted, seemed to require an overwhelming effort. Taking a shower, brushing her teeth, and getting dressed in the morning became virtually impossible.

Sleeping problems are also common, particularly trouble getting to sleep. This disturbance frequently goes hand in hand with cognitive difficulties mentioned earlier. Worried about her endless problems and unable to relax, Cathy found that she would toss and turn for hours before finally falling asleep. Some people also report having difficulty staying asleep throughout the night, and they awaken 2 or more hours before the usual time. Early-morning waking is often associated with particularly severe depression. A less common symptom is for a depressed individual to spend more time sleeping than usual.

Depressed people frequently experience a change in appetite. Although some patients report that they eat more than usual, most reduce the amount that they eat; some may eat next to nothing. Food just doesn't taste good any more. Depressed people can also lose a great deal of weight, even without trying to diet.

People who are severely depressed commonly lose their interest in various types of activities that are otherwise sources of pleasure and fulfillment. One common example is a loss of sexual desire. Depressed people are less likely to initiate sexual activity, and they are less likely to enjoy sex if their partners can persuade them to participate.

Various ill-defined somatic complaints can also accompany mood disorders. Some patients complain of frequent headaches and muscular aches and pains. These concerns may develop into a preoccupation with bodily functions and fear of disease. Styron (1990) described these physical sensations in the following way:

I felt a kind of numbness, an enervation, but more particularly an odd fragility—as if my body had actually become frail, hypersensitive and somehow disjointed and clumsy, lacking normal coordination. And soon I was in the throes of a pervasive hypochondria. Nothing felt quite right with my corporeal self; there were twitches and pains, sometimes intermittent, often seemingly constant, that seemed to presage all sorts of dire infirmities. (p. 43)

Behavioral Symptoms

The symptoms of mood disorders also include changes in the things that people do and the rate at which they do them. The term **psychomotor retardation** refers to several features of behavior that may accompany the onset of serious depression. The most obvious behavioral symptom of depression is slowed movement. Patients may walk and talk as if they are in slow motion. Others become completely immobile and may stop speaking altogether. Some depressed patients pause for very extended periods—perhaps several minutes—before answering a question.

In marked contrast to periods when they are depressed, manic patients are typically gregarious and energetic. Debbie's behavior provided many examples, even after her admission to the psychiatric hospital. Her flirtatious and provocative behavior on the ward was clearly inappropriate. She found it impossible to sit still for more than a moment or two. Virtually everything was interesting to her, and she was easily distracted, flitting from one idea or project to the next. Like other manic patients, Debbie was full of plans that were pursued in a rather indiscriminate fashion. She quit her job without warning in order to visit a friend. She tried to arrange expensive tennis lessons that she could not afford. When she tried to hitch a ride to the tennis club, she was easily persuaded to change these plans and accompany two men to a party. Her impulsive sexual relationships with these men provided another example of her poor judgment.

Jamison's memoir provides vivid descriptions of her own speeded-up behavior:

I was a senior in high school when I had my first attack of manic–depressive illness; once the siege began, I lost my mind rather rapidly. At first, everything seemed so easy. I raced about like a crazed weasel, bubbling with plans and enthusiasm, immersed in sports, and staying up all night, night after night, out with friends, reading everything that wasn't nailed down, filling manuscript books with poems and fragments of plays,

and making expansive, completely unrealistic, plans for my future. The world was filled with pleasure and promise; I felt great. Not just great, I felt *really* great. I felt I could do anything, that no task was too difficult. My mind seemed clear, fabulously focused, and able to make intuitive mathematical leaps that had up to that point entirely eluded me. Indeed, they elude me still. At the time, however, not only did everything make perfect sense, but it all began to fit into a marvelous kind of cosmic relatedness. My sense of enchantment with the laws of the natural world caused me to fizz over, and I found myself buttonholing my friends to tell them how beautiful it all was. They were less than transfixed by my insights into the webbings and beauties of the universe, although considerably impressed by how exhausting it was to be around my enthusiastic ramblings: You're talking too fast, Kay. Slow down, Kay. You're wearing me out, Kay. Slow down, Kay. And those times when they didn't actually come out and say it, I still could see it in their eyes: For God's sake, Kay, slow down. (pp. 36–37)

Other Problems Commonly Associated with Depression

Many people with mood disorders suffer from some clinical problems that are not typically considered symptoms of depression. Within the field of psychopathology, the simultaneous manifestation of a mood disorder and other syndromes is referred to as **comorbidity,** suggesting that the person exhibits symptoms of more than one underlying disorder.

Alcoholism and depression are clearly related phenomena. Many people who are depressed also drink heavily, and many people who are dependent on alcohol—between 33 and 59 percent—eventually become depressed (Merikangas & Gelernter, 1990; Schuckit & Monteiro, 1988). There is also an association between these disorders within families. Alcohol abuse is common among the immediate families of patients with mood disorders. Eating disorders and anxiety disorders are also more common among first-degree relatives of depressed patients than among people in the general population.

Classification

Psychopathologists have proposed hundreds of systems for describing and classifying mood disorders (Grove & Andreasen, 1992). In the following section, we will describe briefly some of the historical figures who played a prominent role in the development of classification systems (Berrios, 1992). This discussion should help place our description of the current diagnostic system, DSM-IV, in perspective.

Brief Historical Perspective

Although written descriptions of clinical depression can be traced to ancient times, the first widely accepted classification system was proposed by the German physician Emil Kraepelin (1921). Kraepelin divided the major forms of mental disorder into two categories: *dementia praecox*, which we now know as schizophrenia (see Chapter 12), and *manic–depressive psychosis*. He based the distinction on age of onset, clinical symptoms, and the course of the disorder (its progress over time). The manic–depressive category included all depressive syndromes, regardless of whether the patients exhibited manic and depressive episodes or simply depression. In comparison to dementia praecox, manic–depression typically showed an episodic, recurrent course with a relatively good prognosis. Kraepelin observed that most manic–depressive patients returned to a normal level of functioning between episodes of depression or mania.

Despite the widespread acceptance and influence of Kraepelin's diagnostic system, other psychiatrists, most notably Adolf Meyer (1866–1950) and Sigmund Freud, proposed alternative approaches. These individuals included milder forms of disorder in their definitions of depression and placed greater emphasis on the role played by environmental events. Meyer, an American psychiatrist, preferred to talk about *depressive reactions* rather than illness. His writings stressed the important roles played by both biological and psychological functions in the process of adapting to environmental circumstances.

Two primary issues have been central in the debate regarding definitions of mood disorders. First, should these disorders be defined in a broad or narrow fashion? Table 5–1 presents a list of considerations that can be used to distinguish clinical depression from normal sadness.

Definitions of depression that incorporate all these criteria tend to be more narrow than those that include only some of them.

The second issue concerns heterogeneity. All depressed patients do not have exactly the same set of symptoms, the same pattern of onset, or the same course over time. Some patients have manic episodes, whereas others experience only depression. Some exhibit psychotic symptoms, such as delusions and hallucinations, in addition to their symptoms of mood disorder;

▼ **Freud's view of depression was built on a consideration of the relation between grief and clinical depression. His observations were concerned particularly with psychological mechanisms in response to loss.**

TABLE 5-1
Important Considerations in Distinguishing Clinical Depression from Normal Sadness

Intensity	The mood change pervades all aspects of the person and impairs social and occupational functions.
Absence of precipitants	The mood may arise in the absence of any discernible precipitant or may be grossly out of proportion to those precipitants.
Quality	The mood change is different from that experienced in normal sadness.
Associated features	The change in mood is accompanied by a cluster of signs and symptoms, including cognitive and somantic features.
History	The mood change may be preceded by a history of past episodes of elation and hyperactivity.

Source: P. C. Whybrow, H. S. Akiskal, and W. T. McKinney, Jr., 1984, *Mood Disorders: Toward a New Psychobiology.* New York: Plenum.

others do not. In some cases, the person's depression is apparently a reaction to specific life events, whereas in others the mood disorder seems to come out of nowhere. Are these qualitatively distinct forms of mood disorder, or are they different expressions of the same underlying problem? Is the distinction among the different types simply one of severity?

Contemporary Diagnostic Systems

The DSM-IV (APA, 1994) approach to classifying mood disorders recognizes several subtypes of depression, placing special emphasis on the distinction between unipolar and bipolar disorders. The overall scheme, outlined in Table 5–2, includes two types of unipolar mood disorder and three types of bipolar mood disorder.

UNIPOLAR DISORDERS

The unipolar disorders include two specific types: major depressive disorder and dysthymia. In order to meet the criteria for major depressive disorder, a person must experience at least one major depressive episode in the absence of any history of manic episodes. Table 5–3 lists the DSM-IV criteria for a major depressive episode. Although some people experience a single, isolated episode of major depression followed by complete recovery, most cases of unipolar depression follow an intermittent course with repeated episodes.

Dysthymia differs from major depression in terms of both severity and duration. Dysthymia represents a chronic mild depressive condition that has been present for many years. In order to fulfill DSM-IV criteria for this disorder, the person must, over a period of at least 2 years, exhibit a depressed mood for most of the day

---

TABLE 5–2

DSM-IV System for Classifying Mood Disorders

UNIPOLAR DISORDERS

Major Depressive Disorders
- One or more major depressive episode
- No manic or unequivocal hypomanic episodes

Dysthymic Disorders
- Depressed mood for at least 2 years
- Never without these symptoms for more than 2 months during this period
- No major depressive episode during first 2 years

BIPOLAR DISORDERS

Bipolar I Disorder
- One or more manic episode

Bipolar II Disorder
- One or more major depressive episode
- At least one hypomanic episode
- No manic episodes

Cyclothymic Disorder
- Numerous periods with hypomanic symptoms and numerous periods with depressed mood for at least 2 years
- Never without these symptoms for more than 2 months during 2-year period
- No major depressive episodes
- No manic episode during first 2 years

TABLE 5-3

Symptoms Listed in DSM-IV for Major Depressive Episode

A. Five or more of the following symptoms have been present during the same 2-week period and represent a change from previous functioning; at least one of the symptoms is either (1) depressed mood, or (2) loss of interest or pleasure.

1. Depressed mood most of the day, nearly every day, as indicated either by subjective report (for example, feels sad or empty) or observation made by others (for example, appears tearful). Note: in children and adolescents, can be irritable mood.

2. Markedly diminished interest or pleasure in all, or almost all, activities most of the day, nearly every day (as indicated either by subjective account or observation by others).

3. Significant weight loss when not dieting or weight gain (for example, a change of more than 5 percent of body weight in a month), or decrease or increase in appetite nearly every day. Note: in children, consider failure to make expected weight gains.

4. Insomnia or hypersomnia nearly every day.

5. Psychomotor agitation or retardation nearly every day (observable by others, not merely subjective feelings of restlessness or being slowed down).

6. Fatigue or loss of energy nearly every day.

7. Feelings of worthlessness or excessive or inappropriate guilt (which may be delusional) nearly every day (not merely self-reproach or guilt about being sick).

8. Diminished ability to think or concentrate, or indecisiveness, nearly every day (either by subjective account or as observed by others).

9. Recurrent thoughts of death (not just fear of dying), recurrent suicidal ideation without a specific plan, or a suicide attempt or a specific plan for committing suicide.

on more days than not. Two or more of the following symptoms must also be present:

1. Poor appetite or overeating
2. Insomnia or hypersomnia
3. Low energy or fatigue
4. Low self-esteem
5. Poor concentration or difficulty making decisions
6. Feelings of hopelessness

These symptoms must not be absent for more than 2 months at a time during the 2-year period. If, at any time during the initial 2-years, the person met criteria for a major depressive episode, the diagnosis would be major depression rather than dysthymia. As in the case of major depressive disorder, the presence of a manic episode would rule out a diagnosis of dysthymia.

The distinction between major depressive disorder and dysthymia is somewhat artificial because both sets of symptoms are frequently seen in the same person. In such cases, rather than thinking of them as separate disorders, it is more appropriate to consider them as two aspects of the same disorder, which waxes and wanes over time (Frances, First, and Pincus, 1995; Keller et al., 1995).

BIPOLAR DISORDERS

All three types of bipolar disorders involve manic or hypomanic episodes. Table 5–4 lists the DSM-IV criteria for a manic episode. The mood disturbance must be severe enough to interfere with occupational or social functioning. A person who

TABLE 5-4

Symptoms Listed in DSM-IV for Manic Episode

A. A distinct period of abnormally and persistently elevated, expansive, or irritable mood, lasting at least 1 week (or any duration if hospitalization is necessary).

B. During the period of mood disturbance, three or more of the following symptoms have persisted (four if the mood is only irritable) and have been present to a significant degree:

1. Inflated self-esteem or grandiosity.

2. Decreased need for sleep—for example, feels rested after only 3 hours of sleep.

3. More talkative than usual, or pressure to keep talking.

4. Flight of ideas or subjective experience that thoughts are racing.

5. Distractibility—that is, attention too easily drawn to unimportant or irrelevant external stimuli.

6. Increase in goal-directed activity (either socially, at work or school, or sexually) or psychomotor agitation.

7. Excessive involvement in pleasurable activities that have a high potential for painful consequences—for example, the person engages in unrestrained buying sprees, sexual indiscretions, or foolish business investments.

---

has experienced at least one manic episode would be assigned a diagnosis of bipolar I disorder. The vast majority of patients with this disorder have episodes of major depression in addition to manic episodes.

Some patients experience episodes of increased energy that are not sufficiently severe to qualify as full-blown mania. These episodes are called **hypomania.** A person who has experienced at least one major depressive episode, at least one hypomanic episode, and no full-blown manic episodes would be assigned a diagnosis of bipolar II disorder. The symptoms that are used in DSM-IV to identify a hypomanic episode are the same as those for manic episode (at least three of the seven symptoms listed in Table 5–4). The differences between manic and hypomanic episodes involve duration and severity. The symptoms need to be present for a minimum of only 4 days to meet the threshold for a hypomanic episode (as opposed to 1 week for a manic episode). The mood change in a hypomanic episode must be noticeable to others, but the disturbance must not be severe enough to impair social or occupational functioning or to require hospitalization.

Cyclothymia is considered by DSM-IV to be a chronic but less severe form of bipolar disorder. It is therefore the bipolar equivalent of dysthymia. In order to meet criteria for cyclothymia, the person must experience numerous hypomanic episodes and numerous periods of depression (or loss of interest or pleasure) during a period of 2 years. There must be no history of major depressive episodes and no clear evidence of a manic episode during the first 2 years of the disturbance.

FURTHER DESCRIPTIONS AND SUBTYPES

The DSM-IV includes several additional ways of describing subtypes of the mood disorders. These are based on two considerations: (1) more specific descriptions of symptoms that were present during the most recent episode of depression (known as *episode specifiers*) and (2) more extensive descriptions of the pattern that the disorder follows over time (known as *course specifiers*).

One episode specifier allows the clinician to describe a major depressive episode as having melancholic features. **Melancholia** is a term that is used to describe a particularly severe type of depression. Some experts believe that melancholia represents a subtype of depression that is caused by different factors than those that are responsible for other forms of depression (Zimmerman & Spitzer, 1989). The presence of melancholic features may also indicate that the person is likely to have a good response to biological forms of treatment, such as electroconvulsive therapy and antidepressant medication (Frances, First, & Pincus, 1995). In order to meet the DSM-IV criteria for melancholic features, a depressed patient must either: (1) lose the feeling of pleasure associated with all, or almost all, activities, or (2) lose the capacity to feel better—even temporarily—when something good happens. The person must also exhibit at least three of the following: (1) the depressed mood feels distinctly different from the depression a person would feel after the death of a loved one; (2) the depression is most often worst in the morning; (3) the person awakens early, at least 2 hours before usual; (4) marked psychomotor retardation or agitation; (5) significant loss of appetite or weight loss; and (6) excessive or inappropriate guilt.

Another episode specifier allows the clinician to indicate the presence of *psychotic features*—hallucinations or delusions—during the most recent episode of depression or mania. The psychotic features can be either consistent or inconsistent with the patient's mood. For example, if a depressed man reports hearing voices that tell him he is a worthless human being who deserves to suffer for his sins, the hallucinations would be considered "mood congruent psychotic features." Depressed patients who exhibit psychotic features are more likely to require hospitalization and treatment with a combination of antidepressant and antipsychotic medication.

Another episode specifier applies to women who become depressed or manic following pregnancy. A major depressive or manic episode can be specified as having a *postpartum onset* if it begins within 4 weeks after childbirth. Because the woman must meet the full criteria for an episode of major depression or mania, this category does not include minor periods of postpartum "blues," which are relatively common.

The DSM-IV course specifiers for mood disorders allow clinicians to describe further the pattern and sequence of episodes, as well as the person's adjustment between episodes. For example, the course of a bipolar disorder can be specified as *rapid cycling* if the person experiences at least four episodes of major depression, mania, or hypomania within a 12-month period. Patients whose disorder follows this problematic course are likely to show a poor response to treatment and are at greater risk than other types of bipolar patients to attempt suicide (Frances, First, & Pincus, 1995).

A mood disorder (either unipolar or bipolar) is described as following a seasonal pattern if, over a period of time, there is a regular relationship between the onset of a person's episodes and particular times of the year. The most typical seasonal pattern is one in which the person becomes depressed in the fall or winter, followed by a full recovery in the following spring or summer.

Researchers refer to a mood disorder in which the onset of episodes is regularly associated with changes in seasons as **seasonal affective disorder.**[†] The episodes most commonly occur in winter, presumably in response to fewer hours of sunlight. Seasonal disorders have attracted considerable interest among mental health professionals since the 1980s (Blehar & Rosenthal, 1989). Seasonal depression is usually characterized by somatic symptoms, such as overeating, carbohydrate craving, weight gain, fatigue, and sleeping more than usual. One study found that, among outpatients who had a history of at least three major depressive episodes, 16 percent met criteria for the seasonal pattern (Thase, 1989). Most patients with seasonal affective disorder have a unipolar disorder, but many would meet criteria for bipolar II disorder. The latter group typically become depressed in the winter followed by a mood reversal to hypomania in the spring. Relatively few have bipolar I disorder (Oren & Rosenthal, 1992).

Course and Outcome

To consider the typical course and outcome of mood disorders, it is useful to study unipolar and bipolar disorders separately. Most studies point to clear-cut differences between these two conditions in terms of age of onset and prognosis (Perris, 1992).

[†] "Affect" and "mood" are sometimes used interchangeably in psychiatric terminology. Depression and mania were called "affective disorders" in DSM-III.

UNIPOLAR DISORDERS

Data regarding the onset and course of unipolar mood disorders must be viewed with some caution because virtually all studies have focused exclusively on the people who have sought treatment for their depression. Very little is known about untreated depressions, but it seems reasonable to assume that they are likely to remit spontaneously in a short period of time.

People with unipolar mood disorders typically have their first episode in middle age; the average age of onset is in the mid-forties. The length of episodes varies widely. DSM-IV sets the minimum duration at 2 weeks, but they can last much longer. In one large-scale follow-up study, 10 percent of the patients had depressive episodes that lasted more than 2 years (Thornicroft & Sartorius, 1993). Most unipolar patients will have at least two depressive episodes. The mean number of lifetime episodes is five or six.

The results of long-term follow-up studies of treated patients indicate that major depressive disorder is frequently a chronic and recurrent condition, in which episodes of severe symptoms may alternate with periods of full or partial recovery (Keller, 1994; Thornicroft & Sartorius, 1993). When a person's symptoms are diminished or improved, the disorder is considered to be in **remission,** or a period of recovery. **Relapse** is a return of active symptoms in a person who has recovered from a previous episode.

Approximately half of all unipolar patients recover within 6 months of the beginning of an episode. The probability that a patient will recover from an episode goes down after 6 months, and 10 to 20 percent have not recovered after 5 years. Among those who recover, 40 percent relapse within 1 year. The risk of relapse goes down as the period of remission increases. In other words, the longer the person remains free of depression, the better his or her chance of avoiding relapse. Older patients tend to relapse more quickly than younger patients, and females relapse more quickly than males.

BIPOLAR DISORDERS

Onset of bipolar mood disorders usually occurs between the ages of 28 and 33 years, which is younger than the average age of onset for unipolar disorders. The first episode is just as likely to be manic as depressive in nature (Coryell & Winokur, 1992). The average duration of a manic episode runs between 2 and 3 months. Bipolar II patients tend to have shorter and less severe episodes (Coryell et al., 1985; Keller, 1987).

The onset of a manic episode is not always sudden. Jamison (1996) noted, for example:

I did not wake up one day to find myself mad. Life should be so simple. Rather, I gradually became aware that my life and mind were going at an ever faster and faster clip until finally, over the course of my first summer on the faculty, they both had spun wildly and absolutely out of control. But the acceleration from quick thought to chaos was a slow and beautifully seductive one. (p. 68)

The long-term course of bipolar disorders is most often episodic, and the prognosis is mixed (Winokur et al., 1994). Most patients have more than one episode, and bipolar patients tend to have more episodes than unipolar patients. The length of intervals between episodes is difficult to predict. The long-term prognosis is mixed for patients with bipolar mood disorder. Although some patients recover and function quite well, others experience continued impairment. Several studies that have followed bipolar patients over periods of up to 10 years have found that 40 to 50 percent of patients are able to achieve a sustained recovery from the disorder. Many patients, however, remain chronically disabled. Rapid cycling patients are less likely to recover from an episode and are more likely to relapse after they do recover (Keller et al., 1993).

Epidemiology

Questions about the frequency and distribution of mood disorders are difficult to answer precisely. One problem is the widespread variation in the definition of clinical depression. Some investigators have adopted a broad approach

to diagnosis, whereas others have focused on a narrow range of severely disturbed patients. The procedure used to identify potential cases is also important. Many of the early epidemiological studies focused on patients treated at hospitals and mental health centers. Unfortunately, large numbers of people experience serious depression without wanting, or being able to seek, professional help. Formal statistics must therefore be considered with caution.

Several large epidemiological studies providing detailed information regarding mood disorders have been completed in recent years. Perhaps most notable among these is the Epidemiologic Catchment Area (ECA) Study, in which nearly 20,000 residents of five U.S. communities were interviewed (Robins & Regier, 1991).

Incidence and Prevalence

Unipolar depression is one of the most common forms of psychopathology. Among people who were interviewed for the ECA study, approximately 3 percent met DSM-III criteria for major depressive episode within a given 6-month period. An additional 3 percent met criteria for dysthymia in the same period. Slightly less than 1 percent met criteria for a manic episode (Weissman et al., 1991). Thus approximately 6 percent of the population in this sample was suffering from a diagnosable mood disorder during a period of 6 months. Unipolar disorders are much more common than bipolar disorders. The ratio of unipolar to bipolar disorders is at least 5:1 (Smith & Weissman, 1992).

Lifetime risk for major depressive disorder was approximately 5 percent, averaged across sites in the ECA program (Weissman et al., 1991). The lifetime risk for dysthymia was approximately 3 percent, and the lifetime risk for bipolar I disorder was close to 1 percent. Almost half the people who met diagnostic criteria for dysthymia had also experienced an episode of major depression at some point in their lives. At each of the sites examined by Robins and her colleagues, the lifetime prevalence of all types of mood disorders combined (about 8 percent) ranked third behind substance use disorders (about 17 percent) and anxiety disorders (about 12 percent). When you consider the magnitude of these numbers, you should also know that other, more recent studies have produced even higher figures for the lifetime prevalence of mood disorders (see Kessler et al., 1994). Therefore the prevalence estimates for mood disorders in the ECA study are probably conservative.

Because the ECA study identified a representative sample of community residents rather than patients already in treatment, it also allows some insight regarding the proportion of depressed people who seek professional help for their problems. Slightly more than 30 percent of those people who met DSM-III criteria for a mood disorder made contact with a mental health professional during the 6 months prior to their interview (Shapiro et al., 1984). These data indicate that a substantial proportion of people who are clinically depressed do not receive professional treatment for their disorders. Finding ways to help these people represents an important challenge for psychologists and psychiatrists who treat mood disorders.

Gender Differences

Women are 2 or 3 times more vulnerable to depression than men are (Nolen-Hoeksema, 1990). This pattern has been reported in study after study, using samples of treated patients as well as community surveys, and regardless of the assessment procedures employed. The increased prevalence of depression among women is apparently limited to unipolar disorders. In the ECA program, for example, the lifetime prevalence rates for major depression were 7 percent in women but only 2.6 percent in men. Relatively large gender differences were also observed for dysthymia, with lifetime prevalence rates of 4.1 percent in women and 2.2 percent in men. Gender differences were not observed, however, for bipolar mood disorders. The lifetime prevalence rates for bipolar I disorder were 0.9 percent for women and 0.7 percent for men (Weissman et al., 1991).

Some observers have suggested that the high rates for unipolar mood disorders in women reflect shortcomings in the data-collection process. Women might simply be more likely than men to seek treatment or to be labeled as being depressed. Another argument holds that culturally determined sanctions make it more difficult for men to admit to subjective feelings of distress such as hopelessness and despair. None of these alternatives has been substantiated by empirical evidence (Nolen-Hoeksema, 1990). Research studies clearly indicate that the higher prevalence of depression among women is genuine.

Cross-Cultural Differences

Questions about the relation between culture and mood disorders were raised early in the twentieth century, when Kraepelin (1921)

▲ **Myrna Weissman, a professor of psychiatry at Columbia University, is one of the leading investigators in the study of the epidemiology of depression.**

visited the island of Java (now part of Indonesia). His impression, based on visits to psychiatric hospitals in that country, was that the disorder that he called "manic–depressive insanity" was just as common in Java as it was in Europe. He also noted, however, that patients in Java suffered "almost exclusively states of excitement and often confusion" (Leff, 1992). Manic episodes apparently were much more common in this culture than were episodes of major depression.

Comparisons of emotional expression and emotional disorder across cultural boundaries encounter a number of methodological problems. One problem involves vocabulary. Each culture has its own ways of interpreting reality, including different styles of expressing or communicating symptoms of physical and emotional disorder (Good & Kleinman, 1985b; Katschnig & Amering, 1990). Words and concepts that are used to describe illness behaviors in one culture might not exist in other cultures. For example, some African cultures have only one word for both anger and sadness. Interesting adaptations are therefore required to translate questions that are supposed to tap experiences such as anxiety and depression. One investigation, which employed a British interview schedule that had been translated into Yoruba—a language spoken in Nigeria—used the phrase "the heart goes weak" to represent depression (Leff, 1988).

We must remember that our own diagnostic categories have been developed within a specific cultural setting; they are not culture-free and are not necessarily any more reasonable than the ways in which other cultures describe and categorize their own behavioral and emotional disorders. One illustration of this principle comes from the study of *neurasthenia*, which is a relatively common problem in China but is rarely diagnosed in Western societies. Although the diagnostic term was not introduced to Chinese physicians until the twentieth century, the concept fits closely with ancient traditions in Chinese folk medicine. Neurasthenic patients present many different complaints that focus primarily on physical symptoms: headaches, insomnia, dizziness, pain, weakness, loss of energy, poor appetite, tingling in the head, and so on. Related psychological symptoms include memory problems, anxiety, disturbing dreams, and poor concentration.

Arthur Kleinman, a psychiatrist and anthropologist at Harvard University, and a group of Chinese psychiatrists studied 100 neurasthenic patients at an outpatient clinic associated with a Chinese medical school (Kleinman, 1982). Interviews were conducted using a translation of an American diagnostic interview schedule, and diagnoses were assigned using DSM-III criteria. In all, 87 of the 100 patients received a diagnosis of major depressive disorder, and 69 received a diagnosis of anxiety disorder. Thus most of the patients fit the criteria for both depression and anxiety.

The cross-cultural differences suggested by Kleinman's study have been confirmed by a number of large-scale research projects, including the World Health Organization's Collaborative Study on Depression (WHO, 1983), which examined cultural variations in symptomatology among depressed patients in Canada, India, Iran,

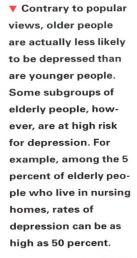

▼ Contrary to popular views, older people are actually less likely to be depressed than are younger people. Some subgroups of elderly people, however, are at high risk for depression. For example, among the 5 percent of elderly people who live in nursing homes, rates of depression can be as high as 50 percent.

Japan, and Switzerland. The WHO study found comparable overall frequencies of mood disorders across all five countries, but the specific symptoms expressed by the patients varied considerably from one culture to the next. For example, depressed patients in Europe and North America were more likely to express feelings of guilt and suicidal ideas, while patients in non-Western countries were more likely to exhibit somatic symptoms.

These cross-cultural comparisons suggest that, at its most basic level, clinical depression is a universal phenomenon that is not limited to Western or urban societies. They also indicate that a person's cultural experiences, including linguistic, educational, and social factors, may play an important role in shaping the manner in which different people express and cope with the anguish of depression. Cross-cultural variations should also be kept in mind when clinicians attempt to identify central or defining features of depression. We will return to this point later in the chapter when we discuss the rationale behind studies that rely on animal models of depression.

Risk for Mood Disorders Across the Life Span

Age is an important consideration in the epidemiology of mood disorders. Some readers might expect that the prevalence of depression would be higher among older people than among younger people. This was, in fact, what many clinicians expected prior to large-scale epidemiological investigations, such as the ECA study. This belief may stem from the casual observation that many older people experience brief episodic states of acute unhappiness, often precipitated by changes in status (for example, retirement, relocation) and loss of significant others (for example, children moving away, deaths of friends and relatives). But brief episodes of sadness and grief are not the same thing as clinical depression.

Although many people mistakenly identify depression with the elderly, data from the ECA project suggest that mood disorders actually are most frequent among young and middle-aged adults. Prevalence rates for major depressive episodes and dysthymia were significantly lower for people over the age of 65. The frequency of bipolar disorders was also low in the oldest age groups. These data are illustrated in Figure 5–1. Notice that rates of both major depression and bipolar I disorder are

lowest in the oldest age group. When unipolar and bipolar mood disorders are combined to examine gender differences and age, the lowest rates are found in the oldest age group for both men and women.

Several explanations have been offered for this pattern. One interpretation is based on the fact that elderly people are more likely to experience memory impairments (see Further Thoughts in Chapter 14). People who are in their 70s and 80s may have more trouble remembering, and therefore may fail to report, episodes of depression that occurred several months before the research interview is conducted. Also, because mood disorders are associated with increased mortality (for example, suicide), many severely depressed people might not have

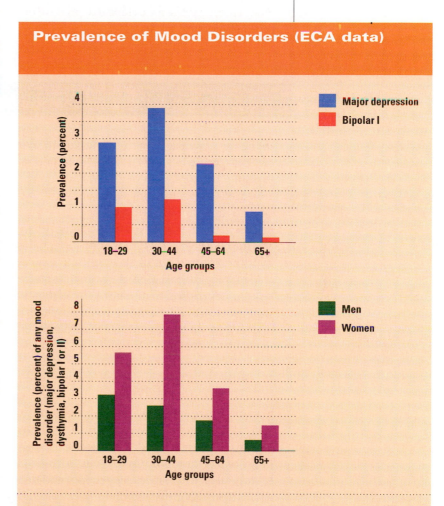

FIGURE 5-1: (*top*) Twelve-month prevalence for unipolar and bipolar mood disorders in different age groups. (*bottom*) Twelve-month prevalence for mood disorder in men and women in different age groups.

Source: M.M. Weissman, M.L. Bruce, P.J. Leaf, L.P. Florio, and C. Holzer, 1991, Affective disorders. In L.N. Robins and D.A. Regier (Eds.), *Psychiatric Disorders in America: The Epidemiologic Catchment Area Study.* New York: Free Press, p. 60.

survived into old age. These are both plausible hypotheses that may have influenced the results of the ECA study and related investigations. Nevertheless, the same pattern has been observed in several studies, and most investigators now believe that the effect is genuine: Clinical depression is less common among elderly people than it is among younger adults (Lewinsohn et al., 1993; Wittchen, Knauper, & Kessler, 1994).

Finally, it should be noted that the frequency of depression is much higher among certain subgroups of elderly people. For example, the prevalence of depression is particularly high among those who are about to enter residential care facilities in comparison to a random sample of elderly people living in the community. One study found that approximately 1 out of 3 elderly applicants for community social services would meet criteria for a clinical depressive disorder (Goldberg, 1970).

Comparisons Across Generations

The ECA findings on age and depression also raise another important question: Has the frequency of depression increased in recent years? The answer is apparently yes. People born after World War II seem to be more likely to develop mood disorders than were people from previous generations. In fact, several studies have reported a consistent trend toward higher lifetime rates of depression in successively younger generations (Lavori et al., 1987; Wittchen, Knauper, & Kessler, 1994). The average age of onset for clinical depression also seems to be younger in people who were born more recently. This kind of pattern is sometimes called a *birth cohort trend*.

Etiological Considerations and Research

In the next few pages we turn our attention to current speculation and knowledge about causes of mood disorders. Several of the hypotheses are based on careful consideration of the specific symptoms of mood disorders—what depressed people say, ways in which they behave, and the effects they have on other people. Other hypotheses grow out of an attempt to explain epidemiological data. Why are women at greater risk for depression than men? Why is depression more prevalent among younger generations? Why do bipolar mood disorders seem to run in families? A truly useful etiological theory must address these questions.

Rather than presenting separate discussions for unipolar and bipolar mood disorders, we have organized the information on etiology according to social, psychological, and biological considerations. Most research on the etiology of bipolar mood disorders has focused on biological factors, especially genetics and neurochemistry. Our discussion of psychological factors will focus exclusively on the etiology of unipolar depression.

Social Factors

It should not be surprising that much of the literature on depression focuses on interpersonal loss and separation. From birth to death, our lives are intertwined with those of other people. We are fundamentally social organisms, and we feel sad when someone close to us dies. Similar feelings occasionally follow major disappointments, such as failure to win acceptance to the school of our choice or being fired from a job. In these cases, rather than losing other people, some clinicians have suggested that we may be losing "social roles" or ways in which we think about ourselves.

Various theories of depression have been built around a consideration of the impact of stressful life events. Beginning around the turn of the century, psychodynamic theories emphasized the central role played by interpersonal relationships and loss of significant others in setting the stage for depression as well as in bringing about a depressive episode.

FREUD'S THEORY OF DEPRESSION
Freud's classic paper on the etiology of depression focused on a comparison of clinical depression with the normal process of grieving (Freud, 1917/1961). Among the various symptoms of depression, Freud was particularly interested in self-reproach and guilt. The fundamental assumption of Freud's view was that depressed people are, in fact, not so much complaining about themselves as they are angry with someone else. The other person is presumably someone with

whom the patient has had a very close relationship and who has either died or been lost in some other way—either in reality or in the patient's imagination. Instead of recognizing and dealing with this anger consciously, depressed people identify with the other person and direct their anger toward themselves.

Freud further argued that the distinction between people who mourn the loss of another and those who become clinically depressed is reflected in the types of interpersonal relationships they form. People predisposed to depression tend to form "narcissistic" relationships in which they depend on the other person to maintain their self-esteem. This dependence invariably leads to negative as well as positive emotions, resulting in an intense ambivalence. The depressed individual cannot express this ambivalence openly, however, for fear of alienating and perhaps losing the other person. When the other person is no longer available, the anger is turned inward and directed toward the self; this expression of inwardly directed anger is presumably depression.

Freud's theory laid the intellectual foundation for many subsequent studies of psychological and social factors in the development and maintenance of unipolar depression. He focused interest on the possibility that stressful life events may precipitate the onset of mood disorders. (We consider contemporary research on this issue in the next section.) Freud's notion of narcissistic relationships also anticipated subsequent studies of social skills in depression and the importance of interpersonal relationships over the course of mood disorders. We will review these considerations in a later section on psychological factors.

STRESSFUL LIFE EVENTS AND UNIPOLAR DISORDERS

Several investigations have explored the relationships between stressful life events and the development of unipolar mood disorders. Do people who become clinically depressed actually experience an increased number of stressful life events? The answer is yes. The experience of stressful life events is associated with an increased probability that a person will become depressed. This correlation has been demonstrated many times (Paykel & Cooper, 1992).

Once the relatively strong relationship between stressful life events and depression was found, difficult methodological issues had to be faced before it could be interpreted. One particularly difficult problem involves the direction of the relationship between life events and mood disorders. For example, being fired from a job might lead a person to become depressed. On the other hand, the onset of a depressive episode, with its associated difficulties in energy and concentration, could easily affect the person's job performance and lead to being fired. Therefore, if depressed people experience more stressful events, what is the direction of effect? Does failure lead to depression, or does depression lead to failure?

The use of prospective research designs, in which subjects are followed over time, has allowed investigators to address the question of cause and effect. Prospective studies have found that stressful life events are useful in predicting the subsequent onset of unipolar depression (Lewinsohn, Hoberman, & Rosenbaum, 1988). This evidence supports the argument that, in many cases, stressful life events contribute to the onset of mood disorders.

Although many kinds of negative events are associated with depression, a special class of circumstances—those involving major losses of important people or roles—seems to play a crucial role in precipitating unipolar depression (Monroe & Simons, 1991). This conclusion is based, in large part, on a series of studies reported by George Brown and his colleagues. Their studies have compared the living circumstances and life experiences of depressed and nondepressed women, regardless of whether they are receiving treatment for their problems.

Brown and Harris (1978) found that "severe" events—those that are particularly threatening and have long-term consequences for the woman's adjustment—increased the probability that a woman would become depressed. The frequency of nonsevere events was roughly equivalent for depressed and nondepressed women. Only 16 percent of the events that were reported by all of the women in the study were considered severe by these standards. Most cases of depression appeared after a single severe event. (The Research Close-Up provides further details regarding the nature of these events.) Brown's data suggest that depression is not caused by an accumulation of ordinary hassles and difficulties to which

▲ Stressful life events and depression are clearly correlated, but the direction of this relationship is not always clear. For example, does the loss of a job lead a person to become depressed? Or does the onset of depression interfere with the person's ability to perform the job, thereby increasing the risk of losing it?

Social Origins of Depression in Women

Some of the most influential studies on the link between depression and stressful life events have been conducted by George Brown, a sociologist, and Tirril Harris, a clinical psychologist, both at the Royal Holloway and New Bedford College (University of London in England). One of their investigations focused on 400 working-class women between the ages of 18 and 50 with children living at home (Brown, Bifulco, & Harris, 1987). This sample was chosen because previous research had demonstrated that women with children living at home are particularly vulnerable to depression (Brown & Harris, 1978).

The study was completed in two phases, separated by approximately 1 year. During the first phase, the investigators asked each woman an extensive series of questions about her psychological adjustment (including symptoms of mental disorders as well as self-esteem) and her living circumstances (including personal relationships and social support). During the second phase, the investigators collected information regarding life events and difficulties that had occurred during the follow-up year. They also inquired, once again, about symptoms of depression and other mental disorders. They identified cases of depression using specific diagnostic criteria that ensured that the symptoms were comparable to those found among patients being treated for mood disorders.

The investigators made a concerted effort to describe each life event and to consider the circumstances in which it occurred. Each interviewer recorded detailed descriptions that were later provided to a panel of judges. The judges in turn rated how threatening each event would be to an average woman under the same living circumstances. Brown and his colleagues were particularly interested in the meaning that the events held for the woman. Judges were allowed to consider all information except the woman's mental status and the actual manner in which she responded to the event.

Results were reported only for the 303 women who were not depressed at the time of the first assessment and who completed the second phase of assessment. Within this sample, 130 women experienced a severe event during the follow-up year. Of these women, 29 (22 percent) became depressed. Among the 173 women who did not experience a severe event, only 3 (2 percent) became depressed. In other words, 29 out of 32 (90 percent) women who became depressed had experienced a severe event in the 6 months prior to onset. This pattern is consistent with other reports that indicate a close association between stressful life events and depression.

Severe events increased the probability of depression, but 78 percent of the 130 women who experienced a severe event in the follow-up year did not become depressed. What is the difference between the circumstances of women who become depressed after a severe event and those who do not? The investigators decided to examine the relationship between severe events and several other aspects of each woman's situation. One consideration involved ongoing difficulties that had been identified at the time of the first interview. Some severe events matched prior difficulties. For example, if a woman's pregnancy was rated as a severe event because she lived in poor housing, the event would have been rated as matching, or linked to, the difficulty. Another consideration involved areas of the woman's commitment, such as children, marriage, and employment, which had also been identified during the first phase of assessment.

The results of these analyses are illustrated in Table 5–5. Remember that all the women had experienced a severe event during the follow-up period. Prior difficulties and prior commitments were both significantly associated with risk for onset of depression after a severe event. In those situations where the severe event matched an ongoing area of difficulty, almost half of the women (16 out of 35) became depressed. An example would be if the woman's husband left home following a history of marital conflict. Only 14 percent of the women became depressed (13 out of 95) if their severe event did *not* match a prior difficulty. Similarly, women who experienced a severe event that matched an area to which they had previously demonstrated marked commitment were almost 3 times more likely to become depressed than those women whose severe events did not match an area of commitment. Of the 11 women who experienced severe events that matched both a prior difficulty and an area of major commitment, 8 became depressed during the 1-year follow-up.

This study is important for two primary reasons. First, the use of a prospective design minimizes questions about the direction of effect. For these women, depression clearly followed their stressful experiences. Second, the data point to a particularly powerful relationship between the onset of depression and certain kinds of stressful life events. The likelihood that a woman will become depressed is especially high if she experiences a severe event in an area of her life that represents a serious commitment and in which she has experienced ongoing difficulties. ■

TABLE 5-5		
Onset of Depression Among 130 Women Who Experienced a Severe Event		
Description of Life Event	**Number of Women**	**Percent Depressed**
Event matches prior difficulty	35	46
Event does not match prior difficulty	95	14
Event matches prior commitment	40	40
Event does not match prior commitment	90	14

Source: G. W. Brown, A. Bifulco, and T. O. Harris, 1987, Life events, vulnerability, and onset of depression: Some refinements, *British Journal of Psychiatry, 150,* 30–42.

most of us are exposed on a daily basis (Monroe & Simons, 1991).

The relationship between stressful life events and depression is not entirely one-way; it runs in both directions. In comparison to women who are not depressed and women with other medical disorders, unipolar depressed women have also been found to generate higher levels of stress, especially with regard to interpersonal circumstances, such as marital conflict (Hammen, 1991). Poor interpersonal problem-solving skills appear to be one important link in this relationship (Davila et al., 1995). This pattern suggests a dynamic process that may lead to an escalation of stress. Independent stressors, which are not caused by the person's own behavior, contribute to the onset of depression. The depressed person then behaves in a maladaptive fashion, leading to even higher levels of stress and perhaps a further deterioration in his or her mood. We will return to our consideration of interpersonal behaviors later in the section on psychological factors.

SOCIAL FACTORS AND BIPOLAR DISORDERS

Most investigations of stressful life events have been concerned with unipolar depression. Considerably less attention has been paid to bipolar mood disorders, but some evidence suggests that the weeks preceding the onset of a manic episode are marked by an increased frequency of stressful life events (Johnson & Roberts, 1995). Stressful life events are also likely to trigger a relapse in bipolar patients who have recovered from previous episodes. Some people with bipolar disorder are less sensitive to stress than others. One study found that bipolar patients whose personality style was extroverted were less likely to relapse, even if they were exposed to a high level of stress (Swendsen, Hammen, Heller, & Gitlin, 1995). This effect might be explained in terms of the ability of extroverted people to construct and maintain a substantial social network that is able to help them cope with difficult experiences.

Aversive patterns of emotional expression and communication within the family can also have a negative impact on the adjustment of people with bipolar mood disorders. David Miklowitz, a clinical psychologist at the University of Colorado, has studied patterns of interaction in the families of bipolar patients (Miklowitz, Goldstein, & Nuechterlein, 1995). One important question in these studies involves the relation between frequency of relapse and the emotional climate within the families. Patients living with family members who are hostile toward or critical of the patient are more likely to relapse shortly after being discharged from the hospital (Miklowitz et al., 1988). This evidence indicates that the course of bipolar mood disorder can be influenced by the social environment in which the person is living.

Psychological Factors

Severe events are clearly related to the onset of depression, but they do not provide a complete account of who will become depressed. Many women who do not become depressed also experience severe events. In the study reported by Brown and Harris (1978), only 1 out of every 5 women who reported a severe event in the preceding year became depressed. Therefore the investigators looked for characteristics that might identify women who were more likely than others to become depressed if they experienced a severe event. They found four such features, which they called "vulnerability factors." These included (1) absence of an intimate, confiding relationship, (2) having several young children at home, (3) lacking employment away from home, and (4) loss of her mother at an early age. Vulnerability factors of this sort presumably reduce the woman's self-esteem and her sense that she will be able to cope successfully in the face of adversity (Brown, Bifulco, & Andrews, 1990). If a threatening event occurs at a time when a woman is less able to be hopeful and to persevere, the probability of serious depression is increased.

Several psychological factors may contribute to a person's vulnerability to stressful life events. In the following pages, we will consider two principal areas that have received attention in the research literature: cognitive factors and social skills. These studies have focused almost exclusively on unipolar mood disorders, so we will not discuss bipolar disorders in this section.

COGNITIVE RESPONSES TO FAILURE AND DISAPPOINTMENT

Cognitive theories concerning the origins of unipolar depression have become extremely influential in recent years. These theories are based on the recognition that humans are not only social organisms; they are also thinking organisms. Cognitive therapists assume that the ways in which people think about and perceive their world have an important influence on the way that they feel. Two people may react very differently to the same event, in large part because they may interpret the event differently.

Beck's Cognitive Model   Aaron Beck, a psychiatrist at the University of Pennsylvania, has been one of the most influential proponents of a cognitive view of depression (see, for example, Beck, 1967, 1974, 1984). Like Freud, Beck began with a primary interest in the things that depressed people say, particularly their self-critical thoughts and their extremely pessimistic views of their environment. He has defined the *depressive triad*—negative, demeaning views of the self, the world, and the future—as being central to our understanding of mood disorders. In contrast to the psychodynamic position, however, Beck has not chosen to view depressed people's critical self-statements as a reflection of their anger toward others. He argues instead that the negative things that depressed people say represent direct manifestations of fundamental cognitive distortions or erroneous ways of thinking about themselves. "The depressed person is overly sensitive to obstacles to goal-directed activity, interprets trivial impediments as substantial, reads disparagement into innocuous statements by others, and, at the same time, devalues himself or herself" (Kovacs & Beck, 1978, p. 242). According to Beck's theory, these pervasive and persistent negative cognitions play a central role in the onset of depression.

Beck has described various types of distortions, errors, and biases that characterize the thinking of depressed people. These include tendencies to assign global, personal meaning to experiences of failure; to overgeneralize conclusions about the self based on negative experiences; to draw arbitrary inferences about the self in the absence of supporting evidence (often in spite of contradictory evidence); to selectively recall events with negative consequences; and to exaggerate the importance of negative events while simultaneously discounting the significance of positive events.

Several research studies have demonstrated that these types of cognitive distortions are indeed more common among depressed people than among people who are not depressed. Most of the evidence suggests, however, that cognitive errors are present during episodes of depression, but they are not readily apparent prior to the onset of an episode or after its resolution (see, for example, Barnett & Gotlib, 1988; Rhode, Lewinsohn, & Seeley, 1990).

How might these self-defeating biases eventually lead to the onset of depression? Why aren't they evident prior to the onset of an episode? According to Beck's theory, cognitive distortions and "depressogenic premises" (for example, "I should be able to endure any hardship with grace," "I should be smart and capable all the time") combine to form a general pattern or cognitive **schema** that guides the ways in which people perceive and interpret events in their environment. Schemas are described as enduring and highly organized cognitive structures—representations of prior experience. Although schemas may be latent—that is, not prominently represented in the person's conscious awareness at any given point in time—they are presumably reactivated when the person experiences a similar event. Depressive schemas increase the probability that the person will overreact to similar stressful events in the future.

Hopelessness Theory Another, related view of the role played by cognitive events has been proposed by Lynn Abramson, Gerald Metalsky, and Lauren Alloy, clinical psychologists at the University of Wisconsin, Lawrence University, and Temple University, respectively. Their theory has evolved out of **learned helplessness theory** (Seligman, 1974, 1975). The original version of learned helplessness theory as proposed by Martin Seligman suggested that depression was similar to the passive behavior shown by animals who had been exposed to inescapable shock in laboratory experiments. The theory argued that people who are depressed do not recognize a contingency between their behavior and outcomes in their environments. In other words, they believe that they are helpless in the sense that they cannot control events in their lives. The theory was revised (Abramson, Seligman, & Teasdale, 1978) to account for various problems that had been noted with the original version. For example, most people do not become depressed when they experience a negative event that is beyond their control.

This perspective has most recently been described in terms of **hopelessness** (Abramson, Metalsky, & Alloy, 1989). According to this view, depression may be associated with the expectation that very desirable events probably will not occur or that aversive events probably will occur regardless of what the person does. Hopelessness refers to the person's negative expectations about future events and the associated belief that these events cannot be controlled. After a negative life event has occurred, the probability that the person will become depressed is a function of the explanations and importance that the person ascribes to these events. These explanations are known as *causal attributions*.

Abramson, Metalsky, and Alloy argue that some people exhibit a general "depressogenic" attributional style that is characterized by a tendency to explain negative events in terms of internal, stable, global factors. For example, after failing an important exam, the person who possesses a depressogenic attributional style would be likely to think that her poor performance was the result of her own inadequacies (internal), which she has recognized for a long time and which will persist into the future (stable), and which are also responsible for her failure in many other important tasks, both academic and otherwise (global). As in Beck's description of negative schemas, attributional style is not seen as a sufficient cause of depression. It does represent an important predisposition to depression, however, to the extent that people with a generalized depressogenic attributional style are more likely to develop hopelessness if they experience a negative life event.

The literature regarding cognitive factors in depression is filled with controversy as well as with interesting speculation (Brewin, 1985; Segal & Dobson, 1992). Research studies provide some support for the argument that attributional style is useful in predicting people's responses to negative events (Metalsky et al., 1993). Furthermore, people who make the type of cognitive errors that are characteristic of depression are also more likely to generate high levels of stress in their own environments (Simons, Angell, Monroe, & Thase, 1993). However, some reviewers have concluded that, although depressed people may present themselves in a negative light on various questionnaires, differences between groups are inconsistent and are smaller than the theories would seem to predict, and cognitive distortions are generally not unique to depressed patients (Coyne, 1992). Although cognitive factors may play an important role in mood disorders, they are only one piece of the etiological puzzle.

INTERPERSONAL FACTORS AND SOCIAL SKILLS

If cognitive factors alone cannot account for the relation between stressful life events and the onset of depression, what other considerations might be important? Several investigators have suggested that, in addition to how we think about negative or stressful experiences, the ways in which we actually respond to these events may also influence the probability that we will become depressed. In other words, it's not just how you think about an event or circumstance but the things that you actually do that will determine its eventual outcome. This focus on overt behavior has been stimulated, in part, by the application of learning theory to the study of depression.

Lewinsohn's Behavioral Model Behavioral psychologists who have studied depression have traditionally focused on the absence of certain behaviors—on reduced activity levels and a withdrawal from social interactions. Peter Lewinsohn (1974), a psychologist at the University of Oregon, proposed an influential behavioral model in which depression is seen as the eventual product of a reduction in response-contingent positive reinforcement. In other words, depressed people presumably become less active because their behavior is not followed by positive reinforcement. The decrease in adaptive behavior, which is produced by this prolonged "extinction schedule," presumably has a negative impact on the person's mood. Thus a vicious cycle is set in motion: Reduced rate of response-contingent positive reinforcement leads to reduced activity, which is followed by a further reduction in reinforcement, and so on.

The behavioral model suggests that the initial reduction in response-contingent positive reinforcement may be the result of several factors, including the range of events that the person finds pleasant, the availability of these events within the person's present environment, and the extent to which the person is able to elicit reinforcement from his or her environment. Lewinsohn has paid considerable attention to the latter category, including the social skills with which people form friendships.

The role of interpersonal relationships is perhaps the most important aspect of this model. According to Lewinsohn, some "depressed behaviors," such as crying, complaining, and criticizing oneself, may be initially reinforced by other people in their attempts to provide comfort and support. By making these social contacts contingent upon the expression of a depressed mood, significant others may unintentionally increase the frequency and stability of their friend's depression. Lewinsohn proposed further that the continued manifestation of depressed behaviors has an aversive impact on other people. Thus the depressed person's few remaining sources of social support will eventually be driven away.

The behavioral model has stimulated interest in the role played by social skills and interpersonal relationships in mood disorders. How does the depressed person cope with stressful events and respond to other people? What types of responses does the patient elicit from others? What are the extent and form of social resources that are available to help support the person during a crisis? Notice that in many ways these questions bring us back to the issue of intimacy, which Brown and Harris identified as one vulnerability factor in their model of depression, as well as the notion of interpersonal dependency, which has been an important consideration in psychodynamic views of depression.

Research on Interpersonal Factors James Coyne, a psychologist at the University of Michigan, has studied the ways in which depressed people interact with those around them (Coyne, 1976; Coyne, Downey, & Boergers, 1993). This interpersonal perspective, which emphasizes the active, reciprocal nature of our social environments, has produced some interesting findings regarding factors that contribute to depression. The assumptions behind this model are quite different from those incorporated in more cognitively oriented theories. For example, Beck might argue that faulty processing of information from their environment leads those who are depressed to believe (erroneously) that their relationships with other people are inadequate. Coyne suggests that depressed people may actually behave in ways that have a genuinely negative effect on other people, thus alienating themselves from friends and family members.

Several research studies have demonstrated that depressed people do indeed have a negative impact on other people's moods and on their nonverbal behavior (Joiner & Metalsky, 1995; Segrin & Abramson, 1994). In addition, depressed people have smaller and less supportive social networks than do people who are not depressed. They know fewer people, interact with them less often, and consider them to be less supportive. Family interactions are generally more negative and argumentative. Perhaps most importantly, these maladaptive patterns of interpersonal relationships are ongoing characteristics of the individual's behavior that persist into periods of symptomatic remission. They are not evident only during active episodes of major depression (Gotlib & Hammen, 1992).

Response Styles and Gender A slightly different aspect of coping behavior may help to explain gender differences in the frequency of depression. Susan Nolen-Hoeksema (1990, 1994), a psychologist at the University of

▲ **Peter Lewinsohn, whose behavioral model of depression inspired much of the research on interpersonal factors in depression. His longitudinal studies have contributed important information regarding the role of cognitive factors and social skills in the development of depression.**

Michigan, has proposed that the manner in which a person responds to the onset of a depressed mood will influence the duration and the severity of the mood. The model emphasizes two different response styles. Some people respond to feelings of depression by turning their attention inward, contemplating the causes and implications of their sadness. Nolen-Hoeksema refers to this as a *ruminative style*. Writing in a diary or talking extensively with a friend about how one feels are indications of a ruminative style. Other people employ a *distracting style* to divert themselves from their unpleasant mood. They work on hobbies, play sports, or otherwise become involved in activities that draw their attention away from symptoms of depression.

The first hypothesis of Nolen-Hoeksema's model is that people who engage in ruminative responses have longer and more severe episodes of depression than do people who engage in distracting responses. Her second hypothesis is that women are more likely to employ a ruminative style in response to depression, whereas men are more likely to employ a distracting style. Because the ruminative style leads to episodes of greater duration and intensity, women are more susceptible to depression than men are.

Research evidence provides some support for both of Nolen-Hoeksema's hypotheses. A ruminative response style tends to be associated with longer and more severely depressed moods, and women are more likely than men to exhibit a ruminative style in response to depressed mood (Butler & Nolen-Hoeksema, 1994; Nolen-Hoeksema, Morrow, & Frederickson, 1993). The model has been tested most extensively with analogue subjects, normal subjects who were experiencing a dysphoric mood. Relatively little information is available regarding its applicability with clinically depressed subjects.

INTEGRATION OF COGNITIVE AND INTERPERSONAL FACTORS

Ian Gotlib, a clinical psychologist at Stanford University, and Constance Hammen, a clinical psychologist at UCLA, have proposed a conceptual framework for understanding unipolar disorders (Gotlib & Hammen, 1992). Their model is especially interesting because it considers depression in terms of several stages: vulnerability, onset, and maintenance. Cognitive factors and interpersonal skills play an important role within each stage. The model emphasizes the importance of ongoing transactions between the person and his or her environment. Adverse events influence a person's mood, but people also play an active role in selecting and shaping their own environments.

Vulnerability to depression is influenced by experiences during childhood, including events such as the loss of a parent. Negative ways of thinking about the world and dysfunctional interpersonal skills are presumably learned early in life. Gotlib and Hammen argue that the combination of cognitive schemas and deficits in interpersonal skills affects the person's social environment in several ways: It increases the likelihood that the person will enter problematic relationships; it diminishes the person's ability to resolve conflict after it occurs; and it minimizes the person's ability to solicit support and assistance from other people.

The *onset* of depression is most often triggered by life events and circumstances. The stressful life events that precipitate an episode frequently grow out of difficult personal and family relationships. Gotlib and Hammen note, at this point, another factor that may make women more likely than men to develop depression. Women are more likely to respond empathically to life events that happen to friends and family members. Men, in contrast, are affected only by things that happen directly to them (Kessler & McLeod, 1984). The impact of these experiences depends on the meanings that people assign to them. People become depressed when they interpret events in a way that diminishes their sense of self-worth.

Depression is *maintained* over an extended period of time, and can escalate to clinical proportions, as a result of persistent

▼ Stressful life events that lead to the onset of depression often involve interpersonal relationships. Women may be more vulnerable to depression than men are because they are likely to respond empathically when something bad happens to their friends or family members.

interpersonal and cognitive problems. Depressed people behave in ways that elicit negative reactions and rejection from others. They are also more likely to be acutely aware of criticism and rejection. Their negative cognitive schemas remain activated, accentuating the impact of stressful circumstances.

Biological Factors

We have considered a number of social and psychological factors that contribute to the etiology of mood disorders. Biological factors are also influential in the regulation of mood. Research conducted since the 1970s has established that certain biological factors are associated with both unipolar and bipolar mood disorders. Various studies suggest that genetic factors are somehow involved, that the process of neural transmission in the brain is dysfunctional in some patients, and that hormonal abnormalities are regularly associated with depression.

GENETICS

In Kraepelin's early writings on manic–depressive psychoses, he noted the presence of a "hereditary taint" in the majority of cases. This inference was based on his observation that many of the patients' relatives exhibited symptoms of the same disorder. Subsequent studies have confirmed his impression that genetic factors are involved in the transmission of mood disorders. They have also provided useful insights regarding the utility of the unipolar/bipolar distinction.

Family Studies   If the development of mood disorders is influenced by genetic factors, these disorders should show a familial pattern of transmission. In other words, they should be more common among the biological relatives of people who are depressed than they are among the general population. First-degree relatives (siblings, parents, and children) of patients with mood disorders should be more vulnerable to the disorder because they share 50 percent of their genes with an affected individual. Several carefully controlled studies have confirmed this hypothesis. Family studies begin with the identification of an individual who has been diagnosed as having a mood disorder, who is known as the *proband*. Researchers obtain as much information as possible about the proband's relatives, either through personal interviews, family informants, or mental health records. They use this information to decide whether each relative fits criteria for mood disorders. They can then compare the lifetime morbid risk among patients' relatives with those figures already established for the general population.

Table 5–6 presents a summary of data from several family studies of mood disorder. An interesting pattern distinguishes unipolar and bipolar mood disorders. Remember that the lifetime risk for major depressive disorder was approximately 5 percent in the ECA study, whereas the lifetime risk for bipolar disorder was approximately 1 percent. With these figures in mind, consider the frequency of disorder among the relatives of unipolar probands. The risk for bipolar disorder among their relatives is close to that seen in the general population, but the risk for unipolar disorder is almost doubled. Among the relatives of bipolar probands, the risk for both bipolar and unipolar disorder is much higher than that seen in the general population. The combined risk for both types of mood disorder is about 19 percent, almost double the combined risk of 10 percent found among the relatives of unipolar probands. Both types of mood disorder are therefore markedly familial. Family studies support the conclusion that bipolar mood disorders should be considered a separate type of mood disorder because the risk for bipolar disorder is elevated only among the families of probands who have bipolar disorders themselves (Winokur et al., 1995).

Twin Studies   The comparison of monozygotic (MZ) and dizygotic (DZ) twin pairs provides a more stringent test of the possible influence of genetic factors (see Chapter 2). Several twin studies of mood disorders have reported

---

TABLE 5-6

Average Morbid Risk for Mood Disorders in First-Degree Relatives of Unipolar and Bipolar Patients

Type of Proband	Relatives' Disorder (% with disorder)	
	Unipolar	**Bipolar**
Unipolar	9.1	0.6
Bipolar	11.4	7.8

Based on 7 studies of relatives of unipolar probands and 12 studies of relatives of bipolar probands. *Source:* R. Katz and P. McGuffin, 1993, The genetics of affective disorders. In L. J. Chapman, J. P. Chapman, and D. Fowles (Eds.), *Progress in Experimental Personality and Psychopathology Research.* New York: Springer.

higher concordance rates among MZ than among DZ twins (Katz & McGuffin, 1993; Moldin, Reich, & Rice, 1991).

One classic study was reported by Axel Bertelson, a Danish psychiatrist, and his colleagues (1977). They used national twin and psychiatric registers in Denmark to identify 110 pairs of same-sexed twins in which at least one member was diagnosed as having a mood disorder. The concordance rates for bipolar disorders in MZ and DZ twins were .69 and .19, respectively. For unipolar disorders, concordance rates for MZ and DZ twins were .54 and .24, respectively. The fact that the concordance rates were significantly higher for MZ than for DZ twins indicates that genetic factors are involved in the transmission of both bipolar and unipolar mood disorders. The fact that the difference between the MZ and DZ rate was somewhat higher for bipolar than for unipolar disorders may suggest that the effects of genes are more important in the case of bipolar disorders. Similar patterns of MZ and DZ concordance rates have been reported subsequently from twin studies of mood disorders conducted in Sweden (Torgersen, 1986) and in England (McGuffin, Katz, Watkins, & Rutherford, 1996).

Twin studies also indicate that environmental factors mediate the expression of a genetically determined vulnerability to depression. The best evidence for the influence of nongenetic factors is the concordance rates in MZ twins, which consistently fall short of 100 percent. If genes told the whole story, MZ twins would always be concordant. Mathematical analyses have been used to estimate the relative contributions of genetic and environmental events to the etiology of mood disorders. The results of these analyses are expressed in terms of *heritability*, which can range from 0 percent (meaning that genetic factors are not involved) to 100 percent (meaning that genetic factors alone are responsible for the development of the trait in question) (see Research Methods in Chapter 17). These analyses indicate that genetic factors are particularly influential in bipolar mood disorders, for which the heritability estimate is 80 percent. Genes and environment contribute about equally to the etiology of major depressive disorder, in which the heritability estimate is 52 percent. The genetic contribution may be relatively minor for dysthymia or neurotic depression, where the heritability estimate is only 10 percent (Katz & McGuffin, 1993).

Genetic Risk and Sensitivity to Stress How do genetic factors and stressful life events interact to bring about depression? The combined effects of genetic and environmental factors can be evaluated by incorporating the investigation of stressful life events into the traditional twin design. One important study that followed this procedure employed approximately 1,000 pairs of female same-sexed twins (590 MZ and 440 DZ pairs) in a study of unipolar mood disorder (Kendler et al., 1995). At two points in time, each separated from the next by approximately a year and a half, the investigators collected information regarding symptoms of depression and the experience of stressful life events. Fourteen percent of the women reported the onset of at least one major depressive episode during the follow-up period.

Kendler and his colleagues found that, within this large sample of twins, stressful life events and genetic factors both influenced the probability that a woman would become clinically depressed. More importantly, they were able to examine the ways in which genetic and environmental events interact. For this analysis, they divided their sample into four groups, based on levels of genetic risk:

- Highest genetic risk: women with a depressed MZ co-twin
- High genetic risk: women with a depressed DZ co-twin
- Low genetic risk: women with a nondepressed DZ co-twin
- Lowest genetic risk: women with a nondepressed MZ co-twin

These groups were further subdivided into those who had experienced a severe life event (death of a close relative, assault, serious marital problems, divorce/breakup) during the follow-up period and those who had not. The data from these comparisons are illustrated in Figure 5–2. Two primary conclusions can be drawn from these results. First, severe life events increase the probability that a person will become depressed, even among those who presumably have a relatively low genetic risk for the disorder. Second, the magnitude of the environmental effect is much larger for people who are genetically predisposed to the development of unipolar depression. Therefore the effects of the environment and genetic factors are not independent. Genetic factors apparently

Factors Affecting Risk for Depression

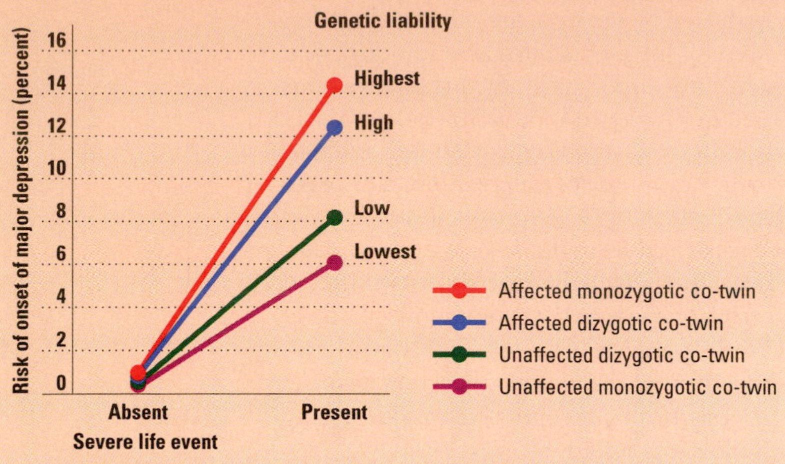

FIGURE 5-2: Risk of onset of major depression as a function of genetic liability and the presence or absence of a severe life event.

Source: K.S. Kendler, R.C. Kessler, E.E. Walters, C. MacLean, M.C. Neale, A.C. Heath, and L.J. Eaves, 1995, Stressful life events, genetic liability, and onset of an episode of major depression in women, *American Journal of Psychiatry, 152,* 838–842.

control the person's sensitivity to environmental events.

Mode of Transmission and Linkage Studies
The family and twin studies indicate that genetic factors play an important role in the development of mood disorders. They have not, however, established the operation of a particular mode of inheritance. Most investigators view mood disorders as being polygenic—they are influenced by several different genes.

In contrast, some investigators favor the single-locus model of inheritance, which holds that one gene at a particular location, or *locus*, on a particular chromosome is responsible for mood disorders. To support their arguments they have searched for evidence of chromosomal linkage between the locus of a known gene and the locus for a gene that is responsible for mood disorders. Two loci are said to be *linked* when they occupy positions that are close together on the same chromosome. Linkage is usually detected by examining the degree of association between two or more traits within specific families (see Research Methods in Chapter 14).

Linkage studies of mood disorders have focused on bipolar patients because the effects of genetic factors appear to be more salient in bipolar than in unipolar disorders, and because

transmission within specific families follows the pattern expected in a simple Mendelian dominant trait. With the introduction of new gene-mapping techniques, our knowledge in this area is expanding dramatically. Thus far, the results are mixed (Berrettini, 1993; Craddock & McGuffin, 1993). One group has reported the detection of linkage with markers on chromosome 11 among Amish people living in Pennsylvania (Egeland et al., 1987). Another found evidence for linkage between bipolar mood disorder and markers on the X (female sex) chromosome such as color blindness (Risch et al., 1986). Several other laboratories, however, have been unable to duplicate these results (Heberbrand, 1992; Mitchell et al., 1991).

The possibility of detecting linkage to known traits is very exciting. This knowledge would enable mental health professionals to identify those individuals who are vulnerable to a disorder before the onset of overt symptoms. At the same time, however, two important cautions should be kept in mind with regard to genetic linkage studies. One problem involves genetic heterogeneity. Within the general population, there may be more than one locus that is capable of producing the trait in question. Mood disorders may be linked to one marker within a certain extended family and to an entirely different marker in another family. Second, it will not be possible to establish linkage unless a single gene of main effect is responsible for the development of a particular disorder. In the case of mood disorders, as we have seen, several genes might be responsible.

NEUROTRANSMITTERS AND DEPRESSION

Chemical activity in the brain is another important biological factor that is undoubtedly involved in the etiology of mood disorders. Over the past several decades, scientists have gathered a great deal of information concerning the neural underpinnings of depression and mania (Delgado, Price, Heninger, & Charney, 1992; Mann & Kupfer, 1993). This information comes from two principal areas: psychopharmacology and neuroscience. Our knowledge in this area initially was based on the accidental discovery of several drugs that have the ability to alter people's moods. Some of the most crucial discoveries occurred within a fairly short period of time during the late 1940s and the 1950s.

Iproniazid was being used to treat people suffering from tuberculosis. Clinicians observed that some patients who took this drug experienced inappropriate mood elevation. Neuroscientists soon determined that iproniazid inhibits the action of monoamine oxidase (MAO), one of the enzymes that break down monoamines, such as norepinephrine and serotonin, in the nerve terminal. Psychiatrists found that this general class of drugs, known as monoamine oxidase (MAO) inhibitors, could be used successfully to treat depressed patients.

A related discovery was made by scientists working for a pharmaceutical company. They were looking for a variant of the phenothiazines, a class of drugs shown to have beneficial effects for people with schizophrenia (see Chapter 13). Imipramine was tested with a variety of psychiatric patients, and although it did not prove useful with schizophrenia, it did appear to have mood-elevating properties and was subsequently shown to be effective with depressed patients. One pharmacological action of imipramine is to block the reuptake of catecholamines (norepinephrine and dopamine) into the nerve terminal. Imipramine and several related compounds form the group of drugs that are known as tricyclic antidepressants (TCAs) because their molecular structures include three rings.

Another drug, reserpine, was identified in 1952 and was soon used widely in the treatment of hypertension. Physicians noticed that approximately 15 percent of hypertensive patients being treated with reserpine developed a major depressive disorder. Scientists subsequently discovered that reserpine depletes stores of norepinephrine and serotonin in the nerve terminal by pushing them out of the vesicles into the cell, where they are broken down.

Based on this evidence, Schildkraut (1965) and Bunney and Davis (1965) proposed a simple biochemical theory—the *catecholamine hypothesis*—to explain the etiology of depression.[†] According to this theory, depression was associated with a decrease in the levels of brain catecholamines, especially norepinephrine. Mania, on the other hand, was presumably associated with an excess of norepinephrine. Shortly thereafter, and based largely on the same pharmacological data, other investigators suggested that serotonin, another neurotransmitter in the central nervous system, might also be related to depression because MAO inhibitors and TCAs affect this neurotransmitter in the same way that they affect norepinephrine. This second theory came to be known as the *indolamine hypothesis*.

Two important considerations have recently led to a somewhat different perspective on neurochemistry and mood disorders. First, several new drugs—known as second-generation or "atypical" antidepressants—have been discovered. These drugs are effective in the treatment of depressed patients, but they have different physiological effects than the classic antidepressant drugs. More specifically, they do not affect the reuptake of monoamines (norepinephrine or serotonin), and they do not inhibit MAO. The second consideration involves the distinction between short-term and long-term drug effects. Antidepressants typically must be taken for 1 to 3 weeks before they have a clinical effect. The catecholamine and indolamine hypotheses were based on evidence regarding the immediate effects of these drugs on cell functioning. If depression is associated with a low level of norepinephrine in certain brain areas, and if TCAs block the uptake of norepinephrine right away, why don't these antidepressants have *immediate* beneficial effects on the patient's mood?

Studies of the *long-term* effects of antidepressants on membrane receptors have cast a new light on the neurochemistry of mood disorders. These studies suggest that the original notions presented in the catecholamine and indolamine hypotheses—that depression was produced by a simple reduction in the amount of norepinephrine or serotonin—were much too simple. Current theories tend to place a greater emphasis on the interactive effects of several neurotransmitter systems, including dopamine (Depue & Iacono, 1989; Kapur & Mann, 1992), as well as serotonin, norepinephrine, and neuropeptides—short chains of amino acids that exist in the brain and appear to modulate the activity of the classic neurotransmitters. These theories focus more on the role of postsynaptic receptor sensitivity and density rather than on a simple deficiency in the amount of neurotransmitter substances that are available (Charney et al., 1991; Potter, Grossman, & Rudorfer, 1993). In essence, they propose that postsynaptic

---

[†] One general class of neurotransmitters in the central nervous system is known as the monoamines, which are organic compounds containing nitrogen in one amino group. The monoamine neurotransmitters contain two important subtypes: catecholamines, which have a catechol portion (such as norepinephrine and dopamine) and indolamines, which have an indole portion (such as serotonin and tryptamine).

receptors are both more sensitive and more dense in depressed patients. These theories are based in part on animal studies that have demonstrated that treatment with antidepressants decreases the sensitivity and density of these receptors (McNeal & Cimbolic, 1986).

THE NEUROENDOCRINE SYSTEM

The endocrine system plays an important role in regulating a person's response to stress. As we saw in Chapter 2, endocrine glands, such as the pituitary, thyroid, and adrenal glands, are located at various sites throughout the body. In response to signals from the brain, these glands secrete hormones into the bloodstream. One important pathway in the endocrine system that may be closely related to the etiology of mood disorders is called the *hypothalamic–pituitary–adrenal (HPA) axis*. Signals from the hypothalamus cause the pituitary gland to secrete a hormone called ACTH, which in turn modulates hormone secretion by the adrenal glands.

Interest in the relation between mood disorders and the endocrine system was stimulated in part by descriptions of Cushing's syndrome, a disease associated with the adrenal glands that results in abnormally high concentrations of the hormone cortisol in the bloodstream. Approximately half of all patients with Cushing's syndrome are also clinically depressed. After Cushing's syndrome is corrected, most patients also recover from their depression. This pattern suggests that abnormally high levels of cortisol may lead to the onset of depression (Checkley, 1992).

An association between the HPA axis and depression is also indicated by evidence regarding the *dexamethasone suppression test (DST)*, which has been used extensively to study endocrine dysfunction in patients with mood disorders (Friedman, Clark, & Gershon, 1992). Dexamethasone is a potent synthetic hormone. People who have taken a test dose of dexamethasone normally show a suppression of cortisol secretion because the hypothalamus is fooled into thinking that there is already enough cortisol circulating in the system (Whybrow, Akiskal, & McKinney, 1984). Approximately half of depressed patients show a failure of suppression in response to the DST. Most of these patients exhibit a normal response on the DST after their clinical condition improves. This pattern is consistent with the hypothesis that a dysfunction of the HPA axis may be involved in the development or maintenance of clinical depression, at least for some people. Relatively high rates of nonsuppression have also been found among patients with anxiety disorders and substance abuse disorders.

In what ways might endocrine problems be related to other etiological factors we have already discussed? Several possibilities exist. In terms of the specific link between the endocrine system and the central nervous system, overproduction of cortisol may lead to a reduced density of serotonin receptors (Roy et al., 1987). At a more general level, hormone regulation may provide a process through which stressful life events interact with a genetically determined predisposition to mood disorder. Stress causes the release of adrenal steroids, such as cortisol, and steroid hormones play an active role in regulating the expression of genes (Checkley, 1992; Haskett, 1993).

The Interaction of Social, Psychological, and Biological Factors

We have considered a variety of social, psychological, and biological factors that appear to be related to the etiology of mood disorders. How can these factors be combined or integrated? Do we need to choose among them, advocating either a radical biological or psychological perspective? Some clinicians have, in fact, argued that some mood disorders are caused by biological factors and others are caused by psychological factors. We favor the systems view, which holds that mood disorders are typically produced by a combination of interacting biopsychosocial systems.

One type of research that illustrates this point has employed an animal model of depression (see Research Methods) based on Seligman's helplessness theory. When laboratory animals are exposed to uncontrollable electric shock, they frequently exhibit behavioral deficits that are similar to (yet obviously not the same as) those seen in depressed humans. The animals develop deficits in motor activity, sleep, and eating behaviors. This type of "stress-induced depression" in laboratory rats is associated with certain neurochemical effects, in particular a large decrease in the concentration of norepinephrine within the locus coeruleus region of the brain. Rats that show this neurochemical consequence following exposure to stress exhibit signs of depression. If the neurotransmitter is not depleted, the rats do not appear to be depressed (Weiss & Simson, 1985).

Furthermore, the administration of antidepressant drugs to these animals has been shown to reverse or prevent the behavioral effects of uncontrollable shock.

This phenomenon illustrates the need to consider the interaction between biological and psychological phenomena. The data on stress-induced depression in rats suggest that neurochemical processes may be reactions to environmental events, such as uncontrollable shock in rats or major stressful events in people. Psychological and biological explanations of depression may be complementary views of the same process, differing primarily in terms of their level of analysis.

RESEARCH METHODS

Analogue Studies of Psychopathology

Many questions about the etiology of psychopathology cannot be addressed using highly controlled laboratory studies with human subjects. Does prolonged exposure to uncontrollable stress cause anxiety disorders? Can the destruction of specific neurotransmitter pathways produce clinical depression? These issues have been addressed using *correlational studies* with people who have the disorders in question, but experiments on these issues cannot be done with human subjects. For important ethical reasons, investigators cannot randomly assign people to endure conditions that are hypothesized to produce full-blown disorders like clinical depression, schizophrenia, or alcoholism. The best alternative is often to study a condition that is similar, or analogous, to the clinical disorder in question. Investigations of this type are called **analogue studies** because they focus on behaviors that resemble mental disorders—or isolated features of mental disorders—that appear in the natural environment.

Many analogue studies depend on the use of *animal models* of psychopathology, which have provided important insights regarding the etiology of conditions such as anxiety, depression, and schizophrenia (Mineka & Zinbarg, 1991). The first influential animal models of psychopathology were developed in Pavlov's laboratory during the 1920s and 1930s. They were concerned with the role of classical conditioning in the etiology of anxiety disorders. In the 1960s, Harry Harlow's research demonstrated that rhesus monkey infants develop despair responses after separation from their mothers. The somatic symptoms exhibited by these monkeys—facial and vocal displays of sadness and dismay, social withdrawal, changes in appetite and sleep, and psychomotor retardation—were remarkably similar to many symptoms of clinical depression in humans.

This *social separation model* of depression has been used to explore several important social variables that may be involved in mood disorders. For example, infant monkeys who have extensive experience with peers and other adults are less likely to become depressed following separation from their mothers. The skills that they learn through social exploration apparently allow them to cope more successfully with stress. The social separation model has also been used to explore neurochemical underpinnings of mood disorders. Drug companies have used the model to evaluate the potential antidepressant effects of new drugs (Mineka & Zinbarg, 1991).

Some clinicians have argued that mental disorders like depression cannot be modeled in a laboratory setting, especially using animals as subjects. Cognitive symptoms—such as Beck's depressive triad—cannot be measured with animals. Do monkeys feel guilty? Can rats experience hopelessness or suicidal ideas? But these symptoms are not necessarily the most central features of the disorder. Cross-cultural studies have shown that in some non-Western societies somatic symptoms are the most prominent symptoms of depression. Many of these aspects of mood disorder are seen in animals. The value of any analogue study hinges, in large part, on the extent to which the analogue condition is similar to the actual clinical disorder. Some models are more compelling than others.

Another type of analogue study is concerned with human behaviors that *resemble* psychopathology. For example, many investigators have studied college students who produce high scores on paper-and-pencil measures of anxiety or depression. The rationale for these studies hinges on the notion that these people experience problems that are similar to anxiety and mood disorders. Perhaps the best known example of this type is the case of Little Albert, the infant who developed a startle response—crying and other nonverbal signs of distress—after the presence of a white rat was repeatedly paired with a loud noise (Watson & Raynor, 1920). Albert's behavior was taken to be an analogue of clinical phobia, intense fear that leads to avoidance of a specific object or situation (see Chapter 6).

Analogue studies have one important advantage over other types of research design in psychopathology: They can employ an experimental procedure. Therefore the investigator can draw strong inferences about cause and effect. The main disadvantage of analogue studies involves the extent to which the results of a particular investigation can be generalized to situations outside the laboratory. If a particular set of circumstances produced a set of maladaptive behaviors in the laboratory, is it reasonable to assume that similar mechanisms produce the actual clinical disorder in the natural environment?

In actual practice, questions about the etiology of disorders like depression will probably depend on converging evidence generated from the use of many different research designs. Theories should be tested using correlational designs with samples of clinical patients as well as experimental designs based on analogue conditions. The combination of results from these complementary research methods has provided important information regarding several disorders that are discussed elsewhere in this book. ■

Treatment

Several procedures, both psychosocial and biological, have proved to be useful in the treatment of mood disorders. We have already mentioned that MAO inhibitors and TCAs can be effective with some depressed patients. Alternative forms of antidepressant medication have also been developed. Current psychological interventions emphasize cognitive patterns and interpersonal skills that are related to the etiological perspectives we have just reviewed. In the following pages we will examine some of the more prominent contemporary approaches to the treatment of unipolar and bipolar mood disorders, as well as the research evidence on their usefulness.

Unipolar Disorders

Most psychological approaches to the treatment of depression owe some debt to psychodynamic procedures and Freud's emphasis on the importance of anger and interpersonal dynamics. According to Freud's view, the primary goal of therapy should be to help the patient understand and express the hostility and frustration that are being directed against the self. These negative emotions are presumably rooted in dysfunctional relationships with other people. Freud also placed considerable emphasis on the apparently irrational beliefs that depressed people hold about themselves and their world. These cognitive factors are also emphasized by cognitive therapists.

COGNITIVE THERAPY

Cognitive therapy has been developed and promoted by Aaron Beck and his colleagues (e.g., Beck et al., 1979). His cognitive model assumes that emotional dysfunction is influenced by the ways in which people interpret events in their environments and the things that they say to themselves about those experiences. Unlike Freud and other proponents of the psychodynamic perspective, Beck did not believe that patients' irrational statements about themselves are actually complaints about other people. He argued instead that these statements are reflections of negative schemas that guide the patient's interpretation of life events.

Cognitive treatments are based on the assumption that the patient's depression will be relieved if these irrational beliefs are changed.

Therefore, instead of probing delicately for the unconscious roots of anger, Beck has encouraged a more directive, rational approach to changing these dysfunctional attitudes. Cognitive therapists focus on helping their patients replace self-defeating cognitions with more rational self-statements.

A specific example may help illustrate this process. Consider the case of Cathy, the depressed attorney whom we introduced at the beginning of the chapter. Cathy focused a great deal of attention on relatively minor negative events at work, blaming herself for anything other than a perfect performance. Her therapist helped her to recognize that she was engaging in a pattern of cognitive distortion that Beck has labeled "selective abstraction." Taking a detail out of context, she would invariably ignore those aspects of her performance that refuted the conclusion that she was professionally incompetent. Her therapist helped her overcome these tendencies by teaching her to question her conclusions and to develop more objective ways of evaluating her experiences.

Cathy also tended to think about herself in absolute and unvarying terms. During the course of therapy, she learned to recognize this pattern and to substitute more flexible self-statements. Instead of saying to herself "I am a hopeless introvert and will never be able to change," she learned to substitute, "I am less comfortable in social situations than some other people, but I can learn to be more confident."

Although Beck's approach to treatment emphasizes the importance of cognitive events, it shares many features with behavioral approaches to intervention. Cognitive therapists are active and directive in their interactions with clients, and they focus most of their attention on their clients' current experience. They also assume that people have conscious access to cognitive events: Our thinking may not always be rational, but we can discuss private thoughts and feelings. Another important aspect of Beck's approach to treatment, and a characteristic that it shares with the behavioral perspective, is a serious commitment to the empirical evaluation of the efficacy of treatment programs. Several studies have found that cognitive therapy is effective in the treatment of nonpsychotic, unipolar depression (Hollon, Shelton, & Davis, 1993). Two direct comparisons of cognitive therapy and behavioral therapy in the treatment of major depressive disorder have found that both types of treatment were effective, with neither being superior to the other (Hollon et al., 1993; Murphy et al., 1984).

INTERPERSONAL THERAPY

Interpersonal therapy is another contemporary approach to the psychological treatment of depression (Klerman et al., 1984). Based originally on traditional psychodynamic notions regarding dependent personality traits and depression, interpersonal therapy focuses primarily on current relationships, especially those involving family members. The therapist helps the patient develop a better understanding of the interpersonal problems that presumably give rise to depression (Gotlib & Hammen, 1992) and attempts to improve the patient's relationships with other people by building communication and problem-solving skills. Therapy sessions often include nondirective discussions of social difficulties and unexpressed or unacknowledged negative emotions as well as role playing to practice specific social skills.

ANTIDEPRESSANT MEDICATIONS

The types of medication that are used most frequently in the treatment of unipolar mood disorders fall into three general categories: tricyclics (TCAs), monoamine oxidase inhibitors (MAO-Is), and selective serotonin reuptake inhibitors (SSRIs).

Tricyclics The **tricyclics,** such as imipramine (Tofranil) and amitriptyline (Elavil), have been in relatively widespread use since the 1950s. They affect brain functions by blocking the uptake of neurotransmitters (for example, norepinephrine and dopamine) from the synapse. Several controlled double-blind studies indicate that tricyclics benefit many depressed patients (Goodwin, 1992), although improvements might not be evident until 2 or 3 weeks after the beginning of treatment. There are several different kinds of tricyclic medication that vary in potency and side effects, but they are generally equal in terms of effectiveness.

Because some depressed patients do not improve after receiving tricyclic medication, considerable research has been devoted to identifying those patients who will show a positive therapeutic response (Joyce, 1992). Although many clinicians believe that a family history of depression and various premorbid personality characteristics are associated with drug response, the empirical evidence has failed to establish any reliable relations among these variables.

▲ **Aaron Beck has developed an influential cognitive theory of depression, emphasizing the importance of distorted ways of thinking about the self. He has pioneered the use of cognitive therapy for the treatment of depression.**

Alternative assessment methods that focus on biological variables, such as the dexamethasone suppression test (Peselow et al., 1989) and EEG patterns during sleep (Rush et al., 1989), have been more encouraging, but their results have not been consistent. At present, the utility of tricyclic medication must still be determined on an individual basis.

Monoamine Oxidase Inhibitors The antidepressant effects of **monoamine oxidase (MAO) inhibitors** were discovered at about the same time as those of the tricyclic drugs. These drugs have not been used as extensively as tricyclics, however, primarily for two reasons. First, patients who use MAO inhibitors and also consume foods containing large amounts of the compound tyramine, such as cheese and chocolate, often develop very high blood pressure. Second, some early empirical evaluations of antidepressant medications suggested that MAO inhibitors are not as effective as tricyclics (see, for example, British Medical Research Council, 1965).

More recent studies have shown that MAO inhibitors are indeed useful in the treatment of depressed patients (Larsen, 1991). They can be used safely when the patient takes the necessary precautions regarding his or her diet. In addition, MAO inhibitors are now widely used in the treatment of certain anxiety disorders, especially agoraphobia and panic attacks (see Chapter 6).

Selective Serotonin Reuptake Inhibitors The **selective serotonin reuptake inhibitors (SSRIs)** are a comparatively new class of antidepressant medication that was developed in the early 1980s (Silverstone, 1992). Unlike the original forms of antidepressant medication, which were discovered by accident, SSRIs were synthesized in the laboratories of pharmaceutical companies on the basis of theoretical speculation regarding the role of serotonin in the etiology of mood disorders. The SSRIs inhibit the reuptake of serotonin into the presynaptic nerve ending and therefore promote neurotransmission in serotonin pathways by increasing the amount of serotonin in the synaptic cleft. They are called "selective" because they seem to have little if any effect on the uptake of other neurotransmitters.

The SSRIs have fewer side effects (such as weight gain, constipation, and drowsiness) than TCAs or MAO inhibitors do, and they are less dangerous if the patient takes an overdose. This does not mean, of course, that they are completely without side effects. Some patients experience nausea, headaches, fatigue, restlessness, and insomnia, although these symptoms are usually mild and short term.

The best known of the SSRIs is fluoxetine (Prozac). Shortly after its introduction (Byerley et al., 1988), Prozac was featured on the covers of national magazines such as *Newsweek* and was inappropriately hailed as a miracle cure for depression. Within months, a backlash occurred in the media, and Prozac became a focus of controversy. A few individual case studies suggested that the drug might reduce inhibitions for violent behavior or increase preoccupation with suicidal ideas (Teicher, Glod, & Cole, 1990). Controlled investigations have subsequently disproved these fears, and Prozac is now a popular form of treatment that is prescribed by psychiatrists more than twice as often as the next most common type of antidepressant drug. Controlled outcome studies indicate that Prozac and other SSRIs are about as effective as traditional forms of antidepressant medication (Greenberg et al., 1994; Stokes, 1993).

THE EFFICACY OF PSYCHOTHERAPY AND TCAS

The Treatment of Depression Collaborative Research Program (TDCRP) was a large-scale study that compared the effectiveness of two types of psychotherapy—cognitive and interpersonal therapy—with that of antidepressant medication (Elkin et al., 1989; Elkin et al., 1996). The study was sponsored by the National Institute of Mental Health (NIMH) and was conducted at three different sites. Unipolar depressed

"...IS IT MY IMAGINATION OR DOES IT SEEM LIKE EVERYONE IS TAKING PROZAC?..."

Courtesy UFS, Inc.

outpatients were assigned to one of four treatment groups: cognitive therapy, interpersonal therapy, antidepressant medication (imipramine, a standard TCA), or placebo plus "clinical management." Patients in the latter group met regularly with a therapist to receive pills that they believed to be antidepressants and also received extensive support and encouragement. Treatment lasted approximately 16 weeks in all conditions.

The results of the TDCRP are extensive and complex, given the large number of measures that were collected on all patients, differences across the three treatment sites, and variability in dropout rates in the different types of treatment. A few major findings stand out. First, all three types of active treatment were superior to the placebo plus clinical management condition in terms of their ability to reduce depression and improve overall levels of functioning. Second, there were no significant differences between cognitive and interpersonal therapy, and both were generally as effective as antidepressant medication. Third, patients improved somewhat more rapidly if they were receiving imipramine, but the rate of improvement in both psychotherapy groups caught up to the drug condition by the end of treatment. Fourth, contrary to expectations, patients who received different forms of psychotherapy did not exhibit improvements in specific psychological domains that were addressed in therapy. In other words, patients who received interpersonal therapy showed as much improvement on measures of cognitive distortion as did the patients who received cognitive therapy.

The three active forms of treatment in the TDCRP appeared to be roughly equivalent on the basis of initial comparisons of all the patients in the study. Subsequent analyses, however, found differences among treatments when the patient sample was subdivided based on how severe their depression was when they entered the study. Among severely depressed patients, those who received imipramine and those who received interpersonal treatment still showed more improvement than the placebo group. Severely depressed patients who received cognitive therapy, however, were not better off than those who received placebo. This result suggests that antidepressant medication and interpersonal therapy are more effective with certain types of depressed patients (Elkin et al., 1996; Jacobson & Hollon, 1996; Klein & Ross, 1993).

The results of the TDCRP were positive over the short run. Unfortunately, follow-up evaluations conducted 18 months after the completion of treatment were less encouraging. By that time, patients in the three active treatment groups were no longer functioning at a higher level than those who received only the placebo and clinical management. Less than 30 percent of the patients who were considered markedly improved at the end of treatment were still nondepressed at follow-up. This aspect of the study's results points to the need for continued efforts to improve currently available treatment methods.

Bipolar Disorders

Lithium   In 1949, the Australian psychiatrist John Cade discovered that the salt *lithium carbonate* was effective in treating bipolar mood disorders. Although lithium was soon widely used throughout Europe, it was temporarily banned by the Food and Drug Administration in the United States before being introduced into clinical practice in the mid-1970s. An extensive literature indicates that lithium carbonate is an effective form of treatment in the alleviation of manic episodes (Abou-Saleh, 1992; Keck & McElroy, 1993). It is also useful in the treatment of bipolar patients who are experiencing a depressive episode. Perhaps most importantly, bipolar patients who continue to take lithium between episodes are significantly less likely to experience a relapse.

Unfortunately, there are also some limitations associated with the use of lithium. Some bipolar patients—perhaps 20 to 25 percent—do not improve when they take lithium (O'Shea, 1993). Nonresponse is particularly common among rapid cycling patients and those who exhibit a mixture of manic and schizophrenic symptoms. Compliance with medication is also a frequent problem; at least half the people for whom lithium is prescribed either fail to take it regularly or stop taking it against their psychiatrist's advice (Goodwin & Jamison, 1990). The main reasons that patients give for discontinuing lithium are negative side effects, including memory problems, weight gain, and impaired coordination.

Anticonvulsant Medications   Often, bipolar patients who do not respond positively to lithium are prescribed anticonvulsant drugs, particularly carbamazepine (Tegretol) or valproic acid (Depakene) (McElroy et al., 1992; O'Shea,

1993). Outcome data suggest that slightly more than 60 percent of bipolar patients respond positively to these drugs (Gerner & Stanton, 1992). Like lithium, carbamazepine and valproic acid can be useful in reducing the frequency and severity of relapse, and they can be used to treat acute manic episodes. Common side effects include gastrointestinal distress (nausea, vomiting, and diarrhea).

Psychotherapy Although medication is the most important method of treatment for bipolar disorders, psychotherapy can be an effective supplement to biological intervention. Both interpersonal therapy and cognitive therapy have been adapted for use with bipolar disorders. In interpersonal therapy with bipolar patients, special emphasis is placed on monitoring the interaction between symptoms (especially the onset of hypomanic or manic episodes) and social interactions. Regulation of sleep and work patterns is also important (Klerman & Weissman, 1992). Cognitive therapy can be used to address both the patient's reactions to stressful life events and his or her reservations about taking medication (Haaga & Beck, 1992).

Relatively little research has been done to evaluate the utility of psychological treatments for bipolar mood disorders. Support for their use hinges, in large part, on clinical intuition and compelling testimonials from grateful patients. Consider, for example, the following personal statement from Kay Jamison (1995), whose descriptions of her own experience with bipolar disorder were cited earlier in this chapter:

At this point in my existence, I cannot imagine leading a normal life without both taking lithium and having had the benefits of psychotherapy. Lithium prevents my seductive but disastrous highs, diminishes my depressions . . . and makes psychotherapy possible. But, ineffably, psychotherapy heals. It makes some sense of the confusion, reins in the terrifying thoughts and feelings, returns some control and hope and possibility of learning from it all. (pp. 88–89)

Unfortunately, enthusiastic endorsements based on personal experience do not constitute strong evidence in favor of a treatment procedure (see Research Methods in Chapter 1). There is an obvious need for more extensive research on the effectiveness of various types of psychosocial treatment for bipolar mood disorders (Goldstein & Miklowitz, 1994; Solomon et al., 1995).

Electroconvulsive Therapy

The procedure known as *electroconvulsive therapy* (or *ECT*) has proved beneficial for many patients suffering from unipolar or bipolar mood disorders (see Chapter 3 for a review of the background of ECT). Electroconvulsive therapy is typically administered in an inpatient setting and consists of a series of treatments given two or three times a week (Abrams, 1993). Many patients show a dramatic improvement after six to eight sessions, but some require more. In current clinical practice, muscle relaxants are always administered before a patient receives ECT. This procedure has eliminated bone fractures and dislocations that were unfortunate side effects of earlier techniques. The electrodes can be placed either bilaterally (on both sides of the head) or unilaterally (at the front and back of the skull on one side of the patient's head). Unilateral placement on the nondominant hemisphere (the right side of the head for right-handed people) may minimize the amount of postseizure memory impairment, but it may also be less effective (Royal College of Psychiatrists, 1989).

Although the mode of action in ECT remains largely a mystery (Kapur & Mann, 1993), empirical studies have demonstrated that it is an effective form of treatment for severely depressed patients (Consensus Conference, 1985). Legitimate reservations regarding the use of ECT center around widely publicized, although apparently infrequent, cases of pervasive and persistent memory loss. No one denies that ECT is an invasive procedure that should usually be reserved

▼ In 1938, two Italian psychiatrists introduced a technique for inducing convulsions through electrical, rather than chemical, methods. In this procedure, electrodes were placed on either side of the patient's head, and an alternating current of 110 volts was passed through the brain for approximately half a second.

for patients who have been resistant to other forms of intervention such as medication and cognitive therapy. Nevertheless, it remains a viable and legitimate alternative for some severely depressed patients, especially those who are so suicidal that they require constant supervision to prevent them from harming themselves. Rapid cycling bipolar patients and depressed patients with psychotic symptoms may also be more responsive to ECT than to medication (Fink, 1993). As always, the risks of treatment must be carefully weighed against those associated with allowing the disorder to follow its natural course.

Seasonal Mood Disorders

The observation that fluctuations in seasons can help bring on episodes of mood disorder leads to the relatively obvious implication that some patients might respond to manipulations of the natural environment. For centuries, physicians have prescribed changes in climate for their depressed clients (Wehr, 1989). The prominent French psychiatrist Jean Esquirol (1772–1840) reportedly advised a patient whose depression appeared when the days grew shorter to move from Belgium to Italy during the winter.

Modern light therapy was introduced in the 1980s (Rosenthal et al., 1984; Oren & Rosenthal, 1992). Typical treatment involves exposure to bright (2,500 lux), broad-spectrum light for 1 to 2 hours every day. Some patients respond positively to shorter periods (30 minutes) of high-intensity (10,000 lux) light (Hill, 1992). This high-intensity light is roughly equivalent to the amount of light that would be generated by a 750-watt spotlight focused on a surface 1 square meter in area. The light source—most often a rectangular box containing fluorescent ceiling fixtures—must be placed close (90 cm) to the patient at eye level. Improvement in the person's mood is often seen within 2 to 5 days.

Outcome studies have found that light therapy is an effective form of treatment for seasonal affective disorder (Terman et al., 1989). The most difficult issue in evaluating this type of treatment has been to control for placebo effects. It is not possible to conduct a true double-blind study because patients know that they are being exposed to light, and they often believe that light will be helpful. The general conclusion is that light therapy is not simply a placebo effect. It is not clear, however, how or why it works (Hill, 1992).

Suicide

Admiral Jeremy (Mike) Boorda was the highest ranking officer in the U.S. Navy when, at the age of 56, he committed suicide (*Newsweek*, May 27, 1996). He was married and the father of four children. Boorda was the first person in the history of the navy to rise from the enlisted ranks to become chief of naval operations. Although his record of leadership was widely admired by fellow officers as well as prominent politicians, he had recently been the subject of journalistic scrutiny. Questions had been raised about whether Boorda had legitimately earned two medals that he displayed on his uniform for several years (small *v*'s that are awarded to people who have shown valor in combat). These public symbols of heroism are a source of considerable status, especially among professional military people. Boorda had stopped wearing the medals after the issue was initially raised, but some members of the media had decided to pursue the issue further. On the morning of his death, Boorda was told that reporters from *Newsweek* magazine wanted to ask him some more questions about his justification for wearing these medals. He never met with them. Telling other officers that he was going home for lunch, Boorda went home and shot himself in the chest with a .38 revolver.

Why would such an enormously successful person choose to end his own life? Suicide is an extremely personal, private, and complicated act. We may never know exactly why Admiral Boorda killed himself, but the circumstances surrounding his death are consistent with a number of facts about suicide. The highest rate of suicide in the United States is found among white males over the age of 50. Within this group, men who have been occupationally successful are more likely to commit suicide, especially if that success is threatened or lost. Notes that the admiral left for his wife and for navy personnel indicated that he could no longer face the public dishonor that might result from *Newsweek*'s investigation. Escape from psychological suffering is often a significant motive in suicide. Did Boorda commit suicide primarily in order to end his own subjective distress? Or was his death intended to avoid bringing disgrace to the navy, which had been plagued by other scandals in recent years. When he was appointed chief of naval operations, several months before his death, it had been hoped that he would restore morale and improve public confidence in the navy. The *Newsweek* probe threatened to negate all of those efforts. Did his death represent a personal sacrifice for the military service that he loved and to which he had devoted 40 years of his life? These difficult questions illustrate the challenges faced by clinicians who must try to understand suicide so that they can more effectively prevent it.

Aides said that Admiral Boorda did not show any signs of being depressed, even on the morning that he died. Nor were there any indications of substance abuse or other mental disorders. In this respect, Boorda's situation was unusual. Although many people who commit suicide do not appear to be depressed, and psychopathology doesn't explain all suicidal behavior, there is undoubtedly a strong relationship between depression and self-destructive acts. The available evidence suggests that at least 50 percent of all suicides occur as a result of, or in the context of, a primary mood disorder (Whybrow, Akiskal, & McKinney, 1984). Moreover, the risk of completed suicide is much higher among people who are clinically depressed than it is among people in the general population. Follow-up studies consistently indicate that 15 to 20 percent of all patients with mood disorders will eventually kill themselves (Goodwin & Jamison, 1990). Thus it seems reasonable to conclude that there is a relatively close link between suicide and depression.

Classification of Suicide

Common sense tells us that suicide takes many forms. The DSM-IV does not address this issue; rather, it lists *suicidal ideation* (thoughts of suicide) only as a symptom of mood disorders. Clinicians and social scientists have proposed a number of systems for classifying subtypes of suicide, based on speculation regarding different motives for ending one's own life. Therefore, in contrast to the principles that were followed in creating DSM-IV, classification systems for suicide are based on *etiological* theories rather than *descriptive* factors.

The most influential system for classifying suicide was originally proposed in 1897 by Emile Durkheim (1858–1917), a French sociologist who is one of the most important figures in the history of that discipline (Coser, 1977). In order to appreciate the nature of this system, you must understand Durkheim's approach to studying social problems. Durkheim was interested in "social facts," such as religious groups and political parties, rather than the psychological or biological features of particular individuals. His scientific studies were aimed at clarifying the social context in which human problems appear, and they were based on the assumption that human passions and ambition are controlled by the moral and social structure of society. One of his most important scientific endeavors involved the comparison of suicide rates among various religious and occupational groups.

In his book *Suicide*, Durkheim (1897/1951) argued that the rate of suicide within a group or a society would increase if levels of social integration and regulation are either excessively low or excessively high (Hankoff, 1982). He identified four different types of suicide, which are distinguished by the social circumstances in which the person is living:

- *Egoistic suicide* (diminished integration) occurs when people become relatively *detached* from society and when they feel that their existence is meaningless. Egoistic suicide is presumably more common among groups such as people who have been divorced and people who are suffering from mental disorders. The predominant emotions associated with egoistic suicide are depression and apathy.
- *Altruistic suicide* (excessive integration) occurs when the rules of the social group dictate that the person must sacrifice his or her own life for the sake of others. One example is the former practice in some Native American tribes of elderly persons who would voluntarily go off by themselves to die after they felt they had become a burden to others.
- *Anomic suicide* (diminished regulation) occurs following a sudden breakdown in social order or a disruption of the norms that govern people's behavior . Anomic suicide explains increased suicide rates that occur following an economic or political crisis or among people who are adjusting to the unexpected loss of a social or

occupational role. The typical feelings associated with *anomie* (a term coined by Durkheim, which literally means "without a name") are anger, disappointment, and exasperation.

- *Fatalistic suicide* (excessive regulation) occurs when the circumstances under which a person lives become unbearable. A slave, for example, might choose to commit suicide in order to escape from the horrible nature of his or her existence. This type of suicide was mentioned only briefly by Durkheim, who thought that it was extremely uncommon.

Durkheim believed that egoistic and anomic suicide were the most common types of suicide in Western industrial societies. Although he distinguished between these two dominant forms, he recognized that they were interconnected and could operate together. Some people may become victims of both diminished integration and ineffective regulation.

Durkheim's system for classifying types of suicide has remained influential throughout the twentieth century (e.g., Travis, 1990). It does have some limitations, however. For example, it does not explain why one person commits suicide while other members of the same group do not. All the people in the group are subject to the same social structures. Another problem with Durkheim's system is that the different types of suicide overlap and may, in some cases, be difficult to distinguish. If the system is used to describe individual cases of suicide, such as that of Admiral Boorda, would clinicians be likely to agree on these subtypes? We are not aware of any attempts to evaluate the reliability of such judgments, but it might be quite low.

Epidemiology of Suicide

In the United States and Canada, the annual rate of completed suicide across all age groups has averaged 12 people per 100,000 population during the twentieth century. More than 30,000 people in the United States kill themselves every year. Suicide rates vary as a function of many factors, including age, gender, and socioeconomic status (see Figure 5-3). The suicide rate among adolescents has increased alarmingly in recent decades (see Chapter 16). Between 1955 and 1980 (years in which "baby boomers" became adults), the suicide rate tripled for young men

between the ages of 15 and 24. The rate for young women in the same age range doubled during the same period (Garland & Zigler, 1993). Rates among other age groups have either fallen or remained steady. Suicide has become the third leading cause of death for people between the ages of 15 and 24, and it is the eighth leading cause of death in the general population (Moscicki, 1995).

Suicide attempts are much more common than are completed suicides. The ratio of attempts to completed suicides in the general population is approximately 10 to 1; among adolescents, the ratio is closer to 100 to 1 (Hendin, 1995). There are important gender differences in rates of attempted suicide versus rates of completed suicide. Females aged 15 to 19 years make 3 times as many suicide attempts as males. Completion rates, however, are 4 times higher among males (Tsuang, Simpson, & Fleming, 1993). The difference in fatalities may be due, in part, to the methods employed. Men and boys are more likely to use violent and lethal methods such as firearms and hanging, whereas women and girls are more likely to take an overdose of drugs, which may allow time for discovery and interventions by other people.

The risk of fatal suicide is highest among older people. Suicide rates have increased dramatically among young adults in recent years, but the highest rates are still found among older

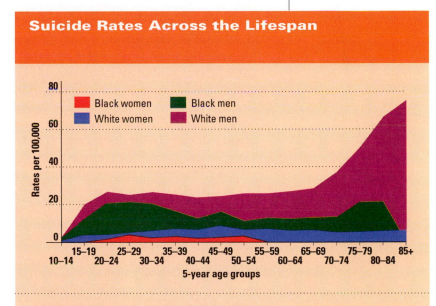

FIGURE 5-3: Suicide rates per 100,000 population by 5-year age group, race, and gender, United States, 1991.

Source: Moscicki, E.K., 1995, Epidemiology of suicidal behavior, *Suicide and Life-Threatening Behavior, 25,* 22-35.

people, especially older white men. Although suicide attempts are most common among younger people, with most being made by those younger than 30, the proportion of suicide attempts that end in death is particularly high among the elderly. It is not clear whether this pattern should be attributed to a difference in method or to decreased physical resilience. Rates of suicide in the United States—broken down by age, race, and gender—are illustrated in Figure 5–3. In 1991, more than 70 percent of all suicides were committed by white men, with the highest rate being among those over the age of 80. The pattern for women is somewhat different. Their risk for suicide increases steadily with age until midlife and then tends to level off.

Etiology of Suicide

Many factors contribute to the etiology of suicide. William Eaton (1994), a distinguished epidemiologist at Johns Hopkins University, offered the following example to illustrate the multiple levels of analysis that can be employed to examine factors leading to suicide:

> Consider a truck driver who commits suicide after finishing a long run. The suicide is at the behavioral level. The depletion of dopamine, which contributed to the suicide, resulted from the rebound effect of taking amphetamines during the run (biological level). At the psychological level, the individual driver may be saddened by a recent death in his family. The drug is available, and regarded as normative, in the driver's peer group (social-psychological level). The driver is able to take the illegal drug because the work is not supervised (social structural). The driver needs to make the run, and take the drug, because the union is less effective in protecting workers from exploitive labor practices (political) which reward drivers for long runs in the face of declining standards of living (economic). (pp. 27–28)

In the following discussion, we consider some of the factors that operate at the level of the individual person—psychological and biological considerations—and are associated with suicidal behavior. We also summarize some contemporary research on social factors that are related to suicide.

PSYCHOLOGICAL FACTORS

Many experts have argued that psychological events lie at the core of suicidal behavior (Schneidman, 1996). Social factors may set the stage for self-destructive acts, but events taking place within the person's mind are most immediately responsible for determining whether a particular individual will attempt to end his or her own life. Prominent among these events are the experience of intense emotional distress and hopelessness. An outline of several psychological variables that are commonly associated with suicide is presented in Further Thoughts.

Schneidman (1996) views suicide as an escape from unbearable psychological pain. According to his perspective, psychological pain is produced by prolonged frustration of psychological needs. Personality theorists have identified a number of fundamental human needs or motives (see Figure 2–7)—needs for achievement, esteem, belongingness, and safety. Frustration in meeting these needs can lead to prolonged, intense, negative emotional states, such as shame, guilt, anger, and grief. Most people who experience these emotions do not attempt suicide. But for some people, suicide appears to offer a solution or a way to end their intolerable distress.

BIOLOGICAL FACTORS

Studies of the connection between neurotransmitters and suicide have focused primarily on reduced levels of serotonin, which might be related to poor impulse control as well as increased levels of violent and aggressive behavior (Asberg, 1994; Hengeveld, 1994; Siever & Trestman, 1993). Analogue studies with animals have found that lesions resulting in serotonin dysfunction lead to increases in aggression and failure to inhibit responses that were previously punished. Dysregulation of serotonin systems has been found among people who attempted suicide, and it has also been found among people who have shown other types of violent and aggressive behavior, such as criminals convicted of murder (Garza-Trevino, 1994).

Serotonin dysfunction has also been linked to depressive disorders. It seems reasonable to wonder whether that connection might explain the findings regarding serotonin and suicide. People who attempt suicide may exhibit abnormal serotonin levels because they are depressed. That might be a reasonable interpretation for some of the data, but the results of other studies indicate that the link to suicide is more direct.

Common Elements of Suicide

Most people who kill themselves are suffering from some form of mental disorder, such as depression, substance dependence, or schizophrenia (Caldwell & Gottssman, 1992). No single explanation can account for all self-destructive behavior. Edwin Shneidman (1996), a clinical psychologist who is a leading authority on suicide, described 10 characteristics commonly associated with completed suicide. Schneidman's list includes features that occur most frequently and may help us understand many cases of suicide:

1. **The common purpose of suicide is to seek a solution.** Suicide is not a pointless or random act. To people who think about ending their own lives, suicide represents an answer to an otherwise insoluble problem or a way out of some unbearable dilemma. It is a choice that is somehow preferable to another set of dreaded circumstances, emotional distress, or disability, which the person fears more than death.

    Attraction to suicide as a potential solution may be increased by a family history of similar behavior. If someone else whom the person admired or cared for has committed suicide, then the person is more likely to do so.

2. **The common goal of suicide is cessation of consciousness.** People who commit suicide seek the end of conscious experience, which to them has become an endless stream of distressing thoughts with which they are preoccupied. Suicide offers oblivion.

3. **The common stimulus (or information input) in suicide is unbearable psychological pain.** Excruciating negative emotions—including shame, guilt, anger, fear, and sadness—frequently serve as the foundation for self-destructive behavior. These emotions may arise from any number of sources.

4. **The common stressor in suicide is frustrated psychological needs.** People with high standards and expectations are especially vulnerable to ideas of suicide when progress toward these goals is suddenly frustrated. People who attribute failure or disappointment to their own shortcomings may come to view themselves as worthless, incompetent, or unlovable. Family turmoil is an especially important source of

frustration to adolescents. Occupational and interpersonal difficulties frequently precipitate suicide among adults. For example, rates of suicide increase during periods of high unemployment (Yang et al., 1992).

5. **The common emotion in suicide is hopelessness-helplessness.** A pervasive sense of hopelessness, defined in terms of pessimistic expectations about the future, is even more important than other forms of negative emotion, such as anger and depression, in predicting suicidal behavior (Weishaar & Beck, 1992). The suicidal person is convinced that absolutely nothing can be done to improve his or her situation; no one else can help.

6. **The common cognitive state in suicide is ambivalence.** Most people who contemplate suicide, including those who eventually kill themselves, have ambivalent feelings about this decision. They are sincere in their desire to die, but they simultaneously wish that they could find another way out of their dilemma.

7. **The common perceptual state in suicide is constriction.** Suicidal thoughts and plans are frequently associated with a rigid and narrow pattern of cognitive activity that is analogous to tunnel vision. The suicidal person is temporarily unable or unwilling to engage in effective problem-solving behaviors and may see his or her options in extreme, all-or-nothing terms. As Shneidman points out, slogans such as "death before dishonor" may have a certain emotional appeal, but they do not provide a sensible basis for making decisions about how to lead one's life.

8. **The common action in suicide is escape.** Suicide provides a definitive way to escape from intolerable circumstances, which include painful self-awareness (Baumeister, 1990).

9. **The common interpersonal act in suicide is communication of intention.** One of the most harmful myths about suicide is the notion that people who really want to kill themselves don't talk about it. Most people who commit suicide have told other people about their plans. Many have made previous suicidal gestures. Schneidman estimates that in at least 80 percent of committed suicides, the people provide verbal or

behavioral clues that indicate clearly their lethal intentions.

10. **The common pattern in suicide is consistency of lifelong styles.** During crises that precipitate suicidal thoughts, people generally employ the same coping responses that they have used throughout their lives. For example, people who have refused to ask for help in the past are likely to persist in that pattern, increasing their sense of isolation. ∎

Consider, for example, a follow-up study of 92 people who were hospitalized following a suicide attempt (Nordstrom et al., 1994). All of the participants met the criteria for a major depressive disorder. The investigators measured levels of a particular serotonin by-product, 5-HIAA (5-hydroxyindoleacetic acid), in each patient's cerebrospinal fluid (CSF) shortly after admission to the hospital. The patients were divided into two groups on the basis of these measurements: those below the median for CSF 5-HIAA and those above the median. In the first year after their attempted suicide, 11 of the 92 patients committed suicide, and 8 of the 11 who died were from the low CSF 5-HIAA group. This result suggests that biochemical measures might be useful for predicting risk for suicide within groups of depressed patients.

Twin studies and adoption studies have found that genetic factors are involved in the transmission of major mood disorders. Do genes contribute to the risk for suicide indirectly by increasing the risk for mental disorders, such as depression, schizophrenia, and substance abuse? Is there a more direct contribution of genetic factors to self-destructive behavior? The answer appears to be "yes" (Mitterauer, 1990; Roy, 1992; Roy et al., 1991). One important investigation examined cases of depression and suicide in a group of large Amish families over a period of 100 years (Egeland & Sussex, 1985). Each family included at least one person who suffered from a mood disorder. Within this sample, there were 26 documented instances of suicide. The vast majority of the suicides (92 percent) occurred in people who had been diagnosed as having a mood disorder. Furthermore, most of the suicides occurred in a small subset of four families.

The investigators suggested that this pattern might be best explained by the existence of a genetic factor that is associated with suicidal behavior, independent of risk for major depression. This factor might be associated with impulsive personality characteristics. Suicide appears to be an especially likely outcome when a person inherits a predisposition to both psychopathology and impulsive or violent behavior.

SOCIAL FACTORS

Durkheim (1897/1951) believed that suicide rates had increased during the nineteenth century because of an erosion of the influence of traditional sources of social integration and regulation, such as the church and the family. Durkheim's own data and subsequent research by other investigators have provided support for the notion that social structures do represent one important consideration with regard to suicide. For example, Pescosolido and Georgianna (1989) found that religious affiliation is significantly related to suicide rates; lowest rates were found among Catholics and Evangelical Baptists, whereas higher rates were found among mainstream Protestant denominations, such as Episcopalians, Presbyterians, and Lutherans. This pattern can be explained in terms of social networks. People who belong to Catholic and conservative Protestant groups are more likely to participate in the various rituals and activities of the church community. These networks become an important source of emotional support during difficult times, protecting the person from the potential influence of self-destructive impulses.

Social policies regulating access to firearms, especially handguns, also have an effect on suicide rates. Guns are a particularly lethal method of suicide, accounting for more than 60 percent of the 30,000 deaths that occur in the United States each year (Hendin, 1995). In states with restrictive gun laws, the suicide rate usually drops, particularly among adolescents (Loftin, McDowall,

▼ Actress Margaux Hemingway killed herself in 1996 at the age of 41 by taking an overdose of a sedative. She was the fifth person in her family to commit suicide. Her grandfather, Ernest Hemingway, had committed suicide 35 years earlier.

Wiersma, & Cottey, 1991). Of course, people who have definitely decided to end their own lives can inevitably find a way to accomplish that goal, but many people who attempt suicide are ambivalent in their intent. Many attempts are made impulsively. Ready access to guns increases the chance that a person who does engage in an impulsive suicide attempt will die, because gunshot wounds are very likely to be fatal.

Prominent television and newspaper coverage of suicidal deaths, especially those of well-known celebrities, can have disastrous consequences by unintentionally encouraging other people to kill themselves. Young people are especially vulnerable to this effect, which is sometimes called *contagious suicide* or a *suicide cluster*. There was, for example, an increase in rates of suicide in both the United States and England in the months immediately after Marilyn Monroe committed suicide (Hendin, 1996). Imitation of this sort may represent a misdirected attempt to lend meaning to a person's life through association with the death of a celebrity. It might also be inspired by the attention that results with increased media coverage that invariably follows in the wake of multiple or sequential suicides. Descriptions of someone else's death may simply reduce some people's resistance to impulsive action.

Treatment of Suicidal People

Efforts to avoid the tragic consequences of suicidal behavior can be organized at several levels. One approach would focus on social structures that affect an entire society. Durkheim's theory of suicide, for example, indicates that the social structure of a society influences suicide rates. The social factors that we have just considered suggest some changes that could be made in contemporary Western societies in an effort to reduce the frequency of suicide. For example, more restrictive gun control laws might minimize access to the most lethal method of self-destruction. More cautious reporting by the media of suicidal deaths might reduce the probability of cluster suicides. These are, of course, controversial decisions, in which many other considerations play an important role. The media, for example, are motivated to report stories in a way that will maximize their popularity with the public. And many people oppose gun control legislation for reasons that have nothing to do with suicide rates. Therefore it may be

unrealistic to hope that these measures, aimed broadly at the level of an entire population, will be implemented widely. Most treatment programs that are concerned with suicidal behavior have been directed toward individual persons and their families.

CRISIS CENTERS AND HOT LINES

Many communities have established crisis centers and telephone hot lines to provide support for people who are distraught and contemplating suicide. The purpose of these programs is typically viewed in terms of *suicide prevention* (Hendin, 1996). Sponsored by various agencies, including community mental health centers, hospitals, and religious groups, these services are often staffed by nonprofessionals, frequently volunteers. They offer 24-hour-a-day access to people who have been trained to provide verbal support for those who are in the midst of a crisis and who may have nowhere else to turn. Rather than provide ongoing treatment, most crisis centers and hot lines help the person through the immediate crisis and then refer him or her to mental health professionals.

Public and professional enthusiasm for suicide prevention centers peaked during the 1960s and '70s. Unfortunately, data that were reported in the 1970s and '80s did not support optimistic claims that these centers were "saving lives." Empirical studies showed that suicide rates do not differ in comparisons of similar communities that either have, or do not have, suicide prevention programs. Creation of crisis centers and hot lines does not seem to reduce suicide rates in communities (Frankish, 1994; Hendin, 1995).

Why don't hot lines reduce suicide rates? The challenges faced by these programs are enormous. Think about the characteristics of people who are driven to contemplate suicide. They are often socially isolated, feeling hopeless, and unable to consider alternative solutions. Many people with the most lethal suicidal ideation will not call a hot line or visit a drop-in crisis center. In fact, most clients of suicide prevention centers are young women; most suicides are committed by elderly men. The primary problem faced by suicide prevention programs is this: The people who they are trying to serve are, by definition, very difficult to reach.

It might be hard to justify the continued existence of crisis centers and hot lines if they are viewed solely in terms of suicide prevention. Only a small proportion of people who call hot lines are seriously suicidal. Most are people who are experiencing serious difficulties and who need to talk to someone about those problems. The value of contact with these individuals should not be underestimated. Crisis centers and hot lines provide support and assistance to very large numbers of people in distress. These services are undoubtedly valuable in their own right, even if serious questions remain about their impact on suicide rates.

PSYCHOTHERAPY WITH SUICIDAL CLIENTS

Psychological interventions with people who are suicidal can take many forms. These include all the standard approaches to psychotherapy, such as cognitive, behavioral, psychoanalytic, and family therapy. These methods address underlying problems that have set the stage for the person's current problems. Additional treatment guidelines are also dictated by the threat of suicide. The following recommendations cover special considerations that are particularly important when clients have expressed a serious intent to harm themselves (adapted from Berman & Jobes, 1994):

1. *Reduce lethality.* The most important task is to reduce the person's experience of psychological pain (see Further Thoughts), from which the person is seeking escape. At a more concrete level, this also involves reducing access to means that could be used to commit suicide, such as guns and pills.
2. *Negotiate agreements.* Therapists frequently ask clients who have threatened to kill themselves to sign a contract, in which the client agrees to postpone self-destructive behavior for at least a short period of time. This kind of written agreement typically includes the client's consent to contact the therapist directly before engaging in any lethal actions. Of course, these agreements can be broken, but they may provide additional brakes to inhibit impulsive actions. The process of negotiating the agreement can also help the clinician determine the severity of the client's suicidal intentions.
3. *Provide support.* It is often useful to make concrete arrangements for social support during a suicidal crisis. Friends and family members are alerted and asked to be available so that the person is not alone.

The presence of others allows the person to discuss his or her problems (if he or she chooses to do so) and also provides supervision that may inhibit dangerous behaviors.

4. *Replace tunnel vision with a broader perspective.* People who are seriously contemplating suicide are typically unable to consider alternative solutions to their problems (see Further Thoughts). Death may strike others as an irrational choice, but to people contemplating suicide, in the midst of the crisis, it seems perfectly logical. The therapist must help potential suicide victims develop or recover a more flexible and adaptive pattern of problem solving.

MEDICATION

Treatment of mental disorders, especially depression and schizophrenia, is an important element of intervention with suicidal clients. The use of various types of medication is often an important part of these treatment efforts. Antidepressant drugs are frequently given to patients who are clinically depressed, and antipsychotic medication is useful with those who meet the diagnostic criteria for schizophrenia (see Chapter 13).

Considerable attention has recently been devoted to the use of selective serotonin reuptake inhibitors (SSRIs), such as fluvoxamine (LuVox) and fluoxetine (Prozac), because of the link between suicide and serotonin dysregulation. Extensive clinical reports suggest that the use of SSRIs in treating depression actually lowers suicide rates (Banki, 1995; Wagner, Zaborny, & Gray, 1994). It should also be noted, however, that placebo-controlled outcome studies have not addressed this specific question. Furthermore, cases have been reported in which treatment with SSRIs has been followed by the developmental of new suicidal ideation (King, Segman, & Anderson, 1994). This pattern suggests that the relation between serotonin and suicide is neither direct nor simple and that caution is warranted in the use of SSRIs in treating suicidal clients.

INVOLUNTARY HOSPITALIZATION

People who appear to be on the brink of committing suicide are often hospitalized, either with their permission or involuntarily (see Chapter 18 for a discussion of the legal issues involved in this process). The primary consideration in such cases is safety. In many cases, commitment to a hospital may be the best way to prevent people from harming themselves. The person's behavior can be monitored continuously, access to methods of harming oneself can be minimized (though perhaps not entirely eliminated), and various types of treatment can be provided by the hospital's professional staff.

Summary

Mood disorders are defined in terms of emotional, cognitive, behavioral, and **somatic symptoms.** In addition to a feeling of pervasive despair or gloom, people experiencing an episode of major **depression** are likely to show a variety of symptoms, such as diminished interest in their normal activities, changes in appetite and sleep, fatigue, and problems in concentration. In contrast, a person in a manic episode feels elated and energetic. Manic patients also exhibit related symptoms, such as inflated self-esteem, rapid speech, and poor judgment.

DSM-IV lists two major categories of **mood disorders.** People with **unipolar mood disorders** experience only episodes of depression. People with **bipolar mood disorders** experience episodes of **mania,** which are most often interspersed with episodes of depression. There are two specific types of unipolar mood disorder in DSM-IV. Major depressive disorder is diagnosed if the person has experienced at least one episode of major depression without any periods of mania. **Dysthymia** is a less severe, chronic form of depression in which the person has been depressed for at least 2 years without a major depressive episode.

A person who has experienced at least one manic episode would receive a diagnosis of bipolar I disorder, regardless of whether he or she has ever had an episode of depression. One episode of major depression combined with evidence of at least one period of **hypomania** would qualify for a diagnosis of bipolar II disorder. **Cyclothymia** is a less severe, chronic form of bipolar mood disorder in which the person has experienced numerous periods of hypomania interspersed with periods of depressed mood.

The validity of the distinction between unipolar and bipolar mood disorders is supported by several types of evidence. Bipolar disorders tend to have an earlier age of onset and a worse prognosis than unipolar disorders.

Mood disorders are among the most common forms of psychopathology. Epidemiological studies have found that the lifetime risk for major depressive disorder is approximately 5 percent and the lifetime risk for dysthymic disorder is approximately 3 percent. Rates for both of these disorders are 2 or 3 times higher among women than among men. The lifetime risk for bipolar I disorder is close to 1 percent. Women and men are equally likely to develop bipolar mood disorder. The prevalence of depression appears to be increasing, with people born after World War II being more likely to become clinically depressed than people born in earlier generations.

The etiology of mood disorders can be traced to the combined effects of social, psychological, and biological factors. Social factors include primarily the influence of stressful life events, especially severe losses that are associated with significant people or significant roles. Some studies show that people who are clinically depressed help to create some of the stressful events that they experience, especially those involving interpersonal relationships.

Two types of psychological factors play an important role in the development of mood disorders: cognitive responses to disappointment and failure and interpersonal skills. Cognitive theories are primarily concerned with the way

KEY TERMS

- affect
- analogue study
- bipolar mood disorder
- comorbidity
- cyclothymia
- depression
- dysphoria
- dysthymia
- emotion
- euphoria
- hopelessness
- hypomania
- learned helplessness theory
- mania
- melancholia
- monoamine oxidase inhibitors (MAO-Is)
- mood
- mood disorder
- psychomotor retardation
- relapse
- remission
- schema
- seasonal affective disorder
- selective serotonin reuptake inhibitors (SSRIs)
- somatic symptoms
- tricyclics
- unipolar mood disorder

in which depressed people experience a severe event. Beck's **schema** model places principal emphasis on cognitive distortions or the erroneous ways in which some people think about themselves and their environments. The **hopelessness** model holds that depression is associated with the expectation that desirable events will not occur or aversive events will occur regardless of what the person does. Furthermore, people will be more likely to become depressed if they attribute negative events to internal, stable, global factors.

Interpersonal theories focus on the ways in which individuals respond to people and events in their environments. Depressed people behave in ways that have a negative impact on other people. In this way they contribute to the stressful nature of their social environment. Coping behaviors may help to explain gender differences in the prevalence of unipolar depression. A ruminative style, in which the person's attention is turned inward, may be associated with longer and more severe episodes of depression. Women may be more likely than men to employ a ruminative style of response to the onset of a depressed mood.

Family and twin studies indicate that genetic factors play an important role in the etiology of both unipolar and bipolar mood disorders. They also indicate that genetic factors may play a stronger role in the development of bipolar than unipolar disorders. Genes may contribute to the development of depression directly through an effect on the central nervous system and indirectly by influencing the person's sensitivity to environmental events, such as severe stress. The mode of genetic transmission in mood disorders has not been identified. Linkage studies may help to find these pathways and could allow clinical scientists to identify individuals who are genetically predisposed to depression.

Neurochemical messengers in the brain also play a role in the regulation of mood and the etiology of mood disorders. Current thinking is focused on serotonin, norepinephrine, and dopamine, although many other neurotransmitter substances may also be involved in depression. Evidence regarding the long-term effects of antidepressant medications points to the importance of sensitivity and density of postsynaptic receptors as well as the interactive effects of multiple neurotransmitter systems.

Several types of psychological and biological treatment have been shown to be effective for mood disorders. Two types of psychotherapy, cognitive therapy and interpersonal therapy, are beneficial for unipolar and dysthymic patients. Three types of antidepressant medication are also useful in the treatment of major depressive disorder: **selective serotonin reuptake inhibitors, tricyclic antidepressants,** and **monoamine oxidase inhibitors.** Medication and psychotherapy are frequently used together. Outcome studies do not consistently favor either psychological or psychopharmacologic treatment.

Three other types of biological treatment are beneficial for specific types of mood disorder. Lithium carbonate and certain anticonvulsant drugs are useful for patients with bipolar mood disorders. Electroconvulsive therapy has been shown to be effective in the treatment of certain depressed patients, and it may be especially useful for patients who are severely suicidal or have failed to respond to other types of treatment. Light therapy seems to be effective for managing seasonal affective disorders.

Suicide is an alarming and complex problem. The suicide rate among adolescents has increased alarmingly in recent years. People commit suicide for many different reasons. Most people who kill themselves are suffering some form of mental disorder, such as depression, substance abuse, or schizophrenia. For some people, suicide represents an escape from unbearable negative emotions or painful self-awareness, which are often the result of frustrated psychological needs. Suicidal ideas are often accompanied by narrow patterns of perception and cognitive activity that make suicide seem like a reasonable solution to an otherwise unbearable dilemma. Serotonin dysfunction and genetic factors seem to contribute to the etiology of suicidal behavior. Social factors that have been studied in relation to suicide include religious affiliation, gun control laws, and media coverage of suicidal deaths. Efforts to prevent suicide include the use of hotlines and crisis centers as well as the provision of psychotherapy and medication for people who are willing or able to seek professional treatment.

Critical Thinking

1. Women are more likely to become depressed at some point during their lives than men are. Can you think of any explanations for this difference? Some data from epidemiological studies suggest that depression is more prevalent among young adults than among elderly persons. Can you explain this fact?

2. Imagine that you're talking to a psychiatrist. She tells you that depression is nothing more than a biochemical imbalance in the brain because certain medications are effective with depressed people. Is she right? What else do we know about the etiology of depression? Suppose a drug changes a neurotransmitter. Does taking that drug eliminate the cause of depression? How do biological factors (neurotransmitters and neurohormones) interact with stress to cause depression? What is the connection?

3. Contemporary psychological views of depression focus on cognitive reactions to negative experiences as well as interpersonal behaviors. Do these theories owe any debt to Freudian theory? How are they similar to Freudian theory? How are they different?

4. What are the relative risks and benefits of (a) medication and (b) cognitive therapy in the treatment of depression? If you were going to be treated, which would seem more useful to you? Imagine that somebody close to you is severely depressed and is threatening suicide. Medication doesn't work. The psychiatrist recommends electroconvulsive therapy but wants your consent. What would you decide? Why?

6
Anxiety Disorders

Anxiety disorders play an important role in the study of abnormal behavior for several reasons. One is the magnitude of the problem. Taken together, the various forms of anxiety disorders—including phobias, obsessions, compulsions, and extreme worry—represent the most common type of abnormal behavior. The National Comorbidity Study found that 17 percent of adults in the U.S. population have at least one type of anxiety disorder in any given year (Kessler et al., 1994). This figure was higher than the 1-year prevalence rates that were observed for mood disorders (11 percent) and substance-use disorders (11 percent). A second reason for the importance of studying anxiety disorders involves history. The anxiety disorders have played a crucial role in the history of psychopathology research and treatment. This influence cuts across theoretical perspectives, from Freud and his followers to learning theorists and proponents of biological hypotheses.

Overview

Anxiety disorders share several important similarities with mood disorders. From a descriptive point of view, both categories are defined in terms of negative emotional responses. Feelings such as guilt, worry, and anger frequently accompany anxiety and depression. There is also considerable overlap between anxiety disorders and major mood disorders such as depression. Many patients who are anxious are also depressed, and similarly, many patients who are depressed are also anxious.

The close relationship between symptoms of anxiety and those for depression suggests that these disorders may share common etiological features. In fact, clinicians and researchers have focused on similar considerations when investigating these disorders. Stressful life events seem to play a role in the onset of both depression and anxiety. Cognitive factors are also important in both types of problems. From a biological point of view, certain neurotransmitters, such as serotonin, are involved in the etiology of various types of anxiety disorders as well as mood disorders. This chapter employs many of the concepts that you

studied in our discussion of mood disorders in an effort to understand the onset and maintenance of anxiety disorders. We address such questions as: Why do some stressful life events lead to mood disorders while others seem to cause chronic anxiety? What is the difference between cognitive factors that contribute to depression and those that are involved in anxiety disorders?

The following case study illustrates the kinds of problems that are included under the heading of anxiety disorders. One feature that should become obvious is the overlap among different features of anxiety disorders, including panic, worry, avoidance, and a variety of alarming somatic sensations. This narrative was written by Johanna Schneller (1988), a freelance writer who has been treated for panic disorder. Her vivid description of her own problems highlights the remarkable clarity of insight that is typical of people with anxiety disorders. *Agoraphobia* refers to an exaggerated fear of being in situations from which escape might be difficult, such as being caught in a traffic jam on a bridge or in a tunnel.

Panic Disorder with Agoraphobia

"Three years have passed since my first panic attack struck, but even now I can close my eyes and see the small supermarket where it happened. I can feel the shoppers in their heavy coats jostling me with their plastic baskets, and once again my stomach starts to drop away.

"It was November. I had just moved to New York City and completed a long search for a job and an apartment. The air felt close in that checkout line, and black fuzz crept into the corners of my vision. Afraid of fainting, I began to count the number of shoppers ahead of me, then the number of purchases they had. The overhead lights seemed to grow brighter. The cash register made pinging sounds that hurt my ears. Even the edges of the checkout counter looked cold and sharp. Suddenly I became nauseated, dizzy. My vertigo intensified, separating me from everyone else in the store, as if I were looking up from underwater. And then I got hot, the kind of hot you feel when the blood seems to rush to your cheeks and drain from your head at the same time.

"My heart was really pounding now, and I felt short of breath, as if wheels were rolling across my chest. I was terrified of what was happening to me. Would I be able to get home? I tried to talk myself down, to convince myself that if I could just stay in line and act as if nothing was happening, these symptoms would go away. Then I decided I wasn't going to faint—I was going to start screaming. The distance to the door looked vast and the seconds were crawling by, but somehow I managed to stay in the checkout line, pay for my bag of groceries and get outside, where I sat on a bench, gulping air. The whole episode had taken ten minutes. I was exhausted.

"At home, I tried to analyze what had happened to me. The experience had been terrifying, but because I felt safe in my kitchen, I tried to laugh the whole thing off—really, it seemed ridiculous, freaking out in a supermarket. I decided it was an isolated incident; I was all right, and I was going to forget it ever happened.

"Two weeks later, as I sat in a movie theater, the uncomfortable buzz began to envelop me again. But the symptoms set in faster this time. I mumbled something to my friends about feeling sick as I clambered over them. It was minutes before I caught my breath, hours before I calmed down completely.

"A month full of scattered attacks passed before they started rolling in like Sunday evenings, at least once a week. I tried to find a pattern: They always hit in crowded places, places difficult to escape. My whole body felt threatened, primed to run during an attack. Ironically, my attacks were invisible to anyone near me unless they knew what to look for—clenched neck muscles, restless eyes, a shifting from foot to foot—and I was afraid to talk to anyone about them, to perhaps hear something I wouldn't want to hear. What if I had a brain tumor? And I was embarrassed, as if it were my fault that I felt out of control. But then one night I had an attack alone in my bed—the only place I had felt safe. I gave in and called a doctor.

"As the weeks passed and the attacks wore on, I began to think maybe I was crazy. I was having attacks in public so often I became afraid to leave my house. I had one on the subway while traveling to work almost every morning—but, luckily, never panicked on the job. Instead, I usually lost control in situations where I most wanted to relax: on weekend trips, or while visiting friends. I felt responsible for ruining other people's good time. One attack occurred while I was in a tiny boat deep-sea fishing with my family; another hit when I was on a weekend canoe trip with my boyfriend. I also suffered a terrifying attack while on my way to see friends, stuck in traffic, merging into a tunnel near Boston's Logan Airport, with no exit ramp or emergency lane in sight.

"I began declining offers I wanted to accept: all I could think was, 'What if I panic in the middle of nowhere?' The times I did force myself to go out, I sat near the doors of restaurants, in aisle seats at movie theaters, near the bathroom at parties. For some reason, I always felt safe in bathrooms, as if whatever happened to me there would at least be easy to clean up.

"On days when I didn't have an actual attack, I could feel one looming like a shadow over my shoulder; this impending panic was almost worse than the real thing. By remembering old episodes, I brought on new ones, and each seemed to pull me closer to a vision I had of my mind snapping cleanly in half, like a stalk of celery." ■

This case illustrates many of the most important features of a panic attack, as well as the manner in which agoraphobia sometimes develops. Johanna's first attack came suddenly and without warning, while she waited in a grocery line. The attack was characterized by various somatic sensations, including breathing difficulties, a pounding heart, nausea, and dizziness. This overwhelming and terrifying experience was over almost as quickly as it had begun. Subsequent attacks caused the author to restrict her social activities, avoiding situations in which she might have another attack. She became fearful of crowded situations from which she might not easily escape.

Johanna's description of her problems raises a number of interesting questions, to which we will return later in the chapter. Was it just a coincidence that her first attack occurred shortly after the difficult experience of moving to a new city, starting a new job, and finding a new apartment? Could the stress of those experiences have contributed to the onset of her disorder? Was there a pattern to her attacks? Why did she feel safe in some situations and not in others? She mentions feeling out of control, as if she were responsible for her attacks. Could she really bring on another attack by remembering one from the past? These questions are related to research studies in the literature on anxiety disorders.

Typical Symptoms and Associated Features

People with anxiety disorders share a preoccupation with, or persistent avoidance of, thoughts or situations that provoke fear or anxiety. Johanna's panic attacks and her dread of crowded theaters and long bridges provide one example. Anxiety disorders frequently have a negative impact on various aspects of a person's life. Johanna found that anxiety and its associated problems constrained both her ability to work and her social relationships. In spite of these problems, most people who knew her probably did not know that she suffered from a mental disorder. In spite of the private terrors that she endured, she was able to carry on most aspects of her life.

In addition to these general considerations, the diagnosis of anxiety disorders depends on several specific types of symptoms, which we discuss in the following sections. We begin by discussing the nature of anxiety, which should be distinguished from more discrete emotional responses, like fear and panic.

Anxiety

Like depression, the term *anxiety* can refer to either a mood or a syndrome. Here, we use the term to refer to a mood. Specific syndromes associated with anxiety disorders are discussed later in the chapter.

Anxious mood is often defined in contrast to the specific emotion of fear, which is more easily understood. **Fear** is experienced in the face of real, immediate danger. It usually builds quickly in intensity and helps organize the person's behavioral responses to threats from the environment (escaping or fighting back). Classic studies of fear among normal adults have often focused on people in combat situations, such as airplane crews during bombing missions over Germany in World War II (Rachman, 1991). In contrast to fear, **anxiety** involves a more general or diffuse emotional reaction—beyond simple fear—that is out of proportion to threats from the environment (Roth & Argyle, 1988). Rather than being directed toward the person's present circumstances, anxiety is associated with the anticipation of future problems.

▼ **Anxiety is not associated with an immediate threat from the environment. People with anxiety disorders anticipate future negative events, even in situations that are not actually dangerous.**

Anxiety can be adaptive at low levels, because it serves as a signal that the person must prepare for an upcoming event (Costello, 1976). When you think about final exams, for example, you may become somewhat anxious. That emotional response may help to initiate and sustain your efforts to study. In contrast, high levels of anxiety become incapacitating by disrupting concentration and performance.

A pervasively anxious mood is often associated with pessimistic thoughts and feelings ("If something bad happens, I probably won't be able to control it"). The person's attention turns inward, focusing on negative emotions and self-evaluation ("Now I'm so upset that I'll never be able to concentrate during the exam!") rather than on the organization or rehearsal of adaptive responses that might be useful in coping with negative events. Taken together, these factors can be used to define maladaptive anxiety, or what David Barlow, a psychologist at Boston University, has called *anxious apprehension*, which consists of (1) high levels of diffuse negative emotion, (2) a sense of uncontrollability, and (3) a shift in attention to a primary self-focus or a state of self-preoccupation (Barlow, 1991).

Excessive Worry

Worrying is a cognitive activity that is associated with anxiety. In recent years psychologists have studied this phenomenon carefully because they consider it to be critical in the subclassification of anxiety disorders (DSM-IV). **Worry** can be defined as a relatively uncontrollable sequence of negative, emotional thoughts and images that are concerned with possible future threats or danger. This sequence of worrisome thoughts is usually self-initiated or provoked by a specific experience or ongoing difficulties in the person's daily life. When excessive worriers are asked to describe their thoughts, they emphasize the predominance of verbal, linguistic material rather than images (Borkovec, 1994). In other words, worriers are preoccupied with "self-talk" rather than unpleasant visual images.

Because everyone worries at least a little bit, you might wonder whether it is possible to distinguish between pathological and normal worry. The answer is yes. The distinction hinges in part on quantity—how often the person worries and about how many different topics the person worries. But it also depends on the quality of worrisome thought. Excessive worriers are more likely than other people to report that the content of their thoughts is negative, that they have less control over the content and direction of their thoughts, and that in comparison to other adults, their worries are less realistic (Craske et al., 1989). This evidence suggests that the crucial features of pathological worrying may be lack of control and negative affect rather than simply the anticipation of future events.

Panic Attacks

A **panic attack** is a sudden, overwhelming experience of terror or fright, like the attack that was experienced by Johanna as she waited in the checkout line. Whereas anxiety involves a blend of several negative emotions, panic is more focused. Some clinicians think of panic as a normal fear response that is triggered at an inappropriate time (Barlow, Brown, & Craske, 1994). In that sense, panic is a "false alarm." Descriptively, panic can be distinguished from anxiety in two other respects: It is more intense, and it has a sudden onset.

Panic attacks are defined largely in terms of a list of somatic or physical sensations, ranging from heart palpitations, sweating, and trembling to nausea, dizziness, and chills. Table 6–1 lists the DSM-IV criteria for a panic attack. A person must experience at least 4 of these 13 symptoms in order for the experience to qualify as a full-blown panic attack. The symptoms must develop suddenly and reach a peak intensity within 10 minutes. The actual numbers and combinations of panic symptoms vary from one person to the next, and they may also change over time within the same person.

People undergoing a panic attack also report a number of cognitive symptoms. They may feel as though they are about to die, lose control, or go crazy. Some clinicians believe that the misinterpretation of bodily sensations lies at the core of panic disorder. Patients may interpret heart palpitations as evidence of an impending heart attack, or racing thoughts as evidence that they are about to lose their minds. Johanna said that she eventually felt as though her mind was going to snap in half.

Panic attacks are further described in terms of the situations in which they occur, as well as the person's expectations about their occurrence. An attack is said to be situationally bound, or *cued*, if it occurs only in the presence of a particular stimulus. For example, someone who is afraid of public speaking might have a cued panic attack if forced to give a speech in front

TABLE 6-1

Diagnostic Criteria for Panic Attack in DSM-IV

A discrete period of intense fear or discomfort, in which four (or more) of the following symptoms developed abruptly and reached a peak within 10 minutes:

1. Palpitations, pounding heart, or accelerated heart rate

2. Sweating

3. Trembling or shaking

4. Sensations of shortness of breath or smothering

5. Feeling of choking

6. Chest pain or discomfort

7. Nausea or abdominal distress

8. Feeling dizzy, unsteady, lightheaded, or faint

9. Derealization (feelings of unreality) or depersonalization (being detached from oneself)

10. Fear of losing control or going crazy

11. Fear of dying

12. Paresthesias (numbness or tingling sensations)

13. Chills or hot flushes

of a large group of people. Unexpected panic attacks, like Johanna's experience in the grocery checkout line, appear without any warning or expectation, as if "out of the blue."

Is there a typical pattern for panic attacks in the natural environment? In one descriptive study, panic disorder patients kept daily diaries describing panic experiences, and they also wore an ambulatory heart rate/physical activity recorder (Margraf et al., 1987). The average (mean) number of panic attacks among these patients was slightly less than one per day, but the number varied considerably across patients. Expected and unexpected panic attacks were experienced in roughly equivalent proportions. Unexpected attacks occurred most frequently at home, whereas situational attacks occurred most frequently in the car, usually while driving on freeways. The timing of unexpected attacks was evenly distributed across the day and night hours, with some occurring while the patient was asleep or

trying to fall asleep. The results of this study and several others indicate that the symptoms and timing of panic attacks can vary widely from one patient to the next (Dukman-Caes, Kraan, & deVries, 1993).

Phobias

In contrast to both diffuse anxiety, which represents a blend of negative emotions, and panic attacks, which are frequently unexpected, **phobias** are persistent, irrational, narrowly defined fears that are associated with a specific object or situation. Avoidance is an important component of the definition of phobias. A fear is not considered phobic unless the person avoids contact with the source of the fear or experiences intense anxiety in the presence of the stimulus. Phobias are also irrational or unreasonable. Avoiding only snakes that are poisonous, or only guns that are loaded, would not be considered phobic.

The most straightforward type of phobia involves fear of specific objects or situations. Different types of specific phobias have traditionally been named according to the Greek words for these objects. Examples of typical specific phobias include fear of heights (acrophobia); fear of enclosed spaces (claustrophobia); fear of small animals (zoophobia); fear of blood or injury; and fear of traveling on airplanes.

Some people experience marked fear when they are forced to engage in certain activities, such as public speaking, initiating a conversation, eating in restaurants, or using public rest rooms, which might involve being observed or evaluated by other people (Liebowitz et al., 1985). Attempts to avoid these feared situations cause serious impairment in the person's social and occupational activities. For example, one young man who was treated by one of the authors of this text was afraid of urinating in public rest rooms. He planned his daily schedule with great care so that he would always be near a rest room with a locking door. Consequently, he was unable to attend movies or eat in restaurants unless they happened to have single-person rest rooms that he could lock from the inside.

AGORAPHOBIA

The most complex and incapacitating form of phobic disorder is known as **agoraphobia,** which literally means "fear of the marketplace (or places of assembly)" and is usually described as fear of public spaces. The case of Johanna provides a brief description of the types of problems experienced by a person suffering from agoraphobia. The fear usually becomes more intense as the distance between the person and his or her familiar surroundings increases, or as avenues of escape are closed off. In that sense, agoraphobia is somewhat different from the other phobias because it is not so much a fear of being close to one specific object or situation (for example, animals, public speaking) as it is of being separated from signals associated with safety.

Typical situations that cause problems include crowded streets and shops, enclosed places like theaters and churches, traveling on public transportation, and driving an automobile on bridges, in tunnels, or on crowded expressways. In any of these situations, the presence of a trusted friend may help the person with agoraphobia feel more comfortable. In the most extreme form of the disorder, agoraphobic patients are unable to venture away from their own homes. Some people with agoraphobia are able to visit public places (for example, shopping malls, theaters), but may remain near exits or aisles so that their escape cannot be easily blocked.

The uncomfortable sensations experienced by people with agoraphobia are similar to those that have already been described for other anxiety disorders. They range from vague feelings of apprehension to specific physical sensations and full-blown panic attacks. People with agoraphobia are frequently afraid that they will experience an "attack" of these symptoms that will be either incapacitating or embarrassing, and that help will not be available to them. Many patients report that they are afraid of becoming dizzy, fainting, losing bladder or bowel control, or having heart problems. In some cases, previous experiences of this sort may have triggered persistent fear of repeated episodes.

Some clinicians have suggested that "fear of fear" is the central feature of agoraphobia (e.g., Goldstein & Chambless, 1978; Klein, 1981). The crucial event that triggers subsequent fears is often a terrifying, unexpected panic attack. Following such an experience, the person may become acutely aware of all internal bodily sensations that may signal the onset of another attack.

THE FAR SIDE By GARY LARSON

Math phobic's nightmare

▼ People with agoraphobia are afraid of crowded places from which they might not be able to escape. They also frequently experience panic attacks that are not cued by particular environmental circumstances.

Obsessions and Compulsions

Obsessions are repetitive, unwanted, intrusive cognitive events that may take the form of thoughts or images or impulses. They intrude suddenly into consciousness and lead to an increase in subjective anxiety. Obsessive thinking can be distinguished from worry in two primary ways: (1) obsessions are usually experienced as coming from "out of the blue," whereas worries are often triggered by problems in everyday living; and (2) the content of obsessions most often involves themes that are perceived as being socially unacceptable or horrific, such as sex, violence, and disease/contamination, whereas the content of worries tends to center around more acceptable, commonplace concerns, such as money and work (Turner, Beidel, & Stanley, 1992).

Compulsions are repetitive behaviors or mental acts that are used to reduce anxiety. These actions are considered by the person who performs them to be senseless or irrational. The person attempts to resist performing the compulsion but cannot. The following case study illustrates many of the most common features of obsessions and compulsions.

CASE STUDY

Obsessive–Compulsive Disorder

Ed, a 38-year-old lawyer, lived with his wife, Phyllis. Most aspects of Ed's life were going well, except for the anxiety-provoking thoughts that lurked beneath his relatively easygoing exterior. One focus of Ed's anxiety was handwriting. He became so tense that his eyes hurt whenever he was forced to write. Feeling exhausted and overwhelmed, Ed avoided writing whenever possible. The problem seemed utterly ridiculous to him, but he couldn't rid himself of his obsessive thoughts.

Sinister meanings had somehow become linked in Ed's imagination to the way in which letters and numbers were formed. The worst letters were *P* and *T* (the first letters in "Phyllis" and in "Tim," his younger brother's name). "Improperly" formed letters reminded Ed of violent acts, especially decapitation and strangulation. If the parts of a letter, such as the two lines in the letter *T*, were not connected, an image of a head that was not attached to its body might pop into his mind. Closed loops reminded him of suffocation, like a person whose throat had been clamped shut. These images were associated with people whose names began with the malformed letter. As a result of these concerns, Ed's handwriting had become extremely awkward and difficult to read.

These writing problems made it very difficult for Ed to complete his work, especially when he was under time pressure. In one particularly upsetting incident, Ed was responsible for completing an important official form that had to be mailed that day. He came to a section in which he needed to write a capital *P* and became concerned that he hadn't done it properly. The loop seemed to be closed, which meant that Phyllis might be strangled! He tore up the first copy and filled it out again. When it was finally done to his satisfaction, Ed sealed the form in an envelope and put it in the box for outgoing mail. After returning to his desk, he was suddenly overwhelmed by the feeling that he had indeed made a mistake with that *P*. If he allowed the form to be mailed, the evil image would be associated forever with his wife. Consumed by fear, Ed rushed back to the mailbox, tore up the envelope, and started a new form. Twenty minutes later, he had the form filled out and back in the mailbox. Then the cycle repeated itself. Each time, Ed became more distraught and frustrated, until he eventually felt that he was going to lose his mind.

In addition to his problems with writing, Ed was also afraid of axes. He would not touch an ax, or even get close to one. Any situation in which he could possibly encounter an ax made him extremely uncomfortable. He refused to shop in hardware stores because they sell axes, and he would not visit museums because their exhibits often contain artifacts such as medieval armor. His fear of axes was quite specific. Ed wasn't afraid of knives, guns, or swords.

One frightening experience seemed to trigger the pervasive anxiety that had plagued Ed for 20 years. When he was 17 years old, some friends persuaded Ed to try smoking marijuana. They told him that it would make him feel high—relaxed, sociable, and perhaps a bit giddy. Unfortunately, Ed didn't react to the drug in the same way that the others had. The physical effects seemed to be the same, but his psychological reaction was entirely different. After sharing two joints with his friends, Ed began to feel lightheaded. Then things around him began to seem unreal, as though he were watching himself and his friends in a movie. The intensity of these feelings escalated rapidly, and panic took over. Frightening thoughts raced through his head. Was he losing his mind? When would it stop? This experience lasted about 2 hours.

The marijuana incident had an immediate and lasting impact. Ed became preoccupied with a fear of accidentally ingesting any kind of mind-altering drug, especially LSD. Every spot on his skin or clothing seemed as though it might be a microscopic quantity of this hallucinogen. He felt compelled to clean his hands and clothes repeatedly to avoid contamination. Intellectually, Ed knew that these concerns were silly. How could a tiny spot on his hand be LSD? It didn't make any sense, but he couldn't keep the thought out of his mind.

The most horrifying aspect of the drug experience was the sensation of being totally out of control of his actions and emotions. The fear of returning to that state haunted Ed. He struggled to resist impulses that he had never noticed before, such as the temptation to shout obscenities out loud in church. He also began to worry that he might hurt his younger brother. He resisted the impulses with all his might. He never acted on them, but they pervaded his consciousness and absorbed his mental energy.

The thoughts were so persistent and unshakable that Ed began to wonder if he might, in fact, be a pathological killer. Could he be as deranged and evil as Richard Speck, who had brutally murdered eight nurses in a Chicago apartment building in 1966? Ed spent many hours reading articles about Speck and other mass murderers. The number 8 came to have special meaning to him because of the number of Speck's victims. Over time, Ed's fears and worries became focused on numbers and letters. The violent images and impulses became a less prominent part of his everyday life, but the writing difficulties escalated proportionately. ∎

Ed's thoughts about violence and death illustrate the anxiety-provoking nature of obsessions. It is not just the intrusive quality of the thought but also the unwanted nature of the thought that makes it an obsession. Some scientists and artists, for example, have reported experiencing intrusive thoughts or inspirational ideas that appear in an unexpected, involuntary way, but these thoughts are not unwanted. Obsessions are unwelcome, anxiety-provoking thoughts. They are also nonsensical; they may seem silly or "crazy." In spite of the recognition that these thoughts do not make sense, the person with full-blown obsessions is unable to ignore or dismiss them.

Examples of typical obsessive thoughts include the following: "Did I kill the old lady?" "Christ was a bastard!" "Am I a sexual pervert?" Examples of obsessive impulses include "I might expose my genitals in public," "I am about to shout obscenities in public," "I feel I might strangle a child." Obsessional images might include mutilated corpses, decomposing fetuses, or a family member being involved in a serious car accident. Although obsessive impulses are accompanied by a compelling sense of reality, obsessive people seldom act upon these impulses (with the possible exceptions of impulses to steal and impulses to molest children; see Rachman & Hodgson, 1980).

Most normal people experience obsessions in one form or another. Between 80 and 90 percent of normal subjects report experiencing intrusive, unacceptable thoughts or impulses that are similar in many ways to those experienced by patients being treated for obsessive–compulsive disorder (Rachman & deSilva, 1978; Salkovskis & Harrison, 1984). These include impulses to hurt other people, impulses to do something dangerous, and thoughts of accidents or disease. In contrast to the obsessions described by people who are not in treatment, those experienced by clinical patients occur more frequently, last longer, and are associated with higher levels of discomfort than normal obsessions. Clinical obsessions are also resisted more strongly, and patients report more difficulty dismissing their unwanted thoughts and impulses. Research evidence suggests that obsessions are relatively common, and that clinical obsessions differ from normal obsessions in degree rather than in nature.

Ed's constricted style of forming letters and his habitual pattern of going back to check and correct his writing illustrate the way in which compulsions are used to reduce anxiety. If he did not engage in these ritualistic behaviors, he would become extremely uncomfortable. His concern about someone being strangled or decapitated if the letters were not properly formed was not delusional, because he readily acknowledged that this was a "silly" idea. Nevertheless, he couldn't shake the obsessive idea that some dreadful event would occur if he was not excruciatingly careful about his writing. He felt as though he had to act, even though he knew that his obsessive thought was irrational. This paradox is extremely frustrating to obsessive–compulsive patients, and it is one of the most common and interesting aspects of the disorder.

Compulsions reduce anxiety, but they do not produce pleasure. Thus some behaviors, such as gambling and drug use, that people describe as being "compulsive" are not considered true compulsions according to this definition.

Although some clinicians have argued that compulsive rituals are associated with a complete loss of voluntary control, it is more accurate to view the problem in terms of *diminished* control. For example, Ed could occasionally manage to resist the urge to write in his compulsive style. The behavior was not totally automatic. But whenever he did not engage in this ritualistic behavior, his subjective level of distress increased dramatically, and within a short period of time he returned to the compulsive writing style.

The two most common forms of compulsive behavior are cleaning and checking. Compulsive cleaning is often associated with an irrational fear of contamination, and in that respect it bears a strong resemblance to certain phobias (Rachman & Hodgson, 1980). There are passive as well as active features of compulsive cleaning. Compulsive cleaners go out of their way to avoid contact with dirt, germs, and other sources of contamination. Then, when they believe that they have come into contact with a source of contamination, they engage in ritualistic cleaning behavior, such as washing their hands, taking showers, cleaning kitchen counters, and so on. These rituals typically involve a large number of repetitions. Some people may wash their hands 50 times a day, taking several minutes to scrub their hands up to the elbow with industrial-strength cleanser. Others take showers that last 2 or 3 hours in which they wash each part of their body in a fixed order, needing to repeat the scrubbing motion an exact number of times.

Compulsive checking frequently represents an attempt to ensure the person's safety or the safety and health of a friend or family member. The person checks things over and over again in an attempt to prevent the occurrence of an imagined, unpleasant, or disastrous event (for example, accidents or sickness).

Classification

To understand the way in which anxiety disorders are currently classified, we must briefly consider the history of these concepts. This general set of problems has been the topic of considerable diagnostic controversy throughout the twentieth century.

Brief Historical Perspective

Anxiety and abnormal fears did not play a prominent role in the psychiatric classification systems that began to emerge in Europe during the second half of the nineteenth century (see Chapter 4). Anxiety disorders were probably left out of these descriptions because the authors were primarily superintendents of large asylums. Their patients were people who were psychotic or so disorganized that they could no longer reside in the larger community (Jablensky, 1985;

Klerman, 1990). People with anxiety problems seldom came to the attention of psychiatrists during the nineteenth century because very few cases of anxiety disorder require institutionalization.

Freud and his followers were responsible for some of the first extensive clinical descriptions of pathological anxiety states. Working primarily with patients who were not hospitalized, Freud had an opportunity to treat and study a variety of anxiety-related problems. He described cases of phobia, generalized anxiety, and obsessive–compulsive behavior. His approach emphasized etiological similarities among the various manifestations of anxiety disorders. The form of specific symptoms (a phobia as compared to a compulsion) was considered to be less important than the underlying causes, which were presumably similar.

PSYCHOANALYTIC THEORY

Freud's psychological explanations for the origins of anxiety disorders have been extremely influential throughout the twentieth century (Frances et al., 1993; Josephs, 1994). Freud focused primarily on the importance of mental conflicts and innate biological impulses (primarily sexual and aggressive instincts) in the etiology of anxiety (see Chapter 2). This perspective played a central role in the way that anxiety disorders were classified in early versions of the DSM. They were grouped with several other types of problems under the general heading of **neurosis,** a term used to describe persistent emotional disturbances, such as anxiety and depression, in which the person is aware of the nature of the problem. Neurotic disorders are distinguished from psychotic disorders, in which the person is often out of touch with reality and unaware of the nature of his or her problems. According to Freud, all the neuroses share a common etiological process.

The basic outline of Freud's theory of anxiety hinges on the notion that the person's ego can experience a small amount of anxiety as a *signal* indicating that an instinctual impulse that has previously been associated with punishment and disapproval is about to be acted on. This usually means that the person is about to do something aggressive or sexual that is considered inappropriate. *Signal anxiety* triggers the use of ego defenses—primarily repression—that prevent conscious recognition of the forbidden impulse, inhibit its expression, and thereby reduce the person's anxiety. When the system works as it should, anxiety is adaptive, and the person's behavior is regulated to conform with social expectations.

Unfortunately, people can still experience pathological levels of anxiety if the system is overwhelmed. Traumatic events or circumstances can lead to extreme levels of free-floating anxiety. The ego is then forced to resort to additional defensive maneuvers that can produce symptoms such as phobias and compulsions. The specific form of overt symptoms is determined by the defense mechanisms that are employed by the ego, but the underlying process is presumably the same across all of the anxiety neuroses.

Consider, for example, a Freudian explanation for the etiology of Ed's obsessive-compulsive disorder. According to this model, the instinctual drive that is most problematic in OCD is aggression. Problems that Ed encountered during early childhood must have left him with serious difficulties in dealing with aggressive impulses, which are coupled with resentment harbored toward his younger brother, Tim. Violent aggressive impulses are unacceptable to the ego, and they have to be dealt with using reaction formation, which is presumably the primary defense in obsessive–compulsive disorder. Rather than attempting to harm his brother (decapitating him or strangling him, as in his violent images), Ed was obliged to spend his time correcting printing errors in order to "protect" Tim or ensure that Tim's name is not forever associated with the image of a violent act. The compulsive rituals are viewed as the product of the defense mechanism that was unconsciously employed to fend off anxiety associated with aggression.

Freud's conceptual model for the anxiety neuroses incorporated several important features, including the importance of biologically based impulses, learning experiences based on interactions with other people, and cognitive (or intrapsychic) events that play an important role in mediating between current and past experience. It was firmly grounded in Freud's observations of his own patients' experiences. Although it served as a useful stimulus to future clinicians and identified many important factors in the etiology of anxiety disorders, his model suffered from a number of weaknesses. Perhaps the major problem was that of measurement. Because Freud's concepts were not linked directly to observable behaviors, his theory of anxiety could not be tested empirically (outside of case studies).

FROM DSM-I TO DSM-IV

Both DSM-I and DSM-II grouped anxiety disorders together under the general heading of neuroses. According to DSM-II, "Anxiety is the chief characteristic of the neuroses. It may be felt and expressed directly, or it may be controlled unconsciously and automatically by conversion, displacement[†] and various other psychological mechanisms" (p. 39). In other words, a person did not have to exhibit obvious signs of anxiety to be considered neurotic. The neurotic

---

[†] Conversion and displacement are, according to psychoanalytic theory, defense mechanisms employed by the ego to combat anxiety. *Conversion* is the symbolic representation of psychic conflict in terms of motor or sensory symptoms (see the discussion of somatoform disorders in Chapter 7). *Displacement* is the process by which emotions are transferred from one object or idea to another or impulses are shifted from one pathway to another.

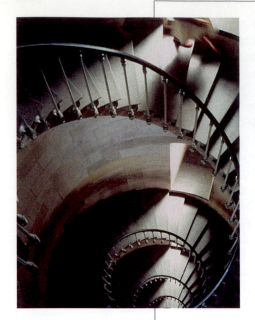

▲ **Specific phobias are irrational fears associated with specific situations that the person avoids. Acrophobia is the name given to fear of heights.**

▲ **Donald Klein, a psychiatrist at Columbia University, suggested that panic disorder should be classified separately from generalized anxiety disorder on the basis of his clinical experience, which indicated that panic attacks could be treated successfully with medication.**

disorders were grouped together on the basis of the common etiological process that they presumably shared (unconscious mental conflicts triggering the use of defense mechanisms, which in turn lead to symptoms). This section of the diagnostic manual remained controversial because many psychologists and psychiatrists did not believe that these psychoanalytic principles were valid.

The authors of DSM-III (APA, 1980) decided to employ a more descriptive approach to classification (see Chapter 4). One of their most significant and controversial changes was to drop the use of the concept *neurosis* as a general organizing principle. Individual forms of neurosis were regrouped into new diagnostic categories based on descriptive features. Most were subsumed under a new class called *anxiety disorders*.

Subclassification

Changes that were made formal with the publication of DSM-III highlight a trend toward greater specificity in the diagnosis of anxiety disorders. Experts who classify mental disorders can be described informally as belonging to one of two groups, "lumpers" and "splitters" (Mack, Forman, Brown, & Frances, 1994). Lumpers argue that anxiety is a generalized condition or set of symptoms without any special subdivisions. Splitters distinguish among a number of conditions, each of which is presumed to have its own etiology. During the first half of the twentieth century, psychiatrists tended to adopt a generalized position with regard to anxiety disorders (see Jablensky, 1985). In other words, they lumped together the various anxiety disorders rather than split them apart into many separate disorders.

The validity of the general category "anxiety neurosis" was challenged by the work of Donald Klein, a psychiatrist at Columbia University. Klein argued that some people who suffered from anxiety neurosis experienced unexpected panic attacks leading to agoraphobia, whereas others did not. Klein's results were reflected in DSM-III, which divided the category of anxiety neurosis into two specific groups: **generalized anxiety disorder (GAD)** and panic

disorder, with or without agoraphobia. People with panic disorder experienced panic attacks; those with GAD did not. Additional evidence that supported the separation of panic disorder from GAD came from the use of medication: Patients with panic disorder responded well to certain drugs that were not effective for patients with GAD.

Another important step in the creation of formal subdivisions within the anxiety disorders was to distinguish between specific phobias and social phobias. In 1966, the British psychiatrists Isaac Marks and Michael Gelder introduced the concept of **social phobia** to describe people who become intensely anxious when they must do something, such as speaking, eating, or writing, in front of other people who in turn might evaluate or scrutinize the person's performance (Marks & Gelder, 1966; Marks, 1969). People with social phobias do not have trouble completing the feared task if they are allowed to do it privately. Marks and Gelder proposed that fears of this type should be distinguished from other types of phobias, noting important differences in terms of age of onset and presenting symptoms. DSM-IV recognizes social phobias as a separate type of anxiety disorder, which may be etiologically distinct from other types of phobias (Judd, 1994; Stein, 1995).

Although it is not currently a popular position, a reasonable argument can still be made in favor of a more unified approach to the classification of anxiety disorders (Andrews, 1996). Consider, for example, the cases of Ed in this chapter and Michael in Chapter 4. Both exhibited a relatively wide range of anxiety symptoms. The high rate of comorbidity among anxiety disorders suggests that these cases are not unusual. Should Ed be considered to have both a phobic disorder (fear of axes) and an obsessive–compulsive disorder? Or are these diverse symptoms best viewed as manifestations of the same anxiety disorder? These are questions about the validity of diagnostic categories (see Chapter 4). Decisions regarding the breadth or specificity of anxiety disorders will ultimately depend on evidence from many areas. Do phobias and OCD show distinct, separate patterns in family studies? Do they respond to different types of treatment? Can we distinguish between them in terms of typical patterns of onset and course? Definitive answers are not yet available. Future research efforts are needed to address these issues.

Contemporary Diagnostic Systems (DSM-IV)

The DSM-IV (APA, 1994) approach to classifying anxiety disorders recognizes several specific subtypes. The overall scheme is outlined in Table 6–2. It includes panic disorder, three types of phobic disorders, obsessive–compulsive disorder, and generalized anxiety disorder, as well as posttraumatic stress disorder (PTSD) and acute stress disorder. (The last two conditions are discussed in Chapter 7.)

To meet the diagnostic criteria for panic disorder, a person must experience recurrent, *unexpected* panic attacks. At least one of the attacks must have been followed by a period of 1 month or more in which the person has either persistent concern about having additional attacks, worry about the implications of the attack or its consequences, or a significant change in behavior related to the attacks. Panic disorder is divided into two subtypes, depending on the presence or absence of agoraphobia.

DSM-IV defines agoraphobia in terms of anxiety about being in situations from which escape might be either difficult or embarrassing. This approach is based on the view that agoraphobia is typically a complication that follows upon the experience of panic attacks (Frances, First, & Pincus, 1995). Avoidance and distress are important elements of the definition. In order to meet the DSM-IV criteria, the person must either avoid agoraphobic situations, such as traveling away from his or her own home; endure the experience with great distress; or insist on being accompanied by another person who can provide some comfort or security. In most cases, the person avoids a wide variety of situations rather than just one specific type of situation.

People who fit this description of agoraphobia without meeting the criteria for panic disorder would be assigned a diagnosis of agoraphobia without history of panic disorder. This category has been the topic of considerable debate. Recent analyses of data from the Epidemiologic Catchment Area study suggest that agoraphobia seldom occurs without panic attacks (Horwath et al., 1993), but the National Comorbidity Study results indicated a 12-month prevalence of 2.8 percent (men and women combined) for this disorder. These discrepancies will undoubtedly be addressed in future research studies.

A *specific phobia* is defined in DSM-IV as "a marked and persistent fear that is excessive or unreasonable, cued by the presence or anticipation of a specific object or situation." Frequently observed types of specific phobia include fear of heights, small animals (such as spiders, bugs, mice, snakes, or bats), tunnels or bridges, storms, illness and injury (including blood), being in a closed place (such as a very small room), and being on certain kinds of public transportation (such as airplanes, buses, or elevators). Exposure to the phobic stimulus must be followed by an immediate fear response.

▲ Social phobias involve a performance element. The person is afraid of being embarrassed in front of other people. Singer Carly Simon has suffered from performance anxiety throughout her successful career.

TABLE 6–2
Categories Listed as Anxiety Disorders in DSM-IV

Panic Disorder
  Without Agoraphobia
  With Agoraphobia
	Obsessive–Compulsive Disorder

Agoraphobia (without history of panic disorder)	Generalized Anxiety Disorder
Specific Phobia	Posttraumatic Stress Disorder
Social Phobia	Acute Stress Disorder

Furthermore, the person must appreciate the fact that the fear is excessive or unreasonable, and the person must avoid the phobic situation. DSM-IV also provides a severity threshold: The avoidance or distress associated with the phobia must interfere significantly with the person's normal activities or relationships with others.

The DSM-IV definition of *social phobia* is almost identical to that for specific phobia, but it includes the additional element of performance. A person with a social phobia is afraid of (and avoids) social situations. These situations fall into two broad headings: doing something in front of unfamiliar people (performance anxiety) and interpersonal interactions (such as dating and parties). Fear of being humiliated or embarrassed presumably lies at the heart of the person's discomfort. Some people have a circumscribed form of social phobia that is focused on one particular type of situation. Examples include giving a speech, playing a musical instrument, urinating in a public rest room, or eating in a restaurant. In other cases, the fear is more generalized, and the person is intensely anxious in almost any situation that involves social interaction. This type of person might be described as being extremely shy. The extensive overlap between generalized social phobia and avoidant personality disorder (see Chapter 10) has created some confusion and has been the topic of numerous research studies (Tran & Chambless, 1995).

Generalized anxiety disorder (GAD) is defined in terms of excessive anxiety and worry that the person finds difficult to control and that lead to significant distress or impairment in occupational or social functioning. The worry must occur more days than not for a period of at least 6 months, and it must be about a number of different events or activities. In order to distinguish GAD from other forms of anxiety disorder, DSM-IV notes that the person's worries should not be focused on having a panic attack (as in panic disorder), being embarrassed in public (as in social phobia), or being contaminated (as in obsessive–compulsive disorder). Finally, the person's worries and "free-floating anxiety" must be accompanied by at least three of the following symptoms: (1) restlessness or feeling keyed up or on edge, (2) being easily fatigued, (3) difficulty concentrating or mind going blank, (4) irritability, (5) muscle tension, and (6) sleep disturbance.

Generalized anxiety disorder remains one of the most controversial anxiety disorders for several reasons. The diagnostic reliability of GAD is often substantially lower than that observed for other types of anxiety disorder (DiNardo et al., 1993; Wittchen, Kessler, Zhao, & Abelson, 1995). As noted in Figure 6–1, GAD has the highest degree of overlap with the other anxiety disorders. The validity of GAD as a separate diagnostic category is therefore open to serious question. Some experts have suggested that it might be more useful to think of GAD as a trait or a vulnerability factor that sets the stage for later development of other specific types of anxiety disorder, such as panic disorder, social phobia, or obsessive–compulsive disorder (Brown, Barlow, & Liebowitz, 1994).

DSM-IV defines *obsessive–compulsive disorder* in terms of the presence of either obsessions or compulsions. Most people who meet the criteria for this disorder actually exhibit both of these symptoms. The person must recognize that the obsessions or compulsions are excessive or unreasonable. Obsessions are described as "recurrent and persistent thoughts, impulses, or images that are experienced, at some time during the disturbance, as intrusive and inappropriate, and cause marked anxiety or distress." The

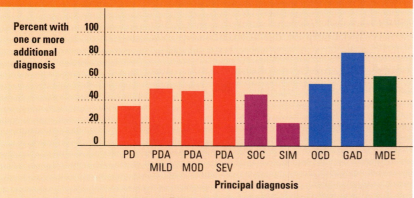

Comorbidity Rates for Anxiety Disorders and Major Depression

PD, panic disorder; PDA, panic disorder with agoraphobia; SOC, social phobia; SIM, simple phobia; OCD, obsessive-compulsive disorder; GAD, generalized anxiety disorder; MDE, major depression

MILD, MOD (moderate), SEV (severe)

FIGURE 6-1: Comorbidity rates for anxiety disorders and major depression (percentage of people who met diagnostic criteria for one anxiety or mood disorder who also qualified for at least one additional diagnosis).

Source: T.A. Brown, 1996, Validity of the DSM-III-R and DSM-IV classification systems for anxiety disorders. In Ronald M. Rapee (Ed.), *Current Controversies in the Anxiety Disorders*, p. 27. New York: Guilford Press.

diagnostic manual specifies further that these thoughts must not be simply excessive worries about real problems. Intrusive thoughts about overdue bills, for example, would not qualify as obsessions. The DSM-IV definition also requires that the person must attempt to ignore, suppress, or neutralize the unwanted thoughts or impulses. Compulsions are defined as "repetitive behaviors or mental acts that the person feels driven to perform in response to an obsession, or according to rules that must be applied rigidly." These behaviors or mental acts must be aimed at reducing or avoiding distress or anxiety.

The line of demarcation between compulsive rituals and normal behavior is often difficult to define. How many times should a person wash her hands in a day? How long should a shower last? Is it reasonable to check more than one time to be sure that the door is locked or the alarm clock is set? DSM-IV has established an arbitrary threshold that holds that rituals become compulsive if they cause marked distress, take more than an hour per day to perform, or interfere with normal occupational and social functioning.

Epidemiology

Some epidemiological studies focus exclusively on treated cases of a disorder, but that strategy can provide a distorted view of the distribution of the disorder within the general population. Many factors can influence whether a person decides to seek treatment. Some cases are less severe than others. Some people treat themselves without consulting a mental health professional. Some people are suspicious of medical facilities, and others are concerned about what other people will think of them if they are treated for a mental disorder. This issue has been a special problem in epidemiological studies of anxiety disorders. Recent evidence indicates that only about 25 percent of people who qualify for a diagnosis of anxiety disorder ever seek psychological treatment. Therefore our estimates of the frequency and severity of these problems must be based on community surveys.

Prevalence

The National Comorbidity Survey (NCS), which included approximately 8,000 people aged 15 to 54 throughout the United States, found that anxiety disorders are more common than any other form of mental disorder (Kessler et al., 1994). The same conclusion had been reached previously in the ECA study (see Table 1–3). Specific phobias are the most common type of anxiety disorder, with a 1-year prevalence of about 9 percent of the adult population (men and women combined). Social phobia is almost as common, with a 1-year prevalence of 8 percent. Agoraphobia without panic disorder and GAD both affect approximately 3 percent of the

population, and 2 percent of adults meet the criteria for panic disorder in any given year. Obsessive–compulsive disorder affects another 2 percent of the population.

Comorbidity

The symptoms of various anxiety disorders overlap considerably. Many people who experience panic attacks develop phobic avoidance, and many people with obsessive thoughts would also be considered chronic worriers. One study found that 50 percent of people who met the criteria for one anxiety disorder also met the criteria for at least one other form of anxiety disorder or mood disorder (Brown & Barlow, 1992). This pattern, broken down by specific types of anxiety disorder, is illustrated in Figure 6–1. The highest rates of comorbidity were found for generalized anxiety disorder (82 percent) and severe cases of panic disorder with agoraphobia (72 percent). The lowest rate was found for cases of specific phobia; only 20 percent of the people with this diagnosis met the criteria for an additional type of anxiety disorder. When a secondary diagnosis was made, what was it? The most common secondary diagnosis was generalized anxiety disorder (23 percent of the cases). Given this pattern of results, it is not surprising that some clinical scientists have argued that the distinction between GAD and other anxiety disorders is not particularly clear (Andrews, 1996). In fact, some scientists wonder whether it should even be considered a separate type of disorder.

Given the emotional bases of both anxiety and depression, it is not surprising that considerable overlap also exists between anxiety disorders and mood disorders. Notice in Figure 6–1 that 61 percent of the people who received a primary diagnosis of major depression also qualified for a secondary diagnosis of some type of anxiety disorder. This extensive overlap raises interesting questions about the relation between these general diagnostic categories (see Further Thoughts). Do people who meet the criteria for both depression and an anxiety disorder really suffer from two distinct syndromes? Or should we think about the existence of three types of disorder: "pure" anxiety disorders, "pure" mood disorders, and a third type of disorder that represents a mixture of anxiety and depression? Reasonable arguments have been made on both sides of this debate, which remains unresolved (Reich et al., 1993).

FURTHER THOUGHTS

A Model of Anxiety and Depression

Anxiety and depression are closely related concepts. Both are defined primarily in terms of negative emotional responses. In actual clinical practice, they often appear together. People who are anxious are also likely to be depressed, and people who are depressed are frequently anxious. What does this overlapping pattern mean? Some clinicians have argued that anxiety and depression are different manifestations of the same underlying problem. Others hold that they are distinctly different disorders, while recognizing that they can appear together. The relationship between the symptoms of anxiety and those of depression has been the focus of many interesting debates.

Lee Anna Clark and David Watson, psychologists at the University of Iowa, have proposed a model of anxiety and depression that helps to explain the distinction between these conditions (Clark & Watson, 1991). Their proposal is based, in part, on the distinction between two dimensions of mood: positive and negative affect[†] (Tellegen, 1985). A person who is experiencing a high level of **negative affect** would be described as being upset, whereas someone whose level of negative affect is low would be considered calm or relaxed. Adjectives that describe negative affect include angry, guilty, afraid, sad, scornful, disgusted, and worried. A person who is experiencing high levels of **positive affect** would be described as energetic or having a zest for life, whereas someone whose level of positive affect is low would be considered tired or sluggish. Adjectives that describe positive affect include active, delighted, interested, enthusiastic, and proud. These dimensions are largely independent. In other words, a person who is high on one is not necessarily low on the other. Some people are high on both dimensions.

Using this concept of emotional responses as a guide, Clark and Watson examined evidence from several studies that tried to distinguish between anxiety and depression in psychiatric patients as well as in nonclinical subjects. They concluded that the data are best explained in terms of three separate elements: (1) *general distress* (high negative affect), which is common to both anxiety and depression; (2) *physiological hyperarousal,* which is specific to anxiety; and (3) *absence of positive affect,* which is specific to depression. All three elements must be considered in order to describe completely the symptoms of anxiety and depression.

General distress is a diffuse combination of several negative emotional responses, including guilt, anger, fear, sadness, and disgust. These responses may be accompanied by related symptoms, such as mild disturbances of sleep and appetite, distractibility, and vague somatic complaints. According to Clark and Watson's model, elevated levels of general distress indicate that the person may be suffering from a mood disorder, an anxiety disorder, or both. To make a diagnosis, the clinician must

---

[†] Clark and Watson use the term "affect" to refer generally to "emotionality," rather than specifically to the observable behaviors associated with emotional responses (see our definition in Chapter 5). Their self-report measure of positive and negative affect, the Positive and Negative Affect Schedule—Expanded Form, includes items tapping subjective feelings as well as interests and behaviors (Watson & Clark, 1990).

take into account the other two elements in their model.

Physiological hyperarousal is presumably associated with anxiety rather than depression. This element of the model is defined in terms of such symptoms as heart palpitations, shortness of breath, excessive sweating, muscular tension and restlessness, shakiness or trembling, and abdominal distress. People with anxiety disorders would presumably exhibit symptoms of somatic hyperarousal as well as high levels of general distress or negative affect.

Absence of positive affect is presumably associated with depression rather than with anxiety. This element of the model is defined in terms of symptoms such as loss of interest in usual activities, inability to experience pleasure (anhedonia), fatigue, and feelings of hopelessness. A patient with a major depressive disorder would be expected to show high levels of negative affect (general distress) in combination with low levels of positive affect.

Anxiety disorders and depression overlap frequently because both conditions are characterized by high levels of general distress. A person who experiences a prolonged period of high negative affect (distress) as well as low levels of positive affect and high levels of somatic symptoms would be likely to report feeling both depressed and anxious.

This model clarifies the phenomenology of anxiety and also explains epidemiological evidence regarding the frequent comorbidity of anxiety and mood disorders. The same three groupings of symptoms (general distress, low positive affect, and somatic arousal) have been found in several different samples of people, ranging from college students to psychiatric patients (Watson et al., 1995a). The fundamental structure of Clark and Watson's model is therefore reliable. The model's validity has also received additional empirical support, because the somatic arousal and positive affect scales have repeatedly been able to distinguish between samples of people who are depressed and people who are anxious (Watson et al., 1995b). ■

Substance dependence is another problem that is frequently associated with anxiety disorders. In one sample of alcoholic patients, Chambless and her colleagues found that 40 percent would have met diagnostic criteria for at least one anxiety disorder at some point during their lives (Chambless et al., 1987). In situations such as these, questions of cause and effect are not clear. Did the person use alcohol in an attempt to control abnormal anxiety, or did the person become anxious after drinking excessively? It can work both ways. Chambless concluded that, in most cases, anxiety was the more longstanding problem. This is especially true for phobic disorders and panic disorder with agoraphobia (Kushner, Sher, & Beitman, 1990).

Gender Differences

There are significant gender differences in several types of anxiety disorders. Pertinent data from the National Comorbidity Survey are summarized in Table 6–3. The gender difference is particularly large for specific phobias, where women are 3 times as likely as men to experience the disorder. Women are about twice as likely as men to experience panic disorder, agoraphobia (without panic

disorder), and generalized anxiety disorder. Social phobia is also more common among women than among men, but the difference is not as striking as it is for other types of phobia. The only type of anxiety disorder for which there does not appear to be a significant gender difference is OCD (Karno & Golding, 1991).

TABLE 6-3

Gender Differences in the 12-Month Prevalence of Anxiety Disorders

Disorder	Women (%)	Men (%)
Any anxiety disorder	22.6	11.8
Panic disorder	3.2	1.3
Agoraphobia without panic disorder	3.8	1.7
Social phobia	9.1	6.6
Specific phobia	13.2	4.4
Generalized anxiety disorder	4.3	2.0
Obsessive–compulsive disorder*	1.9	1.4

*Data on obsessive–compulsive disorder are from the Epidemiologic Catchment Area study (Karno & Golding, 1991) because the National Comorbidity Survey did not ask about obsessions and compulsions.
Source: R. C. Kessler, K. A. McGonagle, S. Zhao, C. B. Nelson, M. Hughes, S. Eshleman, H. Wittchen, & K. S. Kendler, 1994, Lifetime and 12-month prevalence of DSM-III-R psychiatric disorders in the United States: Results from the National Comorbidity Survey, *Archives of General Psychiatry, 51,* 8–19.

The significant gender differences in panic disorder, generalized anxiety disorder, specific phobias, and social phobias must be interpreted in the light of etiological theories, which are considered in the next section. Several explanations remain plausible. Psychological speculation has focused on such factors as gender differences in child-rearing practices or differences in the way in which men and women respond to stressful life events (Cameron & Hill, 1989). Gender differences in hormone functions or neurotransmitter activities in the brain may also be responsible (Yonkers & Gurguis, 1995).

Anxiety Across the Life Span

Data from the ECA study indicate that the prevalence of anxiety disorders is lower among elderly men and women than it is among people in other age groups. This result is perhaps surprising, in light of the fact that many elderly people face problems associated with loneliness, increased dependency, declining physical and cognitive capacities, and changes in social and economic conditions. To explain this result, some scientists speculate that something about the aging process may reduce the probability that stressful or threatening life events will lead to the onset of an anxiety disorder (Flint, 1994; Gurian & Goisman, 1993).

Most elderly people with an anxiety disorder have had the symptoms for many years. It is relatively unusual for a person to develop a new case of panic disorder, specific phobia, social phobia, or obsessive–compulsive disorder at an advanced age. The only type of anxiety disorder that begins with any noticeable frequency in late life is agoraphobia (Flint, 1994).

The diagnosis of anxiety disorders among elderly people is complicated by the need to consider factors such as medical illnesses and other physical impairments and limitations. Respiratory and cardiovascular problems may resemble the physiological symptoms of a panic attack. Hearing losses may lead to anxiety in interpersonal interactions. Subsequent avoidance might be inappropriately attributed to the onset of a social phobia. A frail elderly person who falls down on the street may become afraid to leave home alone, but this may be a reasonable concern rather than a symptom of agoraphobia. For reasons such as these, the diagnosis of anxiety disorders must be done with extra caution in elderly men and women.

Cross-Cultural Comparisons

Peoples in many kinds of cultures experience anxiety disorders. Population surveys suggest that between 1 and 4 people out of 100 experience various types of anxiety disorders in different cultures (Good & Kleinman, 1985). The focus of typical anxiety complaints can vary dramatically across cultural boundaries, however. People in Western societies often experience anxiety in relation to their work performance, whereas in other societies people may be more concerned with family issues or religious experiences. In the Yoruba culture of Nigeria, for example, anxiety is frequently associated with fertility and the health of family members.

Anxiety disorders have been observed in preliterate as well as Westernized cultures. Of course, the same descriptive and diagnostic terms are not used in every culture, but the basic psychological phenomena appear to be similar. Cultural anthropologists have recognized many different culture-bound syndromes that, in some cases, bear striking resemblance to anxiety disorders listed in DSM-IV. Consider the following example of "kayak angst" in an Inuit (Eskimo) hunter. The problem sounds a lot like panic disorder.

> Isak H., aged 34, (was a) hunter fisherman of mixed race from Nugatsiak. He had been quite well before. In 1939 he saw a kayak man drowned and was very much upset. In the summer of 1946, when he was paddling along in his kayak on a calm day with a soft backwash and bright sunshine he suddenly became terrified when looking down to the bottom of the sea. He seemed to feel the kayak filling with water, the point of the kayak being very distant and dim. His head felt queer and he took off his cap. His heart started beating rapidly and he trembled so violently that the kayak shook. Perspiration ran down his face, his heart seemed to turn over and his arms were heavy and numb. He made an effort to reach shore, he vomited, his bowels were loose and he had a strong desire to pass water. Next time he set out in his kayak the same symptoms occurred. He felt more and more terrified of crouching down in his kayak, and he

finally gave up all attempts and stopped fishing by kayak. (From Katschnig & Amering, 1990, pp. 77–78)

Very few epidemiological studies have attempted to collect cross-cultural data using standardized interviews and specific diagnostic criteria. One such study was conducted to evaluate specific drugs for the treatment of panic attacks (Cross-National Collaborative Panic Study, 1992). More than 1,000 patients were treated in 14 different countries across North America, Latin America, and Europe.

Several interesting findings emerged from this study. Panic disorder occurred in all the countries that were included in the study. Nevertheless, some important differences were found among panic patients from different regions. Choking or smothering and fear of dying were more common among patients from southern countries in both the Americas and in Europe. Phobic avoidance was much more common among panic patients seen at clinics in the United States and Canada—9 out of every 10—compared to patients seen at clinics in Latin American countries.

Etiological Considerations and Research

Now that we have discussed the various symptoms associated with anxiety disorders and their distribution within the population, we can consider the origins of these disorders. How do these problems develop? Going back to the cases that were presented at the beginning of the chapter, what might account for the onset of Johanna's panic attacks? Why would Ed find himself plagued by violent images and compelled to form letters in a meticulous fashion?

Current theories regarding the etiology of anxiety disorders often focus on the evolutionary significance of anxiety and fear. These emotional response systems are clearly adaptive in many situations. They mobilize responses that help the person survive in the face of both immediate dangers and long-range threats. Anxiety disorders can be viewed as problems that arise in the regulation of these response systems (Barlow, 1988; Marks & Nesse, 1994). When anxiety becomes excessive, or when intense fear is triggered at an inappropriate time or place, these response systems can become more harmful than helpful. In order to understand the etiology of anxiety disorders, we must consider a variety of psychological and biological systems that have evolved for the purpose of triggering and controlling these alarm responses.

Should we expect to find unique etiological pathways associated with each of the types of anxiety disorder listed in DSM-IV? This seems unlikely, particularly in light of the extensive amount of overlap among the various subtypes. Should we expect that all the different types of anxiety disorders are produced by the same causes? This also seems unlikely. Isaac Marks and

Randolph Nesse (1994) have proposed a broad evolutionary perspective for the etiology of anxiety disorders that suggests a middle ground between these two extremes. They suggest that generalized forms of anxiety probably evolved to help the person prepare for threats that could not be identified clearly. More specific forms of anxiety and fear probably evolved to provide more effective responses to certain types of danger. For example, fear of heights is associated with a freezing of muscles rather than running away, which could lead to a fall. Social threats are more likely to provoke responses such as shyness and embarrassment that may increase acceptance by other people by making the individual seem less threatening. Each type of anxiety disorder can be viewed as a mechanism that has evolved to deal with a particular kind of danger. This model leads us to expect that the etiological pathways leading to various forms of anxiety disorders may be partially distinct but not completely independent.

Social Factors

Our consideration of etiological pathways begins with social factors. We discuss the influence of stressful life events, particularly those involving danger and interpersonal conflict, that trigger the onset of certain types of anxiety disorders. We also consider the role of earlier social experiences. Various aspects of parent–child relationships may leave some people more vulnerable to the development of anxiety disorders when they become adults. Taken together, the evidence bearing on these issues helps explain the relationship between, and the overlap among, anxiety disorders and mood disorders.

STRESSFUL LIFE EVENTS

The relationship between stress and anxiety seems intuitively obvious. Common sense might suggest that people who experience high stress levels are likely to develop negative emotional reactions, which can range from feeling "on edge" to the onset of full-blown panic attacks. In Chapter 5 we reviewed the literature concerning stressful life events and depression. As we have seen, the measurement of stressful events is a complex matter, and it is difficult to establish causal relations between stress and psychological disorders.

Several investigations suggest that stressful life events can influence the onset of anxiety disorders as well as depression. Patients with anxiety disorders are more likely than control subjects to report having experienced a negative event in the months preceding the initial development of their symptoms (Blazer, Hughes, & George, 1987; Monroe & Wade, 1988).

Why do some negative life events lead to depression while others lead to anxiety? The nature of the event may be an important factor in determining the type of mental disorder that appears. This possibility was initially reported by Finlay-Jones and Brown (1981), who interviewed women attending a general medical clinic. This group included women who were depressed, women with anxiety disorders, and women who qualified for a dual diagnosis of anxiety and depression. For the 1-year period immediately preceding the onset of their symptoms, 82 percent of the depressed women, 85 percent of the anxious women, and 93 percent of the anxious/depressed women reported at least one severe event. Only 34 percent of the control group reported a similar event.

The investigators then examined the specific nature of the severe events. The women with anxiety symptoms were much more likely to have experienced an event involving *danger* (lack of security), whereas the women who were depressed were more likely to have experienced a severe *loss* (lack of hope). Mixed cases frequently reported both types of events. This pattern of results has also been found in more recent investigations (Brown, 1993). These studies suggest that different types of environmental stress may lead to different types of emotional symptoms. Those associated with insecurity and danger seem to be mostly closely associated with anxiety disorders.

Further insights regarding the nature of stressful events and the onset of anxiety disorders have focused more specifically on agoraphobia. Serious interpersonal conflicts seem to be especially common prior to the onset of agoraphobia. Consider, for example, the following list of life events, which were all reported with greater frequency by patients being treated for agoraphobia when they were compared to people visiting a general practice physician (Franklin & Andrews, 1989):

- Increase in serious arguments with partner or parents
- Serious problems with a close friend, neighbor, or relative
- Broke off a steady relationship

Each of these events was at least 4 times more common in the agoraphobic group. The relatively high frequency of stressful life events was accompanied by a rather remarkable lack of insight on the part of the agoraphobic patients. When they were asked about their understanding of the development of their disorder, 90 percent said that they found the onset of agoraphobic symptoms "totally baffling and incomprehensible."

CHILDHOOD ADVERSITY

If recent dangers and conflicts can precipitate the full-blown symptoms of an anxiety disorder, do past experiences—those that took place years ago—set the stage for this experience? Further research by George Brown and his colleagues indicates that they can (Brown & Harris, 1993). Their studies of these phenomena focus on measures of *childhood adversity*. This concept included women's recollections of parental indifference (being physically or emotionally neglected by their parents for a period of at least 12 months prior to age 17) and physical abuse (being physically beaten or threatened with violence, usually in an attempt to control or punish the child).

Within a community sample of approximately 400 working-class women, Brown and Harris (1993) found that 25 percent met diagnostic criteria for at least one type of anxiety disorder. The relationship between childhood adversity and the presence of these anxiety disorders is illustrated in Figure 6–2. Women who

▼ Negative life events can precipitate the appearance of anxiety disorders. The onset of agoraphobia is sometimes preceded by serious interpersonal conflicts, including marital discord.

were suffering from most types of anxiety disorder were more likely than women with no disorder to report having been exposed to parental indifference and physical abuse during childhood or adolescence. This pattern was particularly striking for the women with panic disorder. In contrast, women with specific phobias or only mild symptoms of agoraphobia could not be distinguished from the control group on the basis of childhood adversity. This result is consistent with the notion that somewhat different etiological pathways may be associated with specific phobias than with other, frequently more severe forms of anxiety disorder.

ATTACHMENT RELATIONSHIPS AND SEPARATION ANXIETY

The evidence regarding parental adversity is similar to another perspective on the etiology of anxiety disorders that has been concerned with the infant's attachment relationship with caretakers. Attachment theory (see Chapter 2) integrates the psychodynamic perspective with field observations of primate behavior and with laboratory research with human infants (Bretherton, 1992). According to the British psychiatrist John Bowlby, anxiety is an innate response to separation, or the threat of separation, from the caretaker. Those infants who are insecurely attached to their parents are presumably more likely to develop anxiety disorders, especially agoraphobia, when they become adults (Bowlby, 1973, 1980).

Several studies have found that people with agoraphobia are more likely to report that they had problems associated with insecure attachment as children (de Ruiter & van Uzendoorn, 1992; Silove et al., 1993). Anxious attachment as infants may make these individuals more vulnerable, once they are adults, to the threats that are contained in interpersonal conflict—for example, loss of a loved one if a marriage dissolves (Monroe & Wade, 1988). This hypothesis fits nicely with the observation, noted previously, that interpersonal conflict is a relatively frequent triggering event for the onset of agoraphobic symptoms.

Attachment difficulties are not restricted to agoraphobia, however. Rather, studies indicate that they might set the stage for other types of adult anxiety disorders (Lipsitz et al., 1994). Of course, many anxiously attached children do not develop anxiety disorders when they grow up. The suggestion of a causal relationship between childhood attachments and adult anxiety disorders is intriguing, but the evidence

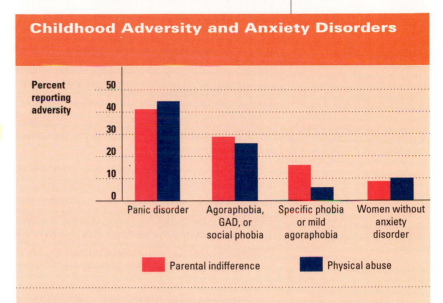

Childhood Adversity and Anxiety Disorders

FIGURE 6-2: **Parental indifference and physical abuse are frequently reported by women who later develop panic disorder. They do not seem to be related to specific phobias.**

Source: G.W. Brown and T.O. Harris, 1993, Aetiology of anxiety and depressive disorders in an inner-city population. 1. Early adversity, *Psychological Medicine, 23,* 143–154.

supporting it will not be convincing until scientists conduct longitudinal studies to test this hypothesis. The same criticism obviously applies to Brown's research on childhood adversity. To test these hypotheses further, psychologists must conduct studies based on direct observations of parent–child relationships rather than on retrospective accounts of childhood behaviors, which are highly subjective and are not always accurate or reliable.

Psychological Factors

Research suggests that stressful life events and childhood adversity contribute to the development of anxiety disorders. But what are the specific mechanisms that link these experiences to specific emotional difficulties such as intense fears, panic attacks, and excessive worry? This question brings our discussion of etiology to a different level of analysis. A number of psychological mechanisms undoubtedly play an important role in helping to shape the development and maintenance of anxiety disorders. These processes include learning processes and cognitive events.

LEARNING PROCESSES

Since the 1920s, experimental psychologists working in laboratory settings have been interested in the possibility that fears might be learned through classical (or Pavlovian) conditioning (see Eysenck, 1979; Mineka, 1985; Mineka & Zinbarg, 1995). The central mechanism in the classical conditioning process is the association between an unconditioned stimulus (UCS) and a conditioned stimulus (CS). The UCS is able to elicit a strong unconditioned emotional response (UR), such as fear. Examples of potential UCSs are painfully loud and unexpected noises, the sight of dangerous animals, and sudden, intense pain. According to psychologists' original views of the classical conditioning process, the CS could be any neutral stimulus that happened to be present when an intense fear reaction was provoked. Through the process of association, the CS would subsequently elicit a conditioned response (CR), which was similar in quality to the original UCR (see Chapter 2).

This explanation for the development of specific phobias fits easily with common sense as well as with clinical experience. Many intense, persistent, irrational fears seem to develop after the person has experienced a traumatic event (Öst & Hugdahl, 1981). An enormous body of research has been conducted on the process of fear acquisition and extinction in laboratory animals and in humans (Davey, 1993; Eysenck, 1979; Rachman, 1991). Evidence from these studies indicates that certain constraints, which appear to be biologically based and may be the result of evolutionary pressures, are associated with the process by which fears are learned. We review these considerations in the next few pages.

Preparedness   Martin Seligman, a psychologist at the University of Pennsylvania, identified several shortcomings of learning theories as explanations for the etiology of phobias. These included the following (Seligman, 1971):

1. Conditioned fear responses that are learned in a laboratory situation are typically easy to extinguish. Phobic responses, on the other hand, are extremely persistent and difficult to change.

2. Phobias that develop after traumatic experiences are typically learned in one trial, but very few laboratory studies have been able to demonstrate one-trial conditioning with fear responses.

3. The original conditioning model held that any neutral stimulus could be used as the CS. If that model is correct, why are phobias associated only with certain types of objects and situations, such as animals, heights, and small enclosed spaces? It is quite unusual for people to develop phobic responses to other types of objects, such as guns, cars, and electrical outlets, even though they are at least as likely to be associated with danger and pain.

In order to account for these difficulties, Seligman proposed that conditioning is governed by a process called **preparedness.** Organisms are assumed to be biologically "prepared," on the basis of neural pathways in their central nervous systems, to learn certain types of associations more quickly than others. According to this perspective, it is not possible to use simply any neutral stimulus as the CS in a classical conditioning paradigm. There are biological constraints on the kinds of associations that members of a particular species are able to make, and these constraints have presumably developed throughout the long process of evolution. Rats, for example, can learn to associate the sensation of nausea (UCS) with the taste of food (CS). They can learn this association in one trial, and once they have developed an aversion to a particular taste, that aversion is highly resistant to extinction.

Seligman argued that human fears that reach phobic proportions may be similar to the taste aversion phenomenon. We may be prepared to develop intense, persistent fears only to a select set of objects or situations. Fear of these stimuli may have conferred a selective advantage upon those people—hundreds of thousands of years ago—who were able to develop fears and consequently avoid certain kinds of dangerous stimuli, such as heights, snakes, and storms. This is not to say that the fears are innate or present at birth, but rather that they can be learned and maintained very easily.

In Chapter 2 we argued that most disorders arise from the interaction of biological, social, and psychological factors. The preparedness model of phobias offers another example of the way in which these factors may combine and interact in the production of specific phobias. The key biological factor is the neurological system, which is prepared to associate quickly certain types of stimuli with intense fear responses. The psychological and social factors in this model involve the nature of the person's developmental history and environmental experience, through which he or she actually learns to associate fear with specific stimuli.

Many investigations have been conducted to test various facets of Seligman's preparedness conditioning model (McNally, 1987; Öhman, 1996). The results of these studies support certain features of the model. For example, Öhman has demonstrated that conditioned responses to fear-relevant stimuli (such as spiders and snakes) are more resistant to extinction than are those to fear-irrelevant stimuli (such as flowers). In addition, they are not affected by verbal instructions; that is, they are more like irrational phobias. Öhman also found that it was possible to develop conditioned fear responses after only one trial of learning.

The process of prepared conditioning may play an important role in the etiology of both social phobias and specific phobias. In specific phobias, the prepared stimuli are things like snakes, heights, storms, and small enclosed places. The prepared stimulus in social phobias might involve other people's faces. Öhman (1986, 1996) has argued that we are prepared to fear faces that appear angry, critical, or rejecting if they are directed toward us. This process is presumably an evolutionary remnant of factors involved in establishing dominance hierarchies, which maintain social order among primates. Animals that are defeated in a dominance conflict are often allowed to remain as part of the group if they behave submissively. The responses of people with social phobias may be somewhat analogous, in the sense that they are afraid of directly facing, or being evaluated by, other people. When a performer makes eye contact with his or her audience, an association may develop very quickly between fear and angry or critical facial expressions.

Observational Learning We all learn many behaviors through imitation. Albert Bandura's early work on modeling, for example, demonstrated that children who observe a model hitting a doll are more likely to behave aggressively themselves when given the opportunity (see Chapter 2). Similar processes may also affect the etiology of intense fear, because some phobias develop in the absence of any direct experience with the feared object. People apparently learn to avoid certain stimuli if they observe other people showing a strong fear response to those stimuli (Rachman, 1990). In other words, the traumatic event does not have to happen to you; it may be enough for you to witness a traumatic event happening to someone else or to watch someone else behave fearfully.

Susan Mineka, a psychologist at Northwestern University, and Michael Cook have conducted a series of intriguing experiments that combine observational learning with the preparedness formulation (e.g., Mineka & Cook, 1993). Their studies have focused on an animal model (see Research Methods in Chapter 5) of phobias: fear reactions among rhesus monkeys. Rhesus monkeys that were raised in their natural environment are markedly afraid of certain kinds of stimuli, such as snakes. Most monkeys reared in the laboratory do not initially react fearfully when they are presented with a toy snake. They quickly acquire this fear, however, after watching a monkey reared in the wild exhibit intense fear in the presence of snakes. The greater the fear exhibited by the wild monkey, the more intense the fears developed by the observer monkey. Further, live observation is not necessary. Monkeys can learn to fear snakes by watching videotapes of other monkeys exhibiting fear reactions.

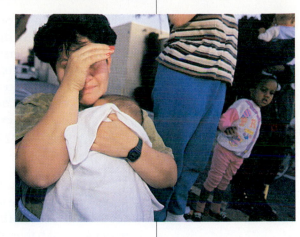

▲ **Vicarious learning can influence the development of strong fear responses. Children who observe adults demonstrating strong emotional responses, like this child in the aftermath of the California earthquakes in 1994, may be likelier to develop phobias.**

Fear of snakes is clearly adaptive, because snakes represent a threat to rhesus monkeys in their natural environment. In Seligman's terms, this could be seen as a prepared association. Will monkeys also learn to avoid nonthreatening and presumably *unprepared* stimuli if they observe a model reacting with intense fear? Is the association between fear and particular stimuli random, or is it selective? Mineka and Cook conducted a series of investigations that proved that the relationship is, in fact, selective: Monkeys are prepared to learn to avoid fear-relevant stimuli (such as snakes and crocodiles) but are not prepared to learn to avoid fear-irrelevant stimuli (such as rabbits or kittens) (Cook & Mineka, 1991).

Learning experiences are clearly important in the etiology of phobias, but their impact often depends on the existence of prepared associations between stimuli. Furthermore, vicarious learning is often as important as direct experience. The importance of the latter factor can be illustrated by considering the development of children's fears during the bombing of London in World War II. When civilian areas were subjected to prolonged and terrifying attacks, families sought safety in underground shelters. If intense fear could be conditioned to any originally neutral stimulus, most of the people subjected to this traumatic experience would develop specific phobic responses in association with whatever stimuli happened to be present during the worst moments of a raid (fear of tunnels, fear of the dark).

In fact, it didn't work that way. Although people showed short-term emotional reactions, very few developed persistent, irrational phobic responses as a result of these terrifying experiences. Anecdotal evidence suggested that children were more likely to become fearful if they had observed their parents exhibiting strong emotional responses during the raids (Rachman, 1990).

COGNITIVE FACTORS

Up to this point, we have talked about the importance of life events and specific learning experiences—variables that can be measured outside the organism. But cognitive events also play an important role as mediators between experience and response. Perceptions, memory, and attention all influence the ways that we react to events in our environments. It is now widely accepted that these cognitive factors play a crucial role in the etiology and maintenance of various types of anxiety disorders. We will focus on four aspects of this literature: perception of controllability and predictability, catastrophic misinterpretation (panic attacks), attentional biases and shifts in the focus of attention, and thought suppression.

Perception of Control   Cognitive theories of emotion have, for many years, emphasized the important relationship between anxiety and the perception of control (for example, Mandler, 1966). People who believe that they are able to control events in their environment are less likely to show symptoms of anxiety than are people who believe that they are helpless.

The importance of this factor can be seen in laboratory studies that have focused on animal models of anxious behavior, sometimes known as "experimental neurosis." Beginning with Pavlov's research on classical conditioning with dogs in the 1920s (see Chapter 2), experimental psychologists have shown that procedures such as extremely difficult discrimination learning tasks (in which an animal is required to make choices between two almost identical stimuli, such as a circle and an ellipse) can produce neurotic behaviors that resemble disorders seen in adult humans. Examples include generalized anxiety and agitation, increased startle responses, and the disruption of purposeful behaviors (such as feeding and harm avoidance). The common feature running through all of these procedures involves repeated exposure to uncontrollable or unpredictable environmental events (Barlow, 1988; Mineka & Kihlstrom, 1978).

An extensive body of evidence supports the conclusion that people who believe that they are less able to control events in their environment are more likely to develop global forms of anxiety (Andrews, 1996), as well as various specific types of anxiety disorder (McNally, 1994). Laboratory research indicates that feelings of lack of control contribute to the onset of panic attacks among patients with panic disorder (see Research Close-Up). The perception of uncontrollability has also been linked to the submissive behavior frequently seen among people with social phobias (Mineka & Zinbarg, 1995), as well as the chronic worries of people with generalized anxiety disorder (Brown, Barlow, & Liebowitz, 1994).

Catastrophic Misinterpretation   A somewhat different type of cognitive dysfunction has been described by David Clark, a psychologist at Oxford University in England. According to this view, panic disorder may be caused by the *catastrophic misinterpretation* of bodily sensations or perceived threat (Clark, 1986b; Clark & Ehlers, 1993). This process is illustrated in Figure 6–3 on p. 224. Although panic attacks can be precipitated by external stimuli, they are usually triggered by internal stimuli, such as bodily sensations, thoughts, or images. On the basis of past experience, these stimuli initiate an anxious mood, which leads to a variety of physiological sensations that typically accompany negative emotional reactions (changes in heart rate, respiration rate, dizziness, and so on). Anxious mood is accompanied by a narrowing of the person's attentional focus and an increased awareness of bodily sensations.

The crucial stage comes next, when the person misinterprets the bodily sensation as a catastrophic event. For example, a person who believes that there is something wrong with his heart might misinterpret a slight acceleration in heart rate as being a sign that he is about to have a heart attack. This reaction ensures the continued operation of this feedback loop, with the misinterpretation enhancing the person's sense of threat, and so on until the process spirals out of control. Thus both cognitive misinterpretation and biological reactions associated with the perception of threat are necessary for a panic attack to occur.

Many research studies have found that the subjective experience of body sensations is, in fact, closely associated with maladaptive self-statements among patients with panic disorder (McNally, 1994). For example, Westling and Öst

Panic and Perception of Control

For many years, psychopathologists have experimented with conditions that are able to produce panic attacks in laboratory situations. If researchers can induce an attack in a lab situation, they might be able to show that the variables that were used to induce panic in the lab are also responsible for inducing it in the real world. Researchers have used several methods to induce artificial panic attacks, including the injection of chemical substances such as lactate. All these procedures produce a range of peripheral somatic sensations, such as palpitations, chest tightness, and light-headedness (Rapee, 1995).

One procedure that has been shown to induce panic attacks in patients with anxiety disorders involves inhaling air that has been enriched with carbon dioxide (CO_2). Sanderson, Rapee, and Barlow (1989) utilized this technique in what is now recognized as a classic study of cognitive factors and panic disorder. Their research design added one crucial variable to the typical panic induction procedure: they manipulated participants' impressions of whether they were in control of the air mixture that they were breathing.

The people who participated in the study all met diagnostic criteria for panic disorder. During the experimental procedure, each person was seated alone in a quiet room. He or she simply breathed the air mixture through a gas mask and provided subjective ratings of his or her anxiety level. The instructions indicated that, while they were breathing the CO_2-enriched air, subjects might experience various emotions, ranging from relaxation to anxiety, and that they might experience some physical sensations. They were also told that they might be able to control the gas mixture:

> During the assessment you will be undergoing, a box in the room may light up. When this box is lit, you will be able to adjust the mixture of CO_2 by using the dial which will be on your lap. You will be able to do this only if the box lights up. We ask that you adjust the mixture only if you find it

necessary, as the assessment would be most useful if the CO_2 remains unchanged.

In fact, the dial that the people held in their hands did not have any effect on the mixture of gas. All patients received 5 minutes of compressed air followed by 15 minutes of CO_2-enriched air. For 10 of the 20 patients (selected at random), the light went on just as the CO_2-enriched air began, and it remained on for the remainder of the session. For the other 10 patients, the light did not go on at all.

Immediately after this procedure, each patient was interviewed to determine whether he or she had experienced a panic attack during the inhalation procedure. The results indicated that the illusion of control had a dramatic impact on the probability that patients would panic. Eight of the 10 patients in the "no illusion group"—those for whom the light did not go on—experienced a panic attack. Most of the people in this group who did panic said that the experience was similar to their naturally occurring panics. Among the "illusion of control group" (patients for whom the light had been illuminated), in contrast, only two of the ten patients experienced a panic attack. Patients in the no illusion group reported more than twice as many symptoms of panic than did patients in the illusion of control group (an average of 9.2 and 4.3 symptoms for each group, respectively). Patients in both groups reported high levels of breathlessness and smothering sensations, dizziness, light-headedness, and pounding or racing heart, but the patients in the illusion of control group were less likely than the no illusion patients to report almost every other type of panic symptom.

The results of this study highlight the interactive nature of biological and psychological events that combine to produce the experience of panic. The biological foundations of the experience—whether precipitated by an "alarm" response to stressful events, the direct administration of lactate, or CO_2 inhalation—are undoubtedly important, but by themselves they are not sufficient. Also important are the person's perceptions of the situation, such as feeling in control. ■

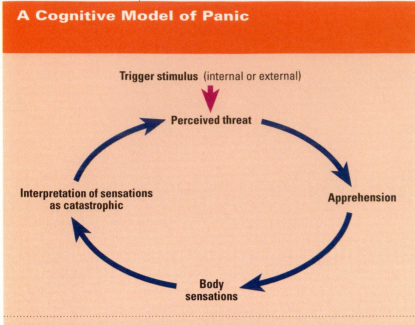

A Cognitive Model of Panic

Trigger stimulus (internal or external)

Perceived threat

Apprehension

Body sensations

Interpretation of sensations as catastrophic

FIGURE 6-3: Diagram of Clark's cognitive model of panic attacks.

Source: D.M. Clark, 1986, A cognitive approach to panic, *Behavior Research and Therapy,* 24, 461–470.

(1993) asked people with panic disorder to keep a daily diary in which they would write down a description of each panic attack they experienced during a 2-week period. Each record was made during the attack or, if that wasn't possible, immediately after it ended. Most of the panic attack descriptions contained catastrophic misinterpretations of bodily sensations (such as "I'm going to suffocate" or "I'm having a heart attack").

This pattern supports the hypothesis that cognitive factors play a central role in many panic attacks. It also indicates, however, that catastrophic misinterpretations cannot account for all instances of panic attacks. For example, patients with panic disorder sometimes experience panic attacks in their sleep (Klein & Klein, 1989). How could that happen if the escalation to panic requires catastrophic misinterpretation of physical sensations? Clearly other factors are also involved.

Attention to Threat and Shifts in Attention

Earlier in the chapter we saw that worry involves negative thoughts and images that anticipate some possible future danger. In recent years, several lines of research have converged to clarify the basic cognitive mechanisms involved in worry. Experts now believe that attention plays a crucial role in the onset of this process. People who are prone to excessive worrying are unusually sensitive to cues that signal the existence of future threats (Mathews, 1990;

Rapee, 1991; Williams, Mathews, & MacLeod, 1996). They attend vigilantly to even fleeting signs of danger, especially when they are under stress. At such times, the recognition of danger cues triggers a maladaptive, self-perpetuating cycle of cognitive processes that can quickly spin out of control.

The threatening information that is generated in this process is presumably encoded in memory in the form of elaborate schemas (see Chapter 5), which are easily reactivated. In comparison with the depressed person, who is convinced that failure will definitely occur, the anxious person is afraid of failure that may occur as a future event, the outcome of which remains uncertain (Beck & Emery, 1985). The threat schemas of anxious people contain a high proportion of "What if" questions, such as "What am I going to do if I don't do well in school this semester?" (Kendall & Ingram, 1989; Vasey & Borkovec, 1992).

Once attention has been drawn to threatening cues, the performance of adaptive, problem-solving behaviors is disrupted, and the worrying cycle launches into a repetitive sequence in which the person rehearses anticipated events and searches for ways to avoid them. The readily accessed network of threat-related schemas then activates an additional series of "What if" questions that quickly leads to a dramatic increase in negative affect.

If worriers are preoccupied with the perception of threat cues and the rehearsal of dangerous scenarios but are unable to reach satisfactory solutions to their problems, why do they continue to engage in this vicious, maladaptive cycle? Thomas Borkovec, a clinical psychologist at Pennsylvania State University, and his students have studied the uncontrollable nature of the worry process. Two of Borkovec's conclusions are particularly important in explaining the self-perpetuating nature of worry: (1) Worry is primarily a verbal-linguistic event (as opposed to visual images), and (2) worry serves the function of avoiding unpleasant somatic activation through the suppression of imagery (Borkovec & Inz, 1990; Roemer & Borkovec, 1993). In other words, some people apparently continue to worry, even though it is not productive, because worrying is reinforced by an immediate (though temporary) reduction in uncomfortable physiological sensations.

Attentional mechanisms also seem to be involved in the etiology and maintenance of social phobias. People who are capable of

▲ **Thomas Borkovec, a clinical psychologist at Penn State University, has conducted extensive research on characteristics of uncontrollable worry and the treatment of anxiety disorders.**

performing a particular task when they are alone (in practice) cannot perform it in front of an audience. Barlow (1988) has argued that this deterioration in skill is caused by anxious apprehension, which is similar to Borkovec's description of the process of worrying. An increase in negative affect presumably triggers a shift toward self-focused attention ("Oh, no, I'm getting really upset") and activates threat schemas ("What if I make a mistake?"). The person becomes distracted by these thoughts, and performance deteriorates. In a sense, the person's fearful expectations become a self-fulfilling prophesy.

Thought Suppression: Obsessive–Compulsive Disorder   The model of worry or anxious apprehension that has been developed by Borkovec, Mathews, and others places primary emphasis on the role of attentional processes. Worrying is unproductive and self-defeating in large part because it is associated with a focus on self-evaluation (fear of failure) and negative emotional responses rather than on external aspects of the problem and active coping behaviors. We may be consciously aware of these processes and simultaneously be unable to inhibit them. The struggle to control our thoughts often leads to a process known as **thought suppression,** an active attempt to stop thinking about something.

It seems simple to say "Stop worrying," but it is virtually impossible for some people to do so. In fact, recent evidence suggests that efforts that are directed toward the control or suppression of unwanted thoughts can frequently have ironic consequences. For example, research by Daniel Wegner (1995), a psychologist at the University of Virginia, has demonstrated that trying to rid your mind of a distressing or unwanted thought can have the unintended effect of making the thought more intrusive. Thought suppression might actually increase, rather then decrease, the strong emotions associated with those thoughts. The bond between a thought and its associated emotion allows activation of one to result in the reinstatement of the other, a kind of dual pathway.

Obsessive–compulsive disorder may be related, in part, to the maladaptive consequences of attempts to suppress unwanted or threatening thoughts that the person has learned to see as being dangerous or forbidden (Barlow, 1988). Remember that obsessive thoughts are a common experience in the general population. They resemble "abnormal" obsessions in form and content (Rachman & deSilva, 1978). However, the obsessions of those in treatment for OCD are more intense and, perhaps most importantly, are more often strongly resisted and more difficult to dismiss. This resistance may be a key component in the association between emotional sensitivity and the development of troublesome obsessive thoughts. People who are vulnerable to the development of OCD apparently react strongly to events that trigger an emotional response (Oltmanns & Gibbs, 1995). These individuals become aware of their exaggerated reactivity and find it unpleasant. In an effort to control their reaction, they attempt to resist or suppress the emotion.

As a result of an individual's attempt to suppress strong emotion, a rebound effect may occur, culminating in a vicious cycle. Thoughts that are present during the instigation of such a cycle become robustly associated with the emotion and may become the content of an obsessive thought. This model may help to explain the episodic nature of obsessive–compulsive symptoms; relapse may be triggered by intense emotional episodes.

Biological Factors

Several pieces of evidence indicate that biological events play an important role in the development and maintenance of the anxiety disorders. In the following pages we review the role of genetic factors and the use of chemicals to induce symptoms of panic. These factors undoubtedly interact with the social and psychological variables that we have considered in the preceding sections.

GENETIC FACTORS

Some of the most useful information about the validity of anxiety disorders comes from studies aimed at identifying the influence of genetic factors. These data address the overlap, as well as the distinctions, among various types of anxiety disorder. They also shed additional light on the relationship between anxiety and depression.

Family Studies   Several studies have focused specifically on the risk for panic disorder among relatives of panic patients. All these studies have found a relatively high rate of panic disorder— between 8 and 21 percent—among the patients' relatives (Weissman, 1993). The patients' relatives are also more likely to experience major depression, even if the probands in the study were originally selected because they had panic disorder without comorbid depression (Maier et al., 1993). These results are consistent with two conclusions: (1) Some people inherit a genetic predisposition to developing panic disorder, and (2) panic disorder and unipolar mood disorders may share some etiological factors.

Family studies of panic disorder also raise interesting questions about subdivisions under the general heading of anxiety disorders. For example, is the split between GAD and panic disorder meaningful? Are the relatives of panic disorder patients at increased risk for generalized anxiety disorder as well as panic disorder? Data from one relevant study are summarized in Table 6–4. They indicate that the relatives of people with panic disorder show an elevated risk of panic disorder themselves but not an elevated risk of generalized anxiety disorder. The same pattern holds for the relatives of people with generalized anxiety disorder: The relatives exhibit a high rate of GAD but not a high rate of panic disorder (Noyes et al., 1987). Similar results have been reported in other studies (Skre et al., 1994). This evidence is consistent with the proposition that panic disorder and GAD are, indeed, etiologically separate disorders.

A family study of social phobia has demonstrated that the *generalized form* of this disorder (where the person is fearful in most types of social situations) is also familial in nature and etiologically distinct from other types of anxiety disorder. The investigators studied first-degree relatives of probands with "pure" social phobia (Fyer et al., 1993; Mannuzza et al., 1995). In other words, they met the criteria for social phobia and had never had any other type of anxiety disorder. Probands in the control group were people who had never had a mental disorder.

The results indicated that the rate of social phobia was particularly high (16 percent) in the relatives of probands whose social phobia was generalized. In contrast, only 5 percent of the relatives in the control group met the diagnostic criteria for social phobia. Moreover, only 6 percent of the relatives of probands with nongeneralized social phobia (in which the person's fear is limited to one particular type of social situation, such as public speaking) had social phobia themselves. This pattern of results suggest that the nongeneralized form of social phobia is not influenced by genetic factors.

Data regarding obsessive–compulsive disorder suggest that a more general vulnerability to anxiety disorders is genetically transmitted through the family. The predisposition can apparently be expressed in different ways, with OCD being only one of them. One study compared the frequency of mental disorders among relatives of patients with OCD to prevalence rates in relatives of normal subjects (Black et al., 1992). The lifetime prevalence of OCD was roughly 2 percent in both groups, no higher than would be expected in the general population. There were significant differences between groups, however, with regard to other types of anxiety disorder. Thirty percent of the patients' relatives met the diagnostic criteria for at least one anxiety disorder, most often GAD. In comparison, only 17 percent of the relatives of the control subjects qualified for a diagnosis of some type of anxiety disorder. The relatives of the OCD probands apparently did not inherit a specific predisposition to this disorder, but they did inherit a more global tendency toward anxiety disorders. The expression of that tendency is presumably influenced by subsequent experience.

The results of the family studies all point toward the potential influence of genetic factors in anxiety disorders. Most of the evidence also supports the validity of the DSM-IV subtypes. Comparisons of panic and GAD support the movement toward splitting these disorders apart in the diagnostic manual. The generalized form of social phobia also seems to be at least somewhat distinct from the other anxiety disorders. On the other hand, data regarding relatives of OCD probands are more consistent with the traditional preference in psychiatric classification for lumping anxiety disorders together.

Twin Studies Family studies do not prove the involvement of genes, because family members also share environmental factors (for example,

---

TABLE 6–4

Frequency of Anxiety Disorders in First-Degree Relatives of Three Types of Subjects

	Percent of Relatives With:		
Proband With:	**Panic Disorder**	**GAD**	**Specific Phobia**
Panic disorder	14.9	5.4	1.7
Generalized anxiety disorder	4.1	19.5	1.6
No psychiatric diagnosis	3.5	3.5	1.8

Source: Adapted from R. Noyes, Jr., et al., 1987, A family study of generalized anxiety disorder, *American Journal of Psychiatry, 144,* 1019–1024.

diet, culture, and so on). Twin studies provide a more stringent test of the genetic hypothesis (see Chapter 2). Kenneth Kendler, a psychiatrist at the Medical College of Virginia, and his colleagues have studied anxiety disorders in a sample of more than 2,000 female–female twin pairs (Kendler et al., 1992a, 1992b). The people who participated in this study were not psychiatric patients; they were living in the community and were identified through a state-wide registry of twins. Diagnoses were assigned following structured diagnostic interviews conducted by the research team.

Table 6–5 summarizes the results of Kendler's study with regard to several types of anxiety disorder. For each type of anxiety disorder in the study, concordance rates were significantly higher for MZ twins than for DZ twins. Nevertheless, the MZ concordance rates were also relatively low (in comparison to MZ concordance rates for bipolar mood disorders, for example). Statistical estimates indicated that anxiety disorders are modestly heritable, with genetic factors accounting for somewhere between 20 and 30 percent of the variance in the transmission of GAD. (See Research Methods in Chapter 16 for a discussion of heritability.) Although all types of phobias appear to be influenced by genetic factors in this study, the greatest genetic influence was found for agoraphobia. The etiology of specific phobias was relatively more influenced by specific environmental factors. Social phobias fell between the other types.

Kendler and his colleagues subsequently examined the influence of both genetic and environmental factors on the etiology of several types of panic disorder, phobia, GAD, and major depression in this same large sample of female twins (Kendler et al., 1995). Their statistical procedures led them to several important conclusions:

1. Genetic risk factors for these disorders are neither highly specific (a different set of genes being associated with each disorder) nor highly nonspecific (one common set of genes causing vulnerability for all disorders).
2. Two genetic factors were identified: one associated with GAD and major depression, and the other with panic disorder and phobias.

TABLE 6-5		
Twin Concordance Rates for Specific Anxiety Disorders		
Disorder	**MZ**	**DZ**
Panic disorder	.24	.11
Agoraphobia	.23	.15
Social phobia	.24	.15
Animal phobia	.26	.11
Generalized anxiety disorder	.28	.17

Source: Data from the Virginia Twin Registry (Kendler et al., 1992a, 1992b).

3. Environmental risk factors that would be unique to individuals also played an important role in the etiology of all of the disorders that were examined. Environmental factors that would be shared by all members of a family did not appear to be influential.
4. Some environmental risk factors appear to be "disorder-specific." This was especially true for phobias (such as "being locked in a trunk by an older brother" or "diving into the water onto a corpse").

NEUROCHEMISTRY

If some people inherit a predisposition that makes them vulnerable to the development of an anxiety disorder, what form does this predisposition take? Considerable speculation has focused on the role of neurochemical factors in this regard, especially in the case of panic disorder. Some clinical scientists have suggested that the central noradrenergic system might be "hyperactive" in people with panic disorder (Ballenger, 1989).

Pharmacological challenge procedures have played a very important role in exploring the neurochemistry of panic disorder. The logic behind this method is simple: If a particular brain mechanism is "challenged" or stressed by the artificial administration of chemicals, and if that procedure leads to the onset of a panic attack, then the neurochemical process that mediates that effect may also be responsible for panic attacks that take place outside the laboratory.

One laboratory procedure that is capable of inducing panic attacks in people who suffer from panic disorder involves the infusion of lactate.[†]

[†] Lactic acid is formed during anaerobic respiration, the phase of cellular respiration that occurs in the absence of oxygen. The respiratory and circulatory systems are usually able to support aerobic respiration when a person is resting. These systems become overloaded when skeletal muscles are used strenuously. Muscle fibers then need to depend on anaerobic respiration to generate energy (Hole, 1984). This process converts glucose to pyruvic acid. As the oxygen supply becomes depleted, pyruvic acid is converted to lactic acid, which accumulates in the bloodstream and is later converted back to glucose by the liver.

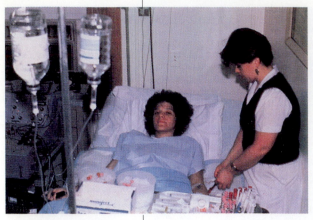

▲ **Clinical scientists have studied factors that influence the onset of panic attacks by using lactate infusion, which can elicit a full-blown panic attack among people who have panic disorder.**

The discovery of this effect was inspired by a few clinical studies, reported in the 1940s and 1950s, that noted that patients with "anxiety neurosis" sometimes experienced an increase in subjective anxiety following vigorous physical exercise. This change in subjective symptoms appeared to be associated with an extremely rapid and excessive increase in lactic acid in the blood.

In order to examine this phenomenon more closely, two psychiatrists at Washington University in St. Louis decided to infuse lactate directly into anxiety disorder patients and a control group of normal subjects (Pitts & McClure, 1967). Each subject was also given a placebo injection on a separate occasion. Subjects in both groups reported few symptoms after the placebo injections. Shortly after the lactate infusion began, however, 13 out of 14 of the anxiety patients experienced an anxiety attack, which they described as being similar to their typical symptoms. In contrast, only 2 of the 10 normal subjects reported an anxiety attack during lactate infusion. Pitts and McClure concluded that a marked increase in lactate production might trigger anxiety symptoms in anyone, but that anxiety patients were especially vulnerable to this effect because of some as-yet-unspecified neurochemical or metabolic difference.

Since the Pitts and McClure experiment, a large number of studies have demonstrated that lactate infusions can provoke panic attacks in anywhere from 50 to 90 percent of patients with anxiety or panic disorders, as compared to only between 0 and 25 percent of normal control subjects (Barlow, 1988). Several other procedures can also be used to induce panic in the laboratory. These include the infusion of other chemicals, such as caffeine, as well as the inhalation of air that has been enriched with carbon dioxide. Some investigators discovered that the administration of certain types of medication, such as MAO inhibitors, could prevent the experience of lactate-induced panic attacks.

The *locus ceruleus*, a small area located in the brain stem, has been the focus of considerable emphasis in research on panic disorder. This area contains a large percentage of the brain's norepinephrine. Neural projections from the locus ceruleus extend to the cerebral cortex as well as the limbic system, which is located in the temporal lobes. Research with monkeys has demonstrated that the firing rate of neurons in the locus ceruleus increases dramatically when a monkey is frightened. Furthermore, electrical stimulation of the locus ceruleus triggers a strong fear response that resembles a panic attack (Redmond, 1985). Several studies of people with panic disorder have pointed toward a dysregulation of the norepinephrine system in some patients, but the evidence is mixed. It does not seem to account for all cases of the disorder (McNally, 1994).

Panic induction procedures allow investigators to monitor brain activities that occur during a panic attack. For example, positron emission tomography, or PET scans, have been used to compare blood flow to various areas of the brain before and after anxiety disorder patients experienced lactate-induced panic attacks. One study found that panic is associated with increased blood flow in the temporal lobes (Reiman et al., 1989), an area that is generally considered to be associated with fear and other emotions (Gray, 1990).

As brain imaging procedures improve, enhancing our ability to isolate anatomic regions, these methods may lead to the localization of specific areas of the brain that mediate symptoms of anxiety. This is an exciting possibility. Information of this sort would tell us where neurological underpinnings of panic are located in the brain. That knowledge, coupled with data regarding social and psychological factors, will help us understand why people experience panic attacks.

FALSE SUFFOCATION ALARMS: AN INTEGRATED SYSTEMS MODEL

Donald Klein has developed an integrated model of panic attacks and agoraphobia that incorporates biological and psychological factors (see Klein, 1981). Klein's interest in these phenomena began in 1959, when he was experimenting with the effects of a new antidepressant drug, imipramine (Tofranil). Some of his hospitalized patients were seriously impaired by agoraphobia and had responded poorly to all attempts at treatment, including psychotherapy, sedative drugs, and ECT. Three weeks after they began taking imipramine, the patients suddenly improved. In contrast to their anxious and clinging behavior prior to this treatment, they began to venture out on their own, away from the ward, especially if they were prompted and encouraged by the hospital staff.

What had happened to these patients? Why, after months and years of fearful confinement, were they suddenly willing to move about in the open environment? To answer these questions, we must recognize that the patients' problems could be divided into two categories: (1) the occasional, ongoing experience of uncued panic attacks, and (2) the fear of having an attack. Careful observations led Klein to conclude that imipramine had a relatively specific effect. It prevented the occurrence of panic attacks. It did not, however, reduce the patients' anticipatory anxiety about possibly having an attack until they left the security of the hospital ward and directly confronted situations that they had learned to fear.

Klein spent the next 30 years developing and revising a theory about the process by which the attacks develop and the ways in which they can be treated. Evidence in support of his theory is drawn primarily from studies regarding both the pharmacological treatment of panic disorder and the provocation of panic in laboratory settings.

Klein (1993) has most recently proposed that the human brain contains a *suffocation monitor*, an adaptive mechanism that increases a person's chances of survival and has evolved with our species. When it detects a threat of suffocation, this monitor triggers distressing feelings associated with breathlessness that in turn provoke urgent efforts to escape to open surroundings. The monitor is sensitive to several different variables, including increased levels of carbon dioxide, that might signal that the person is trapped and being forced to breathe his or her own exhalations (as might happen in a cave-in). An increased level of lactate can also set off the alarm because it acts like carbon dioxide by inducing dilation of cerebral arteries. According to Klein's model, unexpected panic attacks represent a misfire of this system, or a *false suffocation alarm*, which may be triggered by hypersensitivity to carbon dioxide.

The threshold for a person's suffocation alarm can presumably be influenced by a number of biological, social, and psychological factors. Biological factors include hormone levels, which change during pregnancy and may reduce panic among pregnant women by raising the threshold. Social and psychological factors include stressful life events (such as maternal loss) and the development of separation anxiety during childhood, which seem to increase the rate of panic disorder when these children become adults by lowering thresholds.

The false suffocation alarm perspective has received some support from other investigators (McNally, Hornig, & Donnell, 1995; Taylor & Rachman, 1994). These data indicate that there is, in fact, a strong relationship between panic attacks and suffocation sensations. Many other aspects of Klein's model remain to be tested. Perhaps most controversial is his claim that the suffocation alarm is fundamentally a biological mechanism that is not influenced by cognitive factors (Ley, 1994). Relatively little is known about the biological underpinnings of the suffocation alarm, but speculation is focused on specific areas in the brain in which serotonin is the primary neurotransmitter (Klein, 1993).

Treatment

In the following discussion, we review some of the treatment procedures that have been demonstrated to be useful with anxiety disorders. This is one of the areas of psychopathology in which clinical psychologists and psychiatrists are best prepared to improve the level of their clients' functioning. We begin by describing procedures that were used in an effort to help Ed, the person with obsessive–compulsive disorder whose problems were described at the beginning of this chapter.

Ed's psychiatrist gave him a prescription for clomipramine (Anafranil), an antidepressant drug that is also used to treat people with severe obsessions. Weekly psychotherapy sessions continued as the dose was gradually increased. The medication had a beneficial impact after 4 weeks. Ed said that he had begun to feel as though he was trapped at the bottom of a well. After the medication, he no longer felt buried. His situation still wasn't great, but it no longer seemed hopeless or unbearable. He was also less intensely preoccupied by his obsessive violent images. They were still there, but they weren't as pressing. The drug had several annoying, though tolerable, side effects. His mouth felt dry, and he was occasionally a bit dizzy. He also noticed that he became tired more easily. Although Ed was no longer feeling seriously depressed, and the intensity of his obsessions was diminished, they had not disappeared, and he was now avoiding writing altogether.

Because the obsessions were still a problem, Ed's psychiatrist referred him to a psychologist who specialized in behavior therapy for anxiety disorders. He continued seeing the psychiatrist every other week for checks on his medication, which he continued to take. The new therapist told Ed that his fears of particular letters and numbers would be maintained as long as he avoided writing. Ed agreed to begin writing short essays every day, for a period of at least 30 minutes. The content could vary from day to day—anything that Ed felt like writing about—but he was encouraged to include the names of his wife and brother as often as possible. Furthermore, he was instructed to avoid his compulsive writing style, intentionally allowing the parts of letters to be separated or loops to be closed. At the beginning and end of each essay, Ed was required to record his anxiety level so that the therapist could monitor changes in his subjective discomfort. Over a period of 8 to 10 weeks, Ed's handwriting began to change. It was less of a struggle to get himself to write, and his handwriting became more legible.

The final aspect of behavioral treatment was concerned with his fear of axes. Ed and his therapist drew up a list of objects and situations related to axes, arranging them from those that were the least anxiety-provoking through those that were most frightening. They began with the least

▼ Exposure treatments can be administered in imagination or in the person's natural environment. In this photograph, a patient with acrophobia is accompanied to the top of a tall building by a therapist who is conducting exposure therapy.

frightening. In their first exposure session, Ed agreed to meet with the psychologist while a relatively dull, wood-splitting maul was located in the adjoining room. Ed was initially quite anxious and distracted, but his anxiety diminished considerably before the end of their 2-hour meeting. Once that had been accomplished, the therapist helped him to confront progressively more difficult situations. These sessions were challenging and uncomfortable for Ed, but they allowed him to master his fears in an orderly fashion. By the end of the twelfth session of exposure, he was able to hold a sharp ax without fear.

Psychological Interventions

Psychoanalytic psychotherapy has been used to treat patients with anxiety disorders since Freud published his seminal papers at the turn of the century. The emphasis in this type of treatment is on fostering insight regarding the unconscious motives that presumably lie at the heart of the patient's symptoms. Although many therapists continue to employ this general strategy, it has not been shown to be effective in controlled outcome studies.

EXPOSURE: SYSTEMATIC DESENSITIZATION AND FLOODING

Like psychoanalysis, behavior therapy was initially developed for the purpose of treating anxiety disorders, especially specific phobias. The first widely adopted procedure was known as systematic desensitization (see Chapter 3). In desensitization, the client is first taught progressive muscle relaxation. Then the therapist constructs a hierarchy of feared stimuli, beginning with those items that provoke only small amounts of fear and progressing through items that are most frightening. Then, while the client is in a relaxed state, he or she imagines the lowest item on the hierarchy. The item is presented repeatedly until the person no longer experiences an increase in anxiety when thinking about the object or situation. This process is repeated several times as the client moves systematically up the hierarchy, sequentially confronting images of stimuli that were originally rated as being more frightening.

In the years since systematic desensitization was originally proposed (Wolpe, 1958), many different variations on this procedure have been employed. The crucial feature of the treatment involves systematic maintained exposure to the feared stimulus (Marks, 1987; Rachman, 1990).

Positive outcomes have been reported, regardless of the specific manner in which exposure is accomplished. Some evidence indicates that direct ("in vivo") exposure works better than imaginal exposure. A few prolonged exposures can be as effective as a larger sequence of brief exposures. Another variation on exposure procedures, known as *flooding*, begins with the most frightening stimuli rather than working up gradually from the bottom of the hierarchy. All of these variations on the basic procedure have been shown to be effective in the treatment of phobic disorders. Several research studies have demonstrated that exposure therapy leads to clinically meaningful improvement when compared to placebo treatments (see Research Methods). Positive results are typically maintained several months after the end of treatment (O'Sullivan & Marks, 1991). Exposure is often accomplished in the presence of the therapist, but the treatment can be just as effective when the client directs his or her own systematic exposure in the natural environment (Al-Kubaisy et al., 1992).

PROLONGED EXPOSURE AND RESPONSE PREVENTION

The most effective form of psychological treatment for obsessive–compulsive disorder combines prolonged exposure to the situation that

RESEARCH METHODS

Statistical Significance and Clinical Importance

Let's say that an outcome study reveals a statistical difference in the effectiveness of one form of treatment versus another form (or no treatment at all). Does this automatically mean that the difference is clinically significant? The answer is no. We can explain this point by using a hypothetical example. Imagine that you want to know whether exposure-based treatment is effective in the treatment of social phobias. You could conduct a study, using an experimental design, in which 50 patients with this disorder are randomly assigned to receive exposure therapy and another 50 patients—the control group—are not. The latter group might receive a placebo pill or nondirective supportive psychotherapy for purposes of comparison. Measures of anxiety and avoidance are collected before and after treatment for patients in both groups. Your hypothesis is that exposure treatment will lead to more improvement than will placebo or nondirective therapy. In contrast, the *null hypothesis* (see Research Methods in Chapter 1) holds that the two forms of treatment are not truly different. To conclude that exposure therapy is effective, you must reject the null hypothesis.

After collecting your data, you can use statistical tests to help you decide whether you can reject the null hypothesis. These tests assign a probability to that result, indicating how often we would find that result if there are not really differences between the two treatments. Psychologists have adopted the .05 level, meaning that if a difference occurs only by chance, you would find this difference less than 5 times out of every 100 times you repeated this experiment. Differences that exceed the .05 level therefore are assumed to reflect real differences between the variables rather than mere chance. Such results are said to be *statistically significant.*

Statistical significance should not be equated with clinical importance (Jacobson & Truax, 1991). It is possible for an investigator to find statistically significant differences between groups (and therefore reject the null hypothesis) on the basis of relatively trivial changes in the patients' adjustment. Consider the hypothetical example outlined above and suppose that you measured outcome in terms of a rating scale for anxiety whose scores could range from 0 (no symptoms of anxiety) to 100 (highest ratings on all items). Let's also assume that a rating of 50 or higher is typically considered to indicate the presence of important anxiety problems that are often associated with a disruption of the person's social and occupational functioning. Both groups have a mean rating of 85 on the scale prior to treatment. At the end of treatment, the mean rating for the exposure group has dropped to 65, and the mean for the control group is now 75. If you have included enough subjects, and depending on the amount of variation among scores within each group, this difference might reach statistical significance. But is it clinically important? Probably not. The average patient in the exposure group still has a score above the cutoff for identifying meaningful levels of psychopathology.

The investigator must therefore consider carefully not only whether there are statistically significant differences between groups but also the relative amount of change that is observed and the consistency of change across patients within each group. It is also important to employ assessment procedures that measure aspects of behavior that are clinically important (Beidel, Turner, & Cooley, 1993). ∎

increases the person's anxiety with prevention of the person's typical compulsive response (Turner & Beidel, 1988). Neither component is effective by itself. The combination of exposure and response prevention is necessary because of the way in which people with obsessive–compulsive disorder use their compulsive rituals to reduce anxiety that is typically stimulated by the sudden appearance of an obsession. If the compulsive behavior is performed, exposure is effectively cut short.

Consider, for example, the treatment program employed with Ed. His obsessive thoughts and images, which centered around violence, were associated with handwriting. They were likely to pop into his mind when he noticed letters that were poorly formed. In an effort to control these thoughts, Ed wrote very carefully, and he corrected any letter that seemed a bit irregular. By the time he entered behavior therapy, Ed had avoided writing altogether for several months. The therapist arranged for him to begin writing short essays on a daily basis to be sure that he was exposed, for at least 30 minutes each day, to the situation that was most anxiety-provoking. He encouraged Ed to deliberately write letters that did not conform to his compulsive style. In their sessions, for example, Ed was also required to write long sequences of the letter T in which he deliberately failed to connect the two lines. He was not allowed to go back and correct this "mistake." The combination represents prolonged exposure to an anxiety-provoking stimulus and response prevention.

Controlled-outcome studies indicate that this approach is effective with OCD patients (Rachman & Hodgson, 1980). One review of 18 outcome studies found that 51 percent of the OCD patients who had been treated with prolonged exposure and response prevention were either free of symptoms or much improved at the end of treatment; another 39 percent were considered moderately improved. Only 10 percent did not benefit at all (Foa, Steketee, & Ozarow, 1985).

APPLIED RELAXATION

Behavior therapists have used relaxation procedures for many years. Relaxation training usually involves teaching the client alternately to tense and relax specific muscle groups while breathing slowly and deeply (Bernstein & Borkovec, 1973). This process is often described to the client as an active coping skill that can be learned through consistent practice and used to control anxiety and worry.

Outcome studies indicate that relaxation is a useful form of treatment for generalized anxiety disorder. Borkovec and Costello (1993) compared applied relaxation and cognitive behavior therapy to nondirective psychotherapy for the treatment of patients with generalized anxiety disorder (see Research Close-Up in Chapter 3). Patients who received relaxation training and those who received cognitive therapy were more improved at the end of treatment than those who received only nondirective therapy.

COGNITIVE THERAPY

Cognitive therapy is used extensively in the treatment of anxiety disorders. Cognitive treatment procedures for anxiety disorders have been developed by Aaron Beck (Beck & Emery, 1985) and Albert Ellis (1962). They are similar to those employed in the treatment of depression. Therapists help clients identify cognitions that are relevant to their problem; recognize the relation between these cognitions and maladaptive emotional responses (such as prolonged anxiety); examine the evidence that supports or contradicts these beliefs; and teach more useful ways of interpreting events in their environments (Schuyler, 1991).

In the case of anxiety disorders, cognitive therapy is usually accompanied by additional behavior therapy procedures. Barlow's approach to the treatment of panic disorder, for example, includes a cognitive component in addition to applied relaxation and exposure (Barlow & Cerny, 1988). One aspect of the cognitive component involves an analysis of errors in the ways in which people think about situations in their lives. Typical examples of faulty logic include jumping to conclusions before considering all of the evidence, overgeneralizing (basing negative predictions about future performance on a very limited set of previous experiences), all-or-none thinking (assuming that one mistake means total failure), and so on.

A second aspect of Barlow's cognitive component for panic patients is called *decatastrophisizing*. In this procedure, the therapist asks the client to imagine what would happen if his or her worst-case scenario actually happened. The same principles that are used in examining faulty logic are then applied to this situation. The therapist might say, "I don't think that you will fail the exam. But what would happen if you did fail the exam?" The client's initial reaction might be catastrophic ("I would die." "My parents would kill me." "I would flunk out of school."). Upon more careful analysis, however, the client might agree that these negative predictions actually represent gross exaggerations that are based on cognitive errors. Discussions in the therapy session are followed by extensive practice and homework assignments during the week. As one way of evaluating the accuracy of their own hypotheses, clients are encouraged to write down predictions that they make about specific situations and then keep track of the actual outcomes.

Several controlled outcome studies attest to the efficacy of cognitive therapy in the treatment of various types of anxiety disorder, including panic disorder, agoraphobia, social phobia, generalized anxiety disorder, and obsessive–compulsive disorder (Chambless & Gillis, 1993; Clark et al., 1994; Margraf et al., 1993; Zinbarg et al., 1992).

Biological Interventions

Medication is the most effective and most commonly used biological approach to the treatment of anxiety disorders. Several types of drugs have been discovered to be useful. They are often used in conjunction with psychological treatment.

ANTIANXIETY MEDICATIONS

The most frequently used types of minor tranquilizers are from the class of drugs known as benzodiazepines, which includes diazepam (Valium) and alprazolam (Xanax). These drugs reduce many symptoms of anxiety, especially vigilance and subjective somatic sensations, such as increased muscle tension, palpitations, increased perspiration, and gastrointestinal distress. They have relatively less effect on a person's tendency toward worry and rumination (Hoehn-Saric & McLeod, 1991). Benzodiazepines were the most widely prescribed form of psychiatric medication until the 1990s.

Benzodiazepines bind to specific receptor sites in the brain that are ordinarily associated with a neurotransmitter known as gamma-aminobutyric acid (GABA). Benzodiazepines, which inhibit the activity of GABA neurons, fall into two types, based on their rate of absorption and elimination from the body. Some, such as alprazolam and lorazepam (Ativan), are absorbed and eliminated quickly, whereas others, such as diazepam, are absorbed and eliminated slowly.

Benzodiazepines have been shown to be effective in the treatment of generalized anxiety disorders and social phobias (Davidson, Tupler, & Potts, 1994). Drug effects are most consistently evident early in treatment. The long-term effects of benzodiazepines (beyond 6 months of treatment) are not well established (Hoehn-Saric & McLeod, 1991). They are not typically beneficial for patients with phobic disorders or obsessive–compulsive disorder.

Certain high-potency benzodiazepines are also useful for treating panic disorder (Rosenberg, 1993). Alprazolam (Xanax) is considered by some psychiatrists to be the drug of choice for patients with this condition because it produces clinical improvement more quickly than the antidepressants (within 1 to 3 weeks instead of the 8 to 12 weeks that may be required for a full therapeutic response to tricyclic antidepressants) and because it has fewer side effects than antidepressants.

The results of most placebo-controlled outcome studies have been positive. The Cross-National Collaborative Panic Study (CNCPS), which was conducted in two phases, provides some of the best evidence in this regard. The first phase compared alprazolam to a placebo in 500 patients (Ballenger et al., 1988). Among the patients who received alprazolam, 30 percent were markedly improved after 8 weeks of treatment, and another 52 percent were moderately improved. Only 10 percent of the patients who received the placebo were markedly improved after treatment, and another 43 percent in this group were moderately improved.

The second phase of the CNCPS compared alprazolam, imipramine, and placebo treatment in a sample of 1,100 panic disorder patients. The investigators found that alprazolam and imipramine were equally effective in comparison to a placebo. Fewer patients dropped out of the alprazolam group, because the drug had fewer side effects than imipramine. Patients improved faster on alprazolam, but there were no differences between the two drugs after 6 to 8 weeks of treatment.

Some studies have found that many patients with panic disorder and agoraphobia relapse if they discontinue taking medication. For example, one investigation compared four types of treatment over a period of 8 weeks: alprazolam plus exposure; alprazolam plus relaxation;[†] placebo plus exposure; and placebo plus relaxation (Marks et al., 1993). Medication was gradually withdrawn during weeks 8 through 16. Patients were followed up 6 months after the end of treatment. All four groups, including those receiving placebos, showed a significant improvement in terms of diminished number of panic attacks by the end of treatment (8 weeks). On the other measures of anxiety and phobic avoidance, both alprazolam and exposure were effective, but the exposure group exhibited larger gains. The alprazolam group lost therapeutic gains after the medication was withdrawn, whereas patients who received exposure treatment maintained their improvement throughout the follow-up period. The authors concluded that exposure is a preferable form of treatment for patients with a diagnosis of panic disorder with agoraphobia, because of the high relapse rate that was observed after alprazolam was withdrawn.

Common side effects of benzodiazepines include sedation accompanied by mild psychomotor and cognitive impairments. These drugs can, for example, increase the risk of automobile accidents, because they interfere with motor skills. They can also lead to problems in attention and memory, especially among elderly patients.

The most serious adverse effect of benzodiazepines is their potential for addiction. Approximately 40 percent of people who use benzodiazepines for 6 months or more will exhibit symptoms of withdrawal if the medication is discontinued (Sussman & Chou, 1988). Withdrawal reactions include the reappearance of anxiety, somatic complaints, concentration problems, and sleep difficulties. They are most severe among patients who abruptly discontinue the use of benzodiazepines that are cleared quickly from the system, such as alprazolam.

The risk for becoming dependent on benzodiazepines is greatest among people who have a history of abusing other substances, like alcohol.

ANTIDEPRESSANT MEDICATIONS

In the early 1960s, Donald Klein and his research group discovered that tricyclic antidepressant drugs, especially imipramine, can be effective in treating panic attacks in patients with agoraphobia. They recommended that psychological intervention be used to eliminate anticipatory anxiety and avoidant behavior after the medication eliminated the threat of further panic attacks. Some psychiatrists still consider imipramine to be the preferred medication for panic disorder (Agras, 1993; Noyes, 1991) because patients are less likely to become dependent on the drug than they are to high-potency benzodiazepines like alprazolam. In addition, patients experience fewer problems when imipramine is withdrawn. The usual duration of treatment is 6 months. Relapse may occur after medication is withdrawn.

The tricyclic antidepressants produce several unpleasant side effects, including weight gain, dry mouth, and overstimulation (sometimes referred to as an "amphetamine-like" response). Some of the side effects, like palpitations, sweating, and light-headedness, are upsetting to patients because they resemble symptoms of anxiety. Side effects often lead patients to discontinue treatment prematurely. In one study of patients who received long-term treatment with imipramine, 50 percent experienced distressing side effects, including 17 percent who found the effects intolerable (Noyes, Garvey, & Cook, 1989).

Clomipramine (Anafranil), another tricyclic antidepressant, has been used extensively in treating obsessive–compulsive disorder. Several placebo-controlled studies have shown clomipramine to be effective in treating OCD (deVeaugh-Geiss, 1993). One study found that more than 50 percent of the patients who received clomipramine improved to a level of normal functioning over a period of 10 weeks, compared to only 5 percent of the patients in a placebo group (Katz, deVeaugh-Geiss, & Landau, 1990). Patients who continue to take the drug maintain the improvement, but relapse is common if medication is discontinued (Pato et al., 1988).

[†] The investigators considered relaxation to be a psychological placebo with regard to the treatment of panic disorder.

	TABLE 6-6

Treatments of Choice for Anxiety Disorders

Disorder	Drug Treatment		Psychological Treatment
	Generic Name	Trade Name	
Panic Disorder	Imipramine	Tofranil	Cognitive therapy
	Alprazolam	Xanax	
Agoraphobia	Imipramine	Tofranil	Exposure in vivo
			Cognitive therapy
Generalized Anxiety Disorder	Alprazolam	Xanax	Applied relaxation
	Diazepam	Valium	Cognitive therapy
Specific Phobias	Medication not typically recommended		Exposure in vivo
Social Phobia	Propranolol	Inderal	Cognitive therapy
			Social skills training
Obsessive–Compulsive Disorder	Clomipramine	Anafranil	Exposure plus response prevention
	Fluoxetine	Prozac	

Source: Adapted from R. Noyes, Jr., 1991, Treatments of choice for anxiety disorders. In W. Coryell and G. Winokur (Eds.), *The Clinical Management of Anxiety Disorders*. New York; Oxford University Press.

The selective serotonin reuptake inhibitors (SSRIs) have also been employed with anxiety disorders, but they have not been evaluated extensively in double-blind, placebo-controlled studies. Panic disorder and OCD have been treated with SSRIs such as fluvoxamine (Boyer, 1992).

In actual practice, anxiety disorders are often treated with a combination of psychological and biological procedures. The selection of specific treatment components depends on the specific group of symptoms that the person exhibits. Table 6–6 summarizes various types of psychological treatment and specific types of medication that are effective with anxiety disorders. These are not the only types of treatment that are available, but they include those that have been subjected to empirical validation.

Summary

Anxiety disorders are defined in terms of a preoccupation with, or persistent avoidance of, thoughts or situations that provoke **fear** or anxiety. **Anxiety** involves a diffuse emotional reaction that is associated with the anticipation of future problems and is out of proportion to threats from the environment. A pervasive anxious mood is typically associated with pessimistic thoughts and feelings. The person's attention may also turn inward, focusing on negative emotions and self-evaluation rather than on the organization or rehearsal of adaptive responses that might be useful in coping with negative events.

KEY TERMS

- agoraphobia
- anxiety
- compulsion
- fear
- generalized anxiety disorder (GAD)
- negative affect
- neurosis
- obsession
- panic attack
- phobia
- positive affect
- preparedness theory

- social phobia
- thought suppression
- worry

A **panic attack** is a sudden, overwhelming experience of terror or fright. Panic attacks are defined largely in terms of a list of somatic sensations, ranging from heart palpitations, sweating and trembling, to nausea, dizziness, and chills.

Phobias are persistent and irrational narrowly defined fears that are associated with avoidance of a specific object or situation. The most complex and incapacitating form of phobic disorder is **agoraphobia,** which is usually described as fear of public spaces. It is not so much a fear of being close to one specific object or situation as it is a fear of being separated from signals associated with safety.

Obsessions are repetitive, unwanted, intrusive cognitive events that may take the form of thoughts or images or impulses. They intrude suddenly into consciousness and lead to an increase in subjective anxiety. **Compulsions** are repetitive behaviors, considered by the person to be senseless or irrational, that reduce the anxiety associated with obsessions. The person attempts to resist but cannot. The two most common forms of compulsive behavior are cleaning and checking.

DSM-IV recognizes several specific subtypes of anxiety disorders: panic disorders (with or without agoraphobia), phobic disorders (specific phobia, social phobia, and agoraphobia without panic attacks), obsessive–compulsive disorder, and generalized anxiety disorder, as well as posttraumatic stress disorder and acute stress disorder.

The NCS and ECA studies found that anxiety disorders are more common than any other form of mental disorder. Phobias are the most common type of anxiety disorder, with a 1-year prevalence of about 9 percent of the adult population, followed by social phobia (8 percent), generalized anxiety disorder (3 percent), obsessive–compulsive disorder (2 percent), and panic disorder (2 percent). Women are more likely than men to experience specific phobias, social phobias, agoraphobia, panic disorder, and generalized anxiety disorder. Gender differences are less marked in obsessive–compulsive disorder.

Stressful life events can influence the onset of anxiety disorders. Certain kinds of stresses may be differentially associated with particular types of emotional disorders: Severe events involving danger are most often associated with anxiety symptoms, while severe events involving loss are more often associated with depression. Among those people who have developed an anxiety disorder, interpersonal conflict is more characteristic of people with agoraphobia.

The learning model explained the development of phobic disorders in terms of classical conditioning, or the pairing of fear with originally neutral stimuli that happen to be present during a traumatic experience. A modified learning view, known as **preparedness theory,** is based on a recognition that there are biological constraints on the kinds of associations that members of a particular species are able to make. We may be prepared to develop intense, persistent fears only to a select set of objects or situations. People can apparently learn to avoid certain stimuli if they observe other people showing a strong fear response to those stimuli. Studies with infant monkeys support the preparedness model.

Cognitive theorists have argued that panic disorder is caused by the catastrophic misinterpretation of bodily sensations or perceived threat. This theory has the support of several research studies, but there are methodological problems associated with some of the studies. The cognitive theory of panic also has problems explaining some clinical observations regarding panic disorder, such as the fact that some patients experience panic attacks in their sleep.

People who are prone to excessive **worrying** are unusually sensitive to cues that signal the existence of future threats. The recognition of danger cues triggers a maladaptive, self-perpetuating cycle of cognitive processes that can quickly spin out of control. The threatening information that is generated in this process is presumably encoded in memory in the form of elaborate schemas that are easily reactivated. In comparison to the depressed person, who is convinced that failure will definitely occur, the anxious person is afraid of failure that may occur as a future event. Some people apparently continue to worry, even though it is not productive, because worrying is reinforced by an immediate (though temporary) reduction in uncomfortable physiological sensations.

Family studies support the separate classification of panic disorder and **generalized anxiety disorder.** An increased prevalence of panic disorder is found among the relatives of patients with panic disorder. Similarly, an increased prevalence of generalized anxiety is found among the relatives of patients with generalized anxiety disorder. In other words, the two disorders "breed true." This does not seem to be the case for obsessive–compulsive disorder, where patients' relatives show an increased risk for several types of anxiety disorder rather than a specific risk for OCD.

Twin studies indicate that genetic factors are involved in the etiology of several types of anxiety disorder, especially panic disorder. The evidence is inconsistent for generalized anxiety disorder. There appears to be a modest genetic influence on the development of phobic disorders. The influence of environmental events seems to be greatest in specific phobias.

The false suffocation alarm theory explains the etiology of panic disorder in terms of a brain monitor that has evolved specifically for the purpose of detecting threat of suffocation. Unexpected panic attacks presumably represent a misfire of this system. The alarm's threshold can be influenced by a number of biological and psychological factors. Support for this theory comes from studies that provoke panic in a laboratory setting, using procedures such as the infusion of lactate or the inhalation of air that has been enriched with carbon dioxide.

Several psychological approaches to the treatment of anxiety disorders have been shown to be effective. These include the use of exposure and flooding in the treatment of phobic disorders and prolonged exposure and response prevention in the treatment of obsessive–compulsive disorders. Various types of medication are also effective treatments for anxiety disorders. These include benzodiazepines for generalized anxiety disorder, selective serotonin reuptake inhibitors for obsessive–compulsive disorder, and antidepressants for panic disorder.

Critical Thinking

1. What is the difference between being afraid and being anxious? If low levels of anxiety can enhance a person's performance, why and how do high levels of anxiety interfere with that same person's ability to function? What role does worry play in this process?

2. Anxiety and depression frequently appear together. Someone with a diagnosis of clinical depression is also likely to exhibit symptoms of anxiety disorders, and vice versa. In what ways are these maladaptive emotions alike, and how are they different?

3. Stressful life events are correlated with the appearance of both depression and anxiety disorders. Can you think of any ways in which this relationship is different in anxiety than it is in depression? What determines whether a person will become anxious or depressed in response to a serious negative event?

4. How do social, psychological, and biological factors interact in the production of various types of anxiety disorders? Consider the preparedness model of phobias, the suffocation alarm model of panic, and the cognitive model of generalized anxiety.

7

Acute and Posttraumatic Stress Disorders, Dissociative Disorders, and Somatoform Disorders

At times in your life, you may briefly have felt cut off or detached from your usual experience of yourself and the world around you. Perhaps things seemed unreal for a few moments, or you may have had an out of body experience where you seemed to be watching yourself from above. Maybe you have had memories or flashbacks so vivid that it almost seemed as if you were reliving a past event, or perhaps you have had a *déjà vu* experience—feeling as if some interaction has happened before. You probably have been fascinated, and perhaps frightened, by such experiences. If so, you are not alone. Psychological theorists have long speculated and argued about the meaning of these everyday experiences, as well as the meaning of far more severe examples of **dissociation**—the disruption of the normally integrated mental processes involved in memory or consciousness (Spiegel & Cardena, 1991). To a greater or lesser extent, dissociative symptoms characterize all of the intriguing disorders we consider in this chapter: acute and posttraumatic stress disorders, dissociative disorders, and somatoform disorders.

Overview

Acute stress disorder and posttraumatic stress disorder are reactions to **traumatic stress,** exposure to some event that involves actual or threatened death or serious injury to self or others and creates intense fear, helplessness, or horror. Rape, military combat, and exposure to man-made or natural disasters are examples of traumatic stressors. **Acute stress disorder (ASD)** occurs within 4 weeks after exposure to a trauma and is characterized by dissociative symptoms, reexperiencing of the event, avoidance of reminders of the trauma, and marked anxiety or arousal. Like acute stress disorder, **posttraumatic stress disorder (PTSD)** is defined by symptoms of reexperiencing, avoidance, and arousal, but in PTSD the symptoms either are lasting (they persist longer than 1 month) or delayed (the onset of symptoms is 6 months or longer after the traumatic event).

As we noted in Chapter 6, the DSM-IV classifies posttraumatic stress disorder and acute stress disorder with the anxiety disorders. However, we discuss these disorders separately in this chapter, for two main reasons. First, the symptoms of acute and posttraumatic stress disorders include *both* anxiety and dissociation; thus we place them between the two disorders they most resemble—anxiety disorders in Chapter 6 and dissociative disorders in this chapter. In fact, when DSM-IV was being developed, some experts argued that ASD and PTSD should be classified as dissociative disorders (Brett, Spitzer, & Williams, 1988), and others suggested ASD and PTSD should be placed in a separate diagnostic category (Davidson & Foa, 1991). Second, and perhaps more importantly, our separate treatment of acute and posttraumatic stress disorders calls attention to the growing body of research on these very important and distressingly common psychological problems.

Case histories of dissociative and somatoform disorders are fascinating, because they

◄ The record-breaking flooding of the Mississippi River in the summer of 1993 was a traumatic stressor for the families who lived in the flood's path.

challenge many ordinary assumptions about the psyche. **Dissociative disorders** are characterized by persistent, maladaptive disruptions in the integration of memory, consciousness, or identity. You may be familiar with the actual case histories of *multiple personality disorder* (now called *dissociative identity disorder*) explored in the book *Sybil* and in the movie *The Three Faces of Eve*.

Equally intriguing are **somatoform disorders**—problems characterized by unusual physical symptoms that occur in the absence of a known physical illness. The sudden onset of paralysis or blindness without a clear biological cause is a dramatic example of a somatoform disorder. There is no demonstrable physical cause for the symptoms of somatoform disorders. They are somatic in form only—thus their name.†

By definition, dissociative and somatoform disorders involve unconscious mental processes. Memories become inaccessible in dissociative disorders; psychological distress is converted into physical symptoms in somatoform disorders. These transformations occur without intention and often without awareness, an indication

that the mind processes at different levels of consciousness. Although less dramatic, some symptoms of acute and posttraumatic stress disorder also seem to involve unconscious processes, for example, the delayed onset of symptoms in some cases of PTSD.

We already have discussed numerous problems in objectively measuring people's reports about their conscious experience. Imagine, then, the difficulties involved in developing objective, scientific measures of unconscious processes. Our inability to assess unconscious mental processes adequately challenges clinicians as well as research scientists. For skeptical clinicians, one pressing diagnostic question is **malingering:** Could the patient be pretending to have a dissociative, somatoform, or posttraumatic stress disorder in order to achieve some gain, such as a disability payment or avoidance of a legal responsibility? A related diagnostic concern is **factitious disorder,** a feigned condition that, unlike malingering, is motivated primarily by a desire to assume the sick role rather than by a desire for external gain.

---

† The absence of demonstrable physical impairment in somatoform disorders distinguishes them from *psychosomatic illnesses*, stress-related physical disorders that do involve real, organic pathology (see Chapter 8). In everyday language, we sometimes say "his problems are psychosomatic" to indicate that an illness is "all in his head." However, it is somatoform disorders, not psychosomatic disorders, that are purely psychological problems.

Because of the limited assessment and research on dissociative and somatoform disorders, we must be cautious in attempting to explain these problems. At the same time, we cannot help but be captivated and challenged by unusual case studies of the disorders. Throughout the chapter we consider both long and brief case studies, as well as the difficult scientific and clinical questions raised by these intriguing problems. We begin by considering the less controversial and more adequately researched problems of acute and posttraumatic stress disorders.

Acute and Posttraumatic Stress Disorders

Stress is an inevitable, and in some cases a desirable, fact of everyday life. Some stressors, however, are so catastrophic and horrifying that they can cause serious psychological harm. Examples of these *traumatic stressors* include rape, bombings, airplane crashes, earthquakes, major fires, and devastating automobile wrecks. Both the survivors of and witnesses to traumatic stressors are expected to be greatly distressed as a part of their normal response. For some victims, the trauma continues long after the event itself has ended. The horrifying experience leads to general increases in anxiety and arousal, avoidance of emotionally charged situations, and the frequent reliving of the traumatic event. When these symptoms occur in the first 4 weeks after a traumatic stressor, the individual is said to be suffering from *acute stress disorder (ASD)*. When symptoms persist for more than a month or have a delayed onset, the condition is referred to as *posttraumatic stress disorder (PTSD)*. The following case study is a dramatic illustration of the horrors and lasting effects of exposure to traumatic stress.

CASE STUDY

The Lasting Trauma of Sexual Assault

Stephanie Cason was a bright, attractive, and well-adjusted 27-year-old graduate student when she suffered a highly traumatic experience. One spring evening, Stephanie ran outside to investigate a major fire in another building in her apartment complex. While she was outside, Stephanie chatted amiably about the scene with a man who she assumed was a neighbor. After talking with a few other people, Stephanie returned to her apartment. The fire had caused a power outage, but Stephanie found her way upstairs and changed into her nightclothes. When she came back downstairs to check on things, she found the very large man she had met outside standing in the shadows of her darkened apartment. Without saying a word, he raised a tire iron and struck Stephanie across the top of her head—repeatedly, until she fell to the floor and stopped screaming. Stephanie was cut deeply and stunned by the vicious blow, but she attempted to resist as the man began to grab at her breasts and

rip at her clothes. He began to mutter obscenities and told Stephanie he wanted to have sex with her. All Stephanie could think was, "I'm going to be killed."

Somehow Stephanie remained strong enough to think keenly despite the shock of the assault and the blood pouring from her head. She decided she would "agree" to have sex with her assailant, but she told him that she needed to "freshen up" first. Eventually, Stephanie convinced him to let her go to clean up, and as soon as she reached her room, she shoved a bureau in front of the door and screamed frantically out the window for help. Her screams frightened her attacker and brought help to Stephanie. Later, she learned that one of the firefighters tackled and captured the assailant as he tried to run away from the apartment complex.

Stephanie saved herself from being raped, but she could not protect herself from the emotional fallout of her sexual assault. She was tortured by the fear of almost being killed. For days, eventually weeks, she felt intermittently terrified, dazed, and grateful to be alive. She replayed the horror of the evening in her mind repeatedly, and when she managed to fall asleep, she often was wakened by frightening nightmares. Stephanie was terrified to be alone, especially at night but even at many times during the day. She relied on the unwaivering support of her boyfriend and friends to stay nearby and help her cope.

Shortly after the assault, Stephanie sought help from a skilled clinical psychologist, but she fell into a depression despite the therapy. Antidepressant medication helped somewhat with her mood and lethargy, but for months after the trauma she continued to be hypervigilant, to have difficulty concentrating, and to have intermittent feelings of numbness or unreality. In addition, she frequently reexperienced the images and emotions surrounding the dreaded event. She was able to resume her studies at a reduced pace after about 3 months and, within 6 or 8 months she was working fairly regularly, but with considerably less confidence and concentration than formerly. As the anniversary of her assault approached, however, Stephanie grew increasing upset. The calendar and the spring weather—usually a welcome change—reminded her of the terror of the previous spring. Her feelings of unreality and depersonalization returned, and she had flashbacks where she suddenly found herself reliving the dreaded night in her mind. In addition, the nightmares and her fears about being alone reappeared. She again needed the company of friends, especially at night, and she found herself unable to concentrate. Once again, she fell into a depression, although she did not take medication this time. As the dreaded date passed, her reactions eased slowly. After about 2 or 3 months of great emotional disruption, she was able to renew her normal life—as normal as her life could be—with fewer struggles than earlier.

Stephanie found it painful but also helpful to talk about her assault with friends and, over time, more publicly. After the passing of the 1-year anniversary, she actually gave a few lectures about her experiences to classes and to women's groups. She found that talking about the event gave her some relief, and perhaps more importantly, it gave her a sense that some good might come from her trauma. Stephanie also was willing and able to testify at the trial of her assailant, who was convicted of his crimes and sent to prison for 20 years. Although she appeared strong in the courtroom, the trial renewed many of Stephanie's previous symptoms of posttraumatic stress disorder. She again relived the terror of the assault, avoided being alone at night, and became fearful and hypervigilant about potential dangers in her world.

Once the trial was finished and her assailant was sent to prison, Stephanie felt a degree of relief and resolution about the trauma. She also felt some satisfaction and pride in the strength it took to share her experiences with others. Still, she could not fully banish the demons of the traumatic sexual assault. She was disgusted and distressed by thoughts of sexual violation, but Stephanie was most traumatized by the persistent thought that she was almost killed. She again experienced intensely distressing episodes of PTSD for a couple of months surrounding the second and third anniversaries of the sexual assault (which occurred 3½ years prior to this writing). In her heart, she knew the trauma would be with her forever, and she also knew her distress would be most intense near the anniversary of the event. Even at other times, however, Stephanie could unexpectedly fall victim to the terror of her assault. For example, more than 3 years after the assault, her boyfriend (now her husband) silently entered her room after returning home unexpectedly one night. Frightened by his sudden appearance, Stephanie first screamed in terror, then sobbed in uncontrollable fear, and felt numb and unreal for several days afterwards.

Stephanie did not behave like a victim from the moment of the assault, throughout the trial, or in her public discussions of her trauma. But despite her admirable strength, Stephanie could not prevent or control the recurrent terror of PTSD brought on by a violent sexual assault. ∎

Typical Symptoms and Associated Features of ASD and PTSD

As illustrated in Stephanie's terrifying experience, acute and posttraumatic stress disorder both are characterized by (1) reexperienced trauma; (2) marked avoidance of stimuli associated with the trauma; and (3) persistent arousal or increased anxiety. In addition, ASD is characterized by a fourth cluster of problems, namely, dissociative symptoms.

REEXPERIENCING

Like Stephanie, people who have been confronted with a traumatic stressor *reexperience* the event in a number of different ways. Some people experience repeated, distressing images or thoughts of the incident. For example, they visualize the trauma over and over or repeatedly question how they might have acted differently. Other people relive the trauma in horrifying dreams like those that haunted Stephanie. Many people with ASD or PTSD have repeated and intrusive **flashbacks,** sudden memories during which the trauma is replayed in images or thoughts—often at full emotional intensity. In rare cases, reexperiencing occurs as a *dissociative state*, and the person feels and acts as if the trauma actually is recurring in the moment. A combat veteran in a dissociative state might act as if he believes he is back in battle, and he may even take dangerous actions like gathering weapons or barricading himself in his residence. Typically, dissociative states are of short duration, but in unusual cases they can last for days. As we have noted, the alteration in memory and consciousness that characterizes dissociative states resembles symptoms of dissociative disorder.

AVOIDANCE

Marked or persistent avoidance of stimuli associated with the trauma is a second symptom of ASD and PTSD. Trauma victims with these disorders may attempt to avoid thoughts or feelings related to the event, or like Stephanie, they may avoid people, places, or activities that remind them of the trauma. In PTSD, the avoidance also may manifest itself as a general *numbing of responsiveness*. People suffering from PTSD often complain that their feelings seem dampened or even nonexistent, and they frequently withdraw from others, particularly from close relationships. Alternative terms for numbing of responsiveness, such as "psychic numbing" or "emotional anesthesia," convey more dramatically a sense of the nature of the symptom.

AROUSAL OR ANXIETY

Despite their general withdrawal from feelings, people, and painful situations, individuals with ASD and PTSD also experience symptoms that indicate increased arousal and anxiety in comparison to what they felt before the trauma. Stephanie's hypervigilance in searching for dangers in her world is a common symptom of PTSD. Like Stephanie, many trauma victims also have trouble falling or staying asleep or difficulty maintaining their concentration. Other trauma victims feel restless and agitated, and they may be irritable and subject to angry outbursts. A number of people with PTSD or ASD also have an *exaggerated startle response*, excessive fear reactions to unexpected stimuli, such as loud noises. These various symptoms of anxiety and arousal are the reason why traumatic stress disorders are grouped with the anxiety disorders in DSM-IV.

DISSOCIATIVE SYMPTOMS

In addition to reexperiencing, avoidance, and increased arousal, acute stress disorder (but not necessarily PTSD) is characterized by explicit dissociative symptoms. Many people become less aware of their surroundings following a traumatic event. Like Stephanie, they report feeling dazed, and they may seem "spaced out" to other people. Other people experience *depersonalization*, feeling cut off from themselves or their environment. *Derealization* is a related dissociative experience—people feel a marked sense of unreality about themselves or the world around them. ASD also may be characterized by features of *dissociative amnesia*, specifically the inability to recall important aspects of the traumatic experience. (We discuss depersonalization, derealization, and dissociative amnesia in more detail when we review the dissociative disorders later in this chapter.) Finally, the DSM-IV lists a sense of numbing or detachment from others as a dissociative symptom that characterizes acute stress disorder. You might note that a very similar symptom is listed as an indicator of avoidance, not dissociation, in the diagnosis of PTSD (see Table 7–1). This discrepancy in diagnostic criteria reflects some of the broader controversy about whether acute and posttraumatic stress disorders should be classified as dissociative or anxiety disorders (van der Kolk & McFarlane, 1996).

Classification of Acute and Posttraumatic Stress Disorders

BRIEF HISTORICAL PERSPECTIVE

Maladaptive reactions to traumatic stress have long been of interest to the military, where "normal" performance is expected in the face of the trauma of combat. Historically, most of the military's concern has focused on battle dropout, that is, men who leave the field of action as a result of what was called "combat neurosis" (Francis et al., 1995). During the Vietnam War, however, battle dropout was less frequent than in earlier wars, but delayed reactions to the trauma of combat were much more frequent (Figley, 1978). This outcome prompted much interest in posttraumatic stress disorder, a condition first listed in the DSM in 1980 (DSM-III).

CONTEMPORARY CLASSIFICATION

The basic diagnostic criteria for PTSD—reexperiencing, avoidance, and arousal—have remained more or less the same in revisions of the DSM. (See Table 7–1 for a list of DSM-IV diagnostic criteria.) However, the DSM-IV included two significant changes in the classification of

traumatic stress disorders: acute stress disorder was included as a separate diagnostic category and the definition of trauma was altered.

Acute Stress Disorder   The diagnosis of acute stress disorder (ASD) was introduced for the first time in DSM-IV. The symptoms of ASD and PTSD are essentially the same, except that ASD describes reactions occurring in the first 4 weeks after a traumatic stressor, whereas PTSD includes problems extending or beginning at least 1 month subsequent to the traumatic experience. (See

---

TABLE 7-1

DSM-IV Diagnostic Criteria for Posttraumatic Stress Disorder (PTSD)

A. The person has been exposed to a traumatic event in which both of the following were present:
   1. The person experienced, witnessed, or was confronted with an event or events that involved actual or threatened death or serious injury, or a threat to the physical integrity of self or others.
   2. The person's response involved intense fear, helplessness, or horror.

B. The traumatic event is persistently reexperienced in one (or more) of the following ways:
   1. Recurrent and intrusive distressing recollections of the event including images, thoughts, or perceptions
   2. Recurrent distressing dreams of the event
   3. Acting or feeling as if the traumatic event were recurring
   4. Intense psychological distress at exposure to internal or external cues that symbolize or resemble an aspect of the traumatic event
   5. Physiologic reactivity upon exposure to internal or external cues that symbolize or resemble an aspect of the traumatic event

C. Persistent avoidance of stimuli associated with the trauma and numbing of general responsiveness, as indicated by three (or more) of the following:
   1. Efforts to avoid thoughts, feelings, or conversation associated with the trauma
   2. Efforts to avoid activities, places, or people that arouse recollections of the trauma
   3. Inability to recall an important aspect of the trauma
   4. Markedly diminished interest or participation in significant activities
   5. Feeling of detachment or estrangement from others
   6. Restricted range of affect
   7. Sense of a foreshortened future

D. Persistent symptoms of increased arousal, as indicated by two (or more) of the following:
   1. Difficulty falling or staying asleep
   2. Irritability or outbursts of anger
   3. Difficulty concentrating
   4. Hypervigilance
   5. Exaggerated startle response

E. Duration of the disturbance is more than 1 month
   Specify if:
   Acute: If duration of symptoms is less than 3 months
   Chronic: If duration of symptoms is 3 months or more
   Specify if:
   With delayed onset: If onset of symptoms is at least 6 months after the stressor

Table 7–2 for the diagnostic criteria.) Not surprisingly, many people suffer from psychological troubles immediately after a trauma, and the severity of their immediate impairment is a fairly good predictor of whether or not they will have subsequent troubles. The diagnosis of ASD is an attempt to recognize this fact and to prevent the development of PTSD with early treatment. In fact, according to Allen Francis, the chair of the DSM-IV task force, "The diagnosis of acute stress disorder was included in DSM-IV because an ounce of prevention is worth a pound of cure" (Frances et al., 1995, p. 263). The dissociative symptoms were included in the diagnosis of ASD, but not PTSD, because dissociative symptoms are particularly likely to occur in the immediate aftermath of a trauma (Francis et al., 1995).

Traumatic Events Earlier versions of the DSM defined trauma as an event "outside the range of usual human experience," but as we will discuss shortly, research has revealed that, unfortunately, many traumatic stressors are a *common* part of human experience in the United States today. The DSM-IV revised the definition of trauma to reflect this fact, and the manual also attempted to define trauma more precisely (Francis et al., 1995). Thus the DSM-IV developed the two-part definition of trauma that includes (1) the experience of an event involving actual or threatened death or injury to self or others and (2) a response of intense fear, helplessness, or horror in reaction to the event (see Tables 7–1 and 7–2).

Although we can define traumatic stress disorders in general terms, different traumatic stressors can dramatically influence how people

---

TABLE 7–2

DSM-IV Diagnostic Criteria for Acute Stress Disorder (ASD)

A. The person has been exposed to a traumatic event in which both of the following were present:
   1. The person experienced, witnessed, or was confronted with an event or events that involved actual or threatened death or serious injury, or a threat to the physical integrity of self or others.
   2. The person's response involved intense fear, helplessness, or horror.

B. Either while experiencing or after experiencing the distressing event, the individual has three (or more) of the following dissociative symptoms:
   1. A subjective sense of numbing, detachment, or absence of emotional responsiveness
   2. A reduction in awareness of his or her surroundings (e.g., "being in a daze")
   3. Derealization
   4. Depersonalization
   5. Dissociative amnesia (i.e., the inability to recall an important aspect of the trauma)

C. The traumatic event is persistently reexperienced in at least one of the following ways: recurrent images, thoughts, dreams, illusions, flashback episodes, or a sense of reliving the experience; or distress on exposure to reminders of the traumatic event.

D. Marked avoidance of stimuli that arouse recollections of the trauma (e.g., thoughts, feelings, conversations, activities, places, people).

E. Marked symptoms of anxiety or increased arousal (e.g., difficulty sleeping, irritability, poor concentration, hypervigilance, exaggerated startle response, motor restlessness).

F. The disturbance causes clinically significant distress or impairment in social, occupational, or other important areas of functioning or impairs the individual's ability to pursue some necessary task, such as obtaining necessary assistance or mobilizing personal resources by telling family members about the traumatic experience.

G. The disturbance lasts for a minimum of 2 days and a maximum of 4 weeks and occurs within 4 weeks of the traumatic event.

PTSD and the Sexual Assault of Women

The diagnosis of posttraumatic stress disorder is helpful because it highlights many basic similarities in the reactions of victims to different types of traumatic events. Moreover, it calls attention to the fact that extreme distress is a normal response to being a victim of abnormal events. Still, in focusing on the common features of reactions to traumatic stressors, we must not forget that each individual's reaction to particular forms of trauma has certain unique elements as well. This concern is shared by psychologists who are studying the consequences of the sexual assault of women (Goodman, Koss, & Russo, 1993b).

Like many other traumatic stressors, sexual assault is not outside the realm of normal human experience in the United States today. Several surveys have found that approximately 20 percent of U.S. women have been victims of rape. More than 80 percent of these rapes are *acquaintance rapes*: assaults committed by people known to the victim, rather than by strangers (Goodman, Koss, & Russo, 1993a).

The physical consequences of rape cannot be ignored. Thirty-nine percent of rape victims are physically injured on parts of their bodies other than the genitals. A significant proportion of rape victims are infected with a sexually transmitted disease, and about 5 percent of rapes result in pregnancy. Finally, many victims of sexual assault suffer from subsequent gastrointestinal problems, such as nausea.

Most victims of sexual assault show the symptoms of PTSD. Victims may reexperience the horrors of the assault; they may feel numbed in reacting to others, particularly sexual partners; they may avoid any potentially threatening situation; and they may maintain both autonomic hyperarousal and hypervigilance against possible victimization. At the same time, victims of sexual assault also may experience profound relief and fears about simply being alive. They are grateful to be alive, yet fearful that their life could be so threatened. Depression is also common. Sadness, crying, and withdrawal from others often are coupled with sleep and appetite disturbances. Loss of interest in sex, insecurities about sexual identity, sexual dysfunction, and negative feelings toward men also are common.

Another frequent psychological problem is that many victims of sexual assault blame themselves despite the fact that they are the victims. Women may wonder if they unwittingly encouraged their assailant, or they may chastise themselves for not being more cautious in avoiding dangerous circumstances. This irrational self-blame is abetted by cultural myths that women provoke rape or that they actually enjoy it. These myths also may explain why as many as two-thirds of stranger rapes and four-fifths of acquaintance rapes are not reported to authorities. In fact, many women feel that they cannot discuss the sexual assault with anyone, which surely impedes recovery of more normal functioning.

Because sexual assault is difficult to discuss, Goodman, Koss, and Russo (1993a) recommend that all mental and physical health care providers routinely ask their patients whether they have been victims of physical or sexual violence. This is critical information for making a diagnosis of both physical and mental conditions, and questions may encourage some victims to open up about their experiences. There also is the hope that the prevalence of sexual assault can be reduced by increasing awareness of its frequency and its devastating consequences. ■

---

experience PTSD or ASD. Delayed stress reactions to combat experience, particularly among Vietnam War veterans, were the first focus of research on PTSD, but valuable recent efforts have extended research to such traumatic events as rape (Kilpatrick et al., 1989), child sex abuse (Deblinger et al., 1989), spouse abuse (Astin, Ogland-Hand, Coleman, & Foy, 1995), and witnessing disasters (Rubonis & Bickman, 1991). Each of these traumas may result in ASD or PTSD, but, as illustrated by the case of Stephanie, diagnosis and treatment must be extremely sensitive to the unique consequences of different traumatic events (see Further Thoughts).

A particular concern is the experience of **victimization.** Like Stephanie, the victims of violent crimes, particularly sexual assault, have been found to suffer from a number of emotional difficulties, including fear, guilt, self-blame, powerlessness, and lowered self-esteem (see Further Thoughts). Crime victims also have an increased risk for developing affective and anxiety disorders, and as many as one-quarter may develop PTSD. Among rape victims, the rate of PTSD may climb to 50 percent or more (Breslau et al., 1991; Kessler et al., 1995; Kilpatrick et al., 1989).

The psychological effects of exposure to natural disasters, such as the extensive flooding of the Mississippi River in 1993, or man-made disasters, like the Oklahoma City bombing in 1995, also are of concern both to scientists and to public policy makers. A review of 50 studies concluded that a small but significant relation exists between the experience of disasters and the development of psychological problems (Rubonis & Bickman, 1991). Specifically, the risk for a number of different psychological problems was found to be 17 percent higher among those exposed to a disaster. Anxiety and alcohol use were found to be the most common problems, although PTSD was not included as a possible outcome in this review. The highest rates of psychological problems were linked with natural (as opposed to man-made) disasters and to disasters that caused the greatest loss of life (Rubonis & Bickman, 1991).

Differential Diagnosis, Comorbidity, and the Grouping of PTSD/ASD Differential diagnosis can be a major concern in the classification of traumatic stress disorders. ASD and PTSD are distinguished from the diagnosis of *adjustment disorder* both by the nature of the stressor experienced and by the type and severity of the symptoms the stressor causes. Adjustment disorders are caused by "normal" but painful stressors, such as losing a job, and they involve normal (if distressing) emotional, cognitive, and behavioral reactions to these life events (see Chapter 17).

Comorbidity is another issue in differential diagnosis. Many people suffering from PTSD also meet the diagnostic criteria for another mental disorder, particularly depression, anxiety disorders, or substance abuse (Breslau et al., 1991; Kessler et al., 1995). In such cases, the co-occurring disorders must be diagnosed, and they often must be treated separately from the PTSD.

We should reiterate one final issue in the classification of PTSD and ASD. As we have noted, there is controversy about whether these are anxiety disorders, dissociative disorders, or belong in a separate diagnostic category. We expect this controversy to continue, and we anticipate that ASD, PTSD, and adjustment disorders will be grouped together in a separate diagnostic category of stress-related disorders in future revisions of the DSM.

Epidemiology of Trauma and Traumatic Stress Disorders

Only in recent years have experts begun to study the epidemiology of trauma and traumatic stress disorders. One of the first epidemiological studies, focusing on a representative sample of 3,000 individuals living in the St. Louis area, found that 1 percent of the subjects had experienced PTSD at some point in their lives, and approximately 15 percent had experienced at least one symptom of the disorder (Helzer, Robins, & McEvoy, 1987). The most common cause of PTSD among men was participation in the Vietnam War, with 20 percent of wounded veterans having experienced the disorder. For women, physical attack was the most common cause of PTSD, as 4.5 percent of victims experienced the disorder (Helzer, Robins, & McEvoy, 1987). Several more recent studies support the importance of assault and combat exposure in causing PTSD in women and men, respectively, but recent research has documented that the prevalence of PTSD is much higher than previously thought. Most importantly, the National Comorbidity Survey found that nearly 8 percent of people living in the United States will experience PTSD at some point in their lives, including about 10 percent of women and 5 percent of men (Kessler et al., 1995).

A study of a random sample of 1,200 adults living in the Detroit area was the first to offer important details about how many people are exposed to traumatic stress and how many of these people develop PTSD (Breslau et al., 1991). Consistent with the change in the DSM-IV definition of trauma, a high number of adults in this study—39 percent—reported that they had experienced a traumatic stressor. About 25 percent of those exposed to such a stressor later developed PTSD. The disorder was more likely following rape in comparison to other traumas and was less likely following a sudden injury or serious accident. Figure 7–1 illustrates the results of this study, which have been supported by the findings of the National Comorbidity Survey (Kessler et al., 1995).

The Detroit study also documented factors that increased the risk for experiencing trauma and conditions that made PTSD more likely among the trauma victims. Trauma was more likely to be experienced by men, by those with less education, and by people who were more "neurotic" (anxious) or extroverted, who had a history of conduct problems during childhood, and who had a family history of mental disorder. Among victims of traumatic stress, PTSD was more likely to be found among women, the more "neurotic," those with a family history of mental disorder, and people who themselves previously suffered from an emotional problem (Breslau et al., 1991). The same team of investigators replicated many of these findings in a prospective longitudinal study (Breslau, Davis, & Andreski, 1995). Thus, people with a history of emotional problems are more likely both to experience trauma and to suffer PTSD as a consequence.

These findings, and those from other research, raise questions about the role of premorbid personality in experiencing trauma and PTSD. In the St. Louis study, childhood behavior problems also predicted an increased risk of subsequently experiencing a traumatic stressor. In comparison to subjects with few childhood difficulties, people who retrospectively reported having four or more behavior problems before the age of 15 were about twice as likely to have served in Vietnam or to have been beaten or mugged. The St. Louis study further concluded that people with a history of behavior problems were more likely to respond to trauma with PTSD. In fact, the prevalence of PTSD symptoms was about 50 percent higher among those Vietnam veterans or victims of attack who had experienced earlier behavior problems than it was among veterans or victims who were better adjusted during childhood (Helzer, Robins, & McEvoy, 1987). Together, these findings suggest that premorbid maladjustment is not necessary for the development of PTSD, but preexisting psychological problems increase the risk for the disorder in two ways: They increase the

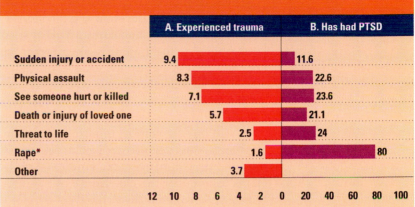

	A. Experienced trauma	B. Has had PTSD
Sudden injury or accident	9.4	11.6
Physical assault	8.3	22.6
See someone hurt or killed	7.1	23.6
Death or injury of loved one	5.7	21.1
Threat to life	2.5	24
Rape*	1.6	80
Other	3.7	

12 10 8 6 4 2 0 20 40 60 80 100

FIGURE 7-1: These bar graphs highlight the prevalence of trauma and the risk for posttraumatic stress disorder. Part (A) illustrates the percentage of the overall population who had experienced a particular trauma (based on a study of 1,200 adults in Detroit between the ages of 21 and 30). Part (B) shows the percentage of people exposed to those traumas who developed PTSD. Note that the rape victims were by far the most likely to experience PTSD.

*The prevalence of rape as reported in this study was much lower than that reported in other studies. We assume that this statistic reflects only the most violent rapes.

Source: Adapted from N. Breslau, G.C. Davis, P. Andreski, and E. Peterson, 1991, Traumatic events and posttraumatic stress disorder in the urban population of young adults, *Archives of General Psychiatry, 48,* 216–22.

likelihood of experiencing trauma, and they diminish the individual's ability to cope with that trauma.

Etiological Considerations and Research on PTSD and ASD

By definition, traumatic experience causes ASD and PTSD, and this identification of a precise etiological agent distinguishes these problems from most disorders listed in the DSM-IV. However, the fact that not everyone who experiences trauma develops ASD or PTSD indicates that the etiology of the disorder is more complex. That is, a given trauma is a necessary but not a sufficient cause of ASD or PTSD.

In general, there are three alternative ways to explain the imperfect relation between the experience of trauma and the development of traumatic stress disorders. *Threshold models* suggest that "everyone has a breaking point." Thus, from this perspective, anyone will develop ASD and/or PTSD when exposed to a sufficiently intense trauma. From the threshold perspective, the most relevant etiological issues concern the nature of the traumatic event and the individual's exposure to it. In contrast, *diathesis-stress models* indicate that trauma is necessary for the development of a traumatic stress disorder, but the disorder will emerge only when combined with other risk factors, such as premorbid personality characteristics. The interaction between risk and trauma is most important from the diathesis-stress perspective. Finally, *illness models* hold that, in many cases, emotional problems found *after* the experience of a trauma actually were present *before* the event occurred. From the illness point of view, the trauma merely leads to the identification or emergence of a preexisting condition. Thus the model has little to say about the specific etiology of ASD or PTSD. It is important to keep in mind these three general models when examining research on specific biological, psychological, and social risk factors.

BIOLOGICAL FACTORS
IN TRAUMATIC STRESS DISORDERS

Biological factors, including genetic influences, may contribute to PTSD and ASD indirectly through their influence on psychological characteristics that increase the risk for the disorders. As we have noted, data indicate that people with preexisting psychological difficulties or personality characteristics are at greater risk for experiencing traumatic events and for developing PTSD than are people without such problems. Consistent with the diathesis-stress model, premorbid personality may (1) increase the risk of experiencing trauma and/or (2) lead to PTSD when combined with the stress of trauma.

In fact, behavior genetic researchers have found that biological factors increase the risk of both experiencing trauma and developing PTSD. A twin study of more than 4,000 Vietnam-era veterans found that MZ twins had a higher concordance rate than DZ twins for experiencing trauma, specifically exposure to combat, and for developing PTSD symptoms (True et al., 1993). Of particular note was the finding that the magnitude of genetic effects differed across symptoms of the disorder. Genetic contributions were greatest in accounting for arousal/anxiety symptoms and least for symptoms of reexperiencing. Conversely, level of exposure to combat predicted symptoms of reexperiencing and avoidance of activities, but exposure did not predict other

symptoms of PTSD (True et al., 1993). Thus, consistent with the diathesis-stress model, it appears that genetic factors contribute to PTSD. However, a preexisting diathesis may contribute more to arousal/anxiety symptoms than to symptoms of reexperiencing, which may be more direct reactions to trauma.

Several different psychological characteristics may account for the increased risk for trauma exposure and for PTSD that has been identified in research in behavior genetics and other areas. Psychological risk factors include antisocial behavior (Helzer, Robins, & McEvoy, 1987; King, King, Foy, & Gudanowski, 1996), depression (Frank et al., 1981), and neuroticism (McFarlane, 1988). One study found that premorbid personality (specifically, a positive family history of psychopathology) was related to PTSD among veterans with low exposure to combat, but it was unrelated to PTSD when combat exposure is high (Foy et al., 1987). This evidence supports both the threshold and the diathesis-stress models. People subjected to intense levels of stress may develop PTSD even in the absence of premorbid personality risk factors, but the risk factors become central in contributing to PTSD when the trauma is less intense.

Biological Effects of Exposure to Trauma   A very different biological approach focuses on the biological *consequences* of exposure to trauma and how these consequences may play a role in the maintenance of PTSD (van der Kolk, 1996; Watson, Hoffman, & Wilson, 1988; Yehuda & McFarlane, 1995). One group of investigators has suggested that trauma alters the activity of particular neurotransmitters in the brain (van der Kolk et al., 1984). According to this theory, trauma increases the production of the neurotransmitter *norepinephrine*. This excess production of norepinephrine in turn causes the increased arousal and anxiety that are symptoms of the disorder. This hypothesis further suggests that excess norepinephrine causes the normal stress response to be activated more intensely and by milder stressors. (See Chapter 8 for a discussion of norepinephrine and the normal stress response.)

Another hypothesis suggests that exposure to traumatic stress increases the production of endogenous (internally produced) *opioids*, chemicals manufactured by the body that have similar effects to exogenous (produced outside the body) opioids like morphine (see Chapter 11). According to this hypothesis, the increase in internally produced opioids causes the numbing that characterizes PTSD (van der Kolk et al., 1984). One interesting study of the hypothesis found that Vietnam veterans with PTSD showed *decreased* pain sensitivity following exposure to a film of combat. No change in pain threshold was found when the veterans were administered naloxone, a chemical that blocks the effects of the opioids, and no changes in pain tolerance—either with or without naloxone—were found among veterans without PTSD (Pitman et al., 1990). The findings of this study are open to several alternative interpretations, but they provide justification for further study of this intriguing hypothesis.

Other research on the biological consequences of exposure to trauma focuses on neuroanatomy rather than on neurophysiology. For example, some researchers have suggested that trauma creates new neural pathways while altering or destroying old ones (Kolb, 1987). This and other biological models of PTSD are supported only by limited research, however. Some evidence supports the suggestion that neurotransmitter levels are higher among those with PTSD, at least as measured in sites peripheral to the brain (Krystal et al., 1989). Moreover, psychophysiological assessment of PTSD veterans indicates higher resting levels of arousal and greater increases in arousal when presented with the sights and sounds of combat (Gerardi, Blanchard, & Kolb, 1989). Still, research on the neurobiological correlates of ASD and PTSD is just beginning, and these tentative findings are only initial leads on the trail to discover the biological contributions to traumatic stress disorders (van der Kolk, 1996).

We also must remember that such biological explanations can be perfectly consistent with psychological and social hypotheses about the development of the disorder. Because every psychological experience has an underlying biological counterpart, ASD and PTSD *must* be accompanied by changes in brain structure or function. The task for psychobiologists and biochemists who wish to understand the effects of psychological trauma is to identify specific brain sites and biochemical actions that are linked with traumatic stress disorders.

PSYCHOLOGICAL FACTORS IN TRAUMATIC STRESS DISORDERS

In addition to the role of premorbid personality, several hypotheses have been offered about how psychological reactions to trauma may play a part in the development of ASD and PTSD.

Psychodynamic formulations emphasize the role of the defenses in protecting the individual against the anxiety created by trauma. Psychodynamic theorists suggest that massive repression plays a role in numbing and withdrawal, a result of the need for strong intrapsychic defenses to cope with intense trauma. Conversely, reexperiencing is thought to result from a breakdown of repression (Oei, Lim, & Hennessy, 1990). Thus, according to the psychodynamic formulation, the essential difficulty in coping with trauma is achieving a homeostatic balance between anxiety and defense.

Psychologist Edna Foa, a leading researcher on social learning causes and treatments for PTSD, has used **two-factor theory** to explain the development of symptoms following a number of traumas (Foa, Steketee, & Rothbaum, 1989). Two-factor theory involves a combination of classical conditioning and operant conditioning. According to Foa and other two-factor theorists, classical conditioning *creates* a number of fears when the terror inherent in trauma is paired with the cues associated with the traumatic event. Operant conditioning, in turn, *maintains* these fears. Specifically, when fear-producing situations are avoided, the avoidance behavior is negatively reinforced by the reduction of aversive anxiety (Keane, Zimering, & Caddell, 1985). For example, Stephanie's fears of being alone at night are understandable both intuitively and from the perspective of classical conditioning. Her avoidance of fearful circumstances, such as being alone, probably helped to maintain her fear in the short run. More importantly, Stephanie's courage in confronting her fears—and her attacker—and her willingness to discuss her experiences surely helped her to learn to overcome her fears, as we discuss in more detail shortly.

Learning theorists suggest that such cognitive processes as self-blame and expectancies of further trauma are also important in the etiology of traumatic stress disorders (Foa, Steketee, & Rothbaum, 1989; Jones & Barlow, 1990). In practice, however, it is difficult to determine whether such factors as self-blame or expectancies are causes of or reactions to (symptoms of) ASD and PTSD. Research indicates that expectancies can be important etiologically, in that people cope with traumatic stress more adequately when they are able to anticipate its onset. For example, pilots with prior training appear to cope more successfully with subsequent helicopter crashes than pilots who have received no

▲ **Edna Foa is a psychologist at the Eastern Pennsylvania Psychiatric Institute in Philadelphia. Foa has done extensive research on the etiology and treatment of PTSD.**

training preparing them for emergency crashes. At the same time, evidence indicates that more severe short-term reactions to trauma—more severe ASD—predicts more severe PTSD in the long term (Shalev, 1996). In fact, research has demonstrated that, among Israeli trauma victims, the degree of dissociation reported within 1 week following a trauma predicted more severe PTSD 6 months later (Shalev et al., 1996). This finding suggests that dissociation may be better conceived as a symptom of traumatic stress disorders and not a (unconscious) coping mechanism. By extension, the finding raises questions about whether other cognitive or emotional processes (e.g., self-blame, anger) are better viewed as reactions to, rather than mediating causes of, ASD and PTSD.

SOCIAL FACTORS
IN TRAUMATIC STRESS DISORDERS

Researchers recently have documented that the risk for PTSD among Vietnam combat veterans increases if they have had a history of family instability or of exposure to prior traumas (King et al., 1996). Thus the predisposition in the diathesis-stress model sometimes may be a past social experience and not just a biological or psychological vulnerability. Most research on social factors in ASD and PTSD has not focused on past events, however, but instead has investigated the role of social factors that occur during or following the trauma. In particular, scientists have studied the extent to which the risk for PTSD is affected by (1) the nature of the traumatic event and the individual's level of exposure to it and (2) the availability of social support following the traumatic event.

Consistent with the threshold model, researchers have found that more intense and life-threatening traumatic events are more likely to result in PTSD. For example, victims of attempted rape are more likely to develop PTSD if the rape is completed, if they are physically injured during the assault, and if they perceive the sexual assault as life-threatening (Kilpatrick et al., 1989). Similarly, PTSD is more prevalent among Vietnam veterans who were wounded, who were involved in the deaths of noncombatants, or who witnessed atrocities (Oei, Lim, & Hennessy, 1990). The importance of the experience of trauma is dramatically underscored by evidence from the same twin study we discussed earlier. Among MZ twin pairs during the Vietnam era, the prevalence of PTSD was found to be 9 times higher for co-twins who served in Vietnam than for their identical twin who did not serve (Goldberg, True, Eisen, & Henderson, 1990). Thus twin research clearly documents the importance of *both* genes *and* experience in causing PTSD.

As with less severe stressors, the availability of social support after the occurrence of the trauma appears to play a crucial role in alleviating long-term psychological damage. Such evidence serves as one rationale for attempts to help the victims of rape become less secretive about their victimization. Many victims of rape mistakenly feel guilty and somehow responsible for being attacked. Rape crisis centers and rape support groups offer social support that helps women recognize that they are not at fault—they are victims of a heinous crime. A lack of social support also is thought to have contributed to the high prevalence of PTSD found among Vietnam veterans (Oei, Lim, & Hennessy, 1990). Rather than being praised as heros, returning veterans often were treated with disdain. This absence of support made it difficult for many veterans to justify the trauma that they had suffered, and it likely increased the number of cases of PTSD as a result.

INTEGRATION
AND ALTERNATIVE PATHWAYS

The combination of evidence suggests some support for all three models, and, in fact, there likely are alternative pathways to the development of ASD and PTSD. In some cases, the threshold model probably is true: Anyone could develop a traumatic stress disorder given a critical level of exposure and a trauma of sufficient intensity. In other cases, the illness model also is likely to be true: A trauma may call attention to or exacerbate preexisting disorders or maladaptive personality characteristics. Notwithstanding these possibilities, evidence indicates that a diathesis-stress model best explains most cases.

▼ **Rape crisis centers offer woman support in dealing with sexual assault.**

Phrased differently, the etiology of ASD and PTSD is best explained by a systems approach. Although trauma is a necessary cause of PTSD, the specific etiology of PTSD typically involves a complex interaction of risk factors that are present before the trauma, during the trauma, and after its occurrence.

Future research should clarify which biological, psychological, and social factors increase the risk for ASD and PTSD, and hopefully scientists also will identify *protective* factors within each of these domains. For example, researchers recently have documented that increased *hardiness*—a personal sense of commitment, control, and challenge in facing stress—predicted lower rates of PTSD among troops in the Persian Gulf War (Sutker, Davis, Uddo, & Ditta, 1995). Research on such protective factors and posttraumatic social support should help us not only to understand better the etiology of ASD and PTSD but also to develop more effective treatments.

Prevention and Treatment of ASD and PTSD

In most cases, the symptoms of traumatic stress disorders begin immediately or shortly after a traumatic event. However, the symptoms of PTSD can begin months or years after the trauma, and the reexperiencing of the trauma can continue for long periods of time. In addition to situations that are reminiscent of the trauma, reminders such as anniversary dates often cause the horror to be relived, as we saw with the case of Stephanie. Because of the variability in onset and duration of symptoms, it is important to distinguish emergency attempts to help trauma victims from longer-term treatment efforts.

EMERGENCY TREATMENT OF TRAUMA VICTIMS

Trauma is a known cause of ASD and PTSD, and this knowledge makes prevention the first consideration in the treatment of the disorders. Early intervention with trauma victims holds the hope of both easing the pain of coping with a horrific event and of preventing the subsequent development of PTSD. The potential for secondary prevention is so important that the Federal Emergency Management Agency, the government agency designated to deal with natural and man-made disasters, is required to provide community mental health centers with special funding during times of local or regional disaster. As we noted earlier, moreover, the potential for preventing the development of PTSD is one reason why acute stress disorder was included in the DSM-IV.

Psychologists and other mental health professionals frequently offer emergency assistance to individual victims of trauma or to groups of people who have experienced a disaster. These emergency treatments range from intensive individual counseling sessions with rape victims to group discussions with children whose school has been destroyed by a tornado. There are many differences in the therapeutic approaches used across such prevention efforts, but offering immediate social support to trauma victims is a common goal of all early interventions (Raphael, Wilson, Meldrum, & McFarlane, 1996).

Little systematic research has been conducted on the effectiveness of most emergency interventions with the victims of trauma (Raphael et al., 1996). The treatment of soldiers in combat is one of the few exceptions where empirical evidence is available. Since World War I, the treatment of soldiers who experience combat stress has been based on the three principles of offering (1) immediate treatment in the (2) proximity of the battlefield with the (3) expectation of return to the front lines upon recovery. The effectiveness of these treatment principles has been long assumed, but they were not studied systematically until 1982, when the Israeli army implemented the practices during the Lebanon war. Evaluation of the emergency services indicated that 60 percent of soldiers who were treated near the front recovered sufficiently to return to battle within 72 hours. Soldiers who expected to return to the front experienced lower rates of PTSD than did those who did not expect to return to battle. In addition, those soldiers who were treated on the front lines were less likely to develop PTSD subsequently when compared to soldiers who were treated in civilian facilities away from the battlefield (Oei, Lim, & Hennessy, 1990).

It seems reasonable to generalize these principles to the treatment of victims of many, but not all (e.g., rape victims), forms of trauma. For example, we would expect that victims of a natural disaster would benefit from immediate treatment near their communities with the expectation of a rapid return to normal life. Perhaps the key to this intervention strategy is the creation of the expectation that extreme distress in the face of trauma is normal, as is recovery from the trauma. This expectation may become a reality when combined with successful, subsequent coping.

TREATMENT OF PTSD

Psychotropic medication is frequently used in the treatment of PTSD, but there is no single medication that has specific effects on the disorder. Rather, various antidepressant and antianxiety medications sometimes are used to treat particular symptoms associated with PTSD (Davidson & van der Kolk, 1996; Marshall & Klein, 1995). For example, one group of investigators found that the antidepressant medication amitriptyline led to improvements in self-reported depression ratings among veterans with PTSD. However, 64 percent of the treated patients continued to meet the diagnostic criteria for PTSD, compared with 72 percent of a control group that was given a placebo (Davidson et al., 1990).

Psychotherapists who specialize in PTSD have suggested some general principles for the psychological treatment of the disorder. In the order in which they are likely to be addressed in therapy, these include (1) establishing a trusting therapeutic relationship, (2) providing education about the process of coping with trauma, (3) stress-management training, (4) encouraging the reexperience of the trauma, and (5) integrating the traumatic event into the individual's experience (Scurfield, 1985).

Therapeutic Reexposure to Trauma   Reexposure to the traumatic event is perhaps the least obvious but most important of these strategies (Frueh, Turner, & Beidel, 1995; Rothbaum & Foa, 1996). Perhaps because the terrifying and uncontrollable reliving of trauma is one of the most distressing symptoms of PTSD, reexperiencing in a controlled treatment setting becomes basic to the therapeutic process. Therapeutic approaches differ widely in how this reexperience is encouraged, yet all treatments encourage the recounting of trauma in some form. The most direct method is **trauma desensitization**. Trauma desensitization is a variation of the well-researched treatment for phobias, systematic desensitization (see Chapter 6). Initially, the client is taught a basic relaxation technique. He or she then relives the traumatic event through discussions with the therapist or through imagining the experience. Exposure to the trauma is gradual, so that the client can maintain a state

of relaxation. The client confronts increasingly distressing details only after he or she can relive less upsetting events while remaining calm.

Little research had been conducted on the effectiveness of trauma desensitization or other treatments for PTSD until recent years, when a few investigations have been completed (Frueh, Turner, & Beidel, 1995; Rothbaum & Foa, 1996). A study conducted in the Netherlands compared the effectiveness of trauma desensitization, hypnotherapy, and psychodynamic therapy in the treatment of people suffering from the effects of a variety of traumatic experiences (Brom, Kleber, & Defares, 1989). Trauma desensitization followed the procedures described above. Hypnotherapy was similar to trauma desensitization, except that hypnosis was used to facilitate the reliving of the traumatic experience. Psychodynamic therapy focused on the intrapsychic conflicts caused by the trauma rather than on the trauma itself.

All treatments produced significantly more positive outcomes in comparison with an untreated control group. Approximately 4 months after an initial assessment, 60 percent of treated subjects exhibited clinically significant improvements in trauma symptoms, in contrast to only 26 percent of untreated controls. The most notable improvements were that subjects were less likely to avoid difficult situations and experienced intrusive thoughts less frequently. Psychodynamic therapy tended to produce the most benefits concerning intrusive thinking; desensitization and hypnotherapy were more effective in treating avoidance behaviors. Overall, however, there were no statistically significant differences among the three alternative treatments (Brom, Kleber, & Defares, 1989).

The similarities in treatment effectiveness may be another indication of the common factors found across different types of psychotherapy (see Chapter 3). In this study, the common factor may have been the reliving of the trauma, whether through desensitization, hypnosis, or discussion of its effects on intrapsychic life. This conclusion is supported by a treatment outcome study of rape victims (Foa et al., 1991). Prolonged exposure involving repeated reliving of the trauma over nine therapy sessions produced more long-term reductions in PTSD symptoms than did three alternatives: (1) stress inoculation training (focusing on relaxation and stress management), (2) supportive counseling (which explicitly omitted exposure procedures), and (3) a wait list control group.

Also of interest was the finding that stress inoculation training produced more short-term benefits, whereas prolonged exposure was more effective in the long run.

One approach to exposure therapy for PTSD, *eye movement desensitization and reprocessing (EMDR)*, has been greeted with considerable clinical enthusiasm—and empirical skepticism. Psychologist Francine Shapiro (1995) "discovered" that rapid back-and-forth eye movements reduced her own anxiety, and she soon applied the eye movement technique to her clients. She and her proponents since have taught EMDR to thousands of practitioners, and case studies (and limited research) attest to the treatment's effectiveness, particularly when used in treating PTSD. However, many experts remain skeptical of EMDR due to the lack of a theoretical basis for the treatment and the absence of sound and objective empirical evidence of its effectiveness (Lohr, et al., 1992).

We share the skepticism about EMDR, although we view reexposure as an essential component in the treatment of traumatic stress disorders. Reliving traumatic events is painful initially, and it may appear to impede progress. However, this painful reexperiencing may be exactly the right therapy (Frueh, Turner, & Beidel, 1995; Rothbaum & Foa, 1996). As illustrated in the case of Stephanie, an important element in overcoming traumatic experience is confronting the experience in memory, in discussions, or, if practical and humane, perhaps in returning to the scene of the trauma.

COURSE AND OUTCOME

Relatively little is known about the long-term course of ASD or PTSD. Evidence indicates, however, that PTSD can be chronic and can interfere with many areas of life functioning. One study of World War II prisoners of war who suffered from PTSD (as diagnosed by retrospective report) found that only about 30 percent were fully recovered, whereas 60 percent continued to have mild to moderate symptoms of the disorder. Another 10 percent either showed no recovery or had a deteriorating course (Kluznik et al., 1986). Given that the follow-up study was conducted 40 years after the imprisonment, these data suggest a poor prognosis, at least for those subjected to the extreme and prolonged trauma of being prisoners of war.

A somewhat more optimistic picture was provided by the findings of the National Comorbidity Survey, which included a much wider range of traumatic experiences. The NCS found that, for many people, PTSD improved fairly quickly during the first year after the trauma, whereas symptoms diminished more gradually over the next several years for most trauma victims (see Figure 7–2). Symptoms were reduced more rapidly among people who received treatment. However, this outcome does not prove the effectiveness of psychological intervention, because clients were not randomly assigned to treatment (see Research Methods in Chapter 3). In fact, regardless of whether they received treatment, over one-third of people who had suffered from PTSD continued to report symptoms of the disorder 6 years after the traumatic event (Kessler et al., 1995). Thus, although most people improve over time, PTSD can become a chronic disorder for many. We need more research on what factors, including prevention and treatment, predict more or less successful life readjustment following ASD and PTSD.

Recovered Memories?   A final issue in consideration of the course and outcome of traumatic stress disorders is the very controversial topic of **recovered memories,** dramatic recollections of a long-forgotten traumatic experience (see Further Thoughts). Is it

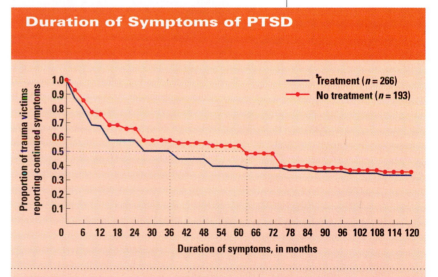

Duration of Symptoms of PTSD

FIGURE 7-2: The symptoms of PTSD decline over time but persist for 10 years among approximately one-third of trauma victims. Treatment may hasten recovery, as victims who received treatment reported significantly more rapid improvement than victims who did not receive treatment. Data are based on the retrospective reports of subjects in the National Comorbidity Survey who had ever experienced PTSD.

Source: R.C. Kessler, A. Sonnega, E. Bromet, M. Hughes, and C.B. Nelson, 1995, Posttraumatic stress disorder in the National Comorbidity Survey, *Archives of General Psychiatry, 52,* 1057.

Recovered Memories?

In 1990, George Franklin was convicted of the brutal murder of an 8-year-old girl. The crime had occurred over 20 years earlier, and the major evidence was the "recovered memory" of Franklin's daughter Eileen. Eileen claimed to have witnessed the rape and murder of her friend by her father, but dissociation pushed the memory of the horrid experience into her unconscious mind. Twenty years later, according to the daughter, the memory returned. In fact, Eileen provided both verifiable and inconsistent accounts of the horrifying event. She recalled a smashed ring on her friend's finger as she raised her hand to protect herself from a blow with a rock. Case records corroborated the memory. On the other hand, Eileen changed her story about the presence of her sister in the van she was riding in that day, and she changed the time of day from morning to afternoon. George Franklin was convicted of murder in 1990, but his conviction was overturned in 1995, and he was released from prison. A U.S. District Court judge did not bar Eileen Franklin's testimony about her recovered memories, but he ruled that the lower court erred in excluding evidence that Eileen could have learned details about the 1969 murder from news articles. Thus the question remains: Was Eileen's memory accurate?

▲ Eileen Franklin at the murder trial of her father, George. Ms. Franklin testified about her "recovered memories" of witnessing her father's rape and murder of an 8-year-old girl. George Franklin was convicted of murder more than 20 years after the girl's death. The conviction was later reversed on appeal, and Franklin was released from prison.

Recovered memories have become an important and controversial issue. Popular books and earnest therapists urge people to unearth past traumas, particularly remembrances of physical and sexual abuse, and an increasing number of people have claimed that they have recovered horrible memories from the past. Many parents faced with accusations about the past suggest, however, that they are being caused to suffer unnecessary pain. They suggest that false memories are being created by misguided, overeager therapists. Are recovered memories examples of dissociation, or are they merely examples of the power of suggestion?

This question has been considered in detail by the psychologist Elizabeth Loftus (1993), a specialist in memories of painful events who has served as an expert witness in numerous trials. Although it is impossible to verify—or disprove—many memories from the distant past, Loftus suggests numerous reasons for skepticism, or at least caution. One area of recovered memories that Loftus clearly disputes are recollections that date to very early childhood. A number of people have claimed to recall trauma dating from infancy or toddlerhood, but such memories are inconsistent with current knowledge of memory in early childhood. Most memories prior to school age are forgotten, and few people can report memories dating back before age 3 or 4. One study found, for example, that few subjects who were under the age of 3 at the time could recall where they were when President Kennedy was assassinated. In contrast, most subjects who had been at least 8 years old at the time of the assassination reported at least some memory of being told about the tragedy (Winograd & Killinger, 1983).

More suspicions emerge from an examination of some case histories of recovered memories. Studies indicate that therapists rarely doubt their clients' recovered memories of the past (Loftus, 1993; Loftus & Ketcham, 1994), but the concern embraces much more than a lack of skepticism. Many therapists and popular books encourage people to search for (create?) memories that they do not recall. Symptoms as common and mild as low self-esteem are sometimes interpreted as indications of past, forgotten trauma. Gaps in memory are also interpreted as a sign of dissociated memories. One example of this approach is noted in the popular book *The Courage to Heal*. The authors state:

> You may think you don't have memories, but often as you begin to talk about what you do remember, there emerges a constellation of feelings, reactions, and recollections that add up to substantial information. To say "I was abused," you don't need the kind of recall that would stand up in a court of law.

> Often the knowledge that you were abused starts with a tiny feeling, an intuition. It's important to trust that inner voice and work from there. Assume your feelings are valid. So far, no one we've talked to thought she might have been abused and then later discovered that she hadn't been. (Bass & Davis, 1988, p. 22)

Could such suggestions lead some people to create memories about events that never happened? We think the answer is yes. Determining the truth in any one case is difficult, sometimes impossible. Nevertheless, several studies supply evidence that memories, even of highly dramatic events, can be inaccurate (Loftus, 1993; Loftus & Ketcham, 1994). In one such study, subjects were interviewed the day after the explosion of the space shuttle *Challenger* and described the circumstances of how they learned of the tragedy. Three years later, the same subjects again were asked how they had learned about the explosion. About one-third of the subjects reported vivid—and grossly inaccurate—memories of what they were doing and how they learned about the *Challenger* tragedy (Neisser & Harsch, 1992).

These observations do not prove that memories of trauma are false. In fact, evidence indicates that memories for emotion-laden events are more accurate than memories for ordinary experiences (Koss, Tromp, & Tharan, 1995). Still, the malleability of memory suggests grounds for skepticism, particularly when a memory is "recovered" after a therapist encourages a client to search for it. In fact, as many as 25 percent of therapists in the United States believe that recovering memories is an important part of their therapy with female clients, and these therapists report using some dubious strategies to help their clients "remember" (Poole, Lindsay, Mamon, & Bull, 1995). A therapist's unwillingness to believe a patient can damage the therapeutic relationship, but false memories also can produce great harm to the client—and to anyone who is falsely accused. Skepticism and clinical sensitivity are not incompatible. There is dramatic and apparently accurate evidence to suggest that traumatic memories sometimes are repressed. Dissociation between experience and memory should not be dismissed merely because it is difficult to demonstrate. At the same time, psychologists must not be overzealous in assuming certain knowledge about topics that inherently involve much uncertainty. ∎

---

possible that some traumatic experiences are so overwhelming that the mind blocks them from conscious awareness? If so, could some experience—perhaps psychotherapy—cause accurate memories of such experiences to resurface into the conscious mind many years later?

This possibility has become a pressing and controversial issue. In recent years, psychologists have vehemently debated the accuracy or even the existence of recovered memories in theory, in therapy, and in courtrooms across the United States. Some therapists and lay enthusiasts have searched so hard to recover their own or others' unconscious memories that psychologists have become concerned that many "memories" may have been created by the power of suggestion.

We believe that proponents have greatly exaggerated the extent and accuracy of recovered memories, although we have no doubt that many memories, including traumatic ones, can become inaccessible over time. In reaching these conclusions, we note three facts (also see Further Thoughts). First, evidence indicates that some people fail to recall traumatic experiences such as childhood sexual abuse that have been documented to occur long ago (Williams, 1994). Second, evidence also indicates that some people report *false memories* of events that are known *not* to have occurred in the past (Loftus, Garry, & Feldman, 1994). Third, psychologists have no reliable and valid method for determining whether, in any given individual case, a "recovered memory" is accurate or false. In any case, the dissociation between traumatic experience and memory provides another link between PTSD and our next topic, dissociative disorders.

Dissociative Disorders

Until recent years, *dissociative disorders*— characterized by persistent, maladaptive disruptions in the integration of memory, consciousness, or identity—were of more interest to theorists and novelists than to empirically oriented mental health professionals. However, there has been an explosion of interest in dissociative disorders since the 1980s. This bodes well for future research. Currently, however, clinical and theoretical approaches to dissociative disorders are controversial, and as you will soon discover, sound empirical evidence on dissociative disorders remains sharply limited.

If the dissociative symptoms found in acute and posttraumatic stress disorders are dramatic, the symptoms of dissociative disorders verge on the unbelievable. The person with a dissociative disorder may be unable to remember many seemingly familiar details about the past; he or she may wander far from home and perhaps assume a new identity; or in extreme cases, two or more personalities may coexist within the same person. We introduce the extraordinary problems found in dissociative disorders in the following case study.

CASE STUDY

Dissociative Fugue

Dallae disappeared mysteriously during final exams during her junior year at a California university. She was reported missing by her roommate, who had last seen Dallae when she was supposed to be studying for her organic chemistry exam. Dallae had been agitated that night. She left her room several times and kept interrupting her roommate, who was cramming for the same exam. Dallae did not take the exam the next day, and she still had not reappeared 2 days later. When she missed two more final exams, her roommate contacted the authorities.

At first, the police suspected foul play, because it did not seem likely that Dallae had left college on her own. None of her personal possessions were missing from her room; even her eyeglasses were still sitting on her desk. However, bank records indicated that Dallae had withdrawn all of her money from her bank account the day before the exam. Investigators also discovered that Dallae had been lying to her parents. She had told them that she had an "A" average in organic chemistry. In fact, she was failing the course, and she had not attended her laboratory section for almost 2 months.

When the local police failed to locate Dallae, they contacted the FBI. After a futile 4-week investigation, Dallae was located in a college town on the East Coast, where she was identified from a missing persons report. She had been brought to a hospital emergency room after she was found wandering on the streets. At the time, she appeared confused and disoriented. She told the emergency room physician that her name was Dawn and that she had been living on the streets and sleeping in dormitory lounges. She said that she had just moved from the West Coast and had come to the town because she hoped eventually to attend the university. She gave a vague and sketchy account about other details of her life. For example, she could not say how she got to the East Coast.

Dallae allowed herself to be voluntarily admitted to the hospital's psychiatric unit. There she talked little and spent most of her time watching television. She told the staff that she was Vietnamese and had been adopted by American parents, but her stories continued to be vague and inconsistent. She said that she didn't remember things, but she did not seem greatly distressed by her memory impairment. A CAT scan and neuropsychological tests detected no physical abnormalities or deficits in short-term memory or motor functioning.

A hospital social worker contacted the local police about the disoriented young patient, and the police were able to identify Dallae from an FBI report. The social worker contacted Dallae's parents shortly thereafter, and her mother immediately flew east to see her. When her mother appeared at the hospital a few days after Dallae had been admitted, Dallae did not recognize her. Her mother was greatly distressed by Dallae's indifference, and she noted other puzzling oddities and inconsistencies. For one thing, Dallae was not Vietnamese, and she was not adopted. She had grown up with her married parents, who were Korean immigrants. Her mother also noted that although Dallae was right-handed, she used her left hand to write a note on the ward. Dallae's consistent use of her left hand was confirmed by the staff and by the neuropsychologist who had tested her.

Two nights after her mother arrived, Dallae's memories apparently returned. That night, she attempted suicide by slashing her wrists, but she was discovered by a hospital staff member, who quickly stopped the bleeding. Dallae was intermittently depressed and extremely agitated for the next several days, especially after seeing her mother. Although she would not talk at length, her conversation indicated that much of her memory was now intact, and she began writing with her right hand again.

During the next 2 weeks, Dallae gradually related details about her life to the psychologist who was treating her. Dallae had been a quiet and obedient girl all through her childhood. Dallae's parents worked very hard, and they had high ambitions for their three children. Dallae's older brother had an MBA and was a very successful young executive. Her older sister currently was editor of the law review at a prestigious law school. Ever since she was a young child, Dallae's parents had planned for her to become a doctor. In fact, all her life her parents had told friends and relatives that Dallae would be a doctor one day.

Dallae worked extremely hard throughout high school and gained admission to a highly regarded public university in her home state despite her mediocre SAT scores. Through continued effort, Dallae had maintained a 3.0 grade point average as a premedical student during her first 2 years of college. Her coursework was becoming overwhelming in her third year, however, and her motivation was evaporating. Dallae now admitted, in fact, that she had never been interested in medicine. She also noted that she had wanted to attend the college in the town where she was found. She was drawn there during her episode for reasons she could not explain, and she still did not recall exactly how she had arrived at her destination. Dallae did note, however, that she felt comforted and somewhat relieved after she had made her way east.

Dallae remained sullen and agitated for several weeks after her mother's arrival, and she continued to talk about wanting to die. During discussions with her therapist, Dallae began to talk more freely about her past. She noted that she had been terrified to tell her parents about her grades and her feelings about studying medicine—especially her father. Her father put endless pressure on Dallae to fulfill what she saw as his dream. She cried at length when relating how he had struck her across the face during the previous Thanksgiving break, when she tried to tell him about her lack of interest in studying medicine.

After spending 6 weeks in the hospital, Dallae was released, and she returned to California with her parents. Her memory was intact at the time of the discharge, except that she continued to have no recollection of her trip across the country or of many of her days living on the streets. She remained uncertain why she thought her name was Dawn, although she did mention being influenced by a television show she had seen about a Vietnamese child who had been adopted. She could not recall the name of the character in the story, but she did remember concluding that she too was Vietnamese and adopted. At the time of Dallae's discharge, her depression had abated somewhat, and she was no longer actively suicidal. She reported being relieved at having told her mother about her feelings about medical school, but she remained very anxious about facing her father's disappointment. ■

Dallae suffered from **dissociative fugue,** a rare and unusual disorder characterized by sudden, unplanned travel, the inability to remember details about the past, and confusion about identity or the assumption of a new identity. Dissociative fugue typically follows a traumatic event. For example, it is sometimes observed among soldiers following a particularly gruesome battle. For Dallae, perhaps her poor grades could be considered to be a trauma, given her father's intense and constant pressure to succeed.

The travel in dissociative fugue is purposeful, despite the memory impairments. Dallae knew where she was going, and she could provide at least a vague explanation about why

▲ **Pierre Janet (1859–1947)** conducted psychological experiments as a professor in Paris, and he later trained as a physician in Jean Charcot's clinic. Janet's views on dissociation were much more circumscribed than those of his rival, Sigmund Freud.

▼ The French neurologist **Jean Charcot (1825–1893)** demonstrating a case of hysteria at the Salpetriere, a famous hospital in Paris. Charcot's work with hysteria and hypnosis greatly influenced the thinking of both Sigmund Freud and Pierre Janet.

she was going there. Purposeful travel is the distinguishing symptom, but the core questions about fugue—and about all dissociative disorders—concern the split between conscious and unconscious psychological experience. How could Dallae be aware of the present but still be unaware of her past? Why didn't all her memories return after she saw her mother? Could she be faking part or all of her "illness"? Several key figures in the history of abnormal psychology have attempted to answer such perplexing questions. In fact, attempts to explain these puzzling disorders resulted in some of the first theories about unconscious psychological processes.

Brief Historical Perspective: Hysteria and Unconscious Mental Processes

Dissociative disorders (and somatoform disorders, which we discuss later in the chapter) once were viewed as expressions of **hysteria,** a term that dates to ancient Greece. In Greek, *hystera* literally means "uterus," and the term *hysteria* reflects ancient speculation that these disorders were caused by frustrated sexual desires, particularly the desire to have a baby. According to the theory, the uterus became detached from its normal location and moved about the body, causing a problem in the location where it eventually lodged. Variants of this fantastic view continued throughout Western history, and as late as the nineteenth century many physicians erroneously believed that hysteria occurred only among women (van der Hart & Friedman, 1989).

New speculation about the etiology of hysteria emerged toward the end of the nineteenth century. The work of Jean Charcot, who used

hypnosis both to treat and to induce hysteria, was particularly important. Charcot greatly influenced the thinking of Freud, who observed Charcot's hypnotic treatments early in his training (see Chapter 2). Charcot also had a strong influence on the work of Freud's contemporary and rival, Pierre Janet (1859–1947). Janet was a French philosophy professor who conducted psychological experiments on dissociation and who later trained as a physician in Charcot's clinic (see Chapter 6).

Both Janet and Freud were eager to explain and treat hysteria, and the problem led both of them to develop theories about unconscious mental processes. The two competitors differed in the specifics of their views about dissociation and the unconscious mind. Janet viewed dissociation as an abnormal process. To him, detachment from conscious awareness occurred only as a part of psychopathology. Thus Janet defined unconscious processes narrowly, consistent with what he observed in dissociative and somatoform disorders. In contrast, Freud viewed dissociation as a normal process, a routine means through which the ego defended itself against unacceptable unconscious thoughts. Freud saw dissociation and repression as similar processes, and, in fact, he often used the two terms interchangeably (Erdelyi, 1990; Perry & Laurence, 1984). Thus Freud considered dissociative and somatoform disorders to be merely one of many expressions of unconscious conflict.

The two theorists criticized each other frequently. Janet thought that Freud greatly overstated the importance of the unconscious; Freud thought that Janet greatly underestimated it. One culmination of their debate was Janet's (1914/1915) famous critique of psychoanalysis in the *Journal of Abnormal Psychology,* one of the leading sources of research on psychopathology in the early—and the late—twentieth century. In this article Janet raised doubts about the originality of many of Freud's ideas. In referring to the famous studies of Joseph Breuer and Freud (see Chapter 3), Janet stated, "At most, these writers only changed some terms in their psychological descriptions; what I called psychological analysis, they called psychoanalysis; where I used 'psychological system,' they used complex. . . .The names were different but all essential conceptions . . . were accepted without modification" (p. 10).

Janet's work influenced a number of investigators, including the U.S. psychologist Morton Prince (1854–1929), who founded the journal in which Janet published his critique

and who wrote several case histories of patients with multiple personalities (Prince, 1906). Janet's work became increasingly obscure, however, as Freudian theory dominated the mental health professions throughout much of the twentieth century. As Freudian influences have declined in recent years, scholars have rediscovered Janet's contributions and his more narrow conception of dissociation and unconscious mental processes.

UNCONSCIOUS PROCESSES AND CONTEMPORARY COGNITIVE SCIENCE

Contemporary psychologists continue to raise important and controversial questions about dissociation and unconscious processes, but they generally agree about two things. First, unconscious processes do exist, and they play a role in both normal and abnormal emotion and cognition (Wegner, 1994). Second, contemporary cognitive scientists carefully distinguish their more restricted view of unconscious processes from Freud's elaborate view of *the* unconscious.

Freud postulated a global unconscious mind, comprising an intricate set of processes (for example, the defenses) and contents (e.g., id impulses). Contemporary cognitive scientists also recognize unconscious contents (e.g., inaccessible memories) and processes (e.g., memory search strategies). In contrast to Freud, however, contemporary scientists view unconscious events as being much less influential in shaping both normal and abnormal behavior (Bowers & Meichenbaum, 1984; Singer, 1990). In the words of one cognitive scientist, the unconscious mind is "dumb," not "smart"; that is, it has a limited influence on human behavior (Loftus & Klinger, 1992).

Typical Symptoms of Dissociative Disorders

We cannot observe unconscious processes, but scientists note that, like many ordinary cognitive procedures, the symptoms of dissociative disorders apparently involve mental processing that occurs outside of conscious awareness. Extreme cases of dissociation include a split in the functioning of the individual's entire sense of self. In dissociative identity disorder, two or more personalities coexist within a single individual, and one or both of the personalities may be unaware of the existence of the other. Unless we assume that the symptom is feigned, dissociative identity disorder would seem to

▲ Soldiers sometimes experience dissociative fugue in response to the trauma of combat.

demonstrate the existence of multiple levels of mental functioning.

Depersonalization is a less dramatic form of dissociation wherein people feel detached from themselves or their social or physical environment. Examples of depersonalization include feeling like a stranger or a "robot" in social interactions, and out-of-body experiences—feelings of detachment from one's physical being. Table 7–3 lists a few examples of depersonalization, as well as several less dramatic examples of dissociation from a frequently used

TABLE 7-3

Sample Items from the Dissociative Experiences Questionnaire

- Some people find that sometimes they are listening to someone talk and they suddenly realize that they did not hear part or all of what was said.

- Some people have the experience of being in a familiar place but finding it strange and unfamiliar.

- Some people have the experience of finding themselves dressed in clothes that they don't remember putting on.

- Some people are told that they sometimes do not recognize friends or family members.

- Some people have the experience of feeling that their body does not seem to belong to them.

- Some people find that in one situation they may act so differently compared with another situation that they feel almost as if they were two different people.

Source: E. M. Bernstein and F. W. Putnam, 1986, Development, reliability, and validity of a dissociation scale, *Journal of Nervous & Mental Disease, 174,* 727–735.

questionnaire measure (Bernstein & Putnam, 1986).

Another dramatic example of dissociation is *amnesia*—the partial or complete loss of recall for particular events or for a particular period of time. Brain injury or disease can cause amnesia (see Chapter 14), but *psychogenic* (psychologically caused) amnesia results from traumatic stress or other sources of emotional distress. Psychogenic amnesia may occur alone or in conjunction with other dissociative experiences. For example, in dissociative identity disorder one personality may not remember the actions—or even the existence—of another (Spiegel & Cardena, 1991).

TRAUMA AND THE ONSET OF DISSOCIATIVE SYMPTOMS

Trauma often plays a role in dissociation and dissociative disorders, another link between these problems and traumatic stress disorders. Fugue and amnesia typically are precipitated by a traumatic event. Moreover, one study found that 80 percent of cases of dissociative identity disorder also met diagnostic criteria for PTSD (Armstrong & Loewenstein, 1990), although dissociative identity disorder presumably is tied with traumas from the past, not in the present. Recovery of functioning usually is rapid in cases of fugue and amnesia where the traumatic onset is clear and sudden, and psychological functioning commonly returns to normal. In dissociative identity disorder, where the onset is more gradual and not clearly linked with a present trauma, the reintegration of cognitive or emotional functioning is less certain or sudden. These more severe cases of dissociative identity disorder also may be accompanied by substantial impairment in life functioning and by a risk of violence toward oneself or others.

▼ This work of art captures one experience of depersonalization: the feeling of being outside your body and watching your actions.

Classification of Dissociative Disorders

BRIEF HISTORICAL PERSPECTIVE

For centuries, theorists considered dissociative and somatoform disorders together as alternative forms of hysteria. However, Freudian proponents, who defined dissociation broadly, classified hysteria as a subtype of *neurosis*—a diagnostic category that also included anxiety and depressive disorders. The category "neurosis" reflected the Freudian view that unconscious conflict was the common cause of each of these apparently different disorders. Still, the historical link between somatoform and dissociative disorders was preserved in many classification systems. For example, the somatoform and dissociative disorders were listed together as subtypes of "hysterical neurosis" in DSM-II (1968).

The descriptive approach to classification introduced in DSM-III (1980) led to the separation of dissociative and somatoform disorders into discrete diagnostic categories. The distinction is preserved in DSM-IV (1994), because the symptoms of the two disorders clearly differ greatly, as we discuss shortly. Consistent with DSM-IV, we review the two problems separately. We nevertheless discuss both problems in a single chapter because of their historical relationship and because both apparently involve unconscious processes.

CONTEMPORARY CLASSIFICATION

The DSM-IV distinguishes four major subtypes of dissociative disorders: dissociative fugue, dissociative amnesia, depersonalization disorder, and dissociative identity disorder. *Dissociative fugue* is characterized by sudden and unexpected travel away from home, an inability to recall the past, and confusion about identity or the assumption of a new identity. The case of Dallae is an example of dissociative fugue.

Dissociative amnesia involves a sudden inability to recall extensive and important personal information that exceeds normal forgetfulness. The memory loss in dissociative amnesia is not attributable to substance abuse, head trauma, or a cognitive disorder, such as Alzheimer's disease. As with fugue, dissociative amnesia typically is characterized by a sudden onset in response to trauma or extreme stress and by an equally sudden recovery of memory. The most common form of amnesia in dissociative disorders is *selective amnesia*, in which patients do not lose their memory completely but instead are unable to remember only selected personal events and information, often events related to a traumatic experience. (See Chapter 14 for a discussion of other types of amnesia found in cognitive disorders.) In one study of 25 patients in a dissociative disorders clinic, 76 percent had selective amnesia (Coons & Milstein, 1988, cited in Spiegel & Cardena, 1991).

Depersonalization disorder is a less dramatic problem that is characterized by severe and persistent feelings of being detached from oneself. Depersonalization experiences include such sensations as feeling as though you are in a dream, or the sensation of floating above your body and observing yourself act. Occasional depersonalization experiences are normal and are reported by about half the population. In depersonalization disorder, however, such experiences are persistent or recurrent, and they cause marked personal distress. The onset of the disorder commonly follows a new or disturbing event, such as drug use. All depersonalization experiences are "as if" feelings, not rigid, delusional beliefs. In fact, some experts question whether depersonalization should be considered a type of dissociative disorder. Unlike other dissociative disorders, depersonalization disorder involves only limited splitting between conscious and unconscious mental processes, and no memory loss occurs (Spiegel & Cardena, 1991).

To many people, the most fascinating subtype of dissociative disorder is **dissociative identity disorder,** a condition that was known as **multiple personality disorder** before DSM-IV. This unusual mental disorder is characterized by the existence of two or more distinct personalities in a single individual. At least two of these personalities repeatedly take control over the person's behavior, and the individual is unable to recall information that is too extensive to be explained by ordinary forgetfulness. The original personality especially is likely to have amnesia for subsequent personalities, which may or may not be aware of the "alternates" (Aldridge-Morris, 1989).

THE THREE FACES OF EVE: THE CASE OF CHRIS SIZEMORE

Perhaps the best-known case history of multiple personality disorder was detailed in Thigpen and Cleckley's (1957) book, *The Three Faces of Eve*, which was made into a motion picture. Thigpen and Cleckley described the case of Eve White, a young mother with a troubled marriage who sought psychotherapy for severe headaches, feelings of inertia, and "blackouts." Eve White was seen for several therapy sessions and was hypnotized during this time as a treatment for her amnesia. Then, during what proved to be a remarkable session, Eve White became agitated and complained of hearing an imaginary voice. As Thigpen and Cleckley wrote, "after a tense moment of silence,

her hands dropped. There was a quick, reckless smile and, in a bright voice that sparkled, she said, 'Hi there, Doc!'" (p. 137). Eve Black had emerged—a carefree and flirtatious personality who insisted upon being called "Miss" and who scorned Eve White, the wife and mother.

Therapy with Eve White, Eve Black, and a third, more calm and mature personality, Jane, lasted over a period of 2½ years. Thigpen used hypnosis to bring out the different personalities in an attempt to understand and reconcile them with one another. He eventually adopted the goal of fading out the two Eves and allowing Jane to take control. Therapy appeared to be successful. According to the psychiatrists' account, treatment ended with one integrated personality in control. This personality was much like Jane, but she decided to call herself "Mrs. Evelyn White."

The end of therapy with Thigpen and Cleckley was not the end of therapy for "Eve." Eve, whose real name is Chris Sizemore, claims to have had a total of 22 different personalities, some of which developed before her treatment with Thigpen and Cleckley and some of which developed afterwards. The personalities always occurred in groups of three, and they always included a wife/mother image, a party girl, and a more normal, intellectual personality (Sizemore & Pittillo, 1977). Sizemore has written several books about her life, and as a well-functioning, unified personality, she has become a spokesperson for mental health concerns. In her book, *A Mind of My Own*, she offers the following observations on her personalities:

Among these twenty-two alters, ten were poets, seven were artists, and one had taught tailoring. Today, I paint and write, but I cannot sew. Yet these alters were not moods or the result of role-playing. They were entities that were totally separate from the personality I was born to be, and am today. They were so different that their tones of voice changed. What's more, their facial expressions, appetites, tastes in clothes, handwritings, skills, and IQs were all different, too. (Sizemore, 1989, p. 9)

▲ Chris Sizemore is "Eve," the patient from the book and movie *The Three Faces of Eve.* Sizemore is now cured and is an advocate for the mentally ill.

The case of Chris Sizemore dramatically illustrates the characteristics of dissociative identity disorder. Sizemore's words also foreshadow controversies about the condition. Some professionals argue that dissociative identity disorder is nothing more than role playing; others assert that multiple personalities are very real and very common.

Epidemiology of Dissociative Disorders

The prevalence of dissociative disorders is difficult to establish. The conditions generally have been considered to be extremely rare. For example, only about 200 case histories of dissociative identity disorder were reported in the entire world literature prior to 1980 (Greaves, 1980). A number of clinicians have diagnosed dissociative identity disorder with much greater frequency in recent years, however. This increase in diagnosis has occurred in conjunction with the recognition of the distressingly high prevalence of child sexual abuse, a traumatic experience that is hypothesized to play a role in the etiology of many dissociative disorders (Kluft, 1987). Thus, in comparison to the 1980 survey, a 1986 report suggested that approximately 6,000 cases of dissociative identity disorder had been diagnosed in North America (Coons, 1986).

Obviously, these more recent figures constitute a dramatic increase in the diagnosis of dissociative identity disorder. In fact, a study of a random, nonclinical sample in Manitoba, Canada, went even further and suggested an unbelievably high prevalence rate. According to diagnoses obtained through a structured, diagnostic interview, over 10 percent of the adult population was designated as suffering from a dissociative disorder! This figure included 7 percent of the population with dissociative amnesia, 3 percent with dissociative identity disorder, 2 percent with depersonalization disorder, and 0.2 percent with dissociative fugue (Ross, 1991). Another study reported that 15 percent of hospitalized psychiatric patients met DSM-III-R criteria for the diagnosis of a dissociative disorder (Saxe et al., 1993).

Clearly, either some investigators have been overzealous in defining dissociative disorders or diagnosticians have been highly inaccurate for years. In fact, a small but vocal and apparently growing group of professionals has argued that most clinicians commonly overlook dissociative disorders. According to this analysis, many patients who are truly suffering from dissociative disorders are misdiagnosed as having schizophrenia, borderline personality disorder, depression, panic disorder, or substance abuse (Gleaves, 1996; Ross, Norton, & Wozney, 1989).

DISORDER OR ROLE ENACTMENT?

Despite such claims, the majority of mental health professionals remain skeptical about the prevalence of dissociative disorders. Although cases have been identified in many cultures (Gleaves, 1996), the diagnosis remains extremely rare in Europe and Japan, perhaps reflecting a North American diagnostic "fad" (Mersky, 1992; Piper, 1994). Some professionals have even raised doubts about the very existence of dissociative identity disorder, arguing that this phenomenon was created by the power of suggestion (Mersky, 1992). The Canadian psychologist Nicholas Spanos (1994) has been a particularly outspoken critic, who has argued that multiple personalties are caused by role playing. Spanos has asserted that patients are influenced by their own and their therapists' goals and expectations about dissociative identity disorder, and, like an actor who loses all perspective, eventually they may come to believe that the role is real.

In support of his sociocognitive model, Spanos and his colleagues have conducted analogue experiments on role playing and the "symptoms" of dissociative identity disorder. These studies were inspired by the case of Kenneth Bianchi, the infamous "Hillside Strangler." In 1979, Bianchi was charged with murdering two college women and was implicated in several other rape-murder cases where victims were left naked on the hillsides of Los Angeles. Considerable evidence supported Bianchi's guilt, but he reported frequent episodes of "blanking out," including an inability to remember events from the night that the murders were committed. At the request of his attorney, Bianchi was seen by a mental health expert, who hypnotized Bianchi and suggested to him, "I've talked a bit to Ken, but I think that perhaps there might be another part of Ken that I haven't talked to, another part that maybe feels somewhat differently from the part I've talked to. And I would like to communicate with that other part" (Watkins, 1984). (See Research Close-up.) Bianchi responded that he was not Ken but Steve. Steve knew of Ken, and he hated him. Steve also confessed to strangling "all of these girls."

Hypnosis: Altered State or the Power of Suggestion?

The nature of **hypnosis** is a matter of continuing debate and uncertainty (Kirsch & Lynn, 1995). On the one hand, there are impressive demonstrations of the power of hypnotic suggestion. For example, in laboratory studies, hypnotized subjects have an increased threshold for pain when given various suggestions, such as that a particular body part is numb and insensate. One particularly interesting aspect of this work has been the identification of what is called the "hidden observer." At some level of consciousness, many hypnotized individuals recognize and can report on their experience of pain, even as they indicate insensitivity to the pain at another level of consciousness (Kihlstrom, 1984).

Not everyone can be hypnotized. People who are most hypnotizable are the same ones who are most powerfully influenced by suggestion. For example, one indicator of hypnotizability is an individual's response to the suggestion to close his or her eyes and imagine a helium balloon being tied to his or her wrist. Subjects whose arm rises with the imagined balloon tend to be more easily hypnotized. This observation has led some researchers to suggest that hypnosis is not an altered state of consciousness. Instead, hypnosis is explained in social-psychological terms as a response to suggestion and expectation (Spanos, 1986).

Miller and Bowers (1986) conducted a study that is difficult to explain in terms of suggestibility alone, however. They identified subjects who were categorized as being either low or high in terms of hypnotizability. Next, they exposed the subjects to three experimental manipulations designed to increase tolerance for pain. Hypnosis was the first condition, and this involved the suggestion that sensitivity to pain would be reduced. The second condition was a cognitive behavioral procedure in which subjects were trained in strategies for coping with pain. The third condition was identical to the second, but the subjects were told that the cognitive coping would involve hypnotic reduction of pain.

Subjects were pretested for pain tolerance using the cold pressor test, which involves immersing one's hands in ice water. No differences among groups were found. The cold pressor test was repeated again after the subjects were taught (and had used) one of the three coping strategies. In fact, all three strategies significantly increased pain tolerance. Members of the cognitive behavioral groups reported using the strategies they had learned, but members of the hypnotic group did not report using similar coping strategies on their own. Importantly, hypnotizability was correlated with increased pain tolerance among the subjects who were hypnotized. The more hypnotizable the subjects were, the more pain they tolerated. Hypnotizability was not related to pain tolerance in the other conditions. These findings suggest that hypnosis, and not susceptibility to suggestion, can lead to increased pain tolerance.

This study does not unequivocally demonstrate that hypnosis is "real," but it makes hypnosis difficult to dismiss out of hand. We are right to remain skeptical about hypnosis, dissociation, and related topics, given the current state of evidence. Our skepticism does not mean, however, that we should dismiss these unusual phenomena. Rather, skepticism should encourage us to devise increasingly sophisticated ways of testing these intriguing ideas. ■

▲ **A person undergoing a hypnotic induction.**

Numerous experts who interviewed Bianchi disagreed about whether his apparent dissociative identity disorder was real or feigned. In fact, the conflicting expert opinion reveals the unreliability of the diagnosis (Aldridge-Morris, 1989). One of the experts was the psychologist and psychiatrist Martin Orne, an internationally recognized authority on hypnosis (see Research Close-Up). Orne tested Bianchi by suggesting new symptoms to him. If Bianchi was faking dissociative identity disorder, he might further the deception by developing the new symptoms. Orne suggested, for example, that if Bianchi really had dissociative identity disorder, he should have a third personality. Sure enough, a third personality, Billy, "emerged" when Bianchi was subsequently hypnotized (Orne, Dinges, & Orne, 1984). While hypnotized, Bianchi also followed Orne's suggestion to hallucinate that his attorney was in the room. Bianchi actually shook hands with the supposed hallucination—a very unusual behavior because tactile hallucinations are rare for someone under hypnosis. Orne concluded from this and other evidence that Bianchi was indeed faking, and that Bianchi actually suffered from antisocial personality disorder (see Chapter 9). Bianchi's insanity defense failed, and he was found guilty of murder.

In testing his role theory, Spanos simulated procedures from the Bianchi case. In one study, undergraduate students played the role of accused murderer and were randomly assigned to one of three conditions. In the "Bianchi" condition, the subjects were hypnotized, and the interviewer asked to communicate with their other part, just as Bianchi's interviewer had asked. Subjects assigned to the second, "hidden part" condition also were hypnotized, but this time it was suggested that hypnosis could get behind the "wall" that hid inner thoughts and feelings from awareness. In the final condition, there was no hypnosis, and subjects simply were told that personality included "walls" between hidden thoughts and feelings.

When subsequently asked, "Who are you?" by the interviewer in the mock murder case, 81 percent of the subjects in the Bianchi condition gave a name different from the one assigned to them in the role play, as did 70 percent of the subjects in the hidden part condition. In contrast, only 31 percent of the subjects in the no-hypnosis condition gave a new name. Increases in amnesia also were found for the two hypnosis conditions in comparison to the control group (Spanos, Weekes, & Bertrand, 1985). These results were replicated in a subsequent study. In this later experiment, hypnotized subjects also provided more "information" on exactly when in the past their alternate personalities had first emerged (Spanos et al., 1986).

These findings certainly raise the caution that the "symptoms" of dissociative identity disorder can be induced through role playing and hypnosis. However, analogue studies cannot prove that role playing causes real cases of multiple personality. Spanos's (1994) sociocognitive model has been criticized on precisely these grounds. The multiple identity enactment created in laboratory studies differs from the multiple identities found in dissociative identity disorder in numerous ways. For example, amnesia is absent in laboratory studies of multiple identity enactment, but it is widely reported in actual cases of dissociative identity disorder (Gleaves, 1996). In fact, the inability to recall important personal information is one diagnostic criterion for the disorder.

Given the current status of research, we reach a cautious conclusion about the epidemiology of dissociative disorders. True dissociative disorders appear to be rare, and although some cases no doubt are misdiagnosed, a much greater problem is the creation of the diagnosis in the minds of clinicians and clients (Mersky, 1992; Piper, 1994). At the same time, we do not doubt the existence of the dissociative disorders. These real but apparently rare psychological problems raise probing questions not only about the disorders themselves but about the very nature of the human psyche.

Etiological Considerations and Research on Dissociative Disorders

Little systematic research has been conducted on the etiology of dissociative disorders. Thus theory and outright speculation dominate discussions of the etiology. One exception is the widely held view that the disorders often are precipitated by trauma, a view that is beginning to find some research support. Trauma may contribute to dissociative disorders, but it clearly is not a sufficient cause. As we have seen, many people experience trauma without developing a dissociative disorder. Thus, consistent with the systems perspective, other biological, psychological, and social factors must contribute to the etiology of these disorders, as we consider in the following sections.

BIOLOGICAL FACTORS

Very little evidence and not much more speculation has been offered about the role of biological factors in the etiology of dissociative disorders (Brown, 1994). Some researchers have theorized that disturbances of the temporal lobe of the brain, including seizure disorders, play a role in dissociative identity disorder (Mesulam, 1981), but this possibility has not been systemically investigated (Brown, 1994). Still, it is known that dissociative states or permanent dissociation can result from biological causes. Examples include the dramatic personality changes that sometimes accompany substance use or abuse (see Chapter 11) and the amnesia that is found in various cognitive disorders associated with aging (see Chapter 14).

A role for a biological contribution to dissociation also is supported by investigations of unusual perceptual disturbances. For example, *prosopagnosia* is an impairment of face recognition that sometimes follows specific forms of brain damage. Patients with prosopagnosia report that they are unable to recognize faces, but indirect testing indicates that recognition occurs at some lower level of perception or consciousness. In particular, patients with prosopagnosia demonstrate the normal preference for viewing faces that are familiar, even though they claim that the face is not familiar to them (Farah, O'Reilly, & Vecera, 1993). This finding implies a dissociation between conscious and unconscious cognitive processes, because recognition must be occurring at some preconscious level.

Such findings have limited direct implications for understanding the etiology of dissociative disorders. In DSM-IV, a diagnosis of dissociative disorders is explicitly excluded if the dissociation occurs in conjunction with substance abuse or organic pathology. However, evidence that biological factors can produce dissociative symptoms has two important implications. First, these findings offer further evidence of the existence of dissociation in cognitive processing. The challenge of explaining unconscious processes is a real one in contemporary science, not merely a remnant of Freudian theory. Second, research on problems like prosopagnosia suggests avenues and methods for future research, particularly subtle assessment strategies that make it easier to detect malingering.

PSYCHOLOGICAL FACTORS

As we noted earlier, professionals agree that trauma can produce dissociative amnesia and fugue, because the onset of the dissociation often can be traced to a specific traumatic experience. A more controversial question is the extent to which trauma plays a role in the etiology of dissociative identity disorder. Many case histories suggest that multiple personalities develop in response to trauma, particularly the trauma of child abuse.

In support of this observation, some researchers have compiled large numbers of case histories from surveys of practitioners. As Table 7–4 indicates, a history of childhood sexual abuse was noted in 79 percent of 236 cases of dissociative identity disorder, according to the results of one survey. Physical abuse was reported in 75 percent of the same cases. Other surveys of clinicians have reported similar results (Gleaves, 1996; Kluft, 1987; Putnam, Curoff, et al., 1986; see Table 7–4). When interpreting these findings, however, be aware that these case observations are based on patients' memories and clinicians' evaluations. They are not objective assessments of the past.

Researchers have raised many concerns about the validity of such *retrospective reports*—evaluations of the past from the vantage point of the present (see Research Methods later in this chapter). A particular concern is that memories may be selectively recalled, may be distorted, or may even be created to conform with

TABLE 7–4

Features Associated with Dissociative Identity Disorder in Two Large-Scale Surveys of Clinicians' Case Histories

Item	Ross[1] N = 236	Putnam[2] N = 100
Average age	30.8	35.8
Percentage of females	87.7%	92.0%
Average years of treatment before diagnosis	6.7	6.8
Average number of personalities	15.7	13.3
Opposite-sex personality present	62.6%	53.0%
Amnesia between personalities	94.9%	98.0%
Past suicide attempt	72.0%	71.0%
History of child physical abuse	74.9%	75.0%
History of child sexual abuse	79.2%	83.9%

[1]Based on data from C. A. Ross, G. R. Norton, and K. Wozney, 1989, Multiple personality disorder: An analysis of 236 cases, *Canadian Journal of Psychiatry, 34,* 413–418.

[2]Based on data from F. W. Putnam, J. J. Curoff, et al., 1986, The clinical phenomenology of multiple personality disorder: Review of 100 recent cases. *Journal of Clinical Psychiatry, 47,* 285–293.

subsequent experiences. An adequate test of the hypothesized relation between child abuse and dissociative disorders requires prospective research following trauma victims from childhood into adult life—and objective assessments of dissociation throughout development.

Assuming for the moment that this relation is real, however, how might child abuse lead to the development of multiple personalities? One theory suggests that the trauma overwhelms children's usual intrapsychic defenses, and dissociation is used as a more dramatic alternative. According to this perspective, over time, dissociation increasingly is used as a means of coping with distress. If the memory of the trauma is not resolved or if the traumatic experience is repeated (as in many cases of child abuse), the recurrent use of dissociation can lead to the development of full, alternative personalities during adolescence (Kluft, 1987).

A similar model of the psychological etiology of multiple personality disorders involves the concept of **state-dependent learning.** Laboratory research has demonstrated that learning that occurs in one state of affect or consciousness is best recalled in the same state of affect or consciousness (Bower, 1990). For example, memories that are acquired when you are sad are more easily recalled during future times when you are sad rather than happy. By extension, some people have hypothesized that experiences that occur during a dissociated state are most easily recalled within the same state of consciousness. Through the repeated experience of trauma, dissociation, and state-dependent learning, more complete and autonomous memories develop over time. Ultimately, this process results in the development of independent personality states that dominate during different states of consciousness (Braun, 1989).

Other speculation has focused on hypnosis as both a cause of, and a treatment for, dissociative disorders. Janet and Freud both were impressed by the similarity in the dissociation experienced during hypnotic states and in hysteria, and at least one contemporary writer has suggested that multiple personality disorder is caused by self-hypnosis (Bliss, 1986). The same questions that have been raised about dissociation can be asked about hypnosis, however. In particular, there is debate about whether hypnosis represents an independent state of consciousness or whether different individuals merely are more or less susceptible to

suggestion and only appear to be "hypnotized" (Frankel, 1990; see Research Close-Up). Obviously, the possible etiological role of hypnosis in the development of dissociation depends on accurate answers to this question.

SOCIAL FACTORS

Few interpersonal or societal factors have been suggested to play a role in the development of dissociative disorders. One exception is that some clinicians have pointed to the risk posed by relationships that are simultaneously abusive and loving. For example, dissociation has been hypothesized to be more common when children are abused by parents. In this circumstance, the child obviously cannot seek parental support in coping with the trauma. Instead, she or he must rely on internal coping mechanisms. According to this speculation, if the conflict between the terror of the abuse and the need for love is great, the child may cope by dissociating these two experiences (Braun, 1989).

A sociological view offers a very different perspective on the etiology of dissociative disorders. At least one theorist has suggested that dissociative disorders are produced by **iatrogenesis,** the manufacture of the dissociative disorders by their treatment. Mersky (1992) reviewed classic case histories of dissociative identity disorder and concluded that many "cases" were created by the expectations of therapists. Mersky does not doubt the pain experienced by the patients in these cases. He argues, however, that the patients developed multiple personalities in response to leading questions asked by their therapists, not as a result of their own defense mechanisms. Thus, consistent with Spanos's (1994) theorizing discussed earlier, Mersky asserts that dissociative identity disorder is little more than a social role. A twist on this reasoning is that perhaps highly hypnotizable people are convinced that they have a dissociative disorder because of their susceptibility to suggestion (Kihlstrom, Glisky, & Angiulo, 1994).

Treatment of Dissociative Disorders

Dating from the time of Janet and Freud, perhaps the central aspect of the treatment of dissociative disorders has been uncovering and recounting past traumatic events. A basic assumption of this approach is that dissociation occurs as a response to unacceptable and overwhelming trauma. Thus it is presumed that if the trauma can be expressed and accepted, then the need for dissociation will disappear (Horevitz & Loewenstein, 1994).

As we have already noted, many clinicians use hypnosis to help patients explore and relive traumatic events. The painful experience is assumed to be more easily recalled while the patient is under hypnosis. These recollections, in turn, are thought to facilitate the integration of the trauma into conscious experience. Unfortunately, no research is available either on *abreaction*, the emotional reliving of a past traumatic experience, or on hypnosis as a treatment for dissociative disorders (Horevitz & Loewenstein, 1994).

In addition to helping patients reexperience trauma, clinical experts emphasize the need to win the trust of the dissociative patient (Braun, 1989; Kluft, 1987). In particular, therapists underscore the importance of establishing rapport with each of the personalities of patients who suffer from dissociative identity disorder. The difficulty of this task can be readily recognized if you recall that, in theory, each personality has developed as a protection against the others.

Clinicians also note that the goal of treatment is not to have one personality triumph over the others. Rather, the objective is to reintegrate the different personalities into a whole. This is not unlike the far less difficult task faced by all of us as we struggle to integrate the different life roles we play into a coherent sense of self.

Antianxiety, antidepressant, and antipsychotic medications also may be used to treat dissociative disorders. The objective in prescribing these medications is to reduce distress, not to cure the disorder. The ultimate goal of reintegrating the dissociated states, memories, or personalities is considered to be more of a psychological than a pharmaceutical task (Horevitz & Loewenstein, 1994).

At this time, little research has been conducted on the effectiveness of any treatment for dissociative disorders, let alone on the comparison of alternative treatments. Advances in therapy await a more accurate description of the disorders and, more generally, a better understanding of the split between conscious and unconscious cognitive processes.

Somatoform Disorders

In addition to dissociative disorders, the ancient diagnostic category *hysteria* included what we now know as somatoform disorders—somatic symptoms in the absence of a physical illness. Indeed, somatoform disorders are synonymous with hysteria in the eyes of many people, because Janet and Freud frequently wrote case histories about patients with unusual and unexplained physical symptoms. For our purposes, we link somatoform disorders with dissociative disorders, because of their historical connection and because somatoform disorders apparently involve a degree of dissociation. In some cases of somatoform disorder, the dissociation is relatively minor; in other cases, it is dramatic.

Typical Symptoms and Associated Features of Somatoform Disorders

All somatoform disorders involve complaints about physical symptoms. In contrast to psychosomatic disorders (see Chapter 8), the symptoms of somatoform disorders cannot be explained by an underlying organic impairment. There is nothing physically wrong with the patient. The symptoms are not feigned, however, as the physical problem is very real in the mind of the person with a somatoform disorder.

The physical symptoms can take a number of different forms. In some dramatic cases, the symptom involves substantial impairment of a somatic system, particularly a sensory or muscular system. The patient will be unable to see, for example, or will report a paralysis in one arm. In other types of somatoform disorder, patients experience multiple physical symptoms rather than a single, substantial impairment. In these cases, patients usually have numerous, constantly evolving complaints about such problems as chronic pain, upset stomach, and dizziness. Finally, some types of somatoform disorder are defined by a preoccupation with a particular part of the body or with fears about a particular illness. The patient may constantly worry that he or she has contracted some deadly disease, for example, and the anxiety persists despite negative medical tests and clear reassurance by a physician.

Unnecessary Medical Treatment

People with somatoform disorders typically do not bring their problems to the attention of a mental health professional. Instead, they repeatedly consult their physicians about their "physical" problems (National Institute of Mental Health, 1990). This often leads to unnecessary medical treatment. In the Epidemiologic Catchment Area study of the prevalence of mental illness in the general population, patients who met the diagnostic criteria for somatization disorder (a subtype of somatoform disorder) had seen a health care provider for an average of more than six visits during the previous 6 months (Swartz et al., 1987). In addition, 25 percent of people diagnosed with somatization disorder had been hospitalized in the past year, compared with 12 percent of the general population (Swartz et al., 1990).

Patients with somatoform disorders often complain about realistic physical symptoms that are difficult to evaluate objectively. Thus physicians frequently do not recognize the psychological nature of the patient's problems, and they sometimes perform unnecessary medical procedures. For example, patients with somatoform disorders have surgery twice as often as people in the general population (Zoccolillo & Cloninger, 1986). In fact, some common surgical procedures are performed with startling frequency on patients with somatoform disorders. One research group concluded that, after discounting cancer surgeries, 27 percent of women undergoing a hysterectomy suffered from somatization disorder (Martin et al., 1980).

Such data are distressing not only because of the risk to the patient but also because of the costs of unnecessary medical treatment. Estimates indicate that anywhere from 20 to 84 percent of patients who consult physicians do so for problems for which no organic cause can be found (Swartz et al., 1990). Such visits may account for as much as half of all ambulatory health care costs (Kellner, 1985). A variety of emotional problems can motivate people to consult their physicians, but much excessive health care utilization is specific to somatoform disorders. Patients with somatization disorder are 3 times more likely to consult physicians than are depressed patients, for example (Morrison & Herbstein, 1988; Zoccolillo & Cloninger, 1986). In fact, health care expenditures for patients with somatization disorder are 9 times the average annual per capita cost of medical treatment (Smith, Monson, & Ray, 1986).

Classification of Somatoform Disorders

The DSM-IV lists five major subcategories of somatoform disorders: (1) conversion disorder, (2) somatization disorder, (3) hypochondriasis, (4) pain disorder, and (5) body dysmorphic disorder.

CONVERSION DISORDER

In many respects, the classic type of somatoform disorder is **conversion disorder.** The symptoms of conversion disorder often mimic those found in neurological diseases, and they can be dramatic. "Hysterical" blindness or "hysterical" paralysis are examples of conversion symptoms. Although conversion disorders often resemble neurological impairments, they sometimes can be distinguished from these disorders because they make no anatomic sense. The patient may complain about anesthesia (or pain) in a way that does not correspond with the innervation of the body part. In some facial anesthesias, for example, numbness begins at the middle of the face; but the nerves involved in sensation do not divide the face into equal halves (see Figure 7–3).

The term *conversion disorder* accurately conveys the central assumption of the diagnosis—the idea that psychological conflicts are converted into physical symptoms. Conversion disorders were the problems that particularly captivated the attention of Charcot, Freud, and Janet and that led them to develop theories about dissociation and unconscious mental processes. The following case is from Janet's writings, and it illustrates his view of hysteria.

> **BRIEF CASE STUDY**
>
> ### A Case Study from Janet
> A girl of nineteen years of age suffered, at the time of her monthly period, convulsive and delirious attacks which lasted several days. Menstruation began

normally, but a few hours after the commencement of the flow the patient complained of feeling very cold and had a characteristic shivering; menstruation was immediately arrested and delirium ensued. In the interval of these attacks the patient had paroxysms of terror with the hallucination of blood spreading out before her, and also showed various permanent stigmata, among others anesthesia of the left side of the face with amaurosis of the left eye.

During a careful study of this patient's history, and particularly of the memories she had conserved of various experiences of her life, certain pertinent facts were ascertained. At the age of thirteen years she had attempted to arrest menstruation by plunging into a tub of cold water with resulting shivering and delirium; menstruation was immediately arrested and did not recur for several years; when it did reappear the disturbance I have just cited took place. Later on she had been terrified by seeing an old woman fall on the stairs and deluge the steps with her blood. At another time, when she was about nine years old, she had been obliged to sleep with a child whose face, on the left side, was covered with scabs, and during the whole night she had experienced a feeling of intense disgust and horror. (Janet, 1914/1915, pp. 3–4) ∎

This case describes symptoms that are consistent with conversion disorder. The numbness on the left side of the face of Janet's young patient is a clear example of a conversion symptom. At the same time, we wonder about other aspects of this classic case. The frightening hallucinations of blood might suggest another diagnosis, perhaps psychotic depression (see Chapter 5) or schizophrenia (see Chapter 13), with the conversion symptom as a secondary aspect of the case. Many alternative diagnoses were not available during the time of Charcot, Janet, and Freud, and this might explain why conversion disorders once were thought to be quite prevalent but are uncommon today.

Detection of Conversion Disorder

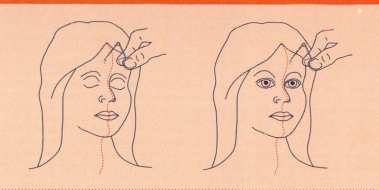

FIGURE 7-3: Conversion disorders are expressed as physical symptoms, but their psychological nature sometimes can be detected when the symptom makes no anatomical sense. As illustrated in this figure, for example, pain insensitivity may be limited to one side of the face in a conversion disorder. However, the nerves involved in pain sensation do not divide the face neatly in half. This symptom thus makes no anatomical sense, suggesting the numbness has a psychogenic origin.

Source: Adapted from D.M. Kaufman, 1985, *Clinical Neurology for Psychiatrists*, 2nd ed., p. 28. Orlando FL: Grune and Stratton.

SOMATIZATION DISORDER

Today, a far more common somatoform disorder is **somatization disorder,** characterized by a history of multiple, somatic complaints in the absence of organic impairments. The extent of the health concerns in somatization disorder is apparent from a cursory examination of the DSM-IV diagnostic criteria. In order to be diagnosed with somatization disorder, the patient must complain of at least eight physical symptoms, as listed in Table 7–5. The complaints must involve multiple somatic systems, moreover, including symptoms of pain, gastrointestinal symptoms (for example, nausea and diarrhea), sexual symptoms (sexual dysfunction, menstrual difficulties), and pseudoneurologic symptoms. Pseudoneurologic symptoms are complaints that mimic neurological diseases—for example, double vision, numbness, seizures, and amnesia (see Table 7–5).

Patients with somatization disorders sometimes present their symptoms in a *histrionic* manner—a vague but dramatic, self-centered, and seductive style (see Chapter 9). Patients also occasionally exhibit **la belle indifférence** ("beautiful indifference"), a flippant lack of concern about the physical symptoms. For example, a

TABLE 7-5

DSM-IV Diagnostic Criteria for Somatization Disorder

A. A history of many physical complaints beginning before age 30 that occur over a period of several years and result in treatment being sought or significant impairment in social, occupational, or other important areas of functioning.

B. Each of the following criteria must have been met, with individual symptoms occurring at any time during the course of the disturbance.

1. Four pain symptoms: A history of pain related to at least four different sites or functions (for example, head, abdomen, back, joints, extremities, chest, rectum, during sexual intercourse, during menstruation, or during urination)

2. Two gastrointestinal symptoms: A history of at least two gastrointestinal symptoms other than pain (for example, nausea, diarrhea, bloating, vomiting other than during pregnancy, or intolerance of several different foods)

3. One sexual symptom: A history of at least one sexual or reproductive symptom other than pain (for example, sexual indifference, erectile or ejaculatory dysfunction, irregular menses, excessive menstrual bleeding, vomiting throughout pregnancy)

4. One pseudoneurologic symptom: A history of at least one symptom or deficit suggesting a neurological disorder not limited to pain (conversion symptoms such as blindness, double vision, deafness, loss of touch or pain sensation, hallucinations, aphonia, impaired coordination or balance, paralysis or localized weakness, difficulty swallowing or lump in throat, difficulty breathing, urinary retention, seizures; dissociative symptoms such as amnesia; or loss of consciousness other than fainting)

▼ Felix Unger, a character from *The Odd Couple,* played here by Jack Lemmon, had numerous hypochondriacal complaints—much to the annoyance of his roommate, Oscar (portrayed by Walter Matthau).

patient may list a long series of somatic complaints in an offhanded and cheerful manner. Although some clinicians have viewed either or both of these styles as defining characteristics of somatization disorders, research indicates that they are found in only a minority of cases (Lipowski, 1988).

In contrast to some stereotypes, somatization disorder is *not* more common among the aged, who consult health care professionals frequently because of chronic and real physical illnesses (National Institute of Mental Health, 1990). In fact, somatization disorder often begins in adolescence, and according to DSM-IV criteria, it must have an onset prior to the age of 30. The problem is sometimes referred to as *Briquet's syndrome*, in recognition of French physician Pierre Briquet, who was among the first to call attention to the multiple somatic complaints found in some "hysterias" (Goodwin & Guze, 1979; National Institute of Mental Health, 1990).

HYPOCHONDRIASIS

Hypochondriasis is a problem characterized by a fear or belief that the individual is suffering from a physical illness. Aspects of this mental disorder surely are familiar to you. The pejorative term *hypochondriac* is a part of everyday language. We all worry about our health, and even unrealistic worries sometimes are normal. Medical students often fear that they have contracted each new disease they encounter in their studies. Many students in abnormal psychology worry that each problem they read about is a perfect description of themselves.

Hypochondriasis is much more serious than these normal and fleeting worries. The preoccupation with fears of disease extends over long periods of time. The worries must last for at least 6 months according to DSM-IV criteria. In addition, in hypochondriasis, a thorough medical evaluation or examination does not alleviate the fear of the disease. The person still worries that the illness may be emerging or that a test was overlooked. Still, the anxiety of hypochondriasis falls short of being delusional. For example, a person may worry excessively about contracting AIDS and therefore may repeatedly go for blood tests. When faced with negative results, however, the person does not delusionally believe that he or she actually has contracted the illness. Nevertheless, the persistent worries that characterize hypochondriasis are severe and preoccupying, and they often lead to substantial impairment in life functioning.

PAIN DISORDER

As its name implies, **pain disorder** is a subtype of somatoform disorder that is characterized by preoccupation with pain. Although there is no objective way to evaluate pain, psychological factors are judged to be significant in creating or intensifying the chronic pain in pain disorder. Complaints seem excessive and apparently are motivated at least in part by psychological factors. Some pain disorder patients may seem to relish the attention their illness brings to them. The DSM-IV distinguishes between pain disorder that occurs with associated problems in general medical conditions and pain disorder that appears in the absence of such problems. For example, low back pain that begins after a physical injury would be differentiated from back pain that cannot be traced to any physical cause.

As with hypochondriasis and somatization disorder, pain disorder can lead to the repeated, unnecessary use of medical treatments. People who experience chronic pain are at a particular risk for developing a dependence on minor tranquilizers or painkillers. The disorder also frequently disrupts social and occupational functioning.

BODY DYSMORPHIC DISORDER

Body dysmorphic disorder is a quite different type of somatoform disorder in which the patient is preoccupied with some imagined defect in appearance. The preoccupation typically focuses on some facial feature, such as the nose or mouth, and in some cases may lead to repeated visits to a plastic surgeon. Preoccupation with the body part far exceeds normal worries about physical imperfections. The endless worry causes significant distress, and in extreme cases, it may interfere with work or social relationships.

Little research has been conducted on body dysmorphic disorder. The problem has received more attention among European and Asian mental health professionals than in the United States, but systematic research has not been conducted anywhere. One controversy is whether the diagnosis should be grouped with other somatoform disorders. In Japan and Korea, body dysmorphic disorder is classified as a type of social phobia (Phillips, 1991). The following brief case history illustrates this unusual type of somatoform disorder.

BRIEF CASE STUDY

Body Dysmorphic Disorder

A 28-year-old single white man became preoccupied at the age of 18 with his minimally thinning hair. Despite reassurance from others that his hair loss was not noticeable, he worried about it for hours a day, becoming "deeply depressed," socially withdrawn, and unable to attend classes or do his schoolwork. Although he could acknowledge the excessiveness of his preoccupation, he was unable to stop it. He saw four dermatologists but was not comforted by their reassurances that his hair loss was minor and that treatment was unnecessary. The patient's preoccupation and subsequent depression have persisted for 10 years and have continued to interfere with his social life and work, to the extent that he avoids most social events and has been able to work only part-time as a baker. He only recently sought psychiatric referral, at the insistence of his girlfriend, who said his symptoms were ruining their relationship (Phillips, 1991, pp. 1138–1139). ■

Epidemiology of Somatoform Disorders

No one knows how prevalent conversion disorders were during the time of Charcot, Janet, and Freud, but the literature of the period suggests that they were common (Shorter, 1992). Today, conversion disorders are rare. For example, one investigation found only a 0.4 percent prevalence of conversion symptoms in an urban community sample (Weissman, Meyers, & Harding, 1978), a figure that probably overestimates the prevalence in the general population.

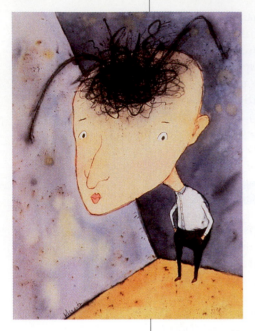

▲ **Body dysmorphic disorder is characterized by a preoccupation with some imagined defect in appearance.**

Ironically, the unusual disorders treated by Freud and Janet appear to have been less enduring than the theories they developed to explain them. This change in prevalence across time may be a result of improved diagnostic practices, as we have suggested, or it may reflect the role of society in the etiology of conversion disorder, a theory that we discuss shortly.

Other somatoform disorders appear to be equally rare, although sound epidemiological research has not been conducted on hypochondriasis, body dysmorphic disorder, or pain disorder. According to the Epidemiologic Catchment Area study, the lifetime prevalence of somatization disorder within the 50 states is only 0.13 percent (Swartz et al., 1990). On the other hand, physical complaints that do not meet all of the diagnostic criteria for somatization disorder are very common. In the same study, 11.6 percent of people were found to suffer from four to six physical symptoms with no identifiable organic cause (fewer than the eight required for the diagnosis of somatization disorder; see Table 7–5) (Swartz et al., 1990).

Hypochondriasis is equally common among men and women, but all other forms of somatoform disorder are more common among women. This is particularly true of somatization disorder, which is 10 times more common among females than among males (Swartz et al., 1990). The disproportionate number of women is consistent with early observations about "hysteria."

Somatization disorder also is more common among lower socioeconomic groups and among people who have less than a high school education. It is 4 times as common among African Americans as among Americans of European heritage, and a considerably higher rate of somatization disorder (0.7 percent) has been reported for Puerto Rico than for the U.S. mainland (Canino, Bird, et al., 1987). Finally, more somatic symptoms are found among people who have lost a spouse through divorce, separation, or death. Never-married adults actually have lower rates than the married population, suggesting that loss may play a role in the etiology of the disorder (Swartz et al., 1990).

COMORBIDITY

An important epidemiological issue is the overlap between somatoform disorders and other psychological problems. People who suffer from somatoform disorders, particularly somatization disorder and hypochondriasis, also frequently suffer from depression (Bridges & Goldberg, 1985; Prestige & Lake, 1987; Rogers et al., 1996; Swartz et al., 1990). The link between depression and somatoform disorders has several possible explanations. Either condition may cause the other, or both could be caused by a third variable, such as life stress. One possibility that primary care physicians must consider more carefully is that some patients may express depression indirectly through their somatic complaints (Lipowski, 1988). In fact, evidence indicates that the majority of depressed people approach their primary care physician first about their problems, but less than half of them are appropriately diagnosed and treated (Prestige & Lake, 1987).

Increased anxiety is also associated with hypochondriasis and somatization disorder (National Institute of Mental Health, 1990; Rogers et al., 1996; Swartz et al., 1990). As with depression, there are several possible explanations for this comorbidity, including some similarities in the defining symptoms of hypochondriasis or somatization disorder and generalized anxiety disorder. A particular concern is the accurate, differential diagnosis of panic disorder (see Chapter 6). Some symptoms of panic, such as dizziness, numbness, and fears about dying, may be dismissed by physicians, or they may be misdiagnosed as either hypochondriasis or somatization disorder (Lipowski, 1988).

Finally, somatization disorder has frequently been linked with antisocial personality disorder, a lifelong pattern of irresponsible behavior that involves habitual violations of social rules (see Chapter 9). The two disorders do not typically co-occur in the same individual, but they often are found in different members of the same family (Lilienfeld, 1992). The problems share other similarities as well. Both begin early in life, have a chronic course, are more common among lower socioeconomic groups, and are associated with marital troubles, substance abuse, and suicide attempts. Because antisocial personality disorder is far more common among men, whereas somatization disorder has the opposite pattern, some have speculated that the two problems are flip sides of the same coin. Antisocial personality disorder is seen as the male expression of high negative emotion and the absence of inhibition, whereas somatization disorder is viewed as the female expression of the same underlying characteristics (Lilienfeld, 1992).

Etiological Considerations and Research on Somatoform Disorders

Little systematic research has been conducted on the etiology of somatoform disorders. Few contemporary hypotheses have been offered about these problems, moreover, despite their historical significance in Janet's and Freud's theories about unconscious psychological processes. We consider perspectives on the etiology of somatoform disorders in the context of the biopsychosocial model. However, the limited evidence prohibits us from offering a complete, systemic model of contributing factors.

BIOLOGICAL FACTORS

An obvious—and potentially critical—biological consideration in somatoform disorders is the possibility of misdiagnosis. A patient may be incorrectly diagnosed as suffering from a somatoform disorder when, in fact, he or she actually has a real physical illness that is undetected or is perhaps unknown. The diagnosis of a somatoform disorder requires that no organic cause of the symptom can be identified. This is very different from the positive identification of a psychological cause of the symptom.

Diagnosis by Exclusion   Because mental health professionals cannot demonstrate psychological causes of physical symptoms objectively and unequivocally, the identification of somatoform disorders involves a process called *diagnosis by exclusion*. The physical complaint is assumed to be a part of a somatoform disorder only when various known physical causes are excluded or ruled out. The possibility always remains, however, that an incipient somatic disease has been overlooked. Some of the problems with diagnosis by exclusion can be appreciated by way of analogy. Consider the difference in certainty between two police lineups, one in which a victim positively identifies a criminal—"That's him!"—versus a second in which an identification is made by ruling out alternatives; "It isn't him or him or him, so it must be that one."

The possibility of misdiagnosis is more than a theoretical concern. Follow-up studies of patients diagnosed as suffering from conversion disorders indicate that somatic illnesses are later detected in some cases (Shalev & Munitz, 1986). Typically, a neurological disease such as epilepsy or multiple sclerosis is the eventual diagnosis. In one classic study, about a quarter of patients diagnosed as having a conversion symptom later were found to develop a neurological disease (Slater, 1965). Thus a significant number of cases of "somatoform disorder" eventually may prove to be real, neurological diseases. This possibility poses a dilemma for diagnosticians. They must weigh the consequences of an incorrect diagnosis of somatoform disorder against the consequences of incorrectly diagnosing a psychological problem as a physical illness.

Perhaps because somatoform disorders are diagnosed only after ruling out numerous potential biological illnesses, few theorists have speculated about biological contributions to somatoform disorders themselves. This is unfortunate, because biological factors may increase the risk for certain somatoform disorders. Even if no biological abnormalities are involved, somatoform disorders pose a challenge for neuroscientists. Brain researchers must explain how neuroanatomy or neurophysiology can account for the dramatic dissociation between psychological and somatic experience found in some of these puzzling problems.

PSYCHOLOGICAL FACTORS

Both Janet and Freud developed psychological theories in an attempt to explain the dissociation between emotional conflicts and physical symptoms. Both theorists initially assumed that a traumatic experience was the starting point for conversion disorder. According to their reasoning, the trauma overwhelmed normal coping efforts, and unconscious coping processes were called into action as a result. Janet viewed this dissociation of experience as an abnormal process. His explanation of conversion disorder followed his account of dissociative disorders, as we discussed earlier in this chapter.

In contrast, Freud came to view dissociation—a term that he used synonymously with repression—as a normal psychological process. He initially viewed traumatic stress as a necessary precondition for conversion disorders (see Research Methods). Later, however, Freud suggested that normal id impulses (particularly sexual urges) were unacceptable to the conscious mind and therefore required

Retrospective Reports

The topic of recovered memories has created great controversy in recent years, but scientists have long been skeptical about the accuracy of people's ongoing memories of the past, even memories that people report readily and confidently. In terms of research methods, particular questions have been raised about the reliability and validity of **retrospective reports**—current recollections of past experiences. Thus, for example, when trying to demonstrate a relationship between current psychopathology and childhood experiences, psychological researchers have called into question the accuracy of the patient's reports of past difficulties. In fact, these concerns about retrospective reports are one of several reasons why investigators prefer prospective, longitudinal studies over retrospective research designs (see Research Methods in Chapter 8).

Concerns about the use of retrospective reports focus on three particular issues that are relevant to abnormal psychology (Brewin, Andrews, & Gotlib, 1993). The first concern addresses normal limitations in memory. As we have noted, scientists doubt the accuracy of everyone's memory, particularly memory for events that occurred long ago and early in life. The second objection is specific to abnormal psychology: Some methodologists have suggested that the memories of people with emotional problems are particularly unreliable. Finally, a third concern is that psychopathology systematically biases people's memories. Investigators have speculated that memory processes are "mood congruent," in that depressed people remember sad experiences better, anxious people tend to recall fearful events, and so on. Thus reported experiences of negative events from the past may reflect a memory bias rather than an actual etiological process.

Brewin, Andrews, and Gotlib (1993) revisited these concerns about retrospective memory in a review of the literature. Their evaluation acknowledges several sound reasons for concern about retrospective reports. They argue, however, that retrospective memories may be less flawed than some methodologists have suggested.

With respect to the reliability and validity of memory in general, Brewin, Andrews, and Gotlib agree that retrospective reports are often inaccurate. They note, for example, that only moderate correlations are found between children's and parents' reports about their past relationships with each other. Moreover, on average, children report more negative memories about the past than do parents, raising the question of whose report is biased. At the same time, the reviewers note that reliability increases to an acceptable level for reports of specific, factual aspects of the past such as the events that occurred around the time of the birth of a sibling. Evidence also supports the validity of many of these specific memories. Thus memory for specific, important events appears to be acceptably reliable and valid, but people may "rewrite" their histories with regard to more global experiences.

Brewin, Andrews, and Gotlib also question the blanket assumption that psychopathology impedes memory. They assert that many flaws are found in research that supposedly documents memory impairments associated with various psychological problems. They conclude that there is no evidence for memory impairments associated with anxiety or depression. They also conclude that research does not support the conclusion that memories are mood congruent. In particular, depressed people do not erroneously recall more than their share of negative events about the past. Thus, with the exception of severe psychopathology, emotional problems do not appear to impair or systematically distort memories.

Evidence that memories are both accurate and inaccurate creates a dilemma in assessing patients' retrospective reports. The quandary was encountered by Sigmund Freud in interpreting his work with "hysterical" patients. Freud initially believed his female patients' reports about their past experience of trauma, particularly sexual abuse. As a result, he concluded that these traumatic experiences caused their conversion symptoms. Freud's patients recounted episodes of childhood sexual abuse with such frequency, however, that he later assumed that the "memories" could not be real. He concluded that his patients were discussing fantasies rather than real memories, and this conclusion led him to develop his theory of childhood sexuality (Freud, 1924/1962). Contemporary researchers, who have found a startlingly high prevalence of childhood sexual abuse in the general population, now assert that Freud's initial position was the accurate one. Perhaps the "fantasies" of Freud's patients were memories after all.

For current research methods, the implication of Brewin, Andrews, and Gotlib's analysis is that retrospective reports should not be dismissed. Serious consideration must be given to studies that link current emotional problems with accounts of past difficulties. Uncertain memories create enough doubt, however, that researchers continue to prefer prospective, longitudinal research designs over retrospective methods (see Research Methods in Chapter 8). Still, memories of specific past events are sufficiently reliable and valid to justify the use of retrospective reports as a first, less expensive research method. ■

---

unconscious coping efforts—that is, the use of intrapsychic defenses.

Primary and Secondary Gain   Freud came to believe therefore that "normal" unconscious processes could lead to the development of hysteria. He assumed that the unacceptable impulse or intolerable memory was unconsciously converted into a physical symptom by intrapsychic defenses (Freud, 1924/1962). The symptom thus served the function of protecting the conscious mind by expressing the psychological conflict unconsciously. In psychoanalytic terminology, this is referred to as the **primary gain** of the symptom. Freud thought that clues about the nature of the primary gain might be found in the symbolism of the specific physical symptom that was expressed. For example, hysterical blindness might result from witnessing some horrifying event.

Freud also recognized that hysterical symptoms could help a patient to avoid work or responsibility or to gain attention and sympathy. He referred to this as the **secondary gain** of the symptom. Cognitive behavioral theorists agree that secondary gain contributes to somatoform disorders, but they use a more direct term to describe the process: reinforcement. More generally, cognitive behaviorists suggest that *learning the sick role* is a part of the etiology of somatoform disorders. In addition to positive reinforcement (extra attention) or negative reinforcement (avoidance of work), social learning theorists suggest that modeling may be involved in learning the sick role (Lipowski, 1988).

Other perspectives on the etiology of somatoform disorders highlight cognitive and social influences in addition to reinforcement and modeling (Kirmayer, Robbins, & Paris, 1994). Key additional factors that contribute to etiology include (1) a tendency to amplify somatic symptoms, (2) *alexithymia*—a deficit in the individual's capacity to recognize and express the emotions signaled by physiological arousal—and (3) the misattribution of normal somatic symptoms.

The sick role and other social learning accounts may partially explain the etiology of pain disorder, hypochondriasis, and somatization disorder. However, they generally fail to account for conversion disorder and the fascinating question of how psychological distress may be converted into physical symptoms. Although the specifics of Freud's or Janet's accounts can be readily criticized, the etiology of conversion disorder seems to require theorizing about unconscious processes. Thus these disorders pose a theoretical challenge for cognitive scientists as well as for neuroscientists.

SOCIAL FACTORS

Social and cultural theorists offer a more straightforward explanation of the physical symptoms of somatization disorder, hypochondriasis, and pain disorder. Theorists assume that patients with these disorders are experiencing some sort of underlying psychological distress. However, the patients describe their problems as physical symptoms, and to some extent experience them that way, because of limited insight into their emotional distress and/or the lack of social tolerance of psychological complaints. Thus sociocultural theorists assume that people with somatoform disorders really are fearful, sad, or uncertain about their life, but they experience, or at least express, these emotional concerns in terms of physical complaints. A simple analogy for this theorizing is a child who complains about an upset stomach, not about fear of failure, before giving a piano recital.

Sociocultural theories of somatoform disorders are based on prevalence data. Somatoform disorders are more common in nonindustrialized countries, and they are more frequent among less educated people in the United States (Kirmayer, 1984; Kirmayer et al., 1994; Mechanic, 1986). The hypothesized explanation for this is that people with less education or financial security do not have the opportunity to learn to describe their inner turmoil in detailed psychological terms (Lipowski, 1988). Similarly, it has been suggested that the apparent reduction in the prevalence of conversion disorders today as compared with 100 years ago is a result of the increased social acceptance of inner feelings (Shorter, 1992).

Treatment of Somatoform Disorders

The sociocultural view of the etiology of somatoform disorders is consistent with the approaches to treatment developed by Charcot, Janet, and Freud. These therapists encouraged their patients to recall and recount psychologically painful events as a way of treating the disorder.

The exploration and uncovering of past or present traumas may free some patients of conversion symptoms, as it apparently did in some classic cases. Nevertheless, no research has been conducted on any "uncovering" therapies for somatoform disorders, and very little systematic research has been conducted on other treatments. The one exception is behavior therapy. Some evidence suggests that cognitive behavior therapy is effective in treating body dysmorphic disorder (Rosen, Reiter, & Orosan, 1995), and researchers have conducted fairly extensive studies of both operant and cognitive behavioral treatments of pain disorders. Operant approaches to chronic pain attempt to alter contingencies that reward "pain behavior" and the sick role. The goal is to reward successful coping and life adaptation instead (Fordyce, 1976). Cognitive behavior therapy typically incorporates operant techniques but also uses cognitive restructuring to address the emotional and cognitive components of pain. Research demonstrates the effectiveness of both variations on behavior therapy in treating chronic lower back pain (Blanchard, 1994).

One reason for the limited research on the psychological treatment of somatoform disorders is that primary care physicians treat most of these patients. Patients with somatoform disorders typically consult physicians about their ailments, and they often insist that their problems are physical even after extensive testing. They are likely to refuse a referral to a mental health professional. Thus primary care physicians often must learn how to manage hypochondriasis, somatization disorder, and related problems in the medical setting.

This can be a difficult task. Primary care physicians may become frustrated by their failure to identify a clear physical problem or may be unsympathetic toward "hypochondriacs" when they have so many patients with "real" problems. Not surprisingly, such reactions can weaken the physician–patient relationship, a consequence that can intensify the problem. In fact, the major recommendation for the medical management of patients with somatization disorder is to establish a strong and consistent physician–patient relationship. Physicians are urged to schedule routine appointments with these patients every month or two and to conduct brief medical exams during this time (National Institute of Mental Health, 1990). This approach not only provides consistent emotional support and medical reassurance but it helps to eliminate the iatrogenic effects of the somatization disorder by reducing unnecessary medical procedures. A physician who is familiar with a patient with somatization disorder is more likely to recognize the psychological origin of the physical complaints and is less likely to order unnecessary medical tests or treatment procedures. In fact, at least one study has documented the effectiveness of this management approach (Smith, Monson, & Ray, 1986).

Whatever the approach to treatment, it is essential for the physician to convey a sense of concern about patients' complaints. There is a place for reassurance and optimism about the patient's good health, but the evaluation is likely to be rejected unless it is coupled with some expression of concern. Patients who do not receive this empathy are likely to ignore the physician's advice and simply recruit a new, more understanding physician (National Institute of Mental Health, 1990).

Referrals to a mental health professional must be made with care by primary health care providers. Patients may believe that the recommendation belittles their problems and may reject it out of hand. When a referral is made successfully, the mental health professional might need to coordinate treatment with the referring physician and perhaps offer treatment in a medical setting.

Summary

To a greater or lesser extent, all the intriguing disorders we consider in this chapter involve **dissociation,** the disruption of the normally integrated mental processes involved in memory or consciousness. Many of the disorders also are known or hypothesized to be reactions to **traumatic stress,** exposure to some event that involves actual or threatened death or serious injury to self or others—and creates intense fear, helplessness, or horror. Sources of traumatic stress include rape, bombings, airplane crashes, earthquakes, major fires, and devastating automobile wrecks.

Traumatic stress disorders include acute stress disorder and posttraumatic stress disorder. **Acute stress disorder (ASD)** is a short-term reaction to trauma that is characterized by symptoms of dissociation, reexperiencing, avoidance, and increased anxiety or arousal. **Posttraumatic stress disorder (PTSD)** is characterized by very similar symptoms—reexperiencing, numbed responsiveness or avoidance, and increased autonomic arousal—but the symptoms either last for longer than 1 month or have a delayed onset in PTSD. Trauma may be reexperienced as a **flashback**—a dissociative state in which the person relives the trauma in the moment. The diminished responsiveness has been referred to as psychic numbing or emotional anesthesia. The increased arousal in ASD or PTSD may include excessive fear, anxiety, or irritability, as well as general psychophysiological arousal.

Scientists have only begun to study the epidemiology of PTSD. Current evidence points to the surprisingly high frequency that people experience some traumatic events. Epidemiology also calls attention to the particularly devastating consequences of rape for women and combat exposure for men.

By definition, the experience of trauma is the central cause of PTSD, but other factors appear to be important in its etiology. Genetic factors increase the risk both for experiencing trauma and for experiencing PTSD following trauma, probably as a result of genetic influences on personality characteristics or psychological disorders. Learning theories also emphasize the importance of **two-factor theory** in the development of PTSD. A number of adverse reactions may be produced by classical conditioning during the experience of trauma, and the reactions can be maintained by operant conditioning as people continue to avoid stressful circumstances. Some short-term reactions may be better conceived as symptoms of ASD, however, and more severe ASD seems to be a fairly good predictor of subsequent PTSD. Finally, the nature and level of exposure to a traumatic event, as well as social support after the occurrence of the trauma, appear to be crucial to facilitating long-term adjustment.

Early intervention with trauma victims can contribute to easing the pain of coping with a horrific event and to preventing the subsequent development of PTSD. Reliving the traumatic event is perhaps the least obvious but most important strategy for subsequent treatment. According to research that is being conducted on therapy outcome, recounting and reexperiencing the trauma in a controlled treatment setting appears to be basic to the therapeutic process. Still, PTSD can have a chronic course in over one-third of all cases. Evidence suggests skepticism, however, that the course of PTSD may include **recovered memories,** the sudden remembering of long-forgotten traumatic experiences.

Dissociative disorders are characterized by persistent, maladaptive disruptions in the integration of memory, consciousness, or identity. **Somatoform disorders** are identified by unusual physical symptoms that occur in the absence of a known physical illness. Memories become inaccessible in dissociative disorders;

KEY TERMS

- acute stress disorder (ASD)
- body dysmorphic disorder
- conversion disorder
- depersonalization disorder
- dissociation
- dissociative amnesia
- dissociative disorders
- dissociative fugue
- dissociative identity disorder
- factitious disorder
- flashback
- hypnosis
- hypochondriasis
- hysteria
- iatrogenesis
- la belle indifference
- malingering
- multiple personality disorder
- pain disorder
- posttraumatic stress disorder (PTSD)
- primary gain
- recovered memories
- retrospective reports
- secondary gain
- somatization disorder
- somatoform disorders
- state-dependent learning
- trauma desensitization
- traumatic stress
- two-factor theory
- victimization

psychological distress is converted into physical symptoms in somatoform disorders. Thus these unusual emotional problems involve unconscious processes by definition, and they challenge psychological theorists to explain those psychological events that occur outside of awareness. In fact, both Freud and Janet developed their influential theories about unconscious processes when attempting to explain these disorders.

The DSM-IV distinguishes four major subtypes of dissociative disorders: fugue, amnesia, depersonalization disorder, and dissociative identity disorder. **Dissociative fugue** is characterized by sudden and unexpected travel away from home, an inability to recall the past, and confusion about identity or the assumption of a new identity. **Dissociative amnesia** involves a sudden inability to recall extensive and important personal information that exceeds normal forgetfulness. As with fugue, dissociative amnesia typically is characterized by a sudden onset in response to trauma or extreme stress and an equally sudden recovery of memory.

Depersonalization disorder is a less dramatic problem that is characterized by severe and persistent feelings of being detached from oneself—sensations such as feeling as if you are in a dream, or as though you are floating above your body and observing yourself act. Occasional depersonalization experiences are normal, but depersonalization disorder involves persistent or recurrent symptoms. Finally, **dissociative identity disorder,** also known as **multiple personality disorder,** is characterized by the existence of two or more distinct personalities in a single individual. At least two of these personalities repeatedly take control over the person's behavior, and some of the personalities have limited or no memory of the others.

Although some investigators suggest that the conditions are pervasive, dissociative disorders appear to be quite rare. A growing body of evidence links the conditions with traumatic experiences, particularly with child abuse. Evidence is weak or nonexistent on other factors that may contribute to the development of the disorder. Similarly, there is no systematic research on the treatment of dissociative disorders, although clinical tradition emphasizes reliving trauma as a way of reintegrating experience.

The DSM-IV lists five major subcategories of somatoform disorders. In many respects, the classic type of somatoform disorder is **conversion disorder.** The term "conversion disorder" accurately conveys the central assumption of the diagnosis—the idea that psychological conflicts are converted into physical symptoms. "Hysterical" blindness or "hysterical" paralysis are examples of conversion symptoms. **Somatization disorder** is characterized by a history of multiple, somatic complaints in the absence of organic impairments. The complaints involve multiple somatic systems, including symptoms of pain, gastrointestinal symptoms, sexual symptoms, and pseudoneurologic symptoms. **Hypochondriasis** is characterized by a fear or belief that the individual is suffering from a physical illness. The persistent worries that characterize hypochondriasis are severe and preoccupying and often result in substantial impairment in life functioning. **Pain disorder** is characterized by preoccupation with pain. Although there is no objective way to evaluate pain, psychological factors are judged to be significant in creating or exacerbating the chronic pain in pain disorder. In **body dysmorphic disorder** the patient is preoccupied with some imagined defect in appearance—a preoccupation that typically focuses on some facial feature, such as the nose or mouth.

True somatoform disorders are rare, although complaints about somatic symptoms that do not have an organic cause are common and represent a significant proportion of medical care. The etiology of somatoform disorders has not been the subject of much research. Etiological concerns include the misdiagnosis of incipient neurological diseases as somatoform disorders; secondary gain or reinforcement for the sick role; cognitive factors, such as a tendency to amplify somatic symptoms; alexithymia—a deficit in the individual's capacity to recognize and express the emotions signaled by physiological arousal; and cultural influences.

Treatment research on somatoform disorders is sorely lacking. Some evidence indicates that behavior therapy is effective in the treatment of body dysmorphic disorder and especially chronic pain. Investigators also are beginning to identify aspects of effective medical management of somatoform disorders. Still, in many ways, these disorders continue to pose as much of a challenge now as they did at the turn of the twentieth century when they attracted the attention of leading figures in the history of abnormal psychology.

Critical Thinking

1. Based on what you have read in this chapter and in Chapter 6, do you think that traumatic stress disorders are more similar to anxiety disorders or to dissociative disorders—or do you see ASD and PTSD as being separate from these two diagnostic categories?

2. Because both are reactions to traumatic stress, ASD and PTSD would seem to be purely "psychological" problems. However, the disorders are best explained by the systems perspective. What biological, psychological, and social risk factors might combine to cause the disorders? What *protective* factors would you hypothesize to lower the likelihood of ASD or PTSD following exposure to trauma?

3. There is much controversy about several of the topics in this chapter, including such issues as recovered memories, dissociative identity disorder, hypnosis, and conversion reactions. These elusive ideas are difficult to evaluate empirically and require a certain amount of "believing" as opposed to "knowing." If you believe in the existence of these phenomena, how could you prove your beliefs to skeptics? If you are a skeptic, what evidence would convince you that the psychic phenomena are "real"?

4. Do you know people who seem to express their psychological concerns through somatic complaints? How do you explain this? Did you express your feelings in this way as a child? Do you still experience or express your emotions in terms of physical sensations or symptoms?

8
Stress and Physical Health

OVERVIEW

Case Study: Stress, lifestyle, and coronary heart disease

Defining stress

TYPICAL SYMPTOMS AND ASSOCIATED FEATURES OF STRESS

Physiological responses to stress

Emotional responses to stress

Research Close-Up: Disclosure of trauma and immunity

Cognitive responses to stress

Behavioral responses to stress

Further Thoughts: Sleep disorders

Illness as a cause of stress

CLASSIFICATION OF STRESS AND PHYSICAL ILLNESS

Brief historical perspective

Contemporary approaches

THE ROLE OF PSYCHOLOGICAL FACTORS IN SOME FAMILIAR ILLNESSES

Cancer

Acquired immune deficiency syndrome (AIDS)

Pain management

CARDIOVASCULAR DISEASE

Typical symptoms and associated features of hypertension and CHD

Epidemiology of CVD

Etiological considerations and research on CVD

Research Methods: Longitudinal research designs

Prevention and treatment of cardiovascular disease

Newspaper stories and magazine articles regularly warn us about the dangers of stress. We are cautioned that stress not only can cause psychological problems but can also lead to physical illnesses ranging from the common cold to heart attacks. Stress is bad, something to be avoided. So many dangers are attributed to stress that it becomes stressful to read about them! Scientific studies support many of the popular concerns about the role of stress in physical illness. As we will see in this chapter, however, scientific evidence is not nearly as clear-cut as is popular belief. In fact, evidence suggests that, under the right conditions, stress can promote "toughness" or *resilience* rather than disorder. A certain amount of stress is adaptive. The key is to maintain a balance between being challenged and being overloaded by stress.

Overview

Stress can be broadly defined as a challenging event that requires physiological, cognitive, or behavioral adaptation. As we discuss shortly, however, scientists disagree about how stress should be defined more precisely for research purposes. Stress may be produced by minor, daily hassles, like the frustration of being trapped in a traffic jam, as well as by major events, such as getting fired from a job or going through a divorce. *Traumatic stress* is caused by exposure to some catastrophic event that involves actual or threatened death or serious injury to oneself or others and creates intense fear, helplessness, or horror (see Chapter 7).

For many years, scientists thought that psychological stress was irrelevant to most physical (or *somatic*) illnesses. Instead, the causes of most physical illnesses were thought to lie "within the skin." This viewpoint was fueled by the discovery of bacteria as a cause of illness and the subsequent development of immunization and antibiotics as successful treatments for bacterial disease. Despite the dominance of "germ theory" throughout much of the twentieth century, some scientists argued that psychological stress

contributed to a limited number of illnesses termed **psychosomatic disorders** (sometimes also called *psychophysiological disorders*). The term *psychosomatic* indicates that a given physical disease is a product of both the *psyche* (mind) and the *soma* (body). Ulcers, migraine headaches, hypertension (high blood pressure), and asthma are examples of physical illnesses that were once called psychosomatic disorders.[†]

The DSM no longer contains a list of psychosomatic disorders, because medical scientists now view *every* physical illness as a product of the interaction between the psyche and soma, mind and body. Contemporary researchers have found that stress plays a role in the onset or exacerbation of all physical illnesses—from a cold to cancer to AIDS. Moreover, evidence indicates that learning more adaptive ways of *coping* can limit the recurrence or improve the course of many physical illnesses. In short, medical scientists now recognize that the distinction between mind and body is a false dualism (see Chapter 2). Theories of the etiology of physical illnesses have adopted—and in many ways have promoted—the systems approach.

[†] In everyday language, we sometimes misuse the term *psychosomatic* to imply that an illness is imagined or not real in a physical sense; for example, "His problems are psychosomatic." Unlike *conversion disorders* (see Chapter 7), psychosomatic disorders *are* very real physical illnesses that involve clear damage to the body.

This holistic view of disease and health has brought about major changes in both psychology and medicine. Of particular note is the rapid development of **behavioral medicine,** a multidisciplinary field that includes both medical and mental health professionals who investigate psychological factors in the symptoms, etiology, and treatment of physical illness and chronic disease. Psychologists who specialize in behavioral medicine often are called *health psychologists*.

Experts in behavioral medicine and health psychology emphasize health rather than just disease. They define disease as "dis-ease," indicating that illness is a departure not only from adaptive biological functioning but also from adaptive social and psychological functioning. In turn, experts view health as successful adaptation to the environment, not merely the absence of somatic illness (Weiner & Fawzy, 1989). Behavioral medicine specialists and health

psychologists therefore study and encourage such healthy behaviors as stress management, proper diet, regular exercise, and avoidance of tobacco use in order to promote positive health among the general public. Examples of treatments for the physically ill include providing education and support to parents of chronically ill children, helping patients cope with chronic pain, and even offering support groups to people with terminal cancer.

In this chapter we discuss a number of innovations in behavioral medicine and health psychology, and we review evidence on the link between stress and a number of different physical illnesses. We also include an extended discussion of hypertension and coronary heart disease in order to illustrate the challenges in studying stress and physical illness. We begin our discussion with a case history of coronary heart disease from our files.

▲ **Stress is a part of everyday life. Stress cannot be avoided, but some ways of coping with life's challenges are more effective than others.**

CASE STUDY

Stress, Lifestyle, and Coronary Heart Disease

One Thursday afternoon, Bob Carter, a salesman for a beer and liquor wholesaler, was completing his regular route, calling on customers. Throughout the morning, he had felt a familiar discomfort in his chest and left arm. As had been happening on occasion for at least a year, that morning he experienced a few fleeting but sharp pains in the center and left side of his chest. This was followed by a dull ache in his chest and left shoulder and a feeling of congestion in the same areas. Breathing deeply made the pain worse, but Bob could manage it as long as he took shallow breaths. The discomfort was not bad enough to interfere with Bob's work, although this time the pain lasted longer than usual. Still, he continued on his route, alternately vowing to see a doctor soon and cursing his aging body for not performing up to his expectations.

After grabbing a hamburger and a beer for lunch, Bob called on a customer who was behind in his payments to the wholesaler. At first, Bob shared a cigarette with the customer and chatted with him in a friendly way. He was a salesman after all. Soon it was time to pressure him about the bill. As Bob was raising his voice in anger, a crushing pain returned to his chest and radiated down his left arm. This was much worse than anything he had experienced before. The pain was so intense that Bob was unable to continue speaking. He slumped forward against the table, but with his right arm he waved away any attempts to help him. After sitting still for about 10 minutes, Bob was able to drag himself to his car and drive to his home 30 miles away. When his wife saw him shuffle into the house looking haggard and in obvious pain, she called for an ambulance. The Carters soon discovered that Bob had suffered a myocardial infarction (a heart attack).

Bob was 49 years old at the time. He was married and the father of three children. His home life was normal and happy, but it also put a lot of pressures on him. His 24-year-old daughter was living at home while her husband was serving in combat duty overseas. Naturally, the entire family was anxious about the son-in-law's well-being. More stress came from Bob's 21-year-old daughter, who had just graduated from college and was getting married in 3 weeks. Finally, Bob's 19-year-old son was home from his first year of college, full of rebellion and ideas that challenged Bob's authority. There was no shortage of family stress.

Bob also put plenty of stress on himself. A former high school athlete, he had always been competitive and hard-driving. He wanted to be the best at whatever he did, and right now his goal was to be the best salesman in his company. Bob worked hard selling beer and liquor. He used his charm, humor, and some not-so-gentle pressure to sell his products, and it worked. But once he had become the best salesman in his wholesaling company, Bob wanted to be the best salesman for the producers whose products he sold. No matter what he accomplished, Bob drove himself hard to meet a new goal.

Bob maintained his drive and competitiveness from his youthful days as a star athlete, but he had not maintained his physical condition. The only exercise he got was playing golf, and he usually rode in a cart instead of walking the course. He was at

least 30 pounds overweight, smoked a pack and a half of cigarettes a day, ate a lot of fatty red meat, and drank heavily. If he had seen a physician earlier, Bob would have been told that he was a good candidate for a heart attack. As it was, he heard this from a cardiologist only after his heart attack.

Bob recuperated quickly in the hospital. He was tired and in considerable pain for a couple of days, but he was telling jokes before the end of a week. His cardiologist explained what had happened to him and gave Bob a stern lecture about how he needed to change his lifestyle. He wanted Bob to quit smoking, lose weight, cut down on his drinking, and gradually work himself back into shape with a careful program of exercise. He urged Bob to slow down at work and told him to quit worrying about his children—they were old enough to take care of themselves.

To underscore these messages, the cardiologist asked a psychologist from the hospital's behavioral medicine unit to consult with Bob. The psychologist reviewed information on coronary risk with Bob and gave him several pamphlets to read on risk factors. The psychologist also explained that the hospital ran several programs that might interest Bob after discharge. These included workshops on stress management, weight reduction groups, and exercise classes. The fees for these programs were minimal, because the hospital ran them primarily as a community service. The psychologist asked Bob if he had other concerns that he wanted to discuss, but Bob said there were none. The psychologist suggested that some issues might come up in the future, and Bob should feel free to raise them with the psychologist or with his cardiologist. The psychologist noted that cardiac patients and their families sometimes had trouble adjusting to the illness and the sudden reminder of the patient's mortality. Bob thanked the psychologist for the information but waved off the professional's offer of assistance much as he had waved off help in the middle of his heart attack.

Bob was discharged from the hospital 10 days after being admitted. Against his doctor's advice, he walked his daughter down the aisle at her wedding the following weekend, and he was back to work within a month. At his 6-week checkup, Bob admitted to his cardiologist that he was smoking again. His weight was unchanged, and his exercise and drinking were only a "little better," according to Bob. When the cardiologist chastised Bob for not following medical advice, Bob promised to renew his efforts. He belied his assertion of commitment, however, by commenting that giving up these small pleasures might or might not make him live any longer, but life surely would seem longer without any indulgences. Clearly, one heart attack was not going to get Bob Carter to slow down. ■

The case of Bob Carter illustrates a number of critical issues and questions about the potential link between stress and physical illness. Most basically, the case strongly suggests that life stress is a factor in the onset of coronary heart disease. Bob's life was full of familiar but stressful pressures that may have increased his risk for myocardial infarction. When added to these chronic sources of stress, the episode of getting angry with his customer appears to have been the "straw that broke the camel's back." In fact, a relation between stress and coronary heart disease has been documented in numerous research studies, as we shall see later in the chapter.

The case of Bob Carter also raises a number of questions about the link between stress and coronary heart disease. What is the physiological mechanism that transforms psychological stress into coronary risk? Is stress the problem, or is the real culprit the unhealthy behaviors that result from stress—smoking, drinking, and overeating? What is more important to the experience of stress—a single major life change, such as the marriage of Bob's daughter, or ongoing hassles like Bob's fighting with his son? What is the role of personality in stress? Bob constantly put pressure on himself, whereas another person might have been more likely to "roll with the punches" on the job and at home. Can someone like Bob be helped to change his lifestyle, and if so, does this lower the risk for future heart attacks? We consider these and related questions in this chapter. First, though, we need to consider more carefully exactly what we mean by "stress."

Defining Stress

In the introduction to this chapter, we defined *stress* as a challenging event that requires physiological, cognitive, or behavioral adaptation. We stand by this definition, but we also note that questions arise when we examine it closely. Is stress the event itself? Some people would relax after becoming the top salesman, but this achievement only produced another, more difficult challenge for Bob Carter. This suggests that perhaps stress should be defined in terms of the individual's reactions to the event. However, our theories indicate that stress causes adverse reactions. Defining stress in terms of these reactions runs the risk of becoming an exercise in circular logic. In fact, scientists continue to debate whether stress is best defined in terms of a life event (a stimulus), an adverse reaction (a response), or a stimulus-response combination.

STRESS AS A STIMULUS

Various efforts to quantify stressful life events have attempted to define stress in terms of a stimulus or *stressor*—a difficult event regardless of the individual's reaction to it. The early work of Holmes and Rahe (1967) was particularly influential. Holmes and Rahe developed the Social Readjustment Rating Scale (SRRS), a list of various troublesome life events. They assigned stress values to life events, basing these ratings on the judgments of a large group of normal adults. Their attempts to measure the amount of stress caused by various life events was both provocative and controversial. Holmes and Rahe concluded that different stressors cause more or less stress, as indexed by what they called *life change units* (see Table 8–1). Thus an individual's total stress is the sum of the life change units for each item that is checked on the scale.

The SRRS and similar instruments have been used frequently in research (Miller, 1989). Not surprisingly, investigators have repeatedly found that more life stress as measured by life change units is associated with a wide variety of physical and psychological disorders. This method of defining stress has been subjected to several criticisms, however. Some critics suggest that people who experience physical or psychological disorders are simply more likely to recall difficult life events than are people who are doing well. Another concern is the limited number of life stressors that are compiled on such scales and the appropriateness of these limited listings for subjects of different ages and ethnic backgrounds. For example, the SRRS includes many

TABLE 8-1

The Social Readjustment Rating Scale

Life Event	Life Change Units
Death of one's spouse	100
Divorce	73
Marital separation	65
Jail term	63
Death of a close family member	63
Personal injury or illness	53
Marriage	50
Being fired at work	47
Marital reconciliation	45
Retirement	45
Change in the health of a family member	44
Pregnancy	40
Sex difficulties	39
Gain of a new family member	39
Business readjustment	39
Change in one's financial state	38
Death of a close friend	37
Change to a different line of work	36
Change in number of arguments with one's spouse	35
Mortgage over $10,000	31
Foreclosure of a mortgage or loan	30
Change in responsibilities at work	29
Son or daughter leaving home	29
Trouble with in-laws	29
Outstanding personal achievement	28
Wife beginning or stopping work	26
Beginning or ending school	26
Change in living conditions	25
Revision of personal habits	24
Trouble with one's boss	23
Change in work hours or conditions	20
Change in residence	20
Change in schools	20
Change in recreation	19
Change in church activities	19
Change in social activities	18
Mortgage or loan of less than $10,000	17
Change in sleeping habits	16
Change in number of family get-togethers	15
Change in eating habits	15
Vacation	13
Christmas	12
Minor violations of the law	11

The SRRS rates different stressors as causing more or less life change for people. More difficult stressors have a higher number of "life change units."

Source: Reprinted with permission from T. H. Holmes and R. H. Rahe, The social adjustment rating scale, *Journal of Psychosomatic Research, 11,* ©1967, Pergamon Press

life events that are irrelevant to most college students—getting divorced, receiving a jail term, obtaining a mortgage. At the same time, the measure omits many of the most relevant stressors that might be experienced by this age group,

such as moving away from home, considering abortion, or changing career plans.

Another objection is that the SRRS includes both positive and negative events as stressors. People may rate getting married and getting fired from a job as being similar in terms of life change units, but the (presumably) positive event of getting married would seem to differ in many important ways from the negative event of being dismissed from a job. Still another objection is the failure to distinguish between transient and chronic life events. Most of the items on the SRRS are not isolated events. Rather, as we shall see in Chapter 17, events such as marital separation or beginning college are major life transitions that have consequences extending into many realms of life and lasting over long periods of time.

The most important objection to instruments like the SRRS is that a given stressor does not always produce the same number of life change units for all individuals in all situations. Different life events have different consequences for different people at different points in their lives. For example, getting pregnant has a very different meaning for an unwed teenager who failed to use birth control than it has for a married couple in their 30s who are eager to conceive a baby.

A study by Dohrenwend and colleagues (1990) illustrates the need to consider individual differences in response to a stressor. Table 8–2 lists the percentage of people who reported that a life event produced either a large, moderate, small, or no amount of change in their lives. The same event clearly had very different effects on different participants in the study. For example, the death of a family member (other than a spouse or child) caused a large change for almost 10 percent of the respondents, but it caused no change for over half of them. Clearly, there are individual differences in the meaning and consequences of similar types of life events. This fact has led many researchers to reject the definition of stress as an event. Instead, they define stress either as a response or a stimulus-response combination.

STRESS AS A RESPONSE

The Canadian physiologist Hans Selye (1907–1982) was an extremely influential stress researcher who defined stress as a response. More precisely, Selye (1956) defined stress in terms of his concept of the **general adaptation syndrome (GAS)**, a specific response to a variety of (nonspecific) stressors. The GAS consists of three stages: alarm, resistance, and exhaustion (see Figure 8–1). The stage of *alarm* involves the mobilization of the body in reaction to perceived threat. The stage of *resistance* is a period of replenishment during which the body becomes physiologically prepared to deal with new threats. *Exhaustion* is the final stage, which occurs if the body's resources are depleted by chronic stress, making further adaptation impossible.

Much of Selye's research was devoted to animal analogue studies of the GAS, and this is one reason why he focused his definition of stress on a response rather than a stimulus. Stressors administered in the laboratory (such as an unpredictable electric shock) are independent variables that are controlled and manipulated by the experimenter (see Research Methods in Chapter 2). Stressful events are clearly defined in a laboratory experiment, where the major interest is the dependent variable—the animal's response to stress.

The laboratory analogue approach to studying stress has tremendous value, and we discuss the biological findings of Selye and other laboratory researchers in more detail shortly. However, by its very nature, the laboratory artificially controls events that are uncontrolled in the real world. As we have noted, all life events do *not* have the same meaning or impact in the everyday, human world, and this fact has forced researchers who study naturalistic stress among people to seek broader definitions of stress.

STRESS AS A STIMULUS-RESPONSE COMBINATION

Richard Lazarus (1966) has been a most effective proponent of the need to define stress in terms of both a stimulus and the individual's response to the stimulus. Lazarus argues that stress arises not from life events themselves but from the individual's **primary appraisal** or cognitive evaluation of the challenge, threat, or harm posed by a particular event (Lazarus & Folkman, 1984). Lazarus asserts that any given life event is a stressor only when it is considered stressful by the individual. For example, an impending exam causes stress when a student feels inadequate in his or her knowledge, but not when he or she feels confident about the subject matter. Lazarus also theorizes that **secondary appraisal,** the assessment of one's abilities and resources for coping with a difficult event, is critical to defining stress. Thus, even if a student believes his or her knowledge is inadequate, the stress caused by an impending exam will be minimized if the student has the time and the ability to study adequately.

		Percentage of Subjects Reporting Each Amount of Change		
Type of Event	**Large**	**Moderate**	**Little**	**None**
Serious physical illness	47.2%	27.8%	8.3%	16.7%
Relations with mate got worse	41.2	47.1	0.0	11.8
Relative died (not child/spouse)	8.3	8.3	29.2	54.2
Close friend died	5.3	15.8	29.8	49.1
Financial loss (not work related)	16.3	44.2	18.6	20.9
Assaulted	18.5	22.2	40.7	18.5
Broke up with a friend	0.0	26.1	37.0	37.0
Laid off	13.3	63.3	13.3	10.0
Had trouble with a boss	17.5	35.0	32.5	15.0
Got involved in a court case	9.5	9.5	28.6	52.4

TABLE 8-2

Variability Across People in the Amount of Change Caused by the Same Life Event

Source: Adapted form B. P. Dohrenwend et al., 1990, Measuring life events: The problem of variability within event categories, *Stress Medicine*, 6, 182.

Lazarus thus defines stress as the combination of a difficult event and a cognitive appraisal of the event as being potentially harmful and exceeding the individual's coping resources. Lazarus's approach solves many of the problems with stimulus or response definitions of stress, but it runs the risk of being *tautological,* or circular. What is stress? An event that causes us to

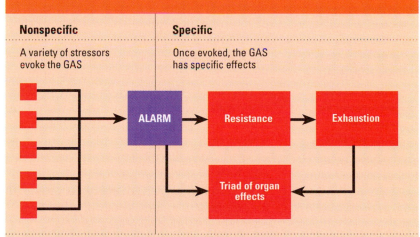

Stress as a Response: Selye's General Adaptation Syndrome (GAS)

Nonspecific

A variety of stressors evoke the GAS

Specific

Once evoked, the GAS has specific effects

ALARM → Resistance → Exhaustion

Triad of organ effects

FIGURE 8-1: Hans Selye defined stress in terms of a response. He assumed that the three stages of the GAS are activated in the same way by different stressors.

Source: Adapted from A. Baum, L.M. Davidson, J.E. Singer, and S.W. Street, 1987, Stress as a psychophysiological response. In A. Baum and J.E. Singer (Eds.), *Handbook of Psychology and Health. Stress,* vol. 5, p. 4. Hillsdale, NJ: Erlbaum.

▲ **Hans Selye (1907–1982) was a physiologist and prolific stress researcher. Selye's concept of the general adaptation syndrome continues to influence contemporary research on the stress response.**

▲ **Walter Cannon (1871–1945) was one of the first scientists to conduct systematic research on stress. Cannon focused on the emergency response, the body's physiological preparation for fight or flight.**

feel threatened and overwhelmed. What causes us to feel threatened and overwhelmed? Stress. We agree with Lazarus that, in naturalistic studies of humans, stress must be defined in terms of both a stimulus and a response (note our definition given earlier). Because of the potential for circularity, however, great caution must be exercised in distinguishing independent variables (stressors) from dependent variables (adverse outcomes) in research on stress.

Typical Symptoms and Associated Features of Stress

In this section we consider short-term physiological, emotional, cognitive, and behavioral responses to stress. We distinguish these immediate reactions from the physical illnesses that stress may cause over longer periods of time.

Physiological Responses to Stress

The American physiologist Walter Cannon (1871–1945) was one of the first researchers to conduct systematic studies of stress, and his profound influence on the field continues to the present day. Cannon (1935) was primarily interested in what he called the *emergency response*, the mobilization of the body in reaction to a perceived threat. According to Cannon, physical or psychological threats produce generalized emotional reactions accompanied by psychophysiological responses, specifically the general arousal of the sympathetic nervous system (see Figure 8–2). When the sympathetic nervous system is aroused, heart and respiration rates increase; blood pressure rises; the pupils dilate; blood sugar levels elevate; and blood flow is redirected in preparation for muscular activity (Baum et al., 1987; Koranyi, 1989).

Cannon argued that these reactions prepare humans (and other animals) for fight or flight in response to threat. Cannon's **fight or flight response** is the reaction you witness when a cat is surprised by a barking dog. At the behavioral level of analysis, the cat can either flee to safety or turn to scratch at the dog. Physiologically, the cat's body becomes prepared for either action. Attention is heightened, energy is provided for sudden action, and its body prepares for the possibility of injury (Sapolsky, 1992).

The fight or flight response has obvious survival value when we are confronted with a physically dangerous threat. Cannon and other theorists have suggested, however, that the human environment may have outpaced our physiological reactions to a threat. Fight or flight seems to be a maladaptive response to many psychological threats that characterize the modern world, such as being reprimanded by your boss, giving a speech before a large audience, or getting caught in a traffic jam. Behavioral fight or flight obviously is inappropriate in such circumstances, and the physiology of the response may be similarly maladaptive. In fact, our physiological reactions to stress may be prolonged precisely because we cannot respond to them with fight or flight. The load on the heart is less, for example, when people can respond to stress with physical activity than when they cannot respond physically (Charvat et al., 1964). Cannon (1935) hypothesized that when stress is intense or chronic, it overwhelms the body's homeostatic mechanisms, and the prolonged arousal of the sympathetic nervous system eventually damages the body. (Cannon, in fact, coined the familiar term *homeostasis*.)

Much like Cannon, Selye identified the stage of exhaustion in his GAS as responsible for converting stress into physical illness (refer back to Figure 8–1). There are subtle differences between the two theories, however. In Selye's view, if stress is sufficiently intense or prolonged, the body can no longer respond appropriately to it. The stress response is exhausted, and the body is damaged by continuous, failed attempts to activate it. An analogy for Cannon's theory is a car in which the engine continues to race instead of idling down after running fast. In contrast, an analogy for Selye's theory is a car that has run out of gas and is damaged because stress keeps turning the key, trying repeatedly and unsuccessfully to restart the engine.

Contemporary researchers suggest that stress may create physical illness through both mechanisms, but a third explanation may be even more important. According to this viewpoint, the problem is that the body cannot perform routine functions such as storing energy or repairing injuries because the stress response demands too much energy and uses the energy inefficiently (Sapolsky, 1992). The result is greater susceptibility to illness. An automotive analogy for the demands of stress in this third model is constantly running a car at high speeds, thus preventing the cooling and lubricant systems from performing their functions.

IMMUNE FUNCTION

Research on stress and the functioning of the immune system is an important illustration of this third theoretical perspective. Numerous studies have found that stress impairs functioning of the immune system, thus weakening the body's ability to fight off infectious disease (Maier, Watkins, & Fleshner, 1994). In fact, research in this area has spawned a new field of study called **psychoneuroimmunology (PNI),** research on the effects of stress on the functioning of the immune system.

Scientists are beginning to document the physiology of how stress weakens immune functioning. Adrenal hormones called *glucocorticoids,* which are secreted in response to stress, inhibit and may even destroy various immune agents, particularly *T cells,* one of the major types of *lymphocytes,* a category of white blood cells that fight off *antigens,* foreign substances like bacteria that invade the body. Experts hypothesize that *immunosuppression,* the decreased production of T cells and other immune agents, makes the body more susceptible to infectious diseases. For example, researchers have found that among medical students during exam periods, T-cell activity diminishes, and rates of various infectious diseases increase (Glaser et al., 1987).

Immunosuppression has also been found among people who are depressed (Herbert & Cohen, 1993), and researchers now link immunosuppression directly to the experience of stress. In one fascinating study, 90 newly married couples were admitted to a hospital research ward where they engaged in a 30-minute discussion of marital problems. Partners who were more hostile or negative during the interaction showed greater immunosuppression over the next 24 hours in comparison to newlyweds who had more positive conversations. (Blood pressure also remained elevated longer following hostile interactions than following friendly interactions.) This research demonstrates that stress has a direct effect on immune functioning. It also revealed that, following a negative marital interaction, newly married women showed more immunosuppression than men (Kiecolt-Glaser, Malarkey, Chee et al., 1993).

Why does stress inhibit immune function? As we noted earlier, stress mobilizes the body

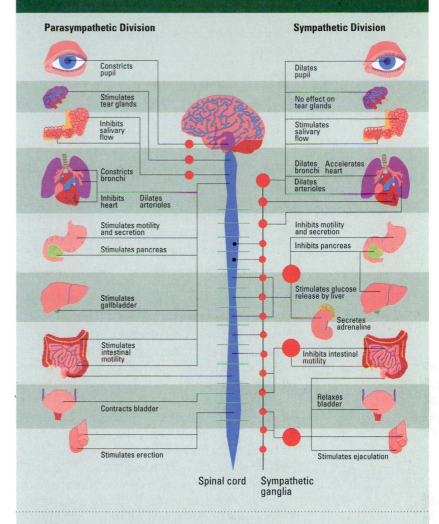

Sympathetic and Parasympathetic Divisions of the Autonomic Nervous System

FIGURE 8-2: The sympathetic nervous system is activated by stress and generally increases arousal. The parasympathetic nervous system typically calms the individual and returns the body to homeostatis.

Source: From *Biology,* 4th ed, by Willis H. Johnson, Louis E. Delanney, Thomas A. Cole, and Austin E. Brooks. Copyright © 1972 by Holt, Rinehart and Winston, Inc.

for fight or flight, and from an evolutionary perspective, it may seem that *heightened* rather than impaired immune function is a more adaptive physiological response to threat. That is, heightened immune functioning might prepare the body for the injury or infection that often follows fight or flight. Maier, Watkins, and Fleshner (1994) argue, however, that the immune response actually impairs action, for example, it creates inflammation, maintains fever, and intensifies pain. Therefore inhibited immune function may be an adaptive reaction to immediate threat from an evolutionary point of view. Consistent with the "energy drain" model discussed at the beginning of this section, Maier and colleagues view fight or flight as competing with the immune response for the body's resources. Thus they argue that stress causes immunosuppression by diverting energy from the immune system to the fight or flight response.

ADRENAL HORMONES AND PHYSIOLOGICAL TOUGHNESS

Stress does not always drain the body's resources. Research indicates that exposure to intermittent stressors of mild or moderate intensity promotes resilience rather than weakness. Much as routine exercise prepares us for intense physical exertion, a moderate level of stress may prepare the body to respond to emergency. Dienstbier (1989) has suggested that, under certain conditions, the result of stress is not a weakening of the organism but a beneficial effect that he calls *physiological toughness*.

In order to explain Dienstbier's theory, we must first review aspects of the stress response. As noted, researchers have documented that one physiological response to stress is increased secretion of hormones from the *adrenal gland*, a part of the endocrine system (see Chapter 2). Two major processes have been identified. One is an increased release of *epinephrine* (also known as *adrenaline*) and *norepinephrine* directly into the bloodstream from the adrenal medulla and other body sites. This was a major focus of Cannon's research. Selye identified a second process, the release of glucocorticoids (Baum et al., 1987; Sapolsky, 1992). Epinephrine, norepinephrine, and the glucocorticoids all stimulate the regulatory systems associated with fight or flight, and they act to inhibit other bodily functions, including reproduction, growth, and the storage of sugar.

Dienstbier's theory suggests that the release of epinephrine and norepinephrine has very different meanings for the stress response than does release of the glucocorticoids. He argues that exposure to moderate amounts of stress increases production of epinephrine and norepinephrine. The result is physiological toughness, as the body is protected against the depletion of epinephrine and norepinephrine during times of more intense or chronic stress. Dienstbier sees no such toughness benefit associated with the release of the glucocorticoids, however. Thus he views glucocorticoid release as an index of physiological stress, whereas he argues that the release of epinephrine and norepinephrine indicates physiological toughness.

DIFFERENT PHYSIOLOGICAL RESPONSES TO DIFFERENT STRESSORS?

Selye and many other stress researchers assumed that all stressors cause the same psychophysiological response. Whatever its nature, Selye believed a stressor would cause the GAS, as long as it was sufficiently intense or prolonged (refer back to Figure 8–1). Because he assumed responses to stress were uniform, he also assumed that all stressors could be grouped together into the single category of stress.

Researchers since Selye have questioned this assumption of *nonspecificity*. For example, Mason (1975) documented that unpredictable stressors produce different patterns of hormonal reactions than do predictable stressors. Thus, although all stressors tend to trigger the release of epinephrine/norepinephrine and glucocorticoids and to impair immune functioning, different categories of stressors appear to cause somewhat different physiological responses.

Emotional Responses to Stress

Some of the physiological reactions to stress may occur without our being aware of them, but others are a part of our conscious experience. For example, consider the familiar psychic experience that accompanies a "rush" of adrenaline. Such responses can be understood at the biological level, but they also can be conceptualized as psychological processes, particularly as emotional reactions. (Recall from Chapter 4 that psychophysiological activity is an indicator of emotional arousal.) In general, the emotions aroused by stress are negative ones (Baum et al., 1987). Anxiety, depression, and anger are the primary affective responses to stressors, although different individuals may experience these emotions as tension, sadness, frustration, numbness, or simply as a somatic symptom like an upset stomach.

Consideration of emotional responses to stress brings us back to the vital topic of coping. A distinction is often made between problem-focused and emotion-focused coping (Lazarus & Folkman, 1984). **Problem-focused coping** is externally oriented and involves attempts to change a stressor. If your job is too stressful, you can look for a new one. In contrast, **emotion-focused coping** is an attempt to alter internal distress. When a romance ends, you may tell yourself that you really don't care.

Emotion-focused coping may involve a deliberate effort to relax or to reevaluate a stressor. Before taking a big exam, you might sit quietly and breathe deeply for several minutes. Other forms of emotion-focused coping may involve unconscious or automatic methods for dampening emotional experience. For example, various intrapsychic defense mechanisms, particularly *repression*, have been hypothesized to alter emotional responses to stress—sometimes with maladaptive consequences. Some experts speculate that repression protects people from consciously experiencing unpleasant emotions, but "repressors" thereby place themselves at greater risk for developing stress-related physical illnesses.

Not surprisingly, the repression hypothesis is difficult to test empirically. Some evidence suggests that people who do not acknowledge their experience of anxiety show exaggerated psychophysiological reactions to stress (Schwartz, 1989). Similar findings have been reported for "defensive-deniers"—subjects who report positive mental health but whom clinicians judge to have emotional problems (Shedler, Mayman, & Manis, 1993). Other research indicates that when people are encouraged to recount very stressful experiences, they show reductions in various psychophysiological indicators of the stress response (Pennebaker, 1990; Petrie et al., 1995). Although the repression hypothesis is difficult to test, talking about your feelings clearly is healthy (see Research Close-Up).

RESEARCH CLOSE-UP

Disclosure of Trauma and Immunity

We have briefly discussed the exciting new field of psychoneuroimmunology, in which scientists study the effects of stress on the functioning of the immune system. We also have mentioned the hypothesis that the risk for stress-related illness is increased by repressing feelings, an observation that implies a dramatic idea: People may be able to lower the risk for physical disease somewhat by talking openly about their troubles. Could the open discussion of feelings actually improve the functioning of the immune system? This was the question asked in an intriguing study conducted by James Pennebaker, Janice Kiecolt-Glaser, and Ronald Glaser (1988).

Subjects in the experimental group in this study were asked to do something fairly simple: write about traumatic events in their lives for 4 consecutive days, preferably about stressors that they had not previously discussed with others. A control group of subjects was told to write about trivial topics for the same time period. All writing took place in the laboratory. Twenty-five psychology undergraduates were randomly assigned to each of these two levels of the independent variable. Dependent variables in the study included self-reported mood before and after writing; measures of autonomic arousal, including blood pressure and heart rate; and immunological assays of the subject's blood before the study, immediately afterwards and 6 weeks later.

The students handed in their writing to the experimenters, and evaluations of the reports indicated that the students in the experimental group had indeed written about very upsetting experiences, including difficulties they had coming to college, serious family conflicts, and problems with the other sex. Writing did not produce an immediate benefit, however, as students who wrote about their troubles reported being more upset immediately after writing than did students who wrote about trivial matters.

Remarkable longer-term benefits were noted even from this brief intervention, however. Students who wrote about personal distress had significantly fewer subsequent medical visits to the student health center and better immune responses than did students in the control group. No differences were found for the measures of autonomic arousal. Further support for the repression hypothesis came from evidence that subjects in the personal writing condition improved more on blood pressure and immunological measures when they wrote about previously undisclosed events rather than events they had discussed with others.

These findings need to be viewed with some caution. Several questions have been raised about aspects of the study's methods (Neale et al., 1988). Clearly, it would be a mistake to draw simplistic conclusions about the complex processes involved in psychoneuroimmunology. Nevertheless, the study and similar findings by the same research group

Cognitive Responses to Stress

In addition to the important issues of primary and secondary appraisal, findings from animal and human research indicate that other aspects of cognition can dramatically alter responses to stress. Two critical issues are the *predictability* of stressors and *control* over them. A rat has a smaller physiological response to a shock that is signaled by the flash of a light than to an unsignaled shock of the same magnitude (Sapolsky, 1992). In one way, predictability is stressful, because the signal elicits a response that is similar to (but weaker than) the response to the actual stressor. However, the signal also decreases negative responding to the actual stressor (Baum et al., 1987). In a sense, predictability allows us to begin to cope even *before* the onset of a stressor.

The importance of control has been documented in much research with animals and humans. Rats who are able to stop a shock by pressing a bar have a smaller stress response than rats exposed to exactly the same shock but who have no opportunity of stopping it through their own actions (Sapolsky, 1992). Even the illusion of control can help to alleviate stress in humans (Mineka & Kihlstrom, 1978), but the perception of being able to control a stressor is not always a good thing. The perception of control can *increase* stress when people believe they can exercise control but are unable to do so, or when they lose control over a formerly controllable stressor (Mineka & Kihlstrom, 1978). Thus control alleviates stress when it can be exercised or even when it is illusory, but failed attempts at control intensify stress.

Behavioral Responses to Stress

Consideration of the costs and benefits of control leads us to a discussion of the behavioral responses to stress. As we have noted, responding to stress with physical activity reduces the physiological reactions of the fight or flight response. In fact, the response need not be directed at the stressor itself, but may include other *outlets for frustration*. For example, rats secrete fewer glucocorticoids if they can attack another rat or run on a running wheel after the administration of an electric shock (Sapolsky, 1992).

As suggested by the literature on control, however, there is a problem with responding to stressors directly: It is often unclear which coping response will be effective, or even whether a stressor can be changed. A difficult class may cause you great stress because you cannot maintain your usual grades. What is the most effective response to this situation? Should you redouble your efforts, drop the course, or accept that this is not your best subject? Problem-focused (behavioral) coping is the appropriate way to conquer many actual stressors, but attempts to change some stressors are doomed to failure. In such cases, efforts at problem-focused coping will increase, not reduce, distress. Thus the only alternative is to accept the stressor for what it is and to use emotion-focused coping to alter your response to it. In short, there is much truth in Reinhold Niebuhr's (1951) "Serenity Prayer":

> God, give us the serenity to accept what cannot be changed;
> Give us the courage to change what should be changed;
> Give us the wisdom to distinguish one from the other.

Calvin and Hobbes by Bill Watterson

HEALTH BEHAVIOR

Behavioral responses to stress are important also because stress may cause illness indirectly, by affecting health behaviors, rather than directly, by altering our physiology (Cohen & Williamson, 1991; see Figure 8–3). **Health behavior** involves activities that are essential to promoting good health. Proper health behavior includes positive actions like eating, sleeping, and exercising adequately, as well as the avoidance of unhealthy activities such as cigarette smoking, excessive alcohol consumption, and drug use. (See Further Thoughts for a discussion of sleep and sleep disorders.) Stress can lead people to engage in less positive and more negative health behavior, and these poor health habits, and not stress, per se, may be responsible for much of the relation between stress and illness (Cohen & Williamson, 1991). In considering the importance of health behavior, you should note that over the last 2 centuries basic health behaviors—personal hygiene, maintaining sanitation, and eating an adequate diet—are more responsible for our vastly increased health and life expectancy than are scientific

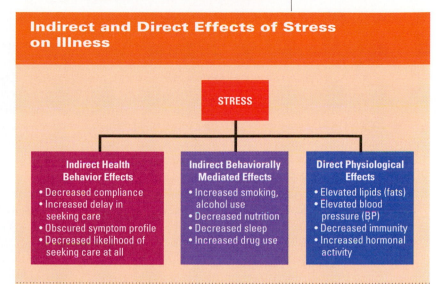

Indirect and Direct Effects of Stress on Illness

STRESS

Indirect Health Behavior Effects
- Decreased compliance
- Increased delay in seeking care
- Obscured symptom profile
- Decreased likelihood of seeking care at all

Indirect Behaviorally Mediated Effects
- Increased smoking, alcohol use
- Decreased nutrition
- Decreased sleep
- Increased drug use

Direct Physiological Effects
- Elevated lipids (fats)
- Elevated blood pressure (BP)
- Decreased immunity
- Increased hormonal activity

FIGURE 8-3: Stress can promote illness both directly through adverse physiological effects and indirectly by undermining positive health behaviors and increasing negative health behaviors.

Source: A. Baum, 1994, Behavioral, biological, and environmental interactions in disease processes. In S. Blumenthal, K. Matthews, and S. Weiss (Eds.), *New Research Frontiers in Behavioral Medicine: Proceedings of the National Conference*, p. 62. Washington, DC: NIH Publications.

FURTHER THOUGHTS

Sleep Disorders

Sleep is very important to good health and psychological well-being, but mental health professionals typically have been concerned with sleep disturbances only as a symptom of some other mental disorder, such as depression or anxiety. This circumstance is changing, however, as more research is being conducted on sleep disturbances. In fact, the DSM-IV is the first edition of DSM to contain a diagnostic category for primary sleep disorder. **Primary sleep disorder** is a condition where the sleeping difficulty is the principal complaint, in contrast to sleep disorders due to general medical condition, another mental disorder, or substance use. Two types of primary sleep disorders are listed in the DSM-IV. *Dyssomnias* are difficulties in the amount, quality, or timing of sleep. *Parasomnias* are characterized by abnormal events that occur during sleep, for example, nightmares.

The dyssomnias include primary insomnia, primary hypersomnia, narcolepsy, breathing-related sleep disorder, and circadian rhythm sleep disorder. *Primary insomnia* involves difficulties initiating or maintaining sleep, or poor quality of sleeping (e.g., restless sleep), that lasts for at least a month and significantly impairs life functioning. Primary insomnia is a common problem, although its exact prevalence is unknown, and it typically is precipitated by stress. *Primary hypersomnia* is excessive sleepiness characterized by prolonged or daytime sleep, lasting at least a month and significantly interfering with life functioning. Primary hypersomnia is similar to *narcolepsy,* irresistible attacks of refreshing sleep, lasting at least 3 months. However, narcolepsy also is characterized by the sudden loss of muscle tone for brief periods of time (usually following intense emotion) and/or intrusive periods of dreaming just before awakening. The "sleep attacks" in narcolepsy are also less resistible than is the general desire to sleep in primary hypersomnia (APA, 1994).

Breathing-related sleep disorder involves the disruption in sleep due to breathing problems such as *sleep apnea,* the temporary obstruction of the respiratory airway. People with sleep apnea typically snore loudly due to an airway that is partially obstructed as a result of obesity or other conditions. Sleep apnea patients will stop breathing for 20 to 30 seconds when the obstruction becomes complete, and this is followed by gasping, body movements, or even louder snoring. Not surprisingly, sleep apnea disrupts not only the patients' sleep but also the sleep of others in their vicinity. *Circadian rhythm sleep disorder* is a mismatch between the patients' 24-hour sleeping patterns and their 24-hour life demands that causes significant life distress. The disorder is found more commonly among adolescents and people who work night shifts (APA, 1994).

The parasomnias include nightmare disorder, sleep terror disorder, and sleepwalking disorder. People with *nightmare disorder* are frequently awakened by terrifying dreams. *Sleep terror disorder* also involves abrupt awakening from sleep, typically with a scream, but it differs from nightmare disorder in important respects. People with nightmare disorder recall their dreams and quickly orient to being awake; people with sleep terror disorder recall little of their dreams, show intense autonomic arousal, and are difficult to soothe. Moreover, a person with sleep terror typically returns to sleep fairly quickly and recalls little, if anything, about the episode the following morning.

Finally, *sleepwalking disorder* involves rising from the bed during sleep and walking about in a generally unresponsive state. In extreme cases, the person may use the bathroom, talk (with a minimum of meaningful dialogue), eat, or even run in a frantic attempt to escape some threat. Upon awakening, however, the person cannot remember the episode. Occasional episodes of sleepwalking are fairly common, especially among children. Like all sleep disorders, sleepwalking disorder tends to be diagnosed only if it causes significant distress or impairs the person's ability to function (APA, 1994). ∎

---

advances like the discovery of penicillin (Starr, 1982).

Stress may also be related to the very important positive health behavior of following medical advice. (Recall that Bob Carter discounted his cardiologist's recommendations to alter his lifestyle.) In fact, as many as 93 percent of all patients *fail* to adhere fully to medical advice (Taylor, 1990). This is a particular problem for illnesses like hypertension (high blood pressure) that usually have no obvious symptoms. In such cases patients may discontinue their medication because it produces no noticeable relief, although it may be controlling a dangerous condition. Stressors such as family conflict also can interfere with adherence to treatments that *do* have clear symptoms. For example, children with insulin-dependent diabetes are less likely to adhere to medical recommendations concerning exercise, diet, testing blood sugars, and the timing and frequency of insulin injections when family conflict is high (Miller-Johnson et al., 1994).

Illness behavior—behaving as if you are sick—also appears to be stress-related. Considerable research indicates that increased stress is correlated with such illness behaviors as making more frequent office visits to physicians or allowing chronic pain to interfere with everyday activities (Taylor, 1990). On the positive side, a happier, less stressful life may motivate people to cope successfully with chronic illness, where effective coping may involve ignoring physical discomfort and living life as normally as possible.

Finally, the fact that many people consult physicians for psychological rather than physical concerns underscores the value of *social support* in coping with stress. Social support can encourage adaptive coping with illness, but research suggests that social support also has direct, physical benefits. For example, one investigation found that stressed monkeys exhibited less immunosuppression when they interacted more often with other monkeys (Cohen et al., 1992). Other findings indicate that increased social support is associated with adaptive functioning of the immune, cardiovascular, and endocrine systems (Uchino, Cacioppo, & Kiecolt-Glaser, 1996)

Illness as a Cause of Stress

Although this chapter is concerned with how stress can help to cause physical illness, the reverse can also be true: Physical illness can cause stress.

The stresses caused by illness may involve minor aggravations like those that accompany a common cold, but some diseases lead to major changes in a person's life. For example, consider the effects of the diagnosis of insulin-dependent diabetes on a 10-year-old boy and his family. In order to maintain a normal range of blood sugars, the child and his parents must frequently test his blood sugars, adjust to giving and receiving one, two, or three injections of insulin daily, and carefully monitor exercise and diet because of their profound effect on blood sugars. In addition, the child and his family must somehow cope with the stigma of being "different" that often accompanies a chronic disease like diabetes, as well as with the possibility of suffering profound, long-term side effects from hyperglycemia (high blood sugars), including kidney dysfunction or blindness. Surely the chronic disease of diabetes causes much stress, particularly when it is first diagnosed.

As with other physical and psychological disorders, however, the link between diabetes and stress is a reciprocal one. That is, diabetes causes stress, but as we have noted, evidence also indicates that stress (family conflict) affects the course of diabetes (Miller et al., 1994). Stress can cause illness, and illness can cause stress.

Classification of Stress and Physical Illness

Now that we have discussed short-term responses to stress, we can consider the relation between stress and more general physical health. We begin with an overview of classification of stress-related physical illnesses

Brief Historical Perspective

Scientific interest in the link between life experience and physical illness was first pursued with vigor by psychoanalytically oriented psychiatrists who helped to establish the field of psychosomatic medicine in the middle of the twentieth century. These early theorists developed a classification of psychosomatic illnesses based on what has become known as the *specificity hypothesis*—the idea that specific personality types cause specific psychosomatic diseases. Specificity theorists (e.g., Alexander, 1950) attempted to classify various psychosomatic illnesses, such as asthma, ulcer, and so on, according to the unique personality type that presumably caused the specific illness. For example, Franz Alexander, one of the most influential of the specificity theorists, wrote:

> The crucial finding in ulcer patients is the frustration (external or internal) of passive, dependent, and love-demanding desires that cannot be gratified in normal relationships. . . . Onset of illness occurs when the intensity of the patient's unsatisfied dependent cravings increases either because of external deprivation or because the patient defends against his cravings by assuming increased responsibilities. The external deprivation often consists in the loss of a person upon whom the patient has been dependent, in leaving home, or in losing money or a position that had given the patient a sense of security. The increased responsibility may take the form of marriage or the birth of a child or the assumption of a more responsible job. (Alexander, French, & Pollock, 1968, p. 16)

Contemporary Approaches

Research does not support the specificity hypothesis, and a more generalized view of stress has come to dominate modern science. As we have noted, contemporary approaches also reject the psychosomatic medicine view that only certain physical illnesses have psychological causes. The DSM-II (1968) contained a list of 10 "psychophysiologic disorders." The DSM-III (1980) included no such list, however, and neither does the DSM-IV. Psyche and soma are now considered to play a role in all physical illnesses; thus a list of "psychosomatic disorders" would contain every known physical illness.

The DSM-IV highlights the essential role of stress in illness by including two separate diagnostic axes, Axis III and Axis IV (see Chapter 4). Physical illnesses that are judged to be relevant to understanding or treating an emotional disorder are coded on Axis III, *general medical conditions*. The only criteria for coding a physical illness on this axis are (1) the disorder involves organic pathology (that is, it is not a

TABLE 8-3

DSM-IV Diagnostic Criteria for Psychological Factors Affecting Medical Condition

A. **A general medical condition (coded on Axis III) is present.**

B. **Psychological factors adversely affect the general medical condition in one of the following ways:**
  1. The factors have influenced the course of the general medical condition as shown by a close temporal association between the psychological factors and the development or exacerbation, or delayed recovery from, the general medical condition.
  2. The factors interfere with the treatment of the general medical condition.
  3. The factors constitute additional health risks for the individual.
  4. Stress-related physiological responses precipitate or exacerbate symptoms of the general medical condition.

somatoform disorder), and (2) the physical illness is related to the Axis I diagnosis in a meaningful way. When the physical illness is the focus of the treatment, the Axis I diagnosis of *psychological factors affecting medical condition* is used in conjunction with the Axis III medical disorder (see Table 8–3). You should note that it is *not* necessary for an Axis I mental disorder to be present in order to use the diagnosis of psychological factors affecting medical condition. In fact, the diagnosis may be used whether the patient has a mental disorder or simply exhibits

TABLE 8-4

DSM- IV Categories of Psychosocial and Environmental Problems

Category	Examples
Problems with primary support group	Death of a family member, family health problems, divorce, sexual abuse, inadequate discipline, family discord, birth of a sibling
Problems related to the social environment	Death or loss of a friend, social isolation, discrimination, adjustment to life cycle transition
Educational problems	Illiteracy, academic problems, discord with teacher, inadequate school environment
Occupational problems	Unemployment, stressful work schedule, job change, discord with boss
Housing problems	Homelessness, unsafe neighborhood, discord with neighbors
Economic problems	Extreme poverty, inadequate finances
Problems with access to health care services	Inadequate health care services, inadequate health insurance
Problems related to interaction with the legal system/crime	Arrest, litigation, incarceration, victim of crime
Other psychosocial problems	Exposure to disasters, war, discord with non-family caregivers

psychological symptoms, personality traits, maladaptive health behaviors, or stress-related physiological responses that might affect his or her medical condition.

The DSM-IV also has a separate axis for coding stressors, Axis IV, *psychosocial and environmental problems*. The DSM makes no attempt to offer an exhaustive listing of potential life stressors for Axis IV. Instead, it simply includes categories of stressors with specific examples under each heading. These categories can be found in Table 8–4.

The DSM-III and DSM-III-R asked clinicians to rate the amount of stress clients had experienced by comparing their life circumstances with a brief list of life events ranked according to their degree of stress. This approach was very similar to the one used by the SRRS (see p. 288), a general method we have already questioned. Researchers found that clinicians were unreliable in rating not only the severity of stress but also the *presence* of difficult life events (Skodol et al., 1990). As a result, the DSM-IV introduced a simplified scheme. The manual makes no attempt to rate the severity of stress. Rather, it asks clinicians simply to rate the presence or absence of difficulties within various categories of life events (see Table 8–4).

As we have noted, scientists have not yet reached consensus about how "stress" should be defined or rated. Perhaps the only certainty for the future is that the DSM definition of stress will change as researchers continue to refine methods of categorizing and quantifying life stressors.

The Role of Psychological Factors in Some Familiar Illnesses

In addition to the emerging medical discoveries of the era, there is a good reason why germ theory dominated medicine at the beginning of the twentieth century. Infectious diseases, specifically influenza, pneumonia, and tuberculosis, were the most common causes of death in the United States in 1900 (Taylor, 1995). Thanks to advances in medical science, and especially in public health, far fewer people die of infectious disease today compared to 100 years ago. As you can see from Figure 8–4, infectious disease is no longer at the top of the list of killers. In fact, lifestyle plays a central role in 7 of the top 10 causes of death in the United States today (Human Capital Initiative, 1996).

Scientists have conducted much promising research on the role of stress in many physical illnesses, including but not limited to the diseases listed in Figure 8–4. In the following sections we briefly review evidence on psychological factors in the etiology, course, and treatment of cancer, HIV infection, and chronic pain. Later, we review research in some detail on the relation between stress and today's number one killer, cardiovascular disease. Our goal is to convey a sense of both the breadth and the depth of research in behavioral medicine.

Cancer

Cancer is the second leading cause of mortality in the United States today, accounting for 23 percent of all deaths. In contrast to the declining rate of death due to cardiovascular disease, moreover, cancer deaths have risen by 20 percent over the last 30 years (American Cancer Society, 1993). At first glance, cancer would seem to be the paramount example of a purely

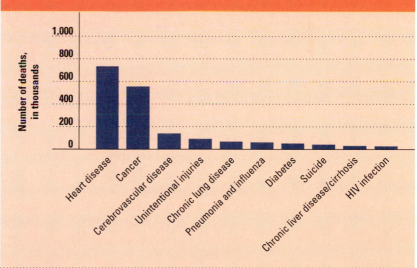

The 10 Leading Causes of Death in the United States in 1990

FIGURE 8-4: Stress and health behavior play a central role in most of the major causes of death in the United States today.

Source: M. McGinnis, 1994, The role of behavioral research in national health policy. In S. Blumental, K. Matthews, and S. Weiss (Eds.), *New Research Frontiers in Behavioral Medicine: Proceedings of the National Conference*, p. 219. Washington, DC: NIH Publications.

▲ A self-help group for patients with cancer. Some evidence suggests that cancer support groups not only improve quality of life, but they may actually help extend the lives of the terminally ill.

biological illness, but the importance of stress and health behavior becomes apparent upon closer examination. To some degree, for example, our actions determine the extent to which we are exposed to various *carcinogens*, cancer-causing agents, such as cigarette smoking.

Stress and health behavior also appear to affect the course of cancer. Not surprisingly, cancer patients often are anxious or depressed, and their negative emotions can lead to increases in negative health behavior (e.g., alcohol consumption) and decreases in positive health behavior (e.g., exercise). Stress or the absence of social support also can undermine compliance with unpleasant but vitally important medical treatments for cancer (Anderson, Kiecolt-Glaser, & Glaser, 1994). Finally, some research indicates that stress *directly* affects the course of cancer. In animal analogue studies, for example, rats exposed to inescapable shock are less able to reject implanted cancer tumors than rats exposed to escapable shock or no stress at all (Visintainer, Seligman, & Volpicelli, 1982). The adverse effects of stress on the immune system may explain how stress may exacerbate the course of cancer. Evidence indicates that immunity plays an important role in limiting the spread of cancerous tumors, and immunosuppression due to stress may disrupt this protective function (Anderson et al., 1994).

A cause and effect relationship between stress and the course of cancer also is implied by some exciting treatment research. Various psychological treatments have been offered to cancer patients in an attempt to improve their quality of life. The type of intervention varies widely, but treatments often include a structured, self-help group. Many of these interventions are successful in improving the quality of life among cancer patients, and a few of the psychological interventions appear to have beneficial *physical* effects (Anderson et al., 1994). For example, one study found that 6 years after treatment, significantly fewer patients who participated in a support group died (9 percent) in comparison to patients who received no psychosocial treatment (29 percent) (Fawzy et al., 1993).

Any number of factors may explain this striking outcome, including lower stress, increased social support, and improved health behavior. We must be cautious not to overinterpret the result, moreover, especially until the finding is replicated widely. Cancer *is* a physical illness. We are hardly arguing that psychological factors alone are responsible for causing cancer, nor are we asserting that the disease should be treated psychologically instead of medically. In fact, many cancer patients have little interest in participating in support groups (Anderson et al., 1994). Still, intervention research dramatically illustrates that psychological factors contribute to the course of one of our most dreaded physical illnesses.

Acquired Immune Deficiency Syndrome (AIDS)

Acquired immune deficiency syndrome (AIDS) is caused by the *human immunodeficiency virus (HIV)*, which attacks the immune system and leaves the patient susceptible to unusual infections. However, people who are HIV positive vary widely in how rapidly they develop AIDS. Some people develop AIDS quickly after HIV infection, whereas others remain symptom-free for 10 years or more. In fact, scientists disagree about whether people who are HIV positive will inevitably develop AIDS, or whether some will escape the dreaded disease (U.S. Department of Health and Human Services, 1993). Because AIDS was first diagnosed in 1981, researchers have yet to answer many questions about the frightening illness. We do know, however, that AIDS is one of the top 10 causes of death in the United States (see Figure 8–4).

We also know that the virus is transmitted through contact with the bodily fluids of an infected individual, particularly blood and semen. Thus behavioral factors play a critical role in the transmission of the disease. Scientists have yet to determine precisely how people become infected with HIV, but researchers have isolated a number of high-risk behaviors, including anal sex between homosexual men and heterosexual vaginal intercourse. The use of condoms greatly reduces the risk of the sexual transmission of HIV, as you undoubtedly have learned from public service announcements in various popular media. Other behaviors that increase the risk for HIV infection include sharing hypodermic needles, and transmission from an infected mother to her unborn child (U.S. Department of Health and Human Services, 1993).

Scientists and policy makers have launched a number of large-scale media campaigns as well as smaller, more intensive efforts to educate the public about HIV and AIDS and to change risky behavior. How effective are these programs? Evidence indicates that although the public has become much more knowledgeable about AIDS, changing behavior is very difficult. For example, practices such as condom use that reduce the risk of infection are now more common among members of high-risk groups such as homosexual men or heterosexual young people with multiple sexual partners. However, unprotected sex is still very common even among members of high-risk groups, and researchers have detected some backsliding in recent years (Taylor, 1995). Strong motivations and the private nature of sexuality make it very difficult to change sexual practices.

Stress causes immunosuppression, but evidence is inconsistent as to whether the course of AIDS is exacerbated by exposure to stress. Similarly, research is contradictory about the benefits of psychological intervention in altering the progression of AIDS. It is clear, however, that social support is extremely important to the AIDS patient's *psychological* well-being. Unfortunately, misunderstanding and fear cause many people, including many health professionals, to distance themselves from AIDS victims rather than offering them understanding, acceptance, and support.

Pain Management

Pain is associated with a number of acute injuries and illnesses, and it often serves the useful functions of alerting people to a problem and motivating them to seek treatment. Pain is not always adaptive, however, and in many cases, pain is *not* a signal of an underlying condition that can be controlled with treatment. Problematic pain can take the form of recurrent acute pain, or pain can be chronic. Headaches are an example of recurrent acute pain, and lower back problems are a common form of chronic pain.

Pain can take a huge toll not only on the sufferer but also on family members—and on the family's and the society's economy. Repeated attempts to treat chronic pain quickly become expensive, and chronic pain can greatly impair work performance. The adverse personal, social, and economic consequences of pain are even more important, because pain is pervasive. In fact, some estimates indicate that as many as 90 million people in the United States suffer from recurrent or chronic pain (Taylor, 1995).

Pain is subjective, and this makes it difficult to evaluate or compare patients' reports about the extent or nature of their pain. Evaluation is especially difficult when pain is not associated with an identifiable injury or illness, as is commonly the case with headaches and lower back pain. Some evidence links reports of increased pain with depression and anxiety (Taylor, 1995). Researchers commonly interpret this finding as indicating that people who are anxious or depressed are more sensitive to pain, less able to cope with it, and more willing to complain than are people who apparently have similar levels of suffering.

Psychologists have tried a number of treatments designed to directly reduce patients' experience of pain. Treatments include a wide range of techniques, such as hypnosis, biofeedback, relaxation training, and cognitive therapy. Researchers report a degree of success with each of these various approaches, but pain reduction typically is modest at best (Taylor, 1995). As a result, most current efforts focus on the *pain management*, not pain reduction. The goal of pain management programs is to help people to cope with pain in a way that minimizes its impact on their lives, even if the pain cannot be eliminated or controlled entirely. Such programs typically include education about pain and its consequences, pain control methods such as relaxation or exercise, attempts to change maladaptive expectations about pain, and social interventions with families or support groups.

Researchers have reported that pain management programs are successful in treating a wide variety of pain problems stemming from

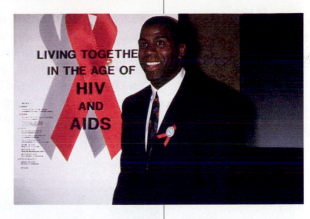

▲ Basketball superstar Ervin (Magic) Johnson became a spokesman for increasing awareness of HIV and AIDS after he tested HIV positive.

various underlying conditions, including headaches, lower back pain, and facial pain. Following treatment, patients report greater satisfaction with their life and relationships, improved employment status, and less reliance on medication. Moreover, patients commonly report that their pain has lessened once they are better able to function in their lives (Taylor, 1995). It is not clear whether improved life functioning actually reduces pain or just reduces patients' awareness of discomfort. In either case, however, these positive results offer strong justification for using behavioral medicine in the treatment of chronic pain.

Cardiovascular Disease

In order to illustrate the complexities of research and treatment relating stress to physical illness, we focus on the very important problem of cardiovascular disease in considerable detail. **Cardiovascular disease (CVD)** is a group of disorders that affect the heart and circulatory system. The most important of these illnesses are **hypertension** (high blood pressure) and **coronary heart disease (CHD).** Hypertension increases the risk for CHD, as well as for other serious disorders, such as stroke. The most deadly and well-known form of coronary heart disease is **myocardial infarction (MI),** commonly called a heart attack.

Cardiovascular disorders are the leading cause of mortality in most industrialized countries, including the United States, where they account for almost half of all deaths. About two-thirds of the deaths due to cardiovascular disorders are caused by coronary heart disease (Jenkins, 1988). Mortality due to CHD is of particular concern because victims of the disease tend to be relatively young. About half of all Americans with CHD and about a quarter of all stroke victims are under the age of 65.

An individual's risk for developing CVD, and particularly CHD, is associated with a number of health behaviors, including weight, diet, exercise, and cigarette smoking, as we saw in the case of Bob Carter. This link between CVD and lifestyle is one reason why health psychology is so important in preventing and treating these disorders. Psychology also is important in understanding hypertension and heart disease, because behavioral and physical risk indicators account for only about half of all cases of CHD (Jenkins, 1988). In addition to health behavior, personality styles, behavior patterns, and forms of emotional expression appear to contribute directly to the development of CVD.

Typical Symptoms and Associated Features of Hypertension and CHD

Hypertension is often referred to as the "silent killer" because it produces no obvious symptoms. For this reason, high blood pressure often goes undetected, and routine blood pressure monitoring is extremely important. The measurement of blood pressure includes two readings. *Systolic* blood pressure is the highest pressure that the blood exerts against the arteries. This occurs when the heart is pumping blood. *Diastolic* blood pressure is the lowest amount of pressure that the blood creates against the arteries. This occurs between heartbeats. Generally, hypertension is defined by a systolic reading above 140 and/or a diastolic reading above 90 when measured while the patient is in a relaxed state.

The most notable symptom of CHD is chest pain. Typically, the pain is centralized in the middle of the chest, and it often extends through the left shoulder and down the left arm. In less severe forms of the disorder, the pain that accompanies CHD is mild, or it may be sharp but brief. The pain during more severe forms of CHD such as myocardial infarction typically is so intense that it is crippling. In fact, MI often results in sudden death. Two-thirds of all deaths from CHD occur within 24 hours of a coronary event (Kamarck & Jennings, 1991). In over half of these sudden deaths, the victim received no previous treatment for CHD, an indication that either there were no warning symptoms or the symptoms were mild enough to have been ignored. Research using portable electrocardiogram monitoring and diary recordings indicates that many episodes of inadequate oxygen supply to the heart occur outside of the patient's awareness (Krantz et al., 1993; Schneiderman, Chesney, & Krantz, 1989).

CLASSIFICATION OF CVD

Myocardial infarction and angina pectoris are the two major forms of coronary heart disease. *Angina pectoris* involves intermittent chest pains that are usually brought on by some form of exertion. Attacks of angina do not damage the heart, but the chest pain can be a sign of underlying pathology that puts the patient at risk for a myocardial infarction. MI (heart attack) does involve damage to the heart, and as noted, it often causes *sudden cardiac death*, which is usually defined as death within 24 hours of a coronary episode.

Hypertension can be primary or secondary. *Secondary hypertension* results from a known problem such as a diagnosed kidney or endocrine disorder. It is called secondary hypertension because the high blood pressure is secondary to—that is, a consequence of —the principal physical disorder. Primary or **essential hypertension** is the major concern of behavioral medicine and health psychology. In the case of essential hypertension, the high blood pressure is the principal disorder. There is no single, identifiable cause of essential hypertension, which accounts for approximately 85 percent of all cases of high blood pressure. Instead, multiple physical and behavioral risk factors are thought to contribute to the primary disorder, elevated blood pressure.

Epidemiology of CVD

Infectious diseases were the leading cause of death in the United States for the first two decades of the twentieth century, but since the 1920s cardiovascular disease has been the nation's leading killer. Cardiovascular disease is also the major cause of death in most other industrialized countries, but some important differences among nations have emerged in recent years. The rate of death due to CVD has declined by 25 percent or more in the United States, Japan, and many Western European countries, whereas mortality rates attributed to CVD have increased in many Eastern European countries. Some of these differences in recent trends seem attributable to changes in diet, cigarette smoking, and blood pressure, but improved health behavior does not fully account for the recent epidemiological differences (Jenkins, 1988). Such differences provide a fascinating challenge for researchers to explain. The increased awareness of the negative effects of stress in the West—and the increased industrialization that may raise maladaptive stress levels in Eastern Europe—may be part of the explanation.

RISK FACTORS FOR CHD

Epidemiological studies have identified several risk indicators for CHD. Men are twice as likely to suffer from CHD as are women; these sex differences are even greater with more severe forms of the disorder. Age is another major risk factor. For men, risk for CHD increases in a linear fashion with increasing age after 40. For women, risk for CHD accelerates more slowly until they reach menopause and increases sharply afterwards. Rates of CHD also are higher among low-income groups, a finding that likely accounts for the higher rates of CHD among black than among white Americans. Finally, a positive family history is also linked to an increased risk for CHD, due at least in part to genetic factors (Jenkins, 1988).

In addition to these background factors, several health behaviors have been linked to CHD. Hypertension increases the risk for CHD by a factor of 2 to 4. The risk for CHD also is 2 to 3 times greater among those who smoke a pack or more of cigarettes a day. Obesity, a fatty diet, elevated serum cholesterol levels, heavy alcohol consumption, and lack of exercise are also related to an increased risk for CHD. Specific risk ratios are difficult to identify for each of these factors, however, because weight, diet, cholesterol, alcohol consumption, and exercise all are closely interrelated (Jenkins, 1988).

Also, it is difficult to calculate the specific risk for CHD associated with psychological characteristics other than health behaviors. This is because of difficulties in measuring some relevant behavioral styles and because of conflicting findings in epidemiologic research. For example, a great deal of research on the psychological contributions to CHD has focused on what is known as the Type A behavior pattern,

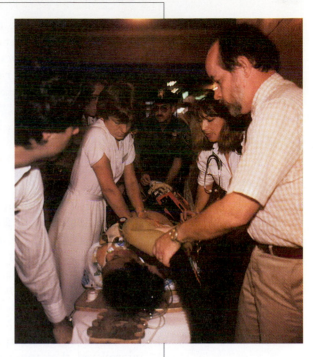

▲ Cardiovascular disease is the leading cause of death in the United States. It is a lifestyle illness that is related to poor health behavior, stress, and anger.

which is a highly driven, competitive personality type. In 1981, the National Heart, Lung, and Blood Institute officially concluded that Type A behavior increased the risk for CHD independently of other health behaviors. However, recent research has challenged this conclusion, as we discuss shortly.

RISK FACTORS FOR HYPERTENSION

About 30 percent of all U.S. adults suffer from hypertension, and many of the same risk factors that predict CHD also predict high blood pressure, including genetic factors, a high salt diet, health behavior, and lifestyle factors. Hypertension is more common in industrialized countries, and in the United States, high blood pressure is found with greater frequency among men, African Americans, low-income groups, and people exposed to high levels of chronic life stress. Although many of these risk factors are interrelated, they appear to have independent effects in increasing the prevalence of hypertension. For example, one study found that hypertension was twice as common among blacks as whites, but among black men who lived in high-stress neighborhoods, the risk was 4 times as great (Roberts & Rowland, 1981).

Etiological Considerations and Research on CVD

BIOLOGICAL FACTORS IN CVD

The immediate cause of CHD is the deprivation of oxygen to the heart muscle. No permanent damage is caused by the temporary oxygen deprivation (*myocardial ischemia*) that accompanies angina pectoris, but part of the heart muscle dies in cases of myocardial infarction. Oxygen deprivation can be caused by temporarily increased oxygen demands on the heart, for example, as a result of exercise. More problematic is when atherosclerosis causes the gradual deprivation of the flow of blood (and the oxygen it carries) to the heart. *Atherosclerosis* is the thickening of the coronary artery wall that occurs as a result of the accumulation of blood lipids (fats) with age. The most dangerous circumstance is when the oxygen deprivation is sudden, as occurs in a *coronary occlusion*. Coronary occlusions result either from arteries that are completely blocked by fatty deposits or from blood clots that make their way to the heart muscle.

The immediate biological causes of hypertension are less well understood, as are the more distant biological causes of both hypertension and CHD. As we noted, a positive family history is a risk factor for both hypertension and CHD, and most experts interpret this association as indicating a genetic contribution to CVD. However, the specific mediating mechanism has yet to be identified. Moreover, research on animal models of CVD suggests that heritable risk interacts with environmental risk. For example, rats prone to develop hypertension do so only when exposed to salty diets or environmental stress (Schneiderman, Chesney, & Krantz, 1989). Other biological risk factors for CVD, such as obesity and elevated serum cholesterol, involve health behaviors, and therefore we consider them as a part of psychological contributions to the disease.

PSYCHOLOGICAL FACTORS IN CVD

The most important of the known psychological contributions to CVD are the wide variety of health behaviors that (1) have a well-documented association with heart disease; (2) decrease the risk for CVD when they are modified; and (3) often are difficult to change. CVD is a *lifestyle disease*, a clear example of the inextricable link between behavior and physical health. Avoiding or quitting smoking, maintaining a proper weight, following a low-cholesterol diet, exercising frequently, monitoring blood pressure regularly, and taking anti-hypertensive medication as prescribed can all reduce the risk of heart disease. Our bodies need routine maintenance, much as any machinery does.

Stress also contributes to CVD, in two different ways. First, stress increases blood pressure and heart rate, thus taxing the cardiovascular system and sometimes precipitating immediate symptoms or broader episodes of CHD. As in the case of Bob Carter, many people report that stress sets off both the minor symptoms of angina pectoris and the major problem of a myocardial infarction. Second, some theories suggest that over the long run the heart can be worn out by constant stress—much like a car that is chronically abused by its driver, especially when routine maintenance is ignored. In the following sections, we consider three areas of research linking stress to cardiovascular disease: (1) cardiovascular reactivity to stress, (2) actual exposure to life stress, and (3) characteristic styles of responding to stress (Krantz et al., 1988).

Cardiovascular Reactivity to Stress Increased blood pressure and heart rate are normal reactions to stress, but researchers have long observed that different people exhibit different

cardiovascular reactivity to stress—greater or lesser increases in blood pressure and heart rate when they are exposed to stress in the laboratory. Are people who show greater cardiovascular reactivity to stress more likely to develop CVD?

The cardiovascular reactivity hypothesis is increasingly supported by research on patients with CHD (Krantz et al., 1988). Patients with coronary disease show greater cardiovascular reactivity to stress than nonpatients (Corse et al., 1982), and diastolic blood pressure reactivity predicted the subsequent development of CHD in one study (Keys et al., 1971). In a recent study of patients with coronary artery disease, patients who reacted to mental stress in the laboratory with greater myocardial ischemia (oxygen deprivation to the heart) had a higher rate of fatal and nonfatal cardiac events over the next 5 years in comparison to their less reactive counterparts. In fact, mental stress was a better predictor of subsequent cardiac events than was physical stress (exercise testing) (Jiang et al., 1996).

In many respects, it is impressive that cardiovascular reactivity in the laboratory predicts subsequent heart disease, because people are exposed to different degrees of stress in their real life. A high-level cardiovascular reactivity will have little effect on an individual if he or she experiences little stress. Thus actual life stress must also be considered in the equation that predicts cardiovascular disease.

Life Stressors and CVD: Job Strain as an Example Considerable evidence does indicate that exposure to chronic stress increases risk for cardiovascular disease (Krantz et al., 1988). For example, researchers have linked increased rates of coronary heart disease with high-stress occupations. A stressful job is more than just a demanding job. What appears to be most important is *job strain*, a situation that pairs high psychological demands with a low degree of decisional control (Karasek et al., 1982). A waitress has relatively high demands and low control, for instance, whereas a forest ranger has relatively few demands and a high degree of control. Figure 8–5 portrays a number of occupations and how they vary in terms of psychological demands and decisional control.

Several studies have found a relationship between job strain and CHD (Krantz et al., 1988). For example, among women who participated in the Framingham Heart Study—a major longitudinal study of the development of coronary

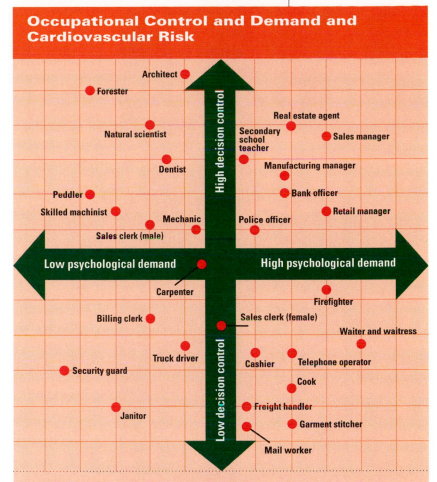

FIGURE 8-5: Occupations classified according to the degree of demand and control that are associated with them. Jobs with low control and high demands are associated with increased cardiovascular risk.

Source: From R.A. Karasek, 1988. Cited in D.S. Krantz, R.J. Contrada, D.R. Hill, and E. Friedler, Environmental stress and biobehavioral antecedents of coronary heart disease, *Journal of Consulting and Clinical Psychology,* 56, 334.

heart disease—the risk for CHD was 1½ times higher among those who were rated as having high job strain based on objective evaluations of their occupations. The risk was 3 times higher among women whose self-reports indicated high job strain (LaCroix & Haynes, 1987).

Such strains are not limited to employment, but include work that is performed in other life roles. In an earlier analysis of women in the Framingham study, women who were employed for more than half of their adult lives were no more likely to develop CHD than were homemakers. However, working women with children were more likely to suffer from heart disease. In fact, the risk for CHD increased with the number of children for working women but not for homemakers (Haynes & Feinleib, 1980). This finding echoes the dilemma of contemporary women who feel strains not only within their occupation but also among their

▲ These stock traders illustrate the Type A behavior pattern. Type A is a personality style characterized by competitiveness, hostility, urgency, impatience, and achievement striving in response to challenge.

various family roles.

Type A Behavior and Hostility Characteristic styles of responding to stress may also increase the risk for CVD. In particular, much research has focused on the increased risks associated with the **Type A behavior pattern**—a competitive, hostile, urgent, impatient, and achievement-striving style of responding to challenge. As originally identified by cardiologists Meyer Friedman and Ray Rosenman (1959), the *Type A* individual is a "superachiever" who knows no obstacle to success and who may sacrifice everything for the sake of achievement (Jenkins, 1988). *Type B* individuals, in contrast, are more calm and content. The case of Bob Carter is an example of someone who is Type A; Bob Carter would not allow anything to beat him, including a heart attack.

Friedman and Rosenman developed a structured interview for identifying Type A behavior. The interviewer not only asks people about their achievement striving, urgency, and hostility but also provokes those very behaviors in the context of a high-stress interview. The classification of Type A based on the interview has predicted CHD in several prospective, longitudinal investigations (see Research Methods), most notably the Western Collaborative Group Study conducted by Rosenman, Friedman, and colleagues (Booth-Kewley & Friedman, 1987). In fact, the National Blood, Heart, and Lung Institute concluded in 1981 that Type A was a risk factor for CHD independent of other risks (e.g., diet).

This official sanction stimulated a great deal of additional research, but many studies conducted since 1980 have failed to support earlier findings (Matthews, 1988). Results across all studies document Type A behavior among 70 percent of middle-aged men with heart disease, whereas 46 percent of men without heart disease exhibit Type A behavior. Research methods may contribute to the conflicting findings. Observation of behavior seems to be an important method, because prediction of heart disease is better when Type A is assessed from Friedman and Rosenman's structured interview than from self-report measures (Miller et al., 1991).

Researchers also have identified a substantive explanation for the conflicting findings. It now appears that only certain elements of Type A behavior increase the risk for CHD. In particular, *hostility* is a more consistent predictor of future heart disease than other aspects of Type A behavior or the pattern as a whole (Booth-Kewley & Friedman, 1987; Matthews, 1988; Miller et al., 1996; Schneiderman, Chesney, & Krantz, 1989). For example, a Finnish investigation found that three items reliably predicted death among men who had a history of CHD or hypertension: ease with which anger was aroused, argumentativeness, and irritability (Koskenvuo et al., 1988).

We should note that hostility and Type A behavior likely interact with both cardiovascular reactivity and exposure to life stress in increasing the risk for heart disease. Evidence indicates that hostile, Type A people are more physiologically reactive to stress (as measured by heart rate and blood pressure) than are their Type B counterparts (Lyness, 1993). We can safely assume that hostile, competitive people also are more likely to create and perhaps seek added stress in their lives, as well as to have less social support available to them (Miller et al., 1996).

SOCIAL FACTORS IN CVD
The research we already have reviewed makes it clear that CVD is affected by both interpersonal relations and broader societal influences. As you may recognize from your own life, social support from friends and family members, as well as from professionals, can encourage a healthy—or an unhealthy—lifestyle (Rook & Dooley, 1985). Interpersonal conflict obviously is a source of much of the anger and hostility that can increase the risk for coronary heart disease. In fact, research demonstrates that economic resources, being married, and/or having a close confidant all predict a more positive prognosis among patients with coronary artery disease (Williams et al., 1992). Finally, the cross-cultural differences in the epidemiology of CVD surely are influenced by a range of societal

Longitudinal Research Designs

We have already reviewed problems with attempting to infer causation from correlation in Research Methods in Chapter 2. Analogue experiments, which were considered in Research Methods in Chapter 5, are one alternative to correlational designs. Analogue experiments are frequently used in stress research. One example that you have already encountered is the analogue experiment with laboratory animals. Animal analogue studies in stress research have the advantages of (1) systematically controlling exposure to stressors and (2) being able to obtain direct measures of physiological and anatomic outcomes. Still, many important questions about stress and illness can be answered only with research on humans; however, ethical and practical constraints often prohibit the use of the experimental method with humans.

The **longitudinal study** is one research design that allows researchers to draw inferences about causation from a correlational study. Subjects are studied over time in a longitudinal study, an approach that contrasts with the more common **cross-sectional study** in which subjects are studied only at one point in time. The basic goal of a longitudinal study is to determine whether hypothesized causes come before their assumed effects. We know that causes must precede effects in time. The bat must be swung before the ball can be hit over the fence. If we can demonstrate that stress comes before heart disease in longitudinal research, this helps scientists to rule out the alternative interpretation (reverse causality) that the illness caused the stress.

As you can easily recognize, a major liability of a longitudinal study is higher cost. It is much less expensive to study both stress and heart disease at one point in time than it is to assess stress now and CHD as it develops over the next 10 years. One way around this problem is to use the *retrospective, or follow-back, study.* In this research design,

scientists look backwards in time either by asking subjects to recall past events or by examining records from the past. The retrospective method is relatively inexpensive, but it is of limited value because of distorted memories and limited records (see Research Methods in Chapter 7).

The **prospective,** or follow-up, **design** is a more effective and more expensive alternative to the follow-back method. In prospective research, supposed causes are assessed in the present, and subjects are then followed to see if the hypothesized effects develop over time. Using the follow-up method, scientists can assess a range of possible predictors more thoroughly and more objectively than in follow-back studies. For example, scientists can use standardized tests to measure a wide variety of personality characteristics like Type A behavior in their subjects over time.

Researchers have used both retrospective and prospective methods fairly often in studying both health and illness and abnormal psychology in general. You will encounter both methods in discussions of a variety of mental health issues throughout this text. When you learn that a finding was supported in prospective longitudinal research, you can have greater confidence in the investigator's hypothesis about causality than if the research was cross-sectional. Remember, however, that correlation does not mean causation, even in a longitudinal study. It remains possible that the supposed "cause" and the "effect" both result from some third variable. For example, a researcher might find that Type A behavior measured at one point in time predicts CHD several years later. But chronic job stress may cause both the Type A behavior and the heart disease. Scientists need many studies utilizing many different types of research methods in order to establish causation. And you need to understand the strengths and weaknesses of research methods, not just the results of a single study, in order to be an informed consumer of scientific information. ■

values, such as attitudes about health behaviors like smoking and cultural norms about competition in the workplace.

Experts recognize the importance of interpersonal and societal influences on CVD and on

physical health in general. A multitude of efforts have been directed toward structuring the *social ecology*—the interrelations between the individual and the social world—in such a way as to promote health (Stokols, 1992). As a child, you were exposed to many of these efforts, such as antismoking campaigns or the awards given in school for physical fitness. Health promotion is a common message in the media, and more and more employers also are encouraging health maintenance. Do these broad-scale efforts work? We address this question and other issues in treating CVD, after briefly discussing the integration of risk factors.

INTEGRATION AND ALTERNATIVE PATHWAYS

Much progress has been made in identifying biological, psychological, and social risk factors for CVD, a prime example of a physical illness that is best explained by the systems approach. An important goal for future research is to integrate knowledge across risk factors. Numerous questions need to be addressed. For example, how do cardiovascular reactivity and the experience of life stress interact in producing risk? How do we distinguish the effects of stress as an immediate, precipitating cause of CHD from its cumulative effects on health over long periods of time? To what extent are the risks associated with stress caused by poor health behavior and not by stress itself? What are the alternative pathways to the development of CHD? What protects those individuals who do not become ill even when they are exposed to multiple risk factors?

In considering these questions, we return to the analogy between the functioning of the cardiovascular system and an automobile. Some cars are built for high performance, some for economy. Some are defective when they leave the factory. Whatever the original condition of the new automobile, its state of repair is affected by how it is driven and how it is maintained. Like make and the wear and tear on different automobiles, the multiple pathways and multiple risk factors that cause CVD combine genetic makeup, an occasional structural defect, maintenance in the form of health behavior, and how hard the heart is driven by stress, coping, and societal standards. Even though some cars and some hearts operate well after being abused, routine maintenance is prudent in all cases. We should attempt to minimize each risk factor associated with CVD. As we noted at the beginning of the chapter, however, avoidance of life's challenges is *not* the way to avoid heart disease. A moderate amount of use is healthy for a car, and a moderate amount of stress may be healthy for the heart.

Prevention and Treatment of Cardiovascular Disease

Several medications known as *antihypertensives* are effective treatments for reducing high blood pressure. Other drugs, called *beta blockers*, reduce the risk of myocardial infarction or sudden coronary death following a cardiac episode (Johnston, 1989). Still other biomedical interventions reduce the risk factors associated with CVD. For example, serum cholesterol can be lowered with medication.

Because many of the risk factors for CVD are linked with health behavior, it may be possible to reduce or prevent heart disease with psychological intervention. In the following sections, we consider efforts to alter lifestyle and to lower the risk for heart disease in terms of the three levels of intervention introduced in Chapter 3: primary, secondary, and tertiary prevention.

PRIMARY PREVENTION

As we have noted, numerous public service advertisements attempt to prevent CVD by encouraging people to quit smoking, eat well, exercise, monitor their blood pressure, and otherwise improve their health behavior. Most of these familiar efforts have not been evaluated systematically, although researchers have conducted a handful of careful studies.

One of the most important studies took place in three small California communities near Stanford University (Farquhar et al., 1977). Media campaigns designed to improve knowledge and change the behavior that makes up CHD risk factors were offered in two towns that formed the experimental groups, whereas no intervention was given in one town that was used as a control group. The media campaigns were supplemented with face-to-face interviews in one of the two towns receiving the intervention. Findings indicated that the media campaigns increased the public's knowledge about CHD in the experimental communities, particularly in the community where face-to-face interviews took place.

Did this increased knowledge lead to actual changes in behavioral? The answer appears to be yes, up to a point. People in the experimental communities improved their diet and lowered their serum cholesterol, but they made only minor changes in their smoking behaviors (Farquhar et al., 1977). The study could not determine whether the interventions helped reduce the incidence of heart disease, but scientists are conducting studies to address this question (Johnston, 1989). (Recall that the rates of CVD have declined in Western countries as health behavior has improved.) Thus it appears that increasing public awareness of risk factors can (slowly) alter health behavior and eventually may lower the risk of heart disease.

SECONDARY PREVENTION

The treatment of essential hypertension is one of the most important attempts at the secondary prevention of CHD, because hypertension is a significant risk factor for heart disease. Treatments of hypertension fall into two categories. One focuses on improving health behavior, and the other emphasizes **stress management,** attempts to teach more effective coping skills.

Improvements in health behavior—including weight reduction, decreased alcohol consumption, and reduced intake of dietary salt—can help lower blood pressure. For many patients these behavioral changes eliminate the need for taking antihypertensive medication (Johnston, 1989). What is less clear is the extent to which psychological intervention brings about improvements in health behavior. Available evidence suggests that psychological intervention is minimally effective at best, in part because many attempts to change health behavior are weak or poorly constructed. For example, physicians may simply encourage their patients to lose weight or give them educational pamphlets to read. More intensive treatments appear to be more effective in changing health behavior, although more research is needed on their effectiveness (Johnston, 1989).

The major form of stress management used with hypertensives is behavior therapy, particularly relaxation training (see Chapter 3) and biofeedback. **Biofeedback** uses laboratory equipment to monitor physiological processes that generally occur outside conscious awareness and to provide the patient with conscious feedback about these processes. Blood pressure may be displayed on a video screen, for example, so that increases or decreases are readily apparent to the patient.

Biofeedback is based on the theory that people can learn to control their autonomic nervous system functions. This is an innovation conceptually and practically, because the functions of the autonomic nervous system traditionally have been viewed as uncontrollable, as conveyed by

the term *autonomic*. During biofeedback, the patient can experiment with various coping strategies and observe whether the techniques are successful in lowering blood pressure (or whatever autonomic response is being monitored).

Both relaxation training and biofeedback produce reliable, short-term reductions in blood pressure. Unfortunately, the reductions are small, are often temporary, and are considerably less than those produced by antihypertensive medications (Andrews et al., 1984). Although these stress management treatments occasionally may be a useful adjunct to medication, they are not an alternative at this point in time. In particular, the viability of biofeedback has not been supported by empirical evidence, and some well-respected investigators have suggested that this technique should be abandoned altogether as a treatment for hypertension (Johnston, 1989).

The Trials of Hypertension Prevention (TOHP) is the most important ongoing study of whether stress management and health behavior interventions succeed in lowering high blood pressure (TOHP Collaborative Research Group, 1992). In this investigation, more than 2,000 women and men with hypertension were randomly assigned to one of seven different treatments. Treatments included three lifestyle interventions—weight reduction, sodium (salt) reduction, and stress management—plus four nutritional supplement conditions. Group meetings were held over several weeks for the three lifestyle interventions. In the nutrition conditions, the patient's ordinary diet was supplemented with dietary agents hypothesized to lower blood pressure: either calcium, magnesium, potassium, or fish oil. Results from Phase I of the study indicated that only the weight reduction and the salt reduction programs were successful in lowering blood pressure over a follow-up period of up to $1\frac{1}{2}$ years. Neither stress management nor any of the dietary supplements produced beneficial effects on blood pressure. The TOHP currently is examining the effects of combined treatments and long-term outcomes, but data from this Phase II of the investigation are not yet available.

Other attempts at the secondary prevention of CHD have tried to change several health behaviors at once rather than focusing on hypertension alone. The Multiple Risk Factor Intervention Trial (MRFIT) is another important investigation. In this study, over 12,000 men with a high risk for developing CHD were assigned at random to intervention and control groups, and the effectiveness of intervention was evaluated over time. Carefully developed intervention programs, including both education and social support, produced improved health behavior, including reduced smoking and lower serum cholesterol. However, during the 7 years following intervention the men randomly assigned to the treatment groups did not have a lower incidence of heart disease than the men in the control group (MRFIT, 1982). An encouraging interpretation of this discouraging outcome is that the failure to find a treatment effect may have been due to the improved health behavior of the men in the control group. The control group had a lower disease rate than was expected based on their risk indicators, and the study was conducted during a time when the public's concern with health increased dramatically.

TERTIARY PREVENTION

Tertiary prevention of CHD targets patients who have already had a cardiac event, typically a myocardial infarction. The hope is to reduce the incidence of recurrence of the illness. Exercise programs are probably the most common treatment recommended for cardiac patients, but evidence of their effectiveness is limited (Johnston, 1989). Some evidence suggests that carefully implemented exercise training programs can reduce the risk for cardiovascular death for up to 3 years (O'Connor et al., 1989). Other researchers have found that treatment programs may dramatically reduce death rates if they are individualized and target multiple health behaviors (Frasure-Smith & Prince, 1985). One patient may benefit from entering a smoking reduction program, a second may be helped by a stress reduction workshop, and a third may be assisted by exercise classes. Together, the findings on successful programs underscore the need to offer behavioral medicine programs that are both highly structured and carefully tailored to the individual (see Blanchard, 1992). Handing out educational pamphlets or delivering stern lectures in the physician's office does little to alter health behavior, as we saw in the case of Bob Carter.

Some of the most optimistic evidence on the treatment of CHD comes from studies of interventions designed to alter the Type A behavior pattern (Friedman et al., 1986), a somewhat surprising circumstance given the controversies about the risk research on Type A we discussed earlier. Intervention with Type A individuals following myocardial infarction is multifaceted. For example, it includes **role playing**—improvisational play acting—to teach patients how to respond to stressful interactions with reduced hostility. In role playing, cardiac patients act out their usual responses to such situations as dealing with a bothersome subordinate, and the therapist models alternative, less hostile means of responding to the frustration. In subsequent role plays, the patients try out the new way of coping. Cognitive therapy designed to alter faulty thought patterns also is a part of the intervention with Type A cardiac patients (Thoresen & Powell, 1992). For example, clinicians may use rational–emotive therapy to challenge patients' beliefs about their self-worth and professional goals (see Chapter 3). At some level, for example, Bob Carter probably believed that he *must* be the best at everything he did in life. One goal of cognitive therapy is to help patients like Bob to develop beliefs and goals that are more realistic—and healthy.

Although evidence is not definitive, studies suggest that Type A behavior can be modified, and this may reduce the subsequent risk for CHD (Nunes, Frank, & Kornfeld, 1987; Thoresen & Powell, 1992). One study of nearly 600 patients found that stress management training reduced the annual incidence of cardiac events by almost 50 percent in comparison to 300 patients who received standard medical care (Friedman et al., 1986). Importantly, subjects who showed the greatest reduction in Type A behavior were 4 times less likely to experience a myocardial infarction during the following 2 years.

As a final note, we should mention that some important psychological treatments focus on the *effects* of heart disease on life stress rather than the other way around. Several investigators have helped cardiac patients cope more successfully with the anxiety and depression that often result from having a heart attack, as well as with the effects of a myocardial infarction on their everyday life. Coronary patients frequently report difficulties with depression, sexuality, marriage and family relationships, and accepting the necessary restrictions on normal activities (Johnston, 1985). In turn, researchers recently have identified depression as a risk factor for subsequent cardiac illness (Carney, Freeland, Rich, & Jaffe, 1995). Psychological treatment can help patients with CHD and their families adjust to the illness. In turn, treating depression and family distress may improve the patient's physical health. The link between stress and physical health clearly is reciprocal, as the systems theory would lead us to expect.

Summary

Stress can be defined broadly as a challenging event that requires physiological, cognitive, or behavioral adaptation. For many years, scientists thought that germs or infectious disease caused most physical illnesses, although some scientists argued that psychological stress contributed to a limited number of **psychosomatic disorders.** However, the DSM no longer contains a list of psychosomatic disorders, because medical scientists now view every physical illness as a product of the interaction between the psyche and soma, mind and body. This holistic view has influenced both psychology and medicine, as is evidenced by the rapid development of **behavioral medicine,** a multidisciplinary field that investigates psychological factors in physical illness.

Scientists disagree about whether stress is best defined in terms of a life event (a stimulus), an adverse reaction (a response), or a stimulus-response combination. Each approach has advantages and disadvantages for research purposes. Despite this controversy, much is known about people's reactions to stress. The **fight or flight response** is a reaction to a threat that is activated by stress and is characterized by intense arousal of the sympathetic nervous system. The **general adaptation syndrome (GAS)** is a more global response to stress that includes the stages of alarm, resistance, and exhaustion. Both responses are mediated by the secretion of hormones from the adrenal gland, including epinephrine/norepinephrine and glucocorticoids. Recent research on **psychoneuroimmunology (PNI)** has identified yet another physiological consequence of stress, less adequate functioning of the immune system.

Emotional responses to stress are especially likely to include increased anxiety, depression, and anger. Coping with these reactions may involve **problem-focused coping,** which is an attempt to change the stressor, or **emotion-focused coping,** which is an attempt to alter distress internally. Critical cognitive processes include **primary appraisal,** the individual's evaluation of the threat posed by a stressor, and **secondary appraisal,** the evaluation of one's ability to cope with a stressor. Predictability and control are other key cognitive evaluations that can greatly facilitate coping.

Behavioral responses to stress include not only attempts to avoid or alter a stressor but also the search for other outlets for frustration. Poor **health behavior** can be another behavioral consequence of stress, including a decrease in positive actions (e.g., exercise) or an increase in negative actions (e.g., alcohol consumption). Illness behavior, behaving as if you were sick, also is stress-related. Finally, it is clear that illness can cause stress, as well as stress causing illness.

The DSM-IV has no list of stress-related or psychosomatic illnesses, because psychological factors are deemed important in all physical illnesses. The essential role of stress in illness is highlighted by the inclusion of two separate diagnostic axes. Physical illnesses that are relevant to mental condition are coded on Axis III,

KEY TERMS

- acquired immune deficiency syndrome (AIDS)
- behavioral medicine
- biofeedback
- cardiovascular disease (CVD)
- cardiovascular reactivity
- coronary heart disease (CHD)
- cross-sectional study
- emotion-focused coping
- essential hypertension
- fight or flight response
- general adaptation syndrome (GAS)
- health behavior
- health psychology
- hypertension
- longitudinal study
- myocardial infarction (MI)
- primary appraisal
- primary sleep disorder
- problem-focused coping
- prospective design
- psychoneuroimmunology (PNI)
- psychosomatic disorder
- role playing
- secondary appraisal
- stress
- stress management
- Type A behavior pattern

general medical conditions, often in association with the Axis I diagnosis of psychological factors affecting medical condition. The DSM-IV also contains a separate axis for coding stressors, Axis IV, psychosocial and environmental problems.

Infectious diseases were the most common causes of death in the United States in 1900, but lifestyle plays a central role in seven of the top 10 causes of death in the United States today. Cancer would seem to be a purely biological illness, but behavior contributes to cancer through exposure to some carcinogens, health behavior, social support in coping with the illness, and perhaps through effects on immune functioning. **Aquired immune deficiency syndrome (AIDS)** is caused by the human immunodeficiency virus (HIV), which is transmitted through risky behaviors, such as unprotected sex and shared hypodermic needles. Psychologists also work to help people cope with chronic pain, most notably through pain management programs.

The complexities of research on stress and physical illness are illustrated by evidence on the number-one killer in the United States today, **cardiovascular disease (CVD),** disorders that affect the heart and circulatory system. Cardiovascular diseases include **essential hypertension** (high blood pressure) and **coronary heart disease (CHD),** particularly **myocardial infarction (MI),** or heart attack. Several health behaviors have been linked to CVD, and other psychological factors may also contribute to CVD. These include **cardiovascular reactivity,** responses to stressors presented in a laboratory; chronic stressors in real life (for example, job strain); and the **Type A behavior pattern,** a characterological response to challenge. Recent evidence suggests that hostility may be the central Type A characteristic related to CHD.

The primary prevention of CHD includes attempts to encourage people to improve their health behaviors. The treatment of hypertension through improved health behaviors or **stress management** is one of the more important attempts at the secondary prevention of CHD. Tertiary prevention of CHD targets patients who have already had a cardiac event, for example, attempting to modify their Type A behavior.

Critical Thinking

1. How do you define stress in your own life? Based on your own experiences, what dimensions of stress do you think are critical for physical and mental health? What about coping? How do you cope with life's struggles? What are your theories about effective and ineffective coping?

2. Like a moderate amount of physical exercise, exposure to a moderate amount of stress may be adaptive. Why might this be the case? How can people find the balance between being challenged and being "stressed-out"?

3. Many of today's most deadly illnesses are "lifestyle diseases," and this raises the issue of responsibility for lifestyle contributions to physical illnesses. For example, cigarette companies increasingly are being sued by people with lung cancer. Is the company responsible, or is the smoker? What about other illnesses like AIDS? What is society's responsibility for altering lifestyle or treating people whose unhealthy lifestyle contributes to their illness?

4. Pause to think about your lifestyle. How has research on stress and health behavior affected your life? Are pressures to live a healthier lifestyle helpful? Stressful? How much have you been influenced by public service campaigns or other messages to lead a healthier life?

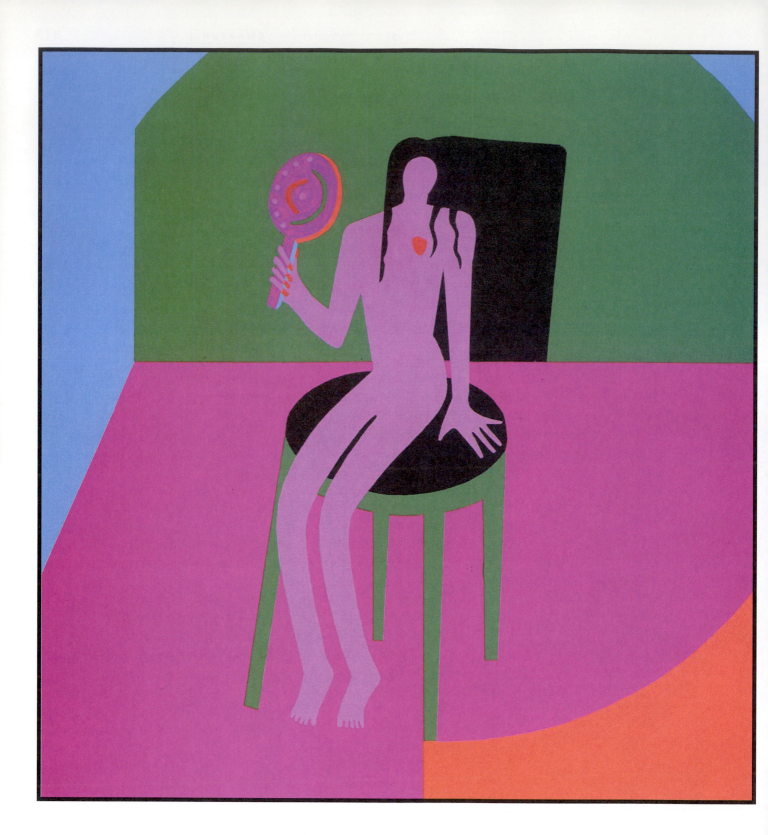

9
Personality Disorders

Personality is an elusive concept that is based largely on our observations of interpersonal behaviors. Most of us find it useful to distinguish between people who are aggressive and those who are not; people who are friendly and outgoing and those who are not; people who are fearful and those who are not. The combination of traits or characteristics that, taken as a whole, describe a person's behavior is considered to be his or her personality. The DSM-IV defines **personality** as "enduring patterns of perceiving, relating to, and thinking about the environment and oneself, which are exhibited in a wide range of important social and personal contexts" (APA, 1994). Without these presumed consistencies in others' behaviors, we would find it difficult to think about and organize our social worlds.

Overview

When these traits bring a person into repeated conflict with others, an individual's personality may be considered disordered. According to the DSM-IV definition of *personality disorder,* the problems must be part of "an enduring pattern of inner experience and behavior that deviates markedly from the expectations of the individual's culture" (APA, 1994). The pattern must be evident in two or more of the following domains: cognition (such as ways of thinking about the self and other people), emotional responses, interpersonal functioning, or impulse control. This pattern of maladaptive experience and behavior must also be:

1. Inflexible and pervasive across a broad range of personal and social situations
2. The source of clinically significant distress or impairment in social, occupational, or other important areas of functioning
3. Stable and of long duration, with an onset that can be traced back at least to adolescence or early adulthood

The impairment associated with most forms of personality disorder causes less personal distress than that found in other types of mental disorder. Some studies estimate that as many as 80 percent of people with personality disorders have never sought professional help for these problems (Samuels et al., 1994).

The personality disorders are among the most controversial categories in the diagnostic system for mental disorders. They are difficult to identify reliably, their etiology is poorly understood, and there is relatively little evidence to indicate that they can be treated successfully. There are important discrepancies between DSM-IV and ICD-10, its European counterpart, in their descriptions of these problems. One type of personality disorder in the U.S. system—narcissistic—is not even included in ICD-10. For all of these reasons, you should think critically about the validity of these categories.

Personality disorders are considered separately from other primary forms of psychopathology in DSM-IV. Most clinical disorders are listed on Axis I, whereas the personality disorders are listed on Axis II. The authors of DSM-IV have organized 10 specific forms of personality disorder into three clusters on the basis of broadly defined characteristics. The specific disorders in each cluster are listed in Table 9–1. The first cluster includes socially isolated people who are odd or eccentric. The second cluster includes flamboyant people, who appear to be excessively dramatic, emotional, or erratic. The third cluster includes people who tend to be anxious and fearful. All of the

TABLE 9-1

Personality Disorders Listed in DSM-IV

Cluster A	Characteristic Features
Paranoid	Distrust and suspiciousness of others
Schizoid	Detachment from social relationships and restricted range of expression of emotions
Schizotypal	Discomfort with close relationships; cognitive and perceptual distortions; eccentricities of behavior

Cluster B	
Antisocial	Disregard for and frequent violation of the rights of others
Borderline	Instability of interpersonal relationships, self-image, emotions, and control over impulses
Histrionic	Excessive emotionality and attention seeking
Narcissistic	Grandiosity, need for admiration, and lack of empathy

Cluster C	
Avoidant	Social inhibition, feelings of inadequacy, and hypersensitivity to negative evaluation
Dependent	Excessive need to be taken care of, leading to submissive and clinging behavior
Obsessive–compulsive	Preoccupation with orderliness and perfectionism at the expense of flexibility

personality disorders are based on exaggerated personality traits that are frequently annoying or disturbing to other people.

The following cases illustrate several of the most important features of personality disorders. Our first case is an example of antisocial personality disorder, which is defined in terms of a pervasive and persistent disregard for, and frequent violation of, the rights of other people. This 21-year-old man was described by Hervey Cleckley in his classic treatise on this topic (Cleckley, 1976). The man had been referred to Cleckley by his parents and his lawyer after his most recent arrest for stealing. The parents hoped that their son might avoid a long prison sentence if Cleckley decided that he was suffering from a mental disorder. Notice that the fundamental features of this man's problems were clearly evident by early adolescence, and they were exhibited consistently over an extended period of time. The stable, long-standing nature of personality disorders is one of their most characteristic features. In this way, they are distinguished from many other forms of abnormal behavior, which are episodic in nature (Hirschfeld, 1993).

CASE STUDY

Antisocial Personality Disorder

Tom looks and is in robust physical health. His manner and appearance are pleasing. In his face a prospective employer would be likely to see strong indications of character as well as high incentive and ability. He is well informed, alert, and entirely at ease, exhibiting a confidence in himself that the observer is likely to consider amply justified. This does not look like the sort of man who will fail or flounder about in the tasks of life but like someone incompatible with all such thoughts.

Evidence of (Tom's) maladjustment became distinct in childhood. He appeared to be a reliable and manly fellow but could never be counted upon to keep at any task or to give a straight account of any situation. He was frequently truant from school. No advice or persuasion influenced him in his acts, despite his excellent response in all discussions. Though he was generously provided for, he stole some of his father's chickens from time to time, selling them at stores downtown. Pieces of table silver would be missed. These were sometimes recovered from those to whom he had sold them for a pittance or swapped them for odds and ends which seemed to hold no particular interest or value for him. He resented and seemed eager to avoid punishment, but no modification in his behavior resulted from it. He did not seem wild or particularly impulsive, a victim of high temper or uncontrollable drives. There was nothing to indicate he was subject to unusually strong temptations, lured by definite plans for high adventure and exciting revolt.

He lied so plausibly and with such utter equanimity, devised such ingenious alibis or simply denied all responsibility with such convincing appearances of candor that for many years his real career was poorly estimated. Among typical exploits with which he is credited stand these: prankish defecation into the stringed intricacies of the school piano, the removal from his uncle's automobile of a carburetor for which he got 75 cents, and the selling of his father's overcoat to a passing buyer of scrap materials.

At 14 or 15 years of age, having learned to drive, Tom began to steal automobiles with some regularity. Often his intention seemed less that of theft than of heedless misappropriation. A neighbor or friend of the family, going to the garage or to where the car was parked outside an office building, would find it missing. Sometimes the patient would leave the stolen vehicle within a few blocks or miles of the owner, sometimes out on the road where the gasoline had given out. After he had tried to sell a stolen car, his father consulted advisers and, on the theory that he might have some specific craving for automobiles, bought one for him as a therapeutic measure. On one occasion while out driving, he deliberately parked his own car and, leaving it, stole an inferior model which he left slightly damaged on the outskirts of a village some miles away.

Private physicians, scoutmasters, and social workers were consulted. They talked and worked with him, but to no avail. Listing the deeds for which he became ever more notable does not give an adequate picture of the situation. He did not every day or every week bring attention to himself by major acts of mischief or destructiveness. He was usually polite, often considerate in small, appealing ways, and always seemed to have learned his lesson after detection and punishment. He was clever and learned easily. During intervals in which his attendance was regular, he impressed his teachers as outstanding in ability. Some charm and apparent modesty, as well as his very convincing way of seeming sincere and to have taken resolutions that would count, kept not only the parents but all who encountered him clinging to hope. Teachers, scoutmasters, the school principal, and others, recognized that in some very important respects he differed from the ordinary bad or wayward youth. (They) made special efforts to help him and to give him new opportunities to reform or readjust.

When he drove a stolen automobile across a state line, he came in contact with federal authorities. In view of his youth and the wonderful impression he made, he was put on probation. Soon afterward he took another automobile and again left it in the adjoining state. It was a very obvious situation. The consequences could not have been entirely overlooked by a person of his excellent shrewdness. He admitted that the considerable risks of getting caught had occurred to him but felt he had a chance to avoid detection and would take it. No unusual and powerful motive or any special aim could be brought out as an explanation.

Tom was sent to a federal institution in a distant state where a well-organized program of rehabilitation and guidance was available. He soon impressed authorities at this place with his attitude and in the way he discussed his past mistakes and plans for a different future. He seemed to merit parole status precociously and this was awarded him. It was not long before he began stealing again and thereby lost his freedom. (Cleckley, 1976, pp. 64–67) ∎

This case provides an excellent example of the senseless nature of the illegal and immoral acts committed by people who meet the diagnostic criteria for antisocial personality disorder. Another puzzling feature of this disorder is the apparent lack of remorse and the inability to learn from experience that accompany such a history of delinquent behavior. It is difficult to understand why someone would behave in this manner. Psychopathologists appeal to the notion of personality disorder to help them understand these irrational behaviors.

The case of Tom also illustrates some other important features of personality disorders. Most other forms of mental disorder, such as anxiety disorders and mood disorders, are *ego-dystonic*; that is, people with these disorders are distressed by their symptoms and uncomfortable with their situations. Personality disorders are usually *ego-syntonic*—the ideas or impulses with which they are associated are acceptable to the person. People with personality disorders frequently do not see themselves as being disturbed. We might also say that they do not have insight into the nature of their own problems. Tom did not believe that his repeated antisocial behavior represented a problem. The other people for whom he created problems were suffering, but he was not. Many forms of personality disorder are defined primarily in terms of the problems that these people create for others rather than in terms of their own subjective distress.

We turn now to another example of personality disorder. The person described in the next case illustrates one of the most important characteristics of personality disorders as they are defined in DSM-IV: overlap among categories. Most people who meet the criteria for one type of personality disorder will also meet the criteria for at least one more. The person in this case met the diagnostic criteria for narcissistic personality disorder and also exhibited some features of histrionic personality disorder. According to DSM-IV, the former is characterized by "grandiosity, lack of empathy, and hypersensitivity to the evaluation of others." The latter is associated with attention seeking and excessive emotionality.

CASE STUDY

Narcissistic Personality Disorder with Histrionic Traits

Lawrence was a 34-year-old professor of English literature at an exclusive private university. He was clever, engaging, and ambitious. The chairperson of the English Department and the university administration considered him to be one of their brightest academic stars, even though he was much younger than most other distinguished faculty members. They treated him with considerable deference, but their efforts were never sufficient to fulfill Lawrence's own expectations for the special consideration that he felt he deserved.

Not surprisingly, Lawrence's colleagues came to view him as pompous and unbearably self-centered. He had a successful record of scholarship for a person of his age, but most of his colleagues in the English Department were similarly productive, and were highly regarded by their peers at other universities. Lawrence refused to acknowledge the accomplishments of his colleagues, and behaved as though he were the only eminent professor in the entire university. Instead of being grateful for the special position he had attained after a series of rapid promotions, Lawrence complained constantly that the university did not know how to treat someone as famous as he. He argued that he was entitled to special privileges. For example, he adamantly refused to teach undergraduate students after he was granted tenure, arguing that undergraduates were not intelligent enough to benefit from the things that he could teach them.

Although Lawrence held an inflated opinion of himself, he also appeared at times to be remarkably insecure. He bombarded colleagues with copies of everything he wrote. His critical reviews and short stories were distributed widely shortly after their publication. His intent was clearly to seek the approval and praise of his peers, who had learned that it was not wise to engage Lawrence by attempting to offer constructive criticism.

Lawrence's personal appearance was also distinctive. Most of his colleagues dressed casually when they were teaching or working in their offices, but Lawrence always insisted on wearing expensive tailored suits. His shirts were carefully pressed and starched, and he wore expensive ties and shoes. His hair was always carefully trimmed and blown dry in a contemporary style that also minimized the effect of his slightly receding hairline and the barely visible thinning patch at the crown of his head. Lawrence was exceedingly sensitive, and responded with surprisingly intense anger if he was teased about these hints that he might be going bald at an early age. He was completely unable to laugh at himself. At the same time, however, he frequently chastised colleagues for the casual way in which they dressed.

Lawrence was married for 10 years before being separated from his wife, Kathleen, and their two young children. The separation had seemed inevitable to everyone who knew the family. Kathleen had always been responsible for all the household chores and for caring for the children, because Lawrence worked at least 12 hours a day, every day of the week. He maintained that this was an eminently fair arrangement because it was Kathleen who had wanted to have children. Given the importance of his academic work, and his unique intellectual talents, he did not believe that his time should be wasted on pedestrian tasks, such as raising his children, that could be accomplished by anyone. He also noted that Kathleen should be happy to have married as handsome and successful a person as he, and that she should be fulfilled simply in being the mother of his children.

One of Lawrence's most annoying characteristics was his complete insensitivity to the feelings of other people. He could be charming and witty, particularly when he was trying to impress someone whom he considered to be (almost) as important as he, but he was also known for his sharp remarks that seemed designed to put other people down. He was particularly likely to say rude things when someone else had become the center of attention and he felt he was being ignored. Parties and celebrations that were called in someone else's honor were particularly difficult for him to handle, especially if the recipient was being honored for an academic achievement. ■

Typical Symptoms and Associated Features

The specific symptoms that are used to define personality disorders represent variations in normal personality traits. Therefore, we must begin our description of typical symptoms with a consideration of several fundamental issues that are involved in the study of normal personality. What is normal personality? Which traits provide the best description of normal personality? And to what extent is personality determined by the culture in which a person is raised? This information will provide a background against which we can then describe the specific symptoms of the 10 types of personality disorder that are included in DSM-IV.

Temperament

By definition, personality disorders are enduring patterns of interacting with one's environment, especially other people. The foundations of these characteristics are presumably evident during childhood. It therefore seems reasonable that our discussion of personality disorders should begin with a brief consideration of interpersonal behaviors during childhood. A critical concept in this consideration is temperament, which refers to characteristic styles of relating to the world, especially those styles that are evident during the first year of life (Campos et al., 1983; Goldsmith et al., 1987). Definitions of temperament typically include response dimensions such as irritability, activity level, and fearfulness. These factors vary considerably in level or degree from one infant to the next and have important implications for later development, such as social and academic adjustment when the child eventually enters school.

Two important qualifications must be made about the development and persistence of individual differences in temperament and personality (Rutter, 1987). First, these differences may not be evident in all situations. Some important personality features may be expressed only under certain challenging circumstances that require or facilitate a particular response. Emotional reactivity is one example.

Some traits are exhibited only when the person is confronted with particular environmental circumstances. Note, for example, that Tom did not always appear to be impulsive. Similarly, Lawrence was not always pompous and overbearing. He could be charming and unpretentious at times, especially when in the presence of an older, distinguished person whom he was trying to impress. His sharp, hostile remarks were most often triggered by situations in which his self-esteem seemed threatened. It was under these circumstances that his narcissistic tendencies could be regularly observed.

The second qualification involves the consequences of exhibiting particular traits. Social circumstances frequently determine whether a specific pattern of behavior will be assigned a positive or negative meaning by other people. Difficult temperament, for example, may serve an adaptive function when it is beneficial for an infant to be demanding and highly visible—for example, during a famine or living in a large institution. On the other hand, in some circumstances, difficult temperament can be associated with an increased risk for certain psychiatric and learning disorders.

Consider the traits that Tom exhibited, especially impulsivity and lack of fear. These characteristics might be maladaptive under normal circumstances, but they could be useful—indeed, admirable—in certain extraordinary settings. War is one extreme example. People in combat situations are frequently called upon to act quickly and decisively, often at great risk to their own physical health. A casual disregard for personal safety might be adaptive under these circumstances. Tom's ability to lie in a calm and convincing fashion was another interesting trait. Again, this might have been a valuable adaptive skill if Tom had been an espionage agent. The meanings that are assigned to particular traits depend on the environment in which they are observed.

Dimensions of Personality

If we grant that there are cross-situational consistencies in some types of behavior, how should these characteristics be described? Experts disagree regarding the basic dimensions of personality (Wiggins & Pincus, 1992). Some theories of normal personality are relatively simple, using only 3 or 4 dimensions. Others are more complicated, and consider as many as 30 or 40 traits.

One widely accepted position is known as the five-factor model of personality (Costa & McCrea, 1992; Goldberg, 1990). The basic traits included in this model are outlined in Table 9–2.

TABLE 9-2		
Brief Description of the Five-Factor Model of Personality		
Global Traits	Characteristics of the High Scorer	Characteristics of the Low Scorer
Neuroticism		
Identifies individuals prone to psychological distress, unrealistic ideas, excessive cravings or urges, and maladaptive coping responses	Worrying, nervous, emotional, insecure, inadequate, hypochondriacal	Calm, relaxed, unemotional, hardy, secure, self-satisfied
Extraversion		
Assesses quantity and intensity of interpersonal interaction; activity level; need for stimulation; and capacity for joy.	Sociable, active, talkative, person-oriented, optimistic, fun-loving, affectionate	Reserved, sober, unexuberant, aloof, task-oriented, retiring, quiet
Openness to Experience		
Assesses proactive seeking and appreciation of experience for its own sake; toleration for and exploration of the unfamiliar.	Curious, broad interests, creative, original, imaginative, untraditional	Conventional, down-to-earth, narrow interests, not artistic, not analytical
Agreeableness		
Assesses the quality of one's interpersonal orientation along a continuum from compassion to antagonism in thoughts, feelings, and actions.	Soft-hearted, good-natured, trusting, helpful, forgiving, gullible, straight-forward	Cynical, rude, suspicious, uncooperative, vengeful, ruthless, irritable, manipulative
Conscientiousness		
Assesses the individual's degree of organization. Contrasts dependable, fastidious people with those who are lackadaisical and sloppy.	Organized, reliable, hardworking, self-disciplined, punctual, scrupulous, neat, ambitious, persevering	Aimless, unreliable, lazy, careless, lax, negligent, weak-willed, hedonistic

Source: Reproduced by special permission of the publisher, Psychological Assessment Resources, Inc., 16204 North Florida Avenue, Lutz, Florida 33549, from the NEO Personality Inventory—Revised by Paul Costa and Robert McCrae, Copyright ® 1978, 1989, 1992 by PAR, Inc. Further reproduction is prohibited without permission of PAR, Inc.

Neuroticism is generally concerned with emotional stability, especially the expression of negative emotions, such as anxiety, depression, and anger. This trait has also been called *negative affectivity* (Watson & Clark, 1984). **Extraversion** describes the person's activity level, especially interest in interacting with other people and the ease with which the person expresses positive emotions. **Openness to experience** involves the

THE FAR SIDE   By GARY LARSON

"The glass is half full!"

"The glass is half empty."

"Half full... No! Wait! Half empty!... No, half... What was the question?"

"Hey! I ordered a cheeseburger!"

The four basic personality types

▼ **Members of different societies have different rules and norms regarding expected social behaviors. Would the DSM-IV descriptions of personality disorders be meaningful for the members of this society in New Guinea?**

person's willingness to consider and explore unfamiliar ideas, feelings, and activities. **Agreeableness** describes the willingness to cooperate and empathize with other people. **Conscientiousness** is a reflection of the person's persistence in the pursuit of goals, ability to organize activities, and dependability in completing expected duties. Taken as a whole, these five dimensions can provide a relatively comprehensive description of any person's behavior.

Many personality disorders are defined in terms of maladaptive variations on the kinds of traits listed in Table 9–2 (Widiger & Costa, 1994). Problems may arise in association with extreme variations in either direction. Consider the following examples. Although most forms of personality disorder are associated with high levels of neuroticism, people with antisocial personality disorder frequently exhibit unusually low levels of anxiety. Similarly, low levels of openness to experience may be associated with rigidity and lack of spontaneity, and high levels of openness may lead to daydreaming, thrill seeking, or preoccupation with bizarre ideas and perceptual illusions. We will return to these dimensions later in this chapter.

Culture and Personality

Personality disorders are presumably defined in terms of behavior that "deviates markedly from the expectations of the individual's culture." In setting this guideline, the authors of DSM-IV recognized that judgments regarding appropriate behavior vary considerably from one society to the next. Some cultures encourage restrained or subtle

displays of emotion, whereas others promote visible, public displays of anger, grief, and other emotional responses. Behavior that seems highly extraverted (or histrionic) in the former cultures might create a very different impression in the latter cultures. Cultures also differ in the extent to which they value *individualism* (the pursuit of personal goals) as opposed to *collectivism* (sharing and self-sacrifice for the good of the group) (Triandis, 1994). Someone who seems exceedingly self-centered and egotistical in a collectivist society might appear to be normal in an individualistic society like the United States.

A number of studies have been conducted regarding normal personality in cross-cultural perspective (Berry, Poortinga, Segall, & Dasen, 1992). These studies emphasize comparisons of *average* or typical personality styles in one society with those in another. Relatively less information is available regarding the extent of *individual differences* within various types of non-Western cultures. The five-factor model, for example, is based primarily on research that has been conducted with college-educated European Americans. It is not clear that these personality dimensions are the most useful way of describing individual differences in personality among people living in other cultures (Lewis-Fernandez & Kleinman, 1994).

The personality disorders may be more closely tied to cultural expectations than any other kind of mental disorder (Frances, First, & Pincus, 1995). More information is needed before we can determine whether the DSM-IV system for describing these problems will be useful in other societies. Two questions are particularly important:

1. In other cultures, what are the personality traits that lead to marked interpersonal difficulties and social or occupational impairment? Are they different than those that have been identified for our own culture?
2. Are the personality disorder syndromes that are defined in DSM-IV (and ICD-10) also found in other cultures?

Some investigators have wondered whether borderline personality disorder and narcissistic personality disorder are unique to Western societies (Lewis-Fernandez & Kleinman, 1994; Tyrer, 1995). Cross-cultural studies that would address this issue must confront a number of difficult methodological problems (see Research Methods). The World Health Organization is sponsoring a large study of personality disorders in 11 countries spanning North America, Europe, Africa, and Asia (Loranger et al., 1994). The results of that study will answer many important questions about the cross-cultural validity of the personality disorders.

RESEARCH METHODS

Cross-Cultural Comparisons

Rules that govern behavior are not the same in all societies. For many years psychologists studied narrowly defined groups of people. Participants in research studies were usually those who were easily recruited, often undergraduate students. Relatively little information was collected from people living in non-Western societies, and even less attention was paid to ethnic and cultural minorities within the United States and other Western countries. Over the past 25 years, psychologists have begun to adopt a broader focus in their consideration of human behavior, including mental disorders.

Culture can be defined as the shared way of life of a group or people (Berry et al., 1992). It is a complex system of accumulated knowledge that helps the people in a particular society to adapt to their environment and also serves to structure interactions among those people. Social traditions that, in combination, make up a culture include patterns of family organization, sex roles, religious beliefs, health care practices, and legal systems. A culture's expectations regarding appropriate forms of behavior are passed down from one generation to the next by a process of social learning.

At the broadest level, culture is a system of meanings that determines the ways in which people think about themselves and their environments. It shapes their most basic view of reality. Consider, for example, the process of bereavement following the death of a close relative. In some Native American cultures, people learn to expect to hear the spirit of the dead person calling to them from the afterworld (Kleinman, 1988). This is a common experience for people in these cultures. It resembles auditory hallucinations (perceptual experiences in the absence of external stimulation) that are seen in people with psychotic disorders. But among some Native American peoples, hearing voices from the dead is a normative response; it is not a sign of dysfunction. Perhaps most importantly, this type of experience is not regularly associated with social or occupational impairment. It would be a mistake therefore to consider these experiences to be symptoms of a mental disorder.

Cross-cultural psychology is the scientific study of ways that human behavior and mental processes are influenced by social and cultural factors (Ho, 1994; Lonner & Malpass, 1994). This field includes the study of *ethnic differences* (among cultural groups living in close proximity within a single nation). Comparison is a fundamental element of any cross-cultural study. Cross-cultural psychologists examine ways in which human behaviors are different, as well as ways in which they are similar, from one culture to the next.

Cross-cultural comparisons are relevant to the study of psychopathology in many ways. One way involves epidemiology—comparisons of the prevalence of disorders across cultures. Investigations aimed at etiological mechanisms, including biological, psychological, and social variables, can also be extremely informative when viewed in cross-cultural perspective. For example, we know that negative patterns of thinking are correlated with depressed mood in middle-class Americans. Is the same relationship found among people living in rural China? Virtually any study of psychopathology would provide useful information if it were replicated in different cultures.

The valuable process of making cross-cultural comparisons can actually be quite difficult. Several complex issues must be faced by investigators who want to study psychopathology in cross-cultural perspective:

1. *Identifying meaningful groups*: The first step in making cross-cultural comparisons

is the selection of participants who are representative members of different cultures. This may be a relatively straightforward process if the comparison is to be made between two small, homogeneous groups (perhaps isolated, rural villages in two very different countries). The situation becomes much more complex if the investigator's goal is to compare ethnic groups within a large, multicultural society such as the United States. Hispanic Americans, for example, include people whose cultural backgrounds can be traced to many different Spanish-speaking homelands with very different cultural traditions, such as Puerto Rico, Mexico, and Cuba. Even greater cultural diversity is found among various Native American peoples. How do we determine which people share a common culture? What is the cultural "unit," and how do we find its boundaries?

2. *Selecting measurement procedures*: Comparison between groups can be valid only if equivalent measurement procedures are used in both cultures (or in all groups). Participants in different cultures often speak different languages (or different dialects). Questionnaires and psychological tests must be cross-validated to ensure that they measure the same concepts in different cultures.

3. *Considering causal explanations*: Suppose that investigators identify a reliable difference between people in two different cultures. They must now decide how to interpret this difference. Is it, in fact, due to *cultural* variables? Would the differences disappear if other variables, such as poverty, education, and age, were held constant between the two groups?

4. *Avoiding culturally biased interpretations*: Investigators, who are often middle-class and white, must interpret cautiously the results of cross-cultural research. In particular, scientists must not interpret *differences* between cultures or ethnic groups as being indicative of *deficits* in minority groups or non-Western cultures. Some cross-cultural psychologists have suggested that it is more important to study developmental processes within cultures or ethnic groups than to compare outcomes between groups. ■

Classification

In the following pages we give brief descriptions of the personality disorder subtypes included in DSM-IV. These brief descriptions provide an overview that will be useful when we review the epidemiology of personality disorders. Later in the chapter we describe in considerably more detail four disorders that are relatively frequent and have been studied extensively: schizotypal, borderline, antisocial, and dependent personality disorders.

Cluster A: Paranoid, Schizoid, and Schizotypal Personality Disorders

Cluster A includes three disorders: paranoid, schizoid, and schizotypal forms of personality disorder. The behavior of people who fit the subtypes in this cluster is typically odd, eccentric, or asocial. All three types share similarity with the symptoms of schizophrenia (see Chapter 13). One implicit assumption in the DSM-IV system is that these types of personality disorder may represent behavioral traits or interpersonal styles that precede the onset of full-blown psychosis. Because of their close association with schizophrenia, they are sometimes called *schizophrenia spectrum* disorders.

Paranoid personality disorder is characterized by the pervasive tendency to be inappropriately suspicious of other people's motives and behaviors. People who fit the description for this disorder are constantly on guard. They expect that other people are trying to harm them, and they take extraordinary precautions to avoid being exploited or injured. Relationships with friends and family members are difficult to maintain because these people don't trust anyone. They frequently overreact in response to minor or ambiguous events to which they attribute hidden meaning.

When they overreact, people with paranoid personality disorder often behave aggressively or antagonistically. These actions can easily create a self-fulfilling prophesy. In other words, thinking (incorrectly) that he or she is being attacked by others, the paranoid person strikes. The other person is, naturally, surprised, annoyed, and perhaps frightened by this behavior, and begins to treat the paranoid person with concern and caution. This response serves to confirm the original suspicions of the paranoid individual, who does not comprehend how his or her own behavior affects others.

Paranoid personality disorder must be distinguished from psychotic disorders, such as schizophrenia and delusional disorder. The pervasive suspicions of people with paranoid personality disorder do not reach delusional proportions. In other words, they are not sufficiently severe to be considered obviously false and clearly preposterous. In actual practice, this distinction is sometimes quite subtle and difficult to make.

Schizoid personality disorder is defined in terms of a pervasive pattern of indifference to other people, coupled with a diminished range of emotional experience and expression. These people are loners; they prefer social isolation to interactions with friends or family. Other people see them as being cold and aloof. By their own report, they do not experience strong subjective emotions, such as sadness, anger, or happiness.

Schizotypal personality disorder centers around peculiar patterns of behavior rather than on the emotional restriction and social withdrawal that are associated with schizoid personality disorder. Many of these peculiar behaviors take the form of perceptual and cognitive disturbance. People with this disorder may report bizarre fantasies and unusual perceptual experiences. Their speech may be slightly difficult to follow because they use words in an odd way or because they express themselves in a vague or disjointed manner. Their affective expressions may be constricted in range, as in schizoid personality disorder, or they may be silly and inappropriate.

In spite of their odd or unusual behaviors, people with schizotypal personality disorder are not psychotic or out of touch with reality. Their bizarre fantasies are not delusional, and their unusual perceptual experiences are not sufficiently real or compelling to be considered hallucinations.

Cluster B: Antisocial, Borderline, Histrionic, and Narcissistic Personality Disorders

Cluster B includes four specific types: antisocial, borderline, histrionic, and narcissistic personality disorders. According to DSM-IV, these

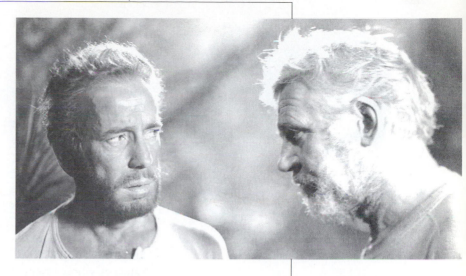

▲ In *The Treasure of the Sierra Madre,* Humphrey Bogart played a prospector whose pervasive paranoia culminated in his murdering his partner and stealing their gold.

disorders are characterized by dramatic, emotional, or erratic behavior, and all are associated with marked difficulty in sustaining interpersonal relationships. The rationale for grouping these disorders together is less compelling than that for Cluster A. In particular, antisocial personality disorder clearly involves something more than just a dramatic style or erratic behavior.

Antisocial personality disorder is defined in terms of a persistent pattern of irresponsible and antisocial behavior that begins during childhood or adolescence and continues into the adult years. The case study of Tom, with which we opened this chapter, illustrates this pattern of behavior. The DSM-IV definition is based on features that, beginning in childhood, indicate a pervasive pattern of disregard for, and violation of, the rights of others. Once the person has become an adult, these difficulties include persistent failure to perform responsibilities that are associated with occupational and family roles. Conflicts with others, including physical fights, are also common. These people are irritable and aggressive with their spouses and children as well as with people outside the home. They are impulsive, reckless, and irresponsible.

We have all read newspaper accounts of famous examples of antisocial personality disorder. These often include people who have committed horrendous crimes against other people, including serial murders. One such person who attracted considerable attention in the national media was Westley Allan Dodd, who was executed after being found guilty of raping, torturing, and killing three young boys. His apparent indifference to the boys' suffering, and his insistence that he would commit similar crimes if he were ever released from prison, led many

▲ **Westley Allan Dodd was hanged in 1991 in the state of Washington for the sadistic rape and murder of three small boys.**

observers to believe that he fit the criteria for antisocial personality disorder. You should not be misled, however, into thinking that only serious criminals meet the criteria for this disorder. Many other forms of persistently callous and exploitative behavior could lead to this diagnosis.

Borderline personality disorder is a diffuse category whose essential feature is a pervasive pattern of instability in mood and interpersonal relationships. People with this disorder find it very difficult to be alone. They form intense, unstable relationships with other people and are often seen by others as being manipulative. Their opinions of significant others frequently vacillate between unrealistically positive and negative extremes. They also exhibit emotional instability. Their mood may shift rapidly and inexplicably from depression to anger to anxiety over a pattern of several hours. Intense anger is common and may be accompanied by temper tantrums, physical assault, or suicidal threats and gestures.

Many clinicians consider identity disturbance to be the diagnostic hallmark of borderline personality disorder. People with this disturbance presumably have great difficulty maintaining an integrated image of themselves that incorporates their positive and negative features. They frequently express uncertainty about such issues as personal values, sexual preferences, and career alternatives. Chronic feelings of emptiness and boredom may also be present.

Histrionic personality disorder is characterized by a pervasive pattern of excessive emotionality and attention-seeking behavior. People with this disorder thrive on being the center of attention. They are self-centered, vain, and demanding, and they constantly seek approval from others. When interacting with other people, their behavior is often inappropriately sexually seductive or provocative. Their emotions tend to be shallow and may vacillate erratically. They frequently react to situations with inappropriate exaggeration.

The concept of histrionic personality is rooted in clinical tradition rather than systematic empirical research (Pfohl, 1995). It overlaps extensively with other types of personality disorder, especially those in Cluster B. From a psychodynamic perspective, histrionic personality disorder has been described as being a less severe form of borderline personality (Kernberg, 1988). People with both disorders are intensely emotional and manipulative. Unlike people with borderline personality disorder, however, people with histrionic personality disorder have an essentially intact sense of their own identity and a better capacity for stable relationships with other people.

There may also be an etiological link between histrionic and antisocial personality disorders. Both may reflect a common, underlying tendency toward lack of inhibition. People with both types of disorder form shallow, intense relationships with others, and they can be extremely manipulative. Family history studies indicate that this predisposition to disinhibition may be expressed as histrionic personality disorder in women and as antisocial personality disorder in men (Pfohl, 1995).

The essential feature of **narcissistic personality disorder** is a pervasive pattern of grandiosity, need for admiration, and inability to empathize with other people. The case of Lawrence, described earlier in this chapter, illustrates this disorder. Narcissistic people have a greatly exaggerated sense of their own importance. They are preoccupied with their own achievements and abilities. Because they consider themselves to be very special, they cannot empathize with the feelings of other people and are often seen as being arrogant or haughty.

There is a considerable amount of overlap between narcissistic personality disorder and borderline personality disorder. Both types of people feel that other people should recognize their needs and do special favors for them. They may also react with anger if they are criticized. The distinction between these disorders hinges on the inflated sense of self-importance that is found in narcissistic personality disorder and the deflated or devalued sense of self found in borderline personality disorder (Ronningstam & Gunderson, 1991).

Cluster C: Avoidant, Dependent, and Obsessive–Compulsive Personality Disorders

Cluster C includes three subtypes: avoidant, dependent, and obsessive–compulsive personality disorders. The common element in all three disorders is presumably anxiety or fearfulness. This description fits most easily with the avoidant and dependent types. In contrast, obsessive–compulsive personality disorder is more accurately described in terms of preoccupation with rules and with lack of emotional warmth than in terms of anxiety.

Avoidant personality disorder is characterized by a pervasive pattern of social discomfort, fear of negative evaluation, and timidity. People with this disorder tend to be socially isolated when outside their own family circles because they are afraid of criticism. Unlike people with schizoid personality disorder, they want to be liked by others, but they are extremely shy—easily hurt by even minimal signs of disapproval from other people. Thus they avoid social and occupational activities that require significant contact with other people.

Avoidant personality disorder is often indistinguishable from generalized social phobia (see Chapter 6). In fact, some experts have argued that they are probably two different ways of defining the same condition (Frances, First, & Pincus, 1995). Others have argued that people with avoidant personality disorder have more trouble than people with social phobia in relating to other people (Millon & Martinez, 1995). People with avoidant personality disorder are presumably more socially withdrawn and have very few close relationships because they are so shy. People with social phobia may have a lot of friends, but they are afraid of performing in front of them. This distinction is relatively clear when social phobia is defined narrowly in terms of a particular kind of situation, such as public speaking. It is much more difficult to make as the social phobia becomes more generalized.

The essential feature of **dependent personality disorder** is a pervasive pattern of submissive and clinging behavior. People with this disorder are afraid of separating from other people on whom they are dependent for advice and reassurance. Often unable to make everyday decisions on their own, they feel anxious and helpless when they are alone. Like people with avoidant personality disorder, they are easily hurt by criticism, extremely sensitive to disapproval, and lacking in self-confidence. One difference between avoidant and dependent personality disorders involves the point in a relationship at which they experience the most difficulty. People who are avoidant have

trouble *initiating* a relationship (because they are fearful); people who are dependent have trouble *separating* after the relationship has gone on for some time.

Obsessive–compulsive personality disorder is defined by a pervasive pattern of orderliness, perfectionism, and mental and interpersonal control, at the expense of flexibility, openness, and efficiency. People with this disorder set ambitious standards for their own performance that frequently are so high as to be unattainable. Many would be described as "workaholics." In other words, they are so devoted to work that they ignore friends, family members, and leisure activities. They are so preoccupied with details and rules that they lose sight of the main point of an activity or project. Intellectual endeavors are favored over feelings and emotional experience. These people are excessively conscientious, moralistic, and judgmental, and they tend to be intolerant of affective behavior in other people.

The central features of this disorder may involve a marked need for control and lack of tolerance for uncertainty (Pollack, 1995). At modest levels, these traits can represent an adaptive coping style, particularly in the face of the demands of our complex, technological society. Very high levels of these characteristics begin to interfere with a person's social and occupational adjustment.

Obsessive–compulsive personality disorder should not be confused with obsessive–compulsive disorder (OCD), which is a type of anxiety disorder (see Chapter 6). A pattern of intrusive, unwanted thoughts accompanied by ritualistic behaviors is used to define OCD. The definition of obsessive–compulsive personality disorder, in contrast, is concerned with personality traits, such as excessively high levels of conscientiousness. Traditional psychodynamic theory has maintained that obsessive–compulsive personality disorder often precedes the onset of OCD, in much the same way that schizotypal personality disorder is presumably an early manifestation of the predisposition to schizophrenia. Research evidence is ambiguous on the issue (Nestadt et al., 1991; Pollack, 1987). In fact, people who meet the criteria for obsessive–compulsive personality

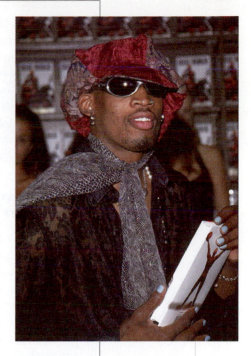

▲ **Basketball star Dennis Rodman is known for his flamboyant style of dress and behavior. Attention seeking is typically not considered abnormal when it is voluntary, especially when it is part of the entertainment industry.**

disorder seem to be at risk for *various* kinds of anxiety disorders, including generalized anxiety disorder and panic disorder as well as OCD. Obsessive–compulsive personality disorder may be more closely related to the form of OCD that involves checking rituals than to the form of OCD that involves washing and cleaning rituals (Gibbs & Oltmanns, 1995).

A Dimensional Perspective on Classification

The DSM-IV treats personality disorders in the same way that it handles other disorders—as discrete categories. For each type of personality disorder, specific criteria are listed. A person who exhibits a sufficient number of the criteria is assumed to have the disorder. Otherwise the disorder is considered to be absent. This approach assumes that there are sharp boundaries between normal and abnormal personalities.

Some clinicians have argued that a dimensional system would be preferable to the categorical approach (Livesley et al., 1994; Watson, Clark, & Harkness, 1994). For example, a frequent complaint about the description of personality disorders is that there is considerable overlap among categories. Many patients meet the criteria for more than one type. It is cumbersome to list multiple diagnoses, especially when the clinician is already asked to list problems on both Axis I and Axis II. In fact, many clinicians are reluctant to make more than one diagnosis on Axis II; consequently, much information is frequently lost. A dimensional system would provide a more complete description of each person, and it would be more useful with patients who fall on the boundaries between different types of personality disorder (Widiger & Costa, 1994).

The relationship between the normal personality traits listed in the five-factor model and the specific categories of personality disorders in DSM-IV is outlined in Table 9–3. Consider the example of paranoid personality disorder. Rather than listing all of the specific symptoms by which this category is described in DSM-IV, a person who exhibits this kind of behavior could also be described as someone who is low on three personality traits: extraversion, openness, and agreeableness (with special emphasis on the latter trait). A person who would meet DSM-IV criteria for obsessive–compulsive personality disorder might be described more easily as being high in conscientiousness (special emphasis), high on neuroticism, and low on extraversion and openness.

TABLE 9-3

Relationship Between the Five-Factor Model of Personality and DSM-IV Personality Disorders

| DSM-IV Category | Personality Traits | | | | |
	Neuroticism	Extraversion	Openness	Agreeableness	Conscientiousness
Paranoid		low	low	**low**	
Schizoid		**low**			
Schizotypal	**high**	**low**	high		
Borderline	**high**	high		low	low
Narcissistic	high	high		**low**	high
Histrionic	high	high	high		low
Antisocial	low			**low**	**low**
Dependent	**high**	high		**high**	
Avoidant	**high**	**low**			
Obsessive–compulsive	high	low	low		**high**

Boldface letters indicate features that are strongly associated with the definition of the disorder (defining features). Letters in regular typeface indicate "associated features" that are frequently associated with the disorder, sometimes based on clinical experience. Blank spaces indicate that the trait is not relevant to this DSM-IV category.
Source: Adapted from T. A. Widiger, 1993, The DSM-III-R categorical personality disorder diagnoses: A critique and an alternative, *Psychological Inquiry, 4,* 83.

Notice that this approach helps to clarify the extent of overlap between DSM-IV categories. The trait descriptions of borderline and histrionic personality disorder are very similar. It is not surprising therefore that studies have found very high rates of comorbidity among these categories. Obsessive–compulsive personality disorder, in contrast, is relatively unique, being one of only two categories that are defined in terms of a high score on the dimension of conscientiousness. This disorder shows much less overlap with the other personality disorders.

Epidemiology

Personality disorders are generally considered to be one of the most common forms of psychopathology, but it is difficult to provide empirical support for that claim (Maier et al., 1992; Weissman, 1993). With the exception of antisocial personality, these disorders did not receive close scrutiny until after the publication of DSM-III, and they have not been included in large-scale epidemiological studies, such as the Epidemiologic Catchment Area study and the National Comorbidity Study.

Prevalence in Community and Clinical Samples

How many people in the general population will meet the criteria for at least one personality disorder? In studies that have examined community-based samples of adults, the overall lifetime prevalence for having any type of Axis II disorder varies between 10 and 14 percent (Weissman, 1993).

Evidence regarding the prevalence of specific types of personality disorder in community samples is summarized in Figure 9–1. This figure presents summary data that have been averaged across a number of studies (Lyons, 1995). Among community samples, the highest prevalence rates are found for schizotypal, histrionic, antisocial, obsessive–compulsive, and dependent personality disorders. Narcissistic personality disorder seems to be the least common form, affecting only 0.2 percent of the population.

The most precise information that is available regarding the prevalence of personality disorders in community samples is concerned specifically with the antisocial type. In both the ECA study and NCS, structured interviews relating to this disorder were conducted with several thousand participants. The overall lifetime prevalence rate for antisocial personality disorder (men and women combined) was 2.6 percent in the ECA study (Robins et al., 1991) and 3.5 in the NCS (Kessler et al., 1994).

Notice that the prevalence rates from the ECA study and NCS are higher than the rate reported in Figure 9–1, which reflects an average across several studies. Some studies have found rates that are much lower than those of the ECA study and NCS. One rigorous investigation of 11,000 people in Taiwan found that only 0.2 percent met the criteria for antisocial personality disorder (Compton et al., 1991). This result might be taken to indicate that antisocial personality disorder is more common in our individualistic society than it is in a society that places greater emphasis on collectivism. But this is only one interpretation. More information is clearly needed before strong conclusions can be drawn. This will be one very interesting question that can be addressed by the

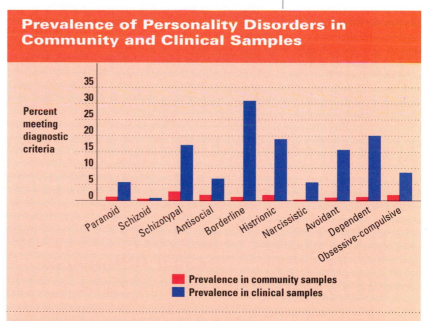

Prevalence of Personality Disorders in Community and Clinical Samples

Percent meeting diagnostic criteria

■ Prevalence in community samples
■ Prevalence in clinical samples

FIGURE 9-1: These estimates of prevalence are based on the median rate for each disorder that has been reported across several different studies.

Source: M.J. Lyons, 1995, Epidemiology of personality disorders. In M.T. Tsuang, M. Tohen, and G.E.P. Zahner (Eds.), *Textbook in Psychiatric Epidemiology*, p. 423. New York: Wiley.

▲ **Vivien Leigh won Academy Awards for her performances as Scarlett O'Hara in *Gone with the Wind* (1940) and Blanche DuBois in *A Streetcar Named Desire* (1952). Both characters exhibit blends of histrionic and narcissistic features that fit stereotyped views of female personality traits.**

international study of personality disorders that is being sponsored by the World Health Organization (Loranger et al., 1994).

One final comment about prevalence rates in community samples: There is considerable overlap among categories in the personality disorders. Most people who meet the diagnostic criteria for one personality disorder also meet the criteria for another disorder (Shea, 1995). Some changes in specific diagnostic criteria that were introduced with the publication of DSM-IV in 1994 were intended to reduce the extent of overlap among the various types of personality disorder, but it is too early to tell whether this effect was achieved. Existing studies on this issue have been based on earlier versions of the diagnostic manual.

The prevalence of personality disorders is much higher among people who are being treated for another mental disorder listed on Axis I of DSM-IV. These data are also summarized in Figure 9–1. Borderline personality disorder appears to be the most common disorder in both inpatient and outpatient settings. Averaged across studies, the evidence suggests that this disorder is found among slightly more than 30 percent of all patients who are treated for psychological disorders. Prevalence rates in clinical samples for dependent, histrionic, schizotypal, or avoidant personality disorder average between 15 and 20 percent. Rates are especially high among those who have been hospitalized, but the specific figures vary considerably from one study to the next.

Gender Differences

The *overall* prevalence of personality disorders is approximately equal in men and women (Weissman, 1993). There are, however, consistent gender differences with regard to at least one specific disorder: Antisocial personality disorder is unquestionably much more common among men than among women. The ECA study found rates of

4.5 percent for men and 0.8 percent for women (Robins, Tipp, & Przybeck, 1991). The NCS reported rates of 5.8 percent for men and 1.2 percent for women (Kessler et al., 1994). Thus antisocial personality disorder is actually an alarmingly common problem among adult males in the United States.

Epidemiological evidence regarding gender differences for the other types of personality disorder is much more ambiguous. Very few community-based studies have been done using standardized interviews as a basis for diagnosis. In one community sample of more than 3,400 adults, the prevalence of histrionic personality disorder was found to be 2.2 percent in both men and women (Nestadt et al., 1990). Almost nothing is known about the extent of potential gender differences for the other types of personality disorder. Borderline personality disorder and dependent personality disorder may be somewhat more prevalent among women than men (Zimmerman & Coryell, 1989). There has been some speculation that paranoid and obsessive–compulsive personality disorders may be somewhat more common among men than women (Bernstein, Useda, & Siever, 1995; Funtowicz & Widiger, 1995).

GENDER BIAS AND DIAGNOSIS

One of the controversies that has surrounded the diagnosis of personality disorders involves the issue of gender bias. Critics contend that the definitions of some categories are based on sex-role stereotypes and therefore are inherently sexist. The dependent type, for example, might be viewed as a reflection of certain traditionally feminine traits, such as being unassertive or putting the needs of others ahead of one's own. It has been suggested that, in DSM-IV, these traits are arbitrarily labeled as being maladaptive. Traditionally masculine traits, such as being unable to identify and express a wide range of emotions, are presumably not mentioned in the manual. This practice arbitrarily assigns responsibility for interpersonal difficulties to the women themselves. Therefore these definitions may turn traditional sex-role behaviors into "disorders" and minimize the extent to which women may simply be trying to cope with unreasonable or oppressive environmental circumstances, including discrimination and sexual abuse (Brown, 1992; Caplan, 1995).

This argument leads to a number of interesting and important questions. One is concerned with the presence of bias within the criterion sets themselves. If the criteria for certain categories are based on stereotypes of feminine traits, is it relatively easy for a woman to meet the criteria for that diagnosis even if she is not experiencing significant distress of impairment in other areas of her life? The answer to that question is tentatively "no" (Funtowicz & Widiger, 1995). In other words, the threshold for assigning a diagnosis of personality disorder does not appear to be lower for those types that are based largely on traits that might be considered traditionally feminine (dependent, histrionic, borderline) than for those that are based on traits that might be considered traditionally masculine (antisocial, paranoid, compulsive).

A second question is concerned with the possibility of gender bias in the ways that clinicians assign diagnoses to their clients, regardless of whether the criteria themselves are biased. Are clinicians more likely to assign diagnoses such as dependent and borderline personality disorder to a woman than to a man, if both people exhibit the same set of symptoms? The answer to this question is tentatively "yes." One study found that both male and female mental health professionals were significantly (though not overwhelmingly) more likely to describe a person as exhibiting symptoms of borderline personality disorder if that person was female rather than male (Becker & Lamb, 1994).

Stability over Time

Temporal stability is one of the most important assumptions about personality disorders. Evidence for the assumption that personality disorders appear during adolescence and persist into adulthood has, until recently, been limited primarily to antisocial personality disorder. A classic follow-up study by Lee Robins

(1966) began with a large set of records describing young children treated for adjustment problems at a clinic during the 1920s. Robins was able to locate and interview almost all of these people, who by then were adults. The best predictor of an adult diagnosis of antisocial personality was conduct disorder in childhood. The people who were most likely to be considered antisocial as adults were boys who had been referred to the clinic on the basis of serious theft or aggressive behavior; who exhibited such behaviors across a variety of situations; and whose antisocial behaviors created conflict with adults outside their own homes. More than half of the boys in Robins's study who exhibited these characteristics were given a diagnosis of antisocial personality disorder as adults.

Another longitudinal study has collected information regarding the prevalence and stability of personality disorders among adolescents (Bernstein et al., 1993). This investigation is particularly important because it did not depend solely on subjects who had been referred for psychological treatment and because it was concerned with the full range of personality disorders. The rate of personality disorders was relatively high in this sample: 17 percent of the adolescents received a diagnosis of at least one personality disorder. While many of these people continued to exhibit the same problems over time, fewer than half of the adolescents who were originally considered to have a personality disorder qualified for that same diagnosis 2 years later. This evidence suggests that maladaptive personality traits are frequently transient phenomena among adolescents. Further details regarding the methods and results of this study are presented in the Research Close-Up.

RESEARCH CLOSE-UP

Stability of Personality Disorders in Adolescents

The first large-scale study of the prevalence and stability of personality disorders among adolescents was conducted by psychologists David Bernstein, Patricia Cohen, and their colleagues at the New York State Psychiatric Institute (Bernstein et al., 1993).

Subjects in this study were identified from a random sample of more than 700 families in upstate New York who had at least one child between the ages of 11 and 21. In families with more than one child in that age range, one child was randomly chosen to become the subject in this study.

The children and their families were broadly representative of people living in the northeastern United States in terms of socioeconomic status. Half the adolescents were male, with an average age of 16 years at the time of the first assessment. Sixty-one percent were from intact families, and 76 percent lived in urban areas. They were less representative with regard to race (91 percent were white) and religious background (56 percent were Catholic).

Each adolescent was assessed at two points in time, separated by 2 years. The investigators collected information about the children's behavior using both structured interviews (conducted independently with both the adolescents and their mothers) and self-report questionnaires (completed only by the adolescents). These data were combined to identify individuals with various types of personality disorder. These individuals were then further classified as having either a moderate or severe form of the disorder.

A total of 31 percent of the adolescents met the criteria for at least one moderate personality disorder, and 17 percent met the criteria for at least one severe personality disorder. The most prevalent form of moderate disorder was obsessive–compulsive personality disorder, which was found in 13 percent of the adolescents. The most prevalent form of severe disorder was narcissistic personality disorder; 6 percent of the adolescents met these criteria. The least common form of personality disorder in this sample was schizotypal, judging by both the moderate and severe diagnostic thresholds.

Only one significant difference was found between boys and girls: Boys were more than twice as likely as girls to qualify for a diagnosis of dependent personality disorder. This result was somewhat surprising in light of the expectation that, in adults, dependent personality disorder is more common among women than among men.

The prevalence of both moderate and severe personality disorders peaked at the age of 12 or 13 years for both boys and girls and then declined. By the time these subjects reached 18 to 21 years of age, the prevalence of severe personality disorder fell to 9 percent for males and 11 percent for females, approximately the same rates found in other epidemiological studies with adult populations.

Less than half the adolescents who received an Axis II diagnosis at the time of the first assessment qualified for a diagnosis at the second assessment. The most persistent forms of personality disorder were the paranoid, narcissistic, obsessive–compulsive, and borderline types. In these categories, 25 to 32 of the cases identified at the first assessment continued to meet diagnostic criteria 2 years later. This pattern indicates that symptoms of personality disorder are frequently unstable during adolescence. They also indicate, however, that a fairly large minority of the adolescents in this study continued to qualify for a diagnosis of personality disorder 2 years after the problem was originally identified.

The results of this study indicate that personality disorders are relatively common among adolescents in the general population. The conclusions with regard to temporal stability are mixed. On the one hand, symptoms of personality disorder usually are not stable over time. On the other hand, adolescents who exhibit a severe personality disorder at one point in time are much more likely than their peers to have similar problems over the next few years. Some of the subjects followed a stable pattern that is consistent with the image of these disorders presented in DSM-IV. Further studies are needed to determine how many of the adolescents whose problems were stable over this initial 2-year period continue to exhibit stable difficulties in subsequent years. ■

Several studies have examined the stability of personality disorders among people who have received professional treatment for their problems, especially those who have been hospitalized for schizotypal or borderline disorders. Many patients who have been treated for these problems are still significantly impaired several years later, but the disorders are not uniformly stable (Perry, 1993). Recovery rates are relatively high among patients with a diagnosis of borderline personality disorder. If patients who were initially treated during their early twenties are followed up when they are in their forties and fifties, only about one person in four would still qualify for a diagnosis of borderline personality disorder (Stone, 1993). The long-term prognosis is less optimistic for schizotypal and schizoid personality disorders. People with these diagnoses are likely to remain socially isolated and occupationally impaired (McGlashan, 1986b, 1992).

Schizotypal Personality Disorder (SPD)

Now that we have reviewed some of the important general issues for the entire set of personality disorders, we consider four specific types of disorder in greater detail. We have decided to focus on schizotypal, borderline, and antisocial types because they have been the subject of extended research and debate in the scientific literature. The discussion of dependent personality disorder is included to illustrate current thinking about one of the Cluster C disorders, even though this disorder has not been studied as extensively as the other three categories.

We begin each of the four sections with a brief case study. We have chosen cases that are prototypes for each disorder. In other words, these are people who exhibit most, if not all, of the features of the disorder. You should not infer from these descriptions that everyone who meets the criteria for these disorders would represent this type of typical case. Remember, also, that many people simultaneously meet the criteria for more than one personality disorder; these cases are relatively simple examples.

The description of the following case, taken from J. Walsh, illustrates some of the most important features of schizotypal personality disorder (SPD).

BRIEF CASE STUDY

Leslie was a 43-year-old unemployed widow fighting to retain custody of her two adolescent children. Shortly after her husband's death from cancer 8 years ago, her parents-in-law accused her of being an unfit mother and successfully acquired temporary custody of the children through the county children's service bureau. Leslie wanted her children with her, and after many appeals the children's bureau was preparing to return them to her. At this time a casual friend suggested to Leslie that getting counseling for herself would further impress the bureau, and this is why she set up her initial appointment. For some unclear reason, however, Leslie chose to keep her counseling experience a secret.

During her early sessions Leslie was quiet, suspicious, and ill at ease. She had no particular agenda for her counseling, only noting in vague terms that she wanted to "get out to the pool." Her affect was constricted, her communications terse and obscure, and her vocabulary rather primitive. Her grooming was haphazard; on some summer days she came dressed in a fur coat, shorts, and hiking boots. Most sessions lasted only 15 to 20 minutes. Leslie would abruptly announce that she had to leave, sometimes to get to work, and quickly walk out, although she always made a point of rescheduling for the following week. Eventually I learned that her work involved collecting tin cans for recycling. Otherwise she spent her time taking long walks in her small town of residence.

Despite her presentation, it eventually became clear that Leslie was not psychotic and in fact was a college graduate with an impressive athletic background. She had married shortly after college when she became pregnant, but had done little since then aside from raising her children as best she could and tolerating an irresponsible husband. Leslie actually felt relieved when he died, saying "Being married never did me any good." She had functioned marginally ever since leaving college. (Walsh, 1990, pp. 45–46). ∎

Brief Historical Perspective

The concept of schizotypal personality disorder is closely tied to the history of schizophrenia as a diagnostic entity (Gottesman, 1987). The term was originally coined as an abbreviation for *schizophrenic phenotype*. These maladaptive personality traits are presumably seen among people who possess the genotype that makes them vulnerable to schizophrenia. The symptoms of schizotypal personality disorder represent early manifestations of the predisposition to develop the full-blown disorder. It has been recognized for many years that a fairly large proportion of the family members of schizophrenic patients exhibit strange or unusual behaviors that are similar to, but milder in form than, the disturbance shown by the patient.

Clinical Features and Comorbidity

The DSM-IV criteria for schizotypal personality disorder are listed in Table 9–4. These criteria represent a blend of those characteristics that have been reported among the relatives of schizophrenic patients and those symptoms that seem to characterize nonpsychotic patients with schizophrenic-like disorders (Siever, Bernstein, & Silverman, 1995). In addition to social detachment, emphasis is placed on eccentricity and cognitive or perceptual distortions.

People who meet the criteria for schizotypal personality disorder frequently meet the criteria for additional Axis II disorders. There is a considerable amount of overlap between schizotypal personality disorder and other personality disorders in Cluster A (paranoid and schizoid), as well as with avoidant personality disorder. This finding is not particularly surprising given the conceptual origins of the schizotypal category. There is also quite a bit of overlap between schizotypal personality disorder and borderline personality disorder. In one study, 33 percent of the patients with schizotypal personality disorder also met the criteria for borderline personality disorder (Morey, 1988).

Etiological Considerations

Most of the interest in the etiology of schizotypal personality disorder has focused on the importance of genetic factors. Is schizotypal personality disorder genetically related to schizophrenia? Family and adoption studies indicate that the answer is "yes" (Thapar & McGuffin, 1993). Twin studies have examined genetic contributions to schizotypal personality disorder from a dimensional perspective in which schizotypal personality traits are measured with questionnaires. This evidence also points to a significant genetic contribution (Nigg & Goldsmith, 1994).

TABLE 9–4

DSM-IV Criteria for Schizotypal Personality Disorder

A. A pervasive pattern of social and interpersonal deficits marked by acute discomfort with, and reduced capacity for, close relationships as well as by cognitive or perceptual distortions and eccentricities of behavior, beginning by early adulthood and present in a variety of contexts, as indicated by five (or more) of the following:

1. Ideas of reference (excluding delusions of reference)
2. Odd beliefs or magical thinking that influences behavior and is inconsistent with subcultural norms (such as superstitiousness, belief in clairvoyance, or telepathy)
3. Unusual perceptual experiences, including bodily illusions
4. Odd thinking and speech (vague, circumstantial, metaphorical, overelaborate, or stereotyped)
5. Suspiciousness or paranoid ideation
6. Inappropriate or constricted affect*
7. Behavior or appearance that is odd, eccentric, or peculiar
8. Lack of close friends or confidants other than first-degree relatives
9. Excessive social anxiety that does not diminish with familiarity and tends to be associated with paranoid fears rather than with negative judgments about self

B. Does not occur exclusively during the course of Schizophrenia, a Mood Disorder with Psychotic Features, another Psychotic Disorder, or a Pervasive Developmental Disorder.

*Inappropriate affect refers to emotional responses that appear to be inconsistent with the social context—for example, uncontrollable giggling at a wake or funeral. Constricted affect refers to the absence of emotional responsiveness, such as lack of facial expressions. See Chapter 12 for a more detailed discussion.

The first-degree relatives of schizophrenic patients are considerably more likely than people in the general population to exhibit schizotypal personality disorder. One large study of this type, the Roscommon Family Study, was conducted in a rural county in the western part of Ireland by Kenneth Kendler and his colleagues. They interviewed more than 1,700 parents and siblings of three groups of probands: 300 schizophrenic patients, 100 patients with major mood disorders, and 150 people with no history of psychiatric disorder. Some of the results of this study are summarized in Table 9–5. The most striking finding was an increased prevalence of schizotypal personality disorder (6.9 percent) among the relatives of the schizophrenic patients. Prevalence rates for paranoid and avoidant personality disorder were also significantly higher among the relatives of the schizophrenic patients. Kendler and his colleagues did not find increased rates of these personality disorders among the relatives of people with mood disorders. These results suggest that these disorders, especially schizotypal personality disorder, are genetically related to schizophrenia. The diagnostic specificity of this finding remains open to question; some studies have reported that schizotypal personality disorder is found with increased frequency among the children of parents with mood disorders (Erlenmeyer-Kimling et al., 1995).

The relationship among schizotypal personality disorder, schizophrenia, and major depression can be better understood through an examination of the specific criteria that are used to define schizotypal personality. One study compared the nonpsychotic first-degree relatives of schizophrenic patients with the first-degree relatives of depressed patients (Torgersen et al., 1993). Some of the features, such as lacking close friends and ideas of reference, were actually more common among the relatives of the depressed patients. Only three features of schizotypal personality disorder were significantly more common among the relatives of the schizophrenic patients than among the relatives of the depressed patients:

- Odd thinking and speech
- Inappropriate or constricted affect
- Excessive social anxiety

The investigators concluded that these three features may represent the core of "true"

schizotypal personality disorder, if that disorder is viewed as a form of personality that is genetically related to schizophrenia.

Treatment

Two important considerations complicate the treatment of people with personality disorders and make it difficult to evaluate the effectiveness of various forms of intervention (Gorton & Akhtar, 1990). The first consideration involves the ego-syntonic nature of many personality disorders. Many people with these disorders do not seek treatment for their problems because they do not see their own behavior as being the source of distress. A related difficulty involves premature termination: A relatively high proportion of personality disorder patients drop out of treatment before it is completed.

When people with personality disorders appear at hospitals or clinics, it is often because they are also suffering from another type of mental disorder, such as depression or substance abuse. This comorbidity is the second consideration that complicates treatment. "Pure forms" of personality disorder are relatively rare. There is tremendous overlap between specific personality disorder categories and other forms of abnormal behavior, including disorders that would be listed on both Axis I and Axis II. Treatment is seldom aimed at problem behaviors that are associated with only one type of personality disorder, and the efficacy of treatment is therefore difficult to evaluate.

The literature regarding treatment of schizotypal personality disorder, like that dealing with its causes, mirrors efforts aimed at schizophrenia. A few studies have focused on the possible

	TABLE 9–5

Familial Relationship Between Schizophrenia and Three Schizophrenia-Related Types of Personality Disorder

	Personality Disorders Diagnosed Among Relatives of the Probands (percent)		
Proband's Diagnosis	Schizotypal	Paranoid	Avoidant
Schizophrenia	6.9	1.4	2.1
Mood disorder	2.3	0.6	0.6
No diagnosis (controls)	1.4	0.4	0.2

Source: K. S. Kendler, M. McGuire, A. M. Gruenberg, A. O'Hare, M. Spellman, and D. Walsh, 1993, The Roscommon Family Study. III. Schizophrenia-related personality disorders in relatives, *Archives of General Psychiatry, 50,* 781–788.

treatment value of antipsychotic drugs, which are effective with many schizophrenic patients. Some studies have found that low doses of antipsychotic medication are beneficial in alleviating cognitive problems and social anxiety in patients who have received a diagnosis of schizotypal personality disorder (for example, Goldberg et al., 1986). There is also some indication that patients with schizotypal personality disorder may respond positively to antidepressant medication (Markovitz et al., 1991). In general, the therapeutic effects of medication are positive, but they tend to be modest (Gitlin, 1993).

Clinical experience seems to suggest that these patients do not respond well to insight-oriented psychotherapy, in part because they do not see themselves as having psychological problems and also because they are so uncomfortable with close personal relationships (Hoch & Polatin, 1949). Some clinicians have suggested that a supportive, educational approach that is focused on fostering basic social skills may be beneficial if the goals of treatment are modest (Stone, 1985; Walsh, 1990). Unfortunately, controlled studies of psychological forms of treatment with schizotypal personality disorder have not been reported.

Borderline Personality Disorder (BPD)

People who meet the criteria for borderline personality disorder (BPD) are typically involved in intense, chaotic relationships. This pattern of interpersonal behavior is reflected in their vacillating attitudes about people. They alternate frequently between viewing themselves and others as all good (*idealizing*) or all bad (*devaluing*). The following case, written by A. Krohn, illustrates many of the features associated with this disorder.

BRIEF CASE STUDY

Miss L. was a 21-year-old, reasonably attractive, slightly overweight woman of medium height who walked with a brusque gait, held herself very erect, seemed aloof, and appeared to know just where she was going. She had a high, loud, and shaky voice that was experienced by many as grating and demanding. Though she did not deliberately behave dramatically, her body movements and speech habits seemed a bit larger than life, like postures or poses, and tended to draw attention to herself.

Following puberty, the patient had developed interests in music and writing that quickly became all-consuming preoccupations. She began to ruminate interminably about her future, became preoccupied with what others thought of her, and became extremely sensitive to the most subtle slights, real or imagined. A fantasy of herself as a great artist alternated with an image of herself as completely worthless. Disgusted by the prospect of a drab, workaday life, she dreamed of living on an exalted plane, continuously achieving and creating—fantasizing inside herself founts of dazzling creativity that would permit her to write, sing, and perform effortlessly.

People often initially experienced the patient as pushy and obnoxious. Her manner made others feel that she was blaming them for her difficulties, that she felt she had been treated unfairly and that she deserved and needed more. What came through in her manner was a gnawing hunger, a sense of being deprived, a demand for recompense, and a haughty demand to be looked up to and respected. The patient initially felt that she was shy, modest, and unnoticed. In consciously trying to compensate for this, she often struck others as trying to impress and boast.

Though she had some friends, she had very few who felt capable of gratifying her intense and continuous needs for support, reassurance, and maternal comfort. She grew enraged even at those who befriended her, because they could not do enough. At moments when she felt people were actually depriving her, she felt a "white-hot rage," involving impulses to murder, smash windows, or throw herself out a window. These rageful episodes frightened her greatly and would make her feel she should kill herself. Alternately, she deprecated herself, feeling like a loathsome, ugly, fat person who contributed nothing to the world, who was a parasite and therefore deserved to be hated.

She would develop clinging, dependent relationships characterized by intense wishes to have the qualities of the other (person), often including intense envy of the (person). (Krohn, 1980, pp. 344–345) ∎

Brief Historical Perspective

The intellectual heritage of borderline personality disorder is quite diverse, and it is more difficult to trace than is the case with schizotypal personality disorder. It is, in fact, rather confusing. Several traditions are important, and in some cases they represent conflicting points of view (Leichtman, 1989).

Otto Kernberg (1967, 1975), a psychiatrist at Cornell University, has developed an explanation of borderline personality that is based on psychodynamic theory. According to Kernberg, borderline disorder is not a specific syndrome. Rather, it refers to a set of personality features or deficiencies that can be found in individuals with various disorders.

In Kernberg's model, the common characteristic of people diagnosed with borderline disorder is faulty development of ego structure. People with this ego weakness frequently try to achieve satisfaction or pleasure through behaviors that normally are associated with infants rather than adults. Especially common are *primary process thinking,* in which the id relieves tensions by imagining the things it desires, and lack of impulse control. Another common feature of people with borderline disorder is *splitting*—the tendency to see people and events alternately as entirely good or entirely bad. Thus a man with borderline disorder might perceive his wife as almost perfect at some times and as highly flawed at other times. The tendency toward splitting helps explain the broad mood swings and unstable relationships associated with borderline personalities.

Kernberg's emphasis on a broadly defined level of pathology, rather than on discrete clinical symptoms, resulted in a relatively expansive definition of borderline personality. Viewed from this perspective, borderline disorder can encompass a great many types of abnormal behavior, including paranoid, schizoid, and cyclothymic personality disorders, impulse control disorders (see Further Thoughts), substance use disorders, and various types of mood disorder. It should not be surprising therefore that the DSM-IV

▲ John Gunderson, a psychiatrist at Harvard University, has played a central role in the development of diagnostic criteria for borderline personality disorder.

FURTHER THOUGHTS

Impulse Control Disorders

Failure to control harmful impulses is associated with several of the disorders listed in DSM-IV. People who meet the criteria for borderline personality disorder and antisocial personality disorder engage in various types of impulsive, maladaptive behaviors (most often self-mutilation in the case of BPD and theft and aggression in the case of ASPD). People in the midst of a manic episode frequently become excessively involved in pleasurable activities that can have painful consequences, such as unrestrained buying or sexual indiscretions. These are examples of impulse control problems that appear as part of a more broadly defined syndrome or mental disorder.

The DSM-IV includes several additional problems under a heading called **impulse control disorders.** Relatively little is known about these problems (Wise & Tierney, 1994). They are defined in terms of persistent, clinically significant impulsive behaviors that are not better explained by other disorders in DSM-IV. They include the following:

- *Intermittent explosive disorder:* Aggressive behaviors resulting in serious assaultive acts or destruction of property. The level of aggression is grossly out of proportion to any precipitating psychosocial stressors.

- *Kleptomania:* Stealing objects that are not needed for personal use or for their financial value. The theft is not motivated by anger or vengeance.

- *Pyromania:* Deliberate and purposeful setting of fires, accompanied by fascination with or attraction to fire and things that are associated with it. The behavior is not motivated by financial considerations (as in arson), social or political ideology, anger, vengeance, or delusional beliefs.

- *Trichotillomania:* Pulling out one's own hair, resulting in noticeable hair loss as well as significant distress or impairment in social or occupational functioning.

- *Pathological gambling:* Repeated maladaptive gambling that is associated with other problems, such as repeated, unsuccessful efforts to stop gambling, restlessness or irritability when trying to stop gambling, lying to family members and friends to conceal the extent of gambling, and committing crimes to finance gambling.

In most cases, the impulsive behavior is preceded by increasing tension and followed by a feeling of pleasure, gratification, or relief. The motivation for these impulsive behaviors is therefore somewhat different than the motivation for *compulsive behavior* (see Chapter 6). Impulsive and compulsive behaviors can be difficult to distinguish. Both types of behavior are repetitious and difficult to resist. The primary difference is that the original goal for impulsive behavior is to experience pleasure, and the original goal for compulsive behavior is to avoid anxiety (Frances, First, & Pincus, 1995).

The most prevalent type of impulse control disorder is pathological gambling, which may affect as many as 9 million people in the United States (McElroy et al., 1995). Men are more likely than women to become pathological gamblers. They tend to be intelligent, well-educated, competitive people who enjoy the challenges and risks involved in betting.

Most gambling is obviously not associated with a mental disorder. Social gambling is a form of recreation that is accepted in most cultures. Professional gambling is an occupation pursued by people whose gambling is highly disciplined. Pathological gambling, in contrast, is out of control, takes over the person's life, and leads to horrendous financial and interpersonal consequences.

The tragic life of Art Schlichter provides a vivid illustration of the devastating impact that persistent, uncontrolled, impulsive gambling can have on a person and his family (Valente, 1996; Keteyian, 1986). Schlichter, an All-American quarterback at Ohio State University, was the first player drafted by the National Football League in 1982. He had been gambling since high school, but the problem became worse after he started playing professional football. His career was disappointing. As the pressures mounted, so did his gambling debts, which eventually reached $1 million. He was cut from several teams in the National Football League and the Canadian Football League, and was ultimately banned from the NFL for betting on professional games. He entered treatment for his compulsive gambling on several occasions, but the results were unsuccessful. His repeated promises to stop gambling went unfulfilled. Schlichter was arrested four times between 1987 and 1994 and served 2 years in jail. The charges against him included unlawful gambling, bank fraud, and writing bad checks. His promising football career was ruined, and his young family was torn apart by his uncontrolled gambling.

The impulse control disorders occupy an interesting and controversial niche in DSM-IV. The implication of impulse control disorders is that people who repeatedly engage in dangerous, illegal, or destructive behaviors *must* have a mental disorder. If they do not, why do they do these things? Unfortunately, this reasoning quickly becomes circular. Why does he gamble recklessly? Because he has a mental disorder. How do you know he has a mental disorder? Because he gambles recklessly. This logical dilemma is particularly evident in the case of impulse control disorders because these problem behaviors do not appear as part of a broader syndrome in which other symptoms of disorder are also present. In other words, the problem behavior *is* the disorder. Until we can step outside this loop, validating the utility of the diagnostic concept by reference to other psychological or biological response systems, we are left with an unsatisfying approach to the definition of these problems. ■

category of borderline personality disorder has been shown to overlap extensively with other forms of personality disorder and with a number of Axis I disorders.

In an effort to foster research on borderline disorders, these psychodynamic views regarding personality organization were translated into more reliable, descriptive terms by several prominent clinicians. John Gunderson (1984, 1994), a psychiatrist at Harvard University, identified a number of descriptive characteristics that are commonly associated with Kernberg's concept of borderline personality. Gunderson and his colleagues developed a structured interview that would allow clinicians to diagnose the condition reliably. Their definition of the concept depends heavily on the presence of intense, unstable interpersonal relationships, manipulative suicide attempts, unstable sense of the self, negative affect, and impulsivity.

Psychiatrist Hagop Akiskal (1992, 1994) maintains a very different view of borderline personality disorder. He has argued that borderline personality disorder is not a valid or meaningful diagnostic concept. According to his view, the borderline personality concept includes a heterogeneous collection of symptoms that are associated with mild forms of brain dysfunction (for example, epilepsy, attention deficit disorder, pregnancy and birth complications), schizophrenic-like conditions, and typical as well as subclinical mood disorders. Akiskal favors the separation of these various conditions into more homogeneous categories. This point of view is shared by some other experts in the field of personality disorders who believe that the boundaries of the borderline concept are too vague and fuzzy for it to be useful diagnostically (Tyrer, 1994).

Clinical Features and Comorbidity

The DSM-IV criteria for borderline personality disorder are presented in Table 9–6. The overriding characteristic of borderline personality

TABLE 9-6

DSM-IV Criteria for Borderline Personality Disorder

A. A pervasive pattern of instability of interpersonal relationships, self-image, and affects, and marked impulsivity beginning by early adulthood and present in a variety of contexts, as indicated by five (or more) of the following:

1. Frantic efforts to avoid real or imagined abandonment.
2. A pattern of unstable and intense interpersonal relationships characterized by alternating between extremes of idealization and devaluation.
3. Identity disturbance: markedly and persistently unstable self-image or sense of self.
4. Impulsiveness in at least two areas that are potentially self-damaging (for example, spending, sex, substance abuse, reckless driving, binge eating).
5. Recurrent suicidal behavior, gestures, or threats, or self-mutilating behavior.
6. Affective instability due to a marked reactivity of mood (such as intense episodic dysphoria, irritability, or anxiety usually lasting a few hours and only rarely more than a few days).
7. Chronic feelings of emptiness.
8. Inappropriate, intense anger or difficulty controlling anger (for example, frequent displays of temper, constant anger, recurrent physical fights).
9. Transient, stress-related paranoid ideation or severe dissociative symptoms.

disorder is a pervasive pattern of instability in self-image, in interpersonal relationships, and in mood. Identity disturbance may be manifested by indecision in such areas as career goals, sexual orientation, and personal values. Chaotic interpersonal relationships are also common. People with borderline personality disorder have a great deal of trouble being alone. Their opinions of significant other people may vacillate from one extreme (overidealization) to the other (devaluation) and back again. Finally, their moods may also shift rapidly and unpredictably from anger to depression and anxiety.

Borderline personality disorder overlaps with several other categories on Axis II, including the histrionic, narcissistic, paranoid, dependent, and avoidant types. There is also a significant amount of overlap between borderline personality disorder and Axis I disorders, especially depression (Trull, 1995; Widiger & Trull, 1993). Many patients with other types of impulse control problems, such as substance dependence and eating disorders, also qualify for a diagnosis of borderline personality disorder.

Follow-up studies suggest many similarities between borderline personality disorder and mood disorders. Akiskal and his colleagues studied a group of 100 outpatients with a diagnosis of borderline personality disorder. During follow-up, 29 percent of the sample developed severe depression. A longitudinal study of patients who were discharged from a private psychiatric hospital is also interesting in this regard. Of the patients with a pure diagnosis of borderline personality disorder (that is, those who did not receive any other diagnosis on Axis I or II), 23 percent developed major depressive episodes in the course of the 15-year follow-up (McGlashan, 1986a).

Etiological Considerations

Genetic factors do not seem to play a central role in the etiology of borderline personality disorder, when it is viewed in terms of the syndrome that is defined in DSM-IV (Torgersen, 1994). It is premature to conclude that genes are irrelevant to the development of this set of problems because neuroticism (one of the personality traits or dimensions that is clearly related to the borderline concept) is influenced by genetic factors (Nigg & Goldsmith, 1994). Nevertheless, most of the discussion regarding causes of borderline

personality disorder has focused on environmental events.

Akiskal elaborated on Kernberg's psychodynamic theory and proposed a similar model for the development of "residual" borderline conditions, those that remain after the exclusion of brain disorders, mood disorders, and schizotypal disorders. He argued that borderline patients suffer from the negative consequences of parental loss during childhood (Davis & Akiskal, 1986). The model is supported by studies of the families of borderline patients and by comparisons with the literature on social development in monkeys that examined the effects of separating infants from their mothers.

The *primate separation model* was originally proposed by other investigators as an analogue for mood disorders in humans. After young monkeys have been separated from their mothers or peers, they experience persistent problems in the area of attachment behavior (see Chapter 2) and negative affect. Their relationships with peers are disrupted—for example, they have difficulty in establishing and maintaining social hierarchies—and they may exhibit self-destructive behaviors. Many of these problems are reminiscent of the interpersonal difficulties of borderline patients.

Studies of patients with borderline personality disorder point toward the influence of widespread problematic relationships with their parents (Guzder et al., 1996). Separation appears to be only one aspect of this complicated picture. Adolescent girls with borderline personality disorder report pervasive lack of supervision, frequent witnessing of domestic violence, and being subjected to inappropriate behavior by their parents and other adults, including verbal, physical, and sexual abuse (Norden et al., 1995; Weaver & Clum, 1993). The extent and severity of abuse vary widely across individuals. Many patients describe multiple forms of abuse by more than a single individual.

We must be careful, however, when we interpret the evidence regarding the relationship between borderline personality disorder and environmental factors, such as separation and abuse. With the exception of the data from primate models, all the evidence is correlational. It is therefore risky to draw causal inferences. What is the direction of effect? It seems likely that this type of family conflict represents the result of a dynamic, transactional process in which children and parents influence each other over an extended period of time (Crowell et al., 1993). Although traumatic experiences are reported frequently by borderline subjects, they are relatively low in severity, and the overall prevalence of this type of environmental event is also relatively high among people with other types of mental disorder (Paris, Zweig-Frank, & Guzder, 1994). A model that attempts to account for the etiology of borderline personality disorder in particular, rather than mental disorder in general, will need to explain why some people develop these specific types of symptoms in response to such experiences as neglect, separation, and abuse and many others do not.

Treatment

Given that the concept of borderline personality disorder is rooted in psychodynamic theory, it should not be surprising that many clinicians have advocated the use of psychotherapy for the treatment of these conditions (Freeman & Gunderson, 1989; Shea, 1991). In psychodynamically based treatment, the transference relationship, defined as the way in which the patient behaves toward the therapist, is used to increase patients' ability to experience themselves and other people in a more realistic and integrated way.

Personality disorders have traditionally been considered to be hard to treat from a psychological perspective, and borderline conditions are among the most difficult. Close personal relationships form the foundation of psychological intervention, and it is specifically in the area of establishing and maintaining such relationships that borderline patients experience their greatest difficulty. Their persistent alternation between overidealization and devaluation leads to frequent rage toward the therapist and can become a significant deterrent to progress in therapy. Not surprisingly, between one-half and two-thirds of all patients with borderline personality disorder discontinue treatment, against their therapists' advice, within the first several weeks of treatment (Kelly et al., 1992).

One promising approach to psychotherapy with borderline patients, called *dialectical behavior therapy* (DBT), has been developed and evaluated by Marsha Linehan (1993), a clinical psychologist at the University of Washington. This procedure combines the use of broadly based behavioral strategies with the more general principles of supportive psychotherapy.

Traditional behavioral and cognitive techniques, such as skill training, exposure, and problem solving, are employed to help the patient improve interpersonal relationships, tolerate distress, and regulate emotional responses. Considerable emphasis is also placed on the therapist's acceptance of patients, including their frequently demanding, manipulative, and contradictory behaviors. This factor is important, because borderline patients are extremely sensitive to even the most subtle signs of criticism or rejection by other people.

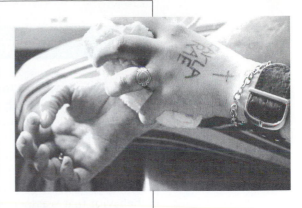

▲ **Some people with borderline personality disorders engage in recurrent suicidal gestures or self-mutilating behaviors.**

A controlled study of dialectical behavior therapy produced encouraging results with regard to some aspects of the patients' behavior (Linehan et al., 1993, 1994). Patients were randomly assigned to receive either DBT or treatment as usual, which was essentially any form of treatment that was available within the community. The adjustment of patients in both groups was measured after 1 year of treatment and over a 1-year period following termination. One of the most important results involved the dropout rate. Almost 60 percent of the patients in the treatment-as-usual group terminated prematurely, whereas the rate in the DBT group was only 17 percent. The patients who received DBT also showed a significant reduction in the frequency and severity of suicide attempts, spent fewer days in psychiatric hospitals over the course of the study, and rated themselves higher on a measure of social adjustment. The groups did not differ, however, on other important measures, such as level of depression and hopelessness. In general, the study suggests that DBT is a promising form of treatment for people with borderline personality disorder.

Psychotropic medication is also used frequently in the treatment of borderline patients. Unfortunately, no disorder-specific drug has been found. Psychiatrists employ the entire spectrum of psychoactive medication with borderline patients, from antipsychotics and antidepressants to lithium and anticonvulsants (Gitlin, 1993; Stein, 1992). Different types of drugs are recommended to treat individual symptoms, but there is no systematic proof that a specific drug is effective for any of the borderline features (Soloff, 1994).

Antisocial Personality Disorder (ASPD)

Antisocial personality disorder (ASPD) has been studied more thoroughly and for a longer period of time than any of the other personality disorders (Blashfield & McElroy, 1989). One case study involving this disorder was presented at the beginning of this chapter. The man in that case illustrated the pattern of repeated antisocial behavior that is associated with the disorder. Emotional and interpersonal problems also play an important role in the definition of antisocial personality disorder. The following case, written by Robert Hare, a clinical psychologist at the University of British Columbia, illustrates the egocentricity that is a central feature of the disorder. It also demonstrates the stunning lack of concern that such people have for the impact of their behavior on other people, especially those who are close to them.

> ### BRIEF CASE STUDY
>
> Terry is 21, the second of three boys born into a wealthy and highly respected family. His older brother is a doctor, and his younger brother is a scholarship student in his second year of college. Terry is a first-time offender, serving 2 years for a series of robberies committed a year ago.
>
> By all accounts, his family life was stable, his parents were warm and loving, and his opportunities for success were enormous. His brothers were honest and hardworking, whereas he simply "floated through life, taking whatever was offered." His parents' hopes and expectations were less important to him than having a good time. Still, they supported him emotionally and financially through an adolescence marked by wildness, testing the limits, and repeated brushes with the law—speeding, reckless driving, drunkenness—but no formal convictions. By age 20 he had fathered two children and was heavily involved in gambling and drugs. When he could no longer obtain money from his family he turned to robbing banks,

> and he was soon caught and sent to prison. "I wouldn't be here if my parents had come across when I needed them," he said. "What kind of parents would let their son rot in a place like this?" Asked about his children, he replied, "I've never seen them. I think they were given up for adoption. How the hell should I know!" (Hare, 1993, p. 167) ∎

The contrast between Terry's willingness to blame his own problems on his parents and his apparent inability to accept responsibility for his own children is striking. It illustrates clearly the callous indifference and shallow emotional experience of the person with antisocial personality disorder.

Brief Historical Perspective

Current views of antisocial personality disorder have been greatly influenced by two specific books. These books have inspired two different approaches to the definition of the disorder itself. The first book, *The Mask of Sanity*, was written by Hervey Cleckley, a psychiatrist at the University of Georgia, and was originally published in 1941. It included numerous case examples of impulsive, self-centered, pleasure-seeking people who seemed to be completely lacking in certain primary emotions, such as anxiety, shame, and guilt. Cleckley used the term **psychopathy** to describe this disorder. According to Cleckley's definition, the *psychopath* is a person who is intelligent and superficially charming but also chronically deceitful, unreliable, and incapable of learning from experience. This diagnostic approach places principal emphasis on emotional deficits and personality traits. Unfortunately, Cleckley's definition was difficult to use reliably because it relied on such elusive features as "incapacity for love" and "failure to learn from experience."

The second book that influenced the concept of antisocial personality disorder was a report by Lee Robins of her follow-up study of children who had been treated many years earlier at a child guidance clinic. The book, *Deviant Children Grown Up* (1966), demonstrated that certain forms of conduct disorder that were evident during childhood, especially among boys, were reliable predictors of other forms of antisocial behavior when these same people became adults. The diagnostic approach inspired by this research study was adopted by DSM-III (APA, 1980). It places principal emphasis on observable behaviors and repeated conflict with authorities, including failure to conform to social norms with respect to lawful behavior. This approach can be used with greater reliability because it is focused on concrete consequences of the disorder, which are often documented by legal records, rather than subjectively defined emotional deficits, such as lack of empathy.

Psychopathy and ASPD are two different attempts to define the same disorder. Yet they are sufficiently different that they certainly do not identify the same people, and they are no longer used interchangeably. Critics argued that DSM-III had blurred the distinction between antisocial personality and criminality. Cleckley's approach had been relatively clear on this point; all criminals are not psychopaths, and all psychopaths are not convicted criminals. The

DSM-III definition made it difficult to diagnose antisocial personality disorder in a person who did not already have a criminal record, such as an egocentric, manipulative, and callous businessperson. It also moved in the direction of including a much larger proportion of criminals within the boundaries of antisocial personality disorder. (Hare, Hart, & Harpur, 1991). The true meaning of the concept might have been sacrificed in DSM-III for the sake of improved reliability.

Clinical Features and Comorbidity

Table 9–7 lists the DSM-IV criteria for antisocial personality disorder. One prominent feature in this definition is the required presence of symptoms of conduct disorder (see Chapter 16) prior to the age of 15, which reflects the impact of Robins' work. The definition also requires the presence of at least three out of seven signs of irresponsible and antisocial behavior after the age of 15. One of these criteria, "lack of remorse," did not appear in DSM-III but was one of Cleckley's original criteria. Its inclusion in DSM-IV clearly signals an attempt to move the definition back toward the original concept.

▲ Robert Hare, a psychologist at the University of British Columbia, is a leading expert on psychopathy. He developed the Psychopathy Checklist, which has become the standard assessment instrument for this disorder.

TABLE 9-7

DSM-IV Criteria for Antisocial Personality Disorder

A. There is a pervasive pattern of disregard for and violation of the rights of others occurring since age 15, as indicated by three (or more) of the following:
  1. Failure to conform to social norms with respect to lawful behavior as indicated by repeatedly performing acts that are grounds for arrest.
  2. Deceitfulness, as indicated by repeated lying, use of aliases, or conning others for personal profit or pleasure.
  3. Impulsivity or failure to plan ahead.
  4. Irritability and aggressiveness, as indicated by repeated physical fights or assaults.
  5. Reckless disregard for safety of self or others.
  6. Consistent irresponsibility, as indicated by repeated failure to sustain consistent work behavior or honor financial obligations.
  7. Lack of remorse, as indicated by being indifferent to or rationalizing having hurt, mistreated, or stolen from another.

B. The individual is at least 18 years old.

C. Evidence of Conduct Disorder with onset before age 15.

Some investigators and clinicians prefer the concept of psychopathy to the DSM-IV definition of antisocial personality. Robert Hare has developed a systematic approach to the assessment of psychopathy, known as the *Psychopathy Checklist (PCL)*, that is based largely on Cleckley's original description of the disorder. The PCL includes two major factors (groups of symptoms): (1) emotional / interpersonal traits and (2) social deviance associated with an unstable or antisocial lifestyle. Key symptoms for both factors are summarized in Table 9–8. The major difference between this definition of psychopathy and the DSM-IV definition of antisocial personality disorder involves the list of emotional and interpersonal traits (although DSM-IV does include being deceitful and failure to experience remorse). Extensive research with the PCL indicates that, contrary to previous experience with Cleckley's criteria, the emotional and interpersonal traits can be used reliably (Hare, Hart, & Harpur, 1991).

The ultimate resolution of this prolonged dispute over the best definition of antisocial personality disorder will depend on systematic comparisons of the two approaches (Lilienfeld, 1994; Widiger & Corbitt, 1995). This situation is a classic example of the issues involved in studying the *validity* of a diagnostic concept (see Chapter 4). How different are these definitions? Which definition is most useful in predicting events such as repeated antisocial behavior following release from prison? The field trial that was conducted when DSM-IV was being prepared represents one large-scale effort of this type (Widiger et al., 1996). That project did not find any major differences in validity between the DSM-based definition of antisocial

personality disorder and a PCL-based definition of psychopathy.

ANTISOCIAL BEHAVIOR OVER THE LIFE SPAN

Not everyone who engages in antisocial behavior does so consistently throughout his or her lifetime. Terrie Moffitt, a clinical psychologist at the University of Wisconsin, has proposed that there are two primary forms of antisocial behavior: transient and nontransient. Moffitt (1993) considers *adolescence-limited antisocial behavior* to be a common form of social behavior that is often adaptive and that disappears by the time the person reaches adulthood. This type presumably accounts for most antisocial behavior, and it is unrelated to antisocial personality disorder.

A small proportion of antisocial individuals, mostly males, engage in antisocial behavior at all ages. Moffitt calls this type *life-course-persistent antisocial behavior*. The specific form of these problems may vary from one age level to the next:

> Biting and hitting at age 4, shoplifting and truancy at age 10, selling drugs and stealing cars at age 16, robbery and rape at age 22, and fraud and child abuse at age 30. The underlying disposition remains the same, but its expression changes form as new social opportunities arise at different points in development (Moffitt, 1993, p. 679).

Many clinicians believe that, among adults, antisocial behavior diminishes with age. Follow-up studies suggest that, in some ways, psychopaths tend to "burn out" when they reach 40 or 45 years of age. These changes are most evident for the impulsive, socially deviant kinds of behavior that are represented in the second factor on Hare's Psychopathy Checklist (Harpur & Hare, 1994). Older psychopaths are, indeed, less likely to exhibit a pathological "need for excitement" or to engage in impulsive, criminal behaviors. In contrast to this pattern, personality traits associated with the emotional-interpersonal factor on the PCL, such as deceitfulness, callousness, and lack of empathy, do *not* become less conspicuous over time. These are apparently more stable features of the disorder.

It is not clear whether the age-related decline in social deviance represents a change in

TABLE 9–8

Key Symptoms of Psychopathy

Emotional/Interpersonal Traits	Social Deviance (Antisocial Lifestyle)
Glib and superficial	Impulsive
Egocentric and grandiose	Poor behavior controls
Lack of remorse or guilt	Need for excitement
Lack of empathy	Lack of responsibility
Deceitful and manipulative	Early behavior problems
Shallow emotions	Adult antisocial behavior

Source: R. D. Hare, 1993, *Without Conscience: The Disturbing World of the Psychopaths Among Us.* New York: Pocket Books.

personality structure (improved impulse control and diminished sensation seeking). Moffitt's theory suggests that, as psychopaths grow older, they may find new outlets for their aggression, their impulsive behavior, and their callous disregard for others. For example, they might resort to fraud or child abuse, for which they are less likely to get caught.

Etiological Considerations

Psychologists have studied etiological factors associated with antisocial personality disorder more extensively than for any of the other personality disorders. Research studies on this topic fall into three general areas. One is concerned with the biological underpinnings of the disorder, especially the possible influence of genetic factors. The second focus of investigation is social factors. The relationship between familial conflict and the development of antisocial behavior in children falls under this general heading. The third group of studies has addressed the nature of the psychological factors that might explain the apparent inability of people with antisocial personality disorder to learn from experience.

BIOLOGICAL FACTORS

Several investigators have employed adoption methods to evaluate the relative contributions of genetic and environmental factors to the development of antisocial personality disorder, and of criminal behavior more generally (Carey & Gottesman, 1996). This strategy is based on the study of *adoptees*: people who were separated from their biological parents at an early age and raised by adoptive families (see Chapter 2). The extent to which the adoptees' behavior resembles that of their biological relatives is taken to be evidence for the influence of genetic factors, and the extent to which their behavior is similar to that of their adoptive relatives presumably reflects the influence of environmental factors.

Several different adoption studies have found that the development of antisocial behavior is determined by an *interaction* between genetic factors and adverse environmental circumstances. In other words, both types of influence are important. The highest rates of conduct disorder and antisocial behavior are found among the offspring of antisocial biological parents who are raised in an adverse adoptive environment.

Consider, for example, the results of one particularly informative study that was conducted by Remi Cadoret, a psychiatrist at the University of Iowa, and several colleagues (Cadoret et al., 1995). The investigators studied men and women who had been separated at birth from biological parents with antisocial personality disorder. This target group was compared to a control group of people who had been separated at birth from biological parents with no history of psychopathology. The offspring and their adoptive parents were interviewed to assess symptoms of conduct disorder, aggression, and antisocial behavior in the offspring. The adversity of the adoptive home environment was measured in terms of the total number of problems that were present, including severe marital difficulties, drug abuse, or criminal activity.

The results of the study by Cadoret and his colleagues indicated that people who were raised in more difficult adoptive homes were more likely to engage in various types of aggressive and antisocial behavior as children and as adults. Further analyses revealed that the harmful effects of an unfavorable environment were more pronounced in the target group than in the control group. In other words, offspring of antisocial parents were much more likely to exhibit symptoms of conduct disorder (truancy, school expulsion, lying, and stealing) as children and exaggerated aggressive behavior as adolescents *if they were raised in an adverse adoptive home environment.* Being raised in an adverse home environment did not significantly increase the probability of conduct disorder, aggression, or antisocial behavior among offspring in the control group. Thus antisocial behavior appeared to result from the interaction of genetic and environmental factors.

SOCIAL FACTORS

Adoption studies indicate that genetic factors interact with environmental events to produce patterns of antisocial and criminal behavior. The combination of a biological predisposition toward antisocial behavior and environmental adversity is particularly harmful. What kinds of events might be involved in this process? One obvious candidate is family conflict.

Robins (1966) found that children raised in families characterized by inconsistent

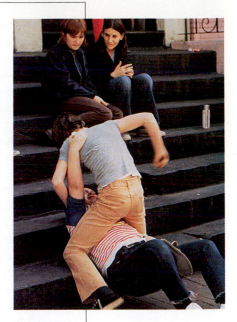

▲ The best predictor of adult antisocial personality disorder in Lee Robins's study was conduct disorder characterized by physical aggression and other rule violations.

discipline or the complete absence of discipline were more likely to receive a diagnosis of antisocial personality disorder when they reached adulthood. She also found that subjects who received a diagnosis of antisocial personality disorder as adults were likely to have had fathers who exhibited antisocial behavior themselves. Her study suggests that parental behaviors can have an important influence on the development of antisocial behavior in their children.

How can the interaction between genetic factors and family processes be explained? Moffitt's explanation for the etiology of life-course-persistent antisocial behavior depends on the influence of multiple, interacting systems. One pathway involves the concept of children's temperament and the effect that their characteristic response styles may have on parental behavior. Children with a "difficult" temperament—whose response style is characterized by high levels of negative emotion or excessive activity—may be especially irritating to their parents and caretakers (Bates, Wachs, & Emde, 1994). They may be clumsy, overactive, inattentive, irritable, or impulsive. Their resistance to disciplinary efforts may discourage adults from maintaining persistent strategies in this regard. This type of child may be most likely to evoke maladaptive reactions from parents who are poorly equipped to deal with the challenges presented by this kind of behavior. Parents may be driven either to use unusually harsh punishments or to abandon any attempt at discipline. This interaction between the child and the social environment fosters the development of poorly controlled behavior. Antisocial behavior is perpetuated when the person selects friends who share similar antisocial interests and problems.

After a pattern of antisocial behavior has been established during childhood, many factors lock the person into further antisocial activities. Moffitt's theory emphasizes two sources of continuity. The first is a limited range of behavioral skills. The person does not learn social skills that would allow him or her to pursue more appropriate responses than behaviors such as lying, cheating, and stealing. Once the opportunity to develop these skills is lost during childhood, they may never be learned. The second source of continuity involves the results of antisocial behavior during childhood and adolescence. The person becomes progressively ensnared by the aftermath of earlier choices. Many possible consequences of antisocial behavior, including being addicted to drugs, becoming a teenaged parent, dropping out of school, and having a criminal record, can narrow the person's options.

PSYCHOLOGICAL FACTORS

Adoption, twin, and family studies provide clues to the types of etiological factors that may cause antisocial personality disorder. Another series of studies, beginning in the 1950s and extending to the present, has been concerned with the psychological mechanisms that may mediate this type of behavior. These investigations have attempted to explain several characteristic features of psychopathy, such as lack of anxiety, impulsivity, and failure to learn from experience, using various types of laboratory tasks.

Subjects in these tasks are typically asked to learn a sequence of responses in order either to receive a reward or avoid an aversive consequence, such as electric shock or loss of money. Although the overall accuracy of psychopaths' performance on these tasks is generally equivalent to that of nonpsychopathic subjects, their behavior sometimes appears to be unaffected by the anticipation of punishment (Lykken, 1957; Kosson & Newman, 1986). Two primary hypotheses have been advanced to explain the poor performance of psychopaths on these tasks.

One point of view is based on Cleckley's argument that psychopaths are emotionally impoverished. Their lack of anxiety and fear is particularly striking. Research support for this hypothesis is based in large part on an examination of physiological responses while subjects are performing laboratory tasks. One particularly compelling line of investigation involves the examination of the eye blink startle reflex. People blink their eyes involuntarily when they are startled by a loud, unexpected, burst of noise. For most people, the magnitude of this response is increased if, at the time they are startled, they are engaged in an ongoing task that elicits fear or some other negative emotional state (such as viewing frightening or disgusting stimuli). The magnitude of the startle response is decreased if the person is engaged in a task that elicits positive emotion. Psychopaths' startle responses follow a different pattern than those observed in normal subjects (Patrick, 1994); they do not show the exaggerated startle response that is indicative of fear in the presence of aversive stimuli. This emotional deficit may explain why psychopaths are relatively insensitive to, or able to ignore, the effects of punishment (Hare, 1993).

The other hypothesis holds that psychopaths have difficulty shifting or reallocating their attention to consider the possible negative consequences of their behavior after a response pattern has been well established. Evidence for this explanation is based in large part on the observation that psychopaths respond normally to punishment in some situations but not in others. This is especially evident in mixed-incentive situations, in which the person's behavior might be either rewarded or punished. The behavior of psychopaths appears to be disinhibited because they are less able than other people to suspend activities that may be rewarded in order to reflect upon the meaning of important, but less salient, cues that indicate that their behavior might lead to punishment (Newman, Kosson, & Patterson, 1992; Patterson & Newman, 1993).

Critics of this line of research have noted some problems with existing psychological explanations for the psychopath's behavior. One limitation is the implicit assumption that most people conform to social regulations and ethical principles because of anxiety or fear of punishment. The heart of this criticism seems to lie in a disagreement regarding the relative importance of Cleckley's criteria for psychopathy. It might be argued that the most crucial features are not low anxiety and failure to learn from experience but lack of shame and pathological egocentricity. According to this perspective, the psychopath is simply a person who has chosen, for whatever reason, to behave in a persistently selfish manner that ignores the feelings and rights of other people. "Rather than moral judgment being driven by anxiety, anxiety is driven by moral judgment" (Levenson, 1992).

Treatment

People with antisocial personalities seldom seek professional mental health services unless they are forced into treatment by the legal system. When they do seek treatment, the general consensus among clinicians is that it is seldom effective (Quality Assurance Project, 1991). This widely held impression is based, in part, on the traits that are used to define the disorder; like people with borderline personality disorder, people with antisocial personality disorder are typically unable to establish intimate, trusting relationships, which obviously form the basis for any treatment program.

The research literature regarding the treatment of antisocial personality disorder is rather sparse (Dolan & Coid, 1993). Very few studies have identified cases using official diagnostic criteria for antisocial personality disorder. Most of the programs that have been evaluated have focused on juvenile delinquents, adults who have been imprisoned, or people otherwise referred by the criminal justice system. Outcome is often measured in terms of the frequency of repeated criminal offenses rather than in terms of changes in behaviors more directly linked to the personality traits that define the core of antisocial personality. The high rate of alcoholism and other forms of substance dependence in this population is another problem that complicates planning and evaluating treatment programs aimed specifically at the personality disorder itself.

Although no form of intervention has proved to be effective for antisocial personality disorder, psychological interventions that are directed toward specific features of the disorder might be useful (Doren, 1993). Examples are behavioral procedures that were originally designed for anger management and deviant sexual behaviors. Behavioral treatments can apparently produce temporary changes in behavior while the person is closely supervised, but they may not generalize to other settings (Freeman & Gunderson, 1989).

Dependent Personality Disorder (DPD)

Dependent personality disorder (DPD) is listed in the third cluster of Axis II in DSM-IV, along with avoidant and obsessive–compulsive personality disorders. Cluster C includes descriptions of various types of people who are anxious or fearful. Those who meet the criteria for DPD assume a submissive role in relationships with other people. They require an extraordinary level of reassurance and support, clinging to others who will take care of them. The following case study, written by I. D. Turkat and C. R. Carlson, illustrates many of the most important features of this disorder.

BRIEF CASE STUDY

The patient, Mrs. S., was a 48-year-old married, Caucasian female. (She) reported numerous decision-making situations which provoke anxiety and attempts to seek reassurance. For example, buying food in the supermarket, deciding what to make for dinner, and buying furniture all provoked anxiety and led Mrs. S. to seek reassurance from her husband. Further, Mrs. S. reported feeling anxious when her husband was not there to reassure her (such as when he was away and Mrs. S. was responsible for trimming the garden bushes and lawn). Finally the patient related numerous anxiety-provoking instances in which decisions she made were initially approved of by an authority figure (such as her husband or physician) and then criticized by an important other (such as after following the instructions of her physician, she was criticized for doing so by a friend).

During school years, Mrs. S. always wanted to be part of the "group," but she felt uncomfortable because no one would assure her explicitly that she "fit in." Moreover, her high school advisor noted on Mrs. S's record that she "lacked initiative."

When the patient went to college, she studied nursing because "a lot of people my age went into nursing." When the time came to choose between a university-based or hospital-based program, she relied largely on her mother's advice.

The patient's first job as a nurse went rather smoothly because her supervisors were readily available. Unfortunately, her second position did not work out well. Apparently, Mrs. S. had trouble adjusting because she did not have

"supportive" supervisors. She left this position after a short time.

Mrs. S. did not have much of a dating history. Her husband was her first and only lover. She was greatly attracted to him because he was "very forceful" and an "independent decision maker." (Turkat & Carlson, 1984, pp. 156–157) ■

Brief Historical Perspective

Dependent personality disorder was introduced as a separate type of mental disorder in DSM-III (APA, 1980). Before then, the concept of dependency was viewed primarily as a personality trait rather than a mental disorder in its own right. It was considered to be a vulnerability factor that increased the person's risk for other types of mental disorder, particularly depression.

Freud proposed that dependent interpersonal relationships set the stage for later onset of depression (see Chapter 5). Contemporary investigators are still very much interested in that hypothesis (e.g., Blatt & Zuroff, 1992). The term *sociotropy* is sometimes used to refer to dependency in that context. According to one version of this theory, people who are dependent, or sociotropic, may be particularly likely to become depressed if they experience a stressful event that is interpersonal in nature. Unfortunately, longitudinal studies have not been able to show that a dependent or sociotropic interpersonal style predicts the later onset of depression (Coyne & Whiffen, 1995).

Clinical Features and Comorbidity

The DSM-IV criteria for dependent personality disorder are listed in Table 9–9. These criteria reflect two underlying components: attachment behaviors and dependency behaviors (Birchnell, 1991; Livesley, 1995). Attachment behaviors reflect the desire to remain close to another person (the "attachment figure") who will provide security and comfort. Dependency behaviors reflect a lack of self-confidence and include actions aimed at eliciting help and approval from others. Unlike attachment behaviors, which are

TABLE 9-9

DSM-IV Criteria for Dependent Personality Disorder

A. **A pervasive and excessive need to be taken care of that leads to submissive and clinging behavior and fears of separation, beginning by early adulthood and present in a variety of contexts, as indicated by five (or more) of the following:**

1. Has difficulty making everyday decisions without an excessive amount of advice and reassurance from others.
2. Needs others to assume responsibility for most major areas of his or her life.
3. Has difficulty expressing disagreement with others because of fear of loss of support or approval (does not include *realistic* fears of retribution).
4. Has difficulty initiating projects or doing things on his or her own (because of lack of self-confidence in judgment or abilities rather than a lack of motivation or energy).
5. Goes to excessive lengths to obtain nurturance and support from others, to the point of volunteering to do things that are unpleasant.
6. Feels uncomfortable or helpless when alone because of exaggerated fears of being unable to care for himself or herself.
7. Urgently seeks another relationship as a source of care and support when a close relationship ends.
8. Is unrealistically preoccupied with fears of being left to take care of himself or herself.

directed toward a specific person, dependency behaviors can be directed toward many different people.

Dependent personality disorder overlaps with several other categories listed on Axis II of DSM-IV. The greatest overlap is with borderline personality disorder. People with both types of personality disorder show fear of being abandoned by other people. The reactions that they show are quite different, however. People with BPD become enraged and manipulative when they think they are being abandoned, whereas people with DPD respond with clinging and submissive behaviors (Hirschfeld, Shea, & Weise, 1995).

Etiological Considerations

Relatively little research has been conducted on the etiology of dependent personality disorder as a separate form of mental disorder. There is, however, a substantial body of evidence concerned with the development of dependency as a *personality trait*. We must therefore use this evidence to draw inferences about pathways leading to dependent personality disorder. The available evidence points toward the importance of social and psychological factors in the development of extreme dependency. Genetic factors seem to

play a relatively minor role (Nigg & Goldsmith, 1994).

Overprotective, authoritarian parents are likely to foster the development of dependency in their children (Bornstein, 1993, 1996). This conclusion is supported by the results of many different types of empirical research. It is also consistent with several different psychological theories, which have emphasized the importance of parent–child relationships in the formation and maintenance of dependent personality traits. For example, according to attachment theory (Ainsworth, 1989; Bowlby, 1973), children have a basic need to form a secure attachment to adults who will care for them (see Chapter 2). Those who are anxiously or insecurely attached as children are likely to become highly dependent during adolescence and adulthood. The process through which this pattern develops presumably involves the child's expectations about the availability of the parent. Children who have little confidence that

▼ **Parental overprotectiveness may encourage dependence and interfere with the child's opportunities to learn skills that are necessary for more independent behavior.**

attachment figures will be easily accessible and responsive when they need something may attempt to remain unusually close to those people, thus behaving in a clinging and dependent manner.

Treatment

There is virtually no literature on the outcome of treatment for dependent personality disorder. Therefore we cannot say whether any therapeutic procedures have been shown to be effective with this type of problem. People with this disorder may be less likely to seek treatment than people with other types of mental disorder. When they enter therapy, it is often because they also have other problems, such as depression, an anxiety disorder, or a substance-use disorder. Whatever information is available on the treatment of this disorder is based on theoretical speculation and clinical experience (rather than empirical research).

Psychodynamic therapists have written most extensively about the treatment of dependent personality disorder. The primary goal in their approach is to help the person recognize the dependent pattern and the negative impact that it has on his or her relationships. Unfortunately, insight into the self-defeating nature of exceedingly dependent relationships may not be sufficient to allow the person to change his or her behavior. Behavior therapists (Goldfried & Davison, 1994) and interpersonal therapists (Benjamin, 1996) emphasize the need to teach skills in assertive communication. The client must learn to communicate feelings (both positive and negative) and desires accurately. The goal is to help the person develop interpersonal skills that will allow him or her to be more independent and self-reliant.

Cognitive therapy may also be beneficial in the treatment of dependent personality disorder. Problem-solving strategies, coupled with regular practice in making decisions, may foster independence and decrease the client's need to depend on other people for reassurance and support in routine situations. Cognitive therapy also addresses irrational or catastrophic self-statements about the potential consequences of behaving more independently or of ending a relationship (Freeman et al., 1990).

Psychopharmacology is not typically used as a specific treatment for dependent personality disorder. When medication is employed with such clients, it is usually aimed at the treatment of comorbid Axis I disorders, such as depression, agoraphobia, and panic disorder (Gitlin, 1993).

Summary

Personality disorders are defined in terms of rigid, inflexible, maladaptive ways of perceiving and responding to oneself and one's environment that lead to social or occupational problems or subjective distress. This pattern must be pervasive across a broad range of situations, and it must be stable and of long duration. Among the hallmark features of personality disorders are major problems in interpersonal relationships. Many of the traits and symptoms that are associated with these problems are ego-syntonic. In other words, many people with personality disorders do not see themselves as being disturbed.

Personality disorders are controversial for a number of reasons, including their low diagnostic reliability, the tremendous overlap among specific personality disorder categories, and the relative absence of effective forms of treatment. They are presumably defined in terms of behaviors that deviate markedly from the expectations of the person's culture.

KEY TERMS

- agreeableness
- antisocial personality disorder
- avoidant personality disorder
- borderline personality disorder
- conscientiousness
- cross-cultural psychology
- culture
- dependent personality disorder
- extraversion
- histrionic personality disorder
- impulse control disorders

Unfortunately, little information is currently available to indicate whether the DSM-IV system for personality disorders will be useful in societies other than the United States, Canada, and Western Europe.

Many systems have been proposed to describe the fundamental dimensions of human **personality.** One that has become quite popular is known as the five-factor model, which includes basic traits known as neuroticism, extraversion, openness to experience, agreeableness, and conscientiousness. Extreme variations in any of these traits—being either pathologically high or low—can be associated with personality disorders.

DSM-IV lists 10 types of personality disorder, arranged in 3 clusters. There is considerable overlap among and between these types. Cluster A includes **paranoid, schizoid,** and **schizotypal personality disorders.** These categories generally refer to people who are seen as being odd or eccentric. Cluster B includes **anti-social, borderline, histrionic,** and **narcissistic personality disorders.** People who fit into this cluster are generally seen as being dramatic, unpredictable, and overly emotional. Cluster C includes **avoidant, dependent,** and **obsessive–compulsive personality disorders.** The common element in these disorders is presumably anxiety or fearfulness.

Dimensional approaches to the description of personality disorder provide an interesting alternative to this categorical system. These procedures provide for rating a person on a number of traits, such as those included in the five-factor model. Dimensional classification systems have the advantage of being better able to account for similarities and differences among people with various combinations of personality traits.

The lifetime prevalence of personality disorders among adults in the general population is between 10 and 14 percent. The overall lifetime prevalence rate for antisocial personality disorder (men and women combined) was 2.6 percent in the ECA study and 3.5 percent in the NCS, with rates being at least 4 times higher in men than in women. The NCS and ECA study did not ask questions about the other specific types of personality disorder. Borderline personality disorder is the most frequently diagnosed form of personality disorder among people seeking mental health services (both inpatients and outpatients).

The disorders listed in Cluster A, especially schizoid and schizotypal personality disorders, have been viewed as possible antecedents or subclinical forms of schizophrenia. They are defined largely in terms of minor symptoms that resemble the hallucinations and delusions seen in the full-blown disorder, as well as peculiar behaviors that have been observed among the first-degree relatives of schizophrenic patients. Research on the etiology of schizotypal personality disorder has focused primarily on studies of its genetic relationship to schizophrenia.

The most important features of borderline personality disorder revolve around a pervasive pattern of instability in self-image, in interpersonal relationships, and in mood. Some investigators believe that borderline personality disorder is an extremely heterogeneous category that should be further subdivided. Research regarding the etiology of borderline personality disorder has focused on two primary areas. One involves the impact of chaotic and abusive families. The other is concerned with the premature separation of children from their parents. Both sets of factors can presumably lead to problems in emotional regulation.

Psychopathy and ASPD are two different attempts to define the same disorder. The DSM-IV definition of antisocial personality disorder (ASPD) places primary emphasis on social deviance in adulthood (repeated lying, physical assaults, reckless and irresponsible behavior). The concept of psychopathy places greater emphasis on emotional and interpersonal deficits, such as lack of remorse, lack of empathy, and shallow emotions. Adoption studies indicate that the etiology of antisocial behavior is determined by an interaction between genetic factors and adverse environmental circumstances. Laboratory studies of people who meet the criteria for psychopathy have focused on two hypothesis. One suggests that psychopaths are emotionally impoverished. The other holds that psychopaths have difficulty shifting their attention in order to avoid punishment.

Treatment procedures for people with personality disorders are especially difficult to design and evaluate, for three principal reasons. First, people with these disorders frequently don't have insight into the nature of their problems. They are therefore unlikely to seek treatment, and if they do, they frequently terminate prematurely. Second, pure forms of personality disorder are relatively rare. Most people with a personality disorder who are in treatment also exhibit comorbid forms of personality disorder and/or comorbid Axis I disorders, such as depression or drug addiction. Third, people with personality disorder have difficulty establishing and maintaining meaningful, stable interpersonal relationships of the sort that are required for psychotherapy.

Treatment for schizotypal and borderline personality disorders often involves the use of antipsychotic medication or antidepressant medication. A few controlled studies indicate that these drugs can be beneficial. Long-term outcome tends to be better for patients with borderline than schizotypal personality disorder. Various types of psychological intervention, including psychodynamic procedures as well as dialectical behavior therapy, have frequently been employed with borderline patients. People with antisocial personality disorder seldom seek treatment voluntarily. When they do, the general consensus among clinicians is that it is seldom effective.

Critical Thinking

1. The DSM-IV lists the personality disorders on a separate axis from the other types of mental disorder. In what ways are these problems different from disorders like depression, schizophrenia, and alcoholism? How are they similar?

2. Imagine that you are a clinical psychologist who is treating a client who is depressed. How would your treatment plan change if you knew that, in addition to a diagnosis of unipolar mood disorder on Axis I, the person also met the DSM-IV criteria for borderline personality disorder? What if the Axis II diagnosis was dependent personality disorder?

3. Think of a typical case of borderline personality disorder, as defined by DSM-IV. How would you describe that person's behavior in terms of the dimensions of the five-factor model? Can you think of any advantages to considering the person's behavior in terms of these dimensions rather than using the DSM-IV category?

4. Imagine that you are a judge who must decide the fate of a 17-year-old male juvenile delinquent who has just been convicted of his first felony offense (theft). You know that he has a long history of truancy from school and of running away from home. His attorney asks you to place him on probation contingent on his entering into psychological treatment, on the grounds that he is suffering from a mental disorder. What would you do? Does that seem like a plausible alternative to jail? Would you respond differently if the man were 40 years old?

10
Eating Disorders

Popular culture in the United States today is obsessed with physical appearance. Every day we are bombarded with media images of people who are perfectly beautiful, perfectly fit, and perfectly thin. We are told that "beauty is only skin deep," but the cosmetic, fashion, and diet industries are eager to convince young people that "looks are everything." The media often project ideal images of men and women. Perfect men are handsome, strong, athletic, and successful. Perfect women are beautiful and thin—often, extremely thin. In fact, women's thinness is equated with beauty, fitness, success, and ultimately with happiness. Given our national obsession with appearance, weight, and diet, is it surprising that many young people, especially young women, become obsessed with food to the point where they develop eating-related disorders?

Overview

Eating disorders are severe disturbances in eating behavior that result from the sufferer's obsessive fear of gaining weight. Some experts have suggested that "dieting disorder" is a more accurate term for these behaviors (Beumont, Garner, & Touyz, 1994), because dread of weight gain and obsession with weight loss are central features of eating disorders. The DSM-IV lists two major subtypes of eating disorders: anorexia nervosa and bulimia nervosa. The most obvious characteristic of **anorexia nervosa** is extreme emaciation, or more technically, the refusal to maintain a minimally normal body weight. The term *anorexia* literally means "loss of appetite," but this is a misnomer. People with anorexia nerovsa *are* hungry, yet they starve themselves nevertheless. Some unfortunate victims literally starve themselves to death. One example is gymnast Christy Heinrich, who died of complications caused by her extreme emaciation. **Bulimia nervosa** is characterized by repeated episodes of binge eating, followed by inappropriate compensatory behaviors such as self-induced vomiting, misuse of laxatives, or excessive exercise. The literal meaning of the term *bulimia* is "ox appetite," but people with bulimia nervosa typically have a normal appetite and maintain a normal weight. In fact, most sufferers view their binge eating as a failure of control, not as an indulgence of their excessive appetites or as a relief from the pressures of dieting. Thus people with bulimia nervosa commonly are ashamed and secretive about their binge eating and purging. Princess Diana is one famous woman who has publicly admitted to struggling with bulimia.

Both anorexia and bulimia are about 10 times more common among females than males, and they develop most commonly among women in their teens and early twenties. The increased incidence among young people reflects both the intense focus on young women's physical appearance and the difficulties many adolescent girls encounter in adjusting to the rapid changes in body shape and weight that begin with puberty (Hsu, 1990). According to the National Centers for Disease Control and Prevention, at any point in time 44 percent of high school females are attempting to lose weight compared with 15 percent of males. In fact, many adolescent boys want to *gain* weight in order to look bigger and stronger (Serdula et al., 1993).

▼ **Images of women in advertising and the popular media often equate thinness with beauty, success, and happiness.**

Moreover, a recent national survey found that almost half of American women have a negative body image, particularly concerning their waist, hips, and/or thighs (Cash & Henry, 1995; see Figure 10–1). Clearly, cultural attitudes about weight, thinness, and appearance play a central role in causing eating disorders.

Because the symptoms of anorexia nervosa differ considerably from those of bulimia nervosa, we consider the typical symptoms of the two disorders separately in this chapter. We combine the two disorders when discussing classification, prevalence, and etiology, however, because they share many developmental similarities. For example, many people with anorexia nervosa also binge and purge on occasion; many people with bulimia nervosa have a history of anorexia nervosa. When discussing treatment, we again discuss the two disorders separately, reflecting the important differences in the focus and effectiveness of therapy for each disorder. We begin our consideration of eating disorders with a case study.

Women's Dissatisfaction with Their Physical Attributes

FIGURE 10-1: Percentage of females reporting that they were "very or mostly dissatisfied" with specific physical attributes in a national sample of women aged 18 to 70 interviewed in 1993.

Source: T.F. Cash and P.E. Henry, 1995, Women's body images: The results of a national survey in the U.S.A., *Sex Roles, 33,* 19-28.

CASE STUDY

Anorexia Nervosa

Seritta was an attractive, well-dressed, and polite 15-year-old high school sophomore who was living in a friendly joint-custody arrangement. She spent alternating weeks living with each of her successful, middle-class parents. Serrita was an excellent student whom her mother described as a "sweet girl who never gave me an ounce of worry—until now." When she was first seen by a clinical psychologist for the treatment of anorexia nervosa, Seritta was 5 feet 2 inches tall and weighed 81 pounds. Seritta's gaunt appearance was painfully obvious to the psychologist and to anyone else who looked at her. Despite her constant scrutiny of her own body, however, Seritta firmly denied that she was too thin. Instead, she asserted that she looked "almost right." Although she weighed only 81 pounds, she was still on a diet, and every day she carefully inspected her stomach, thighs, hips, arms, and face for any signs of fat. Although Seritta was generally pleased with the image she saw in her bathroom mirror, she remained deathly afraid of gaining weight. She monitored her food intake with incredible detail, and

she could recite every item of food she had consumed recently, as well as discuss its caloric and fat content.

Seritta had begun her diet 9 months earlier after visiting her family doctor. At the time, Seritta weighed 108 pounds, a normal weight for her age, height, and body type, although her physician told her that she could stand to lose a pound or two. Seritta claimed that the doctor's comment had motivated her to begin a diet. Previously, Seritta's weight had ranged between 102 and 108 pounds, and she set a goal of getting back to 102. The doctor's suggestion was not the only motivation for Seritta. She said that she also decided to diet because she wanted to look more attractive. Seritta was very interested in fashion and beauty, and she often wished that she looked like the women she saw in her favorite magazines. Seritta felt that her appearance suffered in comparison to her classmates' as well as to fashion models'. She was not part of the "popular crowd," and although she very much wanted to have a boyfriend, she was not dating. She blamed part of her perceived unattractiveness on the fact that she wasn't the "cute, all-American girl." Seritta admitted that she secretly hoped that having a "great body" would help compensate for her perceived inadequacies and make her beautiful in her own eyes and in the eyes of her classmates.

Seritta's diet began normally enough. She was very bright and began to read extensively about food, weight, and diet. She quickly lost the 6 pounds she wanted to lose, and her success was reinforced by her parents' and girlfriends' positive comments. To her knowledge, however, the boys in her school did not notice the change in her appearance, and her social life did not improve. Without really planning to do so, Seritta simply continued her diet. By then, she had developed the habit of scouring her image in the mirror, and she invariably found some spot that was just a bit "too fat." As a result, she was continually setting a new goal to lose another couple of pounds. She weighed herself constantly and said that the bathroom scale became her "best friend." Although her friends and family soon were telling her that she looked too thin, privately Seritta was exhilarated by their comments. To her, the concerned remarks only proved that her diet was working. At last, she had mastered her hunger, eating, and weight.

Seritta's diet was extreme and rigid. She ate breakfast and lunch on her own and adhered obsessively to her routine. Breakfast consisted of one slice of dry wheat toast and a small glass of orange juice. Lunch was either an apple or a small salad without dressing. In between meals, Seritta drank several diet colas, which helped her control her constant, gnawing appetite. Dinner typically was a family meal whether Seritta was at her mom's or her dad's house.

During these meals, Seritta picked at whatever she was served. Often her parents would lecture her or plead with her to eat more, and Seritta typically would eat a bit in an attempt to appease them. On occasion, perhaps once a week, Seritta would force herself to vomit after dinner if she felt that she had been made to eat too much.

Seritta's parents eventually became so concerned about her weight loss that they made her go to see her family physician. The physician also was very concerned about Seritta's low weight, and she discovered that Seritta had not menstruated in over 6 months. The physician detected no other physical problems during her examination, and Seritta did not tell her family doctor about the occasional purging after dinner. The physician raised the possibility that Seritta was suffering from anorexia nervosa. She immediately made a referral to a psychologist as well as to a nutritionist who, the physician hoped, would correct some of Seritta's extreme views about dieting.

In talking with the psychologist, Seritta agreed that she understood why everyone was concerned about her health. She knew about anorexia nervosa, which she realized was a serious problem. Seritta even hinted that she recognized that she herself was suffering from anorexia nervosa. Nevertheless, Seritta steadfastly denied that she needed to gain weight. Although she was happy to talk with the psychologist, she was not prepared to change her eating habits. Seritta was deathly afraid that eating even a little more normally would cause her to "lose control" and "turn into a blimp." Perhaps more importantly, she was *proud* of her mastery of her hunger. She was not about to give up the control she had fought so hard to obtain. ■

Typical Symptoms and Associated Features of Anorexia Nervosa

Seritta showed all the classic symptoms that define anorexia nervosa: extreme emaciation, a disturbed perception of her own body, an intense fear of gaining weight, and the cessation of menstruation (in women). Seritta also exhibited a number of problems that are commonly associated with anorexia nervosa but are not defining symptoms. These include her obsessive preoccupation with food, her occasional purging, and her central and "successful" struggle for control over her persistent hunger.

Finally, Seritta did not suffer from a few important problems that are sometimes associated with anorexia nervosa, particularly mood disturbance, sexual difficulties, a lack of impulse control, and medical problems secondary to the weight loss. The core symptoms of anorexia nervosa are generally the same, but the symptoms and associated features can vary from person to person. Eating disorders among men are especially likely to include unique features, as we examine in Further Thoughts.

Eating Disorders in Males

Both anorexia nervosa and bulimia nervosa are approximately 10 times more common among females than males, but eating disorders *do* occur among males. What do psychologists know about eating disorders among males?

Our culture clearly values extreme thinness far less among males than among females. Adolescent boys often want to be bigger and stronger, not slimmer. Surveys indicate that although the majority of females want to lose weight, males are about equally divided between those who want to lose weight and those who want to gain weight. Another indication of the difference in preferred weights is that women rate themselves as being thin only when they are 90 percent below their ideal body weight. In contrast, men see themselves as thin even when they weigh as much as 105 percent of their expected weight (Drewnowski & Yee, 1987).

The more realistic expectations concerning physical appearance surely contribute to the lower prevalence of eating disorders among males. However, a treatment complication can arise from the fact that men who develop eating disorders deviate far from the expected cultural norm. Peers, therapists, and even females with eating disorders may reject and stigmatize a male who develops an eating problem precisely because his appearance differs so much from the standard for men. The social isolation of a man with an eating disorder can become an important issue in treatment, and it greatly affects one common symptom of anorexia nervosa. As we have discussed, females with anorexia nervosa typically view their appearance and disorder positively, perhaps even with a degree of pride. In contrast, anorexia nervosa is much more likely to have a negative effect on the self-esteem of a male, because weight and/or eating struggles are "unmanly," that is, different from the cultural image of the ideal male (Andersen, 1995).

Eating disorders are more common among certain subgroups of males than in the general population. Male wrestlers have a particularly high prevalence of eating disorders, a result of the intense pressure to "make weight"—to weigh below the weight cutoffs used to group competitors in a wrestling match. Eating disorders also are more common among gay than heterosexual men, although only about 20 percent of men with eating disorders are gay. Finally, men with eating disorders are likelier to have a history of obesity in comparison to women with eating disorders (Andersen, 1995).

Other aspects of eating disorders appear to be similar for males and females, including the age of onset. For both females and males, the disorders typically begin during adolescence or young adulthood. Attempts to predict risk among adolescent boys have not been as successful as among teenage girls, however, in part because prediction is made difficult by the relatively small number of boys with eating problems (Leon et al., 1995; see the Research Close-Up box on p. 373). Still, more research is needed, even though eating disorders are comparatively infrequent among boys. It would be particularly interesting to study the influence of cultural standards and personal ideals for body weight and shape in males. Such research might shed light on the development of eating disorders not only among boys but also among girls. ∎

Refusal to Maintain a Normal Weight

The most obvious and most dangerous symptom of anorexia nervosa is *a refusal to maintain a minimally normal body weight*. As was the case for Seritta, many instances of anorexia nervosa begin with a diet designed to lose just a few pounds. The young woman (or sometimes a man) weighs near or within the range of her healthy body weight, and she may decide to lose a little weight, perhaps to fit into some new clothes or to become more fit. In anorexia nervosa, however, the diet goes awry, and losing weight eventually becomes the key focus of the individual's life. Weight falls below the normal range for age, height, and body type, and it often plummets to dangerously low levels. Another pattern is when a developing adolescent fails to make expected weight gains as a result of dieting.

TABLE 10-1

How Thin Is Too Thin?

Females or males are significantly underweight if they weigh less than the weights given for different heights listed in this table. Weight cutoffs represent a body mass index below 18.

Height[a] (feet, inches)	Weight[b] (pounds)	Height[a] (feet, inches)	Weight[b] (pounds)
4'10"	86	5'8"	118
4'10½"	88	5'8½"	120
4'11"	89	5'9"	121
4'11½"	90	5'9½"	124
5'0"	91	5'10"	125
5'½"	93	5'10½"	127
5'1"	95	5'11"	128
5'1½"	96	5'11½"	131
5'2"	99	6'0"	132
5'2½"	100	6'½"	134
5'3"	101	6'1"	135
5'3½"	103	6'1½"	138
5'4"	105	6'2"	140
5'4½"	106	6'2½"	141
5'5"	108	6'3"	144
5'5½"	109	6'3½"	146
5'6"	112	6'4"	147
5'6½"	113	6'4½"	149
5'7"	114	6'5"	152
5'7½"	117	6'5½"	154

[a]Without shoes.
[b]Without shoes, light indoor clothing.
Source: C. Fairburn, 1995, *Overcoming Binge Eating.* New York: Guilford.

The DSM-IV contains no formal cutoff as to how thin is too thin, but it suggests 85 percent of expected body weight as a rough guideline. The *body mass index*[†], a calculation derived from weight and height, is another useful way to determine whether or not someone is significantly underweight (see Table 10–1). Both the DSM-IV and the body mass cutoffs represent weights well beyond "thin" and into the realm of "emaciated," but weight loss is far more extreme in many cases of anorexia nervosa: The average victim loses 25 to 30 percent of normal body weight (Hsu, 1990). Unlike Seritta, who was fortunate in this sense, some people with anorexia nervosa are not treated until their weight loss becomes

life-threatening. In fact, experts estimate that over 10 percent of people admitted to university hospitals with anorexia nervosa die of starvation, suicide, or medical complications stemming from their extreme weight loss (APA, 1994; Hsu, 1995).

Disturbance in Perceiving or Evaluating Weight or Shape

A second defining symptom of anorexia nervosa involves a perceptual, cognitive, or affective disturbance in evaluating one's weight and shape. Like Seritta, many individuals with anorexia nervosa steadfastly *deny problems with their weight.* Even when confronted with the possibility of medical complications or with their own withered image in a mirror, some people with anorexia nervosa nevertheless insist that their weight is not a problem.

Other people with the disorder apparently suffer from a *disturbance in the way body weight or shape is experienced.* Some experts claim that this symptom stems from a **distorted body image,** an inaccuracy in how people with anorexia nervosa actually perceive their body size and shape. In support of this view, one influential study found that young women with anorexia nervosa overestimated the size of various body parts in comparison to a normal control group (Slade & Russell, 1973). However, dozens of subsequent studies have documented that not all people with anorexia nervosa suffer from a distorted body image, and perhaps more importantly, many people without the disorder inaccurately estimate the size of their body (Garfinkel, Kennedy, & Kaplan, 1995; Thompson, 1996).

Thus not all people with anorexia nervosa have a distorted body image or deny problems with their weight. At a minimum, however, all people with the disorder are *unduly influenced by their body weight or shape in self-evaluation.* Experts agree that, whatever its specific form, a defining characteristic of anorexia nervosa is a disturbance in the way one's body or weight is perceived or evaluated. People with anorexia nervosa do not recognize their emaciation for what it is,

---

[†] You can calculate your own body mass as follows: (1) Multiply your weight in pounds by 700; (2) divide this number by your height in inches; (3) divide this second number by your height in inches. You can interpret the resulting number according to the body mass index: Under 16 = extremely underweight; 16–18 = significantly underweight; 20–25 = healthy weight; 27–30 = overweight; 30–40 = significantly overweight; over 40 = extremely overweight.

a misrepresentation that may continue to perplex victims who have recovered from the disorder. After returning to a more normal weight, many former sufferers recognize their past distortions but can't explain the reasons for their misperception.

Fear of Gaining Weight

An *intense fear of becoming fat* is a third central characteristic of anorexia, as Seritta also demonstrated. The fear of gaining weight presents particular problems for treatment. A therapist's encouragement to eat more can terrify a client with anorexia nervosa. The client fears that relaxing control, even just a little, will lead to a total loss of control. Ironically, the fear of gaining weight is not soothed by the tremendous weight loss. In fact, the fear may grow more intense as the individual loses more weight (APA, 1994).

Cessation of Menstruation

Amenorrhea, the absence of at least three consecutive menstrual cycles, is the fourth and final defining symptom of anorexia nervosa in females. Many people with anorexia nervosa also have sexual difficulties, particularly a lack of interest in sex. The amenorrhea and sexuality symptoms have led to much speculation concerning the role of sex and sexual maturation in the etiology of anorexia nervosa. However, evidence indicates that amenorrhea typically is a *reaction* to the physiological changes produced by anorexia nervosa, specifically a low level of estrogen secretion, and not a symptom that precedes the disorder (APA, 1994). Sexual disinterest also is a common reaction to severe weight loss (Keys et al., 1950).

Medical Complications

Anorexia nervosa can cause a number of *medical complications*. People with anorexia commonly complain about constipation, abdominal pain, intolerance to cold, and lethargy. Some of these complaints stem from the effects of semistarvation on blood pressure and body temperature, both of which may fall below normal. In addition, the person's skin can become dry and cracked, and some people develop *lanugo*, a fine, downy hair, on their face or trunk of their bodies. Broader medical difficulties that can result from anorexia nervosa include anemia, impaired kidney functioning, cardiovascular difficulties,

dental erosion, and osteopenia (bone loss) (Pomeroy, 1996). A particularly dangerous medication complication is an *electrolyte imbalance*, a disturbance in the levels of potassium, sodium, calcium, and other vital elements found in bodily fluids that can lead to cardiac arrest or kidney failure. Anorexia nervosa may begin with the seemingly harmless desire to be a bit thinner or more attractive, but the eating disorder can lead to serious health problems and even death.

Struggle for Control

Although some people with eating disorders act impulsively, clinical accounts and some research indicate that people suffering from anorexia nervosa are likelier to exhibit *excessive conformity* and a paramount *struggle for control*. In one sense, anorexia nervosa is the height of "success" in self-control. The individual with anorexia nervosa has all but conquered one of our most basic biological needs. Consistent with this view, people with anorexia nervosa often take great pride in their self-denial. They feel like masters of control. As we discuss in considering the etiology of the

▲ **Olympic-class gymnast Christy Heinrich with her boyfriend in 1993. After a 5-year struggle with anorexia nervosa, she died of multiple organ failure in 1994. She weighed less than 50 pounds at the time.**

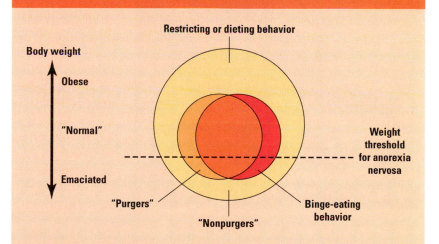

The Overlap in Eating Disorder Symptoms

FIGURE 10-2: Illustration of the relationship between binge eating, purging, and restricting or extreme dieting in eating disorders. All three problematic eating behaviors can be found among people with different body weights.

Source: D.M. Garner, M.V. Garner, and L.W. Rosen, 1993, Anorexia nervosa "restrictors" who purge: Implications for subtyping anorexia nervosa, *International Journal of Eating Disorders, 13,* 182.

disorder, some theorists speculate that the disorder develops out of a desperate pursuit for control. Excessively compliant "good girls" may find that they can govern at least one area of their lives by obsessively regulating their eating behaviors (Bruch, 1982).

Comorbid Psychological Disorders

Anorexia nervosa may be associated with other psychological problems, particularly obsessive–compulsive disorder (Kasvikis et al., 1986), obsessive–compulsive personality disorder (Gillberg, Rastam, & Gillberg, 1995), and depression (Braun, Sunday, & Halmi, 1994). In many cases, however, these comorbid psychological problems may be reactions to anorexia, not causes or associated features of the disorder.

People with anorexia nervosa *are* obsessed with food and diet, and they often follow compulsive rituals around eating. However, a unique study found that obsessive–compulsive behavior can result from starvation rather than cause it. In this study, 32 World War II conscientious objectors fullfilled their military obligation by voluntarily undergoing semistarvation for 24 weeks. (The researchers wanted to learn about the effects of starvation on military personnel in the field.) As the men reduced their food intake and lost more and more weight, they developed extensive obsessions about food and compulsive eating rituals. For many of the

▼ **Conscientious objectors who became subjects in a study of semistarvation during World War II. Many of the men developed symptoms similar to those found in anorexia nervosa.**

men, in fact, the obsessions and compulsions continued long after they returned to their normal weight (Keys et al., 1950). Thus obsessive–compulsive personality disorder may sometimes contribute to anorexia nervosa, but some obsessive–compulsive *behavior* may be a reaction to starvation.

We also need to consider cause and effect carefully when considering the depressive symptoms that commonly accompany anorexia nervosa. Most people with anorexia nervosa show symptoms of mild depression, such as sad mood, irritability, insomnia, social withdrawal, and diminished interest in sex (Braun, Sunday, & Halmi, 1994). Like obsessive–compulsive behavior, however, depression has been found to be a common secondary reaction to starvation. Although mood disturbances sometimes seem to play a role in the development of anorexia nervosa, depression also can be a reaction to the eating disorder (Cooper, 1995; Hsu, 1990).

Finally, we should note that anorexia often co-occurs with the symptoms of bulimia. As we discuss in the following section, the core symptoms that define bulimia are *binge eating*, in which the individual uncontrollably eats vast amounts of food, and *purging*, behaviors designed to eliminate the consumed food from the body (including self-induced vomiting and the misuse of laxatives, diuretics, and enemas). Binge eating and purging are found among a substantial number of people with anorexia nervosa (see Figure 10–2). In some cases of anorexia nervosa, purging follows episodes of binge eating. As with Seritta, however, in other cases purging may be used as a means of further controlling eating that already is dramatically restricted. Finally, in still other cases of anorexia, no binge eating or purging is present. People with anorexia nervosa who do *not* binge eat or purge generally are better adjusted on other measures of their mental health—for example, they have lower rates of depression (Braun et al., 1994).

Typical Symptoms and Associated Features of Bulimia Nervosa

Bulima nervosa and anorexia nervosa share many other similarities in addition to the overlap in the symptoms of binge eating and purging. One important connection is that many people with

bulimia nervosa have a history of anorexia nervosa, as was the circumstance in the following case study.

Bulimia Nervosa

Michelle was a sophomore at a state university when she first sought help for a humiliating problem. Several times a week, she fell into an episode of uncontrollable binge eating followed by self-induced vomiting. The episodes were particularly likely to occur on "bad days," of which Michelle had many. Michelle had enough control to limit her binge eating to periods when her roommate was away. But when Michelle was alone and feeling badly, she typically would buy a half-gallon of ice cream and perhaps a bag of cookies, and bring the food back to her room where she secretly gorged herself. The binge brought her some comfort when she first started eating, but when she was finished, she felt physically uncomfortable, sickened by her lack of control, and terrified of gaining weight. To compensate, she would walk across the street to an empty bathroom in the psychology department. There, she forced herself to vomit by sticking her finger down her throat.

The vomiting brought relief from the physical discomfort and fear of gaining weight, but it did not relieve her shame. Michelle was disgusted by her actions, but she could not stop herself. In fact, the pattern of binge eating and purging had been going on for most of the school year. Michelle decided to seek treatment only when a friend from her psychology class discovered her purging in the bathroom. The friend also had a history of bulimia nervosa, but she had gotten her eating under control. She convinced Michelle to try therapy.

Michelle's eating problems actually began when she was in high school. She had studied ballet since she was 8 years old, and with the stern encouragement of her instructor she had struggled to maintain her willowy figure as she became an adolescent. At first she dieted openly, but her parents constantly criticized her inadequate eating. In order to appease them, Michelle occasionally would eat a normal meal but force herself to vomit shortly afterwards. When she was a junior in high school, Michelle's parents confronted her and brought her to a psychologist, who treated her for anorexia nervosa. She was 5 feet 6 inches tall at the time, but she weighed only 95 pounds. Michelle was furious at her parents and refused to talk in any depth with the therapist. She allowed herself to gain a few pounds—to about 105—only to convince her parents that she did not need treatment.

Michelle's weight eventually stabilized between 105 and 110 pounds—enough of a gain that her parents had allowed her to stop therapy. Even though she was very thin, Michelle continued to plan her diet with great care. She avoided fat with a vengeance. She had not eaten even a lick of ice cream in years. She counted every calorie at every meal every day. Throughout most of her college years, she starved herself all week so she could eat normally on dates during the weekend. Occasionally, she forced herself to vomit after eating too much, but she did not see this as a big problem. Until the previous summer, she had maintained her weight near her goal of 105 pounds. Over the summer, however, Michelle relaxed her diet considerably as she "partied" with old friends. She gained about 15 pounds, a healthy weight for her height and body type. When she returned to college, however, Michelle became disgusted with her appearance and fearful of gaining even more weight.

Michelle was trying to lose weight when she started her current school year, but she met with little success. She started to purge more frequently in an increasingly desperate attempt to lose weight, but she soon found herself binge eating more frequently too. Michelle was extremely frustrated by her "lack of self-control" over her binge eating/purging and her inability to lose weight. Although she now recognized her past problems with anorexia nervosa, Michelle openly longed for the discipline she had once achieved over her hunger and diet.

By all outward appearances, Michelle was a bright, attractive, successful, and happy young woman. Nevertheless, she admitted to her new therapist that she felt like a failure and a "fake." She longed to have a long-term dating relationship, but although she dated a lot, she had never had a real boyfriend. She also was intensely if privately competitive with her girlfriends. She wanted to be more beautiful and intelligent than other girls, but she inevitably felt inferior to one classmate or another.

She had been determined at least to be thinner than her girlfriends, but she felt that she had lost all control over this goal. Michelle also was furious with her parents. Their constant questions about her well-being caused her to feel angry and resentful instead of loved and supported. Michelle viewed her parents as intrusive in their concerns but emotionally distant at the same time. In her mind, they asked all the right questions, but they cared more about the family's image than about Michelle as a person. Michelle pretended to be happy and normal, but inside she felt as though she was going to explode. Secretly, she was miserable. ■

Michelle's frequent struggles with binge eating and purging, her sense of lost control during a binge, and her undue focus on her weight and figure are the core symptoms that define bulimia nervosa. Depression also is commonly associated with the disorder, as it was for Michelle despite her continual struggle to hide her unhappiness from those around her. In addition to depression, substance abuse (see Chapter 11) and personality disorders frequently are comorbid with bulimia nervosa.

Binge Eating

Binge eating is defined in DSM-IV as eating an amount of food in a fixed period of time (e.g., less than 2 hours) that is clearly larger than most people would eat under similar circumstances. There have been some attempts to define a binge more objectively (e.g., eating more than 1,000 calories) or subjectively (e.g., based on the individual's appraisal). Variations in normal eating complicate these alternative definitions, however, as eating a very large number of calories may be normal under certain circumstances and having two cookies may be considered a "binge" by other people. Thus the present DSM-IV definition relies on a clinician's judgment about normal eating patterns (Garfinkel et al., 1995).

Sadly, many of the inappropriate eating behaviors that are symptoms of bulimia nervosa border on being statistically normal—and clearly unhealthy—in our food- and weight-obsessed society. Over 35 percent of people report occasional binge eating. Distressingly large numbers of people also report that they fast (29 percent) and use self-induced vomiting (8 percent) or laxatives (over 5 percent) in an attempt to compensate for their eating (Fairburn & Beglin, 1990).

Binges may be planned in advance, or they may begin spontaneously. In either case, binges typically are secret. Most people with bulimia nervosa are ashamed of their eating problems and often go to elaborate efforts to conceal their binge eating. During a binge, the individual typically eats very rapidly and soon feels uncomfortably full. Although the types of foods that are consumed can vary widely, the person often selects ice cream, cookies, or other foods that are high in calories. Foods also may be selected for smooth texture to make vomiting easier (e.g., ice cream).

Binge eating is commonly triggered by an unhappy mood, which may begin with an interpersonal conflict, self-criticism about weight or appearance, or intense hunger following a period of fasting. The binge initially is comforting and alleviates some of the person's unhappy feelings, but physical discomfort and fear of gaining weight soon override the positive aspects of binge eating (Garfinkel et al., 1995).

A key feature of binge eating is a sense of *lack of control* during a binge. Some individuals experience a binge as a "feeding frenzy," where they lose all control and eat compulsively and rapidly. Others describe the lack of control as a dissociative experience, as if they were watching themselves gorge. It should be noted, however, that people with the disorder do not experience the lack of control as absolute. For example, they can stop if someone unexpectedly interrupts them during an episode of binge eating. In fact, as the disorder progresses, some people feel more in control of their eating during a binge. Nevertheless, they are still unable to stop the broader cycle of binge eating and compensatory behavior.

Inappropriate Compensatory Behavior

The inappropriate compensatory behaviors that follow binge eating can take a number of forms. Almost all people with bulimia nervosa engage in **purging,** designed to eliminate the consumed food from the body. The most common form of purging is self-induced vomiting; as many as 90 percent of people with bulimia nervosa engage in this behavior (APA, 1994). Vomiting brings immediate relief from the physical discomfort caused by a binge, and it reduces morbid fears of gaining weight. Other less common forms of purging include the misuse of laxatives, diuretics (which increase the frequency of urination), and most rarely, enemas. Ironically, purging has only limited effectiveness in reducing caloric intake. Vomiting prevents the absorption of only about half the calories consumed during a binge, and laxatives, diuretics, and enemas have few lasting effects on calories or weight (Kaye et al., 1993).

Compensatory behaviors other than purging include extreme exercise or rigid fasting following a binge. The extent to which these actions actually compensate for binge eating also is questionable, given what we know about the body's biological regulation of weight, a topic we discuss later in this chapter (Brownell & Fairburn, 1995).

Excessive Emphasis on Weight and Shape

People with bulimia nervosa place an *excessive emphasis on body shape and weight* in evaluating themselves, a symptom shared in common with anorexia nervosa (see Table 10–2). Their self-esteem, and much of their daily routine, center

around weight and diet. Some people with bulimia nervosa are exhilarated by positive comments or interest in their appearance, but their esteem crashes and burns if a negative comment is made or if someone else draws more attention. Other people with the disorder constantly criticize their appearance, and the struggle with binge eating and purging only adds to their self-denigration. In either case, the individual's sense of self is linked too closely to appearance instead of personality, relationships, or achievements.

Comorbid Psychological Disorders

Not surprisingly, depression is common among individuals with bulimia nervosa, especially those who self-induce vomiting (APA, 1994). Some individuals clearly become depressed prior to developing the eating disorder, and the bulimia may be a reaction to the depression in some of these cases. In many instances, however, depression begins at the same time as or follows the onset of bulimia nervosa (Braun et al., 1994). In such circumstances, the depression may be a reaction to the bulimia rather than a cause of it. In support of this view, evidence indicates that

▲ **Princess Diana has publicly acknowledged her battle with bulimia nervosa.**

		TABLE 10–2

Anorexia Nervosa and Bulimia Nervosa: Key Differences and Similarities

Issue	Anorexia Nervosa	Bulimia Nervosa
	Differences	
Eating/Weight	Extreme diet; below minimally normal weight	Binge eating/ compensatory behavior; normal weight
View of Disorder	Denial of anorexia; proud of "diet"	Aware of problem; secretive/ashamed of bulimia
Feelings of Control	Comforted by rigid self-control	Distressed by lack of control over binge eating
	Similarities	
Self-Evaluation	Unduly influenced by body weight/ shape	Unduly influenced by body weight/shape
Comorbidity of AN/BN	Some cases of AN also binge and purge	Many cases of BN have history of AN
SES, Age, Gender	Prevalent among high SES, young, female	Prevalent among high SES, young, female

depression often lifts following successful treatment of bulimia nervosa, as we discuss in more detail when considering treatment (Mitchell et al., 1990).

Other psychological disorders that may co-occur with bulimia nervosa include anxiety disorders, personality disorders (particularly borderline personality disorder), and substance abuse, particularly excessive use of alcohol and/or stimulants. Although each of these psychological difficulties presents special challenges in treating bulimia, the comorbidity with depression is the most common and most significant clinical concern (Brewerton et al., 1995).

Medical Complications

A number of medical complications can result from bulimia nervosa. Repeated vomiting can erode dental enamel, particularly on the front teeth, and in severe cases teeth can become chipped and ragged-looking. Repeated vomiting can also produce a gag reflex that is triggered too easily and perhaps unintentionally. One consequence of the sensitized gag reflex—one that is just beginning to be reported in the scientific literature—is *rumination*, the regurgitation and rechewing of food (Parry-Jones, 1994). Another possible medical complication is the enlargement of the salivary glands, a consequence that has the ironic effect of making the sufferer's face appear puffy. As in anorexia nervosa, potentially serious medical complications can result from electrolyte imbalances. Finally, rupture of the esophagus or stomach has been reported in rare cases, sometimes leading to death (Pomeroy, 1996).

Classification of Eating Disorders

Brief Historical Perspective

Isolated cases of eating disorders have been reported throughout history. In fact, the term *anorexia nervosa* was coined in 1874 by a British physician, Sir William Withey Gull (1816–1890). Still, the history of professional concern with the disorders is very brief. References to eating disorders were rare in the literature prior to 1960, and the disorders have received scientific attention only in recent decades (Hsu, 1990; Yates, 1989). In fact, the term *bulimia nervosa* was used for the first time only in 1979 (Russell, 1979).

The diagnoses of anorexia nervosa and bulimia nervosa first appeared in the DSM in 1980 (DSM-III), and although the diagnostic criteria have changed somewhat, the same eating behaviors remain as the central features of these disorders. The only major change in DSM-IV was the creation of a separate diagnostic category for eating disorders. They previously had been listed as a subtype of the Disorders Usually First Diagnosed in Infancy, Childhood, or Adolescence (see Chapter 16), because most eating disorders begin during the teenage years. The new, separate diagnostic grouping reflects the fact that eating disorders sometimes begin during adult life, as well as a more general recognition of the importance of these psychological problems.

Contemporary Classification

ANOREXIA NERVOSA

The DSM-IV contains only two subtypes of eating disorders: anorexia nervosa and bulimia nervosa. Anorexia nervosa is defined by four symptoms: (1) a refusal to maintain weight at or above minimally normal weight for age and height; (2) an intense fear of gaining weight; (3) a disturbance in the way weight or body shape is experienced, undue influence of weight or body shape on self-evaluation, or denial of the seriousness of low body weight; and (4) amenorrhea, the absence of menstruation, in postmenarcheal females (see Table 10–3).

The DSM-IV includes two subtypes of anorexia nervosa. The *restricting type* includes people who rarely engage in binge eating or purging behavior. In contrast, the *binge-eating/purging type* is defined by regular binge eating and purging during the course of the disorder. People with the binge-eating/purging type make up approximately half of those people with anorexia nervosa, and, in comparison to the restricting type, they are likelier to have weighed more before the illness began, to come from families where obesity is more common, to show various problems with impulse control such as substance abuse or impulsive sexual behavior, and to have

TABLE 10-3

DSM-IV Diagnostic Criteria for Anorexia Nervosa

A. **Refusal to maintain body weight at or above a minimally normal weight for age and height (e.g., weight loss leading to maintenance of body weight less than 85 percent of that expected; or failure to make expected weight gain during period of growth, leading to body weight less than 85 percent of that expected)**

B. **Intense fear of gaining weight or becoming fat, even though underweight.**

C. **Disturbance in the way in which one's weight or shape is experienced, undue influence of body weight or shape on self-evaluation, or denial of the seriousness of the current low body weight.**

D. **In postmenarcheal females, amenorrhea, that is, the absence of at least three consecutive menstrual cycles.**

Specify type:
Restricting type: During the current episode, the person has not regularly engaged in binge eating or purging behavior.
Binge-eating/purging type: During the current episode, the person has regularly engaged in binge eating or purging behavior.

---

more personality disorders (Agras, 1987; Garfinkel et al., 1995).

As we noted earlier, however, many people with anorexia nervosa purge following normal or even restricted eating, not following a binge. Should these people be considered the restricting type or the binge-eating/purging type? Evidence suggests that purging, not binge eating, is the key to distinguishing the subtypes. In a study that compared a sample of 116 pure restricters with both binge-purge ($N = 190$) and purge only ($N = 74$) subjects, both of the groups who purged were found to be older, to have had a longer history of anorexia nervosa, to have more obesity in their families, to engage in more impulsive behavior, and to suffer from more psychopathology in comparison to the pure restricters (Garner, Garner, & Rosen, 1993). Thus it is appropriate that the DSM-IV defines the binge-eating/purging subtype in terms of either binge eating *or* purging (see Table 10–3).

BULIMIA NERVOSA

Bulimia nervosa is defined by five symptoms: (1) recurrent episodes of binge eating over which the individual feels a lack of control; (2) recurrent inappropriate compensatory behavior; (3) an average frequency of at least two episodes per week over a period of at least 3 months; (4) undue influence of weight and body shape on self-evaluation; and (5) the disturbance does not occur solely during episodes of anorexia nervosa (see Table 10–4).

Bulimia nervosa also is divided into two subtypes in the DSM-IV. The *purging type* is characterized by the regular use of self-induced vomiting or the misuse of laxatives, diuretics, or enemas. The individual with the *nonpurging type* of bulimia nervosa does not regularly purge but instead attempts to compensate for binge eating with fasting or excessive exercise. The purging subtype of bulimia nervosa is more common and is associated with more frequent binge eating, more psychopathology (particularly depression), and more family dysfunction, including parental discord and child sexual abuse (Garfinkel, Lin, & Goering, in press; McCann et al., Agras, 1991).

BINGE EATING DISORDER AND OBESITY

There has been some debate about whether other eating problems should be included in the DSM-IV list of eating disorders. **Binge eating disorder** is one problem that was given extensive consideration. In fact, provisional diagnostic criteria for binge eating disorder are included in an appendix of DSM-IV for diagnostic categories requiring further study. The proposed disorder

TABLE 10-4

DSM-IV Diagnostic Criteria for Bulimia Nervosa

A. Recurrent epidosdes of binge eating. An episode of binge eating is characterized by both of the following:
   1. Eating, in a discrete period of time (e.g., within any 2-hour period), an amount of food that is definitely larger than most people would eat during a similar period of time and under similar circumstances.
   2. A sense of lack of control over eating during the episode (e.g., a feeling that one cannot stop eating or control what or how much one is eating).

B. Recurrent inappropriate compensatory behavior in order to prevent weight gain, such as self-induced vomiting; misuse of laxatives, diuretics, enemas, or other medications; fasting; or excessive exercise.

C. The binge eating and inappropriate compensatory behaviors both occur, on average, at least twice a week for 3 months.

D. Self-evaluation is unduly influenced by body shape and weight.

E. The disturbance does not occur exclusively during episodes of Anorexia Nervosa.

Specify type:
Purging type: During the current episode, the person has regularly engaged in self-induced vomiting or the misuse of laxatives, diuretics, or enemas.
Nonpurging type: During the current episode, the person has used other inappropriate compensatory behaviors, such as fasting or excessive exercise, but has not regularly engaged in self-induced vomiting or the misuse of laxatives, diuretics, or enemas.

---

involves episodes of binge eating much like those found in bulimia nervosa but without compensatory behavior.

Research has demonstrated that binge eating is associated with a number of psychological and physical difficulties other than anorexia nervosa and bulimia nervosa (Fairburn & Wilson, 1993). Among these problems is **obesity,** or excess body fat, a circumstance that roughly corresponds with a body weight 20 percent *above* the expected weight. A cutoff of 40 percent above normal is a rough marker of severe overweight (Brownell, 1995). Like binge eating, the DSM-IV committee considered classifying obesity as an eating disorder, but too little information was available to justify this move (Garfinkel et al., 1995). Calling obesity a "mental disorder" is controversial, moreover, especially given the high prevalence of overweight individuals in the United States and throughout the world. In fact, some professionals question our society's constant focus on dieting and our castigation of obese people. Obesity is *not* just a lack of "willpower," as biological factors contribute substantially to body shape and weight (Brownell & Rodin, 1994).

Epidemiology of Eating Disorders

Estimates of the epidemiology of anorexia and bulimia vary, but it is clear that the prevalence of both disorders has increased dramatically since the 1960s and 1970s (Hoek, 1995; Kendler et al., 1991). Figure 10–3 illustrates the surge in the number of new cases of anorexia nervosa based on one investigator's compilation of evidence from a number of different studies (Hoek, 1995). According to this summary, the annual *incidence* (i.e., number of new cases each year) of anorexia nervosa rose from 1 case per million people in 1930–1940 to over 50 cases per million people in 1980–1990. Figure 10–3 also suggests that anorexia nervosa is rare in the general population. It is far more common among certain segments of the population, however, particularly among young women. The DSM-IV indicates that anorexia nervosa is found among 0.5 to 1.0 percent of females in adolescence or early adulthood, a figure that is consistent with empirical estimates of the prevalence of the disorder (Hoek, 1995). Anorexia nervosa also occurs among males in this young age group, but it is about 10 times more common among women than men.

Recent decades also seem to have witnessed a torrent of new cases of bulimia nervosa. Changes in the incidence of bulimia nervosa are difficult to document, however, because the diagnostic term was introduced only in 1979. In an attempt to demonstrate the striking increase in bulimia nervosa over time, investigators therefore have examined **cohort effects** in prevalence rates. A **cohort** is a group that shares some feature in common, particularly time of birth; thus cohort effects are differences that distinguish one cohort from another.

Figure 10–4 portrays birth cohort effects in lifetime prevalence rates of bulimia nervosa among a large sample of American women who were born either before 1950, between 1950 and 1959, or in 1960 or after. The figure clearly indicates substantial cohort effects in the prevalence of bulimia nervosa. The lifetime prevalence of bulimia nervosa was far greater among the cohort of women born after 1960 than it was for the cohort of women born before 1950. The risk for women born between 1950 and 1959 was intermediate between these two extremes (Kendler et al., 1991). Thus the recent surge of cases of bulimia nervosa is not due to a general increase among all women but instead results from a flood of cases—some say an epidemic—among women born after 1960.

Figure 10–4 also shows that new cases of bulimia nervosa develop among women in their twenties and their thirties. Still, the risk of developing the disorder declines with increasing age, at least among older cohorts. The curve flattens at older ages, an indication of the discovery of fewer and fewer new cases among older women.

Although the frequency of both disorders has increased dramatically since the 1960s and 1970s, experts agree that bulimia nervosa is far more common than anorexia nervosa (Fairburn, Hay, & Welch, 1993; Hoek, 1995). According to DSM-IV, bulimia nervosa occurs among

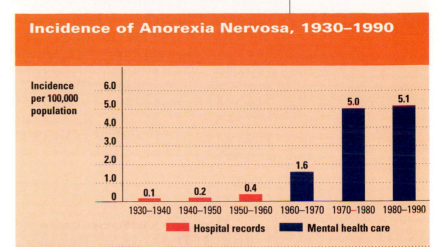

Incidence of Anorexia Nervosa, 1930–1990

FIGURE 10-3: Anorexia nervosa has increased dramatically in recent decades. This figure portrays the annual incidence per 100,000 people in the general population based on data pooled from studies of hospital records and outpatient mental health care. Considerably higher rates are found among population subgroups, particularly young women.

Source: H.W. Hoek, 1995, The distribution of eating disorders. In K.D. Brownell and C.G. Fairbanks (Eds.), *Eating Disorders and Obesity: A Comprehensive Handbook,* p. 209. New York: Guilford.

1 to 3 percent of adolescent and young adult women, a rate that is 2 or 3 times the number of cases of anorexia nervosa in the same age group. As we noted earlier, moreover, the prevalence of subclinical bulimia—occasional binge

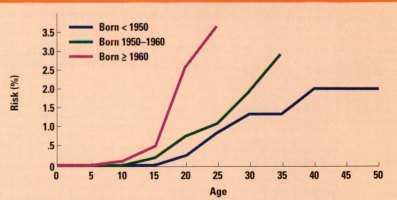

Bulimia Nervosa Among Three Cohorts of Women

FIGURE 10-4: The lifetime cumulative risk for developing bulimia nervosa is far greater for women born after 1960 than for women born before 1950. The risk for developing the disorder decreases with age, at least among the earlier birth cohort. Later birth cohorts have not yet moved through the entire age of risk.

Source: K.S. Kendler, C. MacLean, M. Neale, R. Kessler, A. Heath, and L. Eaves, 1991, The genetic epidemiology of bulimia nervosa, *American Journal of Psychiatry, 148,* 1631.

eating and/or purging—is far greater than the number of cases that meet DSM-IV criteria for bulimia nervosa. Finally, we should note again that there is considerable overlap between anorexia nervosa and bulimia nervosa. About 50 percent of all people with anorexia nervosa engage in episodes of binge eating and purging (Agras, 1987; Garfinkel et al., 1995), and perhaps 30 percent of cases of bulimia nervosa have a history of anorexia nervosa (Yates, 1989).

Gender Differences and Standards of Beauty

Both anorexia and bulimia nervosa are approximately 10 times more common among women than among men. Many commentators and scientists propose that this huge difference is explained by gender roles and standards of beauty (Hsu, 1990; Striegel-Moore, 1995). Popular attitudes about women in the United States often convey the notion that "looks are everything," and thinness is essential to our dominant cultural image of good looks—and happiness. In contrast, young men are valued as much for their achievements as for their appearance, and in any case, the ideal body type for men is considerably larger than for women (Hsu, 1990; Striegel-Moore, 1995).

The growing prevalence of eating disorders in recent decades also may be explained by changing standards of beauty, as beauty increasingly has been equated with thinness. The cultural ideal of beauty is not fixed; it changes over time. For example, Marilyn Monroe, the movie idol of the 1950s, may seem rather chunky by today's standards. In fact, researchers have demonstrated the shift toward thinness in the American view of the "beautiful woman" by examining changes in the dimensions of *Playboy* centerfolds and Miss America Beauty Pageant contestants—cultural icons but dubious models for young women. Between 1959 and 1988, the ratio of weight to height of these "ideal women" has declined dramatically. In fact, 69 percent of *Playboy* centerfolds and 60 percent of Miss America contestants meet one diagnostic criterion for anorexia nervosa: Their body weight is at least 15 percent below expected weight for their height. The body shapes of these idealized women also have become more androgynous over time. Average bust and hip sizes have decreased, while waist sizes have increased slightly (Garner et al., 1980; Wiseman et al., 1992).

Standards of beauty are relative, not absolute. Today, eating disorders are found almost exclusively in North America, Western Europe, and Japan and other industrialized Asian countries; in other cultures, women who are more rounded are considered to be more beautiful (Hsu, 1990; Striegel-Moore, 1995; Yates, 1989). This may reflect a relationship between wealth and standards of beauty. In Third World countries where food is scarce, wealth is positively correlated with body weight. Being larger is a symbol of beauty and success. In industrialized nations where food is plentiful, wealth is negatively correlated with weight (Hsu, 1989). As the Western saying goes, "You can never be too rich or too thin."

Age of Onset

Both anorexia and bulimia nervosa typically begin in late adolescence or early adulthood. A significant minority of cases of anorexia nervosa begin during early adolescence, particularly as young girls approach puberty. The adolescent onset of eating disorders has provoked much speculation about their etiology. Certain characteristics of adolescence have been speculated to cause eating disorders; these include hormonal changes (Garfinkel & Garner, 1982), autonomy struggles (Minuchin, Rosman, & Baker, 1978), and problems with sexuality (Coovert, Kinder, & Thompson, 1989). Other theorists have noted that the young adolescent girl is the most idealized cultural image of beauty (Hsu, 1990; Striegel-Moore, 1995). The natural and normal changes in body shape and weight offer an even more simple explanation of the adolescent onset. Weight gain is normal during adolescence, but the addition of a few pounds can trouble a young woman who is focused on the numbers on her scale. Breast and hip development not only change body shape, but they also affect self-image, social interaction, and the fit of familiar clothes. As we shall see, each of these explanations may have some value in explaining the age of onset of eating disorders.

▼ **Model Kate Moss. Contemporary images of women place a premium on slimness and suggest that women should be judged by their appearance. Both of these messages apparently contribute to the etiology of eating disorders.**

Etiologic Considerations and Research

The regulation of normal eating and body weight results from a combination of biological, psychological, and social factors, and researchers have focused on each of these levels of analysis in attempting to explain the etiology of anorexia and bulimia (see Brownell & Fairburn, 1995). Scientists agree, however, that sociocultural factors are central contributors to the high rate of eating disorders found among young women today. We therefore begin by considering social and cultural factors in the etiology of eating disorders. Of course, not every young woman in the United States or other industrial countries develops an eating disorder. Even within a culture obsessed with weight, diet, and appearance, other social, psychological, and biological risk factors determine who develops anorexia nervosa or bulimia nervosa and who does not.

Social Factors

The image of the ideal woman as extremely thin and the overriding value placed on young women's appearances are basic starting points in searching for the causes of eating disorders. This statement is supported by the epidemiological evidence we have already reviewed, as well as by related findings:

- Eating disorders are far more common among young women than young men (Hoek, 1995; Hsu, 1990).
- The prevalence of eating disorders in the United States has risen dramatically in recent decades, as the image of the ideal woman has increasingly emphasized extreme thinness (Garner et al., 1980; Hoek, 1995; Kendler et al., 1991; Wiseman et al., 1992).
- Eating disorders are even more common among young women working in fields that especially emphasize weight and appearance, such as models, ballet dancers, and gymnasts (Yates, 1989).
- Young women are particularly likely to develop eating disorders during adolescence and young adult life, an age during which our culture places a particular emphasis on appearance, beauty, and thinness (Hsu, 1990; Striegel-Moore, 1995).
- Eating disturbances are more common among young women who report greater exposure to popular media, endorse more gender-role stereotypes, or internalize societal standards towards appearance (Heinberg, Thompson, & Stormer, 1995; Stice et al., 1994).
- Eating disorders are considerably more common among middle- and upper-class whites, who are especially likely to equate thinness with beauty in women. Eating disorders also are increasing among well-to-do African Americans, who increasingly hold to the thinness ideal (Hsu, 1990; Thompson, 1996; Yates, 1989).
- Eating disorders are far more prevalent in industrialized societies, where thinness is the ideal, than in nonindustrialized societies, where a more rounded body type is preferred (Hsu, 1990).
- The prevalence of eating disorders is higher among Arab and Asian women who are living or studying in Western countries than among women living in their native country (Mumford, Whitehouse, & Platts, 1991; Nasser, 1986).

Together, these facts make it clear that adolescent girls and young women are at risk for developing eating disorders in part because they attempt to shape themselves, quite literally, to fit the image of the ideally proportioned, thin woman. A related problem is that the emphasis on appearance lessens the value of other roles filled by girls and women. Researchers have found, for example, that physical *attractiveness* predicts self-esteem among adolescent girls, whereas physical *competence* predicts self-esteem among adolescent boys (Lerner et al., 1986). Our culture needs to do a better job of teaching young women that who you are is much more important than how you look.

▼ **Rounded bodies once were the ideal of beauty for women, as illustrated in** *Turkish Bath* **painted by Jean Auguste Dominique Ingres in 1859–1863 (Louvre, Paris).**

TROUBLED FAMILY RELATIONSHIPS

Not every woman in the United States develops an eating disorder, of course, and some men suffer from anorexia or bulimia nervosa. Other stressors therefore must interact with the cultural diathesis to produce eating disorders. Troubled family relationships may be one such contributing factor, at least in some cases. Researchers have documented family problems in a number of studies, but the typical patterns differ for anorexia nervosa and bulimia nervosa. Young people with bulimia nervosa report considerable conflict and rejection in their families, difficulties that also may contribute to their depression. In contrast, young people with anorexia generally perceive their families as cohesive and nonconflictual (Vandereycken, 1995; Yates, 1989).

Although the families of young people with anorexia nervosa appear to be well functioning, some theorists see the families as being too close—that is, they are **enmeshed families,** or families whose members are overly involved in one another's lives. Young people with anorexia nervosa are obsessed with controlling their eating, and according to the enmeshment hypothesis, this is because eating is the *only* thing they can control in their intrusive families (Minuchin et al., 1978). A relation between measures of conflictual but controlling parent–child relationships and anorexia nervosa has been found in some research (Humphrey, 1987), but it is not clear whether the extensive and intrusive parental concern is a cause or an effect of the eating disorder. It may be that the parents of an adolescent with anorexia nervosa become "enmeshed" as a worried reaction to their daughter's obviously emaciated appearance, not as a cause of it. In either case, family power struggles over eating often become one focus of the treatment of anorexia nervosa.

Child sexual abuse is another family difficulty that might contribute to the development of eating disorders. (See Chapter 18 for a general discussion of child abuse and child sexual abuse.) A number of clinical observers have noted that a disproportionate number of women with eating disorders report a history of sexual abuse, a terrible experience that may explain many of their concerns. Although a report of sexual abuse clearly is an important psychological (and legal) issue in any individual case, recent evidence indicates that sexual abuse does not play a *specific* role in the development of eating disorders. Instead, child sexual abuse apparently increases the risk for a variety of psychological problems during adult life including but not limited to eating disorders. Studies of community samples demonstrate that women with eating disorders are likelier than normal controls to report a history of sexual abuse. However, women with eating disorders are no likelier to report a history of sexual abuse than are women who suffer from other psychological problems (Palmer 1995; Welch & Fairburn, in press).

Finally, we should note that there are many direct ways in which parents may influence children toward developing eating disorders (Pike & Rodin, 1991). Many parents struggle with diet and thinness themselves, and they are models of overconcern for their children; other parents directly encourage their children to be extra thin as a part of the general push to compete with their peers. Parents also may help to shape personality patterns that increase the risk of eating disorders, an issue we discuss in the next section.

Psychological Factors

Researchers have suggested a number of psychological concerns as etiologic factors in eating disorders, including dissatisfaction with body image, various problems with control (including having too little and wanting too much), difficulties with sexuality, fear of autonomy, low self-esteem, perfectionism, reactions to dieting, and a number of comorbid psychological disorders, including various mood disorders, anxiety disorders, and personality disorders. The confusing number of alternative hypotheses reflects two clear facts. First, scientists have not yet identified unequivocal psychological contributors to eating disorders. Second, there will prove to be many alternative pathways to the development of eating disorders, not just one. Here we highlight four of the most promising approaches: control issues, depression/dysphoria, body image dissatisfaction, and reactions to dietary restraint.

A STRUGGLE FOR CONTROL

Hilde Bruch (1904–1984), a physician who fled her native Germany in 1933 to escape the Nazi

▼ Caraline, 28 years old, told a reporter, "I'm not telling you how much I weigh because I'm ashamed I don't weigh less." She later died of complications due to anorexia nervosa.

regime and subsequently settled and studied psychiatry in the United States, was one of the first and most prolific clinical observers of eating disorders. Bruch strongly asserted that a *struggle for control* is the central psychological issue in the development of eating disorders (Bruch, 1982). Bruch observed that girls with eating disorders seem to be exceptionally "good"— conforming and eager to please. She further suggested that these exceptionally "good girls" give up too much of the normal adolescent struggle for autonomy, and instead they attempt to please others, particularly their parents. Bruch thus viewed their obsessive efforts to control eating and weight as a way that overly compliant "good girls" control themselves further. At the same time, she also saw their dieting as an attempt to wrest at least a little control from their parents— control over what they eat. In this struggle for control, young people with anorexia nervosa "succeed" and take considerable pride in their extreme self-control. In contrast, people with bulimia nervosa continually strive—and fail— to gain complete control over eating and weight. The success or failure of control, in turn, may explain the denial that characterizes anorexia nervosa and the humiliation that accompanies bulimia nervosa.

Researchers often use the term *perfectionism* to describe the endless pursuit of control described by Bruch and other clinicians. Perfectionists set unrealistically high standards, are self-critical, and demand a performance from themselves that is higher than is required by a given situation. Research demonstrates that young women with eating disorders endorse perfectionist goals both about eating and weight and about general expectations for themselves (Bastiani et al., 1995; Garner, Olmstead, & Polivy, 1983). Moreover, some evidence indicates that unrealistically high standards persist among women with anorexia nervosa even after they return to a more normal weight (Bastiani et al., 1995).

Young people with eating disorders may also try to control their own emotions excessively, perhaps as a result of their constant attempt to please others instead of themselves (Bruch, 1982). The result may be a lack of **introceptive awareness,** recognition of internal cues including various emotional states as well as hunger. Simply put, people with eating disorders may be unaware of their own needs and feelings. In fact, one of the largest studies of the development of eating disorders found that a measure of lack of introceptive awareness not only predicted the presence of concurrent eating disorders but also predicted the development of eating disorders 2 years in the future (Leon et al., 1993; Leon et al., 1995). (See Research Close-Up.) Thus excessive external control, perfectionism, and a lack of introceptive awareness appear to be one cluster of psychological contributions to the development of eating disorders.

▲ Psychiatrist Hilde Bruch (1904–1984) was an early and prolific clinical observer who viewed the young woman's struggle for control as a central issue in the development of eating disorders.

RESEARCH CLOSE-UP

Risk Factors in the Development of Disordered Eating

University of Minnesota clinical psychologist Gloria Leon and her colleagues have collected data on over 2,000 students in grades 7–10 and assessed 1,640 of them over a period of 3 years in one of the largest and most comprehensive studies of risk factors in the development of eating disorders. Risk factors studied included physical size, pubertal status, eating patterns, attitudes about eating and self, substance use, personality characteristics, multiple self-concept scales, perceived autonomy, and attitudes about sexuality.

In one of the first reports from this large study, the investigators used measures of each of these variables to predict *concurrent* eating difficulties (subclinical problems that were not necessarily eating disorders) among 937 adolescent girls. (The investigators also assessed boys, but too few reported eating difficulties for analysis.) The researchers found that some commonly discussed risk factors, such as depression and lack of autonomy, were related to girls' eating difficulties when considered alone. However, when they tested all variables together, only the following variables proved to be statistically significant risk factors: body dissatisfaction, negative emotionality, low introceptive awareness, hypomania, and low perceived scholastic competence (Leon et al., 1993).

In a subsequent prospective study, the investigators used the same set of variables to predict eating difficulties 3 years later among 843 of the same girls. The only significant predictors of eating difficulties 3 years later were earlier eating difficulties, low introceptive awareness, and white race (Leon et al., 1995). The investigators also tested predictions of eating difficulties among a sample of about 800 boys but failed to identify any significant risk factors other than earlier reports of eating problems.

We need to be careful not to dismiss some of the variables that failed to predict eating difficulties. For example, body image dissatisfaction may not have predicted eating difficulties among the girls, because so many of them reported dissatisfaction with their bodies. In order to be good predictors, variables need to vary.

Although negative findings from the study must be interpreted cautiously, the positive findings for low introceptive awareness are very important. They led the investigators to the following conclusion about the development of eating disorders: "Thus, a combination of poor introceptive awareness and negative emotion (the strongest predictors of risk in our Year 1 cross-sectional findings) could lead to a state of chronic negative arousal. The inability to accurately label one's feelings would then make it difficult to respond adaptively in decreasing this uncomfortable condition. Through a variety of family and cultural influences, severe food restriction or excessive food consumption followed by counteractive measures to rid oneself of the food just eaten may become a learned way of dealing with these negative and indistinct emotional states" (Leon et al., 1995, p. 147). ∎

DEPRESSION, LOW SELF-ESTEEM, AND DYSPHORIA

Depression is another psychological factor that may contribute to eating disorders, particularly to bulimia nervosa. Researchers have found an increased prevalence of depression not only among people with eating disorders but also among the members of their families (Strober, 1995). This has led some experts to speculate that the two problems are etiologically related. In support of this theory, research indicates that antidepressant medications are effective in reducing some symptoms of bulimia nervosa (Mitchell, Raymond, & Specker, 1993).

Other experts suggest, however, that depression may be a reaction to developing bulimia nervosa and especially a reaction to the onset of anorexia nervosa (Hsu, 1990; Yates, 1989). In support of this alternative view, research indicates that depression improves markedly following successful group psychotherapy for bulimia (Mitchell et al., 1990). Moreover, in one large study a measure of depression failed to predict either concurrent or future eating disorders (Leon et al., 1995; see Research Close-Up). Another study of anorexia nervosa found considerable depression at the time of the originial diagnosis but not at a 6-year follow-up (Rastam, Gillberg, & Gillberg, 1995). Thus clinical depression may contribute to the development of eating disorders in a subset of cases, but in most

eating disorders, depression appears to be a secondary problem and not the primary issue.

Despite these conclusions, many researchers and clinicians suggest that depressive *symptoms*, and not necessarily clinical depression, are central factors in various specific aspects of eating disorders. Low self-esteem is a particular concern. More specifically, many observers note that women with eating disorders are preoccupied with their *social self* (Jones, 1985; Striegel-Moore, Silberstein, & Rodin, 1993). The social self includes both how we present ourselves in public and how other people perceive and evaluate us. In eating disorders, preoccupation with the social self may lead to an undue emphasis on physical appearance—a central aspect of young women's self-presentation—as well as considerable anxiety about the social presentation of one's personality. Lacking the confidence and esteem to "be yourself," young people instead may present a facade to the world. Such people may be happy when they get positive reactions from others but distraught when they get negative reactions or no response at all. They may act like "fakes," feel like "frauds," and depend on others' reactions for self-esteem.

Researchers are just beginning to examine these intuitively appealing ideas. Evidence indicates that women with bulimia nervosa or a negative body image report more public self-consciousness, social anxiety, and perceived fraudulence in comparison to other women (Striegel-Moore et al., 1993). Thus some young women with eating disorders appear to be governed more by external appearances than by inner standards.

Depressive symptoms also clearly play a role in maintaining problematic eating behaviors. Dysphoria or negative mood states commonly trigger episodes of binge eating in bulimia nervosa and in the binge-eating/purging subtype of anorexia nervosa. The dysphoria may be brought on by social criticism or conflict, dissatisfaction with eating and diet, or an ongoing depressive episode. Thus, although most cases of clinical depression appear to be reactions to eating disorders, depression, low self-esteem, and periods of dysphoria can contribute to the onset or maintenance of some eating disorder cases.

NEGATIVE BODY IMAGE

A *negative body image*, a highly critical evaluation of one's weight and shape, is another psychological factor that has long been thought to contribute to the development of eating disorders (Bruch, 1962). Psychologists have used a number of techniques to evaluate a negative body image, including self-report measures, callipers or other devices used to directly estimate the size of various body parts, and schematic figures such at the ones in Figure 10–5 (Thompson, 1996).

Early studies of body image in eating disorders focused on a *distorted* body image, a perceptual inaccuracy in judging one's size, particularly in cases of anorexia nervosa. Current research focuses on *dissatisfaction* with one's body image, a negative evaluation of one's body that includes cognitive and affective elements and not just perceptual distortions. Thus one way to assess a negative body image is to compare people's ratings of their "current" and "ideal" size by asking them to pick from the schematics in Figure 10–5. Body image clearly is an important focus for continued research, as several longitudinal studies have found negative evaluations of weight, shape, and appearance to predict the subsequent development of disordered eating (Attie & Brooks-Gunn, 1989; Cattarin & Thompson, 1994; Striegel-Moore et al., 1989).

DIETARY RESTRAINT

Some of the symptoms of eating disorders are likely to be effects of *dietary restraint*, that is, direct consequences of restricted eating (Herman &

Polivy, 1988; Heatherton & Polivy, 1992). This is ironic, because many of the "out-of-control" symptoms of eating disorders appear to be caused by inappropriate efforts to control eating. These symptoms include binge eating, preoccupation with food, and perhaps out-of-control feelings of hunger.

Inappropriate dieting appears to contribute directly to subsequent binge eating. An overly restrictive diet increases hunger, frustration, and lack of attention to internal cues, all of which make binge eating more likely. Moreover, because "quick-fix" diets rarely work, dieters are likely to be left with a sense of failure, disappointment, and self-criticism. The negative affect, in turn, makes further binge eating likely and further lowers the self-esteem of people who already have perfectionistic

▲ **Many women with eating disorders have a distorted body image, as illustrated by this young woman examining her figure in a mirror that gives the illusion of fatness.**

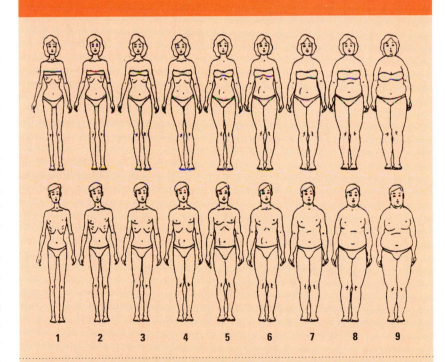

Body Contour Rating Scale

1   2   3   4   5   6   7   8   9

FIGURE 10-5: Schematic figures used to assess body image. The discrepancy between ratings of one's "current" and "ideal" shape/ weight is an index of negative body image.

Source: J.K. Thompson, 1996, Assessing body image disturbance: Measures, methodology, and implementation. In J.K. Thompson (Ed.), *Body Image, Eating Disorders, and Obesity*, p. 79. Washington, DC: American Psychological Association.

standards or a negative body image (Herman & Polivy, 1988; Heatherton & Polivy, 1992). In short, some cases of bulimia nervosa seem to result from the body's rebellion against the individual's attempt to lose an inappropriate amount of weight.

Dietary restraint also may directly cause some of the symptoms of anorexia nervosa. As we noted earlier, military studies during World War II found that obsessive thoughts about food and compulsive eating rituals were one direct consequence of semistarvation (Keys et al., 1950). The same studies also found that during refeeding, many men felt intense, uncontrollable hunger even after eating a considerable amount of food. Perhaps a similar reaction explains some of the intense fear of losing control and gaining weight found in anorexia nervosa.

Biological Factors

Scientists conceptualize normal eating and weight regulation in systems terms, specifically as a result of the interplay among behavior (e.g., energy expenditure, eating), peripheral physiological activity (e.g., digestion, metabolism), and central physiological activity (e.g., neurotransmitter release). Body–brain–behavior relationships are regulated in a way to maintain a homeostatic balance among the metabolism of nutrients, the neural regulation of appetite, and the ingestion of food (Blundell, 1995). Evidence also indicates that homeostatic mechanisms govern the regulation of weight. Specifically, the body maintains weight around certain **weight set points,** fixed weights or small ranges of weight. Maintaining weight near a set point is biologically adaptive. Thus, if weight declines, hunger increases, food consumption goes up, and metabolism slows in an attempt to return weight to its set point (Keesey, 1995). The process is very much like the way a thermostat regulates heating and cooling to maintain air temperature near a given setting.

From this systems perspective, it is clear that, even though they can be conceptualized in psychological terms, the effects of dietary restraint also are biological contributors to the development of eating disorders. The motivations (e.g., hunger) and behaviors (e.g., binge eating) that follow dietary restraint are a part of the body's attempts to maintain weight at a set point through behavioral actions. The body also attempts to maintain weight at a set point through physiological actions. In particular, when food intake is reduced, there is a

slowing in the *metabolic rate*, the rate at which the body expends energy, and movement toward *hyperlipogenesis*, the storage of abnormally large amounts of fat in fat cells throughout the body (Brownell & Fairburn, 1995). All these reactions have obvious survival value and are likely products of evolution. Simply put, the body does not distinguish between intentional attempts to lose weight and potential starvation. Thus some aspects of eating disorders are a result of the individual's struggle against a biological need and binge eating in response to an increasingly urgent biological signal—hunger. (The restricting subtype of anorexia nervosa is an exception.)

Other evidence suggests that biological factors contribute to eating disorders through genetic mechanisms. The most extensive twin study of bulimia nervosa conducted to date found a concordance rate of 23 percent for MZ twins and 9 percent for DZ twins (Kendler et al., 1991). Higher MZ than DZ concordance rates for dysfunctional eating attitudes have also been reported (Rutherford et al., 1993).

It is important to note, however, that MZ–DZ twin differences could be explained by several different heritable mechanisms. It is unlikely that eating disorders are directly inherited, especially given the historically recent surge in prevalence rates. Rather, genetics may influence some personality characteristic that, in turn, increases the risk for bulimia nervosa (Strober, 1995). Or a certain body type or weight set point may be inherited, and this may account for the higher concordance rates found among MZ twins. If so, the well-established genetic contributions to determining weight and body type (Leibel & Hirsch, 1995; Price & Gottesman, 1991) contribute to the development of eating disorders only when combined with cultural expectations about thinness—and with individual concerns about living up to these expectations. Genes clearly affect weight set points and body type, but we cannot mindlessly conclude that eating disorders are "genetic" (see the discussion of behavior genetics in Chapter 2 and Research Methods in Chapter 17).

Finally, we should note that several measures of neurophysiology have been found to be linked with eating disorders, including elevations in endogenous opioids, low levels of serotonin, and diminished neuroendocrine functioning (Yates, 1990). Most of these differences in brain functioning, however, appear to be effects of eating disorders and not causes of them. In extremely rare cases, eating disorders have been linked with a specific biological abnormality, such as a hormonal disturbance or a lesion in the *hypothalamus*, the area of the brain that regulates routine biological functions, including appetite (see Chapter 2). The weight of current evidence suggests, however, that most biological abnormalities associated with eating disorders are either reactions to or indirect contributors to eating disorders.

Integration and Alternative Pathways

Clearly, eating disorders are best understood in terms of a systems approach. Social and cultural values that emphasize thinness, beauty, and appearance over personality are the starting point in understanding eating disorders, particularly among young women. Given the very low prevalence of eating disorders in some cultures and at earlier points in Western history—and their very high prevalence among young women today—social factors come close to being a necessary condition for the development of eating disorders. However, the fact that some cases of eating disorders have been found in other cultures and at other times indicates that societal pressures are not always necessary for eating disorders to develop.

Social forces clearly are not sufficient causes of eating disorders. Although a majority of young women in the United States today are concerned with weight and shape, only a minority actually develop anorexia nervosa or bulimia nervosa. Direct risk factors that distinguish people who develop eating disorders include familial and social pressures to be thin, a negative body image, direct behavioral and biological reactions to dietary restraint, and genetic influences on body weight and shape.

Less obvious risk factors include preoccupation with external evaluation, lack of awareness of internal desires, and preoccupation with conformity and self-control. In some cases, family difficulties may contribute to eating disorders, but in others, parental conflict and concern are better viewed as reactions to a child's frightening loss of weight. Similarly, comorbid mood and anxiety disorders sometimes may cause, but seemingly more often result from, eating disorders.

These latter observations underscore an important point we have emphasized throughout the text: equifinality. There is no one pathway to developing any given emotional problem; rather there are many. Some women who develop eating disorders are naturally thin, but they have perfectionistic standards that drive them to be even thinner. Other women with the disorders may have genetically determined body types that are at or above normal weight, and their eating disorder is a reaction to the social criticism they feel as a result. For some people, an eating disorder is an expression of depression. Other people may develop an eating disorder because they focus too much on outward appearance instead of inner standards.

In considering the development of eating disorders, a key issue that remains unanswered is why some women develop anorexia nervosa and others develop bulimia nervosa. Many social, psychological, and biological elements of the two disorders are similar, although the symptoms and treatment (as we will soon see) of the two conditions differ widely. Future research should help uncover answers to the important question of what factors determine whether a young woman masters her appetite—and becomes emaciated as a result—or whether she continually struggles with frequent binge eating and compensatory behavior.

Treatment of Eating Disorders

The treatments for anorexia nervosa and bulimia nervosa differ in approach and effectiveness. Anorexia nervosa, particularly in severe cases, is more likely to require inpatient treatment, and the initial goal in treating anorexia nervosa is to encourage the sufferer to gain weight. If necessary, coercive methods such as forced feeding may be used in order to reduce the life-threatening consequences of severe emaciation.

Treatment of bulimia nervosa rarely requires such extreme intervention. Most effective approaches to treating bulimia nervosa focus on directly changing eating patterns. Other promising treatments target depression and/or interpersonal difficulties, yet they also help reduce binge eating and compensatory behavior. Recent evidence about the treatment of bulimia nervosa is encouraging, but attempts to treat anorexia nervosa have met with less success. For all these reasons, in the following sections we consider the treatment and course of anorexia nervosa and bulimia nervosa separately.

Treatment of Anorexia Nervosa

The treatment of anorexia nervosa usually focuses on two goals. The first goal is to help the patient gain at least a minimal amount of weight. If weight loss is severe, the patient may be treated in an inpatient setting, where clinicians may use coercive methods, such as tube or intravenous feeding, or introduce strict behavior therapy programs in which rewards (for example, social activities) are contingent on weight gain. Hospitalization also may be needed to prevent suicide, to address severe depression or medical complications, or to remove the patient temporarily from a dysfunctional social circumstance (Garner & Needleman, 1996).

The second goal in treating anorexia nervosa is more general—to address the broader difficulties that may have caused or are maintaining the disorder. Many different forms of treatment may be used to achieve this goal. The clinical literature commonly advocates family therapy. There are many different forms of family therapy, but perhaps the most common is *structural family therapy*, which views parents' interference with adolescent autonomy—and avoidance of their own disagreements—as the central problems in anorexia nervosa. Structural family therapists attempt to redefine the eating disorder as an interpersonal problem, to get the young person with anorexia nervosa out of the sick role, and to encourage parents to confront their own conflicts directly and not through their children (Minuchin et al., 1978). Some evidence indicates that family therapy for anorexia nervosa is more effective than individual treatment, at least when the client is an adolescent (Russell et al., 1987).

Clinicians have also tried a number of different individual therapies for anorexia nervosa. Three approaches of note are (1) Bruch's (1982) modified psychodynamic therapy designed to increase introceptive awareness and correct distorted perceptions of self; (2) cognitive behavioral approaches that aim to alter the belief that "weight, shape, or thinness can serve as the sole or predominant referent for inferring personal value or self-worth" (Garner & Bemis, 1982, p. 142); and (3) *feminist therapies*, which encourage young women to pursue their own values rather than blindly adopting perscribed social roles (Fallon, Katzman, & Wooley, 1994). There is currently little, if any, evidence to show that any of these treatments is effective. Similarly, medication seems to offer no relief for victims of anorexia nervosa (Garner & Needleman, 1996). Keep in mind, however, that the three approaches to individual therapy share the common goal of basing self-esteem more on internal standards and less on external evaluations. Working toward this end is a logical goal in treating and, we believe, in preventing anorexia nervosa.

Course and Outcome of Anorexia Nervosa

Evidence on the course and outcome of anorexia nervosa demonstrates that contemporary treatments are not very effective. At posttreatment follow-up assessments, 50 to 60 percent of patients have a weight within the normal range, 10 to 20 percent remain significantly below their healthy body weight, and the remainder are intermediate in weight (Hsu, 1990; Steinhausen, 1996). Perhaps as many as 10 percent starve themselves to death or die of related complications.

Although important, weight gain is not the only measure of the course of anorexia nervosa. In fact, more than half the women with a history of anorexia nervosa continue to have difficulties with eating notwithstanding gains in weight. Menstruation returns along with weight gain for most women, but preoccupation with diet, weight, and body shape often continues. Moreover, patients may also develop new problems with social life, depression, or bulimia (Hsu, 1990). Predictors of a better prognosis include an early age of onset, conflict-free parent–child relationships, early treatment, less weight loss, and the absence of binge eating and purging (Steinhausen, 1996).

Treatment of Bulimia Nervosa

In recent years, researchers have uncovered promising evidence of the effectiveness of several approaches to treating bulimia nervosa. The most effective forms of treatment include antidepressant medication, cognitive behavior therapy (delivered both individually and in groups), and interpersonal psychotherapy.

ANTIDEPRESSANT MEDICATIONS

All classes of antidepressant medications (see Chapter 5) have been shown to be somewhat effective in treating bulimia nervosa; however, medication is *not* the treatment of choice. Binge eating and compensatory behavior improve only among a minority of people treated with antidepressants, and relapse appears to be common when medication is stopped. Moreover, initial depression or improvement in mood state does not predict improvement in the symptoms of bulimia (Walsh, 1995). Most importantly, medication is not the treatment of choice because several studies have shown psychotherapy to be more effective.

COGNITIVE BEHAVIOR THERAPY

The most thoroughly researched psychotherapy for bulimia nervosa is cognitive behavior therapy. As developed by the British psychiatrist Christopher Fairburn, the cognitive behavioral approach views bulimia as stemming from several maladaptive tendencies, including an excessive emphasis on weight and shape in determining self-esteem; perfectionism; and dichotomous "black or white" thinking (Fairburn, 1996). Fairburn's cognitive behavioral treatment includes three stages: (1) using education and behavioral strategies to normalize eating patterns; (2) addressing broader, dysfunctional beliefs about self, appearance, and dieting; and (3) consolidating gains and preparing strategies for coping with expected relapses in the future (Fairburn, 1995). Overall, cognitive behavior therapy leads to a 70 percent reduction in binge eating and purging across people in treatment. Between one-third and one-half of all clients are able to cease these patterns completely. The majority of individuals maintain these gains at 6-month to 1-year follow-up (Fairburn et al., 1993).

A large study conducted at the University of Minnesota demonstrated that cognitive behavior therapy also is effective in a group format (Mitchell et al., 1990). In this study, 171 women were assigned at random to one of four treatment conditions: (1) placebo only; (2) antidepressant medication only (imipramine); (3) group therapy plus placebo; and (4) group therapy plus medication. The cognitive behavioral groups were short term (10 weeks) but very intensive. The first 2 weeks included two 2-hour group sessions during which the therapists introduced a system for planning meals and explained the cognitive behavior therapy approach. The subjects were encouraged to avoid binge eating and purging during treatment. The groups continued to meet for 3 hours 5 nights per week for the first week in order to monitor eating and provide support for efforts at controlling the bulimia. The frequency of meetings tapered down over time to only one 1½ hour meeting per week near the end of treatment.

Group psychotherapy proved to be an effective treatment that resulted in a 90 percent reduction in episodes of binge eating. Antidepressant medication also reduced binge eating (by 65 percent), but medication was significantly less effective than psychotherapy, and women on medication also were likelier to drop out of the study. Finally, the addition of antidepressant medication (group therapy plus medication versus group therapy plus placebo) did not add significantly to the effectiveness of the group treatment for bulimia nervosa, although it led to some improvement in depression (Mitchell et al., 1990). These results and similar findings indicate that cognitive behavior therapy, not antidepressant medication, is the treatment of choice for bulimia nervosa (Fairburn, 1995; Walsh, 1995).

INTERPERSONAL PSYCHOTHERAPY

Interpersonal psychotherapy, which was originally developed for the treatment of depression (see Chapter 5), may also be an effective treatment for bulimia nervosa. This is surprising because interpersonal therapy does not address eating disorders directly but instead focuses on difficulties in close relationships. Interpersonal therapy for bulimia was initially studied when the treatment was included as a placebo control group in a study of cognitive behavior therapy (see Research Methods). Fairburn and colleagues (1991, 1993) planned to evaluate whether cognitive behavior therapy had specific treatment effects above and beyond the nonspecific, general benefits of receiving psychotherapy (see Chapter 3). The investigators picked interpersonal therapy as a credible placebo treatment because interpersonal problems often are associated with bulimia nervosa. However, they hypothesized that cognitive behavior therapy would outperform the interpersonal approach. The study also included a third condition, a behavior therapy alone group, which essentially was cognitive behavior therapy without the cognitive elements.

When Fairburn and his colleagues (1991) evaluated outcome shortly after treatment, they found that cognitive behavior therapy was more

Effectiveness of Treatments for Bulimia Nervosa over Time

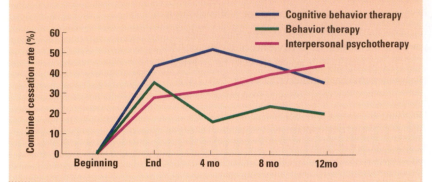

FIGURE 10-6: Percentage of patients who no longer purged or had episodes of bulimia according to objective or subjective reports. Note the decline for the behavior therapy group and continued improvement for the interpersonal therapy group over the 1-year follow-up interval.

Source: C.G. Fairburn, R. Jones, R.C. Peveler, R.A. Hope, and M. O'Connor, 1993, Psychotherapy and bulimia nervosa: Longer-term effects of interpersonal psychotherapy, behavior therapy, and cognitive behavior therapy, *Archives of General Psychiatry, 50,* 423.

effective than interpersonal therapy in changing dieting behavior, self-induced vomiting, and attitudes about weight and shape. Cognitive behavior therapy also was more effective than behavior therapy alone when attitude change was the outcome measure; however, the results of the two behavioral treatments were similar in other respects.

A very different picture emerged at 12-month follow-up (Fairburn et al., 1993) (see Figure 10–6). The improvements brought about by behavior therapy alone deteriorated over time, and a large number of patients dropped out of this group, perhaps reflecting their dissatisfaction with the treatment. In comparison, the improvements in the cognitive behavior therapy group remained fairly stable. Most surprising, however, members of the interpersonal therapy group *continued to improve* in the 12 months following the end of treatment. At 1-year follow-up, in fact, the improvements for interpersonal therapy equaled the improvements for cognitive behavior therapy and outdistanced the behavior therapy alone group.

The continued improvement for the interpersonal therapy group was surprising and impressive, for at least two reasons. First, the interpersonal treatments explicitly excluded direct discussions of eating, diet, and related topics. Second, the investigators had lower expectations for the interpersonal therapy group, and the expectations of experimenters, therapists, and clients often affect treatment outcome (see Research Methods). Some other researchers also have found that interpersonal therapy can be effective in treating bulimia nervosa (Wilfley et al., 1993). Thus interpersonal therapy is emerging as a promising alternative or supplement to cognitive behavior therapy for treating bulimia nervosa.

RESEARCH METHODS

Credible Placebo Control Groups

In Chapter 3, we introduced the concepts of a *placebo,* a treatment that contains no active ingredients for the disorder being treated, and a *placebo control group,* a group of clients who are randomly assigned to receive only a placebo treatment in an outcome study. Scientists must include placebos and placebo control groups in treatment outcome research, because the *expectation* of change can produce many psychological (and physical) improvements in psychological and biomedical treatment research. New treatments work, in part, because the client and the therapist expect them to work.

Placebo treatments are easy to develop when studying medications (but see below). Experimenters give patients a pill that looks real but contains no active chemical ingredients, for example, a "sugar pill." Scientists face a much more challenging task in developing placebos for psychological treatments. How can we create a placebo psychological treatment that contains no active ingredients but increases the client's and the therapist's expectation for change just as much as the real treatment?

As one alternative, experimenters sometimes create a placebo control group by randomly assigning clients to receive an established, alternative therapy that was not designed as a treatment for the specific disorder being studied. In their study of cognitive behavior therapy for bulimia nervosa, for example, Fairburn et al. (1993) thought interpersonal therapy was a credible placebo. The investigators did not believe that interpersonal therapy contained "specific ingredients" for treating bulimia nervosa. They did expect, however, that clients would view it as a legitimate treatment for their problems.

Offering an alternative treatment does not fully resolve the problem of designing a credible placebo, because researchers typically "believe" in their new treatment—otherwise they would not be studying it. In fact, psychologists have identified what has been termed an *allegiance effect*—that is, psychotherapy outcome researchers commonly find a treatment to be more successful when the experimenters ally with that particular form of therapy (Robinson, Berman, & Neimeyer, 1990). The allegiance effect tells us that cognitive behavior therapy should have been more successful in the Fairburn et al. (1993) study, because the investigators were cognitive behavior therapists. In fact, we are particularly impressed by the positive results for the interpersonal therapy group in this study, because interpersonal therapy overcame the allegiance effect. The experimenters did *not* expect interpersonal therapy to be an effective treatment, but it was effective nevertheless.

How can investigators overcome the allegiance effect? This dilemma is resolved in drug treatment research by using a *double-blind study* where neither the patient nor the therapist knows whether the patient is receiving an active treatment or a placebo (see Chapter 3). Unfortunately, specific forms of psychotherapy (or placebo therapies) cannot be disguised. Therefore it is impossible to conduct double-blind studies of psychotherapy. An alternative approach is to include a pill placebo in studies of psychotherapy, a method that also can facilitate comparisons between studies of the effectiveness of drugs and psychotherapy (Klein, 1996). This is a positive step, but even pill placebo effects are not always easy to interpret. For example, evidence indicates that medications, perhaps even placebo medications, are more effective when they produce more side effects (Greenberg et al., 1994). There are at least two possible reasons for this. More disruptive side effects may increase the patient's expectations for change, because the side effects make the drug seem powerful. Or even in a double-blind study, clinicians may be able to determine whether patients are receiving the real medication or a placebo based on the pattern of side effects.

Another way of addressing the allegiance effect in psychotherapy outcome research is to have investigators who hold *opposing* allegiances participate in the same study. Cognitive behavior therapy could be offered by cognitive behavior therapists, interpersonal therapists could deliver interpersonal therapy, and so on. This approach overcomes the allegiance effect, but such studies are more difficult and expensive to conduct—and they create a new problem: Because the same therapists cannot deliver the two different treatments, we cannot control for outcome effects due to the individual therapists (e.g., therapists' personality). Of course, the alternative also has the problem that *neither* treatment is a placebo, at least in theory.

Scientific findings are greatly enhanced by the use of alternative therapies, pill placebos, and competitions between researchers with opposing allegiance, but there is no perfect placebo control group for psychotherapy outcome research. In the absence of a perfect psychological placebo, two conclusions seem clear. First, we must recognize that the expectations of clients, therapists, *and experimenters* can influence the findings of therapy outcome research. Second, we are particularly impressed when, contrary to expectations, a treatment that an experimenter views as a placebo proves to be effective. ■

Course and Outcome of Bulimia Nervosa

Researchers are just beginning to publish findings on the course and long-term outcome of bulimia nervosa. At this point the evidence suggests that the outcome for bulimia nervosa is generally more positive than for anorexia nervosa. About half of clients are free of all symptoms of the disorder following treatment, about one in five continue to meet the diagnostic criteria for bulimia nervosa, and the remainder have occasional relapses or subclinical levels of binge eating and compensatory behavior. Most clients manage to maintain a weight that is generally in the normal range, and—in contrast to anorexia nervosa—mortality is rare. Although data are insufficient, it also appears that comorbid psychological disorders tend to improve with improvements in bulimia nervosa (Hsu, 1995). Few predictors of better or worse outcome have been identified, other than obvious indicators; for example, more frequent purging at the time of

diagnosis predicts a less positive outcome (Olmstead, Kaplan, & Rockert, 1994). In closing, we should note that all these findings on outcome are derived from studies following treatment; essentially no evidence is available on the natural course of bulimia nervosa.

Summary

Eating disorders are severe disturbances in eating behavior that result from the sufferer's obsessive fear of gaining weight. The DSM-IV lists two major subtypes of eating disorders: anorexia nervosa and bulimia nervosa. The defining symptoms of **anorexia nervosa** include extreme emaciation, a disturbed perception of one's body, an intense fear of gaining weight, and the cessation of menstruation (in women). Concerns that commonly characterize anorexia nervosa but are not defining symptoms include obsessive preoccupation with food and an exaggerated struggle for control. Other problems that may be associated with anorexia nervosa include mood disturbance, sexual difficulties, a lack of impulse control, and medical problems secondary to the weight loss. The defining symptoms of **bulimia nervosa** are **binge eating** and compensatory behavior (**purging** or excessive exercise), a sense of lost control during a binge, and undue focus on weight and shape. Depression is commonly associated with bulimia nervosa; substance abuse and personality disorders are to a much lesser degree.

The DSM-IV includes two subtypes of anorexia nervosa. The restricting type includes people who rarely engage in binge eating or purging behavior, whereas the binge-eating/purging type is characterized by regular binge eating and purging. Bulimia nervosa also is divided into two subtypes. The purging type is characterized by the regular use of self-induced vomiting or the misuse of laxatives, diuretics, or enemas. The nonpurging type compensates for binge eating with fasting or excessive exercise. There has been debate about adding to the DSM-IV list of eating disorders. **Binge eating disorder** is included in a special appendix. **Obesity** has been considered for inclusion but rejected.

The prevalence of both anorexia nervosa and bulimia nervosa has increased dramatically in recent years, particularly among young women. Both anorexia and bulimia nervosa are approximately 10 times more common among women than among men, and many scientists blame our society's gender roles and standards of beauty for encouraging eating disorders. Standards of beauty and pubertal changes in body shape and weight also may account for the onset of eating disorders during adolescence and early adulthood.

The regulation of normal eating and weight results from a combination of biological, psychological, and social factors, and researchers

KEY TERMS

- amenorrhea
- anorexia nervosa
- binge eating
- binge eating disorder
- bulimia nervosa
- cohort
- cohort effect
- distorted body image
- eating disorders
- enmeshed family
- introceptive awareness
- obesity
- purging
- weight set point

have focused on each of these levels of analysis in explaining the etiology of anorexia nervosa and bulimia nervosa. Epidemiological evidence highlights the role of social factors. Adolescent girls and young women are at risk, in part, because they attempt to shape themselves to fit the image of the ideal woman. The emphasis on appearances also lessens the value of other roles filled by girls and women. To a lesser extent, family relationships also may influence eating disorders. Four of the most prominent psychological factors in the development of eating disorders are issues of control and perfectionism, dysphoria combined with a lack of **introceptive awareness,** body image dissatisfaction, and reactions to dietary restraint. Biological contributions include the body's attempts to maintain **weight set points,** genetic influences on body weight and shape, and in rare cases a dysfunction of the hypothalamus. Overall, a systems perspective is the best method for conceptualizing eating disorders, and these disorders can develop through several alternative pathways.

Treatments for anorexia nervosa and bulimia nervosa differ in approach and effectiveness. Anorexia nervosa is likelier to require inpatient treatment with the initial goal of gaining weight, even through the use of coercive methods if necessary. Following treatment, 50 to 60 percent of people with anorexia nervosa have a normal weight, and 10 to 20 percent have weights well below normal (the remainder are in between these two groups). About 10 percent of people with the disorder die of starvation, suicide, or medical complications. Changing long-term eating patterns and attitudes in anorexia nervosa is even more difficult than changing weight, and no clearly effective psychological treatment or medication has been identified for the disorder.

Treatments for bulimia nervosa are more promising, particularly cognitive behavior therapy and interpersonal psychotherapy and to a lesser extent antidepressant medication. About half of clients with bulimia nervosa are free of all symptoms following treatment, about one in five continue to meet the diagnostic criteria, and the remainder have occasional relapses or subclinical levels of binge eating and compensatory behavior. Weight is generally in the normal range, and comorbid psychological disorders appear to improve with improvements in bulimia nervosa.

Critical Thinking

1. Many psychologists believe that young women develop eating disorders in part because the popular media portray extremely thin women as beautiful, fit, happy, and successful. Is this perspective consistent with your experience? What changes would you like to see in these images of women?

2. What roles are young women expected to play in their families and in social relationships (including relationships with men and with other women), and how might these roles contribute to the development of eating disorders?

3. What roles are young men expected to play in their families and in social relationships (including relationships with women and with other men), and how might these roles protect men against (or sometimes contribute to) the development of eating disorders?

4. If you had an eating disorder, would you want to be treated with cognitive behavior therapy, interpersonal therapy, or antidepressant medication? What are the reasons for your choice? Why might people who received interpersonal therapy continue to improve over time, whereas people who received behavior therapy often regress?

11
Substance Use Disorders

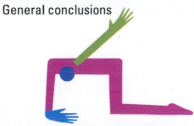

The abuse of alcohol and other drugs is one of the most serious problems facing our society. Alcohol and drug problems receive a great deal of attention in the popular media, as illustrated by former baseball player Mickey Mantle's fatal struggle with alcoholism and the drug-related suicide of Kurt Cobain, leader of the rock group Nirvana. Research efforts, treatment priorities, and national publicity have all helped transform national attitudes toward the abuse of chemical substances. The picture of the drug addict as a homeless derelict whose personality defects and lack of motivation are largely responsible for the problem is being replaced by a new view in which substance abuse is seen to affect people from all walks of life. Experts now locate the causes of substance abuse within a comprehensive biopsychosocial model, and treatment is increasingly included within mainstream health care programs and health insurance (Roman & Blum, 1987).

The costs of substance abuse are astronomical. Alcohol abuse costs the United States $99 billion each year, and abuse of other drugs costs an additional $67 billion. One obvious cost is medical treatment, both for substance use disorders and for the other medical conditions that are associated with these disorders. For example, health care expenditures linked directly to the use of tobacco amount to $50 billion per year (Cooper, 1994). Substance abuse exacts many other costs to society, including lost productivity, aid to families of individuals with substance use disorders, and enforcement of drug laws.

The impact of drug abuse is even more compelling when viewed in terms of its devastation of human lives. More than 75 percent of all foster children are products of alcohol- and/or drug-addicted parents (Children's Defense Fund, 1994). Approximately 15 percent of all deaths in the United States can be attributed to alcohol and drug use (McLellan, Woody, & Metzger, 1996). Tobacco-related diseases (such as cancer and heart disease; see Figure 8–4) kill more than 400,000 people in the United States each year (Kessler et al., 1996). The health problems associated with alcohol use and abuse are also severe. Cirrhosis of the liver, which is frequently the product of chronic alcoholism, is the ninth leading cause of death in the United States. Alcohol is also a major cause of the irreversible memory deficits associated with dementia (see Chapter 14). In addition, alcohol plays a prominent role in many suicides, homicides, and motor vehicle accidents. If all of these problems were combined, alcohol would be the fourth leading cause of death in the United States (Merikangas, 1990).

Overview

The habitual use of various kinds of drugs or chemical substances can create problems that interfere with a person's social and occupational functioning. The DSM-IV uses two terms to describe substance use disorders, which reflect two different levels of severity. **Substance** **dependence,** the more severe of the two forms, refers to a pattern of repeated self-administration that often results in tolerance, the need for increased amounts of the drug to achieve intoxication; withdrawal, unpleasant physical and psychological effects that the person experiences when he or she tries to stop taking the drug; or compulsive drug-taking behavior. **Substance abuse** describes a more broadly conceived, less severe pattern of drug use that is defined in terms of interference with the person's ability to fulfill major role obligations at work or at home, the recurrent use of a drug in dangerous situations, or the experience of repeated legal difficulties that are associated with drug use. People with a substance use disorder frequently abuse several types of drugs; this condition is known as **polysubstance abuse.**

Addiction is another, older term that is often used to describe problems such as alcoholism. The term has been replaced in official terminology by the term *substance dependence*, with which it is synonymous, but it is still used informally by many laypeople. Most people have two principal things in mind when they use the word *addiction*: craving and lack of control. A person who is addicted to something presumably has a compelling need for it and also experiences considerable difficulty regulating behaviors that are associated with it.

When used in this fashion, the notion of addiction can be applied to many forms of behavior that extend well beyond the use of drugs. Many people feel that they are addicted to food. Others have difficulty controlling impulsive behaviors, such as gambling and sex (see Further Thoughts in Chapter 9). In fact, the list could probably be expanded to include such things as watching television, shopping, working, and running. Because of the similarities across these various types of problems, some experts have chosen to view them all as "excessive appetites" (Orford, 1985). These problems have also been called "central activities," which are defined in terms of (1) a puzzling inability to manage the problem behavior, and (2) a self-destructive component (Fingarette, 1988). This is a legitimate and interesting approach to the problems of addiction. For the sake of our discussion, however, we will focus on problems that center on the abuse of chemical substances.

A **drug of abuse**—sometimes called a *psychoactive substance* is a chemical substance that alters a person's mood, level of perception, or brain functioning (Schuckit, 1989). All drugs of abuse can be used to increase a person's psychological comfort level (make you feel "high") or to alter levels of consciousness. The list of chemicals on which people can become dependent is long and seems to be growing

longer. It includes drugs that are legally available in our society, whether over the counter or by prescription only, as well as many that are illegal (see Table 11–1).

The central nervous system (CNS) depressants include alcohol as well as types of medication that are used to help people sleep, called *hypnotics*, and those for relieving anxiety, known as *sedatives* or *anxiolytics*. The CNS stimulants include illegal drugs like amphetamine and cocaine, as well as nicotine and caffeine. The opiates, also called *narcotic analgesics*, can be used clinically to decrease pain. The cannabinoids, such as marijuana, produce euphoria and an altered sense of time. At higher doses, they may produce hallucinations.

One basic question we must address is whether we should view each type of addiction as a unique problem. Experts who answer "yes"

TABLE 11–1

Classification of Psychoactive Drugs

Class	Examples
CNS Depressants	Alcohol
	Hypnotics (barbiturates)
	Anxiolytics (antianxiety drugs)
CNS Stimulants	Amphetamine ("speed")
	Cocaine
	Caffeine
	Nicotine
	Methylphenidate (Ritalin)
	Weight-loss products
Opiates	Heroin
	Morphine
	Methadone
	Prescription painkillers (almost all)
Cannabinoids	Marijuana
	Hashish
Hallucinogens	Lysergic acid diethylamide (LSD)
	Mescaline
	Psilocybin
Solvents	Aerosol sprays
	Glues
	Paint thinner
Over-the-Counter Drugs	Sedatives (sleep aids)
	Weak stimulants
Others	Phencyclidine (PCP)

Source: Adapted from M. A. Schuckit, 1989, *Drug and Alcohol Abuse: A Clinical Guide to Diagnosis and Treatment* (3rd ed.). New York: Plenum.

to this question point out that each class of abused substance seems to affect the body in distinct ways. For example, the long-term use of opiates such as heroin does not seem to cause many chronic physical health problems (Brecher, 1972; Room, 1987), whereas alcohol and tobacco can have a devastating impact on a person's physical health.

Despite these differences, the various forms of substance abuse share many common elements. The psychological and biochemical effects on the user are often similar, as are the negative consequences for both social and occupational behaviors. At the most fundamental level, all forms of abuse represent the inherent conflict between immediate pleasure and longer term harmful consequences (Lang, 1983). The reasons for initial experimentation with a drug, the factors that influence the transition to dependence, and the processes that lead to relapse after initial efforts to change are all similar in many respects. For these reasons, many clinicians and researchers have moved toward a view of substance abuse that emphasizes common causes, behaviors, and consequences (Marlatt et al., 1988; Miller, 1987). In fact, DSM-IV employs a single set of diagnostic criteria that defines dependence for all types of drugs.

The variety of problems associated with substance use disorders can be illustrated using a case study of alcohol abuse. Ernest Hemingway (1899–1961), a Nobel Prize–winning writer, was a chronic alcohol abuser. The following paragraphs, quoted from an article by Paul Johnson (1989), describe the progression of Hemingway's drinking and the problems that it created. They illustrate many typical features of substance dependence, as well as the devastating impact that alcohol can have on various organs of the body. These paragraphs also raise a number of interesting questions about the etiology of this disorder. Most men and women consume alcoholic beverages at some point during their lives. Why do some people become dependent on alcohol while others do not? What factors influence the transition from social drinking to abuse?

CASE STUDY

Ernest Hemingway's Alcohol Dependence

Hemingway began to drink as a teenager, the local blacksmith, Jim Dilworth, secretly supplying him with strong cider. His mother noted his habit and always feared he would become an alcoholic. In Italy he progressed to wine, then had his first hard liquor at the officers' club in Milan. His wound [from World War I] and an unhappy love affair provoked heavy drinking: in the hospital, his wardrobe was found to be full of empty cognac bottles, an ominous sign. In Paris in the 1920s, he bought Beaune by the gallon at a wine cooperative, and would and did drink five or six bottles of red at a meal. He taught Scott Fitzgerald to drink wine direct from the bottle, which, he said, was like "a girl going swimming without her swimming suit." In New York he was "cock-eyed," he said, for "several days" after signing his contract for *The Sun Also Rises,* probably his first prolonged bout.

Hemingway particularly liked to drink with women, as this seemed to him, vicariously, to signify his mother's approval. Hadley [the first of his four wives] drank a lot with him, and wrote: "I still cherish, you know, the remark you made that you almost worshipped me as a drinker." The same disastrous role was played by his pretty 1930s companion in Havana, Jane Mason, with whom he drank gin followed by champagne chasers and huge jars of iced daiquiris; it was indeed in Cuba in this decade that his drinking first got completely out of hand. One bartender there said he could "drink more martinis than any man I have ever seen." On safari, he was seen sneaking out of his tent at 5 A.M. to get a drink. His brother Leicester said that, by the end of the 1930s, at Key West, he was drinking seventeen Scotch-and-sodas a day, and often taking a bottle of champagne to bed with him at night.

At this period, his liver for the first time began to cause him acute pain. He was told by his doctor to give up alcohol completely, and indeed tried to limit his consumption to three whiskeys before dinner. But that did not last. During World War II his drinking mounted steadily and by the mid-1940s he was reportedly pouring gin into his tea at breakfast. A. E. Hotchner, interviewing him for *Cosmopolitan* in 1948, said he dispatched seven double-size Papa Doubles (the Havana drink named after him, a mixture of rum, grapefruit and maraschino), and when he left for dinner took an eighth with him for the drive. And on top of all, there was constant whiskey: His son Patrick said his father got through a quart of whiskey a day for the last 20 years of his life.

Hemingway's ability to hold his liquor was remarkable. Lillian Ross, who wrote his profile for the *New Yorker,* does not seem to have noticed he was drunk a lot of the time he talked to her. Denis Zaphior said of his last safari: "I suppose he was drunk the whole time but seldom showed it." He also demonstrated an unusual ability to cut down his drinking or even to eliminate it altogether for brief periods, and this, in addition to his strong physique, enabled him to survive.

But despite his physique, his alcoholism had a direct impact on his health beginning with his damaged liver in the late 1930s. By 1959, following his last big drinking bout in Spain, he was experiencing both kidney and liver trouble and possibly hemochromatosis (cirrhosis, bronzed skin, diabetes), edema of the ankles, cramps, chronic insomnia, blood-clotting and high blood uremia, as well as his skin complaints. He was impotent and prematurely aged. Even so, he was still on his feet, still alive; and the thought had become unbearable to him. His father had committed suicide because of his fear of mortal illness. Hemingway feared that his illnesses were not mortal: On July 2, 1961, after various unsuccessful treatments for depression and paranoia, he got hold of his best English double-barreled shotgun, put two canisters in it, and blew away his entire cranial vault.

Why did Hemingway long for death [and why did he drink]? . . . He felt he was failing his art. Hemingway had many grievous faults, but there was one thing he did not lack: artistic integrity. It shines like a beacon through his whole life. He set himself the task of creating a new way of writing English, and fiction, and he succeeded. It was one of the salient events in the history of our language and is now an inescapable part of it. He devoted to this task immense resources of creative skill, energy, and patience. That in itself was difficult. But far more difficult, as he discovered, was to maintain the high creative standards he had set himself. This became apparent to him in the mid-1930s, and added to his habitual depression. From then on his few successful stories were aberrations in a long downward slide.

If Hemingway had been less of an artist, it might not have mattered to him as a man: He would simply have written and published inferior novels, as many writers do. But he knew when he wrote below his best, and the knowledge was intolerable to him. He sought the help of alcohol, even in working hours. He was first observed with a drink, a "Rum St. James," in front of him while writing in the 1920s. This custom, rare at first, became intermittent, then invariable. By the 1940s, he was said to wake at 4:30 A.M. [He] "usually starts drinking right away and writes standing up, with a pencil in one hand and a drink in another." The effect on his work was exactly as might be expected, disastrous. Hemingway began to produce large quantities of unpublishable material, or material he felt did not reach the minimum standard he set himself. Some was published nonetheless, and was seen to be inferior, even a parody of his earlier work. There were one or two exceptions, notably *The Old Man and the Sea* (1952), which won him the Nobel Prize, though there was an element of self-parody in that, too. But the general level was low, and falling, and Hemingway's awareness of his inability to recapture his genius, let alone develop it, accelerated the spinning circle of depression and drink. (Johnson, 1989, pp. 58–59) ■

Typical Symptoms and Associated Features

Substance use disorders are associated with a host of problems, many of which are illustrated in the life of Ernest Hemingway. Nevertheless, substance dependence is difficult to define. Alcoholism is one important example. George Vaillant (1995), a psychiatrist at Dartmouth Medical School and the author of an important longitudinal study of alcoholic men, notes that it is difficult to say that one specific problem or set of problems represents the core features of this disorder:

Not only is there no single symptom that defines alcoholism, but often it is not who is drinking but who is watching that defines a symptom. A drinker may worry that he has an alcohol problem because of his impotence. His wife may drag him to an alcohol clinic because he slapped her during a blackout. Once he is at the clinic, the doctor calls him an alcoholic because of his abnormal liver-function tests. Later society labels him a drunk because of a second episode of driving while intoxicated. (p. 24)

The number of problems that a person encounters seems to provide the most useful distinction between people who are dependent on a substance and those who are not. These problems can be sorted loosely into two general areas: (1) patterns of pathological consumption, including psychological and physiological dependence, and (2) consequences that follow a prolonged pattern of abuse, including social and occupational impairment, legal and financial difficulties, and deteriorating medical condition.

It might seem that the actual amount of alcohol that a person consumes would be the most useful index of an alcohol problem. Hemingway, for example, clearly consumed enormous quantities of alcohol over a period of many years. In fact, though, this measure turns out to be of little use in defining alcoholism, because people vary significantly in the amount of alcohol they can consume. Factors such as age, gender, activity level, and overall physical health have a great impact on a person's ability to metabolize alcohol. Some people can drink a lot without developing problems; others drink very little and encounter difficulties.

The Concept of Substance Dependence

Many psychological features or problems are associated with dependence on chemical substances. One such feature involves *craving*. This word is frequently used to describe a forceful urge to use drugs, but the relationship between craving and drug use is actually very complex (Kassel & Shiffman, 1992). People who are dependent on drugs often say that they take the drug to control how they are feeling. They need it to relieve negative mood states or to avoid withdrawal symptoms from previous episodes. They may feel compelled to take the drug as a way to prepare for certain activities, such as public speaking, writing, or sex. Some clinicians refer to this condition as *psychological dependence*. One

useful index of craving is the amount of time that the person spends planning to take the drug. Is access to drugs or alcohol a constant preoccupation? If the person is invited to a party or is planning to eat at a restaurant, does he or she always inquire about the availability of alcoholic drinks? If the person is going to spend a few days at the beach in a neighboring state, will he or she worry more about whether liquor stores will be closed on weekends or holidays than about having enough food, clothes, or recreational equipment?

As the problem progresses, it is not unusual for the person who abuses drugs to try to stop. In the case of alcoholism, for example, it is possible for even heavy drinkers to abstain for at least short periods of time (Fingarette, 1988). Most clinicians and researchers agree that diminished control over drinking is a crucial feature of the disorder. Some experts have described this issue as "freedom of choice." When a person first experiments with the use of alcohol, his or her behavior is clearly voluntary; the person is not compelled to drink. After drinking heavily for a long period of time, most people with a drinking disorder try to stop. Unfortunately, efforts at self-control are typically short-lived and usually fail.

TOLERANCE AND WITHDRAWAL

Two particularly important features of substance dependence are the phenomena known as tolerance and withdrawal. These symptoms are usually interpreted as evidence of *physiological dependence*. **Tolerance** refers to the process through which the nervous system becomes less sensitive to the effects of alcohol or any other substance. A person who has been regularly exposed to alcohol will need to drink increased quantities to achieve the same subjective effect ("buzz," "high," or level of intoxication). The specific mechanisms that are responsible for the development of tolerance are unknown.

Some drugs are much more likely than others to produce a buildup of tolerance (APA, 1994). The most substantial tolerance effects are found among people who are heavy users of opioids, such as heroin, and CNS stimulants, such as amphetamine and cocaine. Pronounced tolerance is also found among people who use alcohol and nicotine. The evidence is unclear regarding tolerance effects and prolonged use of marijuana and hashish. Most people who use cannabinoids are not aware of tolerance effects, but these effects have been demonstrated in animal studies. Hallucinogens (LSD) and phencyclidine (PCP) may not lead to the development of tolerance.

Withdrawal refers to the symptoms experienced when a person stops using a drug. They can go on for several days. For example, alcohol is a CNS depressant, and the heavy drinker's system becomes accustomed to functioning in a chronically depressed state. When the person stops drinking, the system begins to rebound within several hours, producing many unpleasant side effects—hand tremors, sweating, nausea, anxiety, and insomnia. The most serious forms of withdrawal include convulsions and visual, tactile, or auditory hallucinations. Some people develop delirium, a sudden disturbance of consciousness that is accompanied by changes in cognitive processes such as lack of awareness of the environment or inability to sustain attention (see Chapter 13). This syndrome is called *alcohol withdrawal delirium* in DSM-IV (more traditionally known as *delirium tremens*, or *DTs*) if it is induced by withdrawal from alcohol.

The symptoms of withdrawal vary considerably for different kinds of substances. Table 11–2 compares various drugs of abuse in terms of withdrawal and other related characteristics. Unpleasant reactions are most evident during withdrawal from alcohol, opioids, and the general class of sedatives, hypnotics, and anxiolytics (such as Valium). Withdrawal symptoms are also associated with stimulants, such as amphetamine, cocaine, and nicotine, though they are sometimes less pronounced than those associated with alcohol and opioids.

Withdrawal symptoms are not often seen after repeated use of cannabis or hallucinogens, and they have not been demonstrated with phencyclidine. You may be surprised to see in Table 11–2 that, according to DSM-IV, the use of caffeine is not considered to lead to dependence or withdrawal symptoms. Caffeine is the most widely used psychoactive substance in the world. We all know people who crave coffee, especially in the morning. And heavy coffee users often experience discomfort when they stop drinking caffeine. The authors of DSM-IV acknowledged these symptoms, but they decided that the symptoms did not cause clinically significant distress and impairment and therefore should not be included in the manual as a type of mental disorder.

All these problems serve to emphasize the fact that symptoms of substance use disorders fall along a continuum. It is convenient to consider these problems in terms of qualitative distinctions: people who can control their drinking and those who cannot; people who crave alcohol and those who do not; people who have developed a tolerance to the drug and those who have not; and so on. In fact, there are no clear dividing lines on any of these dimensions. For this reason it is extremely difficult to define the nature of substance dependence disorders.

People can become dependent on many different kinds of drugs. Although patterns of dependence are similar in some ways for all drugs, each type of drug also has some unique features. In the next few pages we briefly review some of the most important classes of drugs. For each group, we will describe short-term effects on physiology and behavior as well as the consequences of long-term abuse. Unless otherwise specified, these descriptions are based on information presented by William McKim in his textbook on drugs and behavior (1997).

Alcohol

Alcohol affects virtually every organ and system in the body (Yi, 1991). After alcohol has been ingested, it is absorbed through membranes in the stomach, small intestine, and colon. The rate at which it is absorbed is influenced by many variables, including the concentration of

				TABLE 11-2

Comparison of Various Substances

Substance	Can Produce Dependence	Can Produce Intoxication	Associated Withdrawal	Can Produce Dementia
Alcohol	yes	yes	yes	yes
Amphetamines	yes	yes	yes	no
Caffeine	no	yes	no	no
Marijuana/hashish	yes	yes	no	no
Cocaine	yes	yes	yes	no
Hallucinogens	yes	yes	no	no
Inhalants	yes	yes	no	yes
Nicotine	yes	no	yes	no
Opiates	yes	yes	yes	no
Phencyclidine (PCP)	yes	yes	no	no
Sedatives, hypnotics, and anxiolytics	yes	yes	yes	yes

Source: Based on data from the DSM-IV.

alcohol in the beverage (for example, distilled spirits are absorbed more rapidly than beer or wine), the volume and rate of consumption, and the presence of food in the digestive system. After it is absorbed, alcohol is distributed to all the body's organ systems, with the greatest accumulation occurring in those organs with the largest blood supply and volume of tissue fluid. Almost all the alcohol that a person consumes is eventually broken down or metabolized in the liver. The rate at which alcohol is metabolized varies from person to person, but the average person can metabolize about 1 ounce of 90-proof liquor or 12 ounces of beer per hour (Nathan, 1993). If the person's consumption rate exceeds this metabolic limit, then blood alcohol levels will rise.

Blood alcohol levels are measured in terms of the amount of alcohol per unit of blood. The average 160-pound man who consumes 5 drinks in 1 hour will have a blood alcohol level of 100 milligrams (mg) per 100 milliliters (ml) of blood, or 100 mg percent. There is a relatively strong correlation between blood alcohol levels and CNS intoxicating effects (Verebey, 1991). According to DSM-IV, the symptoms of alcohol intoxication include slurred speech, lack of coordination, an unsteady gait, nystagmus (involuntary to-and-fro movement of the eyeballs induced when the person looks upward or to the side), impaired attention or memory, and stupor or coma.

SHORT-TERM EFFECTS

Some people become intoxicated after drinking relatively small quantities of alcohol, with blood levels less than 10 to 30 mg percent. In most states, the legal limit of alcohol concentration for driving is 100 mg percent. Some state legislatures are considering lowering this limit, because slowed reaction times and interference with other driving skills may occur at lower blood alcohol levels. People with levels of 150 to 300 mg percent will almost always act intoxicated. Neurological and respiration complications begin to appear at higher levels. There is an extreme risk of coma leading to toxic death when blood alcohol levels go above 400 mg percent (Slaby & Martin, 1991).

CONSEQUENCES OF PROLONGED USE AND ABUSE

The long-term abuse of alcohol can have a devastating impact on many areas of a person's life. The disruption of relationships with family and friends can be especially painful. The impact of Hemingway's drinking on his writing career and his family life is clearly evident. Most critics agree that his literary accomplishments were confined primarily to the early stages of his career, before his alcoholism began to interfere with his ability to write. Drinking also took its toll on his marriages, which were characterized by frequent and occasionally furious conflict in public and by repeated episodes of verbal and physical abuse in private (Johnson, 1989).

Many people who abuse alcohol experience blackouts. In some cases, abusers may continue to function without passing out, but they will later be unable to remember their behavior. An example is the person who drives home drunk from a party and in the morning finds a dent in the car bumper but can't remember how it got there. Sometimes problem drinkers will be told by a friend about how they behaved at the previous night's party, but they cannot remember what they did.

Regular heavy use of alcohol is also likely to interfere with job performance. Coworkers and supervisors may complain. Attendance at work may become sporadic. Eventually the heavy drinker may be suspended or fired. Related to job performance is the problem of financial difficulties. Losing one's job is clearly detrimental to one's financial stability, as are the costs of divorce, health care, liquor, and so on.

Many heavy drinkers encounter problems with legal authorities. These problems may include arrests for drunken driving and public intoxication, as well as charges of spouse and child abuse. Many forms of violent behavior are more likely to be committed when a person has been drinking. The association between crime and alcohol is rather strong. In Vaillant's longitudinal study, 61 percent of the men who were dependent on alcohol had been arrested more than twice for alcohol-related offenses (Vaillant, 1995).

On a biological level, prolonged exposure to high levels of alcohol can disrupt the functions of several important organ systems, especially the liver, pancreas, gastrointestinal system, cardiovascular system, and endocrine system. The symptoms of alcoholism include many secondary health problems, such as cirrhosis of the liver, heart problems (in part, the result of being overweight), and various forms of cancer, as well as severe and persistent forms of dementia and memory impairment, or amnestic disorders, such as Korsakoff's syndrome (see Chapter 14). Alcoholism is also associated with nutritional disturbances of many types, because chronic abusers often drink instead of eating balanced meals. Alcohol can suppress a person's appetite, and it can also interfere with normal eating patterns as a result of its effects on the gastrointestinal system. In fact, over an extended period of time, alcohol dependence has more negative health consequences than does abuse of almost any other drug.

Barbiturates and Benzodiazepines

The families of drugs known as barbiturates and benzodiazepines are also known informally as tranquilizers, hypnotics, and sedatives. *Tranquilizers* are used to decrease anxiety or agitation. *Hypnotics* are used to help people sleep. *Sedative* is a more general term that describes drugs that calm people or reduce excitement (other than the relief of anxiety). The **barbiturates,** such as phenobarbital (Nembutal) and amobarbital (Amytal), were discovered in the early twentieth century. They were used widely for many years and for a variety of purposes, ranging from the treatment of chronic anxiety to the prevention of seizures and to relieve pain. The **benzodiazepines** are synthetic drugs whose therapeutic effects were discovered in the 1950s. Some are used in the treatment of anxiety disorders (see Chapter 6), and others are used to relieve sleeping problems. The benzodiazepines, which include diazepam (Valium), alprazolam (Xanax), and triazolam (Halcion), have replaced the barbiturates in medical practice. This is in large part because of their lower potential for producing a lethal overdose.

SHORT-TERM EFFECTS

The barbiturates and benzodiazepines are most often taken orally. They can be used occasionally to achieve a brief period of relaxation or mild euphoria. They can also be used on a regular basis, as prescribed by a physician, to relieve chronic anxiety or to help a person sleep. Speed of action varies considerably among the specific types of benzodiazepines and barbiturates. The faster-acting drugs tend to have a shorter duration of effect. When the drugs are taken orally, they are absorbed from the digestive system much more quickly if the person has also been drinking alcohol. More rapid effects are also achieved if these drugs are injected rather than taken orally. This method of self-administration is more dangerous than oral use, leading to more profound tolerance and withdrawal effects, as well as increased risk of exposure to the human immunodeficiency virus (HIV).

Sedatives and hypnotics can lead to a state of intoxication that is identical to that associated with alcohol. It is characterized by impaired judgment, slowness of speech, lack of coordination, a narrowed range of attention, and disinhibition of sexual and aggressive impulses. Intravenous use of barbiturates can lead quickly to a pleasant, warm, drowsy feeling that is similar to the experience achieved when taking opiates. The anxiolytics (benzodiazepines) can also produce intoxication. Although their main effect is to reduce tension, they sometimes lead to an increase in hostile and aggressive behavior. Some clinicians call this a "rage reaction" or aggressive dyscontrol.

The barbiturates and benzodiazepines seem to work by enhancing the effects of GABA, an inhibitory neurotransmitter in the central nervous system. Their effect therefore is to reduce arousal in many areas of the brain. Higher doses of barbiturates can be used to induce unconsciousness and anesthesia.

CONSEQUENCES OF PROLONGED USE AND ABUSE

People who abruptly stop taking high doses of benzodiazepines may experience symptoms that are sometimes called a "discontinuance syndrome." These symptoms can include a return—and, in some cases, a worsening—of the original anxiety symptoms, if the medication was being used to treat an anxiety disorder. The person may also develop new symptoms that are directly associated with drug withdrawal. These include irritability, paranoia, sleep disturbance, agitation, muscle tension, restlessness, and perceptual disturbances. Withdrawal symptoms are less likely to occur if the medication is discontinued gradually rather than abruptly.

Tolerance and withdrawal can develop after using barbiturates for several weeks. Symptoms of withdrawal include anxiety, insomnia, anorexia, and motor tremors. People who have been taking very high doses of barbiturates are likely to experience motor seizures on the second or third day after they stop taking the drug. They may also develop *delirium*, a cognitive disorder that is characterized by impairment in consciousness, attention, and other cognitive abilities (see Chapter 14). Lethal overdose—either accidental or as an intentional means of suicide—is a very serious risk associated with the use of barbiturates because they can induce respiratory depression.

Opiates

The **opiates** (sometimes called *opioids*) are drugs that have properties similar to *opium*. The natural source of opium is a poppy with a white flower. The main active ingredients in opium are *morphine* and *codeine*. Morphine was first isolated from opium in the early nineteenth century. Morphine and codeine are still widely used in medicine, particularly to relieve pain. They are available legally only by prescription in the United States. In Canada, small quantities of codeine are available without a prescription in over-the-counter painkillers and cough medicines. *Heroin* is a synthetic opiate that is made by modifying the morphine molecule. It was originally marketed as an alternative to morphine when physicians believed, erroneously, that heroin is not addictive.

The opiates can be taken orally, injected, or inhaled. Opium is sometimes eaten or smoked. When morphine is used as a painkiller, it is taken orally so that it is absorbed slowly through the digestive system. People who use morphine for subjective effects most often inject the drug because it leads more quickly to high concentrations in brain tissue. Heroin can be injected, inhaled through the nose in the form of snuff, or smoked and inhaled through a pipe or tube.

SHORT-TERM EFFECTS

The subjective, pleasurable effects of the opiates have been described extensively. The opiates can induce a state of dreamlike euphoria, which may be accompanied by increased sensitivity in hearing and vision. People who inject morphine or heroin also experience a rush—a brief, intense feeling of pleasure that is sometimes described as being like an orgasm in the entire body.

Laboratory studies of mood indicate that the positive, emotional effects of opiates do not last. They are soon replaced by long-term negative changes in mood and emotion. These unpleasant experiences are relieved for 30 to 60 minutes after each new injection of the drug, but they eventually color most of the rest of the person's waking experience.

The opiates can induce nausea and vomiting among novice users, constrict the pupils of the eye, and disrupt the coordination of the digestive system. Continued use of opiates decreases the level of sex hormones in both women and men, resulting in reduced sex drive and impaired fertility.

High doses of opiates can lead to a comatose state, severely depressed breathing, and convulsions. The number of people admitted to hospital emergency rooms for treatment of heroin overdoses increased substantially between 1990 and 1995. Between 3,000 and 4,000 people die from accidental overdoses of heroin in the United States each year (Leland, 1996).

CONSEQUENCES OF PROLONGED USE AND ABUSE

The effects of opiates on occupational performance and health depend in large part on the amount of drug that the person takes. At high doses, people who are addicted to opiates become chronically lethargic and lose their motivation to remain productive. At low to moderate doses, people who use opiates for an extended period of time can remain healthy and work productively in spite of their addiction. This finding is, of course, dependent on the person having easy and relatively inexpensive access to opiates. One possibility is being maintained by a physician on *methadone*, a synthetic opiate that is sometimes used therapeutically as an alternative to heroin.

People who are addicted to opiates become preoccupied with finding and using the drug, in order to experience the rush and to avoid withdrawal symptoms. Tolerance develops rather quickly, and the person's daily dose increases regularly until it eventually levels off and remains steady. The symptoms associated with withdrawal from opiates have been widely exaggerated in popular books and films. Relatively few people are able to take heroin in large enough quantities to cause severe withdrawal symptoms. The withdrawal symptoms associated with alcohol and barbiturates are much more frightening and dangerous than those experienced by people who are withdrawing from heroin.

Most of the severe health consequences of opiate use are the result of the lifestyle of the addict rather than the drug itself. The enormous expenses and difficulties associated with obtaining illegal opiates almost invariably consume all the person's resources. The person typically neglects housing, nutrition, and health care in the search for another fix. Heroin addicts are much more likely than other people in the general population to die from AIDS, violence, and suicide.

Nicotine

Nicotine is the active ingredient in tobacco, which is its only natural source. Nicotine is almost never taken in its pure form because it can be toxic. Very high doses have extremely unpleasant effects. Controlled doses are easier to achieve by smoking or chewing tobacco, which provides a diluted concentration of nicotine. Another way of ingesting nicotine is to inhale snuff into the nostrils. When tobacco smoke is inhaled, nicotine is absorbed into the blood through the mucous membranes of the lungs. This route of administration results in the highest concentrations of nicotine because it is carried directly from the lungs to the heart and from there to the brain.

SHORT-TERM EFFECTS

The effects of nicotine on the peripheral nervous system (see Chapter 2) include increases in heart rate and blood pressure. In the central nervous system, nicotine has pervasive effects on a number of neurotransmitter systems. It stimulates the release of norepinephrine from several sites, producing CNS arousal. Nicotine also causes the release of dopamine and norepinephrine in the mesolimbic dopamine pathway, also known as the reward system of the brain. The serotonin system, which also mediates the effects of antidepressant medication, is influenced by nicotine. In fact, some people

have suggested that nicotine mimics the effects of antidepressant drugs.

Nicotine has a complex influence on subjective mood states. Many people say that they smoke because it makes them feel more relaxed. Some believe that it helps them control their subjective response to stress. This phenomenon is somewhat paradoxical in light of the fact that nicotine leads to increased arousal of the sympathetic nervous system. Various explanations may account for this apparent inconsistency. One involves differences in dosage levels; low doses of nicotine may lead to increased arousal while higher doses lead to relaxation. Another alternative involves withdrawal. Regular smokers may feel relaxed when they smoke a cigarette because it relieves unpleasant symptoms of withdrawal.

CONSEQUENCES OF PROLONGED USE AND ABUSE

Nicotine is one of the most harmful addicting drugs. Considerable evidence points to the development of both tolerance and withdrawal symptoms among people who regularly smoke or chew tobacco (see Further Thoughts). The physiological symptoms of withdrawal from

---

FURTHER THOUGHTS

Governmental Regulation of Tobacco Products

On August 23, 1996, the U.S. Food and Drug Administration (FDA) issued a regulation prohibiting the sale and distribution of tobacco products to children and adolescents (Kessler et al., 1996). Previous efforts to limit smoking focused more narrowly on restricting smoking in public places, eliminating cigarette advertisements on television, and increasing sales taxes. The new rule was much more threatening to the tobacco industry because it asserted that, as a drug, nicotine should be controlled by the government. The decisions behind this regulation raise a number of critical issues with regard to substance use disorders. How does the FDA decide whether a product is a drug? What type of evidence is required to demonstrate that a drug is addicting? Should the government control people's access to addicting drugs? If so, what is the best way to control access?

The FDA invoked the Food, Drug, and Cosmetic Act to justify its jurisdiction over cigarettes and smokeless tobacco. This act authorizes the FDA to regulate drugs, which are defined as "articles (other than food) intended to affect the structure or any function of the body." The agency had conducted an extensive investigation to determine whether tobacco products were *intended* by their manufacturers to deliver nicotine to consumers. Independent research studies, documents from the tobacco industry's own research laboratories, and testimony from former tobacco company scientists and executives pointed to three main conclusions (Dreyfuss, 1996):

1. Nicotine is addictive and has other pharmacological effects on the structure and function of the body. This conclusion was based on overwhelming evidence indicating that people who use tobacco products

clearly develop symptoms of dependence, including tolerance, withdrawal, and a pattern of compulsive use. Heavy smokers consume cigarettes in a manner that serves to maintain a relatively constant level of nicotine in their system.

2. Tobacco manufacturers have known for at least 30 years that consumers use tobacco because of the pharmacological effects of nicotine (Hilts, 1996).

3. Nicotine meets the legal definition of a "drug" because the companies designed their products to have these effects, and they intentionally manipulated nicotine levels to ensure that they did. The agency decided, on the basis of this evidence, that cigarettes are "drug-delivery systems" designed to dispense nicotine in a way that the smoker can readily absorb.

▲ Top executives from seven tobacco companies testified at a congressional hearing that they did not believe that cigarettes were addictive.

Once nicotine was officially recognized to be an addicting drug, what would be the best way to regulate its consumption? The FDA could have chosen to regulate tobacco products as either a *drug* or as a *medical device* (drug-delivery system) (Arno et al., 1996). If it had chosen to pursue its drug-regulation authority, the FDA could have required tobacco companies to demonstrate that cigarettes and smokeless tobacco are safe products. In the absence of such information, these products could have been banned entirely. Another option might have been to require a significant reduction in the amount of nicotine in each cigarette or perhaps a complete elimination of nicotine from cigarettes. The FDA did not consider these options to be practical or politically viable. Because so many adults are already addicted to nicotine, extensive black markets would spring up immediately, similar to those involved with other illegal drugs. An outright ban on nicotine would fail, just as efforts to ban other drugs have failed (Baum, 1996; Brecher, 1972).

The FDA decided instead to approach the nicotine problem by invoking its authority to regulate *medical devices.* The new tobacco regulations imposed by the FDA are prevention efforts designed to break the cycle of addiction to nicotine. The new rule prohibits the sale of tobacco products to anyone less than 18 years old. It also severely restricts advertising, on which the tobacco industry had previously spent $4 billion a year (Cooper, 1994). For example, advertising in the media is limited to black-and-white text, thus eliminating attractive, colorful images that are likely to appeal to children and adolescents. These restrictions are based on recognition of the fact that nicotine addiction almost always begins during adolescence. They are intended to reduce the rate at which young people are recruited to become new smokers and to minimize future health casualties from tobacco use.

The battle about regulation of nicotine is clearly not over. The success or failure of the FDA's efforts will hinge, in large part, on future political and legal decisions. The tobacco industry's $45 billion in annual profits are clearly threatened by this FDA policy. Large tobacco companies are very active in political arenas, and they have filed a massive lawsuit challenging the FDA's authority to regulate tobacco products. The industry has argued that smoking is a voluntary activity, and that smokers assume responsibility for whatever risks are associated with smoking cigarettes. They also contest the authority of the FDA, claiming that it should not have jurisdiction if they do not claim that their tobacco products are therapeutic in some way. Those who favor government regulation respond by pointing to such considerations as the harmful effects of tobacco on nonsmokers (sometimes called *passive smoking*) and the inability of many people to quit smoking after they have become addicted to nicotine.

The FDA policy on nicotine represents a middle-of-the-road approach to this particular drug problem. It is a compromise between two extreme alternatives: allowing completely open access to a dangerous drug or attempting to ban it completely. Public policy will not be able to determine whether adults in our society will use harmful drugs like nicotine. The FDA's new regulation represents one attempt to minimize the risk that children and adolescents will become addicted before they are old enough to make informed decisions about their own health. ■

nicotine include drowsiness, lightheadedness, headaches, muscle tremors, and nausea. People who are attempting to quit smoking typically experience sleeping problems, weight gain, concentration difficulties, and mood swings ranging from anxiety to anger and depression. From a psychological point of view, withdrawal from nicotine is just as difficult as withdrawal from heroin. Many people report that these symptoms disappear after a few months, but some report serious cravings for several years after they quit.

People who smoke tobacco increase their risk of developing many fatal diseases, including heart disease, lung disease (bronchitis and emphysema), and various types of cancer. Eighty percent of all deaths caused by lung cancer can be attributed to smoking tobacco. More than 400,000 people in the United States die prematurely each year as a result of tobacco. Large numbers of people are also killed or injured in fires caused by careless smoking. Women who smoke are also more likely to become infertile. Babies born to mothers who smoked during pregnancy are also likely to weigh less than those born to mothers who do not smoke, and they may be more vulnerable to certain types of birth defects.

Amphetamine and Cocaine

Members of the class of drugs known as **psychomotor stimulants** produce their effects by simulating the actions of certain neurotransmitters, specifically epinephrine, norepinephrine, dopamine, and serotonin. *Cocaine* is a naturally occuring stimulant drug that is extracted from the leaf of a small tree that grows at high elevations, as in the Andes Mountains. The *amphetamines* (such as dexedrine and methamphetamine, also known as "speed," or "ice" in its crystallized form) are produced synthetically.

The stimulants can be taken orally, injected, or inhaled. It is easier to maintain a constant blood level when the drugs are taken orally. They are absorbed more slowly through the digestive system, and their effects are less potent. For many centuries, Indians in the Andes have used cocaine by rolling coca leaves into a ball that can be tucked in the cheek and sucked for an extended period of time. More dramatic effects are achieved by injecting the drug or sniffing it.

Cocaine can also be smoked, using various procedures that have been popularized in the past several years. Some people employ a particularly dangerous procedure called "freebasing," in which the drug is heated and its vapors are inhaled. Many people have been seriously burned when these highly combustible chemicals are accidentally ignited. *Crack* is produced by mixing salt cocaine hydrochloride with a solution of baking soda. The resulting crystallized chunks can be heated in pipes, and the vapors are inhaled. Like freebasing, this process leads to more rapid absorption and a much stronger drug effect.

SHORT-TERM EFFECTS

Cocaine and amphetamines are called stimulants because they activate the sympathetic nervous system. They increase heart rate and blood pressure and dilate the blood vessels and the air passages of the lungs. In fact, after the amphetamines were discovered in the 1880s, they were originally used for the treatment of asthma (to dilate airways and make breathing easier). Stimulants also suppress the appetite and prevent sleep. These effects have been among the reasons for the popularity and frequent abuse of stimulants. They have been used, for example, by truck drivers who want to stay awake on long trips and by students who want to stay awake to study for exams. Unfortunately, in addition to their addicting properties, large doses of amphetamines can also lead to dizziness, confusion, and panic states, which clearly interfere with activities such as driving and studying.

Many people use (and abuse) stimulants because they induce a positive mood state. When they are injected, amphetamines and cocaine produce very similar subjective effects, but the effects of cocaine do not last as long. Low doses of amphetamines make people feel more confident, friendly, and energetic. This effect is most noticeable for a period of 3 to 6 hours after taking the drug. At higher doses, the person is likely to experience a brief, intense feeling of euphoria. The rushes associated with snorting or injecting cocaine are frequently described in sexual terms. Although many people believe that cocaine enhances sexual arousal and pleasure, most of the evidence suggests that prolonged use leads to sexual dysfunction (Jaffe, 1995). Tolerance develops quickly to the euphoric effects of stimulant drugs. The feelings of exhilaration and well-being are typically followed, several

▼ Comedian Richard Pryor suffered from cocaine dependence for many years. He was badly burned in a near-fatal accident while freebasing cocaine.

hours later, by the onset of lethargy and a mildly depressed or irritable mood.

Acute overdoses of stimulant drugs can result in irregular heartbeat, convulsions, coma, and death. The highly publicized overdose deaths of several prominent athletes, such as that of All-American basketball star Len Bias in 1986, indicate that the intense cardiovascular effects of cocaine can be fatal, even among people who are otherwise strong and healthy. The lethal consequences of cocaine seem to stem from a rapid increase in drug levels in the brain. Individual differences in sensitivity to the subjective effects of cocaine may play a role in cocaine-related deaths. In other words, people who are resistant to cocaine-induced euphoria may consume unusually large quantities of the drug while trying to achieve the rush that others have described.

CONSEQUENCES OF PROLONGED USE AND ABUSE

High doses of amphetamines and cocaine can lead to the onset of psychosis. The risk of a psychotic reaction seems to increase with repeated exposure to the drug. This syndrome can appear in people who have no prior history of mental disorder, and it usually disappears a few days after the drug has been cleared. Stimulants can also increase the severity of symptoms among people who had already developed some type of psychotic condition. The symptoms of *amphetamine psychosis* include auditory and visual hallucinations, as well as delusions of persecution and grandeur. The similarity between amphetamine psychosis and paranoid schizophrenia is quite striking. In fact, amphetamine psychosis has been used as an analogue condition in the study of neurochemical factors and schizophrenia (see Chapter 13).

As in the case of other forms of addiction, the most devastating effects of stimulant drugs frequently center around the disruption of occupational and social roles. The compulsion to continue taking cocaine can lead to physical exhaustion and financial ruin. People who are dependent on cocaine must spend enormous amounts of money to support their habit. They may have to sell important assets, such as their homes and cars, in order to finance extended binges.

Prolonged use of amphetamines has also been linked to an increase in violent behavior, but it is not clear whether this phenomenon is due to the drug itself or to the lifestyles with which it is frequently associated. Some violence might be related to a drug-induced increase in paranoia and hostility. Statistics concerning drugs and violent crime are very difficult to interpret. The direct effects of the drug on human behavior are confounded with various economic and social factors that are associated with buying, selling, and using an expensive, illegal drug like cocaine. Other dangers associated with chronic use of psychomotor stimulants, such as an increased risk of exposure to the HIV virus, may be attributed to promiscuous sexual behavior and the exchange of needles that are not sterile.

People who discontinue taking stimulant drugs do not typically experience severe withdrawal symptoms. The most common reaction is depression. Long-term exposure to high doses of amphetamine can lead to a profound state of clinical depression, which is often accompanied by ideas of suicide.

Cannabis

Marijuana and hashish are derived from the hemp plant, *Cannabis sativa*. The most common active ingredient in cannabis is a compound called delta-9-tetrahydro-cannabinol (delta-9-THC, or THC). Because every part of the plant contains THC, cannabis can be prepared for consumption in several ways. **Marijuana** refers to the dried leaves and flowers, which can be smoked in a cigarette or pipe. It can also be baked in brownies and ingested orally. **Hashish** refers to the dried resin from the top of the female cannabis plant. It can be smoked or eaten after being baked in cookies or brownies.

Oral administration of cannabis material leads to slow and incomplete absorption. Therefore the dose must be two or three times larger to achieve the same subjective effect as when it is smoked. When it is smoked, the effects of marijuana and hashish can be felt within a few minutes and may reach a maximum within 30 to 60 minutes. Most of the drug is metabolized in the liver. Blood levels of THC diminish quickly, but traces of its by-products can be detected as long as 30 days after ingestion.

SHORT-TERM EFFECTS

The subjective effects of marijuana are almost always pleasant. "Getting high" on marijuana refers to a pervasive sense of well-being and happiness. Laboratory research has shown that marijuana can have variable effects on a person's mood. Many people begin to feel happy, whereas a few become anxious and paranoid. The mood of other people seems to be especially important. After smoking marijuana, a person's mood may become more easily influenced by the way in which other people are behaving.

Cannabis intoxication is often accompanied by *temporal disintegration*, a condition in which people have trouble retaining and organizing information, even over relatively short periods of time. Conversations may become disjointed because the drug interferes with the people's ability to recall what they have said or planned to say. Lapses in attention and concentration problems are frequent.

CONSEQUENCES OF PROLONGED USE AND ABUSE

The issue of the addictive properties of cannabis remains controversial (Grinspoon & Bakalar, 1993). Some tolerance effects to THC have been observed in laboratory animals. Tolerance effects in humans remain ambiguous. Most evidence suggests that people do not develop tolerance to THC unless they are exposed to high doses over an extended period of time. Some people actually report that they become *more* sensitive (rather than less sensitive) to the effects of marijuana after repeated use. This phenomenon is called *reverse tolerance*. Although reverse tolerance has been reported casually by frequent users, it has not been demonstrated in a laboratory situation, where dosage levels can be carefully controlled. Experienced smokers may believe that they have become more sensitive to the effects of the drug when in fact they have learned to inhale more efficiently (and therefore need to smoke fewer joints to get high).

Withdrawal symptoms are unlikely to develop among people who smoke marijuana occasionally. One investigation found no withdrawal symptoms in a group of people who were required (for the purpose of the study) to smoke one joint a day for 28 days. People who have been exposed to continuous, high doses of THC may experience withdrawal symptoms, such as irritability, restlessness, and insomnia.

Prolonged heavy use of marijuana may lead to certain types of performance deficits on neuropsychological tests, especially those involving sustained attention, learning, and decision making (Pope & Yurgelun-Todd, 1996). These effects should be interpreted cautiously. They might indicate that exposure to high doses of marijuana can have toxic effects on the brain, but they also may be a reflection of residual drug action seen in people who last smoked the drug several hours before taking the tests. Performance deficits may also be an indication of cognitive symptoms of withdrawal rather than permanent intellectual impairment.

Hallucinogens

Drugs that are called **hallucinogens** cause people to experience hallucinations. Although many other types of drugs can lead to hallucinations at toxic levels, hallucinogens cause hallucinations in relatively low doses. There are many different types of hallucinogens, and they have very different neurophysiological effects. The molecular structure of many hallucinogens is similar to the molecular structure of neurotransmitters, such as serotonin and norepinephrine. The most common hallucinogen is a synthetic drug called *LSD* (d-lysergic acid diethylamide), which bears a strong chemical resemblance to serotonin. It acts by blocking serotonin receptors in the brain. *Psilocybin* is another type of hallucinogen whose chemical structure resembles that of serotonin. It is found in different types of mushrooms, which grow primarily in the southern United States and Mexico. *Mescaline* is a type of hallucinogen that resembles norepinephrine. It is the active ingredient in a small, spineless cactus called *peyote*. Mescaline and psilocybin have been used in religious ceremonies by various Native American peoples for many centuries.

Phencyclidine (PCP; also known as *crystal* or *angel dust*) is another synthetic drug that is often classified with the hallucinogens, although its effects are quite different than those associated with LSD and mescaline. It was originally developed as a painkiller. Small doses of PCP lead to relaxation, warmth, and numbness. At higher doses, PCP can induce psychotic behavior, including delusional thinking, catatonic motor behavior, manic excitement, and sudden mood changes. The drug is typically sold in a crystallized form that can be sprinkled on leaves, such as tobacco, marijuana, or parsley, and then smoked. Some people snort it or inject it after dissolving the crystals in water.

▼ **Hallucinogenic drugs distort and intensify visual perceptions.**

SHORT-TERM EFFECTS

The effects of hallucinogenic drugs are difficult to study empirically because they are based primarily in subjective experience. They typically induce vivid, and occasionally spectacular, visual images. During the early phase of this drug experience, the images often take the form of colorful geometric patterns. The later phase is more likely to be filled with meaningful images of people, animals, and places. The images may change rapidly, and they sometimes follow an explosive pattern of movement.

Although these hallucinatory experiences are usually pleasant, they are occasionally frightening. "Bad trips" are a decidely unpleasant experience that can lead to panic attacks and the fear of losing one's mind. People can usually be talked through this process by constantly reminding them that the experience is drug-induced and will be over soon. Some people believe that hallucinogenic drugs can facilitate the process of self-exploration. People who are "tripping" on hallucinogens sometimes report achieving deep insights about their own thoughts and feelings. For this reason, LSD and related chemicals have also been known as *psychedelic* (mind-expanding) drugs.

CONSEQUENCES OF PROLONGED USE AND ABUSE

The use of hallucinogens follows a different pattern than that associated with most other drugs. Hallucinogens—with the possible exception of PCP—are used sporadically and on special occasions rather than continuously. Tolerance develops very quickly to hallucinogens such as LSD, psilocybin, and mescaline (but not to PCP). If these drugs are taken repeatedly within 2 or 3 days, their effects disappear. Most people do not increase their use of hallucinogens over time. People who stop taking hallucinogens after continued use do not experience problems; there seem to be no withdrawal symptoms associated with the hallucinogens that resemble serotonin and norepinephrine.

Most hallucinogens are not particularly toxic. People do not die from taking an overdose of LSD, psilocybin, or mescaline. However, PCP is much more toxic. High doses can lead to coma, convulsions, respiratory arrest, and brain hemorrhage. Death is more likely to occur if the person has also been drinking alcohol and taking barbiturates in addition to using PCP.

The perceptual effects of hallucinogenic drugs almost always wear off after several hours. There are cases, however, in which these drugs have induced persistent psychotic behavior. Most experts interpret these examples as an indication that the drug experience can trigger the onset of psychosis in people who were already vulnerable to that type of disorder. This is, of course, a difficult hypothesis to test because we do not have any independent tests to determine whether a person is vulnerable to psychosis. We can only look back, after the onset of psychotic symptoms, and speculate that some type of predisposition must have been present. PCP is more likely than the other hallucinogens to produce persistent psychotic behavior.

Some people who have taken hallucinogens experience *flashbacks*—brief visual aftereffects that can occur at unpredictable intervals long after the drug has been cleared from the person's body. Scientists do not understand the mechanisms that are responsible for flashbacks. Flashbacks may be more likely to occur when the person is under stress or after the person has used another drug, such as marijuana.

Classification

The problems that we have reviewed in the preceding pages indicate that substance dependence represents an extremely diverse set of problems. Everyone—clinicians and researchers, as well as those who abuse drugs and their families—seems to recognize the existence of a serious psychological disorder. But does it have a core? What is the best way to define it? In the following pages we briefly review some of the ways in which alcoholism and drug abuse have been defined. We must begin with the recognition that alcoholism and other types of addiction have not always been viewed as medical conditions that require treatment.

Brief History of Legal and Illegal Substances

One of the most widely recognized facts about alcohol consumption is that drinking patterns vary tremendously from one culture to the next and, within the same culture, from one point in time to another. Public attitudes toward the consumption of alcohol have changed dramatically during the course of U.S. history. For example, heavy drinking was not generally considered to be a serious problem in colonial times (Levine, 1978). In fact, it seemed to be an integral part of daily life. The average amount of alcohol consumed per person each year was much higher in those days than it is today. A typical American in the eighteenth century drank approximately 4 gallons of alcohol a year; the corresponding figure for our own society is about 2.5 gallons (Fingarette, 1988). Drunkenness was not considered to be either socially deviant or symptomatic of medical illness.

Public attitudes toward alcohol changed dramatically in the United States during the first half of the nineteenth century. Members of the temperance movement preached against the consumption of alcohol in any form. Temperance workers ardently believed that anyone who drank alcohol would become a drunkard. Their arguments were largely moral and religious rather than medical or scientific, and many of their publications included essays on the personality weaknesses that were associated with such morally reprehensible behaviors (Levine, 1978). As a result of their activities, many people who acknowledged problems with drinking made public confessions and took pledges of abstinence. The temperance movement was, in fact, able to persuade many thousands of people to abandon the consumption of alcohol.

The movement finally succeeded in banning the manufacture and sale of alcoholic beverages when Congress approved the Eighteenth Amendment to the Constitution in 1919. During the following years, known as the Prohibition era, the average consumption of alcohol fell substantially, and the incidence of associated medical illnesses, such as cirrhosis of the liver, also declined. Nevertheless, these laws were extremely difficult to enforce, and Prohibition was repealed in 1933.

DSM-IV

The DSM-IV divides addictions into two categories: substance abuse and substance dependence, with the latter being the more severe and advanced form of disorder. This distinction is based, in part, on the recognition that many people who suffer serious impairment from substance abuse do not progress to the level of dependence. The manual lists 11 types of drugs that can lead to problems of abuse and

dependence (refer to Table 11–2). Rather than including separate definitions of dependence and abuse for each class of substance, the manual provides one generic set of criteria for substance dependence and another for substance abuse. These criterion sets can be applied to any type of drug.

The DSM-IV criteria for **substance dependence** are presented in Table 11–3. Tolerance and withdrawal are listed along with five other problems that describe a pattern of compulsive use and loss of control. The person has to exhibit at least three of the seven criteria for a diagnosis of substance dependence to be made. Tolerance and withdrawal are not required for the person to meet this definition of dependence. Their importance is recognized with a subtype designation. If there is evidence of either tolerance or withdrawal (or both), the additional specification of *physiological dependence* is made.

This approach to the definition of substance dependence is convenient because it points to a unified view of addiction. It also has some disadvantages. Perhaps most important is the fact that the use of a single definition of dependence may conceal differences between the kinds of problems that are associated with various classes of drugs (Frances, First, & Pincus, 1995). For example, dependence on opiates almost always involves physiological symptoms of tolerance and withdrawal, whereas dependence on cannabis or hallucinogens almost never does.

Substance abuse is defined in terms of harmful consequences that appear in the absence of tolerance, withdrawal, or a pattern of compulsive use (dependence). The DSM-IV definition of substance abuse is presented in Table 11–4. One difficult issue in defining this condition involves the identification of a boundary between

TABLE 11-3

DSM-IV Criteria for Substance Dependence

A. **A maladaptive pattern of substance use, leading to clinically significant impairment or distress, as manifested by three (or more) of the following, occurring at any time in the same 12-month period:**
1. Tolerance, as defined by either of the following:
   a. A need for markedly increased amounts of the substance to achieve intoxication or desired effect.
   b. Markedly diminished effect with continued use of the same amount of the substance.
2. Withdrawal, as manifested by either of the following:
   a. The characteristic withdrawal syndrome for the substance (criteria sets for withdrawal are listed separately for specific substances).
   b. The same (or a closely related) substance is taken to relieve or avoid withdrawal symptoms.
3. The substance is often taken in larger amounts or over a longer period than was intended.
4. There is a persistent desire or unsuccessful efforts to cut down or control substance use.
5. A great deal of time is spent in activities necessary to obtain the substance (for example, visiting multiple doctors or driving long distances), use the substance (for example, chain-smoking), or recover from its effects.
6. Important social, occupational, or recreational activities are given up or reduced because of substance use.
7. The substance use is continued despite knowledge of having a persistent or recurrent physical or psychological problem that is likely to have been caused or exacerbated by the substance (for example, current cocaine use despite recognition of cocaine-induced depression, or continued drinking despite recognition that an ulcer was made worse by alcohol consumption).

substance abuse and the recreational use of drugs. The diagnostic manual emphasizes the terms *recurrent* and *maladaptive pattern* for this purpose. The problem must be persistent before this diagnosis would be considered. Someone involved in a single drug-related incident would not meet the criteria for this disorder, regardless of how serious the incident might have been (Frances, First, & Pincus, 1995).

Proposed Subtypes

DSM-IV does not recognize any systems for subtyping substance dependence, other than the

TABLE 11-4

DSM-IV Criteria for Substance Abuse

A. **A maladaptive pattern of substance use leading to clinically significant impairment or distress, as manifested by one (or more) of the following, occurring within a 12-month period:**
1. Recurrent substance use resulting in a failure to fulfill major role obligations at work, school, or home.
2. Recurrent substance use in situations in which it is physically hazardous.
3. Recurrent substance-related legal problems.
4. Continued substance use despite having persistent or recurrent social or interpersonal problems caused or exacerbated by the effects of the substance.

B. **The symptoms have never met the criteria of substance dependence for this class of substance.**

presence or absence of physiological symptoms (tolerance or withdrawal). Nevertheless, procedures for subdividing alcoholism have been employed extensively in research studies (Sher, 1991, 1994). One system that is currently influential was proposed by Robert Cloninger (1987), a psychiatrist at Washington University in St. Louis. Cloninger proposed two prototypical varieties of alcoholism. According to this system, Type 1 alcoholism is characterized by a somewhat later onset, prominent psychological dependence (loss-of-control drinking), and the absence of antisocial personality traits. It is found in both men and women. Type 2 alcoholism, which is found almost exclusively among men, typically has an earlier onset and is associated with the co-occurrence of persistent antisocial behaviors. This proposed distinction has been useful in many research studies. On the other hand, the difference between Type 1 and Type 2 alcoholism may be more quanitative than qualitative in nature (Vaillant, 1994). We return to a discussion of these two types when we consider the influence of genetic factors on the etiology of alcoholism.

Course and Outcome

It is impossible to specify a typical course for substance dependence, especially alcoholism. Age of onset varies tremendously, ranging from childhood and early adolescence throughout the life span. Although we can roughly identify stages that intervene between initial exposure to a drug and the eventual onset of tolerance and dependence, the timing with which a person moves through these phases can vary enormously. The best available information regarding the course of substance use disorders comes from the study of alcoholism. The specific course of this problem varies considerably from one person to the next. The only thing that seems to be certain is that periods of heavy use alternate with periods of relative abstinence, however short-lived they may be.

In an effort to examine the natural history of alcoholism, George Vaillant (1996) studied the lives of 456 inner-city adolescents from Boston and 268 former undergraduate students from Harvard University. Initial information was collected in 1940, when the participants were adolescents. Follow-up information was collected every other year by questionnaire and every fifth year by physical examination. The college group has been followed until 70 years of age, and the core city group has been followed

to age 60. At some point during their lives, 21 percent of the college men and 35 percent of the core city men met diagnostic criteria for alcohol abuse, which Vaillant defined as the presence of four or more problems in such areas as employer complaints, marital and family difficulties, medical complications, and legal problems.

As expected, the mortality rate was higher among men who abused alcohol than among those who did not. Heart disease and cancer were twice as common among the alcohol abusers, perhaps in part because they were also more likely to be heavy cigarette smokers.

Most of the alcoholic men went through repeated cycles of abstinence followed by relapse. The life course of alcohol abuse could be charted most clearly for 121 of the core city men

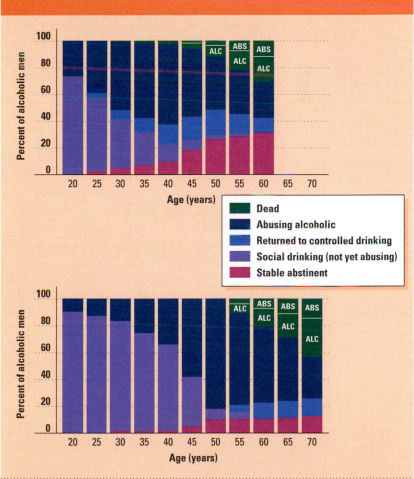

FIGURE 11-1: Results of a long-term follow-up study of two groups of alcoholics: 121 core city men (*top*) and 46 college men (*bottom*). The core city men began abusing alcohol at a younger age and were more likely to achieve stable abstinence by age 60.

Source: G.E. Vaillant, 1996, A long-term follow-up of male alcohol abuse, *Archives of General Psychiatry, 53,* 243-249.

who abused alcohol and remained in the study until age 60 and 46 college men who abused alcohol and remained in the study until age 70. These data are illustrated in Figure 11–1. In the graphs in Figure 11–1, abstinence is defined as less than one drink per month for more than a year. Social drinking refers to problem-free drinking for 10 years or more. Controlled drinking is more than one drink per month for at least 2 years with no reported problem. The main differences between the groups were that the core city men began abusing alcohol at an earlier age, and they were also more likely than the college men eventually to achieve stable abstinence. The average age of onset of alcohol abuse was 40 years for the college men and 29 years for the core city men.

Many men spent the previous 20 years alternating between periods of controlled drinking and alcohol abuse. The proportion of men who continued to abuse alcohol went down after the age of 40. The proportion of alcoholic men in both groups who became completely abstinent went up slowly but consistently during the follow-up period. The longer a man remained abstinent, the greater the probability that he would continue to be abstinent. Vaillant's data indicated that relapse to alcohol abuse was unlikely among men who were able to remain abstinent for at least 6 years.

The relapse process is an important problem for all types of substance dependence. Some evidence suggests that this process may include certain common elements across various types of drugs (Brownell et al., 1986). Most people who have quit using drugs like alcohol or tobacco describe a sequence of circumstances, beginning with cognitive events (contemplating change, making a commitment to change) leading to behavioral outcomes (initial cessation, long-term maintenance).

Many important questions remain to be answered about the relapse process. Is there a "safe point" that separates a period of high risk for relapse from a period of more stable change? Vaillant's data suggest that the 6-year mark may be important for men who abuse alcohol. Will this suggestion be replicated in other studies? And does it generalize to other drugs? Do relapse rates stabilize over time? Is an addicted person more likely to succeed on a later attempt to quit than on an early attempt? Answers to these questions will be useful in the development of more effective treatment programs.

Other Disorders Commonly Associated with Addictions

People who abuse alcohol often exhibit other forms of mental disorder as well. Most prominent among these are antisocial personality disorder, mood disorders, and anxiety disorders (Kushner, Sher, & Beitman, 1990; Merikangas & Gelernter, 1990; Weissman, 1988). The complexity of the association among these problems makes them difficult to untangle. In some cases, prolonged heavy drinking can result in feelings of depression and anxiety. The more the person drinks, the more guilty the person feels about his or her inability to control the drinking. In addition, increased drinking often leads to greater conflict with family members, coworkers, and other people. Sometimes the depression and anxiety precede the onset of drinking. In fact, some people seem to use alcohol initially in a futile attempt to self-medicate for these other conditions. Ultimately, the alcohol makes things worse.

Epidemiology

Drug-related problems are found in most countries around the world. There are interesting variations, however, in patterns of use for specific types of drugs. The maps in Figure 11–2 indicate global variations in the use of opium, cocaine, and cannabis. The use of specific drugs is determined, in part, by their availability. Opium (Figure 11–2a) is used most heavily in Southeast Asia, as well as in some Middle Eastern countries, where the opium poppy is cultivated. Cocaine (Figure 11–2b) is used frequently in certain countries of South America where coca trees grow; it is also imported into North America, particularly the United States. Use of cannabis (Figure 11–2c) is very widespread, in part because the plants can grow in many different climates. In contrast, in Japan, where the amount of land available for cultivation is severely limited, the largest drug problem involves amphetamine, a synthetic drug.

When we consider the epidemiology of drug addiction, we must keep in mind the distinction between use and dependence. People have to use the drug before they can become dependent on it. Patterns of increased use can therefore be alarming. Consider, for example, the evidence presented in Table 11–5, which indicates that the percentage of eighth-grade students who have tried certain kinds of drugs, particularly cocaine, heroin, and marijuana, went up during the early 1990s. These increases are obviously a reason for serious concern; however, most people who occasionally use alcohol and illicit drugs, such as marijuana and cocaine, do not become addicted. Dependence almost always develops slowly after extended exposure to a drug. The average time between initial use of illicit drugs and the onset of symptoms of dependence is between 2 and 3 years (Anthony & Helzer, 1991). The distinction between people who eventually become addicted and those who use drugs without becoming addicted is an important consideration in this field.

Prevalence of Alcohol Abuse and Dependence

Approximately two out of every three males in Western countries drink alcohol regularly, at least on a social basis; less than 25 percent abstain from drinking completely. Among all men and women who have ever used alcohol, roughly 20 percent will develop serious problems at some point in their lives as a consequence of prolonged alcohol consumption (Anthony, Warner, & Kessler, 1994).

The Epidemiologic Catchment Area (ECA) Study provides one detailed picture of the prevalence of alcoholism. The investigators found a lifetime prevalence rate of 13.8 percent for alcoholism (either alcohol abuse or dependence). The 12-month prevalence rate was 6.3 percent. Alcohol-related disorders were the second most common type of mental disorder in the United States—second only to phobias—when men and women were considered together. These problems most often went untreated; only 15 percent of the men and women who were assigned a diagnosis of alcohol abuse or dependence had ever mentioned their symptoms to a doctor. More than half (54 percent) of these people had not experienced symptoms of alcoholism in the past year.

Some occupations are associated with higher rates of alcoholism, perhaps because they provide for regular exposure to alcohol throughout the day or because they lack structured hours, which precludes excessive drinking for other people. The rate of alcoholism among professional writers—especially males—may be

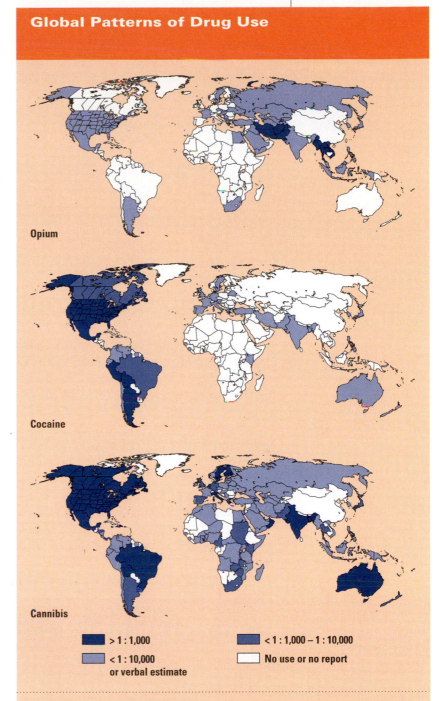

Global Patterns of Drug Use

Opium

Cocaine

Cannibis

> 1 : 1,000   < 1 : 1,000 – 1 : 10,000
< 1 : 10,000 or verbal estimate   No use or no report

FIGURE 11-2: These maps illustrate the prevalence of the use of opium, cocaine, and cannabis around the world. Each drug is used most heavily in regions in which it is most accessible.

Source: J.C. Anthony and J.E. Helzer, 1995, Epidemiology of drug dependence. In M.T. Tsuang, M. Tohen, and G.E.P. Zahner (Eds.), *Textbook in Psychiatric Epidemiology*, pp. 362–64. New York: Wiley.

higher than that in other professions. Of the six American men who have been awarded the Nobel Prize in literature, five have struggled with serious drinking problems (Goodwin, 1991). In addition to Hemingway, the others are Eugene O'Neill, William Faulkner, Sinclair Lewis, and John Steinbeck; the only exception is Saul

TABLE 11-5

Changes in Drug Use: Percent of Eighth-grade Students Who Have Used Drugs in Their Lifetime

Drug	1991	1995
Crack	1.3	2.7
Heroin	1.2	2.3
Marijuana	10.2	19.9
Cocaine	2.3	4.2
Hallucinogens	3.2	5.2
Stimulants	10.5	13.1
Tranquilizers	3.8	4.5
Cigarettes	44.0	46.4
Been drunk	26.7	25.3

Source: University of Michigan, Monitoring the Future Study; SAMHSA Drug Abuse Warning Network (from *Newsweek*, August 26, 1996, p. 56).

Bellow. Neither of the American women who have been awarded the Nobel Prize in literature—Pearl Buck and Toni Morrison—had a drinking problem.

GENDER DIFFERENCES

Approximately 60 percent of women in the United States drink alcohol at least occasionally, but, in comparison to men, relatively few develop alcoholism. Among people who chronically abuse alcohol, men outnumber women by a ratio of approximately 5 to 1 (Robins & Regier, 1991). Recent information suggests that this disparity may be narrower today than it was 20 years ago, especially among younger

TABLE 11-6

Lifetime Prevalence for Drug Dependence Syndromes (NCS Data)

Drug Group	Percent
Tobacco	24.1
Alcohol	14.1
Cannabis	4.2
Cocaine	2.7
Amphetamines	1.7
Barbiturates and benzodiazepines	1.2
Hallucinogens	0.5
Heroin	0.4
Inhalants	0.3

Source: J. C. Anthony, L. A. Warner, and R. C. Kessler, 1994, Comparative epidemiology of dependence on tobacco, alcohol, controlled substances, and inhalants: Basic findings from the national Comorbidity Survey, *Experimental Clinical Psychopharmacology, 2,* 1–24.

people. The National Comorbidity Survey (NCS) found a 12-month prevalence rate for alcohol dependence of 11 percent for men and 4 percent for women (Kessler et al., 1994). Although the rate of alcoholism among younger women appears to be increasing, prevalence is still much higher in men, and the rates do not seem likely to converge. Persistent differences can probably be attributed to biological variables, including the fact that women are, on average, less physically tolerant of alcohol, as well as social variables, such as negative attitudes toward intoxication in women.

American society traditionally has held a negative view of intoxication among women. This pervasive attitude is reflected in opinions voiced by both men and women, including those who are dependent on alcohol (Gomberg, 1988). Social disapproval probably explains why women are more likely than men to drink in the privacy of their own homes, either alone or with another person. Women may be less likely than men to drink heavily because the range of situations in which they are expected to drink, or in which they can drink without eliciting social disapproval, is narrower.

There are also important gender differences in alcohol metabolism. A single standard dose of alcohol, measured in proportion to total body weight, will produce a higher peak blood alcohol level in women than in men (Jones & Jones, 1976). One explanation for this difference lies in the fact that men have a higher average content of body water than women do. A standard dose of alcohol will be less diluted in women because alcohol is distributed in total body water. This may help to explain the fact that women who drink heavily for many years are more vulnerable to liver disorders.

Prevalence of Drug and Nicotine Dependence

The National Comorbidity Study (NCS) surveyed more than 8,000 household residents in the United States between 1990 and 1992. Lifetime prevalence rates generated by this study for specific types of drug dependence are listed in Table 11–6. The combined lifetime prevalence in the NCS for dependence on any type of controlled substance (those that are illegal or available only by prescription) was 7.5 percent. This is approximately half the rate for alcohol dependence. The NCS found a lifetime prevalence of 24 percent for nicotine dependence.

The percentage of people in the United States who smoke tobacco has actually declined since 1964, when the U.S. Surgeon General's Report announced it had found a definite link between smoking and cancer and other diseases. The rate of decline has been greatest among men, who traditionally have smoked more than women. Among teenagers, smoking rates may have stabilized at approximately 10 percent for both males and females (Figure 11–3), but there has been some indication that smoking prevalence among high school seniors had begun to increase again in 1994 and 1995 (Davis, 1996). Furthermore, although tobacco consumption has declined in industrialized countries, it has increased dramatically in the developing countries, where people may be less educated about the health risks associated with smoking (McKim, 1997).

Approximately 32 percent of those people who have ever used tobacco eventually meet the criteria for dependence (Anthony et al., 1994). This statistic might be considered an index of the addicting properties of a drug. In other words, if you use a drug repeatedly, will you develop symptoms of dependence? When viewed from this perspective, nicotine may be among the most addicting drugs that are used in our society (see Further Thoughts). Comparable figures (percentage of users who develop dependence) for other drugs were: anxiolytics and hypnotics, 25 percent; alcohol, 20 percent; heroin, 20 percent; cocaine, 15 percent; marijuana, 15 percent; amphetamines, 10 percent; and hallucinogens, less than 10 percent.

Risk for Addiction Across the Life Span

Older people do not drink as much alcohol as younger people. The proportion of people who abstain from drinking alcohol is only 22 percent for people in their thirties, goes up to 47 percent for people in their sixties, and is approximately 80 percent for people over 80 years of age. Prevalence rates for alcohol dependence are highest among young adults and lowest among the elderly. Most elderly alcohol abusers are people who have had drinking problems for many years (Caracci & Miller, 1991; Ticehurst, 1990).

The use of illegal drugs is relatively infrequent among the elderly (Anthony & Helzer, 1991), but there is a problem associated with their abuse of, and dependence on, prescription drugs and over-the-counter medications,

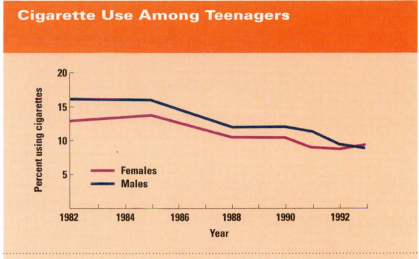

Cigarette Use Among Teenagers

FIGURE 11-3: Rates of cigarette use in 1 month reported by females and males between the ages of 12 and 17, according to the 1993 U.S. National Household Survey.

Source: W.A. McKim, 1997, *Drugs and Behavior*, p. 169. Upper Saddle River, NJ: Prentice Hall.

especially hypnotics, sedatives, anxiolytics, and painkillers. The elderly use more legal drugs than do people in any other age group. One estimate suggested that 25 percent of all people over the age of 55 use psychoactive drugs of one kind or another (Koch & Knapp, 1987). The risk for substance dependence among the elderly is increased by frequent use of multiple psychoactive drugs combined with enhanced sensitivity to drug toxicity (caused by slowed metabolic breakdown of alcohol and other drugs).

The following case illustrates several issues that are associated with substance use disorders among the elderly, including the abuse of alcohol together with abuse of prescription medications, the presence of prominent symptoms

---

BRIEF CASE STUDY

Ms. E is an 80-year-old woman who was brought in for an evaluation by her daughters because they noticed depressive symptoms, appetite disturbance, and memory deficits. She denied all problems related to her daughters' concerns. She had a depressed affect, mild psychomotor agitation, and decrements of recent and remote memory. She was disoriented to time. She verbalized statements of guilt and self-deprecation. She denied ever drinking alcohol, which was corroborated by the daughter with whom she lived but was refuted by her other daughter, who stated that Ms. E drank one or two glasses of brandy almost every day. She had been taking various barbiturates for "nerves" for over 30 years. The dosage she ingested gradually increased over the years, and she frequently took more medications than were prescribed. Because it was unclear if her symptoms were related to her barbiturate use, she reluctantly agreed to be slowly and gradually detoxified. She refused a dementia work-up. Once detoxification was complete, her affect and appetite were improved, but her cognitive deficits were unchanged. Several months later, she and her

family dropped out of treatment. She was reportedly drinking brandy, wine, and "hard liquor" every afternoon and evening, with her hired caregiver mixing the drinks. (Solomon et al., 1993) ■

of anxiety and depression, and the tendency to deny the extent of their use or abuse of drugs.

Diagnostic criteria for substance dependence and abuse are sometimes difficult to apply to the elderly, primarily because drug use has somewhat different consequences in their lives. Tolerance to many drugs is reduced among the elderly, and the symptoms of withdrawal may be more severe and prolonged. They are less likely to suffer occupational impairment because they are less frequently employed than younger people. The probability of social impairment may be reduced because elderly people are more likely to live apart from their families.

Etiological Considerations and Research

Our discussion of etiology will focus primarily on alcohol dependence and abuse. We have chosen this approach because clinical scientists know more about alcohol and its abuse than about any of the other drugs. Research on alcohol abuse illustrates many factors that are also important in the etiology of other forms of substance dependence.

The etiology of substance abuse and dependence represents a clear example of the need for an integrative systems approach to etiology. Most contemporary investigators approach the development of alcoholism in terms of multiple systems. Biological factors obviously play an important role. The addicting properties of certain drugs are crucial: People become addicted to drugs like heroin, nicotine, and alcohol, but they do not become addicted to drugs like the antidepressants or to food additives like Nutrasweet. We must therefore understand how addicting drugs affect the brain in order to understand the process of dependence. At the same time, we need to understand the social and cultural factors that influence how and under what circumstances an individual first acquires and uses drugs. Our expectations about the effects of drugs are shaped by our parents, our peers,

and the media. These are also important etiological considerations.

The etiology of alcoholism is best viewed within a developmental framework that views the problem in terms of various stages: (1) initiation and continuation, (2) escalation and transition to abuse, and (3) development of tolerance and withdrawal (Marlatt & Baer, 1988; Vaillant, 1995). In the following pages we review some of the social, psychological, and biological factors that explain why people begin to drink, how their drinking behaviors are reinforced, and how they develop tolerance after prolonged exposure.

Social Factors

People who don't drink obviously won't develop alcoholism. Therefore one important link in the chain of causal events is the process of initiation. Which people will expose themselves to addictive substances, and why? Among those young people who choose to drink alcohol (or smoke cigarettes, or consume other addictive substances), which ones will eventually develop problems? The development of drug dependence requires continued use, and it is influenced by the manner in which the drug is consumed. In other words, with regard to alcohol, will the person's initial reaction to the drug be pleasant, or will the person become sick and avoid alcoholic beverages in the future? If the person continues drinking, will he or she choose strong or weak drinks, with or without food, with others or alone, and so on?

Several studies have examined social factors that predict substance use among adolescents. Initial experimentation with drugs is most likely to occur among those individuals who are rebellious and extroverted and whose parents and peers model or encourage use (Chassin, 1984). The relative influence of parents and friends varies according to the gender and age of the adolescent as well as the drug in question. For example, parents may have a greater influence over their children's decision to drink alcohol, whereas peers seem to play a more important role in the initial exposure to marijuana.

Parents can influence their children's drinking behaviors in many ways. They can serve as models for using drugs to cope with stressful circumstances. They may also help promote attitudes and expectations regarding the benefits of drug consumption, or they may simply provide access to licit or illicit drugs (Lang & Stritzke, 1993). Adolescents with alcoholic parents are more likely to drink alcohol than those whose parents do not abuse alcohol. This increased risk seems to be due to several factors, including the fact that alcoholic parents monitor their children's behavior less closely, thereby providing more opportunities for illicit drinking. The level of negative affect is also relatively high in the families of alcoholic parents (see Chapter 6). This unpleasant emotional climate, coupled with reduced parental monitoring, increases the probability that an adolescent will affiliate with peers who use drugs (Chassin et al., 1993). Taken together, these considerations indicate that parents' drinking has a definite influence on their children's use of alcohol and that the mechanisms involved in this relationship are quite complex.

Once people begin to drink, why do they continue? Studies that examine the short-term consequences of drinking in normal subjects can help address this question. The effects of acute intoxication vary, but laboratory investigations have found that nonalcoholic drinkers experience several effects that are potentially rewarding or beneficial, including reduced self-awareness, improved mood, and dampened cardiovascular responses to stress (Hull & Bond,

1986; Levenson, 1987). These immediate, positive reactions may encourage some people to continue their use of this drug, in spite of the fact that drinking can lead to dire long-term outcomes.

Biological Factors

Initial physiological reactions to alcohol can have a dramatic negative influence on a person's early drinking experiences. For example, millions of people are unable to tolerate even small amounts of alcohol. These people develop flushed skin, sometimes after only a single drink. They may also feel nauseated, and some experience an abnormal heartbeat. This phenomenon is most common among people of Asian ancestry and may affect 30 to 50 percent of this population. Not coincidentally, the prevalence of alcoholism is unusually low among Asian populations. Research studies indicate a link between these two phenomena. For example, Japanese Americans who experience the fast-flushing response tend to drink less than those who do not flush (Nakawatase et al., 1993). The specific mechanisms involved in this sensitivity reaction to alcohol have not been determined (Newlin, 1989; Wall et al., 1992). The basic evidence suggests that in addition to looking for factors that make some individuals especially vulnerable to the addicting effects of alcohol, it may also be important to identify protective factors that reduce the probability of substance dependence.

A person's initial use of addictive drugs is obviously one important step toward the development of substance dependence, but the fact remains that most people who drink alcohol do not develop alcoholism. What accounts for the next important phase of the disorder? Why do some people abuse the drug while others do not? In the following pages we outline several

▲ **The circumstances in which an adolescent is initially exposed to alcohol can influence the person's pattern of drinking as well as his or her response to the drug. Drinking small amounts of wine with meals on a regular basis may be less likely to lead to alcohol dependence than the sporadic consumption of hard liquor for the purpose of becoming intoxicated.**

additional biological variables. We begin by examining genetic factors, and then we consider the neurochemical effects of the drugs themselves.

GENETICS OF ALCOHOLISM

An extensive literature attests to the fact that patterns of alcohol consumption, as well as psychological and social problems associated with alcohol abuse, tend to run in families. The lifetime prevalence of alcoholism among the parents, siblings, and children of people with alcoholism is at least three to five times higher than the rate in the general population (Merikangas, 1990; Schuckit, 1987). Of course, this elevated risk among first-degree relatives could reflect the influence of either genetic or environmental factors, because families share both types of influence. Therefore we must look to the results of twin and adoption studies in an effort to disentangle these variables.

Twin Studies   Several twin studies have examined patterns of alcohol consumption in nonalcoholic twins. The evidence indicates that both genetic factors and shared environmental factors influence the quantity and frequency of social drinking in normal men and women (Heath, Jardine, & Martin, 1989; Merikangas, 1990; Prescott et al., 1994a).

Other studies have examined twin concordance rates for alcoholism when the proband is identified through a treatment program. Here the focus is on severely disabling drinking problems rather than simply the consumption of alcohol. Several studies have found that concordance rates are higher among MZ than among DZ twin pairs, but in some studies this finding is limited to male subjects. For example, psychologist Matt McGue and his colleagues at the University of Minnesota found concordance rates for DSM-III diagnoses of alcohol abuse or dependence of 77 percent in male MZ twins and 54 percent in male DZ twins (McGue, Pickins, & Svikis, 1992). The corresponding figures for MZ and DZ female twin pairs were 39 percent and 42 percent. This result suggests that different etiological pathways may be responsible for alcoholism in men and women. The possibility is particularly interesting in light of the marked gender differences in the prevalence of alcohol abuse and dependence.

The implications of this disparity between twin study results for males and females are not entirely clear. They may suggest that genetic factors are more important in the development of alcoholism among men. As Merikangas (1990) points out, however, other factors could account for these results. Fewer studies have examined alcoholism in female twins; the sample sizes for female twin pairs tend to be small; and women may be less likely to enter treatment programs through which probands are typically identified. Two studies have examined concordance rates for alcohol abuse in large samples of men and women living in a community. Both found equally strong levels of familial resemblance in male and female twins (Kendler et al., 1992; Prescott et al., 1994b). Thus we cannot conclude definitively on the basis of twin studies that alcoholism among males has a larger genetic element than does alcoholism among females.

Adoption Studies   The strategy followed in an adoption study allows the investigator to separate relatively clearly the influence of genetic and environmental factors. The probands in this type of study are individuals who meet two criteria: (1) they had a biological parent who was alcoholic, and (2) they were adopted away from their biological parents at an early age and raised by adoptive parents.

Two major adoption studies have examined the possible role of genetic factors in the etiology of alcoholism. One investigation was conducted in Denmark by psychiatrist Donald Goodwin of the University of Kansas and his colleagues (Goodwin et al., 1994). This study revealed that by the age of 30, 18 percent of the male offspring of alcoholic biological parents had developed alcoholism, compared to only 5 percent of the control adoptees. The results were quite different for the daughters of alcoholic parents; the risk for alcoholism among female offspring was only 4 percent among both the index cases and the control sample. These data are consistent with the results of McGue's twin study. Genetic factors apparently influence the development of alcoholism among men, but their influence is more ambiguous among women.

A pair of adoption studies was conducted in Sweden by Robert Cloninger and his colleagues (see Research Close-Up). The results of these investigations are consistent with Goodwin's adoption study in pointing toward the influence of genetic factors in the etiology of alcohol abuse and dependence. They also

The Swedish Adoption Studies

Two influential adoption studies suggest that Type 1 and Type 2 alcoholism are distinct forms of disorder that follow different etiological pathways. Genetic and environmental factors apparently interact in different ways for these separate forms of alcohol abuse. The investigations were conducted in Sweden by Robert Cloninger, a psychiatrist at Washington University, Michael Bohman, a Swedish psychiatrist, and Soren Sigvardsson, a Swedish psychologist. The first study included people from Stockholm (Cloninger, 1987). The second study followed the same procedures with men and women from Gothenburg (Sigvardsson, Bohman, & Cloninger, 1996). The fact that the same pattern of findings emerged from both studies lends a great deal of credibility to the investigators' conclusions regarding the etiology of alcoholism.

We will describe the procedures and results of the first study in some detail. The investigators began their initial study with a list of all male children who were born out of wedlock in Stockholm between 1930 and 1949 and who were also adopted away from their biological parents at an early age. At the time of the study, these men were between the ages of 23 and 43. The investigators collected information about the men's adjustment by using official records of local temperance boards, hospital and insurance records, and the national criminal register. They expected this procedure to identify about 70 percent of all people in this population who had a serious drinking problem.

The adoptees were divided into two groups on the basis of the type of alcohol abuse exhibited by their biological parents, using Cloninger's system of Type 1 and Type 2 alcoholism. The subject was considered to have a Type 1 genetic background if the biological father or mother had an adult (later) onset of drinking problems and had not engaged in severe criminal behavior. The subject was classified as having a Type 2 genetic background if the biological father had undergone extensive treatment

for alcoholism or had shown evidence of serious criminal behavior beginning in adolescence or early adulthood.[†]

The top panel of Table 11–7 summarizes the results for adoptees with a Type 1 genetic background. Preliminary analyses indicated that, by itself, the presence of treated alcoholism in the adoptive parents did not increase the risk for alcoholism in the adoptees. The results were different, however, when the investigators combined the effects of an alcoholic parent with family income and social class. The investigators assumed that, in Sweden during that particular time, children who were raised by adoptive fathers with unskilled occupations would be exposed to a pattern of heavy recreational drinking. When the groups were subdivided in this way, Cloninger and his colleagues found that both a

TABLE 11–7
Analysis of Severe Alcohol Abuse in the Swedish Adoption Study

Type 1 Genetic Background	Environmental Background	Male Adoptees Observed	
		Total Sample Size	Severe Abuse (%)
No	No	376	4.3
No	Yes	72	4.2
Yes	No	328	6.7
Yes	Yes	86	11.6

Type 2 Genetic Background	Environmental Background	Male Adoptees Observed	
		Total Size Sample	Type 2 Abuse (%)
No	No	567	1.9
No	Yes	196	4.1
Yes	No	71	16.9
Yes	Yes	28	17.9

[†] They could not find enough mothers with a Type 2 form of alcoholism to include these subjects in the study.

genetic predisposition and environmental factors were necessary to increase the risk for severe alcohol abuse in the offspring of people with Type 1 alcoholism. The presence of either a genetic background for the disorder or a lower social class background did not significantly increase the adoptees' risk for alcoholism. But when an individual experienced both of these vulnerability factors, the risk for alcoholism was significantly increased—approximately double that expected in the general population.

A different pattern emerged among the adoptees with a genetic background associated with Type 2 alcoholism (see the bottom panel of Table 11–7). Here the genetic component was more pronounced. Regardless of the environment provided by the adoptive family, the male offspring in this group were much more likely to abuse alcohol.

Cloninger and his colleagues also examined rates of alcohol abuse among the daughters of biological parents with both types of alcoholism. Female adoptees with a genetic predisposition to Type 1 alcoholism (where either the father or the mother may have abused alcohol) were three times more likely to abuse alcohol than were women in the

control group. It therefore appears that genetic factors influence the development of this form of alcoholism in both men and women. A completely different pattern emerged in daughters of Type 2 alcoholic fathers. They were *not* more likely than the control subjects to abuse alcohol (although they did show an increased risk for somatic anxiety). On the basis of this result, Cloninger and his colleagues have argued that Type 2 alcoholism may be "male-limited."

The distinction between people with Type 1 and Type 2 alcoholism has been incorporated into many other studies. Some aspects of the study have been criticized, however (Searles, 1988, 1990; McGue, 1993). For example, the examination of environmental circumstances in the adoptive homes was quite limited in scope. The interesting interaction of genes and environment in the Type 1 families was based primarily on socioeconomic status, which is a rather crude measure. The investigators were not able to measure specific drinking patterns or attitudes toward alcohol among the adoptive parents. Still, the Swedish adoption studies have generated enormous interest and have served as a catalyst for many other investigations. ■

---

indicate, however, that the manner in which genetic and environmental events combine probably differs from one type of alcoholism to another. The Swedish adoption studies also suggest an explanation for the ambiguous pattern of evidence regarding female alcoholism. Using Cloninger's subtyping system, genetic factors may play a role in the etiology of Type 1 alcoholism in women. The daughters of people with Type 2 alcoholism, on the other hand, are at risk for the development of certain types of anxiety disorders, but they are not more likely to develop alcoholism themselves. Studies that lump together these different types of drinking problems will probably produce less consistent results for women than for men.

What can we conclude from the adoption studies? There are obviously some differences in both methods and results from one study to the next, but there are also consistent indications that genetic factors play some role in the etiology of alcohol abuse and dependence. McGue (1993) conducted a comprehensive review of the adoption study evidence and reached the following general conclusions:

- The offspring of alcoholic parents who are reared by nonalcoholic adoptive parents are more likely than people in the general population to develop drinking problems of their own. Thus the familial nature of alcoholism is at least partially determined by genes.
- Being reared by an alcoholic parent, in the absence of other etiological factors, does not appear to be a critical consideration in the development of the disorder.
- The etiology of alcoholism is probably heterogeneous in nature; that is, there are several pathways to the disorder.
- There is an association between antisocial personality traits, or "behavioral undercontrol," and alcohol abuse or dependence. The exact nature of this relation and the direction of effect have not been determined.

NEUROCHEMICAL MODES OF ACTION

Assuming that some people are genetically more vulnerable to the addicting effects of alcohol than others, what genetic mechanisms are involved, and how do they function? Considerable speculation has focused on brain mechanisms, especially those involving neural transmission (Schuckit, 1994). All of the addicting psychoactive drugs produce changes in the chemical processes by which messages are transmitted in the brain.

Endogenous Opioid Receptors   One promising research area in the neurosciences involves the discovery of the endogenous opioids known as **endorphins.** These relatively short chains of amino acids, or neuropeptides, are naturally synthesized in the brain and are closely related to morphine in terms of their pharmacological properties. Endorphins possess a chemical affinity for specific receptor sites, in the same way that a key fits into a specific lock. More than a dozen endorphins are distributed widely throughout the brain. They appear to be especially important in the activities associated with systems that control pain, emotion, stress, and reward, as well as such biological functions as feeding and growth (Cohen, 1988).

Research studies have demonstrated many interesting features of the endorphins. Laboratory animals can develop tolerance to injections of endorphins, just as they develop tolerance to addicting drugs like morphine, and they also exhibit symptoms of withdrawal if the injections are suddenly discontinued. These studies confirm the pharmacological similarity between endogenous and exogenous opioids, but one crucial difference remains: We don't become addicted to endorphins in normal brain functioning.

Some theorists associate alcoholism with excessive production of endogenous opioids (Blum & Payne, 1991; Gianoulakis, 1993). This hypothesis suggests that common neurochemical mechanisms might account for addiction to alcohol and to opioids such as heroin and morphine. It is based on several observations that indicate that the behavioral and pharmacological effects of alcohol are similar to those of the opioids. For example, laboratory animals that have received injections of small amounts of morphine will increase their consumption of alcohol. Although the relationship between endorphins and alcoholism is intriguing, the hypothesis is also inconsistent with some other facts. The experiences of alcoholics during withdrawal differ markedly from those of heroin addicts (APA, 1994). The endorphin hypothesis would predict that the reactions should be similar because they are caused by common neurochemical processes (Cohen, 1988).

The Serotonin Hypothesis   Addicting drugs probably have widespread effects on the process of neural transmission in the brain, including systems that involve catecholamines (for example, dopamine, norepinephrine, and serotonin) as well as the neuropeptides. Although alcohol does not bind directly to any receptor sites in the brain, it does alter the permeability of neuronal membranes (Yi, 1991). Channels for potassium and chlorine ions are opened, and corresponding channels for sodium and calcium are closed, thus depressing the central nervous system. Concentrations of neurotransmitters, such as serotonin and dopamine, are initially increased. If the person continues to drink heavily over an extended period of time, the drinking produces many effects that are opposite to those of short-term intoxication: The central nervous system becomes excited rather than depressed, and the ion channel events are reversed.

The serotonin theory of the etiology of alcoholism assumes that alcohol dependence is caused by a genetically determined deficiency in serotonin activity in certain areas of the limbic system of the brain (Ferreira & Soares da Silva, 1991; Wallis, Rezazadeh, & Lal, 1993). Some studies have reported that acute intoxication is accompanied by an increase in serotonin activity. When the person sobers up, serotonin activity is reduced to subnormal levels. The serotonin theory suggests that some people begin with a deficiency in serotonin, and the consumption of alcohol initially helps to correct for this deficiency. Unfortunately, prolonged consumption further depletes the system. Therefore the person initially drinks to feel good—alcohol stimulates activity in the reward systems of the brain—but after a while he or she must drink more to avoid feeling worse when serotonin levels are reduced below their initial point.

Evidence supporting this theory comes from several kinds of investigation. First, animals that are bred to exhibit high and low preferences for alcohol exhibit differences in serotonin levels. Those with a high preference for alcohol have lower levels of serotonin in areas of the brain that regulate emotional responses (McBride et al., 1993). Second, serotonin activity differs between two groups of people with alcohol use disorders. Those with an early onset and a family history for the disorder have lower serotonin activity than those with a later onset and no family history for the disorder (Buydens-Branchey et al., 1989). Third, drugs that enhance serotonin transmission (such as selective serotonin reuptake inhibitors or SSRIs; see Chapter 5) can decrease voluntary alcohol consumption in human subjects. The fact that these types of medication are also effective in treating mood disorders, as well as panic and obsessive–compulsive disorder, suggests an etiological link between alcoholism and these disorders (Tollefson, 1991).

Psychological Factors

Genetic factors and pharmacological effects undoubtedly account for many of the problems associated with addicting drugs, but as the systems perspective indicates, biological explanations are not incompatible with psychological ones. In fact, extensive research over the past several decades has found that the progression of substance dependence depends on an interaction between environmental and biological events. One time-honored perspective on the development of alcoholism is the tension-reduction hypothesis. At its most general level, this viewpoint holds that people drink alcohol in an effort to reduce the impact of a stressful environment.

The tension-reduction hypothesis became the focal point for scientific investigation when Conger (1956) adapted formal learning theory to the problem and proposed that alcohol consumption is reinforced by its ability to relieve unpleasant emotional states, especially fear and anxiety. As we will see in the following pages, the relation between stress and alcohol has turned out to be more complex than this theory suggests. Drug effects interact with the person's beliefs and attitudes as well as with the social context in which the drugs are taken.

▼ **Attitudes and expectations about the effects of drugs are shaped, in part, by the beliefs of peers. Many people believe that alcohol makes them more sociable.**

EXPECTATIONS ABOUT DRUG EFFECTS
Placebo effects demonstrate that expectations are an important factor in any study of drug effects (see Chapter 3). During the 1970s, several research studies sought to evaluate the influence of alcohol on various facets of behavior using the *balanced placebo design*. This procedure allows the investigator to separate the direct, biological effects of the drug from the subjects' expectations about how the drug should affect their behavior. The results indicated that expectations can account for many effects that have often been attributed to the drug itself. For example, subjects who believed that they had ingested alcohol but who had actually consumed only tonic water displayed exaggerated aggression and reported enhanced feelings of sexual arousal (Goldman, Brown, & Christiansen, 1987; Goldman et al., 1991; Hull & Bond, 1986). Much less is known about expectancies for drugs other than alcohol, but there is good reason to believe that these cognitive factors also influence the ways in which people respond to cannabis, nicotine, stimulants, anxiolytics, and sedatives (Brandon, Wetter, & Baker, 1996; Brown, 1993).

The results of experiments using the balanced placebo design stimulated considerable thought about the role that alcohol expectancies may play in the etiology of drinking problems. These studies do not manipulate expectancies directly, however. They only lead subjects to believe that they have consumed alcohol when, in fact, they have not. The investigators infer that the subjects believed that alcohol would make them aggressive.

But is that really the case? Subsequent investigations began to examine alcohol expectancies directly (Brown et al., 1980). Investigators asked people, Why do you drink? What do you expect to happen after you have consumed a few beers or a couple of glasses of wine? Answers that subjects provided to these questions fit into six primary categories:

1. Alcohol transforms experiences in a positive way (for example: Drinking makes the future seem brighter).
2. Alcohol enhances social and physical pleasure (for example: Having a few drinks is a nice way to celebrate special occasions).
3. Alcohol enhances sexual performance and experience (for example: After a few drinks, I am more sexually responsive).
4. Alcohol increases power and aggression (for example: After a few drinks it is easier to pick a fight).

5. Alcohol increases social assertiveness (for example: Having a few drinks makes it easier to talk to people).
6. Alcohol reduces tension (for example: Alcohol enables me to fall asleep more easily).

These expectations may constitute one of the primary reasons for continued and increasingly heavy consumption of alcoholic beverages. In fact, expectancy patterns can help predict drinking behaviors. Longitudinal studies have found that adolescents who are just beginning to experiment with alcohol and who initially have the most positive expectations about the effects of alcohol go on to consume greater amounts of alcoholic beverages (Goldman et al., 1991; Smith et al., 1995). This type of demonstration is important because it indicates that, in many cases, the expectations appear before the person begins to drink heavily. Therefore, they may play a role in the onset of the problem rather than being consequences of heavy drinking (see Research Methods).

Risk, Risk Factors, and Studies of High-Risk Samples

We have used the term *risk* informally throughout this book to refer to a hazard—the possibility of suffering harm. In scientific research, a **risk** is a statement about the probability that a certain outcome will occur. For example, the NCS found that the risk that a person in the United States will develop alcoholism at some point in his or her life is about 14 in 100 (see Table 11–6). The combined risk for all types of illegal and controlled substances (such as cannabis, cocaine, heroin, and barbiturates) is about 8 in 100. The concept of risk implies only probability, not certainty. Someone who is "at risk" may or may not suffer harm, depending upon many other events and circumstances.

The concept of relative risk can be used to indicate that people with certain characteristics are more likely than others to develop a disorder. *Relative risk* (or a *risk ratio*) refers to the probability that someone with a certain characteristic will develop a disorder divided by the probability that someone without the same characteristic will develop the same disorder (Zahner, Hsieh, & Fleming, 1995). The higher the number, the greater the risk. For example, the risk for developing alcohol dependence is approximately five times higher among men than among women; thus the relative risk for male gender is 5. This statistic suggests that male gender is a fairly strong risk factor for the development of alcohol dependence. **Risk factors** are variables that are associated with a higher probability of developing a disorder. Notice that this use of the term *risk* implies association, not causality. The concept of risk simply reflects a correlation between the risk factor (in this case, gender) and the disorder.

Some risk factors are demographic variables, such as gender and race. Others are biological and psychological variables. In the case of alcoholism, and many other types of psychopathology, family history of the disorder is an important risk factor. Expectancies about the effects of drugs represent another important risk factor for alcoholism. People who expect that alcohol will reduce tension or transform experiences in a positive way are more likely to drink frequently and heavily than those who have negative expectancies about the effects of alcohol.

In order to determine whether certain risk factors actually play a *causal* role in the development of the disorder, it is often necessary to conduct longitudinal studies (see Research Methods in Chapter 8). The investigator collects information about each person before the onset of the disorder. He or she can therefore determine whether the risk factor is present before or only after the onset of symptoms. Studies of this sort can be extremely expensive and time-consuming. They take several years to complete. Longitudinal studies also require large number of participants because everyone in the study will not go on to develop the disorder in question and because some people inevitably will drop out or be lost from the study before all the follow-ups can be completed.

Some of these shortcomings of longitudinal studies are especially relevant to research on substance abuse disorders. The risk for developing such disorders is quite low in the general population. For example, even though alcoholism is one of the most prevalent forms of mental disorder, a longitudinal study that follows the development of 100 randomly selected people from childhood to middle age will find only about 14 alcoholic adults (based on NCS data). Thus, to collect a useful amount of data, researchers need to study a large population, which can be very expensive.

Recognition of this problem led scientists to develop special methods to increase the productivity of longitudinal research. One important technique is the **high-risk research design.** In high-risk research, subjects are selected from the general population based on some identified risk factor that has a fairly high risk ratio. A number of risk factors might be used to select subjects: positive family history for a given disorder, the presence of certain psychological characteristics, or perhaps a set of demographic variables such as age, gender, and/or race. (An example of a classic high-risk research project on the development of schizophrenia is discussed in the Research Close-Up in Chapter 13.

High-risk studies can address two major goals (Faraone & Tsuang, 1995). First, they can be used to examine the role that risk factors play in the development of a particular disorder. By tracing the relations among psychological, biological, and social variables over time, the investigator may be able to untangle the complex pattern of interactions that ultimately lead to the onset of a mental disorder. Second, they can be used to define *vulnerability indicators* (manifestations of the genotype associated with a mental disorder) in the absence of full-blown symptoms of the disorder. Among the people in the high-risk group, some will eventually develop the disorder and others will not. Looking back at the data collected during childhood or adolescence, investigators may be able to identify signs or markers that are unique to those who eventually become seriously disturbed. ■

Where do these expectations come from, and when do they develop? In some cases they may arise from personal experiences with alcohol, but they can also be learned indirectly. Many adolescents hold strong beliefs about the effects of alcohol long before they take their first drink. These expectations may be influenced by parental and peer attitudes and by the portrayal of alcohol in the mass media. Follow-up studies have demonstrated that adolescents' expectations about the effects of alcohol are useful in predicting which individuals will later develop drinking problems (Christiansen et al., 1989; Stacy, Newcomb, & Bentler, 1991). Positive expectancies about alcohol—which are likely to encourage people to drink—are especially influential. Negative expectancies are associated with diminished use but seem to be less powerful (Leigh & Stacy, 1993; Stacy, Widaman, & Marlatt, 1990).

ATTENTION ALLOCATION

Scientists have studied the behavioral effects of alcohol extensively, especially its influence on anxiety, aggression, sexual responsiveness, and mood. One of the puzzling results of this research is the inconsistency that has emerged from one study to the next. Some papers report that alcohol reduces tension; others conclude that it increases anxiety. Some investigators have found that drinking alcohol can increase self-esteem, whereas others have concluded that it can increase depression. Claude Steele, a psychologist at Stanford University, and Robert Josephs, a psychologist at the University of Texas, have proposed an attention-allocation model of alcohol effects that provides an explanation for these apparent inconsistencies (Steele & Josephs, 1988, 1990).

Steele and Josephs' theory is based on two general factors. First, when alcohol reaches the brain, it interferes with the capacity for controlled and effortful cognitive activities. Intoxicated people focus their attention, by necessity, on immediate internal and external cues and are less able to consider subtle or complex aspects of a problem. Steele and Josephs (1990) call this process *alcohol myopia*—a marked tendency to engage in shortsighted information processing. The second component of the attention-allocation model involves the nature of the immediate environment. The impact of drinking on an intoxicated person's behavior will depend on the specific situation with which the person is confronted.

Steele and Josephs have used this model to study the effects of alcohol on several aspects of human behavior, including drunken excess, the

▼ Drinking increases the risk for aggression and violence. This may be due to expectancies or attention allocation, in addition to the direct effects of alcohol.

tendency for social behavior to become more extreme under the influence of alcohol. The attention-allocation model predicts that alcohol myopia will lead to drunken excess only in situations in which strong cues are pulling for a particular response, but in which that response is also inhibited by higher level cognitive processing. Suppose, for example, that somebody insults you. If you are sober, you might be tempted to respond by punching or slapping the person, but you would also anticipate several negative consequences that might be associated with this choice of action. If you are intoxicated, however, you will be cognitively impaired and therefore less able to invoke these inhibitory cues. Therefore you are more likely to respond in an excessively aggressive fashion.

The attention-allocation theory is an intriguing explanation for the short-term effects of alcohol on human behavior. Of course, as with all theoretical models of psychopathology, the theory conflicts with certain facts. The most important point to be emphasized in considering this approach is that the short-term effects of alcohol on the behavior of nonalcoholic subjects is determined, at least in part, by the disruptive effects of alcohol consumption on cognitive processes (Sayette, 1993).

Integrated Systems

Alcoholism clearly results from an interaction among several types of systems. Various social, psychological, and biological factors influence the person's behavior at each stage in the cycle, from initial use of the drug through the eventual onset of tolerance and withdrawal. The process seems to progress in the following way. Initial experimentation with drugs is influenced by the person's family and peers, who serve as models for the use of drugs. Other people also influence the person's attitudes and expectations about the effects of drugs. Access to drugs, in addition to the patterns in which they are originally consumed, are determined, in part, by cultural factors.

For many people, drinking alcohol leads to short-term positive effects that reinforce continued consumption. The exact psychological mechanisms that are responsible for reinforcing heavy drinking may take several different forms. They may involve diminished self-awareness, stress reduction, or improved mood. These effects of alcohol on behavior and subjective experience are determined, in part, by the person's expectations about the way in which the drug will influence his or her feelings and behavior (Goldman, 1994).

Genetic factors play an important role in the etiology of alcoholism (Schuckit, 1994). There are most likely several different types of genetic influence, as illustrated by the results of the Swedish adoption studies. Genes interact strongly with environmental events for certain types of the disorder. A genetic predisposition to alcohol dependence probably causes the person to react to alcohol in an abnormal fashion. It is not clear whether those who are vulnerable to alcoholism are initially more or less sensitive than other people to the reinforcing effects of alcohol. Research studies have demonstrated both patterns of response (Sher, 1993).

The biological mechanisms responsible for abnormal reactions to alcohol may involve a deficiency in serotonin activity in certain areas of the limbic system. Drinking alcohol initially corrects this problem and increases serotonin activity, but the person eventually begins to feel worse after tolerance develops. Another point of view holds that people who are biologically insensitive to the adverse effects of alcohol are more likely to become alcoholics (Goodwin, 1988).

Drinking gradually becomes heavier and more frequent. The person becomes tolerant to the effects of alcohol and must therefore drink larger quantities to achieve the same reinforcing effects. After the person becomes addicted to alcohol, attempts to quit drinking are accompanied by painful withdrawal symptoms. Prolonged abuse can lead to permanent neurological impairment as well as the disruption of many other organ systems.

Treatment

The treatment of alcoholism and other types of substance use disorders is an especially difficult task. Many people with these problems do not acknowledge their difficulties, and only a relatively small number seek professional help. When they do enter treatment, it is typically with reluctance or on the insistence of friends, family members, or legal authorities. Compliance with treatment recommendations is often low, and dropout rates are high. The high rate of comorbidity with other forms of mental disorder presents an additional challenge, complicating the formulation of a treatment plan. Treatment outcome is likely to be least successful with those people who have comorbid conditions.

The goals of treatment for substance use disorders are a matter of controversy. Some clinicians believe that the only acceptable goal is total abstinence from drinking or drug use. Others have argued that, for some people, a more reasonable goal is the moderate use of legal drugs. Important questions have also been raised about the scope of improvements that might be expected from a successful treatment program. Is the goal simply to minimize or eliminate drug use, or should we expect that treatment will also address the social, occupational, and medical problems that are typically associated with drug problems? If these associated problems are the result of the person's prolonged abuse of alcohol or other drugs, the problems may improve on their own if the person becomes abstinent. However, to the extent that family problems or interpersonal difficulties contribute to the person's use of drugs, it may be necessary to address these difficulties before the drug problem can be resolved (McLellan et al., 1992).

Detoxification and Pharmacotherapy

Treatment of alcoholism and related forms of drug abuse is often accomplished in a sequence of stages, beginning with a brief period of **detoxification**—the removal of a drug on which a person has become dependent—lasting between 3 and 6 weeks (Dackis & Gold, 1991). This process is often extremely difficult, as the person experiences marked symptoms of withdrawal and gradually adjusts to the absence of the drug. For many types of CNS depressants, such as alcohol, hypnotics, and sedatives, detoxification is accomplished gradually. Stimulant drugs, in contrast, can be stopped abruptly (Cohen, 1988). During the detoxification period, medical staff closely monitor the patient's vital signs to prevent seizures and delirium. Although detoxification usually takes place in a hospital, some evidence indicates that it can be accomplished with close supervision on an outpatient basis.

People who are going through alcohol detoxification are often given various types of medication, including anxiolytics, primarily as a way of minimizing withdrawal symptoms (Weddington, 1992). This practice is controversial, in part because many people believe that it is illogical to use one form of drug—especially one that can be abused itself—to help someone recover from dependence on another drug.

Psychiatrists have also used SSRIs, such as Prozac, for the long-term treatment of alcoholic patients. This treatment is based, in part, on evidence from animal studies indicating that the increased availability of serotonin in the brain suppresses alcohol consumption. The effectiveness of this type of pharmacotherapy has not been extensively evaluated (Litten & Allen, 1991).

DISULFIRAM (ANTABUSE)

Disulfiram (Antabuse) is a drug that can block the chemical breakdown of alcohol. It was introduced as a treatment for alcoholism in Europe in 1948 and is still used fairly extensively. If a person who is taking Antabuse consumes even a small amount of alcohol, he or she will become violently ill. The symptoms include nausea, vomiting, profuse sweating, and increased heart rate and respiration rate. People who are taking Antabuse will stop drinking alcohol in order to avoid this extremely unpleasant reaction.

Unfortunately, voluntary compliance with this form of treatment is poor. Many patients discontinue taking Antabuse, usually because they want to resume drinking or because they believe that they can manage their problems without the drug (Børup, Kaiser, & Jensen, 1992). People can drink alcohol without experiencing an unpleasant reaction about 2 or 3 days after they stop taking Antabuse. Treatment therefore requires close medical supervision (Brewer, 1992).

Antabuse is used frequently, especially with patients who are older and highly motivated to stop drinking, but the research evidence regarding its effectiveness is unclear (Kristenson, 1992; Larson et al., 1992). Studies that have employed placebo control groups have found that patients who receive Antabuse are no more likely to remain sober than are those receiving a placebo (Fuller & Roth, 1979). Although most patients eventually relapse, those who are taking Antabuse may be able to stay sober for longer periods of time.

Self-Help Groups: Alcoholics Anonymous

One of the most widely accepted forms of treatment for alcoholism is Alcoholics Anonymous (AA). Organized in 1935, this self-help program is maintained by alcohol abusers for the sole purpose of helping other people who abuse alcohol become and remain sober. Because it is established and active in virtually all communities in

North America and Europe as well as many other parts of the world, AA is generally considered to be "the first line of attack against alcoholism" (Nathan, 1993). Surveys conducted by AA indicate that its membership increased considerably during the 1970s and 1980s. In 1989, there were approximately 1 million members of AA in the United States and Canada (Chappel, 1993). Many members of AA are also involved in other forms of treatment offered by various types of mental health professionals, but AA is not officially associated with any other forms of treatment or professional organizations. Similar self-help programs have been developed for people who are dependent on other drugs, such as opioids (Narcotics Anonymous) and cocaine (Cocaine Anonymous).

The viewpoint espoused by AA is fundamentally spiritual in nature. AA is the original "12-step program." In the first step, the person must acknowledge that he or she is powerless over alcohol and unable to manage his or her drinking. The remaining steps involve spiritual and interpersonal matters such as accepting "a Power greater than ourselves" that can provide the person with direction; recognizing and accepting personal weaknesses; and making amends for previous errors, especially instances in which the person's drinking caused hardships for other people. One principal assumption is that people cannot recover on their own (Bean, 1975; Chappel, 1992).

The process of working through the 12 steps to recovery is facilitated by regular attendance at AA meetings, as often as every day of the first 90 days after the person stops drinking (Chappel, 1992). Most people choose to attend less frequently if they are able to remain sober throughout this initial period. Meetings provide chronic alcohol abusers with an opportunity to meet and talk with other people who have similar problems. New members are encouraged to call older members for help at any time if they experience an urge to drink. There is enormous variability in the format and membership of local AA meetings (Montgomery, Miller, & Tonigan, 1993).

It is difficult to evaluate the effectiveness of AA, for a number of reasons. Long-term follow-up is difficult, and it is generally impossible to employ some of the traditional methods of outcome research, such as random assignment to groups and placebo controls. Early dropout rates are relatively high: About half of all the people who initially join AA drop out in less than 3 months. On the other hand, survival rates (defined in terms of continued sobriety) are much higher for those people who remain in AA. About 80 percent of AA members who have remained sober for between 2 and 5 years will remain sober in the next year (Mäkelä, 1994).

Although the format of AA presents several obstacles to research, some studies indicate that AA does provide important help to many people. In his longitudinal study of alcoholic men, Vaillant (1995) found that attendance at AA meetings was an important predictor of positive outcomes. More recent outcome studies that have examined the effects of AA in combination with other forms of treatment indicate that participation in AA makes a significant positive contribution to treatment outcome (Pisani et al., 1993; Walsh et al., 1991).

Although AA does seem to help people, it is not clear how it helps, or why. Several mechanisms are possible. One explanation centers on the personal growth process that is described in the 12-step program, but the active ingredient may be more social than spiritual. Membership in AA provides people with a stable social network that discourages rather than encourages the use of drugs. Another possible explanation involves personality traits that are present before the person enters treatment. Those people with traits that are compatible with continued membership in a group like AA may be most likely to recover (Pisani et al., 1993). People who exhibit antisocial traits of the type associated with Cloninger's Type 2 alcoholism, who also presumably have an earlier onset and more difficulty abstaining from drinking, may be least likely to benefit from AA.

Controlled Drinking

One psychological approach to the treatment of alcoholism, known as Individualized Behavior Therapy for Alcoholics (IBTA), was developed by psychologists Mark and Linda Sobell (Sobell & Sobell, 1973, 1976). It employed a wide range of therapeutic procedures in an effort to address abusive drinking patterns as well as other types of maladaptive behavior that are associated with alcohol dependence. The latter included training in the use of social skills, which might be used to resist pressures to drink heavily, and problem-solving procedures, which might

▼ Group therapy, like this session from the movie *Clean and Sober,* is an important part of most inpatient treatment programs. It offers an opportunity for patients to acknowledge and confront openly the severity of their problems.

help the person both to identify situations that lead to heavy drinking and to formulate alternative courses of action.

The most controversial aspect of IBTA was its consideration of controlled drinking as a potential goal for people who are dependent on alcohol. This concept refers to the moderate consumption of alcohol in a pattern that avoids drinking to the point of intoxication. Most forms of intervention, including AA, hold firmly to the belief that the only acceptable outcome of treatment is total abstinence. The assumption of this approach is that, for people with alcoholism, a single drink will inevitably lead to complete loss of control. The Sobells set out to teach chronic alcohol abusers to drink in more appropriate ways. Their procedures encouraged patients to choose mixed drinks rather than straight liquor and to take small, intermittent sips rather than gulping drinks quickly. Results suggested that patients who were trained to drink in a controlled fashion had a better outcome, on average, than those in a control group for whom the goal was total abstinence.

The results of the Sobells' IBTA study were subjected to close scrutiny, and they ignited an intense controversy that has lasted for several years (Maltzman, 1989; Peele, 1992; Pendery, Maltzman, & West, 1982; Sobell & Sobell, 1989). Critics claimed, based on their own follow-up assessments, that the patients who had received IBTA did not return successfully to controlled drinking. The general consensus seems to be that, due to methodological problems with the IBTA study, researchers cannot reach definitive conclusions one way or the other.

Relatively few mental health professionals currently consider controlled drinking to be a realistic goal for people who are dependent on alcohol. However, a substantial minority of people who are dependent on alcohol apparently return to alcohol use on a moderate basis. For example, one follow-up study found that approximately 20 percent of a group of people with alcohol use disorders had returned to nonproblem drinking 10 years after receiving inpatient treatment (Finney & Moos, 1991). Therefore treatment aimed at reduced levels of drinking rather than total abstinence may be successful for some people with drinking problems. This approach is perhaps most reasonable with patients who have only recently begun to experience problems associated with alcohol consumption, especially young adults (Donovan & Marlatt, 1993; Kivlahan et al., 1990).

Relapse Prevention

Most people who have been addicted to a drug will say that quitting is the easy part of treatment. The most difficult challenge is to maintain this change after it has been accomplished. Unfortunately, most people will "slip up" and return to drinking soon after they stop. The same thing can be said for people who stop smoking or using any other drug of abuse. These slips often lead to a full-scale return to excessive and uncontrolled use of the drug. Successful treatment therefore depends on making preparations for such incidents.

Alan Marlatt, a clinical psychologist at the University of Washington, and his colleagues have proposed a cognitive behavioral view of the relapse process (Marlatt, 1985, 1996). This process applies to all forms of substance dependence, ranging from alcoholism to nicotine dependence (Shiffman et al., 1996). It has also been applied to other disorders associated with impulsive behavior, such as bulimia and inappropriate sexual behaviors (see Chapters 10 and 12). It places principal emphasis on events that take place after detoxification and the initial efforts at intensive treatment.

The relapse prevention model addresses several important issues that confront the addict in trying to deal with the challenges of life without drugs. The model emphasizes increasing people's belief that they will be able to control their own behavior and events in their lives. The therapist also helps patients learn more adaptive coping responses, such as applied relaxation and social skills, that can be used in situations that formerly might have triggered drug use.

Another important feature of the relapse prevention model is concerned with the *abstinence violation effect,* which refers to the guilt and perceived loss of control that the person feels whenever he or she slips and finds himself or herself having a drink (or a cigarette or whatever drug is involved) after an extended period of abstinence. People typically blame themselves for failing to live up to their promise to quit. They also interpret the first drink as a signal that further efforts to control their drinking will be useless. Marlatt's approach to relapse prevention teaches patients to expect that they may slip occasionally and to interpret these behaviors as a temporary "lapse" rather than a total "relapse."

General Conclusions

In spite of the difficult challenges presented by these disorders, concerted efforts on the part of addicts who have organized self-help groups, and on the part of clinical scientists, have created some promising alternatives that offer hope to people with substance use disorders as well as their families. Comprehensive reviews of the research literature regarding treatment of alcoholism and drug abuse point to several general conclusions (McLellan et al., 1992):

- People who enter treatment for various types of substance abuse and dependence typically show improvement in terms of reduced drug use that is likely to persist for several months following the end of treatment. Unfortunately, relapse is also relatively common.
- There is little if any evidence to suggest that one form of treatment (inpatient or outpatient, professional or self-help, individual or group) is more effective than another (Project Match Research Group, 1997).
- Among those people who are able to reduce their consumption of drugs, or abstain altogether, improvements following treatment are usually not limited to drug use alone but extend to the person's health in general as well as to the person's social and occupational functioning.

Long-term outcome for the treatment of alcoholism is best predicted by the person's coping resources (social skills and problem-solving abilities), the availability of social support, and the level of stress in the environment. These considerations appear to be more important than the specific type of intervention that people receive (Finney & Moos, 1992). Those individuals who are in less stressful life situations, whose families are more cohesive, and who are themselves better equipped with active coping skills are most likely to sustain their improvement for a period of several years.

We must also remember that the vast majority of people with substance use disorders do not receive treatment from professionals or self-help organizations (Kessler et al., 1994). Nevertheless, many people manage to recover on their own. By studying the process of "natural recovery," clinicians may find clues that can be used to develop more effective forms of treatment. For example, the Sobells have compared people who were able to recover from alcohol dependence without the aid of treatment or AA to untreated drinkers who had not recovered (Sobell et al., 1993). More than half of all recoveries were initiated by cognitive events, primarily a reappraisal of the benefits and problems associated with continued drug use. They were not triggered by negative life events, which were frequent in the lives of both groups. Thus, the process of appraising the perceived costs and benefits of continued drinking may play a crucial role in the natural path to recovery.

SUMMARY

DSM-IV uses two terms to describe substance use disorders. **Substance dependence,** the more severe of the two forms, refers to a pattern of repeated self-administration that often results in **tolerance, withdrawal,** or compulsive drug-taking behavior. **Substance abuse** describes a more broadly conceived, less severe pattern of drug use that is defined in terms of interference with the person's ability to fulfill major role obligations at work or at home, recurrent use of a drug in dangerous situations, or the experience of repeated legal difficulties that are associated with drug use.

KEY TERMS

- addiction
- barbiturates
- benzodiazepines
- detoxification
- drug of abuse
- endorphins
- hallucinogens
- hashish
- high-risk research design
- marijuana
- opiates

- polysubstance abuse
- psychological dependence
- psychomotor stimulants
- substance abuse
- substance dependence
- tolerance
- withdrawal

A **drug of abuse**—sometimes called a psychoactive substance—is a chemical substance that alters a person's mood, level of perception, or brain functioning. The list of chemicals on which people become dependent includes drugs that are legally available in the U.S. as well as many that are illegal. Although patterns of dependence are similar in some ways for all drugs, each type of drug also has some unique features.

Prolonged abuse of alcohol can have a devastating impact on social relationships and occupational functioning while disrupting the functions of several important organ systems. Alcohol dependence has more negative health consequences than does abuse of almost any drug, with the possible exception of nicotine.

Barbiturates and **benzodiazepines** can be used, as prescribed by a physician, to decrease anxiety (tranquilizers) or help people sleep (hypnotics). They can also lead to a state of intoxication that is identical to that associated with alcohol. People who abruptly stop taking high doses of benzodiazepines may experience withdrawal symptoms, including a return of the original anxiety symptoms. Tolerance and withdrawal can develop after using barbiturates for several weeks.

Opiates have properties similar to opium and can induce a state of dreamlike euphoria. Tolerance develops quickly to opiates. After repeated use, their positive emotional effects are replaced by long-term negative changes in mood and emotion. Most of the severe health consequences of opiate use are the result of the lifestyle of the addict rather than the drug itself.

Nicotine is one of the most harmful addicting drugs. Recognizing the serious long-term health consequences of exposure to nicotine, the U.S. Food and Drug Administration has prohibited the sale and distribution of tobacco products to children and adolescents. This policy attempts to prevent the development of nicotine addiction rather than trying to ban use of the drug completely.

The **psychomotor stimulants,** such as amphetamine and cocaine, activate the sympathetic nervous system and induce a positive mood state. High doses of amphetamines and cocaine can lead to the onset of psychosis. The most devastating effects of stimulant drugs center around the disruption of occupational and social roles.

Marijuana and **hashish** can induce a pervasive sense of well-being and happiness. People do not seem to develop tolerance to THC (the active ingredient in marijuana and hashish) unless they are exposed to high doses over an extended period of time. Withdrawal symptoms are unlikely to develop among people who smoke marijuana occasionally.

Hallucinogens induce vivid visual images that are usually pleasant, but occasionally frightening. Unlike other drugs of abuse, hallucinogens are used sporadically rather than continuously. Most people do not increase their use of hallucinogens over time, and withdrawal symptoms are not observed.

It is impossible to specify a typical course for substance dependence. The specific pattern varies from one person to the next. In the case of alcoholism, the only thing that seems certain is that periods of heavy use alternate with periods of relative abstinence. Among alcoholic men in one long-term follow-up study, the proportion who become completely abstinent went up slowly but consistently over a period of many years. Relapse to alcohol abuse was unlikely among men who were able to remain abstinent for at least 6 years.

Alcohol dependence and abuse are the most common forms of mental disorder among men, with a lifetime prevalence of 13.8 percent in the ECA study. Among people with alcohol use disorders, men outnumber women by a ratio of approximately 5 to 1. Prevalence rates for alcohol dependence are highest among young adults and lowest among the elderly. According to the NCS, the combined lifetime prevalence for dependence on any type of controlled substance (those that are illegal or available only by prescription) was 7.5 percent.

Research on the etiology of alcoholism illustrates the ways in which various systems interact to produce and maintain drug dependence. The etiology of alcoholism is probably heterogeneous in nature. There are several pathways to the disorder. Social factors are particularly influential in the early phases of substance use. Initial experimentation with drugs is most likely to occur among those adolescents whose parents and peers model or encourage drug use. The culture in which a person lives influences the types of drugs that are used, the purposes for which they are used, and the expectations that people hold for the ways in which drugs will affect their experiences and behavior.

Considerable attention has been paid to the role of biological factors in the etiology of alcoholism, particularly the influence of genetic factors and neurochemical processes. Twin studies indicate that genetic factors influence patterns of social drinking as well as the onset of alcohol dependence. Adoption studies indicate that the offspring of alcoholic parents who are raised by nonalcoholic parents are more likely than people in the general population to develop drinking problems of their own. Genetic factors may be more influential in the development of alcoholism among men than among women.

The influence of genetic factors may vary in different subtypes of alcoholism. The Swedish adoption studies illustrates this possibility, focusing on the proposed distinction between Type 1 and Type 2 alcoholism. The combination of a genetic predisposition to alcoholism and environmental circumstances that encourage heavy drinking may lead to the onset of Type 1 alcoholism (late onset, no antisocial personality). In the case of Type 2 alcoholism (early onset, accompanied by antisocial personality), a genetic contribution increases risk for the disorder regardless of the type of environment in which the person is raised.

One focus of neurochemical research has been the role of endogenous opioids known as **endorphins.** Some theorists have argued that alcoholism is associated with excessive production of endorphins. Another neurochemical hypothesis suggests that alcohol dependence is caused by a genetically determined deficiency in serotonin activity in certain limbic areas of the brain.

Psychological explanations for the etiology of substance use disorders have often focused on the ability of drugs to relieve unpleasant emotional states. Expectations about drug effects have an important influence on the ways in which people respond to alcohol and other drugs. People who believe that alcohol enhances pleasure, reduces tension, and increases social performance are more likely than other people to drink frequently and heavily. The attention allocation theory is based on the recognition that alcohol reduces a person's capacity for cognitive activity. This process helps to explain the short-term effects of alcohol on mood and behavior, which may be reinforcing for some people.

Treatment of substance use disorders is an especially challenging and difficult task in light of the fact that many people with these problems do not recognize or acknowledge their own difficulties. Recovery begins with a process of detoxification. Self-help programs, such as Alcoholics Anonymous, are the most widely used and probably one of the most beneficial forms of treatment.

Critical Thinking

1. What is the difference between the rituals characteristic of obsessive–compulsive disorders and the compulsive drug-taking behaviors associated with substance dependence? Are there any similarities? Do you think that thse disorders should be classified together?

2. Some drugs of abuse are illegal in the United States, whereas others are legally available. What impact does this legal policy have on the definition of substance dependence as well as the probability that a person will receive a DSM-IV diagnosis?

3. Most adults in Western countries drink alcohol on a fairly regular basis, yet relatively few develop alcoholism. Why? There are gender differences and age differences in the prevalence of alcohol dependence. Why would women be less likely than men to become dependent on alcohol?

4. Although most people believe that alcohol makes them feel more relaxed, experimental studies indicate that it sometimes makes people more anxious or more aggressive. Why?

12
Sexual and Gender Identity Disorders

Sex is often a perplexing area of our lives. When something interferes with our ability to function sexually, it can be devastating both to the person who is affected and to the person's partner. Sexual behavior is considered abnormal when it results in personal distress or when it involves nonconsenting partners. Inhibitions of sexual desire and interference with the physiological responses leading to orgasm are called **sexual dysfunctions.** These experiences often lead to anxiety and depression, and they are frequently associated with interpersonal problems, especially marital distress. Another group of sexual disorders is known as the **paraphilias.** This term applies to people who are sexually aroused by unusual things and situations, such as inanimate objects, sexual contact with children, exhibiting their genitals to strangers, and inflicting pain on another person.

A person's sense of being either male or female, known as *gender identity*, is almost always consistent with his or her physical anatomy. In some rare cases, a person develops a strong and persistent identification with the other gender as well as a discomfort with his or her own assigned gender. For example, a person with a penis might insist that, in spite of his genitalia, he is more like a woman than a man. This phenomenon is called **gender identity disorder.**

Overview

Any discussion of sexual disorders requires some frank consideration of normal sexuality. Such openness has been encouraged and promoted by mental health professionals who specialize in the study and treatment of sexual behavior.

William Masters, a physician, and Virginia Johnson, a psychologist, undoubtedly have been the best-known sex therapists and researchers in the United States since the late 1960s (Masters, Johnson, & Kolodny, 1994). Their first book, *Human Sexual Response*, published in 1966, was based on their studies of nearly 700 normal men and women. Observations and physiological recordings were made in a laboratory setting while these individuals engaged in sexual activities, including masturbation and intercourse. Masters and Johnson's research received widespread attention in the popular media and helped make laboratory studies of sexual behavior acceptable.

On the basis of their data, Masters and Johnson described the human sexual response cycle in terms of a sequence of overlapping phases: excitement, orgasm, and resolution. Analogous processes occur in both men and women, but the timing may differ. There are, of course, individual differences in virtually all aspects of this cycle. Variations from the most common pattern may not indicate a problem unless the person is concerned about the response.

Sexual *excitement* increases continuously from initial stimulation up to the point of orgasm. It may last anywhere from a few minutes to several hours. Among the most dramatic physiological changes during sexual excitement are those associated with vasocongestion—engorgement of the blood vessels of various organs, especially the genitals. The male and female genitalia become swollen, reddened, and warmed. Sexual excitement also increases muscular tension, heart rate, and respiration rate. These physiological responses are accompanied by subjective feelings of arousal, especially at more advanced stages of excitement.

The experience of *orgasm* is usually distinct from the gradual buildup of sexual excitement that precedes it. This sudden release of tension is almost always experienced as being intensely pleasurable, but the specific nature of the experience varies from one individual to the next. The female orgasm occurs in three stages, beginning with a "sensation of suspension or stoppage," which is associated with strong genital sensations. The second stage involves a feeling of warmth spreading throughout the pelvic area. The third stage is characterized by sensations of throbbing or pulsating, which are tied to rhythmic contractions of the vagina, the uterus, and the rectal sphincter muscle.

The male orgasm occurs in two stages, beginning with a sensation of ejaculatory inevitability. This is triggered by the movement of seminal fluid toward the urethra. In the second stage, regular contractions propel semen through the urethra, and it is expelled through the urinary opening.

During the *resolution* phase, which may last 30 minutes or longer, the person's body returns to its resting state. Men are typically unresponsive to further sexual stimulation for a variable period of time after reaching orgasm. This is known as the *refractory period*. Women, on the other hand, may be able to respond to further stimulation almost immediately. They are capable of experiencing a series of distinct orgasmic responses that are not separated by a period of noticeably lowered excitement (Andersen & Cyranowski, 1995).

Sexual dysfunctions can involve a disruption of any stage of the human sexual response cycle. The following case study, which was described by Barry McCarthy, is concerned with a man who had difficulty controlling the rate at which he progressed from excitement to orgasm. It illustrates some of the most important features of sexual dysfunction.

CASE STUDY

Premature Ejaculation

Margaret and Bill, both in their late twenties, had been married for 2 years, and they had intercourse frequently. Margaret seldom reached orgasm during these experiences, but she was orgasmic during masturbation. The central feature of their problem was the fact that Bill was unable to delay ejaculation for more than a few seconds after insertion.

Unbeknownst to Margaret, Bill had attempted a "do-it-yourself" technique to gain better control [of ejaculation]. He had bought a desensitizing cream he'd read about in a men's magazine and applied it to the glans of his penis 20 minutes before initiating sex. He also masturbated the day before couple sex.

During intercourse he tried to keep his leg muscles tense and think about sports as a way of keeping his arousal in check. Bill was unaware that Margaret felt emotionally shut out during the sex. Bill was becoming more sensitized to his arousal cycle and was worrying about erection. He was not achieving better ejaculatory control, and he was enjoying sex less. The sexual relationship was heading downhill, and miscommunication and frustration were growing.

Margaret had two secrets that she had never shared with Bill. Although she found it easier to be orgasmic with manual stimulation, she had been orgasmic during intercourse with a married man she'd had an affair with a year before meeting Bill. Margaret expressed ambivalent feelings about that relationship. She felt that the man was a very sophisticated lover, and she had been highly aroused and orgasmic with him. Yet, the relationship had been a manipulative one. He'd been emotionally abusive to Margaret, and the relationship had ended when he accused Margaret of giving him herpes and berated her. In fact, it was probably he who gave Margaret the herpes. Margaret was only experiencing herpes outbreaks two or three times a year, but when they did occur, she was flooded with negative feelings about herself, sexuality, and relationships. She initially saw Bill as a loving, stable man who would help rid her of negative feelings concerning sexuality. Instead, he continually disappointed her with the early ejaculation. Bill knew about the herpes but not about her sexual history and strong negative feelings.

Bill was terribly embarrassed about his secret concerning masturbation, which he engaged in on a twice-daily basis. From adolescence on, Bill had used masturbation as his primary means of stress reduction. For him, masturbation was a humiliating secret (he believed married men should not masturbate). The manner in which he masturbated undoubtedly contributed to the early ejaculation pattern. Bill focused only on his penis, using rapid strokes with the goal of ejaculating as quickly as he could. This was both to prevent himself from being discovered and from a desire to "get it over with" as soon as he could and forget about it.

When it came to his personal and sexual life, Bill was inhibited, unsure of himself, and had particularly low sexual self-esteem. As an adolescent, Bill remembered being very interested sexually, but very unsure around girls. Bill's first intercourse at 19 was perceived as a failure because he ejaculated before he could insert his penis in the woman's vagina. He then tried desperately to insert because the young woman urged him to, but he was in the refractory period (a phenomenon Bill did not understand), and so he did not get a firm erection and felt doubly humiliated. (From McCarthy [1989, pp. 151–159]) ■

The case of Bill and Margaret illustrates several important points. First, sexual problems are best defined in terms of the couple rather than the individual persons involved. Classification systems tend to ascribe psychological impairments to one person, but in the case of sexual dysfunction, this decision is usually arbitrary. Bill would be assigned a diagnosis of premature ejaculation, but both he and Margaret were distressed, and both had important concerns about sex.

Second, although problems in sexual behavior clearly involve basic physiological responses and behavioral skills, mental scripts regarding the meaning of sexual behavior are also extremely important. Sexual behavior usually takes place in the context of a close, personal relationship. The partners need to talk to each other about the things they enjoy as well as about their worries. Failure to communicate is often motivated by feelings of guilt and frustration, which can easily escalate over time.

The classification of sexual disorders has changed dramatically during the twentieth century. Before describing the disorders that are included in DSM-IV, we outline briefly some of the clinical and scientific views on sexuality that laid the foundation for our current system.

Brief Historical Perspective

Early medical and scientific approaches to sexual behavior were heavily influenced by religious doctrines and by prevailing cultural values. The exclusive purpose of sexual behavior was assumed to be biological reproduction; anything that varied from that narrow goal was considered to be a form of psychopathology and was usually subject to severe moral and legal sanctions. For example, throughout the eighteenth and nineteenth centuries, masturbation was widely condemned and was generally considered to be responsible for various physical and mental disorders (Bullough, 1976). Medical authorities were more worried about excessive sexuality and inappropriate or unusual sexual activities than they were about a person's subjective dissatisfaction or impaired sexual performance. This was especially true with regard to the sexual experiences of women, who were, in Victorian society, supposed to remain "pure" and asexual (Heiman & Grafton-Becker, 1989).

Early efforts to develop a classification system for sexual problems were primarily concerned with the definition of "normal" behavior and with a description of *sexual perversions*. The most influential system was proposed by Richard von Krafft-Ebing (1840–1902), a professor of psychiatry and neurology at the University of Vienna and a contemporary of Freud. Krafft-Ebing's classification of sexual problems made only brief mention of sexual dysfunctions, in particular erectile impairment and ejaculatory control. The vast majority of his manual was devoted to the so-called perversions, especially sadism, masochism, fetishism, and homosexuality.

The period between 1890 and 1930 saw many crucial changes in the ways in which society viewed sexual behavior (D'Emilio & Freedman, 1988). A significant number of people

▲ Sexual dysfunctions are best defined in terms of the couple rather than individual persons. They are frequently associated with marital distress.

were beginning to think of sex as something other than a simple procreative function. If the purpose of sexual behavior was to foster marital intimacy or to provide pleasure, then interference with that goal might become a legitimate topic of psychological inquiry. Changes in prevailing social attitudes led to a change in the focus of systems for the classification of sexual problems. Over the course of the twentieth century, there has been a trend toward greater tolerance of sexual variation among consenting adult partners and toward increased concern about impairments in sexual performance and experience.

Several leading intellectuals influenced public and professional opinions regarding sexual behavior during the first half of the twentieth century (Hogan, 1990). The work of Alfred Kinsey (1894–1956), a biologist at Indiana University, was especially significant. In keeping with his conscious adherence to scientific methods, Kinsey adopted a behavioral stance, focusing specifically on those experiences that resulted in orgasm. His research largely ignored subjective experience. In their efforts to describe human sexual behavior, Kinsey and his colleagues interviewed 18,000 men and women between 1938 and 1956. The results of this groundbreaking investigation were published in two seminal volumes, one concerned with men (1948) and the other with women (1953).

The incredible diversity of experiences reported by his subjects led Kinsey to reject the distinction between normal and abnormal sexual behavior (Robinson, 1976). He argued that differences among people are quantitative rather than qualitative. For example, Kinsey argued that the distinction between heterosexual and homosexual persons was essentially arbitrary and fundamentally meaningless. His comments regarding sexual dysfunction reflected a similar view. Kinsey believed that low sexual desire was simply a reflection of individual differences in erotic capacity rather than a reflection of psychopathology (Kinsey et al., 1948).

Orgasm and Emotional Satisfaction

The experience of orgasm is sometimes considered to be the ultimate goal of sexual activity. How important is orgasm? And how frequently do most men and women experience orgasm during sexual activities? How do people evaluate the quality of their sexual relationships? These subjective judgments obviously have an

important impact on each person's commitment to a partnership. Dissatisfaction sometimes leads the couple to seek help from a mental health professional. It is therefore useful to know something about the ways in which normal couples evaluate their own sexual activities before we consider specific types of sexual dysfunction.

The National Health and Social Life Survey (NHSLS) collected extensive information about patterns of sexual activity and satisfaction in the general population (see Research Close-Up). Table 12–1 presents the NHSLS results regarding the proportion of people who said that they always had an orgasm during sexual activity with their primary partner during the past year. Several aspects of these data are worth mentioning. First, there is a very large difference between men and women with regard to the experience of orgasm. Only 29 percent of women reported that they always have an orgasm with this specific partner, compared to 75 percent of men. Second, notice that 44 percent of men reported that their partners always had orgasms during sex. This figure is much higher than the rate reported by women themselves. There are several plausible explanations for this discrepancy. Because female orgasm is sometimes less clearly defined than male orgasm, men may misinterpret some events as signs that their partners have had an orgasm. It may also be the case that women sometimes mislead their partners into thinking that they have reached orgasm so that their partners will feel better about their own sexual prowess.

Perhaps the most important aspect of the data in Table 12–1 involves the participants' ratings of physical and emotional satisfaction. Here the differences between men and women are less marked. Physical and emotional satisfaction in a sexual relationship might reasonably be

▲ On the basis of his extensive interviews, Alfred Kinsey argued that the distinction between normal and abnormal sexual behavior was not useful.

TABLE 12–1
Sexual Satisfaction in Self-Reported Primary Partnership During the Previous Year

Response Category	Men (%)	Women (%)
R always had an orgasm with P	75.0	28.6
P always had an orgasm with R	43.5	78.0
R extremely physically satisfied with P	46.6	40.5
R extremely emotionally satisfied with P	41.8	38.7

R = respondent; P = partner.
Source: E. O. Laumann, J. H. Gagnon, R. T. Michael, S. Michaels, 1994, *The Social Organization of Sexuality: Sexual Practices in the United States.* Chicago: University of Chicago Press.

expected to be influenced by the experience of orgasm, but the relations among these variables are complex. A relationship may be considered intimate and satisfying simply because sexual activity occurs, regardless of whether it always results in orgasm. In fact, a large proportion of both men and women indicated that they were extremely satisfied with their partners, on both the physical and emotional dimensions. Notice in particular that, although only 29 percent of women indicated that they always have an orgasm with their partner, 41 percent of women said that they were extremely physically satisfied with their partners. This pattern suggests that the experience of orgasm is only one aspect of sexual satisfaction, especially for women. Other aspects of the relationship, including tenderness, intimacy, and affection, are also critically important (Tiefer, 1988).

RESEARCH CLOSE-UP

Sexual Activity in the General Population

What kinds of sexual behavior do adults in our society typically practice? Many critical public health issues, including plans for preventing the spread of sexually transmitted diseases, such as AIDS, hinge on answers to this question. Information about the sexual experiences of other people also helps us understand our own feelings and impulses. The most comprehensive information on this topic was collected by a team of investigators headed by Robert Michael, an economist, and Edward Laumann, a sociologist, who are both at the University of Chicago, and John Gagnon, a sociologist at the State University of New York at Stony Brook (Laumann, Gagnon, Michael, & Michaels, 1994). Their study, known as the National Health and Social Life Survey (NHSLS), was the first large-scale follow-up to the Kinsey reports.

The NHSLS research team conducted detailed, face-to-face interviews with nearly 3,500 men and women between the ages of 18 and 59 throughout the United States. Several elements of research design contribute to the overall value of the NHSLS data. Perhaps most important, the investigators used a procedure known as *probability sampling*—sampling in which every member of a clearly specified population has a known probability of selection—to identify their participants. This procedure is absolutely essential in survey research. Without it, conclusions cannot be generalized to the population as a whole (see Research Methods in Chapter 16). Probability sampling provides much more useful information than *convenience sampling,* in which investigators rely on whatever group of participants is readily available (such as introductory psychology students, members of various organizations, or the readers of a magazine who voluntarily respond to a questionnaire). Most of the previously available evidence regarding normal sexual activites was based on convenience samples.

The results of the survey paint a somewhat more conservative picture of sexual activity than some people may have expected. For example, monogamy is by far the most common pattern. In the year of the survey, only 16 percent of the participants had more than one sexual partner; 73 percent had only one partner, and 11 percent had no partner. Among the other key findings are the following:

- Married couples have sex more often than single people.

- Married couples reported more physical pleasure and emotional satisfaction from sex than single people did.

- People in younger generations were more likely than people in older generations to have had premarital sex (84 percent for men and 80 percent for women born between 1963 and 1974).

- One-third of the overall sample said they had sex with a partner at least twice a week; another third had sex with a partner a few times a month; and the remaining third had sex with a partner a few times a year or didn't have sexual partners at all.

Lifetime prevalence rates for specific forms of sexual activity are presented in Figure 12–1.

Masturbation is relatively common among both men and women. Approximately 1 out of every 4 men and 1 out of every 10 women reported masturbating at least once a week. Approximately half of the men and women who masturbated indicated that they felt guilty about it. People without religious affiliations reported less guilt than people with strong religious connections. This pattern provides support for the argument that social factors play a role in shaping normal sexual activities and experiences.

The NHSLS questionnaire also asked about four basic sexual techniques involving partners—vaginal intercourse, fellatio, cunnilingus, and anal intercourse. The lifetime prevalence of these techniques for sexual activities with an opposite-gender partner are illustrated in Figure 12–1 (data for same-gender sexual partnerships were analyzed separately). Virtually all of the men (95 percent) and women (97 percent) had experienced vaginal intercourse at some time during their lives. The investigators concluded that the vast majority of heterosexual encounters focus on vaginal intercourse.

Most of the men and women also reported that they had engaged in oral sexual activities (as both the person giving and receiving oral-genital stimulation). However, the percentage of men and women who indicated that their *most recent* sexual activity involved oral sex was much lower. This pattern suggests that although most people have some experience with oral sex, it is not sufficiently common to be considered a defining feature of sexual encounters between men and women (such as kissing and vaginal intercourse).

Regarding anal intercourse, most men and women in the study reported that they had never engaged in this activity. Anal sex has become a source of concern because it presents a relatively high risk for transmission of HIV. Among those people who had experimented with anal sex, relatively few had incorporated it into their usual sexual experiences.

The use of condoms was more frequent among younger, better-educated people. Men and women who had more than one sexual partner in the past year used condoms more frequently than people involved in stable, monogamous relationships. Nevertheless, some people still engaged in relatively high-risk behaviors. Only 40 percent of the people who had sex with four partners in the past year said that they used a condom during their most recent experience with vaginal intercourse. Many people were reluctant to use condoms during the initial stages of a new sexual relationship, even though this is a time when they are more vulnerable to exposure to sexually transmitted diseases.

We describe other aspects of the NHSLS data at various points throughout this chapter. In addition to the data that we have already discussed, the NHSLS provides valuable information about such critical topics as sexual dysfunction and forced sexual activities. Interested readers are referred to *Sex in America: A Definitive Survey* (Michael et al., 1995) for a description of the results of this study that is written for the layperson. ■

Lifetime Prevalence of Sexual Activities (with an opposite-gender partner)

FIGURE 12-1: This graph illustrates the prevalence of various types of sexual activities, based on responses to the NHSLS questionnaire. Note that vaginal intercourse is the most frequent activity, although masturbation and oral sex are also common.

Source: E.O. Laumann, J.H. Gagnon, R.T. Michael, and S. Michaels, 1994, *The Social Organization of Sexuality: Sexual Practices in the United States.* Chicago: University of Chicago Press.

Sexual Dysfunctions

Sexuality represents a complex behavioral process that can easily be upset. The DSM-IV system places primary emphasis on physiological responses and sexual performance leading to orgasm in its classification of sexual dysfunctions. These problems can arise anywhere, from the earliest stages of interest and desire through the climactic release of orgasm. In some cases these problems take the form of inhibitions of sexual response or diminished pleasure. Some people also experience pain during sexual intercourse.

Although they are not part of the official DSM-IV description of these problems, strong negative emotions, such as anger, fear, and resentment, are often associated with sexual problems. In some cases, these emotional states appear before the onset of the sexual problem, and sometimes they develop later. Given the connection that many cultures make between virile sexual performance and "manhood," it is not surprising that men with erectile difficulties are often embarrassed and ashamed. Their humiliation can lead to secondary problems such as anxiety and depression. Similar feelings frequently accompany premature ejaculation and the recognition that a partner's sexual impulses have not been fulfilled. Women who have trouble becoming aroused or reaching orgasm also frequently experience profound frustration and disappointment. The emotional consequences of sexual problems can be devastating for both partners.

The following sections describe the DSM-IV system for classifying various types of sexual dysfunction.

Typical Symptoms and Associated Features

The DSM-IV subdivides sexual dysfunctions into several types (see Table 12–2). Remember that satisfying sexual activity does not always lead to orgasm. Failure to reach orgasm is not considered a disorder unless it is persistent or recurrent and results in marked distress or interpersonal difficulty. The DSM-IV criteria also require that the sexual dysfunction is not better explained by another Axis I disorder (such as major depression) and is not the direct result of a chemical substance (such as alcohol) or a general medical condition. For many types of disorder, the clinician must decide whether the person has engaged in sexual activities that would normally be expected to produce sexual arousal or orgasm. Diagnostic judgments must take into consideration the person's age, as well as the circumstances in which the person is living, such as the presence of a partner, access to privacy, and so on.

Each of the specific types of sexual dysfunction can be characterized in terms of its pattern of onset and context of occurrence. With regard to pattern of onset, the problem can be either *lifelong*, meaning that the problem has been present since the person's first sexual activities, or it can be *acquired*, meaning that the problem developed only after a period of normal functioning. With regard to context of occurrence, the problem can either be *generalized*, meaning that the dysfunction is not limited to certain situations or partners, or *situational*, meaning that the dysfunction is limited to certain situations or partners.

HYPOACTIVE SEXUAL DESIRE DISORDER

One difficulty that was originally recognized as a type of sexual dysfunction by the sex therapist Helen Singer Kaplan (1979) and is becoming an increasingly common reason for referral to a sex clinic is lack of sexual desire, a condition known as **hypoactive sexual desire.** Sexual desire sets the stage for sexual arousal and precedes the phases of the sexual response cycle outlined by Masters and Johnson. Some clinicians refer to sexual desire as the person's willingness to approach or engage in those experiences that will lead to sexual arousal. Inhibited sexual desire is defined in terms of subjective experiences, such as lack of sexual fantasies and lack of interest in sexual experiences. The absence of interest in sex must be both persistent and pervasive to be considered a clinical problem.

How often should a person be interested in sex? There isn't a definite answer to this question. Although the notion of lack of sexual desire makes intuitive sense, the concept is difficult to define clinically (Beck, 1995; Letourneau & O'Donohue, 1993). The absolute frequency with which a person engages in sex cannot be used as a measure of inhibited sexual desire because the central issue is interest—actively seeking out sexual experiences—rather than participation.

TABLE 12-2

Sexual Dysfunctions Listed in DSM-IV

Hypoactive Sexual Desire Disorder: Persistently or recurrently deficient (or absent) sexual fantasies and desire for sexual activity.

Sexual Aversion Disorder: Persistent or recurrent extreme aversion to, and avoidance of, all (or almost all) genital sexual contact with a sexual partner.

Female Sexual Arousal Disorder: Persistent or recurrent inability to attain, or to maintain until completion of the sexual activity, an adequate lubrication-swelling response of sexual excitement.

Male Erectile Disorder: Persistent or recurrent inability to attain or maintain until completion of the sexual activity, an adequate erection.

Female Orgasmic Disorder: Persistent or recurrent delay in, or absence of, orgasm following a normal sexual excitement phase.

Male Orgasmic Disorder: Persistent or recurrent delay in, or absence of, orgasm following a normal sexual excitement phase during sexual activity.

Premature Ejaculation: Persistent or recurrent ejaculation with minimal sexual stimulation before, on, or shortly after penetration and before the person wishes it.

Dyspareunia: Recurrent or persistent genital pain associated with sexual intercourse in either a male or a female.

Vaginismus: Recurrent or persistent involuntary spasm of the musculature of the outer third of the vagina that interferes with sexual intercourse.

For example, some people acquiesce to their partners' demands, even though they would not choose to engage in sexual activities if it were left up to them. In the absence of any specific standard, the identification of hypoactive sexual desire must depend on a clinician's subjective evaluation of the level of desire that is expected given the person's age, gender, marital status, and many other relevant considerations.

A person's appetite for sexual experience is based on many ingredients. These include the spontaneous appearance of sexual thoughts and feelings, the inclination to seek out sexually arousing stimuli, and the capacity to respond positively to sexual advances from a partner. Almost everyone recognizes that sexual desire fluctuates in intensity over time, sometimes dramatically and frequently, for reasons that we do not understand (Levine, 1987). The fact that hypoactive sexual desire is listed in DSM-IV as a type of disorder should not lead us to believe that it is a unitary condition with a simple explanation. It is, in fact, a collection of many different kinds of problems. People who suffer from low levels of sexual desire frequently experience other mental and medical disorders. Perhaps as many as 85 percent of males and 75 percent of females seeking treatment for hypoactive sexual desire report other forms of sexual dysfunction (Donahey & Carroll, 1993). Men and women with low sexual desire also have high rates of mood disorders (Schreiner-Engel & Schiavi, 1986). The mood disorder typically appears before the onset of low sexual desire. It therefore appears likely that many cases of low sexual desire develop after the person has experienced other forms of psychological distress.

SEXUAL AVERSION DISORDER

Kaplan (1988) also noted that some people develop an active aversion to sexual stimuli and begin to avoid these situations altogether. Some people avoid only certain aspects of sexual behavior, such as kissing, intercourse, or oral sex. This reaction is stronger than simple lack of interest. Fear of sexual encounters can occasionally reach intense proportions. This problem might be viewed as a form of panic disorder because it extends well beyond anxiety about sexual performance.

In clinical practice, the distinction between hypoactive sexual desire and **sexual aversion disorder** is not always easy to make. Consider, for example, the following case from our files. The couple sought help at a psychological clinic in the hope that they might improve their sexual relationship.

BRIEF CASE STUDY

Sexual Aversion Disorder

Doug and Jennifer were both 32 years old. They had been married for 5 years, but they had never had sexual intercourse. They cared for each other very much and described themselves as being like brother and sister. Their inability to have intercourse was upsetting to them both for many reasons. Most important was their mutual desire to have children. Doug also felt that their marriage would be stronger and more enjoyable if they were sexually intimate. Jennifer wasn't interested in sexual activity; she never experienced sexual fantasies or erotic thoughts. She did view sex as her duty, however, and she felt guilty about not fulfilling that part of her "marital obligation." Jennifer's primary concern about the relationship involved a different kind of intimacy; she wished that Doug would spend more time with her—talking, taking walks, and doing things together that did not involve sex.

Neither Doug nor Jennifer had been experienced sexually at the time of their marriage. Jennifer was clearly anxious in the presence of stimuli that were sexual in nature, such as movies or books with a sexual theme, but she did not avoid these situations or sexual interactions altogether. She and Doug had engaged in kissing and gentle touching early in their marriage. Jennifer masturbated Doug to orgasm several times, but she felt disgusted at the sight of semen when he ejaculated. Doug had persuaded her to engage in oral sex on a few occasions. She found it unpleasant and was unable to continue long enough for Doug to reach orgasm. They attempted intercourse once, but Jennifer was unable to become aroused and insertion had been impossible.

Doug and Jennifer gradually lost interest in sexual activities. He was extremely busy with his work and said that he no longer thought about sex very often, although he continued to masturbate. Since their failed attempt at intercourse, Doug had also begun to feel less sexually attracted to Jennifer. They eventually entered treatment in order to explore their feelings for each other and to see if they could do anything to salvage their sexual relationship, primarily in the hope that they would be able to have children.

Several weeks after entering therapy, Jennifer reluctantly confided in her therapist that she had been sexually abused by an uncle with whom she had lived for 2 years as a child. He had forced her to perform oral sex several times when she was about 9 years old. She had never told anyone about the abuse— her parents, her aunt, or Doug—for many reasons. She was ashamed of the experience and frightened of what her uncle might do to her. The memories of this experience were still vivid, especially when she attempted to have sex with her husband. ■

Jennifer's aversion to sexual activity was easily understandable in the context of previous abuse. In terms of diagnostic criteria, however, her symptoms were initially difficult to distinguish from hypoactive sexual desire. She originally reported that she was not interested in sex, and she had not avoided all sexual contact with Doug. The symptoms of sexual aversion disorder are often more pronounced than those that were exhibited by Jennifer. In some people, full-blown symptoms of panic attack may be triggered by exposure to sexual stimuli.

MALE ERECTILE DISORDER

Many men experience difficulties either obtaining an erection that is sufficient to accomplish intercourse or maintaining an erection long enough to satisfy themselves and their partners during intercourse. Both problems are examples of **erectile dysfunction.** Men with this problem may report feeling subjectively aroused, but the vascular reflex mechanism fails, and sufficient blood is not pumped to the penis to make it erect. These difficulties can appear at any time prior to orgasm. Some men have trouble achieving an erection during sexual foreplay, whereas others lose their erection around the time of insertion or during intercourse. This phenomenon used to be called *impotence*, but the term has been dropped because of its negative implications.

Erectile dysfunctions can be relatively transient, or they can be more chronic. Some information suggests that, at some point, around half of the adult male population has experienced problems achieving an erection. Occasional experiences of this type are not considered unusual. When they persist and become a serious source of distress to the couple, however, erectile difficulties can lead to serious problems.

FEMALE SEXUAL AROUSAL DISORDER

Sexual arousal can also be impaired in women, but it is somewhat more difficult to describe and identify than is erectile dysfunction in men. Put simply, a woman is said to experience **inhibited sexual arousal** if she cannot either achieve or maintain genital responses, such as lubrication and swelling, that are necessary to complete sexual intercourse. The desire is there, but the physiological responses that characterize sexual excitement are inhibited.

The capacity for intercourse is somewhat less obvious and more difficult to measure for a woman than for a man, whose erect penis usually serves as a signal of readiness (see Research Methods). Investigators who have studied sexual responses in normal women have reported low correlations between self-reports of subjective arousal and physiological measures, such as the amount of vaginal lubrication or vasocongestion (Morokoff, 1989). Among women who experience sexual difficulties, the problem may more often be decreased subjective arousal rather than impaired physiological responses (Morokoff & Heiman, 1980). Therefore inhibitions in sexual arousal must be defined in terms of this self-report dimension as well as in terms of specific genital responses.

▲ Sexual arousal is somewhat more difficult to measure for women than for men. Women's subjective feelings of arousal are not always directly connected to physiological responses.

RESEARCH METHODS

Hypothetical Constructs and Construct Validity

The term *sexual arousal* refers to the state that precedes orgasm. It is defined in terms of two factors: physiological responses, such as vascular engorgement of the genitals; and subjective feelings of pleasure and excitement. Psychologists refer to sexual arousal as a **hypothetical construct**. Many of the concepts that we have discussed in this book are hypothetical constructs: anxiety, depression, psychopathy, and schizophrenia. Hypothetical constructs are theoretical devices. In the field of psychopathology, they refer to events or states that reside within the person and are proposed to help us understand or explain a person's behavior.

Constructs cannot be observed directly, but in order to be scientifically meaningful they must be defined in terms of observable referents (Cronbach & Meehl, 1955; Kimble, 1989). These referents are all associated with the construct, but they are not perfectly related, and the construct is not exhaustively defined by them. For example, an erect penis is not always accompanied by subjective feelings of sexual excitement, and subjective feelings of arousal are not always associated with physiological responses. In other words, the construct of sexual arousal is anchored by feelings and responses that can be measured directly, but it is more than the sum of these parts.

An **operational definition** is a procedure that is used to measure a theoretical construct. Such a definition usually includes measures of the different components of the construct. For men, one obvious component of sexual arousal is penile erection. The most widely accepted procedure for measuring male sexual arousal uses a device called a *penile plethysmograph* (Barker & Howell, 1992; Harris & Rice, 1996). In this procedure, the man places a thin elastic strain gauge around his penis, underneath his clothing. The rubber loop is filled with a column of mercury that changes in its electrical conductance as the circumference of the penis changes. The wire extending from the strain gauge is connected to a plethysmograph, which amplifies the electrical signal passing through the strain gauge and produces a record reflecting changes in penile tumescence.

The *vaginal photometer,* a device shaped like a tampon and inserted into the vagina, is used to measure female sexual arousal. Like the penile strain gauge, the photometer can be placed in position in private and worn underneath clothing during the assessment procedure. As the woman becomes sexually aroused, the walls of the vagina become congested with blood. Vasocongestion causes changes in the amount of red light that can be transmitted through the tissue. The photometer is sensitive to subtle changes in vaginal tissue and is probably most useful in measuring moderate to low levels of sexual arousal (Geer, Heiman, & Leitenberg, 1984).

Clinical scientists must always think carefully about the meaning of their operational definitions. Although the penile strain gauge and the vaginal photometer measure physiological events that are directly related to sexual arousal, the responses that they measure are not the same thing as sexual arousal. They are reflections of the construct, which has many dimensions (McAnulty & Adams, 1992; McConaghy, 1989). One important goal of scientific studies is to determine more specifically how (and when) these physiological measures are related to the other observable referents of sexual arousal. This process will determine the **construct validity** of the penile strain gauge and the vaginal photometer—that is, the extent to which these specific measures produce results that are consistent with the theoretical construct. ∎

PREMATURE EJACULATION

Some men experience problems with the control of ejaculation. They are unable to prolong the period of sexual excitement long enough to complete intercourse. Once they become intensely sexually aroused, they reach orgasm very quickly. How quickly? As we have noted previously, the human sexual response cycle is quite variable in duration. Some couples are able to prolong sexual intercourse for hours; others are satisfied with relatively brief encounters of several minutes' duration.

There have been many attempts to establish specific, quantitative criteria for this condition, known as **premature ejaculation.** None of the attempts has been entirely satisfactory, but certain boundaries identify conditions that can be problematic. If the man ejaculates before or immediately upon insertion, or after only three or four thrusts, almost all clinicians will identify his response as premature ejaculation (Grenier & Byers, 1995; McCarthy, 1989).

Another way to think about premature ejaculation places emphasis on the couple's satisfaction rather than on the amount of time required to reach orgasm. Masters and Johnson (1970) suggested that premature ejaculation might be present if the man is unable to delay ejaculation until his partner reaches orgasm at least 50 percent of the time. Kaplan (1974) placed primary emphasis on the subjective perception of control. She argued that prematurity should be defined in terms of the reflexive nature of the man's orgasm. If progression to orgasm is beyond the man's voluntary control once he reaches an intense level of sexual arousal, Kaplan would conclude that he has a problem with premature ejaculation.

FEMALE ORGASMIC DISORDER

Some women are unable to reach orgasm even though they apparently experience uninhibited sexual arousal. Women who experience orgasmic difficulties may have a strong desire to engage in sexual relations, they may find great pleasure in sexual foreplay, and they may show all the signs of sexual arousal. Nevertheless, they cannot reach the peak erotic experience of orgasm.

Women whose orgasmic impairment is generalized have never experienced orgasm by any means. Situational orgasmic difficulties occur when the woman is able to reach orgasm in some situations but not in others. That might mean that she is orgasmic during masturbation but not during intercourse, or perhaps she is orgasmic with one partner but not with another.

Orgasmic disorder is somewhat difficult to define in relation to inhibited sexual arousal because the various components of female sexual response are more difficult to measure than are erection and ejaculation in the male. One experienced researcher has described this issue in the following way:

> In my experience, many women who have never reached orgasm present the following set of symptoms: They report that when engaging in intercourse they do not have difficulty lubricating and experience no pain. However, they report no genital sensations (hence the term *genital anesthesia*) and do not appear to know what sexual arousal is. Typically they do not masturbate and often have never masturbated. They do not experience the phenomenon that a sexually functional woman would call sexual desire. . . . Most of these women seek therapy because they have heard from others or have read that they are missing something, rather than because they themselves feel frustrated. (Morokoff, 1989, p. 74)

PAIN DURING SEX

Some people experience persistent genital pain during or after sexual intercourse, which is known as **dyspareunia.** The problem can occur in either men or women, although it is considered to be much more common in women (Quevillon, 1993). The severity of the discomfort can range from mild irritation following sexual activities to searing pain during insertion of the penis or intercourse (Lazarus, 1989). The pains may be sharp and intense, or they may take the form of a dull, aching sensation; they may be experienced as coming from a superficial area near the barrel of the vagina or as being located deep in the lower abdominal area; they may be intermittent or persistent.

The experience of severe genital pain is often associated with other forms of sexual dysfunction. Not surprisingly, many women with dyspareunia develop a lack of interest in, or an aversion toward, sexual activity.

Access to the vagina is controlled by the muscles surrounding its entrance. Some women find that whenever penetration of the vagina is attempted, these muscles snap tightly shut, preventing insertion of any object. This involuntary muscular spasm, known as **vaginismus,** prevents sexual intercourse as well as other activities, such as vaginal examinations and the insertion of tampons. Women with vaginismus may be completely sexually responsive in other respects, fully capable of arousal and orgasm through manual stimulation of the clitoris. Women who seek therapy for this condition often report that they are afraid of intercourse and vaginal penetration (Beck, 1993). The problem can be severe or partial in nature. Some couples report that a mild form of vaginismus occurs from time to time, making intercourse difficult and sometimes painful.

Epidemiology

Surveys conducted among the general population indicate that various forms of sexual dysfunction are relatively common (Ernst et al., 1993; Rosen et al., 1993). We must keep in mind, however, that this impression is based on self-report questionnaires and judgments made by laypersons, which are less technical than those made by experts. Diagnoses made by experienced therapists would take into account the person's age, the context of the person's life, and whether the person had experienced stimulation that would ordinarily be expected to lead to sustained arousal and orgasm. Clinicians would also take into consideration the amount of distress and interpersonal difficulty associated with the problem before arriving at a diagnosis of sexual dysfunction. We must therefore be cautious in our interpretations of these survey data.

The most extensive set of information regarding sexual problems among people living in the community comes from the National Health and Social Life Survey (NHSLS; refer to Research Close-Up). Each participant was asked whether, during the past 12 months, he or she had experienced "a period of *several months or more* when you lacked interest in having sex; had trouble achieving or maintaining an erection or (for women) had trouble lubricating; were unable to come to a climax; came to a climax too quickly; or experienced physical pain during intercourse." For each item, the person was asked for a simple yes or no response. Figure 12–2 indicates the overall percentage of men and

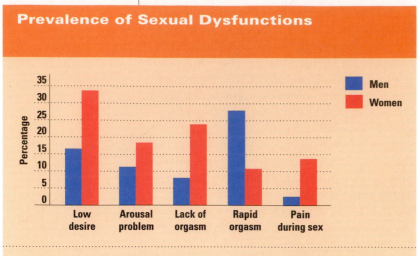

Prevalence of Sexual Dysfunctions

FIGURE 12-2: This graph shows the percentage of NHSLS respondents who reported having sexual difficulties at some time during the previous 12 months. Note the differences in the problems reported by men and women.

women who indicated that they had experienced each of these specific problems. There are obviously significant gender differences in the prevalence of all types of problems. Premature ejaculation is the most frequent form of male sexual dysfunction, affecting almost 1 out of every 3 adult men. All the other forms of

sexual dysfunction are reported more often by women. One-third of women said that they lacked interest in sex, and almost one-quarter indicated that they experienced a period of several months during which they were unable to reach orgasm.

Survey data can be supplemented with information on the prevalence of specific types of sexual dysfunction among people who seek professional treatment for sexual problems (Benet & Melman, 1995; Spector & Carey, 1990). These reports indicate several trends:

- Orgasmic and erectile dysfunction have become more frequent complaints among people seeking treatment.
- Premature ejaculation has become less common as the presenting problem among people seeking treatment for sexual dysfunction.
- The frequency of desire disorders as presenting problems in sex clinics has increased.
- Recently, males have outnumbered females as the person with the presenting problem when couples seek treatment.

SEXUAL BEHAVIOR ACROSS THE LIFE SPAN

Sexual behavior changes with age. Masters and Johnson devoted considerable attention to this topic in their original studies. Their data challenged the myth that older adults are not interested in, or capable of performing, sexual behaviors. The NHSLS data also indicate that many people remain sexually active later in life. Figure 12–3 presents information regarding the percentage of men and women who did not have sex with a partner in the past year. Gender differences become marked in the late fifties, when rates of inactivity increase dramatically for women. Between the ages 70 to 74, 65 percent of men are still sexually active, compared to only 30 percent of women. These differences may be, at least partially, the result of biological factors that are part of the aging process. They may also reflect the influence of a cultural prejudice against sexual activity among older women.

Differences between younger and older people are mostly a matter of degree. As men get older, they tend to achieve erections more slowly, but they can often maintain erections for longer periods of time. Older men find it more difficult to regain an erection if it is lost before orgasm. As women get older, vaginal lubrication

Sexual Activity Across the Life Span

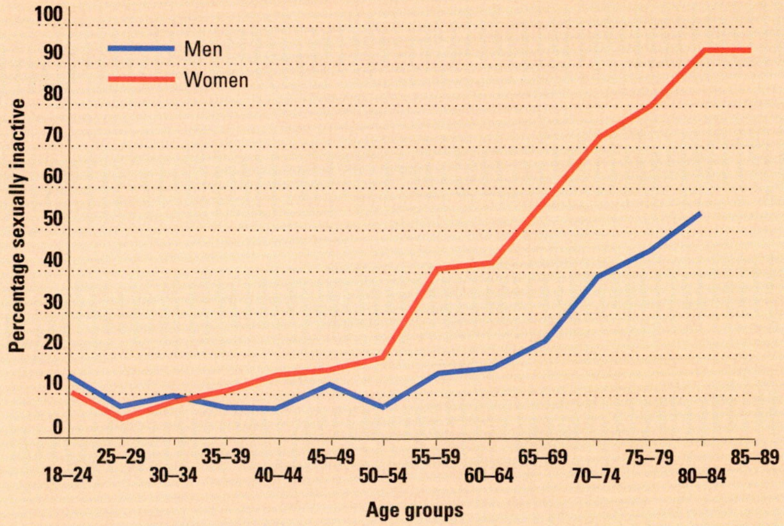

FIGURE 12-3: This figure shows the percentages of male and female NHSLS respondents in each age group who reported being sexually inactive during the previous year.

may occur at a slower rate, but the response of the clitoris remains essentially unchanged. The intensity of the subjective experience of orgasm is decreased for older men and women. For both men and women, healthy sexual responsiveness is most likely to be maintained among those who have been sexually active as younger adults.

The prevalence of certain types of sexual dysfunction increases among the elderly, particularly among men (Feldman et al., 1994). In the NHSLS, for example, the proportion of men reporting erectile problems increased from 6 percent in the 18–24 age range to 20 percent in the 55–59 age range. In contrast, several types of sexual problems actually declined in frequency among older women. Women in the 55–59 age range were less likely than women between the ages of 18 and 24 to report pain during sex or inability to reach orgasm, though they did report a slight increase in trouble with lubrication during sexual activity.

The relation between sexual experience and aging is closely related to other health problems, which increase with age. People who rate their health as being excellent have many fewer sexual problems than people who rate their health as being only fair or poor (Laumann et al., 1994).

Etiology

At each stage of the sexual response cycle, a person's behavior is determined by the interaction of many biological and psychological factors, ranging from vasocongestion in the genitals to complex cognitive events involving the perception of sexual stimuli and the interpretation of sexual meanings. Interference with this system at any point can result in serious problems. In the following pages we review some of the factors that contribute to the etiology of various types of sexual dysfunction.

BIOLOGICAL FACTORS

The experience of sexual desire is partially controlled by biological factors. Among males, sexual desire is influenced by sex hormones, especially testosterone (Davidson, 1990). Men with inadequate levels of sex hormones show an inhibited response to sexual fantasies, but they are still able to have erections in response to viewing explicit erotic films (Bancroft & Wu, 1983). The influence of male sex hormones on sexual behavior is therefore thought to be on sexual appetite rather than on sexual performance. This process probably involves a threshold level of circulating testosterone (Bancroft, 1989). In other words, sexual appetite is impaired if the level of testosterone falls below a particular point (close to the bottom of the laboratory normal range), but above that threshold, fluctuations in testosterone levels will not be associated with changes in sexual desire. The reduction of male sex hormones over the life span probably explains, at least in part, the apparent decline in sexual desire among elderly males.

Among the various types of sexual problems, erectile dysfunction is most often biologically based. We must remember, however, that the distinction between psychological and biological causes is often arbitrary. It is not clear that this simple dichotomy is useful, and in many cases the etiology involves some combination or interaction of many factors (LoPiccolo, 1985).

Therapists at one clinic for sexual disorders reported that more than half the cases of erectile dysfunction they treated could be attributed to vascular, neurological, or hormonal impairment (Melman, Tiefer, & Pedersen, 1988). Erection is the direct result of a threefold increase in blood flow to the penis. Thus it is not surprising that vascular diseases, which may affect the amount of blood reaching the penis, are likely to result in erectile difficulties. Neurological diseases, such as epilepsy and multiple sclerosis, can also produce erectile difficulties, because erection depends on spinal reflexes. Diabetes may be the most common neurologically based cause of impaired erectile responsiveness (Wincze & Carey, 1991).

Other factors that can influence a man's erectile response include various drugs (McCabe et al., 1996). One interesting set of results indicates that men who smoke cigarettes are more likely to experience erectile difficulties than are men in the general population (see Mohr & Beutler, 1990). Many other drugs, including alcohol and marijuana, may have negative effects on sexual arousal. Medication used to treat hypertension can impair erectile responsiveness, and so can various types of antipsychotic and antidepressant drugs.

Many biological factors and physiological diseases can impair a woman's ability to become sexually aroused. Various types of neurological disorder, pelvic disease, and hormonal dysfunction can interfere with the process of vaginal swelling and lubrication. Unfortunately, relatively little research has been conducted on problems of sexual arousal in women

(Andersen & Cyranowski, 1995). These mechanisms are therefore not well understood.

Inhibited orgasm, in both men and women, is sometimes caused by the abuse of alcohol and other drugs. The problem may improve if the person is able to stop drinking and maintain a stable period of sobriety (Schiavi et al., 1995). Orgasm problems can also be associated with the use of prescribed forms of medication. For example, many people who take Prozac (fluoxetine) for the treatment of depression experience delayed ejaculation and orgasmic dysfunction as a side effect (Rothschild, 1995; Segraves, 1988).

SOCIAL FACTORS

Although sexual desire is rooted in a strong biological foundation, social variables also play an important role in the determination of which stimuli a person will find arousing. John Gagnon, Edward Laumann, and William Simon have argued that sexual desire and arousal are determined by mental scripts that we learn throughout childhood and adolescence (Gagnon & Simon, 1973; Laumann & Gagnon, 1995). According to this view, the social meaning of an event is of paramount importance in releasing the biological process of sexual arousal. Both members of the potential couple must recognize similar cues, defining the situation as potentially sexual in nature, before anything is likely to happen.

Beliefs and attitudes toward sexuality, as well as the quality of interpersonal relationships, have an important influence on the development of low sexual desire, especially among women. Women seeking treatment for hypoactive sexual desire report negative perceptions of their parents' attitudes regarding sexual behavior and the demonstration of affection. In comparison to a group of normal women, they also indicate that they feel less close to their husbands, they have fewer romantic feelings, and they are less attracted to their husbands. The quality of the relationship is an important factor to consider with regard to low sexual desire (Stuart, Hammond, & Pett, 1987).

Culturally determined attitudes toward sexual feelings and behaviors can also have a dramatic impact on women's ability to become sexually aroused (Heiman, 1983). Some societies openly encourage female sexuality; others foster a more repressive atmosphere. Within U.S. culture, there are tremendous variations with regard to women's ability to experience and express their sexuality, and some studies have found that different attitudes are associated with different levels of sexual responsiveness. For example, many women feel guilty about having sexual fantasies, in spite of the fact that such fantasies are extremely common. Women who feel guilty about fantasizing while they are having intercourse are more likely to be sexually dissatisfied and to encounter sexual problems, including arousal difficulties (Cado & Leitenberg, 1990).

Social factors are also related to orgasmic difficulties. For example, women who were born in more recent decades are more likely to reach orgasm successfully than are women born in previous decades (Morokoff, 1978). This pattern reflects the fact that public attitudes toward female sexuality, and especially the expectation that women can and should experience orgasm, have changed progressively over the past several decades. Evidence that is consistent with this general hypothesis has been reported by a study that compared patterns of sexual arousal in *anorgasmic* women—those who experience inhibited orgasm—and orgasmic women (Kelly, Strassberg, & Kircher, 1990). The most important factors contributing to failure to reach orgasm involved negative attitudes, feelings of guilt, and failure to communicate effectively, rather than the simple practice of engaging in particular types of stimulation.

PSYCHOLOGICAL FACTORS

Among the psychological factors contributing to impaired sexual arousal, Masters and Johnson (1970) gave primary emphasis to *performance anxiety*, or fear of failure. People who have experienced inhibited sexual arousal on one or two occasions may be likely to have further problems to the degree that these difficulties make them more self-conscious or apprehensive regarding their ability to become aroused in future sexual encounters. Several prominent and experienced sex therapists (for example, Kaplan, 1974) have assumed that anxiety and sexual arousal are incompatible emotional states. People who are anxious will presumably be less responsive to sexual stimuli. And men who have sexual arousal disorders are more likely to report feeling high levels of performance anxiety (Ackerman & Carey, 1995).

Recent evidence suggests that anxiety disrupts sexual performance to the extent that it alters certain perceptual and attentional processes. These cognitive factors have been studied by David Barlow and his colleagues, who have examined the relation between performance concerns and interfering thoughts in men with erectile difficulties. In one study (Cranston-Cuebas et al., 1993), they compared the responses of sexually dysfunctional men with those of control subjects in laboratory settings. Subjects in these studies viewed explicit, erotic films while wearing a penile strain gauge. The experimenters manipulated several variables, such as the subjects' anxiety levels and the extent to which they were distracted by nonsexual stimuli. The results indicated that men who experience erectile failure are less sexually responsive when they are confronted with demands to become sexually aroused; sexually functional men show the opposite effect. Dysfunctional men also tend to be less aware of their level of sexual arousal, and they are more likely to experience negative emotions in the presence of erotic stimuli. The results of the studies by Barlow and coworkers suggest that sexual arousal problems may be mediated by a feedback process in which unpleasant feelings lead to self-distraction and avoidance of erotic stimuli (Barlow, 1986; Cranston-Cuebas & Barlow, 1990).

Relationship factors represent another important consideration in the etiology of sexual dysfunction. Couples that experience communication problems, power conflicts, and an absence of intimacy and trust are more likely than others to experience sexual problems. Lack of assertiveness and lack of comfort talking about sexual activities and pleasures are associated with various types of female sexual dysfunction (Rosen & Leiblum, 1995).

Finally, previous harmful or traumatic experiences can also have an important effect on various aspects of sexual interests and arousal. As we have already discussed in the case of Jennifer, a previous history of sexual abuse can lead to sexual aversion, and it can interfere with a woman's ability to become sexually aroused (Becker, 1989). Premature ejaculation and low sexual desire in men have also been linked to long-lasting, adverse relationships with adults during childhood (Kinzl et al., 1996).

Treatment

Publication of their book *Human Sexual Inadequacy* by Masters and Johnson in 1970 represented a major turning point in the treatment of sexual dysfunctions. Previously, psychological interventions aimed at these problems had focused on long-term therapies directed toward helping couples understand the intrapsychic factors that presumably caused their problems. Masters and Johnson were pioneers in developing

and popularizing a short-term, skills-based approach. Hundreds of couples who visited their clinic in St. Louis went through a 2-week course of assessment and therapy in which they became more familiar with their bodies, learned to communicate more effectively with their partners, and received training in procedures designed to help them diminish their fears about sexuality. The results of this treatment program were very positive and quickly spawned a burgeoning industry of psychosocial treatment for sexual dysfunction.

PSYCHOLOGICAL PROCEDURES

Psychological treatments for sexual dysfunction address several of the etiological factors discussed earlier, especially negative attitudes toward sexuality, failure to engage in effective sexual behaviors, and deficits in communication skills. Sex therapy centers around three primary types of activity: sensate focus and scheduling; education and cognitive restructuring; and communication training (Rosen & Leiblum, 1995; Wincze & Carey, 1991).

The cornerstone of sex therapy is known as **sensate focus,** a procedure developed by Masters and Johnson. Sensate focus involves a series of simple exercises in which the couple spends time in a quiet, relaxed setting, learning to touch each other. They may start with tasks as simple as holding hands or giving each other back rubs. The rationale for sensate focus hinges on the recognition that people with sexual problems must learn to focus on erotic sensations rather than on performance demands. The goal is to help them become more comfortable with this kind of physical sharing and intimacy, to learn to relax and enjoy it, and to talk to each other about what feels good and what does not.

The related facet of psychological approaches to treating sexual dysfunction is *scheduling*. This is, in fact, closely related to sensate focus because the technique of sensate focus requires that people schedule time for sex. Couples need a quiet, relaxed, and private environment in order to engage in pleasurable and satisfying sexual behavior.

The second major aspect of sex therapy involves education and cognitive restructuring—changing the way in which people think about sex. In many cases the therapist needs to help the couple correct mistaken beliefs and attitudes about sexual behavior. Examples are the belief that intercourse is the only true form of sex, that foreplay is an adolescent interest that most adults can ignore, and that simultaneous orgasm is the

▲ **William Masters and Virginia Johnson conducted groundbreaking research on the human sexual response cycle. They have also been pioneers in the field of treatment for sexual dysfunction.**

ultimate goal of intercourse. Providing information about sexual behaviors in the general population can often help alleviate people's guilt and anxiety surrounding their own experiences. Some people are relieved to know that they are not the only ones who fantasize about various kinds of sexual experiences, or that the fact that they fantasize about these things does not mean that they are going to be compelled to behave in deviant ways.

The final element of treatment for sexual dysfunction is communication training. This is another technique that was emphasized by Masters and Johnson in their early work with sexually dysfunctional couples. Many different studies have indicated that people with sexual dysfunction often have deficits in communication skills (for example, Kelly et al., 1990). They find it difficult to talk to their partners about matters involving sex, and they are especially impaired in the ability to tell their partners what kinds of things they find sexually arousing and what kinds of things turn them off. Therefore sex therapists often employ structured training procedures aimed at improving the ways in which couples talk to each other.

The outcome results of psychological treatment programs for sexual disorders have been quite positive. Initial reports from Masters and Johnson's clinic were especially glowing. One summary of their results reported an overall success rate of 85 percent for male patients and 78 percent for female patients. These positive findings offered hope to many couples who had experienced serious difficulties, as well as inspiration to other therapists who became interested in this area of service.

This initial optimism has subsequently been tempered by other studies that have reported less positive results (such as Bancroft et al., 1986).

Important questions have also been raised about the adequacy of the research methods employed in Masters and Johnson's outcome studies (Cole, 1985; Warner & Bancroft, 1986). The overall conclusion is still that psychological treatments for sexual dysfunction are frequently successful (see LoPiccolo & Stock, 1986; O'Donohue & Geer, 1993).

BIOLOGICAL TREATMENTS

Biological treatments are also useful in the treatment of sexual dysfunctions. This is especially true for severe forms of erectile disorder, the most frequent sexual problem for which men seek professional help. One procedure involves surgically inserting a penile implant (or prosthesis), which can be used to make the penis rigid during intercourse (Melman & Tiefer, 1992). Several devices have been used. One option is a semirigid silicone rod that the man can bend into position for intercourse. Another device is hydraulic in nature and can be inflated for the purpose of sexual activity. The man squeezes a small pump, which forces fluid into the inflatable cylinder and produces an erection. The inflatable device is preferred by partners, but it is also more expensive and can lead to more frequent postsurgical complications, such as infection.

Various kinds of medication have been used successfully in the treatment of sexual dysfunction. For example, yohimbine hydrochloride, a drug that enhances the release of norepinephrine, has been shown to be effective in treating men with erectile dysfunction (Mann et al., 1996). Other types of medication that focus on dopamine and serotonin are promising alternatives for the treatment of erectile dysfunction (Rosen & Leiblum, 1995).

Paraphilias

In certain extreme forms of unusual sexual behavior, called *paraphilias*, sexual arousal is associated with atypical stimuli, and the person is preoccupied with or consumed by these activities. Literally translated, paraphilia means "love" (*philia*) "beyond the usual" (*para*). This term refers to conditions that were formerly called perversions or sexual deviations. According to DSM-IV, the central features of all paraphilias

are persistent sexual urges and fantasies that are associated with (1) nonhuman objects, (2) suffering or humiliation of oneself or one's partner, or (3) children or other nonconsenting persons. In the following pages we summarize a few of the most common types of paraphilias, and we consider some of the factors that might influence the development of unusual sexual preferences.

Typical Symptoms and Associated Features

People are capable of becoming sexually aroused by a wide range of stimuli and activities. Some are quite common; others are unusual and perhaps startling. For most people, novel erotic intentions remain limited to fantasies. One hundred years ago, many psychiatrists considered any type of sexual behavior other than heterosexual intercourse to be pathological. Contemporary researchers and clinicians have expanded the boundaries of normal behavior to include a much broader range of sexual behavior. A large proportion of men and women engage in sexual fantasies and mutually consenting behaviors such as oral sex. These experiences enhance their relationships without causing problems (Laumann et al., 1994).

Problems with sexual appetites arise when a pattern develops involving a long-standing, unusual erotic preoccupation that is highly arousing, coupled with a pressure to act on the erotic fantasy. The diagnosis of paraphilia is made only if the person has acted on the urges or is distressed by them. Some people are able to become sexually aroused only by using paraphilic fantasies or stimuli. Others find that they are usually able to respond sexually to "normal" stimuli, and their paraphilic preferences emerge only intermittently, such as during periods of stress. The DSM-IV requires that the erotic preoccupation must have lasted at least 6 months before the person would meet diagnostic criteria for a paraphilia. People with these problems seldom seek treatment unless their behaviors lead to conflict with sexual partners or with other members of society.

It is actually somewhat misleading, or imprecise, to say that paraphilias are defined in terms of reactions to unusual stimuli. The central problem is that sexual arousal is dependent on images that are detached from reciprocal, loving relationships with another adult (Levine, Risen, & Althof, 1990; McConaghy, 1994). Themes of aggression, violence, and hostility are common in paraphilic fantasies, as are impulses involving strangers or unwilling partners. For example, a man might become sexually aroused by images of displaying his erect penis to unsuspecting women, making obscene phone calls, rubbing his genitals against women in a crowded bus, or fondling small children. Rather than focusing on whether the stimuli are common or uncommon, some experts place principal emphasis on the lack of human intimacy that is associated with many forms of paraphilias (Marshall et al., 1996).

Compulsion and lack of flexibility are also important features of paraphilic behaviors. Paraphilias may occupy large amounts of time and consume much of the person's energy. In that sense, they are similar to the addictions. People with paraphilic disorders are not simply aroused by unusual images or fantasies. Their choice of sexual behaviors does not appear to be voluntary. They feel *compelled* to engage in certain acts that may be personally degrading or harmful to others, in spite of the fact that these actions are often repulsive to others and are sometimes illegal. The following case describes some of the central features of paraphilias.

BRIEF CASE STUDY

Paraphilia

For the past 40 years, Jon has masturbated to images of barely clad women violently wrestling each other. Periodically throughout his marriage, he has tried to involve his wife in wrestling matches with her friends and, eventually, with their adolescent daughter. When Jon was drunk, he occasionally embarrassed his wife by trying to pick fights between her and other women. On summer vacations, he sometimes jokingly suggested the women wrestle. During much of his sober life, however, his daydreams of women wrestling were private experiences that preoccupied only him. He amassed a collection of magazines and videotapes depicting women wrestling, to which he would resort when driven by the need for excitement.

Jon presented for help with his inability to maintain his erection with his wife for intercourse. With the exception of procreational sex, he was not able to consummate his long marriage. He was able to (become) erect if his wife described herself wrestling other women while he stimulated his penis in front of her, but he always lost his erection when intercourse was attempted. (Levine, Risen, & Althof, 1990) ■

This case illustrates the way in which paraphilias can interfere with a person's life, especially relationships with other people. Jon's preoccupation with fantasies of women wrestling led him to say and do things that disrupted his marriage and his friendships with other people. Many people with paraphilias experience sexual dysfunction involving desire, arousal, or orgasm during conventional sexual behavior with a partner. This feature is not always present, and it is not included as part of the official diagnostic criteria for paraphilias in DSM-IV. It is, nevertheless, an important consequence of the disorder. The wives of men with paraphilias frequently protest that their husbands are not interested in their sexual relationship. In fact, the husband may be actively engaged in frequent masturbation to paraphilic fantasies. Cases of this sort present an interesting diagnostic challenge to the clinician, who must distinguish a paraphilia from what might otherwise appear to be low sexual desire.

Several researchers have noted that men with paraphilias can typically be described as timid, low in self-esteem, and lacking in social skills (Blair & Lanyon, 1981; Bradford, Bloomberg, & Bourget, 1988). It is, of course, difficult to know whether these characteristics are traits that set the stage for the development of paraphilias or whether they are consequences associated with the performance of sexual behaviors that are considered repugnant by society.

▼ Some gay men who dress in women's clothes refer to themselves as "drag queens." This is different from transvestic fetishism, which applies only to heterosexual men whose cross-dressing is associated with intense, sexually arousing fantasies or urges.

Classification of Paraphilias

Several kinds of paraphilias are described in DSM-IV. Although they are listed as distinct disorders, it might be more useful to think of paraphilia as one diagnostic category, with the variations listed in DSM-IV representing subtypes of this single disorder (Frances, First, & Pincus, 1995). The primary types of paraphalias described in the following pages are the ones most often seen in clinics that specialize in the treatment of sexual disorders. Not surprisingly, they are also the ones that frequently lead to a person being arrested.

FETISHISM

Anthropologists use the word *fetish* to describe an object that is believed to have magical powers to protect or help its owner. In psychopathology, **fetishism** refers to the association of sexual arousal with nonliving objects. The range of objects that can become associated with sexual arousal is virtually unlimited, but fetishism most often involves women's underwear, shoes and boots, or products made out of rubber or leather (Junginger, 1997; Mason, 1997). The person may go to great lengths, including burglary, to obtain certain kinds of fetish objects.

People who fit the description of fetishism typically masturbate while holding, rubbing, or smelling the fetish object. Particular sensory qualities of the object—texture, visual appearance, and smell—can be very important in determining whether or not the person finds it arousing. In addition to holding or rubbing the object, the person may wear, or ask his sexual partner to wear, the object during sexual activity. The person may be unable to become sexually aroused in the absence of the fetish object.

An intense sexual attraction to specific body parts (most often legs or feet, and excluding genitals, breasts, and buttocks) is known as *partialism*. Many experts believe that partialism is a form of fetishism (de Silva, 1993). In DSM-IV, partialism is excluded from fetishism and listed in a miscellaneous category called "paraphilias not otherwise specified" (see Table 12–3).

TRANSVESTIC FETISHISM

A *transvestite* is a person who dresses in the clothing of the other gender. In DSM-IV, **transvestic fetishism** is defined as cross-dressing for the purpose of sexual arousal. It has been described almost exclusively among heterosexual men and should not be confused with the behavior of some gay men known as *drag queens* (for whom cross-dressing has a very different purpose and meaning). People who engage in transvestic fetishism usually keep a collection of female clothes that are used to cross-dress. Some wear only a single article of women's clothing, such as female underwear, covered by male clothing. Others dress completely as women, including makeup, jewelry, and accessories. Cross-dressing may be done in public or only in private. The person masturbates while he is cross-dressed, often imagining himself to be a male as well as the female object of his own sexual fantasy. Aside from their interest in cross-dressing, men with transvestic fetishism are unremarkably masculine in their interests, occupations, and other behaviors. Most of these men get married and have children (Schott, 1995).

The description of transvestic fetishism in DSM-IV suggests that the diagnosis should be ruled out if the cross-dressing occurs exclusively during gender identity disorder. In fact, there is sometimes a complicated relationship between these conditions (Zucker & Blanchard, 1997). Transvestic fetishism usually begins with pretend or secretive cross-dressing during childhood or early adolescence, although these boys are not noted to be particularly feminine in their other behaviors or interests. The motivation for cross-dressing may change gradually over time, with sexual arousal being replaced by a feeling of increased comfort, tension reduction, or relief of a depressed mood. For some men, this process may eventually lead to feelings of dissatisfaction with being male. They may eventually want to live permanently as women. These men, who develop persistent discomfort with their gender role or identity, would be assigned a subtype diagnosis of *transvestic fetishism with gender dysphoria*.

SEXUAL MASOCHISM

People who become sexually aroused when they are subjected to experiencing pain or embarrassment are called masochists. The DSM-IV defines **sexual masochism** as recurrent, intense sexually arousing fantasies, urges, or impulses involving being humiliated, beaten, bound, or otherwise made to suffer. (The experience must be real, not simulated.) People may act on these impulses by themselves or with a partner. In some large cities, clubs

TABLE 12-3

Other Types of Paraphilias

Name	Focus of Sexual Urges and Fantasies
Telephone scatologia	Obscene phone calls
Necrophilia	Corpses
Partialism	One specific part of the body
Zoophilia	Animals
Coprophilia	Feces
Klismaphilia	Enemas
Urophilia	Urine
Stigmatophilia	Piercing; marking body; tattoos

cater to the sexual interests of masochistic men and women, who pay people to punish and abuse them. The goal is usually orgasm, but some people find the experience sexually satisfying without reaching orgasm (Ernulf & Innala, 1995).

The person may become aroused by being bound, blindfolded, spanked, pinched, whipped, verbally abused, forced to crawl and bark like a dog, or in some other way made to experience pain or feelings of shame and disgrace. One relatively common masochistic fantasy takes the form of being forced to display one's naked body to other people. Masochists desire certain types of pain (which are carefully controlled to remain within specified limits, usually unpleasant but not agonizing), but they also go to great lengths to avoid injury during their contrived, often ritualized experiences (Stoller, 1991). They do not enjoy, and are not immune to, painful experiences that lie outside these limited areas of their lives.

Many people who engage in masochistic sexual practices are highly educated and occupationally successful (Levitt, Moser, & Jamison, 1994). Masochists tend to be disproportionately represented among the privileged groups in society. This pattern leads to the suggestion that masochism may be motivated by an attempt to escape *temporarily* from the otherwise constant burden of maintaining personal control and pursuing self-esteem (Baumeister & Butler, 1997).

THE FAR SIDE © 1990, 1996 FARWORKS, INC./Dist. by UNIVERSAL PRESS SYNDICATE.
Reprinted with permission. All rights reserved.

▲ This photo shows the staff at a bondage club in Hollywood. The patrons of such clubs are often highly educated and occupationally successful.

SEXUAL SADISM

Someone who derives pleasure by inflicting physical or mental pain on other people is called a *sadist*. The term is based on the writings of the Marquis de Sade, whose novels described the use of torture and cruelty for erotic purposes. The DSM-IV defines **sexual sadism** in terms of intense, sexually arousing fantasies, urges, or behaviors that involve the psychological or physical suffering of a victim. Sadistic fantasies often involve asserting dominance over the victim; the experience of power and control may be as important as inflicting pain (Hucker, 1997). Some people engage in sadistic sexual rituals with a consenting partner (who may be a sexual masochist) who willingly suffers pain or humiliation. Others act on sadistic sexual urges with nonconsenting partners. In some cases, the severity of the sadistic behaviors escalates over time.

EXHIBITIONISM

The DSM-IV defines **exhibitionism** in the following way: "Over a period of at least 6 months, recurrent, intense sexually arousing fantasies, sexual urges, or behaviors involving exposure of one's genitals to an unsuspecting stranger" (p. 526). This behavior is also known as *indecent exposure*. Many different patterns of behavior fit into this category. About half of these men have erections while exposing themselves, and some masturbate at the time. The others usually masturbate shortly after the experience while fantasizing about the victim's reaction. Their intent usually involves a desire to shock the observer, but sometimes they harbor fantasies that the involuntary observer will become sexually aroused. They rarely attempt to touch or otherwise molest their victims, who are usually women or children (Maletzky, 1997; Murphy, 1997).

Exhibitionism is almost exclusively a male disorder. Most exhibitionists begin to expose themselves when they are teenagers or in their early twenties. As adults, most are either married or living with a sexual partner. Exhibitionism is seldom an isolated behavior; men who engage in this type of behavior tend to do it quite frequently (Abel & Osborn, 1992).

VOYEURISM

The focus of sexual arousal in **voyeurism** is the act of observing an unsuspecting person, usually a stranger, who is naked, in the process of disrobing, or engaging in sexual activity. Many people, especially men, are sexually aroused by the sight of people who are partially clad or naked. As part of a more broadly based, flexible pattern of sexual arousal aimed at a reciprocal, consenting relationship with another adult, this type of behavior is not considered abnormal. The focus of sexual arousal in voyeurism is much more narrow. Voyeurs are not aroused by watching people who know that they are being observed. The process of looking ("peeping") is arousing in its own right. The person might fantasize about having a sexual relationship with the people who are being observed, but direct contact is seldom sought. In fact, the secret nature of the observation and the risk of discovery may contribute in an important way to the arousing nature of the situation. The voyeur reaches orgasm by masturbating during observation or later while remembering what he saw. Most keep their distance from the victim and are not dangerous, but there are exceptions to this rule (King, 1996).

FROTTEURISM

Most people can become sexually aroused through close physical contact with other people, such as dancing with someone whom they find sexually attractive. This contact is not, however, the exclusive goal of the activity. In **frotteurism,** a person who is fully clothed becomes sexually aroused by touching or rubbing his genitals against other, nonconsenting people. The frotteur usually chooses crowded places, such as sidewalks and public transportation, so that he can easily escape arrest. He either rubs genitals against the victim's thighs and buttocks or fondles her genitalia or breasts.

Like exhibitionism, frotteurism is a high-frequency form of paraphilia; interviews with people being treated for frotteurism indicate that they may engage in hundreds of individual paraphilic acts (Abel et al., 1987). People who engage in frotteurism seek to escape as quickly as possible after touching or rubbing against the other person. They are not seeking further sexual contact.

PEDOPHILIA

People who persistently engage in sexual activities with children exhibit what is undoubtedly the most alarming, damaging, and objectionable form of paraphilic behavior: pedophilia. One large-scale survey found that 27 percent of women and 16 percent of men reported that they had experienced some form of sexual abuse as children (Finkelhor et al., 1990). The harmful, long-term consequences of sexual abuse include elevated risk for many of the disorders that we have already considered in this book, including anxiety disorders, mood disorders, personality disorders, substance use disorders, and sexual dysfunction.

Pedophilia entails recurrent, intense, sexually arousing fantasies, sexual urges, or behaviors involving sexual activity with a prepubescent child (generally age 13 years or younger). In order to qualify for a diagnosis of pedophilia in DSM-IV, the person must be at least 16 years of age and at least 5 years older than the child. The terms *pedophile* and *child molester* are sometimes used interchangeably, but this practice confuses legal definitions with psychopathology. A child molester is a person who has committed a sexual offense against a child victim. Therefore the term depends on legal definitions of "sexual offense" and "child victim," which can vary from one state or country to another. In many locations, a child might be anyone under the age of consent, even if that person has reached puberty. All child molesters are not pedophiles. Furthermore, some pedophiles may not have molested children, because the diagnosis can be made on the basis of recurrent fantasies in the absence of actual behavior (Barbaree & Seto, 1997).

Pedophilia includes a great variety of behaviors and sexual preferences (Bradford et al., 1988). Some pedophiles are attracted only to children, whereas others are sometimes attracted to adults. Most pedophiles are heterosexual, and the victims of pedophilia are more often girls than boys. Some offenders are attracted to both girls and boys. Sexual contact with children typically involves caressing and genital fondling. Vaginal, oral, and anal penetration are less common, and physical violence is relatively rare. In many cases, the child willingly and naively complies with the adult's intentions. In most cases, the child knows the person who molests him or her. More than half of all offenses occur in the home of either the child or the offender.

Incestuous relationships, in which the pedophile molests his own children, should perhaps be distinguished from those in which the offender is only casually acquainted with the victim. **Incest** refers to sexual activity between close blood relatives, such as father–daughter, mother–son, or between siblings. The definition may also be expanded to include stepchildren and their stepparents in reconstituted families. Most reported cases of incest involve fathers and stepfathers sexually abusing daughters and stepdaughters (Cole, 1992). Many incest perpetrators would not be considered pedophiles, either because their victims are postpubescent adolescents or because they are also young themselves (such as male adolescents molesting their younger sisters). Perhaps as many as half of the men who commit incest have also engaged in sexual activity with children outside their own families (Abel & Osborn, 1992). This subgroup of pedophilic incest perpetrators may be the most harmful and the most difficult to treat. Their personality style is typically passive and dependent. They are unable to empathize with the plight of their victims, perhaps in part because they were absent or uninvolved in early childcare responsibilities (Williams & Finkelhor, 1990).

RAPE AND SEXUAL ASSAULT

The legal definition of **rape** includes "acts involving nonconsensual sexual penetration obtained by physical force, by threat of bodily harm, or when the victim is incapable of giving consent by virtue of mental illness, mental retardation, or intoxication" (Goodman et al., 1993a). One conservative estimate of rape prevalence based on a national survey indicated that 14 percent of adult women had been raped (National Victims Center, 1992). The actual rate is probably higher—perhaps in the vicinity of 20 percent (Koss, 1992, 1993). The impact of sexual assault on the victim is described in Chapter 7 (Further Thoughts).

The frequency of coercive sex was studied as part of the NHSLS (Laumann et al., 1994). The 3,500 participants were asked whether they had ever been forced to do something sexually that they did not want to do. The question was focused broadly and did not necessarily focus only on acts involving penetration or threats of violence. The prevalence of forced sex is presented separately for men and women in Table 12–4. Slightly more than one out of every five women in the sample reported that they had been forced by a man to engage in some kind

TABLE 12-4

Prevalence of Forced Sexual Activity (Lifetime Occurrence)

Category	Men	Women
Never forced sexually	96.1%	77.2%
Forced by other gender person	1.3	21.6
Forced by same gender person	1.9	0.3
Forced by both men and women	0.4	0.5

Source: E. O. Laumann, J. H. Gagnon, R. T. Michael, and S. Michaels, 1994, *The Social Organization of Sexuality: Sexual Practices in the United States.* Chicago: University of Chicago Press.

of sexual activity against their will. Among those women who had experienced forced sex, 30 percent said that they had been forced sexually by more than one person.

Some rapes are committed by strangers, but many others—known as *acquaintance rapes*—are committed by men who know their victims. Most female victims know the person who raped them (Wiehe & Richards, 1995). Consider, for example, evidence from women in the NHSLS who had been victims of forced sex (excluding those who had been forced by more than one person). Their relationship to the people who forced them to have sex is illustrated in Figure 12–4. Most reported that the person was either someone with whom they were in love or their

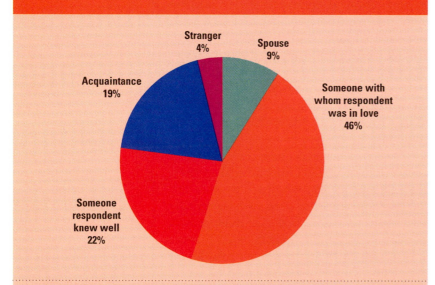

Forced Sex: Relationship to Respondent

Stranger 4%
Spouse 9%
Acquaintance 19%
Someone with whom respondent was in love 46%
Someone respondent knew well 22%

FIGURE 12-4: As this chart shows, most NHSLS respondents who were forced into sexual activity knew the person who coerced them.

Source: Laumann et al., 1994, p. 338.

spouse. Only 4 percent were forced to do something sexual by a stranger.

Rapes are committed by many different kinds of people for many different reasons (Newcomb, 1993). The feminist perspective on rape emphasizes male aggression and violence. The traditional clinical perspective has been concerned with sexual deviance. The authors of DSM-IV considered including rape as a type of paraphilia. This proposal was rejected, primarily because it might imply that rape is always motivated by sexual arousal, and it is not. Nevertheless, the behavior of some rapists does include essential features of paraphilias: recurrent, intense sexually arousing fantasies and urges that involve the suffering of nonconsenting persons. Half the convicted rapists in one study reported a history of other types of paraphilia: pedophilia (24 percent), exhibitionism (19 percent), and voyeurism (17 percent) (Abel & Gouleau, 1990). Current efforts to classify sexual offenders attempt to distinguish between those for whom deviant sexual arousal contributes to the act and those whose behavior is motivated primarily by anger or violent impulses (see Further Thoughts).

Epidemiology

There is very little evidence regarding the frequency of various types of unconventional sexual behavior. This is especially true for victimless or noncoercive forms of paraphilia, such as fetishism, transvestic fetishism, and sexual masochism, because most of these people seldom seek treatment or come to the attention of law enforcement officials. Furthermore, the fact that these forms of behavior are considered deviant or perverse makes it unlikely that people who engage in them will readily divulge their secret urges and fantasies.

With the exception of masochism, paraphilias are almost always male behaviors. Some 95 percent of the people who seek treatment for paraphilic disorders are men (Levine, Risen, & Althof, 1990; Kaplan, 1989).

Paraphilias are seldom isolated phenomena. People who exhibit one type of paraphilia often exhibit others. Gosselin and Wilson (1980) surveyed men who belonged to private clubs that cater to fetishists, sadomasochists, and transvestites, and they found that the members of different clubs often shared the same interests. This overlap is illustrated in Figure 12–5.

This pattern has been called crossing of paraphilic behaviors. Another study categorized a group of approximately 500 sexual offenders

The Classification of Rapists

Raymond Knight, a psychologist at Brandeis University, and Robert Prentky have studied convicted rapists who were imprisoned at the Massachusetts Treatment Center (MTC) for sexually dangerous persons (Knight & Prentky, 1990; Knight, Prentky, & Cerce, 1994). Their research indicates that rape is motivated by both aggressive and sexual components, in varying mixtures. Knight and Prentky developed a classification system for rapists, known as the MTC-R3, that includes four main categories, which are reproduced in Table 12–5.

Two of the categories include men whose motivation for sexual assault is primarily sexual in nature. *Sadistic* rapists exhibit features that are close to the DSM-IV definition of a paraphilia. Their behavior is determined by a combination of sexual and aggressive impulses. The *nonsadistic* category also includes men who are preoccupied with sexual fantasies, but these fantasies are not blended with images of violence and aggression. The sexual aggression of these men may result, in part, from serious deficits in the ability to process social cues, such as the intentions of women (Lipton, McDonel, & McFall, 1987; McFall, 1990).

The other two categories in Knight and Prentky's system describe men whose primary motivation for rape is not sexual. *Vindictive* rapists seem intent on violence directed exclusively toward women. Their aggression is not erotically motivated, as with sadistic rapists. *Opportunistic* rapists are men with an extensive history of impulsive behavior in many kinds of settings and who might be considered psychopaths (see Chapter 9). Their sexual behavior is governed largely by immediate environmental cues. They will use whatever force is necessary to ensure compliance, but they express anger only in response to the victim's resistance.

The utility of the MTC-R3 typology has been examined in a study of rapists who were being treated at a sexual behavior clinic (Barbaree et al., 1994). Most of these men could be placed reliably into one of Knight and Prentky's main categories. Overall, 22 of the men fit the description of the opportunistic rapist, 14 exhibited features of the vindictive type, 15 were described as nonsadistic rapists, and 8 fell into the sadistic category.

The investigators compared rapists in the four major categories on several laboratory measures. Deviant sexual arousal was measured using a penile strain gauge (see Research Methods) while each subject listened to a series of audiotapes describing scenes of mutually consenting sex and of rape. Sadistic and nonsadistic rapists showed greater sexual arousal in response to the rape scenes than did the vindictive and opportunistic rapists. This pattern of results supports the validity of Knight and Prentky's classification system. It indicates that deviant patterns of sexual arousal may play a more important role in the sexual aggression displayed by the sadistic and nonsadistic rapists.

These studies help explain some of the factors that contribute to the disturbing rate of sexual aggression in our society. They may lay the foundation for efforts aimed at the prevention of this form of violence as well as the treatment of rapists. We must

TABLE 12-5

Basic Structure of the MTC Typology for Rapists

Primary Motivation	General Category	Description of Rapists
Aggressive	Vindictive	Actions intended to degrade and humiliate the victim
	Opportunistic	Impulsive, unplanned actions; seeking immediate gratification; indifferent to the victim's plight
Sexual	Sadistic	Preoccupation with sadistic sexual fantasies; actions typically brutal and violent
	Nonsadistic	Distorted views of sexuality and women; feelings of inferiority; poor social skills

Source: Adapted from R. A. Knight and R. A. Prentky, 1990, Classifying sexual offenders. In W. Marshall, D. R. Laws, and H. E. Barbaree (Eds.), *Handbook of Sexual Assault: Issues, Theories, and Treatment of the Offender*, p. 43. New York: Plenum.

keep in mind, however, that this type of research is based almost exclusively on a small subset of rapists—those who have been convicted of their offenses. It would be naive to generalize from this group to all rapists, for several reasons. Most instances of acquaintance rape are not reported. Among those rapes that are reported to the police, less than 10 percent ever lead to conviction. Therefore studies of convicted rapists must be interpreted with caution. We should not conclude that the motivations of all—or even most—rapists are accurately portrayed in these studies. ■

on the basis of many different features: whether or not they touched their victims, whether their victims were relatives, whether their victims were male or female, and whether their victims were children or adults. The data indicated a considerable amount of crossover. Of the offenders who had carried out paraphilic acts against male victims, 63 percent had previously engaged in similar behaviors against female victims; 49 percent of those who had committed acts against adults had previously committed acts against children; and 64 percent of those who committed acts that did not involve touching their victims had previously committed acts that involved touching (Abel & Osborn, 1992).

Etiology

The high rate of overlap among paraphilias indicates that the etiology of these behaviors might be most appropriately viewed in terms of common factors rather than in terms of distinct pathways that lead exclusively to one form of paraphilia or another. Those experiences and conditions that predispose an individual to one form of paraphilia are apparently also likely to lead to another. In the following pages we review a number of proposals regarding the etiology of paraphilias. Some of these have been associated with specific types of paraphilia. For the most part, however, they are concerned more generally with many forms of paraphilias.

The epidemiological evidence suggests another important pattern that must be explained by any theory of paraphilias: They are more prevalent among men than among women. The exception to this rule seems to be masochism, which may be equally common in both genders. We might conclude therefore that the development of masochism may be governed by different factors than those that account for the etiology of other types of paraphilias. Nevertheless, theoretical accounts of most paraphilias must explain why they are more common among men than women.

BIOLOGICAL FACTORS

Most of the evidence regarding the role of biological factors in the etiology of paraphilias has focused on the endocrine system, the collection of glands that regulates sexual responses through the release of hormones (Collaer & Hines, 1995). Some studies of convicted sexually violent offenders have found evidence of elevated levels of testosterone. These reports must be viewed with some skepticism, however, for two reasons. First, the participants in these studies are invariably convicted sexual offenders. It is therefore not clear that the findings can be generalized to all people with paraphilias. Second, there is a high rate of alcoholism and drug abuse among men convicted of sexual crimes. For that reason, we do not know whether biological abnormalities that are observed in these men are causes of their deviant sexual behavior or, instead,

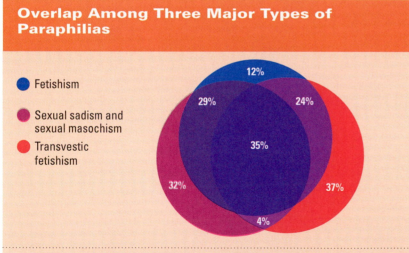

Overlap Among Three Major Types of Paraphilias

- Fetishism
- Sexual sadism and sexual masochism
- Transvestic fetishism

FIGURE 12-5: The extent of overlap in the interests of three major types of paraphilias. Note that only 37 percent of men who practice fetishistic transvestism, 32 percent of men who practice sexual sadism and masochism, and 12 percent of those who practice fetishism exhibited those interests exclusively.

Source: G.D. Wilson, 1987, An ethological approach to sexual deviation. In G.D. Wilson (Ed.), *Variant Sexuality: Research and Theory,* p. 92. London: Croom Helm.

consequences of prolonged substance abuse (Langevin, 1992).

Neurological abnormalities may also be involved in the development of paraphilias. Structures located in the temporal lobes of the brain, especially the amygdala and the hippocampus, appear to play an important role in the control of both aggression and sexual behavior. These limbic structures, in conjunction with the hypothalamus, form a circuit that regulates biologically significant behaviors that sometimes are whimsically called the four F's—feeding, fighting, fleeing, and sexual behavior (Valenstein, 1973). In 1937, two scientists reported that, after extensive bilateral damage to the temporal lobes, rhesus monkeys showed a dramatic increase in sexual activity, as well as a number of related behavioral and perceptual abnormalities. The monkeys apparently tried to copulate with a variety of inappropriate partners, including the investigators. This pattern has subsequently been called the Kluver-Bucy syndrome, named after the scientists who made the original observation.

Inspired by the suggestion that damage to the temporal lobe can lead to unusual patterns of sexual behavior, clinical scientists have studied a number of neurological and neuropsychological factors in convicted sex offenders. Some reports indicate that men with pedophilia and exhibitionism show subtle forms of left temporal lobe dysfunction, as evidenced by abnormal patterns of electrophysiological response and impaired performance on neuropsychological tests (Flor-Henry, 1987; Murphy, 1997).

Some men with fetishism exhibit diffuse signs of neurological impairment, but these are also focused predominantly in the left temporal lobe. Similar findings have been reported for sexually sadistic criminals (Gratzer & Bradford, 1995). Before these results are interpreted too broadly, however, it should also be noted that most people who suffer from temporal lobe epilepsy do not engage in paraphilic behaviors. In fact, the most frequent result of temporal lobe epilepsy is a reduction in sexual activity (Huws, Shubsachs, & Taylor, 1991; Murphy, 1997). It seems reasonable to conclude that some cases of paraphilia are caused, at least in part, by endocrine and neurological abnormalities, but the relations among these factors are not entirely clear.

SOCIAL FACTORS

Some types of paraphilias seem to be distortions of the normal mating process when viewed in a broad, evolutionary context. For male primates, sexual behavior involves a sequence of steps: location and appraisal of potential partners; exchange of signals in which partners communicate mutual interest; and tactile interactions that set the stage for sexual intercourse. Voyeurism, exhibitionism, and frotteurism may represent aberrant versions of these social processes. Kurt Freund and Ray Blanchard, both at the University of Toronto, have described the paraphilias as "courtship disorders" (Freund & Blanchard, 1986, 1993). Something has apparently gone wrong, disrupting whatever mechanisms facilitate the identification of a sexual partner and govern behaviors used to attract a partner.

If people with paraphilias have somehow failed to learn more adaptive forms of courtship behavior, what sort of childhood experiences might have produced such unexpected results? Several background factors have been observed repeatedly among people who engage in atypical sexual behaviors (Wincze, 1989). These include the following:

- Early crossing of normative sexual boundaries through a direct experience (for example, sexual abuse by an adult) or an indirect experience (hearing about a father's atypical sexual behavior)
- Lack of a consistent parental environment in which normative sexual behavior and values were modeled
- Lack of self-esteem
- Lack of confidence and ability in social interactions
- Ignorance and poor understanding of human sexuality

All these factors may increase the probability that a person might experiment with unusual types of sexual stimulation or employ maladaptive sexual behaviors.

Although the most notable feature of paraphilias is sexual arousal, the paraphilias are ultimately problems in social relationships. Interpersonal skills may therefore play as important a role as sexual arousal. William Marshall, a psychologist at Queen's University in Canada, has argued that the core feature of unusual sexual behavior is a failure to achieve intimacy in relationships with other adults (Marshall, 1989; Seidman, Marshall, Hudson, & Robertson, 1994). According to this perspective, people with paraphilias are lonely, insecure, and isolated and have significant deficits in social skills. Offensive sexual behaviors, such as those observed in

▲ John Money, a psychologist at Johns Hopkins University, has written extensively about the etiology of paraphilias. His concept of distorted lovemaps provides an interesting view of their development.

pedophilia, are maladaptive attempts to achieve intimacy through sex. These efforts are invariably unsuccessful and self-defeating in the sense that they serve to isolate the person further from the rest of the community. Paradoxically, the pattern may become deeply ingrained because it results in the momentary pleasure associated with orgasm and because it offers the illusory hope of eventually achieving intimacy with another person.

PSYCHOLOGICAL FACTORS

John Money (1984), a psychologist at Johns Hopkins University, has described the development of paraphilias in somewhat different terms, using a geographic metaphor that he calls a *lovemap*. A lovemap is a mental picture representing a person's ideal sexual relationship. It might also be viewed as the software that encodes his or her sexual fantasies and preferred sexual practices. These "programs" are written early in life, and they are quite persistent. Children learn their lovemaps during sexual play, by imitation of their parents and other adults, and through messages that they digest from the popular media. According to Money, when optimal conditions prevail, the child develops a lovemap that includes intercourse as a preferred form of sexual expression. The child learns that love—romantic attachment to another adult—and lust—erotic attraction—can be directed toward the same person.

The lovemap can be distorted, according to Money's metaphor, if the child learns that romantic attachment and sexual desire are incompatible—that these feelings cannot be directed toward the same person. The inability to integrate these aspects of the lovemap lies at the heart of Money's explanation of paraphilias. One solution to this dilemma would be to avoid or deny sexual expression altogether. That might explain the development of lack of sexual desire. Sexual impulses are powerful, however, and they are not easily denied. In some cases, they are rerouted rather than being shut off completely. Various types of paraphilias represent alternative strategies through which the person finds it possible to express sexual feelings outside of an intimate, loving relationship with another adult. Exhibitionism, voyeurism, and fetishism are therefore partial solutions to the perceived incompatibility of love and lust.

The etiological mechanisms that we have considered thus far seem most applicable to paraphilias that are found predominantly among men, such as fetishes, voyeurism, and exhibitionism. A different story may be necessary to explain masochism, the association of sexual arousal with pain and suffering, because this condition is equally common among women and men.

One intriguing clue regarding the origins of masochism has been reported by Robert Stoller (1991), a psychoanalyst at UCLA who wrote extensively about unusual erotic behaviors. Stoller spent several months conducting detailed interviews with people who were seriously involved in sadomasochistic behaviors with consenting partners. Those who were most committed to physical sadism and masochism had, as children, experienced traumatic physical disease followed by frightening forms of medical treatment. These people described to Stoller how they had "consciously forced themselves to master what at first, in infancy and childhood, was uncontrollable physical agony and terror by taking the pain and working with it in their heads, eventually via daydreams, altered states of consciousness, or genital masturbation, until it was converted into pain-that-is-pleasure" (Stoller, 1991, p. 25). In other words, a strong positive emotion like sexual arousal can be actively employed to control intolerable physical pain. The unfortunate consequence is the development of a persistent association between pain and arousal.

Treatment

The treatment of paraphilias is different from the treatment of sexual dysfunctions in several ways. Perhaps most important is the fact that most people with paraphilias do not enter treatment on a voluntary basis. They are often referred to a therapist by the criminal justice system after they have been arrested for exposing themselves, peeping through windows, or engaging in sexual behaviors with children. Their motivation to change is therefore open to question (Wincze, 1989). Participation in treatment may help them receive reduced sentences or avoid other legal penalties. In many cases, they are being asked to abandon highly reinforcing behaviors in which they have engaged for many years. Their families and other members of society may be much more concerned about change than they are. We mention this issue at the beginning of our discussion because the results of outcome studies in this area are typically less positive than are those concerning the treatment of sexual dysfunctions (Furby, Weinrott, & Blackshaw, 1989; McConaghy, 1990).

AVERSION THERAPY

For the past several decades, the most commonly used form of treatment for paraphilias has been **aversion therapy.** In this procedure, the therapist repeatedly presents the stimulus that elicits inappropriate sexual arousal—such as slides of nude children—in association with an aversive stimulus, such as repulsive smells, electric shock, or chemically induced nausea. Revolting cognitive images are sometimes used instead of tangible aversive stimuli. Whatever the exact procedure, the rationale is to create a new association with the inappropriate stimulus so that the stimulus will no longer elicit sexual arousal. Several research studies have suggested that aversion therapy does produce some positive effects (Kilmann et al., 1982). It has more recently fallen into disfavor, however, because the studies that were used to evaluate it suffered from design flaws.

COGNITIVE-BEHAVIORAL TREATMENT

Alternative treatment programs for paraphilic behaviors reflect a broader view of the etiology of these conditions. There is considerable reason to believe that paraphilias are based on a variety of cognitive and social deficits (Marshall, 1989; McFall, 1990). Marshall, Eccles, and Barbaree (1991) compared two approaches to the treatment of exhibitionists. One was based on aversion therapy, and the other employed cognitive restructuring, social skills training, and stress management procedures. The men who received the second type of treatment were much less likely to return to their deviant forms of sexual behavior than were the men who received aversion therapy. Treatment with aversion therapy was no more effective than was treatment with a placebo. These data suggest that broad-based cognitive and social treatment procedures may ultimately be most useful in the treatment of paraphilias and sexual disorders (Marshall et al., 1996).

Encouraging results have been reported from the Sex Offender Treatment and Evaluation Project (Marques et al., 1993), which was designed for men convicted of either rape or child molestation. Men selected for the treatment program are transferred to a special hospital unit, where they remain for several months. They receive education in human sexuality as well as cognitive behavior therapy, including applied relaxation and social skills training and stress and anger management. Treatment also includes a relapse prevention component that is based on procedures used in the treatment of alcoholism (see Chapter 11). Relapse prevention procedures help the men confront personal, social, and sexual difficulties that may increase their risk of relapse after they are released from prison.

The men in the treatment group are compared to those in two control groups. Outcome is measured in several ways, but the most important consideration is being arrested again for similar crimes. Men in the treatment group were significantly less likely than were men in the control groups to commit new sex offenses during their first 5 years after release (Marques et al., 1994). Results were somewhat more encouraging with men convicted of rape than with those who had molested children. The number of people who had been treated by the time of these reports was still relatively small, so the results should be interpreted with caution. Nevertheless, the data from this program indicate that broadly based behavioral programs that focus on education, social skills, and relapse prevention procedures may be more promising than more traditional forms of therapy.

HORMONES AND MEDICATION

Another approach to the treatment of paraphilias involves the use of drugs that reduce levels of testosterone, on the assumption that male hormones control the sexual appetite (Bradford, 1997). One study reported that treatment of paraphilic men with cyproterone acetate, a drug that blocks the effects of testosterone, produced a significant reduction in some aspects of sexual behavior, expecially sexual fantasies (Bradford & Pawlak, 1993). Among men with pedophilia, the study found a greater reduction of sexual fantasies of children than for images of sex between consenting adults.

Antidepressants and antianxiety drugs have also been used to treat paraphilias. One study found that three patients with paraphilias responded positively to Prozac (Perilstein, Lipper, & Friedman, 1991). The process by which these drugs manage to alter sexual behavior is open to question. For example, medication may reduce social anxiety, which interferes with the ability to enjoy an intimate sexual relationship with another adult (Golwyn & Sevlie, 1992). This hypothesis is consistent with the approach taken by

▲ Leroy Hendricks, a pedophile, was committed to a mental hospital after serving repeated prison terms for molesting children. His challenge to the Kansas sexual predator law will be decided by the U.S. Supreme Court.

Marshall and his colleagues, whose psychological treatment program is aimed at similar types of social deficits.

LEGAL ISSUES

Several states have passed laws that are intended to protect society from people who have been convicted of violent or repeated sexual offenses. These laws fall into two categories. The first includes *community notification laws* (such as "Megan's Law"), which require the distribution of information to the public regarding the presence of child molesters and sexually violent offenders when they are released from prison or placed on parole. These laws are based on two assumptions: (1) notification will reduce the offender's opportunities to commit further crimes, and (2) citizens are better able to protect themselves and their children if they know that a dangerous person lives in their neighborhood. Critics of community notification laws argue that they violate the former offender's constitutional rights by imposing an additional, unfair penalty after his sentence has been served. These laws are popular, but their impact has not been evaluated. It is not clear that people are actually better able to protect themselves after they have been notified. Furthermore, we do not know whether relapse rates are lower among sexual offenders who live in communities where such laws are strictly enforced (Berliner, 1996; Prentky, 1996).

The second category includes *sexual predator laws,* which are designed to keep some criminals in custody indefinitely. For example, a Kansas law passed in 1994 permits authorities to commit certain sex offenders to a mental hospital after their prison terms are over (see the discussion of civil commitment in Chapter 18). Each case is evaluated in a series of steps which end with a civil trial. The person can be hospitalized involuntarily and for an indefinite period of time if the jury decides the person has a "mental abnormality" that will lead him to commit further sexual offenses. Involuntary civil commitment is an infrequent outcome of this law. When it does occur, however, serious questions must be raised about the need to balance public safety against the protection of the offender's constitutional rights. The status of these laws will be determined by many individual cases that are currently under appeal.

Gender Identity Disorders

Our sense of ourselves as being either male or female is known as **gender identity.** Gender identity almost always reflects the child's physical anatomy: Toddlers who possess a penis learn that they are boys, and those with a vagina learn that they are girls. Gender identity is usually fixed by the time a child reaches 2 or 3 years of age (Serbin & Sprafkin, 1987).

Gender identity must be distinguished from **sex roles,** which are characteristics, behaviors, and skills that are defined within a specific culture as being either masculine or feminine. For example, certain aspects of appearance and behavior are more often associated with men than with women. These are considered to be masculine. Those behaviors and appearances that are more often associated with women are considered feminine. In our own culture, masculine and feminine sex roles have changed considerably in recent years, and they overlap to a degree.

Typical Symptoms and Associated Features

Some people are firmly convinced that they are living in the wrong kind of body. In males, this means that they feel strongly that they are women trapped in a man's body. For females, the opposite pattern holds. The DSM-IV categorizes this sense of discomfort with one's anatomical sex as *gender identity disorder.* It has also been called *transsexualism* (Satterfield, 1988) or *gender dysphoria* (Blanchard, 1989). People with gender identity disturbances are not delusional. In other words, they do not literally believe that they are members of the other gender. Rather, they feel that, with the exception of their physical anatomy, they are more like the other gender.

Most transsexuals report that they were aware of these feelings very early in childhood. Many report that they dressed in clothing and adopted sex-role behaviors of the other gender during childhood and adolescence. The intensity of the person's discomfort varies from one individual to the next. Invariably it becomes more intense during adolescence, when the person develops secondary sexual characteristics, such as breasts and wider hips for girls, and facial hair, voice changes, and increased muscle mass for boys. These characteristics make it more difficult for a person to pass for the other gender. Many transsexuals become preoccupied with the desire to change their anatomical sex through surgical procedures.

Gender identity disorders should be distinguished from transvestic fetishism, which is a form of paraphilia in which a heterosexual man dresses in the clothing of the other gender in order to achieve sexual arousal. These are, in fact, very different conditions. Transvestic fetishists do not consider themselves to be women, and transsexuals are not sexually aroused by cross-dressing.

The relation between gender identity disorder and sexual orientation has been a matter of some controversy. Some clinicians have suggested that transsexuals are homosexuals who claim to be members of the other gender as a way to avoid cultural and moral sanctions that discourage engaging in sexual relationships with members of their own sex. This proposal doesn't make sense for two reasons. First, lesbians and gay men are not uncomfortable with their own gender identity. This observation suggests that transsexuals are not simply escaping the stigma of homosexuality. Second, laboratory studies suggest that transsexual and homosexual subjects exhibit different patterns of sexual arousal in response to erotic stimuli (Barr, 1973).

Epidemiology

Gender identity disorders are quite rare in comparison to most of the other disorders that we have considered in this book. Male-to-female transsexuals are apparently more common than female-to-male transsexuals, at least based on the numbers of people who seek treatment at clinics. One study estimated the prevalence figures to be 1 person with gender identity disorder for every 18,000 males and 54,000 females (Eklund, Gooren, & Bezemer, 1988).

Deeply ingrained cross-gender behaviors and attitudes among children occur infrequently in the general population (Zucker, 1985). Mild forms of cross-gender behavior, such as dressing up in the clothes of the other gender or expressing a desire to be a member of the other sex, are relatively common during the preschool years. Extreme forms of these behaviors are relatively rare, however, especially among boys (Achenbach & Edelbrock, 1981).

Etiology

Very little is known about the origins of gender identity in normal men and women, so it is not surprising that the etiology of gender identity disorders is also poorly understood. There is some reason to believe that gender identity is strongly influenced by sex hormones, especially during the prenatal period (LeVay, 1993; Swaab & Gofman, 1995). Much of the research in this area has been done with animals, but an interesting set of data comes from studies of people with a condition that is sometimes called *pseudohermaphroditism*. Individuals with this condition are genetically male, but they are unable to produce a hormone that is responsible for shaping the penis and scrotum in the fetus. Therefore the child is born with external genitalia that are ambiguous in appearance—thus the term *pseudohermaphrodite*.[†]

Many of these children are raised as girls by their families. When they reach the age of puberty, a sudden increase in testosterone leads to dramatic changes in the appearance of the adolescent's genitals. The organ that had previously looked more like a clitoris becomes enlarged and turns into a penis, and testicles descend into a scrotum. The child's voice becomes deeper, muscle mass increases, and the child quickly begins to consider himself to be a man (Imperato-McGinley et al., 1974). The speed and apparent ease with which people with these conditions adopt a masculine gender identity suggest that their brains had been prenatally programmed for this alternative (Hoenig, 1985).

▲ Transsexual Christine Jorgenson (right) in 1952 and the former George Jorgenson (left), an Army veteran from New York. Jorgenson's sex-reassignment surgery, performed in Denmark, attracted worldwide attention.

[†] A hermaphrodite has both male and female reproductive organs.

Treatment

There are two obvious solutions to problems of gender identity: Change the person's identity to match his or her anatomy, or change the anatomy to match the person's gender identity. Various forms of psychotherapy have been used in an effort to alter gender identity, but the results have been fairly negative.

One alternative to psychological treatment is *sex-reassignment surgery,* in which the person's genitals are changed to match the gender identity (Hage, 1995). Medical science can construct artificial male and female genitalia. The artificial penis is not capable of becoming erect in response to sexual stimulation, but structural implants can be used to obtain rigidity. These surgical procedures have been used with thousands of patients over the past 50 or 60 years. Clinics that perform these operations employ stringent selection procedures, and patients are typically required to live for several months as a member of the other gender before they can undergo the surgical procedure.

The results of sex-reassignment surgery have generally been positive. Interviews with patients who have undergone surgery indicate that most are satisfied with the results, and the vast majority believe that they do not have any trouble passing as a member of their newly assumed gender. Psychological tests obtained from patients who have completed surgery indicate reduced levels of anxiety and depression (Bodlund & Kullgren, 1996; Snaith, Michael, & Russell, 1993).

KEY TERMS

- aversion therapy
- construct
- construct validity
- dyspareunia
- erectile dysfunction
- exhibitionism
- fetishism
- frotteurism
- gender identity
- gender identity disorder
- hypoactive sexual desire
- hypothetical construct
- incest
- inhibited sexual arousal
- operational definition
- orgasmic disorder
- paraphilia
- pedophilia
- premature ejaculation
- rape
- sensate focus
- sex roles
- sexual aversion disorder
- sexual dysfunction
- sexual masochism
- sexual sadism
- transvestic fetishism
- vaginismus
- voyeurism

Summary

The DSM-IV recognizes two major forms of sexual disorders. **Sexual dysfunctions** involve an inhibition of sexual desire or disruption of the physiological responses leading to orgasm. **Paraphilias** are defined in terms of extreme forms of unusual sexual behavior, in which sexual arousal is associated with atypical stimuli. The central problem in paraphilias is that sexual arousal has become detached from a reciprocal, loving relationship with another adult.

Sexual dysfunctions are subdivided into several types, based on the stages of the sexual response cycle. These include problems related to sexual desire, sexual arousal, and orgasm. Related difficulties include sexual aversion disorder and **premature ejaculation. Dyspareunia** is defined in terms of persistent genital pain during or after sexual intercourse. **Vaginismus** is an involuntary spasm of the muscles surrounding the entrance to the vagina. All forms of sexual dysfunction can lead to personal distress, including anxiety and depression, as well as interpersonal and marital difficulties.

Sexual behavior is dependent on a complex interaction among biological, psychological, and social factors. These factors include cognitive events related to the perception of sexual stimuli, social factors that influence sexual meanings or intentions, and physiological responses that cause vasocongestion of the genitals during sexual arousal.

Biological factors that contribute to sexual dysfunction include inadequate levels of sex hormones, which can contribute to diminished sexual desire, and a variety of medical disorders. Vascular and neurological diseases are important factors in many cases of erectile disorder. The effects of alcohol, illicit drugs, and some forms of medication can also contribute to erectile disorder in men and to **orgasmic disorder** in men and women.

Several psychological factors are involved in the etiology of sexual dysfunction. Prominent among these are performance anxiety and guilt. Communication deficits can also contribute to sexual dysfunction. Previous experiences, including sexual abuse, play an important role in some cases of sexual dysfunction.

Psychological treatments for sexual dysfunction are quite successful. They focus primarily on negative attitudes toward sexuality, failure to engage in effective sexual behaviors, and deficits in communication skills.

Common characteristics of paraphilias include lack of human intimacy and urges toward sexual behaviors which the person feels compelled to perform. Many people with paraphilias experience sexual dysfunctions during conventional sexual behavior with an adult partner. The diversity and range of paraphilic behavior is enormous. DSM-IV describes a few of the most prominent forms, such as **exhibitionism, fetishism, frotteurism, pedophilia, sexual masochism, sexual sadism, transvestic fetishism,** and **voyeurism.** These are not typically isolated preferences or patterns of behavior; people who exhibit one form of paraphilia often exhibit others.

Treatment outcome is generally less successful with paraphilias than with sexual dysfunction. The most promising approaches to the treatment of paraphilias currently use a combination of cognitive and behavioral procedures to address a broad range of etiological factors, including deficits in social skills and stress and anger management as well as knowledge and attitudes regarding sexuality.

Gender identity disorder represents a disturbance in the person's sense of being either a man or a woman. People with this problem, which is also known as transsexualism, have developed a **gender identity** that is inconsistent with their physical anatomy. These disorders are extremely rare. Very little is known about their etiology. Gender identity seems to be strongly influenced by sex hormones, perhaps during the process of fetal development. Treatment of gender identity disorders may involve sex-reassignment surgery.

Critical Thinking

1. Suppose that you are a therapist who has been contacted by a couple who are concerned that the woman is unable to reach orgasm. What are the first things that you would want to know? Would you want to see each partner alone?

2. Drag queens are gay men who dress up in women's clothing. Their masquerade balls are typically a source of pride and enjoyment. Why wouldn't this type of behavior be considered a sexual disorder? How is their behavior different from transvestic fetishism?

3. Do you think that rape—or some specific subtype of rape—should have been included in DSM-IV under paraphilias? Why or why not?

13
Schizophrenic Disorders

Schizophrenia is a pervasive and sometimes chronic form of abnormal behavior that encompasses what most of us have come to know as "madness." People with schizophrenia exhibit many different symptoms. They may hear voices that aren't there, express absurd ideas and beliefs, or make comments that are difficult, if not impossible, to understand. Their symptoms follow different patterns over time. Some recover fairly quickly, whereas others deteriorate progressively after the initial onset of symptoms. In the face of this marked diversity, many clinicians believe that schizophrenia, or "the group of schizophrenias," may actually include several forms of disorder that have different causes. Others contend that schizophrenia is a single pathological process and that variations from one patient to the next in symptoms and course of the disorder reflect differences in the expression or severity of this process.

Overview

The most common symptoms of schizophrenia include changes in the way a person thinks, feels, and relates to other people and the outside environment. It is a disorder of "multiple handicaps" (Bellack & Mueser, 1993). No single symptom or specific set of symptoms is characteristic of all schizophrenic patients. All of the individual symptoms of schizophrenia can also be associated with other psychological and medical conditions. Schizophrenia is defined by various combinations of psychotic symptoms in the absence of other forms of disturbance, such as mood disorders (especially manic episodes), substance dependence, delirium, or dementia (see Chapter 14).

The symptoms of schizophrenia can be divided into three dimensions: positive symptoms, negative symptoms, and disorganization (Andreasen et al., 1995; Thompson & Meltzer, 1993). **Positive symptoms,** also called *psychotic symptoms*, are assumed to indicate a *distortion of normal functions*. Hallucinations and delusions are considered positive symptoms of schizophrenia. In contrast, **negative symptoms** presumably reflect the *loss of normal functions*—symptoms such as lack of initiative, social withdrawal, and deficits in emotional responding. Some additional symptoms of schizophrenia, such as disorganized speech, do not fit easily into either the positive or negative type. Verbal communication problems and bizarre behavior represent a third symptom dimension, which is sometimes called **disorganization.** Note that these symptom dimensions overlap and combine in various ways within individual patients.

Schizophrenia is not a transient disorder. The DSM-IV definition of schizophrenia requires that the person exhibit symptoms of the disorder for at least 6 months before he or she is considered to meet the diagnostic criteria. If the person displays psychotic symptoms for at least 1 month but less than 6 months, the diagnosis would be *schizophreniform disorder*. The diagnosis would be changed to schizophrenic disorder if the person's problems persisted beyond the 6-month limit.

In the following case studies we describe the experiences of two people who exhibited symptoms of schizophrenia. The DSM-IV divides schizophrenic disorders into several subtypes, based primarily on the type of symptoms that the patient exhibits. Our first case illustrates the paranoid subtype of schizophrenia, which is characterized by a preoccupation with one or more delusions or by frequent auditory hallucinations, most often persecutory.

CASE STUDY

Paranoid Schizophrenia

Ann was 21 years old the first time that she was admitted to a psychiatric hospital. She had completed business college and had worked as a receptionist until she became pregnant with her son, who was born 6 months prior to her admission. She and her husband lived in a small apartment with his 5-year-old daughter from a previous marriage. This was her first psychotic episode.

The first signs of Ann's disturbance appeared during her pregnancy, when she accused her husband of having an affair with her sister. The accusation was based on a conversation that Ann had overheard on a bus. Two women (who were neighbors in Ann's apartment building) had been discussing an affair that some woman's husband was having. Ann believed that this might have been their way of telling her about her husband's infidelity. Although her husband and her sister denied any romantic interest in each other, Ann clung to her suspicions and began to monitor her husband's activities closely. She also avoided talking with her neighbors and friends.

Before this period of time, Ann had been an outgoing and energetic person. Now she seemed listless and apathetic and would often spend days without leaving their apartment. Her husband at first attributed this change in her behavior to the pregnancy, believing that she would "snap out of it" after the baby was born. Unfortunately, Ann became even more socially isolated following the birth of her son. She seldom left her bedroom and would spend hours alone, mumbling softly to herself.

Ann's behavior deteriorated markedly 2 weeks prior to her hospital admission, when she noticed that some photographs of herself and her baby were missing. She told her husband that they had been stolen and were being used to cast a voodoo spell on her. Ann became increasingly preoccupied with this belief in subsequent days. She called her mother repeatedly, insisting that something would have to be done to recover the missing photographs. Her friends and family tried to reassure Ann that the photographs had probably been misplaced or accidentally discarded, but she was totally unwilling to consider alternative explanations.

Ann finally announced to everyone who would listen that someone was trying to kill her and the children. Believing that all the food in the house had been poisoned, she refused to eat and would not feed the children. She became increasingly suspicious, hostile, and combative. Her husband and parents found it impossible to reason with her. She was no longer able to care for herself or the children. The family sought advice from their family physician, who recommended that they contact a psychiatrist. After meeting with Ann briefly, the psychiatrist recommended that she be hospitalized for a short period of time.

After admission, Ann argued heatedly with the hospital staff, denying that she was mentally disturbed and insisting that she must be released so that she could protect her children from the conspiracy. She had no insight into the nature of her problems. ■

The onset of schizophrenia typically occurs during adolescence or early adulthood. The period of risk for the development of a first episode is considered to be between the ages of 15 and 35. The number of new cases drops off slowly after that, with very few people experiencing an initial episode after the age of 55 (Gottesman, 1991).

The subsequent course of the disorder can follow many different patterns. The problems of most patients can be divided into three phases of variable and unpredictable duration: prodromal, active, and residual. Symptoms such as hallucinations, delusions, and disorganized speech are characteristic of the **active phase** of the disorder. The **prodromal phase** precedes the active phase and is marked by an obvious deterioration in role functioning as a student, employee, or homemaker. The person's friends and relatives often view the beginning of the prodromal phase as a change in the person's personality. Prodromal signs and symptoms are similar to those associated with schizotypal personality disorder (see Chapter 9). They include peculiar behaviors (such as talking to one's self in public), unusual perceptual experiences, outbursts of anger, increased tension, and restlessness. Social withdrawal and avolition (indeciveness and lack of willpower) are often seen during the prodromal phase.

The **residual phase** follows the active phase of the disorder and is defined by signs and symptoms that are similar in many respects to those seen during the prodromal phase. At this point, the positive symptoms of psychosis have improved, but the person continues to be impaired in various ways. Negative symptoms, such as impoverished expression of emotions, may remain pronounced during the residual phase.

After the onset of schizophrenia, many people do not return to expected levels of social and occupational adjustment. The man in our second case illustrates this pattern. He is also an example of the disorganized type of schizophrenia. Patients who fit criteria for this category exhibit disorganized speech, disorganized behavior, and flat or inappropriate expression of emotion.

CASE STUDY

Disorganized Schizophrenia

Edward was 39 years old and had lived at home with his parents since dropping out of school after the 10th grade. Edward worked on and off as a helper in his father's roofing business prior to his first psychotic episode at the age of 26. After that time, he was socially isolated and unable to hold any kind of job. He was hospitalized in psychiatric facilities 10 times in the next 14 years. When he was not in the hospital, most of his time at home was spent watching television or sitting alone in his room.

The tenth episode of psychosis became evident when Edward told his mother that he had seen people arguing violently on the sidewalk in front of their house. He believed that this incident was the beginning of World War II. His mother tried to persuade him that he had witnessed an ordinary, though perhaps heated, disagreement between two neighbors, but Edward could not be convinced. He continued to mumble about the fight and became increasingly agitated over the next few days. When he wasn't pacing back and forth from his bedroom to the living room, he could usually be found staring out the front window. Several days after witnessing the argument, he took curtains from several windows in the house and burned them in the street at 2 A.M. A neighbor happened to see what Edward was doing and called the police. When they arrived, they found Edward wandering in a snow-covered vacant lot, talking incoherently to himself. Recognizing that Edward was psychotic, the police took him to the psychiatric hospital.

Although his appearance was somewhat disheveled, Edward was alert and cooperative. He knew the current date and recognized that he was in a psychiatric hospital. Some of his speech was incoherent, and his answers to questions posed by the hospital staff were frequently irrelevant. His expressive gestures were severely restricted. Although he said that he was frightened by the recent events that he reported to his mother, his face did not betray any signs of emotion. He mumbled slowly in a monotonous tone of voice that was difficult to understand. He said that he could hear God's voice telling him that his father was "the Master of the universe" and he claimed that he had "seen the shadow of the Master." Other voices seem to argue with one another about Edward's special calling and whether he was worthy of this divine power. The voices told him to prepare for God's return to earth. At times Edward said that he was a Nazi soldier and that he was born in Germany in 1886. He also spoke incoherently about corpses frozen in Greenland and maintained that he was "only half a person." ∎

Typical Symptoms and Associated Features

In this section we describe in greater detail various types of positive and negative symptoms that are commonly observed among schizophrenic patients and that are currently emphasized by official diagnostic systems, such as DSM-IV. When you are reading these descriptions, remember that all these symptoms can fluctuate in severity over time. Some patients exhibit persistent psychotic symptoms. Others experience symptoms during acute episodes and are better adjusted between episodes.

Hallucinations

Our senses provide us with fundamental information about ourselves and the world in which we live—information that is vital to our notions of who we are, what we are doing, and what others think of us. Many people with schizophrenia experience perplexing and often frightening changes in perception. The most obvious perceptual symptoms are **hallucinations,** or sensory experiences that are not caused by actual external stimuli. Although hallucinations can occur in any of the senses, those experienced by schizophrenic patients are most often auditory. Many patients hear voices that comment on their behavior or give them instructions. Others hear voices that seem to argue with one another. Edward heard the voice of God talking to him. Although Edward's voices were frightening, in some cases hallucinations can be comforting or pleasing to the patient.

Hallucinations should be distinguished from the transient mistaken perceptions that most people experience from time to time (Heilbrun, 1993; Slade & Bentall, 1988). Have you ever turned around after thinking you heard someone call your name, to find that no one was there? You probably dismissed the experience as "just your imagination." Hallucinations, in contrast, strike the person as being real, in spite of the fact that they have no basis in reality. They are also persistent over time. Patients who experience auditory hallucinations often hear the voice (or voices) speaking to them throughout the day and for many days at a time.

Hallucinations are typically associated with other symptoms, particularly delusional beliefs.

▲ Many of the symptoms of schizophrenia, including hallucinations and delusions, can be extremely distressing.

This relation makes considerable intuitive sense. Because hallucinations are vivid perceptual experiences, people who experience them need to explain their origin. These "explanations" often involve delusional beliefs. A patient, like Edward, who hears the voice of God telling him that he has been given divine powers may conclude that he is an important religious figure; this conclusion would be considered a delusion.

Delusional Beliefs

Many schizophrenic patients express **delusions,** or idiosyncratic beliefs that are rigidly held in spite of their preposterous nature. Delusions have sometimes been defined as false beliefs based on incorrect inferences about reality. This definition has a number of problems, including the difficulty of establishing the ultimate truth of many situations. Ann's accusation that her husband was having an affair, for example, could easily become a choice between her word and his. This suspicion would not, on its own, be considered a delusion. The judgment that her beliefs were delusional depended to a large extent on their expansion to more absurd concerns about stolen photographs, voodoo spells, and alleged plots to kill her children.

Several additional characteristics are important in identifying delusions (Harrow,

Rattenbury, & Stoll, 1988). In the most obvious cases, delusional patients express and defend their beliefs with utmost conviction, even when presented with contradictory evidence. For example, Ann's belief that the stolen photographs were being used to cast a spell on her was totally fixed and resistant to contradiction or reconsideration. Preoccupation is another defining characteristic of delusional beliefs. During periods of acute psychosis, many patients like Ann find it difficult, if not completely impossible, to avoid thinking or talking about these beliefs. Finally, delusional patients are typically unable to consider the perspective that other people hold with regard to their beliefs. Ann, for example, was unable to appreciate the fact that other people considered her paranoid beliefs to be ridiculous.

Although delusional beliefs can take many forms, they are typically personal. They are not shared by other members of the person's family or cultural group. Common delusions include the belief that thoughts are being inserted into the patient's head, that other people are reading the patient's thoughts, or that the patient is being controlled by mysterious, external forces. Many delusions focus on grandiose or paranoid content. For example, Edward expressed the grandiose belief that his father was the Master of the universe. Ann clung persistently to the paranoid belief that someone was trying to kill her and her children.

In actual clinical practice, delusions are complex and difficult to define (Maher & Spitzer, 1993; Oltmanns, 1988). Their content is sometimes bizarre and confusing, as in the case of Edward's insistence that he had witnessed the beginning of World War II. Delusions are often fragmented, especially among severely disturbed patients. In other words, delusions are not always coherent belief systems that are consistently expressed by the patient. At various times, for example, Edward talked about being a Nazi soldier and half a person. Connections among these fragmented ideas are difficult to understand.

Disorganized Speech

Another set of schizophrenic symptoms, known as **disorganized speech,** involves the tendency of some patients to say things that don't make sense. Signs of disorganized speech include making irrelevant responses to questions, expressing disconnected ideas, and using words in peculiar ways (Berenbaum & Barch, 1995; Marengo & Harrow, 1993). This symptom is sometimes called *thought disorder* because clinicians have assumed that the failure to communicate successfully reflects a disturbance in the thought patterns that govern verbal discourse. The woman described in the following case exhibited signs of disorganized speech.

CASE STUDY

Schizophreniform Disorder

Marsha was a 32-year-old graduate student in political science. She had never been treated for psychological problems. Marsha called Dr. Higgins, a clinical psychologist who teaches at the university, to ask if she could speak with him about her twin sister's experience with schizophrenia. When she arrived at his office, she was neatly dressed and had a Bible tucked tightly under her arm. The next 3 hours were filled with a rambling discussion of Marsha's experiences during the past 10 years. She talked about her education, her experience as a high school teacher before returning to graduate school, her relationships with her parents, and—most of all—her concern for her identical twin sister, Alice, who had spent 6 of the last 10 years in psychiatric hospitals.

Marsha's emotional expression vacillated dramatically throughout the course of this conversation, which was punctuated by silly giggles and heavy sighs. Her voice would be loud and emphatic one moment as she talked about her stimulating ideas and special talents. At other moments, she would whisper in a barely audible voice or sob quietly as she described the desperation, fear, and frustration that she had experienced watching the progression of her sister's disorder. She said that she had been feeling very uptight in recent months, afraid that she might be "going crazy" like her sister. She had been scared to death to go home because her parents might sense that something was wrong with her. Her behavior was frequently inconsistent with the content of her speech. As she described her intense fears, for example, Marsha occasionally giggled uncontrollably.

Dr. Higgins also found Marsha's train of thought difficult to follow. Her speech rambled illogically from one topic to the next, and her answers to his questions were frequently tangential. For example, when Dr. Higgins asked what she meant by her repeated use of the phrase "the ideal can become real," Marsha replied, "Well, after serving the Word of Christ in California for 3 years, making a public spectacle of myself, someone apparently called my parents and said I had a problem. I said I can't take this anymore and went home. I perceived that Mom was just unbelievably nice to me. I began to think that my face was changing. Something about my forehead resembled the pain of Christ. I served Christ, but my power was not lasting."

At the end of this 3-hour interview, Dr. Higgins was convinced that Marsha should be referred to the mental health center for outpatient treatment. He explained his concerns to Marsha, but she refused to follow his advice, insisting that she did not want to receive the medication with which her sister had been treated. She agreed to return to Dr. Higgins's office in 3 days for another interview, but she did not keep that appointment.

Two weeks later, Marsha called Dr. Higgins to ask if he would talk with her immediately. It was very difficult to understand what she was saying, but she seemed to be repeating in a shrill voice "I'm losing my mind." The door to his office was closed when she arrived, but he could hear her shuffling awkwardly down the hallway, breathing heavily. He opened his door and found Marsha standing in a rigid posture, arms stiffly at her sides. Her eyes were opened wide, and she was staring vacantly at the nameplate on his door. In contrast to her prim and neat appearance at their first meeting, Marsha's hair and clothes were now in disarray. She walked stiffly into the office without bending her knees and sat, with some difficulty, in the chair next to Dr. Higgins's desk. Her facial expression was rigidly fixed. Although her eyes were open and she appeared to hear his voice, Marsha did not respond to any of Dr. Higgins's questions. Recognizing that Marsha was experiencing an acute psychotic episode, Dr. Higgins and one of the secretaries took her to the emergency room at the local hospital. ■

Marsha's speech provides one typical example of disorganized speech. She was not entirely incoherent, but parts of her speech were difficult to follow. Connections between sentences were sometimes arbitrary, and her answers to the interviewer's questions were occasionally irrelevant.

The following excerpt from an interview with another patient illustrates a more extreme form of disorganized speech.

Interviewer: Have you been nervous or tense lately?
Patient: No, I got a head of lettuce.
Interviewer: You got a head of lettuce? I don't understand.
Patient: Well, it's just a head of lettuce.
Interviewer: Tell me about lettuce. What do you mean?
Patient: Well, . . . lettuce is a transformation of a dead cougar that suffered a relapse on the lion's toe. And he swallowed the lion and something happened. The . . . see, the . . . Gloria and Tommy, they're two heads and they're not whales. But they escaped with herds of vomit, and things like that. (Neale & Oltmanns, 1980, p. 102)

When speech becomes this disrupted, it is considered *incoherent*. Notice that this patient did not string words together in a random fashion. His speech followed grammatical rules. He was placing nouns and verbs together in an appropriate order, but they didn't make any sense. His speech conveyed little, if any, meaning, and that is the hallmark of disorganized speech.

Several types of verbal communication disruption contribute to clinical judgments about disorganized speech (Docherty, DeRosa, & Andreasen, 1996). Common features of disorganized speech in schizophrenia include shifting topics too abruptly, called *loose associations* or *derailment*; replying to a question with an irrelevant response, called *tangentiality*; or persistently repeating the same word or phrase over and over again, called *perseveration*. We all say things from time to time that fit these descriptions. It is not the occasional presence of a single feature but, rather, the accumulation of a

▲ **Painting by a young schizophrenic patient, illustrating his hallucinations. He saw monsters, like the one painted here, crawling on the floor. He also believed that the chairs next to his bed had turned into devils. Patient's description of the picture: I was very sick at the time I painted this picture. The head represents my fragmented personality and a feeling of being helpless, hopeless, and off balance and of being in a cocoon of unreality. The bright colored rain and outlines represent the level of intensity of my self. The bright colors provided insulation and protected me. The colors felt like microwaves passing through my control center.**

large number of such features that defines the presence of disorganized speech.

Another type of speech disturbance is called *alogia*, which literally means "speechlessness." The term *alogia* refers to impoverished thinking, which is inferred on the basis of nonfluent or barren speech. In one form of alogia, known as *poverty of speech*, patients show remarkable reductions in the amount of speech. In another form, referred to as *thought blocking*, the patient's train of speech is interrupted before a thought or idea has been completed.

Motor Disturbances

Schizophrenic patients may exhibit various forms of unusual motor behavior, such as the rigidity displayed by Marsha when she appeared for her second interview with Dr. Higgins. *Catatonia* most often refers to immobility and marked muscular rigidity, but it can also refer to excitement and overactivity. For example, some patients engage in apparently purposeless pacing or repetitive movements, such as rubbing their hands over each other in a special pattern for hours at a time. Many catatonic patients exhibit reduced or awkward spontaneous movements. In more extreme forms, patients may assume unusual postures or remain in rigid standing or sitting positions for long periods of time. For example, some patients will lie flat on their backs in a stiff position with their heads raised slightly off the floor as though they were resting on a pillow. Catatonic patients typically resist attempts to alter their position, even though maintaining their awkward postures would normally be extremely uncomfortable or painful.

Catatonic posturing is often associated with a *stuporous state*, or generally reduced responsiveness. The person seems to be unaware of his or her surroundings. For example, during her acute psychotic episode, Marsha refused to answer questions or to make eye contact with others. Unlike people with other stuporous conditions, however, catatonic patients seem to maintain a clear state of consciousness, and it is likely that Marsha could hear and understand everything

that Dr. Higgins said to her. Many patients report, after the end of a catatonic episode, that they were perfectly aware of events that were taking place around them, in spite of their failure to respond appropriately.

Affective and Emotional Disturbances

Schizophrenic patients demonstrate emotional changes of various kinds. Ann, Edward, and Marsha all displayed emotional symptoms. One of the most characteristic phenomena involves a flattening or restriction of the person's nonverbal display of emotional responses that has sometimes been called **blunted affect,** or *affective flattening*. This symptom was clearly present in Edward's case. Blunted patients fail to exhibit signs of emotion or feeling. They are neither happy nor sad, and they appear to be completely indifferent to their surroundings. The faces of blunted patients are apathetic and expressionless. Their voices lack the typical fluctuations in volume and pitch that other people use to signal changes in their mood. Events in their environment hold little consequence for them. They may demonstrate a complete lack of concern for themselves and for others.

Another type of emotional deficit is called **anhedonia,** which refers to the inability to experience pleasure. Whereas blunted affect refers to the lack of outward expression, anhedonia is a lack of positive subjective feelings. People who experience anhedonia typically lose interest in recreational activities and social relationships, which they do not find enjoyable.

Although many schizophrenic patients appear to be emotionally blunted, others exhibit affective responses that are obviously inconsistent with their situation. This symptom is particularly difficult to describe in words. The most remarkable features of **inappropriate affect** are incongruity and lack of adaptability in emotional expression. For example, when Marsha described the private terror that she felt in the presence of her family, she giggled in a silly fashion. The content of Marsha's speech was inconsistent with her facial expression, her gestures, and her voice quality.

Social Withdrawal and Avolition

One of the most important and seriously debilitating aspects of schizophrenia is a malfunction of interpersonal relationships (Meehl, 1993). Many people with schizophrenia withdraw from social relationships. This is, of course, not surprising in light of the extensive cognitive and emotional difficulties that we have considered in the preceding pages. In many cases, however, social isolation develops before the onset of symptoms, such as hallucinations, delusions, and disorganized speech. It can be one of the earliest signs that something is wrong. This was certainly true in Ann's case. She became socially isolated from her family and friends many weeks before she started to talk openly about the stolen pictures and the plot to kill her children. Social withdrawal appears to be both a symptom of the disorder and a strategy that is actively employed by some patients to deal with their other symptoms. They may, for example, attempt to minimize interactions with other people in order to reduce levels of stimulation that can exacerbate perceptual and cognitive disorganization (Walker, Davis, & Baum, 1993).

The withdrawal seen among many schizophrenic patients is accompanied by indecisiveness, ambivalence, and a loss of willpower. This symptom is known as **avolition** (lack of volition or will). A person who suffers from avolition becomes apathetic and ceases to engage in purposeful actions.

▲ These dementia praecox patients, treated by Emil Kraepelin in the late nineteenth century, display "waxy flexibility," a feature of catatonic motor behavior. "They were put without difficulty in the peculiar positions and kept them, some with a sly laugh, others with rigid seriousness."

Classification

The broad array of symptoms outlined in the previous section have all been described as being part of schizophrenic disorders. The specific organization of symptoms has been a matter of some controversy for many years. Schizophrenic disorders have been defined in many different ways. In the following pages we briefly review some of the more prominent trends that led up to the DSM-IV description of these disorders.

Brief Historical Perspective

Descriptions of schizophrenic symptoms can be traced far back in history, but they were not considered to be symptoms of a single disorder until late in the nineteenth century (Gottesman, 1991). At that time, Emil Kraepelin, a German psychiatrist, suggested that several types of problems that previously had been classified as distinct forms of disorder should be grouped together under a single diagnostic category called **dementia praecox.** This term referred to psychoses that ended in severe intellectual deterioration (dementia) and that had an early or premature (praecox) onset, usually during adolescence. Kraepelin argued that these patients could be distinguished from those suffering from other disorders (most notably manic–depressive psychosis) largely on the basis of changes that occurred as the disorder progressed over time, primarily those changes involving the integrity of mental functions.

In 1911, Eugen Bleuler (1857–1939), a Swiss psychiatrist and a contemporary of Kraepelin, published an extremely influential monograph in which he agreed with most of Kraepelin's suggestions about this disorder. He did not believe, however, that the disorder always ended in profound deterioration or that it always began in late adolescence. Kraepelin's term *dementia praecox* was therefore unacceptable to him. Bleuler suggested a new name for the disorder— *schizophrenia.* This term referred to the *splitting of mental associations*, which Bleuler believed to be the fundamental disturbance in schizophrenia. One unfortunate consequence of this choice of terms has been the confusion among laypeople of schizophrenia with dissociative identity disorder (also known as multiple

▲ The Swiss psychiatrist Eugen Bleuler coined the term *schizophrenia* in his 1911 monograph on the disorder.

personality), a severe form of dissociative disorder (see Chapter 7). The two disorders actually have very little in common.

Many other suggestions have been made in subsequent years regarding the description and diagnosis of schizophrenia (Neale & Oltmanns, 1980). Some clinicians have favored a broader definition, whereas others have argued for a more narrow approach. These differences of opinion have focused on a number of issues.

One such issue has been the relative importance of specific types of symptoms in establishing a diagnosis of schizophrenia. Are some symptoms more useful than others in predicting the course of the disorder or the patient's response to treatment? Many clinicians have disagreed with Bleuler's choice of fundamental symptoms. One prominent alternative opinion was offered by Kurt Schneider (1959), a German psychiatrist, whose diagnostic system for schizophrenia placed primary emphasis on a set of specific types of hallucinations, delusions, and perceptual distortions that he considered to be "first-rank symptoms." Examples include thought broadcasting, in which the person believes that his or her thoughts are being transmitted so that others know what he or she is thinking; voices commenting, in which the person hears someone else's voice provide a running commentary that describes or criticizes his or her behavior; and somatic passivity, in which the person believes that he or she is a passive, unwilling recipient of physical sensations imposed by some outside force (see Further Thoughts).

FURTHER THOUGHTS

First-Person Accounts of Schizophrenia

The subjective experiences of people who struggle with schizophrenia are an important source of knowledge about this complex and disabling disorder. Some of the most fundamental elements of psychosis involve private events that cannot be observed directly by others. Fortunately, many articulate patients have provided compelling accounts of their own internal struggles. The following paragraphs were written by a patient who was being treated for schizophrenia. She describes experiences that fit Kurt Schneider's list of first-rank symptoms for this disorder.

"At the beginning of my last year at (the university), 'feelings' began to descend on me. I felt distinctly different from my usual self. I would sit for hours on end staring at nothing, and I became fascinated with drawing weird, disconnected monsters. I carefully hid my drawings, because I was certain I was being watched. Eventually I became aware of a magical force outside myself that was compelling me in certain directions. The force gained power as time went on, and soon it made me take long walks at 2 or 3 o'clock in the morning down dark alleys in my high-crime neighborhood. I had no power to disobey the force. During my walks I felt as though I was in a different, magical, four-dimensional universe. I understood that the force wanted me to take those walks so that I might be killed.

"I do not clearly understand the relationship between the force and the Alien Beings (alas, such a name!), but my universe soon became populated with them. The Alien Beings were from outer space, and of all the people in the world, only I was aware of them. The Alien Beings soon took over my body and removed me from it. They took me to a faraway place of beaches and sunlight and placed an Alien in my body to act like me. At this point I had the distinct impression that I did not really exist, because I could not make contact with my kidnapped self. I also saw that the Aliens were starting to take over other people as well, removing them from their bodies and putting Aliens in their place. Of course, the other people were unaware of what was happening; I was the only person in the world who had the power to know it. At this point I determined that the Aliens were involved in a huge conspiracy against the world.

"The Alien Beings were gaining strength and had given me a complex set of rules. The rules were very specific and governed every aspect of my behavior. One of the rules was that I could not tell anyone else about the Aliens or the rules, or else the Aliens would kill me. Another of the rules was that I had to become utterly, completely mad. So now I was living in a world of great fear.

"I had a number of other symptoms as well. I felt as though I had been pushed deep within myself, and I had little or no reaction to events or emotions around me. Almost daily the world became unreal to me. Everything outside of me seemed to fade into the distance; everything was miles away from me. I came to feel that I had the power to influence the behavior of animals; that I could, for instance, make dogs bark simply by hooking up rays of thought from my mind to theirs. Conversely, I felt that certain people had the capacity to read my mind. I became very frightened of those people and tried my best to avoid them. Whenever I saw a group of two or three people, I was sure they were talking about me. Paranoia is a very painful emotion! But when I saw crowds of people (as in a shopping mall), I felt an acute longing to wander among them, singing hymns and nursery rhymes" (Payne, 1992, pp. 726–727).

The long-term emotional impact of this disorder on parents and families has been described by a woman whose daughter, then in her mid-thirties, had exhibited symptoms of schizophrenia for 17 years. Her statement also indicates that even the most severely disturbed patients may eventually show signs of improvement.

"The saddest thing of all is to realize that the stories of family life and previous achievements that were a part of the past lives of each of these people are no longer important to them. Nothing in (our daughter's) growing up years could have prepared us for the shock and devastation of seeing this normal, happy child become totally incapacitated by schizophrenia. Coming to grips with the thought of your child living in a mental hospital, possibly for many years, leaves you with a gnawing sense of helplessness that never really dissipates.

"In the past year, a new Cindy has emerged. Where once there was a rather unfriendly, often unpleasant girl, there is now an amiable, more responsive person. Cindy smiles more these days, something a person with schizophrenia doesn't do very often. For years her face was a solemn mask, and she could neither give nor receive affection. She knew something terrible had happened to her and could not understand why no one would rescue her from the hell in her head. In the past few months she has become quite loving, and the smiles that now light her face light mine as well" (Smith, 1991, pp. 690–691). ■

DSM-IV

The current U.S. approach to the diagnosis of schizophrenic disorders gives primary consideration to three types of symptoms: positive (psychotic) symptoms, negative symptoms, and disorganized speech and behavior. The DSM-IV definition includes a more restricted range of symptoms than Bleuler's description of the disorder, which placed less emphasis on the presence of persistent psychotic symptoms such as hallucinations and delusions. The inclusion of negative symptoms does represent, however, a remnant of Bleuler's influence.

The DSM-IV lists several specific criteria for schizophrenia (see Table 13–1). The first requirement (Criterion A) is that the patient must exhibit two (or more) active symptoms for at least 1 month. Notice that only one of the characteristic symptoms is required if that symptom is a bizarre delusion or hallucination that fits Schneider's description of first-rank symptoms. Negative symptoms, such as blunted affect, avolition, and social withdrawal, play a relatively prominent role in the DSM-IV definition of schizophrenia, although some concern has been expressed about the reliability with which they are measured. The work group that developed DSM-IV considered negative symptoms vital both to determining the causes of the disorder and to treating it successfully (Andreasen & Carpenter, 1993).

The DSM-IV definition also takes into account social and occupational functioning as well as the duration of the disorder (Criteria B and C). These criteria reflect the influence of Kraepelin, who argued that the disorder is accompanied by marked impairment in functioning as well as a chronic, deteriorating course. The DSM-IV definition requires evidence of a decline in the person's social or occupational functioning as well as the presence of disturbed behavior over a continuous period of at least 6 months. Active phase symptoms do not need to be present for this entire period. The total duration of disturbance is determined by adding together continuous time during which the person has

---

TABLE 13-1

DSM-IV Diagnostic Criteria for Schizophrenia

A. Characteristic Symptoms: Two (or more) of the following, each present for a significant portion of time during a 1-month period (or less if successfully treated):
1. Delusions
2. Hallucinations
3. Disorganized speech (such as frequent derailment or incoherence)
4. Grossly disorganized or catatonic behavior
5. Negative symptoms, such as affective flattening, alogia, or avolition

(Note: Only one A symptom is required if delusions are bizarre or hallucinations consist of a voice keeping up a running commentary on the person's behavior or thoughts, or two or more voices conversing with each other.)

B. Social/Occupational Dysfunction: For a significant portion of the time since the onset of the disturbance, one or more major areas of functioning such as work, interpersonal relations, or self-care is markedly below the level achieved prior to the onset.

C. Duration: Continuous signs of the disturbance persist for at least 6 months. This 6-month period must include at least 1 month of symptoms that meet criterion A (active phase symptoms), and may include periods of prodromal or residual symptoms. During these prodromal or residual periods, the signs of the disturbance may be manifested by only negative symptoms or two or more symptoms listed in Criterion A present in an attenuated form (such as odd beliefs, unusual perceptual experiences).

---

exhibited prodromal, active, and residual symptoms of schizophrenia.

The final consideration in arriving at a diagnosis of schizophrenia involves the exclusion of related conditions, especially mood disorders. According to the DSM-IV, active phase symptoms of schizophrenia must appear in the absence of a major depressive or manic episode. If symptoms of depression or mania are present, their duration must be brief relative to the duration of the active and residual symptoms of schizophrenia.

Subtypes

Schizophrenia is a heterogeneous disorder with many different clinical manifestations and levels of severity. The title of Bleuler's classic text referred to "the group of schizophrenias" in an effort to draw attention to the varied presentations of the disorder. It is not clear, however, how best to think about the different forms of schizophrenia. Many clinicians and investigators believe that schizophrenia is a general term for a group of disorders, each of which may be caused by a completely different set of factors. Other clinicians believe that the numerous

symptoms of schizophrenia are most likely varying manifestations of the same underlying condition (Gottesman, 1991). Given the current state of evidence, it is not possible to choose between these conceptual options. Nevertheless, most investigators agree that we should at least consider the possibility that there are distinct forms.

DSM-IV SUBCATEGORIES

Kraepelin's definition of dementia praecox was based on an integration of three patterns of symptoms that had previously been considered separate syndromes: hebephrenia, catatonia, and dementia paranoides. He argued that they were all manifestations of a single disorder, and since that time they have been considered symptomatic subtypes of schizophrenia. They represent three of the five subtypes that are recognized in DSM-IV.

The subtypes are used to describe the clinical state of the patient during the most recent examination. Only one subtype can be assigned at any point in time. The five subtypes are arranged in a hierarchy so that patients who exhibit symptoms of different subtypes can be diagnosed. The catatonic type is at the top of the hierarchy. Patients who fit this description are diagnosed as catatonic even if they show additional symptoms that are characteristic of other subtypes. The remaining subtypes, in descending order, are the disorganized subtype, the paranoid subtype, the undifferentiated subtype, and the residual subtype.

The **catatonic type** is characterized by symptoms of motor immobility (including rigidity and posturing) or excessive and purposeless motor activity. In some cases, the person may be resistant to all instructions or refuse to speak, for no apparent reason. Catatonic patients may also show a decreased awareness of their environment and a lack of movements and activity. If her disorder lasted more than 6 months, Marsha would probably have received a diagnosis of schizophrenic disorder, catatonic type, on the basis of her prominent motor symptoms and stuporous behavior.

Hebephrenia is now known as the **disorganized type** of schizophrenia because it is characterized by disorganized speech, disorganized behavior, and flat or inappropriate affect. All three features must be present to make this diagnosis. Social impairment is usually quite marked in these patients. The patient's speech is frequently incoherent, and, if delusions or hallucinations are present, their content is usually not well organized. Consider, for example, the delusions expressed by Edward. At various times, he talked about Nazi soldiers and World War II, frozen corpses in Greenland, being "half a person," and having special powers because he was the son of God. These fragmented and bizarre ideas were clearly delusional, but they were not woven into a coherent framework.

The most prominent symptoms in the **paranoid type** are systematic delusions with persecutory or grandiose content. Preoccupation with frequent auditory hallucinations can also be associated with the paranoid type. Ann would have received a diagnosis of schizophrenic disorder, paranoid type, because of her preoccupation with the systematic delusion about the photographs that had been stolen and the attempt to harm her children. Patients who exhibit disorganized speech, disorganized behavior, flat or inappropriate affect, or catatonic behavior are excluded from a diagnosis of paranoid schizophrenia and would fall into one of the other subtypes.

Two additional subtypes are described in DSM-IV, presumably to cover those patients who do not fit one of the traditional types. The **undifferentiated type** of schizophrenia includes schizophrenic patients who display prominent psychotic symptoms and either meet the criteria for several subtypes or otherwise do not meet the criteria for the catatonic, disorganized, or paranoid types. They often exhibit some disorganized symptoms together with hallucinations and/or delusions.

The **residual type** includes patients who no longer meet the criteria for active phase symptoms but nevertheless demonstrate continued signs of negative symptoms or attenuated forms of delusions, hallucinations, or disorganized speech. They are in "partial remission."

EVALUATION OF TRADITIONAL SUBTYPES

The usefulness of the traditional subtypes has been debated extensively. Clinicians who advocate the use of subtype diagnoses claim that these categories are moderately stable over time (McGlashan & Fenton, 1993). Although traditional subtypes do not strongly predict either the course of the disorder or response to treatment, there is some evidence indicating that patients who fit descriptions of the catatonic and paranoid subtypes have the best prognosis, whereas those in the disorganized subtype may have the worst prognosis (Deister & Marneros, 1994; McGlashan & Fenton, 1991).

Critics respond by noting that the subtypes have relatively poor diagnostic reliability and are frequently unstable over time. Patients who fit a traditional subcategory during one psychotic episode may satisfy criteria for a different subtype diagnosis during a subsequent disturbance (Kendler, Gruenberg, & Tsuang, 1985). Perhaps most important is the fact that studies of extended families suggest that the traditional subtypes of schizophrenia are not etiologically distinct syndromes (Kendler et al., 1994).

Manfred Bleuler (1978), a Swiss psychiatrist and the son of Eugen Bleuler, treated and observed more than 200 schizophrenic patients over a long period of time. His experience suggested that distinctions among subtypes become blurred over time. Bleuler's follow-up data and much of the other research evidence

▲ People with schizophrenia sometimes exhibit disorganized behavior, like this hospitalized woman.

support the hypothesis that symptomatic subtypes are a reflection of varying stages of a single disorder or varying levels of severity of the disorder (Gottesman, 1991; Goldberg & Weinberger, 1995).

Related Disorders

The U.S. concept of schizophrenia is relatively narrow. The boundaries of the disorder have been refined by excluding patients with certain types of psychotic symptoms from a diagnosis of schizophrenic disorder. The DSM-IV lists three disorders other than schizophrenia that are characterized by prominent psychotic symptoms.

Schizoaffective disorder is an ambiguous and somewhat controversial category (Frances, First, & Pincus, 1995). It describes the symptoms of patients who fall on the boundary between schizophrenia and mood disorder with psychotic features. This diagnosis applies only to the description of a particular episode of disturbance; it does not describe the overall lifetime course of the person's disorder. Schizoaffective disorder is defined by an episode in which the symptoms of schizophrenia partially overlap with a major depressive episode or a manic episode. The key to making this diagnosis is the presence of delusions or hallucinations for at least 2 weeks in the absence of prominent mood symptoms. If the delusions and hallucinations are present only during a depressive episode, for example, the diagnosis would be major depressive episode with psychotic features. Schizoaffective disorder will continue to be a vague diagnostic category until progress is made in unraveling the etiological distinction between mood disorders and schizophrenia.

People with **delusional disorder** do not meet the full symptomatic criteria for schizophrenia, but they are preoccupied for at least 1 month with delusions that are not bizarre. These are beliefs about situations that could occur in real life, such as being followed or poisoned. Ann's delusion, for example, might have fit this description. She believed that someone was trying to kill her and her children and that someone was trying to cast a voodoo spell on them. Ann would not be assigned a diagnosis of delusional disorder, however, because she also displayed negative symptoms, such as avolition. The presence of hallucinations, disorganized speech, catatonic behavior, or negative symptoms rules out a diagnosis of delusional disorder. The definition of delusional disorder also holds that the person's behavior is not bizarre and that social and occupational functioning are not impaired except for those areas that are directly affected by the delusional belief.

Brief psychotic disorder is a category that includes those people who exhibit psychotic symptoms—delusions, hallucinations, disorganized speech, or grossly disorganized or catatonic behavior—for at least 1 day but no more than 1 month. An episode of this sort is typically accompanied by confusion and emotional turmoil, often (but not necessarily) following a markedly stressful event. After the symptoms are resolved, the person returns to the same level of functioning that had been achieved prior to the psychotic episode. This diagnosis is not assigned if the symptoms are better explained by a mood disorder, schizophrenia, or substance abuse. This category is used infrequently, and very little research has been conducted with people who have this disorder.

Course and Outcome

Traditionally, schizophrenia has been considered a severe, progressive disorder that most often begins in adolescence and typically has a poor outcome. In fact, Kraepelin considered the deteriorating course to be one of the principal defining features of the disorder. Recent evidence suggests that this view may be unnecessarily pessimistic. Many patients in fact experience a good outcome (Harding, Zubin, & Strauss, 1992). For example, Manfred Bleuler (1978) studied a sample of 208 schizophrenic patients who had been admitted to his hospital in Switzerland during 1942 and 1943. After a follow-up period of 23 years, 53 percent of the patients were either recovered or significantly improved.

In order to describe more completely the various patterns that patients followed over time, Bleuler identified two types of onset (acute or gradual), two types of course (undulating or simple), and two types of outcome (recovered/mild impairment or moderate/severe impairment). When combined, these elements form eight basic patterns for the onset and course of schizophrenic disorders, which are illustrated in Figure 13–1.

A long-term follow-up study of schizophrenia, reported by Swiss psychiatrist Luc Ciompi (1980), provided useful information about the proportion of patients whose disorder fits into the types of onset, course, and outcome that Bleuler proposed. Ciompi found that approximately half of the 228 patients in his study suffered an acute onset of symptoms during their initial episode. Again, during the intermediate stages of the disorder, half of the patients followed an undulating course, whereas the others exhibited relatively stable symptoms. By the time the patients had reached the end state of their disorder, half had recovered (or showed only mild residual symptoms), whereas the other half continued to experience moderate or severe impairment. The proportions of patients in Ciompi's study who fit different combinations of onset, course, and outcome are indicated in Figure 13–1.

Follow-up studies of schizophrenic patients have found that the description of outcome can be a complicated process. Many factors must be taken into consideration other than whether the person is still in the hospital. Is the person still exhibiting symptoms of the disorder? Does he or she have any other problems, such as depression or anxiety? Is the person employed? Does she have any friends? How does he get along with other people? The evidence indicates that different dimensions of outcome, such as social adjustment, occupational functioning, and symptom severity, are only loosely correlated. As in most situations where psychologists attempt to predict future behavior, the outcome data regarding schizophrenia suggest that the best predictor of future social adjustment is previous social adjustment. Similarly, the best predictor of symptom severity at follow-up is severity of psychotic symptoms at initial assessment (Carpenter & Strauss, 1991; Strauss & Carpenter, 1978, 1981).

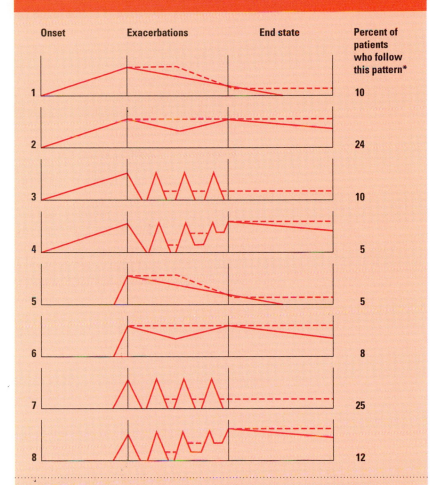

Course and Outcome in Schizophrenia (8 types)

FIGURE 13-1: Patterns identified in long-term follow-up studies. The horizontal axis represents time and the vertical axis represents severity of disturbance. Dotted lines represent slight variations on the overall pattern.

*Data from Ciompi, 1980.

Source: C.M. Harding, 1988, Course types in schizophrenia: An analysis of European and American studies, *Schizophrenia Bulletin, 14,* 633–643.

Epidemiology

One of the most informative ways of examining the frequency of schizophrenia is to consider the *lifetime morbid risk*—that is, the proportion of a specific population that will be affected by the disorder at some time during their lives. Most studies in Europe and the United States have reported lifetime morbid risk figures of approximately 1 percent (Jablensky, 1986). In other words, approximately 1 out of every 100 people will experience or display schizophrenic symptoms at some time during

their lives. Of course, prevalence rates depend on the diagnostic criteria that are used to define schizophrenia in any particular study, as well as the methods that are used to identify cases in the general population. Investigators who have used more narrow or restrictive criteria for the disorder typically report lower morbid risk figures.

Data from the Epidemiologic Catchment Area (ECA) study are consistent with figures reported earlier (Keith, Regier, & Rae, 1991).

Using DSM-III criteria for the disorder, the investigators found a lifetime prevalence of 1.3 percent for schizophrenia and 0.2 percent for schizophreniform disorder. The mean age of onset was 20 years, and 71 percent of the people who met criteria for schizophrenia had experienced their first symptoms by the age of 25. For those persons who no longer exhibited active symptoms at the time of the interview, the mean duration of the disorder was 15 years.

Gender Differences

Most epidemiological studies have reported that, across the life span, men and women are equally likely to be affected by schizophrenia (Gottesman, 1991; Keith, Regier, & Rae, 1991). This conclusion has been challenged in recent years, however, by studies that suggest that, among new cases of schizophrenia, men may outnumber women by a ratio of at least 2:1 (e.g., Iacono & Beiser, 1992). This pattern seems to depend on the breadth of the diagnostic criteria that are employed to identify cases of the disorder; studies that employ broader, more inclusive sets of diagnostic criteria are more likely to find equivalent rates of schizophrenia in men and women (Goldstein, 1995a).

The controversy surrounding gender differences in incidence may reflect, at least in part, gender differences in more specific aspects of schizophrenia. There are some interesting and widely recognized differences between male and female patients with regard to patterns of onset, symptomatology, and course of the disorder. For example, the average age at which

schizophrenic males begin to exhibit overt symptoms is younger by about 4 or 5 years than the average age at which schizophrenic women first experience problems (Hafner et al., 1994). A summary of proposed gender differences in schizophrenia is presented in Table 13–2. Male patients are more likely than female patients to exhibit negative symptoms, and they are also more likely to follow a chronic, deteriorating course.

Gender differences in the age of onset and symptomatic expression of schizophrenia can be interpreted in several ways. The alternatives fall into two types of hypotheses (Castle et al., 1995; Goldstein, 1995b; Lewine & Seeman, 1995). One approach assumes that schizophrenia is a single disorder and that its expression varies in men and women. A common, genetically determined vulnerability to schizophrenia might be expressed differently in men than in women. Mediating factors that might account for this difference could be biological differences between men and women—perhaps involving certain hormones—or different environmental demands, such as the timing and form of stresses associated with typical male and female sex roles. An alternative approach suggests that there are two qualitatively distinct subtypes of schizophrenia: one with an early onset that affects men more often than women, and another with a later onset that affects women more often than men. Both approaches fit the general diathesis-stress model. The available evidence does not allow us to favor one of these explanations over the other.

Cross-Cultural Comparisons

Schizophrenia has been observed in virtually every culture that has been subjected to careful scrutiny. Of course, the formal term *schizophrenia* is not used in societies that have not adopted modern medical practices, but the symptoms of the disorder are nevertheless present (see Research Close-Up in Chapter 1).

Two large-scale epidemiological studies, conducted by teams of scientists working for the World Health Organization (WHO), indicate that the incidence of schizophrenia is relatively constant across different cultural settings. The International Pilot Study of Schizophrenia (IPSS) began in the 1960s and was conducted in nine countries in Europe, North America, South America, Africa, and Asia. It

---

TABLE 13-2

Typical Gender Differences in Schizophrenia

Variable	Men	Women
Age of onset	Earlier (18–25)	Later (25–35)
Premorbid adjustment	Poor social functioning; more schizotypal traits	Good social functioning; fewer schizotypal traits
Typical symptoms	More negative symptoms; more withdrawn and passive	More hallucinations and paranoia; more emotional and impulsive
Course	More often chronic; poorer response to treatment	Less often chronic; better response to treatment

Source: Based on J. M. Goldstein, 1995, The impact of gender on understanding the epidemiology of schizophrenia. In M. V. Seeman (Ed.), *Gender and Psychopathology*, pp. 159–199. Washington, DC: American Psychiatric Press.

included 1,200 patients who were followed for 5 years after their initial hospitalization. The Collaborative Study on the Determinants of Outcome of Severe Mental Disorders (DOS) was conducted a few years later in six of the same countries that had participated in the IPSS, plus four others. The DOS study included more than 1,500 patients. Both the IPSS and DOS projects examined rural and urban areas in both Western and non-Western countries. For purposes of cultural comparison, the countries were divided into those that were "developing" and those that were already "developed" on the basis of prevailing socioeconomic conditions. All the interviewers were trained in the use of a single, standardized interview schedule, and all employed the same sets of diagnostic criteria.

The IPSS results indicated that patients who exhibited characteristic signs and symptoms of schizophrenia were found in all of the study sites. Comparisons of patients across research centers revealed more similarities than differences in clinical symptoms at the time of entry into the study, which was always an active phase of disorder that required psychiatric treatment.

Using a relatively narrow set of diagnostic criteria, scientists found that the incidence of schizophrenia did not differ significantly among the research centers. The IPSS investigators also found that clinical and social outcomes at 2- and 5-year follow-up were significantly better for schizophrenic patients in developing countries than in developed countries, such as the United States, England, and Russia (Leff et al., 1992). The DOS study confirmed those results (Jablensky et al., 1992).

Taken together, the WHO studies provide compelling support for the conclusion that schizophrenia occurs with similar frequency and presents with similar symptoms in different cultures. The more favorable clinical outcome that was observed in India and Nigeria has been interpreted as being a product of the greater tolerance and acceptance that are extended to people with psychotic symptoms in developing countries. This conclusion is consistent with evidence regarding the relationship between frequency of relapse and patterns of family communication, which we consider later in this chapter in the section on expressed emotion.

Etiological Considerations and Research

Having considered the defining characteristics of schizophrenia, ways in which it has been classified, and some basic information regarding its distribution within the general population, we now review the evidence regarding factors that might contribute to the development of the disorder, as well as its course and outcome.

Biological Factors

Many of the early investigators who originally defined schizophrenia at the beginning of the twentieth century believed that the disorder was the product of a biological dysfunction. At that time, very little was known about human genetics or the biochemistry of the brain. Research in the areas of molecular genetics and the neurosciences has progressed at an explosive rate in the past decade. Much of what we know today about the biological substrates of schizophrenia has emerged from advances that have taken place in other sciences.

GENETICS

The role of genetic factors has been studied more extensively with regard to schizophrenia than with any other type of mental disorder. The existing data are based on sophisticated methods that have been refined over many years. The cumulative weight of this evidence points clearly toward some type of genetic influence in the transmission of this disorder (Gottesman & Moldin, 1997).

Family Studies   Figure 13–2 illustrates the lifetime risk for schizophrenia for various types of relatives of a person with schizophrenia. Irving Gottesman, a psychologist at the University of Virginia, created this figure by pooling data from 40 European studies that were published between 1920 and 1987 (Gottesman, 1991). All of the studies employed conservative diagnostic criteria for the disorder.

Consider the data for first-degree relatives and second-degree relatives. On average,

▲ **Irving Gottesman, Sherrell J. Aston Professor of Psychology at the University of Virginia, is one of the world's leading experts on genetic factors and schizophrenia.**

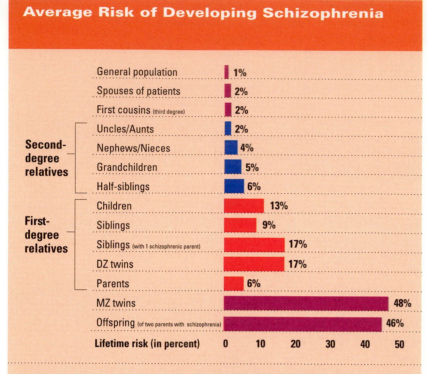

FIGURE 13-2: Average risk of schizophrenia among biological relatives of a schizophrenic proband.

Source: I.I. Gottesman, 1991, *Schizophrenia Genesis: The Origins of Madness,* p. 96. New York: Freeman.

siblings and children share 50 percent of their genes with the schizophrenic proband; nieces, nephews, and cousins share only 25 percent. The lifetime morbid risk for schizophrenia is much greater among first-degree relatives than it is among second-degree relatives. The risk in the second-degree relatives is greater than the 1 percent figure that is typically reported for people in the general population. As the degree of genetic similarity increases between an individual and a schizophrenic patient, the risk to that person increases. The family history data are consistent with the hypothesis that the transmission of schizophrenia is influenced by genetic factors. They do not prove the point, however, because family studies do not separate genetic and environmental events (see Chapter 2).

Twin Studies   Several twin studies have examined concordance rates for schizophrenia. The results of these studies are also summarized in Figure 13–2. The average concordance rate for MZ twins is 48 percent, whereas the comparable figure for DZ twins is 17 percent. One study from Norway, published after Gottesman computed average rates for his figure, found a concordance rate of 48 percent among MZ twins

and only 4 percent among DZ twins (Onstad et al., 1991). Although the specific rates vary somewhat from study to study, all of the published reports have found that MZ twins are significantly more likely than DZ twins to be concordant for schizophrenia. This pattern suggests strongly that genetic factors play an important role in the development of the disorder.

It should also be pointed out, however, that none of the twin studies of schizophrenia has found a concordance rate that even approaches 100 percent, which would be expected if genetic factors were entirely responsible for schizophrenia. Thus the twin studies also provide compelling evidence for the importance of environmental events. Some people apparently inherit a predisposition to the development of schizophrenia. Among that select group of vulnerable individuals, certain environmental events must determine whether a given person will eventually exhibit the full-blown symptoms of the disorder.

Adoption Studies   Studies of children who were adopted away from their biological parents and reared by foster families provide this type of clear distinction between genetic and environmental influence. The first adoption study of schizophrenia was reported by Leonard Heston (1966), a psychiatrist at the University of Washington. He began by identifying records for a group of 49 children who were born between 1915 and 1945 while their mothers were hospitalized for schizophrenia. All the children were apparently normal at birth and were separated from their mothers within 3 days of birth. To rule out possible exposure to the environment associated with the mother's psychosis, any child who had been in contact with maternal relatives was excluded from the study. A control group of children was selected using the admission records of foundling homes where many of the target children had originally been placed. These children were matched to the patients' children on a number of variables, including age, sex, type of eventual placement, and length of institutionalization.

Heston was able to locate and interview most of the offspring, the majority of whom were then in their mid-thirties. Five of the adult offspring of schizophrenic mothers received a diagnosis of schizophrenia. Correcting for the fact that most of the participants were still within the period of risk for the disorder, this resulted in a lifetime morbidity risk for schizophrenia of

16.6 percent in the target group, which is almost exactly the rate observed among children of schizophrenic parents who were raised by their biological parents (see Figure 13–2). In contrast, none of the adult offspring in the control group received a diagnosis of schizophrenia. Because the only difference between the two groups was the genetic relationship between the target offspring and their schizophrenic biological mothers, Heston's data indicate that genetic factors play a role in the development of the disorder. Several other adoption studies have been concerned with schizophrenia, and all reach the same conclusion as Heston's original report (see Gottesman, 1991, and Kendler & Diehl, 1993, for reviews of this literature).

The Spectrum of Schizophrenic Disorders Results from adoption and twin studies have also provided interesting clues regarding the boundaries of the concept of schizophrenia. Several types of psychotic disorders and personality disorders resemble schizophrenia in one way or another, including schizoaffective disorder, delusional disorder, and schizotypal personality disorder. Are these conditions a reflection of the same genetically determined predisposition as schizophrenia, or are they etiologically distinct disorders? If they are genetically related, then investigators should find that the biological relatives of schizophrenic adoptees are more likely to exhibit these conditions as well as schizophrenia. Table 9–6 (p. 339) presents one set of data from this type of study. The overall pattern of results suggests that vulnerability to schizophrenia is sometimes expressed as schizophrenia-like personality traits and other types of psychosis that are not specifically included in the DSM-IV definition of schizophrenia (Kendler & Diehl, 1993).

Linkage Studies The combined results from twin and adoption studies indicate that genetic factors are involved in the transmission of schizophrenia. This conclusion does not imply, however, that the manner in which schizophrenia develops is well understood. We know little beyond the fact that genetic factors are involved in some way. The mode of transmission has not been identified. Some clinical scientists believe that a single dominant gene is involved. Others believe that schizophrenia is a polygenic characteristic, which means that it is the product of a reasonably large number of genes rather than a single gene (see Chapter 2).

One of the most exciting areas of research on genetics and schizophrenia focuses on the search for genetic linkage (see Research Methods in Chapter 14 for an explanation of this process). Studies of this type are designed to identify the location of a specific gene that is responsible for the disorder (or some large component of the disorder).

Linkage analysis has not yet produced any firm conclusions or replicable findings. Kendler and Diehl (1993) reviewed more than 30 genetic linkage studies of schizophrenia. None of the subsequent studies has found strong support for linkage to any genetic locus. Supporters of linkage analysis contend that the absence of definitive discoveries is not necessarily surprising when we consider that there are probably tens of thousands of genes that influence activities in the brain. They feel that the search for a particular gene that causes schizophrenia will take much time. Critics respond that schizophrenia is a polygenic disorder, and therefore we will never trace its etiology to a single gene. There is good reason to believe that polygenic models provide the best explanation for the distribution of the disorder within families (Gottesman & Moldin, 1997; Vogler et al., 1990).

PREGNANCY AND BIRTH COMPLICATIONS

People with schizophrenia are more likely than the general population to have been exposed to various problems during pregnancy and to have suffered birth injuries. Problems during pregnancy include the mother's contracting various types of diseases and infections. Birth complications include extended labor, breech delivery, forceps delivery, and the umbilical cord wrapped around the baby's neck. These events may be harmful, in part, because they impair circulation or otherwise reduce the availability of oxygen to developing brain regions. Birth records indicate that the mothers of people who later develop schizophrenia experienced more complications at the time of labor and delivery (McNeil, Cantor-Graae, Sjostrom, et al., 1994; McNeil, Cantor-Graae, Torrey, Sjostrom, et al., 1994).

It is not clear whether the effects of pregnancy and birth complications interact with genetic factors (Gottesman, 1991). They may produce neurodevelopmental abnormalities that result in schizophrenia regardless of family history for the disorder. Conversely, a fetus that is genetically predisposed to schizophrenia may be more susceptible to brain injury following certain kinds of obstetric difficulties.

Dietary factors may also play a role in the etiology of the disorder. Severe maternal malnutrition in the early months of pregnancy leads to an increased risk of schizophrenia among the offspring. This conclusion is based on a study of medical and psychiatric records of people who were born in the western part of the Netherlands between 1944 and 1946 (Susser et al., 1996). The Nazi blockade of ports and other supply routes in this area led to a severe famine at the end of World War II. People who were conceived during the worst months of the famine were twice as likely to develop schizophrenia as were people whose mothers became pregnant at other times, including the early months of the famine. These results suggest that prenatal nutritional deficiencies may disrupt normal development of the fetal nervous system.

VIRAL INFECTIONS

Some speculation has focused on the potential role that viral infections may play in the etiology of schizophrenia (Gupta, 1993; Torrey & Yolken, 1995). One indirect line of support for this hypothesis comes from studies indicating that people who develop schizophrenia are somewhat more likely than other people to have been born during the winter months (Bradbury & Miller, 1985; Huttunen, Machon, & Mednick, 1994; Pulver et al., 1992). Some clinicians interpret this pattern to mean that, during their

pregnancies, the mothers were more likely to develop viral infections, which are more prevalent during the winter. This possibility has received considerable attention in the research literature and remains an important topic of debate. Support for the hypothesis remains indirect, however. No evidence has been found to confirm a direct link between viral infections and schizophrenia (Kirch, 1993).

NEUROPATHOLOGY

One important step toward understanding the etiology of schizophrenia would be to identify its neurological underpinnings. If people with schizophrenia suffer from a form of neurological dysfunction, shouldn't it be possible to observe differences between the structure of their brains and those of other people? This is a very challenging task. Scientists have invented methods to create images of the living human brain (see Chapter 4). Some of these procedures provide static pictures of various brain structures at rest, just as an X ray provides a photographic image of a bone or some other organ of the body. More recently, sophisticated methods have enabled us to create functional images of the brain while a person is performing different tasks. Studies using these techniques have produced evidence indicating that a number of brain areas are involved in schizophrenia (Gur & Pearlson, 1993; Van Horn, Berman, & Weinberger, 1996). You may want to review the description of brain structures in Chapter 2 (Figure 2–4) and consult Figure 13–3 as well as Figure 14–3 before reading the next sections of this chapter.

Structural Brain Imaging Many investigations of brain structure in people with schizophrenia have employed computerized tomographic (CT) scanning, which produces a series of two-dimensional images at sequential slices or planes of the brain (see Chapter 4 for an explanation of this process). The most consistent result across a large number of CT-scan studies has been the finding that some people with schizophrenia have mildly to moderately enlarged *lateral ventricles*, the cavities on each side of the brain that are filled with cerebrospinal fluid (Raz & Raz, 1990; Kotrla & Weinberger, 1995). These differences seem to reflect a natural part of the disorder rather than a side effect of treatment with antipsychotic medication. In fact, some studies have found enlarged ventricles in young schizophrenic patients before they have been exposed to any form of treatment. One

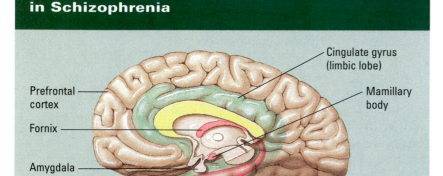

Areas of the Brain Implicated in Schizophrenia

Cingulate gyrus (limbic lobe)

Mamillary body

Prefrontal cortex

Fornix

Amygdala

Parahippocampal gyrus (limbic lobe)

Temporal lobe

Hippocampus

FIGURE 13-3: Brain imaging studies have suggested that specific components of the limbic system, including the hippocampus and the amygdala, may be dysfunctional in schizophrenia.

Source: Adapted from F. Martini and M. Timmons, 1995, *Human Anatomy*, p. 318. Upper Saddle River, NJ: Prentice Hall.

important study has also found enlarged ventricles prior to the onset of symptoms (see Research Close-Up). Significantly, these differences do not appear to become more marked as time goes on. The structural changes seem to occur early in the development of the disorder and therefore may play a role in the onset of symptoms.

RESEARCH CLOSE-UP

The Danish High-Risk Project

Our ability to understand the etiology of schizophrenia is limited by a lack of information regarding patients' developmental histories. Once a person has become psychotic, it is difficult to reconstruct events from previous years. Furthermore, comparisons between schizophrenic patients and other groups are difficult to interpret because the patients have already been exposed to treatment. For these reasons, it would be extremely useful if systematic data could be collected before the onset of the disorder.

In 1962, Sarnoff Mednick, now a psychologist at the University of Southern California, and Fini Schulsinger, a Danish psychiatrist, began in Denmark a longitudinal study of biological children of parents with schizophrenia (Mednick & Schulsinger, 1968). These people were selected because, in comparison to members of the general population, they are at **high risk** for schizophrenia. Roughly 13 percent of the high-risk group would be expected to develop the disorder as adults (see Figure 13–2). The project included 207 high-risk children whose biological mothers had been diagnosed as schizophrenic and 104 low-risk children to serve as a comparison group. The families of the low-risk children had been free of mental illness for at least three generations. When the study was begun, none of the children had exhibited any overt signs of psychological disorder. The family environments (for example, social class, rural or urban residence) were similar in both groups.

Mednick and his colleagues have collected an enormous amount of information in order to describe the developmental histories of children in both groups, from birth to adulthood. They relied on hospital records to determine the frequency of pregnancy and delivery complications associated with each subject's birth. The investigators conducted follow-up assessments, including structured diagnostic interviews, with each person at two principal times: in the early 1970s and again in the late 1980s, when the participants' average age was 42 years. The latter assessment included the use of CT scans to detect structural brain pathology.

It has been more than 30 years since the Danish study began, and 31 of the high-risk offspring have developed schizophrenia (Parnas et al., 1993). Age-corrected morbid risk rates for schizophrenia in the high- and low-risk groups are 17 percent and 3 percent, respectively. The high-risk offspring were also more likely than the low-risk offspring to meet the criteria for schizotypal personality disorder (18 percent compared to 5 percent). Rates of mood disorders were similar in both groups, suggesting that the high-risk group was predisposed to schizophrenia-spectrum disorders in particular rather than to serious mental disorders in general.

The most important data in this project involve factors that may precede the onset of schizophrenic symptoms. Several intriguing findings have been reported. For example, researchers noted a correlation between delivery complications and enlarged ventricles among people in the high-risk group but not among people in the low-risk group (Cannon et al., 1993). In addition, an earlier report indicated that, in comparison to members of the high-risk group who did not become schizophrenic, those high-risk individuals who did develop schizophrenia had experienced more pregnancy and birth complications (Cannon, Mednick, & Parnas, 1990). This was especially true for people who developed negative symptoms of the disorder. Thus far, the overall pattern of results suggests that vulnerability to schizophrenia may be associated with a pattern of fetal brain development that is especially sensitive to disruptions caused by delivery complications. The combination of genetic risk and problems in delivery seems to be especially relevant. Data from the Danish high-risk project are also consistent with the hypothesis that neurodevelopmental problems in schizophrenia are antecedents rather than consequences of the disorder. ■

Many questions remain to be answered regarding the relation between enlarged ventricles and schizophrenia. Does the pattern reflect a generalized deterioration of the brain, or is it the result of a defect in specific brain sites? We don't know. Is the presence of enlarged ventricles consistently found in some subset of schizophrenic patients? Some investigators have reported an association between this type of neuropathology and other factors, such as negative symptoms, poor response to medication, and absence of family history of the disorder. These are all interesting possibilities, but none has been firmly established (Torrey et al., 1994).

With *magnetic resonance imaging (MRI)*, investigators are able to identify clearly many specific smaller structures within the brain that were not clearly visible using CT scans. The temporal lobes have been studied rather extensively using MRI scans. Several studies have reported decreased size of the hippocampus, the amygdala, and the thalamus, which are all parts of the limbic system (Buchsbaum et al., 1996; Gur & Pearlson, 1993). These areas of the brain (located in the temporal lobes; see Figure 13–3) play a crucial role in the regulation of emotion as well as the integration of cognition and emotion. Decreased size of these structures in the limbic area of the temporal lobes may be especially noticeable on the left side of the brain, which plays an important role in the control of language. One interesting study found that schizophrenic patients who exhibited the greatest degree of disorganized speech were most likely to show a decrease in the size of left temporal lobe structures (Shenton et al., 1992).

Results for several other brain areas have been less consistent than the data regarding ventricles, the hippocampus, and the amygdala. Some studies have reported significant differences between people with schizophrenia and comparison groups with regard to areas of the frontal cortex and the basal ganglia (Kotrla & Weinberger, 1995; Sharif, Gewirtz, & Iqbal, 1993).

Another set of findings is focused on the planum temporale, an area of the temporal cortex that is involved in the processing of auditory stimuli (Clarke, 1994; see Figure 2–4). Normal men show marked *hemispheric asymmetry* for this structure; it is larger in the left hemisphere of the brain than in the right hemisphere. Women are less likely to show asymmetry with regard to the size of the planum temporale (Kulynych et al., 1994). Studies using MRI technology indicate that hemispheric asymmetry in the size of this brain structure may be reversed in men with schizophrenia; that is, it is larger in the right hemisphere (McCarley et al., 1993; Petty et al., 1995). This neurological irregularity may be related to their difficulties in verbal communication, as language skills seem to be regulated by the left hemisphere of the brain.

Functional Brain Imaging   In addition to CT- and MRI-scan procedures, which provide static pictures of brain structures, clinical scientists are also using techniques that provide dynamic images of brain functions. One of these procedures involves the measurement of *regional cerebral blood flow (rCBF)*. Images can be generated while the subject is at rest or performing a specific task. Visual stimulation will produce increased cerebral blood flow in the visual cortex; people performing a simple motor task exhibit increased flow in the motor cortex.

Studies using the measurement of rCBF have found differences between people with schizophrenia and others, particularly in the frontal regions of the brain (Weinberger & Lipska, 1995). Daniel Weinberger, a psychiatrist at the National Institute of Mental Health, and his colleagues have measured rCBF in the prefrontal cortex while participants perform an abstract problem-solving task that presumably requires cognitive abilities that are mediated in the frontal lobes. Normal people show an increase in blood flow to the frontal regions of the brain when they are engaged in this task. Many schizophrenic patients, in contrast, do not show this same increase. This decrease in frontal lobe activity is sometimes called *hypofrontality*. Studies of brain metabolism and blood flow have also identified functional changes in the temporal lobes and basal ganglia in many persons with schizophrenia.

Another dynamic brain imaging technique is *positron emission tomography (PET)* scanning. Like rCBF, it can reflect changes in brain activity as the person responds to various task demands. The results of PET-scan

▼ **3-D MRI of the brains of a normal adult and a schizophrenic patient, illustrating structural changes. The cerebrum appears in red. In the patient's brain (right) the hippocampus (yellow) is shrunken and the fluid-filled ventricles (grey) are enlarged.**

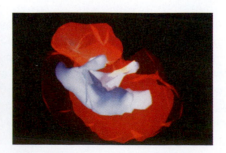

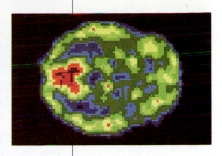

studies are consistent with rCBF results and suggest dysfunction in the frontal cortex as well as the temporal lobes (Goldman-Rakic, 1996; Gur et al., 1995). These problems are also observed among patients with major mood disorders.

The role of neurological abnormalities in schizophrenia has been highlighted by a study of identical twins conducted by a group of investigators at the National Institute of Mental Health (NIMH). Participants included 27 pairs of twins discordant for schizophrenia and 13 pairs that were concordant for the disorder. Changes in brain structure, measured by MRI, and changes in brain function, measured by cerebral blood flow, were prominent in the twins who had developed schizophrenia. Their well co-twins also exhibited more neurological impairment than a group of normal control participants, but these abnormalities were less marked than those found in the probands. Among discordant monozygotic pairs, the schizophrenic twin typically had the smaller hippocampus and smaller amygdala. The schizophrenic twins always showed reduced frontal lobe rCBF activity compared with their unaffected co-twins. Results for enlarged ventricles were less consistent. In general, neurological dysfunction seemed to be associated with the overall severity of the disorder rather than being indicative of an etiologically distinct subgroup of patients (Torrey et al., 1994).

General Conclusions   The primary conclusion that can be drawn from existing brain imaging studies is that schizophrenia is associated with diffuse patterns of neuropathology. The most consistent findings point toward structural as well as functional irregularities in the limbic areas of the temporal lobes, which play an important role in cognitive and emotional processes. The neural network connecting these areas with the frontal cortex may be fundamentally disordered in schizophrenia.

Speculation regarding disruptions in neural circuitry must also be tempered with caution. Evidence of neuropathology does not seem to be unique to schizophrenic patients. Many patients with other psychiatric and neurological disorders show similar changes in brain structure and function. Furthermore, a specific brain lesion has not been identified, and it is unlikely that one will be found. As Paul Meehl (1990) has argued, it is unlikely that a disorder as complex as schizophrenia will be traced to a single

site in the brain. The various symptoms and cognitive deficits that have been observed in schizophrenic patients may be linked to a host of subtle disruptions in neurological functions (M. Strauss, 1993).

It should also be emphasized that brain imaging procedures are not diagnostically meaningful tests for mental disorders. For example, a CT scan showing enlarged ventricles does not prove that a patient has schizophrenia. Brain imaging procedures have identified interesting *group* differences, but they do not predict the presence of schizophrenia for *individuals*. The group differences that have been observed are quite subtle in comparison to the levels of neuropathology found in disorders such as Alzheimer's disease and Huntington's disease (see Chapter 14). Some schizophrenic patients do not show abnormalities in brain structure or function.

A dramatic example of this point was found in the NIMH study of discordant MZ twins. In one pair, the well twin was a successful businessman who had never had any problems with mental disorder. His twin brother had been severely impaired with schizophrenia for 20 years. The well twin had ventricles that were five times larger than those of the schizophrenic twin. Thus we should approach all these hypotheses with caution and skepticism.

NEUROCHEMISTRY

The neurological underpinnings of schizophrenia may not take the form of changes in the size or organization of brain structures. They may be even more subtle, involving alterations in the functioning of particular parts of the brain. As we saw in Chapter 2, the process of chemical transmission in the brain is an active, dynamic system. Neurons regulate the synthesis and release of neurotransmitters as they monitor levels of these chemicals in the system. Too much dopamine in the synapse can result

▲ **Photo on left shows a PET scan of the brain of a normal person, and photo on right shows a PET scan of a person with a schizophrenic disorder who was not taking antipsychotic medication at the time. The images were made while the people were engaged in performing a continuous-performance task. Higher rates of metabolic activity are indicated by colors in the yellow-red end of the spectrum; colors in the blue-green range indicate lower rates. Notice the relatively higher frontal metabolism in the normal person's brain and the higher posterior metabolism in the patient's brain.**

in decreased synthesis in the cell body. Similarly, insufficient amounts of dopamine can result in the synthesis of extra postsynaptic receptors. These dynamic properties are important in understanding the way in which antipsychotic drugs affect abnormal behavior.

The Dopamine Hypothesis of Schizophrenia   Scientists have proposed various neurochemical theories to account for the etiology of schizophrenia (Iqbal & van Praag, 1995; Kahn & Davidson, 1995). The most influential theory, known as the *dopamine hypothesis*, focuses on the function of specific dopamine pathways in the limbic area of the brain. The original version of the dopamine hypothesis proposed that the symptoms of schizophrenia are the product of excessive levels of dopaminergic activity. This hypothesis grew out of attempts to understand how antipsychotic drugs, also known as *neuroleptics*, improve the adjustment of many schizophrenic patients. Animals who receive doses of neuroleptic drugs show a marked increase in the production of dopamine. In 1963, Arvid Carlsson, a Swedish pharmacologist, suggested that neuroleptics block postsynaptic dopamine receptors. The presynaptic neuron recognizes the presence of this blockade and increases its release of dopamine in a futile attempt to override it (Carlsson & Lindqvist, 1963).

Further support for the dopamine hypothesis came from two additional observations. First, patients who receive neuroleptic medication for an extended period of time often develop motor side effects that resemble the symptoms of Parkinson's disease, which is produced by the destruction of dopamine in certain brain pathways (see Chapter 14). It therefore seemed likely that schizophrenia was associated with an initially overactive dopamine system and that treatment with antipsychotic medication corrected this problem.

The second observation involves the effect of chronic amphetamine use. Amphetamine is a dopamine agonist. In other words, it is able to stimulate firing by dopamine neurons. People who take amphetamines for an extended period of time often develop a form of paranoid psychosis that is very similar to schizophrenia. This suggests that the natural form of schizophrenia may also be associated with overactivity in these neural pathways.

If the dopamine system is dysfunctional in schizophrenic patients, what is the specific form of this problem? One possibility that has received a great deal of attention in the past few years is concerned with the number of postsynaptic dopamine receptors. The potency of various types of antipsychotic drugs is specifically related to their ability to block one type of dopamine receptor, known as D_2 *receptors* (Creese, Burt, & Snyder, 1976). Autopsy studies of schizophrenic patients' brains have found that some patients have an excessive number of D_2 receptors in the striatum, while the number of D_1 receptors is apparently normal (Kornhuber et al., 1989).

With regard to etiology, the most important question is whether an increased number of D_2 receptors is present before schizophrenic patients are treated with neuroleptic medication. The results of autopsy studies may simply reflect the fact that treatment with antipsychotic drugs produces an increase in the number of D_2 receptors. The density of dopamine receptors can be measured in the brains of living patients using PET scanning procedures. One laboratory has reported that untreated, first-episode schizophrenic patients have significantly more D_2 receptors when compared to a group of normal volunteers, but other studies have failed to replicate this result (Farde et al., 1995).

Current Neurochemical Models   The original dopamine hypothesis stimulated an enormous amount of research, and it has been an extremely useful model from that point of view. At least for some patients, a dysfunction of certain dopamine tracts in the brain is somehow involved in the disorder. On the other hand, biologically minded investigators now generally agree that this model was too simple. It failed to account for many different aspects of the disorder, including the following: Some patients do not respond positively to drugs that block dopamine receptors; the effects of antipsychotic drugs require several days to become effective, but dopamine blockage begins immediately; research studies that examined the by-products of dopamine in cerebrospinal fluid were inconclusive at best.

Current neurochemical hypotheses regarding schizophrenia focus on a broad array of neurotransmitters, including GABA, acetylcholine, serotonin, and neuropeptides. Special interest has been focused on serotonin pathways since the introduction of a new class of antipsychotic drugs such as clozapine (Clozaril) that are useful in treating patients who were resistant to traditional neuroleptic drugs. (See our later section on treatment.) These "atypical" antipsychotics apparently work by producing a strong blockade of serotonin receptors and only a weak blockade of D_2 receptors. This pattern leads to speculation that the neurochemical substrates of schizophrenia may involve a complex interaction between serotonin and dopamine pathways in the brain (Kapur & Remington, 1996; Meltzer, 1993).

Social Factors

There is little question that biological factors play an important role in the etiology of schizophrenia, but twin studies also provide compelling evidence for the importance of environmental events. The disorder is expressed in its full-blown form only when vulnerable individuals experience some type of environmental event, which might include anything from nutritional variables to stressful life events (Fowles, 1992). What sorts of nongenetic events interact with genetic factors to produce schizophrenia? Specific answers are not available at the present time. We can, however, review some of the hypotheses that have been proposed and studied.

SOCIAL CLASS

One general indicator of a person's status within a community's hierarchy of prestige and influence is social class. People from different social classes are presumably exposed to different levels of environmental stress, with those people in the lowest class being subjected to the most hardships. More than 50 years ago, social scientists working in Chicago found that the highest prevalence of schizophrenia was found in neighborhoods of the lowest socioeconomic status (Faris & Dunham, 1939). Many research studies have subsequently confirmed this finding in several other geographic areas (Neale & Oltmanns, 1980). The evidence supporting an inverse relationship between social class and schizophrenia is substantial.

There are two ways to interpret the relationship between social class and schizophrenia. One holds that harmful events associated with membership in the lowest social classes, which might include many factors ranging from stress and social isolation to poor nutrition, play a causal role in the development of the disorder. This is often called the *social causation hypothesis*. It is also possible, however, that low social class is an outcome rather than a cause of schizophrenia. Those people who develop schizophrenia may be less able than others to complete a higher-level education or hold a well-paying job. Their cognitive and social impairments may cause downward social mobility. In other words, regardless of the social class of their family of origin, many schizophrenic patients may gradually drift into the lowest social classes. This view is sometimes called the *social selection hypothesis*.

Research studies have found evidence supporting both views. The social selection hypothesis is supported by studies that have compared the occupational roles of male schizophrenic patients with those of their fathers. The patients are frequently less successful than their fathers, whereas the opposite pattern is typical of men who do not have schizophrenia (Goldberg & Morrison, 1963; Jones et al., 1993). It is also true, however, that a disproportionately high percentage of the fathers of schizophrenic patients were from the lowest social class (Turner & Wagonfeld, 1967). The latter finding is consistent with the social causation hypothesis.

Other support for the social causation hypothesis has been found using different research strategies. For example, one unique study considered the relation between economic conditions (employment rates) and rates of psychiatric hospitalization in the state of New York between 1852 and 1967 (Brenner, 1973). Throughout this extended period of time, increases in the rate of unemployment were followed closely, usually within a year, by sharp increases in the number of patients admitted to mental hospitals. The strongest relationship was found for schizophrenia and bipolar mood disorders. If we assume that the rate of hospitalization is a reflection of the incidence of these problems in the community, then these data support the social causation hypothesis.

In general, the evidence regarding socioeconomic status and schizophrenia indicates that the disorder is, to a certain extent, influenced by social factors. Adverse social and economic circumstances may increase the probability that persons who are genetically predisposed to the disorder will develop its clinical symptoms (Cohen, 1993; Freeman, 1994). The literature on social class has identified this relationship in very general terms. Some of the specific details have been examined in studies that are considered in the next section of this chapter.

Psychological Factors

Psychodynamic views of psychopathology encouraged the consideration of family interactions and patterns of interpersonal communication in the etiology of schizophrenia. Several clinicians proposed that schizophrenia was caused by deviant patterns of interaction between patients and their parents, typically while the patient was still a small child. These hypotheses were particularly popular in the United States during the 1950s and 1960s. Variations on this general theme were widely cited and became the subject of numerous empirical investigations (Goldstein, 1988; Miklowitz, 1995).

FAMILY INTERACTION

One particularly influential hypothesis was advanced by Lyman Wynne and Margaret Singer (1963), who were concerned with the relationship between thought disorder in young schizophrenic patients and communication problems exhibited by their parents. Wynne and Singer proposed that the parents of schizophrenic patients are often unable to communicate clearly. This deficiency results in disrupted conversations and confusion on the part of their intended listener, most often the child. Wynne and Singer argued that the child is caught between parents who are locked in conflict and subsequently fails to develop either a secure identity or conventional forms of thinking and speaking. These problems eventually result in the onset of schizophrenic symptoms.

Hypotheses regarding family communication and the etiology of schizophrenia were tested extensively during the 1960s and 1970s. Some investigators approached the problem by bringing young patients and their parents into a laboratory and directly observing the manner in which they communicated with one another (Mishler & Waxler, 1968). Results typically indicated that the families of schizophrenic patients communicated less effectively than did the families of control participants.

Wynne and Singer used a somewhat different method. Rather than observing parent–child interactions directly, they studied the parents' cognitive and linguistic abilities by examining their responses to standard psychological tests, most often the Rorschach and the Thematic Apperception Test (TAT; see Chapter 4). Wynne and Singer asked the parents to interpret ambiguous stimuli such as inkblots. They then scored the responses for various forms of *communication deviance (CD)*, such as peculiar statements, difficulty in completing answers, and other types of disruptive verbal behavior during the test. Consistent with their hypothesis, Singer and Wynne (1965) found that the parents of offspring with schizophrenia produced more instances of CD than did the parents of adolescents without mental disorders or the parents of offspring with other forms of psychological disturbance, such as borderline personality or anxiety disorders.

Family communication problems appear to be related to schizophrenia, but do these difficulties play a causal role in the onset of the disorder? Most of the data are correlational in nature: Schizophrenic patients tend to have parents who perform in unusual ways on psychological tasks and communicate less effectively than other parents. The direction of this relationship is not clear (Onstad, Skre, Torgersen, & Kringlen, 1994). Figure 13–4 illustrates several possible explanations. Singer and Wynne's data might indicate that subtle communication impairment among the parents may eventually cause their children to develop schizophrenia (Model 1 in Figure 13–4). Later studies also found, however, that parents of schizophrenic patients do not communicate in an unusual way when they are observed interacting with their offspring who did not become schizophrenic. Furthermore, parents whose offspring are all normal will also begin to exhibit communication problems if they interact with a schizophrenic patient in a laboratory setting (Liem, 1974). This pattern suggests that the children influence their parents, rather than the other way around (Model 2 in Figure 13–4).

A third explanation suggests that problems in verbal communication are symptoms of the genetically transmitted predisposition to schizophrenia. If that is the case, many of the patients' parents would speak in a disorganized

Causal Pathways Involving Communication Problems and Schizophrenia

Model 1: Parent problems cause children's disorder.
    Parental Communication Problems ⟶ **Child's Schizophrenia**

Model 2: Child's adjustment problems cause parents' problems.
    Child's Schizophrenia ⟶ **Parental Communication Problems**

Model 3: Both the child's disorder and the parents' communication problems reflect the common genetic influence.

    Genotype for Schizophrenia ⟶ **Parental Communication Problems**
                                     ⟶ **Child's Schizophrenia**

FIGURE 13-4: Research has indicated that communication problems between parents are related to schizophrenia among their children, but the nature of this relationship remains unclear. This figure illustrates three possible explanations for this relationship.

or confusing way because they are predisposed to schizophrenia, even though they have not developed the full-blown disorder (Model 3 in Figure 13–4). According to this interpretation, the parents' communication problems may not directly influence the development of their children's disorder.

More complex research strategies are required to distinguish among the pathways illustrated in Figure 13–4. For example, the first and third models could be compared using families like the ones in Heston's adoption study. If schizophrenia is produced by exposure to deviant parental communication, then the adoptive parents of people who develop schizophrenia should exhibit problems similar to those that Singer and Wynne observed among the biological parents of schizophrenic patients. On the other hand, if high levels of CD reflect a genetically determined vulnerability to the disorder, then the speech of the adoptive parents should not differ from that of parents of normal offspring; communication problems would be most common among the biological parents of the adoptees.

A large adoption study that is being conducted in Finland is concerned with issues of this sort. Pekka Tienari, Lyman Wynne, and their colleagues have identified 155 people, called *index cases*, who were adopted away at an early age from parents with schizophrenia. All were born between 1960 and 1979. Their comparison group is composed of 186 people, called *control cases*, who were adopted away from parents who never had a psychotic disorder. The investigators used Singer and Wynne's assessment procedure to examine levels of communication deviance among the adoptive parents of these individuals. They combined that information with data collected during interviews with the adoptive parents to produce global ratings of each family's level of functioning. This study offers a unique opportunity to examine the possible interaction of genetic factors and environmental events. All the index cases are genetically vulnerable to the disorder. The probability that these people will develop schizophrenia can be evaluated as a function of the presence of communication problems in the adoptive parents.

Preliminary reports from the Finnish Adoptive Family Study indicate that 14 of the adoptees have some type of psychosis: 13 of these people are the offspring of mothers with schizophrenia, and 1 is in the control group[†] (Tienari et al., 1994). This pattern is consistent with earlier adoption studies, reflecting a genetically determined predisposition to the disorder. Tienari also found that, among those who were genetically predisposed, the people who became psychotic were most often those whose adoptive families were also rated as being disturbed. Very few cases of severe psychopathology were found among the people who were raised by healthy adoptive families, regardless of whether their biological mothers had schizophrenia. In other words, the *combination* of genetic and environmental factors seems to be especially harmful.

These results must be viewed with caution. By the time the investigators conducted their initial assessments of the adoptive families, some of the index cases had already become psychotic. In these cases, either of the first two models in Figure 13–4 provides a plausible explanation of the relation between family disturbance and mental disorders in their offspring. Tienari's data cannot be explained in terms of the third model in the figure because the adoptive parents were no more genetically predisposed to the disorder than were people in the general population.

The most important part of the Finnish Adoptive Family Study remains to be completed. The youngest adoptees had not entered the primary age of risk for schizophrenia when the family assessments were completed. These people are now being followed prospectively. The longitudinal data from this part of the study will address the distinction between Models 1 and 2 in Figure 13–4 because the investigators will be able to determine whether the parents' communication problems appeared *before* the onset of psychopathology in their adoptive children.

EXPRESSED EMOTION

A related body of research indicates that the family environment has a significant impact on the course (as opposed to the etiology) of schizophrenia. These studies do not address the original onset of symptoms. Instead, they are concerned with the posttreatment adjustment of patients who have already exhibited schizophrenic symptoms.

The original observations in this area were reported by George Brown, John Wing, and their

---

[†] Within the group of 13 index cases who had become psychotic, 7 were diagnosed with schizophrenia, 2 with schizophreniform disorder, 2 with delusional disorder, and 2 with bipolar mood disorder with psychotic features.

colleagues at the University of London. Their early studies, conducted during the 1950s, were concerned with the adjustment of schizophrenic patients who were discharged after being treated in a psychiatric hospital for at least 2 years. The investigators found that men with schizophrenia were much more likely to return to the hospital within the next 9 months if they went to live with their wives or parents than if they went to live in other lodgings or with their siblings. Furthermore, patients who returned to live with their mothers were particularly likely to relapse if both they and their mothers were unemployed. Although these results could be interpreted in a number of ways, the investigators chose to focus on the effects of interpersonal interactions. More specifically, they hypothesized that many of the patients who relapsed were reacting negatively to some feature of their close relationship with their wives or mothers. The data suggested that the family environment had an effect on the course of the patient's disorder.

Subsequent research by the same group confirmed this initial impression (Brown, Birley, & Wing, 1972; Vaughn & Leff, 1976). These studies were particularly important because they assessed the emotional characteristics of the family directly and followed the patients' adjustment prospectively for a period of several months. The investigators interviewed relatives of schizophrenic patients prior to the patients' discharge from the hospital. Many of the relatives expressed hostility toward the patient or repeatedly criticized the patient's behavior. Others appeared to

be overprotective or too closely identified with the patient. This general collection of negative or intrusive attitudes was referred to as **expressed emotion (EE).** If at least one of a patient's relatives was hostile, critical, or emotionally overinvolved, the family environment was considered *high in expressed emotion.* Patients who returned to live in a home with at least one member who was high in EE had a 51 percent relapse rate in the first 9 months after discharge. Only 13 percent of the patients from low EE homes relapsed during the same period of time.

This result has been replicated many times as investigators have gradually expanded our understanding of this phenomenon. More than 25 studies have been conducted in several different countries. Approximately half of the schizophrenic patients in these studies lived in families that were rated as being high in EE. Average relapse rates—defined primarily in terms of the proportion of patients who show a definite return of positive symptoms in the first 9 to 12 months following hospital discharge—are 50 percent for patients in high EE families and 21 percent for patients in low EE families. Among the various types of comments that can contribute to a high EE rating, criticism is usually most strongly related to patients' relapse. Observations of family interaction have shown that relatives who express hostility or criticism during an assessment interview with the research team also make more critical comments directly to the patient (Bebbington & Kuipers, 1994; Kavanagh, 1992).

Another interesting result that has emerged from the studies of high EE families is concerned with the effect of face-to-face contact between patients and other family members. Most investigators divide patients into two groups for this purpose. Those who spend more than 35 hours per week with a high EE relative are placed in the "high-contact" category; less than 35 hours per week is considered "low contact." The relationship between family contact and patients' relapse rates is illustrated in Figure 13–5. This figure is based on a reanalysis of data from 25 studies, with a combined sample of more than 800 patients (Bebbington & Kuipers, 1994). Close contact with relatives increases the risk of relapse for schizophrenic patients living with a high EE relative. The opposite pattern is seen in low EE families, where increased contact with relatives seems to have a protective influence.

The influence of expressed emotion is not unique to schizophrenia. Patients with

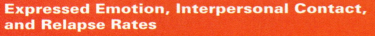

Expressed Emotion, Interpersonal Contact, and Relapse Rates

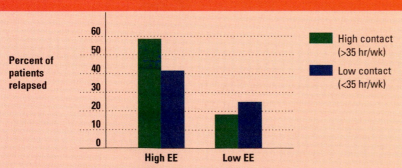

FIGURE 13-5: Close contact increases the risk of relapse for schizophrenic patients living with a high-EE relative. In low-EE families, increased contact has a protective effect.

Source: P. Bebbington and L. Kuipers, 1994, The predictive utility of expressed emotion in schizophrenia: An aggregate analysis, *Psychological Medicine, 24,* 707–718.

unipolar and bipolar mood disorders are also more likely to relapse following discharge if they are living with a high EE relative (Hooley & Teasdale, 1989; Miklowitz et al., 1988). The extension of this phenomenon to other disorders should not be taken to mean that it is unimportant or that the social context of the family is irrelevant to our understanding of the maintenance of schizophrenia (see Research Methods). It may indicate, however, that this aspect of the etiological model is shared with other forms of psychopathology. The specific shape of the person's symptoms may hinge on the genetic diathesis.

RESEARCH METHODS

Comparison Groups in Psychopathology Research

Research studies in the field of psychopathology typically involve comparisons among two or more groups of participants. One group, sometimes called "cases," includes people who already meet the diagnostic criteria for a particular mental disorder, such as schizophrenia. Comparison groups are composed of people who do not have the disorder in question. This approach is sometimes called the *case control design* because it depends on a contrast between cases and control participants. If the investigators find a significant difference between groups, they have demonstrated that the dependent variable is correlated with the disorder (see Research Methods in Chapter 2). They often hope to conclude that they have identified a variable that is relevant to understanding the etiology of this condition. Causal inferences are risky, however, in correlational research. Our willingness to accept these conclusions hinges in large part on whether the investigators selected an appropriate comparison group.

People conducting correlational research, then, must make every effort to identify and test a group of people who are just like the cases except that they do not have the disorder in question (Gehlbach, 1988). This typically means that the people in both groups should be similar with regard to such obvious factors as age, gender, and socioeconomic background. If the investigators find differences between people who have the disorder and those who do not, they want to attribute these differences to the disorder itself. Two main types of comparison groups are used in psychopathology research: people with no history of mental disorder, sometimes called "normal participants," and people who have some other form of mental disorder, sometimes called "patient controls."

Selecting normal comparison groups is not as simple as it might seem. In fact, researchers must make several basic decisions (Kendler, 1990). Does "normal" mean that the person has never had the disorder in question, or does it mean a complete absence of any type of psychopathology? Should people be included as normal control participants if they have a family history of the disorder, even though they do not have the disorder themselves?

A second research strategy involves comparing patients with one type of disorder to those who have another form of psychopathology. Investigators usually employ this strategy to determine whether the variable in question is specifically related to the disorder that they are studying. Are enlarged lateral ventricles or family communication problems unique to people with schizophrenia? Lack of specificity may raise questions about whether this variable is related to the cause of the disorder. It might suggest that this particular variable is, instead, a general consequence of factors such as hospitalization, which the patient control group has also experienced.

Many of the etiological variables that we have discussed in this chapter are not unique to schizophrenia. Expressed emotion predicts relapse among patients with mood disorders as well as among those with schizophrenia. Should this result be taken to mean that EE does not play an important role in the etiology of schizophrenia? Not necessarily. The answer to this question depends on the specific causal model that is being considered (Garber & Hollon, 1991). All forms of psychopathology depend on the interaction of multiple factors spanning biological, social, and psychological systems. Some of these may be specific to the disorder being studied, and others may be general. The development of schizophrenia may depend on a specific genetically determined predisposition. The environmental events that are responsible for eventually causing vulnerable people to express this disorder might be nonspecific. The course of schizophrenia is clearly influenced by the social context in which the patient lives. The fact that similar factors influence people with mood disorders should not be taken to mean that EE is not an important factor in the complex chain of events that explain the etiology and maintenance of schizophrenia.

For all these reasons, the selection of meaningful comparison groups can be a complex and difficult process. There are no perfect solutions to these issues. The research strategy selected in any particular study will depend on the specific questions that the investigators are trying to answer. ■

High EE seems to be related, at least in part, to relatives' knowledge and beliefs about their family member's problems. Relatives find it easier to accept positive symptoms as being the product of a mental disorder (Brewin et al., 1991). They show less tolerance toward negative symptoms, such as avolition and social withdrawal, perhaps because the patient may appear to be simply lazy or unmotivated. Fortunately, relatives' negative attitudes can change. Ratings of relatives' EE can fluctuate over time and are often highest while the patient is hospitalized. Six months after the patient's discharge, roughly half of the people who were originally rated as being high EE are considered to be low EE (Leff et al., 1990).

Cross-cultural studies suggest that high EE may be more common in Western or developed countries than in non-Western or developing countries. This observation might help explain why the long-term course of schizophrenia is typically less severe in developing countries (Jablensky et al., 1992). Speculation has focused on the possibility that people in developing countries may be more tolerant of eccentric behavior among their extended family members (Kuipers & Bebbington, 1988; Lefley, 1992). These attitudes may create environments similar to those found in low EE homes in the West.

We must be cautious to avoid a narrow view of this phenomenon. The EE studies raise extremely sensitive issues for family members, who have too frequently been blamed for the problems of people with schizophrenia. Expressed emotion is not the only factor that can influence the course of a schizophrenic disorder. Some patients relapse in spite of an understanding, tolerant family environment. Furthermore, research studies have shown that the relationship between patients' behavior and relatives' expressed emotion is a transactional or reciprocal process. In other words, patients influence their relatives' attitudes at the same time that relatives' attitudes influence patients' adjustment. Persistent negative attitudes on the part of relatives appear to be perpetuated by a negative cycle of interactions in which patients play an active role (Cook et al., 1989; Miklowitz et al., 1989).

The EE concept has stimulated a great deal of research on the family and schizophrenia (Hooley & Richters, 1995; Kuipers, 1992). Interest in EE has inspired innovative psychosocial treatment programs aimed at the family context in which schizophrenia is treated (see later section on treatment). It is not clear that the emotional climate of the family contributes to the original onset of schizophrenic symptoms, but it is clearly one factor that can influence the course of the disorder. EE has been a broadly defined concept that includes many different attitudes and behaviors, ranging from hostility and criticism to emotional overinvolvement. One goal of current and future research is to employ measures that will help us understand more specific components of family dynamics and the pathways by which they combine with other factors to influence the patient's adjustment (Halford, 1991; Nuechterlein et al., 1992).

Integrated Systems and Multiple Pathways

The combined results of many twin and adoption studies point strongly toward the influence of genetic factors in the etiology of schizophrenia. It is also clear, however, that these genetic factors do not provide a complete explanation for the disorder, because MZ twins are not always concordant for schizophrenia. In fact, the concordance rate for MZ twins is approximately 50 percent. A useful etiological model must therefore provide for the interaction of genetic factors and environmental events.

The heterogeneous nature of the disorder, in terms of symptoms as well as course, also suggests that schizophrenia should be explained in terms of multiple pathways. Some forms of the disorder may represent the product of a strong genetic predisposition acting in combination with relatively common psychosocial experiences, such as stressful life events or disrupted communication patterns. For other people, relatively unusual circumstances, such as severe malnutrition during pregnancy, may be responsible for neurodevelopmental abnormalities that eventually lead to the onset of psychotic symptoms in the absence of genetic vulnerability.

Paul Meehl has proposed a theory of schizophrenia that provides a useful guide to investigators who are trying to understand this complex disorder. According to Meehl (1962, 1990, 1993), individuals who are predisposed to schizophrenia inherit a subtle neurological defect of unknown form. Meehl referred to this condition as **schizotaxia.** As a result of the interaction between this defect and inevitable learning experiences, schizotaxic individuals develop odd or eccentric behaviors, which he called *schizotypic signs*. Most prominent among these behaviors are "associative loosening," which is similar to the cognitive symptoms emphasized by Bleuler, and "aversive drift," in which the individual withdraws from interpersonal relationships because they are associated with negative affect. These are relatively subtle behaviors in comparison to the full-blown symptoms of psychosis. Only a small proportion of schizotypic persons will eventually become overtly schizophrenic.

Various kinds of environmental events have been linked to the etiology of schizophrenia. Some may operate in interaction with the genotype for schizophrenia; others may be sufficient to produce the disorder on their own. Considerable speculation has focused recently on biological factors, such as viral infections and nutritional deficiencies. Psychosocial factors, such as adverse economic circumstances and dysfunctional patterns of family communication, may also be involved. These events may be particularly harmful to those individuals who are genetically predisposed to the disorder.

Individual cases of schizophrenia undoubtedly represent various combinations of these genetic and environmental factors. Irving Gottesman (1991) has developed a sketch of a few hypothetical trajectories that might be followed by people who eventually develop symptoms of the disorder. His illustration is presented in Figure 13–6. The horizontal axis represents time, beginning at the point of conception. The vertical axis represents the person's "combined liability" to the disorder—the probability of exhibiting overt symptoms of the disorder. Liability is determined by ongoing, dynamic interactions between genotype and environmental. Figure 13–6 is based on a *threshold model*, in which liability is viewed as lying along a continuum, but the probability that certain symptoms will be present changes dramatically as the person crosses a threshold. Two thresholds are represented in the figure: one for symptoms of schizophrenia spectrum disorders (which might also be viewed as prodromal and residual symptoms) and a second for active symptoms of schizophrenia, such as delusions and hallucinations.

The figure illustrates three hypothetical genotypes (two twin pairs and one individual) and the trajectories that they might follow over the life span. Consider first the simplest case, which involves twins C and D. They both start life with a genetic predisposition (G_3) that places them relatively close to the threshold for schizophrenia. Both develop schizoid personality disorder and become concordant for schizophrenia

▲ **Paul Meehl, Regents Professor Emeritus of Psychology at the University of Minnesota, is the only clinical psychologist ever elected to the National Academy of Science. His theory of schizophrenia has guided research efforts to discover signs of vulnerability to the disorder.**

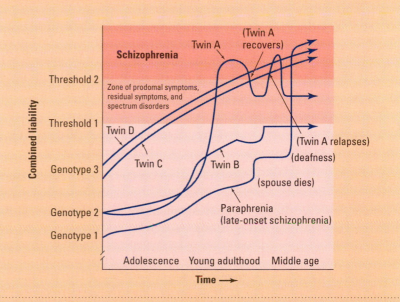

The Interaction Between Heredity and Environment in Cases of Schizophrenia

FIGURE 13-6: Hypothetical pathways illustrating interactions between genetic predisposition and environmental factors in schizophrenia over time. The lines show one individual with late-onset delusional disorder, as well as a discordant MZ twin pair (Twins A and B) and a concordant MZ pair (Twins C and D).

Source: I.I. Gottesman, 1991, *Schizophrenia Genesis: The Origins of Madness*, p. 224. New York: Freeman.

during adolescence. Moderately stressful experiences, which might be relatively harmless for other people, may help to precipitate their disorder.

The person illustrated by the line beginning at G_1 follows a very different pathway that results in the relatively unusual late onset of schizophrenic symptoms. His genotype places him at a relatively low risk for schizophrenia, and he remains relatively distant from the hypothetical threshold for spectrum disorders until he encounters some unfortunate experiences during middle age. Loss of his spouse sets the stage for an acute onset of psychosis, which is precipitated when he unexpectedly becomes completely deaf.

The last situation illustrated in Figure 13–6 involves identical twins A and B, who begin life with a genotype (G_2) placing them at average risk for schizophrenia. Twin A experiences more stress during infancy, moving her closer than twin B to the first threshold. The onset of her first psychotic episode occurs after she experiments with hallucinogenic drugs in college. Successful treatment leads to improvement in her condition (with residual symptoms), followed by relapse when she discontinues her medication. Her twin sister never develops the disorder, in spite of the fact that her combined liability brings her close to the threshold for prodromal symptoms.

Gottesman's sketch and hypothetical cases illustrate the need to consider multiple pathways to schizophrenia, as well as the many ways in which genetic and environmental events can interact to produce this disorder.

The Search for Markers of Vulnerability

Some people apparently inherit a predisposition to schizophrenia. It would obviously be useful to be able to identify those people. Genetic linkage studies may provide the answer, if one gene (or a small set of genes) is found to be responsible for the disorder. But that possibility is open to question.

If we are looking for observable signs of vulnerability that can be detected among individuals who are genetically predisposed to schizophrenia, where should we look? What form will these signs take? We might also frame this question in terms of liability to the disorder (see Figure 13–6). Is it possible to detect signs of vulnerability among individuals who approach the threshold for schizophrenia

spectrum disorders but have not exhibited any kind of overt symptoms? This issue has attracted considerable attention, but we don't have any firm answers to these questions (Gooding & Iacono, 1995).

According to Meehl's theoretical model, people who are vulnerable to schizophrenia might be detected by developing measures that could detect the underlying biological dysfunction (schizotaxia) or by developing sensitive measures of their subtle eccentricities of behavior (schizotypal traits). The range of possible markers is therefore quite large.

Assume that we have selected a specific measure, such as a biochemical assay or a psychological test, and we are interested in knowing whether it might be useful in identifying people who are vulnerable to schizophrenia. What criteria should a **vulnerability marker** fulfill? First, the proposed marker must distinguish between people who already have schizophrenia and those who do not. Second, it should be a stable characteristic over time. The more dramatic, psychotic symptoms of schizophrenia may come and go over the person's lifetime, but vulnerability is presumably a persistent trait that is present on a continuous basis. Third, the proposed measure of vulnerability should identify more people among the biological relatives of schizophrenic patients than among people in the general population. For example, it should be found among the discordant MZ twins of schizophrenic patients, even if they don't exhibit any symptoms of schizophrenia. Fourth, the trait measured by the test should be transmitted genetically. Finally, the proposed measure of vulnerability should be able to predict the future development of schizophrenia among those who have not yet experienced a psychotic episode (Iacono & Clementz, 1993; Meehl, 1990; Zubin & Spring, 1977).

Although reliable measures of vulnerability have not been identified, they are being actively pursued by many investigators with a wide variety of measurement procedures (Faraone et al., 1995). In the following pages we will outline some of the psychological procedures that have been shown to be among the most promising possibilities.

ATTENTION AND COGNITION

Many investigators have pursued the search for signs of vulnerability by looking at measures of performance in which schizophrenic patients differ from other people. Some of these studies have focused on cognitive tasks that evaluate information processing, selective attention, and working memory (Holzman, 1994; Park, Holzman, & Goldman-Rakic, 1995). The assumption that cognitive factors are central to this disorder can be traced to Bleuler's original suggestion that the disorder should be defined in terms of a splitting of mental functions.

One important set of results regarding attentional dysfunction is based on use of the Continuous Performance Task (CPT). In one version of this task, the subject is required to pick out a letter or sequence of letters from among a larger sequence of letters that is presented very briefly (less than 1 second per letter) on a computer screen. Whenever the subject notices the target, he or she is supposed to press a button. Several dependent measures can be collected using this procedure, including the number of correct button presses, the number of times the button was pressed when the target was not present, and the number of times the button was not pressed when the target was present.

Numerous studies have demonstrated that schizophrenic patients are less accurate than normal people and other psychiatric patients in their performance on the CPT (Nuechterlein, Buchsbaum, & Dawson, 1994). This seems to be a stable characteristic that does not fluctuate over time. Furthermore, the attentional deficits tapped by the CPT are found with increased prevalence among the unaffected first-degree relatives of schizophrenic persons (Cornblatt & Keilp, 1994; Lenzenweger et al., 1991).

Especially intriguing are the results of studies that have examined the performance of children with a biological parent who has schizophrenia. Many offspring of schizophrenic parents exhibit problems on the CPT that are similar to those seen in adult patients (Erlenmeyer-Kimling & Cornblatt, 1992). There is also some reason to believe that this problem may be specific to schizophrenia, because it is not as common among the offspring of mothers with mood disorders or among hyperactive children. Finally, within a group of children of schizophrenic parents, those who exhibited attentional deficits at approximately 10 years of age were more likely to develop maladaptive personality traits, such as social insensitivity and social indifference, in early adulthood (Cornblatt, Lenzenweger, Dworkin, & Erlenmeyer-Kimling, 1992). The CPT measure appears to fulfill several of the criteria for an index of vulnerability. The research results support the possibility that measures of attentional problems may be useful signs of vulnerability to schizophrenia.

EYE-TRACKING DYSFUNCTION

Another promising line of exploration involves impairments in eye movements—specifically, difficulty in tracking the motion of a pendulum or a similarly oscillating stimulus. When people with schizophrenia are asked to track a moving target, like an oscillating pendulum, with their eyes, a substantial number of them show dysfunctions in smooth-pursuit eye movement (Levy, Holzman, Matthysse, & Mendell, 1994). Instead of reproducing the motion of the pendulum in a series of smooth waves, their tracking records show frequent interruptions of smooth-pursuit movements by numerous rapid movements. Examples of normal tracking records and those of schizophrenic patients are presented in Figure 13–7. Only about 8 percent of normal people exhibit the eye-tracking dysfunctions illustrated in part (c) of Figure 13–7, although some studies have reported higher figures (Scarone et al., 1987).

The fascinating part of the eye-tracking story involves the performance of family members of people with schizophrenia. Approximately 50 percent of the first-degree relatives of schizophrenic persons show similar smooth-pursuit impairments (Iacono, 1993). Although the same eye movement problems are seen in many patients with bipolar affective disorder, only 10 percent of their parents exhibit eye-tracking dysfunctions, and the eye-tracking problems of the patients themselves appear to be side effects of treatment with lithium carbonate. The overall pattern of results seen in people with schizophrenia and their families suggests that poor

Eye-Tracking Patterns

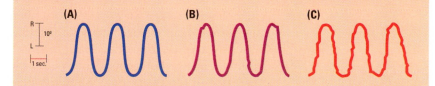

FIGURE 13-7: This illustration contrasts smooth-pursuit eye-tracking patterns of normal subjects with those of schizophrenic patients. Part (A) shows the actual target. Part (B) illustrates the pattern of normal subjects, and part (C) shows the pattern for people with schizophrenia.

Source: From D.L. Levy et al., 1993, Eye-tracking dysfunction and schizophrenia: A critical perspective, *Schizophrenia Bulletin, 19,* 462.

▲ **This woman is attached to equipment used to record smooth-pursuit eye movements. Sensors inside the helmet are positioned in front of her right eye. Eye movements are recorded while she watches a dot of light move back and forth on a computer screen. The electronic equipment behind her records and amplifies the ocular signals.**

tracking performance may be associated with the predisposition to schizophrenia. That conclusion becomes even more interesting in light of evidence from additional studies suggesting that tracking ability is influenced by genetic factors and is apparently a stable trait (Gooding, Iacono, & Beiser, 1994; Iacono & Clementz, 1993).

Several other interesting patterns have emerged from an extended program of eye-tracking research conducted by University of Minnesota psychologists William Iacono, William Grove, and Brett Clementz (Clementz et al., 1992; Iacono et al., 1992). Eye-tracking dysfunction is not found in all individuals with schizophrenia. Rather, it is present in 50 to 60 percent of all families in which at least one person has the disorder. Among those families in which eye-tracking problems have been

identified, smooth-pursuit impairments tend to be found among those relatives who also exhibit schizotypic signs, such as odd interpersonal behaviors, and who perform deviantly on the CPT (Grove et al., 1991). These findings led Iacono and Grove (1993) to suggest that eye-tracking problems and attentional impairment are markers for one form of schizophrenia, which accounts for approximately half of all cases of this disorder. According to this model, in patients whose families do not exhibit eye-tracking anomalies, schizophrenia is caused by a different etiological mechanism.

It is not yet possible to identify people who are specifically predisposed to the development of schizophrenia, but research studies have identified potential vulnerability markers. The real test, of course, will center around predictive validity. Can any of these measures, such as smooth-pursuit eye-tracking impairment or attentional dysfunction, predict the later appearance of schizophrenia in people whose scores indicate possible vulnerability? High-risk studies will be useful in providing this type of evidence (see Research Close-Up).

If valid vulnerability markers can be found, clinical scientists may be able to design early treatment programs that prevent the eventual onset of full-blown schizophrenic symptoms. Until that time, treatment efforts must be directed toward the resolution of acute episodes of the disorder, reducing the frequency and severity of relapse, and improving the level of functioning among patients in the residual phase of schizophrenia. We review these possibilities in the next section.

Treatment

Schizophrenia is a complex disorder that often must be treated over an extended period of time. Clinicians must be concerned about the treatment of acute psychotic episodes as well as the prevention of future episodes. A multifaceted approach to treatment is typically required. Neuroleptic medication is the primary mode of treatment for this disorder. Because many patients remain impaired between episodes, long-term care must often involve the provision of housing and social support. People with impaired occupational and social skills need special types

of training. The treatment of schizophrenia requires attention on all of these fronts and is necessarily concerned with the cooperative efforts of many types of professionals.

Neuroleptic Medication

The antipsychotic properties of a class of drugs known as the phenothiazines were discovered quite accidentally in the early 1950s by a French neurosurgeon who was using them as a supplement to anesthesia. They were not effective for the purpose he intended, but they did have a calming effect on the patients. This experience prompted psychiatrists to try using the same drugs with their patients. Early reports of success in treating chronic psychotic patients quickly led to the widespread use of phenothiazines, such as chlorpromazine (Thorazine), in psychiatric hospitals throughout Europe and the United States. The discovery of these drugs quickly changed the way in which schizophrenia was treated. Large number of patients who had previously been institutionalized could be discharged to community care (but see Chapter 18 on the effects of deinstutionalization).

Several related types of drugs have been developed in subsequent years. They are called *antipsychotic drugs* because they have a relatively specific effect—to reduce the severity of, and sometimes eliminate, psychotic symptoms. Antipsychotics are also known as **neuroleptic** drugs[†] because they also induce side effects that resemble the motor symptoms of Parkinson's disease. Traditional forms of neuroleptic medication act by blocking D_2 dopamine receptors in the cortical and limbic areas of the brain (Marder et al., 1993). The antipsychotic efficacy of various types of neuroleptic drugs is directly proportional to their ability to block D_2 receptors.

Beneficial effects are sometimes noticed within a week after the patient begins taking neuroleptics, but it often takes several weeks before improvement is seen. Among the traditional or standard types of neuroleptic medication, there is no convincing evidence to indicate that one is more effective than another (Kane & Marder, 1993). The possible exception to this conclusion involves clozapine (Clozaril), an atypical form of antipsychotic medication, which we will discuss after a brief review of the traditional neuroleptics.

The enthusiasm that followed the introduction of neuroleptics was soon confirmed by double-blind, placebo-controlled studies that evaluated the effectiveness of antipsychotic drugs in the treatment of patients who are acutely psychotic. Literally thousands of studies have addressed this issue over a period of almost 40 years (Ellenbroek, 1993; Marder et al., 1993). These studies provide substantial support for the effectiveness of neuroleptic medication. Most studies find that about half of the patients who receive neuroleptic medication are rated as being much improved after 4 to 6 weeks of treatment. Further improvements may continue beyond that point for some patients. In contrast, patients treated with placebos exhibit much smaller rates of improvement, and many of them actually deteriorate.

Neuroleptic drugs may be more useful for certain types of symptoms than for others (Kane, 1995). Positive symptoms, such as hallucinations, seem to respond better to medication than negative symptoms, such as alogia and blunted affect. This differential effect is not entirely clear-cut, however. For example, some patients who are socially withdrawn become less isolated when taking neuroleptics.

Unfortunately, a substantial minority of schizophrenic patients, perhaps 25 percent, do not improve on neuroleptic medication (Lewander, 1992). Another 30 to 40 percent might be considered partial responders: Their condition improves, but they do not show a full remission of symptoms. Investigators have been unable to identify reliable differences between patients who improve on medication and those who do not. Some experts have suggested that the more severe the symptoms, the less the improvement brought about by medication (Farmer & Blewett, 1993).

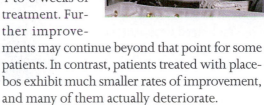

▲ Lionel Aldridge was a defensive lineman for the Green Bay Packers when they won the first Super Bowl in 1965. He later developed schizophrenia. With the help of antipsychotic medication, his disorder is now in remission. Aldridge is a spokesman for the needs of people who suffer from schizophrenia.

SIDE EFFECTS

Most neuroleptic drugs produce several unpleasant side effects. Consequently, patients frequently dislike taking these medications, and some discontinue using them, against their psychiatrist's advice. Side effects come in varying degrees and affect different patients in different ways. The most obvious and troublesome are called *extrapyramidal symptoms (EPS)* because they are

---

[†] The word *neuroleptic* is derived from the Greek, meaning "that takes hold of the nerves." It is defined operationally as drugs that produce a syndrome of side effects similar to those associated with chlorpromazine (Ellenbroek, 1993). The terms *antipsychotic* and *neuroleptic* are used interchangeably, but they do not have exactly the same meaning. Many newer forms of antipsychotic medication (usually called *atypical neuroleptics*) might not be neuroleptics from a technical standpoint because they do not produce motor side effects. We have decided to follow convention and use the term *neuroleptic* because it is used most often in the literature.

mediated by the extrapyramidal neural pathways that connect the brain to the motor neurons in the spinal cord. These symptoms include an assortment of neurological disturbances, such as muscular rigidity, tremors, restless agitation, peculiar involuntary postures, and motor inertia. EPS may diminish spontaneously after 3 or 4 months of continuous treatment. Additional drugs, such as benztropine (Cogentin), can be used to minimize the severity of EPS during the first few months of treatment. Unfortunately, some patients exhibit persistent signs of EPS in spite of these efforts.

Prolonged treatment with neuroleptic drugs frequently leads to the development of **tardive dyskinesia (TD).** This syndrome consists of abnormal involuntary movements of the mouth and face, such as tongue protrusion, chewing, and lip puckering, as well as spasmodic movements of the limbs and trunk of the body. The latter include writhing movements of the fingers and toes and jiggling of the legs, as well as jerking movements of the head and pelvis. Taken as a whole, this problem is distressing to patients and their families. The TD syndrome is induced by neuroleptic treatment, and it is irreversible in some patients, even after

neuroleptics have been discontinued. In fact, in some patients, TD becomes worse if neuroleptic medication is withdrawn.

The incidence of TD increases steadily with continued use of neuroleptic medication. Roughly 5 percent of patients will develop TD during the first year of neuroleptic treatment. Approximately 20 percent of patients develop TD after long-term treatment with neuroleptic drugs (Kane, 1995).

MAINTENANCE MEDICATION

After patients recover from acute psychotic episodes, there is a high probability that they will have another episode. The relapse rate may be as high as 65 to 70 percent in the first year after hospital discharge if patients discontinue medication. Continued treatment with neuroleptic drugs can reduce this rate to approximately 40 percent (Hogarty, 1993). Therefore the great majority of schizophrenic patients continue to take medication after they recover from psychotic episodes, although usually at lower dosages. The need for maintenance medication is less clearly defined among patients who have had only one episode of schizophrenia. The relapse rate for these patients is lower than among those who have had multiple episodes.

Figure 13–8 illustrates general relapse rates for schizophrenic outpatients. The estimated rates presented in this figure were generated by analyzing data from several outcome studies (Weiden & Olfson, 1995). They apply to outpatients who have experienced more than one episode, have responded positively to neuroleptics, and are not receiving active psychosocial treatments (discussed later in the chapter). The "best-case" scenario represents expected relapse rates for patients who are receiving an optimal neuroleptic dose and who continue taking the medication on a regular basis. Under these circumstances, slightly more than half of schizophrenic outpatients will relapse and require rehospitalization within 2 years of discharge. The "real-world" scenario in Figure 13–8 indicates that actual relapse rates are even higher because some patients stop taking medication, often to avoid unpleasant side effects (Fleischhacker, Meise, Gunther, & Kurz, 1994).

Some patients who have had more than one psychotic episode can also avoid relapse without taking medication on a maintenance basis. Approximately 20 percent of chronic schizophrenic patients can avoid rehospitalization without taking neuroleptics and can function at least

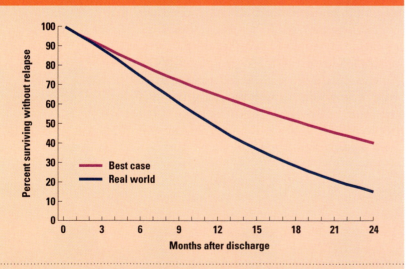

Relapse Rates for Schizophrenic Patients Taking Maintenance Medication

FIGURE 13-8: Estimated relapse rates for patients receiving optimal doses of standard neuroleptic medication while not receiving active psychosocial treatments. Real world: Assumes some noncompliance with medication. Best case: Assumes complete compliance with medication.

Source: P.J. Weiden and M. Olfson, 1995, Cost of relapse in schizophrenia, *Schizophrenia Bulletin, 21,* 425.

as well as they would on medication (Johnstone & Geddes, 1994). Unfortunately, we do not know how to distinguish these patients from those who need continued pharmacological treatment, other than through trial and error.

ATYPICAL ANTIPSYCHOTICS

Some relatively new forms of antipsychotic medication are known as **atypical antipsychotics** because they do not produce EPS and may not be associated with increased risk of TD. In addition, at least 30 percent of schizophrenic patients who were previously treatment resistant improve after taking atypical antipsychotic drugs (Buchanan, 1995). Treatment resistance is usually defined as failure to improve on at least three different types of classic neuroleptic medication after 6 weeks on moderate to high doses.

The best known of the atypical drugs, clozapine (Clozaril), was first manufactured in the 1959s and has been used extensively throughout Europe since the 1970s. Use of clozapine was delayed for several years in the United States because it can produce a lethal blood condition known as agranulocytosis in about 1 percent of patients. It was approved for use by the U.S. Food and Drug Administration in 1990, with the requirement that patients receive weekly monitoring of their white-blood-cell levels. Controlled-outcome studies indicate that clozapine has beneficial effects on positive symptoms of schizophrenia without inducing unpleasant motor side effects. Some reports have also noted improvements in negative symptoms among previously treatment-resistant patients, but other studies have not found this effect. Clozapine would probably be the treatment of choice for all schizophrenic patients if it were not for the risk of agranulocytosis (Buchanan, 1994; Carpenter et al., 1995).

Risperidone (Risperdal) is another atypical antipsychotic drug, which was first marketed in the United States in 1994. Several double-blind studies indicate that risperidone is at least as effective as classic neuroleptics in the treatment of schizophrenic patients who are in the active phase of the disorder (Umbricht & Kane, 1995). Like clozapine, risperidone is associated with a very low rate of adverse motor side effects. Some studies have reported that risperidone may be more effective than classic neuroleptics in treating patients with prominent negative symptoms. Relatively little empirical evidence is available regarding the effectiveness of risperidone

during maintenance treatment or in use with treatment-resistant patients.

Clozapine and risperidone produce different neurochemical actions in the brain than do the classic neuroleptic drugs. Clozapine produces a relatively strong blockade of serotonin receptors and a relatively weak blockade of D_2 dopamine receptors (Lieberman, 1994; Meltzer, 1993). Its reduced affinity for dopamine receptors is presumably the reason for its failure to produce significant EPS. The fact that clozapine has well-documented beneficial effects for schizophrenic patients and that its site of action in the brain involves serotonin pathways has required important revisions to the original dopamine hypothesis. Risperidone resembles the classic neuroleptic drugs in terms of its ability to block D_2 receptors. Like clozapine, however, it also produces a relatively strong blockade of serotonin receptors. Further progress in the pharmacological treatment of schizophrenia will undoubtedly produce new drugs that have varying mechanisms of neurochemical action.

Psychosocial Treatment

Several forms of psychological treatment have proved to be effective for schizophrenic patients. These procedures address a wide range of problems that are associated with the disorder. In contrast to pharmacological approaches, psychological approaches place relatively little emphasis on the treatment of acute psychotic episodes. Instead, they concentrate on long-term strategies (Bellack & Mueser, 1993).

FAMILY-ORIENTED AFTERCARE

Studies of expressed emotion have inspired the development of innovative family-based treatment programs (Goldstein, 1994). Family treatment programs attempt to improve the coping skills of family members, recognizing the burdens that people often endure while caring for a family member with a chronic mental disorder. Patients are maintained on antipsychotic medication on an outpatient basis throughout this process. There are several different approaches to this type of family intervention. Most include an educational component that is designed to help family members understand and accept the nature of the disorder. One goal of this procedure is to eliminate unrealistic expectations for the patient, which may lead to harsh criticism. Behavioral family management also places considerable emphasis on the improvement of communication and problem-solving skills, which may enhance the family members' ability to work together and thereby minimize conflict.

Several empirical studies have evaluated the effects of family interventions. Most have found dramatic reductions in relapse rates for people receiving family treatment. In the first year of treatment, relapse rates for patients who receive family treatment plus medication are typically below 20 percent, compared with 40 or 50 percent for those receiving medication alone (Leff, 1995; Tarrier & Barrowclough, 1995). Relapse rates increase in the next year for both groups, with rates ranging from 17 to 44 percent for family interventions and 59 to 83 percent for control patients. Family-based treatment programs can delay relapse, but they do not necessarily prevent relapse in the long run. The beneficial effects of treatment may be lost shortly after treatment ends (Hogarty, 1993). In the case of a disorder such as schizophrenia, which is often chronic, treatment programs must be available to patients and their family members on a continuous basis.

SOCIAL SKILLS TRAINING

Many patients who avoid relapse and are able to remain in the community continue to be impaired in terms of residual symptoms. They also experience problems in social and occupational functioning. For these patients, drug therapy must be supplemented by psychosocial programs that address residual aspects of the disorder. The need to address these problems directly is supported by evidence that shows that deficits in social skills are relatively stable in schizophrenic patients and relatively independent of other aspects of the disorder, including both positive and negative symptoms (Mueser et al., 1991).

Social skills training (SST) is a structured, educational approach to these problems that involves modeling, role playing, and the provision of social reinforcement for appropriate behaviors (Liberman, DeRisi, & Mueser, 1989). Controlled-outcome studies indicate that, in combination with neuroleptic medication, SST leads to improved performance on measures of social adjustment. It is not clear, however, that SST has any beneficial effects on relapse rates (Penn & Mueser, 1996). This may not be surprising in light of evidence regarding the course of this disorder, which suggests that various aspects of outcome, including symptom severity and social adjustment, tend to be relatively independent.

INSTITUTIONAL PROGRAMS

Although schizophrenic persons can be treated with medication on an outpatient basis, various types of institutional care continue to be important. Most patients experience recurrent phases of active psychosis (Eaton et al., 1992). Brief periods of hospitalization (usually 2 or 3 weeks) are often beneficial during these times.

Some patients are chronically disturbed and require long-term institutional treatment. Social learning programs, sometimes called *token economies*, can be useful for these patients. In these programs, specific behavioral contingencies are put into place for all of the patients on a hospital ward. The goal is to increase the frequency of desired behaviors, such as appropriate grooming and participation in social activities, and to decrease the frequency of undesirable behaviors, such as violence or incoherent speech. Staff members monitor patients' behavior throughout the day. Each occurrence of a desired behavior is praised and reinforced by the presentation of a token, which can be exchanged for food or privileges, such as time to watch television. Inappropriate behaviors are typically ignored, but occasional punishment, such as loss of privileges, is used if necessary.

Gordon Paul, a clinical psychologist at the University of Houston, and his colleagues conducted an extensive evaluation of behavioral treatment with chronic schizophrenic patients (Paul & Lentz, 1977). They compared two inpatient programs in the treatment of severely disturbed patients who had been continuously hospitalized for many years. One program followed a carefully designed and closely supervised social learning model, and the other followed a more traditional approach. These experimental treatments were compared to a group of similar patients who continued to reside in their original hospital wards. The patients' adjustment was evaluated at 6-month intervals over a period of approximately 6 years.

Both groups of patients who received treatment showed significant improvement, especially during the first 6 months of the study. This finding highlights the possibility for improvement, even among chronically disturbed patients. Patients in the social learning program showed even more improvement than those in the traditional group, especially with regard to social functioning and self-care. These

▲ **Gordon Paul, a clinical psychologist at the University of Houston, has developed behavioral assessment and treatment procedures for psychotic behaviors. His research demonstrated that social learning programs can significantly improve the adjustment of seriously disturbed patients.**

benefits were maintained throughout the duration of the treatment program. Perhaps most impressive was the fact that, by the end of the first 4 years of active treatment, 11 percent of the patients in the social learning program were discharged to independent living in the community without being readmitted to the hospital. In contrast, none of the patients in the standard hospital comparison group was released to independent living. This study indicates that carefully structured inpatient programs, especially those that follow behavioral principles, can have important positive effects for chronic schizophrenic patients.

Summary

People who meet the diagnostic criteria for **schizophrenia** exhibit many types of symptoms that represent impairments across a broad array of cognitive, perceptual, and interpersonal functions. These symptoms can be roughly divided into three types. **Positive symptoms** include hallucinations and delusions. **Negative symptoms** include **blunted affect,** alogia, **avolition,** and social withdrawal. Symptoms of **disorganization** include verbal communication problems and bizarre behavior.

The onset of *schizophrenia* is typically during adolescence or early adulthood. The disorder can follow different patterns over time. Some people recover fairly quickly from schizophrenia, whereas others deteriorate progressively after the initial onset of symptoms.

The disorder was originally defined by Emil Kraepelin, who emphasized the progressive course of the disorder in distinguishing it from manic-depressive psychosis. Eugen Bleuler coined the term *schizophrenia*, proposing that disturbances in speech and emotion are the fundamental symptoms of the disorder. Many clinicians believe that schizophrenia actually includes several types of disorder with different causes. Others believe that it is a single pathological process with variations in symptomatic expression and course.

The negative symptoms of schizophrenia have been given increased emphasis in DSM-IV. The manual requires evidence of a decline in the person's social or occupational functioning, as well as the presence of disturbed behavior over a continuous period of at least 6 months. The DSM-IV recognizes several subtypes of schizophrenia, such as **paranoid, catatonic,** and **disorganized types,** that are based on prominent symptoms. These subtypes have relatively poor diagnostic reliability and are frequently unstable over time.

The lifetime prevalence of schizophrenia is approximately 1 or 2 percent in virtually all areas of the world. Men and women are equally likely to be affected, although the onset of the disorder appears at an earlier age in males. Male patients are more likely than female patients to exhibit negative symptoms, and they are also more likely to follow a chronic, deteriorating course. Two large cross-cultural studies found patients who exhibited characteristic signs and symptoms of schizophrenia in all of the study sites. Comparisons of patients across centers revealed more similarities than differences in clinical symptoms.

Genetic factors clearly play a role in the development of schizophrenia. Risk for developing the disorder is between 10 and 15 percent among first-degree relatives of schizophrenic patients. Concordance rates are approximately 48 percent in MZ twins compared to only 17 percent in DZ pairs. Adoption studies have found that approximately 15 percent of the offspring of a schizophrenic parent will eventually develop the disorder themselves, even if they are separated from their biological parent at an early age and are raised by adoptive families. Twin and

KEY TERMS

- active phase
- anhedonia
- atypical antipsychotic
- avolition
- blunted affect
- brief psychotic disorder
- catatonic type
- delusion
- delusional disorder
- dementia praecox
- disorganization
- disorganized speech
- disorganized type
- expressed emotion (EE)
- hallucination
- high risk research design
- inappropriate affect
- negative symptoms
- neuroleptic
- paranoid type
- positive symptoms
- prodromal phase
- residual phase
- residual type
- schizoaffective disorder
- schizophrenia
- schizotaxia
- tardive dyskinesia (TD)
- undifferentiated type
- vulnerability marker

adoption studies also indicate that the disorder has variable expressions, sometimes called the *schizo-phrenia spectrum*. Related disorders include schizotypal personality disorder and **schizoaffective disorder.** Linkage studies have not found consistent evidence for a specific gene of major influence.

Advances in brain imaging technology have allowed extensive study of structural and functional brain abnormalities in schizophrenia. A specific brain lesion has not been identified, and it is unlikely that a disorder as complex as schizophrenia will be traced to a single site in the brain. Structural images of schizophrenic patients' brains reveal enlarged ventricles as well as decreased size for parts of the limbic system. Studies of brain metabolism and blood flow have identified functional changes in the frontal lobes, temporal lobes, and basal ganglia in many persons with schizophrenia. Current evidence points toward a subtle and diffuse type of neuropathology in schizophrenia.

The discovery of antipsychotic medication stimulated interest in the role of neurochemical factors in the etiology of schizophrenia. The dopamine hypothesis provided the major unifying theme in this area for many years, but it is now considered too simple to account for the existing evidence. Current neurochemical hypotheses regarding schizophrenia focus on a broad array of neurotransmitters, with special emphasis on serotonin.

The importance of environmental events in the etiology of schizophrenia is evident in the results of twin studies, which show that concordance rates in MZ twins do not approach 100 percent. Several social and psychological factors have been shown to be related to the disorder. Social class is inversely related to the prevalence of schizophrenia. In some cases, low levels of socioeconomic achievement represent a consequence of the disorder. Several kinds of research studies have also found, however, that social factors appear to make a causal contribution to the

disorder. Disturbed patterns of family communication have been presumed to be related to the etiology of schizophrenia for many years. There is no evidence to indicate that the behavior of family members contributes to the original onset of schizophrenic symptoms. Recent efforts on this topic have examined the relation between the social context of the family and the long-term course of the disorder. Patients from families that are high in expressed emotion are more likely to relapse than those from low EE families. Expressed emotion is the product of an ongoing interaction between patients and their families, with patterns of influence flowing in both directions.

The evidence regarding etiology supports a diathesis-stress model. It should be possible to develop **vulnerability markers** that can identify individuals who possess the genetic predisposition to the disorder. Promising research in this area is concerned with a broad range of possibilities, including smooth-pursuit eye-tracking movements and laboratory measures of sustained attention.

The central aspect of treatment for schizophrenia is antipsychotic medication. These drugs help to resolve acute psychotic episodes. They can also delay relapse and improve the level of patients' functioning between episodes. Unfortunately, they often produce troublesome side effects, and a substantial minority of schizophrenic patients are resistant to classic types of antipsychotic medication. The **atypical antipsychotics** are able to help some patients who do not respond to other drugs, and they produce fewer unpleasant motor side effects.

Various types of psychosocial treatment also provide important benefits to schizophrenic patients and their families. Prominent among these are family-based treatment for patients who have been stabilized on medication following discharge from the hospital. Social skills training can also be useful in improving the level of patients' role functioning.

Critical Thinking

1. The typical course of schizophrenia may be less chronic in developing countries than in developed countries. How would you explain these differences? Why would the disorder tend to be more long-lasting among people living in the United States than in people living in rural India, for example?

2. Clinical scientists have been unable to identify a specific type of environmental event that is responsible for triggering the original onset of symptoms of schizophrenia. Where would you look if you were conducting research on the "stress" end of the diathesis-stress model?

3. How can we identify people who are vulnerable for schizophrenia? Would you place greater emphasis on studying behavioral markers or biological markers?

4. Imagine that you are the director of a large mental health center that provides services for all types of disorders. If you have limited resources, which aspects of schizophrenia would receive highest priority in your programs? Medication for the resolution of acute psychotic episodes? Support to family members? Alternative housing? Social skills training?

Where did I put my

14

Dementia, Delirium, and Amnestic Disorders

ost of us are absentminded from time to time. We may forget to make a phone call, run an errand, or complete an assignment. Occasional lapses of this sort are part of normal experience. Unfortunately, some people develop severe and persistent memory problems that disrupt their everyday activities and their interactions with other people. Imagine that you have lived in the same house for many years. You go for a short walk, and then you can't remember how to get home. Suppose you are shown a photograph of your parents, and you don't recognize them. These are some of the fundamental cognitive problems experienced by people with **dementia,** a gradually worsening loss of memory and related cognitive functions, including the use of language, as well as reasoning and decision making. It is a clinical syndrome that involves progressive impairment of many cognitive abilities (Cummings, 1995).

Overview

Dementia and delirium are the most frequent disorders found among elderly psychiatric patients. Both conditions involve memory impairments, but they are quite different in other ways. **Delirium** is a confusional state that develops over a short period of time and is often associated with agitation and hyperactivity. The most important symptoms of delirium are disorganized thinking and a reduced ability to maintain and shift attention (Tueth & Cheong, 1993). Delirium and dementia are produced by very different processes. Dementia is a chronic, deteriorating condition that reflects the gradual loss of neurons in the brain. Delirium is usually the result of medical problems, such as infection, or of medication side effects. If diagnosed and properly treated, delirium is typically short-lived. It can, however, result in serious medical complications, permanent cognitive impairment, or death if the causes go untreated.

People with **amnestic disorders** experience memory impairments that are more limited than those seen in dementia or delirium. The person loses the ability to learn new information or becomes unable to recall previously learned information, but other higher-level cognitive abilities—including the use of language—are unaffected.

Dementia, delirium, and amnestic disorders are listed as Cognitive Disorders in DSM-IV. Cognitive processes, including perception and attention, are related to many types of mental disorders that we have already discussed, such as depression, anxiety, and schizophrenia. In most forms of psychopathology, however, the cognitive problems are relatively subtle—mediating factors that help us understand the process by which clinical symptoms are produced. They are not considered to be the central, defining features of the disorder. In dementia, memory and other cognitive functions are the most obvious manifestations of the problem. As dementia progresses, the person's attention span, concentration, judgment, planning, and decision making become severely disturbed.

Dementia and amnestic disorders are often associated with specific identifiable changes in brain tissue (Wise & Gray, 1996). Many times these changes can be observed only at autopsy, after the patient's death. For example, in Alzheimer's disease, which is one form of dementia, microscopic examination of the brain reveals the presence of an unusual amount of debris left from dead neurons, called plaque, and neurofibrillary tangles indicating that the connections between nerve cells had become disorganized. We describe the neuropathology of Alzheimer's disease later in this chapter.

Because of the close link between cognitive disorders and brain disease, patients with these problems are often diagnosed and treated by **neurologists,** physicians who deal primarily with diseases of the brain and the nervous system. Multidisciplinary clinical teams are concerned with studying and providing care for people with dementia and amnestic disorders. Direct care to patients and their families is usually provided by nurses and social workers. **Neuropsychologists** have particular expertise in the assessment of specific types of cognitive impairment. This is true for clinical assessments as well as for more detailed laboratory studies for research purposes.

The following two case studies illustrate the variety of symptoms and problems that are included in the general category of dementia. The first case describes the early stages of dementia.

CASE STUDY

Dementia

Jonathan was a 61-year-old physician who had been practicing family medicine for the past 30 years. His wife, Alice, worked as his office manager. A registered nurse, Kathryn, had worked with them for several years. Four months earlier, Alice and Kathryn both noticed that Jonathan was beginning to make obvious errors at work. On one occasion, Kathryn observed Jonathan prescribe the wrong medication for a patient's condition. At about the same time, Alice became concerned when she asked Jonathan about a patient whom he had seen the day before. Much to her surprise, he did not remember having seen the patient, in spite of the fact that he spent almost half an hour with her, and she was a patient whom he had treated for several years.

Jonathan's personality also seemed to change in small but noticeable ways. For example, Jonathan had always been a gentle and easygoing man. He had a special fondness and tolerance for small children. One day, one of his patients was accompanied to the office by her 2-year-old son. As Jonathan was talking with the mother, the little boy accidentally pushed some bottles of pills off a counter. No harm was done, but Jonathan screamed loudly at the boy, chastising him for being so clumsy and careless. The mother was quite embarrassed. So were Kathryn and Alice, who witnessed Jonathan's sudden and uncharacteristic display of temper.

Although Alice tried to convince herself that these were isolated incidents, she finally decided to discuss them with Kathryn. Kathryn agreed that Jonathan's memory was failing. He had trouble recognizing patients whom he had known for many years, and he had unusual difficulty making treatment decisions. These problems had not appeared suddenly. Over the past year or two, both women had been doing more things for Jonathan than they had ever done in the past. They needed to remind him about things that were routine parts of his practice. As they pieced together various incidents, the pattern of gradual cognitive decline became obvious.

Alice talked seriously with Jonathan about the problems that she and Kathryn had observed. He said that he felt fine, but he reluctantly allowed her to make an appointment for him to be examined by a neurologist, who also happened to be a friend. Jonathan admitted to the neurologist that he had been having difficulty remembering things. He believed that he had been able to avoid most problems, however, by writing notes to himself—directions, procedures, and so on. The results of psychological testing and brain imaging procedures, coupled with Jonathan's own description of his experiences and Alice's account of his impaired performance at work, led the neurologist to conclude that Jonathan was exhibiting early signs of dementia, perhaps Alzheimer's disease. He spoke directly with Jonathan regarding his diagnosis and recommended firmly that Jonathan retire immediately. A malpractice suit would be devastating to his medical practice. Jonathan agreed to retire.

Although Jonathan was no longer able to cope with his demanding work environment, his adjustment at home was not severely impaired. The changes in his behavior remained relatively subtle for many months. In short conversations, his cognitive problems were not apparent to his friends, who still did not know the real reason for his retirement. His speech was fluent, and his memory for recent events was largely intact, but his comprehension was diminished. Alice noticed that Jonathan's emotional responses were occasionally flat or restricted. At other times, he would laugh at inappropriate times when they watched television programs together. If Alice asked him about his reaction, it was sometimes apparent that Jonathan did not understand the plot of even the simplest television programs.

Jonathan had become increasingly literal-minded. If Alice asked him to do something for her, she had to spell out every last detail. For example, he began to have trouble selecting his clothes, which had been a source of pride before the onset of his cognitive problems. Alice found that she had to sew labels into Jonathan's collars to distinguish for him the clothes that he wore to work in the yard from those that he wore if they were going shopping or out to eat. His judgment about what was appropriate to wear in different situations had disappeared altogether.

It had also become difficult for Jonathan to do things that required a regular sequence of actions or decisions, even if they were quite simple and familiar. Routine tasks took longer than before, usually because he got stuck part of the way through an activity. He had, for example, always enjoyed making breakfast for Alice on weekends. After his retirement, Alice once found him standing in the kitchen with a blank expression on his face. He had made a pot of coffee and some toast for both of them, but he ran into trouble when he couldn't find coffee cups. That disrupted his plan, and he was stymied. ■

▼ **People with dementia can remain active longer by using signs to prompt their behavior. This man is reminded to lock the door when he leaves his apartment.**

Jonathan's case illustrates many of the early symptoms of dementia, as well as the ways in which the beginnings of memory problems can severely disrupt a person's life. The onset of the disorder is often difficult to identify precisely because forgetfulness increases gradually. Problems are most evident in challenging situations, as in Jonathan's medical practice, and least noticeable in familiar surroundings.

Changes in emotional responsiveness and personality typically accompany the onset of memory impairment in dementia. These changes may be consequences of the cognitive problems. Jonathan's irritability might easily have been aggravated by his own frustration with himself for being forgetful and indecisive. His emotional responses may have seemed unusual sometimes because he failed to comprehend aspects of the environment that were obvious to his wife and other people.

Our next case illustrates more advanced stages of dementia, in which the person can become extremely disorganized. Memory impairment progresses to the point where the person no longer recognizes his or her family and closest friends. People in this condition are unable to care for themselves, and they become so disoriented that the burden on others is frequently overwhelming. This case also provides an example of delirium superimposed on dementia. Up to 50 percent of dementia patients who are admitted to a hospital are also delirious. It is important for the neurologist to recognize the distinction between these conditions because the cause of the delirium (which might be an infection or a change in the patient's medications) must be treated promptly (Tueth & Cheong, 1993).

Dementia (and Delirium)

Mary was an 84-year-old retired schoolteacher who had grown up in the same small, rural community in which she still lived. Never married, she lived with her parents most of her life, except for the years when she was in college. Her parents had died when Mary was in her early sixties. After her retirement at age 65, Mary continued living in her parents' farmhouse. She felt comfortable there, in spite of its relative isolation, and liked the fact that it had plenty of space for animals, including her dog, which she called "my baby," several cats, and a few cows that were kept in the pasture behind the house. Mary's niece, Nancy, who was 45 years old and lived an hour's drive away, stopped to visit her once every 2 or 3 months.

Over the past year, Nancy had noticed that Mary was becoming forgetful, as well as more insistent that her routines remain unchanged. Bills went unpaid—in fact, the telephone had been disconnected for lack of payment—and the mail wasn't brought in from the roadside box. Nancy had suggested to Mary that she might be better off in a nursing home, but Mary was opposed to that idea.

At her most recent visit, Nancy was shocked to find that conditions at Mary's home had become intolerable. Most distressing was the fact that some of her animals had died because Mary forgot to feed them. The dog's decomposed body was tied to its house, where it had starved. Conditions inside the house were disgusting. Almost 30 cats lived inside the house, and the smell was unbearable. Mary's own appearance was quite disheveled. She hadn't bathed or changed her clothes for weeks. Nancy contacted people at a social service agency, who arranged for Mary's admission to a nursing home. Mary became furious, refusing to go and denying that there was anything wrong with her own home. Nancy was soon declared her legal guardian because Mary was clearly not competent to make decisions for herself.

Mary grew progressively more agitated and belligerent during the few weeks that she lived at the nursing home. She was occasionally disoriented, not knowing where she was or what day it was. She shouted and sometimes struck people with her cane. She had trouble walking, a problem that was compounded by visual and spatial judgment difficulties. After she fell and broke her hip, Mary was transferred to a general hospital.

Mary became delirious in the hospital, apparently as a result of medication she was given for her injury. She appeared to be having visual hallucinations and often said things that did not make sense. These periods of incoherence fluctuated in severity throughout the course of the day. During her worst moments, Mary did not respond to her name being spoken, and her speech was reduced primarily to groans and nonsense words. This clouding of consciousness cleared up a few days after her medication was changed. She became less distractible and was once again able to carry on brief conversations. Unfortunately, her disorientation became more severe while she was immobilized in the hospital. When her hip eventually healed, she was moved to a psychiatric hospital and admitted to the geriatric ward.

Although Mary was no longer aware of the date or even the season of the year, she insisted that she did not have any problems with her mind. For the first 6 weeks at the psychiatric hospital, she would be surprised that she was not in her own home when she woke up each morning. After that time, she acknowledged that she was in a hospital, but she did not know why she was there, and she did not understand that the other patients on the unit were also demented. She didn't recognize hospital staff members from one day to the next. She was completely unable to remember anything that had happened recently. Nevertheless, her memory for events that had happened many years earlier was quite good. Mary repeated stories about her childhood over and over again.

Nurses on the unit were bombarded continuously with her complaints about being removed from her home. Every 20 minutes or so, Mary would approach the nurses' station, waving her cane and shouting, "Nurse, I need to go home. I have to get out of here. I have to go home and take care of my dog." The hospital staff would explain to her that she would have to stay at the hospital, at least for a while longer, and that her dog had died several months earlier. This news would usually provoke sadness, but she seemed unable to remember it long enough to complete the grieving process. Several minutes later, the whole scene would be repeated. Mary also became paranoid, claiming to anyone who would listen that people were trying to steal her things. The most common focus of her concern was her purse. If it was out of her sight, she would announce loudly that someone had stolen it.

In the midst of these obvious problems, Mary retained many other intellectual abilities. She was a well-educated and intelligent woman. Her attention span was reduced, but she was still able to do crossword puzzles and enjoyed reading short stories. Poetry had always been one of her special interests, and she was still able to recite many of her favorite poems beautifully from memory. In a quiet room, it was often possible to talk with her and pursue a meaningful conversation. Unfortunately, these lucid periods were interspersed with times of restless pacing and shouting. Her agitation would escalate rapidly unless staff members distracted her, taking her to a quiet room, talking to her, and getting her to read or recite something out loud. ■

Delirium: Typical Symptoms and Associated Features

The DSM-IV criteria for delirium are listed in Table 14–1. The primary symptom of delirium is clouding of consciousness in association with a reduced ability to maintain and shift attention. The disturbance in consciousness might also be described as a reduction in the clarity of a person's awareness of his or her surroundings. Memory deficits may occur in association with impaired consciousness and may be the direct result of attention problems. The person's thinking appears disorganized, and the person may speak in a rambling, incoherent fashion. Fleeting perceptual disturbances, including visual hallucinations, are also common in delirious patients (Liptzin, 1996).

The symptoms of delirium follow a rapid onset—from a few hours to several days—and typically fluctuate throughout the day. The person may alternate between extreme confusion and periods in which he or she is more rational and clearheaded. Symptoms are usually worse at night. The sleep/wake cycle is often disturbed.

TABLE 14–1

DSM-IV Criteria for Delirium

A. **Disturbance of consciousness (i.e., reduced clarity of awareness of the environment) with reduced ability to focus, sustain, or shift attention.**

B. **A change in cognition (such as memory deficit, disorientation, language disturbance) or the development of a perceptual disturbance that is not better accounted for by a preexisting, established, or evolving dementia.**

C. **The disturbance develops over a short period of time (usually hours to days) and tends to fluctuate during the course of the day.**

Daytime drowsiness and lapses in concentration are often followed by agitation and hyperactivity at night. If the condition is allowed to progress, the person's senses may become dulled, and he or she may eventually lapse into a coma. The delirious person is also likely to be disoriented with relation to time ("What day, month, or season is it?") or place ("Where are we? What is the name of this place?"). However, identity confusion (What is your name?) is rare.

The underlying mechanisms that are responsible for the onset of delirium undoubtedly involve neuropathology and neurochemistry (Francis, 1995; Trzepacz, 1994). The incidence of delirium increases among elderly people, presumably because the physiological effects of aging make elderly people more vulnerable to medication side effects and cognitive complications of medical illnesses. Delirium can be caused by many different kinds of medication, including the following:

- Psychiatric drugs (especially antidepressants, antipsychotics, and benzodiazepines)
- Drugs used to treat heart conditions
- Painkillers
- Stimulants (including caffeine)

Delirium also develops in conjunction with a number of metabolic diseases, including pulmonary and cardiovascular disorders (which can interfere with the supply of oxygen to the brain), as well as endocrine diseases (especially thyroid disease and diabetes mellitus). Various kinds of infection can lead to the onset of delirium. Perhaps the most common among elderly people is urinary tract infection, which

	TABLE 14-2

Distinguishing Features of Dementia and Delirium

Characteristic	Delirium	Dementia
Onset	Sudden	Slow
Duration	Brief	Extended
Course	Fluctuating	Nonfluctuating
Attention	Impaired	Intact
Hallucinations	Visual/tactile/vivid	Rare
Insight	Lucid intervals	Consistently poor
Sleep	Disturbed	Less disturbed

Source: M. J. Tueth and J. A. Cheong, 1993, Delirium: Diagnosis and treatment in the older patient, *Geriatrics, 48,* 75–81.

can result from the use of an indwelling urinary catheter (sometimes necessary with incontinent nursing home patients).

It isn't always easy to recognize the difference between dementia and delirium, especially when they appear simultaneously in the same patient. Table 14–2 summarizes several considerations that are useful in making this diagnostic distinction (Tueth & Cheong, 1993). One important consideration involves the period of time over which the symptoms appear. Delirium follows a rapid onset, whereas dementia develops in a slow, progressive manner. In dementia, the person usually remains alert and responsive to the environment. Speech is most often coherent in demented patients, at least until the end stages of the disorder, but it is typically confused in delirious patients. Finally, delirium can be resolved, whereas dementia cannot.

Dementia: Typical Symptoms and Associated Features

The cases at the beginning of this chapter illustrate the changing patterns that emerge as dementia unfolds. Jonathan's cognitive symptoms were recognized at a relatively early stage of development, in part because of his occupational situation and because of his close relationships with other people. Mary's situation was much different, because she lived in a relatively isolated setting without close neighbors or friends. By the time Nancy recognized the full severity of Mary's problems, the cognitive impairment had progressed so far that Mary was no longer able to appreciate the nature of her own difficulties. In the following pages we describe in more detail the types of symptoms that are associated with dementia.

Cognitive Symptoms

Dementia appears in people whose intellectual abilities have previously been unimpaired. Both of the people in our case studies were bright, well educated, and occupationally successful before the onset of their symptoms. The earliest signs of dementia are often quite vague. They include difficulty remembering recent events and the names of people and familiar objects. These are all problems that are associated with normal aging, but they differ from that process in order of magnitude (see Further Thoughts). The distinguishing features of dementia include cognitive problems in a number of areas, ranging from memory and learning to language and abstract thinking. By the final stages of dementia, intellectual and motor functions may disappear almost completely (Cummings, 1992).

FURTHER THOUGHTS

Memory Changes in Normal Aging

Changes in cognitive abilities are part of the normal aging process. Most elderly adults complain more frequently about memory problems than younger adults do, and they typically perform less efficiently than younger adults on laboratory tests of memory (Chalfonte & Johnson, 1996; Light, 1991). There are, of course, individual differences in the age at which cognitive abilities begin to decline, as well as in the rate at which these losses take place (Berkman et al., 1993). Nevertheless, some types of memory impairment are an inevitable consequence of aging.

In order to understand more clearly the cognitive changes associated with aging, it is useful to distinguish between two aspects of mental functioning. Paul Baltes, a cognitive psychologist at the Max Planck Institute in Germany, divides intellectual abilities into *mechanics* (also known as fluid intelligence) and *pragmatics* (sometimes called crystallized intelligence). Baltes uses the computer as a metaphor to explain this distinction. Cognitive mechanics are "the hardware of the mind." These functions are concerned with the speed and accuracy of such basic processes as perception, attention, and memory. The proficiency of mechanics depends on neurophysiological processes and on the structural integrity of the person's brain.

Cognitive pragmatics represent the "culture-based software of the mind." Reading and writing skills, as well as knowledge about the self and ways of coping with environmental challenges, are examples of pragmatics. They represent information about the world that is acquired continually throughout the person's lifetime. Wisdom is a reflection of cognitive pragmatics.

According to Baltes (1993), mechanics and pragmatics follow different trajectories over the normal human life span. Both develop continuously during childhood and adolescence, reaching a point of optimal efficiency during young adulthood. After that point, mechanics follow a gradual pattern of decline. Pragmatics, on the other hand, remain unimpaired as the person reaches old age. The erosion of cognitive mechanics over time is presumably due to subtle atrophy of brain regions such as the hippocampus that take place during normal aging (Golomb et al., 1993).

Several research studies support this general conclusion. One laboratory task designed to measure cognitive mechanics requires subjects to remember long lists of words in their correct order. Even after many training and practice sessions, most adults in their sixties and seventies are unable to achieve the level of performance shown by young adults after a small number of practice sessions (Baltes & Kliegl, 1992). Age-related deficits are found even among those normal elderly persons who are selected for study because of their experience with and talent for similar cognitive tasks.

Different measurement procedures have been used to explore the relationship between aging and cognitive pragmatics. In one procedure, subjects are presented with a life dilemma, such as "A 15-year-old girl wants to get married right away. What should she consider and do?" The subjects' task is to think aloud about each dilemma. Responses are scored in terms of the amount of knowledge that the person displays with regard to facts, values, and procedures that must be considered in each circumstance. In contrast to the results of research on mechanics, studies of pragmatics have found no change in performance between the ages of 30 and 70. Elderly people are just as likely as younger adults to produce the best scores on this type of task.

Baltes (1993) suggested that "the aging mind" depends on the coordination of gains and losses. The elderly person strikes a balance through a process that Baltes calls *selective optimization with compensation.* Arthur Rubinstein, the brilliant pianist who performed concerts well into his eighties, provides an example of this process. Rubinstein described three strategies that he employed in his old age: (1) he was *selective,* performing fewer pieces, (2) he *optimized* his performance by practicing each piece more frequently, and (3) he *compensated* for a loss of motor speed by utilizing pieces that emphasized contrast between fast and slow segments so that his playing seemed faster than it really was. Successful aging is based on this dynamic process. The person compensates for losses in cognitive mechanics by taking advantage of pragmatics—increased knowledge and information.

The fact that an older person begins to experience subtle memory problems does not necessarily indicate that he or she is becoming demented. Where can we find the line between normal aging and dementia? Is this distinction simply a matter of degree, or is there a qualitative difference between the expected decline in cognitive mechanics and the onset of cognitive pathology? These issues present an important challenge for future research. ■

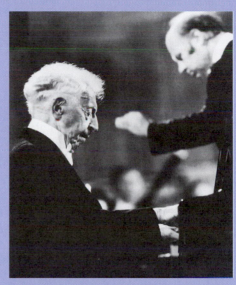

▲ **Piano virtuoso Arthur Rubinstein performed concerts in his 80s by reducing the number of pieces that he played and by practicing them more often.**

MEMORY AND LEARNING

Memory loss is the diagnostic hallmark of dementia. In order to describe the various facets of memory impairment, it is useful to distinguish between old memories and the ability to learn new things. **Retrograde amnesia** refers to the loss of memory for events prior to the onset of an illness or the experience of a traumatic event. **Anterograde amnesia** refers to the inability to learn or remember new material after a particular point in time.

Anterograde amnesia is usually the most obvious problem during the beginning stages of dementia. Consider, for example, the case of Jonathan. Alice eventually noticed that he sometimes could not remember things that he had done the previous day. Mary, the more severely impaired person, could not remember for more than a few minutes that her dog had died. Long-term memories are usually not affected until much later in the course of the disorder. Even in advanced stages of dementia, a person may retain some recollections of the past. Mary was able to remember, and frequently described, stories from her childhood.

VERBAL COMMUNICATION

Language functions can also be affected in dementia. **Aphasia** is a term that describes various types of loss or impairment in language that are caused by brain damage (Benson, 1992). Language disturbance in dementia is sometimes relatively subtle, but it can include many different kinds of problems. Patients often remain verbally fluent, at least until the disorder is relatively advanced. They retain their vocabulary skills and are able to construct grammatical sentences. They may have trouble finding words, naming objects, and comprehending instructions.

In addition to problems understanding and forming meaningful sentences, the demented person may also have difficulty performing purposeful movements in response to verbal commands, a problem known as **apraxia.** The person possesses the normal strength and coordination to carry out the action and is able to understand the other person's speech, but is nevertheless unable to translate the various components into a meaningful action.

Some aspects of the communication problems associated with dementia are captured in the following passage from a novel by J. Bernlef titled *Out of Mind,* which provides an insightful and poignant description of the subjective experiences of a man from Holland, named Maarten, who is becoming demented. In this passage, Maarten is listening to his wife, Vera, as she discusses his situation with their physician.

"Sometimes he's like a stranger to me. I can't reach him. It's a terrible, helpless feeling. He hears me but at such times I don't think he understands me. He behaves as if he were on his own."

I know exactly what she means. Like it was just then, when it all went wrong. All of a sudden I had to translate everything into English first, before I could say it. Only the forms of sentences came out, fragments, the contents had completely slipped away.

Furiously I glare into the front room. I seem to lose words like another person loses blood. And then suddenly I feel terribly frightened again. The presence of everything! Every object seems to be heavier and more solid than it should be (perhaps because for a fraction of a second I no longer know its name). I quickly lie down on the settee and close my eyes. A kind of seasickness in my mind, it seems. Under this life stirs another life in which all times, names and places whirl about topsy-turvy and in which I no longer exist as a person.

"Curious," I say to Vera as she enters the room. "Sometimes I just have to lie down for a moment. I never used to."

"It doesn't matter. Have some time to yourself." She sits down, picks up a book.

"Have some time to yourself." I repeat the phrase because it appears strange to me.

She turns the pages but she isn't reading. I can tell from the look in her eyes that she doesn't understand me.

"It should be: have some time in yourself. That describes the situation better."

"Is that how you feel?"

"Less and less so."

"What do you mean?"

"Like a ship," I say, "A ship, a sailing vessel that is becalmed. And then suddenly there is a breeze, I am sailing again. Then the world has a hold on me again and I can move along with it." (Bernlef, 1988, pp. 54–55)

Some of the things that Maarten says in this passage reflect subtle problems in verbal communication. His description of the sailing ship, however, is a remarkable analogy that captures the intermittent quality of the cognitive impairment.

PERCEPTION

Some patients with dementia have problems identifying stimuli in their environments. The technical term for this phenomenon is **agnosia,** which means "perception without meaning." The person's sensory functions are unimpaired, but he or she is unable to recognize the source of stimulation. Agnosia can be associated with visual, auditory, or tactile sensations, and it can be relatively specific or more generalized. For example, visual agnosia is the inability to recognize certain objects or faces. Some people with visual agnosia are able to identify inanimate stimuli but are unable to recognize human faces.

It is sometimes difficult to distinguish between aphasia and agnosia. Imagine, for example, that a clinician shows a patient a toothbrush and asks, "What is this object?" The patient may look at the object and be unable to name it. Does that mean that the person cannot think of the word "toothbrush"? Or does it mean that the person cannot recognize the object at all? In this case, the distinction could be made by saying to the person, "Show me what you do with this object." A person suffering from aphasia would take the toothbrush in his hand and make brushing movements in front of his mouth, thereby demonstrating that he recognizes the object but cannot remember its name. A person with agnosia would be unable to indicate how the toothbrush is used.

ABSTRACT THINKING

Another manifestation of cognitive impairment in dementia is loss of the ability to think in abstract ways. The person may be bound to concrete interpretations of things that other people say. It may also be difficult for the person to interpret words that have more than one meaning (for example, "pen") or to explain why two objects are alike ("Why are a basketball and a football helmet alike?" Because they are both types of sporting equipment.)

In our opening case, Jonathan became increasingly literal-minded in his conversations with other people. After he retired, he had much more time to become involved in routine tasks around the home. Alice found that she had to give him very explicit instructions if she wanted him to do anything. For example, if she asked him to mow the grass, he would do exactly that—nothing more. This was unusual for Jonathan, because he had always enjoyed taking care of their lawn and took great pride in their bushes and flower gardens. Previously, "mowing the grass" would have been taken to include trimming, pulling weeds, raking leaves out from under bushes, and all sorts of related details. Now Jonathan interpreted this instruction in concrete terms.

JUDGMENT AND SOCIAL BEHAVIOR

Related to deficits in abstract reasoning is the failure of social judgment and problem-solving skills. In the course of everyday life, we must acquire information from the environment, organize and process it, and then formulate and perform appropriate responses by considering these new data in the light of past experiences. The disruption of short-term memory, perceptual skills, and higher-level cognitive abilities obviously causes disruptions of judgment. Examples from Jonathan's case include problems deciding which clothes to wear for working around his home as opposed to going out in public, as well as his inability to understand the humor in some television programs. Impulsive and careless behaviors are often the product of the demented person's poor judgment. Activities such as shopping, driving, and using tools can create serious problems.

Assessment of Cognitive Impairment

There are many ways to measure the level of cognitive impairment that a person displays. One is the Mini-Mental State Exam, which is outlined in Table 14–3. We include it here to give you an idea of the types of questions that a clinician might ask in order to elicit the cognitive problems of dementia. Some are directed at the person's orientation to time and place. Others are concerned with anterograde amnesia, such as the ability to remember the names of objects for a short period of time (items 3 and 5). Agnosia, aphasia, and apraxia are addressed by items 6, 7, and 8, respectively. Perceptual difficulties are tapped by the last item.

Neuropsychological assessment can be used as a more precise index of cognitive impairment. This process involves the evaluation of performance on psychological tests to indicate whether a person has a brain disorder. Neuropsychological tests can sometimes be used to infer the location of a brain lesion. The best-known neuropsychological assessment procedure is the Halstead-Reitan Neuropsychological Test Battery, which includes an extensive series of tests that tap sensorimotor, perceptual, and speech functions. For example, in the tactile performance test, the person is blindfolded and then required to fit differently shaped blocks into spaces in a form board. The time

---

TABLE 14-3

Mini-Mental State Examination

1. What is the (year, season, date, day, month)?
2. Where are we (state, city, hospital)?
3. Name three objects (pen, sky, dog), then ask patient to repeat them.
4. Spell "world" backwards.
5. Ask for names of three objects given in question #3.
6. Point to a pencil and a watch. Ask the patient to name each as you point.
7. Ask the patient to repeat, "No ifs, ands, or buts."
8. Three-stage command: "Take this paper in your right hand. Fold the paper in half. Put the paper on the floor."
9. Ask the patient to read and obey the following (write on card in large letters): "CLOSE YOUR EYES."
10. Have the patient write a sentence of his or her choice.
11. Have the patient copy two intersecting pentagons.

Source: M. F. Folstein, S. E. Folstein, and P. R. McHugh, 1975, Mini-mental state: A practical method for grading the cognitive state of patients for the clinician, *Journal of Psychiatric Research, 2,* 189–198.

---

needed to perform this test reflects one specific aspect of the person's motor skills.

Some neuropsychological tasks require the person to copy simple objects or drawings. The drawings illustrated in Figure 14–1 demonstrate this process and the type of impairment typically seen in a patient during the relatively early stages of Alzheimer's disease. The patient was asked to reproduce a drawing. This was done initially while the original figure was still in sight and then repeated after it had been covered up. The performance of the patient in this

Neuropsychological Test Performances

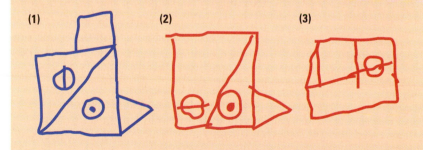

FIGURE 14-1: These drawings represent part of the neuropsychological test performance of a 59-year-old woman with a diagnosis of Alzheimer's disease. The figure at the left (1) was drawn by the psychologist, who then handed the piece of paper to the patient and asked her to make an exact copy of the figure next to the original. After the patient had completed her replica (2), the piece of paper was turned over and she was asked to draw the figure again, this time from memory. The figure that she drew based on memory is presented at the right (3).

▲ **One of the tests in the Halstead-Reitan Neuropsychological Test Battery is the Tactual Performance Task, in which the person must place differently shaped blocks of wood into holes without seeing the pieces or the board in which they are placed.**

figure indicates two problems associated with the disorder. First, inconsistencies between drawings 1 and 2 reflect perceptual difficulties. Second, the drastic deterioration from drawing 2 to drawing 3 indicates that the patient had a great deal of difficulty remembering the shape of the figure for even a few brief moments.

Associated Features

Personality changes, emotional difficulties, and motivational problems are frequently associated with dementia. Some patients also exhibit symptoms of psychosis, such as hallucinations and delusions. These problems may not contribute to the diagnosis of the disorder, but they do have an impact on the person's adjustment. They can also create additional burdens for people who care for demented patients.

EMOTION

The emotional consequences of dementia are quite varied. Some demented patients appear to be apathetic or emotionally flat. Their faces are less expressive, and they appear to be indifferent to their surroundings. Alice noticed, for example, that something seemed a bit vacant in Jonathan's eyes. At the same time, emotional reactions may become exaggerated and less predictable. The person may become fearful or angry in situations that would not have aroused strong emotion in the past. Jonathan's sudden rage at the boy who pushed bottles off the counter in his office provides one example. Changes like this often lead others to believe that the person's personality has changed.

Depression is another problem that is frequently found in association with dementia (Migliorelli et al., 1995). In many ways, feelings of depression are understandable. The

realization that your most crucial cognitive abilities are beginning to fail, that you can no longer perform simple tasks or care for yourself, would obviously lead to sadness and depression. Mary's case illustrates one way in which cognitive impairment can complicate depression: Her inability to remember from one day to the next that her dog had died seemed to interfere with her ability to grieve for the loss of her pet. Each time that she was reminded of his death was like the first time that she had heard the news.

MOTOR BEHAVIOR

Motor behavior may become agitated in demented persons, who may pace restlessly or wander away from familiar surroundings. In the later stages of the disorder, patients may develop problems in the control of the muscles by the central nervous system. Some patients develop muscular rigidity, which can be accompanied by painful cramping. Others experience epileptic seizures, which consist of involuntary, rapidly alternating movements of the arms and legs.

Some specific types of dementia are associated with involuntary movements or **dyskinesia**—tics, chorea, tremors. These motor symptoms help to distinguish among different types of dementia. We return to this area later in the chapter when we discuss the classification of differentiated and undifferentiated dementias. *Chorea* is a type of motor dysfunction that involves jerky, semipurposeful movements of the person's face and limbs (Cutting & McClelland, 1991).

PSYCHOTIC SYMPTOMS

Hallucinations and delusions are seen in about 20 percent of dementia cases (Bolger, Carpenter, & Strauss, 1994). The delusional beliefs are typically understandable consequences of the person's disorientation or anterograde amnesia. They are most often simple in nature and are relatively short-lived. Mary's frequent insistence that someone had stolen her purse is a typical example. Other common themes are phantom house guests and personal persecution (Harvey, 1996).

Amnestic Disorder: Typical Symptoms and Associated Features

Some cognitive disorders involve more circumscribed forms of memory impairment than those seen in dementia. In amnestic disorders,

a person exhibits a severe impairment of memory while other higher-level cognitive abilities are unaffected. The memory disturbance interferes with social and occupational functioning and represents a significant decline from a previous level of adjustment. Subtypes of amnestic disorder are diagnosed on the basis of evidence, acquired from the patient's history, from a physical examination, or from laboratory tests, regarding medical conditions or substance use that is considered to be related to the onset of the memory impairment.

The following case, written by Oliver Sacks (1985), illustrates a form of amnestic disorder, involving severe anterograde amnesia, that developed after the patient had been dependent on alcohol for several years.

Alcohol-Induced Persisting Amnestic Disorder

Jimmie G. was admitted to our Home for the Aged near New York City early in 1975, with a cryptic transfer note saying, "Helpless, demented, confused and disoriented." Jimmie was a fine-looking man, with a curly bush of grey hair, a healthy and handsome 49-year-old. He was cheerful, friendly, and warm.

"Hiya, Doc!" he said. "Nice morning! Do I take this chair here?" He was a genial soul, very ready to talk and to answer any questions I asked him. He told me his name and birth date, and the name of the little town in Connecticut where he was born. He described it in affectionate detail, even drew me a map. He spoke of the houses where his family had lived—he remembered their phone numbers still. He spoke of school and school days, the friends he'd had, and his special fondness for mathematics and science. He talked with enthusiasm of his days in the navy—he was 17, had just graduated from high school when he was drafted in 1943. With his good engineering mind he was a "natural" for radio and electronics, and after a crash course in Texas found himself assistant radio operator on a submarine. He remembered the names of various submarines on which he had served, their missions, where they were stationed, the names of his shipmates. He remembered Morse code, and was still fluent in Morse tapping and touch-typing.

A full and interesting early life, remembered vividly, in detail, with affection. But there, for some reason, his reminiscences stopped. He recalled, and almost relived, his war days and service, the end of the war, and his thoughts for the future. He had come to love the navy, thought he might stay in it. But with the GI Bill, and support, he felt he might do best to go to college.

With recalling, reliving, Jimmie was full of animation; he did not seem to be speaking of the past but of the present, and I was very struck by the change of tense in his recollections as he passed from his school days to his days in the navy. He had been using the past tense, but now used the present—and (it seemed to me) not just the formal or fictitious present tense of recall, but the actual present tense of immediate experience.

A sudden, improbable suspicion seized me. "What year is this, Mr. G.?" I asked, concealing my perplexity under a casual manner.

"Forty-five, man. What do you mean?" He went on, "We've won the war, FDR's dead, Truman's at the helm. There are great times ahead."

"And you, Jimmie, how old would you be?"

Oddly, uncertainly, he hesitated a moment, as if engaged in calculation. "Why, I guess I'm 19, Doc. I'll be 20 next birthday."

Looking at the grey-haired man before me, I had an impulse for which I have never forgiven myself—it was, or would have been, the height of cruelty had there been any possibility of Jimmie's remembering it.

"Here," I said, and thrust a mirror toward him. "Look in the mirror and tell me what you see. Is that a 19-year-old looking out from the mirror?"

He suddenly turned ashen and gripped the sides of the chair. "Jesus Christ," he whispered. "Christ, what's going on? What's happened to me? Is this a nightmare? Am I crazy? Is this a joke?"—and he became frantic, panicked.

"It's okay, Jimmie," I said soothingly. "It's just a mistake. Nothing to worry about. Hey!" I took him to the window. "Isn't this a lovely spring day. See the kids there playing baseball?" He regained his color and started to smile, and I stole away, taking the hateful mirror with me.

Two minutes later I re-entered the room. Jimmie was still standing by the window, gazing with pleasure at the kids playing baseball below. He wheeled around as I opened the door, and his face assumed a cheery expression.

"Hiya, Doc!" he said. "Nice morning! You want to talk to me—do I take this chair here?" There was no sign of recognition on his frank, open face.

"Haven't we met before, Mr. G.?" I asked casually.

"No, I can't say we have. Quite a beard you got there. I wouldn't forget you, Doc!"

"Why do you call me 'Doc'?"

"Well, you are a doc, ain't you?"

"Yes, but if you haven't met me, how do you know what I am?"

"You talk like a doc. I can see you're a doc."

"Well, you're right, I am. I'm the neurologist here."

"Neurologist? Hey, there's something wrong with my nerves? And 'here'—where's 'here'? What is this place anyhow?"

"I was just going to ask you—where do you think you are?"

"I see these beds, and these patients everywhere. Looks like a sort of hospital to me. But hell, what would I be doing in a hospital—and with all these old people, years older than me. I feel good, I'm strong as a bull. Maybe I work here. . . . Do I work? What's my job? . . . No, you're shaking your head, I see in your eyes I don't work here. If I don't work here, I've been put here. Am I a patient, am I sick and don't know it, Doc? It's crazy, it's scary. . . . Is it some sort of joke?" (Sacks, 1985, pp. 22–25) ∎

The preceding case illustrates the most common type of amnestic disorder, alcohol-induced persisting amnestic disorder, also known as *Korsakoff's syndrome*. In this disorder, which is caused by chronic alcoholism, memory is impaired but other cognitive functions are not. More detailed examinations of the patients' cognitive abilities, using neuropsychological tests, have found evidence of more widespread cognitive deficits, especially those related to visuo-perceptual skills and abstract thinking (Jacobson, Acker, & Lishman, 1990).

One theory regarding this condition holds that lack of vitamin B_1 (thiamine) leads to atrophy of the medial thalamus, a subcortical structure of the brain, and mammillary bodies, which are illustrated in Figure 13–3 (see p. 478). There is also some evidence that prolonged exposure to alcohol may have direct toxic effects on cortical tissue that are independent of vitamin deficiencies. Alcohol apparently can cause brain damage regardless of the person's nutritional habits (Langlais, 1995).

Classification

Cognitive disorders have been classified by a somewhat different process than most other forms of psychopathology because of their close link to specific types of neuropathology. Description of specific cognitive and behavioral symptoms has not always been the primary consideration. In the following pages we describe the ways in which these disorders have been defined and some of the considerations that influence the way in which they are classified.

Brief Historical Perspective

Alois Alzheimer (1864–1915) was a German psychiatrist who worked closely in Munich with Emil Kraepelin, who is often considered responsible for modern psychiatric classification (see Chapters 4, 5, and 12). Alzheimer's most famous case involved a 51-year-old woman who had become delusional and also experienced a severe form of recent memory impairment, accompanied by apraxia and agnosia. This woman died 4 years after the onset of her dementia. Following her death, Alzheimer conducted a microscopic examination of her brain and made a startling discovery: bundles of neurofibrillary tangles and senile plaques. Alzheimer presented the case at a meeting of psychiatrists in 1906 and published a three-page paper in 1907. Emil Kraepelin began to refer to this condition as *Alzheimer's disease* in the eighth edition of his famous textbook on psychiatry, published in 1910. He distinguished between this form of dementia, which is characterized by an early onset, and senile dementia, which presumably has an onset after the age of 65.

For many years, there was an argument about the distinction between senile and presenile dementia. As more and more evidence accumulated regarding these conditions, questions were raised about the value of the distinction. For example, several cases were reported in which two siblings developed dementia, but one had the presenile form and the other had the senile form. Clinical symptoms and brain pathology in the siblings were often the same. Katzman (1976) proposed that both types are forms of Alzheimer's disease, which may have either an early or a late onset, and that they are distinctly different from normal aging. Age of onset may be a reflection of the severity of the disorder. Most clinicians and researchers still believe that Alzheimer's disease is a heterogeneous category, and the genetic literature supports that contention.

DSM-IV

Until recently, the diagnostic manual classified the various forms of dementia as Organic Mental Disorders because of their association with known brain diseases. That concept has fallen into disfavor because it is founded on an artificial dichotomy between biological and psychological processes. If we call dementia an organic mental disorder, does that imply that other types of psychopathology are not organically based (Spitzer et al., 1992)? Obviously not. Therefore, in order to be consistent with the rest of the diagnostic manual, and so as to avoid falling into the trap of simplistic mind–body dualism, dementia and related clinical phenomena are now classified as Cognitive Disorders in DSM-IV. These disorders are divided into three major headings: deliria, dementias, and amnestic disorders (see Table 14–4).

Many specific disorders are associated with dementia. They are distinguished primarily on the basis of known neuropathology—specific brain lesions that have been discovered throughout this century. These disorders can be subclassified into primary and secondary forms of dementia (Heston & White, 1991). A *primary dementia* is one in which the cognitive impairment is produced by the direct effect of a disease on brain tissue. A *secondary dementia* is one in which the cognitive impairment is a by-product or side effect of some other type of biological or psychological dysfunction. Secondary dementias include those associated with vascular disease, infections, and substance abuse (such as chronic alcoholism). The distinction between primary and secondary dementias is important, in large part because the treatment outlook may be more positive for some forms of secondary dementias.

The primary dementias are further subdivided into *undifferentiated* and *differentiated* types. In the differentiated dementias, such as Huntington's disease and Parkinson's disease, cognitive deficits are most often accompanied by disturbances of muscular control. These types of dementia are much less common than the undifferentiated dementias. The undifferentiated dementias, such as Alzheimer's disease and Pick's disease, cannot be distinguished from one another on the basis of manifest symptoms (thus the term *undifferentiated*). Microscopic examination of brain tissue upon autopsy is necessary. Neuropsychological tests also suggest some important differences.

The DSM-IV lists several different categories of dementia. The criteria for cognitive deficits of dementia are the same for each type, and they

▲ **Alois Alzheimer (left) on a pleasure cruise with his friend Emil Kraepelin. The form of dementia that Alzheimer described in his famous case was named after him in part because of the influence of Kraepelin's textbook.**

TABLE 14-4	
Cognitive Disorders Listed in DSM-IV	
Delirium	Delirium due to a general medical condition
	Substance-induced delirium
	Delirium due to multiple etiologies
Dementia	Dementia of the Alzheimer's type
	Vascular dementia
	Dementia due to other general medical conditions
	HIV disease
	Head trauma
	Parkinson's disease
	Huntington's disease
	Pick's disease
	Creutzfeldt-Jakob disease
	Substance-induced persisting dementia
	Dementia due to multiple etiologies
Amnestic disorders	Amnestic disorder due to a general medical condition
	Substance-induced persisting amnestic disorder

are listed in Table 14–5. In order to qualify for a diagnosis of dementia, the person must exhibit memory impairment (either anterograde or retrograde amnesia) and at least one other type of cognitive disturbance, such as aphasia, apraxia, agnosia, or problems in abstract thinking. There must also be evidence that the person's cognitive impairment interferes with his or her social or occupational functioning. Finally, for all forms of dementia, DSM-IV notes that the cognitive problems must be above and beyond anything that could be attributed solely to delirium.

Specific Disorders

DEMENTIA OF THE ALZHEIMER'S TYPE

Alzheimer's disease (primary undifferentiated dementia) is distinguished from the other types of dementia listed in DSM-IV on the basis of speed of onset. In this disorder, the cognitive impairment appears gradually, and the person's cognitive deterioration is progressive. If the person meets these criteria, the diagnosis is then made on the basis of excluding other conditions such as vascular disease, Huntington's disease, Parkinson's disease, and chronic substance abuse.

A definite diagnosis of Alzheimer's disease requires the observation of two specific types of brain lesions: neurofibrillary tangles and senile plaques. The brain is composed of millions of neurons. Part of the internal structure of each neuron is composed of *neurofibrils*, which provide structural support for the cell and help transport chemicals that are used in the production of neurotransmitters (Kolb & Whishaw, 1990). In the normal cell, neurofibrils are organized symmetrically. In Alzheimer's disease, the structural network of some neurofibrils becomes highly disorganized. Because these areas look like a tangled mass under the microscope, they are known as **neurofibrillary tangles.** They are found in both the cerebral cortex and the hippocampus. Cells with this appearance cannot function properly and are probably dead (Heston & White, 1991). Neurofibrillary tangles have also been found in adults with Down syndrome and patients with Parkinson's disease.

The other type of lesion in Alzheimer's disease is known as **senile plaques,** which consist of a central core of homogeneous protein material known as **beta-amyloid** surrounded by clumps of debris left over from destroyed neurons. These plaques are located primarily in the cerebral cortex. They are found in large numbers in the brains of patients with Alzheimer's disease, but they are not unique to that condition. The brains of normal elderly people, especially after the age of 75, often contain some neurofibrillary tangles and senile plaques. A few widely scattered cells of this type do not appear to interfere with normal cognitive functioning.

PICK'S DISEASE

Pick's disease is a form of primary dementia that is associated with atrophy of the frontal and temporal lobes of the brain. It is very similar to

---

TABLE 14–5

DSM-IV Criteria for Dementia of the Alzheimer's Type

A. **The development of multiple cognitive deficits manifested by both:**
    1. Memory impairment (impaired ability to learn new information or to recall previously learned information)
    2. One (or more) of the following cognitive disturbances:
        a. Aphasia (language disturbance)
        b. Apraxia (impaired ability to carry out motor activities despite intact motor function)
        c. Agnosia (failure to recognize or identify objects despite intact sensory function)
        d. Disturbance in executive functioning (that is, planning, organizing, sequencing, abstracting)

B. **The cognitive deficits each cause significant impairment in social or occupational functioning and represent a significant decline from a previous level of functioning.**

C. **The course is characterized by gradual onset and continuing cognitive decline.**

Alzheimer's disease in terms of both behavioral symptoms and cognitive impairment. Patients with both disorders display problems in memory and language. Early personality changes that precede the onset of cognitive impairment are more common among Pick patients. In comparison to Alzheimer patients, Pick patients are also more likely to engage in impulsive sexual actions, roaming and aimless exploration, and other types of disinhibited behavior (Mendez et al., 1993).

A detailed examination of brain tissue from patients with Pick's disease reveals the presence of *Pick's bodies*, a distinctive ballooning of nerve cells. The neurofibrillary tangles and senile plaques found in Alzheimer's disease are no more common in patients with Pick's disease than in normal people of the same age.

HUNTINGTON'S DISEASE

Huntington's disease is distinguished from the undifferentiated types of dementia by the presence of unusual involuntary muscle movements known as **chorea** (from the Greek word meaning "dance"). These movements are relatively subtle at first, with the person appearing to be restless or fidgety. As the disorder progresses, sustained muscle contractions become difficult. Movements of the face, trunk, and limbs eventually become uncontrolled, leaving the person to writhe and grimace. A large proportion of Huntington's patients also exhibit a variety of personality changes and symptoms of mental disorders, including primarily depression and anxiety. Between 5 and 10 percent develop psychotic symptoms (Shoulson, 1990). The symptoms of mental disorder may be evident before the appearance of motor or cognitive impairment.

The movement disorder and the cognitive deficits are produced by progressive neuronal degeneration in the basal ganglia (Chesselet & Delfs, 1996). This is a group of nuclei, including the caudate nucleus, the putamen, and the globus pallidus, that form a collaborative system of connections between the cerebral cortex and the thalamus (see Figure 14–2).

Dementia appears in all Huntington's disease patients, although the extent of the cognitive impairment and the rate of its progression vary widely. Impairments in recent memory and learning are the most obvious cognitive problems. Patients have trouble encoding new information. Higher-level cognitive functions are typically well preserved, and insight

is usually intact. Unlike the pattern of dementia seen in Alzheimer's disease, patients with Huntington's do not develop aphasia, apraxia, or agnosia (Morris, 1995; see Research Close-Up).

The diagnosis of Huntington's disease depends on the presence of a positive family history for the disorder. It is one of the few disorders that are transmitted in an autosomal dominant pattern with complete penetrance. In other words, the person must only inherit one gene—from either parent—to be vulnerable, and an individual who inherits the problematic gene will always develop the disorder.

PARKINSON'S DISEASE

Parkinson's disease is primarily a disorder of the motor system that is caused by a degeneration of a specific area of the brain stem known as the substantia nigra and loss of the neurotransmitter dopamine, which is produced by cells in this area. Typical symptoms include tremors, rigidity, postural abnormalities, and reduction in voluntary movements (Lishman, 1987). Unlike people with Huntington's disease, most patients with Parkinson's disease do not become demented. Follow-up studies suggest that approximately 20 percent of elderly patients with Parkinson's disease will develop symptoms of dementia.

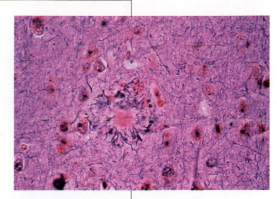

▲ This microscopic photograph illustrates senile plaques, which are found throughout the cortex and hippocampus of patients with Alzheimer's disease.

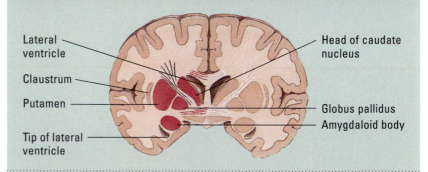

Areas of the Brain Implicated in Huntington's Disease

Lateral ventricle

Claustrum

Putamen

Tip of lateral ventricle

Head of caudate nucleus

Globus pallidus

Amygdaloid body

FIGURE 14-2: Huntington's disease involves deterioration of the basal ganglia (also known as the cerebral nuclei). The primary units of this system are the caudate nucleus, putamen, globus pallidus, and the claustrum.

Source: Adapted from F. Martini and M. Timmons, 1995, *Human Anatomy*, p. 378. Upper Saddle River, NJ: Prentice Hall.

Memory Differences in Alzheimer's Disease and Huntington's Disease

The cognitive deficits that are displayed by patients with dementia represent an important challenge as well as a unique opportunity for psychologists (Butters, 1992; Poon, Kaszniak, & Dudley, 1992). The challenge is to define more specifically the nature of the cognitive impairments associated with different types of dementia. If scientists can develop laboratory tests that identify specific types of cognitive impairment, these tests might be useful for several purposes: as early signs of the onset of dementia; as diagnostic tools to help clinicians distinguish among various types of dementia; and as measures of adjustment to mark the progression of the disorder or the response to treatment.

The opportunity is to find clues to the brain mechanisms that are responsible for different aspects of memory and information processing by studying individuals who have naturally occurring neurological dysfunctions. Carefully studied individual cases have given psychologists some insight regarding neurological underpinnings regarding the organization of memory in the brain. For example, one 52-year-old man, called R.B., developed severe amnesia in 1978 after the blood supply to his brain was temporarily interrupted during open-heart surgery. For the next 5 years, R.B.'s memory problems were studied extensively. His other cognitive functions were well preserved. After R.B.'s death in 1983, examination of his brain revealed extensive bilateral damage to the hippocampus (see Figure 13–3, p. 478) (Zola-Morgan, Squire, & Amaral, 1986).

This case, together with many other types of data, supports the hypothesis that the hippocampus is essential to a specific kind of memory, which is sometimes called *declarative* or *explicit memory* (Squire, 1992). In tasks that require explicit memory, subjects are asked to remember and later retrieve or recognize target information, such as words, letters, and symbols. In an implicit memory task, the subject's performance may be enhanced by prior experience with target information, even though the subject was not explicitly asked to remember it.

Comparisons between the cognitive performance of patients with specific types of dementia and normal people of the same age may provide us with insights that are similar to those gleaned from case studies like R.B.'s. One especially intriguing study involved a comparison among patients with dementia of the Alzheimer's type, patients with Huntington's disease, and elderly normal control subjects. Each subject performed two implicit memory tasks. In the motor learning task, they were seated in front of a rotating turntable upon which a small metallic disk was located. They were asked to

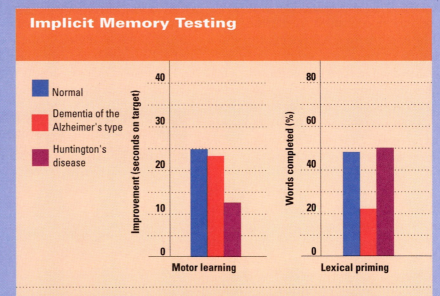

FIGURE 14-3: Comparison of patients with dementia and normal subjects on two tests of implicit memory: a pursuit-rotor learning task and a lexical priming task.

Source: Adapted from W.C. Heindel et al., 1989, Neuropsychological evidence for multiple implicit memory systems. A comparison of Alzheimer's, Huntington's, and Parkinson's disease patients, *Journal of Neuroscience, 9,* 586.

maintain contact between a stylus, which they held in their preferred hand, and the rotating disk. The investigators kept track of "time on target," and improvement was measured over three series of eight trials.

In the lexical priming task, the subjects were shown a sequence of 10 words (for example, MOTEL, ABSTAIN). Each word was printed on a small card, and the subjects were asked to rate how much they liked each word. These ratings were completed twice in order to increase the subjects' exposure to the target words. They were not asked to remember the words. When the second set of ratings was completed, the subjects were asked to complete one final task. They were presented with a sequence of three-letter stems (for example, MOT, ABS) and asked to complete each stem with the first word that came to mind. The index of implicit memory was the percentage of word stems completed with words that they had been asked to rate previously.

The results of this study are illustrated in Figure 14-3. The Alzheimer's patients were impaired on the lexical priming task, but their performance on the motor learning task was indistinguishable from that of the normal control subjects. The opposite pattern was found for patients with Huntington's disease. These data led to some interesting conclusions. First, although the cognitive symptoms associated with different forms of dementia may be difficult to distinguish on a clinical basis, laboratory tasks indicate that they may be associated with more specific types of cognitive impairment. Second, different types of implicit memory may be dependent on distinct brain mechanisms. Further, different mechanisms might be affected in varying ways by different disorders. ■

Their risk is approximately double the risk of dementia found among people of similar age who do not have Parkinson's disease (Marder et al., 1995; Tison et al., 1995).

VASCULAR DEMENTIA

Many conditions other than those that attack brain tissue directly can also produce symptoms of dementia. These are known as *secondary dementias*. The central agent in these problems can be either medical conditions or other types of mental disorder. Diseases that affect the heart and lungs, for example, can interfere with the circulation of oxygen to the brain. Substance abuse can also interfere with brain functions.

One of the leading causes of secondary dementia is vascular or blood vessel disease, which affects the arteries responsible for bringing oxygen and sugar to the brain (Skoog et al., 1996). A stroke, the severe interruption of blood flow to the brain, can produce various types of brain damage, depending on the size of the affected blood vessel and the area of the brain that it supplies. The area of dead tissue produced by the stroke is known as an **infarct.** The behavioral effects of a stroke are usually obvious and can be distinguished from dementia on several grounds: (1) they appear suddenly rather than gradually; (2) they affect voluntary movements of the limbs and gross speech patterns as well as more subtle intellectual abilities; and (3) they often result in unilateral rather than bilateral impairment, such as paralysis of only one side of the body. There are instances, however, in which the stroke affects only a very small artery and may not have any observable effect on the person's behavior. If several of these small strokes occur over a period of time, and if their sites are scattered in different areas of the brain, they may gradually produce cognitive impairment.

The DSM-IV refers to this condition as **vascular dementia.** Another commonly used term for this condition is *multi-infarct dementia.* The cognitive symptoms of vascular dementia that are listed in the diagnostic manual are the same as those for Alzheimer's disease, but DSM-IV does not require a gradual onset for vascular dementia, as it does for dementia of the Alzheimer's type. In addition, the diagnosis of vascular dementia depends on the presence of either focal neurological signs and symptoms associated with the experience of stroke, such as gait abnormalities or weakness in the extremities, or laboratory evidence of blood vessel disease.

DEMENTIA VERSUS DEPRESSION

Depression is another condition that can be associated with symptoms of dementia, especially among the elderly. There are, indeed, many areas of overlap between these disorders. Approximately 25 percent of patients with a diagnosis of dementia also exhibit symptoms of major depressive disorder (Lobo et al., 1995). The

TABLE 14-6

Signs and Symptoms Distinguishing Depression from Dementia

Depression	Dementia
Uneven progression over weeks	Even progression over months or years
Complains of memory loss	Attempts to hide memory loss
Often worse in morning, better as day goes on	Worse later in day or when fatigued
Aware of, exaggerates disability	Unaware or minimizes disability
May abuse alcohol or other drugs	Rarely abuses drugs

Source: Adapted from I. I. Heston and J. A. White, 1991, *The Vanishing Mind: A Practical Guide to Alzheimer's Disease and Other Dementias.* New York: Freeman.

symptoms of depression include a lack of interest in, and withdrawal of attention from, the environment. People who are depressed often have trouble concentrating, they appear preoccupied, and their thinking is labored. These cognitive problems closely resemble some symptoms of dementia. Some depressed patients exhibit poverty of speech and restricted or unchanging facial expression. A disheveled appearance, due to self-neglect and loss of weight, in an elderly patient may contribute to the impression that the person is suffering from dementia.

Despite the many similarities, there are important differences between depression and dementia. These are summarized in Table 14–6. Experienced clinicians can usually distinguish between depression and dementia by considering the pattern of onset and associated features (Allen & Blazer, 1991). In those cases where the distinction cannot be made on the basis of these characteristics, response to treatment may be the only way to establish a differential diagnosis. If the person's condition, including cognitive impairments, improves following treatment with antidepressant medication or electroconvulsive therapy, it seems reasonable to conclude that the person was depressed. These procedures can also be somewhat dangerous, because the cognitive symptoms of patients who are actually suffering from dementia may become exaggerated in response to medication (Horvath et al., 1991).

The relationship between depression and dementia has been the topic of considerable debate. Is depression a consequence of dementia, or are the symptoms of dementia a consequence of depression? Some clinicians have used the term *pseudodementia* to describe the condition of patients with symptoms of dementia whose cognitive impairment is actually produced by a major depressive disorder. There is no doubt that cases of this sort exist (Bulbena & Berrios, 1991). In fact, depression and dementia are not necessarily mutually exclusive disorders. We know that these conditions coexist more often than would be expected by chance, but we do not know why (Carpenter, Strauss, & Kennedy, 1995; Teri & Wagner, 1992).

Epidemiology of Dementia

Cognitive disorders represent one of the most pressing health problems in our society. Dementia is an especially important problem among elderly people. Although it can appear in people as young as 40 to 45, the average age of onset is much later. The incidence of dementia will be much greater in the near future, because the average age of the population is increasing steadily (see Chapter 17). People over the age of 80 represent one of the fastest growing segments of our population. By the year 2040, more than 9 million people in the United States will be affected by Alzheimer's disease (Max, 1993). The personal and economic impact of dementia on patients, their families, and our society clearly warrants serious attention from health care professionals, policymakers concerned with health care reform, and clinical scientists seeking more effective forms of treatment.

Epidemiological studies must be interpreted with caution, of course, because of the problems associated with establishing a diagnosis of dementia. Mild cases are difficult to identify reliably. At the earliest stages of the disorder, symptoms are difficult to distinguish from forgetfulness, which can increase in normal aging (see Further Thoughts). Definitive diagnoses depend on information collected over an extended period of time so that the progressive nature of the cognitive impairment, and deterioration from an earlier, higher level of functioning, can be documented. Unfortunately, this kind of information is often not available in a large-scale epidemiological study.

You should also bear in mind the fact that the diagnosis of specific subtypes of dementia, such as dementia of the Alzheimer's type and dementia due to Pick's disease, requires microscopic examination of brain tissue after the person's death. Again, these data are not typically available to epidemiologists. With these limitations in mind, we now consider what is known about the frequency of dementia in the general population.

Incidence and Prevalence by Age Group

The incidence and prevalence of dementia increase dramatically with age. Longitudinal studies of community samples indicate that the annual incidence of dementia is 1.4 percent in people over the age of 65 and 3.4 percent for people over the age of 75 (Brayne, 1993). Because dementia is most often a progressive disorder from which patients do not recover, we would expect that prevalence rates would be much higher than incidence rates. Most studies have reported a prevalence rate of about 5 percent for moderate or severe dementia among all people over the age of 65 years. Beginning with a rate of approximately 1 percent in the age group 60 to 64 years, the rate doubles approximately every 5 years. Almost 40 percent of people over 90 years of age exhibit symptoms of moderate or severe dementia (Gussekloo et al., 1995; Hafner, 1990; Johansson & Zarit, 1995).

Survival rates are reduced among demented patients. In Alzheimer's disease, for example, the average time between onset of the disorder and the person's death is approximately 8 years. Those with an earlier age of onset tend to live for a shorter period of time; the average survival period is only 4.5 years for those with an onset before age 45 (Heston & White, 1991). There is considerable variability in these figures. Some patients have survived more than 20 years after the first appearance of obvious symptoms.

There are no obvious differences between men and women with regard to the overall prevalence of dementia, broadly defined (Fichter et

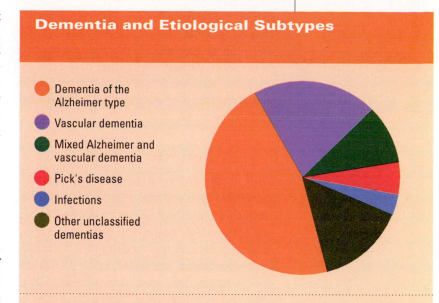

Dementia and Etiological Subtypes

- ● Dementia of the Alzheimer type
- ● Vascular dementia
- ● Mixed Alzheimer and vascular dementia
- ● Pick's disease
- ● Infections
- ● Other unclassified dementias

Figure 14-4: Proportions of dementia that can be attributed to different etiological subtypes.

Source: Adapted from L.L. Heston and J.A. White, 1991, *The Vanishing Mind: A Practical Guide to Alzheimer's Disease and Other Dementias.* New York: Freeman.

al., 1995; Kokmen et al., 1993). It seems, however, that dementia in men is more likely to be associated with vascular disease or to be secondary to other medical conditions or to alcohol abuse (Brayne, 1993).

Prevalence by Subtypes

The studies we have already reviewed refer to cross-sectional examinations of populations, which do not allow diagnosis of specific subtypes of dementia. Some clinical studies, based on hospital populations, have allowed investigators to look at the frequency of specific subtypes of dementia (Kaye, 1995). These data are summarized in Figure 14–4. Dementia of the Alzheimer's type appears to be the most common form of dementia, followed by dementia produced by vascular disease. Pick's disease is much less common. Huntington's disease, which is not included in this figure, is quite rare by comparison. It affects only 1 person in every 20,000 (O'Shea & Falvey, 1988; Shoulson, 1990).

Dementia: Etiological Considerations and Research

In discussing the classification of dementia and other cognitive disorders, we have touched on many of the factors that contribute to the etiology of these problems. Most of the other disorders listed in DSM-IV are classified on the basis of symptoms alone. The classification of dementia is sometimes determined by specific knowledge of etiological factors, even though these may be determined only after the patient's death, as in Alzheimer's disease. In the following discussion we consider in greater detail a few of the specific pathways that are known to lead to dementia.

Genetic Factors

Neurologists who treat demented patients have recognized for many years that the disorder often runs in families. Until recently, twin studies have not been used extensively to evaluate the influence of genetic factors in dementia because of the comparatively late age of onset of these disorders. By the time a proband develops symptoms of dementia, his or her co-twin may be deceased. A few recent studies have capitalized on national samples to find an adequate number of twin pairs. They confirm the impression, based on family studies, that genetic factors play an important role in the development of dementia. One Swedish study, for example, found that the concordance rate in monozygotic twins was over 50 percent, more than double the dizygotic rate (Pedersen & Gatz, 1991). A U.S. study, based on a registry of aging twin veterans of World War II and the Korean War, found an MZ concordance rate of 35 percent in 24 male pairs. None of the 16 DZ pairs was concordant at the time of the report (Breitner et al., 1993).

Most of the research concerned with genetic factors and Alzheimer's disease has focused on genetic linkage strategies. The astounding advances that have been made in molecular genetics since 1980 (see Research Methods) have been applied to Alzheimer's disease with fruitful results (Heston, 1997; Pollen, 1993). Some studies confirm an association between Alzheimer's disease and Down syndrome (see Chapter 15). It has been known for many years that senile plaques and neurofibrillary tangles are also found in the brains of all people who have Down syndrome. This similarity led investigators to search for a link between the gene for Alzheimer's disease and known markers on chromosome 21, because people with Down syndrome possess three copies of chromosome 21 in every cell instead of the normal two. Several research groups have independently confirmed this association. Within some families, the gene for Alzheimer's disease is located on chromosome 21. It has also been established that the gene responsible for producing proteins that serve as precursors to beta-amyloid, found in the core of senile plaques, is also located on chromosome 21.

RESEARCH METHODS

Genetic Linkage Analysis

It is one thing to say that genetic factors "are involved" in the transmission of a disorder, and quite another to identify the specific mode of inheritance. Discovery of the gene that is responsible for a disorder would be an exciting step toward explaining the etiology of the disorder. It would also have crucial implications for people who are known to be at increased risk for the disorder. Developments in the field of molecular genetics have allowed scientists to begin the search for such genes and, in some cases, to find them. The dementias, especially Huntington's disease, are one area in which important advances have been made in this regard.

The mode of inheritance in Huntington's disease has been relatively clear for many years because it follows an obvious Mendelian pattern: Almost exactly 50 percent of an affected person's first-degree relatives will also have the disorder. It is therefore considered to be an *autosomal dominant trait.* The term *autosomal* means that the gene is not located on one of the sex chromosomes. The knowledge that one gene, or a single locus on a particular chromosome, is apparently responsible for Huntington's disease made it an obvious candidate for genetic linkage analysis.

A gene is a strand of DNA, composed of a vast sequence of pairs of nucleic acid bases. These are the rods that lend a stairlike appearance to the familiar double helix structure of DNA, described by James D. Watson and Francis Crick in 1953. We all possess 46 chromosomes (23 pairs), which, taken together, contain 3 billion of these base pairs. Locating a gene on a chromosome can be accomplished by demonstrating **genetic linkage** between the genetic locus associated with the disorder and the locus for a known gene, a chromosome marker. Two loci are said to be linked when they are sufficiently close together on the same chromosome. Because of this physical association, the alleles at the two loci do not segregate independently during meiosis, the cell division process that results in the formation of sperm and egg cells.

In order to identify linkage, an investigator must study a large extended family in which several members have been affected by the disorder in question. Samples of cells are collected from everyone in the family. If all (or almost all) of the family members who have the disorder also have the marker in question, and if all (or almost all) of the unaffected members do not have the marker, then genetic linkage has been established (Heston & White, 1991).

The concept of genetic linkage was introduced early in the twentieth century by Thomas Hunt Morgan. Progress toward establishing genetic linkage in human disorders was extremely limited, however, because very few markers were available. In the late 1970s, recombinant DNA procedures led to the discovery of *restriction fragment-length polymorphisms (RFLPs),* fragments of DNA that are not associated with any recognized phenotypic trait but nevertheless provide useful landmarks for DNA segments. RFLPs are scattered across all the chromosomes.

In 1983, a group of scientists reported that the gene responsible for Huntington's disease was located on the short arm of chromosome 4 (Gusella et al., 1983). The data for their investigation came from a large extended family living in several remote villages on the northern coast of Venezuela. An unusually large number of the people in this family are victims of Huntington's disease. This is exactly the kind of pedigree required for genetic linkage analysis. Using blood samples collected from affected and unaffected members of the Venezuelan family, the investigators began looking for linkage with approximately a dozen RFLP markers. They were extremely lucky. The third marker that they tested produced a score indicating that the odds in favor of linkage between the Huntington's disease gene and this probe were over 200 million to 1. The probe was obviously located in very close proximity to the gene for which they were searching. Ten years later, the Huntington's Disease Collaborative Research Group (1993) announced that it had found the specific gene. ∎

The link to chromosome 21 is tentative, however. Other labs have failed to find an association between Alzheimer's disease and chromosome 21, and some have reported linkage with other chromosomes. In some families, an unidentified gene on chromosome 14 appears to be responsible for a late-onset form of the disorder (Schellenberg et al., 1993). Experts now assume that Alzheimer's disease is genetically heterogeneous. In other words, there are several forms of the disorder, and each may be associated with a different gene or set of genes (Folstein & Folstein, 1997).

Neurotransmitters

In patients suffering from dementia, the process of chemical transmission of messages within the brain is probably disrupted, but the specific mechanisms that are involved have not been identified. We know that Parkinson's disease, which is sometimes associated with dementia, is caused by a degeneration of the dopamine pathways in the brain stem. This dysfunction is responsible for the motor symptoms seen in patients with that disorder. It is not entirely clear, however, that the intellectual problems experienced by patients with Parkinson's disease are directly related to dopamine deficiencies.

Other types of dementia have also been linked to problems with specific neurotransmitters. Huntington's disease may be associated with deficiencies in gamma-aminobutyric acid (GABA), and a decrease in the availability of acetylcholine, another type of neurotransmitter, has been implicated in Alzheimer's disease (Newhouse, 1997; Raskind & Peskind, 1997).

Viral Infections

Some forms of primary dementia are known to be the products of "slow" viruses—infections that develop over a much more extended period of time than do most viral infections. *Creutzfeldt-Jakob disease* is one example. Susceptibility to infection by a specific virus can be influenced by genetic factors. The demonstration that a condition is transmitted in a familial fashion does not rule out the involvement of viral infection. In fact, familial transmission has been demonstrated for the forms of dementia that are known to be associated with a specific virus.

Immune System Dysfunction

The immune system is the body's first line of defense against infection. It employs antibodies to break down foreign materials, such as bacteria and viruses, that enter the body. The regulation of this system allows it to distinguish between foreign bodies that should be destroyed and normal body tissues that should be preserved. The production of these antibodies may be dysfunctional in some forms of dementia, such as Alzheimer's disease. In other words, the destruction of brain tissue may be caused by a breakdown in the system that regulates the immune system.

The presence of beta-amyloid at the core of senile plaques provides one important clue to the possible involvement of immune system dysfunction. This protein is the breakdown product of a structural component of brain cells. It is made and eliminated constantly as part of normal brain functioning. For some reason, which probably involves genetic factors, some people develop problems with the elimination of beta-amyloid. Clumps of beta-amyloid accumulate. Some clinical scientists believe that immune cells in the brain attempt to destroy these senile plaques and inadvertently harm neighboring, healthy brain cells. Some research evidence supports this hypothesis (McGeer & McGeer, 1996; Richardson, 1996).

Environmental Factors

Epidemiological investigations have discovered several interesting patterns that suggest that some types of dementia, especially Alzheimer's disease, may be related to environmental factors. One example is exposure to aluminum, a chemical that is abundant in the natural environment. Experimental studies with animals have demonstrated that exposure to aluminum can induce brain lesions that resemble the neurofibrillary tangles found in Alzheimer's disease. Excess levels of aluminum have also been found at autopsy in the brains of some victims of Alzheimer's disease. Some epidemiological evidence indicates a correlation between levels of aluminum in the water supply and rates of dementia and cognitive impairment in the local population. Other studies have failed to replicate this result (Brayne, 1993; Jacqmin et al., 1994). The possible link between aluminum and dementia is both questionable and controversial, but it is still a topic of serious research efforts (Copestake, 1993; Rifat, 1994).

In addition to the aluminum connection, other studies have reported significant relationships between Alzheimer's disease and two other variables that seem to operate as protective factors: cigarette smoking and level of education. Some reports indicate, for example, that people who have smoked cigarettes actually have a lower risk for developing Alzheimer's disease (Brenner et al., 1993). These data are interesting in light of the fact that autopsies of Alzheimer's victims have found a reduced density of nicotinic receptors in the brain. Some investigators have speculated that the experience of smoking cigarettes may reduce the risk for dementia of the Alzheimer's type by increasing the density or sensitivity of nicotinic receptors.

The final correlation we will consider is between dementia of the Alzheimer's type and educational attainment. Several investigators have found that people who have achieved high levels of education are less likely to develop Alzheimer's disease than are people with less education (Friedland, 1993; Stern, Gurland, Tatemichi, et al., 1994). Snowdon et al. (1989), for example, found that among elderly Catholic nuns, those who had graduated from college were much less likely to be cognitively impaired than were those who had less than a college education. There are several ways to interpret this relationship. One suggests that increased "brain work" leads to a facilitation of neuronal activation, increased cerebral blood flow, and higher levels of glucose and oxygen consumption in the brain. This experience may reduce the

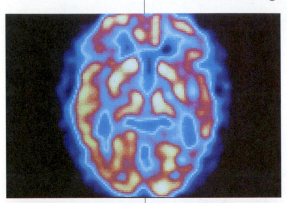
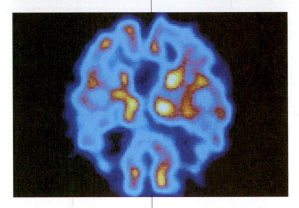

▲ **PET scan of the brain (basal ganglia level) of a normal person and a patient with Alzheimer's disease. The scans show brain activity from low (blue) to high (yellow). Normal brain metabolic activity produces a roughly symmetrical pattern in the yellow areas of the left and right hemispheres (top). The patchy appearance of the patient's scan indicates degeneration of brain tissue.**

person's risk for later neuronal deterioration in much the same way that higher levels of environmental stimulation can facilitate neural growth during early development in young animals (Greenough, 1987).

Although these findings are thought-provoking, a strong word of caution is in order. It is not clear whether these correlations indicate a causal relationship between these variables and dementia (Heston & White, 1991; Katzman, 1993). The correlations could easily be due to any number of third variables. Directionality is also a problem. For example, aluminum might become concentrated in brain tissue after the death of nerve cells, which is caused by some other factor. It is certainly the case that many people who have been exposed to comparatively high levels of aluminum— metalworkers, people who take certain medications, and people who drink large quantities of tea, which is high in aluminum—have not become demented.

Treatment and Management

The most obvious consideration with regard to treatment of the cognitive disorders is accurate diagnosis (Cummings, 1995; Wise & Gray, 1996). The distinction between delirium and dementia is important because many conditions that cause delirium can be treated. Delirium must be recognized as early as possible so that the source of the problem, such as an infection or some other medical condition, can be treated. Some types of secondary dementia can also be treated successfully. For example, if the patient's cognitive symptoms are the products of depression, there is a relatively good chance that he or she will respond positively to antidepressant medication or electroconvulsive therapy.

When the person clearly suffers from a primary type of dementia, such as dementia of the Alzheimer's type, a return to previous levels of functioning is extremely unlikely. No form of treatment is presently capable of improving cognitive functioning in dementia of the Alzheimer's type (Growdon, 1992). Realistic goals include helping the person to maintain his or her level of functioning for as long as possible in spite of cognitive impairment and minimizing the level of distress experienced by the person and the person's family. Several treatment options are typically used in conjunction, including medication, management of the patient's environment, behavioral strategies, and providing support to caregivers (Banazak, 1996).

Medication

We do not yet have specific drugs that can reverse the process of cell loss in the brain that is responsible for dementia. There are, however, a number of clues available regarding the nature of the neurochemical abnormalities involved in dementia of the Alzheimer's type. For the past decade, these clues have stimulated attempts to treat Alzheimer's patients with experimental types of medication (Arneric et al., 1995; Newhouse, 1997). It has been demonstrated, for example, that levels of the transmitter acetylcholine (ACh) may be reduced in this disorder. The production of ACh in the brain is controlled by an enzyme known as choline acetyl transferase, and some studies have found that activity levels of this enzyme are reduced in the brains of people suffering from dementia of the Alzheimer's type (Raskind & Peskind, 1997).

Evidence regarding ACh and choline acetyl transferase generated many efforts to stimulate increased production of ACh in the hope that it would lead to an improvement in cognitive functioning. Unfortunately, the earliest treatment studies of this sort were largely unsuccessful (Davis & Haroutunian, 1993). A few patients showed modest improvement, but most did not, and the side effects of the drugs were quite unpleasant. More recently, investigators have continued to pursue new types of medication that are intended primarily to increase levels of ACh in the brain. One specific drug, tracine (THA), has shown promising results in terms of its ability to improve the immediate signs and symptoms of dementia of the Alzheimer's type (Davis et al., 1995; Soares & Gerson, 1995). The drug provides temporary symptomatic improvement for some patients. It is not clear, however, whether THA can actually slow down the rate at which the disorder progresses (Giacobini, 1994).

Although the cognitive deficits associated with primary dementia cannot be completely reversed with medication, neuroleptic medication can be used to treat the subset of patients who develop psychotic symptoms (Beckson & Cummings, 1992; Devanand & Levy, 1995). Low doses are preferable because demented patients are especially vulnerable to the side effects of neuroleptics. These are the same drugs that are used to treat schizophrenia. Their pharmacological action is focused on blocking postsynaptic dopamine receptors.

Environmental and Behavioral Management

Patients with dementia experience fewer emotional problems and are less likely to become agitated if they follow a structured and predictable daily schedule (Kettl, 1993; Stewart, 1995). Activities such as eating meals, exercising, and going to bed are easier and less anxiety-provoking if they occur at regular times. The use of signs and notes may be helpful reminders for patients who are in the earlier stages of the disorder. As the patient's cognitive impairment becomes more severe, even simple activities, such as getting dressed or eating a meal, must be broken down into smaller and more manageable steps. Directions have to be adjusted so that they are appropriate to the patient's level of functioning. Patients with apraxia, for example, may not be able to perform tasks in response to verbal instructions. Caregivers need to adjust their expectations and assume increased responsibilities as patients' intellectual abilities deteriorate.

Severely impaired patients often reside in nursing homes and hospitals. The most effective residential treatment programs combine the use of medication and behavioral interventions with an environment that is specifically designed to maximize the level of functioning and minimize the emotional distress of patients who are cognitively impaired. Several goals guide the design of such an environment (Kettl, 1993; Lawton, 1989). These

include considerations that enhance the following aspects of the patient's life.

- *Knowledge of the environment:* For example, rooms and hallways must be clearly labeled, because patients frequently cannot remember directions.
- *Negotiability:* In the case of dementia, psychological accessibility is at least as important as physical accessibility. For example, spaces that the person would use (a commons area or the dining room) should be visible from the patient's room if they cannot be remembered.
- *Safety and health:* For example, access to the setting must be secured so that patients who would otherwise wander away can remain as active as possible.

One important issue related to patient management involves the level of activity expected of the patient. It is useful to help the person remain active and interested in everyday events. Patients who are physically active are less likely to have problems with agitation, and they may sleep better. Engaging in pleasant activities may also minimize the frequency and severity of depression among patients with dementia (Teri & Gallagher-Thompson, 1991). Nevertheless, expectations regarding the patient's activity level may have to be reduced in proportion to the progression of cognitive impairment. Efforts should be made to preserve familiar routines and surroundings in light of the inevitable difficulties that are associated with learning new information and recalling past events. Helping the person to cope with these issues may minimize the emotional turmoil associated with the increasing loss of cognitive abilities.

Social interactions are often troublesome for patients with dementia. An example of this type of problem was described in the case of Mary at the beginning of this chapter. After Mary had been admitted to the hospital, she frequently approached the nurses insisting that she had to go home to take care of her dog, which had in fact died. Creative problem-solving strategies that accommodate the patient's distorted view of reality are sometimes useful in this type of situation. Imagine, for example, a patient who continually insists that he must go to his former place of employment. It might be more effective to inform him each morning that his office called to say that he was not needed until the next day, rather than engaging in futile and

▼ Residential programs attempt to keep patients with dementia as active as possible.

upsetting arguments about whether he had, in fact, retired for medical reasons—a fact that he is incapable of remembering (Zarit et al., 1990).

Support for Caregivers

A final area of concern is the provision of support to people who serve as caregivers for demented patients. In the United States, spouses and other family members provide primary care for more than 80 percent of people who have dementia of the Alzheimer's type (Rabins, 1997). Their burdens are often overwhelming, both physically and emotionally. Consider, for example, the situation described by Bernlef in *Out of Mind*. In the following passage, Maarten describes the experience of listening to his wife, Vera, describe to a young woman (whom Vera has hired to help care for Maarten) how she has felt while attempting to cope with his progressive cognitive deterioration:

I hear Vera. "More than 40 years I have been married to him. And then suddenly this. Usually these things happen more slowly, gradually. But with him it came all at once. I feel it has been sprung on me. It's cruel and unfair. Sometimes I get so angry and rebellious when I see him looking at me as if from another world. And then again I feel only sad and I would so much like to understand him. Or I just talk along with him and then I feel ashamed afterwards. I'm glad you're here because it really gets on top of me at times, when I just can't bear watching it any more. At least now I'll be able to get out occasionally."

There is a moment of silence. I feel the tears running under my eyelids and down my cheeks.

"And sometimes, sometimes his face radiates perfect peace. As if he's happy. Like a child can be. Those moments are so brief I sometimes think I imagine them. But I know only too well what I see at such moments: someone who looks exactly like my husband of long ago. At your age it's difficult to understand that. But people like us live by their memories. If they no longer have those there's nothing left. I am afraid he is in the process of forgetting his whole life. And to live alone with those memories while he sits there beside me . . . empty."
(Bernlef, 1988, pp. 80–81)

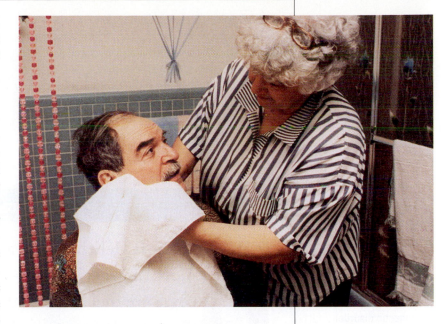

▲ **Individuals who care for people with dementia assume an enormous burden. Respite programs attempt to provide assistance to these individuals.**

In addition to the profound loneliness and sadness that caregivers endure, they must also learn to cope with more tangible stressors, such as the patient's incontinence, functional deficits, and disruptive behavior. Relationships among other family members and the psychological adjustment of the principal caregiver are more disturbed by caring for a demented person than by caring for someone who is physically disabled (Brody, 1989). Guilt, frustration, and depression are common reactions among the family members of patients.

Some treatment programs provide support groups as well as informal counseling and ad hoc consultation services for spouses caring for patients with Alzheimer's disease. The New York University Aging and Dementia Research Center has evaluated the effects of this approach, which attempts to help the caregiver survive the spouse's illness and to postpone the need to place the patient in a nursing home (Mittelman et al., 1997). Compared to caregivers in a control group, those who participated in the special support program were able to delay for a longer time placing the Alzheimer's patient in a nursing home. They were also less likely to become depressed and more likely to express satisfaction with the social support that they received from their families.

Some treatment programs arrange for direct assistance in addition to social support. *Respite programs* provide caregivers with temporary periods of relief away from the patient. One model program was designed and evaluated by M. Powell Lawton and his colleagues at the

Philadelphia Geriatric Center (Brody, Saperstein, & Lawton, 1989). They either would send someone to the patient's home to relieve the caregiver or, in more severe cases, would temporarily institutionalize the patient if the caregiver needed to be away from home for an extended period. In some cases, these services were planned in advance so that the caregiver could take a short vacation,

attend special events, or make his or her own medical appointments. Respite care was also available in response to unexpected circumstances, such as the illness of the caregiver. This type of flexible, comprehensive program is clearly needed to relieve the enormous burden that is faced by people who care for demented patients.

Summary

Dementia, delirium, and amnestic disorders are listed as Cognitive Disorders in DSM-IV. Disruptions of memory and other cognitive functions are the most obvious symptoms of these disorders. Dementia and amnestic disorders are often associated with specific forms of neuropathology. These changes in brain tissue can often be observed only at autopsy, after the person's death. Until recently, the DSM referred to the Cognitive Disorders as Organic Mental Disorders because of their association with known brain diseases. That expression has been abandoned because it implies an artificial dichotomy between biological and psychological processes.

Dementia is defined as a gradually worsening loss of memory and related cognitive functions, including the use of language as well as reasoning and decision making. **Aphasia** and **apraxia** are among the most obvious problems in verbal communication. Perceptual difficulties, such as **agnosia,** are also common.

In amnestic disorder, the memory impairment is more circumscribed. The person may experience severe **anterograde amnesia,** but other higher-level cognitive abilities remain unimpaired. **Delirium** is a confusional state that develops over a short period of time and is often associated with agitation and hyperactivity.

Dementia can be associated with many different kinds of neuropathology. The most common form of dementia is associated with **Alzheimer's disease.** It accounts for approximately half of all diagnosed cases of dementia. Another 20 percent of cases are produced by vascular disease. Several small strokes over a period of time can produce **infarcts** scattered in different areas of the brain and can lead to the gradual onset of cognitive impairment. Less common forms of dementia are associated with Pick's

disease, Huntington's disease, and Parkinson's disease.

A definitive diagnosis of Alzheimer's disease can be made only after the patient's death. It requires the observation of two specific types of brain lesions: **neurofibrillary tangles** and **senile plaques,** which are found throughout the cerebral cortex. Neurofibrillary tangles are also found in the hippocampus, an area of the brain that is crucial for memory.

The incidence and prevalence of dementia increase dramatically with age. The annual incidence of dementia is 1.4 percent in people over the age of 65 and 3.4 percent for people over the age of 75. Almost 40 percent of people over 90 years of age exhibit symptoms of moderate or severe dementia. Men and women are equally vulnerable to these disorders.

The etiology of dementia depends on many different factors. Some types of dementia are produced by viral infections and dysfunction of the immune system. Environmental toxins also may contribute to the onset of cognitive impairment.

KEY TERMS

- agnosia
- Alzheimer's disease
- amnestic disorder
- anterograde amnesia
- aphasia
- apraxia
- beta-amyloid
- chorea
- delirium
- dementia
- dyskinesia
- genetic linkage
- infarct
- neurofibrillary tangles
- neurologist
- neuropsychological assessment
- neuropsychologist
- retrograde amnesia
- senile plaques
- vascular dementia

Genetic factors clearly play a role in the etiology of some forms of dementia. Considerable research efforts have been devoted to the study of genetic linkage in Alzheimer's disease. Chromosome 21 has been examined closely because people with Down syndrome, who possess three copies of chromosome 21 in every cell, also have senile plaques and neurofibrillary tangles like those found in the brains of Alzheimer's patients. Within some families, the gene for Alzheimer's disease is located on chromosome 21. This pattern of linkage is not found for all families, however. Experts now assume that there are several forms of Alzheimer's disease, and each may be associated with a different gene or set of genes.

Delirium can often be resolved successfully by treating the infection or some other medical condition. In some types of secondary dementia, the person can be restored to his or her original level of cognitive functioning. The intellectual deficits in primary forms of dementia are progressive and irreversible. The treatment goals in these disorders are more limited. They include maintaining the person's level of functioning for as long as possible while minimizing the level of distress experienced by the patient and the family, especially caregivers. Medication can produce modest cognitive benefits for some patients with dementia, but not all patients respond to such treatment, and the clinical significance of these changes is extremely limited. Drugs can be used to control motor dysfunctions associated with primary differentiated forms of dementia, such as Huntington's disease and Parkinson's disease.

Behavioral and environmental management are important aspects of any treatment program for demented patients. They allow patients to reside in the least restrictive and safest possible settings. Respite programs provide much-needed support to caregivers, usually spouses and other family members, who can easily be overwhelmed by the demands of caring for a person with dementia.

Critical Thinking

1. Suppose you know an elderly person who is beginning to show memory problems. Does that necessarily mean that he or she is developing dementia? What sort of measures might be used to distinguish normal aging from dementia?

2. Dementia and amnestic disorders are classified as cognitive disorders in DSM-IV. Many clinicians also talk about the role of cognitive factors in the development of disorders such as anxiety and depression. What is the difference between cognitive impairments seen in dementia and those seen in other forms of psychopathology?

3. Why has the etiology of Alzheimer's disease received increased attention in recent years? Why do clinical scientists consider this disorder to be one of the most pressing health problems in our society?

4. If dementia is an irreversible process, how can it be treated? To which considerations would you give the highest priority in addressing the needs of patients and their families?

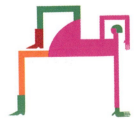

15

Mental Retardation and Pervasive Developmental Disorders

Mental retardation is a common and familiar problem. Many of us attended schools where students with mental retardation were "mainstreamed" into regular classes, and we often encounter mental retardation in everyday life. Despite its prevalence, psychologists—and the popular media—often pay scant attention to mental retardation. Perhaps this is changing. We recently have been uplifted by the triumphs of characters like Forrest Gump (from the Academy Award–winning movie), and Benny from the discontinued television show "L.A. Law." Technically, neither of these characters suffered from mental retardation. Mental retardation is characterized by significantly subaverage intellectual functioning *and* deficits in adaptive life skills. The mythic figure of Forrest Gump clearly adapted successfully to life despite his apparently low intelligence. The far more realistic character Benny also might not be considered to have mental retardation, because his adaptive skills were recognized and utilized.

Overview

Most triumphant of all is the television character of Corky Thatcher played by Christopher Burke, who has Down syndrome, one of the most common causes of mental retardation. Burke recently wrote about his condition:

> My name is Chris Burke and I live an exciting and happy life. That's because I am living my dreams. I love entertaining people and being an actor, and I like to help my fellow handi-capables. Many people recognize me from my role as Corky Thatcher on "Life Goes On," an ABC-TV series for many years. Corky has Down syndrome and so do I. Only I call it Up syndrome, because having Down syndrome has never made me feel down. I'm always up. One reason it is uplifting is because of the tremendous support I have received from my family and all the people in my life. My teachers, my friends, and the people I have worked with are very important to me, just like I am important to them. (Burke, 1995, p. ix)

Many people would not consider someone like Chris Burke to have mental retardation, apparently including Chris Burke. When people with significantly subaverage intelligence are able to adapt well in everyday life, we recognize their strengths and no longer label them as having a mental disorder.

Pervasive developmental disorders are far less common than mental retardation; thus few of us encounter these disturbances in everyday life. Pervasive developmental disorders are distinguished by unusual symptoms, including severe and pervasive impairments in communication, social interaction, and stereotyped behavior. Dustin Hoffman's role as Raymond in the movie *Rain Man* is perhaps the most familiar portrayal of a pervasive developmental disorder, specifically autistic disorder (autism). Although pervasive developmental disorders are less common than mental retardation, psychologists and the public have devoted disproportionate attention to them. Perhaps this is because some theorists have argued that pervasive developmental disorders are emotional problems, not intellectual ones. It has been suggested, for example, that people with pervasive developmental disorders are of normal or perhaps even superior intelligence, but their intellectual skills are masked by their emotional problems (see Happe, 1995). Unfortunately, this hopeful speculation is not supported by research evidence. Although there are intriguing exceptions, the majority of people who suffer from a pervasive developmental disorder also have mental retardation. Still, pervasive developmental disorders continue to be viewed largely as mental health problems.

In contrast, mental retardation commonly is seen as an educational problem, and its treatment often falls within the domain of special educators instead of mental health professionals. As a result of this focus on intellectual difficulties, practitioners often have overlooked the Axis I emotional problems found among people with mental retardation. In order to correct this bias, mental retardation is coded on Axis II in the DSM-IV (see Chapter 4). In addition to the fact that significantly subaverage IQ is enduring, the placement on Axis II should call attention to Axis I mental disorders among people with mental retardation.

Both mental retardation and pervasive developmental disorders typically either are present at birth or begin early in life. Both disorders are characterized by serious disruptions in many areas of functioning, sometimes including the ability to care for oneself independently. For these reasons we consider the two conditions together in a single chapter. We discuss mental retardation before reviewing the pervasive developmental disorders, because as we have noted, most people with pervasive developmental disorders also have mental retardation.

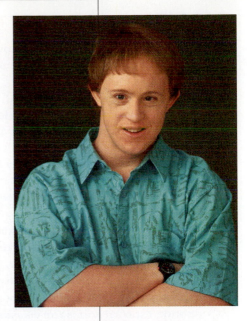

▲ **Christopher Burke, a boy with Down syndrome, starred as Corky Thatcher in the television show "Life Goes On."**

Mental Retardation

Mental retardation is a diverse diagnostic category. All people with mental retardation have impaired intellectual abilities, but they vary widely in academic ability and functioning. People with mental retardation also differ substantially in their ability to communicate, to master social situations, and to participate in their own care. Some people with profound retardation require total care and live their entire lives in institutions. However, the vast majority of people with mental retardation learn the self-care and vocational skills needed to allow them to live in the community.

Despite stereotypes to the contrary, much can be done about mental retardation. Although there are limits, early intervention can bring about substantial improvements in the lives of people with mental retardation, and many cases of mental retardation can be prevented by careful planning and health care. We begin our consideration of this important problem with a case from our files.

CASE STUDY

A Mother with Mild Mental Retardation

Karen Cross was a 41-year-old woman with three children when child protective services referred her and her husband, Mark, for a family evaluation. Two months earlier, the Cross's 16-year-old daughter, Lucy, had called the police following a family fight. Lucy and her mother had been arguing about Lucy's excessive use of the telephone, and when Mr. Cross entered the dispute, he cuffed Lucy across her mouth in anger. Lucy was not seriously hurt, and the social workers who visited with the Cross family following the incident found no history of physical abuse. They were concerned about the adequacy of the Crosses' parenting, however, and the agency strongly recommended an evaluation for the family.

At the time of the referral, Mr. Cross was employed as a custodian at an elementary school where he had been working for 15 years. Testing indicated that he had an IQ of 88, and there was no sign of serious psychopathology based on a diagnostic interview or an MMPI. Both Mr. Cross and his wife admitted that he had exhibited increasingly frequent, angry outbursts, but they both denied any history of violence toward the children or Mrs. Cross.

Mrs. Cross was a homemaker who cared for Lucy and a 12-year-old daughter, Sue. The Cross's 19-year-old son was serving in the Army. Mrs. Cross had a tested IQ of 67, and she reported that she had attended special education classes throughout her schooling. She married at the age of 19 and lived a normal life with her husband and children, but their low income barely kept the family out of poverty. Although Mrs. Cross demonstrated many adaptive skills in caring for her family, her coping currently was impaired by a severe depression. During the interview, Mrs. Cross's speech and body movements were slowed, and she reported feeling constantly tired. She did not describe herself as "depressed," but she felt unhappy and unable to cope with her children. She was not sure what had caused her troubles, but Mr. Cross traced the onset of her problems to her mother's death a year earlier.

Mrs. Cross cried repeatedly when recalling the loss of her mother. She described her mother as her best friend. They had lived in the same trailer park, and mother and daughter spent most of their days together. Mrs. Cross's mother offered her much practical support, especially in raising the children. Now the children ignored their mother's directions, and Mr. Cross was of little help. Mrs. Cross felt that her husband was too harsh, and she often contradicted him when he tried to punish the girls.

A family interview with the parents and the two teenagers together confirmed the impressions given by the parents. Lucy looked distracted and bored throughout the interview, and Sue frequently looked toward and imitated her older sister. The girls paid more attention briefly when their father got angry, but this ended when Mr. and Mrs. Cross started fighting over his tone of voice.

School records indicated that the girls were obtaining mostly C grades. Standardized test scores from the school indicated that the girls' academic abilities were in the normal range, although their scores were below average. Telephone calls to each of their homeroom teachers indicated that Sue was not much of a behavior problem in school, but Lucy had lately become very disruptive.

Based on the data obtained from multiple sources, the psychologists made several recommendations to the family and to child protective services. They suggested an evaluation for antidepressant medication for Mrs. Cross, a referral to the school counselor for Lucy, and a brief course of family therapy that would always include Mr. Cross and Mrs. Cross and sometimes would include the girls. The family therapy was designed to help the parents agree on a set of rules for the girls and enforce discipline with a clear system of rewards and punishments that would focus on the loss of privileges. Therapy also would be used to evaluate Mr. Cross's anger further and to monitor Mrs. Cross's depression. One possibility for the future for Mr. Cross was individual therapy focused on controlling his anger. Finally, an attempt would be made to identify services in the community for Mrs. Cross with the goal of helping her build a new system of support. ■

The case of Karen Cross and her family illustrates some important features of mental retardation. One issue is the adequacy of her functioning. Despite her recent struggles, Karen Cross had succeeded in living a happy, productive life. Many people in her community would not consider her to have mental retardation. Another feature is Karen Cross's depression. Many people with mental retardation suffer from emotional difficulties, a fact that is overlooked all too often. Finally, the case of Karen Cross raises concerns about children reared in disadvantaged environments, as well as questions about how society can be supportive but not intrusive in family life. We consider each of these issues in this chapter, but first we examine more closely the definition of mental retardation.

Typical Symptoms and Associated Features

The American Association on Mental Retardation (AAMR), the leading organization for professionals concerned with mental retardation, offers the following definition of **mental retardation:**

> Mental retardation refers to substantial limitations in present functioning. It is characterized by significantly subaverage intellectual functioning, existing concurrently with related limitations in two or more of the following applicable adaptive skill areas: communication, self-care, home living, social skills, community use, self-direction, health and safety, functional academics, leisure, and work. Mental retardation manifests before age 18. (AAMR, 1992, p. 1)

The AAMR's definition of mental retardation differs somewhat from the one found in DSM-IV (see Table 15–1), and we highlight some of the differences and controversies between the two systems later in the chapter. Fortunately, however, both definitions generally agree on the major criteria for mental retardation.

Each definition has three major parts. "Significantly subaverage intellectual functioning" refers to an IQ of approximately 70 or below as measured by an individually administered intelligence test. The DSM and AAMR differ somewhat on the exact cutoff score, as the DSM notes "approximately 70" whereas the AAMR designates a range of 70 to 75. This seemingly small difference can have some important practical implications, as we discuss shortly. "With related limitations in two or more . . . adaptive skill areas" refers to deficits in life skills. People who have an IQ below 75 but who

function well in life are not considered to have mental retardation. The criterion "Mental retardation manifests before age 18" excludes people whose deficits begin during adult life. When factors such as injury or degenerative brain disease produce significantly subaverage IQ after the age of 18, dementia, and not mental retardation, may be the appropriate diagnosis (see Chapter 14).

SIGNIFICANTLY SUBAVERAGE IQ

The AAMR and the DSM both define subaverage intellectual functioning in terms of a score on an individualized *intelligence test*, a standardized measure for assessing intellectual ability. Commonly used intelligence tests include the Wechsler Intelligence Scale for Children—Revised (WISC-R) and the Wechsler Adult Intelligence Scale—Revised (WAIS-R). Intelligence tests yield a score called the **intelligence quotient,** or **IQ,** the test's rating of an individual's intellectual ability.

Measurement of Intelligence Defining *intelligence* can be controversial, and definitions and measures of intellectual ability have changed over the years. Early versions of intelligence tests derived an IQ by dividing the individual's "mental age" by his or her chronological age. Mental age was determined by comparing an individual's test results with the average obtained for various age groups. For example, someone who answered the same number of items correctly as the average 10-year-old would be given a mental age of 10. Mental age next was divided by chronological age, and the ratio was multiplied by 100 to yield an IQ score.

TABLE 15–1

DSM-IV Diagnostic Criteria for Mental Retardation

A. Significantly subaverage intellectual functioning: an IQ of approximately 70 or below on an individually administered IQ test (for infants, a clinical judgment of significantly subaverage intellectual functioning).

B. Concurrent deficits or impairments in present adaptive functioning (i.e., the person's effectiveness in meeting the standards expected for his or her age by his or her cultural group) in at least two of the following skill areas: communication, self-care, home living, social/interpersonal skills, use of community resources, self-direction, functional academic skills, work, leisure, health and safety.

C. Onset is before age 18 years.

The Normal Distribution of IQ Scores and the IQ Cutoff Score for Mental Retardation

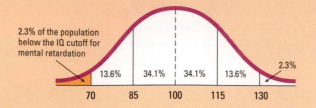

2.3% of the population below the IQ cutoff for mental retardation

13.6%   34.1%   34.1%   13.6%   2.3%

70   85   100   115   130

FIGURE 15–1: Many theories assume a normal distribution of intelligence in the population. Contemporary IQ tests have a mean of 100 and a standard deviation of 15. The IQ cutoff for mental retardation is two standard deviations below the mean.

Contemporary intelligence tests have abandoned the concept of mental age and instead adopt the concept of the "deviation IQ." According to this theory, intellectual ability follows the **normal distribution** in the population, a common bell-shaped frequency distribution that is illustrated in Figure 15–1. As is the case with height and weight, both of which follow the normal distribution, most people are assumed to be near average in intelligence, while a few people are thought to be exceptionally low or exceptionally high in their intellectual abilities. The individual's IQ is determined based on how the person scores on an intelligence test relative to the norms for his or her age group. Narrow age ranges are used in creating norms for children, because cognitive abilities and knowledge acquisition change rapidly with age. In contrast, all adults are treated as a part of the same age group.

Intelligence tests are normed to have a mean (average) IQ score of 100 and a **standard deviation** of 15. (See the Research Methods box for a definition and calculation of standard deviation.) Thus, by definition, given a normal distribution of IQ scores, about two-thirds of the population has an IQ within one standard deviation of the mean—between 85 and 115. The cutoff score for mental retardation is approximately two standard deviations below the average. About 2 percent of the population falls below this cutoff in the normal distribution (see Figure 15–1).

IQ tests are widely used, and they have demonstrated value for predicting performance in school. Moreover, IQ is a trait that is stable over time. Preschool measures of intelligence tend to be unstable, but the IQ scores of school-age children are good predictors of IQ scores later in life. This is true for people with mental retardation as well as for those with IQs in the normal range (Baroff, 1986). A school-age child who has a significantly subaverage IQ is likely to continue to score below the cutoff point for mental retardation throughout life.

RESEARCH METHODS

Central Tendency, Variability, and Standard Scores

We can explain the nature and meaning of IQ scores more fully by describing a few, basic statistics. A *frequency distribution* simply is a way of arranging data according to the frequencies of different possible scores. For example, we might obtain the following frequency distribution of ages in a group of ten college students:

Age	Frequency
17	1
18	4
19	1
20	2
21	2

The **mean** is the arithmetic average of a distribution of scores, as defined by the formula:

$$M = \frac{\text{sum of scores}}{N}$$

where *M* is the mean, and *N* is the number of scores. Thus, the mean of the frequency distribution of ages listed above is:

$$M = \frac{17+18+18+18+18+19+20+20+21+21}{10} = 19$$

The mean is the most commonly used of various *measures of central tendency,* which are single scores that summarize and describe a frequency distribution. Other important and commonly used measures of central tendency are the median and the mode. The **median** is the midpoint of a frequency distribution, that is, the score that half of all subjects fall above and half of all subjects fall below. In the above example, 19 is the median age. Finally, the **mode** is the most frequent score in a distribution. In our example, the mode is 18. The mean, median, and mode are often different, and each may be more or less useful depending on the characteristics of a particular frequency distribution.

In addition to measures of central tendency, measures of variability also provide useful summary information about a frequency distribution. The *range* is a simple measure of variability that includes the lowest and highest scores in a frequency distribution. In our example, the range of ages is 17 to 21. As a more complex measure of variability, we may wish to compute the average distance of each individual score from the overall mean (21 - 19, 17 - 19, etc). However, when we subtract each score in a frequency distribution from the mean of the distribution, the positive and negative numbers always add up to zero. (Try this in our example.) As a way of compensating for this inevitability, statisticians have created a statistic called the **variance** in which the differences from the mean are squared (to eliminate negative numbers) before they are added together. The variance is a very useful measure of variability that is defined by the following formula:

$$V = \frac{\text{sum of (score} - M)^2}{N}$$

where V is the variance, M is the mean, and N is the number of scores. The variance in our example is 1.8. You may want to calculate this statistic yourself to aid your understanding.

The variance is an extremely useful measure, but the variance is expressed as a different unit of measurement from the mean (because the scores have been squared). This problem is easily solved by taking the square root of the variance, which results in a statistic called the *standard deviation*. Formally, the standard deviation is defined as the square root of the variance, but you can also view the standard deviation as roughly representing the average distance of scores in a frequency distribution from the mean of the distribution. The standard deviation is defined by the formula:

$$SD = \sqrt{V}$$

where SD is the standard deviation and V is the variance. In our example, the standard deviation is 1.34 or the square root of 1.8 (the variance).

In order to make summary information about scores even more useful, statisticians often convert frequency distributions into **standard scores** by subtracting each score from the mean and dividing the difference by the standard deviation. Standard scores, or *z-scores*, as they are often called, are computed according to the following formula:

$$z = \frac{(\text{score} - M)}{SD}$$

where z is the standard score, M is the mean, and SD is the standard deviation. Because of the nature of the statistic, z-scores always have a mean of zero and a standard deviation of 1. This brings us back to the deviation IQ, which is nothing more or less than a standard score. The reason why IQ scores have a mean of 100 and a standard deviation of 15 is because the z-scores are first multiplied by 15 and then a constant of 100 is added to the product. For example, a standard score of 1 translates into a deviation IQ score of 115 ($[1 \times 15] + 100$) or a standard score of -2 translates into a deviation IQ score of 70 ($[-2 \times 15] + 100$).

The mean and the standard deviation are basic statistics for creating deviation IQ scores. The two statistics also are central to understanding numerous other psychological concepts. For example, you should now be better able to understand the discussion of standard deviation units in relation to the meta-analysis (see Chapter 3). We recommend that you read back through the discussion and calculate the statistics yourself if you are at all confused about these concepts. ■

Controversies About Intelligence Tests   Despite the value of IQ tests in predicting academic performance, a number of important questions have been raised about them. One of the most controversial questions is whether intelligence tests are "culture-fair." In the United States, the average IQ scores of African Americans and Latinos are lower than those obtained by Caucasians and Asians, and more members of these groups are classified as having mental retardation. Some of these differences among groups have been attributed to bias in the composition of intelligence tests; some test items seem geared toward the language and the experience of majority groups. Because of the possibility of cultural bias, the AAMR explicitly notes that the valid

Sample Items from the Vineland Adaptive Behavior Scales

Daily Living Skills

Age   1: Drinks from a cup.
Age   5: Bathes or showers without assistance.
Age 10: Uses a stove for cooking.
Age 15: Looks after own health.

Socialization

Age   1: Imitates simple adult movements like clapping.
Age   5: Has a group of friends.
Age 10: Watches television about particular interests.
Age 15: Responds to hints or indirect cues in conversation.

Source: S. S. Sparrow, D. A. Balla, and D. V. Cicchetti, 1984, *Vineland Adaptive Behavior Scales.* Circle Pines, MN: American Guidance Service.

assessment of intelligence should consider cultural and linguistic diversity (AAMR, 1992).

Another controversy about intelligence tests is how well intelligence is measured among people with mental retardation. Many people with mental retardation have sensory or physical disabilities that impede their performance on standard IQ tests; thus they must take tests that are not influenced by their particular disability. Despite the difficulties involved in assessment, evidence indicates that, if anything, the IQ test scores of people with mental retardation are more reliable and more valid than IQ scores in the normal range (Baroff, 1986).

The most basic concern about intelligence tests is the most important one: What is intelligence? Intelligence tests measure precisely what their original developer, Alfred Binet, intended them to measure: potential for school achievement. And IQ tests predict school achievement fairly well. In fact, IQ scores correlate 0.4 to 0.7 with school achievement (Baroff, 1986). However, school achievement is not the same as "intelligence." Common sense, social sensitivity, and so-called "street smarts" are also part of what most of us would consider to be intelligence, and they are not measured by IQ tests. There would be less controversy if IQ tests were labeled appropriately as measures of academic aptitude.

LIMITATIONS IN ADAPTIVE SKILLS

Both the AAMR and DSM recognize that intelligence is more than an IQ score; thus they include adaptive skills as a part of the definition of mental retardation. The AAMR (1992) suggests that adaptive skills include both practical intelligence and social intelligence. *Practical intelligence* refers to the ability to manage the ordinary activities of daily living, and *social intelligence* indicates the ability to understand how to conduct oneself in social situations. More specifically, the AAMR and the DSM identify 10 critical, adaptive skills: communication, self-care, home living, social skills, community use, self-direction, health and safety, functional academics, leisure, and work.

Adaptive skills are difficult to quantify—there is no summary measure of "practical IQ" or "social IQ." However, some useful, standardized instruments have been developed, such as the Vineland Social Maturity Scale—Revised (see Table 15–2). As with academic aptitude, adaptive skills must be judged within the context of age. Among preschoolers, adaptive skills include the acquisition of motor abilities, language, and self-control. Key skills during the school-age years include adequate academic performance and developing social relationships with peers. In adult life, adaptive skills include the ability to manage oneself, live independently, and assume adult interpersonal roles.

An argument has been made for defining retardation solely on the basis of intelligence testing, because current measures of adaptive skills are imprecise (MacMillan, Gresham, & Siperstein, 1995). Moreover, the intellectual limitations of mental retardation imply that adaptive skills will necessarily be limited (Zigler & Hodapp, 1986). Since 1959, however, deficits in adaptive behavior have been an essential part of the AAMR's definition of mental retardation (Heber, 1959). The adaptive skills criterion highlights the importance of assessing life functioning in borderline cases, as well as the need for services among people with mental retardation (AAMR, 1992). Many people with significantly subaverage IQs, like Chris Burke, lead lives that are not only normal but exciting. Moreover, deficits in adaptive behavior are less stable over time than are IQ limitations, especially as life demands change from school to the more diverse world of work. Thus mental retardation can be "cured" in the sense that adaptive skills can be taught or environmental demands can be shaped to match an individual's unique abilities and experiences.

ONSET BEFORE AGE 18 YEARS

The third criterion for defining mental retardation is an onset before 18 years of age. This excludes people whose deficits in intellect and adaptive skills begin later in life as a result of brain injury or disease. Besides differences in etiology, the most important aspect of this criterion is the experience of normal development. The cognitive development, social relationships, and life experiences of people who have lived normal lives into adulthood differentiate them from people with mental retardation in numerous important ways. People with mental retardation have not lost skills they once had mastered, nor have they experienced a notable change in their condition. Unfortunately, this means that their retardation may be perceived as "who they are" and not as something that has "happened to them." As one small step toward recognizing the personhood of people with mental retardation, some advocates argue for putting the "person first" in our language—refer to the "person with mental retardation," not to the "mentally retarded person." We have tried to follow this convention throughout this chapter.

Classification

Academic aptitude was less necessary to successful living in earlier, agrarian societies than it is in our modern, technological world. Thus many people seen as having mild mental retardation today would not have been viewed as having notable problems in the past. Even today, mental retardation is defined differently in more industrialized countries than in less industrialized ones because of the educational and technological requirements for work in the industrialized countries (Scheerenberger, 1982).

BRIEF HISTORICAL PERSPECTIVE

Severe mental retardation has been recognized as an abnormality throughout history, but few special efforts were directed toward helping people with the disorder. Until late in the Middle Ages, no distinction was made between mental illness and mental retardation in terms of treatment. Both "lunatics" and "idiots," as people with mental illness and mental retardation were called from the Middle Ages through the nineteenth century, were either abandoned to roam the streets, sheltered inadequately in poorhouses, or warehoused in institutions (see Chapter 18). Socially, people with mental retardation often were derided because of their disabilities. Such pejorative terms as "idiot," "fool," "moron," and "imbecile" actually were used in formal diagnostic or legal terminology well into the twentieth century (Grossman, 1983).

The work of the French physician Jean Marc Itard (1774–1838) was instrumental in spurring efforts to develop special education programs for children with mental retardation. Itard worked extensively with a feral child, whom he named "Victor," found living in the woods near Aveyron, France, in 1799. Itard worked with the "wild boy of Aveyron" for 5 years in an attempt to educate and socialize him. In the end, Itard felt that he had failed in his efforts, but his work nevertheless encouraged others to develop special programs for educating children with mental retardation (Patton, Beirne-Smith, & Payne, 1990).

The beginnings of contemporary classifications of mental retardation can be traced to the second half of the nineteenth century. In 1866, the British physician Langdon Down first described a subgroup of children with mental retardation who had a characteristic appearance. Their faces reminded Down of the appearance of Mongolians, and he used the term "mongolism" to describe them. Despite this offensive terminology, Down's classification helped subsequent scientists to establish a specific etiology for what we now know as Down syndrome.

The creation of IQ tests in the early twentieth century also greatly furthered the classification of mental retardation. The French psychologists Alfred Binet (1856–1911) and Theophile Simon developed the first successful intelligence test in 1905 in response to a French government effort to identify children in need of special educational services. The Binet scale was refined further by the American psychologist Lewis Terman of Stanford University, and these efforts resulted in the Stanford-Binet intelligence tests. The first Wechsler intelligence test was developed by David Wechsler in 1939, and revisions of Wechsler's individualized intelligence tests continue to dominate contemporary intellectual assessment.

As intelligence tests developed into reliable and valid measures, controversy grew about what IQ score cutoff should define mental retardation. The debate reached a climax in 1959 when the AAMR greatly expanded the definition of retardation. In an attempt to help more people in need of services, the IQ cutoff was shifted from two standard deviations below the mean to one standard deviation below the mean. Anyone who scored 85 or lower was considered to have mental retardation, a criterion that included almost 15 percent of the U.S. population. This well-intentioned change included far too many well-functioning individuals, and it distracted attention from those most in need of help. Thus the AAMR returned to the two-standard-deviation cutoff of 70 in 1973 (Grossman, 1983).

In 1983, the AAMR introduced the range of 70 to 75 as a way of accommodating measurement error and of acknowledging the fact that IQ scores are continuous rather than categorical differences. A child with an IQ score of 71 is not notably different from a child with an IQ of 69. However, some controversy surrounds the AAMR's use of a range of scores. Critics note that a cutoff of 70 includes 2.3 percent of the population in a normal distribution, but a cutoff of 75 doubles the size of the group to 4.7 percent (MacMillan, Gresham, & Siperstein, 1995). The DSM currently uses the somewhat less ambiguous criterion of "approximately 70."

CONTEMPORARY CLASSIFICATION

Today, mental retardation can be classified according to two different criteria. One criterion is based on IQ scores; the other is according to known or presumed etiology. Both approaches are reliable, and each is valid for different

purposes, demonstrating that different classification systems can have value for different purposes (see Chapter 4).

The value of both approaches is seen in some conflicts between the AAMR and the DSM-IV definitions of mental retardation. The AAMR (1992) now uses a multiaxial diagnosis of mental retardation in which etiology is rated on a separate dimension from the primary diagnosis of mental retardation. This is an important step, because many specific causes of mental retardation have been identified. Additional axes in the new AAMR definition also rate emotional problems, physical health, and environmental characteristics. The new AAMR subclassification also includes ratings of four levels of intensity of needed support (see Table 15–3). Support intensities are not assumed to be global. Instead, needed supports are rated separately for different areas of functioning. This focus is intended to convey the diversity of skills and needs among people with mental retardation. For example, one person with an IQ of 65 may need more assistance with self-care and community living, whereas a second person with the same IQ may need to be employed in a carefully structured setting. Although this approach is sensitive to individual needs, some professionals question its reliability and validity (MacMillan, Gresham, & Siperstein, 1995).

The DSM-IV does not include these multidimensional ratings. Instead, DSM-IV follows an earlier AAMR scheme and divides mental retardation into four levels based primarily on IQ scores: mild, moderate, severe, and profound. Although the AAMR's concerns about individualized assessment are important, we highlight the DSM-IV subclassification because it has been the focus of considerable research.

Mild mental retardation is the designation for those with IQ scores between 50–55 and 70. This category accounts for about 85 percent of people with mental retardation. People with mild mental retardation typically have few, if any, physical impairments, generally reach the sixth-grade level in academic functioning, acquire vocational skills, and typically live in the community with or without special supports.

People with *moderate mental retardation* have IQs between 35–40 and 50–55; they make up about 10 percent of those with mental retardation. They may have obvious physical abnormalities such as the features of Down syndrome. Academic achievement generally reaches to the

---

TABLE 15–3

AAMR Definitions of Intensities of Needed Support

Intermittent

Supports on an "as needed basis." Characterized by episodic nature, person not always needing the support(s), or short-term supports needed during lifespan transitions (e.g., job loss or acute medical crisis). Intermittent supports may be high or low intensity when provided.

Limited

An intensity of supports characterized by consistency over time, time-limited but not of an intermittent nature, may require fewer staff members and less cost than more intense levels of support (e.g., time-limited employment training or transitional supports during the school to adult provided period).

Extensive

Supports characterized by regular involvement (e.g., daily) in at least some environments (such as work or home) and not time-limited (e.g., long-term support and long-term home living support).

Pervasive

Supports characterized by their constancy, high intensity; provided across environments; potential life-sustaining nature. Pervasive supports typically involve more staff members and intrusiveness than do extensive or time-limited supports.

Source: From American Association on Mental Retardation, 1992, *Mental Retardation: Definition, Classification, and Systems of Support,* 9th ed., p. 26. Washington, DC: AAMR.

second-grade level, work activities require close training and supervision, and special supervision in families or group homes is needed for living in the community.

Severe mental retardation is defined by IQ scores between 20–25 and 35–40. This category accounts for 3 to 4 percent of people with mental retardation. At this severity level, motor development typically is abnormal, communicative speech is sharply limited, and close supervision is needed for community living.

About 1 to 2 percent of people with mental retardation have *profound mental retardation*. This severity level is characterized by an IQ below 20–25. Motor skills, communication, and self-care are severely limited, and constant supervision typically is required in the community or in institutions.

Epidemiology

Because IQ theoretically is distributed according to the normal curve, approximately 2.3 percent of the population should have IQs of 70 or below. In reality, however, more than the expected number of people are below the 70 cutoff. Departures from the normal distribution are particularly large for lower IQ scores, a result of the various biological conditions that produce mental retardation (Grossman, 1983). It is useful therefore to think of two IQ distributions. One is the normal distribution of IQ scores. The second is the distribution of IQs of people with biological disorders known to cause mental retardation (Zigler, 1967). These two theoretical distributions are portrayed in Figure 15–2.

Despite the fact that the number of people below the 70 cutoff point is lower than expected, IQ distributions actually overestimate the observed prevalence rates of mental retardation. The main reason for this is that mental retardation involves deficits in adaptive behavior as well as low IQ. The most widely accepted estimate is that approximately 1 percent of the population in the United States—not 2 or 3 percent—has mental retardation at any given point in time. This lower figure is a result of several factors. For one, IQs cannot be adequately assessed among very young children, who therefore are omitted from prevalence figures. Also, many adults with low IQs are not designated as having mental retardation because they do not have deficits in the adaptive skills needed for work and community living. As an indication of these influences, studies show that

twice as many school-age children as preschoolers have mental retardation, but the prevalence rates drop again among adults (Grossman, 1983).

Mental retardation in the United States is more common among the poor and, as a result, among certain ethnic groups. However, the increased prevalence is not found for all subtypes of retardation. Mental retardation with a specific, known organic cause (for example, Down syndrome) generally has an equal prevalence among all social classes, whereas retardation of nonspecific etiology is more common among families living in poverty (Patton, Beirne-Smith, & Payne, 1990). This epidemiological fact is the source of much controversy, as we discuss in the following sections.

Etiological Considerations and Research

As we have noted, the etiology of mental retardation can be grouped into two broad categories: cases caused by known biological abnormalities, and cases resulting from normal variations in IQ. We review known biological causes before considering the debate about the causes of the largest category of mental retardation, those cases at the extreme end of the normal IQ distribution.

BIOLOGICAL FACTORS

About one-quarter of all cases of mental retardation are caused by known biological abnormalities (Grossman, 1983). In contrast to cases of unknown origin, known biological causes

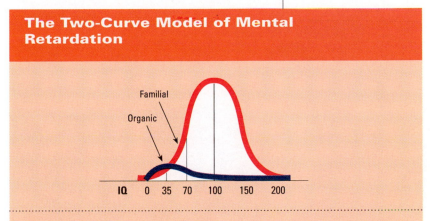

The Two-Curve Model of Mental Retardation

FIGURE 15–2: The two-curve model of mental retardation distinguishes between the normal distribution of IQ scores and the IQ scores for people with known biological causes of mental retardation.

Source: E. Zigler, 1967, Familial mental retardation: a continuing dilemma. *Science 155*, pp. 292–98. Copyright 1967 by the American Association for the Advancement of Science.

more often lead to retardation of moderate to profound severity and are associated with physical handicaps. Of the over 250 known biological causes (AAMR, 1992), we focus only on several major ones here.

Chromosomal Disorders The most common known biological cause of mental retardation is the chromosomal disorder **Down syndrome.** People with Down syndrome have a distinctively abnormal physical appearance. They have slanting eyes with an extra fold of skin in the inner corner, a small head and short stature, a protruding tongue, and a variety of organ, muscle, and skeletal abnormalities. They also have physical handicaps and limited speech (Thapar, Gottesman, Owen, O'Donovan, & McGuffin, 1994).

The cause of Down syndrome is the presence of an extra chromosome. Children with Down syndrome have 47 chromosomes instead of the normal 46. The extra chromosome is attached to the 21st pair; thus the disorder often is referred to as *trisomy 21*.

The incidence of Down syndrome is related to maternal age. For women under the age of 30, about 1 in 1,000 births are Down syndrome infants. The incidence rises to 1 in 750 births for mothers between ages 30 and 34, 1 in 300 between 35 and 39, and over 1 in 100 after age 40. Increasing paternal age also is associated with Down syndrome and is thought to cause about 25 percent of the cases (Magenis et al., 1977). Down syndrome can be detected by testing during pregnancy.

In general, children and adults with Down syndrome function within the moderate to severe range of mental retardation. They exhibit substantial variation in their intellectual level, however, and research suggests that intensive intervention can lead to higher achievement and greater independence. Institutionalization once was commonly recommended, but home or community care is now the rule. In fact, many experts who have worked with people with Down syndrome report that they are especially sociable and eager to help, although research findings on their distinctive personality traits are not conclusive (Cicchetti & Beegly, 1990).

A potentially important recent discovery is that, by their thirties, the majority of adults with Down syndrome develop brain pathology similar to that found in Alzheimer's disease. About one-third also exhibit the symptoms of dementia (Thase, 1988). Death in mid-adult life is common, although some adults with Down syndrome live into their fifties and sixties.

Another chromosomal abnormality, **fragile-X syndrome** (Lubs, 1969), is the second most common biological cause of mental retardation. Fragile-X syndrome is indicated by a weakening or break on one arm of the X sex chromosome (see Figure 15–3), and it is transmitted genetically. In fact, the specific gene responsible for the disorder, the fragile-X mental retardation (FMR-1) gene, was identified recently (Warren & Ashley, 1995). The disorder occurs in 1 out of every 1,500 male births and about 1 in 2,500 females (Bregman et al., 1987; Warren & Ashley, 1995).

Not all boys or girls with the fragile-X abnormality have mental retardation. Girls with fragile-X syndrome are considerably less likely to have mental retardation than are boys (Warren & Ashley, 1995). For children with fragile-X syndrome who have retardation, the clinical picture varies considerably. Intellectual functioning ranges from moderate mental retardation to normal. Among those with normal intelligence, learning disabilities are common. Most of those who display intellectual abnormalities have a characteristic facial appearance that includes an elongated face, high forehead, large jaw, and large, underdeveloped ears (Bregman et al., 1987). Although most fragile-X children behave fairly normally, some display the symptoms of autism. Recent advances make it possible to detect fragile-X in the fetus during pregnancy.

Several other chromosomal abnormalities have been linked to mental retardation. As in

▼ **This girl with Down syndrome shows that children with mental retardation can join in many normal childhood activities.**

fragile-X syndrome, abnormalities of the sex chromosomes are particularly notable. *Klinefelter syndrome*, found in about 1 in 1,000 live male births, is characterized by the presence of one or more extra X chromosomes in males. The most common chromosome configuration is XXY. With Klinefelter syndrome, IQ functioning typically is in the low normal to the mild range of mental retardation. Another chromosomal abnormality, *XYY syndrome*, once was thought to increase criminality (see Chapter 9), but the syndrome is now recognized to be linked with only minor social deviance and a mean IQ about 10 points lower than average. The syndrome occurs in 1–2 out of 2,000 male births. *Turner syndrome*, the XO configuration in females, is characterized by a missing X chromosome. Girls with Turner syndrome are small, fail to develop sexually, and generally have intelligence near or within the normal range. The disorder occurs in about 1 in every 2,200 live female births (Thapar et al., 1994).

Genetic Disorders Few cases of mental retardation result from dominant genetic inheritance, because such a mutation is unlikely to remain in the gene pool. However, mental retardation is known to be caused by several recessive gene pairings. **Phenylketonuria,** or **PKU,** is one of these. Geneticists estimate that about 1 in every 54 normal people carries a recessive gene for PKU, but the two genes are paired only in 1 of every 11,500 births.

PKU is caused by abnormally high levels of the amino acid *phenylalanine*, usually due to the absence of *phenylalanine hydroxylase*, an enzyme that metabolizes phenylalanine. Children with PKU have normal intelligence at birth. However, as they eat foods containing phenylalanine early in life, the amino acid builds up in their system. This *phenylketonuria* produces brain damage that eventually results in mental retardation. Retardation typically progresses to the severe to profound range. PKU sometimes results in the behavioral symptoms of autism, as does the extremely rare dominant-gene disorder *tuberous sclerosis*, characterized by white growths in the ventricles of the brain that appear tuberous.

Fortunately, PKU can be detected by blood testing in the first several days after birth. (The musty odor of the infant's urine is a much less exact but notable clinical indicator of PKU.) Early detection is very important, because

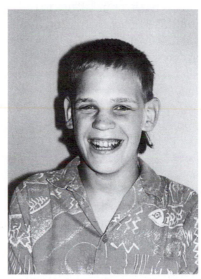

intellectual and behavioral impairments are diminished dramatically if the child maintains a diet low in phenylalanine. In such cases the child is likely to have normal to mildly impaired intelligence. For this reason, all state laws now require routine screening of newborns for PKU. In order to maximize the benefits of the diet, the child should maintain it for as long as possible (Lancet, 1991). This is very difficult because phenylalanine is found in most foods and many food additives. Take a look at the labels of some of the foods you have at home (e.g., diet sodas). You will notice a warning about phenylalanine on many of the labels.

Other relatively rare recessive-gene disorders also can cause mental retardation. *Tay-Sachs disease* is a particularly severe disorder that eventually results in death during the infant or preschool years. The recessive gene that causes Tay-Sachs is particularly common among Jews of Eastern European heritage. *Hurler syndrome*, or *gargoylism*, results in gross physical abnormalities, including dwarfism, humpback, bulging

FIGURE 15-3 Weaknesses or breaks characterize fragile-X chromosomes. Top: The fragile-X syndrome can be identified by a gap (arrow) near the distal end of the long arm of the X chromosome. Bottom: This adolescent boy with mental retardation suffers from fragile-X syndrome. He has an elongated face and prominent forehead and ears, features that characterize many people with this disorder.

Source (top): S.T. Warren and D.L. Nelson, 1994, Advances in molecular analysis of fragile-X syndrome, JAMA, 271, 536–542.

head, and clawlike hands. Children with this disorder usually do not live past the age of 10. *Lesch-Nyhan syndrome* is most notable for the self-mutilation that accompanies the mental retardation. Children with this disorder bite their lips and fingers, often causing tissue loss. As with Down syndrome and fragile-X syndrome, many of these genetic abnormalities can be detected during pregnancy.

Infectious Diseases   Mental retardation can also be caused by various infectious diseases. Damaging infections may be contracted during pregnancy, at birth, or in infancy to early childhood. Among the diseases passed from mother to fetus during pregnancy are *cytomegalovirus*, the most common fetal infection (and one that is usually harmless), and *toxoplasmosis*, a protozoan infection contracted from ingestion of infected raw meats or from contact with infected cat feces. No widely accepted treatments for these diseases exist.

Rubella (German measles) is a viral infection that may produce few symptoms in the mother but can cause severe mental retardation and even death in the developing fetus, especially if it is contracted in the first 3 months of pregnancy. Fortunately, rubella can be completely prevented by vaccination of prospective mothers before pregnancy. Vaccination against rubella is now a part of routine health care.

Syphilis is a bacterial disease that is transmitted through sexual contact. Infected mothers can pass the disease to the fetus. If untreated, syphilis produces a number of physical and sensory handicaps in the fetus, including mental retardation. The adverse consequences are avoided by testing the mother and administering antibiotics when an infection has been detected. Because penicillin crosses the placental barrier, treating the mother also will cure the disease in the fetus.

Another sexually transmitted disease, *genital herpes*, can be transmitted to the infant during birth. Herpes is a viral infection that produces small lesions on the genitals immediately following the initial infection and intermittently thereafter. Generally, the disease can be transmitted only when the lesions are present. If there is an outbreak of genital lesions near or at the time of delivery, a cesarean section can be performed, thus preventing infection of the newborn. About half of all infants delivered genitally in the presence of active lesions are infected, resulting in a number of very serious problems, including mental retardation, blindness, and possible death.

Two infectious diseases that occur after birth, primarily during infancy, can cause mental retardation. *Encephalitis* is an infection of the brain that produces inflammation and permanent damage in about 20 percent of all cases. *Meningitis* is an infection of the *meninges*, the three membranes that line the brain. The inflammation creates intracranial pressure that can irreversibly damage brain tissues. Encephalitis and meningitis can be caused by a variety of infectious diseases. Cases resulting from bacterial infections can usually be treated successfully with antibiotics. In other cases, the outcome of both encephalitis and meningitis is unpredictable. Neuromuscular problems, sensory impairments, and mental retardation are possible.

Toxins   Exposure to a variety of environmental toxins also can cause mental retardation. Like infectious diseases, toxic chemicals can produce mental retardation when exposure occurs either before or after birth, but exposure during pregnancy creates the greatest risk.

Both licit and illicit drugs pose a risk to the developing fetus. Because of its frequent use, alcohol presents the greatest threat. About 1–2 of every 1,000 births is a baby with **fetal alcohol syndrome.** This disorder is characterized by retarded physical development, a small head, narrow eyes, cardiac defects, and cognitive impairment. Intellectual functioning ranges from mild mental retardation to normal intelligence accompanied by learning disabilities.

Women who drink heavily during pregnancy (an average of 5 ounces of alcohol per day) are twice as likely to have a child with the syndrome as are women who average 1 ounce of alcohol per day or less (Baroff, 1986). Controversy continues about the risk for difficulties associated with drinking in the intermediate range. Because of possible adverse effects of even low or moderate consumption, many experts recommend that pregnant women abstain from alcohol altogether.

Illicit drugs also are a cause of considerable concern. Although heroin and methadone addiction have not been directly linked with mental retardation, they do result in the serious problems of low birth weight and drug addiction for the newborn. Particular concern has been raised recently about the use of crack cocaine by pregnant women. "Crack babies" are more likely to be born prematurely, to have a lower than normal birth weight, and to have a smaller than normal head circumference. These adverse conditions have been linked in other research to an increased risk for mental retardation, but the long-term intellectual and psychological outcomes for crack babies have yet to be adequately documented (Hawley & Disney, 1992).

Toxins also present a potential hazard to intellectual development after birth. *Mercury poisoning* is known to produce severe physical, emotional, and intellectual impairments, but it does not present a major public health problem because few children are exposed to mercury. Much more threatening to the public health is **lead poisoning.** Until banned by federal legislation, the lead commonly used in paint and produced by automobile emissions exposed hundreds of thousands of children to a potentially serious risk. Although controversy continues about the effects of exposure to low levels of lead, at toxic levels lead poisoning can produce a number of adverse behavioral and cognitive impairments, including mental retardation. Despite federal bans on lead-based paints and leaded gasoline, lead poisoning continues to pose a particular risk to children reared in dilapidated housing who may eat peeling, lead-based paint chips (Tesman & Hills, 1994).

Other Biological Abnormalities   A variety of pregnancy and birth complications also can cause mental retardation. One major complication is *Rh incompatibility*. The Rh factor is a protein found on the surface of red blood cells, and it is a dominant hereditary trait. People who possess this protein are known as Rh-positive; people who don't are Rh-negative. Rh incompatibility can occur when the mother is Rh-negative and the father is Rh-positive. In such cases the mother can develop antibodies that attack the blood cells of her Rh-positive fetus. The antibodies destroy oxygen-carrying red blood cells in the developing fetus, with a number of adverse consequences including possible mental retardation.

Rh-negative women develop antibodies only after exposure to their infant's Rh-positive blood. If this exposure occurs at all, it usually does not happen until delivery. Thus the risk of Rh incompatibility in first births is minimal; the greatest risk is for subsequent pregnancies. This risk can be largely prevented, however, by the administration of the antibiotic RhoGAM to the mother within 72 hours after birth of the first child. RhoGAM prevents the mother's body from developing internal antibodies against the Rh-positive factors. This eliminates most of the risk for a future pregnancy. In the event that an Rh-negative mother develops antibodies against Rh-positive factors during pregnancy, a fetal blood transfusion must be carried out to replace the destroyed red blood cells.

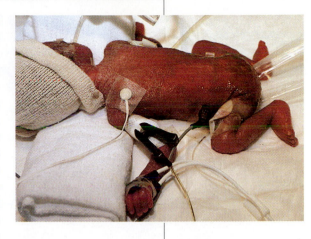

▲ **A newborn of a mother who used crack cocaine. Crack babies often are premature and have low birth weights, and they are typically irritable and difficult to soothe.**

Another pregnancy and birth complication that can cause intellectual deficits is *premature birth*. Premature birth is defined either as birth before 38 weeks of gestation or a birth weight of less than 5½ pounds. There are many potential causes of prematurity, including the hereditary, infectious, and toxic factors already discussed. Other risk factors include poor maternal nutrition, maternal age of less than 18 years or more than 35 years, maternal hypertension or diabetes, and damage to the placenta. The effects of prematurity on the infant are variable, ranging from few or no deficits to sensory impairments, poor physical development, and mental retardation. More serious consequences occur at lower birth weights, and infant mortality is common at very low weights.

Other known biological causes of mental retardation include extreme difficulties in delivery, particularly *anoxia*, or oxygen deprivation; severe *malnutrition* (which is rare in the United States but a major problem in less developed countries); and the seizure disorder *epilepsy*. The intellectual difficulties associated with each of these causes vary but are potentially significant.

Normal Genetic Variation   All of the biological causes of mental retardation discussed so far are clear abnormalities in development. The last biological factor we consider, however, focuses on the tail of the normal IQ distribution (see Figure 15–1). These are the cases of mental retardation of unknown etiology—what is often referred to as **cultural-familial retardation.** As the term suggests, cultural-familial retardation tends to run in families and is linked with poverty. A controversial issue is whether this typically mild form of mental retardation is caused primarily by genes or by psychosocial disadvantage.

TABLE 15-4

Correlations Between the IQ Scores of Pairs of Relatives Reared Together or Apart

Type of Relative	Reared Together		Reared Apart	
	Correlation	(N)	Correlation	(N)
Monozygotic twins	.86	(4,672)	.72	(65)
Dizygotic twins	.60	(5,546)	—	
Biological siblings	.47	(26,473)	.24	(203)
Adoptive siblings	.34	(369)	—	
Parent–child	.42	(8,633)	.22	(814)
Adoptive parent–child	.19	(1,397)	—	

Source: Adapted from T. J. Bouchard, Jr., and M. McGue, 1981, Familial studies of intelligence: A review, *Science*, *212*, 1055–1059. Copyright ® 1981 by the American Association for the Advancement of Science.

Normal genetic variation clearly contributes to individual differences in intelligence (Thapar et al., 1994). As summarized in Table 15–4, numerous family, twin, and adoption studies have been conducted on IQ. All of this research points to a substantial genetic contribution to intelligence. For example, the IQs of adopted children are more highly correlated to the IQs of their biological parents than to those of their adoptive ones (Horn, Loehlin, & Willerman, 1979; Plomin & Daniels, 1987).

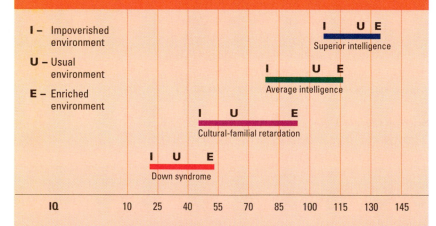

Theoretical Reaction Ranges of IQ Scores for Groups with Differing Genetic Predispositions

I – Impoverished environment

U – Usual environment

E – Enriched environment

FIGURE 15-4: Theoretical reaction ranges of IQ scores. According to the model, genes set different limits on IQ, and environment determines variation within the limits. Note also that the usual environmental contribution to intelligence differs among the four groups.

Source: G.S. Baroff, 1986, *Mental retardation: Nature, cause, and management.* p. 151. Washington D.C.: Hemisphere.

How much of intelligence is inherited? Behavior geneticists have calculated indices to measure the extent of genetic contribution to a characteristic, called *heritability ratios*. Estimates generally indicate that about 50 percent of the normal range of intelligence is attributable to genetics, but there has been no good research on genetic contributions to cultural-familial retardation (Thapar et al., 1994). We should note, moreover, that heritability ratios can be misleading, because they imply a false dichotomy between genes and environment (see Research Methods in Chapter 17).

The concept of **reaction range** better conveys how genes and environment interact together to determine IQ (Gottesman, 1963). The reaction range concept proposes that heredity determines the upper and lower limits of IQ, and experience determines the extent to which people fulfill their genetic potential. Figure 15–4 portrays some theoretical reaction ranges for children with Down syndrome, cultural-familial retardation, normal intelligence, and superior intelligence. This figure illustrates the key point that genetics and environment determine intelligence together, not independently (Turkheimer, 1991).

PSYCHOLOGICAL FACTORS

Many people misinterpret evidence on the genetic contributions to intelligence and mistakenly conclude that environment matters little or not at all. Environment does matter, as is illustrated by reaction range and by other evidence. For example, it is theoretically important to note that grossly abnormal environments can produce gross abnormalities in intelligence. This apparently is what happened with Itard's "wild boy," and environmentally caused mental retardation has been documented in some horrific case studies.

An example is Koluchova's (1972) case study of the effects of the abuse and deprivation experienced by two identical twin boys. Until they were discovered at the age of 6, the twins lived in a closet in almost total isolation. Apparently, they were beaten regularly throughout their early life. When discovered, the twins could barely walk, had extremely limited speech, and showed no understanding of abstractions, like photographs. Over several years of intervention, however, their measured intelligence moved from moderate mental retardation when first discovered to the normal range by the age of 11.

Fortunately, cases of such torturous abuse are rare. They illustrate the theoretical contribution of experience to intelligence more than the actual contribution. Awareness of this theoretical contribution is important, however, because contemporary research on intelligence necessarily reflects the effects of a limited range of environments (see Research Methods in Chapter 17). As a social ideal, Americans hope to provide all citizens with an equally advantaged environment. In working toward this laudable goal, we can overlook the fact that heritability increases as environmental variation decreases. In fact, the heritability of intelligence would be 1.0 if everyone had exactly the same environmental advantages. Ironically, if we strive to create a nurturing and stimulating world for every child, we run the risk of concluding that "environment doesn't matter" if we misunderstand concepts like heritability.

SOCIAL FACTORS

Today, the range of environments in the United States still includes many undesirable circumstances for children. Millions of children are reared in psychosocial disadvantage in our cities and in the equally unstimulating environments found among the rural poor. In fact, children are the most impoverished age group in this country. In 1992, 22 percent of U.S. children were living in poverty, and since the 1980s the number of children in poverty has been rising (Hogan & Lichter, 1995).

Cultural-familial retardation is found far more frequently among the poor. Part of this association certainly is due to the fact that lower intelligence can cause lower social status. People with a below-average IQ will generally make less money in our society; thus they will remain in, or move into, lower socioeconomic classes. However, part of the link between poverty and cultural-familial retardation is caused by the effects of psychosocial disadvantage in lowering IQ scores.

Impoverished environments lack the *stimulation* and *responsiveness* required to promote children's intellectual development. A stimulating environment challenges children's developing intellectual skills. Toys and other playthings make the toddler's environment interesting to explore. A responsive environment offers encouragement for their pursuits. Parents or siblings mimic the infant's first sounds and words.

Studies of adopted children demonstrate the positive effects of stimulating and responsive environments (Turkheimer, 1991). A famous early study by Skodak and Skeels (1949) demonstrated that children who were adopted away from unfortunate circumstances early in life achieved IQ scores at least 12 points higher on average than those of their biological mothers. More recent studies have found similarly dramatic increases (Capron & Duyme, 1989; Schiff et al., 1982). The potential for increasing IQ by 10 to 15 points obviously holds important implications for prevention and intervention. Many people with cultural-familial retardation could function normally if stimulating and responsive environments helped them to achieve their potential to function near the upper end of their reaction range.

Treatment: Primary, Secondary, and Tertiary Prevention and Normalization

Three major categories of intervention are essential in the treatment of mental retardation. First, many cases of both organic and cultural-familial mental retardation can be prevented through adequate maternal and child health care, as well as through early psychoeducational programs. Second, educational, psychological, and biomedical treatments can help people with mental retardation to raise their achievement levels. Third, the lives of people with mental retardation can be normalized through mainstreaming in public schools and promoting care in the community.

PRIMARY PREVENTION

The availability and use of good maternal and child health care is one major step toward the primary prevention of many biological causes of mental retardation. Health care measures include specific actions, such as vaccinations for rubella and the detection and treatment of infectious diseases like syphilis. In addition, an adequate diet and abstinence from alcohol, cigarettes, and other drugs are essential to the health of pregnant women and the welfare of the developing fetus.

Planning for childbearing can also help prevent mental retardation. Pregnancy and birth complications are notably more common among mothers younger than 18 and older than 35. Although most babies born to women outside this age range are healthy and normal, many women are aware of the statistical

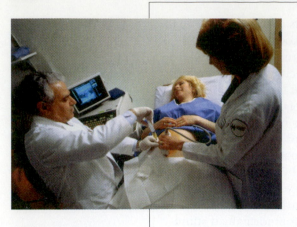

▲ During amniocentesis, amniotic fluid is extracted from the sac protecting the fetus. Tests of the amniotic fluid can detect some genetic and chromosomal defects that cause mental retardation.

risks and attempt to time their pregnancies accordingly. Children of teenage mothers also face a much greater threat of a life of poverty—a pressing issue, given that almost 8 percent of all children in the United States are born to adolescent mothers (Select Committee on Children, Youth, and Families, 1989).

A more controversial means of preventing retardation is through diagnostic testing and selective abortion. One diagnostic procedure is **amniocentesis,** in which fluid is extracted from the amniotic sac that protects the fetus during pregnancy. As we have noted, some chromosomal and genetic defects in the fetus can be determined from testing the amniotic fluid, leaving parents with the extremely difficult decision of whether to terminate the pregnancy if an abnormality is found. Despite the emotional turmoil that such a decision can provoke, many parents opt for amniocentesis. The procedure is particularly common among older women, whose infants are at a greatly increased risk for having Down syndrome.

SECONDARY PREVENTION

In addition to medical and health care measures, early social and educational interventions can lead to the secondary prevention of cultural-familial retardation. The most important current secondary prevention effort is Head Start, a federal intervention program begun in 1964. The goals of Head Start include providing preschool children living in poverty with early educational experiences, nutrition, and health care monitoring. Evidence indicates that Head Start produces short-term increases in IQ (5 to 10 points) and achievement. The academic advantages diminish or disappear within a few years after intervention ends, but data indicate that children who participate in Head Start are less likely to repeat a grade or to be placed in special education classes. They also are more likely to graduate from high school (McKey et al., 1985; Zigler & Styfco, 1993). These data indicate that Head Start undoubtedly reduces the prevalence of cultural-familial retardation through its influence on adaptive behavior if not on IQ itself.

More specific evidence on preventing mental retardation through early intervention comes from two research programs—the Carolina Abcedarian Project (Ramey & Bryant, 1982) and the Milwaukee Project (Garber, 1988). Both interventions offered a variety of services to children of mothers with below-average IQs, and both used control groups to assess the effectiveness of intervention. Gains of 20 or more points in IQ have been reported for experimental versus control children in the Milwaukee Project (Garber, 1988), but questions about the methods of this study suggest that they be interpreted with caution (Baroff, 1986). More modest gains of 5 to 10 IQ points have been reported for the Abcedarian Project (Ramey & Bryant, 1982). Regardless of the magnitude of change, these projects, together with adoption studies and findings from Head Start, indicate that at least some cases of familial retardation can be prevented through increasing environmental stimulation and responsiveness.

TERTIARY PREVENTION

A huge array of services has been developed for the tertiary prevention and treatment of the various cognitive, socioemotional, and medical difficulties faced by people with mental retardation from birth through adult life. Given the volumes of work devoted to the subject, we can only touch on a few treatments here.

One of the most important aspects of tertiary prevention is careful assessment early in life. Medical screening is essential for certain conditions such as PKU, as is the early detection of mental retardation through cognitive tests. Unfortunately, many cases of mental retardation are not detected early, as the doubling in prevalence during the school years indicates. Public screening of children's academic potential typically is not conducted until school age, and as we have noted, the intelligence tests available for infants and preschoolers are of questionable reliability and validity.

Accurate detection is important, because early interventions can benefit children diagnosed with mental retardation. Intervention with infants typically takes place in the home and focuses on stimulating the infant, educating parents, and promoting good parent–infant relationships (Shearer & Shearer, 1976). During the preschool years, special instruction may take place in child development centers, which also offer respite care for the parents who need relief from the added demands of rearing a child with mental retardation.

Treatment of the social and emotional needs of people with mental retardation is an essential component of their care. Treatment may include teaching basic self-care skills, such as feeding, toileting, and dressing, during the younger ages and various "life-survival" skills at later ages. Children with mental retardation may also need treatment for unusual behaviors, such as self-stimulation or aggressiveness. In general, research indicates that operant behavior therapy is the most effective treatment approach (Matson & Frame, 1986). Still, the effectiveness of behavioral approaches in absolute terms has been questioned, because problem behavior may remain despite some improvements (Scotti et al., 1991).

Medical care for physical and sensory handicaps is critical in the treatment of certain types of mental retardation. In addition, medications are helpful in treating disorders such as epilepsy that may co-occur with mental retardation. Medication is not especially helpful in treating the intellectual or socioemotional problems of people with mental retardation. Nevertheless, estimates indicate that 30 to 50 percent of institutionalized people with mental retardation are prescribed medication, often inappropriately, to control their behavior problems (Singh, Guernsey, & Ellis, 1992).

Neuroleptics (discussed in Chapter 13) are used with particular frequency to treat aggressiveness or other uncontrolled behavior in institutions (Grossman, 1983). In some institutional settings, these drugs have been used primarily to sedate patients, and various public exposés have raised broad questions about their misuse (Scheerenberger, 1983). The use of neuroleptics with mental retardation is especially questionable because behavior therapy provides a safe treatment alternative (Matson & Frame, 1986).

NORMALIZATION

Normalization is a major focus of the treatment of mental retardation. Normalization means that people with mental retardation are entitled to live as much as possible like other members of society. Major goals of normalization include mainstreaming children into public schools and promoting a role in the community for adults with mental retardation.

Schooling is of great importance to children with mental retardation. Prior to 1975, however, only about half of all children with mental retardation received an education at public expense. That year Congress passed the Education for All Handicapped Children Act, also known as Public Law 94-142, which affirmed that all handicapped children have a right to a free and appropriate education in the "least restrictive environment." Within the limits set by the handicapping condition, services are to be provided in a setting that restricts personal liberty as little as possible.

For many children with mental retardation, particularly those with mild retardation, providing the least restrictive environment means **mainstreaming** them into regular classrooms. Rather than being taught in special classes, children with mental retardation enter the mainstream and receive as much of their education as possible in normal classrooms. Unfortunately, there are broad inconsistencies in the extent of mainstreaming and in the quality of support services provided to children with mental retardation across school districts and across states. The lack of consistent quality is a matter of concern, because some evidence indicates that children with mental retardation who are mainstreamed into regular classrooms learn as much as or more than they do in special classes. More broadly, advocates argue that children with mental retardation have a right to education in the least restrictive environment, irrespective of the academic outcome of mainstreaming (Baroff, 1986; see Chapter 18).

The *deinstitutionalization* movement that began in mental hospitals in the 1960s (see Chapter 18) also has greatly helped to normalize the lives of people with mental retardation. Between 1970 and 1981, the number of people with mental retardation living in institutions dropped from 190,000 to 126,000. Deinstitutionalization has been particularly rapid for those with milder forms of mental retardation. Of those now living in institutions, 7.1 percent have mild, 13.0 percent have moderate, 24.4 percent have severe, and 55.5 percent have profound levels of retardation (Baroff, 1986). Evidence indicates that people with mental retardation who move from institutions to the community receive better care and function at a higher level. Despite some continued fear and prejudice, it is clear that people with mental retardation contribute to communities through their work, their play, and their relationships with all of us.

Autistic Disorder and Pervasive Developmental Disorders

The **pervasive developmental disorders** are unusual problems that begin early in life and involve severe impairments in a number of areas of functioning. People with pervasive developmental disorders exhibit profound disturbances in relationships, engage in repetitive, stereotyped activities, and typically have substantial communication difficulties. These difficulties are pronounced in **autistic disorder** (also known as **autism**), the most carefully researched form of pervasive developmental disorder. The dictionary definition of the word *autism* is "absorption in one's own mental activity," but the term understates the profound social disturbances that accompany the disorder.

Autistic disorder was brought to the public's awareness by Dustin Hoffman's stirring portrayal of Raymond in the movie *Rain Man*. The portrayal misrepresented some aspects of autism; for example, no one with autism can count hundreds of toothpicks as they fall to the floor. As we discuss shortly, however, some people with autism have highly unusual, specialized talents, and the character of Raymond was an accurate portrait of other aspects of a *good* adult outcome for autism. (Some professionals believe that Raymond really suffered from Asperger's disorder, a disturbance similar to autism except that the individual functions on a much higher level.) Because pervasive developmental disorders have been the subject of considerable theorizing and research, most of our discussion focuses on autistic disorder and its counterpart, Asperger's disorder. We begin with a case study.

CASE STUDY

A Child with Autistic Disorder

John was 3½ years old when he was first seen at a treatment center that specialized in autism. He spoke very little, and most of what he said wasn't meaningful. He used no names for himself or for others. If asked "What is your name?" he repeated "Name?" rather than answering "John." John would sometimes respond "you, you" as an affirmative answer to the question "Do you want something to eat?" This odd response was one of his few verbalizations that conveyed any meaning.

John's relationships were equally troubling. He literally showed no interest in other people. His parents reported that he never did such everyday things as seeking them out for play or sitting in their laps just to cuddle. In fact, John sometimes would throw a violent tantrum when he was touched. His mother said that when she tried to hug him, John frequently screamed in apparent pain and twirled away from her. She touched him rarely because of these horrible reactions. John was equally uninterested in his 6-year-old sister, who was functioning normally. He didn't tease her or follow her around like most little brothers. In fact, he didn't even seem to know she existed. John also was terrified of the gentle family dog. The dog was kept tied up when John was awake, because its attempts to play with John provoked fearful tantrums.

According to his parents, John was most content when he was by himself in the family room at home. He liked to have the television set turned on, although his parents felt that he didn't really watch or understand the shows. He would sit on the floor near the set and rock back and forth for hours. He spent several hours like this every day.

John's parents could remember no particular incident that marked the beginning of his problems. They became aware of them gradually as John failed to meet some normal developmental milestones. They recalled that John had been an easy baby, but they now felt that his meager need for attention may have been an early sign of his problems. His parents were concerned by his very limited speech and odd behavior as a toddler, but they were reassured by the fact that he had learned to walk at the appropriate age and otherwise seemed normal physically. John's pediatrician also had been reassuring about the boy's apparently delayed development until his annual checkup at age 3. That was when the pediatrician suggested that John might have mental retardation. After subsequent visits to several mental health professionals in their community, John's parents were referred to a treatment center that specialized in autism.

John was diagnosed by members of the center staff as suffering from autistic disorder. The center had an inpatient program for children with autism that used intensive behavior modification, but John's parents wanted him to remain with them. The center staff gave the parents extensive information about autism and about behavior modification programs, and they referred the family to a child development center in his community. The center offered preschool programs for children with mental retardation, and the staff would help the parents attempt to teach John language and self-care skills. The center also would give John's parents a break from the demands of caring for him. The staff warned John's parents, however, that without intensive inpatient treatment or truly heroic efforts on their part, John would continue to have severe difficulties with language, social relationships, and age-appropriate activities. ■

Typical Symptoms and Associated Features

The case of John illustrates several of the central characteristics of autistic disorder and its diagnosis. Like John, most children with autistic disorder are normal in physical appearance. Some observers have even suggested that they are especially attractive youngsters. Although they sometimes have unusual actions and postures (Wing, 1988), their body movements are not grossly uncoordinated, and their physical growth and development is generally normal. Judging from physical appearance alone, one would not expect children with autistic disorder to have severe psychological impairments.

Early onset is another feature of autism illustrated by the case of John. Autism begins early in life, and in retrospect many parents recall abnormalities that seem to date back to birth. Because many infants with autism make few demands and have a normal physical appearance, the condition may not be accurately diagnosed for a few years. In the majority of cases, however, parents become aware that their child is profoundly disturbed by the age of 3 (Short & Schopler, 1988). By this time, parents have noted the child's impaired communication abilities, one of the three classic symptoms of autism. The other two central symptoms are impairments in social interaction and stereotyped patterns of behavior, interests, and activities. In the following sections we discuss disturbances in terms of these three defining symptoms. We also discuss other notable symptoms commonly found among people with autism and other pervasive developmental disorders, specifically apparent sensory deficits, self-injurious behavior, and savant performance—highly specialized abilities found in some rare but fascinating cases.

IMPAIRED SOCIAL INTERACTION

Many mental health professionals view the inability to relate to others as the central feature of autistic disorder. A contemporary viewpoint argues that people with autism lack a *theory of mind*, that is, they fail to appreciate that other people have a point of reference that differs from their own (Baron-Cohen, Tager-Flusberg, & Cohen, 1993). The concept of theory of mind is best illustrated by the "Sally-Ann task" (see Figure 15–5). In the Sally-Ann task, the test child is shown two dolls, Sally, who has a basket, and Ann, who has a box. Sally puts a marble in her basket and then leaves. While Sally is gone, Ann takes the marble out of Sally's basket and puts it into her own box. When Sally returns, the question is: Where will she look for her marble?

Sally should look for the marble in her basket where she left it, because she did not see Ann hide it. However, children with autism typically fail to appreciate Sally's perspective—they lack a theory of mind. In one early study, 80 percent of children with autism said Sally would search in Ann's box, whereas only 14 percent of children with Down syndrome made the same error (Baron-Cohen, Leslie, & Frith, 1985).

The Sally–Ann Task

FIGURE 15–5: Where will Sally (on left) look for the marble? Many children with autism answer "in the box," evidence that they may lack a "theory of mind."

Source: U. Frith, 1989, *Autism: Explaining the Enigma*, p. 41. Oxford: Basil Blackwell.

Theory of mind has proved to be a useful, overarching concept for understanding social disturbances in autistic disorder (Happe, 1995; Rutter, 1996), but more specific problems also are important to note. Social impairments range from relatively mild oddities, such as a lack of social or emotional reciprocity, to extreme difficulties in which there is little awareness of the existence of others, let alone of their perspective. Some children and adults with pervasive developmental disorders treat other people as if they were confusing and foreign objects rather than as sources of protection, comfort, and reciprocal stimulation.

Many people with pervasive developmental disorders appear to be missing the basic, inborn tendency to form attachments with other people. As infants, they do not show the attachment behaviors that help normal children form a special bond with their caregivers. In retrospect, many parents remember that their children did not seek them out in times of distress, nor were they comforted by physical contact. Many children with autism find normal hugs and kisses disturbing, even painful, rather than reassuring.

Social impairments continue as the infants become toddlers and preschoolers. Children with pervasive developmental disorder show little interest in their peers. They do not engage in spontaneous social play, and they fail to develop friendships as they grow older. They also exhibit *gaze aversion*; that is, they actively avoid eye contact.

Even those adults who achieve exceptionally good outcomes continue to show severely disturbed social emotions and understanding. Consider the remarkable case of Temple Grandin, a woman who achieved what may be the most successful outcome of autism on record.

Temple Grandin: An Anthropologist on Mars

Temple Grandin, a woman who is now in her forties, suffered from the classic symptoms of autism as a child. She had not developed language by the age of 3, and she threw wild tantrums in response to social initiations, even gentle attempts to give her a hug. Grandin spent hours staring into space, playing with objects, or simply rocking or spinning herself. She also engaged in other

▲ Temple Grandin, who suffers from autism, has achieved remarkable success both as an advocate for autistic disorder and as an animal scientist who has developed more humane methods of slaughtering cattle.

unusual behaviors, such as repeatedly smearing her own feces. With the extensive help of her parents and teachers, and with her own determination, however, Grandin developed complex strategies to help her compensate for, and cope with, her severe psychological impairments. Remarkably, she even earned a Ph.D. in animal science and has developed widely used techniques for managing cattle. In stark contrast to Grandin, the majority of people with autism spend most of their adult life in institutions.

One of Grandin's most complex coping strategies is "computing" how other people feel and how she should react in social circumstances. Like the characters of Data or Mr. Spock from the "Star Trek" series—with whom she identifies—Grandin does not experience normal human emotions and motivations. Rather, she describes herself as "an anthropologist on Mars." Like an anthropologist in a strange culture, she has had to learn how to relate to the human species through careful observation of "their" behavior. Grandin details her struggles with social situations and other aspects of autism in two autobiographies, *Emergence: Labelled Autistic* and *Thinking in Pictures.* The neurologist Oliver Sacks has also written a detailed case study about Grandin. The following excerpt from Sacks's observations illustrates some of her social struggles.

"I can tell if a human being is angry," she told me, "or if he's smiling." At the level of the sensorimotor, the concrete, the unmediated, the animal, Temple has no difficulty. But what about children, I asked her. Were they not intermediate between animals and adults? On the contrary, Temple said, she had great difficulties with children—trying to talk with them, to join in their games (she could not even play peekaboo with a baby, she said, because she would get the timing all wrong)—as she had had such difficulties herself as a child. Children, she feels, are already far advanced, by the age of three or four, along a path that she, as an autistic person, has never advanced far on. Little children, she feels, already "understand" other human beings in a way she can never hope to. (Sacks, 1995, p. 270)

Although she feels that she lacks even children's understanding of social motivations, Grandin apparently has residual traces of human needs, such as the need for physical contact. Still, she finds human touch—hugging—overwhelming. As a result, Grandin developed another remarkable strategy to compensate for her deep-seated aversion to human touch. She developed a "squeeze machine," a device that gives her a soothing, mechanical hug. In *Thinking in Pictures,* Grandin describes her development of her squeeze machine:

From as far back as I can remember, I always hated to be hugged. I wanted to experience the good feeling of being hugged, but it was just too overwhelming. It was like a great all-engulfing tidal wave of stimulation, and I reacted like a wild animal. . . . After visiting my aunt's ranch in Arizona . . . I watched cattle being put in the squeeze chute for their vaccinations, I noticed some of them relaxed. . . . I asked Aunt Ann to press the squeeze sides against me and to close the head restraint bars around my neck. I hoped it would calm my anxiety. At first there were a few moments of sheer panic as I stiffened up and tried to pull away from the pressure. . . . Five seconds later I felt a wave of relaxation. . . . I copied the design and built the first human squeeze machine out of plywood panels when I returned to school. (Grandin, 1995, pp. 62–63) ■

We have numerous descriptions of the unusual behavior of people with autistic disorder, as in our earlier case study of John. But social and communicative impairments of autism typically prevent us from learning about the inner world of autism. Temple Grandin offers us a compelling exception to the rule. Throughout the remainder of this chapter, we quote from *Thinking in Pictures* in an attempt to offer some insight into autism from the inside.

IMPAIRED COMMUNICATION

In addition to their dramatic social isolation, people with pervasive developmental disorders suffer from a variety of impairments in communication. (The one exception is Asperger's disorder.) The communication problems often are severe, but there can be a range of difficulties. Some children fail to speak at all between the ages of 1 and 2, the time when normal children typically learn their first words. Others learn a few rudimentary words such as "Mama" and then suddenly lose their language abilities. Still other children progress further in acquiring language, but they either lose their abilities or stop progressing at the normal rate of language acquisition (Schreibman, 1988). Many children with autism remain mute, and about half never acquire functional language (Rutter, 1978a; Volkmar et al., 1994). According to field studies conducted for DSM-IV, 54 percent of patients with autism remain mute, compared with 35 percent of patients with other pervasive developmental disorders (Volkmar et al., 1994).

Many unusual features are found in the language of people with pervasive developmental disorders who do learn to speak. For one, the subtleties of speaking style often are unusual, a problem referred to as *dysprosody*. In dysprosody, speech production is disturbed in its rate, rhythm, and intonation. This makes the disturbed child or adult sound highly unusual to the normal listener, even when the speech content is normal.

Echolalia is another common language problem. People with autism or other pervasive developmental disorders frequently repeat phrases that are spoken to them, or sometimes repeatedly echo a phrase they heard at an earlier time. As with other problems, there is a dramatic contrast with normal development. When the mother of a 1½-year-old points to herself and says, "Who is this?," normal toddlers will respond with "Mama." A 10-year-old child with autism and echolalia will respond to the same question by repeating "Who is this?"

Another common language problem is *pronoun reversal*. Children and adults with pervasive developmental disorder are especially likely to confuse the pronoun "you" with the pronoun "I." They say "You want a cookie" when they mean "I want a cookie." Some have speculated that this speech error reveals profound emotional confusion. According to one interpretation, pronoun reversal indicates that children with autism have failed to individuate, to become a separate person (Bettelheim, 1967). Another explanation is that pronoun reversal demonstrates a lack of understanding of speech. In hundreds of everyday conversations, people with pervasive developmental disorders are referred to as "you." Lacking a deeper understanding of the meaning of pronouns, they refer to themselves as "you," not "I."

The speech difficulties found in autism and other pervasive developmental disorders are not the products of auditory or other sensory problems, nor are they simply disturbances in the mechanics of speech. Rather, the difficulties stem from basic disturbances in the ability to communicate, and even more basically, in the ability to imitate or reciprocate interactions. Unlike infants and toddlers who are deaf or mute, children with autism do not use gestures as substitutes for speech. In fact, some children do not engage in the social imitation that is essential for learning basic skills, let alone for building relationships. Once again, theory of mind offers a possible explanation for these deficits. In many respects, children with autism seem to lack the essential motivation for communicating with others. Their communication difficulties convey the failure to appreciate the perspective—or even the existence—of other minds (Tager-Flusberg, 1996).

Even high-functioning people with pervasive developmental disorders who imitate others and have relatively well-developed language skills nevertheless demonstrate a limited ability to communicate about or understand abstractions. They may fail to generate unique or imaginative speech, and they have difficulty comprehending abstractions like metaphors. Thus the language problems in the pervasive developmental disorders apparently involve restrictions in thinking, not just in expression. Here is how Temple Grandin describes her struggles with language and abstraction:

I can remember the frustration of not being able to talk at age three. This caused me to throw many a tantrum. I could understand what people said to me, but I

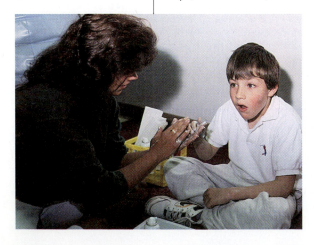

▼ **Children with autistic disorder, like the child in this picture, are normal in physical appearance. The communication problems, autistic aloneness, and need to preserve sameness are readily apparent among children with autism, however.**

could not get my words out. It was like a big stutter, and starting words was difficult. My first few words were very difficult to produce and generally had only one syllable, such as "bah" for "ball." (p. 45)

Autistics have problems learning things that cannot be thought about in pictures. The easiest words for an autistic child to learn are nouns, because they directly related to pictures. . . . Spatial words such as "over" and "under" had no meaning for me until I had a visual image to fix them in my memory. Even now, when I hear the word "under" by itself, I automatically picture myself getting under the cafeteria tables at school during an air-raid drill, a common occurrence on the East Coast during the early fifties. . . . When I read, I translate written words into color movies or I simply store a photo of the written page to be read later. When I retrieve material, I see a photocopy of the page in my imagination. I can then read it like a TelePrompTer. . . . When I am unable to covert text to pictures, it is usually because the text has no concrete meaning. Some philosophy books and articles about cattle futures market are simply incomprehensible. (pp. 29–31)

STEREOTYPED BEHAVIOR, INTERESTS, AND ACTIVITIES

The third major symptom of autism and other pervasive developmental disorders is restricted, repetitive, and stereotyped patterns of behavior, interests, and activities. Many children with autistic disorder literally spend hours spinning a top or flapping a string in front of their eyes. Others might become uncontrollably agitated if the arrangement of furniture in a room is changed even slightly. Compulsively rigid adherence to daily routines is yet another aspect of these restricted activities and interests.

Not surprisingly, these odd preoccupations and rituals create social complications. People unfamiliar with the disorder are likely to find such behavior bizarre and perhaps frightening. The ritualistic behavior also causes numerous problems for those who are trying to manage and educate children with autism. How do you educate a child who is totally preoccupied with flapping a string in front of his or her face for hours?

What purpose does such stereotyped behavior serve for the disturbed individual? Rituals such as flapping a string or spinning a top seem to serve no other function than to provide sensory feedback. Thus they are often referred to as *self-stimulation*. The common interpretation of self-stimulation is that the child with autism receives too little sensory input, and that the ritual self-stimulation increases sensation to a more desirable level. We prefer an alternative interpretation. The stimulation of everyday environments has been described as overwhelming by several high-functioning people with pervasive developmental disorders. Perhaps self-stimulation reduces rather than increases sensory input by making the stimulation monotonously predictable. This alternative interpretation suggests, in fact, that all of the stereotyped behavior found in pervasive developmental disorders can be viewed as a form of compulsive ritual. The repetitive actions may serve the function of making a terrifying world more constant and predictable and therefore less frightening. Again, here are some comments by Temple Grandin on the topic:

When left alone, I would often space out and become hypnotized. I could sit for hours on the beach watching sand dribbling through my fingers. I'd study each individual grain of sand as it flowed between my fingers. Each grain was different, and I was like a scientist studying the grains under a microscope. As I scrutinized their shapes and contours, I went into a trance which cut me off from the sights and sounds around me.

Rocking and spinning were other ways to shut out the world when I became overloaded with too much noise. Rocking made me feel calm. It was like taking an addictive drug. The more I did it, the more I wanted to do it. My mother and my teachers would stop me so I would get back in touch with the rest of the world. (pp. 44–45)

APPARENT SENSORY DEFICITS

Some people with autism or other pervasive developmental disorders respond to auditory, tactile, or visual sensations in highly unusual and idiosyncratic manners. For example, some people with autistic disorder occasionally respond as if they were deaf, even though their hearing is intact. This unresponsiveness is an example of an *apparent sensory deficit* (Lovaas et al., 1971). There is no impairment in the sense organ, but the individual's responding makes it appear otherwise. Even more puzzling is that the same person who fails to be startled by a sudden crack

▲ **Nadia, a girl with autism, drew this picture of a horse and rider when she was 5½ years old. Nadia's savant drawing ability diminished as she began to learn to communicate and relate to others.**

of thunder may scream in apparent pain in reaction to a small sound like the scratch of chalk on a blackboard (Schreibman, 1988). This inconsistency suggests that the problem lies at some higher level of perception rather than at a lower level of sensation. The sensory apparatus is intact, but some cortical abnormality in integrating and perceiving sensory input creates these unusual and varied reactions to sounds, sights, and touches. Temple Grandin has argued that psychological researchers have not paid sufficient attention to this aspect of autistic disorder. Here are some of her comments on her own experience:

When I was little, loud noises were also a problem, often feeling like a dentist's drill hitting a nerve. They actually caused pain. I was scared to death of balloons popping, because the sound was like an explosion in my ear. Minor noises that most people can tune out drove me to distraction. When I was in college, my roommate's hair dryer sounded like a jet plane taking off. (p. 67)

SELF-INJURY

Self-injurious behavior is one of the most bizarre and dangerous difficulties that can accompany autism and other pervasive developmental disorders. The most common forms of

self-injury are repeated head banging and biting of the fingers and wrists (Rutter, Greenfield, & Lockyer, 1967). The resultant injuries may involve only minor bruises, or they can be severe enough to cause broken bones, brain damage, and even death. It is important that this self-injury not be misinterpreted as suicidal behavior. The child with autism does not have enough self-awareness to be truly suicidal. Instead, self-injury seems to have several possible causes, the most widely accepted of which is self-stimulation (Carr, 1977). Fortunately, self-injury can be treated effectively with behavior modification techniques, as we discuss later.

SAVANT PERFORMANCE

One of the most intriguing characteristics of autism and pervasive developmental disorders is the occasional child who shows **savant performance**—an exceptional ability in a highly specialized area of functioning. Savant performance typically involves artistic, musical, or mathematical skills. The image on this page portrays the savant artistic abilities of Nadia, a girl with autism who drew numerous, highly sophisticated pictures during her preschool and early school-aged years. Nadia's artistic abilities are impressive and fascinating, especially if you pause to consider the usual drawings of a 5-year-old child. Even more puzzling is that Nadia's artistic abilities deteriorated as her symptoms improved following intensive therapy (Selfe, 1977; see Further Thoughts).

No one has an adequate theory, let alone an explanation, for savant performance. Unfortunately, one thing does seems clear. Despite what many people had hoped, the existence of savant performance does not indicate that children with autistic disorder have superior intelligence. Most children with autism do not exhibit these special abilities, and savant performance sometimes is observed among people with mental retardation or brain injury. More specifically, approximately a quarter of children with autism have IQs below 55, about half have IQs between 55 and 70, and only one-fourth have IQs over 70 (Volkmar et al., 1994; see Table 15–5). Moreover, the IQ scores of children with autistic disorder behave like the IQs of normal children: They are stable over time, and they predict future educational attainment (Schreibman, 1988). We should note, however, that people with Asperger's disorder generally have normal intelligence.

TABLE 15–5

IQ Scores for Patients with Autism and Other Pervasive Developmental Disorders Based on DSM-IV Field Trials

IQ Score	Autism		Other Pervasive Developmental Disorder	
	N	Percent	N	Percent
>70	118	26.0	122	50.8
55–69	197	43.4	61	25.4
<20–54	114	25.1	53	22.1
Unspecified	25	5.5	4	1.7

Source: Based on F. R. Volkmar et al., 1994, Field trial for autistic disorder in DSM-IV, *American Journal of Psychiatry, 151,* 1361–1367.

Savant Performance

Savant performance is one of the most intriguing observations in abnormal psychology. Several hundred cases of savant performance have been documented throughout the world in the last century. Such notable figures as Langdon Down and Alfred Binet wrote about one or more of their patients with savant abilities. Incredible, specialized abilities have been found among a small percentage of people with autism, mental retardation, and brain injuries (Treffert, 1988). The abilities are not just unusual relative to the mental disturbance or low IQ of the savant individual, but they far exceed normal performance in a highly specialized area of functioning.

There seem to be a limited number of categories of savant performance. Mathematical facility and calendar calculation are among the most commonly noted areas of ability. Some savants can perform incredibly rapid mental arithmetic; others are able to recite the day of the week for virtually any past or future date in a matter of several seconds. Astonishing memory skills are another type of savant ability. Cases have been reported, for example, in which people with mental retardation could accurately recall the weather for any particular day extending back for years in time. Musical talents are a third type of savant ability. Several cases have been reported in which people of limited intelligence could play back entire complicated compositions after hearing them only once (Treffert, 1988). Finally, some savants possess advanced drawing abilities, as exemplified by the sketch by Nadia.

Nadia was 6½ years old when she was first seen by the British therapist Lorna Selfe (1977), who documented her drawing abilities. According to her mother, Nadia had begun to produce complex drawings by the age of 3½. Nadia drew frequently and quickly, working with her left hand while holding her face very close to the sheet of paper. She used no colors in her drawings, and she did not copy from picturebooks. Rather, Nadia typically would see a picture in a book, often a simple one, and a day or two later she would begin to draw a similar but more complex version of it. Her favorite subjects for drawing were horses, roosters, and human figures.

At the time she was first seen, Nadia had severely restricted language skills and met the criteria for a diagnosis of autism. She later entered a school for children with autism at the age of 7½, and she had made some progress by the age of 9. For example, she learned to return a greeting rather than echo "Hello Nadia" when greeted by others. A puzzling and somewhat sad consequence of her education was that her drawing interest and ability waned as her other skills developed (Selfe, 1977).

What allows savants like Nadia to perform their seemingly magical feats? Savants themselves are of little help in answering this question. They typically cannot describe their own mental processes. Scientific explanations are not much more satisfying. Some theorists have speculated that savant abilities are attributable to exceptional eidetic imagery or visual memory. Others have hypothesized that savant ability is a result of genetic influences. Finally, several theorists have suggested that savant performance is a way of compensating for sensory deprivation or limited cognitive abilities. One compensatory hypothesis is that damage to the left cerebral hemisphere heightens the functioning of the spatial and mathematical abilities localized in the right hemisphere of the brain.

Each of these speculations is far from being adequately developed or researched. At present, savant performance remains a fascinating and unexplained phenomenon. It poses a challenge both to abnormal psychologists and to cognitive scientists, who must somehow account for these unusual abilities in theories of normal cognitive abilities. ■

Classification

BRIEF HISTORICAL PERSPECTIVE

The history of the classification of the pervasive developmental disorders is very brief. The syndrome of "early infantile autism" was first described in 1943 by the psychiatrist Leo Kanner (1894–1981) of Johns Hopkins University. Kanner reported on 11 children whose unusual symptoms were strikingly similar and whose

▲ Leo Kanner (1894–1981) was a U.S. psychiatrist who promoted the study of psychological problems among children. Kanner was noted for his identification of autism as a distinct psychological disorder.

difficulties were dramatically different from those of other emotionally disturbed children. Among the characteristics that Kanner noted were an inability to form relationships with others, delayed or noncommunicative speech, a demand for sameness in the environment, stereotyped play activities, and lack of imagination (Kanner, 1943). To Kanner's credit, contemporary diagnostic criteria are very similar to the symptoms he described.

Whereas Kanner's contributions are well known, mental health professionals have only recently recognized that the Viennese psychiatrist Hans Asperger (1944/1991) identified a very similar condition to autism at virtually the same time as Kanner. One important difference, however, was that Asperger's patients exhibited higher intellectual functioning. The distinction between Kanner's and Asperger's patients has been introduced into the formal diagnostic nomenclature in DSM-IV. **Asperger's disorder** is now listed as a subtype of pervasive developmental disorder. Descriptively, it is identical to autism, with the exception that the disorder involves no clinically significant delay in language.

Kanner's and Asperger's observations have stood the test of time. In contrast, another event in the history of the classification of autism is memorable for the misunderstanding that it caused. For several decades, the term *childhood schizophrenia* was used to classify autism together with other severe forms of childhood psychopathology (Bender, 1947). However, the symptoms of autism and schizophrenia differ dramatically, and evidence indicates that autism and schizophrenia remain different over time (Rutter, Greenfield, & Lockyear, 1967). Moreover, the pervasive developmental disorders have an onset in the preschool years, whereas the incidence of schizophrenia does not become notable until the teen years. Some professionals continue to use the misleading term *childhood schizophrenia*, but it has been appropriately abandoned by most investigators.

CONTEMPORARY CLASSIFICATION

The diagnostic criteria for autistic disorder have evolved somewhat in the DSM, but the basic symptoms of the disorder have remained the same. The major change in the DSM-IV criteria, which are summarized in Table 15–6, was to define the symptoms more narrowly in order to reduce the high rate of false-positive diagnoses produced by earlier DSM criteria (Volkmar, 1996).

More generally, the DSM-IV has introduced some important changes in its list of pervasive developmental disorders. As noted, Asperger's disorder refers to people who show the symptoms of autism but do not have major problems in communication and generally function higher in other areas as well. Professionals differ, however, about whether Asperger's disorder is best viewed as categorically different from autistic disorder or on a continuum with it (Volkmar et al., 1994). *Childhood disintegrative disorder* refers to a poorly understood and somewhat controversial condition (Rutter, 1996) characterized by problems in social interaction and communication, in addition to stereotyped behavior. The onset occurs after at least 2 years of normal development, and previously acquired skills are lost. Finally, *Rett's disorder* is a clearly distinct condition characterized by at least 5 months of normal development followed by (1) a deceleration in head growth, (2) loss of purposeful hand movements, (3) loss of social engagement, (4) poor coordination, and (5) a marked delay in language. Rett's disorder is found only among females.

Inexperienced clinicians are not especially reliable in distinguishing among various pervasive developmental disorders, but clinicians who have experience with these syndromes have proved very reliable (Volkmar et al., 1994). Experienced clinicians also can reliably distinguish pervasive developmental disorders from related conditions, such as *developmental aphasia*, a disorder characterized by delayed or absent speech. Children with developmental aphasia attempt to communicate through nonverbal signals, and they have normal social interests. Sociability also distinguishes the pervasive developmental disorders from mental retardation. As noted earlier, inexperienced clinicians may fail to recognize autism and misdiagnose the disorder as mental retardation.

Epidemiology

Autism is an extremely rare disorder. Traditional estimates indicated that only 4–5 of every 10,000 children qualify for the diagnosis, although some recent statistics suggest 1 in 1,000 children are affected by the disorder (Bryson, 1996). Even the combined prevalence of autism and other pervasive developmental disorders is extremely low, perhaps 20 out of every 10,000 children (Wing & Gould, 1979).

At one time experts believed that autism was more common among the higher social

TABLE 15-6

DSM-IV Diagnostic Criteria for Autistic Disorder

A. **A total of six (or more) items from (1), (2), and (3), with at least two from (1), and one each from (2) and (3):**

1. Qualitative impairment in social interaction, as manifested by at least two of the following:
   a. marked impairment in the use of multiple nonverbal behaviors such as eye-to-eye gaze, facial expression, body postures, and gestures to regulate social interaction
   b. failure to develop peer relationships appropriate to developmental level
   c. a lack of spontaneous seeking to share enjoyment, interests, or achievements with other people
   d. lack of social or emotional reciprocity

2. Qualitative impairments in communication as manifested by at least one of the following:
   a. delay in, or total lack of, the development of spoken language (not accompanied by an attempt to compensate through alternative modes of communication such as gesture or mime)
   b. in individuals with adequate speech, marked impairment in the ability to initiate or sustain a conversation with others
   c. stereotyped and repetitive use of language or idiosyncratic language
   d. lack of varied, spontaneous make-believe play or social imitative play appropriate to developmental level

3. Restricted repetitive and stereotyped patterns of behavior, interests, and activities, as manifested by at least one of the following:
   a. encompassing preoccupation with one or more stereotyped and restricted patterns of interest that is abnormal either in intensity or focus
   b. apparently inflexible adherence to specific, nonfunctional routines or rituals
   c. stereotyped and repetitive motor mannerisms
   d. persistent preoccupation with parts of objects

B. **Delays or abnormal functioning in at least one of the following areas, with onset prior to age 3 years: (1) social interaction, (2) language as used in social communication, or (3) symbolic or imaginative play**

---

classes, but research reveals that the apparent relation was created by referral bias (Gillberg & Schaumann, 1982). Parents with fewer resources may accept an initial misdiagnosis of mental retardation, but wealthier and better-educated parents continue to seek opinions from specialized professionals, who eventually recognize the autism (Schopler, Andrews, & Strapp, 1979). This referral bias creates a misleading correlation between social class and autism. The majority of children seen at prestigious specialty clinics have wealthy, educated parents; thus it may seem that the disorder is related to social class. However, no association is found when the general population is examined. This methodological problem is important, because it resulted in some misleading substantive conclusions. The supposed relation between autism and social status has been used as "evidence" to support the false views that children with autism have superior intellects and that the disorder is caused by successful but cold and distant parents.

A more promising epidemiological finding is that the risk for autism increases dramatically among the siblings of children with autistic disorder. The prevalence of autism among the overall population is about .05 percent, whereas the prevalence among children with a sibling with autism is 2 to 5 percent, a 50- to 100-fold increase (Smalley, Asarnow, & Spence, 1988; Smalley & Collins, 1996). Although these statistics don't prove that autism has a genetic cause, they have encouraged research in this area. Finally, the fact that autism is 3 to 4 times more common among boys than among girls has prompted a search for a gender-linked etiology.

Etiological Considerations and Research

Autism appears to have multiple causes. Several problems that we have already discussed as causes of mental retardation also appear to cause autism. In addition, recent findings suggest that genetic factors play an important role in the etiology of the disorder. Before discussing evidence on biological etiologies of autism, we first briefly consider—and reject—environmental explanations.

PSYCHOLOGICAL AND SOCIAL FACTORS

For many years after Kanner identified autism, a number of professionals asserted that the disorder was caused by poor parenting. In particular, the disorder was said to be caused by parents who were cold, distant, and subtly rejecting of their children. This view was once so popular that, in 1960, *Time* published an account of these "refrigerator parents." The article claimed that the parents of children with autism "just happened to defrost long enough to produce a child" (Schreibman, 1988).

Hypothesizing about a psychological etiology began with Kanner (1943) himself. To his credit, however, Kanner consistently argued that autism was caused by a combination of biological and psychosocial factors (Eisenberg & Kanner, 1956). Other theorists focused exclusively on parenting. Theories of parental causation ranged from purely psychoanalytic speculations that autism was a result of the infant's defense against maternal hostility (Bettelheim, 1967) to purely behavioral views that the disorder was caused by inappropriate parental reinforcement (Ferster, 1961).

Evidence to support these speculations either has crumbled or failed to emerge. The observation that many parents of children with autism came from higher socioeconomic backgrounds once formed a major part of the justification for theories about "refrigerator parents." But, as we saw earlier, research has demonstrated that autism is not associated with high parental intelligence and social status. More directly, researchers have found no differences in the child-rearing styles of the parents of children with autism when compared with those of the parents of normal children (Cantwell, Baker, & Rutter, 1979).

The view that "refrigerator parents" cause autism also can be seriously challenged on logical grounds. How could a parent's emotional distance create such an extreme disturbance so early in life? As we saw in our discussion of mental retardation, even the heinous abuse of infants does not cause symptoms that approach the form or severity of the problems found among children with autism. And no one has ever suggested that children with autism suffer anything approaching traumatic abuse. Moreover, if parents are emotionally distant from their disordered children, could this be a reaction to their children's gross disturbances? Attachment behaviors are maintained by reciprocal interaction. If an infant shows no normal interest in cuddling or mimicking, is it surprising if the parent becomes a bit distant?

Speculation that autism is caused by poor parenting can never be completely disproved. However, logic, the lack of empirical support for psychological hypotheses, and mounting research on biological causes suggest with virtual certainty that autism does not have a psychological cause. More basically, the rules of science require scientists to prove their hypotheses and not to force others to disprove them (see Research Methods in Chapter 1). Parents have been unfairly blamed for causing autism, and we greet further assertions that poor parenting causes autism with extreme skepticism.

BIOLOGICAL FACTORS

A number of findings indicate that biological abnormalities play an important role in the etiology of autism. These include the following:

- Nearly half of all children with autistic disorder develop seizure disorders by adolescence or early adult life (Tsai, 1996; Wing, 1988).

- Substantial increases in the prevalence of autism are found among children who have certain known genetic and infectious diseases (Reiss, Feinstein, & Rosenbaum, 1986).

- The prevalence of autism is higher among immediate relatives of individuals with autism than among the general population. Prevalence is particularly high among twin pairs (Smalley et al., 1988; Bailey et al., 1995).

- A disproportionate number of neurological abnormalities have been identified among children with autism by a variety of techniques ranging from evidence of pregnancy and birth complications to abnormal EEGs to findings based on postmortem examination of the brain (Bauman, 1996; Schreibman, 1988).

Autism as a Consequence of Known Biological Disorders One view of these diverse findings is that autism has several different biological causes (Reiss, Feinstein, & Rosenbaum, 1986).

In support of this view, one epidemiological study found that over half the cases of autism were associated with various known biological difficulties or disorders (Wing, 1988). These illnesses include many established causes of mental retardation, in particular fragile-X syndrome, tuberous sclerosis, PKU, rubella, and encephalitis (Reiss, Feinstein, & Rosenbaum, 1986). Other causes of mental retardation, however, are not associated with an increased prevalence of autism. For example, autism is not related to Down syndrome, the most common biological cause of mental retardation. Thus there are many brain pathologies that cause mental retardation but only a few specific disturbances that may cause both mental retardation and autism.

A Strongly Genetic Disorder?   In recent years a handful of studies have suggested that genetic factors also play an important role in the etiology of many, if not all, cases of autism. The prevalence of autism is as much as 100 times higher among the siblings of a proband with autism, and researchers have found higher concordance rates for autism among MZ than DZ twins (Smalley et al., 1988; Smalley & Collins, 1996). In one investigation, the concordance rate for MZ twins was reported to be 95.7 percent, in contrast to 23.5 percent for DZ twins (Ritvo et al., 1985). This result may have overestimated the true concordance rate, however, as the investigators recruited subjects through a national newsletter to parents, and parents with twins who are concordant for autism are more likely to respond to this method of recruitment (Le Couteur, 1988). Nevertheless, another report found a concordance rate of 91 percent for autism among MZ twin pairs in contrast to 0 percent among DZ twins (Steffenburg et al., 1989).

Somewhat different results have been reported by a group of British investigators who conducted two major studies of the behavior genetics of autism. In the first report, the concordance rate for autism was found to be 36 percent for MZ twins and 0 percent for DZ twins (Folstein & Rutter, 1977). Importantly, however, the MZ–DZ comparison jumped to 82 percent versus 10 percent when concordance for any form of cognitive or learning difficulty was computed. From these results, the investigators concluded that autism was an extreme manifestation of an underlying cognitive disorder that was strongly heritable.

This research group replicated and expanded these findings in a recent investigation that included a reevaluation of the original sample and recruitment of a new group of twins

(Bailey et al., 1995). In this largest study to date, concordance rates for autism were 60 percent for MZ twins and 0 percent for DZ twins. Concordance rates for a social or cognitive disorder were 92 percent for MZ pairs and 10 percent for DZ pairs. Importantly, all twins in this new study were carefully screened for known heritable conditions (like fragile-X) that may have distorted the results of earlier studies. The fact that only a few conditions were detected by screening suggests that most cases of autism are caused by a genetic abnormality that has yet to be detected, not by known genetic or infectious illnesses (Bailey et al., 1995). If so, autism is strongly but not completely genetic.

Integration: Multiple Pathways to a Brain Disorder   Even if autism does not have a single specific etiology, it still may be produced by a common underlying brain pathology. That is, genetics, PKU, and tuberous sclerosis may be different routes to the same destination in that they produce similar abnormalities in brain function, structure, or development. In fact, different brain abnormalities may cause different symptoms of the disorder, and perhaps this accounts for differences in the presentation of pervasive developmental disorders (for example, autism versus Asperger's disorder). Detecting a common pathology could lead to the development of more effective means of preventing or treating the disorder. Toward these ends, researchers have developed several promising leads in understanding the neurophysiology and neuroanatomy of autism.

Neurophysiology and Autism   With respect to abnormal brain function, theorizing has focused on two major neurophysiological processes. The first theory concerns the neurotransmitter serotonin. About one-third of children with autism have elevated blood levels of serotonin (Kohler, 1988). However, elevated levels of neurotransmitters in the blood or other peripheral sites do not necessarily indicate higher levels in the brain.

A potentially more important finding concerns the effect of the medication *fenfluramine* in the treatment of autism. Commonly used as a diet aid in the general population, fenfluramine has been demonstrated to reduce brain serotonin levels in animals, and some pilot research suggested that the drug alleviates some symptoms of autism (Geller et al., 1982). Subsequent investigation of the clinical effectiveness of fenfluramine has produced much more mixed results, however, as we shall see in the treatment section. At this time the relationship of serotonin levels to autism is uncertain and requires further investigation.

Recent research has also focused on the possible role of endorphins in the neurophysiology of autism. Some evidence indicates that endorphin levels are elevated among people with autistic disorder and that elevated blood levels of endorphins are associated with decreased pain sensitivity among children with autism. (Recall from Chapter 11 that the internally produced endorphins have effects similar to those of externally administered opiate drugs like morphine.) This suggests that elevated endorphin levels may be responsible for some unusual symptoms exhibited by children with autism, particularly their self-destructive behavior (Gillberg, 1988).

Neuroanatomy and Autism   Other research has searched for abnormalities in brain structure among people with autism. Perhaps certain structures of the brain are damaged or develop abnormally in children with autism. The question is: Where are the abnormalities located?

Early theorizing suggested that the left cerebral hemisphere was a likely site of brain damage in autism, because speech typically is controlled by left hemisphere structures. Many experts have rejected this view, however, because the communication deficits that characterize autism are more basic than problems in language expression or comprehension. Based on this observation, it has been suggested that damage is more likely to be found in subcortical brain structures (Wing, 1988).

Consistent with this reasoning, some research suggests that people with autism may have abnormalities in parts of the limbic system—the area of the brain that regulates emotions—and also

in areas of the cerebellum, where sensorimotor input is integrated (Bauman, 1996; Schreibman, 1988). The abnormalities are considerably more subtle than the brain damage associated with most known organic causes of mental retardation or with Rett's disorder, where the brain is approximately 25 percent smaller than its expected size (Bauman, 1996). More evidence on specific abnormalities will come from research that uses new brain imaging techniques, as well as from further postmortem examination of brains of people who suffered from the disorder.

A Disorder of Brain Development   As investigators search for sites of brain damage, one thing seems clear: Any structural abnormalities are likely to be the result of abnormal brain development, not of specific damage or lesions. This is because *plasticity* is a basic characteristic of the development of the infant's brain. If damage occurs in one area of the infant's brain, another area often takes over the function of the damaged site. Because most cases of autism begin at an age when the brain is still plastic, specific brain damage or lesions are unlikely causes (Rutter, 1978a, 1996).

Treatment

Some controversy exists about the degree to which treatment can alter the prognosis for children with autistic disorder. Some people are optimistic about the possibilities of new or established treatments, whereas others are far more skeptical (see Research Close-Up). Everyone acknowledges, however, that there is no cure for autism. Thus the effectiveness of treatment must be compared against the natural course and outcome of the disorder.

RESEARCH CLOSE-UP

A Study of Facilitated Communication

Facilitated communication is a technique that has created both excited optimism and deep skepticism concerning the possibilities for treating autism. In facilitated communication, a "facilitator" supports the hand and arm of a disabled individual, thus allowing the child to type on a keyboard. The technique was developed in Australia by the educator Rosemary Crossley, who originally used it with people with motor disabilities such as cerebral palsy (Crossley & McDonald, 1980). It was brought to the United States by the Australian special educator Douglas Biklen, who has used the technique with autism. Biklen (1992) has claimed that the technique allows people with autism to express themselves. He reports that people with autism show insight, awareness, and literary talent. He also maintains that they sometimes report traumatic experiences during facilitated communication.

Many popular media sources, including nationally televised programs, have portrayed facilitated communication enthusiastically and uncritically. Eager for a breakthrough cure, many relatives of people with autism have embraced the technique. Is facilitated communication a legitimate breakthrough?

Whereas Biklen (1992) argues for a case study approach to facilitated communication and invariably finds positive results, independent investigators have conducted more systematic studies of the technique. One such study was carried out by Eberlin, McConnachie, Igel, and Volpe (1993), who investigated facilitated communication in 21 adolescents diagnosed with autism and 10 adult facilitators who were enthusiastic about the technique.

The research study involved four primary procedures. First, in the baseline condition the adolescents with autism were asked a variety of questions and allowed to type or otherwise communicate their answers to the best of their abilities. A special, alphabetically configured keyboard was used for typing in this and all other conditions. Second, in the pretest the adolescents responded to the same questions as in the first condition, but they were encouraged to type their answers with the aid of the facilitator, who was screened from hearing or seeing the questions being asked. Third, in the free response condition the adolescents were asked to respond to questions with the aid of the facilitator after the facilitator had received 20 hours of training in the technique. In this condition, the facilitator could see and hear the questions being asked. Finally, in the posttest the adolescents were asked to respond to the identical questions as in the first and second conditions with the aid of the facilitator. The facilitators were screened again in this last condition.

Test questions included items from an intelligence test and personal questions like "What is your favorite food?" Results indicated that responses to the questions were *worse* during the facilitated communication pretest than they had been during baseline. (Some of the adolescents were able to communicate with words or gestures on their own, at least to a minimal degree.) For example, 14 of 21 subjects were able to answer at least one personal question correctly during the baseline, but only 3 subjects did so with facilitated communication at pretest. (A few subjects could type accurately on their own, thus explaining the correct answers.) Scoring of correct answers was very liberal. For example, a response of "APPXYZ" was judged to be the correct answer "apple" on the pretest.

Results obtained from a few subjects during the free response condition contrasted dramatically with the pretest findings. For example, before facilitated communication, one subject was able to communicate only by using two manual signs. When asked to define emotion during free response, however, with the aid of a facilitator this same subject typed "EMOTION ZOME-THIN* FEEL EXPREZ."

This response and other improvements with facilitated communication surely would be more impressive if we did not know the results of the next phase of study. Responses during the facilitated communication posttest, when facilitators were screened from the questions, were again significantly *worse* than baseline. Only five subjects answered at least one question correctly.

▲ A teacher attempting facilitated communication with a student with autistic disorder. Evidence indicates that the technique does *not* allow us to communicate with people with autistic disorder.

Apparently, the facilitators were experiencing something akin to the effect of a Ouija board. Their own thoughts subtly influenced the "response" they "facilitated." In fact, the Science Working Group on Facilitated Communication of the American Psychological Association recently reviewed numerous studies of the technique and concluded that no evidence supports the effectiveness of facilitated communication (Jacobson, Mulick, & Schwartz, 1995).

"Breakthrough" treatments like facilitated communication have a ready audience. Mentally ill people and their relatives, frustrated professionals, and the popular media often are desperate for dramatic advances and therefore are uncritical and susceptible to inadequately documented claims. Although we share the desire for spectacular and successful treatments, once again we urge you to be healthy skeptics. The burden of proof falls upon the shoulders of the proponent of a treatment (see Research Methods in Chapter 1). When a truly effective new treatment is discovered, it will not be difficult to demonstrate its effectiveness using sound scientific methods. ■

COURSE AND OUTCOME

Unfortunately, autism is a lifelong disorder. In one study of 63 children with autism who were followed into adulthood, only 1 was functioning in what could be considered the normal range. Another 22 children achieved fair to good adjustment as adults. Even this group exhibited social isolation and odd behavior, however, and required some form of specialized supervision. The remainder of the people with autism in the study (over 60 percent) were living in institutions or other special settings at the time of follow-up (Rutter, 1970). This gloomy picture is consistent with the findings painted by several similar longitudinal investigations (Schreibman, 1988), although Asperger's disorder has a more optimistic prognosis (Gillberg, 1991).

Two developmental periods are especially important to the course of autism: the early preschool years and early adolescence. Children who have developed language skills by the age of 5 or 6 have a significantly more positive prognosis than do those who have no or severely limited speech at this age. Not surprisingly, higher IQ as measured during the early school years also is a positive prognostic indicator (Schreibman, 1988).

The other key developmental period in autism is early adolescence. During the early teen years, the cognitive and social skills of some children with autism improve notably, whereas those of others decline. Scientists cannot yet predict which path any given child will follow. Adolescence is also important because as many as half of all teenagers with autism develop seizure disorders (Wing, 1988).

Case studies offer a sobering view of even good outcomes for autism. One example is the case of Jerry, a 31-year-old man who had been diagnosed with autism by Kanner (Bemporad, 1979). At the time of the case study, Jerry was living by himself in an apartment near his parents' home. Watching television was Jerry's only leisure activity, and he spent most of his free time in front of the set. At the time of the interview, Jerry was nearing completion of a college degree. He also held a part-time job. However, he needed extremely detailed instructions in order to complete his work, because he had great difficulty thinking of an original way to attack a problem.

At 31, Jerry had no friends and only a vague interest in social relationships. People seemed frightening to him, not so much because he feared ridicule or rejection, but because they were so unpredictable. Jerry compulsively needed routine, and people did not repeat identical behaviors over and over again. He apparently had little insight into his social isolation, blaming his social problems on the evils of society.

Other aspects of his early symptoms also continued into adult life. Although Jerry could communicate well, his imagination was severely constrained. He reported no fantasies or daydreams. His earlier need for sameness also stayed with him into adulthood. Much of his day was filled with rituals. It took him 2 hours to take a shower, for example, because of his need to arrange things just right. On occasion, he would still lose himself in self-stimulation, rocking back and forth repeatedly.

Jerry's memories of his childhood are especially interesting. Although he had been seriously disturbed, Jerry was a high-functioning child. When he was 8 years old, his IQ was measured at 101. Here are some of the interviewer's comments on Jerry's recollection of his childhood:

> His childhood experience could be summarized as consisting of two predominant experiential states: confusion and terror. The recurrent theme that ran through all of Jerry's recollections was that of living in a frightening world presenting painful stimuli that could not be mastered. Noises were unbearably loud, smells overpowering. Nothing seemed constant; everything was unpredictable and strange. Animate beings were a particular problem. Dogs were remembered as eerie and terrifying. As a child, he believed they were somehow humanoid (since they moved of their own volition, etc.), yet they were not really human, a puzzle that mystified him. . . . He was also frightened of other children . . . he could never predict or understand their behavior. . . . He said that he realized he was a burden to his family because he stuttered so much. Obviously, among all of his problems the stuttering caused the least concern to his parents; yet, after all these years, Jerry could still not judge the relative significance of his various problems. (Bemporad, 1979, pp. 192–193)

Despite his many successes, Jerry continued to be isolated from other people and frightened and puzzled by much of the world around him. Still, he achieved a life that is far superior to the typical course of autism. Can treatment help other children with pervasive developmental disorders to lead more normal lives?

MEDICATION

A huge variety of medications have been used to treat autism, including antipsychotics, antidepressants, amphetamines, psychedelics, and megavitamins. Unfortunately, none of these medications is an effective treatment for autism, and few show much promise.

Of all the medications, fenfluramine has generated the most excitement. Fenfluramine was used initially as an experimental treatment for autism based on the hypothesis that some symptoms of autism are caused by excess levels of serotonin (Geller et al., 1982). In several studies by the UCLA group that first experimented with the drug, fenfluramine was reported to reduce blood serotonin levels and to improve the cognitive performance and social behavior of children with autism (Geller et al., 1982; Ritvo et al., 1984).

Some investigators replicated the positive findings of the UCLA group (e.g., Campbell et al., 1986). Unfortunately, other researchers have found few positive benefits and several side effects associated with fenfluramine treatment. Fenfluramine does reduce serotonin blood levels, but several independent researchers have not found improved functioning among children with autism as a result (Ekman et al., 1989; Sherman et al., 1989). In any case, the effects of fenfluramine clearly are not dramatic. This fact, together with side effects that include the possibility of brain damage, has led some experts to recommend against further use of fenfluramine in treating autistic disorder (McDougle, Price, & Volkmar, 1994).

Other medications may help alleviate aspects of some symptoms of autism. Certain antipsychotic medications, particularly haloperidol (Haldol), help the management and education of children with autism. Recently, medications used in treating obsessive–compulsive disorder (e.g., clomipramine; see Chapter 6) have been found to help with some stereotyped behavior in autistic disorder (Lewis, 1996). However, all medications fall far short of "curing" autism (Lewis, 1996; Schreibman, 1988).

PSYCHOTHERAPY: INTENSIVE BEHAVIOR MODIFICATION

Several theorists and clinicians have attempted to treat autism with various types of psychodynamic therapy. Based on the "refrigerator parent" hypothesis, many of these treatments attempted to provide nurturing, supportive environments that would allow children with autism to form attachments with surrogate caretakers (e.g., Bettelheim, 1967). Rejection of theories of psychological etiology, together with evidence on the ineffectiveness of psychodynamic therapies (Bartak & Rutter, 1973), have caused responsible professionals to abandon this avenue of treatment.

Intensive behavior modification using operant conditioning techniques is a much more promising approach. Behavior therapists have focused on treating the specific symptoms of autism, including communication deficits, self-care skills, and self-stimulatory or self-destructive behavior. Even within these different symptom areas, behavior modification emphasizes very specific and small goals. In attempting to teach language, for example, the therapist might spend hours, days, or weeks teaching the pronunciation of a specific syllable. Months of intensive effort may be needed to teach a small number of words and phrases. The lack of imitation among many children with autism is one reason why so much effort goes into achieving such modest goals.

If the first goal of behavior modification is to identify very specific target behaviors, the second is to gain control over these behaviors through the use of reinforcement and punishment. Unlike normal children, who are reinforced by social interest and approval, children with autism do not understand ordinary praise, or they may find all social interaction unpleasant. For these reasons, the child's successful efforts must be rewarded repeatedly with primary reinforcers such as a favorite food, at least in the beginning phases of treatment.

An example helps to illustrate the level of detail of behavior modification programs. A common goal in treating echolalia is to teach the child to respond by answering questions rather than repeating them. As an early step in treatment, a target behavior might be to teach the child to respond to the question "What is your name?" with the correct answer "Joshua."

In order to bring this specific response under the control of the therapist, initially it may be necessary to reward the child for simply echoing. Therapist: "What is your name?" Child: "What is your name?" Reward. This first step may have to be repeated hundreds of times over the course of several days.

A logical next step would be to teach the child to echo both the question and the response. Therapist: "What is your name? . . . Joshua." Child: "What is your name? . . . Joshua." Reward. Again, hundreds of repetitions may be necessary.

Gradually, the behavior therapist sets slightly more difficult goals, rewarding only increasingly accurate approximations of the correct response. One such intermediate step might be to echo the question "What is your name?" in a whisper and repeat the response "Joshua" in a normal tone of voice. Over a period of days, even weeks, the child learns to respond "Joshua" to the question, "What is your name?"

Similar detailed strategies are used to teach children with autism other language skills. In the hope of speeding the process, some therapists have used sign language to teach

communication to children with autism (Carr, 1982). Unfortunately, this method has not led to a breakthrough. The communication deficits in autism apparently are more basic than receptive or expressive problems with spoken language. Behavior modification remains a painfully slow process that differs greatly from the way in which children normally learn to speak. The intensity and detail of these necessary efforts remind us that normal children come into the world remarkably well equipped to acquire language.

In addition to teaching communication skills, behavior therapists who work with children with pervasive developmental disorders have concentrated on reducing the excesses of self-stimulation, self-injurious behavior, and general disruptiveness, as well as teaching new skills to eliminate behavioral deficits in self-care and social behavior (Schreibman, 1988). Behavior modification programs have been successful with some behavioral excesses, particularly self-injury, but the treatments are controversial because they typically rely on punishment. A slap or a mild electric shock can reduce or eliminate such potentially dangerous behaviors as head banging, but are such aversive treatments justified? Obviously, we all would prefer an alternative that did not involve punishment, but this option is currently not available. What is the appropriate ethical choice? Should a self-injurious child with autism be punished as a means of eliminating head banging, or is it preferable to use restraints (such as having the child wear a helmet) to deal with the behavior? This is a question that confronts therapists, parents, and others concerned with the treatment and protection of children with autism. Which option would you choose?

In other areas of intervention, behavior therapists have been fairly successful in teaching self-care skills and less successful in teaching social responsiveness. As Schreibman (1988) noted in her review of attempts to modify the social isolation of children with autistic disorder, "It is perhaps prophetic that the behavior characteristic which most uniquely defines autism, is also the one that has proven the most difficult to understand and treat" (p. 118).

Although behavior therapy often focuses on specific target behaviors, ultimately the important question is: To what extent does treatment

▲ O. Ivar Lovaas, a psychologist at UCLA, is a leader in using behavior modification to treat children with autistic disorder.

improve the entire syndrome of autism? Research has demonstrated that children with autism can learn specific target behaviors, but do intensive training efforts bring about improvements that are clinically significant?

An optimistic answer to this question has been provided by O. Ivar Lovaas, a psychologist at UCLA who is an acknowledged leader in behavior modification for autism. In a comprehensive report on the efforts of his research team, Lovaas (1987) compared the outcomes of three groups of children with autism: 19 children who received intensive behavior modification; 19 children who were referred to the program but who received less intensive treatment due to the unavailability of therapists; and 21 children who were seen elsewhere. In this study, all children received independent diagnoses of autism. Children with extremely low IQ scores were excluded, and treatment began before the children were 4 years of age. The children in the treatment group received the types of interventions described above, including both reinforcement and punishment procedures. In fact, they were treated 40 hours a week for a period of more than 2 years.

No differences among the three groups of children were found before treatment began. Assessments following treatment were conducted between the ages of 6 and 7, at the time when the children ordinarily would have finished the first grade. In the intensive behavior modification group, 9 children (47 percent) completed first grade in a normal school. Eight more children (42 percent) passed first grade in a special class for children who cannot speak. In comparison, only 1 child (2 percent) in the two control groups completed first grade in a normal classroom. In addition, 18 children (45 percent) in the control groups completed first-grade classes for aphasic children. Data on these findings are summarized in Table 15–7. In examining this table, you should note the strong relation between IQ and classroom placement. You also should note the low mean IQ levels of the children, despite the investigators' attempts to screen out the most severely impaired children.

These data provide a reason for some optimism, and we applaud the efforts of Lovaas and others who have used behavior therapy to teach skills to children with autism. Despite the fact that autism seems to be caused by neurological abnormalities, the most effective

Group	Classroom	N	(%)	Mean IQ
Intensive Behavior Modification	Normal	9	(47)	107
	Aphasic	8	(42)	74
	Retarded	2	(11)	30
Limited Treatment	Normal	0	(0)	—
	Aphasic	8	(42)	74
	Retarded	11	(58)	36
No Treatment	Normal	1	(5)	99
	Aphasic	10	(48)	67
	Retarded	10	(48)	44

TABLE 15-7

Educational Placement and IQ of Children with Autistic Disorder Following Behavior Modification or Alternative Treatments

Source: From O. I. Lovaas, 1987, Behavioral treatment and normal educational and intellectual functioning in young autistic children, *Journal of Consulting and Clinical Psychology, 55,* 3–9.

treatment for the disorder is highly structured and intensive operant behavior therapy (Rutter, 1996; Schreibman, 1988). Still, cautions must be raised. Are the children who passed first grade functioning normally in other respects? Would treatment have been as effective if it had not begun so early in life? Because pretreatment IQ predicted outcome (Lovaas, 1987), does behavior modification produce dramatic changes only with children who are high-functioning? What about the 53 percent of children who received intensive therapy but who were not in normal classrooms? Why have other researchers and clinicians found much more modest benefits following intensive behavior modification?

Perhaps the most important question about the effectiveness of behavior modification is its cost. Remember that the children in the intensive behavior modification group were treated for 40 hours per week for a period of more than 2 years. At the same time, children in the "limited treatment" control group received almost 10 hours of weekly treatment, yet they showed few improvements. The expenses associated with early but effective treatment clearly are far less than those involved in a lifetime of care (Lovaas, 1987). Still, our question is this: How do we, as a society, justify devoting large amounts of resources to the rare problem of autism, when in comparison we neglect intervention efforts with the much more common—and in many ways more treatable—problem of mental retardation?

Summary

Mental retardation is defined by (1) significantly subaverage intellectual functioning, (2) existing concurrently with related limitations in adaptive skills, and (3) an onset before age 18. Intellectual functioning must be determined by an individualized IQ test. Many important criticisms have been raised about IQ tests, but the tests are reliable and valid (if imperfect) predictors of academic performance. Many people who have significantly subaverage IQs function adequately in the world, however, because they show no deficits in adaptive behavior. Such people are not considered to have mental retardation.

The DSM-IV divides **mental retardation** into four levels based on IQ scores. People with mild mental retardation complete their education at the sixth-grade level and live in the community with little or no support. This is by far the most common category of mental retardation. People with moderate mental retardation reach a second-grade level of academic performance and require careful supervision in independent living. Severe mental retardation is characterized by major limitations in development and communication and necessitates close supervision. Finally, profound mental retardation often is accompanied by many physical handicaps and sharply restricted development, and it demands constant supervision in the community or in institutions.

The etiology of mental retardation can be grouped into cases caused by known biological abnormalities and cases resulting from normal variations in IQ. **Down syndrome,** which is caused by an extra chromosome on the 21st pair, is the most common of the known biological causes of mental retardation. **Fragile-X syndrome,** the second leading biological cause, is a genetic disorder indicated by a weakening of the X sex chromosome. Other known biological causes include **phenylketonuria (PKU),** an inherited metabolic deficiency; infectious diseases transmitted to the fetus during pregnancy or birth, such as rubella, syphilis, and genital herpes; excessive maternal alcohol consumption or drug use during pregnancy; Rh

incompatibility; and malnutrition, premature birth, and low birth weight.

So-called **cultural-familial retardation** comprises most cases of mental retardation. Retardation typically is mild, and there is no known specific etiology. An important debate about cultural-familial retardation is the relative importance of normal genetic variation and deprived psychosocial environments in its development.

Many cases of mental retardation can be prevented by adequate health care before and during pregnancy. Testing for chromosomal or genetic abnormalities in the fetus and considering selective abortion is a more controversial means of preventing retardation. Early psychoeducational programs also may prevent some cases of mental retardation by improving adaptive behavior if not by increasing IQ scores. Treatments for mental retardation include preschool stimulation programs, medical treatment of physical handicaps, and specialized educational services in school. Finally, a major policy goal is to **normalize** the lives of people with mental retardation through **mainstreaming** in public schools and promoting care in the community.

The **pervasive developmental disorders** involve profound disturbances in relationships, stereotyped activities, and communication difficulties. **Autistic disorder** is the most widely researched pervasive developmental disorder. Social impairments in autism may be relatively mild oddities, but they also may include extreme difficulties in which there is little awareness of the existence of others. One unifying perspective on the social deficits suggests that children with autism lack a "theory of mind." About half of all children with autism fail to develop communicative speech, and the remainder have either highly restricted language abilities or striking oddities in speech. Finally, many people with autism spend hours engaging in self-stimulation or compulsively adhere to rigid daily routines.

Other difficulties associated with autism and the pervasive developmental disorders include apparent sensory deficits and self-injurious behavior. **Savant performance** is an exceptional ability at performing mental feats such as rapid mathematical calculations. Despite such unusual abilities, most people with pervasive developmental disorders do not have exceptional intelligence; rather, they have mental retardation. One exception is **Asperger's disorder,** characterized by the same difficulties that are found in autism except that language acquisition is not impaired.

The pervasive developmental disorders are rare conditions, and they almost certainly are caused by biological abnormalities. Several known causes of mental retardation may also cause pervasive developmental disorders (for example, fragile-X syndrome). Recent evidence also suggests that genetics plays an important role. At this time, there is no easy, effective treatment for these conditions. Intensive behavior modification has shown much promise as a treatment, but the expense and effort involved are considerable. Without intensive treatment over a prolonged period of time, the prognosis for the pervasive developmental disorders is a gloomy one. The majority of people with these conditions require intensive, lifelong care, often within an institution.

Critical Thinking

1. The concept of intelligence can be quite controversial. Is academic performance the same thing as intelligence? How would you define social or practical intelligence? Do you agree that people should be considered mentally retarded only if they have a significantly sub-average IQ *and* deficits in adaptive skills?

2. In some states, children with autism are able to receive more subsidized mental health services than are children with mental retardation. In part, this is because autism is often viewed as an illness that can be cured, whereas mental retardation is seen as an unchangeable characteristic of the person. Do you agree with these views? Do you think it is justifiable to spend more money per child to treat autism than to treat mental retardation?

16

Psychological Disorders of Childhood

s it normal to lie on the floor, kick, scream, and cry if you don't get your way? This certainly is not normal behavior for a 19-year-old college student. However, it is normal, though sometimes obnoxious, for a 2-year-old child to throw a temper tantrum. Similarly, fears of monsters are developmentally normal at the age of 4, but not at the age of 14. We judge abnormal behavior by making comparisons with normal behavior, but what is considered normal changes rapidly during the first 20 years of life. Thus, in evaluating whether a child's behavior is normal or abnormal, the first question we must ask is: How old is the child? Psychologists become concerned only when a child's behavior deviates substantially from age-appropriate *developmental norms*.

Overview

Children and adolescents may suffer from most of the disorders we have covered in earlier chapters. For example, children sometimes develop mood disorders, anxiety disorders, or schizophrenia. With the exception of mental retardation and pervasive developmental disorders, however, all of the psychological disorders we have discussed so far are far more prevalent among adults than among children. An important implication of this epidemiological fact is that children who do suffer from an "adult" disorder depart considerably from developmental norms. Thus their disorder may be especially severe.

Psychological problems that arise more commonly among children than adults are listed in the DSM-IV category Disorders Usually First Diagnosed in Infancy, Childhood, or Adolescence. Other than mental retardation and pervasive developmental disorders (see Chapter 15), the most important disorders in this category are the various **externalizing disorders.** Externalizing disorders create difficulties for the child's external world. They are characterized by children's failure to control their behavior according to the expectations of others—parents, siblings, peers, teachers, and legal authorities.

Perhaps the most familiar externalizing disorder is **attention-deficit/hyperactivity disorder (ADHD),** a prevalent behavior problem that is particularly noticeable in school and is characterized by inattention, overactivity, and impulsivity. ADHD is commonly treated with medication and is typically viewed as having a biological cause. As such, ADHD often is contrasted with **oppositional defiant disorder (ODD),** an externalizing disorder characterized by negative, hostile, and defiant behavior that also is prevalent among school-aged children. **Conduct disorder (CD)** is a problem similar to oppositional defiant disorder, except the rule violations are much more serious in conduct disorder, which is more common among adolescents than younger children. In contrast to ADHD, conventional wisdom views ODD (and CD) as a psychological problem that requires psychological treatment. We consider the assumed and actual distinctions between ADHD and ODD at some length in this chapter, and we highlight the complication of comorbidity: Many schoolchildren have *both* ADHD and ODD. For now, you simply should know that externalizing disorders are the most commonly diagnosed disorders of childhood, accounting for about half of all children in treatment (Kazdin, 1995). For these

▼ Temper tantrums are a normal part of child development during the "terrible twos." Awareness of developmental norms is essential for evaluating abnormal behavior in children.

reasons, we focus most of this chapter on externalizing disorders.

Internalizing disorders are psychological problems that primarily affect the child's internal world—for example, excessive anxiety or sadness. The DSM-IV does not list internalizing disorders as separate psychological disorders of childhood; rather, it notes that children may qualify for many "adult" diagnoses, such as anxiety or mood disorders. However, we think it is important to take a *developmental psychopathology* approach (see Chapter 2) and highlight children's unique experience of anxiety and depression. Children do not interpret events or express emotions in the same manner as adults; developmental norms change rapidly with age; and the family, peer, and school contexts typically affect children more dramatically than they affect adults. Thus we suggest that children's mood and anxiety disorders are not simply miniature versions of adult diagnoses.

In this chapter we also introduce many of the 26 *additional* diagnoses included in the DSM-IV's list of disorders usually first diagnosed during childhood. An important and familiar example of these psychological problems are **learning disorders,** substantial discrepancies between academic achievement and intellectual ability.

Our coverage of many of these other childhood disorders is necessarily limited, not only by their shear number but also by questions we have about the appropriateness of several of these diagnostic categories.

Few children or adolescents identify themselves as having a psychological problem. Instead, some adult, often a parent or teacher, decides that a child is emotionally troubled. Not surprisingly, children often disagree with the parent's or teacher's evaluation. Some children are unable to recognize or admit to their disturbed feelings. In other cases, however, the child may be right, and the adult may be wrong. In a sense, children sometimes serve as "projective tests" for adults—depressed parents may overinterpret the significance of children's normal moodiness, or intolerant teachers may see normal misbehavior as a sign of an externalizing disorder. Not only do children and adults often see things differently, but different adults also frequently disagree in their evaluation of a child's behavior. Such conflicting perceptions on the normality or abnormality of children's behavior challenge the assessment and classification of childhood disorders, because it is often unclear who is objective and who is biased, as illustrated in the following case study.

CASE STUDY

Conflicts About Externalizing Behavior

Jeremy W., an 8-year-old boy, was brought to a clinical psychologist by his mother following the recommendations of his second-grade teacher and a school counselor. Mrs. W. came to the psychologist reluctantly, because she was not sure if she agreed with the suggestions of the school personnel. In fact, Mrs. W. wasn't sure if she agreed with her husband about what was going on with Jeremy.

According to Mrs. W., Jeremy was constantly in trouble at school. His teacher reprimanded Jeremy daily for disrupting the class, not paying attention, and failing to finish his work. The teacher felt that her attempts at discipline had little effect. Sometimes Jeremy would listen for awhile, but soon he was pestering another child, talking out of turn, or simply staring off into space. Lately, Jeremy had begun to talk back when he was disciplined, and his

teacher had sent him to the principal's office several times in the past month.

The psychologist confirmed this information in a subsequent telephone call to the school. At that time, the teacher also noted that Jeremy had no real friends in school, and that other kids thought of him as a "pain." The teacher had referred Jeremy to a school counselor, who gave him several academic tests. According to an individualized intelligence test, Jeremy had an IQ of 108. However, his achievement test scores indicated that he was achieving at a first-grade level, almost a year behind his current grade level. The school counselor suspected that Jeremy might have a learning disorder, but she also thought that his behavior problems were interfering with his learning. She concluded that Jeremy should remain in his regular classroom for the present. As a first step, the counselor recommended therapy for Jeremy and perhaps for his parents. After treatment, she would reevaluate him for possible placement in a "resource room," a special class for students with learning problems.

Mrs. W. was frightened by the counselor's suggestion that Jeremy might be "emotionally disturbed" or "learning disordered." According to his mother, Jeremy was somewhat difficult to manage at home, but she had never considered the possibility that he needed psychological help. Jeremy had been a handful ever since the "terrible twos," but in her view, he had never been a bad child. Instead, Mrs. W. thought that Jeremy expressed himself better through actions than words. In this respect, he was the opposite of his 11-year-old sister, who was an A and B student. Mrs. W. was not convinced that Jeremy's teacher was the best person to work with him, but she did agree that he was having problems in school. In her mind, Jeremy was developing low self-esteem, and many of his actions were attempts to get attention.

According to Mrs. W., Jeremy's father spent very little time with him. Mr. W. worked long hours on his construction job, and he often was off with his friends on weekends. Mrs. W. said that her husband was of little help even when he was home. He would tell his wife that it was her job to take care of the kids—he needed his rest. With tears in her eyes, Mrs. W. said that she needed a rest, too.

In any case, Mr. W. was not concerned about Jeremy's behavior or his schoolwork. Instead, he thought that Jeremy was just "all boy" and not much of a student—just like Mr. W. was as a child. He refused to take time off from work to see a psychologist.

In confidence, Mrs. W. said that she too saw a lot of his father in Jeremy—too much of him, in fact. She got no support from her husband in disciplining Jeremy or in encouraging him in his schoolwork. She blamed her husband for Jeremy's problems, and she was secretly furious with him. She knew that Jeremy had to do well in school in order to live a better life, and she felt like a failure as a mother. She was willing to try anything to help Jeremy, but she doubted that there was anything she could do without her husband's support. ∎

The case of Jeremy W. illustrates many of the complicated issues that arise in assessing and treating children's psychological problems. Is Jeremy a disobedient child, as his teacher thinks? A learning-disordered child, as suggested by the school counselor? An emotionally disturbed child, as his mother fears? Or is he simply "all boy," as his father claims? What about Jeremy? How does he feel about himself, about his family, and about his schoolwork and his friendships at school?

Mental health professionals who treat children are constantly vexed by such difficult questions, and treatment often begins with an attempt to achieve consensus about the nature of a child's problem. The overriding goal is to reach an accurate diagnosis, but another goal is to reduce the conflicts between adults that often contribute to a child's misbehavior. In Jeremy's case, Mr. and Mrs. W. may need to learn to support each other and to present a "united front" to Jeremy, and to do so they may need to resolve issues in their marriage. Because it is so important for adults to work together, many psychologists prefer to see children in *family therapy* rather than treat children alone. Many psychologists also work to coordinate treatment between the home and the school and to establish better communication and cooperation between parents and teachers.

Of course, Jeremy is also at least part of the problem. If we can trust his teacher's report—and experienced child clinical psychologists do trust teachers—Jeremy clearly has some type of externalizing problem. The question is: What is the problem, and why does he have it? Perhaps Jeremy's behavior is simply a reaction to his parents' conflicts, and he will get better if they work out their differences. Or perhaps Jeremy is a troubled child who is causing some of these conflicts, not just reacting to them. Mr. and Mrs. W. both felt that Jeremy and his father were a lot alike. Could Jeremy have learned or inherited some of his father's characteristics? As we have alluded, different answers to these questions are implied by the diagnosis of attention-deficit/hyperactivity disorder versus oppositional defiant disorder. We can begin to understand this important distinction for Jeremy and for other children by considering the typical symptoms of externalizing disorders.

Typical Symptoms: Externalizing Disorders

Externalizing disorders may be characterized by a broad range of specific transgressions ranging from defying rules at home to daydreaming and earning poor grades in school to committing very serious criminal acts like robbery, rape, or murder. Psychologists organize these many, specific problem behaviors into broader categories of symptoms, including rule violations; negativity, anger, and aggression; impulsivity; hyperactivity; and attention deficits. Rule violations and negativity, anger, and aggression are more characteristic of oppositional defiant disorder and related conduct problems. Impulsivity, hyperactivity, and attention deficits are symptoms of attention-deficit/hyperactivity disorder.

Rule Violations

Many externalizing symptoms are characterized by violations of age-appropriate social rules. Rule violations may include disobeying parents or teachers, violating social or peer group norms (e.g., annoying others), and perhaps violating the law. All children violate at least some social rules, of course, and we often admire an innocent and clever rule breaker. For example, Mark Twain's fictional character Tom Sawyer broke all kinds of rules, but we still view Tom as the prototypical "all-American boy." Tom Sawyer decidedly was not a candidate for psychotherapy! Similarly, we see Calvin of the Calvin and Hobbes cartoons as devilish, but he is not really "bad," and we certainly do not view him as "sick."

SERIOUSNESS OF CHILDREN'S RULE VIOLATIONS

Some misconduct is normal, perhaps even healthy, for children. However, the rule violations found in externalizing disorders are not trivial and are far from "cute." Many schoolteachers lament that they spend far too much time disciplining children—a circumstance that is frustrating to teachers and unfair to well-behaved youngsters in the classroom. Even more serious, the FBI reports that 29 percent of arrests for index offenses—major crimes including murder, forcible rape, and robbery—are of juveniles under the age of 18 (FBI, 1992). Other evidence indicates that the worst 5 percent of juvenile offenders account for about half of all juvenile arrests (Farrington, Ohlin, & Wilson, 1986).

Several factors influence how we evaluate the seriousness of children's rule violations. Externalizing behavior is a far greater concern when it is frequent, intense, lasting, and pervasive. That is, externalizing behavior is more problematic when it is part of a *syndrome*, or cluster of problems, than when it is a *symptom* that occurs in isolation. The existence of an externalizing syndrome has been demonstrated consistently by statistical analysis (factor analysis) of checklists on which parents or teachers rate children's psychological symptoms. Moreover, agreement among adult raters typically is fairly high for this externalizing dimension (Achenbach, McConaughy, & Howell, 1987).

CHILDREN'S AGE AND RULE VIOLATIONS

Children of different ages are likely to violate very different rules. A preschooler with an externalizing problem is likely to be disobedient to his parents and uncooperative with other children. During the school years, he or she is more likely to be disruptive in the classroom, uncooperative on the playground, or defiant at home. By adolescence, the problem teenager may be failing in school, ignoring all discipline at home, hanging out with delinquent peers, and perhaps violating the law.

Children's age is also important to consider in relation to the timing as well as the nature of rule violations. All children violate rules, but children with externalizing problems violate rules at a younger age than is developmentally normal (Loeber, 1988). For example, most young people experiment with smoking, alcohol, or sexuality, but children with externalizing disorders do so at a notably younger age.

Calvin and Hobbes by Bill Watterson

ADOLESCENCE-LIMITED VERSUS LIFE-COURSE-PERSISTENT EXTERNALIZING BEHAVIOR

We must be especially aware of the developmental norms for committing rule violations during the teen years, as adolescence is a stage of normal development that borders on the abnormal—at least from the perspective of adults. Teenagers often violate the rules laid down by parents, teachers, and society as a means of asserting their independence and perhaps of conforming to the rules of their peer group (see Figure 16–1). Because of this normative increase in externalizing behavior, it is essential to distinguish between externalizing behavior that is *adolescent-limited*—that ends along with the teen years—and *life-course-persistent* antisocial behavior that continues into adult life (Moffitt, 1993).

In fact, externalizing problems that begin *before* adolescence are more likely to persist over the individual's life course than are problems that begin *during* adolescence. It is counterintuitive, but true, that scientists are better able to predict adult antisocial behavior from information obtained during childhood than from information obtained during adolescence (Farrington, Ohlin, & Wilson, 1986; Loeber, 1988; Moffitt, 1993).

The vast majority of antisocial adults do have a history of adolescent social and legal rule violations (see Chapter 9). However, so many teenagers violate at least some rules that, in order to distinguish life-course-persistent antisocial behavior, scientists need to look back in time to a stage of development (childhood) when conformity, not rebellion, was the norm (Moffitt, 1993).

Negativity, Anger, and Aggression

Negativity, anger, and aggression also are symptoms of oppositional defiant disorder and related externalizing problems. These symptoms range from oppositional behavior, stubbornness, and uncooperativeness, particularly among younger children, to hostility, threats, and causing physical injury to others, particularly among adolescents. In addition to the harmful effects of interpersonal aggression, these symptoms are important because they shed light on the motivations of a child with an externalizing disorder. We may chuckle at the innocent adventures of a Calvin or a Tom Sawyer, but we judge externalizing behavior harshly if the perpetrator is uncaring, angry, and callous.

The reason for this is that children's negativity, anger, and aggression strongly influence our judgments about their *intent* and *remorse*. As in our legal system, we judge externalizing behavior more harshly when the actions are selfishly motivated and when perpetrators express little regret about the consequences of their actions. You might wonder about Jeremy W.'s private motivations, for example, and judge him differently based on whether he is an angry child who cares little about being "bad" or an impulsive child who tries but just cannot consistently be "good." Externalizing behavior that is motivated by anger is very different from externalizing behavior that is more innocent or impulsive, not only for rendering social judgments but also in distinguishing between attention-deficit/hyperactivity disorder and oppositional defiant disorder.

Impulsivity

Impulsivity is acting before thinking, and it is a symptom that characterizes ADHD rather than ODD. Children with ADHD often fail, and seem unable, to control many of their impulses. They may have trouble waiting their turn, blurt out answers in class, intrude into the activities of other children, or cause accidents around the

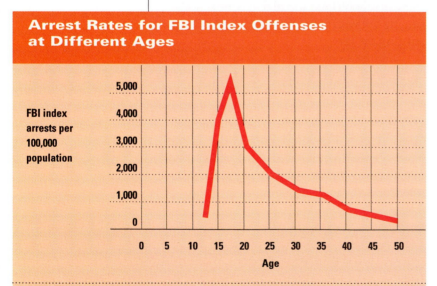

Arrest Rates for FBI Index Offenses at Different Ages

FBI index arrests per 100,000 population

FIGURE 16-1: Arrest rates across age for the Federal Bureau of Investigation's index offenses in 1980, which include homicide, forcible rape, robbery, aggravated assault, burglary, larceny, and auto theft.

Source: A. Blumstein, J. Cohen, and D.P. Farrington, 1980, Criminal career research: Its value for criminology, *Criminology, 26,* 11.

house, school, or playground. Such actions certainly are annoying and disruptive to others, but the impulsive behavior in ADHD is more innocent than the negativity and anger in ODD. In fact, the impulsive behavior of the youngster with ADHD is much the opposite of intentional aggression. Children with ADHD generally want to be "good," not "bad," but they seem unable to control their behavior according to situational demands.

At least one leading researcher has asserted that impulsive tendencies may be *the* hallmark symptom of attention-deficit/hyperactivity disorder (Barkley, 1990). However, impulsivity has been studied much less frequently than the two primary symptoms of ADHD, hyperactivity and attention deficits.

Hyperactivity

Hyperactivity, the most obvious symptom of ADHD, often is manifested as squirming, fidgeting, or restless behavior. Children with this symptom are described as being in constant motion, and they have difficulty engaging in quiet activities, even leisure ones like watching television. Hyperactivity is found across situations, even during sleep, but it is much more notable in structured settings than in unstructured ones (Barkley, 1988, 1990). In particular, hyperactive behavior is much more noticeable in the classroom than in other circumstances, and this is one reason why ADHD typically is diagnosed for the first time during the early school years.

Situational influences can complicate the evaluation of hyperactivity, because children who are extremely active in the classroom may be relatively controlled in the pediatrician's or the psychologist's office. In one study, only 20 percent of children with attention-deficit/hyperactivity disorder were overly active during an examination in the pediatrician's office (Sleator & Ullmann, 1981). Consequently, reports from teachers are critical in identifying hyperactive behavior. The Conners Teacher Rating Scale is a measure commonly used by pediatricians and other professionals in order to assess teacher ratings of hyperactivity and other symptoms of ADHD in the classroom (see Figure 16–2).

ATTENTION DEFICITS

Attention deficit or inattention is the third classic symptom of attention-deficit/

hyperactivity disorder. Attention deficits are characterized by distractibility, frequent shifts from one uncompleted activity to another, careless mistakes, poor organization or effort, and general "spaciness," for example, not listening well or responding to questions. A particular attentional problem is "staying on task," or what has been termed difficulties with *sustained attention* (Douglas & Peters, 1979). Numerous studies have documented that children with ADHD perform poorly on the *continuous performance test,* a laboratory task that requires the subject to monitor and respond to numbers or letters presented on a computer screen (Douglas, 1983; see Chapter 12). As with impulsivity, the ADHD child's inattention is not intentional or oppositional; rather, it reflects an inability to maintain a focus despite an apparent desire to do so.

Brief Conners Teacher Rating Scale for Attention-Deficit/Hyperactivity Disorder

Observation	Degree of Activity			
CLASSROOM BEHAVIOR	**(0)** Not At All	**(1)** Just a Little	**(2)** Pretty Much	**(3)** Very Much
Constantly fidgeting				
Demands must be met immediately— easily frustrated				
Restless or overactive				
Excitable, impulsive				
Inattentive, easily distracted				
Fails to finish things he starts— short attention span				
Cries often and easily				
Disturbs other children				
Mood changes quickly and drastically				
Temper outbursts; explosive and unpredictable behavior				

FIGURE 16-2: Psychologists often ask teachers to complete this ten-item scale as a screening device for ADHD. A total score of 15 (mean of 1.5) or greater suggests that a child may have ADHD.

Source: C.K. Conners, 1969, A teacher rating scale for use with drug studies with children, *American Journal of Psychiatry, 126,* 884–888.

Typical Symptoms: Internalizing Disorders

Children's *internalizing symptoms* include sadness, fears, and somatic complaints, as well as other indicators of mood and anxiety disorders—for example, feeling worthless or tense. As we have noted, the DSM-IV does not have a separate category for children's internalizing disorders, but the manual does identify some unique ways in which children experience the symptoms of mood and anxiety disorders. When diagnosing major depressive episodes among children and adolescents, for example, the manual allows the clinician to substitute "irritable mood" for "depressed mood." The manual's authors realized that children sometimes act angry when they are feeling sad, and, more generally, that children may express their feelings in unique ways, or they may hide their true emotions, especially when talking to adults.

Another example of how the DSM deals with symptoms in children involves the diagnosis of phobia. In contrast to adults, children are not required to recognize that their fears are unreasonable. This suggests that children may have limited insight into their problems. More generally, young children may lack the *cognitive capacity* to experience some of the internalizing symptoms found among adults with the same or similar disorder.

Internalizing Symptoms and Normal Development: A Challenge for Research

These provisions in the DSM-IV recognize that children's capacity to recognize emotions emerges over the course of development, as does their ability to express—and to mask—their own feelings (Lewis & Michalson, 1983). Unfortunately, the course of children's normal emotional development is not well charted, because it is extremely difficult to assess children's feelings. Children, especially at younger ages, typically are not reliable or valid informants about their internal life, and it is much more difficult for adults to evaluate children's inner experiences than it is to observe their externalizing behavior.

Research on depressed children illustrates some of the problems in assessing internalizing symptoms. In one study of children hospitalized for depression, for example, clinicians found a correlation of *zero* between children's and parents' ratings on identical measures of the children's depression (Kazdin, French, & Unis, 1983). In another study, children's and parents' ratings of depression were correlated with very different associated features. Children linked depression with other indices of their internal distress—feelings of hopelessness, low self-esteem, internal attributions for negative events, and external locus of control. In contrast, parents' ratings of children's depression were correlated with ratings of children's externalizing behavior—not with measures of children's internal distress (Kazdin, 1989). Finally, and perhaps of greatest concern, evidence indicates that parents systematically underestimate the extent of depression reported by their children and adolescents (Kazdin & Petti, 1982; Rutter, 1989).

Given parents' and children's widely differing perceptions, psychologists are rightly concerned about a child's depression if *either* a parent *or* a child notes problems. In assessing children's internalizing problems, mental health professionals must obtain information from *multiple informants*—parents, teachers, and the children themselves. More generally, our understanding of children's internalizing symptoms would be aided greatly by better evidence on the normal course of emotional development, a future challenge for developmental psychopathology research.

Children's Fears in Developmental Perspective

Evidence on children's fears offers an example of how research on normal development could improve our understanding of internalizing symptoms in children. Although children cannot identify many of their inner feelings, they are often able to identify their fears, and adults also can observe much of children's fearful behavior. Thus research on the development of children's fears is more advanced than it is for other internalizing symptoms.

▼ **Depression becomes much more common during adolescence, especially among teenage girls.**

Three findings from fear research are especially helpful. First, children develop different fears for the first time at different ages, and the onset of new fears may be sudden and have no apparent cause in the child's environment. For example, infants typically develop a fear of strangers in the months just before their first birthday; preschoolers develop fears of monsters and the dark between the ages of 2 and 4; and children between ages 5 and 8 often develop fears related to school. (To cite one curious example, if you ever dreamed of going to school in your underwear or partially dressed, you are not alone. Such dreams are surprisingly common among school-aged children.) In short, many fears, even those that seem odd or arise suddenly, are developmentally normal, a conclusion that can be reassuring to parents and perhaps to children. A second finding of importance is that some fears, particularly fears of uncontrollable events, are both common and relatively stable across different ages. Third, many other fears, especially specific ones, decline in frequency as children grow older (King et al., 1989). Apparently, children "outgrow" many of their fears, probably by gradually confronting them in everyday life.

Separation Anxiety Disorder and School Refusal

We can illustrate the importance of these three findings by considering the special case of separation anxiety. *Separation anxiety* is distress expressed following separation from an attachment figure, typically a parent or other close caregiver. It is a normal fear that begins to develop around 8 months and peaks around 15 months (Kagan, Kearsley, & Zelazo, 1978). An infant who has tolerated separations in the past may suddenly start to cling, cry, and scream whenever a parent tries to leave, even for a brief separation. Children's upset lessens over time, but even toddlers and preschoolers typically experience distress upon separation,

Calvin and Hobbes   by Bill Watterson

CALVIN AND HOBBES © Watterson. Dist. by UNIVERSAL PRESS SYNDICATE. Reprinted with permission. All rights reserved.

particularly when left in an unfamiliar circumstance.

Although it is a normal response at younger ages, excessive separation anxiety can become a serious problem at older ages if children fail to "outgrow" the reaction. In fact, the DSM-IV contains a diagnosis for **separation anxiety disorder,** which is defined by symptoms such as persistent and excessive worry for the safety of an attachment figure, fears of getting lost or being kidnapped, nightmares with separation themes, and refusal to be alone. For a child to be diagnosed with this disorder, he or she must exhibit three or more of these symptoms for at least 4 weeks.

Separation anxiety disorder is especially problematic when it interferes with school attendance. **School refusal,** also known as *school phobia*, is characterized by an extreme reluctance to go to school and is accompanied by various symptoms of anxiety, such as stomachaches and headaches. Some children are literally school phobic—they are afraid of school or specific aspects of attending school. But in many cases, school refusal can be traced to separation anxiety disorder (Last & Strauss, 1990). Whatever its origins, school refusal is a serious problem that has been reported to account for more than two-thirds of referrals to an anxiety disorders clinic for children.

▼ **Separation anxiety is a normal fear that typically develops just before a baby's first birthday. Toddlers and preschoolers continue to show a degree of distress even during routine separations from their attachment figures.**

Additional Symptoms of Childhood Disorders

In addition to internalizing and externalizing symptoms, it is important to note additional symptoms of children's psychological disorders. We highlight two of the many other symptoms children may experience: troubled peer relationships and specific developmental deviations or delays.

Troubled Peer Relationships

Children with internalizing or externalizing problems often have troubled peer relationships. In fact, research shows that peer relationship difficulties predict future, as well as current, psychological problems among children (Parker & Asher, 1987; Rutter, 1989). Simply put, children who are aggressive and disobedient or shy and withdrawn often are not well liked by their peers. However, different patterns of difficulties relating to peer relationship have been found among children with internalizing and externalizing problems.

Many recent research findings on psychological problems and peer relationships have used the peer sociometric method to assess children's relationships. **Peer sociometrics** evaluate children's relationships by obtaining information on who is "liked most" and who is "liked least" from a large group of children who know one another (for example, children in a classroom). Statistical procedures are then used to group children into one of five categories based on the ratings of their peers. *Popular* children receive many "liked most" and few "liked least" ratings. *Average* children also receive few "liked least" ratings, but they receive fewer "liked most" ratings than popular children. *Neglected* children receive few of either type of rating, and *rejected* children are the opposite of popular children: They receive many "liked least" ratings and few "liked most" nominations. Finally, *controversial* children receive many positive and many negative ratings from their peers (Coie & Kupersmidt, 1983; Newcomb, Bukowski, & Pattee, 1993).

The neglected and rejected classifications are especially relevant to the present discussion.

Rejected children are considerably more likely to have externalizing problems in comparison to the other four peer status groups (Patterson, Kupersmidt, & Griesler, 1990). Still, it is important to note that children with externalizing problems are not completely isolated. They usually have some close friends, but unfortunately their friends are likely to be other children with conduct problems (Olweus, 1984).

Neglected children also have more troubles than popular, average, and controversial children. Not surprisingly, neglected children are likely to have internalizing symptoms such as loneliness (Asher & Wheeler, 1985). An optimistic research finding about the neglected sociometric status is that it is not particularly stable over time and across situations (Coie & Kupersmidt, 1983; Newcomb, Bukowski, & Pattee, 1993). Apparently, children who are left out of one social group often succeed in finding friends in new social circumstances.

Specific Delays or Deviations in Development

A number of troubling symptoms of children's psychological disorders are best understood as specific *developmental delays* or *developmental deviations*, significant departures from age-appropriate norms in some specific area of functioning. In fact, some developmental delays or deviations are considered disorders in their own right. Specific deviations in reading, writing, or arithmetic are considered to be learning disorders if the deviation is substantial, as judged against both peer norms and the individual child's intellectual ability (see Further Thoughts). Similarly, once a child is past the age when most children toilet appropriately, delays in

---

FURTHER THOUGHTS

Learning Disorders

The classification *learning disorder* (or *learning disability*) refers to a heterogeneous group of problems in which academic performance differs noticeably from academic aptitude. There are numerous ways of defining learning disabilities more specifically, but each method presents difficulties (Lyon, 1996; Wicks-Nelson & Israel, 1991). The most common definition compares scores on intelligence tests, which measure academic aptitude, with scores on *academic achievement tests*—measures of performance in some academic subject area. Typically, a learning disorder is defined as a difference of one or two standard deviations between aptitude and achievement. Thus, according to this definition, a child would be considered to have a learning disorder if he or she scored a standard deviation above the mean on an intelligence test (an IQ of 115) but a standard deviation below the mean in reading (scoring well below the average for his or her grade level).

The DSM-IV includes learning disorders in its list of mental disorders. The DSM-IV also includes subcategories of learning disorders in reading, arithmetic, and written expression. Learning disorders typically are diagnosed by school professionals, however, and they almost always are treated in academic settings. Thus mental health professionals typically work with children with learning disorders only when the problems co-occur with other psychological disorders. In fact, there is a high degree of comorbidity between learning disabilities and both attention-deficit/hyperactivity disorder and oppositional defiant disorder (Barkley, 1990).

The origins of learning disorders have been traced to a number of problems, including perceptual distortions, attentional problems, language difficulties, and poor cognitive strategies. Typically, etiology is attributed to some biological cause, and considerable research has been conducted on brain functions in learning disorders. This research, however, has not identified any psychological deficit or biological cause that is common to all learning disorders (Wicks-Nelson & Israel, 1991).

Tremendous efforts have gone into attempts to treat learning disorders. Interventions in schools were given great impetus in 1975 when Congress passed the Education for All Handicapped Children Act. This law mandated that local school systems must provide special resources for educating handicapped children, including children with learning disorders. The federal legislation dramatically increased the number of children identified as having a learning disorder (see Figure 16–3). However, this increase has led some commentators to question

whether we are using overly broad definitions of learning disorders (Lyon, 1996). Even more critically, it is not clear that the identification of students with learning problems has led to more effective education for these students. Numerous interventions have been attempted, including intensive tutoring, individually or in small groups; behavior therapy programs in which academic success is systematically rewarded; psychostimulant medication; counseling for related problems (for example, low self-esteem); and various special efforts such as training in visual-motor skills. Unfortunately, no treatment has demonstrated consistent success (Lyon, 1996; Wicks-Nelson & Israel, 1991).

We can conclude that a substantial number of children in the United States—perhaps 5 percent of all schoolchildren—do not achieve at a level consistent with their abilities (Lyon, 1996). Learning disorders are "real" in the sense that these children seem to have the ability and motivation to perform better in school, yet they still perform well below their abilities. Nevertheless, the identification of the discrepancy between ability and performance has not solved the puzzle of learning disorders. Controversy and uncertainty remain about their definition, cause, and treatment. ■

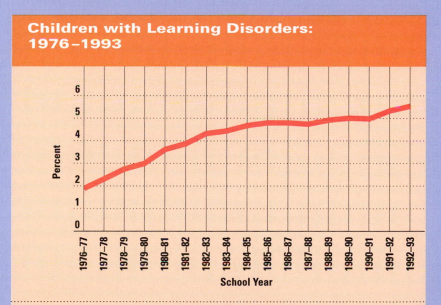

Children with Learning Disorders: 1976–1993

FIGURE 16-3: Federal legislation greatly increased the diagnosis of learning disorders. Some commentators attribute the increase to social, economic, and political factors—not to better intervention with children.

Source: Office of Special Education Programs, 1993, *Implementation of the Individuals with Disabilities Education Act: Fifteenth Annual Report to Congress.* Washington, DC: U.S. Department of Education.

developing bladder or bowel control are considered to be abnormal. Of course, we can only determine if a child is delayed in his or her development if we know what is normal for children of the same age. Developmental norms are essential in assessing abnormal behavior in children.

Classification of Psychological Disorders of Childhood

Brief Historical Perspective

The beginnings of child clinical psychology as a discipline can be traced to 1896. In that year, the psychologist Lightner Witmer (1867–1956) of the University of Pennsylvania established the first psychological clinic for children in the United States. Witmer's efforts stemmed from the emergence of psychology as a discipline, but his clinic also reflected major changes in societal attitudes toward children. Prior to the nineteenth century, life was harsh for children, who were expected to act and work (beginning around the age of 7) like little adults (Aries, 1962). Beginning in the latter half of the nineteenth century, however, child labor laws were passed, schooling became mandatory, and special juvenile courts were created. In short, U.S. society began to recognize that children require special protection and nurturance.

Despite the early origins of child clinical psychology, children were largely ignored in early classifications of mental disorders (Garber, 1984). The DSM-I (1952) contained only two separate diagnoses for children, and DSM-II (1968) listed only seven childhood disorders. Prompted by the Group for Advancement of Psychiatry (GAP, 1966) and the World Health Organization (Rutter, Shaffer, & Shepherd, 1975), DSM-III recognized a much wider range of childhood disorders (1980). In fact, the DSM-III contained a proliferation of diagnostic categories for children, 40 in all. Although laudable, the new effort was overly ambitious. Many of the new diagnoses were severely criticized and subsequently were dropped.

Contemporary Classification: Some Strengths and Weaknesses in DSM-IV

Table 16–1 summarizes the childhood disorders contained in DSM-IV (1994). Many of the DSM-IV diagnoses in Table 16-1 may be unfamiliar to you, in part, because some of them are rare and unusual problems. We can consider most of these disorders only briefly. *Pica* is the persistent eating of nonnutritive substances, such as paint or dirt. Many infants and toddlers put nonnutritive substances in their mouths, but the feeding disorder pica is rarely diagnosed, except among mentally retarded children. *Rumination disorder,* the repeated regurgitation and rechewing of food, is another infrequent feeding disorder. Rumination disorder is found primarily among infants, and it can be a serious problem that causes very low weight gain and can even lead to death.

Tourette's disorder is a rare problem (4 to 5 cases per 10,000 people) that is characterized by repeated motor and verbal tics. The tics can be voluntarily suppressed only for brief periods of time, and they can interfere substantially with life functioning. Other tic disorder classifications reflect the facts that children may develop verbal or motor tics in isolation, and that children's tics often last for only a brief period of time (see Table 16–1). *Stereotypic movement disorder* is self-stimulation or self-injurious behavior that is serious enough to require treatment, as may be the case in mental retardation or pervasive developmental disorder (see Chapter 15).

Selective mutism involves the consistent failure to speak in certain social situations (for example, in school), while speech is unrestricted in other situations (for example, at home). Selective mutism is found among less than 1 percent of the children treated for mental health disorders. *Reactive attachment disorder* is another rarely diagnosed problem, although it may be more prevalent than we would hope. Reactive attachment disorder is characterized by severely disturbed and developmentally inappropriate social relationships. Children may resist comfort and cuddling, for example, or they may "freeze" and watch others from a safe distance. Reactive attachment disorder is caused by parenting that is so grossly neglectful that the infant or preschooler fails to develop a selective attachment relationship. (In Chapter 18, we discuss the topics

TABLE 16-1

DSM-IV Disorders Usually First Diagnosed in Infancy, Childhood, or Adolescence[a]

Attention-Deficit and Disruptive Behavior Disorders
Attention-deficit/hyperactivity disorder
    Combined type
    Predominantly inattentive type
    Predominantly hyperactive-impulsive type
Conduct disorder
Oppositional defiant disorder

Learning Disorders
Reading disorder
Mathematics disorder
Disorder of written expression

Motor Skills Disorder
Developmental coordination disorder

Communication Disorders
Expressive language disorder
Mixed receptive-expressive language disorder
Phonological disorder
Stuttering

Feeding and Eating Disorders of Infancy or Early Childhood
Pica
Rumination disorder
Feeding disorder of infancy or early childhood

Tic Disorders
Tourette's disorder
Chronic motor or vocal tic disorder
Transient tic disorder

Elimination Disorders
Encopresis
    With constipation and overflow incontinence
    Without constipation and overflow incontinence
Enuresis

Other Disorders of Infancy, Childhood, and Adolescence
Separation anxiety disorder
Selective mutism
Reactive attachment disorder of infancy or early childhood
Stereotypic movement disorder

[a]*Note:* This listing does not include mental retardation or pervasive developmental disorders, which we discussed in Chapter 15. It also does not include "Not Otherwise Specified" (NOS) subtypes of the diagnoses. NOS subtypes exist for many of the disorders listed here, and they are used when a child meets many but not all of the diagnostic criteria for the specific disorder.

of child abuse and neglect, social problems that unfortunately are not rare.)

In contrast to many of these childhood disorders, **encopresis** and **enuresis** are common problems. The terms refer respectively to inappropriately controlled defecation and urination. According to DSM-IV, enuresis may be considered abnormal beginning at age 5, as most children have developed bladder control by this age. Bedwetting is found among approximately 5 percent of 5-year-olds, 2 to 3 percent of 10-year-olds, and 1 percent of 18-year-olds. Encopresis may be diagnosed beginning at age 4, and it is a much less common problem. Encopresis is found among approximately 1 percent of all 5-year-olds and fewer older children.

Encopresis and enuresis typically are causes of, not reactions to, psychological distress. That is, symptoms that sometimes accompany enuresis or encopresis, for example, shyness or social anxiety, generally disappear once children learn to control their bowels or bladders. Encopresis and especially enuresis can be effectively treated with various biofeedback devices. The best-known such treatment is the *bell and pad*, a device that awakens children by setting off an alarm as they begin to wet the bed during the night. Research indicates that the bell and pad is about 75 percent effective in treating bedwetting among young school-aged children (Houts, 1991).

OVERINCLUSIVE LISTING OF DISORDERS

Another reason some of the disorders listed in Table 16–1 may be unfamiliar is the questionable nature of their status as "mental disorders." A number of commentators believe that, beginning with DSM-III, the manual became overinclusive in its listing of childhood disorders. That is, the manual included too many "disorders" that are not in fact mental disorders (Garmezy, 1978). Many disorders were dropped from DSM-III and DSM-III-R, but there seem to be other ways in which the list should be shortened.

"Developmental coordination disorder" is perhaps the most obvious example of overinclusion in DSM-IV. The manual defines this problem as follows: "Performance in daily activities that require motor coordination is substantially below that expected given the person's chronological age and measured intelligence" (p. 54). In poking fun at such diagnostic overzealousness, two pediatricians proposed a new diagnostic category they called "sports deficit disorder." The major diagnostic criterion for this "disorder" is always being the last one chosen for a sports team (Burke & McGee, 1990).

The "learning disorders" and "communication disorders" are more controversial examples of possible overinclusion in DSM-IV. Educators call these childhood problems learning disabilities (see Further Thoughts) and speech and hearing problems, respectively. Learning disabilities and speech and hearing problems both are common and serious difficulties experienced by children, but we question their status as mental disorders. We view both problems as involving educational more than mental health concerns.

SUBCLASSIFICATION OF EXTERNALIZING DISORDERS

DSM-IV lists three major subtypes of disruptive behavior disorders: attention-deficit/hyperactivity disorder (ADHD), oppositional defiant disorder (ODD), and conduct disorder (CD). The appropriate subclassification of externalizing disorders is an important, controversial, and frequently studied issue. The distinction between attention-deficit/hyperactivity disorder and oppositional defiant disorder is particularly important.

Attention-Deficit/Hyperactivity Disorder Attention-deficit/hyperactivity disorder is characterized by hyperactivity, attention deficit, and impulsivity (see Table 16–2). Although they have been given equal billing in DSM-IV, at earlier points in time the symptoms of hyperactivity and attention deficit each have been viewed as the central characteristic of ADHD. In fact, DSM-II called the disorder *hyperkinesis*, a synonym for "hyperactivity," whereas DSM-III referred to it as *attention-deficit disorder*, or *ADD*. We are not concerned whether "attention deficit" or "hyperactivity" gets top billing in labeling a condition with an ever-changing series of names, but we are concerned about two facts. First, contrary to what has been asserted by some professionals, hyperactivity is not merely a consequence of inattention or vice versa (Barkley, 1990). Each is an independent symptom. Second, some children have problems primarily with only one of the two symptoms, as is evident in the subtypes of ADHD listed in DSM-IV (see Table 16–2).

Oppositional Defiant Disorder Oppositional defiant disorder is defined as a pattern of negative, hostile, and defiant behavior. The rule violations in ODD typically involve rather minor transgressions, however, such as refusing to obey adult requests, arguing, and acting angry (see Table 16–3). Such behavior may be developmentally normal among adolescents, but it is a cause for concern among school-aged children. Childhood ODD may foreshadow the development of much more serious antisocial behavior during adolescence and adult life.

TABLE 16-2

DSM-IV Diagnostic Criteria for Attention-Deficit/Hyperactivity Disorder

A. Either (I) or (II):

(I) Inattention: Six (or more) of the following symptoms of inattention have persisted for at least 6 months to a degree that is maladaptive and inconsistent with developmental level:
1. Often fails to give close attention to details or makes careless mistakes in schoolwork, work, or other activities.
2. Often has difficulty sustaining attention in tasks or play activities.
3. Often does not seem to listen when spoken to directly.
4. Often does not follow through on instructions and fails to finish schoolwork, chores, or duties in the workplace.
5. Often has difficulty organizing tasks and activities.
6. Often avoids, dislikes, or is reluctant to engage in tasks that require sustained mental effort.
7. Often loses things necessary for tasks or activities.
8. Is often easily distracted by extraneous stimuli.
9. Is often forgetful of daily activities.

(II) Hyperactivity and Impulsivity: Six (or more) of the following symptoms of hyperactivity-impulsivity have persisted for at least 6 months to a degree that is maladaptive and inconsistent with developmental level:

Hyperactivity
1. Often fidgets with hands or feet or squirms in seat.
2. Often leaves seat in classroom or in other situations in which remaining seated is expected.
3. Often runs about or climbs excessively in situations in which it is inappropriate.
4. Often has difficulty playing or engaging in leisure activities quietly.
5. Is often "on the go" or often acts as if "driven by a motor."
6. Often talks excessively.

Impulsivity
7. Often blurts out answers before questions have been completed.
8. Often has difficulty awaiting turn.
9. Often interrupts or intrudes on others.

B. Some hyperactive-impulsive or inattentive symptoms that caused impairment were present before age 7 years.

C. Some impairment from the symptoms is present in two or more settings.

D. There must be clear evidence of clinically significant impairment in social, academic, or occupational functioning.

Code Based on Type

Combined Type: Criteria for I and II are met for past 6 months.

Predominantly Inattentive Type: Criteria for I are met but Criteria for II are not met for past 6 months.

Predominantly Hyperactive-Impulsive Type: Criteria for II are met but Criteria for I are not met for past 6 months.

DSM-IV Diagnostic Criteria for Oppositional Defiant Disorder

A. A pattern of negativistic, hostile, and defiant behavior lasting at least 6 months, during which four (or more) of the following are present:
1. Often loses temper.
2. Often argues with adults.
3. Often actively defies or refuses to comply with adults' requests or rules.
4. Often deliberately annoys people.
5. Often blames others for his or her mistakes or misbehavior.
6. Is often touchy or easily annoyed by others.
7. Is often angry and resentful.
8. Is often spiteful and vindictive.

B. The disturbance in behavior causes clinically significant impairment in social, academic, or occupational functioning.

ADHD versus ODD Professionals have long debated whether oppositional defiant disorder is distinct from attention-deficit/hyperactivity disorder. Some professionals have argued that the two conditions are distinct not only in symptomatology but also in terms of etiology and effective treatment. Others have asserted that the distinction between ADHD and ODD is false and is wrongly used to justify treating troubled children with medication. Researchers have struggled to test these widely opposing viewpoints, but they have been hampered by diagnostic difficulties. Differential diagnosis cannot be easily made with a high level of reliability; thus it is difficult or impossible to determine whether investigators are studying subjects with ADHD, ODD, or both disorders (Hinshaw, 1987, 1994).

The current consensus is that the two disorders are best conceived as separate but overlapping problems (Barkley, 1990; Hinshaw, 1987, 1994; see Figure 16–4). Oppositional defiant disorder and attention-deficit/hyperactivity disorder can be differentiated, but they are highly comorbid conditions. As many as half of all children with one disorder also have the other problem (Hinshaw, 1994). Unfortunately, such a circumstance makes it difficult to interpret past research, as researchers have only recently recognized the comorbidity problem. Scientists are hopeful, however, that future research can help to untangle the web of confusing findings by studying cases of "pure" ODD and ADHD, that is, by studying cases where there is no comorbidity. In so doing, it also is essential to distinguish cases with comorbid learning disorders, since as many as 25 percent of children with ODD and ADHD also have a learning disorder (Hinshaw, 1994).

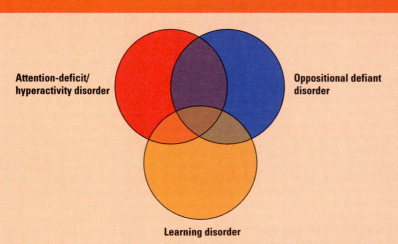

Comorbidity Among Attention-Deficit/ Hyperactivity Disorder, Oppositional Defiant Disorder, and Learning Disorder

Attention-deficit/ hyperactivity disorder

Oppositional defiant disorder

Learning disorder

FIGURE 16-4: Attention-deficit/hyperactivity disorder and oppositional defiant disorder are distinct but overlapping conditions. As many as half of all children with one disorder also suffer from the other problem. To a lesser extent, ADHD and ODD also overlap with learning disorders.

ADHD with and without Hyperactivity The subtyping of ADHD into cases with and without hyperactivity is another important and sometimes controversial distinction. Consistent with the DSM-IV, researchers generally accept the distinction between ADHD with and without hyperactivity, but confusion arises when we consider all subtypes together. For example, are there cases of ADHD with hyperactivity *and* comorbid ODD, and are there other cases of ADHD with hyperactivity but *no* comorbid ODD? We cannot answer this question definitively, but as summarized in Table 16–4, evidence suggests that ADHD *with* hyperactivity might be akin to—or the same thing as—ADHD with comorbid oppositional defiant disorder. In reviewing the evidence summarized in Table 16–4, note that ADHD with hyperactivity is linked with many of the same factors associated with ODD, such as antisocial behavior and rejection by peers.

Conduct Disorder   Conduct disorder (CD) is similar to oppositional defiant disorder, except the aggression and rule violations are far more serious in conduct disorder. Conduct disorder is defined primarily by rule violations that are illegal as well as antisocial, for example, assault or robbery (see Table 16–5). Consistent with research we reviewed earlier, the DSM-IV notes that the ODD and CD often are developmentally related. Oppositional defiant disorder is diagnosed primarily among school-aged children, and may develop into a more serious conduct disorder during preadolescence or adolescence (Loeber, Lahey, & Thomas, 1991). You should note that the DSM-IV also includes a notation for age of onset in defining conduct disorders— a distinction between the adolescent- limited versus life- course patterns of antisocial behavior, as we discussed earlier (see Table 16–5).

You may think of what DSM-IV calls conduct disorder as being equivalent to juvenile delinquency. Many of the symptoms of conduct disorder do indeed involve *index offenses*— that is, crimes against people or property that are illegal at any age. Other diagnostic criteria are comparable to **status offenses**— acts that are illegal only because of the youth's status as a minor. Examples are running away from home and truancy from school. However, **juvenile delinquency** is a legal classification, not a mental health term. Technically, youths are not classified as delinquent until they are found to be delinquent by a judge. In the United States, juvenile court judges may

▲ **Boys breaking into school lockers. Juveniles commit many minor and many very serious illegal acts.**

	TABLE 16-4

Differences Found in Research Comparing ADHD with and without Hyperactivity

Feature	ADHD without Hyperactivity	ADHD with Hyperactivity
Family history of psychopathology	Internalizing-spectrum disorders; learning disabilities	Antisocial-spectrum disorders and ADHD
Symptomatology	Distinct pattern of attention problems (sluggish, daydreaming; some evidence for internalizing problems)	Oppositional and aggressive behaviors
Peer problems	Social isolation, peer neglect	Active peer rejection
Academic achievement	Some evidence for higher rates of learning disabilities	Higher rates of school suspension and special education placement
Neuropsychological deficits	Suggestion of slow automatization, similar to children with learning disabilities	Mixed evidence for frontal/prefrontal deficits
Course	Few extant data	Risk for antisocial outcomes and negative course; disinhibitory behaviors are predictors
Treatment response	Tend to respond to lower stimulant dosages	Tend to respond to moderate stimulant dosages

Source: S. P. Hinshaw, 1994, *Attention Deficits and Hyperactivity in Children*, p. 72. Thousand Oaks, CA: Sage.

TABLE 16-5

DSM-IV Diagnostic Criteria for Conduct Disorder

A. A repetitive and persistent pattern of behavior in which the basic rights of others or major age-appropriate societal norms or rules are violated, as manifested by the presence of three (or more) of the following criteria in the past 12 months, with at least one criterion present in the past 6 months:

Aggression to People and Animals
1. Often bullies, threatens, or intimidates others.
2. Often initiates physical fights.
3. Has used a weapon that can cause serious physical harm to others.
4. Has been physically cruel to people.
5. Has been physically cruel to animals.
6. Has stolen while confronting a victim.
7. Has forced someone into sexual activity.

Destruction of Property
8. Has deliberately engaged in fire setting with the intention of causing serious damage.
9. Has deliberately destroyed others' property.

Deceitfulness or Theft
10. Has broken into someone else's house, building, or car.
11. Often lies to obtain goods or favors to avoid obligations.
12. Has stolen items of nontrivial value without confronting a victim.

Serious Violations of Rules
13. Often stays out at night despite parental prohibitions, beginning before age 13 years.
14. Has run away from home overnight at least twice while living in parental or parental surrogate home.
15. Is often truant from school, beginning before age 13 years.

B. The disturbance in behavior causes clinically significant impairment in social, academic, or occupational functioning.

Specify Type Based on Age at Onset

Childhood-Onset Type: Onset of at least one criterion characteristic of Conduct Disorder prior to age 10 years.

Adolescent-Onset Type: Absence of any criteria characteristic of Conduct Disorder prior to age 10 years.

---

find a youth to be delinquent for committing either criminal or status offenses, although adjudication for status offenses is increasingly rare.

Contextual Classifications for Abnormal Child Behavior?

As a final note on classification, we remind you that children's behavior is intimately linked with the family, school, and peer contexts. Because of this, some commentators have suggested that diagnosing individual children is misleading and misguided (Kazdin, 1989). Instead, children's psychological problems could be classified within the context of key interpersonal relationships. As you saw in the case of Jeremy, parents, teachers, and peers often are part of a child's "individual" problem. Given current research and theory, we have followed the traditional approach to classification in this chapter. However, future research should attempt to classify children's problem behavior in the social context and compare the reliability and validity of the contextual approach with the individual classifications used in DSM-IV.

Epidemiology of Psychological Disorders of Childhood

A panel of experts assembled by the National Academy of Sciences (1989) concluded that at least 12 percent of the 63 million children living in the United States suffer from a mental disorder. The panel found that a minimum of $1.5 billion was spent annually for the direct mental health treatment of children—and this figure excluded the additional costs of treating children's emotional problems in general medical settings, schools, welfare agencies, and juvenile courts. Clearly, children's mental health is a major national problem, but epidemiological evidence is valuable for reasons other than documenting the extent of children's psychological difficulties. Factors correlated with higher prevalence rates identify subgroups of children at risk, and this information suggests possible causes of children's psychological disorders (see Research Methods).

RESEARCH METHODS

Samples and Sampling

Psychologists are very concerned with the samples that they study, and samples are often described in great detail in psychological research—a fact attested to by numerous examples throughout this text. However, psychologists often do not consider it necessary to obtain a **representative sample**—a sample that accurately represents some larger group of people. Instead, psychologists and other mental health researchers often obtain *convenience samples*—groups of people who are easily recruited and studied. In research in abnormal psychology, people who have sought psychological treatment often comprise the convenience sample.

The use of a convenience sample does not create problems for many of the questions that psychologists wish to study. For example, there is no need to obtain a representative sample to study the effectiveness of medication for treating most psychological disorders. For other purposes, obtaining representative samples is essential. For example, researchers who have studied children in clinical settings have found that a disproportionate number of these children come from single-parent families.

From this evidence, they conclude that single parenting causes the children's psychological problems. When more representative samples are studied, however, it becomes evident that the great majority of children from single-parent families do *not* have psychological problems. Therefore single parenting alone cannot cause the children's troubles. A relationship exists between family status and children's psychological adjustment, but it is not nearly as strong in representative samples as it appears to be in convenience samples (Emery, 1988).

Our concern with sampling is one reason why we have systematically addressed the topic of epidemiology throughout this text. When studying risk factors like family status, often it is informative to be able to *generalize*—to make accurate statements that extend beyond a specific sample to a larger population group. How do scientists select representative samples that allow them to generalize to a larger population? Theoretically, the methods for obtaining a representative sample are straightforward. First, the researcher must identify the *population* of interest, the entire group of people to whom the researcher wants to generalize—for example, children under the age of 18 living in the United States. Second, the researcher must *randomly select* research subjects from the sample and obtain a large enough sample to ensure that the results are statistically reliable. These two procedures allow researchers to make generalizations that sometimes seem remarkable, such as when the outcome of a political election is accurately predicted by polling a relatively small number of voters.

Errors can occur in either step of the process of selecting a representative sample. One of the most famous errors in sampling occurred in 1948 when newspaper headlines heralded Thomas E. Dewey's election over Harry S. Truman in the U.S. presidential election. Ultimately, Truman won the election. Where did the pollsters go wrong? They made a mistake in identifying the population of voters. The researchers sampled randomly and appropriately from the population of voters who owned telephones. In 1948, however, many less affluent people did not own telephones, and the less wealthy voted overwhelmingly for Truman, a Democrat.

Political scientists have become much more sophisticated in their sampling strategies since 1948, but psychologists sometimes repeat earlier errors. Thus, as you read about psychological research, we urge you to think critically about samples and sampling methods. A fortunate trend in the study of child psychopathology is that sociologists and psychologists are beginning to collaborate in epidemiological research. An example is Nicholas Zill, a researcher who was trained as a psychologist but who conducts demographic studies with population samples. In a report on findings from a survey of 17,110 children—a representative sample of U.S. children 17 years of age and younger taken in 1988—the following data were obtained (Zill & Schoenborn, 1990):

1. Nearly 20 percent of young people in the United States between the ages of 3 and 17 had a learning, behavioral, or developmental disorder. About 4 percent had delays in growth or development, 6.5 percent had a learning disorder, and 13.4 percent had significant emotional or behavioral problems. (The percentages add up to more than 20 percent, because some children had more than one problem.)

2. About 2 percent of children received treatment or counseling for developmental delays, 5 percent for learning problems, and more than 10 percent for psychological problems.

3. Learning and emotional or behavior problems were associated with family income, but the relationship was a modest one. For example, 15.8 percent of the children whose parents earned under $10,000 a year had an emotional or behavior problem, compared with 12.8 percent of children whose parents earned over $40,000.

4. Black and Latino parents reported fewer problems among their children than did white parents. This finding may be attributable to underreporting among members of these ethnic groups. Blacks and Latinos have lower average incomes than whites, and therefore more, not fewer, problems are expected among minority children. In fact, this is exactly what was found according to data taken from school records instead of parents' observations.

These findings are important in their own right, and they also illustrate the broader value of obtaining representative samples of the general population in some psychological research. Clinical and convenience samples are decidedly not representative of the general population. There often are compelling reasons for studying these unrepresentative groups, but researchers who rely on such samples must exercise great caution in generalizing to the larger population. Such inferences only can be drawn from studies of representative samples. ■

Gender Differences in Externalizing and Internalizing Problems

Gender is one risk factor for psychological problems, but the risk associated with gender reverses across the course of development. More boys than girls are treated for psychological problems, but more women than men enter into therapy. Where is the turning point, and what is the explanation for this phenomenon? We can begin to answer this question by examining gender differences in externalizing and internalizing problems.

Epidemiological studies consistently find that, after the first few years of life, boys have far more externalizing disorders than girls (Keenan & Shaw, in press; National Academy of Sciences, 1989; Rutter, 1989). From 3 to 5 percent of children are estimated to have attention-deficit/hyperactivity disorder, and anywhere from 5 to 15 percent of youths may have oppositional defiant disorder and/or conduct disorder. These problems are 2 to

10 times more common among boys than among girls.

Except for the normative increase during adolescence, the prevalence of externalizing behavior generally declines with age, although it declines at much earlier ages for girls (age 4 or 5) than for boys (Keenan & Shaw, in press). In contrast, the prevalence of internalizing problems increases with age. In particular, depression begins to emerge in preadolescence and adolescence (Achenbach & Edelbrock, 1981; Fleming & Offord, 1990; National Academy of Sciences, 1989; Rutter, 1989), and mood disorders become one of the most common psychological problems of adult life (see Chapter 5). Thus we can offer this explanation for the changing status of gender as a risk factor across age: Parents, teachers, and other adults seek treatment for younger boys' externalizing behavior, but the increase in depression among teenagers, especially adolescent girls, begins to balance the relationship between gender and the prevalence of psychological problems (Lewinsohn et al., 1994). By early adult life, more females than males report psychological problems.

Family Risk Factors

The prevalence of psychological disorders among children is related to several factors in addition to gender. Family adversity is a particularly important risk factor, as has been highlighted by the British psychiatrist Michael Rutter, an international authority on the epidemiology of child psychopathology. Rutter's (1978b, 1989) family adversity index includes six family predictors of behavior problems among children: (1) low income, (2) overcrowding in the home, (3) maternal depression, (4) paternal antisocial behavior, (5) conflict between the parents, and (6) removal of the child from the home. Rutter found that the risk for externalizing problems did not increase substantially when only one family risk factor was present. However, the risk increased fourfold when two family adversity factors were present. The risk for children's antisocial behavior increased even further with three or more sources of family adversity.

Other epidemiological findings underscore the relationship between children's psychological problems and social disadvantage. For example, psychological disorders are found among over 20 percent of children living in inner-city neighborhoods (National Academy of Sciences, 1989) and are associated with divorce

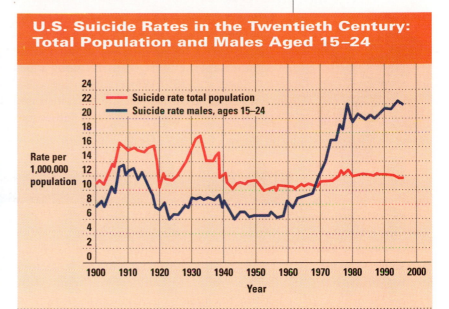

U.S. Suicide Rates in the Twentieth Century: Total Population and Males Aged 15–24

FIGURE 16-5: Teen suicide rates tripled during the 1960s and 1970s.

Source: H. Hendin, 1995, *Suicide in America*, p. 53. New York: Norton.

and single parenting (see Further Thoughts in Chapter 18). Family dysfunction and stressful life events are associated with both internalizing and externalizing problems (Fleming & Offord, 1990). For these reasons, family adversity is a substantial concern in the etiology of children's psychological problems.

Suicide Among Children and Adolescents

Because of their prevalence and disruptiveness, externalizing problems are the focus of much psychological attention. Adults also need to be sensitive to children's internal distress, however, as the evidence on suicide underscores in a dramatic fashion. Suicide is the third leading cause of death among teenagers, trailing only automobile accidents and natural causes. Teenage suicide is of special concern because adolescent suicide rates have tripled since the 1960s (see Figure 16–5). Suicide is extremely rare among children under the age of 10, but the rate of suicide also has increased among younger age groups (Hawton, 1986).

In comparison to adult suicide attempts, suicide attempts among adolescents are more impulsive, are more likely to

▼ Mourners at the wake of three teenagers who committed suicide together.

follow a family conflict, and are more often motivated by anger rather than depression (Hawton, 1986). Cluster suicides are also more common among teenagers than among adults (Spirito et al., 1989). When one teenager commits suicide, his or her peers are at an increased risk for suicide attempts. The risk sometimes stems from suicide pacts, but in addition, the death may make suicide seem more acceptable to other teenagers. As suggested by some accounts of reactions to the 1994 suicide of rock star Kurt Cobain, some adolescents may view a peer's suicide as understandable, even romantic.

▲ **Michael Rutter, a British psychiatrist, is an international authority on child psychopathology. Rutter was knighted by the queen of England in recognition of his many contributions.**

▲ **The Canadian-American psychologist Mary Ainsworth is an internationally reknowned expert on infant–caregiver attachments. Her empirical studies grounded and expanded attachment theory.**

Etiological Considerations and Research

We begin our review of the etiology of childhood disorders with a discussion of parenting, family relationships, and other social factors, because parenting and the family context are critical to children's psychological adjustment. As we have noted repeatedly throughout the text, however, bear in mind that families share genes as well as the family environment. Also bear in mind that, as with other topics we have reviewed, the preponderance of research focuses on the development of externalizing disorders. Most research on the causes of mood and anxiety disorders among children is based on the same theories of etiology we have discussed in relation to adults (Puig-Antich, 1986; see Chapters 5 and 6). Evidence simply is lacking or inadequate on the development of many other psychological problems of childhood. In discussing etiology, we follow our developmental psychopathology approach and begin each section with a brief consideration of normal development. In discussing social factors, we highlight the development of attachments and the socialization of children as central issues in normal development and in developmental psychopathology.

Social Factors

ATTACHMENT RELATIONSHIPS

The major task of social development during the first year of life is the formation of a close bond, an *attachment*, between an infant and his or her caregivers (see Chapter 2). The British psychiatrist and theorist John Bowlby (1969, 1973, 1980) and the Canadian-American psychologist and empiricist Mary Ainsworth (1979) together have developed *attachment theory*, a set of proposals about the normal development of attachments and the adverse consequences of troubled attachment relationships. Troubled attachments may include the failure to develop a selective attachment early in life; the development of an insecure attachment; or multiple, prolonged separations from (or the permanent loss of) an attachment figure.

Reactive Attachment Disorder As we noted earlier, extreme parental neglect deprives infants of the opportunity to form a selective attachment. Such neglect can cause *reactive attachment disorder*, or what attachment researchers sometimes call *anaclitic depression*—the lack of social responsiveness found among infants who do not have a consistent attachment figure (Sroufe & Fleeson, 1986). Research on the consequences of extreme neglect for children is strongly buttressed by evidence from animal analogue research. Nonhuman primates who are raised in isolation without a parent or a substitute attachment figure have dramatically troubled social relationships (Suomi & Harlow, 1972). Thus it has been clearly established that psychological problems can be caused by the failure to form an attachment relationship.

Insecure Attachments Attachment theory also predicts that variations in the quality of early attachments are associated with normal or maladjustment among children. Attachment quality can be broadly divided into secure (healthy) and anxious attachments. Infants with *secure attachments* separate easily and explore away from their attachment figures, but they quickly seek proximity and comfort when they are threatened or distressed. Infants with **anxious attachments** are fearful about exploration and are not easily comforted by their attachment figures, who respond inadequately or inconsistently to the child's needs (Ainsworth et al., 1978; Carlson & Sroufe, 1995). Anxious attachments are further subcategorized into (1) *anxious avoidant attachments*, where the infant is generally unwary of strange situations and shows little preference for the attachment figure over others; (2) *anxious resistant attachments*, where the infant is wary of exploration, not easily soothed by the attachment figure, and angry or ambivalent about contact; and (3) *disorganized attachments*, where the infant responds inconsistently because of conflicting feelings toward an inconsistent caregiver who is the potential source of either reassurance or fear (Carlson & Sroufe, 1995).

A number of longitudinal studies have demonstrated that secure versus anxious attachments during infancy foreshadow difficulties in children's social and emotional adjustment throughout childhood. However, an insecure attachment does not seem to result in the development of any particular emotional disorder. Rather, insecure attachments predict a number of internalizing and social difficulties, including lower self-esteem, less competence in peer interaction, and increased dependency on others (Cassidy, 1988; Carlson & Sroufe, 1995; Sroufe & Fleeson, 1986). Recent research demonstrates, moreover, that stable, anxious attachments during infancy also predict externalizing behavior at 3 years of age (Shaw & Vondra, 1995). Thus, anxious attachments appear to be a general rather than a specific risk factor for children's subsequent psychological problems.

Separation and Loss Separation or loss is another disruption in attachment—one that clearly causes distress among children, at least in the short run. Children move through a four-stage process akin to grief when they are separated from or lose an attachment figure. The process includes (1) numbed responsiveness, (2) yearning and protest, (3) disorganization and despair, and ultimately (4) reorganization and detachment or loss of interest in the former attachment figure (Bowlby, 1979). However, there is considerable controversy about the consequences of separation, loss, and detachment. Bowlby (1972) asserted that detachment causes dependence, which, in turn, increases the risk for depression as the child's needs go unfulfilled in subsequent relationships. Critics have suggested, however, that what Bowlby called detachment is really an indication of children's adjustment to the new circumstances (Rutter, 1981). This interpretation highlights children's **resilience** or ability to "bounce back" from adversity. It is consistent with research that has failed to find a relationship between childhood loss and depression during adult life (Crook & Eliot, 1980; Tennant, Bebbington, & Hurry, 1980).

SOCIALIZATION

Socialization is the process of shaping children's behavior and attitudes to conform to the expectations of parents, teachers, and society as a whole (Hetherington & Parke, 1986). Many psychologists believe that parental explanation, example, and appropriate discipline are most important in socializing children, but other influences cannot be ignored. Peer groups exert strong if sometimes subtle conformity pressures that increase as children grow older. School and television also are powerful socialization agents.

Ineffective Discipline and Parenting Styles Parental discipline, a major socialization tool, is sometimes mistakenly viewed as the polar opposite of attachment or loving children. In fact, parents need not choose between being strict and loving. Secure attachments facilitate parenting by making discipline both less necessary and more effective (Shaw & Bell, 1993). For example, attachment research indicates that babies are not "spoiled" when they are picked up, cuddled, and loved in other ways. Such natural interactions make infants easier, not more difficult, to manage (Ainsworth, 1979).

But love alone is not enough as children grow older. **Authoritative parenting,** parenting that is both loving and firm, is most effective in rearing well-adjusted children. In fact, developmental psychologists classify parenting into four styles by combining the two dimensions of warmth and control (see Figure 16–6). In contrast to authoritative parents, *authoritarian* parents lack warmth, and while their

▲ Together with Mary Ainsworth the British psychiatrist John Bowlby (1907–1990) can be credited with developing attachment theory, a set of proposals about the importance of close parental relationships to children's psychological development.

A Classification of Parenting Styles

	Accepting, Responsive, Child-centered	Rejecting, Unresponsive, Parent-centered
Demanding, controlling	Authoritative	Authoritarian
Undemanding, low in control attempts	Indulgent	Neglectful

FIGURE 16-6: Four styles of parenting, based on dimensions of parental warmth and discipline efforts.

Source: E.E. Maccoby and J.A. Martin, 1983, Socialization in the context of the family: Parent-child interaction. In E.M. Hetherington (Ed.), *Socialization, Personality, and Social Development, Vol. 4, Handbook of Child Psychology*, pp. 1-101. New York: Wiley.

▲ Clinical psychologist Gerald Patterson is a leader in studying children's aggression from a social learning perspective.

discipline is strict, it is often harsh and undemocratic. Children of authoritarian parents generally are compliant, but they also may be anxious. *Indulgent* parents are the opposite of authoritarian parents—affectionate but lax in discipline. The children of indulgent parents tend to be impulsive and noncompliant, but they are not extremely antisocial. Finally, *neglectful* parents are unconcerned either with their children's emotional needs or with their needs for discipline. Children with serious conduct problems often have neglectful parents (Baumrind, 1971; Loeber & Dishion, 1983; Maccoby & Martin, 1983; see Figure 16–6).

Coercion More specific problems in parenting also appear to contribute to the development of children's externalizing problems. The psychologist Gerald Patterson's (1982) concept of coercion is one of the most important examples of this line of research. **Coercion** occurs when parents *positively* reinforce children's misbehavior by giving in to their demands. The children, in turn, *negatively* reinforce their parents by ending their obnoxious behavior as soon as their parents capitulate. Thus coercion describes a system of interaction in which parents and children reciprocally reinforce child misbehavior and parent capitulation. The concept is illustrated in the following brief case study.

BRIEF CASE STUDY

Ms. B. finally admitted that she had lost all control of her 4-year-old son, Billy. Ms. B. was a single parent who was exhausted by her routine of working from 8 to 5:30 every day and managing Billy and the household in the evenings and on weekends. She had no parenting or financial support from Billy's father or anyone else, and Ms. B. was worn down. When it came time to discipline Billy, she usually gave in—either because this was the easiest thing to do, or because she felt too guilty to say no.

Ms. B. described many difficult interactions with Billy. One example stood out in the mind of the psychologist she consulted. Ms. B. would often stop at the grocery store with Billy after work,

---

and he inevitably gave her trouble while they were shopping. Dealing with the candy aisle was a recent problem. Billy had asked for some candy when they first approached the aisle. Ms. B. told him no, but in an increasingly loud voice Billy protested, "I WANT CANDY!" Ms. B. attempted to stick to her guns, but soon she was embarrassed by the disapproving looks on the faces of other mothers. Feeling both resentful and resigned, she grabbed a bag of M&Ms and gave it to Billy. This gave her a few minutes of peace and quiet while she completed her shopping. ■

Clearly, Ms. B. rewarded Billy for his misbehavior in this interaction. As suggested by the coercion construct, Billy also negatively reinforced his mother by quieting down when she gave in to his demands. Because both parties were reinforced, the coercive interaction is predicted to continue over time (Patterson, 1982).

The coercion concept is appealing, in part, because it has direct, practical implications. Parents need to break the pattern of interaction by ignoring the misbehavior (extinction), punishing it, or rewarding more positive actions (Forehand & McMahon, 1981). We discuss such treatments of noncompliant behavior later in the chapter. In Billy's case, the psychologist recommended the use of **time-out,** the technique of briefly isolating a child following misbehavior. The next time Billy acted up in the grocery store, Ms. B. left her shopping cart, and she and Billy sat in the car until he quieted down. She then completed her shopping. Several trips to the car were needed the first day, but Billy's behavior improved so that soon no time-outs were needed. He quickly was earning rewards for being good—not for being bad—while shopping.

The Importance of Parental Love The coercion concept underscores the importance of parental discipline in managing children's behavior. As we have noted, however, children are better behaved when their parents are loving as well as firm. Why is this so? Attachment theory suggests that children who feel secure and valued by their parents are more compliant because they value their parents in return. That is, children *identify* with parents who are loving to them (Waters, Hay, & Richters, 1986).

More generally, children's noncompliance may not always stem from a lack of discipline. Sometimes children misbehave as a way of getting attention rather than as a way of getting what they want. Consider the concept of *negative attention*, the idea that attempts at punishment sometimes accidentally reinforce children's misbehavior. Imagine, for example, the teacher who scolds the "class clown" for misbehaving. In some circumstances, the scolding increases rather than decreases the child's misbehavior; that is, the attempt at punishment actually serves as a reinforcement. Rather than trying to find a truly effective punishment, we think it is essential to understand *why* negative attention is reinforcing. We believe that many children are reinforced by negative attention because they are not getting enough positive attention—enough love. If so, increasing parental affection should be a better way of treating their externalizing behavior than increasing parental discipline (Emery, 1992).

Conflict and Inconsistent Discipline Inconsistent discipline is another frequent correlate of children's externalizing problems (Patterson, DeBaryshe, & Ramsey, 1989). Inconsistency can involve frequent changes in the style and standards of one parent, or two parents may be inconsistent in their differing expectations and rules for a child. For example, inconsistency between mothers and fathers often becomes a problem when parents have conflicts in their own relationship—as when they are unhappily married, divorced, or experience other forms of family adversity (Shaw & Emery, 1988; Shaw et al., 1994). In these circumstances, parents may deliberately undermine each other's discipline.

Yet another problem occurs when parents' actions are inconsistent with their words. For example, consider the contradiction inherent in angry and harsh physical punishment. On the one hand, such discipline teaches children to follow the rules. On the other hand, it teaches children that anger and aggression are acceptable means of solving problems. Parents socialize children by modeling appropriate behavior as well as by disciplining them, and children often imitate what their parents do, not what they say (Bandura, 1973).

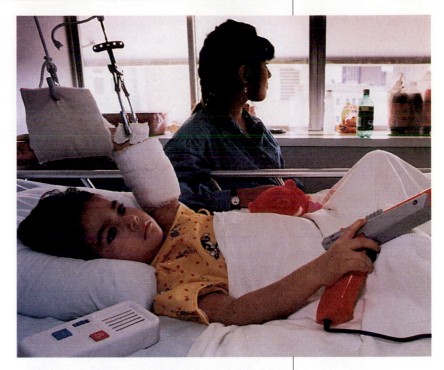

▲ Societal influences on children's behavior are pervasive. This 3-year-old boy suffered a gunshot wound during a drive-by shooting. Still, the boy plays with a toy pistol while recuperating in his hospital bed.

Broader Social Influences: Peers, Neighborhoods, Television, and Society Parents are not solely responsible for socializing children. Violence is continually modeled on television, for example, and longitudinal evidence indicates that children learn aggression from television programs (Eron, 1982). Peer groups also can teach antisocial behavior. In fact, some researchers have suggested that socialized delinquency, in which criminal acts occur in the company of others, is an important subtype of externalizing disorders (Kazdin, 1995).

A number of neighborhood and societal factors also play a role in the etiology of internalizing and especially externalizing problems. As we noted earlier, more psychological problems are found among children who grow up in poor inner-city neighborhoods (Rutter, 1978b, 1989; Shaw & Emery, 1988; Shaw et al., 1994). Professionals who wish to promote children's mental health therefore need to be concerned about poverty, inadequate schooling, and violence (Caspi & Moffitt, 1995; Dishion, French, & Patterson, 1995).

Cross-cultural evidence also points to broad societal influences on externalizing behavior. Citizens of other countries often are horrified and puzzled by the extent of teenage crime in the United States, and there is good reason for their shock and fear (see Figure 16–7). Robbery, sexual offenses, assault, and burglary are far more common in the United States than in Europe or

Rates of Violent Crime Victimization in the United States, Japan, and Europe, 1988

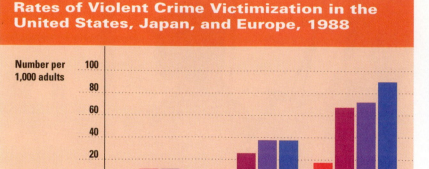

FIGURE 16-7: Delinquent and criminal behaviors are influenced by broad social forces, as well as the immediate family and peer contexts.

Source: J.P. Van Dijk and M.K. Mayhew, 1992, *Experiences of Crime Across the World: Key Findings of the 1989 International Crime Society.* Boston: Kluewer.

Note: Figure included here was reprinted in M.A. Jones and B. Krisberg, 1994, *Images and reality: Juvenile crime, youth violence, and public policy.* San Francisco: National Council on Crime and Delinquency.

Japan. As we have noted, many of these crimes are committed by juveniles. According to many politicians, crime is widespread because the United States is "soft on crime." In fact, far *more* people are imprisoned in the United States than in Europe, Canada, or Japan (see Figure 16–8).

Child Poverty, Crime, and Prison Use in the United States, Japan, Europe, and Canada

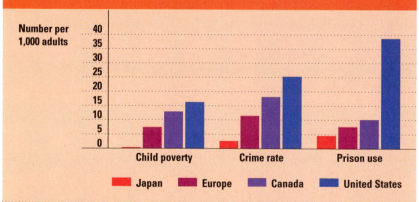

FIGURE 16-8: Prison use indicates that the United States is not "soft on crime" in comparison to other countries. Other factors, such as the higher rate of poverty, may explain the high crime rate in the United States.

Source: United Nations Interregional Crime and Justice Research Institute.

Note: Figure included here was reprinted in M.A. Jones and B. Krisberg, 1994, *Images and reality: Juvenile crime, youth violence, and public policy.* San Francisco: National Council on Crime and Delinquency.

This suggests that other aspects of U.S. culture, such as higher poverty rates or lack of gun control, may account for the societal influences on juvenile crime (Jones & Krisberg, 1994).

Social Factors in Attention-Deficit/Hyperactivity Disorder When discussing the etiology of externalizing disorders, we have not distinguished between the development of oppositional defiant disorder or conduct disorder and attention-deficit/hyperactivity disorder. In fact, none of the above findings purports to explain the unique development of ADHD. Scientists who study psychological factors in the development of externalizing problems seem to fall into one of two camps. One camp makes no diagnostic distinction between ADHD and ODD, and these scientists therefore apply all the findings to both problems. Another camp views ADHD as a biological problem, and these scientists therefore apply the findings only to oppositional defiant disorder and conduct disorder. In other words, there are essentially no theories of how social factors might play a unique role in the development of attention-deficit/hyperactivity disorder (Hinshaw, 1994).

Some researchers have found that the parents of children with ADHD are less effective than other parents. For example, mothers of children with ADHD have been observed to be more critical, demanding, and controlling when compared to the mothers of normal children (Mash & Johnston, 1982). However, problems in parenting may be a reaction to the children's troubles and not a cause of them.

Researchers have used a clever technique to document that mothers do react negatively to their children's ADHD. Scientists have compared the interactions between mothers and their children under two conditions: placebo versus medication. That is, the experimenter administers either a psychostimulant medication (discussed shortly) or a placebo in a triple-blind study (neither the child, the mother, nor the experimenter knows who received the real medication), and mother–child interactions are subsequently observed. Because psychostimulant medication directly alters children's hyperactive behavior, any differences between mother–child interactions in the two conditions must be caused by changes in the children's behavior.

In fact, children with ADHD become more attentive and compliant while on medication, and their mothers' behavior "improves" as well. In comparison to the placebo group, mothers become less negative and less controlling when their children are medicated (Barkley et al., 1984; Danforth, Barkley, & Stokes, 1991). Children with ADHD make social interactions more difficult. Still, troubled parenting surely intensifies their problems.

Biological Factors

All children require some socialization to control their selfish or aggressive behavior (Caspi & Moffit, 1995; Dishion et al., 1995). All children do not come into the world with the same behavioral tendencies, however, as any parent of two children will attest. In this section we consider four biological influences on individual differences related to the development of psychological disorders among children: temperament, behavior genetics, neuropsychological abnormalities, and the ingestion of food additives and sugar.

TEMPERAMENT

Temperament refers to a child's inborn behavioral characteristics, such as activity level, emotionality, and sociability (Buss, 1991). Temperament researchers disagree about exactly what qualities comprise children's temperamental characteristics (Goldsmith et al., 1987), but Thomas and Chess's (1977) grouping into easy, difficult, and slow-to-warm-up categories is one clear and enduring categorization of temperamental styles. *Easy* children quickly form social relationships and follow discipline; *difficult* children challenge parental authority; *slow-to-warm-up* children tend to be shy and withdrawn. Many theorists have argued that a difficult temperament is a risk factor for later externalizing disorders, an assertion that has been supported by some recent research on infants and toddlers (Shaw, Keenan, & Vondra, 1994).

Some of the most exciting recent research on children's temperament has been conducted by the psychologist Jerome Kagan and colleagues (Kagan & Snidman, 1991), who have studied a temperamental style that they call *inhibited to the unfamiliar*, which is similar to the slow-to-warm-up grouping. As opposed to uninhibited infants, infants who are inhibited to the unfamiliar cry easily and often in response to novel toys, people, or circumstances, and their psychophysiological responses (e.g., heart rate acceleration) also indicate their fearfulness. About 10 percent of babies consistently show inhibition to unfamiliar circumstances during the first 2 years of life (Kagan & Snidman, 1991). Most important for present purposes, researchers have linked behavioral inhibition with an increased risk for anxiety disorders among children and their parents or other relatives. More specifically, the prevalence of anxiety disorders is higher among parents and biological relatives of children who have been identified as inhibited than it is among the general population (Biederman, Rosenbaum, Chaloff, & Kagan, 1995).

BEHAVIOR GENETIC RESEARCH

Genes not only affect general temperamental characteristics, but they also may contribute more specifically to the development of children's psychological disorders. Few behavior genetic studies have been conducted on internalizing disorders, except for some recent research documenting genetic influences on childhood onset obsessive–compulsive disorder (March, Leonard, & Swedo, 1995).

Many scientists believe that genetics plays an especially important role in the etiology of attention-deficit/hyperactivity disorder (Barkley, 1990). Even among normal children genetic factors partly determine activity levels and attentional capacities (Scarr, 1966; Willerman, 1973). Researchers recently have identified a specific genetic disorder (that produces generalized resistance to thyroid hormone) that is strongly related to ADHD but not to other mental disorders (Hauser et al., 1993). However, only a tiny proportion of children with ADHD has this genetic disorder; thus it accounts for very few cases. In broader samples, researchers have found a 51 percent concordance rate for ADHD among MZ twins, compared with a 33 percent concordance rate for DZ pairs (Goodman & Stevenson, 1989). These data demonstrate that genes contribute to ADHD, but the moderate concordance for MZ twins indicates that nongenetic factors must be involved as well (Hinshaw, 1994).

Evidence also indicates that genetic factors influence the development of antisocial behavior. It is important to note, however, that genetic factors are much more important in the development of life-course-persistent than adolescent-limited antisocial behavior. Presumably, this is because of the strong social pressures to violate rules during the teen years (Gottesman & Goldsmith, 1994).

We noted earlier in the chapter that conventional wisdom views ADHD as a biological problem and ODD and conduct disorder as psychological problems. However, behavior genetics studies raise two basic problems with this conventional view. First, it oversimplifies etiology by pitting genes against the environment. In contrast, the systems approach acknowledges multiple contributions and multiple pathways to the development of externalizing disorders. Second, conventional wisdom confuses etiology with some basic symptoms of ADHD and ODD. Children with ADHD try but fail to control their behavior; they are impulsive. Children with ODD or CD seem like they are not trying to control their behavior; they have aggressive intentions and show lack of remorse. Such symptoms may seem to be related to biological versus psychological causation, but the relationship is only a superficial one.

If genes contribute to the development of externalizing disorders, an essential question is: What is the inherited mechanism? Hyperactivity or inattention may be directly inherited but rule violations surely are not. No one has suggested that there is a "crime gene," let alone an "argue with your teacher gene!" One inherited tendency that may contribute to ODD or CD is chronic underarousal of the autonomic nervous system. That is, children with externalizing problems may be less emotionally reactive than other children. As a result, they may be more likely to engage in stimulation-seeking and less likely to learn from punishment (Quay, 1965, 1993).

NEUROPSYCHOLOGICAL ABNORMALITIES

Findings from neuropsychological research suggest other biological contributions to externalizing disorders, particularly to attention-deficit/hyperactivity disorder. We have already noted that brain damage can produce overactivity and inattention, but *hard signs* of brain damage, such as an abnormal CT scan, are found in less than 5 percent of cases of ADHD (Rutter, 1983). Neurological *soft signs*, such as delays in fine motor coordination (as may be evident in poor penmanship) also have been found with greater frequency among children with ADHD. However, many children with ADHD do not have soft signs of neurological difficulties, and soft signs are found among many normal children who do not have neurological abnormalities (Barkley, 1990). Thus the implications of the presence of soft signs are unclear both in general and in cases of ADHD.

Minor anomalies in physical appearance, delays in reaching developmental milestones, and a history of pregnancy and birth complications also appear more commonly among children with ADHD than normal children. Thus several findings suggest that neuropsychological problems contribute to ADHD, but no clear marker of biological vulnerability has been identified. Two promising avenues for further investigation are the search for dopamine deficits and the possibility that impairments are localized in the prefrontal region of the right cerebral hemisphere, an area of the brain that may underlie attentional abilities and behavioral inhibition (Barkley, 1990).

FOOD ADDITIVES AND SUGAR

A number of people have speculated that diet and food additives can cause ADHD. However, with the exception of lead poisoning (see Chapter 15), research has failed to find a relation between diet and ADHD. Consider research on the so-called "Feingold diet." In a popular book written for parents, the physician Benjamin Feingold (1975) proposed that ADHD was caused by ingestion of food additives, particularly the *salicylates*, which are commonly found in processed foods. Feingold asserted that children would become better behaved if they avoided salicylates, and tens of thousands of parents of children with ADHD embraced his recommendation. The Feingold diet became so popular that Congress considered a ban on salicylates.

Many parents reported notable benefits of the Feingold diet, and they became staunch advocates despite the tremendous inconvenience of searching out natural foods. But the parents' great effort presented a problem. Could the diet simply have been a placebo? The answer to this question was "yes," according to researchers who randomly assigned the families of 36 boys with ADHD either to the Feingold diet or to a sham diet that required a similar effort (Harley et al., 1978). With few exceptions, the investigators found no differences between the alternative diets on parent ratings or on observations of the children's behavior in a laboratory setting. Other research has found that these dietary substances do not cause ADHD, although a small subgroup of children may respond adversely to certain food additives (Conners, 1980).

Food additives are not the only aspect of children's diets that have been suspected of causing ADHD. Parents and teachers often blame refined sugar, and physicians often recommend sugar-restricted diets to the parents of children with ADHD (Bennett & Sherman, 1983). Existing studies indicate that sugar does not cause hyperactive behavior, however, nor does the restriction of sugar lead to behavioral improvement (Milich, Wolraich, & Lindgren, 1986).

Psychological Factors

SELF-CONTROL AND EXTERNALIZING DISORDERS

Child development proceeds from the external to the internal control of emotion and behavior. For example, parents initially control children's behavior with discipline, but *self-control*, the internal regulation of behavior, is the ultimate goal of this socialization. Not surprisingly, several investigators have found problems with self-control among children with externalizing disorders.

One area of research on self-control has focused on *delay of gratification*—the adaptive ability to defer smaller but immediate rewards for larger long-term benefits. (An example of delay of gratification is studying for an exam rather than going out with friends.) In general, children with externalizing problems have been found to be lacking in the ability to delay gratification. They are more oriented to the present than are other children. They opt for immediate rewards rather than for long-term goals, a maladaptive characteristic for achieving educational and career goals (Mischel, 1983).

Children with externalizing problems also may fail to exert self-control because they misinterpret the intentions of others, particularly in ambiguous social situations. Several studies by psychologist Ken Dodge and his colleagues have indicated that aggressive children overinterpret the aggressive intentions of their peers (Dodge & Frame, 1982; Crick & Dodge, 1994). In a sense, some children with externalizing problems seem to believe that they need to "get you before you get me."

More broadly, some psychologists question the moral reasoning of children with externalizing problems. In particular, psychologist Lawrence Kohlberg (1985) created a hierarchy of moral reasoning based on the explanations children give to justify their actions. Research indicates that children use increasingly abstract and sophisticated moral principles as they grow older. For example, a young boy may say that the reason he behaves well is because "Mommy will get mad." An older boy may explain that the reason he behaves well is because "You need

to follow the rules." A teenager might explain that he behaves well because "It is the right thing to do."

According to Kohlberg, higher moral principles are based on values regarding appropriate conduct rather than on the immediate consequences of misbehavior. He has hypothesized that these more sophisticated guidelines, in turn, lead to more prosocial behavior. In support of his theorizing, some evidence indicates that aggressive children follow the hedonic principles commonly used by children at younger ages (Kohlberg, 1985). They exhibit less self-control, or to put it in familiar terms, they may have less of a "conscience" than their peers.

EMOTION REGULATION AND INTERNALIZING BEHAVIOR

Although less obvious than the regulation of behavior, the regulation of children's emotions also progresses from external to internal control across the course of development. For example, attachment relationships offer security and soothe anxiety for infants and toddlers. As children grow older, however, they develop internal *working models* or expectations about relationships as extensions of their early attachment experiences (Carlson & Sroufe, 1995). *Emotion regulation* is a more general process as children learn to identify, evaluate, and control their feelings based on the reactions, attitudes, and advice of their parents and others in their social world.

As noted earlier, our understanding of children's emotional development is far from complete, and only scattered efforts have attempted to link troubles with emotion regulation to children's internalizing disorders. One exciting example comes from the research of psychologist Carolyn Zahn-Waxler, who has conducted several studies of children of depressed mothers. Children of depressed mothers are at an increased risk for depression themselves, and Zahn-Waxler hypothesizes that troubled parenting is one contributing cause. More specifically, she believes these children take excessive responsibility in caring for their mothers, rather than being cared for by them. One problematic result of this role reversal can be excessive feelings of guilt on the part of the children. In fact, Zahn-Waxler and colleagues (1990) found excessive guilt among 5- to 6-year-old children of depressed mothers and indications of defensiveness against excessive guilt among 7- to 9-year-olds. Studies have not determined whether children's feelings of responsibility and guilt increase the risk for subsequent childhood depression, but future research should address this question. More generally, research should focus on how children are socialized to regulate various emotions and the extent to which problems in emotion regulation contribute to the development of internalizing disorders.

Integration and Alternative Pathways

How can we integrate evidence on the diverse contributions to the development of psychological disorders of childhood? Two conclusions seem clear. First, childhood disorders have many etiological pathways, not one. Obviously, different factors contribute to causing internalizing versus externalizing disorders or to causing subtypes of disorders such as ADHD versus ODD. However, there also are different pathways to the development of the *same* disorder. An example is the different pathways to externalizing behavior during adolescence. Life-course-persistent and adolescent-limited antisocial behavior cannot be distinguished based on their appearance, but the two problems clearly reflect different etiological pathways: long-standing biological and socialization problems in the former cases, and short-term rebellion and peer influences in the latter cases (Moffitt, 1993).

Second, biological, psychological, and social factors clearly interact in causing children's psychological disorders. Temperament theorists note, for example, that the *goodness of fit* between a child's temperament and the family environment may be of greatest importance to healthy psychological development (Shaw & Bell, 1993). A difficult child should benefit from firm, consistent, patient, and loving discipline, whereas the combination of a difficult temperament and family adversity may result in ODD and eventually conduct disorder (Kasen, Cohen, Brook, & Hartmark, 1996).

Can more precise etiological mechanisms be identified in the future? Perhaps, but only if scientists can identify more specific categories of children's abnormal behavior. Current diagnostic categories are very *heterogeneous*; there is much variation in the nature and severity of the symptoms across cases. Future research may succeed in identifying specific subtypes of childhood disorders, some of which may have very specific causes such as the thyroid resistance already identified among a very small proportion of children with ADHD (Hauser et al., 1993). We believe, however, that multifactorial causality and equifinality—the systems approach—will continue to be the best explanations of the etiology of most childhood disorders.

Treatment

Treatment of Internalizing Disorders

Until recently, children were expected to "outgrow" most of their internalizing problems. Thus few treatments for anxiety or mood disorders have been developed or studied specifically as they apply to children (Kazdin, 1994). Recent findings indicate, however, that the disorders are not "outgrown"—they persist across time, sometimes into adult life (Harrington et al., 1990). Children's internalizing problems therefore require treatment, and treatments need to be developed and modified to meet children's unique needs.

Some findings are beginning to emerge on the treatment of children's internalizing disorders. For example, it may surprise you to

learn that antidepressant medications are no more effective than placebos in treating depression among children and adolescents (DeVane & Sallee, 1996; Geller et al., 1992). More optimistically, children with obsessive–compulsive disorders respond positively to clomipramine, the same medication that is effective with adults (Leonard et al., 1989). Moreover, some forms of cognitive behavior and family therapy for children's internalizing problems show promise (Barrett, Dadds, & Rapee, 1996; Kendall, 1994; see Research Close-Up). Still, the most accurate conclusion about the treatment of children's internalizing disorders is that research is needed on the effects of psychological and psychopharmacological interventions.

Family Treatment of Childhood Anxiety

Few controlled studies have been conducted on the treatment of children's anxiety disorders. In fact, Barrett, Dadds, and Rapee (1996) cite their recent research on this topic as only the *second* randomized treatment study of anxiety disorders in children. An earlier study by Kendall (1994) found that cognitive behavior therapy, which included cognitive coping strategies (e.g., self-talk) and modeling, relaxation training, and exposure to feared situations, produced significant improvements among children with a diagnosed anxiety disorder. In the Kendall study, 64 percent of children no longer met diagnostic criteria for an anxiety disorder following treatment. Barrett and colleagues reasoned that family involvement in treatment might produce higher rates of improvement, as well as facilitate the maintenance of treatment gains over time.

The family treatment developed by Barrett and colleagues has three major components. First, the investigators taught parents to reward their children's courageous behavior and to ignore (extinguish) excessive complaining or fearful behavior. More specifically, the therapists taught parents to respond empathically the first time children expressed fear but to ignore subsequent complaints while encouraging and praising successful coping. Second, therapists taught parents to become more aware of their own anxiety, to cope with their own emotions, and to model successful coping with fear. Third, the therapists taught parents some basic communication and problem-solving skills so they could continue working with their children following the end of treatment.

In order to conduct the research, the investigators identified 79 children aged 7 to 14 who met diagnostic criteria for separation anxiety disorder, social phobia, or generalized anxiety disorder. They assigned children at random to either cognitive behavior therapy (CBT), cognitive behavior therapy plus family treatment (CBT + FAM), or a waitlist control group that did not receive treatment until after the study was completed. The two treatment groups received therapy for 12 sessions of 60 to 80 minutes each. The investigators completed follow-up assessments immediately following treatment, 6 months after treatment, and 12 months following the end of therapy.

The investigators replicated the results of Kendall's (1994) study and found that 57 percent of children treated with cognitive behavior therapy alone no longer met diagnostic criteria at the end of treatment. However, they found that the addition of family treatment produced better results than cognitive behavior therapy alone. Following treatment, 84 percent of children in the CBT + FAM group no longer could be diagnosed with an anxiety disorder, and the improvement rate jumped to 95 percent 1 year following treatment (compared with 70 percent for CBT alone). These differences between CBT + FAM and CBT alone were statistically significant, and both groups improved significantly more than the waitlist control group.

These findings are very promising for the treatment of children's anxiety disorders. In fact, the improvement rates, if replicated, are notably higher than improvement rates found in the treatment of anxiety disorders among adults (see Chapter 6). The fact that children's anxiety improves over time also distinguishes them from adults, among whom the benefits of treatment tend to diminish as time passes. The reason for these differences is not clear because we know little about the natural course of children's anxiety disorders. Treatment may be especially effective and enduring with children as compared to adults with anxiety disorders, or, as with many specific fears, some symptoms of anxiety disorders among children may diminish with time. Regarding the role of the passage of time, we note that 26 percent of the waitlist control group no longer met diagnostic criteria following a waiting period of roughly 3 months—a high rate of spontaneous remission but an improvement rate well below those of the two treatment groups. At a minimum, Barrett and colleagues have demonstrated the effectiveness of therapy in hastening the elimination of children's anxiety disorders. Hopefully, their optimistic findings will spur further research on both the natural course and the successful treatment of anxiety disorders among children. ■

Treatment of Externalizing Disorders

In contrast to internalizing disorders, numerous treatments have been developed for children's externalizing disorders. Unfortunately, however, these problems are difficult to change (Kazdin, 1987, 1995). The most promising treatments include psychostimulants for attention-deficit/hyperactivity disorder, behavioral family therapy for oppositional defiant disorder, and various family and residential programs for treating conduct disorders and delinquent youth.

PSYCHOSTIMULANTS AND ADHD

Every year more than 600,000 children in the United States—between 1 and 2 percent of the school-age population—are treated with **psychostimulants** for attention-deficit/hyperactivity disorder (Safer & Krager, 1988). These numbers may startle you, but medication is an inexpensive, carefully researched, and effective treatment for the disorder (Barkley, 1990; Henker & Whalen, 1989). Psychostimulants produce immediate and noticeable improvements in the behavior of about 75 percent of children with ADHD. Still, these conclusions must be qualified on several grounds. Psychostimulants have only limited effects on learning; it is not clear whether they produce long-term benefits; and they have several side effects. Finally, the effectiveness of psychostimulants is not specific to ADHD. We examine each of these issues, but first we must consider a long-held and mistaken view about psychostimulants and ADHD.

The "Paradoxical Effect" Paradox Psychostimulants are medications that heighten energy and alertness when taken in small dosages, and they lead to restless, even frenetic, behavior in larger dosages. (The effects of large doses are accurately conveyed by the street name for the drugs, "speed.") The U.S. psychiatrist Charles Bradley (1937) was one of the first to observe that stimulants seemingly have an ironic effect on overactive children. Psychostimulants speed up normal adults, but they slow down hyperactive children. For many years, professionals believed that psychostimulants therefore have a "paradoxical effect" on children with ADHD. In fact, this evidence was used to support the conclusion that ADHD had biological causes, including minimal brain dysfunction (MBD). The real irony, however, is that the idea of a paradoxical effect was, and is, wrong.

There is a simple reason why professionals mistakenly believed in the paradoxical effect for so long. It was deemed unethical to give experimental dosages of psychostimulants to normal children—even though it was accepted practice to prescribe the same medication to millions of "abnormal" children with ADHD. However, a group of researchers at the National Institute of Mental Health eventually found a clever way to address the ethical problem. They obtained permission from colleagues in the medical and mental health communities to study the effects of psychostimulants on their exceptionally competent children. The researchers found that the psychostimulants affected the normal children in the same way that they affected overactive children. The medication improved the normal children's attention and decreased their motor activity (Rapoport et al., 1978). In fact, psychostimulants have the same effects on adults when taken in comparably small dosages. There is no paradoxical effect of psychostimulants on children with ADHD.

Usage and Effects Paradox or not, psychostimulants are effective in treating ADHD. The most commonly prescribed psychostimulants are known by the trade names of Ritalin, Dexedrine, and Cylert. Each medication has the effect of increasing alertness and arousal. Psychostimulants usually are prescribed by pediatricians, who typically are consulted following a child's difficulties in the early years of school. The central nature of school-related problems is evident in the fact that psychostimulants typically are prescribed around the school day. A pill is taken before school in the morning, and because the effects of the medication last only 3 or 4 hours, another pill is taken at the lunch hour. A third pill may or may not be taken after school, but the medication typically is not taken on weekends or during school vacations because of concerns about side effects.

Children take psychostimulants for years, not days or weeks. Traditionally, medication was discontinued in early adolescence, because it was believed that the problem was "outgrown" by that age. However, follow-up studies indicate that problems with inattention, impulsivity, and hyperactivity continue through adolescence and into adult life (Thorley, 1984; Weiss et al., 1985). Thus the current trend is to continue psychostimulants through the teen years and perhaps into adulthood (Barkley, 1991; Campbell, Green, & Deutsch, 1985).

Psychostimulants indisputably improve children's attentiveness and decrease their disruptiveness (Barkley, 1991; Pelham et al., 1993). These benefits have been demonstrated in numerous double-blind, placebo-controlled studies, but they also are demonstrated more informally. Many teachers who are unaware of the new treatment send notes home about the improved behavior of one of their "problem" pupils. The benefits of psychostimulants for learning are less certain. On the one hand, psychostimulants lead to improved schoolwork, evident in more accurate completion of reading, spelling, and arithmetic assignments (Pelham et al., 1985). On the other hand, grades and achievement test scores do not improve dramatically, if they improve at all (Henker & Whalen, 1989; O'Leary, 1980).

Research on **dose-response effects,** the response to different dosages of medication, was once thought to explain the different effects on behavior and learning. Sprague and Sleator (1977) found that a lower dosage of psychostimulants produced maximum gains in learning, but the medication *interfered* with learning at higher dosages. These same higher doses produced maximum improvements in behavior, suggesting that some children received too much medication, because medication typically is increased gradually or *titrated* until maximum behavioral improvements are reached.

Dose-response effects have been inconsistent in subsequent research, however, and different children often respond uniquely to different dosages of medication (Tannock, Schachar, & Logan, 1995). Although more research is needed on dose-response effects, it is uncertain why improved attention and behavior in the classroom do not translate into notably improved grades and achievement. An even more troubling and puzzling fact is that psychostimulants have not been found to lead to long-term improvements in behavior, learning, or other areas of functioning (Barkley, 1991; Dulcan, 1986; Hinshaw, 1994).

Side Effects   The side effects of psychostimulants also are somewhat troubling. Some side effects are relatively minor, such as decreased appetite, increased heart rate, and sleeping difficulties. Evidence that psychostimulants can slow physical growth is of much greater concern. Children maintained on psychostimulants fall somewhat behind expected gains in height and weight, although rebounds in growth occur when the medication is stopped. This is one reason why the medication often is

discontinued when children are out of school. Still, careful monitoring of cases is necessary because of possible individual differences in growth effects (Campbell, Green, & Deutsch, 1985).

Another side effect that concerns some psychologists is that parents, teachers, and children often credit the pills, not the child, for the improved behavior (Whalen et al., 1976). When they are having an "off" day, for example, many children with ADHD are asked, "Did you take your pill today?" Some research indicates that ADHD children on psychostimulants do not credit "the pill"; they make internal attributions for their positive behavior (Hoza et al., 1993). Still, the question about attributions may reflect a more general concern: Should children's misbehavior be corrected with medication?

This is an important and reasonable question to ask, especially considering that the effects of psychostimulants are not specific to attention-deficit/hyperactivity disorder. Medication improves oppositional and defiant behavior as well (Klorman et al., 1994). ADHD has not been proved to be a unique biological problem with a specific biological treatment. At the same time, psychostimulants are an inexpensive and effective treatment, especially in comparison with the alternatives. Many parents and professionals identify medication as the treatment of choice for ADHD; others are fearful that we are overmedicating schoolchildren.

Antidepressant Medication for ADHD   Psychostimulants clearly are the medication of choice for treating ADHD. However, a number of children with ADHD have been treated with antidepressant medication in recent years. Although depression and ADHD often do co-occur, this is not the rationale for the treatment. Rather, the antidepressants are thought to affect ADHD symptoms directly for reasons that are not yet clear. What is clear, however, is that antidepressants are a second-line treatment for ADHD. Their use is justified only following the failure of psychostimulants (DeVane & Sallee, 1996; Biederman et al., 1989).

▲ **Psychostimulants are effective treatments of ADHD, but concern is rising that medication may be given too quickly to too many children.**

BEHAVIORAL FAMILY THERAPY

Behavioral family therapy is the major alternative treatment for ADHD, as well as a common treatment for other externalizing problems. There are several variations of behavioral family therapy, but all approaches train parents and perhaps teachers to use the principles of operant conditioning to improve discipline in children's daily life.

Behavioral family therapy typically begins with *parent training*. Parents are taught to identify specific problematic behaviors, list preferred alternative behaviors, and set consequences for appropriate and inappropriate behavior. Parents also may be told to make a "star chart" for recording children's progress and perhaps to develop a "daily report card" that the child will carry home from school as a way of coordinating discipline in both settings.

Other aspects of parent training may include teaching parents about punishment strategies, such as the time-out technique. Conventional wisdom in parent training holds that punishment should be firm but not angry, and that rewards should far outweigh punishments as a strategy of discipline. These are reasonable goals, but some experts feel that parent training should directly emphasize increasing warmth as well as discipline in parent–child relationships. From this perspective, the goal of parent training is to teach parents to be authoritative.

Research with younger (Forehand, Wells, & Griest, 1980) and older (Patterson, 1982) children with oppositional defiant disorders supports the short-term effectiveness of behavioral family therapy. Some evidence also indicates that improvements are sustained over the course of a year (Patterson & Fleischman, 1979). A comprehensive review concluded that parent training was "one of the more promising treatments for conduct disorders" (Kazdin, 1987, p. 191). The same reviewer argued, however, that conduct disorders are chronic diseases that require intensive and repeated treatment. Behavior therapy leads to short-term improvements, but because externalizing problems are often chronic, treatment may need to be repeated over time.

A positive evaluation of behavioral family therapy is tempered further by several studies that have compared the treatment with psychostimulants in working with children with ADHD. Medication has consistently been found to be more effective, although a combination of medication and behavior therapy may be better than either alone (Henker & Whalen, 1989; Pelham et al., 1993). In considering the challenges for behavioral family therapy, you should recall that the parents of children with externalizing problems are often living in adverse circumstances that make it difficult to alter their parenting (Emery, Fincham, & Cummings, 1992). In fact, parent training has been found to be less effective when family troubles are greater (Kazdin, 1995). Parents can be effective in changing children's behavior, but psychologists need to develop more effective ways of helping parents to cope with difficult family environments.

TREATMENT OF CONDUCT DISORDERS AND JUVENILE DELINQUENCY

Numerous programs have been developed to treat conduct disorders and juvenile delinquency. In fact, exciting claims about the effectiveness of new programs for difficult youth commonly are reported in the popular media. You should be cautious as you learn about these new approaches. Research indicates that conduct disorders among adolescents are even more resistant to treatment than are externalizing problems among younger children (Kazdin, 1994, 1995).

Some behavioral family therapy approaches have shown promise in treating young people with family or legal problems (Alexander & Parsons, 1982). These treatments are based on principles similar to those in programs for younger children, such as parent training. An important difference is that *negotiation*—a process in which young people are actively involved in defining rules—is central to behavioral family therapy with adolescents. An obvious reason for the negotiation strategy is that parents have less direct control over adolescents than over younger children. Because of diminishing parental control, many mental health professionals also advocate treating externalizing problems prior to adolescence.

Multisystemic therapy is another approach to family intervention that has received increasing attention (Henggeler & Borduin, 1990). In recognition of the diverse causes of externalizing behavior, multisystemic therapy combines family treatment with coordinated interventions in other important contexts of the troubled child's life, including peer groups, schools, and neighborhoods. Multisystemic therapy has not yet been adequately evaluated by independent research groups, but initial evidence is promising for improving family relationships and school attendance while reducing arrest rates among youth with conduct disorders (Borduin et al., 1995; Henggeler, 1994).

Residential Programs and Juvenile Courts A significant number of adolescents are treated in residential programs outside the home, because their conduct problems are severe, their families are dysfunctional, or they have been determined by the courts to be juvenile delinquents. One of the most actively researched residential programs is *Achievement Place*, a group home that operates according to highly structured behavior therapy principles. Achievement Place homes, like many similar residential programs, are very effective in improving aggression and noncompliance while the adolescent is living in the treatment setting. For this reason, professionals working in residential or inpatient settings are wise to adopt similar behavioral strategies. Unfortunately, the programs do not prevent **recidivism,** or repeat offending, once the adolescent leaves the residential placement (Emery & Marholin, 1977; Kazdin, 1987, 1995). Delinquent adolescents typically return to family, peer, and school environments that do not consistently reward prosocial behavior or monitor and punish antisocial behavior.

Of course, many delinquent youths are treated in the juvenile justice system, and treatment or *rehabilitation* is the explicit goal of most legal interventions with minors. The philosophy of the juvenile justice system in the United States is based on the principle of *parens patriae*—the state as parent. In theory, juvenile courts are designed to help troubled youth, not to punish them. This lofty goal is belied by research indicating that **diversion**—keeping problem youths out of the juvenile justice system—is a promising "treatment" (Davidson et al., 1987). The juvenile justice system often seems to create delinquency instead of curing it, and evidence indicates that recidivism is lower when delinquents are diverted away from the courts.

Our overview of the treatment of externalizing disorders is realistic, but we do not intend it to be pessimistic. Externalizing disorders are of vast importance for children, families, and society, and the difficulties in treating antisocial youth should be seen as a challenge and not a defeat. Perhaps the best hope is to prevent some of these problems from developing in the first place by helping to ease some of the sources of family adversity that help to create them.

Course and Outcome

Do children "outgrow" psychological disorders? Parents ask this question frequently, and the answer, obviously, is important for treatment planning. Unfortunately, the most simple answer to the question is "no," but we should briefly consider some important differences in the course and outcome of different psychological disorders of childhood.

Until recently, psychologists believed that children outgrew internalizing problems. Prospective research demonstrates, however, that certain internalizing disorders often persist over time. Specific fears tend to be relatively short-lived, but more complex disorders, such as depression (Harrington et al., 1990; Kovacs et al., 1984) and obsessive–compulsive disorder (March, Leonard, & Swedo, 1995), are likely to continue from childhood into adolescence and adult life. Thus the prognosis is not optimistic for a child who has a full-blown mood or anxiety disorder.

Externalizing disorders also are stable over the course of development, but the pattern is much the opposite as it is for internalizing disorders. Roughly half of all children with externalizing disorders continue to have problems with antisocial behavior into adulthood, but antisocial behavior rarely begins during adult life (Hinshaw, 1994; Kazdin, 1995). Somewhat different patterns of continuity hold for various subtypes of externalizing disorders. As we noted earlier, antisocial behavior that begins during adolescence has a *better* adult prognosis than antisocial behavior that begins during childhood (Moffit, 1993). Similarly, the prognosis of attention-deficit/hyperactivity disorder depends on whether there is comorbid oppositional-defiant disorder or conduct disorder. In such cases, the patients are more likely to develop problems with substance abuse, criminality, and other forms of antisocial behavior (Hinshaw, 1994).

The continuity of childhood disorders clearly underscores the need for more and better research on the etiology and effective treatment of psychological disorders of childhood. If we can do better in helping children, we will succeed in preventing a number of psychological disorders among adults.

Summary

Psychological problems that arise more commonly among children than adults are listed in the DSM-IV category "Disorders Usually First Diagnosed in Infancy, Childhood, or Adolescence." The most important disorders in this category are the various **externalizing disorders.** Externalizing disorders create difficulties for the child's external world. They are characterized by children's failure to control their behavior according to the expectations of others. The most familiar externalizing disorder is **attention-deficit/hyperactivity disorder (ADHD),** a prevalent behavior problem that is particularly noticeable in school and is characterized by inattention, overactivity, and impulsivity. ADHD often is contrasted with **oppositional defiant disorder (ODD),** an externalizing disorder characterized by negative, hostile, and defiant behavior that is also prevalent among school-aged children. **Conduct disorder (CD)** is a similar problem to ODD, except the rule violations are much more serious and conduct disorder is more common among adolescents than younger children.

Internalizing disorders are psychological problems that primarily affect the child's internal world, for example, excessive anxiety or sadness. The DSM-IV does not list internalizing disorders as separate psychological disorders of childhood but instead notes that children may qualify for many "adult" diagnoses, such as anxiety or mood disorders. The DSM does include 26 additional childhood disorders, such as **learning disorder** and **separation anxiety disorder.** Some of these additional disorders are relatively rare conditions; other DSM categories are questionable in terms of their status as "mental disorders."

At least 12 percent of the 63 million children living in the United States suffer from a mental disorder. Gender is one risk factor noted in epidemiological research: Boys are more likely to be identified as having psychological problems during childhood, but girls are found to have more difficulties in adolescence and early adult life. Apparently, adults seek treatment for children's externalizing behavior, which is more common among boys, but the increase in depression among teenagers, especially adolescent girls, begins to balance the relationship between gender and the prevalence of psychological problems. Family adversity is a particularly important risk factor for externalizing problems, and epidemiological data indicate that suicide has been a growing problem among teens.

Troubled attachments are one of the social factors that may play a role in causing children's emotional problems. Other research indicates that parents are most effective when they are **authoritative:** loving and firm in disciplining their children. **Coercion** is a more specific parenting problem that occurs when parents reinforce children's misbehavior by giving in to their demands. Conflict and inconsistent discipline are other parenting problems that may arise when parents are unhappily married or divorced. Other social factors that contribute to the etiology of internalizing and especially of externalizing problems include television violence, deviant peer groups, poverty, and societal attitudes.

Biological factors are thought to be more critical to attention-deficit/hyperactivity disorder than to oppositional defiant disorder; these include **temperament,** genetics, and neuropsychological abnormalities. However, researchers have failed to identify a specific biological etiology of ADHD, and it is clear that biological factors contribute to ODD and CD, as well as to some internalizing disorders. The comorbidity of ADHD and ODD makes it difficult to interpret past research, and both problems are heterogeneous disorders that may require further subclassification.

Biological risks and problems in **socialization** may combine to produce psychological factors that cause or maintain children's psychological disorders. Lack of self-control, a tendency to overattribute aggressive intentions to others, and less developed moral reasoning are some of the psychological characteristics related to externalizing disorders. Insecure working models of attachment or problems with emotion regulation may foreshadow the development of internalizing problems.

Few treatments for anxiety or mood disorders have been developed specifically for children, with the exception of some encouraging research on the combination of family and cognitive-behavior therapy. The most promising treatments for externalizing disorders include **psychostimulants** for attention-deficit/hyperactivity disorder, **behavioral family therapy** for oppositional defiant disorder, and multisystemic family therapy for treating conduct disorders and delinquent youth. The difficulty of changing externalizing problems is underscored by the limited success of numerous attempts to treat conduct disorders and **juvenile delinquency** in families, in group homes, and in the juvenile justice system. Data demonstrating the continuity of both externalizing and internalizing disorders underscore the need to develop more effective treatments for troubled children.

Critical Thinking

1. Under what circumstances do you think a parent or teacher might be especially biased or inaccurate in assessing a child's problem behavior? Do you think depressed, anxious, or angry parents or teachers sometimes project their own concerns on to children? How could you detect such inaccuracies, either for individual cases or on standardized instruments?

2. Family adversity is a risk factor for various externalizing problems, but many children are resilient in the face of adversity. What factors do you think help to make children resilient in the face of difficult life circumstances?

3. What are your personal thoughts on the use of psychostimulant medication? Do you think it is appropriate to use medication to help children behave in school? How might your feelings change if you had a child with attention-deficit/hyperactivity disorder?

17

Adjustment Disorders and Difficult Life Events: Life-Cycle Transitions

Epidemiological evidence tells us that at least one out of every four people who consult a mental health professional have *never* met the criteria for the diagnosis of a mental disorder (Kessler et al., 1994). What issues bring these people into treatment? Many people enter psychotherapy in the hope that it will help them cope with familiar struggles, such as making critical life decisions, marital conflict, child-rearing problems, divorce, loneliness, and bereavement. Most of these "problems in living" are listed in the DSM-IV, but they receive scant attention in the manual. Like many scientists and practitioners, we are concerned by this limited coverage. We need a more thorough understanding of difficulties that can be traced to *person–environment interactions*, psychological problems that are found not within the individual but in the relationship between the individual and his or her world.

Overview

The DSM-IV has two ways of categorizing life problems (other than mental disorders) that may cause people to seek the assistance of a mental health professional. First, the manual includes a diagnostic category for **adjustment disorders,** the development of clinically significant symptoms in response to stress that are not severe enough to warrant classification as another mental disorder. Second, the DSM-IV includes a diverse list of *other conditions that may be a focus of clinical attention*, which includes such difficulties as "partner relational problem," "bereavement," and "phase of life problem." The DSM provides only brief descriptions for both adjustment disorders and other conditions that may be the focus of treatment; it does not offer a common set of symptoms for either of these conditions; and it includes little in the way of an empirical or theoretical rationale for the classifications.

There are good reasons for these shortcomings in the DSM-IV. Different people may face a very wide array of life problems, and psychologists have not reached a consensus about how best to classify either difficult life events or people's reactions to stress (see Chapter 8). Still, psychologists have made progress in studying commonalities in difficult life experiences. In fact, scientists from a number of disciplines increasingly conduct research on **life-span development,** continuities and changes in behavior from infancy through the last years of life. As we have noted throughout this text, knowledge of normal development is essential to an understanding of abnormal behavior.

A unique aspect of the field of life-span development is its emphasis on *adult development*, the occurrence of fairly predictable challenges in relationships, work, life goals, and personal identity during adult life. Researchers have only loosely identified the ages and events that best mark the stages of adult development. In fact, we use the term *stage* tentatively, because adult development is not characterized by a sequence of time-limited and qualitatively different experiences, as the term implies. Nevertheless, several theorists divide adult development into three periods—early, middle, and later life.

Consistent with this division of adult development, we highlight three major **life-cycle transitions** in this chapter. Life-cycle transitions are struggles in the process of moving from one social or psychological stage of adult development into a new one. They are times of change that often cause interpersonal conflict and emotional distress. During a life-cycle transition,

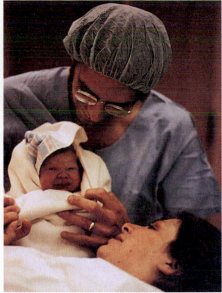

people may set their life course in a more adaptive—or maladaptive—direction. The *transition to adult life* in the late teens and early twenties is a time for grappling with the major issues related to identity, career, and relationships. *Family transitions* in the middle years of life may include very happy events, like the birth of the first child, or very unhappy ones, like a difficult divorce. The *transition to later life* may involve major changes in life roles (e.g., retirement), grief over the death of loved ones, and more abstract issues that accompany the inevitable processes of aging and facing our own mortality.

We have several reasons for discussing life-cycle transitions in a text on abnormal psychology. First, as we have noted, many people seek psychological help that either directly addresses the life problem (e.g., couples therapy) or helps the individual to adjust to the stressor. Second, a more thorough consideration of life-cycle transitions can further our understanding of the etiology of mental disorders, since life stress (or inadequate coping) may contribute to the development of individual psychopathology. Finally, we consider life-cycle transitions in order to suggest new ways of conceptualizing and treating emotional problems. The DSM is an evolving classification system, and we expect that future editions will include more *interpersonal diagnoses*—the classification of psychological problems that reside within the context of human relationships and not just within the individual (McLemore & Benjamin, 1979). We begin our consideration of adjustment disorders and difficult life events with a case study from our files.

▲ **Development continues throughout the adult life cycle. "Stages" of adult development often are marked by key transitions in family relationships and academic or work roles.**

CASE STUDY

Divorce in Midlife

Chuck M. was 51 years old when his wife told him she wanted a divorce. Chuck and his wife had been married for 27 years, and he was totally unprepared for her pronouncement. He knew that his marriage was not perfect, but he had thought of his wife's complaints as normal "nagging." He had never thought of his marriage as either particularly troubled or particularly happy. He just had not thought about his marriage much at all. Chuck was content in his lifestyle, and he could not fathom what his wife was thinking. After serving in the Navy for 20 years, Chuck was collecting a pension and working as a technician for an electronics company. His two children were grown, the family was financially secure, and Chuck was planning to retire to Florida in another 10 or 15 years. His life was on the course he had set long ago.

At first, Chuck simply did not believe what was happening. His wife said that she had been unhappy for years, and that she only recently got the courage to leave him. This account clashed with Chuck's view of the history of their marriage. He openly wondered if the real problem was his wife's menopause, or what he called "the change of life."

Reality began to hit Chuck a few weeks after his wife moved out of their house and into an apartment. Chuck's wife said that she wanted a friendly divorce, and she telephoned him a few times a week just to talk. Chuck did not want a divorce, and if it was going to come to a divorce, he certainly did not want to be "friends." He was furious with his wife, but he still worked to avoid conflicts and keep his anger under control. Chuck wanted to avoid hard feelings, at least until he figured out what was going on with his wife and his marriage. Although he saw no need for it, he consulted a clinical psychologist at his wife's suggestion. She had been seeing a counselor, and she had found their discussions very helpful.

Chuck remained stoic throughout the first several therapy sessions. He freely discussed the events of his life and admitted that he now realized that he had taken his wife for granted. He grudgingly acknowledged that he was a "little upset" and "pretty angry," but he could not or would not describe his emotions with more intensity or much more detail. Mostly, he wanted the therapist to try to help him to figure out what was really going on with his wife.

Chuck's feelings came flooding out in therapy a few weeks later when his wife told him that she was in love with another man. Chuck raged to the therapist about how he felt used and cheated. He was stunned, but he was not going to let his wife get away with this. He immediately contacted a lawyer—he wanted to make sure that his wife "didn't get a dime" out of the divorce settlement. Chuck also called his children and told them all of the details about what had happened. He seemed bent on revenge.

Chuck admitted to his therapist that, in addition to anger, he felt intense hurt and pain—real, physical pain as though someone had just punched him in the chest. When the therapist asked Chuck if any of these emotions were familiar to him, Chuck eventually recalled his feelings when he was 17 years old. His father died suddenly that year, and Chuck remembered feeling intense grief over the loss. He had controlled his feelings at the time, so he was surprised by the strong emotions he now felt in recalling the unfortunate event over 30 years later. His current feelings about his marital separation reminded him a lot of his sadness at his father's death, but his present grief was more volatile and he was much more angry than before.

Chuck began to talk more about his intense loneliness and sadness as therapy continued over the next few months and as it became clearer that his marriage really was ending. He kept up his daily routine at home and at work, but he said that it seemed as if he was living in a dream. In the midst of his grief, he sometimes wondered if his entire marriage, maybe his entire life, had been a sham. How could he have been so blind? Who was this woman he had been married to? What was he supposed to do with himself and his life plans if the divorce really happened? ■

Typical Symptoms and Associated Features of Life-Cycle Transitions

Are Chuck's reactions typical "symptoms" of adjustment to divorce?[†] Various life-cycle transitions differ greatly, and it is also true that different people respond to the same stressor in unique ways (see Chapter 8). Thus Chuck's reactions may have little in common with the feelings of other people who are getting divorced, let alone with people who are experiencing other major life changes.

At a more abstract level, however, there are some similarities across diverse life-cycle transitions. The psychologist Erik Erikson (1902–1994) highlighted *conflict* as the common theme. In fact, Erikson organized each of his eight stages of psychosocial development around a central conflict, or what he termed a *crisis of the healthy personality* (Erikson 1959, 1980; see Chapter 2). According to Erikson, the

[†] We discuss normal reactions to life-cycle transitions in this chapter; thus we often use the term *experience* instead of *symptom*. We continue to use *typical symptoms* in chapter headings for consistency with earlier chapters.

conflict inherent in change creates both intrapsychic and interpersonal tension, as the comfortable but predictable known is pitted against the fearsome but exciting unknown.

Like Erikson, we also view conflict as a commonality across different life-cycle transitions. By definition, transitions involve change, and conflict is a frequent consequence of change. Conflict is not necessarily bad; in fact, conflict may be necessary in order for change to occur. Nevertheless, conflict and change often are psychologically distressing.

Thus we view conflict as a common "symptom" or theme across very different life-cycle transitions. In discussing conflict in this chapter, we often consider its behavioral, emotional, and cognitive components. At a behavioral level, interpersonal conflicts often increase in frequency during life-cycle transitions, particularly conflicts in close relationships. Chuck's growing conflict with his former wife is an obvious example. Emotional conflicts are characterized by uncertain and opposing feelings. Chuck felt many contradictory emotions, especially conflicts between holding on to hope for his marriage, becoming angry with his wife, and feeling sad over the separation and loss. Cognitive conflicts may involve a number of challenges to self-esteem, including broad doubts about what Erikson (1968) called *identity*, our global sense of self (see Chapter 2). Psychologists typically associate identity conflicts with adolescence and early adult life, but different life-cycle transitions can cause people to reexamine basic assumptions about who they are (Waterman & Archer, 1990). Chuck certainly faced an identity crisis, as the marital separation undercut many of his assumptions about his wife, his life course, and ultimately his sense of self.

Classification of Life-Cycle Transitions

The DSM-IV includes two ways of classifying life issues that are not considered to be mental disorders but bring people to the attention of mental health professionals. *Adjustment disorders* are defined by the development of clinically significant symptoms in response to stress, but the symptoms are not severe enough to warrant classification as a mental disorder (see Table 17–1). Adjustment disorders are similar to *acute stress disorders* and *posttraumatic disorders* (see Chapter 7), because stress is an etiological factor in all three conditions. However, an adjustment disorder can be a reaction to a stressor of *any* severity, not just traumatic stress. In addition, the traumatic stress disorders share a common set of symptoms, but adjustment disorders may involve a wide array of different symptoms—anxiety, depression, conduct disturbance, or some other symptom may predominate (Frances et al., 1995). In fact, the DSM-IV offers only a very general description of the symptoms needed for a diagnosis.

▲ The psychologist Erik Erikson (1902–1994) characterized development in terms of stages extending throughout the life span. A central conflict defines the transition between each of his stages of psychosocial development.

TABLE 17–1

DSM-IV Diagnostic Criteria for Adjustment Disorder

A. The development of emotional or behavioral symptoms in response to an identifiable stressor(s) occurring within 3 months of the onset of the stressor(s).

B. These symptoms or behaviors are clinically significant as evidenced by either of the following:
1. Marked distress that is in excess of what would be expected from exposure to the stressor
2. Significant impairment in social or occupational (academic) functioning

C. The stress-related disturbance does not meet the criteria for another specific Axis I disorder and is not merely an exacerbation of a preexisting Axis I or Axis II disorder.

D. The symptoms do not represent bereavement.

E. Once the stressor (or its consequences) has terminated, the symptoms do not persist for more than an additional 6 months.

The DSM-IV also contains a list of *other conditions that may be a focus of clinical attention*, sometimes referred to as "V codes."[†] This list is not a conceptually coherent summary of life difficulties (see Table 17–2), and the DSM-IV offers only very brief descriptions of each problem. For example, here is the manual's *entire* coverage of *partner relational problem*: "This category should be used when the focus of clinical attention is a pattern of interaction between spouses or partners characterized by negative communication (e.g., criticisms), distorted communication (e.g., unrealistic expectations), or noncommunications (e.g., withdrawal) that is associated with clinically significant impairment in individual or family functioning or the development of symptoms in one or both partners" (DSM-IV, p. 681). Because of the limitations in the DSM-IV, we focus on other attempts to categorize life struggles during the course of adult development.

BRIEF HISTORICAL PERSPECTIVE

The concept of adult development is a very recent idea when viewed from a historical perspective. Erikson (1959, 1980) first highlighted the notion in his work on the eight stages of psychosocial development from birth until death (see Table 2–4). Erikson's model includes four stages of adult development: (1) identity versus role confusion, (2) intimacy versus self-absorption, (3) generativity versus stagnation, and (4) integrity versus despair. Erikson viewed *identity versus role confusion* as the major challenge of adolescence and young adulthood. The young person's goal is to integrate various role identities into a global sense of self. The resolution of the **identity crisis,** this period of basic uncertainty about self, provides the first complete answer to the question "Who am I?" In Erikson's view, the resolution of the identity crisis allows young adults to embark on a journey toward achieving long-term life goals.

[†] The term V *code* has no special meaning; it refers to the letter of an appendix in the International Classification of Disease where the codes were once listed.

TABLE 17-2

DSM-IV Listing of Other Conditions That May Be a Focus of Clinical Attention*

Relational Problems

Relational problem related to a mental disorder or general medical condition
Parent–child relational problem
Partner relational problem
Sibling relational problem

Additional Conditions That May Be a Focus of Clinical Attention

Noncompliance with treatment
Malingering
Adult antisocial behavior
Child or adolescent antisocial behavior
Borderline intellectual functioning
Age-related cognitive decline
Bereavement
Academic problem
Occupational problem
Identity problem
Religious or spiritual problem
Acculturation problem
Phase of life problem

*The category also includes the subgroups of *psychological factors affecting medical conditions* (see Chapter 8), *medication induced movement disorders* (see Chapter 13), and *problems related to abuse or neglect* (see Chapter 18).

According to Erikson, one life goal is to form an intimate relationship early in adulthood. In his second stage of adult development, *intimacy versus self-absorption*, Erikson described the challenge in establishing intimate relationships as achieving a balance between closeness and independence. Self-absorption characterizes people who either become dependent in intimate relationships or remain aloof from others. Of course, people can remain aloof either inside or outside of close relationships.

People who succeed in establishing a truly intimate relationship are better prepared for their family and work lives. According to Erikson, they nevertheless eventually encounter the third crisis of adult life, *generativity versus stagnation*. Generativity is defined by accomplishments in middle adult life. These accomplishments include career achievements, but success in rearing children also is critical from Erikson's perspective. People who stagnate may have both a family and a job, but they steer their life course without a sense of purpose or direction in either of these principal areas of adult life.

Erikson's last stage of psychosocial development involves the conflict between *integrity and despair*. People can look back on their lives either with a sense of acceptance or a sense of despair or anger. Integrity comes from pride in life accomplishments and, more importantly, from the acceptance of personal history. Despair comes from the impossible desire to change the past and from yearning for a second chance at life.

CONTEMPORARY CLASSIFICATION OF LIFE-CYCLE TRANSITIONS

Erikson's views continue to be used to classify and comprehend life-cycle transitions. He focused largely on the psychological side of psychosocial development, however, whereas many contemporary approaches emphasize the social aspects of life-span changes. For example, some contemporary researchers study the **family life cycle**—the developmental course of family relationships throughout life. Table 17–3 offers an example of one such approach to classifying the family life cycle.

Family life cycle theorists classify adult development based on the tasks and transitions of family life rather than on the psychological challenges of adulthood. Their efforts to delineate the family life cycle typically define stages around major changes in children's developmental status, because shifts in children's development create marked changes not only for children

as individuals but also for the family as a whole. In reviewing these important and familiar transitions in family life, you should note that these stages of family development are not the same for everyone, and they focus mainly on the experience of white, middle-class families in the United States. We consider both common themes and diversity in family transitions in more detail later in this chapter.

Another example of a greater emphasis on social rather than purely psychological tasks of adult development has been offered by psychologist Daniel Levinson. Levinson (1986) emphasized three major (and many more minor) transitions between broad "eras" or "seasons" in adult life. The *early adult transition* involves moving away from family and assuming adult roles. In Levinson's view, the *midlife transition* is a time for becoming less driven by internal and

TABLE 17–3
The Family Life Cycle

Stage	Family Developmental Tasks
1. **Married Couple**	Establishing a mutually satisfying marriage; adjusting to pregnancy and the promise of parenthood; fitting into kin network
2. **Childbearing**	Having, adjusting to, and encouraging the development of infants; establishing a satisfying home for both parents and infants
3. **Preschool Age**	Adapting to the critical needs and interests of preschool children in stimulating, growth-promoting ways; coping with energy depletion and lack of privacy as parents
4. **School Age**	Fitting into the community of school-aged families in constructive ways; encouraging children's educational achievement
5. **Teenage**	Balancing freedom with responsibility as teenagers mature and emancipate themselves; establishing postparental interests and careers
6. **Launching Center**	Releasing young adults into work, military service, college, marriage, and so forth with appropriate rituals and assistance; maintaining a supportive home base
7. **Middle-Aged Parents**	Rebuilding the marriage relationship; maintaining kin ties with older and younger generations
8. **Aging Family Members**	Coping with bereavement and living alone; closing the family home or adapting to aging; adjusting to retirement

Source: E. M. Duvall and B. C. Miller, 1985, *Marriage and Family Development*, p. 62. New York: Harper & Row.

Life Transitions During the Adult Years

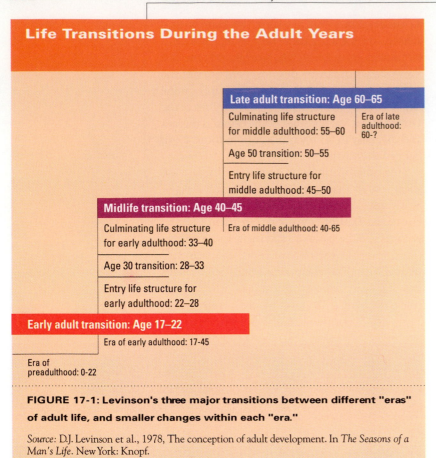

Late adult transition: Age 60–65

Culminating life structure for middle adulthood: 55–60 | Era of late adulthood: 60–?

Age 50 transition: 50–55

Entry life structure for middle adulthood: 45–50

Midlife transition: Age 40–45

Culminating life structure for early adulthood: 33–40 | Era of middle adulthood: 40–65

Age 30 transition: 28–33

Entry life structure for early adulthood: 22–28

Early adult transition: Age 17–22

Era of early adulthood: 17–45

Era of preadulthood: 0–22

FIGURE 17-1: Levinson's three major transitions between different "eras" of adult life, and smaller changes within each "era."

Source: D.J. Levinson et al., 1978, The conception of adult development. In *The Seasons of a Man's Life.* New York: Knopf.

external demands and for developing more compassion for ourselves and others. This is his somewhat controversial idea of a "midlife crisis." The *late adult transition,* according to Levinson, is characterized by the changing roles and relationships of later life (see Figure 17–1).

All these models of adult development are intriguing, but they must be considered with some caution. One caution is that history, culture, and personal values strongly influence views about which tasks are "normal" during the course of adult development. For example, Erikson's writing dates to the middle of the twentieth century. One reflection of cultural and historical influences on his model is that he assumed that normal adult development included forming an intimate heterosexual relationship and remaining in a lifelong partnership. We can readily question his implicit assumption that deviations from this pattern were "abnormal" by pointing to the more diverse lifestyles and demographics of our times. In contrast to Erikson's perspective, contemporary life-span psychology notes that many diverse paths may be traveled in the journey through normal adult life.

Another caution is that transitions or "crises" may not be as predictable as the models imply. Some people may not pass through a particular stage of development. For example, not everyone experiences an identity crisis during the transition to adult life, and nor do all people have a midlife crisis when they turn 40. In addition, once a crisis is resolved, it is not necessarily resolved permanently. Still, the outlines offered by Erikson, Levinson, and family life cycle theorists do capture broad commonalities in the experiences of a great many people. At the very least, we all develop **social clocks**—age-related goals for ourselves—and we evaluate our achievements to the extent that we are "on time" or "off time," according to our individual social clocks.

The Transition to Adulthood

In the United States, the transition to adult life typically begins late in the teen years, and it may continue into the middle twenties or even later. During this age range, young adults assume increasing independence, and many leave their family home. By the end of the transition, young adults have begun life roles in the central areas of adult development: love and work.

Typical Symptoms and Associated Features of the Adult Transition

In writing about the transition to adult life, Erikson (1959, 1980) argued that, in order to assume successful and lasting adult roles, young people need a **moratorium,** a time of uncertainty about themselves and their goals. In his words:

> The period can be viewed as a *psychosocial moratorium* during which the individual through free role experimentation may find a niche in some section of his society, a niche which is firmly defined and yet seems to be uniquely made for him. In finding it the young adult gains an assured sense of inner continuity and social sameness which will bridge what he *was* as a child and what he is *about to become,* and will reconcile his *conception of himself* and his community's

recognition of him. (pp. 119–120, italics in original)

IDENTITY CRISIS

As conveyed by this quotation, Erikson focused on the identity crisis as the central psychological conflict during the transition to adult life. Identity conflicts are epitomized by the searching and repeated question "Who am I?" Erikson's focus on identity has much intuitive appeal, as it seems to capture many familiar experiences. In fact, the identity crisis is a frequent theme in novels like J. D. Salinger's *The Catcher in the Rye* and movies such as *Reality Bites*. At this time of multiple changes in life roles, many of us feel unable to decide on a career, and our tentative choices are uncertain and volatile. We question our values and loyalties about religion, sex, relationships, and morality. We often doubt our ability to succeed in work or in relationships. Significantly, we also lack perspective on our experience. We feel as though we are confronting fundamental questions about who we are rather than merely passing through a stage.

CHANGES IN ROLES AND RELATIONSHIPS

Other things besides a person's identity change during the transition to adulthood. Young adults must make decisions about whether and where to go to college and what career paths to pursue. Such major decisions can permanently alter the course of life.

New boundaries also must be negotiated in the relationships between young adults and their parents. Finding the right balance between autonomy and relatedness is difficult (Allen & Hauser, in press). Conflicts in parent–child relationships increase during adolescence, as young people interpret parental control as an infringement on their independence (Smetana, 1989).

The theories of the ego psychologist Karen Horney (1939) are helpful to an understanding of conflicted relationships between parents and young adults, as well as other relationship difficulties throughout the adult life cycle. Horney theorized that people have competing needs to move toward, to move away from, and to move against others. *Moving toward* others fulfills needs for love and acceptance. *Moving away* from others is a way of establishing independence and efficacy. *Moving against* others meets the individual's need for power and dominance. According to Horney, relationship difficulties come from conflicts among these three basic

needs. Young adults want their parents' support; they also want their own independence; and at the same time, they may also want to outdo their parents.

Conflicts often increase in relationships with peers as well as with parents during the transition to adult life. Young adults become less certain about their friends as they become less certain about themselves. In fact, a sense of certainty about personal identity is correlated with both greater intimacy and the relative lack of conflict in peer relationships, including loving relationships (Fitch & Adams, 1983). Another important change is that relationships, especially intimate relationships, take on new meanings during the transition to adult life. Young adults seriously consider the possibility of making a lifelong commitment, a prospect that puts new pressures on love relationships.

The number of changing roles and relationships suggests that the search for self during the transition to adulthood may be less of an attempt to define a single "me" and more of a struggle to integrate new role identities with old ones. Given all of the real and practical changes during the transition to adult life, it is not surprising that many of us ask: "Who am I?"

EMOTIONAL TURMOIL

Emotional conflicts also mark the transition to adult life, as well as earlier adolescent transitions (Paikoff & Brooks-Gunn, 1991). Research has shown that young people experience more intense and volatile emotions than adults do. In a clever series of studies, "beepers" were used to signal adolescents and adults at various times during the day and night in order to assess their activities and emotional states. In comparison to adults, young people between the ages of 13 and 18 reported emotions that were more intense, shorter lived, and more subject to change (Csikszentmihalyi & Larson, 1984; Larson, Csikszentmihalyi, & Graef, 1980).

Anxiety and depression often increase somewhat during the transition to adult life, but in our view many emotional conflicts stem from uncertainty about relationships. In particular, Horney's conflicting needs to move toward, away from, and against others may be experienced as emotional conflicts. That is, young people often

▲ Uncertainty about identity, relationships, and life goals is common during the transition to adult life. The movie *Reality Bites* offered a contemporary portrayal of the struggles involved in assuming adult roles.

experience the conflicting feelings of love (moving toward), sadness (moving away from), and anger (moving against). Their emotional struggles may stem from both conflicts among these competing feelings and the intensity with which young people feel each of these emotions.

Classification of Identity Conflicts

The DSM-III-R listed "identity disorder" as a psychological disorder of childhood, but the DSM-IV has wisely moved identity problems to the section on "other conditions that may be a focus of clinical attention" (see Table 17–2). As with all of these life problems, the description of identity problems in the DSM-IV is much briefer than the detailed consideration of mental disorders. There is one sentence: "This category can be used when the focus of clinical attention is uncertainty about multiple issues relating to identity such as long-term goals, career choice, friendship patterns, sexual orientation and behavior, moral values, and group loyalties" (p. 685).

Other classification efforts have divided identity conflicts according to a progression of stages in achieving an independent sense of self. Based on Erikson's concepts, Marcia (1966) proposed several categories of identity conflict. Young people who have questioned their childhood identities but who are not actively searching for new adult roles fall into the category of *identity diffusion*. *Identity foreclosure* describes young adults who never question themselves or their goals but who instead proceed along the predetermined course of their childhood commitments. People who are in the middle of an identity crisis and who are actively searching for adult roles fall into a grouping called *identity moratorium*. Finally, young people who have questioned their identities and who have successfully decided on their own long-term goals have reached the stage of *identity achievement*.

Some research supports the validity of these categories (Marcia, 1994). For example, the percentage of students classified as identity achievers increases between the first and last years of college (Waterman, Geary, & Waterman, 1974), and the percentage continues to increase in the years after college graduation (Waterman & Goldman, 1976). Consistent with Erikson's theory, identity achievers also are less conforming and more confident in social interaction than others are (Adams et al., 1985; Adams, Abraham, & Markstrom, 1987). At the same time,

researchers have failed to detect a clear developmental sequence in Marcia's four categories; they do not appear to be actual stages of identity formation. What is most notable, however, is the general neglect of empirical research on the development of identity.

Epidemiology of Identity Conflicts

The epidemiology of the transition to adult life is easy to characterize. Given sufficient time, everyone eventually becomes an adult! More serious questions can be asked about this process: How many people experience significant distress during this phase of development? How many people never fully assume the responsibility of adult roles? To what extent are identity conflicts influenced by cultural expectations?

Unfortunately, psychologists have few empirical answers to these crucial questions. Perhaps the most important epidemiological evidence pertains to cultural influences on identity formation. For example, research conducted during the 1960s, a time of social and political strife, particularly for college students, suggested that a new identity status was common during this historical period: *alienated identity achievement*. Young people with this status assumed an adult identity (they were identity achievers), but their definition of self was alienated; it conflicted with many values held by the larger society (Marcia, 1980). These people chose new adult roles that differed from traditional ones.

College students may be less alienated today than they were in the 1960s. Instead, demographic data suggest more reasons for alienation among a different group of young adults. The William T. Grant Foundation's Commission on Work, Family, and Citizenship (1988) brought particular attention to the status of the "forgotten half"—youth who do not attend college and who often assume marginal roles in U.S. society. The commission concluded:

Our 2-year study of 16- to 24-year-olds has convinced us that, as young Americans navigate the passage from youth to adulthood, far too many flounder and ultimately fail in their efforts. Although rich in material resources, our society seems unable to ensure that *all* our youth will mature into young men and women able to face their futures with a sense of confidence and security. This is especially true of the 20 million non-college-bound young people we have termed the Forgotten Half. . . . Opportunities for today's young workers who begin their careers with only a high school diploma or less are far more constrained than were those of their peers of 15 years ago. Typically, they cope with bleak job prospects by delaying marriage and the formation of their families. Many stop looking for work altogether. Disappointed in their ambitions and frustrated in their efforts to find a satisfying place in their communities, an unacceptably high number of young Americans give little in return to their families, their schools, and their work. (p. 1)

The report about the "forgotten half" highlights the influence of society on the transition of adult life. Young adults cannot form an enduring identity in their occupations if there are few attractive job opportunities. Identity diffusion may be a consequence of unresolved psychological conflicts, but delays in making commitments to work and family can also result from the limited opportunities available to some members of society.

Etiological Considerations and Research on the Adult Transition

Few psychologists have attempted to predict empirically who will have more difficulties with the transition to adulthood. Nevertheless, the broad influences of family and society appear to be of central importance (Oosterwegel & Wicklund, 1995). Psychological research suggests that the most successful young adults have parents who strike a balance between continuing to provide support and supervision of their children and allowing them increasing independence (Hill & Holmbeck, 1986). Identity achievers often grow up in such families, whereas identity diffusers may have rejecting and distant families, and identity foreclosers may have overprotective families (Adams & Adams, 1989; Marcia, 1994). Moreover, young people who come from troubled families are more successful when they have developed a close and supportive relationship with some other adult (Werner & Smith, 1982).

Is the absence of an identity crisis a problem that foreshadows identity conflicts later in life? Little research has been conducted on this important question, but cross-cultural considerations imply that avoiding an identity crisis may not be a problem. In fact, some commentators have suggested that the struggles of the transition to adult life are a consequence of the affluence, education, and alternative roles available to young people in industrialized societies. In less developed countries, people's life course may be determined by parental authority or economic necessity, neither of which allows for an identity crisis. In considering this, you should also note that adult roles were assumed at much younger ages in the United States in the not-too-distant past, as they still are in many nonindustrialized societies.

Gender roles also appear to influence the resolution of the identity crisis and the formation of identity. Erikson's theories have been criticized for focusing on men to the exclusion of women. As an alternative, it has been suggested that women often form identities based more on family relationships than on instrumental success in a career (Gilligan, 1982). Consistent with this perspective, some evidence indicates that the process of developing an identity is different among women with traditional gender-role orientations than it is among others. Men may form an identity *before* entering into lasting relationships with others. Women in traditional roles, however, may define themselves in terms of their significant relationships with other people; that is, their identity develops out of their relationships, not vice versa. For these women, relationship intimacy may be fused with identity rather than being a consequence of it (Dyk & Adams, 1990).

Treatment During the Transition to Adult Life

No research has been conducted on alternative treatments for people who are experiencing distress during the transition to adult life. Clinical reports indicate that many young adults seek therapy at this time, an observation bolstered by the frequent utilization of college counseling services. As discussed in the clinical literature, treatment goals include validating the young person's distress and helping him or her to understand and clarify difficult life choices. In addition, it may be helpful to "normalize" the experience of identity conflict; that is, to conceptualize the individual's struggle as a part of the difficult but normal confusion that results from the search for self. Finally, many clinicians suggest that supportive, nondirective therapy is a particularly appropriate treatment approach, because seeking autonomy is a recurring theme of the transition to adulthood. Each of these observations holds intuitive appeal, but firm conclusions await empirical validation.

Family Transitions

Family transitions are major changes in family life and family relationships. They typically involve the addition or loss of members of a family household. Among the major transitions are the transitions to marriage, parenting, and the *empty nest*—the adjustment that occurs when adult children leave the family home. Other family transitions may involve only changes in relationships and not in household composition, such as when an adolescent assumes more independence. Divorce and remarriage also are common family transitions in the United States today, an observation that underscores the fact that families extend beyond the boundaries of one household.

Clearly, there are many different types of families, including married families, single-parent families, divorced families, remarried families, gay and lesbian families, childless families, and extended family groups. Nevertheless, social scientists find it helpful to consider the family life cycle, a fairly predictable sequence of development in family relationships across time (see Table 17–3). In fact, changes in family relationships are the focus of many of the key transitions in adult development in the middle years of life.

Typical Symptoms and Associated Features of Family Transitions

All family transitions are characterized by change—changes in time demands, changing expectations, and changes in the degree of control or warmth in family relationships. Early in marriage, newlyweds must directly or indirectly negotiate their expectations about time together, emotional closeness, and who will assume authority and responsibility for performing different tasks inside and outside the household. The roles that couples assume in the first years of their marriage often set a pattern that lasts for a lifetime. Nevertheless, aspects of the marital roles must be renegotiated when children are born. Children place numerous demands on each partner's time, energy, and patience. Although it is a joyous event for many young couples, the birth of the first child also challenges the marital relationship. A spouse's needs may become second priority to the demands of parenting, and the birth of children also confronts young adults with the substantial dilemma of choosing between priorities in work and family (Cowan & Cowan, 1993).

As children grow older, parents must gradually allow their relationships with their children to change in order to meet the children's developmental needs. Maintaining warmth while loosening the reins of control is the overriding theme of change in parent–child relationships. When children leave the family home, adults must discover or rediscover interests inside

"Do you want to tell him he's taking all the fun out of our marriage or shall I?"

their marriage and outside the home. These patterns are again altered by the birth of grandchildren, retirement, and other family transitions of later life.

FAMILY CONFLICT

Increased family conflict is a common consequence of all of these changes in family relationships. The increase in conflict is illustrated by research on the relationship between children's age and parents' marital satisfaction. On average, marital satisfaction declines following the birth of the first child and does not rise again until the family nest begins to empty (Anderson, Russell, & Schumm, 1983; Rutter & Rutter, 1993).

Family members may fight about hundreds of different issues. However, psychologists generally have been more concerned with the process than with the content of family conflicts. One analysis suggests that all disputes during family transitions ultimately involve either power struggles or intimacy struggles. *Power struggles* are attempts to change dominance relations, whereas *intimacy struggles* are attempts to alter the degree of closeness in a relationship (Emery, 1992). Uncertainty about the **boundaries** or rules of the relationship may make conflicts particularly difficult during family transitions. Each dispute takes on added importance because it sets a precedent for the new roles that are being defined in the relationship. As family members move through the transition, they eventually negotiate new boundaries for their relationship. Conflict is reduced as they reach this broader understanding.

Increased conflict may be a normal part of family transitions, but conflict creates great difficulties for some families. One of the most consistent findings in the study of family interactions concerns the **reciprocity** or social exchange of cooperation and conflict (Jacobson, Follette, & McDonald, 1982; Margolin, 1981; Patterson, 1982). Family members who have happy relationships reciprocate each other's positive actions, but they overlook negative behavior. A grouchy remark is dismissed as part of a "bad day," whereas a compliment is readily returned. In contrast, family members who have troubled relationships are caught in negative cycles of interaction. They ignore positive initiations but reciprocate negative ones. Pleasant comments may be seen as manipulative or may simply be ignored, whereas a sarcastic comment elicits retaliation in a game of one-upsmanship. In

fact, the reciprocity of conflict can escalate into episodes of family violence (Cordova, et al., 1993; see Chapter 18).

A particular problem in marital conflict is the *demand and withdrawal* pattern, where the wife becomes increasingly demanding and the husband withdraws further and further as time passes. Conflicts go unresolved, and the couple's relationship grows increasingly distant. Evidence indicates that demand and withdrawal interactions predict future marital disatisfaction, especially among women (Heavey, Christensen, & Malamuth, 1995). Other evidence indicates that conflicts in troubled families are more likely to continue over time and to spill over into other family relationships (Margolin, Christensen, & John, 1996). For example, marital conflicts may lead to fights between parents and children, perhaps because of the parents' negative affect or because the children become another focus of an ongoing marital dispute.

EMOTIONAL DISTRESS

Whether family conflict is expressed through explosive outbursts, constant bickering, or the "silent treatment," fighting often causes emotional distress for all family members. In fact, differences in emotional arousal between men and women may explain the demand and withdrawal pattern of interaction. Research on psychophysiological arousal during marital conflict indicates that men experience high psychophysiological (emotional) arousal as negative, whereas women do not (e.g., Levenson, Carstensen, & Gottman, 1994). That is, women appear to be comfortable with the emotion produced by marital disputes, but men are uncomfortable with their strong emotions. As a result, men may withdraw from marital disagreements as a way of regulating their own affect. The reduction in emotional arousal, in turn, negatively reinforces men's disengagement; thus the pattern of withdrawal is likely to continue. In contrast, women's emotions do not interfere with marital interaction; thus they may appear demanding as they

▲ The movie *Mrs. Doubtfire* conveyed some of the emotional conflict of divorce. In order to maintain contact with his children, the character played by Robin Williams dressed as an older woman and became a housekeeper for his children and former wife.

continue to attempt to resolve the dispute (Gottman & Levenson, 1988).

Arguments not only upset the opponents in a dispute, but they can reverberate throughout the family (Cummings & Davies, 1994). For example, children are often upset by their parents' conflicts even when there is no spillover of marital hostility. In fact, researchers have found that children's psychophysiological arousal increases in response to observing their parents' fighting (Gottman & Katz, 1989).

Increased emotional distress may be only a temporary, if trying, consequence of family transitions. However, unresolved conflicts may lead to more serious emotional problems. Ongoing family conflict, particularly marital conflict, is closely linked with depression, especially among women (Beach, Sandeen, & O'Leary, 1990). Marital distress also is associated with an increased risk for agoraphobia (Barlow, O'Brien, & Last, 1984), and parental conflict predicts increased behavior problems among children (Emery, 1982). As we saw in the case of Chuck M., moreover, emotional turmoil is a clear and painful consequence of separation and divorce. Significantly, women are more likely to become depressed in response to marital conflict, whereas men are more likely to experience depression following a divorce (Gotlib & McCabe, 1990). (See Further Thoughts in Chapter 18 for a discussion of children and divorce.)

COGNITIVE CONFLICTS

Cognitive conflicts also may accompany difficult family transitions. Attribution of blame for family distress is one specific source of cognitive conflict. For example, happily married couples blame their marital disputes on difficult but temporary circumstances. In contrast, among unhappily married couples each partner tends to blame the conflict on difficulties in the other partner's personality (Bradbury & Fincham, 1990).

Family transitions also can cause broader cognitive conflicts. Identity conflicts may be renewed, especially because identity often is closely linked with family roles. For example, a divorce may challenge a woman's identity, especially if much of her sense of self is based on her roles as wife and mother. Marriage, childbirth, and the empty nest also lead to role changes that may lead to a broad redefinition of self. In addition to challenges to personal identity, we often are confronted by a fundamental conflict between *acceptance and change* when moving through a life transition or when attempting to reconcile ongoing problems with a family member (Jacobson & Christensen, 1996). Our ability to mold our children, parents, or partners—or ourselves—is not limitless. We all must learn to accept those things we cannot change in our loved ones if we want to maintain harmony and happiness within our families and ultimately within ourselves.

Classification of Troubled Family Relationships

Family transitions can be classified according to different stages in the family life cycle (see Table 17–3), but some family theorists have developed very different typologies of family difficulties. For example, psychologist Lorna Benjamin (1993) has proposed that Sullivan's interpersonal theory of personality (see Chapter 3) can be used to classify personality disorders within the context of key relationships. Benjamin argues that there are two key dimensions of relationships, an affiliation dimension and an interdependence dimension. Her *affiliation* continuum is anchored by attack at one end and active love at the opposite extreme. Her *interdependence* dimension has control and emancipation at the two opposite extremes. From these two dimensions, she derives four basic styles of relationships, as portrayed in Figure 17–2.

Yet another way of classifying family relationships comes from the clinical literature on family therapy. This more informal approach categorizes constellations or patterns of family

A Classification of Relationship Types

| Hostile differentiation | Friendly differentiation |
| Hostile enmeshment[†] | Friendly enmeshment[†] |

FIGURE 17-2: Four types of relationships derived from Benjamin's dimensions of affiliation and interdependence. Benjamin's proposal is an example of an attempt to classify troubled relationships instead of troubled individuals.

[†] Enmeshment refers to overly involved relationships.

Source: L.S. Benjamin, 1993, *Interpersonal Diagnosis and Treatment of Personality Disorders,* p. 59. New York: Guilford.

relationships. The scapegoating pattern is a commonly discussed example of this approach to family typology. A *scapegoat* is a family member who is held to blame for all of a family's troubles. The concept of scapegoating is akin to the idea of the "common enemy" in international relations. Common enemies can create alliances between enemies, as occurred in World War II when the United States and the Soviet Union joined forces in opposing Nazi Germany. Scapegoating in families is thought to serve a similar function. For example, unhappily married parents may unite in their mutual blaming of family difficulties on a scapegoated child. The scapegoat is treated like an outsider in a family, as illustrated in Figure 17–3, which portrays a boy's view of his family.

These and other approaches to classifying family relationships hold some appeal, but current attempts to classify family problems are inadequate both conceptually and empirically. Researchers first must demonstrate the reliability and validity of family classifications. Ultimately, they must prove that the family approach to classification is superior to categorizing individuals, at least in some areas of functioning. Such empirical efforts seem worthwhile, because many sources of emotional distress may be more adequately conceptualized within the context of key family relationships.

Epidemiology of Family Transitions

Epidemiological evidence is scant on the percentage of families who have difficulties with many life transitions. However, sound data are available on the number of people who pass through various family transitions with or without troubles. In fact, such data are considered to be so important to our national well-being that they often are collected by the U.S. Census Bureau.

Alternative lifestyles notwithstanding, evidence clearly indicates that most adults in the United States—over 90 percent—get married during their adult lives. Age at first marriage has increased in recent years, and nearly half of all people who get married today report a history of cohabitation prior to marriage (Cherlin, 1992). About five out of every six married women in the United States bear a child, but childbirth increasingly takes place outside marriage. In 1990, about 33 percent

Miguel's "Sculpture" of His Family

FIGURE 17–3: Miguel arranged family members in this way when asked to make a "sculpture" of his family during a family therapy session. Miguel put himself behind the table and apart from his siblings and parents, a clue to his status as the family scapegoat.

Source: Illustration by Gaston Weisz. In R. Sherman and N. Fredman, 1986, *Handbook of Structured Techniques in Marriage and Family Therapy*, p. 76. New York: Brunner/Mazel.

of all first-time mothers were unmarried, including 74 percent of blacks and 26 percent of whites. Only 18 percent of first-time, unmarried mothers are over the age of 25; about 50 percent are teenagers (Cherlin, 1992; Hernandez, 1993).

Although probably very few people live "happily ever after," at any point in time most people report their marriage is happy. One national survey of the parents of children aged 7 to 11 found that 69 percent reported their marriage to be "very happy," 28 percent said it was "fairly happy," and 3 percent admitted it was "not too happy" (Zill, 1978). The extent to which marital happiness fluctuates is not known, nor do we know the number of couples who become extremely dissatisfied with their marriage at some point.

Divorce rates have increased dramatically in the United States since the 1960s, and much research has focused on this important topic. Estimates indicate that about half of all existing marriages will end in divorce. Most divorces occur early in a marriage, moreover, so that about half of all divorces take place within the first 7 years of marriage. Divorce is likely to be followed by remarriage, especially among whites. About three out of four whites, and perhaps one out of two blacks, remarry following a divorce. In addition, a large number of divorced adults also cohabit either before or instead of remarrying (Cherlin, 1992).

Etiological Considerations and Research on Family Transitions

Most theories of the causes of difficulties in family transitions emphasize psychological and social factors. This focus is not surprising, given that family life obviously is an environmental event.

However, it is also true that individuals make their own environments; thus environments are partially *heritable* (see Research Methods). For these reasons, it is important that we briefly examine biological contributions to family transitions after we consider psychological and social factors.

RESEARCH METHODS

The Concept of Heritability

Behavior genetics is the study of genetic contributions to complex behavior like psychopathology (see Chapter 2). The twin study is the most common method used in behavior genetics. We have reviewed numerous examples of twin research throughout this text, and we have noted that the evidence indicates numerous genetic contributions to abnormal behavior. When researchers find that MZ twins have higher concordance rates for a particular behavioral characteristic than do DZ twins, they rightly conclude that genes contribute to the development of the characteristic.

The value of twin studies for identifying genetic contributions to behavior is widely accepted, but it is less commonly recognized that twin studies also yield important information about environmental contributions to behavior. In particular, environmental factors are implicated in the etiology of a disorder when the concordance rate for MZ twins is less than 100 percent. Concordance rates for MZ twins would have to be perfect if a disorder was purely genetic, because MZ twins are genetically identical. Thus imperfect MZ concordance rates demonstrate environmental contributions to the development of a behavioral characteristic—provided that the characteristic has been measured reliably and validly.

Because twin studies yield information about the contributions of both genes and environments, behavior geneticists have developed ways of measuring **heritability,** the relative contribution of genes to behavioral characteristics. Defined more formally, heritability is the

proportion of variance in a trait that is attributable to genetic factors. Researchers often measure heritability by a statistic called the **heritability ratio,** which can be described according to the following simple formula:

$$\text{Heritability ratio} = \frac{\text{Variance due to}}{\text{Total variance in a}}$$
$$\text{genetic factors}$$
$$\text{behavioral characteristic}$$

where

Total variance = Variance due to genetic factors + Variance due to environmental factors + Variance due to the interaction of genes and environment[†]

The heritability ratio is a commonly used statistic for summarizing the genetic contributions to behavioral characteristics. It can be a useful summary when it is interpreted cautiously. You should particularly note two cautions. First, recall that the systems perspective indicates that genes and environments work together, not separately. Thus, in one sense it is erroneous even to attempt to calculate heritability, because all behavior is the product of genes *and* environments. That is, some experts view the heritability ratio as representing a false dichotomy. Second, any estimate of heritability is necessarily limited to the particular sample in a study. That is, we cannot generalize heritability estimates from one investigation to the population as a whole. When a researcher finds a heritability of 50 percent for some trait, this does not mean that the trait has

---

[†] The variance due to environments can be further divided into shared and unique (non-shared) environmental components. An example of a shared environment is family income; an example of a nonshared environment is being the favorite child.

the same heritability in the population as a whole or that heritability ratios are unchangeable.

This second point leads into a broader caution. Heritability estimates do not reflect the range of environments that are *theoretically* possible. Consider this point. One political goal in the United States is to provide everyone with the same rich and fullfilling environment. If we ever achieved the goal of providing everyone with the identical environment, all differences between people would be caused by genetics. You can see this by setting the variance due to environmental factors to zero in the above equation. In this case, heritability always equals 1.0. In short, heritability estimates in contemporary studies underestimate potential environmental contributions to a behavior. Although there are dramatic and frightening exceptions, contemporary environments vary relatively little from one another compared to what is possible in theory.

The practical implication of this theoretical point is that environments may matter more than we are able to detect in contemporary research. Consider, for example, that the environmental variation found in today's research does not include those historical changes in the average expected environment that have produced notable increases in life expectancy, education, and material resources for the population as a whole. Dramatic changes have occurred in the average expected environment in the United States in the past century or two. Thus estimates of heritability in today's samples may be high in part because there is relatively limited environmental variation, notwithstanding ongoing social problems like poverty, racism, and sexism. Regardless of heritability estimates, both genes and environment are important to behavioral development, as we discuss further in the Research Close-Up in this chapter. ■

PSYCHOLOGICAL FACTORS

Family therapists and family researchers often blame difficulties in negotiating family transitions on problems with *communication*. Family members must be able to communicate their feelings and wishes in order to renegotiate family roles and relationships during routine times as well as during times of change. Communication includes not only direct conversation but also nonverbal behaviors, such as posture, voice tone, and affect that can convey hidden meanings. Think of the different meanings you can attach to a simple statement like "You look great today." Depending on your tone of voice, emphasis, and nonverbal gestures, the same statement might be an honest complement, a sarcastic insult, a sexual innuendo, or a disinterested observation.

Communication Problems There are many potential problems in communication. Based on his extensive studies of marital interaction, John Gottman (1994), a clinical psychologist and noted marital interaction researcher, has identified four basic communication problems: criticism, contempt, defensiveness, and stonewalling. *Criticism* involves attacking someone's personality rather than his or her actions. According to Gottman, a criticism is a statement like, "You are unimaginative and boring!" A more adaptive complaint is, "I wish we could do something different once in a while." *Contempt* is an insult that may be motivated by anger and is

intended to hurt the other person. *Defensiveness* is a form of self-justification, such as denying responsibility, blaming the other person, or "yes-butting"—for example, "Okay, I understand how you feel, but. . . ." Finally, *stonewalling* is a pattern of isolation and withdrawal. Complaints are ignored, and for all practical purposes, communication is nonexistent.

Gottman's research has focused on married couples, but similar patterns of problematic communication would seem to apply to other intimate partners, to parents and children, and even to divorced partners. Other researchers in the area of family interaction have focused on different problems in communication, but their findings share a basic conclusion: Communication difficulties distinguish distressed from nondistressed family relationships.

Family Roles Broader family roles may also be responsible for the development of some distressed family relationships. Many people believe, for example, that pressures to fulfill traditional marital roles—the wife as homemaker and the husband as breadwinner—cause difficulties in some marriages. In studies of unhappily married couples, women often complain of feeling unsupported in their marriages, whereas men often report feeling disengaged from their family life. In contrast, one study found that *androgynous* couples—couples in which both husbands and wives scored high on measures of masculinity and femininity—had marriages that were happier and less distressed than more traditional unions (Baucom et al., 1990). Although nontraditional gender roles may lead to better long-term outcomes, it probably is also true that androgyny creates more conflict during the transition to marriage. Nontraditional couples must define the terms of their own relationship rather than assume clearly defined social roles; that is, the boundaries of their relationship are not defined by tradition.

SOCIAL FACTORS

Gender roles can be conceptualized in psychological terms, but they also reflect the influence of society on family relationships. Numerous other social influences contribute to the development of family distress. Poverty, crowded living conditions, and limited social support systems all can cause substantial distress in family life and family relationships. In fact, many family problems are major social concerns in the United States today. Teenage pregnancy, nonmarital childbirth, divorce, and family violence are social issues, not just psychological ones.

BIOLOGICAL FACTORS

Although their importance may be less obvious, biological factors also contribute to problematic family transitions. In fact, the potential contribution of biological factors to difficult family transitions bears on a central debate about individual development and family distress: Is family distress caused by dysfunctional individuals, or do troubled family relationships cause individual psychological problems? Clearly, family and individual problems are correlated, but it is not easy to determine the direction of causality or to rule out third variables. For example, marital status and marital distress are associated with an increased risk for individual psychopathology. More specifically, people who have never been married, who are divorced or widowed, or who have conflictive marital relationships are more likely to have psychological problems than happily married partners. This correlation has several potential explanations, however. Marital distress may cause psychopathology, or marital happiness might protect individuals against it. Furthermore, people with emotional disorders may be less likely to get married or to remain in a marriage (Gotlib & McCabe, 1990).

Psychological research does not have any simple answers to untangling this and other correlations between individual and family distress. Rather, evidence points to different explanations for different disorders, and to reciprocal influences, such that each problem contributes to the other. It is clear, however, that biological factors contribute to family distress. For example, evidence even indicates that there are genetic contributions to family transitions such as divorce (McGue & Lykken, 1992). As we discuss in the Research Close-Up, this empirical finding should lead you not only to think more deeply about the causes of family distress but also to rethink the meanings and the methods of behavior genetic research.

Treatment During Family Transitions

A wide array of therapies have been developed for the treatment of family distress. These include both marital and family therapies and a variety of community action projects designed to prevent family problems. In the following sections we introduce a few of these efforts.

RESEARCH CLOSE-UP

The Genetics of Divorce

Quite obviously, family transitions like marriage and divorce are changes that occur in the environment. For this reason, family transitions are commonly assumed to be determined purely by psychological and social factors.

However, behavior geneticists have increasingly emphasized that people make their own environments (Scarr & McCarthy, 1982). That is, environmental events do not occur at random. Rather, different people are more or less likely to seek out unique environments or to respond to common environments in unique ways. For example, some people are risk takers who constantly seek thrills in experience; others are risk-adverse, and they seek stable, predictable environments. Thus family transitions like marriage and divorce may be partially determined by a person's personality, and personality and other individual characteristics may be influenced by genetic factors. In this way, family transitions may be partly determined by biology; in this sense, divorce may be genetic.

In fact, behavior genetics researchers have found genetic contributions to environmental experience. A study conducted by psychologists Matt McGue and David Lykken (1992) of the University of Minnesota provides one example of this line of evidence. They gathered a sample of more than 1,500 MZ and DZ twin pairs to test the extent to which genetic factors play a role in divorce, a life event that few of us have typically conceived of as being "genetic."

These investigators found dramatically higher concordance rates for divorce among MZ than among DZ twin pairs. Overall, MZ twins with divorced co-twins were more than six times as likely to be divorced as MZ twins with never-divorced probands. For DZ twins, the risk of divorce also was greater if the co-twin was divorced, but the risk was less than two times higher than when the DZ proband was never divorced. In fact, the investigators calculated that the heritability of divorce was .525 in their sample. This estimate is all the more remarkable because the researchers studied only one marital partner. Presumably, the twins' various spouses also contributed to marital longevity or divorce. Thus genetic contributions to divorce may be even stronger than indicated by the heritability estimate.

How could divorce be genetic? Clearly, there is no divorce gene. Rather, McGue and Lykken speculated that divorce may be a consequence of personality factors that are partially shaped by genetics—for example, a tendency toward antisocial behavior. This is a very important suggestion. It implies, for instance, that researchers who compare children from married and divorced families are, to some extent, comparing apples and oranges. Divorce does not occur at random; thus children from divorced and married families differ in more ways than their parents' marital status. Genetically determined personality characteristics probably are among the differences between the two groups of children.

This intriguing study raises questions about research on the consequences of family environments. At the same time, however, it also raises questions about the interpretation of behavior genetics research. One question concerns whether genes and environment should be separated in calculating heritabilities or in conceptualizing etiology in any other way. Divorce rates in the United States 100 years ago were close to zero, and they still are in some parts of the world (for example, Ireland, where the issue of legalizing divorce is still being debated). We certainly would be hard-pressed to explain such historical and cultural changes in divorce rates in terms of genetics. What does it mean to calculate the heritability of divorce when historical changes in the course of 100 years can change divorce rates from zero to over 50 percent? Genes may be important in determining who gets divorced, but environmental thresholds can eliminate divorce, or perhaps even increase divorce rates to 100 percent! In short, the issue is genes *and* environment, not genes *or* environment.

The findings also highlight the important question of explaining the *mechanisms* of genetic effects. Personality may be the genetically determined mechanism that explains these findings, as suggested by McGue and Lykken. The findings may also be explained by a host of other genetically determined factors, however, ranging from physical attractiveness to age at marriage. Finally, the findings raise questions about whether MZ and DZ twins always share the same trait-relevant environment, an essential assumption of the twin study method (see Chapter 2). Social influences may explain some of the difference in concordance rates in this study. For example, divorce often occurs in clusters, suggesting a process of social disinhibition. McGue and Lykken's findings may partially reflect that process. People may find divorce to be more socially acceptable if their identical rather than their fraternal co-twin has been divorced previously.

These observations are not intended as specific criticisms of the study by McGue and Lykken. In fact, the investigators themselves raised several of these issues in their important scientific report. Rather, the observations are intended to encourage you to think more deeply both about genetic contributions to environmental events—and about environmental contributions to behavior genetic findings. ■

PREVENTION PROGRAMS

Programs designed to prevent marital distress have a long and informal history. Perhaps the most common attempts to promote successful marriages have been offered by various religious groups. As a requirement before performing a wedding, some religions encourage or require engaged couples to attend counseling sessions or discussion groups about family life. Unfortunately, little systematic research has been conducted on the effectiveness of most of these programs, and available data indicate that traditional efforts offer modest benefits at best (Sullivan & Bradbury, 1996, in press).

Some research has been conducted on more psychologically oriented prevention efforts. One example is the Premarital Relationship Enhancement Program (PREP), a program originally designed from research with college students. PREP participants meet in small groups of couples, where they freely discuss their expectations about marital relationships, including difficult topics such as sexuality. Couples also learn specific communication and problem-solving skills as a part of the training. In one study, couples randomly assigned to participate in PREP maintained their marital satisfaction 3 years later, while the marital happiness of control couples declined during this time (Markman et al., 1988). Even 5 years after the intervention, PREP couples maintained their improved communication and reported lower rates of marital violence than control couples (Markman et al., 1993).

The evidence on the success of the PREP is encouraging for the prevention of marital distress, but the systematic research illustrated by this study is of broader importance. Formal and informal prevention programs have been developed to help family members at nearly every transition in the family life cycle. There are childbirth programs, parenting programs, and support groups for parents whose children are infants, preschoolers, school-aged, or teenagers. Courts have programs for helping parents cope with separation, divorce, and remarriage (see Chapter 18). Creativity in developing programs is not lacking. What often is missing, however, is systematic research on the effectiveness of prevention efforts.

COUPLES THERAPY AND FAMILY THERAPY

Couples therapy and *family therapy* both focus on changing relationships, rather than on changing individuals. The couples or family therapist acts as an objective outsider who helps family members to identify and voice their disagreements, improve their communication, solve some specific problems, and ultimately alter and enhance troubled family relationships. This very different approach to therapy is illustrated in the following brief case study.

BRIEF CASE STUDY

Conflict and Communication in Marital Therapy

Jan and Bill were seeking therapy for long-standing troubles in their marriage. Jan, a wife and homemaker, complained that Bill did not give her enough help with running the household or raising the couple's three children. More poignantly, Jan felt unloved because Bill did not seem to enjoy being around her and the children. Bill countered that he loved being with his children, but that Jan was a constant nag who did not appreciate the demands of his job as an insurance salesman. He also said that she was a "bottomless pit" in demanding his love and attention. The couple had been seen for several sessions when the following interaction occurred:

Jan: As you suggested, Bill and I were supposed to be working on a schedule so that he would only call on clients two evenings last week. But just like I knew would happen, Bill didn't follow through. (Jan begins to cry.) I just knew you wouldn't do it! Is that so much to ask? Couldn't you be home a few evenings during the week? Couldn't you at least tell me when you have to go out?

Bill: (in a monotone) I got some new clients this week, and there's a sales push on. I couldn't reschedule. Next week will be better.

Jan: Next week won't be any different! Or the week after that. You aren't going to change. Why should you? You have everything your way!

Therapist: I can see you're upset, Jan, but let's give Bill a chance. Do you know your schedule for next week?

Bill: Pretty much, but you never know.

Therapist: Do you want to make a

commitment to Jan right now about what nights you will be home in the evening next week?

Bill: I suppose I can be home around six or so on Tuesday . . .

Jan: You suppose! Go ahead and . . .

Therapist: One second, Jan. OK, Bill. Tuesday is a start, but do you see what your tone of voice says to Jan?

Bill: But she's always complaining about something! I said that I'd be home, OK? What else do you want me to do?

Jan: I want you to *want* to be home.

Therapist: Now we're getting to the real issue. Part of this is about schedules and time together, but part of this is about what it means to fight about these things. Jan, when it seems like Bill doesn't want to be around you and the kids, you feel unloved.

Jan: That's what I just said. You heard me, but he didn't.

Therapist: Bill, you feel controlled when Jan asks you about your work schedule. You have a lot to balance between work and home, and maybe you really don't want to be with Jan when you feel like she's forcing you to come home.

Bill: That's exactly how I feel.

Therapist: I want the two of you to talk with each other about these feelings. Then we will get back to work on the schedule—that might help to solve some practical problems. Jan, tell Bill how you feel—and Bill, I only want you to listen to her feelings. Try to understand what she says, and don't worry about a rebuttal. In a few minutes, we'll try this the other way around. ■

Several aspects of marital therapy are evident in this brief exchange with Jan and Bill. At the most specific level, the goal was to help them solve the important problem of work and family schedules. Even an imperfect schedule might reduce some of the couple's conflict, because it would give them some clarity. Another goal was to break the couple's negative cycle of interaction by interrupting some fights, ignoring provocations, and encouraging Jan and Bill to talk about their own, deeper feelings. The

discussion of feelings should be helpful in its own right. It also might allow the couple to develop a schedule, which, in turn, would alleviate some hard feelings. If they could mutually agree on a plan, Jan would have one less reason to feel rejected, and Bill would have one less reason to feel dominated.

Behavioral Marital Therapy Most research on marital therapy has examined behavior therapy approaches, the approach illustrated in the case of Bill and Jan. **Behavioral marital therapy** emphasizes the couple's moment-to-moment interaction, particularly their exchange of positive and negative behaviors, their style of communication, and their strategies for solving problems. Systematic research comparing the effectiveness of behavioral marital therapy versus no treatment indicates that marital therapy leads to significant, short-term improvements in marital satisfaction in about half of all couples treated. Still, approximately half of couples seen in behavioral marital therapy do not improve significantly. Relapse at follow-up is also common, and other treatment approaches appear to be about as effective as behavioral marital therapy (Alexander, Holtzworth-Munroe, & Jameson, 1994).

Thus there clearly is a need to expand on behavioral marital therapy and perhaps to integrate it with other approaches. Clinically, behavioral marital therapists are beginning to address emotion, the core issue for Jan and Bill (Margolin, 1987), and the acceptance of disputes or differences that cannot be changed (Jacobson & Christensen, 1996). These innovations bode well for future treatment research. There is also a need to extend research efforts to include treatments for other difficult family transitions—for example, coping with divorce (Emery, 1994).

Treating Individual Problems with Couples Therapy or Family Therapy Couples therapy increasingly has been used not only to improve marriages but also as an alternative to individual therapy in the treatment of psychological disorders. Couples or family therapy has been attempted as a primary or adjunctive treatment for almost every mental disorder, but most empirical work has focused on couples treatment for depression, anxiety, and alcoholism. In each area, research suggests that an improved marriage helps to alleviate individual disorders, particularly depression (Beach, Sandeen, & O'Leary, 1990; Jacobson,

Holtzworth-Munroe, & Schmaling, 1989). These findings not only are important for treatment outcome, but they also underscore the reciprocal nature of individual and family relationships. In some cases, successful marital therapy removes the cause of an individual spouse's psychopathology. In other cases, successful marital therapy enables well-adjusted spouses to understand and cope with their partner's psychological troubles.

Aging and the Transition to Later Life

In the United States today, we commonly think of "old" as beginning at the age of 65, but aging and the transition to later life does not begin—or end—at this age. In fact, the aging transition extends over many years, and such issues as changes in appearance, health, family, friendships, work, and living arrangements become more or less salient at different ages. In addition, the nature, timing, and meaning of the transition to later life often differ for men and women.

Typically, adults become increasingly aware of aging in their forties and fifties. Middle-aged men often worry about their physical performance in athletics and sex. Men in their forties and fifties also become more concerned about their physical health, especially as they learn of events like a friend's unexpected heart attack. Women also worry about their physical performance and appearance in middle age, but women often are more concerned with their husbands' than with their own physical health. Men have a notably shorter life expectancy than women—7 years shorter on average. Thus, even as they encourage their husbands to follow good health practices, many middle-aged wives begin a mental "rehearsal for widowhood" (Neugarten, 1990).

Concerns about physical health increase for both men and women in their sixties, seventies, and eighties. Chronic diseases such as hypertension become common, all five sensory systems decline in acuity, and some cognitive abilities diminish with advancing age (see Chapter 14). All of these physical changes occur gradually throughout adult life, although the decline in functioning accelerates on average beginning around the age of 75. Major social transitions also take place during the later adult years. Most people retire from lifelong occupations in their early to middle sixties, a transition that is eagerly anticipated by many people but dreaded by some. Whether retirement is seen as the end of a valued career or the beginning of a new life, it requires a redefinition of family roles as husbands and wives have more time and expectations for each other. Parent–child relationships also change with age. Parents become more of a "friend" as their children become adults, and as parents become grandparents, older adults offer children and grandchildren practical support and a sense of continuity in family life. As older adults move through their seventies and enter into their eighties, children—who are now middle-aged themselves—increasingly find themselves worrying about and caring for their parents.

Death is an inevitability that confronts all of us but is especially relevant for older adults. With advancing age, we all must face both the abstraction of our own mortality and our specific fears about a painful and prolonged death. Bereavement is a part of life for older adults, as friends fall ill and die. Because of differences in life expectancy, women are particularly likely to become widows in their sixties, seventies, and eighties.

Ageism

Declining physical health and death are inevitabilities of aging, but this does not mean that older adults are unhappy or that the transition to later life is without rewards. As we will see shortly, older adults generally are as satisfied with their lives as are younger adults. In fact, older adults report *more* satisfaction is some areas of life. In considering the transition to later life, we must be careful not to fall prey to stereotypes about "old people." Older adults confront a form of social prejudice known as **ageism,** a term that encompasses a number of misconceptions and prejudices about aging (Pasupathi, Carstensen, & Tsai, 1995). For example, young Americans, even mental health professionals, tend to view older adults as stubborn, irritable, bossy, and complaining (Thomas, 1980). Older adults are more different than they are alike, however, and stability rather than change in personality seems to be the rule across the transition to later life. Some research indicates that adults become more inwardly focused as they enter later life, but the major finding is that personality is consistent from middle age to old age (Clarke-Stewart, Perlmutter, & Friedman, 1988).

Typical Symptoms and Associated Features of the Transition to Later Life

We must be selective in reviewing typical issues related to aging, because later life encompasses a large age range as well as numerous social and psychological transitions. In the following sections, we highlight only a few of the more important topics, including changes in physical functioning and health; general psychological well-being, work, and relationships; bereavement and grief; and mental health.

PHYSICAL FUNCTIONING AND HEALTH

Physical functioning and health decline with age, but the loss of health and vigor is not nearly as rapid as our stereotypes suggest. Men and women can and do remain healthy and active well into their seventies and eighties. In fact, physical activity and physical health are among the better predictors of psychological well-being among older adults.

Menopause Menopause, the cessation of menstruation, is an important physical focus for middle-aged women. (Men do not experience a similar change in reproductive functioning.) Women in the United States have their last period at an average age of 51 years old, although menstruation typically is erratic for at least 2 or 3 years prior to its complete cessation. Many women experience physical symptoms such as "hot flashes" during menopause, and some experience emotional swings as well. For example, they may find themselves crying for no apparent reason. Episodes of depression also increase during menopause.

Psychological adjustments to aging and the loss of fertility contribute to emotional volatility during menopause, but so do the physical symptoms that result from fluctuations in the female sex hormone **estrogen.** In fact, *hormone replacement therapy,* the administration of artificial estrogen, alleviates many of the adverse physical symptoms of menopause. This eases some of the psychological strains associated with these symptoms. Hormone replacement

therapy also reduces the subsequent risk for heart and bone disease, but it is a controversial treatment because it simultaneously increases the risk for cancer.

Hormone replacement therapy has no direct effect on depression, which is unrelated to estrogen levels during menopause, or on other broad psychological consequences of the "change of life" (Rutter & Rutter, 1993). Many women struggle with the challenges to identity that accompany the very real changes in their bodies and family lives near the time of menopause. Still, we should note that for many other women menopause is *not* a trying time. For example, women may find the freedom from fear of pregnancy liberating. Moreover, many middle-aged women enjoy the "empty nest"—they value the increased time they have for themselves as children move away from home (Rutter & Rutter, 1993).

Sensation and Physical Movement Menopause is a rather "sudden" event in comparison to other physical changes that occur with age.

▲ The transition to later life is *not* a time of despair for most people. Older adults who remain physically active and socially involved have better mental and physical health.

For example, the functioning of all sensory systems declines gradually throughout adult life. Visual acuity declines slowly with age, as does the ability of the lens to accommodate from focusing on an object that is near to one that is far away. The eye also adapts to darkness or to light more slowly with age. In addition, hearing loss is gradual throughout adult life, particularly the ability to hear high tones. Sensitivity to taste, smell, and touch also decreases with advancing age, although, as with losses in vision and hearing, declines in these senses typically are gradual until the seventies, when loss of sensitivity may accelerate notably (Cavanaugh, 1993).

The amount of muscle in our bodies also declines with age, but, like sensory function, the loss is gradual until advanced age. A 70-year-old retains 80 percent of his or her young adult muscle strength, but the loss may double in the next 10 years. Bone loss also occurs with advancing age, with women experiencing bone loss at twice the rate of men. After menopause, women are especially susceptible to the development of *osteoporosis*, a condition in which bones become honeycombed and can be broken easily. Many older adults develop other chronic illnesses, especially arthritis, cardiovascular diseases, cancer, diabetes, and sleep disorders (Longino & Mittelmark, 1996; see Chapter 8).

LIFE SATISFACTION, WORK, AND RELATIONSHIPS

The fact that aging is accompanied by gradual declines in physical health does *not* mean that older adults experience similar declines in psychological well-being. In fact, older adults report *more* positive relationships and a *greater* sense of mastery over their environment than do adults who are young or in midlife. On the other hand, older adults do report feeling less of a sense of

purpose in life and less satisfaction with personal growth in comparison to younger adults (Ryff, 1995).

Older adults also report greater satisfaction with their jobs than younger people, but this may be a result of self-selection. Older adults may find and remain in a satisfying occupation, while younger adults may change jobs or perhaps leave the labor force. Despite their generally positive appraisal of work, most adults view retirement positively. Retirement clearly leads to a loss of income and perhaps of status, but on average these costs are outweighed by the added benefits of increased leisure and freedom (Cavanaugh, 1993).

Integrity versus Despair Erik Erikson suggested that the conflict between integrity and despair was a common psychological struggle during the transition to later life. Experience suggests that many older adults do struggle with the broad issue of the meaning of their lives when they look back from the perspective of their later years. Identity conflicts also may accompany less monumental tasks, such as the changes that come from becoming a grandparent or retiring from a long-term occupation. Unfortunately, little research has been conducted on Erikson's interesting conceptualization of the major psychosocial conflict of later life (see Further Thoughts).

Relationships People have more friendships as young adults than during later life, but the quality of relationships is more important than the number. The presence of a supportive close relationship is an important predictor of psychological well-being during adult life. In fact, one reason why older adults have fewer friendships is because they

---

FURTHER THOUGHTS

Reminiscence Among Older Adults

It is difficult to operationalize and conduct research on the abstractions of Erikson's stages of psychosocial development, including his stage of integrity versus despair. Some researchers have made innovative attempts in this direction, however, by studying a common phenomenon among older adults: *reminiscence*—the recounting of personal memories of the distant past. In fact, reminiscence may be helpful in facilitating adjustment during later life, and many senior centers in the community offer life-history discussion groups as a part of their services.

All memories of the past are not equal, as suggested by Erikson's conflict between integrity and despair. Older adults may recall their journey through life with pride and acceptance or with disappointment and regret. As a way of studying the manner in which memories of the past mark adjustment during later life, Canadian psychologists Paul Wong and Lisa Watt developed a taxonomy of six different categories of reminiscence.

Integrative reminiscence is an attempt to achieve a sense of self-worth, coherence, and reconciliation with the past. It includes a discussion of past conflicts and losses, but it is characterized by an overriding acceptance of events. *Instrumental reminiscence* involves the review of goal-directed activities and attainments. It reflects a sense of control and success in overcoming life's obstacles. *Transitive reminiscence* serves the function of passing on cultural heritage and personal legacy, and it includes both direct moral instruction and storytelling that has clear moral implications. *Escapist reminiscence* is full of glorification of the past and deprecation of the present, a yearning for the "good old days." *Obsessive reminiscence* includes preoccupation with failure and is full of guilt, bitterness, and despair. Finally, *narrative reminiscence* is descriptive rather than interpretive. It involves "sticking to the facts" and does not serve clear intrapsychic or interpersonal functions.

Each of these styles of discussing the past has been found among older adults. In fact, evidence has found that integrative reminiscence and instrumental reminiscence are related to successful aging, whereas obsessive reminiscence is associated with less successful adjustment in later life (Wong & Watt, 1991). Reminiscence may have limited value as an intervention, however, because researchers have not found any differences in the amount of time that successful and unsuccessful older adults spend discussing the past. Perhaps we are limited in the extent to which we can "rewrite" our personal histories in a more favorable light. ■

become more selective in their companions. That is, older adults actively chose to spend their time with only the people they care for most, perhaps because they believe their time is limited and more precious (Lang & Carstensen, 1994).

Family relationships are of key importance to psychological well-being throughout the life span. Of course, relationships with children are very important to older adults. In addition, sibling relationships often take on renewed practical and emotional importance later in life (Cohler & Nakamura, 1996). Of course, the marital relationship remains centrally important. If anything, marital satisfaction increases in later life, and conflicts become less embedded or intense. Unfortunately, the loss of loved ones, including the loss of a spouse, is a fact of life for older adults, particularly for older women, as illustrated in the following case study.

BRIEF CASE STUDY

Losing a Love of a Lifetime

Mrs. Sylvia J. was 78 years old when she consulted a clinical psychologist for the first time in her life. Mrs. J. was physically fit, intellectually sharp, and emotionally vital. She remained terribly distressed by her husband's death, however. Eighteen months earlier, the 83-year-old Mr. J. had suffered a stroke. After a few weeks in the hospital, he was transferred to a nursing home, where his recuperation progressed slowly over the course of several months. According to his wife, Mr. J.'s care in the nursing home bordered on malpractice. He died as a result of infections from pervasive bedsores that he developed lying in the same position for hours on end. The staff was supposed to shift his position frequently in order to prevent bedsores from developing, but according to Mrs. J., they simply ignored her husband.

Mrs. J. was uncertain how to handle her grief, because she was stricken by many conflicting emotions. She had literally waited a lifetime to find the right man—she had married for the first time at the age of 71 after a long and successful career as a schoolteacher. She had been content throughout her life, but her marriage was bliss. She felt intensely sad over the loss of her husband, and she continued to make him part of her life. She would talk aloud to his picture when she awoke in the morning, and she visited his grave daily except when the weather was very bad.

Mrs. J. cried freely when discussing her loss, but she also chastised herself for not doing better in "getting on with her life." She had several female friends with whom she played bridge several times a week. Mrs. J. enjoyed the company of her friends, who also were widowed and who seemed more accepting of their losses.

A greater problem than acceptance was the intense anger Mrs. J. often felt but rarely acknowledged. She was furious at the nursing home, and she was vaguely considering legal action against the institution. During her career as a teacher, she had never tolerated incompetence, and the incompetence of the nursing home had robbed her of her happiness. She was confused, however, because her minister said that her anger was wrong. He said that she should forgive the nursing home and be happy to know that her husband was in heaven. Mrs. J. wanted to follow her minister's advice, but her emotions would not allow it. She wanted the psychologist to tell her if her feelings were wrong. ■

Clearly, it was not wrong for Mrs. J. to be distraught over her husband's death, but were some of her other reactions abnormal? Having constant thoughts of another person might seem obsessional in some circumstances, and talking out loud to a picture might indicate delusions or hallucinations. Mrs. J. was showing normal reactions to grief, however, as similar responses are common among other grief-stricken older people. Frequent thoughts of a loved one are a normal part of grief, and it also is normal for intense grief to continue for a year or two, or perhaps longer. But what about Mrs. J.'s anger? Whether she should forgive the nursing home or sue depends on many factors, of course, but she was not wrong—abnormal—for feeling angry. Evidence indicates that anger too is a common part of grief, and grief is a frequent experience among older adults.

GRIEF AND BEREAVEMENT

Grief is the emotional and social process of coping with a separation or a loss. **Bereavement** is a specific form of grieving in response to the death of a loved one. The process of grieving in bereavement is commonly described as proceeding in a series of stages. For example, Elisabeth Kübler-Ross (1969) developed a popular model of bereavement in her work with terminally ill medical patients. She described their grief as occurring in five stages: (1) denial, (2) anger, (3) bargaining, (4) depression, and (5) acceptance.

Kübler-Ross's model is similar to Bowlby's (1979) four-stage outline of children's responses to separation or loss (see Chapter 16). The stage of bargaining, a period of attempting to negotiate for a longer life, is the only major difference between the two models. Perhaps bargaining is a unique reaction found among terminally ill patients, who understandably hope for some miracle cure. For our purposes, you should note that anger is a part of both models of grief. Importantly, Bowlby's attachment theory offers an explanation for why someone might feel angry in the middle of intense sadness over a loss. Yearning and searching (his second stage of grief) is a pursuit of, and a signal to, the missing attachment figure—an attempt to bring about reunion. Of course, a reunion is impossible following the death of a loved one, as bereaved people understand intellectually. However, emotions, specifically anger, may not be rational at a time of loss.

Stage theories of grief have considerable intuitive appeal, but researchers have questioned whether bereavement follows any clear-cut series of stages. According to available evidence, few people experience grief in a fixed sequence of stages, but mourners instead vacillate among different emotions—for example, moving back and forth between sadness and anger. Many people apparently do not experience several of the stages described by Bowlby or Kübler-Ross, and still other people show few observable reactions to bereavement—they suffer in silence. In short, although denial, sadness, and anger may be normal reactions to loss, there is no one "right" way to grieve, nor should people be forced to express their unexpressed grief. In fact, research indicates that *less* intense bereavement predicts *better* long-term adjustment (Wortman & Silver, 1988). In general, bereavement is more intense when a loss is "off time"—for example, when the loss of a mate occurs early in adult life or when a child dies before a parent (Cohler & Nakamura, 1996). There is no "good" time to lose a loved one, of course, but we all are more prepared for the death of aged family members, and we often can find some solace in their long life.

Returning to the case study, we believe that Mrs. J's grief *was* a normal reaction to the loss of her husband, but there are cases where grief becomes problematic. Theorists have created some systems for classifying normal and abnormal grief. For example, Worden (1996) divided bereavement responses into normal, chronic, delayed, exaggerated, and masked grief. A recent study found that clinicians were more reliable when using this system to classifiy case vignettes than when applying potentially appropriate DSM diagnoses to the same cases (e.g., depression, PTSD) (Marwit, 1996). This research is only a preliminary step toward studying abnormal grief, but we are encouraged to see new empirical research on this important topic.

Epidemiological evidence indicates that the prevalence of mental disorders is *lower*, not higher, among adults 65 years of age and older. Contrary to some stereotypes, later life is *not* a time of fear, disappointment, dejection, and despair. With the exception of the cognitive disorders, which do increase with age (see Chapter 14), mood and anxiety disorders are the most common emotional problems among older adults. Affective disorders are less than half as common among older as among younger adults, however, and anxiety disorders also are less prevalent (Gurland, 1996).

Despite the lower prevalence rates, psychological disorders are an important concern among older adults. This is especially true of depression, which may be more profound, lasting, and debilitating among older than younger adults. Suicide risk is a particular concern; adults over the age of 65 have the highest rate of completed suicide of any age group. The risk for completed suicide is notably higher among older white males, and, in fact, suicide is one of the top 10 causes of death among older adults (Koenig & Blazer, 1990). Many experts view the increase in suicide as a consequence not only of the emotional problems and adverse social circumstances found among older adults but also as a result of chronic pain, physical disease, and the prospect of a long terminal illness.

Classification of Aging

Classification of adults in later life typically divides categories based on age and/or health status. In **gerontology,** the multidisciplinary study of aging, it is common to distinguish between the young-old, the old-old, and the oldest-old.

The *young-old* are adults roughly between the ages of 65 and 75. However, the category is defined less by age than by health and vigor. Notwithstanding the normal physical problems of aging, the young-old are in good health and are active members of their communities. The majority of older adults belong to this group.

The *old-old* are adults between the ages of approximately 75 and 85 who suffer from major physical, psychological, or social (largely economic) problems. They require some routine assistance in living, although only about 6 percent of Americans in this age group live in a nursing home. Despite advanced age, a healthy and active 80-year-old adult would be considered to be young-old instead of old-old.

Finally, the *oldest-old* are adults 85 years old or older. People in this category are a diverse group and include some adults who maintain their vigor and others in need of constant assistance. Widowed women and low-income groups are found disproportionately among the oldest-old. Twenty-two percent of the oldest-old live in nursing homes (Neugarten, 1990).

Epidemiology of Aging

In 1994, approximately 1 out of every 8 persons living in the United States—over 33 million people—were 65 years of age or older. Approximately 10 percent, or 3.5 million, of these older adults were the oldest-old—people 85 years old or older (U.S. Census Bureau, 1996). Both the proportion and the absolute number of older Americans are expected to increase through the middle of the twenty-first century. The increase will occur partly as a result of medical advances but primarily due to the aging of the post–World War II "baby boom" generation (see Figure 17–4).

The Growing Number of Older Adults

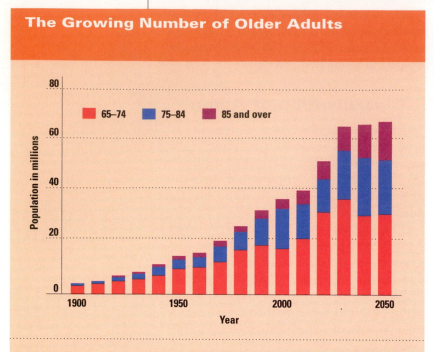

FIGURE 17-4: The actual and projected number of older adults in the United States aged 65 or older. Note the particularly dramatic increase in the oldest-old population.

Source: U.S. Bureau of the Census, 1983, American in transition: An aging society. *Current Population Reports*, Series P23-128. Washington, DC: U.S. Government Printing Office.

The Proportion of Men to Women Among Older Adults

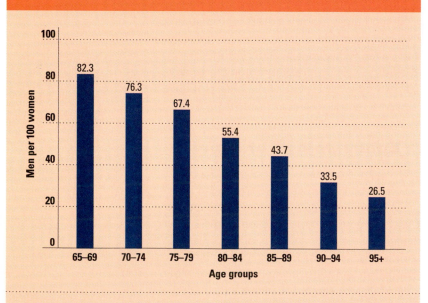

FIGURE 17-5: The number of men per 100 women in the United States in 1994. Women live longer than men; therefore, the ratio of men to women shrinks with increasing age.

Source: U.S. Bureau of the Census, 1996, 65+ in the United States. *Current Population Reports*, Series P23-190, p. 2-10. Washington, DC: U.S. Government Printing Office.

The proportion of the U.S. population 65 years of age or older should peak around the year 2030. At that time, 1 out of every 5 Americans will be at least 65 years old. During these years, increases in the prevalence of older adults in the United States will be most dramatic among the oldest of the old. In fact, the proportion and absolute number of adults in the oldest-old grouping will continue to rise until halfway through the twenty-first century. By the year 2050, the oldest-old may comprise one-fourth of the population of older adults (U.S. Census Bureau, 1986).

Most older Americans are women, and the ratio of women to men increases at older ages. Among adults 65 years of age or older, women outnumber men by 3 to 2, but women outnumber men 2 to 1 at the age of 85 or older (U.S. Census Bureau, 1996; see Figure 17–5). One important consequence of gender differences in longevity is that the majority of older men (75 percent) are married, whereas the majority of older women (60 percent) live alone (Longino & Mittelmark, 1996). Census data also indicate that poverty rates are higher among older Americans than among younger age groups (except children), and the percentage of older Americans living in poverty increases with advancing age. This is due, in part, to the lower economic status of widowed women.

Etiological Considerations and Research on the Aging Transition

Biological, psychological, and social factors all contribute to the quality of adjustment during the transition to later life. There is little doubt that the most important biological contribution to psychological well-being in later life is good physical health (Cohler & Nakamura, 1996). In fact, a study of adults over the age of 70 found that both men and women listed poor health as the most common contribution to a negative quality of life in their later years (Flanagan, 1982).

Health behavior is particularly important to the physical well-being of older adults. Increased vigor and good health in later life are associated with proper diet, continued exercise, weight control, and the avoidance of cigarette smoking and excessive alcohol use (Bromley, 1990). More generally, it has been suggested that the overriding goal of gerontology in industrialized societies should be to promote healthy and active lifestyles among older adults and to decrease the period of illness and infirmity that precedes death (Fries, 1990). In industrialized societies, current life expectancies probably are very close to the biological limits of the human species; therefore, increasing longevity may not be a realistic goal. Still, it may be possible to extend the number of vigorous and healthy years of life.

In addition to appropriate health behavior, important psychological contributions to adjustment in later life include the availability of close relationships and the experience of loss. Among men over the age of 70 the most frequently listed positive contributions to quality of life include relationships with spouses, friends, and children. Because so many women over the age of 70 are widowed, women mention relationships with spouses far less frequently than men in describing contributions to their positive quality of life. However, they list relationships with friends and children, as well as general socializing (Flanagan, 1982).

As we discussed earlier in this chapter, marital satisfaction is more closely related to women's than to men's mental health among younger adults, whereas marital status is more closely linked with men's than women's emotional well-being. Evidence on widowhood suggests that the pattern continues into later life. Bereavement and living alone are more strongly related to depression among men than among women (Siegel & Kuykendall, 1990). Men apparently benefit more from marriage, and women benefit more from happy relationships.

Numerous social factors are linked with a happier transition to later life, especially material well-being and participation in recreational activities. Religion is also very important to many older adults, and religious affiliations have been found to moderate the ill-effects of bereavement, particularly among men (Siegel & Kuykendall, 1990). Other research indicates that integration into a community is a major contribution to adjustment to later life. For example, rates of mental illnesses, particularly depression and cognitive disorders, are notably higher among residents of nursing homes (Koenig & Blazer, 1990).

Treatment of Psychological Problems in Later Life

The availability and adequacy of medical care are of great importance to older adults, not only for treating disease but also for promoting physical health and psychological well-being. Because health behavior is critical to the quality of life among older adults, experts view health psychology and behavioral medicine as central components of medical care. In fact, a new subdiscipline of these fields called **behavioral gerontology** has been developed specifically for studying and treating the behavioral components of health and illness among older adults (Bromley, 1990).

The same psychological and biological therapies used to treat emotional disorders among younger adults can be used to treat these problems among the aged. However, older adults may have misconceptions about psychotherapy. Thus education about the process can be critical to its success. Some evidence also indicates that certain biological treatments may be more effective among older than among younger adults, particularly electroconvulsive therapy in the treatment of unremitting depression. In general, however, research is insufficient on the effectiveness of alternative treatments for mental disorders among older adults. Mental services designed specifically for this population also are inadequately developed.

Summary

At least one out of every four people who consult a mental health professional have never met the criteria for the diagnosis of a mental disorder, and many of these people are seeking help with some difficult life problem. DSM-IV categorizes such problems either as **adjustment disorders,** clinically significant symptoms in response to stress, or as part of a

KEY TERMS

- adjustment disorder
- ageism
- behavioral gerontology
- behavioral marital therapy
- bereavement
- boundaries

general list of other conditions that may be a focus of clinical attention. We prefer to view life problem in terms of **life-cycle transitions,** struggles in moving from one stage of adult development into a new one. Life-cycle transitions are decidedly not mental disorders, but they are important to study because (1) they are a frequent focus of treatment, (2) they may be important to the etiology of specific emotional disorders, and (3) they suggest new ways of conceptualizing psychological problems.

The experiences associated with diverse life-cycle transitions differ greatly, but there are some similarities. Conflict is one common theme. Many conflicts during life-cycle transitions are interpersonal; others reflect a search for identity, our global sense of self; and still others involve emotions.

The concept of adult development is a recent idea that was first highlighted by Erik Erikson's work on psychosocial development. In contrast, family life cycle theorists classify adult development in terms of transitions in family life, and other theorists emphasize the social as well as the psychological nature of adult development.

The transition to adult life begins late in the teen years and may continue into the middle twenties. The **identity crisis** is a central psychological conflict during the transition to adult life, a conflict epitomized by the question "Who am I?" Many things other than identity change during the transition to adulthood, however, including parent–child relationships, educational and career paths, and peer relationships. Emotional conflicts also mark the transition to adult life, as young people experience more intense and rapidly changing emotions than adults do.

Family transitions are major changes in family relationships that typically involve the addition or loss of members of a family household. Family members who have troubled relationships get caught in negative interactions. Ongoing family conflict is closely linked with individual psychological problems, especially among women. Some emotional distress may be better conceptualized within the context of family relationships, but classification of family types is only beginning.

Epidemiological evidence on family transitions is collected by the U.S. Census Bureau. This evidence indicates that about 90 percent of people get married; five out of six married people have children; an increasing proportion of children are born outside of marriage; and divorce (which occurs in 50 percent of marriages) and remarriage are common transitions today. Family researchers often blame difficulties in negotiating family transitions on problems with communication, but broader family roles, such as traditional gender roles, also may be responsible for distressed family relationships. Social factors like poverty and even genetics also contribute to difficulties in family transitions. Both marital and family therapies and a variety of community action projects have been used to treat or prevent family problems.

Declining physical health and death are inevitabilities of aging, but this does not mean that older adults are unhappy or that the transition to later life is without rewards. Older adults confront a form of social prejudice known as **ageism,** a term that encompasses a number of misconceptions and prejudices about aging.

Menopause, the cessation of menstruation, is an important physical focus for middle-aged women; women in the United States have their last period at an average age of 51 years old. Menopause is a "sudden" event in comparison to other physical changes that occur with age. The functioning of all sensory systems declines gradually throughout adult life, as do physical strength and general health.

The gradual declines in physical health does *not* mean that older adults experience similar declines in psychological well-being. Despite their generally positive appraisal of work, most adults also view retirement positively. Relationships with children are very important, and sibling relationships often taken on renewed importance later in life. Marital satisfaction increases in later life, and conflicts become less embedded or intense. Unfortunately, the loss of loved ones, including the loss of a spouse, is a fact of life for older adults, particularly for older women. **Bereavement** is **grief** in response to the death of a loved one that is commonly described as proceeding in a series of stages. Finally, the prevalence of mental disorders is lower, not higher, among adults 65 years of age and older.

Young-old adults are between the ages of 65 and 75, are in good health, and are active members of their communities. The old-old are adults between 75 and 85 who suffer from major physical, psychological, or social problems. The oldest-old are adults 85 years old or older. Approximately one out of every eight persons living in the United States is 65 years

of age or older, and both the proportion and the absolute number of older Americans are expected to increase through the middle of the twenty-first century.

The most important biological factor in psychological well-being in later life is good physical health, which is dependent on positive health behavior. Psychological factors include the availability of close relationships and the experience of loss. Social factors include material well-being, participation in recreational activities, religious affiliation, and integration into the community. **Behavioral gerontology** is a central component of medical care for older adults, and the same therapies can be used to treat psychological disorders among younger and older adults.

Critical Thinking

1. What are some of the benefits and limitations of a broad model like Erikson's stages of psychosocial development? Can psychologists ever hope to develop a clear model of adult development, or are the tasks of adult life too diverse to study systematically?

2. What are your personal thoughts about identity conflicts? Do you experience uncertainties about yourself or observe them in your friends? Do you think a moratorium is necessary for healthy development? Do you worry about people who vigorously pursue their childhood career paths?

3. Is communication overrated by psychologists? Are some things better left unsaid and some conflicts better left unresolved? Do gender differences exist in communication interests and styles?

4. What can the United States do to prepare for the aging of its population? Are the country's social, medical, and economic resources sufficient to provide for the coming "boom" in the population of older adults?

18
Mental Health and the Law

You already have encountered many of the topics considered in this chapter—perhaps even in this morning's newspaper. The *insanity defense* may be the most familiar of the intriguing and often controversial issues found at the intersection of abnormal psychology and the law. Under certain circumstances, a person with a mental illness may be found not guilty by reason of insanity. When judges or juries determine that defendants are insane, perpetrators are not held to be legally responsible for their actions, even though they have committed a crime. Instead of going to jail, insane defendants are likely to be confined in a mental institution. But what is insanity, and how does it differ from mental illness? As we address these and other questions in this chapter, you will learn that the legal system views abnormal behavior very differently from the way it is understood by mental health professionals.

Overview

▼ **One of several notes that John Hinckley wrote to actress Jodie Foster. Hinckley believed that he could win Foster's love by gaining notoriety, a delusion that apparently motivated him to attempt to assassinate former President Ronald Reagan.**

In addition to the insanity defense and related questions of criminal responsibility, the topics considered in this chapter include several issues related to mental hospitals, especially involuntary commitment, deinstitutionalization, and the rights of mental patients. The confinement of an individual against his or her will is a serious action that must balance broad societal values against the needs and rights of the individual. In order to gain a glimpse of the magnitude of this decision, recall that many political dissidents in the former Soviet Union were confined to institutions to "treat" their "mental illnesses."

We also discuss legal intervention in families in this chapter, with an emphasis on the issues of child abuse and custody disputes after divorce. Concerns about serious mental illness are the exception, not the rule, in custody and abuse cases. However, predictions about children's emotional well-being often are vital to decisions in these cases—and the legal decisions, in turn, can have far-reaching implications for children's emotional and physical health.

Finally, we consider some of the legal responsibilities of mental health professionals to their clients, especially confidentiality and the limitations on it. Confidentiality and other topics in psychology and the law are not only of interest to legal and mental health professionals, but they also have broad implications for society. The manner in which we treat the most disturbed members of our society often marks the boundaries that define some of our most basic legal rights and responsibilities as citizens.

As a way of introducing the topic of mental health and the law, we consider an infamous

and successful use of the insanity defense: the acquittal of John Hinckley. In 1981 Hinckley attempted to assassinate Ronald Reagan, the president of the United States. Our account is based on information in two detailed books on the assassination attempt (Clarke, 1990; Low, Jeffries, & Bonnie, 1986), and it is summarized in the following case study.

CASE STUDY

John Hinckley and the Insanity Defense

On March 30, 1981, John Hinckley stood outside the Washington Hilton hotel, drew a revolver from his raincoat pocket, and fired six shots at President Ronald Reagan. The president and three other men were wounded. The president rapidly recovered from his potentially fatal wound, but the presidential press secretary, James Brady, was permanently crippled by a shot that struck him just above the left eye. Hinckley was charged with attempted assassination, but his trial resulted in a verdict of "not guilty by reason of insanity."

Hinckley, who came from a wealthy family, had never been convicted of a crime. He had a history of unusual behavior, however, and had expressed violent intentions. Hinckley had read several books on famous assassinations and had joined the American Nazi Party. In fact, he was expelled from the Nazi Party in 1979 because of his continual advocacy of violence. A particular oddity was Hinckley's obsession with the actress Jodie Foster, whom he had seen play the role of a child prostitute in the movie *Taxi Driver.* In an attempt to win her favor, Hinckley adopted much of the style of Foster's movie rescuer, Travis Bickle. This included acquiring weapons similar to those used by the movie character and stalking the president, much as the movie character had stalked a political candidate.

Hinckley repeatedly tried to contact Foster in real life and succeeded a few times, but his approaches were consistently rejected. He came to believe that the only way to win her over was through dramatic action. Less than 2 hours before he shot the president, he completed a letter to Foster, which said:

> Jodie, I would abandon this idea of getting Reagan in a second if I could only win your heart and live out the rest of my life with you, whether it be in total obscurity or whatever.
>
> I will admit to you that the reason I'm going ahead with this attempt now is because I just cannot wait any longer to impress you. I've got to do something now to make you understand, in no uncertain terms, that I am doing all of this for your sake! By sacrificing my freedom and possibly my life, I hope to change your mind about me. This letter is being written only an hour before I leave for the Hilton Hotel. Jodie, I'm asking you to please look into your heart and at least give me the chance, with this historical deed, to gain your respect and love.

Hinckley's trial centered on the question of his sanity, or as one author put it, whether he was "mad" or merely angry (Clarke, 1990). Both the defense and the prosecution called numerous expert witnesses to determine whether Hinckley was legally sane or insane. According to the federal law that was in effect at the time, the prosecution had to prove "beyond a reasonable doubt" that Hinckley was indeed sane. That is, the prosecution had to establish that mental disease had not either (1) created an irresistible impulse that made it impossible for Hinckley to resist attempting to kill the president, or (2) so impaired Hinckley's thinking that he did not appreciate the wrongfulness of his actions. (The burden of proof and the definition of insanity in the federal law subsequently were changed because of Hinckley's acquittal, as we discuss later in this chapter.)

All the prosecution's experts concluded that Hinckley was sane; all the defense's experts concluded that Hinckley was insane. The prosecution's experts called attention to the fact that Hinckley's actions were planned in advance and to Hinckley's awareness that his actions would have consequences, including possible imprisonment or death. He chose six deadly "devastator" bullets from an abundance of ammunition, and he fired them all accurately in less than 3 seconds. Defense experts emphasized his erratic behavior, particularly his obsession with Jodie Foster. One psychiatrist suggested, for example, that the president and other victims were merely "bit players" in Hinckley's delusion that through his "historic deed" he would be united with Foster in death.

Hinckley was found not guilty by reason of insanity. We don't know what factors influenced the jury to come to this decision or whether they found him insane based on the "irresistible impulse" or the "right from wrong" part of the insanity defense. In any event, the verdict meant that Hinckley received no prison sentence. Instead, he was ordered into a mental hospital to be treated in confinement for an unspecified period of time. As of now, Hinckley remains confined in St. Elizabeth's Hospital outside Washington, D.C. Theoretically, he could be released if he is considered by the hospital staff no longer to be dangerous to himself or to others. On the other hand, Hinckley could remain confined to the hospital for the rest of his life. In fact, he has unsuccessfully petitioned for release on several occasions. ■

John Hinckley obviously was emotionally disturbed, and legally he was determined to be insane when he shot the president. As is illustrated in this case study, however, the insanity defense is an area of conflict between mental health and the law. One conflict involves the unreliability of expert testimony, as different mental health experts often disagree about a given defendant's sanity, thus creating a "battle of the experts" (Low, Jeffries, & Bonnie, 1986). A more basic conflict centers on the difference between the legal concept of sanity and the psychological concept of mental disorder, as we discuss shortly. An even more fundamental conflict involves the opposing assumptions that the legal and mental health systems make about the causes of and responsibility for human behavior—that is, free will versus determinism.

Free Will versus Determinism

Criminal law assumes that human behavior is the product of **free will,** the capacity to make choices and freely act on them. Because behavior is assumed to be a product of free will, in the eyes of the law people are responsible for their own actions. When a person violates the law, the individual is held accountable. This is the legal concept known as **criminal responsibility.**

In contrast, mental health professionals assume that human behavior is determined by biological, psychological, and social forces. This assumption, known as **determinism,** is made by all psychologists (except humanists; see Chapter 2), but it is particularly obvious in the study of abnormal behavior. Mental disorders and the actions that stem from them are not viewed as choices but as conditions that are outside of voluntary control. Just as the concept of responsibility follows from an assumption of free will, a consequence of the deterministic view is that no one is ultimately "responsible" for his or her actions.

The assumption of determinism is not arbitrary. Rather, it is essential if psychology is to be a science. The causes of human behavior cannot be studied without assuming that behavior is determined by factors that can be measured and perhaps controlled. To draw an analogy, if meteorologists assumed that hurricanes were caused by "free will," they would have nothing to study. Imagine a weather forecast in which the meteorologist says, "Well, I wonder where Hurricane Bob will choose to head tonight." If meteorologists wish to have a scientific discipline, they must assume that the path of a hurricane is determined, that it is caused by forces that are potentially knowable. Similarly, free will is a concept that is foreign to psychologists when they are thinking as scientists, because it is an unscientific concept.

Assumptions about free will and determinism come into particular conflict in the case of the insanity defense. In the U.S. law, **insanity** is an exception to criminal responsibility. The legally insane individual is assumed *not* to be acting out of free will. As a result, like John Hinckley, the legally insane are held not to be criminally responsible for their actions. Ironically, the insanity defense reaffirms the legal system's view that people are responsible for their actions by calling attention to the rare exceptions when they are not.

Thus debates about the insanity defense involve a broad conflict of philosophies, as well as differences about the specifics of a given case. Is human behavior a product of free will, or is it determined by biological, psychological, and social forces? Are people with mental disorders responsible for their actions, or are they not responsible?

IS MENTAL ILLNESS A MYTH?

American psychiatrist Thomas Szasz (1963, 1970) has adopted a provocative and controversial position about free will, mental illness, and the insanity defense. Szasz abandons the traditional deterministic view held by behavioral scientists and embraces a humanistic philosophy that puts free will at the center of human behavior. In fact, Szasz asserts that the concept of mental illness is a myth. According to Szasz, abnormal behavior must be defined relative to some social or moral standard. Because there is no objective standard, there can be no objective mental disease. Thus Szasz argues that mental disorders are subjective "problems in living," not objective diseases.

The logical conclusion of Szasz's view of free will is that all people—even people with emotional disorders—*are* responsible for their actions. Consistent with this position, Szasz has argued that the insanity defense should be abolished (Szasz, 1963). It also follows from Szasz's view that other exceptions made for mentally disturbed people in the legal system should be eliminated—for example, commitment to mental hospitals against their will (Moore, 1975).

RIGHTS AND RESPONSIBILITIES

In arguing for a broader concept of responsibility, Szasz also fights for broader recognition of human dignity and individual rights. In the law, rights and responsibilities go hand in hand. When responsibilities are lost, rights are lost too. When responsibilities are assumed, rights are gained. Thus, while opposing the insanity defense, Szasz simultaneously supports greater recognition of the rights of mental patients who become involved in either the legal or the mental health system. The basic, human rights of mental patients sometimes have been trampled on, and much concern has been raised about their better protection. Szasz argues that the mentally ill should be treated identically to the mentally healthy in terms of both social responsibility and social dignity.

Szasz's concerns about the "myth of mental illness" extend beyond the individual to broad social abuses. He asserts that the concept of mental illness can be invoked to obscure the logic of behavior that runs counter to social standards and to blame social deviance on disease instead of on society. This clearly happened in the former Soviet Union, where some dissidents were judged insane for holding political beliefs that conflicted with those of the Communist Party. Their "diagnosis" justified their confinement to mental hospitals. Szasz asserts that similar, albeit far more subtle abuses of the "myth of mental illness" occur in the United States.

Not surprisingly, Szasz's view that mental illness is a myth is generally seen as an extreme—and inaccurate—position (Appelbaum, 1994). Nevertheless, Szasz has contributed greatly to issues in mental health and the law by cutting to the heart of philosophical assumptions. Differences in basic assumptions about free will and determinism inevitably create conflicts between the legal and mental health systems. Many debates about the rights and responsibilities of people with a mental disorder ultimately turn on contrasting views about whether or how much mental illness impairs free will. As we will see in numerous examples in this chapter, the core of the dilemma is how to reconcile concepts of individual rights and responsibilities, which follow from an assumption of free will, with the deterministic view that is at the core of a scientific approach to understanding human behavior.

▲ The psychiatrist Thomas Szasz has called attention to fundamental conflicts about individual rights and responsibilities in the philosophies of the legal and mental health systems.

Mental Health, Criminal Responsibility, and Procedural Rights

Criminal law assumes that mental disorders sometimes may affect an individual's capacity to exercise his or her rights and responsibilities. Defendants who are judged *incompetent to stand trial* are thought to be unable to exercise their right to participate in their own trial defense. Defendants who are found not guilty by reason of insanity are determined not to be criminally responsible for their actions. We consider each of these issues in this section.

The Insanity Defense

The idea that mental disability should limit criminal responsibility dates back to ancient Greek and Hebrew traditions and was evident in early English law. Records indicate cases where

English kings pardoned murderers because of "madness," and later judicial decisions similarly excused some criminals who were "madmen" or "idiots" (Reisner & Slobogin, 1990). The emerging rationale underlying many of these insanity acquittals was that the defendant lacked the capacity to distinguish "good from evil" or what eventually became known as the inability to distinguish right from wrong. This ground for the **insanity defense** was codified in 1843, after Daniel M'Naghten was found not guilty of murder by reason of insanity.

M'NAGHTEN TEST

M'Naghten was a British subject who claimed that the "voice of God" had ordered him to kill Prime Minister Robert Peel, but who mistakenly murdered Peel's private secretary instead. His insanity acquittal raised considerable controversy and caused the House of Lords to devise the following insanity test:

> To establish a defense on the ground of insanity, it must be clearly proved that, at the time of the committing of the act, the party accused was laboring under such a defect of reason, from disease of the mind, as not to know the nature and quality of the act he was doing; or, if he did know it, that he did not know he was doing what was wrong. [*Regina v. M'Naghten*, 8 Eng. Rep. 718, 722 (1843)]

Subsequently known as the *M'Naghten test*, this rule clearly articulated the "right from wrong" principle for determining insanity. If at the time a criminal act is committed a mental disease or defect prevents a criminal from knowing the wrongfulness of his or her actions, the criminal can be found to be *not guilty by reason of insanity (NGRI)*. The "right from wrong" ground established in the M'Naghten case continues to be the major focus of the insanity defense in U.S. law today. However, subsequent developments first broadened and later narrowed the grounds for determining insanity.

IRRESISTIBLE IMPULSE AND THE PRODUCT TEST

Later in the nineteenth century, the insanity defense was broadened in the United States when a second ground for determining insanity was introduced—the so-called *irresistible impulse test*. The irresistible impulse test determined that defendants also could be found insane if they were unable to control their actions because of mental disease. *Parsons v. State* was one of the first cases in which the irresistible impulse test was adopted [81 Ala. 577, 596, 2 So. 854 (1886)]. In this 1886 case, an Alabama court ruled that defendants could be judged insane if they could not "avoid doing the act in question" because of mental disease. The rationale for the irresistible impulse test was that when people are unable to control their behavior, the law can have no effect on deterring crimes. *Deterrence*, the idea that people will avoid committing crimes because they fear being punished for them, is a major public policy goal of criminal law. In the *Parsons* case, however, the court reasoned that convicting people for acts that they could not control would serve no deterrence purpose. In such cases, a finding of NGRI was justified.

A 1954 ruling by the Washington, D.C., federal circuit court in *Durham v. United States* further broadened the insanity defense [214 F.2d 862 (D.C. Cir. 1954)]. Known as the *product test*, the Durham opinion indicated that an accused is not criminally responsible if his or her unlawful act was the product of mental disease or defect. The ruling made no attempt to define either "product" or "mental disease." In fact, the terms were purposely designed to be very broad. The vague product test was justified as a way of allowing mental health professionals wide discretion in using their expertise in determining insanity and testifying in court.

Problems arose in applying the product test, however, including the fact that some mental health professionals decided to include psychopathy (antisocial personality disorder in DSM-IV) as one of the "mental diseases" that could be used as a basis for an insanity defense. This created a circular problem: Antisocial personality disorder is defined primarily by a pattern of criminal behavior, yet the same criminal behavior could be used to substantiate that the perpetrator was insane (Campbell, 1990). This and other problems with the definition of mental disease under the product test came to a halt when the *Durham* decision was overruled in 1972 (Reisner & Slobogin, 1990).

LEGISLATIVE ACTIONS

In 1955, a year after the original *Durham* decision, the American Law Institute drafted model legislation designed to address various problems with the previous rules for determining insanity. The model legislation is important because it subsequently was adopted by the majority of states. The rule indicates that:

> A person is not responsible for criminal conduct if at the time of such conduct as a result of mental disease or defect he lacks substantial capacity either to appreciate the criminality [wrongfulness] of his conduct or to conform his conduct to the requirements of the law.

This definition of insanity combines the M'Naghten rule and the irresistible impulse test, although it softens the requirements somewhat with the term *substantial capacity*. (Compare this with the language used in the M'Naghten rule.) A second component of the American Law Institute's model legislation, which also has been enacted by many states, excluded a history of criminal behavior from being used to define "mental disease or defect." This eliminates the problem of circularity caused by the antisocial personality disorder diagnosis.

The most recent developments in the law governing the insanity defense occurred as a result of the acquittal of John Hinckley. Following the controversy over this case, both the American Bar Association and the American Psychiatric Association recommended the elimination of the irresistible impulse component of the insanity defense. These organizations judged this strand of the insanity defense to be more controversial and unreliable than the right from wrong standard (Mackay, 1988). Consistent with these recommendations, federal law was changed when the Insanity Defense Reform Act was passed in 1984 and defined the insanity defense as follows:

> It is an affirmative defense to a prosecution under any federal statute that, at the time of the commission of acts constituting the offense, the defendant, as a result of severe mental disease or defect, was unable to appreciate the nature and quality or the wrongfulness of his acts. Mental disease or defect does not otherwise constitute a defense. (Title 18 of the United States Code)

GUILTY BUT MENTALLY ILL

Several states have since echoed this change in federal law by enacting similar legislation. Another change prompted by the Hinckley case was the promotion of the new verdict of *guilty but mentally ill (GBMI)*, which has been enacted by 13 states (American Bar Association, 1995). Defendants can be found guilty but mentally ill if it is demonstrated that they are guilty of the crime, were mentally ill at the time it was committed, but were not legally insane at that time. The GBMI verdict was designed as a compromise to NGRI. The GBMI verdict holds defendants criminally responsible for their crimes but acknowledges their mental disorder and helps ensure that they receive treatment (Mackay, 1988). Thus a defendant found GBMI can be sentenced in the same manner as any criminal, but the court can order treatment for the mental disorder as well. Some evidence indicates, however, that rather than replace NGRI verdicts, the GBMI verdict is most often used in cases in which defendants simply would have been found guilty in the past (Smith & Hall, 1982).

Recent developments clearly represent a move toward restricting the insanity defense. The furor surrounding the high-profile Hinckley case was not unlike the controversy that surrounded the high-profile M'Naghten case more than 100 years earlier. Ironically, the Hinckley case also caused the insanity defense to be revised to resemble the original M'Naghten test (Mackay, 1988). As it was for a time after 1843, the most common contemporary standard for determining legal insanity is the inability to distinguish right from wrong (see Table 18–1).

BURDEN OF PROOF

In addition to the definition of insanity, the *burden of proof* substantially influences the meaning and likely success of the insanity defense. Under U.S. criminal law, the defendant is assumed to be innocent until proven guilty "beyond a reasonable doubt." The burden of proof thus rests with the prosecution, and the *standard of proof* is a very high one—beyond a reasonable doubt. But must the prosecution also prove beyond a reasonable doubt that a defendant is sane?

In fact, about one-third of all states require the prosecution to prove a defendant's sanity beyond a reasonable doubt, and until the Insanity Defense Reform Act was passed in 1984, this also was the practice in federal courts. In the Hinckley trial, the prosecution was obliged to prove that Hinckley was sane beyond a reasonable doubt, a case they failed to make. Changes implemented in federal law following the Hinckley case shifted the burden of proof. In federal courts the defense now must prove defendants' insanity rather than the prosecution having to

TABLE 18-1

Developments in the Insanity Defense

Right from Wrong

Defendants may be found NGRI if they lacked the capacity to distinguish right from wrong at the time of committing a crime due to mental disease or defect. Formally defined in the M'Naghten case, this standard for defining insanity remains in effect today.

Irresistible Impluse

Defendants may be found NGRI if they were unable to control their actions at the time of committing a crime due to mental disease or defect. Developed in the nineteenth century, this standard has been eliminated in several states following the Hinckley case.

Product Test

Defendants may be found NGRI if their behavior was a product of mental disease or defect. Established in *Durham* in 1954, this means of determining insanity was overturned and eliminated in 1972.

American Law Institute Definition

Defendants may be found NGRI by either the right from wrong or the irresistible impulse test, but a history of antisocial behavior is insufficient evidence of mental disease. Developed by the American Law Institute in 1955 to eliminate ambiguities in previous rules, this definition of insanity has been adopted by many states.

Guilty but Mentally Ill

Defendants may be found guilty but also mentally ill at the time of the crime; thus treatment as well as punishment may be ordered. Developed in recent years, more states have enacted this defense since the Hinckley case.

prove their sanity. Insanity must be proven by the standard of "clear and convincing evidence," a stringent standard but not as exacting as "beyond a reasonable doubt." About two-thirds of states also now place the burden of proof on the defense, but the standard of proof typically is less restrictive than that found in federal law—"the preponderance of the evidence." Thus the insanity defense has been narrowed even further by shifting the burden of proof from the prosecution to the defense in federal law and in many states (American Bar Association, 1995).

DEFINING "MENTAL DISEASE OR DEFECT"

An issue of obvious importance to the mental health professions is the precise meaning of the term *mental disease or defect*, which is used in one form or another in all the legal definitions of insanity. The American Law Institute's proposal specifically excludes antisocial personality disorder, but would any other diagnosis listed in the DSM qualify? The 1984 federal legislation indicates that the mental disease must be "severe," but what does this mean?

The question of which mental disorders qualify for the "mental disease or defect" component of the insanity defense is unresolved, although the legal definition of "mental disease" generally is more restrictive than the mental health definition (Campbell, 1990). Some legal and mental health professionals would allow any disorder listed in the DSM to qualify for the insanity defense, however, provided that the other criteria for the legal definition of insanity also were met. Others have argued that some especially difficult circumstances—for example, being a victim of repeated violence—should qualify defendants for the "mental disease or defect" component of the insanity defense, even if the problems are not listed as DSM diagnoses (see Further Thoughts). Still other commentators would sharply restrict the mental diseases or defects that can be used as a part of the insanity defense. One suggestion is to confine the insanity defense to mental retardation, schizophrenia, mood disorders, and cognitive disorders, excluding cognitive disorders induced by substance use or abuse (Applebaum, 1994). Finally, the American Psychiatric Association has stated that mental diseases or defects are limited to "those severely abnormal mental conditions that grossly and demonstrably impair a person's perception or understanding of reality that are not attributable primarily to the voluntary ingestion of alcohol or other psychoactive substances" (APA, 1983).

MENTAL HEALTH PROFESSIONALS AS EXPERT WITNESSES

Whether testifying about a defendant's sanity or about other mental health matters, mental health experts for the prosecution and the defense often present conflicting testimony. Such a "battle of the experts" can be an embarrassment to the profession and can raise questions about professional ethics. For example, a commonly asked question is whether an expert's testimony has been "bought" by one side or the other. This possibility sometimes seems feasible to juries when they learn about the fees paid to **expert witnesses,** specialists who are

The Battered Woman Syndrome as a Defense

For centuries large numbers of women have been physically beaten by their husbands or lovers. This fact is easy to document, because wife battering has been institutionalized for much of Western history—and it remains an accepted practice in parts of the world today. For example, the familiar phrase "rule of thumb" refers to the size of the stick, no thicker than a man's thumb, with which men were legitimately allowed to beat their wives according to common law.

Nevertheless, spousal abuse has been recognized as a social problem only in the last few decades. During these years, laws have been passed that for the first time protect wives from their husbands' physical and sexual abuse. Even today, however, in some states a husband cannot be charged with raping his wife no matter what the circumstances of forced sex might be. American laws have protected people from assaults by strangers much more stringently than they have protected people from assault by members of their own family.

The prevalence of spouse abuse in the United States today is a matter of political and scientific debate, in large part because of disagreements about what constitutes abuse. Some startling facts about family violence cannot be disputed, however. For example, FBI statistics indicate that approximately one-third of all female murder victims are killed by a husband or a boyfriend.

Battered women often remain in the abusive relationship for incomprehensibly long periods of time. To outsiders, the battered woman's reluctance to leave the relationship seems foolish, even masochistic. To the battered woman herself, however, leaving the relationship often seems wrong or impossible. She may feel trapped in an abusive relationship by finances or out of concern for her children; chronic abuse may cause her to lose perspective on the extent of her maltreatment; or she simply may see no viable alternative to subjecting herself to repeated abuse. Some women who have been constantly threatened, intimidated, and beaten by their husbands or boyfriends eventually escape the abuse only by killing their tormentors. According to

a report of the American Psychological Association (1995), approximately 1,000 women kill their current or former batterer each year. (A similar circumstance arises when an abused child kills a parent or stepparent.) Is this violence in response to violence ever justified?

The killing of an abuser clearly is justified in the U.S. law when the victim's life is in immediate danger. In such a circumstance, the action can easily be construed as self-defense. In other cases, however, the killing of a batterer takes place when the threat of abuse may be looming in the background but is not immediate. In this situation, a woman might still plead self-defense. According to contemporary trial practice, the defense may depend heavily on what has been called the battered woman syndrome.

The **battered woman syndrome** is a term coined by the psychologist Lenore Walker (1979) to describe her observations about the psychological effects of being chronically abused by a husband or lover. Two aspects of the syndrome are especially crucial to its use as a defense. First, Walker discusses what she calls the "cycle of violence," which includes three stages: (1) a tension-building phase leading up to violence; (2) the battering incident itself; and (3) a stage of loving contrition, during which the batterer apologizes and attempts to make amends for his actions. A second crucial aspect of Walker's battered woman syndrome is her view that the abused woman experiences learned helplessness (see Chapter 5). Walker assumes that learned helplessness makes it impossible for some battered women to leave an abusive relationship. These two assertions are essential to a successful defense, because they imply that the battered woman expects to be beaten repeatedly but becomes immobilized and unable to leave the relationship.

Expert testimony on the battered woman's syndrome apparently has been influential in successfully defending a number of battered women who have killed abusive men. Walker (1989) reported that members of her firm had testified in over 160 cases where a battered woman had killed her abuser. This defense has become controversial, however. A number of courts have determined that expert testimony on the battered woman syndrome is inadmissible on various grounds, although the trend appears to be toward increasing acceptance of such testimony by the legal system (Brown, 1990). Others have questioned the scientific status of the battered woman syndrome, doubting the coherence of the theory and the evidence that supports it (Faigman, 1986). One question that has been asked, for example, is: How can someone who is suffering from learned helplessness bring herself to kill?

Questions like this can make it difficult to plead self-defense based on the battered woman syndrome. A defense of *temporary insanity* is an alternative that may be more easily proved in court. The legal definition of insanity refers to a defendant's mental state at the time of committing the criminal act; thus it is possible for a defendant to suffer from "temporary insanity." An argument for temporary insanity based on the battered woman syndrome could be made on the basis of either the right from wrong or the irresistible impulse strand of the insanity defense. The essence of such an argument would be that the stress of the physical abuse so impaired the battered woman's thinking that either

she was unable to appreciate the consequences of her actions or she was driven to the point where she could no longer control her behavior (Cipparone, 1987).

The questions of whether the woman was imminently threatened and why she did not leave the relationship usually play a lesser role in a temporary insanity defense than in a plea of self-defense. However, in cases where women have killed their batterers, temporary insanity pleas appear to be used less frequently than self-defense. Perhaps this is because the temporary insanity defense is less palatable. This defense carries the stigma of an insanity determination, as well as the possibility of confinement in a mental institution. More broadly, advocates for battered women feel strongly that abused women are in a vulnerable and dangerous situation, and they wish to establish that the victims' actions are legitimate acts of self-defense. A successful insanity defense relieves one woman of criminal responsibility for her actions. In contrast, the successful use of self-defense makes a broader political statement—that women have a right to take extreme actions to protect themselves against chronic battering (Walker, 1989). ■

allowed to testify about specific matters of opinion (not just fact) that lie within their area of expertise.

In fact, some psychologists have argued that mental health professionals should not be allowed to offer expert testimony at all. These critics assert that the mental health questions posed by the legal system cannot be answered with adequate reliability or validity. They also deny that mental health experts help judges and juries reach more accurate decisions (Faust & Ziskin, 1988). Reflect for a moment about the many concerns about diagnostic reliability raised throughout this textbook. If mental health professionals often disagree about the presence or absence of a carefully defined mental disorder, is it any wonder that they frequently disagree about the presence or absence of a poorly defined concept like insanity? And if the reliability of the insanity diagnosis is poor, is it unethical for an

expert witness to testify about its presence or absence?

In considering these questions, we must recognize that the procedures and goals of the legal system differ from those familiar to psychologists. Expert witnesses are expected to offer informed opinion, not to present the "truth" to the court. Lawyers expect questions to be raised about the credibility of an expert witness's testimony, and they also expect conflicting testimony to be presented by the opposing side's experts (Fitch, Petrella, & Wallace, 1987). The duty of the attorneys for the prosecution and for the defense is to present the most convincing case for their side, which is not the same thing as presenting the most objective case. Although courtroom procedure rules do not excuse inaccurate "expert testimony," they do leave room for testimony even in the face of imperfect empirical evidence. The end product of a trial is a judgment about truth made by a judge or a jury, not the establishment of a scientific fact.

Mental health professionals who act as expert witnesses serve their profession and the legal system best if their testimony adheres closely to

▼ A member of the "Framingham Eight," eight women imprisoned for killing their abusers. The women petitioned for early release from prison, claiming they acted in self-defense.

their expertise. In insanity cases, for example, the mental health experts' job is to testify about defendants' mental health and state of mind, not to determine their sanity. The determination of a defendant's sanity is a decision to be made by a judge or a jury, not by the expert witness. In fact, the American Psychological Association specifically recommends that "since it is not within the professional competence of psychologists to offer conclusions on matters of law, psychologists should resist pressure to offer such conclusions" (Monahan, 1980). A lawyer may ask for the expert's opinion about the "ultimate issue" of insanity, but many commentators believe that expert witnesses have an obligation not to answer such questions of law because these questions exceed their expertise.

USE AND CONSEQUENCES
OF THE INSANITY DEFENSE

Given the tremendous controversy and important philosophical issues that surround the insanity defense, you might be surprised to learn how infrequently this strategy is used. Evidence suggests that the insanity defense is put forward in only about 1 percent of all criminal cases in the United States, and only about 25 percent of defendants who offer the defense are actually found to be NGRI (Callahan et al., 1991; Steadman, Pantle, & Pasewark, 1983). Furthermore, over 90 percent of these acquittals result from plea bargains rather than jury trials (Callahan et al., 1991). In England, where the M'Naghten rule still stands, the insanity defense is virtually nonexistent. It is used in only a handful of cases each year (Mackay, 1988).

Does a successful insanity defense result in a shorter amount of time spent incarcerated? Some defendants found NGRI have been incarcerated in mental institutions for much shorter periods of time than they would have served if they had been sentenced to jail. However, many defendants have actually been incarcerated for much longer periods of time—yet another reminder that rights are lost when responsibilities are not assumed. Research indicates that, on average, NGRI acquittees spend approximately the same amount of time in mental institutions as they might have served in prison (Pantle, Pasewark, & Steadman, 1980). Currently, some state laws actually limit the length of confinement following an NGRI verdict to the maximum sentence the acquittee would have served if convicted. However, the U.S. Supreme Court has ruled that longer confinements are permitted because treatment, not punishment, is the goal of commitment following an NGRI verdict (American Bar Association, 1995).

Competence and Criminal Proceedings

Another important link between mental health and criminal law is the issue of competence. **Competence** concerns defendants' ability to understand the legal proceedings that are taking place against them and to participate in their own defense. If defendants have no such understanding—that is, if they are *incompetent*—the legal proceedings must be suspended until such time as they can be understood by the defendant. Competence has been defined as follows by the U.S. Supreme Court in *Dusky v. United States* [363 U.S. 402, 80 S. Ct. 788, 4 L. Ed.2d. 824 (1960)]:

> The test must be whether he [the defendant] has sufficient present ability to consult with his attorney with a reasonable degree of rational understanding and a rational as well as factual understanding of proceedings against him.

You should note several features of the legal definition of competence. First, competence refers to the defendant's current mental state, whereas the insanity defense refers to the defendant's state of mind at the time of committing a crime. Second, as with insanity, the legal definition of incompetence is not the same as the psychologist's definition of mental illness. Even a psychotic individual may possess enough rational understanding to be deemed competent in the eyes of the law. Third, competence refers to the defendant's ability to understand criminal proceedings, not willingness to participate in them. For example, a defendant who simply refuses to consult with a court-appointed lawyer is not incompetent. Finally, the "reasonable degree" of understanding needed to establish competence is generally acknowledged to be fairly low. That is, only those who suffer from severe emotional disorders are likely to be found incompetent (Melton et al., 1987).

Unlike the various definitions of insanity, the legal definition of incompetence contains no reference to "mental disease or defect." The role of expert witnesses in determining competency is therefore quite different from their

TABLE 18-2

Abilities Related to Competence to Stand Trial

Competence to stand trial may involve the defendant's ability to:

1. Understand his or her current legal situation.
2. Understand the charges against him or her.
3. Understand the facts relevant to his case.
4. Understand the legal issues and procedures in his case.
5. Understand legal defenses available in his behalf.
6. Understand the dispositions, pleas, and penalties possible.
7. Appraise likely outcomes.
8. Appraise the roles of defense counsel, the prosecuting attorney, the judge, the jury, the witnesses, and the defendant.
9. Identify and locate witnesses.
10. Relate to defense counsel.
11. Trust and communicate relevantly with his counsel.
12. Comprehend instructions and advice.
13. Make decisions after receiving advice.
14. Maintain a collaborative relationship with his attorney and help plan legal strategy.
15. Follow testimony for contradictions or errors.
16. Testify relevantly and be cross-examined if necessary.
17. Challenge prosecution witnesses.
18. Tolerate stress at the trial and while awaiting trial.
19. Refrain from irrational and unmanageable behavior during the trial.
20. Disclose pertinent facts surrounding the alleged offense.
21. Protect himself and utilize the legal safeguards available to him.

Source: Group for Advancement of Psychiatry, 1974, *Misuse of Psychiatry in the Criminal Courts: Competency to Stand Trial*, pp. 896–897.

role in determining sanity. The evaluation focuses much more on specific behaviors and capacities than on DSM disorders. One listing of the specific capacities that should be considered in a competency evaluation has been compiled by the Group for the Advancement of Psychiatry. These areas of inquiry are summarized in Table 18–2.

The most common finding of incompetence occurs when defendants are found incompetent to stand trial, but the issue of incompetence may arise at several stages of the criminal process. Defendants must be competent to understand the *Miranda warning* issued during their arrest. (The Miranda warning details the suspect's rights to remain silent and to have an attorney present during police questioning.) Defendants also must be competent at the time of their sentencing, which takes place after they have been convicted of a crime. Finally, recent rulings indicate that defendants sentenced to death must be competent at the time of their execution, or the death sentence cannot be carried out.

Many more people accused of crimes are institutionalized because of findings of incompetence than because of insanity rulings. However, incompetence has received far less attention from both legal and mental health scholars. This may reflect the fact that competence determinations raise few broad social and philosophical issues, unlike the insanity defense.

The goal of ensuring fairness forms the rationale for requiring that defendants are competent before criminal actions can proceed. Unfortunately, determinations of incompetence have sometimes produced what would seem to be very unfair results. Defendants who are judged to be incompetent are confined to mental institutions until they are competent to understand the criminal proceedings, at which time the proceedings resume. In some cases, the length of time that defendants have been confined while awaiting their return to competence has greatly exceeded the time that they would have served if they had been convicted. Although there is little doubt that defendants who are found incompetent have severe mental disorders, people who are hospitalized because of incompetence do not always receive the same protections as people who are hospitalized through civil commitment procedures, the topic we turn to next.

Mental Hospitals and the Law

Mental health issues are important in civil law as well as in criminal law. In particular, the involuntary hospitalization of the severely mentally impaired raises questions of major importance in civil law. Three issues are of special relevance: (1) civil commitment, the legal process of sending someone to a mental hospital against his or her will; (2) patients' rights, especially their right to treatment, their right to treatment in the least restrictive alternative environment, and their right to refuse certain treatments; and (3) deinstitutionalization, the movement to treat patients in their communities instead of in mental hospitals. We begin our consideration of involuntary hospitalization with a brief review of the history of mental hospitals in the United States.

Brief Historical Perspective: U.S. Mental Hospitals

In 1842, the famous British author Charles Dickens toured the United States and visited several mental institutions while on his tour. In *American Notes and Pictures from Italy* (1842/1970), he wrote the following about one of the institutions that he visited:

> I cannot say that I derived much comfort from the inspection of this charity. The different wards might have been cleaner and better ordered; I saw nothing of that salutary system which had impressed me so favorably elsewhere; and everything had a lounging, listless, madhouse air, which was very painful. The moping idiot, cowering down with long dishevelled hair; the gibbering maniac, with his hideous laugh and pointed finger; the vacant eye, the fierce wild face, the gloomy picking of the hands and lips, and munching of the nails: there they were all without disguise, in naked ugliness and horror. In the dining-room, a bare, dull, dreary place, with nothing for the eye to rest on but the empty walls, a woman was locked up alone. She was bent, they told me, on committing suicide. If anything could have strengthened her in her resolution, it would certainly have been the insupportable monotony of such an existence. (p. 93)

Such cruel care of the mentally disturbed has been a problem throughout the course of history. In Europe during the Middle Ages, "lunatics" and "idiots," as the mentally ill and mentally retarded were commonly called, were given marginal care. Some were kept at home by their families, while others roamed freely as beggars. Mentally disturbed people who were violent or appeared dangerous often were imprisoned with criminals. A few were tried as witches. Those who could not subsist on their own were housed in almshouses for the poor.

In the 1600s and 1700s, *insane asylums* were established to house the mentally disturbed. The first asylum in the United States was founded in Williamsburg, Virginia, in 1773. Early asylums were little more than human warehouses, but as the nineteenth century began, the **moral treatment** movement led to improved conditions in at least some mental hospitals. Founded on a basic respect for human dignity and the belief that humanistic care would help to relieve mental illness, moral treatment reforms were instituted by such leading mental health professionals as Benjamin Rush in America, Phillippe Pinel in France, and William Tuke in England. Rather than simply confining mental patients, moral treatment offered support, care, and a degree of freedom.

Many of the large mental institutions that still dot the U.S. countryside were built in the nineteenth century to fulfill the philosophy of moral treatment. In the middle of the 1800s, mental health advocate Dorothea Dix gave particular impetus to this trend. Dix argued that treating the mentally ill in mental hospitals was both more humane and more economical than caring for them haphazardly in their communities, and she urged that special facilities be built to house mental patients. Dix and like-minded reformers were successful in their efforts. In 1830, there were only four public mental hospitals in the United States that housed a combined total of under 200 patients. By 1880, there were 75 public mental hospitals, with a total population of more than 35,000 residents (Torrey, 1988; see Chapter 1).

Despite laudable intentions, hospitalization cured few patients. As the moral treatment movement faded, many mental institutions simply became larger and more grotesque human warehouses. The number of patients living in mental hospitals continued to grow rapidly in the first half of the twentieth century, and the problems of large mental institutions grew along with their populations. The squalid conditions in state mental hospitals began to be revealed to the public shortly after World War II. Many conscientious objectors who worked in mental hospitals instead of serving in the armed forces observed their horrors and brought the terrible conditions to the attention of politicians and the popular media (Torrey, 1988).

As can be seen in Figure 18–1, the number of patients living in mental hospitals began to shrink dramatically in the 1950s. This was due in large part to the discovery of antipsychotic medications and to the *deinstitutionalization movement*—the attempt to care for the mentally ill in their communities—which owed no small debt to the public outcry started by the World War II conscientious objectors. Even today, however,

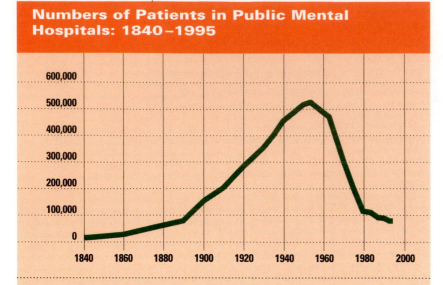

Numbers of Patients in Public Mental Hospitals: 1840–1995

FIGURE 18-1: The number of patients living in mental hospitals increased from the last part of the 1800s, when large mental hospitals were built, and declined from the 1950s to the present with the development of antipsychotic medication and deinstitutionalization.

Source: E.F. Torrey, 1988, *Nowhere to Go: The Tragic Odyssey of the Homeless Mentally Ill*, p. 3. New York: HarperCollins; and E.F. Torrey, 1997, *Out of the Shadows*, p. 9. New York: Wiley.

some large institutions continue to offer inadequate care. Moreover, the laudable deinstitutionalization movement, which had the opposite goals of Dix's institutionalization efforts, has many problems, as we will soon see.

Libertarianism versus Paternalism in Treating Mental Patients

What are society's legal and philosophical rationales for hospitalizing people against their will? As a general matter, debates about involuntary hospitalization highlight the philosophical tension between *libertarian* views, which emphasize protecting the rights of the individual, and *paternalist* approaches, which emphasize the state's duty to protect its citizens. This tension is evident in contemporary rationales for committing mental patients to institutions. For example, the involuntary hospitalization of someone who appears to be dangerous to others serves a protective, paternalist goal. Yet civil libertarians note that *preventive detention*—confinement before a crime is committed—can lead to substantial abuse. With the exception of **civil commitment**—the involuntary hospitalization of the mentally ill—our laws prohibit the confinement of someone simply on the suspicion

that he or she is about to commit a crime, no matter how strong or how realistic this suspicion may be.

Many scholars have become embroiled in the debate between the libertarian and paternalist philosophies. Some of these scholars recognize few justifications for civil commitment (Durham & LaFond, 1988), whereas others argue that many such justifications exist (Torrey, 1988). Despite a recent swing of the pendulum back in the direction of paternalism, the major trend over the past several decades has been a libertarian one, including a closer scrutiny of civil commitment procedures, an increasing recognition of patients' rights, and the deinstitutionalization of patients from mental hospitals (Appelbaum, 1994). Note that this increased concern for the rights of patients has run parallel to the increased emphasis on their criminal responsibility in the insanity defense. Rights and responsibilities do indeed go hand in hand.

Civil Commitment

American law contains two broad rationales for civil commitment. The first rationale is based on the state's *parens patriae* authority, the philosophy that the government has a humanitarian responsibility to care for its weaker members. (The literal translation of the Latin phrase *parens patriae* is the "state as parent.") The concept of *parens patriae* dates back to ancient Rome and has influenced U.S. law through English traditions. Under the state's *parens patriae* authority, civil commitment may be justified when the mentally disturbed are either dangerous to themselves or unable to care for themselves (Myers, 1983–84). In addition to the confinement of the mentally ill, the concept of *parens patriae* is used to justify the state's supervision of minors and physically incapacitated adults.

The second rationale for civil commitment is based on the state's *police power*—its duty to protect the public safety, health, and welfare. Our government restricts individual liberties for the public good in many ways. For the safety of others, we are restricted from yelling "Fire!" in a crowded theater or from driving an automobile at 100 miles an hour. The civil commitment of people who are dangerous to others is justified by similar police power rationales. Civil commitment obviously involves a dramatic restriction in individual liberty, however, as it constitutes confinement without having committed a crime. Thus this severe restriction on individual liberty requires the highest degree of scrutiny.

The police power rationales for civil commitment have been invoked throughout the history of U.S. law, even in colonial times, as the "furiously insane" could be detained in order to prevent them from doing harm to others (Myers, 1983–84). In contrast, commitment under *parens patriae* rationales was virtually unknown in the United States until large mental institutions were built in the 1800s. Some evidence suggests that civil commitment standards were very lax during the same historical period that mental institutions were being built (Appelbaum, 1994). For example, an 1842 New York state statute required the confinement of all "lunatics" irrespective of whether they were dangerous or able to care for themselves. The law commissioned "assessors" to round up lunatics and have them confined for a period of no less than 6 months (Reisner & Slobogin, 1990).

Legislation that more carefully defined the grounds for civil commitment and protected at least some of the rights of the mentally ill was not adopted until the latter part of the nineteenth century; its adoption was due in large part to the efforts of Mrs. E.P.W. Packard (Myers, 1983–84). Mrs. Packard was committed to a mental hospital by her husband under an Illinois law that allowed a man to commit his children or his wife to a mental hospital against their will and without the usual evidence of insanity. The commitment of Mrs. Packard was questionable at best. In presenting evidence in favor of her commitment, for example, one doctor noted that Mrs. Packard was rational but she was a "religious bigot" (Reisner & Slobogin, 1990). Following her release 3 years after being committed, Mrs. Packard campaigned to revise commitment standards to prevent such abuses, and she succeeded in influencing the laws in many states.

Following the reforms begun by Mrs. Packard, civil commitment laws remained largely unchanged from the late 1800s until the 1960s and 1970s. During more recent years, several notable cases set important precedents that have affected civil commitment laws and procedures. These developments are discussed shortly, but first we consider civil commitment procedures and philosophies in more detail.

GROUNDS AND PROCEDURES

Most states provide two types of civil commitment procedures: emergency procedures and formal procedures. *Emergency commitment procedures* allow an acutely disturbed individual to be temporarily confined in a mental hospital, typically for no more than a few days. Various states designate physicians, mental health professionals, or even police officers as being qualified to determine whether an emergency commitment is required. Obviously, such action is taken only when a mental disorder is very serious, and the risk that the patient is dangerous to self or others appears to be very high.

Formal commitment procedures can lead to involuntary hospitalization that lasts for much longer periods of time than an emergency commitment, and it can be ordered only by a court. An adversary hearing must be available to mental patients who object to involuntary hospitalization; all of their usual due process rights must be protected in formal commitment procedures, and the need for hospitalization typically must be demonstrated by "clear and convincing" evidence. Furthermore, once an individual is involuntarily committed to a mental institution through formal procedures, his or her case often is automatically reviewed after a set period of time—for example, every 6 months.

Because civil commitment is a matter of state law, the specific grounds for involuntary hospitalization vary from state to state. Still, three grounds tend to dominate commitment laws: (1) inability to care for self, (2) being dangerous to self, and (3) being dangerous to others. The broadest of these is *inability to care for self*. In some states, mental patients may be hospitalized against their will if they are unable to care for themselves adequately in the community or if they do not have family or friends who will care for them. The intention of this commitment standard is benevolent, but because it has been abused in some cases, newly articulated patient rights have been used to attack the "inability to care for self" ground for civil commitment (Appelbaum, 1994; Durham & LaFond, 1988). Debates continue in courtrooms and in state legislatures. Is it better to be paternalist and sacrifice some individual rights by involuntarily committing mental patients who do not want but who clearly need inpatient treatment? Or is it better to protect civil liberties by not committing patients who obviously are severely disturbed but who manage to survive on their own outside of mental hospitals?

The two other grounds for justifying civil commitment generally have not been attacked

▲ **John Monahan, a psychologist at the University of Virginia School of Law, is a leader in the study of psychology and the law. Monahan is particularly noted for his work on the prediction of violence.**

on philosophical grounds. Few civil libertarians object to hospitalizing people against their will when they clearly are either *dangerous to self* or *dangerous to others*, provided that the danger is "imminent." Thus a commonly accepted standard for civil commitment is "clear and convincing evidence of imminent danger to oneself or others." Questions have been raised about the ability of mental health professionals to predict dangerousness, however.

PREDICTING DANGEROUSNESS AND SUICIDAL RISK

The first question to ask about civil commitment and the prediction of dangerousness is: Are mentally disturbed people more dangerous than other people? To many laypeople, the obvious answer to this question is yes. Until recently, however, psychological research has suggested the opposite answer. John Monahan (1992), a psychologist and law professor and the leading authority on the prediction of dangerousness, once concluded that there was no evidence that violence and mental illness were related. Recently, he has modified his position.

Monahan (1992) argues that more recent, methodologically sophisticated research suggests that violence and serious mental illness are related after all. In addressing the question about the link between violence and mental illness, he examines both the rate of violence among the mentally ill and the rate of mental disorder among criminals. Whichever way the question is asked, evidence supports the conclusion that the two problems are associated. The prevalence of bipolar disorder, major depression, and schizophrenia has been found to be several times as high among prison inmates as among the general population. Similarly, the rate of violence is about five times higher among people diagnosed with one of these major mental disorders than among those with no diagnosis. People who abuse alcohol or drugs are even more likely to engage in violent behavior (see Table 18–3).

Research documenting the increased risk of dangerousness to others is important, but for several reasons this evidence does not directly translate into a policy of confining the mentally ill. For one, the data indicate that the risk for violence among the mentally ill is far lower than is publicly perceived. In fact, approximately 90 percent of the mentally disturbed have *no* history of violence (Monahan, 1992). Second, other research indicates that although current psychotic symptoms predict violence, a past history of psychosis is not associated with an increased risk (Link, Cullen, & Andrews, 1990). Third, the presence of a mental illness is unrelated to future arrests for violent crime among jail detainees, although the rate of recidivism is high among this group as a whole (Teplin, Abram, & McClelland, 1994). Finally and most importantly, numerous factors other than mental illness are known to predict an increased risk for violence, but they obviously do not justify involuntary confinement. For example, research has documented that people who live in poverty or who have a history of criminal behavior are more likely to be violent. Would anyone suggest that such a statistical risk justifies involuntary hospitalization?

Clinical Assessment and the Prediction of Dangerousness   If mental illness is a relatively poor and philosophically problematic predictor of violence, our second question becomes: Can clinical assessments of the dangerousness of mental patients improve prediction?

TABLE 18-3
Mental Illness and Violence

Current Prevalence of Mental Disorders Among Convicted Criminals and Community Controls

Diagnosis	Percentage with Diagnosis	
	Chicago Jail Detainees	Controls
Schizophrenia	2.7	0.9
Major depression	3.9	1.1
Mania or bipolar disorder	1.4	0.1
Any severe disorder	6.4	1.8

Prevalence of Violence Among People with or without a Mental Disorder

Diagnosis	Percentage Violent
No disorder	2.1
Schizophrenia	12.7
Major depression	11.7
Mania or bipolar disorder	11.0
Alcohol abuse/dependence	24.6
Substance abuse/dependence	34.7

Sources: Adapted from J. Monahan, 1992, Mental disorder and violent behavior: Perceptions and evidence, *American Psychologist*, 47, 516, 518; L. Teplin, 1990, The prevalence of severe mental disorder among male urban jail detainees, *American Journal of Public Health*, 80, 665; and J. Swanson et al., 1990, Violence and psychiatric disorder in the community, *Hospital and Community Psychiatry*, 41, 765.

Researchers have concluded that clinical predictions that someone will be violent are wrong approximately two out of three times (Ennis & Emery, 1978; Monahan, 1981; see Research Close-Up). That is, the false-positive rate of a prediction of violence is about 67 percent. In fact, several commentators have asserted that it is unethical for mental health experts to offer predictions about dangerousness to the courts, because the clinical prediction of violence is so inaccurate (Ewing, 1991; Foot, 1990; Melton et al., 1987).

RESEARCH CLOSE-UP

The Accuracy of Predictions of Violence

Researchers have concluded that the clinical prediction of violence to others is inaccurate, but most studies of this topic are older and are flawed in various ways. Many studies, for example, assumed that the clinician had predicted violence only in cases where the patient was committed to a hospital. Clinicians do not commit every patient who they fear may be violent, however, and they sometimes commit patients who have a low likelihood of violence. Moreover, some dangerous patients allow themselves to be hospitalized voluntarily. Another problem with past research is the measurement of subsequent violence. Studies have used police reports, court records, and medical files to assess subsequent violence, but many acts of violence are not documented in these official records.

An important study by Lidz, Mulvey, and Gardner (1993) sought to assess clinical predictions of violence more thoroughly than in past research. These investigators studied 714 cases seen in the psychiatric emergency room of a large teaching hospital in an urban area. Half the cases were predicted to have some potential for violence by two clinicians who interviewed them (including at least one psychiatrist), and the other half were comparison cases that were not predicted to be violent by the clinicians. Clinicians were asked directly about their predictions, and the two groups of patients were matched on their age, sex, and race, as well as on whether they were admitted to the hospital. Thus any differences in actual violence between the groups had to be a result of the predictions, not of either the background factors or whether the patient was hospitalized.

The investigators later interviewed both patients and someone who knew them about subsequent episodes of violence. This step represented another improvement over past research, which had used only official records of hospitals, courts, and/or the police to document violence. (These records were also checked in the present study.) The investigators conducted at least three interviews with all 714 cases in the 6 months following their contact with the emergency room. Violence was judged to have occurred if, according to any source of information, a patient laid hands on another person with a violent intent or threatened another person with a weapon.

The investigators found that 53 percent of the predicted cases engaged in a subsequent episode of violence versus 36 percent of the comparison cases, a statistically significant difference. Clinicians were equally good at predicting violence among members of different ethnic groups and among people of different ages. Predictions of violence among women were less accurate than predictions for men, however. In fact, the clinical predictions of violence among women were no better than chance, as the clinicians greatly underestimated the base rate of violence among women (see Research Methods).

Among patients who had no prior history of violent behavior, clinical prediction still was found to be above chance levels. Apparently the clinicians made some accurate judgments based on information other than past behavior. Surprisingly, however, the accuracy of the clinical predictions was no greater when the risk of violence in a patient was judged to be higher versus lower. The critical distinction was the decision of whether the potential for violence was present or absent.

This research indicates that the clinical prediction of violence does have some value after all.

Many inaccuracies are found in clinical prediction, but at least among men, clinicians were able to beat chance in predicting the potential for violence. A challenge for future research will be to find ways to improve the prediction of violence. This is an especially important goal given the damage wrought by both false positives—wrongly hospitalizing someone who is not dangerous—and by false negatives—releasing someone who is dangerous to others. ■

In arguing in support of the expert prediction of dangerousness, other commentators have noted that the prediction of violence is above chance levels despite inaccuracies in prediction (Monahan, 1981). At first glance, being wrong in predicting violence two out of three times may seem *worse* than chance. This is not the case, however, as one must take **base rates** or population frequencies into account. When predicting an event that has a very low frequency, a false-positive rate of two-thirds is, in fact, better than chance (see Research Methods). This is an important if somewhat difficult point. The U.S. Supreme Court Justice Harry Blackmun failed to grasp the concept of base rates when he considered evidence on the prediction of violence in a real case that was heard before the court. He wrongly claimed that a coin flip would be more accurate than clinical prediction (Reisner & Slobogin, 1990).

RESEARCH METHODS

Base Rates and Predictions

The validity with which an outcome like violence can be predicted depends on a number of factors. One obvious influence is the magnitude of the relation between the predictor and the outcome. The stronger the relation, the better the prediction. Thus the clinical prediction of violence seems highly flawed when we learn that clinicians are wrong two-thirds of the time that they predict that a patient will be violent. However, the validity of prediction also is affected by some conditions that are not obvious. Base rates or population frequencies are another very important influence (Meehl & Rosen, 1955).

We can use the prediction of violence to illustrate the general influence of base rates on the validity of prediction. We construct a hypothetical example in which we assume that (1) future, serious violence in our population has a base rate of 3 percent, (2) clinicians predict that violence will occur among 6 percent of the population, and (3) the clinical prediction of violence is wrong two-thirds of the time. These assumptions are portrayed in the following contingency table:

	Actually Violent	Actually Not Violent
Predicted Violent	2% (true positive)	4% (false positive)
Predicted Not Violent	1% (false negative)	93% (true negative)

A quick check of the figures will confirm that they meet all our assumptions. The base rate of actual violence is 3 percent; the clinicians predict violence in 6 percent of the cases; and the prediction that patients will be violent is wrong two-thirds of the time. But let us examine the prediction a bit more closely. The hypothetical example yields a *sensitivity* (true positives over the sum of true positives and false negatives) of 67 percent and a *specificity* (true negatives divided by the sum of the true negatives and false positives) of 96 percent. Even though the predictions of violence are wrong two-thirds of the time, it is also true that the clinicians *correctly* detect 67 percent of violent patients and 96 percent of nonviolent patients in our hypothetical example.

Now let us compare these figures with another hypothetical example: Supreme Court Justice Harry Blackmun's prediction that a coin flip is as accurate as the clinical prediction of violence (see accompanying text). Justice Blackmun assumed that a coin flip would be right half of the time—it would come up heads or tails—while clinical prediction was right only one-third of the time. The statistics are not as simple as Justice Blackmun assumed, however, as we can easily illustrate. For this example, we will assume that (1) the base rate of future, serious violence remains at 3 percent, (2) the coin will predict violence (heads) 50 percent of the time, and (3) the coin flip produces random predictions. These assumptions are portrayed in the following contingency table:

	Actually Violent	Actually Not Violent
Predicted Violent	1.5%	48.5%
Predicted Not Violent	1.5%	48.5%

Unlike what Justice Blackmun asserted, the coin flip does not beat clinical prediction in these hypothetical examples. Both the sensitivity and specificity of the coin flip are 50 percent. These figures indicate random prediction, and they are considerably lower than those obtained for clinical prediction. The coin flip method correctly detected only 50 percent of violent patients (versus 67 percent) and 50 percent of nonviolent patients (versus 96 percent). More simply, the percentage of false positives is much higher using Justice Blackmun's method than using clinical prediction (48.5 percent versus 4 percent). In our first example, the clinical prediction of violence was wrong 67 percent of the time, as we forced it to be. In our second example, however, Justice Blackmun's coin flip was not wrong in predicting violence 50 percent of the time. It was wrong in predicting violence 97 percent of the time [48.5/ (48.5 + 1.5)].

A key to understanding Justice Blackmun's error is to recognize that base rates affect the percentage of false positives and false negatives. The base rate of predicting violence using the clinical method (6 percent) was fairly close to the base rate of the actual occurrence of violence (3 percent). However, the base rate of predicting violence using the coin flip (50 percent) was much higher than its actual occurrence. In general, the statistical potential for accurate prediction is maximized when the predictor variable and the outcome variable have more similar base rates (Meehl & Rosen, 1955).

A low base rate is one reason why serious violence and other infrequent events are so difficult to predict. Predictions that the infrequent event will occur typically have a higher base rate than the actual outcomes. As a final illustration of how these differing base rates affect prediction, we return to the coin flip example but alter one aspect of it. We set the base rate of the occurrence of violence as identical to the base rate with which it is predicted to occur (50 percent). This is illustrated in the following contingency table:

	Actually Violent	Actually Not Violent
Predicted Violent	50%	50%
Predicted Not Violent	50%	50%

The association between the coin flip and the occurrence of violence clearly is random in this example, as indicated by its specificity and sensitivity, which remain at 50 percent. In this hypothetical example, however, the coin flip "beats" the clinical prediction of violence. The coin flip is wrong in predicting violence only half of the time, which is better than being wrong two-thirds of the time. But this is only a hypothetical example. In the real world, violence is a low-frequency event, and for statistical reasons alone, this makes it more difficult to predict validly (Meehl & Rosen, 1955). The clinical prediction of violence is far from perfect, but it is better than chance. Justice Blackmun did not understand the influence of base rates. We hope that you do now. ■

Another consideration is that the prediction of violence may be better in the short term than in the long run. This is an important distinction, because most research examines long-term outcomes (Monahan, 1981). Specifically, research indicates that two out of three people who are involuntarily hospitalized are not violent after they are released. This does not mean that they would not have been violent if they had never been committed. Obviously, clinicians commit only those people who they strongly believe will become violent imminently, and they release the same people only if they are convinced that these people will not become violent. Such urgent, real-life decisions make it impossible to conduct unequivocal research. For obvious ethical reasons, no one has done or ever will do the true experiment that would best test the validity of short-term clinical predictions: release or confine potentially violent people at random and compare their rates of actual violence with clinical predictions about violence.

In reconciling the conflicting viewpoints on the prediction of violence, perhaps the best advice comes from those who point to differences between the definitions and goals of the legal system and the mental health system. As with insanity assessments, clinicians who perform expert assessments of violence do best when they restrict their evaluation to their area of expertise. Research and clinical evidence can be used to determine a reasonable assessment of the likelihood of violence. However, it is the job of the legal system, not the mental health profession, to translate such probabilities into decisions about whether a given individual is "dangerous" in the legal sense of the term (Grisso & Appelbaum, 1992). In clinical settings, evidence indicates that patients perceive hospital admissions to be less coercive if they feel they have a greater "voice" in the decision. That is, even if patients object to the ultimate decision, they are more likely to accept hospitalization if they feel they have been respectfully included in the decision-making process (Lidz et al., 1995).

Assessing Suicide Risk   Identical concerns apply to civil commitment and the assessment of suicide risk as to the assessment of dangerousness to others. As we discussed in Chapter 5, mental disorders, particularly depression, are related to an increased risk of suicide, but the risk of suicide clearly is far too small to justify civil commitment simply because of the presence of a mental disorder. Similarly, evidence on the clinical prediction of suicide risk also indicates very high false-positive rates (Pokony, 1983). These findings again raise concerns about the accuracy of clinical prediction, but we can be reassured by the actual procedures used to evaluate patients for civil commitment under either of the two dangerousness standards. In many cases in which a patient is involuntarily hospitalized, patients freely and directly acknowledge their intention to commit suicide or to physically harm others (Appelbaum, 1994).

COMMITMENT OF MINORS

The caution that accompanies the civil commitment of adults stands in marked contrast to the process of institutionalizing juveniles who do not wish to be hospitalized. Technically, the involuntary hospitalization of minors is not a civil commitment issue because most minors are classified as "voluntary" patients even when they are hospitalized against their wishes. This is because parents, not minor children, have the right to commit children to hospitals. According to the 1979 Supreme Court ruling in *Parham v. J.R.* [442 U.S. 584 (1979)], minors, unlike adults, are not entitled to a full hearing before they can be committed to a mental hospital. Although state laws may add requirements, according to *Parham* parents can commit a minor against the minor's wishes, as long as an independent fact finder agrees. The staff of the hospital where parents have applied for admission qualify as independent fact finders, even though they have clear financial incentives to find reasons why inpatient care is needed (Weithorn, 1988).

Paternalists and libertarians find themselves in hot debate over the commitment of minors. Civil libertarians argue for an increased recognition of children's rights, whereas paternalists are reluctant to interfere with parents' rights or family autonomy. Perhaps the strongest libertarian argument is that too many minors are committed to mental hospitals merely because they are troublesome to their parents—and because hospitalization is profitable to private psychiatric hospitals.

Clinical psychologist and attorney Lois Weithorn (1988) assembled some impressive evidence in support of this perspective based on trends that occurred during the 1980s. Among the facts that she documented are the following:

- Between 1980 and 1984 the number of juveniles admitted to private psychiatric hospitals increased by 450 percent.
- Advertisements suggesting hospitalization as an option for difficult or troubled adolescents were common in the popular media during the 1980s.
- The National Association of Private Psychiatric Hospitals adopted guidelines suggesting that hospitalization of teenagers is justified by "sexual promiscuity" and perhaps even by a preference for punk rock music over scout or church group activities.

- Less than one-third of all hospitalized adolescents suffered from severe disorders, such as psychosis or serious depression.
- The number of status offenders adjudicated in the juvenile justice system declined sharply during the same years that hospital admissions rose.

Weithorn concluded that these facts indicated that the former status offender (see Chapter 16) became the new adolescent inpatient in the 1980s. The managed care environment of the 1990s may reverse this trend, as insurance coverage for inpatient treatment of adolescents becomes more restrictive in order to contain insurance costs. Even so, we find Weithorn's concerns to be compelling. She sees the shift from the juvenile justice system to the mental health system as a worrisome change of emphasis from "badness" to "sickness" in dealing with troublesome adolescents. From her perspective, a basic problem with this shift is the lack of protection of the due process rights of minors who are hospitalized. Due process rights for teenagers accused of crimes were won in the juvenile courts in the 1960s, but, as the *Parham* decision made clear, adolescents are not entitled to the same procedural protections as adults in the mental health system. This lack of protection is a particular concern because many of the difficulties that lead to the hospitalization of adolescents do not seem to be "mental disorders" but instead seem like "problems in living with a teenager," to paraphrase Szasz.

The Rights of Mental Patients

Several important court cases have clarified the rights of mental patients following their civil commitment to a mental hospital. These rights include the right to treatment; the right to treatment in the least restrictive alternative environment; and the right to refuse treatment.

THE RIGHT TO TREATMENT

Two of the most significant cases for establishing that hospitalized mental patients have a constitutional right to treatment were *Wyatt v. Stickney* and *O'Connor v. Donaldson*.

Wyatt v. Stickney *Wyatt v. Stickney* (1972) began as a dispute over the dismissal of 99 employees from Bryce Hospital in Tuscaloosa, Alabama. The state mental hospital had been built in the 1850s and housed nearly 5,000 patients when the much-needed staff members were released due to budget cuts. All accounts indicate that conditions in the hospital were very bad even before the layoffs. The buildings were fire hazards, the food was inedible, sanitation was neglected, avoidable sickness was rampant, abuse of patients was frequent, and confinement of patients with no apparent therapeutic goal occurred regularly.

Litigation was filed on behalf of Ricky Wyatt, a resident in the institution, as part of a class action suit against the Alabama mental health commissioner, Dr. Stickney. The suit argued that institutionalized patients had a right to treatment that Bryce Hospital failed to fulfill. The commissioner was in the somewhat unusual position of being a proponent of a suit against him, as he wanted to improve the care of the mentally ill in the state but was faced with budget problems. The case was tried and appealed several times, and the patients' suit was upheld.

The victory forced the state of Alabama to provide services, but *Wyatt* had a broader impact that influenced mental patients and mental hospitals throughout the country. The judicial rulings clearly established that hospitalized mental patients have a right to treatment. Specifically, a federal district court ruled that at a minimum, public mental institutions must provide (1) a humane psychological and physical environment, (2) qualified staff in numbers sufficient to administer adequate treatment, and (3) individualized treatment plans [334 F. Supp. 1341 (M.D. Ala. 1971) at 1343]. The court also ordered that the implementation of changes needed to fulfill these patients' rights could not be delayed until funding was available.

The *Wyatt* decision helped focus national attention on the treatment of the mentally ill and the mentally retarded and led to the filing of numerous "right to treatment" cases. The threat of litigation impelled the staff of numerous other mental hospitals to improve patient care. *Wyatt* also helped to spur the deinstitutionalization movement, because the level of care required by the ruling is impossible to provide in large, overcrowded institutions (Myers, 1983–84). As we shall see, however, this has meant that some mental patients simply were released to the community without adequate care there either (Appelbaum, 1994; Torrey, 1997).

O'Connor v. Donaldson The Supreme Court acknowledged the right of mental patients to treatment in another landmark case, *O'Connor v. Donaldson* [422 U.S. 563 (1975)]. Kenneth Donaldson had been confined in a Florida mental hospital for nearly 15 years, despite his repeated requests for release based on his claims that he was not mentally ill, was not dangerous to himself or others, and was receiving no treatment in the hospital. Eventually, he sued the hospital's superintendent, Dr. J. B. O'Connor, for release, based on the assertion that he had been deprived of his constitutional right to liberty.

The evidence presented at the trial indicated that Donaldson was not and never had been dangerous to himself or others. Testimony also revealed that reliable individuals and agencies in the community had made several offers to care for Donaldson, but superintendent O'Connor had repeatedly rejected them. O'Connor had insisted that Donaldson could be released only to the custody of his parents, who were very old and unable to care for him. O'Connor's position on Donaldson's supposed inability to care for himself was puzzling, because Donaldson was employed and had lived on his own for many years before being committed to the hospital. Other evidence documented that Donaldson had received nothing but custodial care while he was hospitalized.

After a series of trials and appeals, the Supreme Court eventually ruled that Donaldson was not dangerous either to himself or others. It further ruled that a state could not confine him as being in need of treatment and yet fail to provide him with that treatment. Specifically, it ordered that "the State cannot constitutionally confine . . . a non-dangerous individual who is capable of surviving safely in freedom by himself or with the help of willing and responsible family members or friends." Thus *O'Connor* and similar cases not only underscored a patient's right to treatment, but they also set limitations on civil commitment standards. Commitment based on dangerousness to self or others remained unquestioned, but commitment based on inability to care for self became much more controversial, especially if institutionalization offered little treatment or therapeutic benefit.

▼ **Kenneth Donaldson proudly displays a copy of the U.S. Supreme Court ruling in his case. The Court held that nondangerous mental patients cannot be confined against their will, a decision that freed Donaldson and set an important precedent for other hospitalized mental patients.**

TREATMENT IN THE LEAST RESTRICTIVE ALTERNATIVE ENVIRONMENT

The patient's right to be treated in the least restrictive alternative environment was first developed in the 1966 case of *Lake v. Cameron* [364 F. 2d 657 (D.C. Cir. 1966)], decided by the Washington, D.C., Circuit Court of Appeals. Catherine Lake was 60 years old when she was committed to St. Elizabeth's Hospital because of "a chronic brain syndrome associated with aging." A particular problem was her tendency to wander away from her home, which posed a threat to her life through exposure to the elements and other dangers.

In contesting the commitment, Mrs. Lake did not object to her need for treatment, but she argued that appropriate treatment was available in a less restrictive setting. The court agreed, suggesting several less restrictive alternatives to institutionalization. These alternatives ranged from having Mrs. Lake carry an identification card to treating her in a public nursing home.

Several additional cases following *Lake* firmly established the doctrine of the least restrictive alternative. Litigation was quickly followed by legislation, as numerous states incorporated the right to treatment in the least restrictive alternative environment into their mental health statutes (Hoffman & Foust, 1977). Although the concept was quickly embraced, no one was or is absolutely certain what the expression "least restrictive alternative" means.

In theory, the least restrictive alternative can be seen as an attempt to balance paternalist and libertarian concerns in the involuntary treatment of the mentally ill. The state provides mandatory care, but that care must restrict individual liberties to the minimal degree possible. Questions arise about how to define and implement the theory. Who should determine what alternative is the least restrictive? Is this the job of the mental health professional who is making treatment decisions? Should the court monitor the consideration of alternatives? Should an independent party supervise these decisions? The practical answer to these important questions generally has been to place the decisions in the hands of mental health professionals. Ironically, this was the arrangement before *Lake*; thus the case did not lead to the development of new procedural safeguards.

Perhaps the most important issue about the least restrictive alternative concerns the problem that developed in the original *Lake* case: Less restrictive alternatives to institutionalization often are not available. No suitable community care was found for Mrs. Lake, who was returned to the institution. If a less restrictive alternative treatment is not available, must such treatment be developed and provided by the community? Some early cases suggested that the courts would mandate such a solution, but this trend quickly faded. Thus *Lake* both established patients' right to treatment in the least restrictive alternative environment and foreshadowed the problem of insufficient alternative treatments in the community. The development of community resources has not kept up with the release of patients from mental hospitals (Hoffman & Foust, 1977). This is especially unfortunate, given that data suggest that community treatment can be more effective than inpatient care (Kiesler, 1982).

THE RIGHT TO REFUSE TREATMENT

The third and most recent development in litigation involving people committed to mental hospitals is the *right to refuse treatment*, particularly the right to refuse psychotropic medication. Several courts and state legislatures have concluded that mental health patients have the right to refuse certain treatments under certain conditions, although this right is on less firm ground than the other two rights we have discussed. In particular, the Supreme Court has yet to establish whether there is a constitutional basis for the right to refuse treatment.

The very concept of a patient refusing treatment is problematic in that involuntary hospitalization itself is treatment against a patient's will. The patient who is committed involuntarily to a mental hospital has refused inpatient treatment but is receiving it anyway. On what grounds can subsequent treatment decisions be refused if the decision about hospitalization already has been taken out of the patient's hands? Many mental health professionals have noted this contradiction, and they argue that patients lose their right to refuse treatment once they are involuntarily hospitalized (Appelbaum, 1994; Gutheil, 1986; Torrey, 1997). After all, a mental health professional is in an awkward position if a patient is committed to a hospital for treatment yet retains the right to refuse medication. How can mental health professionals do their job in such a circumstance?

The question of the right to refuse treatment often turns on the issue of informed consent, one of several legal doctrines that can be used to justify a patient's refusal of mental health (or medical) treatments (Hermann, 1990). **Informed consent** requires that (1) a clinician tell a patient about a procedure and its associated risks, (2) the patient understands the information and freely consents to the treatment, and (3) the patient is competent to give consent. When the patient's competence to provide consent is in question, a common approach is to appoint an independent guardian who offers a *substituted judgment*, deciding not what is best for the patient but what the patient would have been likely to do if he or she were competent (Gutheil, 1986).

The rationales for and parameters of patients' right to refuse treatment are still being debated in litigation and legislation. Several courts have ruled that patients retain their competence to make treatment decisions even if they have been committed through civil procedures. Moreover, half the states have recognized the right to refuse psychotropic medications provided that patients are not dangerous to themselves or others (Hermann, 1990). The Supreme Court first ruled on this topic in the 1990 case of *Washington v. Harper* [110 S. Ct. 1028 (1990)]. This case involved a Washington state prison that overrode a patient's refusal of psychotropic medications. The court decided in favor of the prison, ruling that the prison's review process sufficiently protected the patient's right to refuse treatment. This process stipulated that the patient's wishes could be overruled only after review by a three-member panel consisting of a psychologist, a psychiatrist, and a deputy warden. The Supreme Court's decision may signal a greater willingness on the part of the courts to limit patients' right to refuse treatment.

Almost a Revolution   Overall, the cases and legislation of the 1960s, 1970s, and 1980s served an essential function in articulating and increasing awareness of patients' rights. Recently, however, the swing toward libertarianism has begun to be balanced by important paternalist concerns—the need to protect the public from the violently mentally ill and especially the need to treat severely disturbed patients who lack insight into their condition (Appelbaum, 1994; Torrey, 1997). Serious mental illness is *not* a myth, and mental health professionals—and the state—have a duty to provide care for those who cannot care for themselves. Libertarians help ensure that treatments do not become overly paternalistic, but the paternalist position embraces legitimate and benevolent goals. Thus, in the words of one commentator, the libertarian changes in mental health law have produced "almost a revolution" (Appelbuam, 1994).

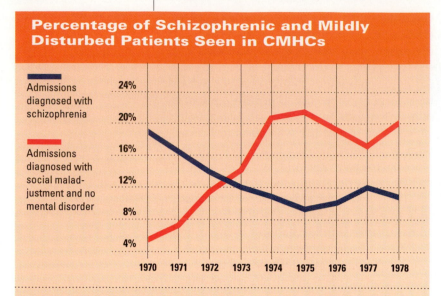

Percentage of Schizophrenic and Mildly Disturbed Patients Seen in CMHCs

Admissions diagnosed with schizophrenia

Admissions diagnosed with social maladjustment and no mental disorder

FIGURE 18-2: The decline in the number of schizophrenic patients and rise in the number of mildly disturbed patients is one indication of the failure of community mental health centers (CMHCs) to compensate for deinstitutionalization.

Source: E.F. Torrey, 1988, *Nowhere to Go: The Tragic Odyssey of the Homeless Mentally Ill,* p. 3. New York: HarperCollins.

Deinstitutionalization

Legal cases have restricted the inpatient treatment of the mentally ill, but a broader influence has been the **deinstitutionalization** movement—the philosophy that many of the mentally ill and mentally retarded can be better cared for in their community than in large mental hospitals. Bertram Brown, a former director of the National Institute for Mental Health, defined the goals of deinstitutionalization as "(1) the prevention of inappropriate mental hospital admissions through the provision of community alternatives for treatment, (2) the release to the community of all institutionalized patients who have been given adequate preparation for such a change, and (3) the establishment and maintenance of community support systems for noninstitutionalized people receiving mental health services in the community" (Braun et al., 1981).

The establishment of mental health centers in communities was part of the effort to achieve these three goals. In 1963, Congress passed the Community Mental Health Centers (CMHC) act with the strong support of President John F. Kennedy.[†] The act provided for the creation of community care facilities for the seriously mentally ill as alternatives to institutional care.

This law began a broad change in the way mental health services are delivered in the United States. There were no community mental health centers in operation in 1965, but by 1981 nearly 800 were in existence (Torrey, 1988).

Deinstitutionalization has occurred in dramatic fashion. In 1955, more than 500,000 people in the United States were confined to mental hospitals, but by 1994 that number had shrunk to less than 72,000 (Torrey, 1997). The effects of deinstitutionalization are even greater than these numbers suggest, because the overall population grew from 164 million in 1955 to 260 million in 1994. Thus, almost 900,000 people would be in institutions today if the 1955 proportion of inpatients to the total population had remained unchanged (Torrey, 1997). Unfortunately, CMHCs have not achieved many of their goals in helping deinstitutionalized patients. In fact, CMHCs generally have not focused their services on former inpatients with serious mental illness. As can be seen in Figure 18–2, the percentage of schizophrenic patients served by CMHCs is small and declining, while the percentage of patients with mild problems is larger and growing. In fact, many CMHCs do not even offer services for the seriously mentally ill, such as emergency treatment or inpatient care, despite the fact that they are mandated to do so by legislation (Torrey, 1988, 1997). Other community resources, such as halfway houses, simply have not been implemented in adequate numbers.

Other problems with the deinstitutionalization movement are evident. As public hospitalization has declined, the number of mental patients living in nursing homes and other for-profit institutions has grown (Goldman, Adams, & Taube, 1983; Torrey, 1988). More people with a mental illness also are being confined in jail. In fact, about 10 percent of the prison population suffers from a serious mental illness (Appelbaum, 1994; Torrey, 1997). In addition, a *revolving door* phenomenon has developed in which more patients are admitted to psychiatric hospitals more frequently but for shorter periods of time. For example, one study found that 24 percent of inpatients in New York City had 10 or more previous admissions (Karras & Otis, 1987). Moreover, the deinstitutionalized mentally ill constitute a large part of the homeless population (Fischer & Breakey, 1991; Torrey, 1997). One study found that 31 percent

---

[†] President Kennedy had a special interest in mental health because of his sister Rosemary. She was mildly mentally retarded as a child, but she became psychotic as a young adult and underwent a failed lobotomy that left her so impaired that she had to be confined to a nursing home.

of the homeless were in need of mental health services (Roth & Bean, 1986). In his stirring and disturbing book *Nowhere to Go*, psychiatrist E. Fuller Torrey (1988) notes eight major problems with deinstitutionalization:

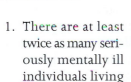

1. There are at least twice as many seriously mentally ill individuals living on streets and in shelters as there are in public mental hospitals.
2. There are increasing numbers of seriously mentally ill individuals in the nation's jails and prisons.
3. Seriously mentally ill individuals are regularly released from hospitals with little or no provision for aftercare or follow-up treatment.
4. Violent acts perpetrated by untreated mentally ill individuals are increasing in number.
5. Housing and living conditions for mentally ill individuals in the community are grossly inadequate.
6. Community mental health centers, originally funded to provide community care for the mentally ill so that these individuals would no longer have to go to state mental hospitals, are almost complete failures in this regard.
7. Laws designed to protect the rights of the seriously mentally ill primarily protect their right to remain mentally ill.
8. The majority of mentally ill individuals discharged from hospitals have been officially lost. Nobody knows where they are.

HAS THE PENDULUM SWUNG TOO FAR?
Some advocates for the mentally ill, particularly those in mental health professions, feel that the pendulum between paternalism and libertarianism has swung too far in the direction of patients' rights. Many mental patients who

clearly are in need of treatment cannot be committed under existing statutes. Some of the problems of the deinstitutionalized mentally ill are compounded by restrictive civil commitment laws. One commentary graphically described the situation as one in which patients were "rotting with their rights on" (Appelbaum & Gutheil, 1979). Torrey (1988) argues, "Freedom to be insane is an illusory freedom, a cruel hoax perpetrated on those who cannot think clearly by those who will not think clearly" (p. 34).

As a means of balancing paternalist and libertarian concerns, some experts have suggested that more paternalism is needed in committing patients, but that commitment should be to involuntary treatment in the least restrictive environment, such as mandatory outpatient care (Myers, 1983–84). Hospitalization would be required only as a last resort. Others call for the involuntary treatment of inpatients but only following careful review. In addition to providing procedural safeguards, the increased supervision of treatment decisions should benefit patients in state institutions where care often is less than ideal (Appelbaum, 1994). Other commentators support more paternalism in civil commitment laws but argue that a broader reorientation is needed in the thinking—and funding—of mental health professionals. Most psychiatrists, clinical psychologists, and social workers treat only the "worried well," and perhaps new incentives are needed to direct more of their efforts toward helping the seriously mentally ill (Torrey, 1988, 1997).

▲ **These contrasting photos illustrate how mental patients often are neglected both inside and outside of institutions. The photo on the left, taken several decades ago, shows some of the depressing and dehumanizing conditions that characterized many institutions for the mentally ill. The photo on the right depicts the contemporary problem of homelessness. Many homeless people are deinstitutionalized mental patients.**

Mental Health and Family Law

Both the insanity defense and civil commitment primarily involve people who have a serious mental illness. In contrast, mental health

professionals who are involved with *family law* issues typically work with people whose problems are less severe, and they often are consulted about issues related to normal development. This is evident in the major issues that form the focus of family law: divorce, spousal abuse, foster care, adoption, juvenile delinquency, child custody disputes, and child abuse and neglect. Any one of these problems can involve serious psychopathology, but they more commonly involve family members who are only mildly disturbed or are functioning normally.

We consider both family law and mental health law issues together in this chapter, because the opinions and advice of mental health professionals are frequently sought by legal professionals working in both areas. However, family and mental health law are distinct in the legal system. The two areas have different roots and practices, and attorneys may specialize in one or the other area but rarely both. In fact, family law cases typically are tried in different courts than are mental health law cases. These separate courts, known variously as "juvenile courts," "domestic relations courts," or "family courts," were first created at the turn of the century and adhere to a different philosophy than other U.S. courts. Much of mental health law is based on the state's police power obligations, but virtually all of family law is premised on the government's *parens patriae* duties.

In theory, the functions of juvenile and family courts are to help and protect children and families. Thus the goals of family courts historically have been more psychological than legal. In fact, the authors of a recent, comprehensive overview of the role of psychologists in the courts concluded, "Perhaps nowhere in the legal system is there as much deference to mental health professionals as in the juvenile court" (Melton et al., 1987, p. 291).

The importance of mental health professionals is particularly evident in the two family law topics considered in this chapter—child custody disputes following divorce and cases of child abuse and neglect. Mental health professionals and psychological findings are of great importance not only because of the family court's philosophy but also because terms like *child abuse* are poorly defined in the law. The laws governing judicial dispositions of these family concerns are similarly vague. In fact, the guiding principle for judicial decision making is the very general directive to make determinations according to what is in the "child's best interest" (Mnookin, 1975). Not surprisingly, family court judges frequently turn to mental health professionals for practical guidance in defining a given child's "best interests."

Balancing the Interests of Children, Parents, and the State

A general dilemma in family law is how to balance the potentially competing interests of children, parents, and the state (Mnookin, 1985). We alluded to this three-sided problem in our earlier discussion of the *Parham* decision on the commitment of minors to mental hospitals. People involved with such cases must address a number of difficult questions: Are children entitled to the same due process rights as adults? Should parental authority be respected above and beyond the wishes of either children or the state? Or should the state's *parens patriae* obligation overrule the desires of both children and parents?

One set of answers to these questions comes from advocates for children who consistently argue that children, or at least adolescents, are entitled to the same basic rights as adults. Advocates for this position were upset by *Parham*, for example, because they want minors to have the same due process rights as adults. Different rationales come from paternalists who believe that children need vigorous protection by the state. Paternalists do not favor *Parham* either, because it limits state supervision by giving parents the power to make decisions about hospitalizing minors. A paternalist might instead advocate for increased government regulation of private mental hospitals. The winners in *Parham* were those people who hold a third position as advocates for parental rights or "family autonomy." Proponents of family autonomy want to minimize the involvement of the state in the family, whether that intrusion comes from state supervision or broader rights for children.

The tension among the rights and responsibilities of children, parents, and the state pervades controversies about child custody and child abuse. Advocates for children's rights want children to have a voice in the outcome of custody disputes and the disposition of abuse cases. Advocates for family autonomy want parents to resolve custody disputes themselves and to narrow the definition of abuse and neglect in order to minimize state intervention in the family. Advocates for state intervention want judges to determine custody arrangements, and they argue for earlier and more vigorous intervention in cases of child abuse.

Child Custody Disputes Following Divorce

Divorce is a common experience for children living in the United States (see Further Thoughts on children of divorce). Every year, approximately 2 percent of U.S. children experience a divorce (SCCYF, 1989), and demographers have estimated that 38 percent of white children and 75 percent of black children born to married parents will experience a parental divorce by the age of 16 (Bumpass, 1984). **Child custody** is one of the issues that must be decided when parents divorce. Although the legal terminology differs from state to state, in effect custody decisions involve two determinations: *physical custody*, or where the children will live at what times; and *legal custody*, or how the parents will make separate or joint decisions about their children's lives. *Sole custody* refers to a situation in which only one parent retains physical or legal custody of the children; in contrast, in *joint custody* both parents retain custody.

The majority of custody decisions are made outside of court by attorneys who negotiate for the parents. A growing number of custody decisions are being made by parents themselves, however, typically with the help of a *mediator*—a neutral third party who facilitates the parents' discussions. Finally, a small but significant percentage of custody disputes are decided in court by a judge (Maccoby & Mnookin, 1992). Mental health professionals may be involved in providing recommendations during attorney negotiations, they may provide expert testimony in court, or they may act as mediators themselves.

FURTHER THOUGHTS

The Psychological Health of Children of Divorce

The state's *parens patriae* duty to protect children is a major justification for its role in automatically assuming supervision over child custody following divorce. (Even though most custody disputes are settled out of court, in theory, all agreements are subject to judicial review and could be overturned by a judge.) Obviously, this role was assumed long before psychological research was available on the question of how divorce affects children's emotional well-being. Still, considerable research has been conducted on children from divorced families, and findings raise questions about the child protection justification for state intervention.

The psychological consequences of divorce for children have been and continue to be debated. Some studies suggest that children successfully cope with divorce, and others conclude that divorce has severe, lasting, and damaging emotional consequences. However, empirical research clearly documents two important facts about the adjustment of children from divorced families: (1) on various measures of their psychological functioning, they differ only to a small degree from children whose parents are married, and (2) a substantial portion of the difficulties found among children after divorce actually begin long before the marital separation occurs.

Numerous studies have compared the psychological functioning of children whose parents have divorced with that of children whose parents remain married. Many of these investigations were included in a quantitative meta-analysis of 92 studies of divorce that involved more than 13,000 children (Amato & Keith, 1991a). When all studies of children from married and divorced families were compared on all measures, an average effect size of only .14 standard deviation units was found to distinguish the two groups of children, a difference that is equivalent to an IQ of 100 compared to an IQ of 102. The reviewers found that the largest effect size for any area of psychological difficulty was .23 standard deviation units for children's conduct problems.

The effect sizes attributable to divorce may be even smaller than those suggested by cross-sectional studies, because differences in children's psychological health may be present before divorce. This is exactly what several studies have found. The possibility was first documented in a small but intensive longitudinal study of normal children and their families (Block, Block, & Gjerde, 1986). The finding was confirmed in an investigation of two large, nationally representative samples, one of 14,476 British children and the second of 2,279 American children (Cherlin et al., 1991). Data were available on the behavior problems of children before and after divorce, thus allowing the investigators to compare children's adjustment following divorce with their adjustment prior to divorce. In fact, when various predivorce differences in children's functioning and family life were statistically controlled, the postdivorce differences were reduced to the point that they were no longer statistically reliable, even in these very large samples.

An independent analysis of the national sample of British children confirmed that problems found among children after divorce actually began long before the marital separation (Elliott & Richards, 1991). To the extent that they do, these problems cannot be "consequences of divorce." Together with the small mean differences found in the psychological adjustment of children from divorced and married families, this evidence raises questions about why courts automatically assume supervision of children whose parents divorce through their *parens patriae* powers. The state may have a legitimate role in regulating divorce, but on average, divorce has only a modest negative effect on children's mental health. ■

EXPERT WITNESSES IN CUSTODY DETERMINATIONS

Mental health professionals who conduct custody evaluations typically consider a number of factors in evaluating a child's best interests. These include the quality of the child's relationship with each parent, the family environment provided by each parent, each parent's mental health, the relationship between the parents, and the child's expressed wishes, if any (Emery & Rogers, 1991; Emery, 1994). Mental health professionals face a tremendous obstacle in conducting a custody evaluation, however. The law that governs custody disputes, the *child's best interests standard*, is unclear about what a child's future best interests are, how they can be determined, or how they can be achieved. As law professor Robert Mnookin (1975) has pointed out:

> Deciding what is best for a child poses a question no less ultimate than the purposes and values of life itself. Should the judge be primarily concerned with the child's happiness? Or with the child's spiritual and religious training? Should the judge be concerned with the economic "productivity" of the child when he grows up? Are the primary values of life in warm interpersonal relationships, or in discipline and self-sacrifice? Is stability and security for a child more desirable than intellectual stimulation? These questions could be elaborated endlessly. And yet, where is the judge to look for the set of values that should inform the choice of what is best for the child? (pp. 260–261)

Because the child's best interests standard is so vague, Mnookin has argued further that it increases the likelihood that custody hearings will be acrimonious. Virtually any information that makes one parent look bad and the other look good may be construed as helping a parent's case—and people who have been married have much private and potentially damaging information about each other. The likelihood that the best interests standard increases acrimony is a particular problem, because a wide range of research indicates that conflict between parents is strongly related to maladjustment among children following divorce (Emery, 1982, 1997; Grych & Fincham, 1990). This raises the sad irony that parents and the legal system may be undermining a child's best interests by fighting for them in a custody battle (Emery & Wyer, 1987). For this reason, many mental health professionals feel that they serve children and the legal system better if they help parents to settle custody disputes outside of court rather than providing testimony in court.

CUSTODY MEDIATION

Mental health professionals, as well as many family lawyers, have begun to serve a new role in helping parents who dispute custody by working as divorce and custody mediators. In **divorce mediation,** parents meet with a neutral third party who helps them to identify, negotiate, and ultimately resolve their disputes. The role of mediator is very different from the role that mental health professionals have traditionally fulfilled in evaluating children in custody disputes. Mediation also is a major change in the practice of the law, as mediators adopt a cooperative approach to dispute resolution rather than the usual adversary procedures (Emery & Wyer, 1987; Emery, 1994).

Custody mediation has been embraced rapidly in the United States, and a number of states and many county or local jursidictions require that mediation be attempted before a custody dispute will be heard in court (Hendricks, 1993–94). Evidence consistently indicates that mediation dramatically reduces the number of custody hearings in court, helps parents reach decisions more quickly, and is viewed more favorably than litigation by parents, especially fathers (Emery, 1994; Emery, Matthews, & Wyer, 1991; Emery, Matthews, & Kitzmann, 1994). Perhaps the most significant contribution of custody mediation, however, is that it suggests that mental health professionals need not limit their involvement in the legal system to providing evaluations. Rather, mental health professionals can help to develop alternatives to legal procedures when these procedures create undue distress for the people involved.

Child Abuse

The legal trend in child custody disputes is toward more family autonomy, but the state's role in regulating child abuse clearly has grown dramatically. Like spousal abuse (see Further Thoughts on battered women), historically child abuse was common and condoned, and only recently has it been "discovered" to be a problem. The first child protection efforts in the United States did not begin until 1875. A much publicized case of foster parents who physically beat a young girl in their care led to the founding of the New York Society for the Prevention of Cruelty to Children. The society was given the power to police child abuse, and other states rapidly followed New York's example by establishing similar organizations and legislation (Lazoritz, 1990).

Although state governments assumed some jurisdiction over child abuse in the nineteenth century, consistent public attention was not brought to bear on the problem until 1962, when the physician Henry Kempe wrote about the "battered child syndrome." Kempe documented tragic cases of child abuse in which children suffered repeated injuries, fractured bones, and, in a substantial number of cases, death (Kempe et al., 1962). Kempe's influential article prompted legislation that defined child abuse and required physicians to report

suspected cases. This reporting requirement continues today, and in most states it extends to include mental health professionals, schoolteachers, and other professionals who have regular contact with children. In fact, mental health professionals not only can but they must break the confidentiality of psychotherapy if they suspect child abuse (Melton & Limber, 1989).

Four forms of **child abuse** generally are distinguished by mental health professionals and are treated separately in the law: physical abuse, sexual abuse, neglect, and psychological abuse (American Psychological Association, 1995). *Physical child abuse* involves the intentional use of physically painful and harmful actions. The definition of physical abuse is complicated by the fact that corporal punishments like spanking are widely accepted discipline practices (Emery, 1989; Wolfe, 1987). Only about 10 percent of physically abused children whose caretakers are reported to social service agencies sustain injuries serious enough to require professional care, but the danger to children can be considerable nevertheless. Estimates indicate that 2,000 to 5,000 children die every year because of maltreatment (Zigler & Hall, 1989).

Child sexual abuse involves sexual contact between an adult and a child. Reports of child sexual abuse have increased astronomically in recent years, as this important problem has been fully recognized only since the 1980s (Haugaard & Reppucci, 1988). The sexual abuse of children is now known to be far more prevalent than would have been believed a short time ago. For example, one survey of adult women living in an urban area found that 2.5 percent said that they had been coerced into oral, anal, or genital intercourse with their father,

▼ A memorial for Elisa Izquierdo, a 6-year-old girl who was beaten to death by her mother. The child had been repeatedly abused by her mother and stepfather, but overwhelmed social service agencies found at least two reports of her abuse to be "unfounded."

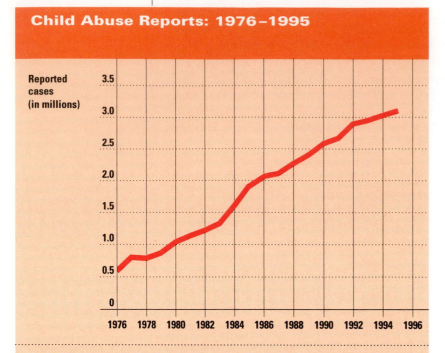

Child Abuse Reports: 1976–1995

Reported cases (in millions)

FIGURE 18-3: Reports of child abuse made to social service agencies have increased sharply. Experts disagree about what has increased— actual abuse or the awareness and reporting of abuse.

Source: Based on data from C.T. Lanf and D. Daro, 1996, *Current Trends in Child Abuse Reporting and Fatalities: The Results of the 1995 Annual State Survey,* Working Paper 808. Washington, DC: National Committee on the Prevention of Child Abuse.

stepfather, or brother before the age of 18 (Russell, 1983).

Child neglect, the most commonly reported form of child abuse, involves placing children at risk for serious physical or psychological harm by failing to provide basic and expected care. Some children are severely neglected, and they experience extreme failure in their growth and development as a result (Wolfe, 1987). Some children also suffer *psychological abuse*— repeated denigration in the absence of physical harm.

The number of reported cases of child abuse has increased dramatically since the 1970s and into the 1990s. As indicated in Figure 18–3, the number of reports of child abuse made to social service agencies climbed from 669,000 in 1976 to 3,111,000 in 1995 (Lang & Daro, 1996). Experts debate the reasons for the increased number of reports. The rate of child abuse could be increasing, but the real increase may be in reports of abuse (Besharov, 1992; Besharov & Laumann, 1996; Finkelhor, 1992). Over half of all reports of abuse are found to be unsubstantiated after an investigation, and some experts have

suggested that the percentage of unsubstantiated reports is growing. One reason for this, according to some critics, is that the concept of neglect is applied too broadly (Besharov, 1986, 1988, 1992).

The increasing number of reports of child abuse and the large percentage of less severe cases that are unsubstantiated may create two problems. First, if social service agencies are overwhelmed with more minor cases, they are less able to deal with children who are living in circumstances of clear danger. Second, intervention in less severe cases may actually do more harm than good. Overwhelmed social service agencies may stigmatize and disrupt families that are troubled but coping—and offer them relatively little treatment in return (Besharov, 1986, 1988, 1992).

When an allegation of abuse is substantiated, one of the major questions is whether to remove the child from the home. Over 100,000 maltreated children are placed in *foster care* each year. Foster care obviously benefits children who are in physical danger, but as many as half of all children placed in foster care are in no immediate danger of physical injury (Besharov, 1988). Stable foster care can offer children psychological benefits, as well as physical protection (Wald, Carlsmith, & Leiderman, 1985). However, half of the children placed in foster care remain there for at least 2 years, almost one-third are separated from their parents for over 6 years, and a substantial proportion live in many different foster homes during this time (Besharov, 1986).

As with child custody decisions, judicial determinations about foster care and other possible dispositions of child abuse cases are guided by the "child's best interest" standard. Psychologists frequently play a role in these legal proceedings by investigating allegations of abuse in interviews with children, making recommendations to the court about appropriate placements for children, and providing treatment to children and families (Becker et al., 1995; Melton & Limber, 1989). The ambiguity in defining abuse, and the uncertainty about the benefits and costs of intervention, suggest perhaps a more important role psychologists can play in abuse cases: conducting more research that can be used to clarify and guide legal decision making in this important area.

Professional Responsibilities and the Law

The regulation of the mental health professions is the final area of psychology and the law that we consider in this chapter. Psychiatrists, clinical psychologists, and social workers all have **professional responsibilities** to meet the ethical standards of their profession and to uphold the laws of the states in which they practice. The duties of mental health professionals are numerous and varied, and we focus on only two important and illustrative professional issues: negligence and confidentiality.

Professional Negligence and Malpractice

Negligence occurs when a professional fails to perform in a manner that is consistent with the level of skill exercised by other professionals in the field. Simply put, negligence is substandard professional service. *Malpractice* refers to situations in which professional negligence results in harm to clients or patients. In the law, malpractice is demonstrated when (1) a professional has a duty to conform to a standard of conduct, (2) the professional is negligent in that duty, (3) the professional's client experiences damages or loss, and (4) it is reasonably certain that the negligence caused the damages (Reisner & Slobogin, 1990). When professionals are found to be guilty of malpractice, they are subject to disciplinary action both from their professional organizations and through state licensing boards, as well as to civil suits and possibly to criminal actions.

Whereas medical malpractice claims are common, malpractice claims against mental health professionals are relatively infrequent. For example, one survey found that claims against psychiatrists accounted for only 0.3 percent of all malpractice suits filed in the state of California between 1974 and 1978 (Slawson & Guggenheim, 1984). The inappropriate use of electroconvulsive therapy (ECT) and medication are two of the more common reasons for malpractice claims against mental health professionals. These treatments are clearly defined, research on their appropriate use is more clearcut than is psychotherapy research, and the treatments can result in physical as well as psychological damages. In other words,

malpractice is easier to demonstrate for these treatments.

The existence of a sexual relationship between therapists and their clients is another common ground for successful malpractice suits. Although specific damages can be difficult to prove, it has become commonly accepted that sexual relationships between therapists and their clients are harmful in and of themselves. This is evident in the ethical codes of the American Psychological Association and the American Psychiatric Association, both of which prohibit sexual relationships between therapists and their clients. Other claims of professional negligence stem from the failure to prevent suicide, failure to prevent violence against others, and violations of confidentiality (Leesfield, 1987). Each of these areas of professional negligence is significant, and together they dominate the malpractice claims that have been filed against mental health professionals. As the field continues to evolve, a new area of professional negligence may become important: the failure to offer adequate treatment and to inform clients about treatment alternatives.

INFORMED CONSENT ON THE EFFICACY OF ALTERNATIVE TREATMENTS

Patients may be given a wide range of alternative treatments for the same mental disorder. From the patient's perspective, the choice of treatment hinges, in part, on chance factors such as the profession of the therapist or his or her "theoretical orientation." Only psychiatrists can prescribe medication, and they surely are more likely to recommend this treatment than are psychologists and social workers. Similarly, behavior therapists are likely to offer behavior therapy, and psychoanalysts to offer psychoanalysis.

As we have argued throughout this text, however, the goal of research is to identify specific treatments for specific disorders. This scientific approach has been successful in identifying some approaches that are more effective than others in treating particular disorders. If evidence points to the superiority of one treatment over another, several questions arise. Does the mental health professional have an obligation to offer the more effective treatment, make a referral to another professional who can provide it, or at a minimum, obtain informed consent to pursue an alternative course of therapy?

Osheroff v. Chestnut Lodge This issue was raised in *Osheroff v. Chestnut Lodge* [62 Md. App. 519, 490 A. 2d. 720 (Md. App. 1985)]. In 1979, Dr. Rafael Osheroff, an internist, admitted himself to Chestnut Lodge, a private psychiatric hospital in Maryland that had long been famous as a center for psychoanalytic psychotherapy. Dr. Osheroff had a history of depression and anxiety, problems that previously had been treated on an outpatient basis with some success using tricyclic antidepressant medication. Apparently, Dr. Osheroff had not been taking his medication prior to his admission to Chestnut Lodge, and his condition had worsened. He was diagnosed by hospital staff as suffering primarily from a narcissistic personality disorder and secondarily from manic–depressive illness (Klerman, 1990; Malcolm, 1987).

Hospital staff did not offer medication to Dr. Osheroff during his hospitalization because they hoped that he could achieve what they viewed as "more basic" changes in his personality through psychotherapy. As an alternative to medication, Dr. Osheroff was seen in individual psychoanalytic psychotherapy 4 times a week, and he participated in group therapy as well. During Dr. Osheroff's 7 months of hospitalization, his condition did not improve and actually may have deteriorated somewhat. After this time, his family discharged him from Chestnut Lodge and admitted him to another private psychiatric hospital, Silver Hill in Connecticut. At Silver Hill, Dr. Osheroff was diagnosed as suffering from a psychotic depressive reaction, and he was treated with phenothiazines and tricyclic antidepressants. He began to improve within 3 weeks after treatment began, and he was discharged from the hospital within 3 months. Although he continued to experience some problems, following his discharge Dr. Osheroff was able to resume his medical practice with the help of outpatient psychotherapy and antidepressants (Klerman, 1990; Malcolm, 1987).

In 1982, Dr. Osheroff sued Chestnut Lodge for negligence. His claim stated that Chestnut Lodge had misdiagnosed his condition, failed to offer appropriate treatment, and failed to offer him informed consent about treatment alternatives (Malcolm, 1987). He argued that research available in 1979 provided clear support for the use of medication in the treatment of severe depression but offered no support for the use of psychoanalytic psychotherapy in the treatment of either depression or narcissistic personality disorder. As required by state law in Maryland, the matter was first heard by an arbitration panel. The panel initially awarded Dr. Osheroff $250,000 in damages, but it later reduced the amount of the award. Both sides appealed the decision of the arbitration board, but the matter was eventually settled out of court (Klerman, 1990).

The private settlement of this case limits its precedent-setting value. Nevertheless, it suggests that mental health professionals will be held to increasingly higher standards in offering alternative treatments, or at least in informing patients about the risks and benefits of various treatments. As researchers demonstrate that certain approaches are more or less effective in treating particular disorders, offering informed consent about treatment alternatives is likely to become a routine practice for mental health professionals. Informed consent means providing accurate information about risks and benefits in an understandable and noncoercive manner.

WHO IS THE CLIENT?

An issue closely related to the choice of a therapeutic approach is the choice of who is to receive treatment. Many psychological problems are closely linked with family difficulties, as we have discussed in previous chapters. Researchers continue to debate whether particular disorders cause family distress or whether family distress causes particular disorders, but some degree of reciprocal causality surely operates even for severe disorders like schizophrenia (Gotlib & McCabe, 1990). This raises the question of who should be targeted to receive psychological treatment as well as what sort of treatment they should receive.

The issue is not a minor one. Not only are certain treatments more effective than others for certain disorders, but the choice of a treatment can convey subtle but important messages about the cause of psychological problems and the responsibility for changing them. For example, individual therapy with a troubled child or a depressed wife can communicate both to the clients and their families that the problem rests within the individual, even though the difficulties might be a reaction to poor parenting or to an abusive marriage. Similarly, family therapy can falsely convey the impression that schizophrenia is caused by inadequate child rearing. Some of these impressions can be corrected by direct feedback from a therapist, but some are unavoidable consequences of the focus of treatment.

Another problem arises when therapists are unclear about who their client is. To whom do therapists owe confidentiality? Should information that therapists obtain from children be held in confidence, or are parents entitled to know what their children are saying in therapy? If a couple divorces after marital therapy, can a therapist testify at the request of one spouse and over the objection of the other? If a therapist sees a client in court-ordered treatment, must (or can) information on therapy be shared with the court? There are no easy solutions to such dilemmas. Clearly, the best approach is for therapists to decide who their client is before the question of disclosure arises and to share their position on confidentiality with all involved parties. Confidentiality, however, is not an all-or-none proposition.

Confidentiality

Confidentiality—the ethical obligation not to reveal private communications—is basic to psychotherapy. The therapist's guarantee of privacy is essential to facilitating the disclosure of important, clinically relevant information, and the maintenance of confidentiality with past clients is essential to gaining the trust of future clients. For these reasons, confidentiality standards are a part of the professional ethics of all of the major mental health professions, and they are frequently addressed in state licensing regulations as well.

Despite the overriding importance of confidentiality, mental health professionals sometimes may be compelled by law to reveal confidential information. For example, all states require mental health professionals to break confidentiality and report suspected cases of child abuse. *Privileged communications* are confidential exchanges that legislation explicitly protects from being revealed. Various state statutes extend some privileged communication to psychologists and psychiatrists, as they do to physicians, lawyers, and the clergy (Morse, 1990), but child abuse must be reported in all states. This requirement can create dilemmas for therapists (Smith & Meyer, 1985). In order to provide fully informed consent, must a therapist make the limits on confidentiality clear before beginning therapy? If therapists tell their clients

that their disclosures of child abuse will be reported to social service agencies, does this encourage clients to be something less than honest? Does reporting child abuse undermine the therapeutic relationship that might benefit an abused child?

Confidentiality also must be broken when clients are dangerous to themselves or others, so that civil commitment can proceed. The influential case of *Tarasoff v. Regents of the University of California* [551 P.2d 334 (1976)] identified another obligation that therapists may assume when a client expresses violent intentions: the duty to warn the potential victim.

TARASOFF AND THE DUTY TO PROTECT POTENTIAL VICTIMS

On October 27, 1969, a young woman named Tatiana Tarasoff was killed by Prosenjit Poddar, a foreign student at the University of California at Berkeley. Poddar had pursued a romantic relationship with Tarasoff, but after having been repeatedly rejected by her, he sought treatment at the Berkeley student health facility. Poddar was diagnosed as suffering from paranoid schizophrenia, and the clinical psychologist who treated Poddar concluded that he was dangerous to himself and others. After consulting with two psychiatrists, the psychologist decided to pursue civil commitment. He notified the campus police of his concerns, and asked them to detain Poddar for the purpose of an emergency commitment. The police concluded that Poddar was not dangerous, however, and released him after he agreed to stay away from Tarasoff. Poddar subsequently discontinued therapy, and no one notified Tarasoff that Poddar posed a threat to her life. Poddar had never mentioned Tatiana Tarasoff by name, but the information he related to the psychologist was sufficient to deduce her identity. Two months after the police had questioned him, Poddar murdered Tarasoff after being rejected by her once more.

Tarasoff's parents sued the university, the therapists, and the police for negligence. The California Supreme Court ruled that the defendants were liable for failing to warn the woman of the impending danger. Specifically, the court ruled that therapists are liable if (1) they should have known about the dangerousness based on

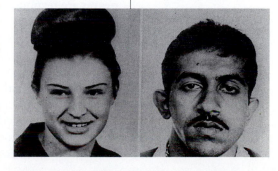

▼ Tatiana Tarasoff and Prosenjit Poddar, the man who killed her. The California Supreme Court ruled that Poddar's therapist should have warned Tarasoff that her life might be in danger.

accepted professional standards of conduct, and (2) they failed to exercise reasonable care in warning the potential victim. Subsequent California cases have limited the duty to protect to cases that involve a specific, identifiable target of potential violence. A general statement of intended violence invokes no duty to protect (Goodman, 1985).

The *Tarasoff* case prompted subsequent litigation, and almost 20 states have enacted laws that outline therapists' duty to protect potential victims of violence (Appelbaum, 1994; Geske, 1989). Guidelines for evaluating and documenting assessments of dangerousness to others are rapidly becoming as important as policies for assessing suicide risk (Monahan, 1993). Still, the issues raised by *Tarasoff* are far from resolved. For example, we can easily foresee future cases in which questions will be raised about therapists' duty to protect the unwitting sexual partners of their clients who have AIDS.

Summary

The U.S. legal system assumes that behavior is the product of free will, the capacity to make choices and freely act on them. The law therefore holds people responsible for their own actions. Scientific psychology rejects the notion of **free will** and instead emphasizes **determinism,** the idea that behavior is caused by biological, psychological, and social forces. Assumptions about free will and determinism conflict strongly in the **insanity defense.** The legally insane individual is not assumed to be acting out of free will and therefore is not held responsible for his or her actions.

The M'Naghten test is one rule for finding a person not guilty by reason of **insanity.** According to this rule, legal insanity is established if a mental disease or defect prevents a criminal from knowing the wrongfulness of his or her actions. A second major rule, the irresistible impulse test, indicates that defendants are insane if they were unable to control their actions because of mental disease or defect. Controversies about the insanity defense have caused some states to drop the irresistible impulse test, as well as to shift the burden of proof from the prosecution to the defense. Professionals who serve as **expert witnesses** are responsible only for offering opinions about psychological well-being. The court, not the expert witness, is responsible for determining the ultimate issue of insanity.

Competence is the defendant's ability to understand legal proceedings and to participate in his or her own defense. Many more people accused of crimes are institutionalized because of findings of incompetence than because of insanity. Incompetence has received far less attention, perhaps because, unlike the insanity defense, competence determinations raise few broad philosophical issues about responsibility.

The issue of **civil commitment**—hospitalizing people against their will—reflects philosophical tensions within the law. Libertarian views, which emphasize protecting the rights of the individual, often conflict with paternalist approaches, which emphasize the state's duty to protect its citizens. Three grounds dominate commitment laws: (1) inability to care for self, (2) dangerous to self, and (3) dangerous to others. Controversies abound, but a relation between mental illness and "dangerousness" does exist, and mental health professionals can predict dangerousness with some accuracy. The fact that violence has a low **base rate** in the population is a major contributor to inaccurate prediction.

Paternalists and libertarians disagree concerning the commitment of minors who can be hospitalized by their parents. Admissions of adolescents to mental hospitals have increased

KEY TERMS

- base rates
- battered woman syndrome
- child abuse
- child custody
- civil commitment
- competence
- confidentiality
- criminal responsibility
- deinstitutionalization
- determinism
- divorce mediation
- expert witness
- free will
- informed consent
- insanity
- insanity defense
- moral treatment
- professional responsibilities

dramatically, and some critics have suggested that many minors are committed to mental hospitals merely because they are troublesome to their parents and because hospitalization is profitable to private psychiatric hospitals.

The rights of mental patients have received increased attention since the 1970s. The right to treatment indicates that hospitalized patients must receive therapy and not just custodial care. The right to treatment in the least restrictive environment indicates that therapy should be provided in community settings when it is possible and appropriate. The right to refuse treatment indicates that patients cannot be forced to receive certain treatments (for example, taking medications) without **informed consent** or a careful substituted judgment. Concerns about patients' rights also have given impetus to the **deinstitutionalization** movement, the philosophy that many of the mentally ill and mentally retarded can be better cared for in their community than in large mental hospitals. Unfortunately, the lack of follow-up care in the community has undermined this laudable goal.

Family law and mental health law have different roots, and cases involving one are typically tried in different courts than are cases involving the other. A general dilemma in family law is how to balance the potentially competing interests of children, parents, and the state.

Child custody must be decided when parents divorce. These decisions involve determinations about both physical custody—where the children will live—and legal custody—how the parents will make decisions about their children. Custody decisions are based on the child's best interests standard, a vague directive that requires judgments as to what the child's best interests are and what the future will bring. Parents often make determinations about their own children's best interests privately in **divorce mediation** or elsewhere.

Child abuse may involve physical abuse, sexual abuse, neglect, or psychological abuse. Reports of child abuse have increased greatly in recent years, but neither the law nor mental health professionals have reached consensus on how best to fulfill children's best interests in these cases.

Psychiatrists, clinical psychologists, and social workers all have **professional responsibilities** to meet the ethical standards of their profession and to uphold the laws of the states in which they practice. Key professional issues include obtaining informed consent about alternative treatment procedures, clearly identifying whom the professional is serving, and maintaining **confidentiality.** A relatively new concern is the duty to warn potential victims when a client reveals violent intentions.

Critical Thinking

1. What is your view on the insanity defense? Should we hold mentally ill criminals fully responsible for all of their actions? What about battered women who kill their husbands?

2. What is your position on deinstitutionalization? Has the pendulum swung too far in the direction of releasing mental patients into communities with inadequate services? How would you feel if a group home for the mentally ill was being planned for your neighborhood?

3. What are your own views on the consequences of divorce for children and how the legal system can better serve divorcing families? Do you think laws should make it harder for spouses with children to get divorced?

4. Do you think it is unethical for mental health professionals to offer treatments they prefer even when research indicates that other approaches are more effective?

Glossary

Abnormal psychology The application of psychological science to the study of mental disorders. Includes investigation of the causes and treatment of psychopathological conditions.

Abstinence violation effect The guilt and perceived loss of control that the person feels whenever he or she slips and finds himself or herself returning to drug use after an extended period of abstinence.

Acquired immune deficiency syndrome (AIDS) A disease caused by the human immunodeficiency virus (HIV) that attacks the immune system and leaves the patient susceptible to unusual infections.

Active phase In schizophrenia, the period of time during which the person exhibits obvious psychotic symptoms, such as hallucinations and delusions.

Actuarial interpretation Analysis of test results based on an explicit set of rules derived from empirical research.

Acute stress disorder (ASD) A new category of mental disorder in DSM-IV that is defined as a reaction occurring within 4 weeks following a traumatic experience and is characterized by dissociative symptoms, reexperiencing, avoidance, and marked anxiety or arousal. Contrasts with posttraumatic stress disorder, which either lasts longer or has a delayed onset.

Addiction A term used to describe substance use problems such as alcoholism. Replaced in official terminology by the term *substance dependence*, with which it is synonymous.

Adjustment disorder A DSM-IV classification designating the development of clinically significant symptoms in response to stress in which the symptoms are not severe enough to warrant classification as another mental disorder.

Affect The pattern of observable behaviors that are associated with subjective feelings. People express affect through changes in their facial expressions, the pitch of their voices, and their hand and body movements.

Ageism A number of misconceptions and prejudices about aging and older adults.

Agnosia ("perception without meaning") The inability to identify objects. The person's sensory functions are unimpaired, but he or she is unable to recognize the source of stimulation.

Agoraphobia An exaggerated fear of being in situations from which escape might be difficult. Literally means "fear of the marketplace," and is sometimes described as fear of public spaces.

Agreeableness A dimension of personality that describes the person's willingness to cooperate and empathize with other people.

Allegiance effect A characterization of psychotherapy outcome research such that investigators commonly find the most effective treatment is the one to which they hold a theoretical allegiance.

Alogia A form of speech disturbance found in schizophrenia. Can include reductions in the amount of speech (poverty of speech) or speech that does not convey meaningful information (poverty of content of speech).

Alzheimer's disease A form of dementia in which cognitive impairment appears gradually and deterioration is progressive. A definite diagnosis of Alzheimer's disease requires the observation of two specific types of brain lesions: neurofibrillary tangles and senile plaques.

Amenorrhea The absence of at least three consecutive menstrual cycles; a defining symptom of anorexia nervosa in females.

Amnestic disorder A form of cognitive disorder characterized by memory impairments that are more limited or circumscribed than those seen in dementia or delirium.

Amniocentesis The extraction of fluid from the amniotic sac in order to test for chromosomal and genetic defects in the developing fetus.

Analogue study A research procedure in which the investigator studies behaviors that resemble mental disorders or isolated features of mental disorders. Usually employed in situations in which the investigator hopes to gain greater experimental control over the independent variable.

Androgyny The possession of both "female" and "male" gender-role characteristics.

Anhedonia The inability to experience pleasure. In contrast to blunted affect, which refers to the lack of outward expression, anhedonia is a lack of positive subjective feelings.

Anorexia nervosa A type of eating disorder characterized by the refusal to maintain a minimally normal body weight along with other symptoms related to eating and body image.

Anterograde amnesia The inability to learn or remember new material after a particular point in time.

Antisocial personality disorder A pervasive and persistent disregard for, and frequent violation of, the rights of other people. Also known as *psychopathy*. In DSM-IV, it is defined in terms of a persistent pattern of irresponsible and antisocial behavior that begins during childhood or adolescence and continues into the adult years.

Anxiety A diffuse emotional reaction that is out of proportion to threats from the environment. Rather than being directed toward the person's present circumstances, anxiety is typically associated with the anticipation of future problems.

Anxious attachment An insecure relationship in which an infant or child shows ambivalence about seeking reassurance or security from an attachment figure.

Aphasia The loss or impairment of previously acquired abilities in language comprehension or production that cannot be explained by sensory or motor defects or by diffuse brain dysfunction.

Apraxia The loss of a previously acquired ability to perform purposeful movements in response to verbal commands. The problem cannot be explained by muscle weakness or simple incoordination.

Asperger's disorder A subtype of pervasive developmental disorder (new in DSM-IV) that is identical to autism (oddities in social interaction, stereotyped behavior), with the exception that there is no clinically significant delay in language.

Assessment The process of gathering and organizing information about a person's behavior.

Attachments Selective bonds that develop between infants and their caregivers, usually their parents, and are theorized to be related to later development. Analogous to the process imprinting which has been observed in many animals.

Attention deficit Inattention characterized by distractibility, frequent shifts from one uncompleted activity to another, careless mistakes, and/or poor organization or effort. A key symptom of attention-deficit/hyperactivity disorder.

Attention-deficit/hyperactivity disorder A psychological disorder of childhood characterized by hyperactivity, inattention, and impulsivity. Typically has an onset by the early school years.

Attribution Perceived causes; people's beliefs about cause–effect relations.

Atypical antipsychotic A type of medication that is beneficial for psychotic patients but does not produce extrapyramidal motor side effects and may not be associated with increased risk of tardive dyskinesia.

Authoritative parenting A style of parenting that is both loving and firm and is often used by parents of well-adjusted children.

Autistic disorder A severe form of pervasive developmental disorder characterized by oddities in social interaction (autistic aloneness), communication impairments, and stereotyped behavior, interests, and activities.

Autism Literally, "absorption in one's own mental activity." Formally, a severe pervasive developmental disorder characterized by profound problems in social interaction, communication, and stereotyped behavior, interests, and activities (see also autistic disorder).

Autonomic nervous system The division of the peripheral nervous system that regulates the functions of various bodily organs such as the heart and stomach. The actions of the autonomic nervous system are largely involuntary, and it has two branches, the sympathetic and parasympathetic nervous systems.

Aversion therapy A classical conditioning technique for attempting to eliminate unwanted behavior by pairing an unpleasant (aversive) stimulus with the behavior—for example, inducing nausea when alcohol is consumed.

Avoidant personality disorder An enduring pattern of thinking and behavior that is characterized by pervasive social discomfort, fear of negative evaluation, and timidity. People with this disorder tend to be socially isolated outside of family circles. They want to be liked by others, but they are easily hurt by even minimal signs of disapproval from other people.

Avolition (lack of volition or will) A negative symptom of schizophrenia involving a loss of willpower, indecisiveness, and ambivalence. The person becomes apathetic and ceases to engage in purposeful actions.

Axon The trunk of the neuron where messages are transmitted outward toward other cells with which a given neuron communicates.

Balanced placebo design A research design that combines the placebo and antiplacebo methods. It can be used to assess the effect of alcohol, the effect of expectations, and the interaction of alcohol by expectation.

Barbiturates Drugs that depress activities of the central nervous system; mostly for sedation.

Base rates Population frequencies. Relative base rates set statistical limits on the degree to which two variables can be associated with each other.

Battered woman syndrome A controversial classification of the common psychological effects of spousal abuse. Includes a tension-building phase leading up to violence, the battering incident itself, and a stage of loving contrition, during which the batterer apologizes. According to some experts, this induces learned helplessness in battered women.

Behavioral approach A paradigm that focuses on observable behavior as the subject of psychology. Also emphasizes learning through classical conditioning, operant conditioning, modeling, and perhaps cognitive processes.

Behavioral coding system (also known as a formal observation schedule) An observational assessment procedure that focuses on the frequency of specific behavioral events.

Behavioral family therapy A form of family treatment that may include several variations, but always trains parents to use operant conditioning as a way of improving child discipline.

Behavioral gerontology A subspecialty within behavioral medicine developed specifically for studying and treating the behavioral components of illness among older adults.

Behavioral marital therapy A variation on couples therapy that emphasizes the partners' moment-to-moment interaction, particularly their exchange of positive and negative behaviors, their style of communication, and their strategies for solving problems.

Behavioral medicine A multidisciplinary field concerned with studying and treating the behavioral components of physical illness.

Behavior genetics The study of broad genetic contributions to the development of normal and abnormal behavior.

Behaviorism The belief within scientific psychology that observable behaviors, not unobservable cognitive or emotional states, are the appropriate focus of psychological study.

Behavior therapy An approach to psychotherapy that focuses on behavior change in the present; includes a diverse array of techniques, many of which were developed from basic, psychological research.

Benzodiazepines Group of drugs that have potent hypnotic, sedative, and anxiolytic action (also called antianxiety drugs).

Bereavement Grieving in response to the death of a loved one.

Beta-amyloid Protein material that forms the core of senile plaques, a type of brain lesion found in patients with Alzheimer's disease.

Binge eating Eating an amount of food in a fixed period of time that is clearly larger than most people would eat under similar circumstances. One part of the eating disorder of bulimia nervosa.

Binge eating disorder A controversial diagnosis defined by repeated episodes of binge eating but in the absence of compensatory behavior; included in an appendix of DSM-IV.

Biofeedback Behavioral medicine treatment that uses laboratory equipment to monitor physiological processes (that generally occur outside of conscious awareness) and provide feedback about them. Hypothesized to help patients to gain conscious control over problematic physiological processes such as hypertension.

Biological reductionism The assumption that biological explanations are more useful than psychological explanations because they deal with smaller units—with brain chemistry, for example, instead of emotional experience.

Biomedical approach A paradigm for conceptualizing abnormal behavior that focuses on biological causation and the analogy between physical and psychological illnesses. Sometimes referred to as the "medical model."

Biopsychosocial model A view of the etiology of mental disorders which assumes that disorder can best be understood in terms of the interaction of biological, psychological, and social systems.

Bipolar mood disorder A form of mood disorder in which the person experiences episodes of mania as well as episodes of depression.

Blunted affect A flattening or restriction of the person's nonverbal display of emotional responses. Blunted patients fail to exhibit signs of emotion or feeling.

Body dysmorphic disorder A type of somatoform disorder characterized by constant preoccupation with some imagined defect in physical appearance.

Body image A cognitive and affective evaluation of one's weight and shape, often a critical one.

Borderline personality disorder An enduring pattern of thinking and behavior whose essential feature is a pervasive instability in mood, self-image, and interpersonal relationships. Manifestations of this disorder include frantic efforts to avoid real or imagined abandonment. People who fit this description frequently hold opinions of significant others that vacillate between unrealistically positive and negative extremes.

Boundaries Rules defining a relationship, particularly the rules that separate a third person from an individual or another relationship. For example, the boundary of the marital relationship is defined, in part, by the limited discussion of intimate topics outside the relationship.

Brief psychotic disorder A diagnostic category in DSM-IV that includes people who exhibit psychotic symptoms for at least 1 day but no more than 1 month. After the symptoms are resolved, the person returns to the same level of functioning that had been achieved prior to the psychotic episode.

Bulimia nervosa A type of eating disorder characterized by repeated episodes of binge eating followed by inappropriate compensatory behaviors (such as self-induced vomiting) together with other symptoms related to eating and body image.

Cardiovascular disease (CVD) A group of disorders that affect the heart and circulatory system. Hypertension (high blood pressure) and coronary heart disease are the most important forms of CVD.

Cardiovascular reactivity A measure of the intensity of an individual's cardiovascular reactions to stress in the laboratory; a predictor of future cardiovascular disease.

Case study A careful description and analysis of the problems experienced by one person.

Catatonia Motor symptoms that can include either immobility and marked muscular rigidity or excitement and overactivity.

Catatonic type A subtype of schizophrenia that is characterized by symptoms of motor immobility (including rigidity and posturing) or excessive and purposeless motor activity.

Categorical approach to classification A view of classification based on the assumption that there are qualitative differences between normal and abnormal behavior as well as between one form of abnormal behavior and other forms of abnormal behavior.

Catharsis The release of pent-up feelings; presumed by Freud and others to be a means of reducing the psychic strain caused by unexpressed emotions.

Central nervous system The major communication system in the body, which comprises the brain and the spinal cord.

Cerebellum Part of the hindbrain that serves as a control center in helping to coordinate physical movements. The cerebellum receives information on body movements and integrates this feedback with directives about desired actions from higher brain structures.

Cerebral cortex The uneven surface of the brain that lies just underneath the skull, and controls and integrates sophisticated memory, sensory, and motor functions.

Cerebral hemispheres The two major structures of the forebrain and the site of most sensory, emotional, and cognitive processes. The functions of the cerebral hemispheres are lateralized. In general, the left cerebral hemisphere is involved in language and related functions, and the right side is involved in spatial organization and analysis.

Child abuse A legal decision that a parent or other responsible adult has inflicted damage or offered inadequate care to a child; may include physical abuse, sexual abuse, neglect, and psychological abuse.

Child custody A legal decision, especially common in separation and divorce, that involves determining where children will reside and how parents will share legal rights and responsibilities for child rearing.

Chorea Unusual, involuntary muscle movements associated with disorders such as Huntington's disease.

Chromosomes Chainlike structures found in the nucleus of cells that carry genes and information about heredity. Humans normally have 23 pairs of chromosomes.

Civil commitment The involuntary hospitalization of the mentally ill; the decision typically is justified based on dangerousness to self or others (or inability to care for self).

Classical conditioning Pavlov's form of learning through association. A conditioned response eventually is elicited by a conditioned stimulus after repeated pairings with an unconditioned stimulus (which produces an unconditioned response).

Classification system A system for grouping together objects or organisms that share certain properties in common. In psychopathology, the set of categories in DSM-IV that describes mental disorders.

Client-centered therapy Carl Rogers's humanistic therapy that follows the client's lead. Therapists offer warmth, empathy, and genuineness, but clients solve their own problems.

Clinical psychology The profession and academic discipline that is concerned with the application of psychological science to the assessment and treatment of mental disorders.

Coercion A pattern of interaction in which unwitting parents positively reinforce children's misbehavior (by giving in to their demands), and children negatively reinforce parents' capitulation (by ending their obnoxious behavior).

Cognitive behavior therapy The expansion of the scope of behavior therapy to include cognition and research on human information processing. Includes various general techniques, such as Beck's cognitive therapy and Ellis's RET.

Cognitive therapy A psychotherapy technique and important part of cognitive behavior therapy that was developed specifically as a treatment

for depression by Aaron Beck. Beck's cognitive therapy involves challenging negative cognitive distortions through a technique called collaborative empiricism.

Cohort A group that shares some feature in common, particularly their date of birth.

Cohort effect Differences that distinguish one cohort from another. Cohorts share some feature in common, especially their date of birth, and cohort effects often distinguish people born in one time period (e.g., the 1960s) from those born in another.

Community psychology An approach within clinical psychology that attempts to improve individual well-being by promoting social change.

Comorbidity The simultaneous manifestation of more than one disorder.

Competence Defendants' ability to understand legal proceedings and act rationally in relation to them. Competence evaluations can take place at different points in the legal process, but competence to stand trial (the ability to participate in one's own defense) is particularly important.

Compulsion A repetitive, ritualistic behavior that is aimed at the reduction of anxiety and distress or the prevention of some dreaded event. Compulsions are considered by the person to be senseless or irrational. The person feels compelled to perform the compulsion; he or she attempts to resist but cannot.

Concordance Agreement. In behavior genetic studies, concordance occurs when a relative has the same disorder as a proband (index case); for example, when twin pairs either both have the same disorder or both are free from the disorder.

Conditioned response A response that is elicited by a conditioned stimulus; similar to but weaker than the unconditioned response. Central in classical conditioning.

Conditioned stimulus A neutral stimulus that, when repeatedly paired with an unconditioned stimulus, comes to produce a conditioned response. In Pavlov's experiments, the bell was the conditioned stimulus. Central in classical conditioning.

Conduct disorder (CD) A psychological disorder of childhood that is defined primarily by behavior that is illegal as well as antisocial.

Confidentiality The ethical obligation not to reveal private communications in psychotherapy and in other professional contacts between mental health professionals and their clients.

Conscientiousness A dimension of personality that reflects the person's persistence in the pursuit of goals, the ability to organize activities, and dependability in completing expected duties.

Construct (or hypothetical construct) A theoretical device that refer to events or states that reside within a person and are proposed to help understand or explain a person's behavior.

Construct validity The overall strength of the network of relations that have been observed among variables that are used to define a

construct. The extent to which the construct possesses some systematic meaning.

Contingency management A form of operant behavior therapy that focuses on directly changing rewards and punishments in order to increase desired and decrease undesired behavior. A contingency is the relationship between a behavior and its consequences; contingency management involves changing this relationship.

Control group The group of participants in an experiment that receives no treatment or perhaps a placebo treatment. Participants in the control group are compared with participants in the experimental group (who are given an active treatment).

Controlled drinking A controversial goal for some alcohol abusers. This concept refers to moderate consumption of alcohol in a pattern that avoids drinking to the point of intoxication.

Conversion disorder A type of somatoform disorder characterized by physical symptoms that often mimic those found in neurological diseases, such as blindness, numbing, or paralysis. The symptoms often make no anatomic sense.

Coronary heart disease (CHD) A group of diseases of the heart that includes angina pectoris (chest pains) and myocardial infarction (heart attack).

Correlational study A scientific research method in which the relation between two factors (their co-relation) is studied in a systematic fashion. Has the advantage of practicality, as correlations between many variables can be studied in the real world, but also has the disadvantage that "correlation does not mean causation."

Correlation coefficient A number that always ranges between -1.00 and $+1.00$ and indicates the strength and direction of the relation between two variables. A higher absolute value indicates a stronger relation, while a correlation coefficient of 0 indicates no relation. The sign indicates the direction of the correlation.

Countertransference The therapist's own feelings toward the client, particularly as described in psychoanalysis.

Couples therapy Partners who are involved in an intimate relationship are seen together in psychotherapy; sometimes called marital therapy or marriage counseling. Improving communication and negotiation are common goals.

Creutzfeldt-Jakob disease A type of dementia caused by a specific viral infection.

Criminal responsibility A legal concept that holds a person responsible for committing a crime if he or she (a) has been proven to have committed the act and (b) was legally sane at the time.

Cross-cultural psychology The scientific study of ways that human behavior and mental processes are influenced by social and cultural factors.

Cross-sectional study A research design in which subjects are studied only at one point in time. (Contrast with longitudinal study.)

Cultural-familial retardation Typically mild mental retardation that runs in families and is linked with poverty. Thought to be the most common cause of mental retardation. There is controversy about the relative roles of genes or psychosocial disadvantage.

Culture The shared way of life of a group or people; a complex system of accumulated knowledge that helps the people in a particular society adapt to their environment.

Cybernetics A communication and control process that uses feedback loops in order to adjust progress toward a goal, for example, the operation of a thermostat.

Cyclothymia A chronic, less severe form of bipolar disorder. The bipolar equivalent of dysthymia.

Defense mechanisms Unconscious processes that service the ego and reduce conscious anxiety by distorting anxiety-producing memories, emotions, and impulses, for example, projection, displacement, or rationalization.

Deinstitutionalization The movement to treat the mentally ill and mentally retarded in communities rather than in large mental hospitals.

Delirium A confusional state that develops over a short period of time and is often associated with agitation and hyperactivity. The primary symptom is clouding of consciousness or reduced awareness of one's surroundings.

Delusion An obviously false and idiosyncratic belief that is rigidly held in spite of its preposterous nature.

Delusional disorder Describes persons who do not meet the full symptomatic criteria for schizophrenia, but they are preoccupied for at least 1 month with delusions that are not bizarre.

Dementia A gradually worsening loss of memory and related cognitive functions, including the use of language as well as reasoning and decision making.

Dementia praecox Kraepelin's original term for the disorder now known as schizophrenia. It referred to psychotic disorders that ended in severe intellectual deterioration (dementia) and that had an early or premature (praecox) onset, usually during adolescence.

Dendrites "Branches" from the soma of the neuron that serve the primary function of receiving messages from other cells.

Dependent personality disorder An enduring pattern of dependent and submissive behavior. These people are exceedingly dependent on other people for advice and reassurance. Often unable to make everyday decisions on their own, they feel anxious and helpless when they are alone.

Dependent variable The outcome that is hypothesized to vary according to manipulations in the independent variable in an experiment.

Depersonalization disorder A type of dissociative disorder characterized by severe and persistent feelings of being detached from oneself (depersonalization experiences). For example, the repeated and profound sensation of floating above your body and observing yourself act.

Depression Can refer to a *symptom* (subjective feelings of sadness), a *mood* (sustained and pervasive feelings of despair), or to a clinical *syndrome* (in which the presence of a depressed mood is accompanied by several additional symptoms, such as fatigue, loss of energy, sleeping difficulties, and appetite changes).

Determinism The philosophical assumption (made by all psychologists except humanistic psychologists) that behavior is a potentially predictable consequence of biological, psychological, and social factors. Contrasts with the assumption that behavior is the product of free will.

Detoxification The process of short-term medical care (medication, rest, diets, fluids, and so on) during removal of a drug upon which a person has become dependent. The aim is to minimize withdrawal symptoms.

Developmental psychopathology A new approach to abnormal psychology that emphasizes the importance of normal development to understanding abnormal behavior.

Developmental stage A distinct period of development focused on certain central "tasks" and marked by boundaries defined by changing age or social expectations.

Diagnosis The process of determining the nature of a person's disorder. In the case of psychopathology, deciding that a person fits into a particular diagnostic category, such as schizophrenia or major depressive disorder.

Diathesis A predisposition to disorder. Also known as *vulnerability*. A diathesis only causes abnormal behavior when it is combined with a stress or challenging experience.

Diathesis-stress model A general view of the etiology of mental disorder that assumes that a disorder is produced by an interaction between some type of predisposition and a precipitating event.

Dimensional approach to classification A view of classification based on the assumption that behavior is distributed on a continuum from normal to abnormal. Also includes the assumption that differences between one type of behavior and another are quantitative rather than qualitative in nature.

Disorganization A type of symptom, such as disorganized speech and bizarre behavior, found in schizophrenic disorders that does not fit easily into either the positive or negative category of symptoms.

Disorganized speech (also known as *formal thought disorder*) Severe disruptions of verbal communication, involving the form of the person's speech.

Disorganized type A subtype of schizophrenia (formerly known as hebephrenia) that is characterized by disorganized speech, disorganized behavior, and flat or inappropriate affect. If delusions or hallucinations are present, their content is not well organized.

Dissociation The separation of mental processes such as memory or consciousness that normally are integrated. Normal dissociative experiences include fleeting feelings of unreality and *deja vu* experiences—the feeling that an event has happened before. Extreme dissociative experiences characterize dissociative disorders.

Dissociative amnesia A type of dissociative disorder characterized by the sudden inability to recall extensive and important personal information. The onset often is sudden and may occur in response to trauma or extreme stress.

Dissociative disorders A category of psychological disorders characterized by persistent, maladaptive disruptions in the integration of memory, consciousness, or identity. Examples include dissociative fugue and dissociative identity disorder (multiple personality).

Dissociative fugue A rare dissociative disorder characterized by sudden, unplanned travel, the inability to remember details about the past, and confusion about identity or the assumption of a new identity. The onset typically follows a traumatic event.

Dissociative identity disorder An unusual dissociative disorder characterized by the existence of two or more distinct personalities in a single individual (also known as multiple personality disorder). At least two personalities repeatedly take control over the person's behavior, and some personalities have limited or no memory of the other.

Distorted body image A perceptual inaccuracy in evaluating body size and shape that sometimes is found in anorexia nervosa.

Diversion A practice of directing problem youth away from the juvenile justice system and into some alternative treatment or program. For example, a juvenile offender may be referred to counseling instead of having a hearing held in court.

Divorce mediation A procedure in which former partners attempt to resolve child custody or other disputes that arise from a divorce with the help of an impartial third party (a mediator).

Dizygotic (DZ) twins Fraternal twins produced from separate fertilized eggs. Like all siblings, DZ twins share an average of 50 percent of their genes.

Dominance The hierarchical ordering of a social group into more and less powerful members. Dominance rankings are indexed by the availability of uncontested privileges.

Dose-response effects Different treatment responses to different dosages of a medication.

Double blind, placebo-controlled study A study in which neither the therapist nor the patient knows whether the patient receives the real treatment (for example, a medication) or a placebo.

Down syndrome A chromosomal disorder that is the most common known biological cause of mental retardation. It is caused by an extra chromosome (usually on the 21st pair) and associated with a characteristic physical appearance.

Drug of abuse (also called a *psychoactive substance*) A chemical substance that alters a person's mood, level of perception, or brain functioning.

Dualism The philosophical view that the mind and body are separate. Dates to the writings of the philosopher René Descartes, who attempted to balance the dominant religious views of his times with emerging scientific reasoning. Descartes argued that many human functions have biological explanations, but some human experiences have no somatic representation. Thus, he argued for a distinction—a dualism—between mind and body.

Dyskinesia Involuntary movements, such as tics, chorea, or tremors, that are often associated with certain types of dementia.

Dyspareunia Persistent genital pain during or after sexual intercourse. The problem can occur in either men or women.

Dysphoria Unpleasant mood, often associated with depression.

Dysthymia One of the mood disorders; a form of mild depression characterized by a chronic course (the person is seldom without symptoms).

Eating disorders A category of psychological disorders characterized by severe disturbances in eating behavior, specifically anorexia nervosa and bulimia nervosa.

Eclectic An approach of picking different treatments according to the needs of individual disorders and individual clients.

Ego One of Freud's three central personality structures. In Freudian theory, the ego must deal with reality as it attempts to fulfill id impulses as well as superego demands. The ego operates on the reality principle, and much of the ego resides in conscious awareness.

Ego analysis Originated in the work of different therapists trained in Freudian psychoanalysis, but who focus much more on the ego than on the id. Ego analysts are concerned with the patient's dealings with the external world.

Electra complex Freud's hypothesis of "penis envy," girls yearn for something their fathers have and that they are "missing." In Freudian theory, girls resolve the Electra complex by identifying with their mothers.

Electroconvulsive therapy (ECT) A treatment that involves the deliberate induction of a convulsion by passing electricity through one or both hemispheres of the brain. Modern ECT uses restraints, medication, and carefully controlled electrical stimulation to minimize adverse consequences. Can be an effective treatment for severe depression, especially following the failure of other approaches.

Emotion A state of arousal that is defined by subjective feeling states, such as sadness, anger, and disgust. Emotions are often accompanied by physiological changes, such as in heart rate and respiration rate.

Emotion-focused coping Internally oriented coping in an attempt to alter one's emotional or cognitive responses to a stressor.

Empathy Emotional understanding. Empathy involves understanding others' unique feelings and perspectives. Highlighted by Roger's but basic to most forms of psychotherapy.

Encopresis Inappropriately controlled defecation among children old enough to maintain control of their bowels.

Endocrine system A collection of glands found at various locations throughout the body, including the ovaries or testes and the pituitary, thyroid, and adrenal glands. Releases hormones that sometimes act as neuromodulators and affect responses to stress. Also important in physical growth and development.

Endorphin The term is a contraction formed from the words *endogenous* (meaning "within") and *morphine*. Endorphins are relatively short chains of amino acids, or neuropeptides, that are naturally synthesized in the brain and are closely related to morphine (an opioid) in terms of their pharmacological properties.

Enmeshed family Families whose members are overly involved in one another's lives.

Enuresis Inappropriately controlled urination (during sleep or while awake) among children old enough to maintain control of their bladder.

Epidemiology The scientific study of the frequency and distribution of disorders within a population.

Equifinality A concept from systems theory that states that the same outcome (e.g., a psychological disorder) may have different causes. That is, there may be not one cause but multiple pathways that lead to a given outcome (disorder).

Erectile dysfunction Difficulty experienced by a man in obtaining an erection that is sufficient to accomplish intercourse or maintaining an erection long enough to satisfy himself or his partner during intercourse.

Essential hypertension A form of high blood pressure in which the hypertension is the principal disorder, as opposed to hypertension that is secondary to a known illness such as a kidney disorder.

Estrogen The female sex hormone.

Etiology The causes or origins of a disorder.

Euphoria An exaggerated feeling of physical and emotional well-being, typically associated with manic episodes in bipolar mood disorder.

Exclusion criteria Symptoms or conditions that are used to exclude the presence of a particular disorder. For example, in most DSM-IV disorders, the diagnosis is ruled out if the person's symptoms represent the direct physiological effects of a drug of abuse or a general medical condition.

Exhibitionism One of the paraphilias, characterized by distress over, or acting on, urges to expose one's genitals to an unsuspecting stranger.

Experiment A powerful scientific method that allows researchers to determine cause and effect relations. Key elements include random assignment, the manipulation of the independent variable, and careful measurement of the dependent variable.

Experimental group The group of participants in an experiment that receives a treatment that is hypothesized to cause some measured effect. Participants in the experimental group are compared with untreated participants in a control group.

Experimental hypothesis A new prediction made by an investigator to be tested in an experiment.

Expert witness An individual stipulated as an expert on some subject matter who, because of his or her expertise, is allowed to testify about matters of opinion and not just matters of fact. For example, mental health professionals may serve as expert witness concerning a defendant's sanity.

Expressed emotion (EE) A concept that refers to a collection of negative or intrusive attitudes sometimes displayed by relatives of patients who are being treated for a disorder. If at least one of a patient's relatives is hostile, critical, or emotionally overinvolved, the family environment typically is considered high in expressed emotion.

Externalizing disorders An empirically derived category of disruptive child behavior problems that create problems for the external world (for example, attention-deficit/hyperactivity disorder).

External validity Whether the findings of an experiment generalize to other people, places, and circumstances, particularly real-life situations.

Extinction The gradual elimination of a response when learning conditions change. In classical conditioning, extinction occurs when a conditioned stimulus no longer is paired with an unconditioned stimulus. In operant conditioning, extinction occurs when the contingent is removed between behavior and its consequences.

Extraversion A dimension of personality that describes a person's activity level, especially interest in interacting with other people, and the ease with which the person expresses positive emotions.

Factitious disorder A feigned condition that, unlike malingering, is motivated by a desire to assume the sick role, not by a desire for external gain.

Family life cycle The developmental course of family relationships throughout life; most family life-cycle theories mark stages and transitions with major changes in family relationships and membership.

Family therapy Treatment that might include two, three, or more family members in the psychotherapy sessions. Improving communication and negotiation are common goals, although family therapy also may be used to help well members adjust to a family member's illness.

Fear An unpleasant emotional reaction experienced in the face of real, immediate danger. It builds quickly in intensity and helps to organize the person's responses to threats from the environment.

Fetal alcohol syndrome A disorder caused by heavy maternal alcohol consumption and repeated exposure of the developing fetus to alcohol. Infants have retarded physical development, a small head, narrow eyes, cardiac defects, and cognitive impairments. Intellectual functioning ranges from mild mental retardation to normal intelligence with learning disabilities.

Fetishism The use of nonliving objects as a focus of sexual arousal.

Fight or flight response A response to a threat in which psychophysiological reactions mobilize the body to take action against danger.

Fixation The psychodynamic concept that psychological development is arrested at a particular age or stage. The person stops growing emotionally.

Flashbacks Reexperienced memories of past events, particularly as occurs in posttraumatic stress disorder or following use of hallucinogenic drugs.

Flooding A treatment for fears and phobias that involves exposure to the feared stimulus at full intensity. Works through extinction.

Fragile-X syndrome The second most common known biological cause of mental retardation. Transmitted genetically and indicated by a weakening or break on one arm of the X sex chromosome.

Free association A basic technique in Freudian psychoanalysis in which patients are encouraged to speak freely about whatever thoughts cross their mind; presumed to give insight into the unconscious.

Free will The capacity to make choices and freely act upon them. A philosophical counterpoint to determinism, which is the scientific assumption that behavior is a predictable consequence of internal and external events. Humanistic psychology and the American legal system assume people act out of free will.

Frontal lobe A region of the brain located just behind the forehead that is involved in controlling a number of complex cognitive functions including reasoning, planning, emotion, speech, and movement.

Frotteurism One of the paraphilias, characterized by recurrent, intense sexual urges involving touching and rubbing against a nonconsenting person; it often takes place in crowded trains, buses, and elevators.

Gender identity A person's sense of himself or herself as being either male or female.

Gender identity disorder A strong and persistent identification with the opposite sex coupled with a sense of discomfort with one's anatomic sex.

Gender roles Roles associated with social expectations about gendered behavior, for example, "masculine" or "feminine" activities.

General adaptation syndrome (GAS) Selye's three stages in reaction to stress: alarm, resistance, and exhaustion.

General paresis (general paralysis) A set of severe symptoms including dementia, delusions of grandeur, and paralysis caused by the sexually transmitted disease syphilis. Discovery of the cause of general paresis spurred the biological model of mental illness.

Generalization Making accurate statements that extend beyond a specific sample to a larger population.

Generalized anxiety disorder One of the anxiety disorders, which is characterized by excessive and uncontrollable worry about a number of events or activities (such as work or school performance) and associated with symptoms of arousal (such as restlessness, muscle tension, and sleep disturbance).

Genes Ultramicroscopic units of DNA that carry information about heredity. Located on the chromosomes.

Genetic linkage A close association between two genes, typically the genetic locus associated with a disorder or a trait and the locus for a known gene. Two loci are said to be linked when they are sufficiently close together on the same chromosome.

Genotype An individual's actual genetic structure, most of which cannot be observed directly at this time.

Gerontology The multidisciplinary study of aging and older adults.

Gestalt therapy A variation of the humanistic approach to psychotherapy that underscores affective awareness and expression, genuineness, and experiencing the moment (living in the "here and now").

Grief The emotional and social process of coping with a separation or a loss, often described as proceeding in stages.

Group therapy The treatment of three or more people in a group setting, often using group relationships as a central part of therapy.

Hallucination A perceptual experience in the absence of external stimulation, such as hearing voices that aren't really there.

Hallucinogens Drugs that produce hallucinations.

Harmful dysfunction A concept used in one approach to the definition of mental disorder. A condition can be considered a mental disorder if it causes some harm to the person and if the condition results from the inability of some mental mechanism to perform its natural function.

Hashish The dried resin from the top of the female cannabis plant. Ingestion of hashish leads to a feeling of being "high" (see marijuana).

Health behavior A wide range of activities that are essential to promoting good health, including positive actions such as proper diet and the avoidance of negative activities such as cigarette smoking.

Health psychology A subspecialty in psychology concerned with the study and promotion of healthy behavior.

Heritability The variability in a behavioral characteristic that is accounted for by genetic factors.

Heritability ratio A statistic for computing the proportion of variance in a behavioral characteristic that is accounted for by genetic factors in a given study or series of studies.

High-risk research design A longitudinal study of persons who are selected from the general population based on some identified risk factor that has a fairly high risk ratio.

Histrionic personality disorder An enduring pattern of thinking and behavior that is characterized by excessive emotionality and attention-seeking behavior. People with this disorder are self-centered, vain, and demanding. Their emotions tend to be shallow and may vacillate erratically.

Holism The assumption that the whole is more than the sum of its parts. A central tenet of systems theory, and counterpoint to reductionism.

Homeostasis The tendency to maintain a steady state. A familiar concept in biology that also is widely applicable in psychology.

Hopelessness theory A theory regarding the role of cognitive events in the etiology of depression; depression is associated with the expectation that very desirable events probably will not occur and that aversive events probably will occur regardless of what the person does.

Hormones Chemical substances that are released into the bloodstream by glands in the endocrine system. Hormones affect the functioning of distant body systems and sometimes act as neuromodulators.

Humanistic psychology A paradigm for conceptualizing abnormal behavior that rejects determinism and argues that human behavior is the product of free will—how people choose to act. Also adopts an explicitly positive view of human nature.

Humanistic psychotherapy An approach that assumes that the most essential human quality is the ability to make choices and freely act on them (free will). Promoted as a "third force" to counteract the deterministic views of psychodynamic and the behavioral approaches to psychotherapy.

Huntington's disease A primary, differentiated dementia characterized by the presence of unusual involuntary muscle movements. Many Huntington's patients also exhibit a variety of personality changes and symptoms of mental disorders, including primarily depression and anxiety.

Hyperactivity A symptom of attention-deficit/hyperactivity disorder (ADHD), often manifested as squirming, fidgeting, or restless behavior. Found across situations but particularly notable in structured settings.

Hypertension High blood pressure.

Hypnosis An altered state of consciousness during which hypnotized subjects are particularly susceptible to suggestion. There is considerable debate as to whether hypnosis is a unique state of consciousness or merely a form of relaxation.

Hypoactive sexual desire Diminished desire for sexual activity and reduced frequency of sexual fantasies.

Hypochondriasis A type of somatoform disorder characterized by a person's preoccupying fear or belief that he or she is suffering from a physical illness.

Hypomania An episode of increased energy that is not sufficiently severe to qualify as a full-blown manic episode.

Hypothalamus A part of the limbic system that plays a role in sensation, but more importantly it controls basic biological urges, such as eating, drinking, and sexual activity, as well as much of the functioning of the autonomic nervous system.

Hypothesis A prediction about the expected findings in a scientific study.

Hypothetical construct (see construct)

Hysteria An outdated but influential diagnostic category that included both somatoform and dissociative disorders. Attempts to treat hysteria had a major effect on Charcot, Freud, and Janet, among others. In Greek, *hysteria* means "uterus," a reflection of ancient speculation that hysteria was restricted to women and caused by frustrated sexual desires.

Iatrogenesis A creation of a disorder by an attempt to treat it.

Id One of Freud's three central personality structures. In Freudian theory, the id is present at birth and is the source of basic drives and motivations. The id houses biological drives (such as hunger), as well as Freud's two key psychological drives, sex and aggression. Operates according to the pleasure principle.

Identification A process wherein children not only imitate adults but also want to be like them and adopt their values. In Freudian theory, identification is the resolution to the Oedipal and Electra conflicts. In developmental psychology, a similar but broader concept than modeling.

Identity Erikson's term for the broad definition of self; in his view, identity is the product of the adolescent's struggle to answer the question "Who am I?"

Identity crisis Erikson's period of basic uncertainty about self during late adolescence and early adult life. A consequence of the psychosocial stage of identity versus role confusion.

Impulse control disorder A disorder characterized by failure to resist an impulse or a temptation to perform some pleasurable or tension-releasing act that is harmful to oneself or others; examples are pathological gambling, setting fires, and stealing.

Inappropriate affect A form of emotional disturbance seen in schizophrenia. The central features of inappropriate affect are incongruity and lack of adaptability in emotional expression.

Incest Sexual activity between close blood relatives, such as father-daughter, mother-son, or siblings.

Incidence The number of new cases of a disorder that appear in a population during a specific period of time.

Inclusion criteria Symptoms or characteristic features that must be present in order for a person to meet the diagnostic criteria for a particular disorder

Independent variable The variable in an experiment that is controlled and deliberately manipulated by the experimenter (for example, whether or not a subject receives a treatment). Affects the dependent variable.

Infarct The area of dead tissue produced by a stroke.

Informed consent A legal and ethical safeguard concerning risks in research and in treatment. Includes (a) accurate information about potential risks and benefits, (b) competence on the part of subjects/patients to understand them, and (c) the ability of subjects/patients to participate voluntarily.

Inhibited sexual arousal Difficulty experienced by a woman in achieving or maintaining genital responses, such as lubrication and swelling, that are necessary to complete sexual intercourse.

Insanity A legal term referring to a defendant's state of mind at the time of committing a crime. An insane individual is not held legally responsible for his or her actions because of a mental disease or defect.

Insanity defense An attempt to prove that a person with a mental illness did not meet the legal criteria for sanity at the time of committing a crime. The inability to tell right from wrong and an "irresistible impulse" are the two most common contemporary grounds for the defense.

Insight Self-understanding; the extent to which a person recognizes the nature (or understands the potential causes) of his or her disorder. In psychoanalysis, insight is the ultimate goal, specifically, to bring formerly unconscious material into conscious awareness.

Intelligence quotient (IQ) A measure of intellectual ability that typically has a mean of 100 and a standard deviation of 15. An individual's IQ is determined by comparisons with norms for same-aged peers.

Internalizing disorders An empirically derived category of psychological problems of childhood that affect the child more than the external world (for example, depression).

Internal validity Whether changes in the dependent variable can be accurately attributed to changes in the independent variable in an experiment, that is, there are no experimental confounds.

Interpretation A tool in psychotherapy and psychoanalysis in which the therapist suggests new meanings about a client's accounts of his or her past and present life.

Introceptive awareness Recognition of internal cues including various emotional states as well as hunger.

In vivo desensitization A treatment for overcoming fears and phobias that involves gradual exposure to feared stimuli in real life while simultaneously maintaining a state of relaxation. Contrast with systematic desensitization.

Juvenile delinquency A legal term that refers to a minor who has violated the law and been judged responsible for the lawbreaking.

Kappa A statistical index of reliability (diagnostic agreement between clinicians) that reflects the proportion of agreement that occurred above and beyond that which would have occurred by chance.

Korsakoff's syndrome An amnestic disorder sometimes associated with chronic alcoholism. Memory is impaired but other cognitive functions are not.

Labeling theory A perspective on mental disorders that is primarily concerned with the social context in which abnormal behavior occurs. Labeling theory is more interested in social factors that determine whether or not a person will be given a psychiatric diagnosis than in psychological or biological reasons for the behaviors.

La belle indifference A flippant lack of concern about physical symptoms that may accompany somatoform disorders.

Lateralization The specialized functioning of each cerebral hemisphere. In general, the left hemisphere is involved in language and related functions, and the right side is involved in spatial organization and analysis.

Lead poisoning Ingestion of toxic levels of lead (mainly through environmental pollutants) that can cause brain damage and a number of adverse behavioral and cognitive impairments, including mental retardation.

Learned helplessness theory A theory that holds that depressed people do not recognize a contingency between their behavior and outcomes in their environments.

Learning disorders A heterogenous group of educational problems characterized by academic performance that is notably below academic aptitude.

Life-cycle transitions Movements from one social or psychological "stage" of adult development into a new one; often characterized by interpersonal, emotional, and identity conflict.

Life-span development The study of continuities and changes in behavior, affect, and cognition from infancy through the last years of life.

Limbic system A variety of brain structures, including the thalamus and hypothalamus, that are central to the regulation of emotion and basic learning processes.

Linkage A process used to locate the position of a gene on a particular chromosome. Two genetic loci are said to be linked if they are close together on the same chromosome.

Longitudinal study A type of research design in which subjects are studied over a period of time (contrasts with the cross-sectional approach of studying subjects only at one point in time). Longitudinal studies attempt to establish whether hypothesized causes precede their putative effects in time.

Mainstreaming The educational philosophy that mentally retarded children should be taught, as much as possible, in regular classrooms rather than in "special" classes.

Malingering Pretending to have a psychological disorder in order to achieve some external gain such as insurance money or avoidance of work.

Mania A disturbance in mood characterized by such symptoms as elation, inflated self-esteem, hyperactivity, and accelerated speaking and thinking. An exaggerated feeling of physical and emotional well-being.

Marijuana The dried leaves and flowers of the female cannabis plant. "Getting high" on marijuana refers to a pervasive sense of well-being and happiness.

Mean The arithmetic average of a distribution of scores; the sum of scores divided by the number of observations.

Median The midpoint of a frequency distribution; half of all subjects fall above and half fall below the median.

Medulla The part of the hindbrain that controls various body functions involved in sustaining life, including heart rate, blood pressure, and respiration.

Melancholia A particularly severe type of depression. In DSM-IV, melancholia is described in terms of a number of specific features, such as loss of pleasure in activities and lack of reactivity to events in the person's environment that are normally pleasurable.

Menopause The cessation of menstruation and the associated physical and psychological changes that occur among middle-aged women (the so-called "change of life").

Mental retardation Substantial limitations in present functioning characterized by significantly subaverage intellectual functioning (IQ of 70 to 75 or below), concurrent limitations in adaptive skills, and an onset before age 18.

Midbrain Part of the brain between the hindbrain and forebrain that is involved in the control of some motor activities, especially those related to fighting and sex.

Minimal brain damage (MBD) Damage to the brain too slight to be detected with objective instruments but sometimes inferred from behavior. Was once held to be the cause of attention-deficit/hyperactivity disorder, but now widely rejected.

Mode The most frequent score in a frequency distribution.

Modeling A social learning concept describing the process of learning through imitation. Contrasts with the broader concept of identification.

Monoamine oxidase inhibitors A group of antidepressant drugs that inhibit the enzyme monoamine oxidase (MAO) in the brain and raise the levels of certain neurotransmitters, such as norepinephrine, dopamine, and serotonin.

Monothetic class A category that is defined in terms of features that are necessary and sufficient to identify members of the class.

Monozygotic (MZ) twins Identical twins produced from a single fertilized egg; thus MZ twins have identical genotypes.

Mood A pervasive and sustained emotional response that, in its extreme, can color the person's perception of the world.

Mood disorders A broad category of psychopathology that includes depressive disorders and bipolar disorders. These conditions are defined in terms of episodes in which the person's behavior is dominated by either clinical depression or mania.

Moral treatment A historically important movement in the treatment of the mentally ill that led to improved hospital conditions. This movement was based on the belief that the mentally ill deserve adequate care and that good care would promote their recovery.

Moratorium A period of allowing oneself to be uncertain or confused about identity. Erikson advocated a moratorium as an important step in the formation of an enduring identity.

Multiaxial classification system A classification system in which the person is rated with regard to several separate aspects of behavior or adjustment.

Multifactorial causes The etiology of a disorder results from a combination of biological, psychological, and social factors rather than from a single cause.

Multiple personality disorder An unusual dissociative disorder characterized by the existence of two or more distinct personalities in a single individual (called dissociative identity disorder in DSM-IV).

Myocardial infarction (MI) Commonly known as a heart attack, this most deadly form of coronary heart disease is caused by oxygen deprivation to the heart and results in the death of at least some heart tissue.

Narcissistic personality disorder An enduring pattern of thinking and behavior that is characterized by pervasive grandiosity. Narcissistic people are preoccupied with their own achievements and abilities.

Nature–nurture controversy The debate that pits genetic and biological factors against life experience as causes of abnormal behavior.

Negative affect One of two mood dimensions (compare positive affect) employed by Tellegen as well as Watson and Clark in their theories of personality. Adjectives that describe negative affect include angry, guilty, afraid, and sad.

Negative reinforcement Occurs when the cessation of a stimulus increases the frequency of behavior (for example, a friend's nagging ends when you give in).

Negative symptoms (of schizophrenia) Include flat or blunted affect, avolition, alogia, and anhedonia.

Neurofibrillary tangles A type of brain lesion found in the cerebral cortex and the hippocampus in patients with Alzheimer's disease. A pattern of disorganized neurofibrils, which provide structural support for the neurons and help transport chemicals that are used in the production of neurotransmitters.

Neuroleptic A type of antipsychotic medication that also induces side effects that resemble the motor symptoms of Parkinson's disease.

Neurologist A physician who deals primarily with diseases of the brain and nervous system.

Neuromodulators Chemicals such as endorphins that may be released from neurons or from endocrine glands. Neuromodulators can influence communication among many neurons, and they often affect regions of the brain that are quite distant from where they were released.

Neuron The nerve cells that form the basic building blocks of the brain. Each neuron is composed of the soma or cell body, the dendrites, the axon, and the terminal buttons.

Neuropsychological assessment Assessment procedures focused on the examination of performance on psychological tests to indicate whether a person has a brain disorder. An example is the Halstead-Reitan Neuropsychological Test Battery.

Neuropsychologist A psychologist who has particular expertise in the assessment of specific types of cognitive impairment, including those associated with dementia and amnestic disorders.

Neurosis A traditional term, often associated with psychoanalytic theory, that describes maladaptive behavior resulting from the ego's failure to control anxiety resulting from unconscious conflicts. In DSM-I and DSM-II, neurotic disorders were defined as those in which anxiety is the chief characteristic. Anxiety presumably could be felt and expressed directly, or it could be controlled unconsciously by defense mechanisms.

Neuroticism A dimension of personality that is concerned with emotional stability, especially the expression of negative emotions, such as anxiety, depression, and anger.

Neurotransmitters Chemical substances that are released into the synapse between two neurons and carry signals from the terminal button of one neuron to the receptors of another.

Nonshared environment The component of a sibling's environment inside or outside the family that is unique to that sibling, for example, being a favorite child or one's best friend.

Contrasts with the shared environment, family experiences that are common across siblings.

Normal distribution A frequency distribution represented by a bell-shaped curve—the normal curve—that is important for making statistical inferences. Many psychological characteristics (e.g., intelligence) are assumed to follow the normal distribution.

Normalization The philosophy that mentally retarded or mentally ill people are entitled to live as much as possible like other members of the society. Often associated with deinstitutionalization in providing custodial care and mainstreaming in education.

Null hypothesis The prediction that an experimental hypothesis is not true. Scientists must assume that the null hypothesis holds until research contradicts it.

Obesity Excess body fat, a circumstance that roughly corresponds with a body weight 20 percent above the expected weight.

Obsession A repetitive, unwanted, intrusive cognitive event that may take the form of thoughts, images, or impulses. Obsessions intrude suddenly into consciousness and lead to an increase in subjective anxiety.

Obsessive–compulsive personality disorder An enduring pattern of thinking and behavior that is characterized by perfectionism and inflexibility. These people are preoccupied with rules and efficiency. They are excessively conscientious, moralistic, and judgmental.

Occipital lobe A region of the brain located behind the temporal lobe that receives and interprets visual information.

Oedipal conflict Freud's view that boys harbor forbidden sexual desires for their mothers, and they typically resolve the dilemma between the ages of 4 and 6 by identifying with their fathers.

Openness to experience A dimension of personality that describes the person's willingness to consider and explore unfamiliar ideas, feelings, and activities.

Operant conditioning A learning theory asserting that behavior is a function of its consequences. Specifically, behavior increases if it is rewarded, and it decreases if it is punished.

Operational definition A procedure that is used to measure a theoretical construct.

Opiates (sometimes called opioids) Drugs that have properties similar to opium. The main active ingredients in opium are morphine and codeine.

Oppositional defiant disorder A psychological disorder of childhood characterized by persistent but relatively minor transgressions, such as refusing to obey adult requests, arguing, and acting angry.

Orgasmic disorder A sexual disorder in which the person has recurrent difficulties reaching orgasm after a normal sexual arousal.

Pain disorder A type of somatoform disorder characterized by preoccupation with pain, and complaints are motivated at least in part by psychological factors.

Panic attack A sudden, overwhelming experience of terror or fright. While anxiety involves a blend of several negative emotions, panic is more focused.

Paradigm A set of assumptions both about the substance of a theory and about how scientists should collect data and test theoretical propositions. The term was applied to the progress of science by Thomas Kuhn, an influential historian and philosopher.

Paranoid personality disorder An enduring pattern of thinking and behavior characterized by a pervasive tendency to be inappropriately suspicious of other people's motives and behaviors. People who fit the description for this disorder expect that other people are trying to harm them, and they take extraordinary precautions to avoid being exploited or injured.

Paranoid type A subtype of schizophrenia that is characterized by systematic delusions with persecutory or grandiose content. Preoccupation with frequent auditory hallucinations can also be associated with the paranoid type.

Paraphilias Forms of sexual disorder that involve sexual arousal in association with unusual objects and situations, such as inanimate objects, sexual contacts with children, exhibiting their genitals to strangers, and inflicting pain on another person.

Parasympathetic nervous system The branch of the autonomic nervous system that generally controls the slowing of psychophysiological arousal and energy conservation.

Parietal lobe A region of the brain located at the top and back of the head that receives and integrates sensory information and also plays a role in spacial reasoning.

Parkinson's disease A disorder of the motor system that is caused by a degeneration of a specific area of the brain stem known as the *substantia nigra* and loss of the neurotransmitter dopamine, which is produced by cells in this area.

Pedophilia One of the paraphilias, characterized by marked distress over, or acting on urges involving, sexual activity with a prepubescent child.

Peer sociometrics A method of assessing children's social relationships and categorizing children's social standing by obtaining information on who is "liked most" and who is "liked least" from a group of children who know each other.

Peripheral nervous system Nerves that stem from the central nervous system and connect to the body's muscles, sensory systems, and organs. Divided into two subdivisions, the somatic and the autonomic nervous systems.

Personality The combination of persistent traits or characteristics that, taken as a whole, describe a person's behavior. In DSM-IV, personality is defined as "enduring patterns of perceiving, relating to, and thinking about the environment and oneself, which are exhibited in a wide range of important social and personal contexts."

Personality disorder Inflexible and maladaptive patterns of personality that begin by early adulthood and result in either social or occupational problems or distress to the individual.

Personality inventory Sometimes called an *objective personality test*, it consists of a series of straightforward statements that the person is required to rate or endorse as being either true or false in relation to himself or herself.

Pervasive developmental disorders A category of unusual psychological problems that begin early in life and involve severe impairments in a number of areas of functioning. Autistic disorder is one example.

Phenomenology The study of events and symptoms (including subjective experiences) in their own right rather than in terms of inferred causes.

Phenotype The observed expression of a given genotype or genetic structure, for example, eye color.

Phenylketonuria (PKU) A cause of mental retardation transmitted by the pairing of recessive genes that results in the deficiency of the enzyme that metabolizes phenylalanine. Infants have normal intelligence at birth, but the ingestion of foods containing phenylalanine causes phenylketonuria and produces brain damage. Can be prevented with a phenylalanine-free diet.

Phobia A persistent and irrational narrowly defined fear that is associated with a specific object or situation.

Pick's disease A form of primary dementia that is associated with atrophy of the frontal and temporal lobes of the brain. Very similar to Alzheimer's disease in terms of both behavioral symptoms and cognitive impairment.

Placebo In medicine, pills that are pharmacologically inert; more broadly, any type of treatment that contains no known "specific ingredients" for treating a given condition.

Placebo control group A group of subjects given a treatment with no known specific ingredients for the purpose of comparison with alternative treatments that are thought to contain specific, therapeutic benefits.

Placebo effect The improvement in a condition produced by a placebo (sometimes a substantial change). An overriding goal of scientific research is to identify treatments that exceed placebo effects.

Polygenic Caused by more than one gene. Characteristics become normally distributed as more genes are involved in the phenotypic expression of a trait.

Polysubstance abuse (also known as *multidrug abuse*) A disorder characterized by the abuse of at least three different psychoactive drugs (not including nicotine or caffeine). No single substance predominates in the pattern of abuse.

Polythetic class A category that is defined in terms of a set of criteria that are neither necessary nor sufficient. Each member of the category must possess a certain minimal number of the defining features, but none of the features has to be found in each member of the category.

Pons Part of the hindbrain that serves various functions in regulating stages of sleep.

Population The entire group of people about whom a researcher wants to generalize.

Positive affect One of two mood dimensions (compare negative affect) employed by Tellegen as well as Watson and Clark in their theories of personality. Adjectives that describe positive affect include active, delighted, enthusiastic, and proud.

Positive reinforcement Occurs when the onset of a stimulus increases the frequency of behavior (for example, you get paid for your work).

Positive symptoms (of schizophrenia) Include hallucinations, delusions, disorganized speech, inappropriate affect, and disorganized behavior.

Posttraumatic stress disorder (PTSD) A psychological disorder characterized by recurring symptoms of numbing, reexperiencing, and hyperarousal following exposure to a traumatic stressor.

Prefrontal lobotomy A psychosurgery technique introduced in 1935 by Egas Moniz in which the two hemispheres of the brain were severed. Moniz won a Nobel Prize for the treatment, which now is discredited.

Premature ejaculation A type of sexual disorder, in which a man is unable to delay ejaculation long enough to accomplish intercourse.

Premorbid history A pattern of behavior that precedes the onset of an illness. Adjustment prior to the disorder.

Preparedness theory The notion that organisms are biologically prepared, on the basis of neural pathways in their central nervous systems, to learn certain types of associations (also known as *biological constraints on learning*).

Prevalence An epidemiological term that refers to the total number of cases that are present within a given population during a particular period of time.

Primary appraisal The cognitive evaluation of the challenge, threat, or harm posed by a stressful life event.

Primary gain A psychoanalytic concept that a conversion symptom protects the mind by unconsciously expressing a psychological conflict. For example, a physical symptom (paralysis) may symbolize some underlying conflict (a desire to hurt someone). Contrasts with secondary gain or the direct reinforcement of a symptom.

Primary prevention An attempt to prevent new cases of disorder by improving the environment; promotes health, not just the treatment of illness.

Primary sleep disorder A condition where a sleeping difficulty is the principal complaint. In DSM-IV, either a dyssomnia—a difficulty in the amount, quality, or timing of sleep, or a parasomnia—an abnormal event that occurs during sleep; for example, nightmares.

Probands Index cases. In behavior genetic studies, probands are family members who have a disorder, and the relatives of the index cases are examined for concordance.

Problem-focused coping Externally oriented coping in an attempt to change or otherwise control a stressor.

Prodromal phase Precedes the active phase of schizophrenia and is marked by an obvious deterioration in role functioning. Prodromal signs and symptoms are less dramatic than those seen during the active phase of the disorder.

Professional responsibilities A professional's obligation to follow the ethical standards of his or her profession and to uphold the laws of the states in which he or she practices, for example, confidentiality.

Prognosis Predictions about the future course of a disorder with or without treatment.

Projective tests Personality tests, such as the Rorschach inkblot test, in which the person is asked to interpret a series of ambiguous stimuli.

Prospective design A research design in which people are studied longitudinally and forward in time. Supposed causes of future outcomes are assessed in the present, and subjects are then followed to see if the hypothesized effects develop over time.

Psychiatry The branch of medicine that is concerned with the study and treatment of mental disorders.

Psychoactive drugs Various drugs—ranging from alcohol, tobacco, and caffeine to controlled substances—that affect the individual's psychological state.

Psychoactive substance A drug that alters a person's mood, level of perception, or brain functioning.

Psychoanalysis Freud's orthodox form of psychotherapy that is practiced rarely today because of its time, expense, and questionable effectiveness in treating mental disorders. Freud viewed the task of psychoanalysis as promoting insight by uncovering the unconscious conflicts and motivations that cause psychological difficulties.

Psychoanalytic theory A paradigm for conceptualizing abnormal behavior based on the concepts and writings of Sigmund Freud. Highlights unconscious processes and conflicts as causing abnormal behavior and emphasizes psychoanalysis as the treatment of choice.

Psychodynamic A variation on the Freudian approach that searches for unconscious conflicts and motivations, but does not adhere to Freud literally as in psychoanalysis.

Psychodynamic psychotherapy An "uncovering" form of psychotherapy in which the therapist typically is more engaged and directive; the process is considerably less lengthy than in psychoanalysis.

Psychological dependence A term used to describe forceful, subjective urges to use drugs, often as a means of relieving negative mood states.

Contrasts with the term "physiological dependence," which involves symptoms of tolerance and withdrawal.

Psychology The science, profession, and academic discipline concerned with the study of mental processes and behavior in humans and animals.

Psychometric approach A method of classification that forms diagnostic categories from statistical analysis of symptom checklists. Particularly used in classifying externalizing and internalizing disorders of childhood.

Psychomotor retardation A generalized slowing of physical and emotional reactions. The slowing of movements and speech; frequently seen in depression.

Psychomotor stimulants Drugs such as amphetamine and cocaine that produce their effect by simulating the effects of certain neurotransmitters, specifically epinephrine, norepinephrine, dopamine, and serotonin.

Psychoneuroimmunology (PNI) Research on the effects of stress on the functioning of the immune system.

Psychopathology The manifestations of (and the study of the causes of) mental disorders. Generally used as another term to describe abnormal behavior.

Psychopathy Another term for antisocial personality disorder. Usually associated with Cleckley's definition of that concept, which included features such as disregard for the truth, lack of empathy, and inability to learn from experience.

Psychopharmacology The study of the effects of psychoactive drugs on behavior. Clinical psychopharmacology involves the expert use of drugs in the treatment of mental disorders.

Psychophysiology The study of changes in the functioning of the body that result from psychological experiences.

Psychosis A term that refers to several types of severe mental disorder in which the person is out of contact with reality. Hallucinations and delusions are examples of psychotic symptoms.

Psychosomatic disorder A term indicating that a physical disease is a product both of the psyche (mind) and the soma (body).

Psychostimulants Medications that heighten energy and alertness when taken in small dosages, but lead to restless, even frenetic, behavior when misused. Often used in the treatment of attention-deficit/hyperactivity disorder.

Psychosurgery A controversial treatment that involves the surgical destruction of specific regions of the brain. Modern psychosurgery involves relatively little destruction of brain tissue, unlike the discredited prefrontal lobotomy.

Psychotherapy The use of psychological techniques in an attempt to produce change in the context of a special, helping relationship.

Punishment Occurs when the onset of a stimulus decreases the frequency of behavior (for example, your parents scold you).

Purging An intentional act designed to eliminate consumed food from the body. Self-induced vomiting is the most common form.

Random assignment Any of several methods of ensuring that each subject has a statistically equal chance of being exposed to any level of an independent variable.

Random selection A method of selecting samples from a larger population that ensures that each subject has a statistically equal chance of being selected.

Rape Acts involving nonconsensual sexual penetration obtained by physical force, by threat of bodily harm, or when the victim is incapable of giving consent by virtue of mental illness, mental retardation, or intoxication.

Rating scale An assessment tool in which the observer is asked to make judgments that place the person somewhere along a dimension.

Rational–emotive therapy (RET) A cognitive behavior therapy technique designed to challenge irrational beliefs about oneself and the world. Developed by Albert Ellis as a treatment for anxiety, depression, and related problems.

Reaction range A behavior genetic concept for conceptualizing the joint influence of genes and environment; specifically, that heredity determines the upper and lower limits of a trait and experience determines the extent to which people fulfill their genetic potential.

Reactivity The influence of an observer's presence on the behavior of the person who is being observed.

Receptors Sites on the dendrites or soma of a neuron that are sensitive to certain neurotransmitters.

Recidivism Repeat offending in violating the law.

Reciprocal causality The concept of causality as bidirectional (or circular). Interaction is a process of mutual influence, not separable causes and effects.

Reciprocity The social exchange of cooperation and conflict. Family members with happy relationships reciprocate positive actions; family members with troubled relationships reciprocate negative ones.

Recovered memories Dramatic recollections of long-forgotten traumatic experiences; a controversial topic because the "memories" often are impossible to validate and many such memories may be created rather than recovered.

Reductionism The scientific perspective that the whole is the sum of its parts, and that the task of scientists is to divide the world into its smaller and smaller components.

Regression A return or retreat to an earlier stage or style of coping or behaving.

Relapse The reappearance of active symptoms following a period of remission (such as a return to heavy drinking by an alcoholic after a period of sustained sobriety).

Reliability The consistency of measurements, including diagnostic decisions. One index of reliability is agreement among clinicians.

Remission A stage of disorder characterized by the absence of symptoms (i.e., symptoms that were previously present are now gone).

Representative sample A sample that accurately represents the larger population of an identified group (e.g., a representative sample of all children in the United States).

Residual phase Follows the active phase of a disorder such as schizophrenia. At this point, psychotic symptoms have improved, but the person continues to be impaired in various ways. Negative symptoms may be more pronounced during the residual phase.

Residual type A subtype of schizophrenia that includes patients who no longer meet the criteria for active phase symptoms but nevertheless demonstrate continued signs of negative symptoms or attenuated forms of delusions, hallucinations, or disorganized speech.

Resilience The ability to "bounce back" from adversity despite life stress and emotional distress.

Response cost Occurs when the removal of a stimulus decreases the frequency of behavior (for example, your parents take away the use of the car).

Reticular activating system Located in the midbrain, but extending into the pons and medulla as well. Regulates sleeping and waking and sexual behavior.

Retrograde amnesia The loss of memory for events prior to the onset of an illness or the experience of a traumatic event.

Retrospective reports Recollections about past experiences that are often questioned in terms of reliability and validity.

Reuptake The process of recapturing some neurotransmitters in the synapse before they reach the receptors of another cell and returning the chemical substances to the terminal button. The neurotransmitter then is reused in subsequent neural transmission.

Reverse causality Indicates that causation could be operating in the opposite direction: Y could be causing X instead of X causing Y. A threat to interpretation in correlational studies, and a basic reason why correlation does not mean causation.

Risk A statement about the probability that a certain outcome will occur

Risk factor A variable that is associated with a higher probability of developing a disorder

Role playing Improvisational play acting that may be used in therapy to teach clients alternative ways of acting in problematic situations.

Savant performance An exceptional ability in a highly specialized area of functioning typically involving artistic, musical, or mathematical skills.

Schema A general cognitive pattern that guides the way a person perceives and interprets events in his or her environment.

Schizoaffective disorder A disorder defined by a period of disturbance during which the symptoms of schizophrenia partially overlap with a major depressive episode or a manic episode.

Schizoid personality disorder An enduring pattern of thinking and behavior characterized by pervasive indifference to other people, coupled with a diminished range of emotional experience and expression. People who fit this description prefer social isolation to interactions with friends or family.

Schizophrenia A type of (or group of) psychotic disorders characterized by positive and negative symptoms and associated with a deterioration in role functioning. The term was originally coined by Eugen Bleuler to describe the *splitting of mental associations*, which he believed to be the fundamental disturbance in schizophrenia (previously known as *dementia praecox*).

Schizophrenic spectrum A group of disorders that, on the basis of family history and adoption study data, are presumed to be genetically related to schizophrenia. These disorders may include schizotypal personality disorder, schizoaffective disorder, and delusional disorder.

Schizophreniform disorder A condition characterized by the same symptoms as schizophrenia, in which the patient has exhibited symptoms for less than the 6-month period required by DSM-IV for a diagnosis of schizophrenia.

Schizotaxia According to Paul Meehl's theoretical model for schizophrenia, a subtle neurological defect of unknown form that is inherited by all individuals who are predisposed to schizophrenia.

Schizotypal personality disorder An enduring pattern of discomfort with other people coupled with peculiar thinking and behavior. The latter symptoms take the form of perceptual and cognitive disturbances. Considered by some experts to be part of the schizophrenic spectrum.

School refusal (*school phobia*) Extreme reluctance to go to school, accompanied by various symptoms of anxiety such as stomachaches and headaches. May be a fear of school or an expression of separation anxiety disorder.

Scientist-practitioner model A model of training and professional activity, particularly influential in clinical psychology, that emphasizes the integration of science and practice.

Seasonal affective disorder A type of mood disorder (either unipolar or bipolar) in which there has been a regular temporal relation between onset (or disappearance) of the person's episodes and a particular time of the year. For example, the person might become depressed in the winter.

Secondary appraisal The assessment of one's abilities and resources for coping with a stressful life event.

Secondary gain The psychoanalytic concept that conversion (or other somatoform)

symptoms can help a patient avoid responsibility or receive attention (reinforcement).

Secondary prevention Focuses on the early detection of emotional problems (for instance, "at risk" groups) in an attempt to prevent problems from becoming more serious and difficult to treat.

Selective serotonin reuptake inhibitors (SSRIs) A group of antidepressant drugs that inhibit the reuptake of serotonin into the presynaptic nerve endings and therefore promote neurotransmission in serotonin pathways.

Self-control Appropriate behavior guided by internal (rather than external) rules.

Self-efficacy Albert Bandura's central cognitive concept, the belief that one can achieve desired goals.

Self-instruction training A cognitive behavior therapy technique for teaching children self-control that involves modeling and imitation of self-statements.

Senile plaques A type of brain lesion found in Alzheimer's disease that consists of a central core of homogeneous protein material known as *amyloid* surrounded by clumps of debris left over from destroyed neurons.

Sensate focus A procedure for the treatment of sexual dysfunction that involves a series of simple exercises in which the couple spends time in a quiet, relaxed setting, learning to touch each other.

Separation anxiety disorder A psychological disorder of childhood characterized by persistent and excessive worry for the safety of an attachment figure and related fears such as getting lost, being kidnapped, nightmares, and refusal to be alone. Distinct from normal separation anxiety, which typically develops shortly before an infant's first birthday.

Sex roles Characteristics, behaviors, and skills that are defined within a specific culture as being either masculine or feminine.

Sexual aversion disorder A form of sexual dysfunction in which a person has an extreme aversion to, and avoids, genital sexual contact with a partner.

Sexual dysfunctions Forms of sexual disorder that involve inhibitions of sexual desire or interference with the physiological responses leading to orgasm.

Sexual masochism A form of paraphilia in which sexual arousal is associated with the act of being humiliated, beaten, bound, or otherwise made to suffer.

Sexual sadism A form of paraphilia in which sexual arousal is associated with desires to inflict physical or psychological suffering, including humiliation, on another person.

Shared environment The component of the family environment that offers the same or highly similar experiences to all siblings, for example, socioeconomic status. Stands in contrast to the nonshared environment, experiences inside

and outside the family that are unique to one sibling.

Socialization The process of shaping children's behavior and attitudes to conform to the expectations of parents, teachers, and society.

Social clocks Age-related goals people set for themselves and later use to evaluate life achievements.

Social phobia A type of phobic disorder in which the person is persistently fearful of social situations that might expose him or her to scrutiny by others, such as fear of public speaking.

Social skills training A behavior therapy technique in which clients are taught new skills that are desirable and likely to be rewarded in the everyday world.

Social support The emotional and practical assistance received from others.

Social work A profession whose primary concern is how human needs can be met within society.

Soma The cell body and largest part of the neuron where most of the neuron's metabolism and maintenance are controlled and performed.

Somatic symptoms Symptoms of mood disorders that are related to basic physiological or bodily functions, including fatigue, aches and pains, and serious changes in appetite and sleep patterns.

Somatization disorder A type of somatoform disorder characterized by multiple, somatic complaints in the absence of organic impairments.

Somatoform disorders A category of psychological disorders characterized by unusual physical symptoms that occur in the absence of a known physical pathology. Examples include hypochondriasis and conversion disorder. Somatoform disorders are somatic in form only, thus their name (note the distinction from psychosomatic disorders, which do involve real physical pathology).

Standard deviation A measure of dispersion of scores around the mean. Technically, the square root of the variance.

Standard scores A standardized frequency distribution in which each score is subtracted from the mean and the difference is divided by the standard deviation.

State-dependent learning Learning that occurs in one state of affect or consciousness is best recalled in the same state of affect or consciousness.

Status offense An act that is illegal only because of a youth's status as a minor, for example, running away from home, truancy from school.

Stress An event that creates physiological or psychological strain for the individual. Stress has been defined differently by various scientists.

Stress management A treatment used in behavioral medicine and health psychology to teach more effective coping skills, reduce adverse reactions to stress, and improve health behavior.

Substance abuse The less severe form of substance use disorder listed in DSM-IV. Describes a pattern of drug use that is defined in terms of interference with the person's ability to fulfill major role obligations, the recurrent use of a drug in dangerous situations, or the experience of repeated legal difficulties that are associated with drug use.

Substance dependence The more severe form of substance use disorder listed in DSM-IV. Refers to a pattern of repeated self-administration that results in tolerance, withdrawal, or compulsive drug-taking behavior.

Superego One of Freud's three central personality structures, roughly equivalent to the "conscience." In Freudian theory, the superego contains societal standards of behavior, particularly rules that children learn from identifying with their parents. The superego attempts to control id impulses.

Sympathetic nervous system The branch of the autonomic nervous system that generally controls psychophysiological activities associated with increased arousal and energy expenditure.

Synapse A small gap filled with fluid that lies between the axon of one neuron and a dendrite or soma of another neuron.

Syndrome A group of symptoms that appear together and are assumed to represent a specific type of disorder.

Systematic desensitization A treatment for overcoming fears and phobias developed by Joseph Wolpe. Involves learning relaxation skills, developing a fear hierarchy, and systematic exposure to imagined, feared events while simultaneously maintaining relaxation.

Systems theory An innovation in the philosophy of conceptualizing and conducting science that emphasizes interdependence, cybernetics, and especially holism—the idea that the whole is more than the sum of its parts. Often traced to the biologist and philosopher Ludwig von Bertalanffy.

Tardive dyskinesia (TD) A motor syndrome produced as a side effect of neuroleptic medication. Consists of abnormal involuntary movements of the mouth and face, such as tongue protrusion, chewing, and lip-puckering, as well as spasmodic movements of the limbs and trunk of the body.

Temperament Characteristic styles of relating to the world that are often conceptualized as inborn traits. Generally emphasizes the "how" as opposed to the "what" of behavior.

Temporal lobe A region of the brain located beneath much of the frontal and pariental lobes that processes sound and smell, regulates emotions, and is involved in some aspects of learning, memory, and language.

Terminal buttons Buds found on the small branches at the end of the axon where messages are sent from one neuron to other neurons.

Tertiary prevention Involves treatment for a disorder, but also attempts to address some of the adverse consequences of mental illness (such as unemployment).

Thalamus A part of the limbic system that is involved in receiving and integrating sensory information both from the sense organs and from higher brain structures.

Third variable An unmeasured factor that may account for a correlation observed between any two variables. A threat to interpretation in correlational studies, and a basic reason why correlation does not mean causation.

Thought suppression An active attempt to stop thinking about something; a form of mental control that often leads to paradoxical effects, such as an increase in strong emotions associated with unpleasant thoughts.

Threshold model A perspective on etiology that holds that people can exhibit characteristics of a disorder without experiencing any adverse impact on their adjustment until they pass a critical threshold. Beyond that level, there is presumably a dramatic increase in the number of problems that are encountered.

Time-out A discipline technique that involves briefly isolating a child as a punishment for misbehavior.

Token economy A type of contingency management program that has been adopted in many institutional settings. Desired and undesired behaviors are identified, contingencies are defined, behavior is monitored, and rewards or punishments are given according to the rules of the economy.

Tolerance The process through which the nervous system becomes less sensitive to the effects of a psychoactive substance. As a result, the person needs to consume increased quantities of the drug to achieve the same subjective effect.

Transference In psychoanalysis, the process whereby patients transfer feelings about a key figure in their life onto the analyst. In psychotherapy, the client's feelings toward the therapist.

Transsexualism A severe form of gender identity disorder in adults.

Transvestic fetishism A form of paraphilia in which sexual pleasure is derived from dressing in the clothing of the opposite gender.

Trauma desensitization A treatment for posttraumatic stress disorder where the client is first taught to relax, and while maintaining a state of relaxation, he or she gradually relives the traumatic event through discussions or fantasies.

Traumatic stress A catastrophic event that involves real or perceived threat to life or physical well-being.

Tricyclics A group of antidepressant drugs that block the uptake of neurotransmitters, such as norepinephrine and dopamine, from the synapse.

Two-factor theory A combination of classical conditioning and operant conditioning that is hypothesized to explain the acquisition and maintenance of fear. Fears are acquired through classical conditioning and maintained through operant conditioning (the reduction in anxiety that stems from avoidance).

Type A behavior pattern A characterological response to challenge that is competitive, hostile, urgent, impatient, and achievement-striving. Linked to an increased risk for coronary heart disease.

Unconditioned response An automatic reaction to an event (unconditioned stimulus), as when an animal salivates in response to the sight of meat. Central in classical conditioning.

Unconditioned stimulus A stimulus that elicits an automatic reaction (an unconditioned response), as when the sight of meat produces salivation. Central in classical conditioning.

Unconscious Mental processes or contents that reside outside of awareness. In Freudian theory, the seat of many hidden memories, motivations, and defenses.

Undifferentiated type A subtype of schizophrenia that includes patients who display prominent psychotic symptoms and either meet the criteria for several subtypes or otherwise do not meet the criteria for the catatonic, paranoid, or disorganized types.

Unipolar mood disorder A form of mood disorder in which the person experiences episodes of depression but has never experienced an episode of mania or hypomania.

Vaginismus A form of sexual dysfunction in which the outer muscles of the vagina snap tightly shut when penetration is attempted, thus preventing insertion of any object.

Validity The meaning or systematic importance of a construct or a measurement.

Variance A measure of dispersion of scores around the mean. Technically, the average squared difference from the mean (see also standard deviation).

Vascular dementia (also known as *multi-infarct dementia*) A type of dementia associated with vascular disease. The cognitive symptoms of vascular dementia are the same as those for Alzheimer's disease, but a gradual onset is not required.

Ventricles Four connected chambers in the brain filled with cerebrospinal fluid. The ventricles are enlarged in some psychological and neurological disorders.

Victimization A pattern of responses often observed among victims of violent crimes, particularly rape, that includes fear, guilt, self-blame, powerlessness, and lowered self-esteem.

Voyeurism A form of paraphilia (also known as *peeping*) in which a person becomes sexually aroused by observing unsuspecting people (usually strangers) while they are undressing or engaging in sexual activities.

Vulnerability marker A specific measure, such as a biochemical assay or a psychological test, that might be useful in identifying people who are vulnerable to a disorder such as schizophrenia.

Weight set point Fixed weights or small ranges of weight around which the body regulates weight, for example, by increasing or decreasing metabolism.

Withdrawal The constellation of symptoms that are experienced shortly after a person stops taking a drug after heavy or prolonged use.

Worry A relatively uncontrollable sequence of negative, emotional thoughts and images that are concerned with possible future threats or danger.

References

Abel, G.G., Becker, J.V., Mittelman, M., Cunningham-Rathner, J. et al. (1987). Self-reported sex crimes of nonincarcerated paraphiliacs. *Journal of Interpersonal Violence*, 2, 3–25.

Abel, G.G., & Gouleau, J.L. (1990). Male sex offenders. In M.E. Thase, B.A. Edelstein, & M. Hersen (Eds.), *Handbook of outpatient treatment of adults: Nonpsychotic mental disorders*, pp. 271–290. New York: Plenum.

Abel, G.G., & Osborn, C. (1992). The paraphilias: The extent and nature of sexually deviant and criminal behavior. *Psychotic Clinics of North America*, 15, 675–687.

Abou-Saleh, M.T. (1992). Lithium. In E.S. Paykel (Ed.), *Handbook of affective disorders*, 2nd ed., pp. 369–386, New York: Guilford.

Abrams, R. (1993). ECT technique: Electrode placement, stimulus type, and treatment frequency. In C.E. Coffey (Ed.), *The clinical science of electroconvulsive therapy*, pp. 17–28. Washington, DC: American Psychiatric Press.

Abramson, L.Y., Metalsky, G.I., & Alloy, L.B. (1989). Hopelessness depression: A theory based-subtype of depression. *Psychological Review*, 96, 358–372.

Abramson, L.Y., Seligman, M.E.P., & Teasdale, J. (1978). Learned helplessness in humans: Critique and reformulation. *Journal of Abnormal Psychology*, 87, 49–74.

Achenbach, T.M. (1985). *Assessment and taxonomy of child and adolescent psychopathology*. Beverly Hills, CA: Sage.

Achenbach, T.M., & Edelbrock, C.S. (1981). Behavioral problems and competencies reported by parents of normal and disturbed children aged four through sixteen. *Monographs of the Society for Research in Child Development*. Series No. 188.

Achenbach, T.M., Howell, C.T., Quay, H.C., & Conners, C.K. (1991). National survey of problems and competencies among four- to sixteen-year-olds. *Monographs of the Society for Research in Child Development*, 56, no. 3, Series No. 225.

Achenbach, T.M., McConaughy, S.H., & Howell, C.T. (1987). Child/adolescent behavioral and emotional problems: Implications of cross-information correlations for situational specificity. *Psychological Bulletin*, 101, 213–232.

Ackerman, M.D., & Carey, M.P. (1995). Psychology's role in the assessment of erectile dysfunction: Historical precedents, current knowledge, and methods. *Journal of Consulting and Clinical Psychology*, 63, 862–876.

Adams, G.R., Abraham, K.G., & Markstrom, C.A. (1987). The relation among identity development, self-consciousness and self-focusing during middle and late adolescence. *Developmental Psychology*, 23, 292–297.

Adams, G.R., & Adams, C.M. (1989). Developmental issues. In L.K.G. Hsu & M. Hersen (Eds.), *Recent developments in adolescent psychiatry*, pp. 13–30. New York: Wiley.

Adams, G.R., Ryan, J.H., Hoffman, J.J., Dobson, W.R., & Nielsen, E.C. (1985). Ego identity status, conformity behavior and personality in late adolescence. *Journal of Personality and Social Psychology*, 47, 1091–1104.

Agras, W.S. (1987). *Eating disorders: Management of obesity, bulimia, and anorexia nervosa*. Elmsford, NY: Pergamon.

Agras, W.S. (1993). The diagnosis and treatment of panic disorder. *Annual Review of Medicine*, 44, 39–51.

Ainsworth, M.D.S. (1979). Infant-mother attachment. *American Psychologist*, 34, 932–937.

Ainsworth, M.D.S. (1989). Attachments beyond infancy. *American Psychologist*, 44, 709–716.

Ainsworth, M.D.S., Blehar, M., Waters, E., & Wall, S. (1978). *Patterns of attachment*. Hillsdale, NJ: Erlbaum.

Akiskal, H.S. (1985). Anxiety: Definition, relationship to depression, and proposal for an integrative model. In A.H. Tuma and J.D. Maser (Eds.), *Anxiety and the anxiety disorders*. Hillsdale, NJ: Erlbaum.

Akiskal, H.S. (1992). Borderline: An adjective still in search of a noun. In D. Silver & M. Rosenbluth (Eds.), *Handbook of borderline disorders*, pp. 155–176. Madison, CT: International Universities Press.

Akiskal, H.S. (1994). The temperamental borders of affective disorders. *Acta Psychiatrica Scandinavica*, 89 (suppl. 379), 32–37.

Akiskal, H.S., Chen, S.E., Davis, G.C., Puzantian, V.R., Kashgarian, M., & Bolinger, J.M. (1985). Borderline: An adjective in search of a noun. *Journal of Clinical Psychiatry*, 46, 41–48.

Aldridge-Morris, R. (1989). *Multiple personality: An exercise in deception*. Hillsdale, NJ: Erlbaum.

Alessi, G. (1992). Models of proximate and ultimate causation in psychology. *American Psychologist*, 47, 1359–1370.

Alexander, F. (1950). *Psychosomatic medicine: Its principles and applications*. New York: Norton.

Alexander, F., & French, T.M. (1947). *Psychoanalytic therapy*. New York: Ronald Press.

Alexander, F., French, T.M., & Pollock, G.H. (1968). *Psychosomatic specificity*. Chicago: University of Chicago Press.

Alexander, J.F., Holtzworth-Munroe, A., & Jameson, P.B. (1994). The process and outcome of marital and family therapy: Research, review, and evaluation. In A.E. Bergin & S.L. Garfield (Eds.), *Handbook of psychotherapy and behavior change*, 4th ed., pp. 595–630. New York: Wiley.

Alexander, J.F., & Parsons, B.V. (1982). *Functional family therapy*. Monterey, CA: Brooks/Cole.

Al-Kubaisy, T., Marks, I.M., Logsdail, S., Marks, M.P., Lovell, K., Sungur, M., & Araya, R. (1992). Role of exposure homework in phobia reduction: A controlled study. *Behavior Therapy*, 23, 599–621.

Allan, C.A., & Cooke, D.J. (1985). Stressful life events and alcohol misuses in women: A critical review. *Journal of Studies on Alcohol*, 46, 147–152.

Allen, A., & Blazer, D.G. (1991). Mood disorders. In J. Sadavoy, L.W. Lazarus, & L.F. Jarvik (Eds.), *Comprehensive review of geriatric psychiatry*, pp. 337–351. Washington, DC: American Psychiatric Press.

Allen, J.P., & Hauser, S.T. (in press). Autonomy and relatedness in adolescent-family interactions as predictors of young adults' states of mind regarding attachment. *Development and Psychopathology*.

Alloy, L.B., Abramson, L.Y., Metalsky, G.I., & Hartlage, S. (1988). The hopelessness theory of depression: Attributional aspects. *British Journal of Clinical Psychology*, 27, 5–21.

Amato, P.R., & Keith, B. (1991a). Parental divorce and the well-being of children: A meta-analysis. *Psychological Bulletin*, 110, 26–46.

Amato, P.R., & Keith, B. (1991b). Parental divorce and adult well-being: A meta-analysis. *Journal of Marriage and the Family*, 53, 43–58.

American Association on Mental Retardation (1992). *Mental retardation: Definition, classification, and systems of support*, 9th ed. Washington, DC.

American Bar Association (1995). *Mental disability law*, 5th ed. Washington, DC.

American Cancer Society (1994). *Cancer facts and figures— 1993*. New York.

American Psychiatric Association (1980). *Psychiatric glossary*. Washington, DC: American Psychiatric Press.

American Psychiatric Association (1983). American Psychiatric Association statement on the insanity defense. *American Journal of Psychiatry*, 140, 681–688.

American Psychiatric Association (1994). *Diagnostic and statistical manual of mental disorders*, 1st ed. 1952; 2nd ed. 1968; 3rd ed. 1980; rev. 3rd ed. 1987; 4th ed. 1994. Washington, DC.

American Psychological Association (1991). The definition and description of clinical psychology. *Clinical Psychologist*, 44, 5–11.

American Psychological Association (1995). *Violence in the family*. Washington, DC.

Ames, M.A., & Houston, D.A. (1990). Legal, social, and biological definitions of pedophilia. *Archives of Sexual Behavior*, 19, 333–342.

Anastasi, A. (1986). Evolving concepts of test validation. *Annual Review of Psychology*, 37, 1–15.

Andersen, A.E. (1995). Eating disorders in males. In K.D. Brownell & C.G. Fairburn (Eds.), *Eating disorders and obesity: A comprehensive handbook*, pp. 177–182. New York: Guilford.

Andersen, B.L., & Cyranowski, J.M. (1995). Women's sexuality: Behaviors, responses, and individual differences. *Journal of Consulting and Clinical Psychology*, 63, 891–906.

Anderson, A.A., Russell, C.S., & Schumm, W.R. (1983). Perceived marital quality and family life cycle categories: A further analysis. *Journal of Marriage and the Family*, 45, 127–139.

Anderson, B.L., Kiecolt-Glaser, J.K., & Glaser, R. (1994). A biobehavioral model of cancer stress and disease course. *American Psychologist*, 49, 389–404.

Anderson, N.B., & McNeilly, M. (1991). Age, gender, and ethnicity as variables in psychophysiological assessment: Sociodemographics in context. *Psychological Assessment*, 3, 376–384.

Andreasen, N.C. (1984). *The broken brain: The biological revolution in psychiatry*. New York: Harper & Row.

Andreasen, N.C. (1988). Brain imaging: Applications in psychiatry. *Science*, 239, 1381–1388.

Andreasen, J.C. (Ed.). (1989). *Brain imaging: Applications in psychiatry*. Washington, D.C.: American Psychiatric Press.

Andreasen, N.C., Arndt, S., Alliger, R., Miller, D., & Flaum, M. (1995). Symptoms of schizophrenia: Methods, meanings, and mechanisms. *Archives of General Psychiatry*, 52, 341–351.

Andreasen, N.C., & Carpenter, W.T., Jr. (1993). Diagnosis and classification of schizophrenia. *Schizophrenia Bulletin*, 19, 199–214.

Andreasen, N.C., Flaum, M., Swayze, V.W.II. Tyrell, G., & Arndt, S. (1990). Positive and negative symptoms in schizophrenia: A critical reappraisal. *Archives of General Psychiatry*, 47, 615–621.

Andreasen, N.C., & Olsen, S. (1982). Negative v. positive schizophrenia: Definition and validation. *Archives of General Psychiatry*, 39, 789–794.

Andrews, G. (1996). Comorbidity in neurotic disorders: The similarities are more important than the differences. In Ronald M. Rapee (Ed.), *Current controversies in the anxiety disorders*, pp. 3–20. New York: Guilford.

Andrews, G., MacMahon, S.W., Austin, A., & Byrne, D.G. (1984). Hypertension: Comparison of drug and non-drug treatments. *British Medical Journal*, 284, 1523–1530.

Anthony, J.C., & Helzer, J.E. (1991). Syndromes of drug abuse and dependence. In L.N. Robins & D.A. Regier (Eds.), *Psychiatric disorders in America: The Epidemiologic Catchment Area Study*, pp. 116–154. New York: Free Press.

Anthony, J.C., & Helzer, J.E. (1995). Epidemiology of drug dependence. In M.T. Tsuang, M. Tohen, & G.E.P. Zahner (eds.), *Textbook in psychiatric epidemiology*, pp. 361–406. New York: Wiley-Liss.

Anthony, J.C., Warner, L.A., & Kessler, R.C. (1994). Comparative epidemiology of dependence on tobacco, alcohol, controlled substances, and inhalants: Basic findings from the National Comorbidity

Survey. *Experimental and Clinical Psychopharmacology, 2,* 1–24.

Appelbaum, P.S. (1994). *Almost a revolution: Mental health law and the limits of change.* New York: Oxford University Press.

Appelbaum, P.S., & Gutheil, T.G. (1979). Rotting with their rights on: Constitutional theory and clinical reality in drug refusal by psychiatric patients. *Bulletin of the American Academy of Psychiatry and Law, 7,* 308–317.

Arato, M., Frecska, E., Tekes, K., MacCrimmon, D.J. (1991). Serotonergic interhemispheric asymmetry: Gender differences in cortex. *Acta Psychiatrica Scandinavica, 84,* 110–111.

Archer, R.P. (1992). Review of the Minnesota Multiphasic Personality Inventory-2. In J.J. Kramer & J.C. Conoley (Eds.), *The eleventh mental measurements yearbook.* Lincoln: University of Nebraska Press.

Aries, P. (1962). *Centuries of childhood: A social history of family life.* New York: Vintage.

Armstrong, J., & Loewenstein, R.J. (1990). Characteristics of patients with multiple personality and dissociative disorders on psychological testing. *Journal of Nervous and Mental Disease, 178,* 448–458.

Arneric, S.P., Sullivan, J.P., Decker, M.W., Brioni, J.D., et al. (1995). Potential treatment of Alzheimer disease using cholinergic channel activators with cognitive enhancement, anxiolytic-like, and cytoprotective properties. *Alzheimer Disease and Associated Disorders, 9* (suppl. 2), 50–61.

Arno, P.S., Brandt, A.M., Gostin, L.O., & Morgan, J. (1996). Tobacco industry strategies to oppose federal regulation. *Journal of the American Medical Association, 275,* 1258–1263.

Asberg, M. (1994). Monoamine neurotransmitters in human aggressiveness and violence: A selected review. *Criminal Behaviour and Mental Health, 4,* 303–327.

Asher, S.R., & Wheeler, V.A. (1985). Children's loneliness: A comparison of rejected and neglected peer status. *Journal of Consulting and Clinical Psychology, 53,* 500–505.

Asperger, H. (1944/1991). "Autistic psychopathy" in childhood. In U. Frith (Ed. and Trans), *Autism and Asperger syndrome* (pp. 37–92). Cambridge, UK: Cambridge University Press. (Original published in 1944).

Astin, M.C., Ogland-Hand, S.M., Coleman, E.M., & Foy, D.W. (1995). Posttraumatic stress disorder and childhood abuse in battered women: Comparisons with maritally distressed women. *Journal of Consulting and Clinical Psychology, 63,* 308–312.

Atkinson, D.R., Morten, G., & Sue, D.W. (1993). *Counseling American minorities: A cross-cultural perspective,* 4th ed Dubuque, IA: William C. Brown.

Attie, I., & Brooks-Gunn, J. (1989). Development of eating problems in adolescent girls: A longitudinal study. *Developmental Psychology, 25,* 70–79.

Babor, T.F. (1992). Cross-cultural research on alcohol: A quoi bon? In J.E. Helzer & G.J. Canino (Eds.), *Alcoholism in North America, Europe, and Asia,* pp. 33–52. New York: Oxford University Press.

Baer, L., Rauch, S.L., Ballantine, T., et al. (1995). Cingulotomy for intractable obsessive-compulsive disorder: Prospective long-term follow-up of 18 patients. *Archives of General Psychiatry, 52,* 384–392.

Bailey, A., Le Couteur, A., Gottesman, I., Bolton, P., Simonoff, E., Yuzda, E., & Rutter, M. (1995). Autism as a strongly genetic disorder: Evidence from a British twin study. *Psychological Medicine, 25,* 63–77.

Baker, C.D., & de Silva, P. (1988). The relationship between male sexual dysfunction and belief in Zilbergeld's myths: An empirical investigation. *Sexual and Marital Therapy, 3,* 229–238.

Baker, T.B., Morse, E., & Sherman, J.E. (1986). The motivation to use drugs: A psychobiological analysis of urges. *Nebraska Symposium on Motivation, 34,* 257–323.

Baker, T.B., & Tiffany, S.T. (1985). Morphine tolerance as habituation. *Psychological Review, 92,* 78–108.

Ballenger, J.C. (1989). Toward an integrated model of panic disorder. *American Journal of Orthopsychiatry, 59,* 284–293.

Ballenger, J.C. (1991). Long-term pharmacologic treatment of panic disorder. *Journal of Clinical Psychiatry, 52* (suppl. 2), 18–23.

Ballenger, J.C., Burrows, G.D., DuPont, R.L., Lesser, I.M., Noyes, R., et al. (1988). Alprazolam in panic disorder and agoraphobia: Results from a multicenter trial. I. Efficacy in short term treatment. *Archives of General Psychiatry, 45,* 413–422.

Baltes, M.M., Kuhl, K.P., & Sowarka, D. (1922). Testing for limits of cognitive reserve capacity: A promising strategy for early diagnosis of dementia? *Journal of Gerontology: Psychological Sciences, 47,* P165–P167.

Baltes, P.B. (1993). The aging mind: Potential and limits. *Gerontologist, 33,* 580–594.

Baltes, P.B., & Kliegl, R. (1992). Further testing of limits of cognitive plasticity: Negative age differences in a mnemonic skill are robust. *Developmental Psychology, 28,* 121–125.

Banazak, D.A. (1996). Difficult dementia: Six steps to control problem behaviors. *Geriatrics, 51,* 36–42.

Bancroft, J. (1989). *Human sexuality and its problems,* 2nd ed. Edinburgh: Churchill Livingstone.

Bancroft, J., Dickerson, M., Fairburn, C.G., Gray, J., Greenwood, J., Stevenson, N., & Warner, P. (1986). Sex therapy outcome research: A reappraisal of methodology. I. A treatment study of male sexual dysfunction. *Psychological Medicine, 16,* 851–863.

Bancroft, J., & Wu, F.C.W. (1983). Changes in erectile responsiveness during androgen therapy. *Archives of Sexual Behavior, 12,* 59–66.

Bandura, A. (1973). *Aggression: A social learning analysis.* Englewood Cliffs, NJ: Prentice Hall.

Bandura, A. (1977). Self-efficacy: Toward a unifying theory of behavior change. *Psychological Review, 84,* 191–215.

Bandura, A., & Walters, R.H. (1963). *Social learning and personality development.* New York: Ronald Press.

Banki, C.M. (1995). Prophylactic potential of selective reuptake inhibitors in suicidal patients. *International Clinical Psychopharmacology, 9* (suppl. 4), 61–65.

Barbaree, H.E., & Seto, M.C. (1997). Pedophilia: Assessment and treatment. In D.R. Laws & W.T. O'Donohue (Eds.), *Handbook of sexual deviance: Theory and application.* New York: Guilford.

Barbaree, H.E., Seto, M.C., Serin, R.C., Amos, N.L., & Preston, D.L. (1994). Comparisons between sexual and nonsexual rapist subtypes: Sexual arousal to rape, offense precursors, and offense characteristics. *Criminal Justice and Behavior, 21,* 95–114.

Barker, J.G., & Howell, R.J. (1992). The plethysmograph: A review of recent literature. *Bulletin of the American Academy of Psychiatry and the Law, 20,* 13–25.

Barkley, R.A. (1988). The effects of methylphenidate on the interactions of preschool ADHD children with their mothers. *Journal of the American Academy of Child and Adolescent Psychiatry, 27,* 336–341.

Barkley, R.A. (1990). *Attention-deficit hyperactivity disorder: A handbook for diagnosis and treatment,* 2nd ed. New York: Guilford.

Barkley, R.A., Karlsson, J., Strzelecki, E., & Murphy, J.V. (1984). Effects of age and Ritalin dosage on the mother-child interactions of hyperactive children. *Journal of Consulting and Clinical Psychology, 52,* 750–758.

Barlow, D.H. (1986). Causes of sexual dysfunction: The role of anxiety and cognitive interference. *Journal of Consulting and Clinical Psychology, 54,* 140–148.

Barlow, D.H. (1988). *Anxiety and its disorders: The nature and treatment of anxiety and panic.* New York: Guilford.

Barlow, D.H. (1991). Disorders of emotion. *Psychological Inquiry, 2,* 58–71.

Barlow, D.H., Brown, T.A., & Craske, M.G. (1994). Definitions of panic attacks and panic disorder in the DSM-IV: Implications for research. *Journal of Abnormal Psychology, 103,* 553–564.

Barlow, D.H., & Cerny, J.A. (1988). *Psychological treatment of panic.* New York: Guilford.

Barlow, D.H., & Craske, M.G. (1988). The phenomenology of panic. In S. Rachman & J.D. Maser (Eds.), *Panic: Psychological perspectives.* Hillsdale, NJ: Erlbaum.

Barlow, D.H., O'Brien, G.T., & Last, C.G. (1984). Couples treatment of agoraphobia. *Behavior Therapy, 15,* 41–58.

Barnett, P.A., & Gotlib, I.H. (1988). Psychosocial functioning and depression: Distinguishing among antecedents, concomitants, and consequences. *Psychological Bulletin, 104,* 97–126.

Baroff, G.S. (1986). *Mental retardation: Nature, cause, and management,* 2nd ed. Washington, DC: Hemisphere.

Baron-Cohen, S., Leslie, A.M., & Frith, U. (1985). Does the autistic child have a "theory of mind"? *Cognition, 21,* 37–46.

Baron-Cohen, S., Tager-Flusberg, H., & Cohen, D.J. (Eds.) (1993). *Understanding other minds.* Oxford: Oxford University Press.

Barondes, S.H. (1993). *Molecules and mental illness.* New York: Scientific American.

Barr, R.F. (1973). Responses to erotic stimuli of transsexual and homosexual males. *British Journal of Psychiatry, 123,* 579–585.

Barrett, P.M., Dadds, M.R., & Rapee, R.M. (1996). Family treatment of childhood anxiety: A controlled trial. *Journal of Consulting and Clinical Psychology, 64,* 333–342.

Bartak, L., & Rutter, M. (1973). Special educational treatment of autistic children: A comparative study. I. Design of study and characteristics of units. *Journal of Child Psychology and Psychiatry, 14,* 217–222.

Baruth, L.G., & Huber, C.H. (1984). *An introduction to marital theory and therapy.* Monterey, CA: Brooks/Cole.

Basoglu, M., Lax, T., Kasvikis, Y., & Marks, I. (1988). Predictors of improvement in obsessive-compulsive disorder. *Journal of Anxiety Disorders, 2,* 299–317.

Bass, E., & Davis, L. (1988). *The courage to heal.* New York: Harper & Row.

Bastiani, A.M., Rao, R., Weltzin, T., & Kaye, W.H. (1995). Perfectionism in anorexia nervosa. *International Journal of Eating Disorders, 17,* 147–152.

Bates, J.E., Wachs, T.D., & Emde, R.N. (1994). Toward practical uses for biological concepts of temperament. In J.E. Bates & T.D. Wachs (Eds.), *Temperament: Individual differences at the interface of biology and behavior,* pp. 275–306. Washington, DC: American Psychological Association.

Baucom, D.H., & Epstein, N. (1990). *Cognitive-behavioral marital therapy.* New York: Brunner/Mazel.

Baucom, D.H., Notarius, C.I., Burnett, C.K., & Haefner, P. (1990). Gender differences and sex-role identity in marriage. In F.D. Fincham & T.N. Bradbury (Eds.), *The psychology of marriage: Basic issues and applications,* pp. 150–171. New York: Guilford.

Baum, A., Davidson, L.M., Singer, J.E., & Street, S.W. (1987). Stress as a psychophysiological response. In A. Baum & J.E. Singer (Eds.), *Handbook of psychology and health. Stress,* vol. 5, pp. 1–24. Hillsdale, NJ: Erlbaum.

Baum, D. (1996). *Smoke and mirrors: The war on drugs and the politics of failure.* Boston: Little Brown.

Bauman, M.L. (1996). Neuroanatomic observations of the brain in pervasive developmental disorders. *Journal of Autism and Developmental Disorders, 26,* 199–203.

Baumeister, R.F. (1990). Suicide as escape from self. *Psychological Review, 97,* 90–113.

Baumeister, R.F., & Butler, J.L. (1997). Sexual masochism. In D.R. Laws & W.T. O'Donohue (Eds.), *Handbook of sexual deviance: Theory and application.* New York: Guilford.

Baumrind, D. (1971). Current patterns of parental

authority. *Developmental Psychology Monograph, 4,* (1, Pt. 2).

Bayer, R. (1981). *Homosexuality and American psychiatry: The politics of diagnosis.* New York: Basic Books.

Beach, S.R.H., Sandeen, E.E., & O'Leary, K.D. (1990). *Depression in marriage: A model for etiology and treatment.* New York: Guilford.

Bean, M.H. (1975). Alcoholics anonymous: AA. *Psychiatric Annals, 5,* 83–91.

Bebbington, P., & Kuipers, L. (1994). The predictive utility of expressed emotion in schizophrenia: An aggregate analysis. *Psychological Medicine, 24,* 707–718.

Bech, P. (1992). Symptoms and assessment of depression. In E.S. Paykel (Ed.), *Handbook of affective disorders,* 2nd ed., pp. 3–14. New York: Guilford.

Beck, A.T. (1967). *Depression: Clinical, experimental, and theoretical aspects.* New York: Harper & Row.

Beck, A.T. (1974). The development of depression. In R.J. Friedman & M.M. Katz (Eds.), *The psychology of depression: Contemporary theory and research,* pp. 3–20. New York: Winston-Wiley.

Beck, A. (1976). *Cognitive therapy and the emotional disorders.* New York: International Universities Press.

Beck, A.T. (1984). Cognition and therapy. *Archives of General Psychiatry, 41,* 1112–1114.

Beck, A.T., & Emery, G. (1985). *Anxiety disorders and phobias: A cognitive perspective.* New York: Basic Books.

Beck, A.T., Rush, A.J., Shaw, B.F., & Emery, G. (1979). *Cognitive therapy of depression.* New York: Guilford.

Beck, A.T., Steer, R.A., & Garbin, M.G. (1988). Psychometric properties of the Beck Depression Inventory: Twenty-five years of evaluation. *Clinical Psychology Review, 8,* 77–100.

Beck, J.G. (1993). Vaginismus. In W. O'Donohue & J.H. Geer (Eds.), *Handbook of sexual dysfunctions: Assessment and treatment,* pp. 381–397. Boston: Allyn & Bacon.

Beck, J.G. (1995). Hypoactive sexual desire disorder: An overview. *Journal of Consulting and Clinical Psychology, 63,* 919–927.

Becker, D., & Lamb, S. (1994). Sex bias in the diagnosis of borderline personality disorder and posttraumatic stress disorder. *Professional Psychology: Research and Practice, 25,* 55–61.

Becker, J.V. (1989). Impact of sexual abuse on sexual functioning. In S.R. Lieblum & R.C. Rosen (Eds.), *Principles and practice of sex therapy,* 2nd ed. New York: Guilford.

Becker, J.V., Alpert, J.L., BigFoot, D.S., Bonner, B.L., Geddie, L.F., Henggeler, S.W., Kaufman, K.L., & Walker, C.E. (1995). Empirical research on child abuse treatment: Report by the Child Abuse and Neglect Treatment Working Group, American Psychological Association. *Journal of Clinical Child Psychology, 24,* 23–46.

Beckson, M., & Cummings, J.L. (1992). Psychosis in basal ganglia disorders. *Neuropsychiatry, Neuropsychology & Behavioral Neurology, 5,* 126–131.

Beidel, D.C., Turner, S.M., & Cooley, M.R. (1993). Assessing reliable and clinically significant change in social phobia: Validity of the social phobia and anxiety inventory. *Behaviour Research and Therapy, 31,* 331–337.

Belar, C.D., & Perry, N.W. (1992). The national conference on scientist-practitioner education and training for the professional practice of psychology. *American Psychologist, 47,* 71–75.

Bell, R.Q. (1968). A reinterpretation of the direction of effects in studies of socialization. *Psychological Review, 75,* 81–95.

Bellack, A.S., & Mueser, K.T. (1993). Psychosocial treatment for schizophrenia. *Schizophrenia Bulletin, 19,* 317–336.

Bemporad, J.R. (1979). Adult recollections of a formerly autistic child. *Journal of Autism and Developmental Disorders, 9,* 179–197.

Bender, L. (1947). Childhood schizophrenia, clinical study of one hundred schizophrenic children. *American Journal of Orthopsychiatry, 17,* 40–56.

Benet, A.E., & Melman, A. (1995). The epidemiology of erectile dysfunction. *Urologic Clinics of North America, 22,* 699–709.

Benjamin, L.S. (1974). Structural analysis of social behavior. *Psychological Review, 81,* 392–425.

Benjamin, L.S. (1993). *Interpersonal diagnosis and treatment of personality disorders.* New York: Guilford.

Benjamin, L.S. (1996). *Interpersonal diagnosis and treatment of personality disorders,* 2nd ed. New York: Guilford.

Bennett, F.C., & Sherman, R. (1983). Management of childhood "hyperactivity" by primary care physicians. *Journal of Developmental and Behavioral Pediatrics, 4,* 88–93.

Benson, D.F. (1992). Neuropsychiatric aspects of aphasia and related language impairments. In S.C. Yudofsky & R.E. Hales (Eds.), *Textbook of neuropsychiatry,* 2nd ed., pp. 311–327. Washington, DC: American Psychiatric Press.

Berenbaum, H., & Barch, D. (1995). The categorization of thought disorder. *Journal of Psycholinguistic Research, 24,* 349–376.

Berg, I. (1993). Aspects of school phobia. In C.G. Last (Ed.), *Anxiety across the lifespan: A developmental perspective,* pp. 78–93. New York: Springer.

Berkman, L.F., Seeman, T.E., Albert M., Blazer, D., Kahn, R., Mohs, R., Finch, C., Schneider, E., Cotman, C., McClearn, G., Nesselroade, J., Featherman, D., Garmezy, N., McKhann, G., Brim, G., Praeger, D., & Rowe, J. (1993). High, usual, and impaired functioning in community-dwelling older men and women: Findings from the MacArthur Foundation research network on successful aging. *Journal of Clinical Epidemiology, 46,* 1129–1140.

Berman, A.L., & Jobes, D.A. (1994). Treatment of the suicidal adolescent. In A.A. Leenaars, J.T. Maltsberger, & R.A. Neimeyer (Eds.), *Treatment of suicidal people,* pp. 89–100. Washington, DC: Taylor & Francis.

Bernlef, J. (1988). *Out of mind.* London: Faber.

Berliner, L. (1996). Community notification of sex offenders: A new tool or a false promise? *Journal of Interpersonal Violence, 11.* 294–296.

Bernstein, D.A., & Borkovec, T.D. (1973). *Progressive relaxation training: A manual for the helping professions.* Champaign, IL: Research Press.

Bernstein, D.P., Cohen, P., Velez, C.N., Schwab-Stone, M., Siever, L.J., & Shinsato, L. (1993). Prevalence and stability of the DSM-III-R personality disorders in a community-based survey of adolescents. *American Journal of Psychiatry, 150,* 1237–1243.

Bernstein, D.P., Useda, D., & Siever, L.J. (1995). Paranoid personality disorder. In W.J. Livesley (Ed.) *The DSM-IV personality disorders.* New York: Guilford, pp. 45–57.

Bernstein, E.M., & Putnam, F.W. (1986). Development, reliability, and validity of a dissociation scale. *Journal of Nervous & Mental Disease, 174,* 727–735.

Berrettini, W.H. (1993). The molecular genetics of bipolar disease. In J.J. Mann & D.J. Kupfer (Eds.), *Biology of depressive disorders, Part A: A systems perspective,* pp. 189–204. New York: Plenum.

Berrios, G.E. (1989). Obsessive-compulsive disorder: Its conceptual history in France during the 19th century. *Comprehensive Psychiatry, 30,* 283–295.

Berrios, G. (1990). Memory and the cognitive paradigm of dementia during the 19th century: A conceptual history. In R.M. Murray & T.H. Turner (Eds.), *Lectures on the history of psychiatry.* Oxford: Gaskell/Royal College of Psychiatrists.

Berrios, G.E. (1990). Alzheimer's disease: A conceptual history. *International Journal of Geriatric Psychiatry, 5,* 355–365.

Berrios, G.E. (1992). Research into the history of psychiatry. In C. Freeman & P. Tyrer (Eds.), *Research methods in psychiatry: A beginner's guide,* 2nd ed. London: Gaskell.

Berrios, G.E., & Hauser, R. (1988). The early development of Kraepelin's ideas on classification: A conceptual history. *Psychological Medicine, 18,* 813–821.

Berry, J.W., Poortinga, Y.H., Segall, M.H., & Dasen, P.R. (1992). *Cross-cultural psychology: Research and applications.* New York: Cambridge University Press.

Bertelson, A., Harvald, B., & Hauge, M. (1977). A Danish twin study of manic-depressive disorders. *British Journal of Psychiatry, 130,* 330–351.

Besharov, D.J. (1986). The misuse of foster care: When the desire to help children outruns the ability to improve parental functioning. *Family Law Quarterly, 20,* 213–231.

Besharov, D.J. (1988). How child abuse programs hurt poor children: The misuse of foster care. *Clearinghouse Review, 20,* 219–227.

Besharov, D.J. (1992). A balanced approach to reporting child abuse. *Child, Youth, and Family Services Quarterly, 15,* 5–7.

Besharov, D.J., & Laumann, L.A. (1996). Child abuse reporting: The need to shift priorities from more reports to better reports. In I. Garfinkel, J.L. Hochschild, & S.S. McLanahan (Eds.), *Social policies for children,* pp. 257–274. Washington, DC: Brookings Institution.

Bettelheim, B. (1967). *The empty fortress.* New York: Free Press.

Beumont, P.J.V., Garner, D.M., & Touyz, S.W. (1994). Diagnoses of eating or dieting disorders: What may we learn from past mistakes? *International Journal of Eating Disorders, 16,* 349–362.

Beutler, L.E., Crago, M., & Arizmendi, T.G. (1986). Therapist variables in psychotherapy process and outcome. In S.L. Garfield & A.E. Bergin (Eds.), *Handbook of psychotherapy and behavior change,* 3rd ed., pp. 257–310. New York: Wiley.

Beutler, L.E., Machado, P.P.P., & Neufeldt, S.A. (1994). Therapist variables. In A.E. Bergin & S.L. Garfield, *Handbook of psychotherapy and behavior change,* 4th ed., pp. 229–269. New York: Wiley.

Bianchi, S. (1991). Family disruption and economic hardship: The short-run picture for children. *Current Population Reports* (Series P-70, No. 23). Washington, DC: U.S. Government Printing Office.

Bickel, H. (1980). Phenylketonuria: Past, present, future. *Journal of Inherited Metabolic Disease, 3,* 123–312.

Biederman, J., Baldessarini, R.J., Wright, V., Knee, D., & Harmatz, J.S. (1989). A double-blind placebo controlled study of desipramine in the treatment of ADD. I. Efficacy. *Journal of the American Academy of Child and Adolescent Psychiatry, 28,* 903–911.

Biederman, J., Rosenbaum, J.F., Chaloff, J., & Kagan, J. (1995). Behavioral inhibition as a risk factor. In J.S. March (Ed.), *Anxiety Disorders in Children and Adolescents,* pp. 61–81. New York: Guilford.

Biggins, C.A., Boyd, J.L., Harrop, F.M., Madeley, P., Mindham, R.H.S., Randall, J.I., & Spokes, E.G.S. (1992). A controlled, longitudinal study of dementia in Parkinson's disease. *Journal of Neurology, Neurosurgery, and Psychiatry, 55,* 566–571.

Biklen, D. (1992). Autism orthodoxy versus free speech: A reply to Cummins and Prior. *Harvard Educational Review, 62,* 242–256.

Billings, A.G., & Moos, R.H. (1982). Psychosocial theory and research on depression: An integrative framework and review. *Clinical Psychology Review, 2,* 213–237.

Billy, J.O.G., Tanfer, K., Grady, W.R., & Klepinger, D.H. (1993). The sexual behavior of men in the United States. *Family Planning Perspectives, 25,* 52–60.

Bingham, W.V.D., & Moore, B.V. (1924). *How to interview.* New York: Harper & Row.

Binswanger, L. (1963). *Being-in-the-world: Selected papers of Ludwig Binswanger.* New York: Basic Books.

Birtchnell, J. (1991). The measurement of dependence by questionnaire. *Journal of Personality Disorders, 5*, 281–295.

Black, D.W., Noyes, R., Goldstein, R.B., & Blum, N. (1992). A family study of obsessive-compulsive disorder. *Archives of General Psychiatry, 49*, 362–368.

Blackburn, R. (1988). On moral judgments and personality disorders: The myth of psychopathic personality revisited. *British Journal of Psychiatry, 153*, 505–512.

Blader, J.C., & Marshall, W.L. (1989). Is assessment of sexual arousal in rapists worthwhile? A critique of current methods and the development of a response compatibility approach. *Clinical Psychology Review, 9*, 569–587.

Blair, C.D., & Lanyon, R.I. (1981). Exhibitionism: Etiology and treatment. *Psychological Bulletin, 89*, 439–463.

Blanchard, E.B. (Ed.) (1992). Special issue on behavioral medicine. *Journal of Consulting and Clinical Psychology, 60*.

Blanchard, E.B. (1994). Behavioral medicine and health psychology. In A.E. Bergin & S.L. Garfield (Eds.), *Handbook of psychotherapy and behavior change*, 4th ed., pp. 701–733. New York: Wiley.

Blanchard, R. (1989). The classification and labeling of nonhomosexual gender dysphorias. *Archives of Sexual Behavior, 18*, 315–334.

Blashfield, R.K. (1973). An evaluation of the DSM-II classification of schizophrenia as a nomenclature. *Journal of Abnormal Psychology, 82*, 382–389.

Blashfield, R.K. (1982). Feighner et al., invisible colleges, and the Matthew Effect. *Schizophrenia Bulletin, 8*, 1–6.

Blashfield, R.K. (1984). *The classification of psychopathology: Neo-Kraepelinian and quantitative approaches.* New York: Plenum.

Blashfield, R.K., & Draguns, J.G. (1976). Evaluative criteria for psychiatric classification. *Journal of Abnormal Psychology, 85*, 140–150.

Blashfield, R.K., & McElroy, R.A. (1987). The 1985 literature on the personality disorders. *Comprehensive Psychiatry, 28*, 536–546.

Blashfield, R.K., & McElroy, R.A. (1989). Ontology of personality disorder categories. *Psychiatric Annals, 19*, 126–131.

Blashfield, R.K., Sprock, J., Haymaker, D., & Hodgin, J. (1989). The family resemblance hypothesis applied to psychiatric classification. *Journal of Nervous and Mental Disease, 177*, 492–497.

Blatt, S.J., & Zuroff, D.C. (1992). Interpersonal relatedness and self-definition: Two prototypes for depression. *Clinical Psychology Review, 12*, 527–562.

Blazer, D., Hughes, D., & George, L.K. (1987). Stressful life events and the onset of a generalized anxiety syndrome. *American Journal of Psychiatry, 144*, 1178–1183.

Blehar, M.C., & Rosenthal, N.E. (1989). Seasonal affective disorders and phototherapy: Report of a National Institute of Mental Health-sponsored workshop. *Archives of General Psychiatry, 46*, 469–474.

Bleuler, M. (1978). *The schizophrenic disorders: Long-term patient and family studies.* New Haven, CT: Yale University Press.

Bliss, E.L. (1986). *Multiple personality, allied disorders, and hypnosis.* New York: Oxford University Press.

Bloch, S., & Crouch, E. (1987). *Therapeutic factors in group psychotherapy.* New York: Oxford University Press.

Block, J.H., Block, J., & Gjerde, P.F. (1986). The personality of children prior to divorce: A prospective study. *Child Development, 57*, 827–840.

Blum, K., & Payne, J.E. (1991). *Alcohol and the addictive brain: New hope for alcoholics from biogenetic research.* New York: Free Press.

Blume, S.B. (1991). Women, alcohol, and drugs. In N.S. Miller (Ed.), *Comprehensive handbook of drug and alcohol addiction*, pp. 147–177. New York: Marcel Dekker.

Blumenthal, S., Matthews, K., & Weiss, S. (Eds.), *New research frontiers in behavioral medicine: Proceedings of the National Conference.* Washington, DC: NIH Publications.

Blundell, J.E. (1995). The psychobiological approach to appetite and weight control. In K.D. Brownell & C.G. Fairburn (Eds.), *Eating disorders and obesity: A comprehensive handbook*, pp. 13–20. New York: Guilford.

Bodlund, O., & Kullgren, G. (1996). Transsexualism—General outcome and prognostic factors: A five-year follow-up study of nineteen transsexuals in the process of changing sex. *Archives of Sexual Behavior, 25*, 303–317.

Bolger, J.P., Carpenter, B.C., & Strauss, M.E. (1994). Behavior and affect in Alzheimer's disease. *Clinics in Geriatric Medicine, 10*, 315–337.

Booth-Kewley, S., & Friedman, H.S. (1987). Psychological predictors of heart disease: A quantitative review. *Psychological Bulletin, 101*, 343–362.

Borduin, C.M., Mann, B.J., Cone, L.T., Henggeler, S.W., Fucci, B.R., Blaske, D.M., & Williams, R.A. (1995). Multisystemic treatment of serious juvenile offenders: Long-term prevention of criminality and violence. *Journal of Consulting and Clinical Psychology, 63*, 569–578.

Borkovec, T.D. (1994). The nature, functions, and origins of worry. In G.C.L. Davey & F. Tallis (Eds.), *Worrying: Perspectives in theory, assessment and treatment*, pp. 5–33. London: Wiley.

Borkovec, T.D., & Costello, E. (1993). Efficacy of applied relaxation and cognitive-behavioral therapy in the treatment of generalized anxiety disorder. *Journal of Consulting and Clinical Psychology, 61*, 611–619.

Borkovec, T.D., & Inz, J. (1990). The nature of worry in generalized anxiety disorder: A predominance of thought activity. *Behavior Research and Therapy, 28*, 153–158.

Borkovec, T.D., Shadick, R., & Hopkins, M. (1990). The nature of normal versus pathological worry. In R. Rapee & D.H. Barlow (Eds.), *Chronic anxiety and generalized anxiety disorder.* New York: Guilford.

Bornstein, R.F. (1993). *The dependent personality.* New York: Guilford.

Bornstein, R.F. (1996). Dependency. In C.G. Costello (Ed.), *Personality characteristics of the personality disordered*, pp. 120–145. New York: Wiley-Interscience.

Bornstein, R.F., Klein, D.N., Mallon, J.C., & Slater, J.F. (1988). Schizotypal personality disorder in an outpatient population: Incidence and clinical characteristics. *Journal of Clinical Psychology, 44*, 322–325.

Børup, C., Kaiser, A., & Jensen, E. (1992). Long-term Antabuse treatment: Tolerance and reasons for withdrawal. *Acta Psychiatrica Scandinavica, 86*, 47–49.

Boss, M. (1963). *Daseinsanalysis and psychoanalysis.* New York: Basic Books.

Bower, G.H. (1990). Awareness, the unconscious, and repression: An experimental psychologist's perspective. In J.L. Singer (Ed.), *Repression and dissociation*, pp. 209–232. Chicago: University of Chicago Press.

Bowers, K.S., & Meichenbaum, D. (Eds.) (1984). *The unconscious reconsidered.* New York: Wiley.

Bowlby, J. (1969). *Attachment.* New York: Basic Books.

Bowlby, J. (1973). *Separation: Anxiety and anger.* New York: Basic Books.

Bowlby, J. (1979). *The making and breaking of affectional bonds.* London: Tavistock Publications.

Bowlby, J. (1980). *Loss: Sadness and depression.* New York: Basic Books.

Bowlby, J. (1982). Attachment and loss: Retrospect and prospect. *American Journal of Orthopsychiatry, 52*, 664–678.

Boyer, W.F. (1992). Potential indications for the selective serotonin reuptake inhibitors. *International Clinical Psychopharmacology, 6*, suppl. 5, 5–12.

Bradbury, T.N., & Fincham, F.D. (1990). Attributions in marriage: Review and critique. *Psychological Bulletin, 107*, 3–33.

Bradbury, T.N., & Miller, G.A. (1985). Season of birth in schizophrenia: A review of evidence, methodology, and etiology. *Psychological Bulletin, 98*, 569–594.

Bradford, J. (1997). Medical interventions in sexual deviance. In D.R. Laws & W.T. O'Donohue (Eds.), *Handbook of sexual deviance: Theory and application.* New York: Guilford.

Bradford, J.M.W., Bloomberg, B.A., & Bourget, D. (1988). The heterogeneity/homogeneity of pedophilia. *Psychiatric Journal of the University of Ottawa, 13*, 217–226.

Bradford, J.M.W., Boulet, J., & Pawlak, A. (1992). The paraphilias: A multiplicity of deviant behaviours. *Canadian Journal of Psychiatry, 37*, 104–107.

Bradford, J.M.W., & Pawlak, A. (1993). Double-blind placebo cross-over study of cyproterone acetate in the treatment of paraphilias. *Archives of Sexual Behavior, 22*, 383–402.

Bradley, C. (1937). The behavior of children receiving benzedrine. *American Journal of Psychiatry, 94*, 577–585.

Brandon, T.H., Wetter, D.W., & Baker, T.B. (1996). Affect, expectancies, urges, and smoking: Do they conform to models of drug motivation and relapse? *Experimental and Clinical Psychopharmacology, 4*, 29–36.

Braun, B.G. (1989). Psychotherapy of the survivor of incest with a dissociative disorder. *Psychiatric Clinics of North America, 12*, 307–324.

Braun, D.L., Sunday, S.R., & Halmi, K.A. (1994). Psychiatric comorbidity in patients with eating disorders. *Psychological Medicine, 24*, 859–867.

Braun, P., Kochansky, G., Shapiro, R., et al. (1981). Overview: Deinstitutionalization of psychiatric patients: A critical review of outcome studies. *American Journal of Psychiatry, 138*, 736–749.

Brayne, C. (1993). Research and Alzheimer's disease: An epidemiological perspective. *Psychological Medicine, 23*, 287–296.

Brecher, E.M., & the editors of *Consumer Reports.* (1972). *Licit and illicit drugs.* Boston: Little, Brown.

Breggin, P.R. (1994). *Talking back to Prozac.* New York: St. Martin's Press.

Bregman, J.D., Dykens, E., Watson, M., Ort, S.I., & Leckman, J.F. (1987). Fragile-X syndrome: Variability of phenotypic expression. *Journal of the American Academy of Child and Adolescent Psychiatry, 26*, 463–471.

Breier, A., Buchanan, R.W., Irish, D.I., & Carpenter, W.T., Jr. (1993). Clozapine treatment of outpatients with schizophrenia: Outcome and long-term response patterns. *Hospital and Community Psychiatry, 44*, 1145–1149.

Breitner, J.C.S., Gatz, M., Bergem, A.L.M., Christian, J.C., Mortimer, J.A., McClearn, G.E., Heston, L.L., Welsh, K.A., Anthony, J.C., Folstein, M.F., & Radebaugh, T.S. (1993). Use of twin cohorts for research in Alzheimer's disease. *Neurology, 43*, 261–267.

Brenner, D.E., Kukull, W.A., van Belle, G., Bowen, J.D., McCormick, W.C., Teri, L., & Larson, E.B. (1993). Relationship between cigarette smoking and Alzheimer's disease in a population-based case-control study. *Neurology, 43*, 293–300.

Brenner, M.H. (1973). *Mental illness and the economy.* Cambridge, MA: Harvard University Press.

Breslau, N., Davis, G.C., & Andreski, P. (1995). Risk factors for PTSD-related traumatic events: A prospective analysis. *American Journal of Psychiatry, 152*, 529–535.

Breslau, N., Davis, G.C., Andreski, P., and Peterson, E. (1991). Traumatic events and posttraumatic stress disorder in an urban population of young adults. *Archives of General Psychiatry, 48*, 216–222.

Bretherton, I. (1985). Attachment theory: Retrospect and prospect. In I. Bretherton & E. Waters (Eds.), *Growing points in attachment theory and research. Monographs of the Society for Research in Child Development, 56*, 1–14.

Bretherton, I. (1992). The origins of attachment theory: John Bowlby and Mary Ainsworth. *Developmental Psychology, 28*, 759–775.

Brett, E.A., Spitzer, R.L., & Williams, J.B.W. (1988).

DSM-III-R criteria for posttraumatic stress disorder. *American Journal of Psychiatry, 145,* 1232–1235.

Brewer, C. (1992). Controlled trials of Antabuse in alcoholism: The importance of supervision and adequate dosage. *Acta Psychiatrica Scandinavica, 86,* 51–58.

Brewerton, T.D., Lydiard, R.B., Herzog, D.B., Brotman, A.W., O'Neil, P.M., & Ballenger, J. (1995). Comorbidity of Axis I psychiatric disorders in bulimia nervosa. *Journal of Clinical Psychiatry, 56,* 77–80.

Brewin, C.R. (1985). Depression and causal attributions: What is their relation? *Psychological Bulletin, 98,* 297–309.

Brewin, C.R., Andrews, B., & Gotlib, I.H. (1993). Psychopathology and early experience: A reappraisal of retrospective reports. *Psychological Bulletin, 113,* 82–98.

Brewin, C.R., MacCarthy, B., Duda, K., et al. (1991). Attributions and expressed emotion in the relatives of patients with schizophrenia. *Journal of Abnormal Psychology, 100,* 546–554.

Bridges, R.N., Goldberg, D.P. (1985). Somatic presentation of DSM-III psychiatric disorders in primary care. *Journal of Psychosomatic Research, 29,* 563–569.

British Medical Research Council (1965). Clinical trial of the treatment of depressive illness. *British Medical Journal, 1,* 881–886.

Brody, E.M. (1989). The family at risk. In E. Light & B.D. Lebowitz (Eds.), *Alzheimer's disease treatment and family stress: Directions for research.* U.S. Department of Health and Human Services, DHHS Publication No. (ADM) 89-1569, pp. 2–49.

Brody, E.M., Saperstein, A.R., & Lawton, M.P. (1989). A multi-service respite program for caregivers of Alzheimer's patients. *Journal of Gerontological Social Work, 14,* 41–75.

Brom, D., Kleber, R.J., & Defares, P.B. (1989). Brief psychotherapy for posttraumatic stress disorders. *Journal of Consulting and Clinical Psychology, 57,* 607–612.

Bromley, D.B. (1990). *Behavioral gerontology: Central issues in the psychology of ageing.* New York: Wiley.

Bronfenbrenner, U. (1979). *The ecology of human development.* Cambridge, MA: Harvard University Press.

Brown, G.W. (1993). Life events and affective disorder: Replications and limitations. *Psychosomatic Medicine, 55,* 248–259.

Brown, G.W., Bifulco, A., & Andrews, B. (1990). Self-esteem and depression. III. Aetiological issues. *Social Psychiatry and Psychiatric Epidemiology, 25,* 235–243.

Brown, G.W., Bifulco, A., & Harris, T.O. (1987). Life events, vulnerability and onset of depression: Some refinements. *British Journal of Psychiatry, 150,* 30–42.

Brown, G.W., Birley, J.L.T., & Wing, J.K. (1972). Influence of family life on the course of schizophrenic disorders: A replication. *British Journal of Psychiatry, 121,* 241–258.

Brown, G.W., & Harris, T.O. (1978). *Social origins of depression: A study of psychiatric disorder in women.* London: Tavistock.

Brown, G.W., & Harris, T.O. (1993). Aetiology of anxiety and depressive disorders in an inner-city population. 1. Early adversity. *Psychological Medicine, 23,* 143–154.

Brown, L.S. (1992). A feminist critique of the personality disorders. In L.S. Brown & M. Ballou (Eds.), *Personality and psychopathology: Feminist reappraisals.* New York: Guilford.

Brown, P. (1994). Toward a psychobiological model of dissociation and post-traumatic stress disorder. In S.J. Lynn & J.W. Rhue (Eds.), *Dissociation: Clinical and theoretical perspectives,* pp. 94–122. New York: Guilford.

Brown, R. (1990). Limitations on expert testimony on the battered women syndrome in homicide cases: The return of the ultimate issue rule. *Arizona Law Review, 32,* 665–689.

Brown, S.A. (1993). Drug effect expectancies and addictive behavior change. *Experimental and Clinical Psychopharmacology, 1,* 55–67.

Brown, S.A., Goldman, M.S., Inn, A., & Anderson, L. (1980). Expectations of reinforcement from alcohol: Their domain and relation to drinking patterns. *Journal of Consulting and Clinical Psychology, 48,* 419–426.

Brown, T.A. (1996). Validity of the DSM-III-R and DSM-IV classification systems for anxiety disorders. In Ronald M. Rapee (Ed.), *Current controversies in the anxiety disorders,* pp. 21–45. New York: Guilford.

Brown, T.A., & Barlow, D.H. (1992). Comorbidity among anxiety disorders: Implications for treatment and DSM-IV. *Journal of Consulting and Clinical Psychology, 60,* 835–844.

Brown, T.A., Barlow, D.H., & Liebowitz, M.R. (1994). The empirical basis of generalized anxiety disorder. *American Journal of Psychiatry, 151,* 1272–1280.

Brown, W.A. (1990). Is light treatment a placebo? *Psychopharmacology Bulletin, 26,* 527–530.

Brownell, K.D. (1995). Definition and classification of obesity. In K.D. Brownell & C.G. Fairburn (Eds.), *Eating disorders and obesity: A comprehensive handbook,* pp. 386–390. New York: Guilford.

Brownell, K.D., & Fairburn, C.G. (Eds.) (1995). *Eating disorders and obesity: A comprehensive handbook.* New York: Guilford.

Brownell, K.D., Marlatt, G.A., Lichtenstein, E., & Wilson, G.T. (1986). Understanding and preventing relapse. *American Psychologist, 41,* 765–782.

Brownell, K.D., & Rodin, J. (1994). The dieting maelstrom: Is it possible and advisable to lose weight? *American Psychologist, 49,* 781–791.

Bruch, H. (1962). Perceptual and conceptual disturbances in anorexia nervosa. *Canadian Journal of Psychiatry, 26,* 187–194.

Bruch, H. (1982). Anorexia nervosa: Therapy and theory. *American Journal of Psychiatry, 132,* 1531–1538.

Buck, R. (1984). *The communication of emotion.* New York: Guilford.

Bryson, S.E. (1996). Epidemiology of autism. *Journal of Autism and Developmental Disorders, 26,* 165–167.

Buchanan, R.W. (1995). Clozapine: Efficacy and safety. *Schizophrenia Bulletin, 21,* 579–591.

Buchsbaum, M.S., Someya, T., Teng, C.Y., Abel, L., et al. (1996). PET and MRI of the thalamus in never-medicated patients with schizophrenia. *American Journal of Psychiatry, 153,* 191–199.

Bulbena, A., & Berrios, G.E. (1986). Pseudodementia: Facts and figures. *British Journal of Psychiatry, 148,* 87–94.

Bulbena, A. & Berrios, G.E. (1991). Cognitive function in the affective disorders: A prospective study. *Psychopathology, 26,* 6–12.

Bullough, V.L. (1976). *Sexual variance in society and history.* New York: Wiley.

Bumpass, L., (1984). Children and marital disruption: A replication and update. *Demography, 21,* 71–82.

Bunney, W.E., & Davis, J.M. (1965). Norepinephrine in depressed reactions. *Archives of General Psychiatry, 13,* 483–494.

Burke, B.L., & McGee, D.P. (1990). Sports deficit disorder. *Pediatrics, 85,* 1118.

Burke, C. (1995). Foreword. In L. Nadel & D. Rosenthal (Eds.), *Down syndrome: Living and learning in the community,* p. ix. New York: Wiley.

Burlingame, M. (1994). *The inner world of Abraham Lincoln.* Urbana and Chicago: University of Illinois Press.

Busby, W.J., Campbell, A.J., Borrie, M.J., & Spears, G.F.S. (1988). Alcohol use in a community-based sample of subjects aged 70 years and older. *Journal of the American Geriatrics Society, 36,* 301–305.

Buss, A. (1991). The EAS theory of temperament. In J. Strelau & A. Angleitner (Eds.), *Explorations in temperament.* New York: Plenum.

Buss, A.H., & Plomin, R. (1986). The EAS approach to temperament. In R. Plomin & J. Dunn (Eds.), *The study of temperament: Changes, continuities, and challenges.* Hillsdale, NJ: Erlbaum.

Buss, D.M. (1992). Mate preference mechanisms: Consequences for partner choice and intrasexual competition. In J.H. Barkow, L. Cosmides, & J. Tooby (Eds.), *The adapted mind: Evolutionary psychology and the generation of culture.* New York: Oxford University Press.

Butcher, J.N., Graham, J.R., & Ben-Porath, Y.S. (1995). Methodological problems and issues in MMPI, MMPI-2, and MMPI-A research. *Psychological Assessment, 7,* 320–329.

Butler, L.D., & Nolen-Hoeksema, S. (1994). Gender differences in responses to depressed mood in a college sample. *Sex Roles, 30,* 331–346.

Butters, N. (1992). Memory remembered: 1970–1991. *Archives of Clinical Neuropsychology, 7,* 285–295.

Buydens-Branchey, L., Branchey, M.H., Noumair, D., & Lieber, C.S. (1989). Age of alcoholism onset. II. Relationship to susceptibility to serotonin precursor availability. *Archives of General Psychiatry, 46,* 231–236.

Byerley, W.F., Reimherr, F.W., Wood, D.R., & Grosser, B.I. (1988). Fluoxetine, a selective serotonin uptake inhibitor, for the treatment of outpatients with major depression. *Journal of Clinical Psychopharmacology, 8,* 112–115.

Cacioppo, J.T., & Bernston, G.G. (1992). Social psychological contributions to the decade of the brain: Doctrine of multilevel analysis. *American Psychologist, 47,* 1019–1028.

Cado, S., & Leitenberg, H. (1990). Guilt reactions to sexual fantasies during intercourse. *Archives of Sexual Behavior, 19,* 49–63.

Cadoret, R.J., Yates, W.R., Troughton, E., Woodworth, G., & Stewart, M.A. (1995). Genetic-environmental interaction in the genesis of aggressivity and conduct disorders. *Archives of General Psychiatry, 52,* 916–924.

Cairns, R.B., & Green, J.A. (1979). How to assess personality and social patterns: Observations or ratings? In R.B. Cairns (Ed.), *The analysis of social interactions: Methods, issues, and illustrations.* Hillsdale, NJ: Erlbaum.

Caldwell, C., & Gottesman, I.I. (1992). Schizophrenia—A high-risk factor for suicide: Clues to risk reduction. *Suicide and Life-Threatening Behavior, 2,* 479–493.

Caldwell-Smith, G. (1990). First-person account: A mother's view. *Schizophrenia Bulletin, 16,* 687–690.

Callahan, L.A., Steadman, H.J., McGreevy, M.A., & Robbins, P.C. (1991). The volume and characteristics of insanity defense pleas: An eight-state study. *Bulletin of the American Academy of Psychiatry and the Law, 19,* 331–338.

Calvocoressi, L., Lewis, B., Harris, M., Trufan, S.J., Goodman, W.K., McDougle, C.J., & Price, L.H. (1995). Family accommodation in obsessive-compulsive disorder. *American Journal of Psychiatry, 152,* 441–443.

Cameron, H.M., & McGoogan, E. (1981). A prospective study of 1152 hospital autopsies. II. Analysis of inaccuracies in clinical diagnoses and their significance. *Journal of Pathology, 133,* 285–300.

Cameron, N., & Rychlak, J.F. (1985). *Personality development and psychopathology: A dynamic approach.* Boston: Houghton Mifflin.

Cameron, O.G., & Hill, E.M. (1989). Women and anxiety. *Psychiatric Clinics of North America, 12,* 175–186.

Campbell, E. (1990). The psychopath and the definition of "mental disease of defect" under the Model Penal Code test of insanity: A question of psychology or a question of law? *Nebraska Law Review, 69,* 190–229.

Campbell, M., Green, W.H., & Deutsch, S.I. (1985). *Child and adolescent psychopharmacology.* Beverly Hills, CA: Sage.

Campbell, M., Perry, R., Polonsky, B.B., Deutsch, S.I., Palij, M., & Lukashok, D. (1986). An open study of fenfluramine in hospitalized young autistic children. *Journal of Autism and Developmental Disorders, 16,* 494–505.

Campos, J.J., Barrett, K.C., Lamb, M.E., Goldsmith, H.H., & Sternberg, C. (1983). Socioemotional development. In M.M. Haith & J. Campos (Eds.), *Infancy and developmental psychobiology,* Vol. 2, *Mussen's handbook of child psychology.* New York: Wiley.

Canino, G.L., Bird, H.R., et al. (1987). Prevalence of specific psychiatric disorders in Puerto Rico. *Archives of General Psychiatry, 44,* 727–735.

Cannon, T.D., Mednick, S.A., & Parnas, J. (1990). Antecedents of predominantly negative and predominantly positive-symptom schizophrenia in a high-risk population. *Archives of General Psychiatry, 47,* 622–632.

Cannon, T.D., Mednick, S.A., Parnas, J., Schulsinger, F., Praestholm, J., & Vestergaard, A. (1993). Developmental brain abnormalities in the offspring of schizophrenic mothers. I. Contributions of genetic and perinatal factors. *Archives of General Psychiatry, 50,* 551–564.

Cannon, W.B. (1935). Stress and strains of homeostasis. *American Journal of Medical Science, 189,* 1–14.

Cantwell, D.P. (1988). DSM-III studies. In M. Rutter, A.H. Tuma, & I.S. Lann (Eds.), *Assessment and diagnosis in child psychopathology,* pp. 3–36. New York: Guilford.

Cantwell, D.P., Baker, L., & Rutter, M. (1979). Families of autistic and dysphasic children. I. Family life and interactions patterns. *Archives of General Psychiatry, 36,* 682–687.

Caplan, G. (1964). *Principles of preventive psychiatry.* New York: Basic Books.

Caplan, P.J. (1995). *They say you're crazy: How the world's most powerful psychiatrists decide who's normal.* Reading: MA: Addison-Wesley.

Capron, C., & Duyme, M. (1989). Assessment of effects of socioeconomic status on IQ in a full cross-fostering study. *Nature, 340,* 552–554.

Caracci, G., & Miller, N.S. (1991). Alcohol and drug addiction in the elderly. In N.S. Miller (Ed.), *Comprehensive handbook of drug and alcohol addiction,* pp. 179–191. New York: Marcel Dekker.

Carey, G., & Gottesman, I.I. (1978). Reliability and validity in binary ratings: Areas of common misunderstanding in diagnosis and symptom rating. *Archives of General Psychiatry, 35,* 1454–1459.

Carey, G., & Gottesman, I.I. (1981). Twin and family studies of anxiety, phobic, and obsessive disorders. In D.F. Klein & J.G. Rabkin (Eds.), *Anxiety: New research and changing concepts.* New York: Raven Press.

Carey, G., & Gottesman, I.I. (1996). Genetics and antisocial behavior: Substance versus sound bytes. *Politics and the Life Sciences,* March, 88–90.

Carlson, E.A., & Sroufe, A. (1995). Contribution of attachment theory to developmental psychopathology. In D. Cicchetti & D.J. Cohen (Eds.), *Developmental psychopathology,* vol. 1, pp. 581–617. New York: Wiley.

Carlsson, A. (1988). The current status of the dopamine hypothesis of schizophrenia. *Neuropsychopharmacology, 1,* 179–186.

Carlsson, A., & Lindqvist, M. (1963). Effect of chlorpromazine and haloperidol on the formation of 3-methoxytyramine and normetanephrine in mouse brain. *Acta Pharmacology, 20,* 140.

Carney, R.M., Freeland, K.E., Rich, M.W., & Jaffe, A.S. (1995). Depression as a risk factor for cardiac events in established coronary heart disease: A review of possible mechanisms. *Annals of Behavioral Medicine, 17,* 142–149.

Carpenter, B.D., Strauss, M.E., & Kennedy, J.S. (1995). Personal history of depression and its appearance in Alzheimer's disease. *International Journal of Geriatric Psychiatry, 10,* 669–678.

Carpenter, W.T., Conley, R.R., Buchanan, R.W., Breier, A., et al. (1995). Patient response and resource management: Another view of clozapine treatment of schizophrenia. *American Journal of Psychiatry, 152,* 827–832.

Carpenter, W.T., & Strauss, J.S. (1991). The prediction of outcome in schizophrenia. IV. Eleven-year follow-up of the Washington IPSS cohort. *Journal of Nervous and Mental Disease, 179,* 517–525.

Carr, E.G. (1977). The motivation of self-injurious behavior: A review of some hypotheses. *Psychological Bulletin, 84,* 800–816.

Carr. E.G. (1982). *How to teach sign language to developmentally disabled children.* Lawrence, KS: H & H Enterprises.

Carroll, M.A., Schneider, H.G., & Wesley, G.R. (1985). *Ethics in the practice of psychology.* Englewood Cliffs, NJ: Prentice Hall.

Casas, J.M. (1995). Counseling and psychotherapy with racial/ethnic minority groups in theory and practice. In B. Bongar & L.E. Beutler (Eds.), *Comprehensive handbook of psychotherapy,* pp. 311–335. New York: Oxford University Press.

Cash, T.F., & Henry, P.E. (1995). Women's body images: The results of a national survey in the U.S.A. *Sex Roles, 33,* 19–28.

Caspi, A., Elder, G.H., & Bem, D.J. (1988). Moving away from the world: Life-course patterns of shy children. *Developmental Psychology, 24,* 824–831.

Caspi, A., & Moffitt, T.E. (1995). The continuity of maladaptive behavior: From description to understanding in the study of antisocial behavior. In D. Cicchetti & D.J. Cohen (Eds.), *Developmental psychopathology,* vol. 1, pp. 472–511. New York: Wiley.

Cassidy, J. (1988). Child-mother attachment and the self in six-year-olds. *Child Development, 59,* 121–134.

Castle, D.J., Abel, K., Takei, N., & Murray, R.M. (1995). Gender differences in schizophrenia: Hormonal effect or subtypes? *Schizophrenia Bulletin, 21,* 1–12.

Cattarin, J.A., & Thompson, J.K. (1994). A three-year longitudinal study of body image, eating disturbance, and general psychological functioning in adolescent females. *Eating Disorders: The Journal of Treatment and Prevention, 2,* 114–125.

Cavanaugh, J.C. (1993). *Adult development and aging,* 2nd ed. Pacific Grove, CA: Brooks/Cole.

Chalfonte, B.L., & Johnson, M.K. (1996). Feature memory and binding in young and older adults. *Memory and Cognition, 24,* 403–417.

Chalkey, A.J., & Powell, G.E. (1983). The clinical description of forty-eight cases of sexual fetishism. *British Journal of Psychiatry, 142,* 292–295.

Chambless, D.L., Cherney, J., Caputo, G.C., & Rheinstein, B.J. (1987). Anxiety disorders and alcoholism: A study with inpatient alcoholics. *Journal of Anxiety Disorders, 1,* 29–40.

Chambless, D.L., & Gillis, M.M. (1993). Cognitive therapy of anxiety disorders. *Journal of Consulting and Clinical Psychology, 61,* 248–260.

Chambless, D.L., Sanderson, W.C., Shoham, V., et al. (1996). An update on empirically validated therapies. *Clinical Psychologist, 49,* 5–18.

Chappel, J.N. (1992). Effective use of Alcoholics Anonymous and Narcotics Anonymous in treating patients. *Psychiatric Annals, 22,* 409–418.

Chappel, J.N. (1993). Long-term recovery from alcoholism. *Psychiatric Clinics of North America, 16,* 177–187.

Charney, D.S., Delgado, P.L., Price, L.H. & Heninger, G.R. (1991). The receptor sensitivity hypothesis of antidepressant action: A review of antidepressant effects on serotonin function. In S. Brown and H.M. van Praag (Eds). *The role of serotonin in psychiatric disorders.* New York: Brunner/Mazel, pp. 27–56.

Charvat, J., Dell, P.P., Golkow, P., & Folkow, B. (1964). Mental factors in cardiovascular disease. *Cardiology, 44,* 124–141.

Chassin, L. (1984). Adolescent substance use and abuse. In P. Karoly & J.J. Steffen (Eds.), *Adolescent behavior disorders: Foundations and contemporary concerns* [*Advances in Child Behavioral Analysis and Therapy* (vol. 3)]. pp. 99–152.

Chassin, L., Pillow, D.R., Curran, P.J., Molina, B.S.G., & Barrera, M., Jr. (1993). Relation of parental

alcoholism to early adolescent substance use: A test of three mediating mechanisms. *Journal of Abnormal Psychology, 102,* 3–19.

Checkley, S. (1992). Neuroendocrine mechanisms and the precipitation of depression by life events. *British Journal of Psychiatry, 160* (suppl. 15). 7–17.

Chen, C.S. (1972). A further note on studies of acquired behavioral tolerance to alcohol. *Psychopharmacologia, 27,* 265–274.

Cherlin, A.J. (1991). *Marriage, divorce, remarriage,* 2nd ed. Cambridge, MA: Harvard University Press.

Cherlin, A.J. (1992). *Marriage, divorce, remarriage,* 2nd ed. Cambridge, MA: Harvard University Press.

Cherlin, A.J. (1996). *Public and private families.* New York: McGraw-Hill.

Cherlin, A.J., Furstenberg, F.F., Chase-Lansdale, P.L., Kiernan, K.E., Robins, P.K., Morrison, D.R., & Teitler, J.O. (1991). Longitudinal studies of effects of divorce on children in Great Britain and the United States. *Science, 252,* 1386–1389.

Chess, S., & Thomas, A. (1984). *Origins and evolution of behavior disorders.* New York: Bruner-Mazel.

Chesselet, M., & Delfs, J.M. (1996). Basal ganglia and movement disorders: An update. *Trends in Neurosciences, 19,* 417–423.

Christensen, A., & Jacobson, N.S. (1994). Who (or what) can do psychotherapy: The status and challenge of nonprofessional therapies. *Psychological Science, 5,* 8–14.

Christiansen, B.A., Smith, G.T., Roehling, P.V., & Goldman, M.S. (1989). Using alcohol expectancies to predict adolescent drinking behavior after one year. *Journal of Consulting and Clinical Psychology, 57,* 93–99.

Ciarnello, R.D., Aimi, J., Dean, R.R., Morilak, D.A., Porteus, M.H., & Cicchetti, D. (1995). Fundamentals of molecular neurobiology. In D. Cicchetti & D. Cohen (Eds.), *Developmental psychopathology* (pp. 109–160). New York: Wiley.

Cicchetti, D., & Beegly, M. (1990). *Children with Down syndrome: A developmental perspective.* New York: Cambridge University Press.

Cicchetti, D., & Cohen, D. (Eds.) (1995). *Developmental psychopathology,* Vols. 1 & 2. New York: Wiley.

Ciompi, L. (1980). Catamnestic long-term study on the course of life and aging of schizophrenics. *Schizophrenia Bulletin, 6,* 606–618.

Cipparone, R.C. (1987). The defense of battered women who kill. *University of Pennsylvania Law Review, 135,* 427–452.

Clark, D.B., & Sayette, M.A. (1993). Anxiety and the development of alcoholism: Clinical and scientific issues. *American Journal on Addictions, 2,* 59–76.

Clark, D.M. (1986a). A cognitive approach to panic. *Behaviour Research and Therapy, 24,* 461–470.

Clark, D.M. (1986b). Cognitive therapy for anxiety. *Behavioral Psychotherapy, 14,* 283–294.

Clark, D.M., & Ehlers, A. (1993). An overview of the cognitive theory and treatment of panic disorder. *Applied and Preventive Psychology, 2,* 131–139.

Clark, D.M., Salkovskis, P.M., Hackmann, A., Middleton, H., Anastasiades, P., & Gelder, M. (1994). A comparison of cognitive therapy, applied relaxation and imipramine in the treatment of panic disorder. *British Journal of Psychiatry, 164,* 759–769.

Clark, L.A., McEwen, J.L., Collard, L.M., & Hickok, L.G. (1993). Symptoms and traits of personality disorder: Two new methods for their assessment. *Psychological Assessment, 5,* 81–91.

Clark, L.A., & Watson, D. (1991). Tripartite model of anxiety and depression: Psychometric evidence and taxonomic implications. *Journal of Abnormal Psychology, 100,* 316–336.

Clark, L.A., Watson, D., & Reynolds, S. (1995). Diagnosis and classification of psychopathology: Challenges to the current system and future directions. *Annual Review of Psychology, 46,* 121–153.

Clarke, J.M. (1994). Neuroanatomy: Brain structure

and function. In D.W. Zaidel (Ed.), *Neuropsychology. Handbook of perception and cognition*, 2nd ed., pp. 29–52. San Diego, CA: Academic Press.

Clarke, J.W. (1990). *On being mad or merely angry*. Princeton, NJ: Princeton University Press.

Clarke-Stewart, A., Perlmutter, M., & Friedman, S. (1988). *Lifelong human development*. New York: Wiley.

Cleckley, H. (1976). *The mask of sanity*, 5th ed. St. Louis: Mosby.

Clementz, B.A., & Iacono, W.G. (1993). Nosology and diagnosis. In A.S. Bellack & M. Hersen (Eds.), *Psychopathology in adulthood*, pp. 3–20. Boston: Allyn & Bacon.

Clementz, B.A., Grove, W.M., Iacono, W.G., & Sweeney, J.A. (1992). Smooth-pursuit eye movement dysfunction and liability for schizophrenia: Implications for genetic modeling. *Journal of Abnormal Psychology*, 101, 117–129.

Clementz, B.A., & Sweeney, J.A. (1990). Is eye movement dysfunction a biological marker for schizophrenia? A methodological review. *Psychological Bulletin*, 108, 77–92.

Cloninger, C.R. (1987). Neurogenetic adaptive mechanisms in alcoholism. *Science*, 236, 410–416.

Cloninger, C.R., & Gottesman, I.I. (1987). Genetic and environmental factors in antisocial behavior disorders. In S.A. Mednick, T.E. Moffitt, & S.A. Stack (Eds.), *The causes of crime: New biological approaches*, pp. 92–109. Cambridge: Cambridge University Press.

Cloninger, C.R., Sigvardsson, S., Bohman, M., & von Knorring, A.L. (1982). Predisposition to petty criminality in Swedish adoptees. II. Cross-fostering analysis of gene-environment interaction. *Archives of General Psychiatry*, 39, 1242–1249.

Cohen, C.I. (1993). Poverty and the course of schizophrenia: Implications for research and policy. *Hospital and Community Psychiatry*, 44, 951–958.

Cohen, S. (1988). *The chemical brain: The neurochemistry of addictive disorders*. Irvine, CA: CareInstitute.

Cohen, S., Kaplan, J.R., Cunnick, J.E., Manuck, S.B., & Rabin, B.S. (1992). Chronic social stress, affiliation, and cellular immune response in nonhuman primates. *Psychological Science*, 3, 301–304.

Cohen, S., & Williamson. G.M. (1991). Stress and infectious disease in humans. *Psychological Bulletin*, 109, 5–24.

Cohen, S., & Wills, T.A. (1985). Stress, social support, and the buffering process. *Psychological Bulletin*, 98, 310–357.

Cohler, B.J., & Nakamura, J.E. (1996). In J. Sadavoy, L.W. Lazarus, L.F. Jarvik, & G.T. Grossberg (Eds.), *Comprehensive review of geriatric psychiatry—II*, pp. 153–194. Washington, DC: American Psychiatric Press.

Coie, J., & Kupersmidt, J., (1983). A behavioral analysis of emerging social status in boys' groups. *Child Development*, 54, 1400–1416.

Colby, K.M. (1975). *Artificial paranoia: A computer simulation of paranoid processes*. New York: Pergamon.

Cole, M. (1985). Sex therapy—A critical appraisal. *British Journal of Psychiatry*, 147, 337–351.

Cole, W. (1992). Incest perpetrators: Their assessment and treatment. *Psychiatric Clinics of North America*, 15, 689–701.

Coleman, P. (1993). Overview of substance abuse. *Primary Care: Clinics in Office Practice*, 20, 1–18.

Collaer, M.L., & Hines, M. (1995). Human behavioral sex differences: A role for gonadal hormones during early development. *Psychological Bulletin*, 118, 55–107.

Comfort, A. (1987). Deviation and variation. In G.D. Wilson (Ed.), *Variant sexuality: Research and theory*, pp. 1–20. London: Croom Helm.

Conger, J.J. (1956). Alcoholism: Theory, problem, and challenge. II. Reinforcement theory and the dynamics of alcoholism. *Quarterly Journal of Studies on Alcohol*, 17, 296–305.

Conners, C.K. (1980). Artificial colors and the diet of disruptive behavior: Current status of research. In R.M. Knights & D.J. Bakker (Eds.), *Treatment of hyperactive and learning disabled children*. Baltimore: University Park Press.

Consensus Conference on Electroconvulsive Therapy. (1985). *JAMA*, 254, 103–108.

Consumer Reports (1995, November). Mental health: Does therapy help? pp. 734–739.

Cook, D.R. (1985). Craftsman versus professional: Analysis of the controlled drinking controversy. *Journal of Studies on Alcohol*, 46, 433–442.

Cook, M., & Mineka, S. (1989). Observational conditioning of fear to fear-relevant versus fear-irrelevant stimuli in Rhesus monkeys. *Journal of Abnormal Psychology*, 98, 448–459.

Cook, M., & Mineka, S. (1991). Selective associations in the origins of phobic fears and their implications for behavior therapy. In P.R. Martin (Ed). *Handbook of behavior therapy and psychological science: An integrative approach*. New York: Pergamon. pp. 413–434.

Cook, W.L., Strachan, A.M., Goldstein, M.J., & Miklowitz, D.J. (1989). Expressed emotion and reciprocal affective relationships in families of disturbed adolescents. *Family Process*, 28, 337–348.

Coons, P. (1986). The prevalence of multiple personality disorder. *Newsletter of the International Society for the Study of Multiple Personality and Dissociation*, 4, 6–8.

Coons, P., & Milstein, V. (1988). Psychogenic amnesia: A clinical investigation of 25 consecutive cases. Unpublished data cited in D. Spiegel & E. Cardena (1991). Disintegrated experience: The dissociative disorders revisited. *Journal of Abnormal Psychology*, 100, 366–378.

Cooper, J.E., Kendell, R.E., Gurland, B.J., Sharpe, L., Copeland, J.R.M., & Simon, R. (1972). *Psychiatric diagnosis in New York and London*. London: Oxford University Press.

Cooper, M.H. (1994). Regulating tobacco: Can the FDA break America's smoking habit? *CQ Researcher*, 4, 843–858.

Cooper, P.J. (1995). Eating disorders and their relationship to mood and anxiety disorders. In K.D. Brownell & C.G. Fairburn (Eds.), *Eating disorders and obesity: A comprehensive handbook*, pp. 159–164. New York: Guilford.

Coovert, D.L., Kinder, B.N., & Thompson, J.K. (1989). The psychosexual aspects of anorexia nervosa and bulimia nervosa: A review of the literature. *Clinical Psychology Review*, 9, 169–180.

Copestake, P. (1993). Aluminum and Alzheimer's disease: An update. *Food and Chemical Toxicology*, 31, 670–683.

Cordova, J.V., Jacobson, N.S., Gottman, J.M., Rushe, R., & Cox, G. (1993). Negative reciprocity and communication in couples with a violent husband. *Journal of Abnormal Psychology*, 102, 559–564.

Cornblatt, B.A., & Kelip, J.G. (1994). Impaired attention, genetics, and the pathophysiology of schizophrenia. *Schizophrenia Bulletin*, 20, 31–46.

Cornblatt, B.A., Lenzenweger, M.F., Dworkin, R.H., & Erlenmeyer-Kimling, L. (1992). Childhood attentional dysfunctions predict social deficits in unaffected adults at risk for schizophrenia. *British Journal of Psychiatry*, 16 (suppl. 18) 59–64.

Corning, W.C. (1986). Bootstrapping toward a classification system. In T. Millon & G. Klerman (Eds.), *Contemporary directions in psychopathology: Toward the DSM-IV*, pp. 279–306. New York: Guilford.

Corse, C.D., Manuck, S.B., Cantwell, J.D., Giordani, B., & Matthews, K.A. (1982). Coronary-prone behavior pattern and cardiovascular response in persons with and without coronary heart disease. *Psychosomatic Medicine*, 44, 449–459.

Coryell, W., Endicott, J., Andreasen, N., & Keller, M. (1985). Bipolar I, bipolar II, and nonbipolar major depression among the relatives of affectively ill probands. *American Journal of Psychiatry*, 142, 817–821.

Coryell, W., & Winokur, G. (1992). Course and outcome. In E.S. Paykel (Ed.), *Handbook of affective disorders*, 2nd ed., pp. 89–110. New York: Guilford.

Coser, L.A. (1977). *Masters of sociological thought: Ideas in historical and social context*. San Diego: Harcourt Brace Jovanovich.

Costa, P.T., & McCrea, R.R. (1992). The five-factor model of personality and its relevance to personality disorders. *Journal of Personality Disorders*, 6, 343–359.

Costello, C.G. (1976). *Anxiety and depression: The adaptive emotions*. Montreal: McGill-Queen's University Press.

Costello, C.G. (1982). Fears and phobias in women: A community study. *Journal of Abnormal Psychology*, 91, 280–286.

Costello, C.G. (1992). Problems in recent tests of two cognitive theories of panic. *Behaviour Research and Therapy*, 30, 1–5.

Costello, C.G. (1993). Advantages of the symptom approach to schizophrenia. In C.G. Costello (Ed.), *Symptoms of schizophrenia*, pp. 1–26. New York: Wiley.

Cowan, C.P. & Cowan, P.A. (1992). *When partners become parents*. New York: Basic Books.

Coyne, J. (1976). Toward an interactional description of depression. *Psychiatry*, 39, 28–40.

Coyne, J. (1985). Ambiguity and controversy: An introduction. In J. Coyne (Ed.), *Essential papers on depression*. New York: New York University Press.

Coyne, J.C. (1992). Cognition in depression: A paradigm in crisis. *Psychological Inquiry*, 3, 232–235.

Coyne, J.C., Downey, G., & Boergers, J. (1993). Depression in families: A systems perspective. In D. Cichetti & S.L. Toth (Eds.), *Rochester Symposium on Developmental Psychopathology, Vol. 4, Developmental approaches to the affective disorders*. Rochester, NY: University of Rochester.

Coyne, J.C., & Gotlib, I.H. (1983). The role of cognition in depression: A critical appraisal. *Psychological Bulletin*, 94, 472–505.

Coyne, J.C., & Whiffen, V.E. (1995). Issues in personality as diathesis for depression: The case of sociotropy-dependency and autonomy-self-criticism. *Psychological Bulletin*, 118, 358–378.

Craddock, N., & McGuffin, P. (1993). Approaches to the genetics of affective disorders. *Annals of Medicine*, 317–322.

Cranston-Cuebas, M.A., & Barlow, D.H. (1990). Cognitive and affective contributions to sexual functioning. In J. Bancroft, D.M. Davis, & D. Weinstein (Eds.), *Annual review of sex research, Vol. 1, An integrative and interdisciplinary review*, pp. 119–161. Lake Mills, IA: Stoyles Graphic Services.

Cranston-Cuebas, M.A., Barlow, D.H., Mitchell, W., & Athanasiou, R. (1993). Differential effects of a misattribution manipulation on sexually functional and dysfunctional men. *Journal of Abnormal Psychology*, 102, 525–533.

Craske, M.G., Sanderson, W.C., & Barlow, D.H. (1987). The relationships among panic, fear, and avoidance. *Journal of Anxiety Disorders*, 1, 153–160.

Craske, M.G., Rapee, R.M., Jackel, L., & Barlow, D.H. (1989). Qualitative dimensions of worry in DSM-III-R generalized anxiety disorder subjects and nonanxious controls. *Behaviour Research and Therapy*, 27, 397–402.

Creese, I., Burt, D.R., & Snyder, S.H. (1976). Dopamine receptor binding predicts clinical and pharmacological potencies of antischizophrenic drugs. *Science*, 192, 481–483.

Crick, N.R., & Dodge, K.A. (1994). A review and reformulation of social information-processing mechanisms in children's social adjustment. *Psychological Bulletin*, 115, 74–101.

Critelli, J.W., & Neumann, K.F. (1984). The placebo: Conceptual analysis of a construct in transition. *American Psychologist*, 39, 32–39.

Crocker, J., & Major, B. (1989). Social stigma and self-esteem: The self-protective properties of stigma. *Psychological Review, 96,* 608–630.

Cronbach, L.J., & Meehl, P.E. (1955). Construct validity in psychological tests. *Psychological Bulletin, 52,* 281–302.

Crook, T., & Eliot, J. (1980). Parental death during childhood and adult depression: A critical review of the literature. *Psychological Bulletin, 87,* 252–259.

Cross-National Collaborative Panic Study. Second Phase Investigators. (1992). Drug treatment of panic disorder: Comparative efficacy of alprazolam, imipramine, and placebo. *British Journal of Psychiatry, 160,* 191–202.

Crossley, R., & McDonald, A. (1980). *Annie's coming out.* New York: Penguin.

Crow, T.J. (1980). Molecular pathology of schizophrenia: More than one disease process? *British Medical Journal, 280,* 66–68.

Crow, T.J. (1985). The two-syndrome concept: Origins and current status. *Schizophrenia Bulletin, 11,* 471–486.

Crowell, J.A., Waters, E., Kring, A., & Riso, L.P. (1993). The psychosocial etiologies of personality disorders: What is the answer like? *Journal of Personality Disorders,* suppl., 118–128.

Csikszentmihalyi, M. & Larson, R. *Being adolescent.* New York: Basic Books.

Cummings, E.M., & Davies, P. (1994). *Children and marital conflict.* New York: Guilford.

Cummings, J.L. (1992). Neuropsychiatric aspects of Alzheimer's disease and other dementing illnesses. In S.C. Yudofsky & R.E. Hales (Eds.), *Textbook of neuropsychiatry,* 2nd ed., pp. 605–620. Washington, DC: American Psychiatric Press.

Cummings, J.L. (1995). Dementia: The failing brain. *Lancet, 345,* 1481–1485.

Cutting, J. (1986). *The psychology of schizophrenia.* London: Churchill Livingstone.

Cutting, J., & McClelland, R. (1986). Psychiatric manifestations of organic illness. In P. Hill, R. Murray, & A. Thorley (Eds.), *Essentials of postgraduate psychiatry,* 2nd ed. pp. 461–493. London: Grune & Stratton.

Dackis, C.A., & Gold, M.S. (1991). Inpatient treatment of drug and alcohol addiction. In N.S. Miller (Ed.), *Comprehensive handbook of drug and alcohol addiction,* pp. 1233–1244. New York: Marcel Dekker.

Dadds, M.R., Schwartz, S., & Sanders, M.R. (1987). Marital discord and treatment outcome in behavioral treatment of child conduct disorders. *Journal of Consulting and Clinical Psychology, 55,* 396–403.

Danforth, J.S., Barkley, R.A., & Stokes, T.F. (1991). Observations of parent-child interactions with hyperactive children: Research and clinical implications. *Clinical Psychology Review, 11,* 703–727.

Daniel, D.G., Zigun, J.R., & Weinberger, D.R. (1994). Brain imaging in neuropsychiatry. In S.C. Yudofsky & R.E. Hales (Eds.), *Synopsis of neuropsychiatry,* pp. 143–156. Washington, DC: American Psychiatric Press.

Darkes, J., & Goldman, M.S. (1993). Expectancy challenge and drinking reduction: Experimental evidence for a mediational process. *Journal of Consulting and Clinical Psychology, 61,* 344–353.

Davey, G.C.L. (1989). UCS revaluation and conditioning models of acquired fears. *Behaviour Research and Therapy, 27,* 521–528.

Davey, G.C.L., de Jong, P.J., & Tallis, F. (1993). UCS inflation in the aetiology of a variety of anxiety disorders: Some case histories. *Behaviour Research and Therapy, 31,* 495–498.

Davidson, J., Kudler, H., Smith, R., Mahorney, S.L., Lipper, S., Hammett, E., Saunders, W.B., & Cavenar, J.O. (1990). Treatment of posttraumatic stress disorder with amitriptyline and placebo. *Archives of General Psychiatry, 47,* 259–266.

Davidson, J.M. (1989). Sexual emotions, hormones and behavior. *Advances* (Institute for the Advancement of Health), 6, 56–58.

Davidson, J.R., & Foa, E.B. (1991). Diagnostic issues in posttraumatic stress disorder: Considerations for the DSM-IV. *Journal of Abnormal Psychology, 100,* 346–355.

Davidson, J.R.T., Tupler, L.A., & Potts, N.L.S. (1994). Treatment of social phobia with benzodiazepines. *Journal of Clinical Psychiatry, 55* (suppl. 6), 28–32.

Davidson, J.R.T., & van der Kolk, B.A. (1996). The psychopharmacological treatment of posttraumatic stress disorder. In B.A. van der Kolk, A.C. McFarlane, & L. Weisaeth (Eds.), *Traumatic stress,* pp. 510–524. New York: Guilford.

Davidson, M. (1982). *Uncommon sense: The life and thought of Ludwig von Bertalanffy (1901–1972), father of general systems theory.* Boston: Houghton Mifflin.

Davidson, W.S., Redner, R., Blakely, C.H., Mitchell, C.M., & Emshoff, J.G. (1987). Diversion of juvenile offenders: An experimental comparison. *Journal of Consulting and Clinical Psychology, 55,* 68–75.

Davila, J., Hammen, C., Burge, D., Paley, B., et al. (1995). Poor interpersonal problem solving as a mechanism of stress generation in depression among adolescent women. *Journal of Abnormal Psychology, 104,* 592–600.

Davis, G.C., & Akiskal, H.S. (1986). Descriptive, biological, and theoretical aspects of borderline personality disorder. *Hospital and Community Psychiatry 37,* 685–692.

Davis, J.P., Chesney, P.J., Wand, P.J., Laventure, M., et al. (1980). Toxic-shock syndrome: Epidemiological features, recurrence, risk factors, and prevention. *New England Journal of Medicine, 303,* 1429–1435.

Davis, K.L., & Haroutunian, V. (1993). Strategies for the treatment of Alzheimer's disease. *Neurology, 4* (suppl. 4), S52–S55.

Davis, K.L., Kahn, R.S., Ko, G., & Davidson, M. (1991). Dopamine in schizophrenia: A review and reconceptualization. *American Journal of Psychiatry, 148,* 1474–1486.

Davis, R.E., Coyle, P.D., Carroll, R.T., Emmerling, M.R., & Jaen, J. (1995). Cholinergic therapies for Alzheimer's disease. Palliative or disease altering? *Arzneimittel-Forschung, 45,* 425–431.

Davis, R.H. (1978). Review of the Rorschach test. In O.K. Burros (Ed.), *Mental measurements yearbook,* 8th ed., p. 1045. Highland Park, NJ: Gryphon Press.

Davis, R.M. (1996). The ledger of tobacco control: Is the cup half empty or half full? *Journal of the American Medical Association, 275,* 1281–1285.

Davis, V.E., & Walsh, M.J. (1970). Alcohol, amines and alkaloids: A possible biochemical basis for alcohol addiction. *Science, 167,* 1005–1007.

Dawes, R.M. (1994). *House of cards: The collapse of modern psychotherapy.* New York: Free Press.

Dawes, R.M., Faust, D., & Meehl, P.E. (1989). Clinical versus actuarial judgment. *Science, 243,* 1668–1674.

Day, N.L. (1995). Epidemiology of alcohol use, abuse, and dependence. In M.T. Tsuang, M. Tohen, & G.E.P. Zahner (Eds.), *Textbook in psychiatric epidemiology,* pp. 345–360. New York: Wiley-Liss.

Deblinger, E., McLeer, S.V., Atkins, M.S., Ralphe, D., & Foa, E. (1989). Post-traumatic stress in sexually abused, physically abused, and nonabused children. *Child Abuse and Neglect, 13,* 403–408.

Deister, A., & Marneros, A. (1994). Prognostic value of initial subtype in schizophrenic disorders. *Schizophrenia Research, 12,* 145–157.

DeLeon, P.H., Sammons, M.T., & Sexton, J.L. (1995). Focusing on society's real needs: Responsibility and prescription privileges. *American Psychologist, 50,* 1022–1032.

Deltito, J.A., & Perugi, G. (1986). A case of social phobia with avoidant personality disorder treated with MAOI. *Comprehensive Psychiatry, 27,* 255–258.

D'Emilio, J., & Freedman, E.B. (1988). *Intimate matters: A history of sexuality in America.* New York: Harper & Row.

Delgado, P.L., Price, L.H., Heninger, G.R., & Charney, D.S. (1992). Neurochemistry. In E.S. Paykel (Ed.). *Handbook of affective disorders,* 2nd ed. New York: Guilford.

Depue, R.A., & Iacono, W.G. (1989). Neurobehavioral aspects of affective disorders. *Annual Review of Psychology, 40,* 457–492.

de Ruiter, C., & van Uzendoorn, M.H. (1992). Agoraphobia and anxious-ambivalent attachment: An integrative review. *Journal of Anxiety Disorders, 6,* 365–381.

de Silva, P. (1993). Fetishism and sexual dysfunction: Clinical presentation and management. *Sexual and Marital Therapy, 8,* 147–155.

de Silva, P. (1988). Phobias and preparedness. Replication and extension. *Behaviour Research and Therapy, 26,* 97–98.

Deutsch, A. (1949). *The mentally ill in America: A history of their care and treatment from colonial times.* New York: Columbia University Press.

Deutsch, M. (1973). *The resolution of conflict.* New Haven, CT: Yale University Press.

Devanand, D.P., & Levy, S.T. (1995). Neuroleptic treatment of agitation and psychosis in dementia. *Journal of Geriatric Psychiatry and Neurology, 8,* (suppl.), S18–S27.

DeVane, C.L., & Sallee, F.R. (1996). Serotonin selective reuptake inhibitors in child and adolescent psychopharmacology: A review of published evidence. *Journal of Clinical Psychiatry, 57,* 55–66.

DeVeaugh-Geiss, J. (1993). Diagnosis and treatment of obsessive-compulsive disorder. *Annual Review of Medicine, 44,* 53–61.

Dickens, C. (1842/1970). *American notes and pictures from Italy.* New York: Oxford University Press.

Dienstbier, R.A. (1989). Arousal and physiological toughness: Implications for mental and physical health. *Psychological Review, 96,* 84–100.

Dijkman-Caes, D.I., Kraan, H.F., & DeVries, M.W. (1993). Research on panic disorder and agoraphobia in daily life: A review of current studies. *Journal of Anxiety Disorders, 7,* 235–247.

DiLalla, L.F., & Gottesman, I.I. (1990). Heterogeneity of causes for delinquency and criminality: Lifespan perspectives. *Development and Psychopathology, 1,* 339–349.

DiNardo, P.A., Moras, K., Barlow, D.H., Rapee, R.M., & Brown, T.A. (1993). Reliability of DSM-III-R anxiety disorder categories: Using the Anxiety Disorders Interview Schedule-Revised (ADIS-R). *Archives of General Psychiatry, 50,* 251–256.

DiNardo, P.A., O'Brien, G.T., Barlow, D.H., Waddell, M.T., & Blanchard, E.B. (1988). *Anxiety Disorders Interview Schedule—Revised (ADIS-R).* Albany: State University of New York at Albany, Phobia and Anxiety Disorders Clinic.

Dishion, T.J., French, D.C., & Patterson, G.R. (1995). The development and ecology of antisocial behavior. In D. Cicchetti & D.J. Cohen (Eds.), *Developmental psychopathology,* vol. 1, pp. 421–471. New York: Wiley.

Docherty, N.M., DeRosa, M., & Andreasen, N.C. (1996). Communication disturbances in schizophrenia and mania. *Archives of General Psychiatry, 53,* 358–364.

Dodge, K.A., & Frame, C.L. (1982). Social-cognitive biases and deficits in aggressive boys. *Child Development, 53,* 620–635.

Dohrenwend, B.P., Levav, I., Shrout, P.E., Schwartz, S., Naveh, G., Link, B.G., Skodol, A.E., & Stueve, A. (1992). Socioeconomic status and psychiatric disorders: The causation-selection issue. *Science, 255,* 946–952.

Dohrenwend, B.P., Link, B.G., Kern, R., Shrout, P.E., & Markowitz, J. (1990). Measuring life events: The problem of variability within event categories. *Stress Medicine, 6,* 179–187.

Dolan, B. (1991). Cross-cultural aspects of anorexia

nervosa and bulimia: A review. *International Journal of Eating Disorders, 10,* 67–78.

Dolan, B., & Coid, J. (1993). *Psychopathic and antisocial personality disorders: Treatment and research issues.* London: Gaskell/Royal College of Psychiatrists.

Donahey, K.M., & Carroll, R.A. (1993). Gender differences in factors associated with hypoactive sexual desire. *Journal of Sex and Marital Therapy, 19,* 25–40.

Donovan, D.M., & Marlatt, G.A. (1993). Behavioral treatment. In M. Galanter, H. Begleiter, D. Deitrich, et al. (Eds.), *Recent developments in alcoholism,* Vol. 11: *Ten years of progress,* pp. 397–411. New York: Plenum.

Doren, D.M. (1993). Antisocial personality disorder. In R.T. Ammerman & M. Hersen (Eds.), *Handbook of behavior therapy with children and adults: A developmental and longitudinal perspective,* pp. 263–276. Boston: Allyn & Bacon.

Douglas, V.I. (1983). Attention and cognitive problems. In M. Rutter (Ed.), *Developmental neuropsychiatry,* pp. 280–329. New York: Guilford.

Douglas, V.I., & Peters, K.G. (1979). Toward a clearer definition of the attentional deficit of hyperactive children. In G.A. Hale & M. Lewis (Eds.), *Attention and the development of cognitive skills,* pp. 173–248. New York: Plenum.

Draguns, J.G. (1980). Psychological disorders of clinical severity. In H.C. Triandis & J.G. Draguns (Eds.), *Handbook of cross-cultural psychology: Psychopathology,* vol. 6, pp. 99–174. Boston: Allyn & Bacon.

Draguns, J.G. (1994). Pathological and clinical aspects. In L.L. Adler & U.P. Gielen (Eds.), *Cross-cultural topics in psychology,* pp. 165–178. Westport, CT: Praeger.

Drake, R.E., & Vaillant, G.E. (1985). A validity study of Axis II of DSM-III. *American Journal of Psychiatry, 142,* 553–558.

Drewnoski, A., & Yee, D.K. (1987). Men and body image: Are males satisfied with their body weight? *Psychosomatic Medicine, 49,* 626–634.

Dreyfuss, R. (1996). Tobacco enemy number 1. *Mother Jones, 21,* 42–48.

Dryden, W., & DiGiuseppe, R. (1990). *A primer on rational-emotive therapy.* Champaign, IL: Research Press.

Dulcan, M.K. (1986). Comprehensive treatment of children and adolescents with attention deficit disorders: The state of the art. *Clinical Psychology Review, 6,* 539–569.

Durham, M.L., & LaFond, J.Q. (1988). A search for the missing premise of involuntary therapeutic commitment: Effective treatment of the mentally ill. *Rutgers Law Review, 40,* 303–368.

Durham, R.C., & Allan, T. (1993). Psychological treatment of generalized anxiety disorder: A review of the clinical significance of results in outcome studies since 1980. *British Journal of Psychiatry, 163,* 19–26.

Durkheim, E. (1897/1951). *Suicide: A study in sociology.* New York: Free Press.

Dyk, P.H., & Adams, G.R. (1990). Identity and intimacy: An initial investigation of three theoretical models using cross-lag panel correlations. *Journal of Youth and Adolescence, 19,* 91–110.

D'Zurilla, T., & Goldfried, M. (1971). Problem solving and behavior modification. *Journal of Abnormal Psychology, 78,* 107–126.

Eagle, M., & Wolitzky, D.L. (1988). Psychodynamics. In C.G. Last & M. Hersen (Eds.), *Handbook of anxiety disorders.* New York: Pergamon.

Eaton, W.W. (1994). Social facts and the sociological imagination: The contributions of sociology to psychiatric epidemiology. *Acta Psychiatrica Scandinavica, 90* (suppl. 385), 25–38.

Eaton, W.W., Dryman, A., & Weissman, M.M. (1991). Panic and phobia. In L.N. Robins & D.A. Regier (Eds.), *Psychiatric disorders in America: The epidemiologic Catchment Area Study,* pp. 155–179. New York: Free Press.

Eaton, W.W., Mortensen, P.B., Herrman, H., Freeman, H., et al. (1992). Long-term course of hospitalization for schizophrenia. I. Risk for rehospitalization. *Schizophrenia Bulletin, 18,* 217–228.

Eberlin, M., McConnachie, G., Igel, S., & Volpe, L. (1993). Facilitated communication: A failure to replicate the phenomenon. *Journal of Autism and Developmental Disorders, 23,* 507–530.

Edelbrock, C., & Costello, A.J. (1984). Structured psychiatric interviews for children and adolescents. In G.R. Goldstein & M. Hersen (Eds.), *Handbook of psychological assessment,* pp. 276–290. London: Pergamon.

Edmonstone, Y., Austin, M.P., Prentice, N., Dougall, N., Freeman, C.P.L., Ebmeier, K.P., & Goodwin, G.M. (1994). Uptake of 99mTc-exametazime shown by single photon emission computerized tomography in obsessive-compulsive disorder compared with major depression and normal controls. *Acta Psychiatrica Scandinavica, 90,* 298–303.

Egeland, J.A., Gerhard, D.S., Pauls, D.L., Sussex, J.N., Kidd, K.K., Allen, C.R., Hostetter, A.M., & Housman, D.E. (1987). Bipolar affective disorders linked to DNA markers on chromosome 11. *Nature, 325,* 783–787.

Egeland, J.D., & Sussex, J.N. (1985). Suicide and family loading for affective disorders. *Journal of the American Medical Association. 254,* 915–918.

Ehrenfest, H. (1926). Birth injuries of the child. *Gynecological and Obstetrical Monographs.* New York: Appleton.

Ehrman, R., Ternes, J., O'Brien, C.P., & McLellan, A.T. (1992). Conditioned tolerance in human opiate addicts. *Psychopharmacology, 108,* 218–224.

Eisenberg, L. (1995). The social construction of the human brain. *American Journal of Psychiatry, 152,* 1563–1575.

Eisenberg, L., & Kanner, L. (1956). Early infantile autism: 1943–1955. *American Journal of Orthopsychiatry, 26,* 55–65.

Eisenthal, S., Emery, R., Lazare, A., & Udin, H. (1979). "Adherence" and the negotiated approach to patienthood. *Archives of General Psychiatry, 36,* 393–398.

Eklund, P.L.E., Gooren, L.J.G., & Bezemer, P.D. (1988). Prevalence of transsexualism in the Netherlands. *British Journal of Psychiatry, 152,* 638–640.

Ekman, G., Miranda-Linne, F., Gillberg, C., Garle, M., & Wetterberg, L. (1989). *Journal of Autism and Developmental Disorders, 19,* 511–531.

Elkin, I., Gibbons, R.D., Shea, M.T., Sotsky, S.M., Watkins, J.T., Pilkonis, P.A., & Hedeker, D. (1996). Initial severity and differential treatment outcome in the NIMH Treatment of Depression Collaborative Research Program. *Journal of Consulting and Clinical Psychology, 64.*

Elkin, I., Shea, T., Watkins, J.T., Imber, S.D., Sotsky, S.M., Collins, J.F., Glass, D.R., Pikonis, P.A., Leber, W.R., Docherty, J.P., Fiester, S.J., & Parloff, M.B. (1989). National Institute of Mental Health treatment of depression collaborative research program: General effectiveness of treatments. *Archives of General Psychiatry, 46,* 971–982.

Ellenbroek, B.A. (1993). Treatment of schizophrenia: A clinical and preclinical evaluation of neuroleptic drugs. *Pharmacological Therapy, 57,* 1–78.

Elliott, B.J., & Richards, M.P.M. (1991). Children and divorce: Educational performance and behaviour before and after parental separation. *International Journal of Law and the Family, 5,* 258–276.

Elliott, G. (1989). Stress and illness. In S. Cheren (Ed.), *Psychosomatic medicine: Theory, physiology, and practice,* Vol. 1, pp. 45–90. Madison, CT: International Universities Press.

Ellis, A. (1962). *Reason and emotion in psychotherapy.* New York: Lyle Stuart.

Ellis, A. (1970). *Reason and emotion in psychotherapy.* New York: Lyle Stuart.

Ellis, A. (1973). *Humanistic psychotherapy: The rational-emotive approach.* New York: McGraw-Hill.

Emery, R.E. (1982). Interparental conflict and the children of discord and divorce. *Psychological Bulletin, 92,* 310–330.

Emery, R.E. (1988). *Marriage, divorce, and children's adjustment.* Newbury Park, CA: Sage.

Emery, R.E. (1989). Family violence. *American Psychologist, 44,* 321–328.

Emery, R.E. (1992). Family conflict and its developmental implications: A conceptual analysis of deep meanings and systemic processes. In C.U. Shantz & W.W. Hartup (Eds.), *Conflict in child and adolescent development,* pp. 270–298. London: Cambridge University Press.

Emery, R.E. (1994). *Renegotiating family relationships: Divorce, child custody, and mediation.* New York: Guilford.

Emery, R.E. (1997). *Marriage, divorce, and children's adjustment* (2nd ed.). Thousand Oaks, CA: Sage Publications.

Emery, R.E., Fincham, F.D., & Cummings, E.M. (1992). Parenting in context: Systemic thinking about parental conflict and its influence on children. *Journal of Consulting and Clinical Psychology, 60,* 909–912.

Emery, R.E., & Marholin, D. (1977). An applied behavior analysis of delinquency: The irrelevancy of relevant behavior. *American Psychologist, 32,* 860–873.

Emery, R.E., Matthews, S., & Kitzmann, K. (1994). Child custody mediation and litigation: Parents' satisfaction and functioning a year after settlement. *Journal of Consulting and Clinical Psychology, 62,* 124–129.

Emery, R.E., Matthews, S., & Wyer, M.M. (1991). Child custody mediation and litigation: Further evidence on the differing views of mothers and fathers. *Journal of Consulting and Clinical Psychology, 59,* 410–418.

Emery, R.E., & Rogers, K.C. (1990). The role of behavior therapists in child custody cases. In M. Hersen & R.M. Eisler (Eds.), *Progress in behavior modification,* pp. 60–89. Beverly Hills: Sage.

Emery, R.E., & Wyer, M.M. (1987). Divorce mediation. *American Psychologist, 42,* 472–480.

Emmelkamp, P.M.G., & Beens, H. (1991). Cognitive therapy with obsessive-compulsive disorder: A comparative evaluation. *Behaviour Research and Therapy, 29,* 293–300.

Engel, G.L. (1977). The need for a new medical model: A challenge for biomedicine. *Science, 196,* 129–136.

Ennis, B., & Emery, R. (1978). *The rights of mental patients.* New York: Avon.

Epstein, S. (1979). The stability of behavior. I. On predicting most of the people much of the time. *Journal of Personality and Social Psychology, 37,* 1097–1126.

Epstein, S. (1980). The stability of behavior. II. Implications for psychological research. *American Psychologist, 35,* 790–806.

Erdelyi, M.H. (1990). Repression, reconstruction, and defense: History and integration of the psychoanalytic and experimental frameworks. In J.L. Singer (Ed.), *Repression and dissociation,* pp. 1–32. Chicago: University of Chicago Press.

Erikson, E.H. (1959, 1980). *Identity and the life cycle.* New York: Norton.

Erikson, E.H. (1968). *Identity: Youth and crisis.* New York: Norton.

Erlenmeyer-Kimling, L., Squires-Wheeler, E., Adamo, U.H., Bassett, A.S., Cornblatt, B.A., Kestenbaum, C.J., Rock, D., Roberts, S.A., & Gottesman, I.I. (1995). The New York high-risk project: Psychoses and cluster A personality disorders in offspring of schizophrenic parents at 23 years of follow-up. *Archives of General Psychiatry, 52,* 857–865.

Erlenmeyer-Kimling, L., & Cornblatt, B.A. (1992). A summary of attentional findings in the New York high-risk project. *Journal of Psychiatric Research, 26,* 405–426.

Ernst, C., Foldenyi, M., & Angst, J. (1993). The Zurich study. XXI. Sexual dysfunctions and disturbances in young adults. *European Archives of Psychiatry and Clinical Neuroscience, 243, 179–188.*

Ernulf, K.E., & Innala, S.M. (1995). Sexual bondage: A review and unobtrusive investigation. *Archives of Sexual Behavior, 24, 631–655.*

Eron, L.D. (1982). Parent-child interaction, television violence, and aggression in children. *American Psychologist, 37, 197–211.*

Ewing, C. (1991). Preventive detention and execution: The constitutionality of punishing future crimes. *Law and Human Behavior, 15, 139–163.*

Exner, J.E. (1986). *The Rorschach: A comprehensive system,* vol. 1, 2nd ed. New York: Wiley.

Eysenck, H.J. (1952/1992). The effects of psychotherapy: An evaluation. *Journal of Consulting Psychology, 16, 319–324.*

Eysenck, H.J. (1979). The conditioning model of neurosis. *Behavioral and Brain Sciences, 2, 155–199.*

Fabrega, H. (1991). The culture and history of psychiatric stigma in early modern and modern Western societies: A review of recent literature. *Comprehensive Psychiatry, 32, 97–119.*

Faigman, D.L. (1986). The battered woman syndrome and self-defense: A legal and empirical dissent. *Virginia Law Review, 72, 619–647.*

Fairburn, C.G. (1996). *Overcoming binge eating.* New York: Guilford.

Fairburn, C.G. (1995). Short-term psychological treatments for bulimia nervosa. In K.D. Brownell & C.G. Fairburn (Eds.), *Eating disorders and obesity: A comprehensive handbook,* pp. 344–348. New York: Guilford.

Fairburn, C.G., & Beglin, S.J. (1990). Studies of the epidemiology of bulimia nervosa. *American Journal of Psychiatry, 147, 401–480.*

Fairburn, C.G., Hay, P.J., & Welch, S.L. (1993). Binge eating and bulimia nervosa: Distribution and determinants. In C.G. Fairburn & G.T. Wilson (Eds.), *Binge eating: Nature, assessment, and treatment,* pp. 123–143. New York: Guilford.

Fairburn, C.G., Jones, R., Peveler, R.C., Carr, S.J., Solomon, R.A., O'Connor, M.E., Burton, J., & Hope, R.A. (1991). Three psychological treatments for bulimia nervosa. *Archives of General Psychiatry, 48, 463–469.*

Fairburn, C.G., Jones, R., Peveler, R.C., Hope, R.A., & O'Connor, M. (1993). Psychotherapy and bulimia nervosa: Longer-term effects of interpersonal psychotherapy, behavior therapy, and cognitive behavior therapy. *Archives of General Psychiatry, 50, 419–428.*

Fairburn, C.G., & Wilson, G.T. (Eds.) (1993). *Binge eating: Nature, assessment, and treatment.* New York: Guilford.

Falloon, I., Boyd, J.L., & McGill, C.W. (1985). *Family care of schizophrenia.* New York: Guilford.

Fallon, P., Katzman, M.A., & Wooley, S.C. (1994). *Feminist perspectives on eating disorders.* New York: Guilford.

Farah, M.J., O'Reilly, R.C., & Vecera, S.P. (1993). Dissociated overt and covert recognition as an emergent property of a lesioned neural network. *Psychological Review, 100, 571–588.*

Faraone, S.V., Kremen, W.S., Lyons, M.J., Pepple, J.R., et al. (1995). Diagnostic accuracy and linkage analysis: How useful are schizophrenia spectrum phenotypes? *American Journal of Psychiatry, 152, 1286–1290.*

Faraone, S.V., & Tsuang, M.T. (1995). Methods in psychiatric genetics. In M.T. Tsuang, M. Tohen, & G.E.P. Zahner (Eds.), *Textbook in psychiatric epidemiology,* pp. 81–134. New York: Wiley-Liss.

Farde, L., & Nordstrom, A.L. (1992). PET analysis indicates atypical central dopamine receptor occupancy in clozapine-treated patients. *British Journal of Psychiatry, 160 (suppl. 17), 30–33.*

Farde, L., Nordstrom, A., Karlsson, P., Halldin, C., & Sedvall, G. (1995). Positron emission tomography studies on dopamine receptors in schizophrenia. *Clinical Neuropharmacology, 18 (suppl. 1), S121–S129.*

Faris, R.E.L., & Dunham, H.W. (1939). *Mental disorders in urban areas: An ecological study of schizophrenia and other psychoses.* Chicago: University of Chicago Press.

Farmer, A.E., & Blewett, A. (1993). Drug treatment of resistant schizophrenia: Limitations and recommendations. *Drugs, 45, 374–383.*

Farmer, A.E., & Griffiths, H. (1992). Labeling and illness in primary care: Comparing factors influencing general practitioners' and psychiatrists' decisions regarding patient referral to mental illness services. *Psychological Medicine, 22, 717–723.*

Farmer, A.E., McGuffin, P., & Gottesman, I.I. (1984). Searching for the split in schizophrenia: A twin study perspective. *Psychiatry Research, 13, 109–118.*

Farmer, A.E., McGuffin, P., & Gottesman, I.I. (1987). Twin concordance for DSM-III schizophrenia: Scrutinizing the validity of the definition. *Archives of General Psychiatry, 44, 634–641.*

Farquhar, J.W., Macoby, N., Wood, P.D., et al. (1977). Community education for cardiovascular health. *Lancet, i, 1192–1195.*

Farrington, D., Ohlin, L., & Wilson, J.Q. (1986). *Understanding and controlling crime.* New York: Springer.

Faust, D., & Ziskin, J. (1988). The expert witness in psychology and psychiatry. *Science, 241, 31–35.*

Fawcett, J., Clark, D.C., & Busch, K.A. (1993). Assessing and treating the patient at risk for suicide. *Psychiatric Annals, 23, 244–255.*

Fawzy, F.I., Fawzy, N.W., Hyun, C.S., Gutherie, D., Fahey, J.L., & Morton, D. (1993). Malignant melanoma. Effects of an early structured psychiatric intervention, coping, and affective state on recurrence and survival six years later. *Archives of General Psychiatry, 50, 681–689.*

Federal Bureau of Investigation. (1992). *Crime in the United States, 1992.* Washington, DC: U.S. Department of Justice.

Feingold, B.F. (1975). *Why your child is hyperactive.* New York: Random House.

Feldman, H.A., Goldstein, I., Hatzichristou, D.G., Krane, R.J., & McKinlay, J.B. (1994). Impotence and its medical and psychosocial correlates: Results of the Massachusetts Male Aging Study. *Journal of Urology, 151, 54–61.*

Ferreira, L., & Soares-da-Silva, P. (1991). 5-hydroxytryptamine and alcoholism. *Human Psychopharmacology: Clinical and Experimental, 6 (suppl.), 21–24.*

Ferster, C.B. (1961). Positive reinforcement and behavioral deficits of autistic children. *Child Development, 32, 437–456.*

Fichter, M.M., Meller, I., Schroppel, H., & Steinkirchner, R. (1995). Dementia and cognitive impairment in the oldest old in the community: Prevalence and comorbidity. *British Journal of Psychiatry, 166, 621–629.*

Figley, C.R. (1978). *Stress disorders among Vietnam veterans.* New York: Brunner/Mazel.

Fillmore, K.M. (1987). Women's drinking across the adult life course as compared to men's *British Journal of Addiction, 82, 801–811.*

Fincham, F.D., & Bradbury, T.N. (1987). The impact of attributions in marriage: A longitudinal analysis. *Journal of Personality and Social Psychology, 53, 510–517.*

Fincham, F.D., & Bradbury, T.N. (1990). *The psychology of marriage: Basic issues and applications.* New York: Guilford.

Fingarette, H. (1988). *Heavy drinking: The myth of alcoholism as a disease.* Berkeley: University of California Press.

Fink, M. (1992). Electroconvulsive therapy. In E.S. Paykel (Ed.), *Handbook of affective disorders,* 2nd ed., pp. 359–367. New York: Guilford.

Fink, M. (1993). Who should get ECT? In C.E. Coffey (Ed.), *The clinical science of electroconvulsive therapy,* pp. 3–15. Washington, DC: American Psychiatric Press.

Fink, P.J., & Tasman, A. (Eds.) (1992). *Stigma and mental illness.* Washington, DC: American Psychiatric Press.

Finkelhor, D. (1992). New myths about the child welfare system. *Child, Youth, and Family Services Quarterly, 15, 3–5.*

Finkelhor, D., Hotaling, G., Lewis, I.A., & Smith, C. (1990). Sexual abuse in a national sample of adult men and women: Prevalence, characteristics, and risk factors. *Child Abuse and Neglect, 14, 19–28.*

Finlay-Jones, R., & Brown, G.W. (1981). Types of stressful life event and the onset of anxiety and depressive disorders. *Psychological Medicine, 11, 803–815.*

Finney, J.W., & Moos, R.H. (1991). The long-term course of treated alcoholism. I. Mortality, relapse and remission rates and comparisons with community controls. *Journal of Studies on Alcohol, 52, 44–54.*

Finney, J.W., & Moos, R.H. (1992). The long-term course of treated alcoholism. II. Predictors and correlates of 10-year functioning and mortality. *Journal of Studies on Alcohol, 53, 142–153.*

Fisher, P.J., & Breakey, W.R. (1991). The epidemiology of alcohol, drug, and mental disorders among homeless persons. *American Psychologist, 46, 1115–1128.*

Fitch, S.A., & Adams, G.R. (1983). Ego-identity and intimacy status: Replication and extension. *Developmental Psychology, 19, 839–845.*

Fitch, W.L., Petrella, R.C., & Wallace, J. (1987). Legal ethics and the use of mental health experts in criminal cases. *Behavioral Sciences and the Law, 5, 105–117.*

Flanagan, J.C. (1982). *New insights to improve the quality of life at age 70.* Palo Alto, CA: American Institutes for Research.

Fleischhacker, W.W., Meise, U., Gunther, V., & Kurz, M. (1994). Compliance with antipsychotic drug treatment: Influence of side effects. *Acta Psychiatrica Scandinavica, 89 (suppl. 382), 11–15.*

Fleming, J.E., & Offord, D.R. (1990). Epidemiology of childhood depressive disorders: A critical review. *Journal of American Academy of Child and Adolescent Psychiatry, 29, 571–580.*

Flint, A.J. (1994). Epidemiology and comorbidity of anxiety disorders in the elderly. *American Journal of Psychiatry, 151, 640–649.*

Flor-Henry, P. (1987). Cerebral aspects of sexual deviation. In G.D. Wilson (Ed.), *Variant sexuality: Research and theory,* pp. 49–83. Baltimore: Johns Hopkins University Press.

Foa, E.B., & Kozak, M.J. (1995). DSM-IV field trial: Obsessive-compulsive disorder. *American Journal of Psychiatry, 152, 90–96.*

Foa, E.B., Rothbaum, B.O., Riggs, D.S., & Murdock, T.B. (1991). Treatment of posttraumatic stress disorder in rape victims: A comparison between cognitive-behavioral procedures and counseling. *Journal of Consulting and Clinical Psychology, 59, 715–723.*

Foa, E.B., & Steketee, G. (1989). Obsessive-compulsive disorder. In C. Lindemann (Ed.), *Handbook of phobia therapy: Rapid symptom relief in anxiety disorders,* pp. 183–206. Northvale, NH: Jason Aronson.

Foa, E.B., Steketee, G., & Rothbaum, B.O. (1989). Behavioral/cognitive conceptualizations of posttraumatic stress disorder. *Behavior Therapy, 20, 155–176.*

Folstein, M.F., & Folstein, S.E. (1977). Clinical, pathological, and genetic heterogeneity of Alzheimer's disease. In L. Heston (Ed.), *Progress in Alzheimer's disease and similar conditions.* Washington, DC: American Psychiatric Press.

Folstein, S., & Rutter, M. (1977). Infantile autism: A genetic study of 21 twin pairs. *Journal of Child Psychology and Psychiatry, 18, 291–321.*

Foot, P. (1990). Ethics and the death penalty: Participation of forensic psychiatrists in capital trials. In R. Rosner & R. Weinstock (Eds.), *Ethical practice in psychiatry and the law,* pp. 202–217. New York: Plenum.

Ford, C., & Beach, F. (1951). *Patterns of sexual behavior.* New York: Harper & Row.

Ford, D.H., & Lerner, R.M. (1992). *Developmental systems theory: An integrative approach.* Newbury Park, CA: Sage.

Fordyce, W.E. (1976). *Behavioral methods for chronic pain and illness*. St. Louis: Mosby.

Forehand, R., & McMahon, R.J. (1981). *Helping the noncompliant child: A clinician's guide to parent training*. New York: Guilford.

Forehand, R., Wells, K., & Griest, D. (1980). An examination of the social validity of a parent training program. *Behavior Therapy, 11*, 488–502.

Foster, S.L., & Cone, J.D. (1986). Design and use of direct observation procedures. In A.R. Ciminero, K.S. Calhoun, & H.E. Adams (Eds.), *Handbook of behavioral assessment*, 2nd ed. New York: Wiley.

Foster, S.L., & Cone, J.D. (1995). Validity issues in clinical assessment. *Psychological Assessment, 7*, 248–260.

Fowles, D.C. (1992). Schizophrenia: Diathesis-stress revisited. *Annual Review of Psychology, 43*, 303–336.

Fox, K., Merrill, J.C., Chang, H.H., & Califano, J.A., Jr. (1995). Estimating the costs of substance abuse to the Medicaid hospital care program. *American Journal of Public Health, 85*, 48–54.

Foy, D.W., Resnick, H.S., Sipprelle, R.C., & Carroll, E.M. (1987). Premilitary, military, and post-military factors in the development of combat-related post-traumatic stress disorder. *Behavior Therapist, 10*, 3–9.

Frances, A. (1980). The DSM-III personality disorders section: A commentary. *American Journal of Psychiatry, 137*, 1050–1054.

Frances, A., First, M.B., & Pincus, H.A. (1995). *DSM-IV guidebook*. Washington, DC: American Psychiatric Press.

Frances, A., Miele, G.M., Widiger, T.A., Pincus, H.A., Manning, D., & Davis, W.W. (1993). The classification of panic disorders: From Freud to DSM-IV. *Journal of Psychiatric Research, 27* (suppl. 1), 3–10.

Frances, A.J., Widiger, T.A., & Pincus, H.A. (1989). The development of DSM-IV. *Archives of General Psychiatry, 46*, 373–375.

Francis, J. (1995). A half-century of delirium research: Time to close the gap. *Journal of the American Geriatrics Society, 43*, 585–586.

Frank, E., Anderson, C., & Rubenstein, D. (1978). Frequency of sexual dysfunction in normal couples. *New England Journal of Medicine, 299*, 111–115.

Frank, J.D. (1961). *Persuasion and healing*. Baltimore: Johns Hopkins University Press.

Frank, J.D. (1973). *Persuasion and healing*, 2nd ed. Baltimore: Johns Hopkins University Press.

Frank, J.D., & Frank, J.B. (1991). *Persuasion and healing*, 3rd ed. Baltimore: Johns Hopkins University Press.

Frank, E., Turner, S.M., Stewart, B.D., Jacob, M., & West, D. (1981). Past psychiatric symptoms and the response to sexual assault. *Comprehensive Psychiatry, 22*, 479–487.

Frankel, F.H. (1990). Hypnotizability and dissociation. *American Journal of Psychiatry, 147*, 823–829.

Frankish, C.J. (1994). Crisis centers and their role in treatment: Suicide prevention versus health promotion. In A.A. Leenaars, J.T. Maltsberger, & R.A. Neimeyer (Eds.), *Treatment of suicidal people*, pp. 33–44. Washington, DC: Taylor & Francis.

Franklin, J.A., & Andrews, G. (1989). Stress and the onset of agoraphobia. *Australian Psychologist, 24*, 203–219.

Frasure-Smith, N., & Prince, R. (1985). Long-term follow-up of the ischemic heart disease life stress monitoring program. *Psychosomatic Medicine, 51*, 485–513.

Freeman, A., Pretzer, J., Fleming, B., & Simon, S.M. (1990). *Clinical applications of cognitive therapy*. New York: Plenum.

Freeman, H. (1994). Schizophrenia and city residence. *British Journal of Psychiatry, 164* (suppl. 23), 39–50.

Freeman, P.S., & Gunderson, J.G. (1989). Treatment of personality disorders. *Psychiatric Annals, 19*, 147–153.

Freud, S. (1894/1957). On the grounds for detaching a particular syndrome from neurasthenia under the description "anxiety neurosis." In J. Strachey (Ed.), *Standard edition of the complete psychological works of Sigmund Freud*, vol. 1. London: Hogarth Press.

Freud, S. (1912/1957). Recommendations for physicians on the psycho-analytic method for treatment. *Standard Edition*, vol. 12, pp. 109–120. London: Hogarth Press.

Freud, S. (1917/1955). A difficulty in the path of psychoanalysis. J. Strachey (Ed. & Trans.), *The standard edition of the complete psychological works of Sigmund Freud*, vol. 17. London: Hogarth Press.

Freud, S. (1917/1961). Mourning and melancholia. In J. Strachey (Ed. and Trans.), *The standard edition of the complete psychological works of Sigmund Freud*, vol. 14. London: Hogarth Press.

Freud, S. (1924/1962). The aetiology of hysteria. In J. Strachey (Ed. and Trans.), *The standard edition of the complete psychological works of Sigmund Freud*, vol. 3, pp. 191–221. London: Hogarth Press.

Freud, S. (1926/1959). Inhibitions, symptoms, and anxiety. In J. Strachey (Ed.), *Standard edition of the complete psychological works of Sigmund Freud*, vol. 20. London: Hogarth Press.

Freud, S. (1930/1961). Civilization and its discontents. In J. Strachey (Ed. and Trans.), *The standard edition of the complete psychological works of Sigmund Freud*, vol. 21. London: Hogarth Press.

Freud, S. (1940/1969). *An outline of psycho-analysis*. New York: Norton.

Freund, K., & Blanchard, R. (1986). The concept of courtship disorder. *Journal of Sex and Marital Therapy, 12*, 79–92.

Freund, K., & Blanchard, R. (1993). Erotic target location errors in male gender dysphorics, paedophiles, and fetishists. *British Journal of Psychiatry, 162*, 558–563.

Freund, K., & Watson, R.J. (1991). Assessment of the sensitivity and specificity of a phallometric test: An update of phallometric diagnosis of pedophilia. *Psychological Assessment, 3*, 254–260.

Friedland, R.P. (1993). Epidemiology, education, and the ecology of Alzheimer's disease. *Neurology, 43*, 246–248.

Friedman, E.S., Clark, D.B., & Gershon, S. (1992). Stress, anxiety, and depression: Review of biological, diagnostic, and nosologic issues. *Journal of Anxiety Disorders, 6*, 337–363.

Friedman, M., & Rosenman, R.H. (1959). Association of specific overt behavior pattern with blood and cardiovascular findings: Blood cholesterol level, blood clotting time, incidence of arcus senilis and clinical coronary artery disease. *Journal of the American Medical Association, 169*, 1286–1296.

Friedman, M., Thoresen, C.D., Gill, J.J., et al. (1986). Alteration of Type A behavior and its effect on cardiac recurrences in post-myocardial infarction patients: Summary results of the recurrent coronary prevention project. *American Heart Journal, 112*, 653–665.

Fries, J.F. (1990). Medical perspectives upon successful aging. In P.B. Baltes & M.M. Baltes (Eds.), *Successful aging: Perspectives from the behavioral sciences* (pp. 35–49). Cambridge, MA: Cambridge University Press.

Frueh, B.C., Turner, S.M., & Beidel, D.C. (1995). Exposure therapy for combat-related PTSD: A critical review. *Clinical Psychology Review, 15*, 799–817.

Fuller, R.K., & Roth, H.P. (1979). Disulfiram for the treatment of alcoholism: An evaluation of 128 men. *Annals of Internal Medicine, 90*, 901–904.

Funder, D.C., & Colvin, C.R. (1991). Explorations in behavioral consistency: Properties of persons, situations, and behaviors. *Journal of Personality and Social Psychology, 60*, 773–794.

Funtowicz, M.N., & Widiger, T.A. (1995). Sex bias in the diagnosis of personality disorders: A different approach. *Journal of Psychopathology and Behavioral Assessment, 17*, 145–165.

Furby, L., Weinrott, M.R., & Blackshaw, L. (1989). Sex offenders recidivism: A review. *Psychological Bulletin, 105*, 3–30.

Fyer, A.J., Mannuzza, S., Chapman, T.F., Liebowitz, M.R., & Klein, D.F. (1993). A direct interview family study of social phobia. *Archives of General Psychiatry, 50*, 286–293.

Gagnon, J.H., & Simon, W. (1973). *Sexual conduct: The social sources of human sexuality*. Chicago: Aldine.

Garber, H.I. (1988). *The Milwaukee project: Preventing mental retardation in children at risk*. Washington, DC: American Association on Mental Retardation.

Garber, J. (1984). Classification of childhood psychopathology: A developmental perspective. *Child Development, 55*, 30–48.

Garber, J., & Hollon, S.D. (1991). What can specificity designs say about causality in psychopathology research? *Psychological Bulletin, 110*, 129–136.

Garfield, S.L. (1989). *The practice of brief psychotherapy*. New York: Pergamon.

Garfield, S., & Kurtz, R. (1974). A survey of clinical psychologists: Characteristics, activities, and orientations. *Clinical Psychologist, 28*, 7–10.

Garfinkel, P.E., & Garner, D.M. (1982). *Anorexia nervosa: A multidimensional perspective*. New York: Basic Books.

Garfinkel, P.E., Lin, B., & Goering, P. (in press). Purging and nonpurging forms of bulimia nervosa in a community sample. *International Journal of Eating Disorders*.

Garfinkel, P.E., Kennedy, S.H., & Kaplan, A.S. (1995). Views on classification and diagnosis of eating disorders. *Canadian Journal of Psychiatry, 40*, 445–456.

Garland, A.F., & Zigler, E. (1993). Adolescent suicide prevention: Current research and social policy implications. *American Psychologist, 48*, 169–182.

Garmezy, N. (1978). DSM-III: Never mind the psychologists; Is it good for the children? *Clinical Psychologist, 31*, 1–6.

Garner, D.M., & Bemis, K.M. (1982). A cognitive-behavioral approach to anorexia nervosa. *Cognitive Therapy and Research, 6*, 123–150.

Garner, D.M., Garfinkel, P.E., Schwartz, D., & Thompson, M. (1980). Cultural expectations of thinness in women. *Psychological Reports, 47*, 483–491.

Garner, D.M., Garner, M.V., & Rosen, L.W. (1993). Anorexia nervosa "restrictors" who purge: Implications for subtyping anorexia nervosa. *International Journal of Eating Disorders, 13*, 171–185.

Garner, D.M., & Needleman, L.D. (1996). Stepped-care and decision-tree models for treating eating disorders. In J.K. Thompson, *Body image, eating disorders, and obesity*, pp. 225–252. Washington, DC: American Psychological Association.

Garner, D.M., Olmstead, M.P., & Polivy, J. (1983). The Eating Disorder Inventory: A measure of cognitive-behavioral dimensions of anorexia nervosa and bulimia. In P.L. Darby, P.E. Garfinkel, D.M. Garner, & D.V. Coscina (Eds.), *Anorexia nervosa: Recent developments in research*, pp. 173–184. New York: Liss.

Garza-Trevino, E. (1994). Neurobiological factors in aggressive behavior. *Hospital and Community Psychiatry, 45*, 690–699.

Gaylord, S.A., & Zung, W.W.K. (1987). Affective disorders among the aging. In L.L. Carstensen & B.A. Edelstein (Eds.), *Handbook of clinical gerontology*. New York: Plenum.

Geer, J., Heiman, J., & Leitenberg, H. (1984). *Human sexuality*. Englewood Cliffs, NJ: Prentice Hall.

Gehlbach, S.H. (1988). *Interpreting the medical literature: Practical epidemiology for clinics*, 2nd ed. New York: Macmillan.

Geller, B., et al. (1992). Pharmacokinetically designed double-blind placebo-controlled study of nortriptyline in 6- to 12-year-olds with major depressive disorder. *Journal of the American Academy of Child and Adolescent Psychiatry, 31*, 34–44.

Geller, E., Ritvo, E.R., Freeman, B.J., & Yuwiler, A. (1982). Preliminary observations on the effect of fenfluramine on blood serotonin and symptoms in three autistic boys. *New England Journal of Medicine, 307*, 165–169.

Gerardi, R.J., Blanchard, E.B., & Kolb, L.C. (1989). Ability of Vietnam veterans to dissimulate a psychophysiological assessment for posttraumatic stress disorder. *Behavior Therapy, 20,* 229–244.

Gerner, R.H., & Stanton, A. (1992). Algorithm for patient management of acute manic states: Lithium, valproate, or carbamazepine? *Journal of Clinical Psychopharmacology, 12* (suppl. 1). 57S–63S.

Gerstley, L., McLellan, T., Alterman, A.I., Woody, G.E., Luborsky, L., & Prout, M. (1989). Ability to form an alliance with the therapist: A possible marker of prognosis for patients with antisocial personality disorder. *American Journal of Psychiatry, 146,* 508–512.

Geske, M.R. (1989). Statutes limiting mental health professionals' liability for the violent acts of their patients. *Indiana Law Journal, 64,* 391–422.

Giacobini, E. (1994). Therapy for Alzheimer's disease: Symptomatic or neuroprotective? *Molecular Neurobiology, 9,* 115–118.

Gianoulakis, C. (1993). Endogenous opioids and excessive alcohol-consumption. *Journal of Psychiatry and Neuroscience, 18,* 148–156.

Gibbs, N.A., & Oltmanns, T.F. (1995). The relation between obsessive-compulsive personality traits and subtypes of compulsive behavior. *Journal of Anxiety Disorders, 9,* 397–410.

Gilbert, D.G., Hagen, R.L., & D'Agostino, J.A. (1986). The effects of cigarette smoking on human sexual potency. *Addictive Behaviors, 11,* 431–434.

Gillberg, C. (1988). The role of the endogenous opioids in autism and possible relationships to clinical features. In L. Wing (Ed.), *Aspects of autism: Biological research,* pp. 31–37. London: Gaskell.

Gillberg, C. (1991). Outcome in autism and autistic-like conditions. *Journal of the American Academy of Child and Adolescent Psychiatry, 30,* 375–382.

Gillberg, C., Rastam, M., & Gillberg, C. (1995). Anorexia nervosa 6 years after onset. I. Personality disorders. *Comprehensive Psychiatry, 36,* 61–69.

Gillberg, C., & Schaumann, H. (1982). Social class and infantile autism. *Journal of Autism and Developmental Disorders, 12,* 223–228.

Gilligan, C. (1982). *In a different voice.* Cambridge, MA: Harvard University Press.

Gitlin, M.J. (1993). Pharmacotherapy of personality disorders: Conceptual framework and clinical strategies. *Journal of Clinical Psychopharmacology, 13,* 343–353.

Gittelman-Klein, R. (1988). Questioning the clinical usefulness of projective psychological tests for children. *Developmental and Behavioral Pediatrics, 7,* 378–382.

Glaser, R., Rice, J., Sheridan, J., Fertel, R., Stout, J., Speicher, C.E., Pinsky, D., Kotur, M., Post, A., Beck, M., & Kiecolt-Glaser, J.K. (1987). Stress-related immune suppression: Health implications. *Brain, Behavior, and Immunity, 1,* 7–20.

Gleaves, D.H. (1996). The sociocognitive model of dissociative identity disorder: A reexamination of the evidence. *Psychological Bulletin, 120,* 42–59.

Gleick, J. (1987). *Chaos: Making of a new science.* New York: Viking.

Goldberg, E.M. (1970). *Helping the aged: A field experiment in social work.* London: Allen & Unwin.

Goldberg, E.M., & Morrison, S.L. (1963). Schizophrenia and social class. *British Journal of Psychiatry, 109,* 785–802.

Goldberg, J., True, W.R., Eisen, S.A., & Henderson, W.G. (1990). A twin study of the effects of the Vietnam War on posttraumatic stress disorder. *Journal of the American Medical Association, 263,* 2725–2729.

Goldberg, L.R. (1990). An alternative "description of personality": The big five factor structure. *Journal of Personality and Social Psychology, 59,* 1216–1229.

Goldberg, L.R. (1993). The structure of phenotypic personality traits. *American Psychologist, 48,* 26–34.

Goldberg, S. (1991). Recent developments in attachment theory and research. *Canadian Journal of Psychiatry, 36,* 393–400.

Goldberg, S.C., Schulz, S.C., Schulz, P.M., et al. (1986). Borderline and schizotypal personality disorders treated with low-dose thiothizene vs placebo. *Archives of General Psychiatry, 43,* 680–686.

Goldberg, T.E., & Weinberger, D.R. (1995). A case against subtyping in schizophrenia. *Schizophrenia Research, 17,* 147–152.

Goldblatt, M.J. (1994). Hospitalization of the suicidal patient. In A.A. Leenaars, J.T. Maltsberger, & R.A. Neimeyer (Eds.), *Treatment of suicidal people,* pp. 153–165. Washington, DC: Taylor & Francis.

Goldfried, M.R. (Ed.) (1982). *Converging themes in psychotherapy.* New York: Springer.

Goldfried, M.R., & Castonguay, L.G. (1993). Behavior therapy: Redefining strengths and limitations. *Behavior Therapy, 24,* 505–526.

Goldfried, M.R., & Davison, G.C. (1994). *Clinical behavior therapy,* 2nd ed. New York: Wiley-Interscience.

Goldfried, M.R., & Kent, R.N. (1972). Traditional versus behavioral personality assessment: A comparison of methodological and theoretical assumptions. *Psychological Bulletin, 77,* 409–420.

Goldman, H.H., Adams, N.H., & Taube, C.A. (1983). Deinstitutionalization: The data demythologized. *Hospital and Community Psychiatry, 34,* 129–134.

Goldman, H.H., Skodol, A.E., & Lave, T.R. (1992). Revising Axis V for DSM-IV: A review of measures of social functioning. *American Journal of Psychiatry, 149,* 1148–1156.

Goldman, M.S., Brown, S.A., & Christiansen, B.A. (1987). Expectancy theory: Thinking about drinking. In H.T. Blane & K.E. Leonard (Eds.), *Psychological theories of drinking and alcoholism,* pp. 181–226. New York: Guilford.

Goldman, M.S. (1994). The alcohol expectancy concept: Applications to assessment, prevention, and treatment of alcohol abuse. *Applied and Preventive Psychology, 3,* 131–144.

Goldman, M.S., Brown, S.A., Christiansen, B.A., & Smith, G.T. (1991). Alcoholism and memory: Broadening the scope of alcohol-expectancy research. *Psychological Bulletin, 110,* 137–146.

Goldman-Rakic, P. (1996). Dissolution of cerebral cortical mechanisms in subjects with schizophrenia. In S.J. Watson (Ed.), *Biology of schizophrenia and affective disease,* pp. 113–127. Washington, DC: American Psychiatric Press.

Goldsmith, H. (1988). Roundtable: What is temperament? Four approaches. *Child Development, 58,* 505–529.

Goldsmith, H.H., Buss, A.H., Plomin, R., Rothbart, M., Klevjord, T., Thomas, A., Chess, S., Hinde, R.A., & McCall, R.B. (1987). Roundtable: What is temperament? Four approaches. *Child Development, 58,* 505–552.

Goldstein, A.J., & Chambless, D.L. (1978). A reanalysis of agoraphobia. *Behavior Therapy, 9,* 47–59.

Goldstein, J.M. (1995a). The impact of gender on understanding the epidemiology of schizophrenia. In M.V. Seeman (Ed.), *Gender and psychopathology,* pp. 159–199. Washington, DC: American Psychiatric Press.

Goldstein, J.M. (1995b). Gender and the familial transmission of schizophrenia. In M.V. Seeman (Ed.), *Gender and psychopathology,* pp. 201–226. Washington, DC: American Psychiatric Press.

Goldstein, M.J. (1988). The family and psychopathology. *Annual Review of Psychology, 39,* 283–299.

Goldstein, M.J. (1994). Psychoeducational and family therapy in relapse prevention. *Acta Psychiatrica Scandinavica, 89* (suppl. 382), 54–57.

Goldstein, M.J., & Kant, H.S. (1973). *Pornography and sexual deviance.* Berkeley: University of California Press.

Goldstein, M.J., & Miklowitz, D.J. (1994). Family intervention for persons with bipolar disorder. In A. Hatfield (Ed.), *Family interventions in mental illness.* San Francisco: Jossey-Bass.

Golomb, J., de Leon, M.J., Kluger, A., George, A.E., Tarshish, C., & Ferris, S.H. (1993). Hippocampal atrophy in normal aging: An association with recent memory impairment. *Archives of Neurology, 50,* 967–973.

Golub, E.S. (1994). *The limits of medicine: How science shapes our hope for the cure.* New York: Random House.

Golwyn, D.H., & Sevlie, C.P. (1992). Paraphilias, nonparaphilic sexual addictions, and social phobia. *Journal of Clinical Psychiatry, 53,* 330.

Gomberg, E.S.L. (1987). Drug and alcohol problems of elderly persons. In T.D. Nirenberg & S.A. Maisto (Eds.), *Developments in the assessment and treatment of addictive behaviors.* Norwood, NJ: Ablex.

Gomberg, E.S.L. (1988). Alcoholic women in treatment: The question of stigma and age. *Alcohol and Alcoholism, 23,* 507–514.

Gomberg, E.S.L. (1993). Women and alcohol: Use and abuse. *Journal of Nervous and Mental Disease, 181,* 211–219.

Good, B., & Kleinman, A. (1985a). Culture and anxiety: Cross-cultural evidence for the patterning of anxiety disorders. In A.H. Tuma & J. Maser (Eds.), *Anxiety and the anxiety disorders.* Hillsdale, NJ: Erlbaum.

Good, B., & Kleinman, A. (1985b). Culture and depression. In A. Kleinman & B. Good (Eds.), *Culture and depression: Studies in the anthropology and cross-cultural psychiatry of affect and disorder,* pp. 491–506. Berkeley: University of California Press.

Gooding, D.C., & Iacono, W.G. (1995). Schizophrenia through the lens of a developmental psychopathology perspective. In D. Cicchetti & D.J. Cohen (Eds.), *Developmental psychopathology. Vol. 2. Risk, disorder, and adaptation,* pp. 535–580. New York: Wiley.

Gooding, D.C., Iacono, W.G., & Beiser, M. (1994). Temporal stability of smooth-pursuit eye tracking in first-episode psychosis. *Psychophysiology, 31,* 62–67.

Goodman, L.A., Koss, M.P., & Russo, N.F. (1993a). Violence against women: Physical and mental health effects. Part I. Research findings. *Applied and Preventive Psychology, 2,* 79–89.

Goodman, L.A., Koss, M.P., & Russo, N.F. (1993b). Violence against women: Mental health effects. Part II. Conceptualizations of posttraumatic stress. *Applied and Preventive Psychology, 2,* 123–130.

Goodman, L.A., Koss, M.P., Fitzgerald, L.F., Russo, N.F., & Keita, G.P. (1993). Male violence against women: Current research and future directions. *American Psychologist, 48,* 1054–1058.

Goodman, R., & Stevenson, J. (1989). A twin study of hyperactivity. II. The aetiological role of genes, family relationships, and perinatal adversity. *Journal of Child Clinical Psychology and Psychiatry, 30,* 691–709.

Goodman, T.A. (1985). From Tarasoff to Hopper: The evolution of the therapist's duty to protect third parties. *Behavioral Sciences and the Law, 3,* 195–225.

Goodman, W.K., Price, L.H., Rasmussen, S.A., Mazure, C., Fleischman, R.L., Hill, C.L., Heninger, G.R., & Charmey, D.S. (1989). The Yale-Brown Obsessive Compulsive Scale. 1. Development, use, and reliability. *Archives of General Psychiatry, 46,* 1006–1011.

Goodwin, D.W. (1991). The genetics of alcoholism. In P.R. McHugh & V.A. McKusick (Eds.), *Genes, brain, and behavior.* New York: Raven Press.

Goodwin, D.W. (1984a). Speculations on the cause(s) of alcoholism. *Journal of Clinical Psychiatry, 45,* 491–493.

Goodwin, D.W. (1984b). Studies of familial alcoholism: A review. *Journal of Clinical Psychiatry, 45,* 14–17.

Goodwin, D.W. (1988). *Alcohol and the writer.* New York: Penguin.

Goodwin, D.W., & Guze, S.B. (1979). *Psychiatric diagnosis,* 2nd ed. New York: Oxford University Press.

Goodwin, D.W., Knop, J., Jensen, P. Gabrielli, W.F., Schulsinger, F., & Penick, E.C. (1994). Thirty-year follow-up of men at high risk for alcoholism. *Annals of the New York Academy of Sciences, 708,* 97–101.

Goodwin, F.K., & Jamison, K.R. (1990). *Manic-depressive illness.* New York: Oxford University Press.

Goodwin, G.M. (1992). Tricyclic and newer

antidepressants. In E.S. Paykel (Ed.), *Handbook of affective disorders*. 2nd ed. pp. 327–344. New York: Guilford.

Gorenstein, E.E. (1992). *The science of mental illness*. San Diego: Academic Press.

Gorton, G., & Akhtar, S. (1990). The literature on personality disorders, 1985–88: Trends, issues, and controversies. *Hospital and Community Psychiatry, 41*, 39–51.

Gosselin, C.C., & Wilson, G.D. (1980). *Sexual variations*. London: Faber & Faber.

Gotlib, I.H., & Colby, C.A. (1987). *Treatment of depression: An interpersonal systems approach*. New York: Pergamon.

Gotlib, I.H., & Hammen, C. (1992). *Psychological aspects of depression: Toward a cognitive-interpersonal integration*. New York: Wiley.

Gotlib, I.H., & McCabe, S.B. (1990). Marriage and psychopathology. In F.D. Fincham & T.N. Bradbury (Eds.), *The psychology of marriage: Basic issues and applications*, pp. 226–257. New York: Guilford.

Gotlib, I.H., & Meltzer, S.J. (1987). Depression and the perception of social skill in dyadic interaction. *Cognitive Therapy and Research, 11*, 41–53.

Gotlib, I.H., & Robinson, L.A. (1982). Responses to depressed individuals: Discrepancies between self-report and observer-rated behavior. *Journal of Abnormal Psychology, 91*, 231–240.

Gottesman, I.G. (1963). Genetic aspects of intelligent behavior. In N. Ellis (Ed.), *The handbook of mental deficiency: Psychological theory and research*, pp. 253–296. New York: McGraw-Hill.

Gottesman, I.I. (1987). The psychotic hinterlands or, the fringes of lunacy. *British Medical Bulletin, 43*, 1–13.

Gottesman, I.I. (1991). *Schizophrenia genesis: The origins of madness*. New York: Freeman.

Gottesman, I.I., & Goldsmith, H.H. (1994). Developmental psychopathology of antisocial behavior: Inserting genes into its ontogenesis and epigenesis. In C.A. Nelson (Ed.), *Threats to optimal development: Integrating biological, psychological, and social risk factors*, pp. 69–104. Hillsdale, NJ: Erlbaum.

Gottesman, I.I., McGuffin, P., & Farmer, A. (1987). Clinical genetics as clues to the "real" genetics of schizophrenia. *Schizophrenia Bulletin, 13*, 23–47.

Gottesman, I.I., & Moldin, S.O. (1997). Genes, experience, and chance in schizophrenia: Positioning for the 21st century. *Schizophrenia Bulletin, 23*.

Gottfries, C.G. (1991). Classifying organic mental disorders and dementia—A review of historical perspectives. *International Psychogeriatrics, 3* (suppl.), 9–17.

Gottman, J.M. (1985). Observational measures of behavior therapy outcome: A reply to Jacobsen. *Behavioral Assessment, 7*, 317–321.

Gottman, J.M. (1994). *Why marriages succeed or fail*. New York: Simon & Schuster.

Gottman, J.M., & Katz, L.F. (1989). Effects of marital discord on young children's peer interaction and health. *Developmental Psychology, 25*, 373–381.

Gottman, J.M., & Levenson, R.W. (1986). Assessing the role of emotion in marriage. *Behavioral Assessment, 8*, 31–48.

Gottman, J.M., & Levenson, R.W. (1988). The social psychophysiology of marriage. In P. Noller & M.A. Fitzpatrick (Eds.), *Perspectives on marital interaction*, pp. 182–200. Clevedon, England: Multilingual Matters.

Gottman, J.M., & Levenson, R.W. (1992). Marital processes predictive of later dissolution: Behavior, physiology, and health. *Journal of Personality and Social Psychology, 63*, 221–233.

Gottman, J., Notarius, C., Gonso, J., & Markman, H. (1976). *A couple's guide to communication*. Champaign, IL: Research Press.

Goudie, A.J. (1990). Conditioned opponent processes in the development of tolerance to psychoactive drugs. *Progress in Neuro-Psychopharmacology and Biological Psychiatry, 14*, 675–688.

Gould, M.S. (1990). Suicide clusters and media exposure. In S.J. Blumenthal, and D.J. Kupfer (Eds.), *Suicide over the life cycle: Risk factors, assessment, and treatment of suicidal patients*. Washington, D.C.: American Psychiatric Press. pp. 517–532.

Gove, W.R. (1970). Societal reaction as an explanation of mental illness: An evaluation. *American Sociological Review, 35*, 873–884.

Gove, W.R. (1990). Labeling theory's explanation of mental illness: An update of recent evidence. In M. Nagler (Ed.), *Perspectives on disability*. Palo Alto, CA: Health Markets Research.

Gove, W.R., Hughes, M., & Styles, C.B. (1983). Does marriage have positive effects on the psychological well-being of the individual? *Journal of Health and Social Behavior, 24*, 122–132.

Graham, J.R. (1990). *MMPI-2. Assessing personality and psychopathology*. New York: Oxford University Press.

Grant, William T., Foundation. (1988). *The forgotten half: Pathways to success for America's youth and young families*. Washington, DC: Youth and America's Future: William T. Grant Foundation Commission on Work, Family and Citizenship.

Grandin, T. (1995). *Thinking in pictures and other reports from my life with autism*. New York: Doubleday.

Granville-Grossman, K. (1983). Mind and body. In M.H. Lader (Ed.), *Handbook of psychiatry 2: Mental disorders and somatic illness*, pp. 5–13. London: Cambridge University Press.

Gratzer, T., & Bradford, J.M.W. (1995). Offender and offense characteristics of sexual sadists: A comparative study. *Journal of Forensic Sciences, 40*, 450–455.

Gray, J.A. (1990). Brain systems that mediate both emotion and cognition. *Cognition and Emotion, 4*, 269–288.

Greaves, G.B. (1980). Multiple personality disorder: 165 years after Mary Reynolds. *Journal of Nervous and Mental Disease, 168*, 577–596.

Greenberg, L.S., Elliott, R.K., & Lietaer, G. (1994). In A.E. Bergin & S.L. Garfield, *Handbook of psychotherapy and behavior change*, 4th ed., pp. 509–542. New York: Wiley.

Greenberg, R.P., Bornstein, R.F., Zborowski, M.J., Fisher, S., & Greenberg, M.D. (1994). A meta-analysis of fluoxetine outcome in the treatment of depression. *Journal of Nervous and Mental Disease, 182*, 547–551.

Greene, R.L. (1991). *The MMPI-2/MMPI: An interpretive manual*. Boston: Allyn and Bacon.

Greenough, W.T. (1987). Experience effects on the developing and the mature brain: Dendritic branching and synaptogenesis. In N.A. Krasnegor, E.M. Blass & M.A. Hofer (Eds.), *Perinatal development: A psychobiological perspective*, pp. 195–221. Orlando, FL: Academic Press.

Grenier, G., & Gyers, E.S. (1995). Rapid ejaculation: A review of conceptual, etiological and treatment issues. *Archives of Sexual Behavior, 24*, 447–471.

Griffitt, W. (1987). Females, males, and sexual responses. In K. Kelley (Ed.), *Females, males, and sexuality*. Albany: State University of New York Press.

Grinspoon, L., & Bakalar, J.B. (1993). *Marihuana: The forbidden medicine*. New Haven, CT: Yale University Press.

Grisso, T., & Appelbaum, P.S. (1992). Is it unethical to offer predictions of future violence? *Law and Human Behavior, 16*, 621–633.

Grob, G.N. (1994). *The mad among us: A history of the care of America's mentally ill*. Cambridge, MA: Harvard University Press.

Grossman, H.J. (1983). *Classification in mental retardation*. Washington, DC: American Association on Mental Deficiency.

Grotevant, H.D., & Carlson, C.I. (1989). *Family assessment: A guide to methods and measures*. New York: Guilford.

Group for Advancement of Psychiatry (1966). *Psychopathological disorders of childhood: Theoretical considerations and a proposed classification*. Report 62. New York: Mental Health Memorials Center.

Grove, W.M., & Andreasen, N.C. (1992). Concepts, diagnosis and classification. In E.S. Paykel (Ed.), *Handbook of affective disorders*, 2nd ed., pp. 25–42. New York: Guilford.

Grove, W.M., Andreasen, N.C., McDonald-Scott, P., Keller, M.B., & Shapiro, R.W. (1981). Reliability studies of psychiatric diagnosis. *Archives of General Psychiatry, 38*, 408–413.

Grove, W.M., Andreasen, N.C., Young, M., Endicott, J., Keller, M.B., Hirschfeld, R.M.A., & Reich, T. (1987). Isolation and characterization of a nuclear depressive syndrome. *Psychological Medicine, 17*, 471–484.

Grove, W.M., Clementz, B.A., Iacono, W.G., & Katsanis, J. (1992). Smooth pursuit ocular motor dysfunction in schizophrenia: Evidence for a major gene. *American Journal of Psychiatry, 149*, 1362–1368.

Grove, W.M., Lebow, B.S., Clementz, B.A., Cerri, A., et al. (1991). Familial prevalence and coaggregation of schizotypy indicators: A multitrait family study. *Journal of Abnormal Psychology, 100*, 115–121.

Grove, W.M., & Tellegen, A. (1991). Problems in the classification of personality disorders. *Journal of Personality Disorders, 5*, 31–41.

Growdon, J.H. (1992). Treatment for Alzheimer's disease? *New England Journal of Medicine, 327*, 1306–1308.

Grych, J.H., & Fincham, F.D. (1990). Marital conflict and children's adjustment: A cognitive-contextual framework. *Psychological Bulletin, 101*, 267–290.

Guggenmoos-Holzmann, I. (1993). How reliable are chance-corrected measures of agreement? *Statistics in Medicine, 12*, 2191–2205.

Gunderson, J. (1984). *Borderline personality disorder*. Washington, DC: American Psychiatric Press.

Gunderson, J.G. (1994). Building structure for the borderline construct. *Acta Psychiatrica Scandinavica, 89* (suppl. 379), 12–18.

Gunderson, J., Kolb, J., Austin, V. (1981). The diagnostic interview for borderline patients. *American Journal of Psychiatry, 138*, 896–903.

Gunderson, J.G., & Singer, M.T. (1975). Defining borderline patients: An overview. *American Journal of Psychiatry, 132*, 1–10.

Gupta, S. (1993). Can environmental factors explain the epidemiology of schizophrenia in immigrant groups? *Social Psychiatry and Psychiatric Epidemiology, 28*, 263–266.

Gur, R.E. (1985). Regional cerebral blood flow in schizophrenia. In M. Alpert (Ed.), *Controversies in schizophrenia: Changes and constancies*. New York: Guilford.

Gur, R.E., Mozley, D., Resnick, S.M., Mozley, L.H., et al. (1995). Resting cerebral glucose metabolism in first-episode and previously treated patients with schizophrenia relates to clinical features. *Archives of General Psychiatry, 52*, 657–667.

Gur, R.E., & Pearlson, G.D. (1993). Neuroimaging in schizophrenia research. *Schizophrenia Bulletin, 19*, 337–353.

Gurian, B., & Goisman, R. (1993). Anxiety disorders in the elderly. *Generations, 17*, 39–42.

Gurland, B.J. (1976). The comparative frequency of depression in various adult age groups. *Journal of Gerontology, 31*, 283–392.

Gurland, B. (1996). Epidemiology of psychiatric disorders. In J. Sadavoy, L.W. Lazarus, L.F. Jarvik, & G.T. Grossberg (Eds.), *Comprehensive review of geriatric psychiatry—II*, pp. 3–42. Washington, DC: American Psychiatric Press.

Gurman, A.S., & Kniskern, D.P. (Eds.) (1991). *Handbook of family therapy*, vol. II. New York: Brunner/Mazel.

Gusella, J.F., Wexler, N.S., Conneally, P.M., Naylor, S.L., Anderson, M.A., Tanzi, R.E., Watkins, P.C., Ottina, K., Wallace, M.R., Sakaguchi, A.Y., Young, A.B., et al. (1983). A polymorphic DNA marker genetically linked to Huntington's disease. *Nature, 306*, 234–238.

Gussekloo, J., Heeren, T.J., Izaks, G.J., Ligthart, G.J., et al. (1995). A community based study of the incidence of dementia in subjects aged 85 years and over. *Journal of Neurology, Neurosurgery, & Psychiatry, 59,* 507–510.

Gutheil, T.G. (1986). The right to refuse treatment: Paradox, pendulum and the quality of care. *Behavioral Sciences and the Law, 4,* 265–277.

Guzder, J., Paris, J., Zelkowitz, P., & Marchessault, K. (1996). Risk factors for borderline psychology in children. *Journal of the American Academy of Child and Adolescent Psychiatry, 35,* 26–33.

Guze, S.B., & Robins, E. (1970). Suicide and primary affective disorders. *British Journal of Psychiatry, 117,* 437–438.

Haaga, D.A.F., & Beck, A.T. (1992). Cognitive therapy. In E.S. Paykel (Ed.), *Handbook of affective disorders,* 2nd ed., p. 511–523. New York: Guilford.

Hafner, H. (1990). Primary dementia of Alzheimer's type—Epidemiology and risk factors. *Psychiatria Fennica, 21,* 145–162.

Hafner, H., Maurer, K., Loffler, W., Fatkenheuer, B., an der Heiden, W., Riecher-Rossler, A., Behrens, S., & Gattaz, W.F. (1994). The epidemiology of early schizophrenia: Influence of age and gender on onset and early course. *British Journal of Psychiatry, 164* (suppl. 23), 29–38.

Hage, J.J. (1995). Medical requirements and consequences of sex reassignment surgery. *Medicine, Science and the Law, 35,* 17–24.

Halford, W.K. (1991). Beyond expressed emotion. Behavioral assessment of family interaction associated with the course of schizophrenia. *Behavioral Assessment, 13,* 99–123.

Hall, G.C. (1995). Sexual offender recidivism revisited: A meta-analysis of recent treatment studies. *Journal of Consulting and Clinical Psychology, 63,* 802–809.

Hamilton, M. (1982). Symptoms and assessment of depression. In E.S. Paykel (Ed.), *Handbook of affective disorders,* pp. 3–11. New York: Guilford.

Hammen, C. (1991). The generation of stress in the course of unipolar depression. *Journal of Abnormal Psychology, 100,* 555–561.

Hankoff, I.D. (1982). Suicide and attempted suicide. In E.S. Paykel (Ed.), *Handbook of affective disorders,* pp. 416–428. New York: Guilford.

Hanson, D.R., Gottesman, I.I., & Heston, L.L. (1976). Some possible childhood indications of adult schizophrenia inferred from children of schizophrenics. *British Journal of Psychiatry, 129,* 142–154.

Hanson, D.R., Gottesman, I.I., & Heston, L.L. (1990). Long range schizophrenia forecasting: Many a slip twixt cup and lip. In J. Rolf, K. Nuechterlein, A. Masten, & D. Cicchetti (Eds.), *Risk and protective factors in the development of schizophrenia,* pp. 424–444. New York: Cambridge University Press.

Happe, F. (1995). *Autism.* Cambridge, MA: Harvard University Press.

Harding, C.M. (1988). Course types in schizophrenia: An analysis of European and American studies. *Schizophrenia Bulletin, 14,* 633–643.

Harding, C.M., Zubin, J., & Strauss, J.S. (1992). Chronicity in schizophrenia: Revisited. *British Journal of Psychiatry, 161* (suppl. 18), 27–37.

Hare, R.D. (1983). Diagnosis of antisocial personality disorder in two prison populations. *American Journal of Psychiatry, 140,* 887–890.

Hare, R.D. (1985). Comparison of procedures for the assessment of psychopathy. *Journal of Consulting and Clinical Psychology, 53,* 7–16.

Hare, R.D. (1993). *Without conscience: The disturbing world of the psychopaths among us.* New York: Pocket Books.

Hare, R.D., Hart, S.D., & Harpur, T.J. (1991). Psychopathy and the DSM-IV criteria for antisocial personality disorder. *Journal of Abnormal Psychology, 100,* 391–398.

Harley, J.P., Ray, R.S., Tomasi, L., Eichman, P.L., Matthews, C.G., Chun, R., Cleeland, C.S., & Traisman, E. (1978). Hyperkinesis and food additives: Testing the Feingold hypothesis. *Pediatrics, 6,* 818–828.

Harpur, T.J., & Hare, R.D. (1994). Assessment of psychopathy as a function of age. *Journal of Abnormal Psychology, 103,* 604–609.

Harrington, R., Fudge, H., Rutter, M., Pickles, A., & Hill, J. (1990). Adult outcomes of childhood and adolescent depression. I. Psychiatric status. *Archives of General Psychiatry, 47,* 465–473.

Harris, G.T., & Rice, M.E. (1996). The science in phallometric measurement of male sexual interest. *Current Directions in Psychological Science, 5,* 156–160.

Harris, G.T., Rice, M.E., Quinsey, V.L., Chaplin, T.C., et al. (1992). Maximizing the discriminant validity of phallometric assessment data. *Psychological Assessment, 4,* 502–511.

Harris, T., Brown, G.W., & Bifulco, A. (1986). Loss of parent in childhood and adult psychiatric disorder: The role of lack of adequate parental care. *Psychological Medicine, 16,* 641–659.

Harrow, M., Rattenbury, F., & Stoll, F. (1988). Schizophrenic delusions: An analysis of their persistence, of related premorbid ideas, and of three major dimensions. In T.F. Oltmanns & B.A. Maher (Eds.), *Delusional beliefs,* pp. 184–211. New York: Wiley.

Hartmann, H., Kris, E., & Loewenstein, R.W. (1947). Comments on the formation of psychic structure. In A. Freud et al. (Eds.), *The psychoanalytic study of the child.* New York: International Universities Press.

Harvey, R.J. (1996). Review: Delusions in dementia. *Age and Ageing, 25,* 405–409.

Haskett, R.F. (1993). The HPA axis and depressive disorders. In J. John Mann & David J. Kupfer (Eds.), *Biology of depressive disorders, Part A: A systems perspective,* pp. 171–188. New York: Plenum.

Haugaard, J.J., & Reppucci, N.D. (1988). *The sexual abuse of children.* San Francisco: Jossey-Bass.

Hauser, P., Zametkin, A.J., Martinez, P., Vitiello, B., Matochik, J.A., Mixson, A.J., & Weintraub, B.D. (1993). Attention deficit-hyperactivity disorder in people with generalized resistance to thyroid hormone. *New England Journal of Medicine, 328,* 997–1001.

Havighurst, R.J. (1952). *Developmental tasks and education.* New York: McKay.

Hawley, T.L., & Disney, E.R. (1992). Crack's children: The consequences of maternal cocaine abuse. *Social Policy Report: Society for Research in Child Development, 6,* 1–22.

Hawton, K. (1986). *Suicide and attempted suicide among children and adolescents.* Beverly Hills, CA: Sage.

Hayes, S.C., Nelson, R.O., & Jarrett, R.B. (1987). The treatment utility of assessment: A functional approach to evaluating assessment quality. *American Psychologist, 42,* 963–974.

Haynes, S.G., & Feinleib, M. (1980). Women, work, and coronary heart disease: Prospective findings from the Framingham heart study. *American Journal of Public Health, 70,* 133–141.

Heath, A.C., Jardine, R., & Martin, N.G. (1989). Interactive effects of genotype and social environment on alcohol consumption in female twins. *Journal of Studies on Alcohol, 50,* 38–48.

Heath, D.B. (1991). Uses and misuses of the concept of ethnicity in alcohol studies: An essay in deconstruction. *International Journal of the Addictions, 25,* 607–628.

Heatherton, T.F. & Polivy, J. (1992). Chronic dieting and eating disorders: A spiral model. In J. Crowther, S.E. Hobfall, M.A.P. Stephens, & D.L. Tennenbaum (Eds.), *The etiology of bulimia: The individual and familial context* (pp. 135–155). Washington, D.C.: Hemisphere.

Heavey, C.L., Christensen, A., & Malamuth, N.M. (1995). The longitudinal impact of demand and withdrawal during marital conflict. *Journal of Consulting and Clinical Psychology, 63,* 797–801.

Heber, R. (1959). A manual on terminology and classification in mental retardation. *American Journal on Mental Deficiency, 64* (Monograph Supplement).

Heberbrand, J. (1992). A critical appraisal of X-linked bipolar illness. Evidence for the assumed mode of transmission is lacking. *British Journal of Psychiatry, 160,* 7–11.

Heilbrun, A.B., Jr. (1993). Hallucinations. In C.G. Costello (Ed.), *Symptoms of schizophrenia,* pp. 56–91. New York: Wiley.

Heiman, J.R. (1983). Women and sexuality: Loosening the double binds. In G.W. Albee, S. Gordon, & H. Leitenberg (Eds.), *Promoting sexual responsibility and preventing sexual problems.* Hanover, NH: New England Press.

Heiman, J.R. (1980). Female sexual response patterns: Interactions of physiological, affective, and contextual cues. *Archives of General Psychiatry, 37,* 1311–1316.

Heiman, J.R., & Grafton-Becker, V. (1989). Orgasmic disorders in women. In S.R. Leiblum & R.C. Rosen (Eds.), *Principles and practice of sex therapy: Update for the 1990s,* 2nd ed., pp. 51–88. New York: Guilford.

Heimberg, R.G., Holt, C.S., Schneier, F.R., Spitzer, R.L., & Liebowitz, M.R. (1993). The issue of subtyping in the diagnosis of social phobia. *Journal of Anxiety Disorders, 7,* 249–269.

Heinberg, L.J., Thompson, J.K., & Stormer, S. (1995). Development and validation of the sociocultural attitudes towards appearance questionnaire. *International Journal of Eating Disorders, 17,* 81–89.

Heindel, W.C., Salmon, D.P., Shults, C.W., Walicke, P.A., & Butters, N. (1989). Neuropsychological evidence for multiple implicit memory systems: A comparison of Alzheimer's, Huntington's, and Parkinson's disease patients. *Journal of Neuroscience, 9,* 582–587.

Heitler, S.M. (1992). *From conflict to resolution: Strategies for diagnosis and treatment of distressed individuals, couples, and families.* New York: Norton.

Helmes, E., & Reddon, J.R. (1993). A perspective on developments in assessing psychopathology: A critical review of the MMPI and MMPI-2. *Psychological Bulletin, 113,* 453–471.

Helzer, J.E. (1987). Epidemiology of alcoholism. *Journal of Consulting and Clinical Psychology, 55,* 284–292.

Helzer, J.E., Bucholz, K., & Robins, L.N. (1992). Five communities in the United States: Results of the Epidemiologic Catchment Area Survey. In J.E. Helzer & G.J. Canino (Eds.), *Alcoholism in North America, Europe, and Asia.* pp. 71–95. New York: Oxford University Press.

Helzer, J.E., Burnam, A., & McEvoy, L.T. (1991). Alcohol abuse and dependence. In L.N. Robins & D.A. Regier (Eds.), *Psychiatric disorders in America: The Epidemiologic Catchment Area Study,* pp. 81–115. New York: Free Press.

Helzer, J.E., & Canino, G.J. (Eds.) (1992). *Alcoholism in North America, Europe, and Asia.* New York: Oxford University Press.

Helzer, J.E., Robins, L.N., & McEvoy, L. (1987). Posttraumatic stress disorder in the general population: Findings of the Epidemiologic Catchment Area Survey. *New England Journal of Medicine, 317,* 1630–1634.

Hempel, C.G. (1961). Introduction to problems of taxonomy. In J. Zubin (Ed.), *Field studies in the mental disorders.* New York: Grune & Stratton.

Hendin, H. (1995). *Suicide in America.* New York: Norton.

Hendricks, C.L. (1993–94). The trend toward mandatory mediation in custody and visitation disputes of minor children: An overview. *Journal of Family Law, 32,* 491–510.

Hengeveld, M.W. (1994). Serotonin in attempted suicide. *Journal of Psychosomatic Research, 38,* 639–641.

Henggeler, S.W. (1994). *Treatment manual for family*

preservation using multisystemic therapy. Charleston: Medical University of South Carolina.

Henggeler, S.W., & Borduin, C.M. (1990). *Family therapy and beyond: A multisystemic approach to treating the behavior problems of children and adolescents.* Pacific Grove, CA: Brooks/Cole.

Henker, B., & Whalen, C.K. (1989). Hyperactivity and attention deficits. *American Psychologist, 44,* 216–223.

Herbert, T.B., & Cohen, S. (1993). Depression and immunity: A meta-analytic review. *Psychological Bulletin, 113,* 472–486.

Herdt, G.H., & Davidson, J. (1988). The Sambia "Turnim-Man": Sociocultural and clinical aspects of gender formation in male pseudohermaphrodites with 5-alpha-reductase deficiency in Papua New Guinea. *Archives of Sexual Behavior, 17,* 33–56.

Herdt, G., & Stoller, R.J. (1990). *Intimate communications: Erotics and the study of culture.* New York: Columbia University Press.

Herman, C.P. & Polivy, J. (1988). Excess and restraint in bulimia. In K. Pirke, W. Vandereycken, & D. Ploog (Eds.), *The psychobiology of bulimia* (pp. 33–41). Munich: Springer-Verlag.

Hermann, D.H.J. (1990). Autonomy, self determination, the right of involuntarily committed persons to refuse treatment, and the use of substituted judgment in medication decisions involving incompetent persons. *International Journal of Law and Psychiatry, 13,* 361–385.

Hernandez, D.J. (1993). *America's children: Resources from family, government, and the economy.* New York: Russell Sage.

Hesselbrock, V., & Hesselbrock, M. (1990). Behavioral/social factors that may enhance or attenuate genetic effects. In C.R. Cloninger & H. Begleiter (Eds.), *Genetics and biology of alcoholism,* pp. 75–86. Cold Spring Harbor, NY: Cold Spring Harbor Laboratory Press.

Heston, L.L. (1966). Psychiatric disorders in foster home reared children of schizophrenic mothers. *British Journal of Psychiatry, 112,* 819–825.

Heston, L.L. (1997). The future is now (provided we recognize it). In L. Heston (Ed.), *Progress in Alzheimer's disease and similar conditions.* Washington, DC: American Psychiatric Press.

Heston, L.L., & White, J.A. (1991). *The vanishing mind: A practical guide to Alzheimer's disease and other dementias.* New York: Freeman.

Hetherington, E.M., & Parke, R.D. (1986). *Child psychology: A contemporary perspective.* New York: McGraw-Hill.

Hibbs, E.D., Hamburger, S.D., Kruesi, M.J.P., & Lenane, M. (1993). Factors affecting expressed emotion in parents of ill and normal children. *American Journal of Orthopsychiatry, 63,* 103–112.

Hill, J., & Holmbeck, G. (1986). Attachment and autonomy during adolescence. In G. Whitehurst (Ed.), *Annals of child development,* Vol. 3, pp. 145–189. Greenwich, CT: JAI.

Hill, M.A. (1992). Light, circadian rhythms, and mood disorders: A review. *Annals of Clinical Psychiatry, 4,* 131–146.

Hilts, P.J. (1996). *Smoke screen: The truth behind the tobacco industry coverup.* Reading, MA: Addison-Wesley.

Hinde, R.A. (1992). Developmental psychology in the context of other behavioral sciences. *Developmental Psychology, 28,* 1018–1029.

Hinshaw, S.P. (1987). On the distinction between attentional deficits/hyperactivity and conduct problems/aggression in child psychopathology. *Psychological Bulletin, 101,* 443–463.

Hinshaw, S.P. (1994). *Attention deficits and hyperactivity in children.* Thousand Oaks, CA: Sage.

Hirschfeld, R.M.A. (1993). Personality disorders: Definition and diagnosis. *Journal of Personality Disorders,* suppl., 9–17.

Hirschfeld, R.M.A., Shea, M.T., & Weise, R. (1995). Dependent personality disorder. In W.J. Livesley (Ed.), *The DSM-IV personality disorders,* pp. 239–256. New York: Guilford.

Hite, S. (1976). *The Hite report.* New York: Macmillan.

Ho, D.Y. (1994). Introduction to cross-cultural psychology. In L.L. Adler & U.P. Gielen (Eds.), *Cross-cultural topics in psychology,* pp. 3–14. Westport, CT: Praeger.

Hoch, P.H., & Polatin, P. (1949). Pseudoneurotic forms of schizophrenia. *Psychiatric Quarterly, 23,* 248–276.

Hoehn-Saric, R., & NcLeod, D.R. (1991). Clinical management of generalized anxiety disorder. In W. Coryell & G. Winokur (Eds.), *The clinical management of anxiety disorders,* pp. 79–100. New York: Oxford University Press.

Hoek, H.W. (1995). The distribution of eating disorders. In K.D. Brownell & C.G. Fairburn (Eds.), *Eating disorders and obesity: A comprehensive handbook,* pp. 207–211. New York: Guilford.

Hoenig, J. (1985). Etiology of transsexualism. In B.W. Steiner (Ed.), *Gender dysphoria: Development, research, management,* pp. 33–74. New York: Plenum.

Hoffman, P.B., & Foust, L.L. (1977). Least restrictive treatment of the mentally ill: A doctrine in search of its senses. *San Diego Law Review, 14,* 1100–1154.

Hogan, D.R. (1990). Sexual dysfunctions: A historical perspective. In C.E. Walker (Ed.), *History of clinical psychology,* pp. 279–309. Pacific Grove, CA: Brooks/Cole.

Hogan, D.P., & Lichter, D.T. (1995). Children and youth: Living arrangements and welfare. In R. Farley (Ed.), *State of the union: America in the 1990s.* New York: Russell Sage.

Hogarty, G.E. (1993). Prevention of relapse in chronic schizophrenic patients. *Journal of Clinical Psychiatry, 54* (suppl.), 18–23.

Hogarty, G.E., Anderson, C.M., Reiss, D.J., et al. (1991). Family psychoeducation, social skills training, and maintenance chemotherapy in the aftercare treatment of schizophrenia. II. Two-year effects of a controlled study on relapse and adjustment. *Archives of General Psychiatry, 48,* 340–347.

Hole, J.W., Jr. (1984). *Human anatomy and physiology,* 3rd ed. Dubuque, IA: Wm C. Brown.

Hollin, C.R. (1997). Sexual sadism: Assessment and treatment. In D.R. Laws & W.T. O'Donohue (Eds.), *Handbook of sexual deviance: Theory and application.* New York: Guilford.

Hollon, S.D., & Beck, A.T. (1986). Cognitive and cognitive-behavior therapies. In S.L. Garfield & A.E. Bergin (Eds.), *Handbook of psychotherapy and behavior change: An empirical analysis,* 3rd ed., pp. 443–482. New York: Wiley.

Hollon, S.D., DeRubeis, R.J., & Evans, M.D. (1987). Causal medication of change in treatment for depression: Discriminating between nonspecificity and noncausality. *Psychological Bulletin, 102,* 139–149.

Hollon, S.D., Shelton, R.C., & Davis, D.D. (1993). Cognitive therapy for depression: Conceptual issues and clinical efficacy. *Journal of Consulting and Clinical Psychology, 61,* 270–275.

Holman, J.E., & Caston, R.J. (1987). Interorganizational influences on mental health diagnoses: A macro-level study of labeling processes. *Sociological Perspectives, 30,* 180–200.

Holmes, T.H., & Rahe, R.H. (1967). The Social Readjustment Rating Scale. *Journal of Psychosomatic Research, 11,* 213–218.

Holzman, P.S. (1994). Parsing cognition: The power of psychology paradigms. *Archives of General Psychiatry, 51,* 952–954.

Holtzworth-Munroe, A., & Jacobson, N.S. (1991). Behavioral marital therapy. In A.S. Gurman & D.P.

Kniskern (Eds.), *Handbook of family therapy,* Vol. II, pp. 96–133. New York: Brunner/Mazel.

Holzman, P.S. (1989). The use of eye movement dysfunctions in exploring the genetic transmission of schizophrenia. *European Archives of Psychiatry and Neurological Sciences, 239,* 43–48.

Hooley, J.M. (1985). Expressed emotion: A review of the critical literature. *Clinical Psychology Review, 5,* 119–139.

Hooley, J.M. (1986). Expressed emotion and depression: Interactions between patients and high- versus low-expressed emotion spouses. *Journal of Abnormal Psychology, 95,* 237–246.

Hooley, J.M., & Richters, J.E. (1995). Expressed emotion: A developmental perspective. In D. Cicchetti & S.L. Toth (Eds.), *Emotion, cognition, and representation, Rochester symposium on developmental psychopathology,* Vol. 6, pp. 133–166. Rochester, NY: University of Rochester Press.

Hooley, J.M., & Teasdale, J.D. (1989). Predictors of relapse in unipolar depressives: Expressed emotion, marital distress, and perceived criticism. *Journal of Abnormal Psychology, 98,* 229–235.

Hopps, J.G., & Pinderhughes, E.B. (1987). Profession of social work: Contemporary characteristics. In A. Minehan (Ed.), *Encyclopedia of social work,* 18th ed. Silver Spring, MD: National Association of Social Work.

Horevitz, R., & Loewenstein, R.J. (1994). The rational treatment of multiple personality disorder. In S.J. Lynn & J.W. Rhue (Eds.), *Dissociation: Clinical and theoretical perspectives,* pp. 289–316. New York: Guilford.

Horn, J.M., Loehlin, J.C., & Willerman, L. (1979). Intellectual resemblance among adoptive and biological relatives: The Texas Adoption Project. *Behavior Genetics, 9,* 177–205.

Horney, K. (1939). *New ways in psychoanalysis.* New York: International Universities Press.

Horvath, T.B., Siever, L.J., Mohs, R.C., & Davis, K. (1991). Organic mental syndromes and disorders. In H.I. Kaplan & B.J. Sadock (Eds.), *Comprehensive textbook of psychiatry,* 5th ed., Vol. 1, pp. 599–641. Baltimore, MD: Williams & Wilkins.

Horwath, E., Lish, J.D., Johnson, J., Hornig, C.D., & Weissman, M.M. (1993). Agoraphobia without panic: Clinical reappraisal of an epidemiologic finding. *American Journal of Psychiatry, 150,* 1496–1501.

Hotchner, A.E. (1966). *Papa Hemingway: A personal memoir.* New York: Random House.

Houts, A.C. (1991). Nocturnal enuresis as a biobehavioral problem. *Behavior Therapy, 22,* 133–151.

Howard, K.I., Cornille, T.A., Lyons, J.S., Vessey, J.T., Lueger, R.J., & Saunders, S.M. (1996). Patterns of mental health service utilization. *Archives of General Psychiatry, 53,* 696–707.

Howard, K.I., Kopta, S.M., Krause, M.S., & Orlinsky, D.E. (1986). The dose-effect relationship in psychotherapy. *American Psychologist, 41,* 159–164.

Hoza, B., Pelham, W.E., Milich, R., Pillow, D., & McBride, K. (1993). The self-perceptions and attributions of attention deficit hyperactivity disordered and nonreferred boys. *Journal of Abnormal Child Psychology, 21,* 271–286.

Hsu, L.K. (1989). The gender gap in eating disorders: Why are the eating disorders more common among women? *Clinical Psychology Review, 9,* 393–407.

Hsu, L.K.G. (1990). *Eating disorders.* New York: Guilford.

Hsu, L.K.G. (1995). Outcome of bulimia nervosa. In K.D. Brownell & C.G. Fairburn (Eds.), *Eating disorders and obesity: A comprehensive handbook,* pp. 238–244. New York: Guilford.

Hucker, S.J. (1997). Sexual sadism: Theory and psychopathology. In D.R. Laws & W.T. O'Donohue

(Eds.), *Handbook of sexual deviance: Theory and application.* New York: Guilford.

Hughes, P.H., Canavan, K.P., Jarvis, G., & Aris, A. (1983). Extent of drug use: An international review with implications for health planners. *World Health Statistics Quarterly, 36,* 394–497.

Hughes, P.L., Wells, L.A., Cunningham, C.J., & Ilstrup, D.M. (1986). Treatment of bulimia with desipramine: A double-blind, placebo-controlled study. *Archives of General Psychiatry, 43,* 182–186.

Hull, J.G., & Bond, C.F., Jr. (1986). Social and behavioral consequences of alcohol consumption and expectancy: A meta-analysis. *Psychological Bulletin, 99,* 347–360.

Human Capital Initiative. *Doing the right thing: A research plan for healthy living.* Washington, DC: American Psychological Society.

Humphrey, L.L. (1987). Comparison of bulimic-anorexic and nondistressed families using structural analysis of social behavior. *Journal of the American Academy of Child and Adolescent Psychiatry, 26,* 248–255.

Huntington's Disease Collaborative Research Group (1993). A novel gene containing a trinucleotide repeat that is expanded and unstable on Huntington's disease chromosomes. *Cell, 72,* 971–983.

Hurt, S.W., Reznikoff, M. & Clarkin, J.F. (1991). *Psychological assessment, psychiatric diagnosis, and treatment planning.* New York: Brunner/Mazel.

Huston, A.C. (1983). Sextyping. In E.M. Hetherington (Ed.), *Socialization, personality, and social development,* Vol. 4, *Handbook of child psychology,* pp. 388–467. New York: Wiley.

Huttunen, M.O., Machon, R.A., & Mednick, S.A. (1994). Prenatal factors in the pathogenesis of schizophrenia. *British Journal of Psychiatry, 164* (suppl. 23), 15–19.

Huws, R., Shubsachs, A.P.W., & Taylor, P.J. (1991). Hypersexuality, fetishism and multiple sclerosis. *British Journal of Psychiatry, 158,* 280–281.

Hyler, S.E., Williams, J.B.W., & Spitzer, R.L. (1982). Reliability in the DSM-III field trials. *Archives of General Psychiatry, 39,* 1275–1278.

Iacono, W.G. (1985). Psychophysiologic markers of psychopathology: A review. *Canadian Psychology, 26,* 96–112.

Iacono, W.G. (1991). Psychophysiological assessment of psychopathology. *Psychological Assessment, 3,* 309–320.

Iacono, W.G. (1993). Smooth pursuit oculomotor dysfunction as an index of schizotaxia. In R.L. Cromwell & C.R. Snyder (Eds.), *Schizophrenia: Origins, processes, treatment, and outcome,* pp. 76–97. New York: Oxford University Press.

Iacono, W.G., & Beiser, M. (1992). Are males more likely than females to develop schizophrenia? *American Journal of Psychiatry, 149,* 1070–1074.

Iacono, W.G., & Clementz, B.A. (1993). A strategy for elucidating genetic influences on complex psychopathological syndromes. In L.J. Chapman, J.P. Chapman, & D. Fowles (Eds.), *Progress in experimental personality and psychopathology research,* pp. 11–65. New York: Springer.

Iacono, W.G., & Grove, W.M. (1993). Schizophrenia reviewed: Toward an integrative genetic model. *Psychological Science, 4,* 273–276.

Iacono, W.G., Moreau, M., Beiser, M., Fleming, J.A., et al. (1992). Smooth-pursuit eye tracking in first-episode psychotic patients and their relatives. *Journal of Abnormal Psychology, 101,* 104–116.

Imperato-McGinley, J., Guerrero, L., Gautier, T., & Peterson, R.E. (1974). Steroid 5a-reductase deficiency in man: An inherited form of male pseudohermaphroditism. *Science, 186,* 1213–1215.

Insel, T.R. (1992). Toward a neuroanatomy of OCD. *Archives of General Psychiatry, 49,* 739–744.

Iqbal, N., & van Praag, H.M. (1995). The role of serotonin in schizophrenia. In J.A. Den Boer, H.G. Westenberg, & H.M. van Praag (Eds.), *Advances in the neurobiology*

of schizophrenia: Wiley series on clinical and neurobiological advances in psychiatry, Vol. 1, pp. 221–243. Chichester, England: Wiley.

Jablensky, A. (1985). Approaches to the definition and classification of anxiety and related disorders in European psychiatry. In A.H. Tuma & J. Maser (Eds.), *Anxiety and the anxiety disorders.* Hillsdale, NJ: Erlbaum.

Jablensky, A. (1986). Epidemiology of schizophrenia: A European perspective. *Schizophrenia Bulletin, 12,* 52–73.

Jablensky, A., Sartorius, N., Ernberg, G., Anker, M., Korten, A., Cooper, J.E., Day, R., & Bertelsen, A. (1992). Schizophrenia: Manifestations, incidence and course in different cultures: A World Health Organization ten-country study. *Psychological Medicine,* Monograph Suppl., 20, 1–97.

Jacobson, E. (1938). *Progressive relaxation.* Chicago: University of Chicago Press.

Jacobson, J.W., Mulick, J.A., & Schwartz, A.A. (1995). A history of facilitated communication: Science, pseudoscience, and antiscience. *American Psychologist, 50,* 750–765.

Jacobson, N.S. (1985). The role of observational measures in behavior therapy outcome research, *Behavioral Assessment, 7,* 297–308.

Jacobson, N.S., & Christensen, A. (1996). *Integrative couple therapy: Promoting acceptance and change.* New York: Norton.

Jacobson, N.S., Follette, W.C., & McDonald, D.W. (1982). Reactivity to positive and negative behavior in distressed and nondistressed married couples. *Journal of Consulting and Clinical Psychology, 50,* 706–714.

Jacobson, N.S., & Hollon, S.D. (1996). Cognitive-behavior therapy versus pharmacotherapy: Now that the jury's returned its verdict, it's time to present the rest of the evidence. *Journal of Consulting and Clinical Psychology, 64,* 74–80.

Jacobson, N.S., Holtzworth-Munroe, A., & Schmaling, K.B. (1989). Marital therapy and spouse involvement in the treatment of depression, agoraphobia, and alcoholism. *Journal of Consulting and Clinical Psychology, 57,* 5–10.

Jacobson, N.S., & Truax, P. (1991). Clinical significance: A statistical approach to defining meaningful change in psychotherapy research. *Journal of Consulting and Clinical Psychology, 59,* 12–19.

Jacobson, R.R., Acker, C.F., & Lishman, W.A. (1990). Patterns of neuropsychological deficit in alcoholic Korsakoff's syndrome. *Psychological Medicine, 20,* 321–334.

Jacoby, R., & Bergmann, K. (1986). The psychiatry of old age. In P. Hill, R. Murray, & A. Thorley (Eds.), *Essentials of postgraduate psychiatry,* 2nd ed., pp. 495–526. London: Grune & Stratton.

Jacqmin, H., Commenges, D., Letenneur, L., Barbergergateau, P., & Dartigues, J.F. (1994). Components of drinking water and risk of cognitive impairment in the elderly. *American Journal of Epidemiology, 139,* 48–57.

Jamison, K.R. (1995). *An unquiet mind: A memoir of moods and madness.* New York: Knopf.

Jaffe, J.H. (1995). Pharmacological treatment of opioid dependence: Current techniques and new findings. *Psychiatric Annals, 25,* 369–375.

Janet, P. (1915/1915). Psychoanalysis. *Journal of Abnormal Psychology,* 1–35, 187–253.

Jarvis, T.J. (1992). Implications of gender for alcohol treatment research: A quantitative and qualitative review. *British Journal of Addiction, 87,* 1249–1261.

Jellinek, E.M. (1952). Phases of alcohol addiction. *Quarterly Journal of Studies on Alcohol, 13,* 673–684.

Jellinek, E.M. (1960). *The disease concept of alcoholism.* New Haven, CT: Hillhouse Press.

Jenkins, C.D. (1988). Epidemiology of cardiovascular diseases. *Journal of Consulting and Clinical Psychology, 56,* 324–332.

Jeste, D.V., & Caligiuri, M.P. (1993). Tardive dyskinesia. *Schizophrenia Bulletin, 19,* 303–316.

Jiang, W., Babyak, M., Krantz, D.S., Waugh, R.A., et al.

(1996). Mental stress-induced myocardial ischemia and cardiac events. *Journal of the American Medical Association, 275,* 1651–1656.

Johansson, B., & Zarit, S.H. (1995). Prevalence and incidence of dementia in the oldest old: A longitudinal study of a population-based sample of 84–90-year-olds in Sweden. *International Journal of Geriatric Psychiatry, 10,* 359–366.

Johnson, D. (1990). Long-term drug treatment of psychosis: Observations on some current issues. *International Review of Psychiatry, 2,* 341–353.

Johnson, P. (1989). Hemingway: Portrait of the artist as an intellectual. *Commentary, 87,* 49–59.

Johnson, S.L., & Roberts, J.E. (1995). Life events and bipolar disorder: Implications from biological theories. *Psychological Bulletin, 117,* 434–449.

Johnston, D.W. (1985). Psychological interventions in cardiovascular disease. *Journal of Psychosomatic Research, 29,* 447–456.

Johnston, D.W. (1989). Prevention of cardiovascular disease by psychological methods. *British Journal of Psychiatry, 154,* 183–194.

Johnstone, E.C., & Geddes, J. (1994). How high is the relapse rate in schizophrenia? *Acta Psychiatrica Scandinavica, 89* (suppl. 382), 6–10.

Joiner, R.E., & Metalsky, G.I. (1995). A prospective test of an integrative interpersonal theory of depression: A naturalistic study of college roommates. *Journal of Personality and Social Psychology, 69,* 778–788.

Jones, B.M., & Jones, M.K. (1976). Women and alcohol: Intoxication, metabolism, and the menstrual cycle. In M. Greenblatt & M.A. Schuckit (Eds.), *Alcohol problems in women and children,* pp. 103–136. New York, Grune & Stratton.

Jones, D.M. (1985). Bulimia: A false self identity. *Clinical Social Work, 13,* 305–316.

Jones, J.C., & Barlow, D.H. (1990). The etiology of post-traumatic stress disorder. *Clinical Psychology Review, 10,* 299–328.

Jones, M.A., & Krisberg, B. (1994). *Images and reality: Juvenile crime, youth violence, and public policy.* San Francisco: National Council on Crime and Delinquency.

Jones, P.B., Bebbington, P., Foerster, A., Lewis, S.W., et al. (1993). Premorbid social underachievement in schizophrenia: Results from the Camberwell Collaborative Psychosis Study. *British Journal of Psychiatry, 162,* 65–71.

Jones, R.R., Reid, J.B., & Patterson, G.R. (1975). Naturalistic observation in clinical assessment. In P. McReynolds (Ed.), *Advances in psychological assessment,* vol. 3. San Francisco: Jossey-Bass.

Josephs, L. (1994). Psychoanalytic and related interpretations. In B.B. Wolman & G. Stricker (Eds.), *Anxiety and related disorders: A handbook,* pp. 11–29. New York: Wiley-Interscience.

Josephs, R.A., & Steele, C.M. (1990). The two faces of alcohol myopia: Attentional mediation of psychological stress. *Journal of Abnormal Psychology, 99,* 115–126.

Joyce, P. (1992). Prediction of treatment response. In E.S. Paykel (Ed.), *Handbook of affective disorders,* 2nd ed., pp. 453–462. New York: Guilford.

Judd, L.L. (1994). Social phobia: A clinical overview. *Journal of Clinical Psychiatry, 55* (suppl. 6), 5–9.

Junginger, J. (1997). Fetishism. In D.R. Laws and W.T. O'Donohue (Eds), *Handbook of sexual deviance: Theory and application.* New York: Guilford.

Kagan, J. (1958). The concept of identification. *Psychological Review, 65,* 296–305.

Kagan, J, Kearsley, R., & Zelazo, P.R. (1978). *Infancy: Its place in human development.* Cambridge, MA: Harvard University Press.

Kagan, J., Reznick, S., & Snidman, N. (1987). The physiology and psychology of behavioral inhibition in children. *Child Development, 58,* 1459–1473.

Kagan, J., & Snidman, N. (1991). Temperamental

factors in human development. *American Psychologist,* 46, 856–862.

Kahn, R.S., & Davidson, M. (1995). Dopamine in schizophrenia. In J.A. Den Boer, H.G. Westenberg, & H.M. van Praag (Eds.). *Advances in the neurobiology of schizophrenia: Wiley series on clinical and neurobiological advances in psychiatry,* Vol. 1, pp. 204–220. Chichester, England: Wiley.

Kallman, W.M., & Feuerstein, M.J. (1986). Psychophysiological procedures. In A.R. Ciminero, K.S. Calhoun, and H.E. Adams (Eds.), *Handbook of behavioral assessment,* 2nd ed. New York: Wiley-Interscience. pp. 325–350.

Kamarck, T., & Jennings, J.R. (1991). Biobehavioral factors in sudden cardiac death. *Psychological Bulletin,* 109, 42–75.

Kane, J.M. (1995). Current problems with the pharmacotherapy of schizophrenia. *Clinical Neuropharmacology,* 18 (suppl. 1), S154–S160.

Kane, J.M., & Marder, S.R. (1993). Psychopharmacologic treatment of schizophrenia. *Schizophrenia Bulletin,* 19, 287–302.

Kane, J.M., Woerner, M., & Lieberman, J. (1985). Tardive dyskinesis: Prevalence, incidence and risk factors. In D.E. Casey, T.N. Chase, A.V. Christensen, & J. Gerlach (Eds.), *Dyskinesis: Research and treatment,* pp. 72–78. Berlin: Springer.

Kane, J.M., Woerner, M., Lieberman, J., & Rabiner, C.J. (1984). Studies on the long-term treatment of schizophrenia. *Psychiatric Hospital,* 15, 179–183.

Kanner, L. (1943). Autistic disturbances of affective contact. *Nervous Child,* 2, 217–250.

Kaplan, H.S. (1974). *The new sex therapy: Active treatment of sexual dysfunctions.* New York: Brunner/Mazel.

Kaplan, H.S. (1979). *Disorders of sexual desire and other new concepts and techniques in sex therapy.* New York: Brunner/Mazel.

Kaplan, H.S. (1988). Anxiety and sexual dysfunction. *Journal of Clinical Psychiatry,* 49, 21–25.

Kaplan, L.J. (1989). *Female perversions: The temptations of Emma Bovary.* New York: Doubleday.

Kapur, S., & Mann, J.J. (1992). Role of the dopaminergic system in depression. *Biological Psychiatry,* 32, 1–17.

Kapur, S., & Mann, J.J. (1993). Antidepressant action and the neurobiologic effects of ECT: Human studies. In C.E. Coffey (Ed.), *The clinical science of electroconvulsive therapy,* pp. 235–250. Washington, DC: American Psychiatric Press.

Kapur, S., & Remington, G. (1996). Serotonin-dopamine interaction and its relevance to schizophrenia. *American Journal of Psychiatry,* 153, 466–476.

Karasek, R.A., Theorell, T.G., Schwartz, J., Pieper, C., & Alfredsson, L. (1982). Job, psychological factors and coronary heart disease: Swedish prospective findings and U.S. prevalence findings using a new occupational inference method. *Advances in Cardiology,* 29, 62–67.

Karler, R., Calder, L.D., Chaudhry, I.A., & Turkanis, S.A. (1989). Blockade of "reverse tolerance" to cocaine and amphetamine by MK-801. *Life Sciences,* 45, 599–606.

Karno, M., & Golding, J.M. (1991). Obsessive-compulsive disorder. In L.N. Robins & D.A. Regier (Eds.), *Psychiatric disorders in America: The Epidemiologic Catchment Area Study.* New York: Free Press.

Karras, A., & Otis, D.B. (1987). A comparison of inpatients in an urban state hospital in 1975 and 1982. *Hospital and Community Psychiatry,* 38, 963–967.

Kasen, S., Cohen, P., Brook, J.S., & Hartmark, C. (1996). A multiple-risk interaction model: Effects of temperament and divorce on psychiatric disorders in children. *Journal of Abnormal Child Psychology,* 24, 121–150.

Kass, F., Charles, E., Klein, D.F., & Cohen, P. (1983). Discordance between the SCL-90 and therapists' psychopathology ratings: Implications for clinical assessment. *Archives of General Psychiatry,* 40, 389–392.

Kassel, J.D., & Shiffman, S. (1992). What can hunger teach us about drug craving? A comparative analysis of the two constructs. *Advances in Behaviour Research and Therapy,* 14, 141–167.

Kasvikis, Y.G., Tsakiris, F., Marks, I.M., Basogulu, M., & Noshirvani, H.V. (1986). Past history of anorexia nervosa in women with obsessive-compulsive disorders. *International Journal of Eating Disorders,* 5, 1069–1075.

Katon, W., & Roy-Byrne, P.P. (1991). Mixed anxiety and depression. *Journal of Abnormal Psychology,* 100, 337–345.

Katsanis, J., & Iacono, W.G. (1991). Clinical, neuropsychological, and brain structural correlates of smooth-pursuit eye tracking performance in chronic schizophrenia. *Journal of Abnormal Psychology,* 100, 526–534.

Katschnig, H., & Amering, M. (1990). Panic attacks and panic disorder in cross-cultural perspective. In J.C. Ballenger (Ed.), *Clinical aspects of panic disorder.* New York: Wiley.

Katz, R., & McGuffin, P. (1993). The genetics of affective disorders. In D. Fowles (Ed.), *Progress in experimental personality and psychopathology research.* New York: Springer.

Katz, R.J., DeVeaugh-Geiss, J., & Landau, P. (1990). Clomipramine in obsessive-compulsive disorder. *Biological Psychiatry,* 28, 401–414.

Katzman, R. (1976). The prevalence and malignancy of Alzheimer's disease. *Archives of Neurology,* 33, 217–218.

Katzman, R. (1993). Education and the prevalence of dementia and Alzheimer's disease. *Neurology,* 43, 13–20.

Kaul, T.J., & Bednar, R.L. (1986). Experimental group research: Results, questions, and suggestions. In S.L. Garfield & A.E. Bergin (Eds.), *Handbook of psychotherapy and behavior change,* 3rd ed., pp. 671–714. New York: Wiley.

Kavanagh, D.J. (1992). Recent developments in expressed emotion and schizophrenia. *British Journal of Psychiatry,* 160, 601–620.

Kaye, D.W.K. (1995). The epidemiology of age-related neurological disease and dementia. *Reviews in Clinical Gerontology,* 5, 39–56.

Kaye, W.H., Weltzin, T.E., Hsu, L.K.G., McConahan, C.W., & Bolton, B. (1993). Amount of calories retained after binge eating and vomiting. *American Journal of Psychiatry,* 150, 969–971.

Kazdin, A.E. (1987). Treatment of antisocial behavior in children: Current status and future directions. *Psychological Bulletin,* 102, 187–203.

Kazdin, A.E. (1989). Identifying depression in children: A comparison of alternative selection criteria. *Journal of Abnormal Child Psychology,* 17, 437–455.

Kazdin, A.E. (1990). Childhood depression. *Journal of Child Psychology and Psychiatry,* 31, 121–160.

Kazdin, A.E. (1994). Psychotherapy for children and adolescents. In A.E. Bergin & S.L. Garfield (Eds.), *Handbook of psychotherapy and behavior change,* 4th ed., pp. 543–594. New York: Wiley.

Kazdin, A.E. (1994). Methodology, design, and evaluation in psychotherapy research. In A.E. Bergin and S.L. Garfield (Eds.), *Handbook of psychotherapy and behavior change* (4th ed., pp. 19–71). New York: Wiley.

Kazdin, A.E. (1995). *Conduct disorders in childhood and adolescence,* 2nd ed. Thousand Oaks, CA: Sage.

Kazdin, A.E., French, N.H., & Unis, A.S. (1983). Child, mother, and father evaluations of depression in psychiatric inpatient children. *Journal of Abnormal Child Psychology,* 11, 167–180.

Kazdin, A.E., & Petti, T.A. (1982). Self-report and interview measures of childhood and adolescent depression. *Journal of Child Psychology and Psychiatry,* 23, 437–457.

Kazdin, A.E., & Wilcoxon, L.A. (1976). Systematic desensitization and nonspecific treatment effects: A methodological evaluation. *Psychological Bulletin,* 83, 729–758.

Keane, T.M., Fairbank, J.A., Caddell, J.M., & Zimering, R.T. (1989). Implosive (flooding) therapy reduces symptoms of PTSD in Vietnam combat veterans. *Behavior Therapy,* 20, 245–260.

Keane, T.M., Zimering, R.T., & Caddell, J.M. (1985). A behavioral formulation of posttraumatic stress disorder in Vietnam veterans. *Behavior Therapist,* 8, 9–12.

Keck, P.E., & McElroy, S.L. (1993). Current perspectives on treatment of bipolar disorder with lithium. *Psychiatric Annals,* 23, 64–69.

Keenan, K., & Shaw, D. (in press). Developmental and social influences on young girls' early problem behavior. *Psychological Bulletin.*

Keesey, R.E. (1995). A set-point model of body weight regulation. In K.D. Brownell & C.G. Fairburn (Eds.), *Eating disorders and obesity: A comprehensive handbook,* pp. 46–50. New York: Guilford.

Keith, S.J., Regier, D.A., & Rae, D.S. (1991). Schizophrenic disorders. In L.N. Robins & D.A. Regier (Eds.), *Psychiatric disorders in America: The Epidemiologic Catchment Area Study,* pp. 33–52. New York: Free Press.

Keller, M. (1970). Tribute to E.M. Jellinek. In R.E. Popham (Ed.), *Alcohol & Alcoholism,* pp. xi–xvi. Toronto: University of Toronto Press.

Keller, M.B. (1987). Differential diagnosis, natural course and epidemiology of bipolar disorder. *American Psychiatric Association Annual Review,* 6.

Keller, M.B. (1988). Diagnostic issues and clinical course of unipolar illness. *American Psychiatric Association Annual Review,* 6.

Keller, M.B. (1994). Depression: A long-term illness. *British Journal of Psychiatry,* 165 (suppl. 26), 9–15.

Keller, M.B., Lavori, P.W., Coryell, W., Endicott, J., & Mueller, T.I. (1993). Bipolar I: A five-year prospective follow-up. *Journal of Nervous and Mental Disease,* 181, 238–245.

Kellner, R. (1985). Functional somatic symptoms in hypochondriasis. *Archives of General Psychiatry,* 42, 821–833.

Kelly, M.P., Strassberg, D.S., & Kircher, J.R. (1990). Attitudinal and experiential correlates of anorgasmia. *Archives of Sexual Behavior,* 19, 165–177.

Kelly, T.A. (1990). The role of values in psychotherapy: A critical review of process and outcome effects. *Clinical Psychology Review,* 10, 171–186.

Kelly, T., Soloff, P.H., Cornelius, J., George, A., Lis, J.A., & Ulrich, R. (1992). Can we study (treat) borderline patients? Attrition from research and open treatment. *Journal of Personality Disorders,* 6, 417–433.

Kempe, C.H., Silverman, F., Steele, B., Droegueller, W., & Silver, H. (1962). The battered child syndrome. *Journal of the American Medical Association,* 181, 17–24.

Kendall, P.C. (1994). Treating anxiety disorders in children: Results of a randomized clinical trial. *Journal of Consulting and Clinical Psychology,* 62, 100–110.

Kendall, P.C., & Ingram, R.E. (1989). Cognitive-behavioral perspectives: Theory and research on depression and anxiety. In P.C. Kendall & D. Watson (Eds.), *Anxiety and depression: Distinctive and overlapping features,* pp. 27–53. San Diego, CA: Academic Press.

Kendall, P.C., & Watson, D. (Eds.) (1989). *Anxiety and depression: Distinctive and overlapping features.* San Diego: CA: Academic Press.

Kendell, R.E. (1968). *The classification of depressive illnesses.* London: Oxford University Press.

Kendell, R.E. (1975). *The role of diagnosis in psychiatry.* Oxford: Blackwell.

Kendell, R.E. (1976). The classification of depression: A review of contemporary confusion. *British Journal of Psychiatry,* 129, 15–28.

Kendell, R.E. (1981). The present status of electroconvulsive therapy. *British Journal of Psychiatry,* 139, 265–283.

Kendell, R.E. (1984). Reflections on psychiatric

classification—For the architects of DSM-IV and ICD-10. *Integrative Psychiatry, 2,* 43–47.

Kendell, R.E. (1989). Clinical validity. *Psychological Medicine, 19,* 45–55.

Kendell, R.E. (1991). Relationship between the DSM-IV and the ICD-10. *Journal of Abnormal Psychology, 100,* 297–301.

Kendler, K.S. (1988). Familial aggregation of schizophrenia and schizophrenia spectrum disorders. *Archives of General Psychiatry, 45,* 377–383.

Kendler, K.S. (1990). The super-normal control group in psychiatric genetics: Possible artifactual evidence for coaggregation. *Psychiatric Genetics, 1,* 45–53.

Kendler, K.S., & Diehl, S.R. (1993). The genetics of schizophrenia: A current, genetic-epidemiologic perspective. *Schizophrenia Bulletin, 19,* 261–285.

Kendler, K.S., Gruenberg, A.M., & Tsuang, M.T. (1985). Subtype stability in schizophrenia. *American Journal of Psychiatry, 142,* 827–832.

Kendler, K.S., Heath, A.C., Neale, M.C., Kessler, R.C., & Eaves, L.J. (1992). A population-based twin study of alcoholism in women. *Journal of the American Medical Association, 268,* 1877–1882.

Kendler, K.S., Kessler, R.C., Neale, M.C., Heath, A.C., & Eaves, L.J. (1993). The prediction of major depression in women: Toward an integrated etiologic model. *American Journal of Psychiatry, 150,* 1139–1148.

Kendler, K.S., Kessler, R.C., Walters, E.E., MacLean, C., Neale, M.C., Heath, A.C., & Eaves, L.J. (1995). Stressful life events, genetic liability, and onset of an episode of major depression in women. *American Journal of Psychiatry, 152,* 833–842.

Kendler, K.S., MacLean, C., Neale, M., Kessler, R., Heath, A., & Eaves, L. (1991). The genetic epidemiology of bulimia nervosa. *American Journal of Psychiatry, 148,* 1627–1637.

Kendler, K.S., McGuire, M., Gruenberg, A.M., O'Hare, A., Spellman, M., & Walsh, D. (1993). The Roscommon Family Study. III. Schizophrenia-related personality disorders in relatives. *Archives of General Psychiatry, 50,* 781–788.

Kendler, K.S., McGuire, M., Gruenberg, A.M., & Walsh, D. (1994). Outcome and family study of the subtypes of schizophrenia in the west of Ireland. *American Journal of Psychiatry, 151,* 849–856.

Kendler, K.S., McGuire, M., Gruenberg, A.M., & Walsh, D. (1995). Schizotypal symptoms and signs in the Roscommon Family Study. *Archives of General Psychiatry, 52,* 296–303.

Kendler, K.S., Neale, M.C., Kessler, R.C., Heath, A.C., & Eaves, L.J. (1992a). Generalized anxiety disorder in women: A population-based twin study. *Archives of General Psychiatry, 49,* 267–272.

Kendler, K.S., Neale, M.C., Kessler, R.C., Heath, A.C., & Eaves, L.J. (1992b). The genetic epidemiology of phobias in women: The interrelationship of agoraphobia, social phobia, situational phobia, and simple phobia. *Archives of General Psychiatry, 49,* 273–281.

Kendler, K.S., Neale, M.C., Kessler, R.C., Heath, A.C., & Eaves, L.J. (1993). A longitudinal twin study of 1-year prevalence of major depression in women. *Archives of General Psychiatry, 50,* 843–852.

Kennedy, J.L., Giuffra, L.A., Moises, H.W., Cavalli-Sforza, L.L., Pakstis, A.J., Kidd, J.R., Castiglione, C.M., Sjorgren, B., Wetterberg, L., & Kidd, K.K. (1988). Evidence against linkage of schizophrenia to markers on chromosome 5 in a northern Swedish pedigree. *Nature, 336,* 167–170.

Kenrick, D.T., & Funder, D.C. (1988). Profiting from controversy: Lessons from the person-situation debate. *American Psychologist, 43,* 23–34.

Kent, T.A., Campbell, J.R., & Goodwin, D.W. (1985). Blood platelet uptake of serotonin in men alcoholics. *Journal of Studies on Alcohol, 46,* 357–359.

Kernberg, O.F. (1967). Borderline personality

organization. *Journal of the American Psychoanalytic Association, 15,* 641–685.

Kernberg, O.F. (1975). *Borderline conditions and pathological narcissism.* New York: Aronson.

Kernberg, O. (1988). Hysterical and histrionic personality disorders. In A. Cooper, A. Frances, & M. Sacks, (Eds.), *The personality disorders and neuroses.* Philadelphia: Lippincott.

Kessel, J.B., & Zimmerman, M. (1993). Reporting errors in studies of the diagnostic performance of self-administered questionnaires. *Psychological Assessment, 5,* 395–399.

Kessler, R.C. (1995). The national comorbidity survey: Preliminary results and future directions. *International Journal of Methods in Psychiatric Research, 5,* 139–151.

Kessler, R.C., McGonagle, K.A., Zhao, S., Nelson, C.R., Highes, M., Eshleman, S., Wittchen, H., & Kendler, K.S. (1994). Lifetime and 12-month prevalence of DSM-III-R psychiatric disorders in the United States: Results from the National Comorbidity Survey. *Archives of General Psychiatry, 51,* 8–19.

Kessler, R.C., & McLeod, J.D. (1984). Sex differences in vulnerability to undesirable life events. *American Sociological Review, 49,* 620–631.

Kessler, R.C., Sonnega, A., Bromet, E., Hughes, M., & Nelson, C.B. (1995). Posttraumatic stress disorder in the National Comorbidity Survey. *Archives of General Psychiatry, 52,* 1048–1060.

Keteyian, A. (1986). The straight-arrow addict: Compulsive gambling of A. Schlichter. *Sports Illustrated,* March 10, 74–77.

Kettl, P.A. (1993). 10 basic rules for managing dementia. *Patient Care 27,* 79–86.

Kety, S.S. (1987). The significance of genetic factors in the etiology of schizophrenia: Results from the national study of adoptees in Denmark. *Journal of Psychiatric Research, 21,* 423–429.

Kety, S.S., Rosenthal, D., Wender, P.H., Schulsinger, F., & Jacobsen, B. (1975). Mental illness in the biological and adoptive families of adopted individuals who have become schizophrenic: A preliminary report based on psychiatric interviews. In R.R. Fieve, D. Rosenthal, & H. Brill (Eds.), *Genetic research in psychiatry.* Baltimore: Johns Hopkins University Press.

Keys, A., Brozek, J., Henschel, A., Mickelsen, O., & Taylor, H.L. (1950). *The biology of human starvation,* 2 vols. Minneapolis: University of Minnesota Press.

Keys, A., Taylor, H.L., Blackburn, H., Brozek, J., Anderson, H., & Simonson, E. (1971). Mortality and coronary heart disease among men studied for 23 years. *Archives of Internal Medicine, 128,* 201–214.

Kiecolt-Glaser, J.K., Malarkey, W.B., Chee, M., Newton, T., Cacioppo, J.T., Mao, H., & Glaser, R. (1993). Negative behavior during marital conflict is associated with immunological down-regulation. *Psychosomatic Medicine, 55,* 395–409.

Kiesler, C. (1982). Mental hospitals and alternative care: Noninstitutionalization as potential public policy for mental patients. *American Psychologist, 37,* 349–360.

Kihlstrom, J.F. (1984). Conscious, subconscious, unconscious: A cognitive perspective. In K.S. Bowers & D. Meichenbaum (Eds.), *The unconscious reconsidered,* pp. 149–211. New York: Wiley.

Kihlstrom, J.F., Glisky, M.L., & Angiulo, M.J. (1994). Dissociative tendencies and dissociative disorders. *Journal of Abnormal Psychology, 103,* 117–124.

Kihlstrom, J.F., & Hoyt, I.P. (1990). Repression, dissociation, and hypnosis. In J.L. Singer (Ed.), *Repression and dissociation,* pp. 181–208. Chicago: University of Chicago Press.

Kilmann, P.R., et al. (1982). The treatment of sexual paraphilias: A review of the outcome research. *Journal of Sex Research, 18,* 193–252.

Kilpatrick, D.G., Saunders, B.E., Amick-McMullan, A.,

Best, C.L., Veronen, L.J., & Resnick, H.S. (1989). Victim and crime factors associated with the development of crime-related posttraumatic stress disorder. *Behavior Therapy, 20,* 199–214.

Kimble, G.A. (1989). Psychology from the standpoint of a generalist. *American Psychologist, 44,* 491–499.

King, B.M. (1996). *Human sexuality today.* Upper Saddle River, NJ: Prentice Hall.

King, D.W., King, L.A., Foy, D.W., & Gudanowski, D.M. (1996). Prewar factors in combat-related posttraumatic stress disorder: Structural equation modeling with a national sample of female and male Vietnam veterans. *Journal of Consulting and Clinical Psychology, 64,* 520–531.

King, N.J., Ollier, K., Iacuone, R., Schuster, S., Bays, K., Gullone, E., & Ollendick, T.H. (1989). Fears of children and adolescents: A cross-sectional Australian study using the Revised-Fear Survey Schedule for Children. *Journal of Child Psychology and Psychiatry, 30,* 775–784.

King, R.A., Segman, R.H., & Anderson, G.M. (1994). Serotonin and suicidality: The impact of acute fluoxetine administration. I. Serotonin and suicide. *Israel Journal of Psychiatry and Related Sciences, 31,* 271–279.

Kinsey, A.C., Pomeroy, W.B., & Martin, C.E. (1948). *Sexual behavior in the human male.* Philadelphia: Saunders.

Kinsey, A.C., Pomeroy, W., Martin, C., & Gebhard, P. (1953). *Sexual behavior in the human female.* Philadelphia: Saunders.

Kinzl, J.F., Mangweth, B., Traweger, C., & Biebl, W. (1996). Sexual dysfunction in males: Significance of adverse childhood experiences. *Child Abuse and Neglect, 20,* 759–767.

Kirch, D.G. (1993). Infection and autoimmunity as etiologic factors in schizophrenia: A review and reappraisal. *Schizophrenia Bulletin, 19,* 355–370.

Kirk, S.A., & Kutchins, H. (1992). *The selling of DSM: The rhetoric of science in psychiatry.* New York: Aldine.

Kirmayer, L.J. (1984). Culture, affect and somatization. *Transcultural Psychiatric Research Review, 21,* 159–188.

Kirmayer, L.J., Robbins, J.M., & Paris, J. (1994). Somatoform disorders: Personality and the social matrix of somatic distress. *Journal of Abnormal Psychology, 103,* 125–136.

Kirsch, I., & Lynn, S.J. (1995). The altered state of hypnosis: Changes in the theoretical landscape. *American Psychologist, 50,* 846–858.

Kivlahan, D.R., Marlatt, G.A., Fromme, K., Coppel, D.B., & Williams, E. (1990). Secondary prevention with college drinkers: Evaluation of an alcohol skills training program. *Journal of Consulting and Clinical Psychology, 58,* 805–810.

Kleiger, J.H. (1992). A conceptual critique of the EA:es comparison in the Comprehensive Rorschach System. *Psychological Assessment, 4,* 288–296.

Klein, D.F. (1981). Anxiety reconceptualized. In D.F. Klein & J. Rabkin (Eds.), *Anxiety: New research and changing concepts,* pp. 235–263. New York: Raven Press.

Klein, D.F. (1993). False suffocation alarms, spontaneous panics, and related conditions: An integrative hypothesis. *Archives of General Psychiatry, 50,* 306–317.

Klein, D.F. (1995). Psychopharmacological practice and health reform. *Psychiatric Annals, 25,* 79–83.

Klein, D.F. (1996). Preventing hung juries about therapy studies. *Journal of Consulting and Clinical Psychology, 64,* 81–87.

Klein, D.F., & Klein, H.M. (1989). The definition and psychopharmacology of spontaneous panic and phobia. In P. Tyrer (Ed.), *Psychopharmacology of anxiety.* New York: Oxford University Press.

Klein, D.F., & Ross, D.C. (1993). Reanalysis of the National Institute of Mental Health Treatment of Depression Collaborative Research Program General Effectiveness Report. *Neuropsychopharmacology, 8,* 241–251.

Kleinman, A. (1982). Neurasthenia and depression: A

study of somatization and culture in China. *Culture, Medicine, and Psychiatry, 6,* 117–189.

Kleinman, A. (1988). *Rethinking psychiatry: From cultural category to personal experience.* New York: Free Press.

Klerman, G.L. (1984). The advantages of DSM-III. *American Journal of Psychiatry, 141,* 539–545.

Klerman, G.L. (1990a). History and development of modern concepts of anxiety and panic. In J. Ballenger (Ed.), *Clinical aspects of panic disorder,* pp. 3–12. New York: Wiley.

Klerman, G. (1990b). The psychiatric patient's right to effective treatment: Implications of Osheroff vs. Chestnut Lodge. *American Journal of Psychiatry, 147,* 409–418.

Klerman, G.L. (1986). Historical perspectives on contemporary schools of psychopathology. In T. Millon & G. Klerman (Eds.), *Contemporary directions in psychopathology: Toward the DSM-IV.* New York: Guilford.

Klerman, G.L., & Weissman, M.M. (1992). Interpersonal psychotherapy. In E.S. Paykel (Ed.), *Handbook of affective disorders,* 2nd ed., pp. 501–510. New York: Guilford.

Klerman, G.L., Weissman, M.M., Markowitz, J.C., Glick, I., Wilner, P.J., Mason, B., & Shear, M.K. (1994). Medication and psychotherapy. In A.E. Bergin & S.L. Garfield (Eds.), *Handbook of psychotherapy and behavior change,* 4th ed., pp. 734–782. New York: Wiley.

Klerman, G.L., Weissman, M.M., Rounsaville, B.J., & Chevron, E.S. (1984). *Interpersonal psychotherapy of depression.* New York: Basic Books.

Klorman, R., Brumaghim, J.T., Fitzpatrick, P.A., Borgstedt, A.D., & Strauss, J. (1994). Clinical and cognitive effects of methylphenidate on children with attention deficit disorder as a function of aggression/oppositionality and age. *Journal of Abnormal Psychology, 103,* 206–221.

Kluft, R.P. (1987). An update on multiple personality disorder. *Hospital and Community Psychiatry, 38,* 363–373.

Kluznik, J.C., Speed, N., Van Valkenburg, C., & Magraw, R. (1986). Forty-year follow-up of United States prisoners of war. *American Journal of Psychiatry, 143,* 1443–1446.

Knight, R.A., & Prentky, R.A. (1990). Classifying sexual offenders: The development and corroboration of taxonomic models. In W.L. Marshall, D.R. Laws, & H.E. Barbaree (Eds.), *Handbook of sexual assault: Issues, theories, and treatment of the offender.* New York: Plenum.

Knight, R.A., Prentky, R.A., & Cerce, D.D. (1994). The development, reliability, and validity of an inventory for the multidimensional assessment of sex and aggression. *Criminal Justice and Behavior, 21,* 72–94.

Koch, H., & Knapp, D.E. (1987). Highlights of drug utilization in office practice. National Ambulatory Medical Survey, 1885. *Advance data from vital and health statistics,* No. 134, U.S. Department of Health and Human Services Publication No. (PHS) 87-1250.

Koenig, H.G., & Blazer, D.G. (1990). Depression and other affective disorders. In C.K. Cassel, D.E. Riesenberg, L.B. Sorenson, & J.R. Walsh (Eds.), *Geriatric medicine,* 2nd ed., pp. 473–489. New York: Springer.

Kohlberg, L. (1985). *The psychology of moral development.* San Francisco: Harper & Row.

Kohler, J.A. (1988). The role of serotonin in autism. In L. Wing (Ed.), *Aspects of autism: Biological research,* pp. 53–58. London: Gaskell.

Kohut, J. (1971). *The analysis of the self.* New York: International Universities Press.

Kohut, J. (1977). *The restoration of the self.* New York: International Universities Press.

Kokmen, E., Beard, C.M., O'Brien, P.C., Offord, K.P., & Kurland, L.T. (1993). Is the incidence of dementing illness changing? A 25-year time trend study in Rochester, Minnesota (1960–1984). *Neurology, 43,* 1887–1993.

Kolb, B., & Whishaw, I.Q. (1990). *Fundamentals of human neuropsychology,* 3rd ed. New York: Freeman.

Kolb, L.C. (1987). A neuropsychological hypothesis explaining posttraumatic stress disorder. *American Journal of Psychiatry, 144,* 989–995.

Koluchova, J. (1972). Severe deprivation in twins: A case study of marked IQ change after age 7. *Journal of Child Psychology and Psychiatry, 13,* 107–114.

Kopta, S.M., Howard, K.I., Lowry, J.L., & Beutler, L.E. (1994). Patterns of symptomatic recovery in psychotherapy. *Journal of Consulting and Clinical Psychology, 62,* 1009–1016.

Koran, L.J. (1975). The reliability of clinical methods, data and judgments. *New England Journal of Medicine, 293,* 642–646, 695–701.

Koranyi, E.K. (1989). Physiology of stress reviewed. In S. Cheren (Ed.), *Psychosomatic medicine: Theory, physiology, and practice,* Vol. 1, pp. 241–278. Madison, CT: International Universities Press.

Kornhuber, J., Riederer, P., et al. (1989). 3H-spiperone binding sites in post-mortem brains from schizophrenic patients: Relationship to neuroleptic drug treatment, abnormal movements, and positive symptoms. *Journal of Neural Transmission, 75,* 1–10.

Koskenvuo, M., Kaprio, J., Rose, R.J., Kesaniemi, A., Sarna, S., Heikkila, K., & Langinvainio, H. (1988). Hostility as a risk factor for mortality and ischemic heart disease in men. *Psychosomatic Medicine, 50,* 330–340.

Koss, M.P. (1992). The underdetection of rape. *Journal of Social Issues, 48,* 63–75.

Koss, M.P. (1993). Rape: Scope, impact, interventions, and public policy responses. *American Psychologist, 48,* 1062–1069.

Koss, M.P., & Butcher, J.M. (1986). Research on brief psychotherapy. In S.L. Garfield & A.E. Bergin (Eds.), *Handbook of psychotherapy and behavior change,* 3rd ed., pp. 627–670. New York: Wiley.

Koss, M.P., Tromp, S., & Tharan, M. (1995). Traumatic memories: Empirical foundations, forensic, and clinical implications. *Clinical Psychology: Science and Practice, 2,* 111–132.

Kosson, D.S., & Newman, J.P. (1986). Psychopathy and the allocation of attentional capacity in a divided-attention situation. *Journal of Abnormal Psychology, 95,* 257–263.

Kotrla, K.J., & Weinberger, D.R. (1995). Brain imaging in schizophrenia. *Annual Review of Medicine, 46,* 113–122.

Kovacs, M., Feinberg, T.L., Crouse-Novak, M.A., Paulaukas, S., Pollock, M., & Finkelstein, R. (1984). Depressive disorders in childhood. II. A longitudinal study of the risk for a subsequent major depression. *Archives of General Psychiatry, 41,* 643–649.

Kovelman, J.A., & Scheibel, A.B. (1986). Biological substrates of schizophrenia. *Acta Neurologica Scandinavica, 73,* 1–32.

Kozel, N.J., & Adams, E.H. (1986). Epidemiology of drug abuse: An overview. *Science, 234,* 970–974.

Kraepelin, E. (1921). *Manic-depressive insanity and paranoia.* Edinburgh: Livingstone.

Krafft-Ebing, R. (1892). *Psychopathia sexualis, with especial reference to contrary sexual instinct: A medico-legal study.* (translation of the 7th edition). Philadelphia: Davies.

Krantz, D.S., Contrada, R.J., Hill, D.R., & Friedler, E. (1988). Environmental stress and biobehavioral antecedents of coronary heart disease. *Journal of Consulting and Clinical Psychology, 56,* 333–341.

Krantz, D.S., Gabbay, F.H., Hedges, S.M., Leach, S.G., Gottdiener, J.S., & Rozanski, A. (1993). Mental and physical triggers of silent myocardial ischemia: Ambulatory studies using self-monitoring diary methodology. *Annals of Behavioral Medicine, 15,* 33–40.

Kristenson, H. (1992). Long-term antabuse treatment of alcohol-dependent patients. *Acta Psychiatrica Scandinavica, 86,* 41–45.

Krohn, A. (1980). Some clinical manifestations of

structural defects in a borderline personality. *International Journal of Psychoanalytic Psychotherapy, 8,* 337–362.

Krystal, J.H., Kosten, T.R., Southwick, S., Mason, J.W., Perry, B.D., & Giller, E.L. (1989). Neurobiological aspects of PTSD: Review of clinical and preclinical studies. *Behavior Therapy, 20,* 199–214.

Kubler-Ross, E. (1969). *On death and dying.* New York: MacMillian. Levinson, D.J. (1986). A conception of adult development. *American Psychologist, 41,* 3–13.

Kuhn, T.S. (1962). *The structure of scientific revolutions.* Chicago: University of Chicago Press.

Kuiper, B., & Cohen-Kettenis, P. (1988). Sex reassignment surgery: A study of 141 Dutch transsexuals. *Archives of Sexual Behavior, 17,* 439–457.

Kuipers, L. (1992). Expressed emotion research in Europe. *British Journal of Clinical Psychology, 31,* 429–443.

Kuipers, L., & Bebbington, P. (1988). Expressed emotion research in schizophrenia: theoretical and clinical implications. *Psychological Medicine, 18,* 893–909.

Kulynych, J.J., Vladar, K., Jones, D.W., & Weinberger, D.R. (1994). Gender differences in the normal lateralization of the supratemporal cortex: MRI surface-rendering morphometry of Heschl's gyrus and the lanum temporale. *Cerebral Cortex, 4,* 107–118.

Kupfer, D.J., & Thase, M.E. (1989). Laboratory studies and validity of psychiatric diagnosis: Has there been progress? In L.N. Robins & J.E. Barrett (Eds.), *The validity of psychiatric diagnosis,* pp. 177–197. New York: Raven Press.

Kushner, M.B., Sher, K.J., & Beitman, B.D. (1990). The relation between alcohol problems and the anxiety disorders. *American Journal of Psychiatry, 147,* 685–695.

Kutchins, H., & Kirk, S.A. (1986). The reliability of DSM-III: A critical review. *Social Work Research and Abstracts, 22,* 3–12.

L'Abate, L., & Bagarozzi, D.A. (1993). *Sourcebook of marriage and family evaluation.* New York: Brunner/Mazel.

Lacey, J.I. (1967). Somatic response patterning and stress: Some revisions of activation theory. In M.H. Appley & R. Trumball (Eds.), *Psychological stress.* New York: McGraw-Hill.

LaCroix, A.Z., & Haynes, S.G. (1987). Gender differences in the stressfulness of workplace roles: A focus on work and health. In R. Barnett, G. Baruch, & L. Biener (Eds.), *Gender and stress,* pp. 96–121. New York: Free Press.

Lamb, M.E., Thompson, R.A., & Gardner, W.P., et al. (1984). Security of infantile attachment as assessed in the "strange situation": Its study and biological interpretation. *Behavioral and Brain Sciences, 7,* 127–147.

Lambert, M.J., Shapiro, D.A., & Bergin, A.E. (1986). The effectiveness of psychotherapy. In S.L. Garfield & A.E. Bergin (Eds.), *Handbook of psychotherapy and behavior change,* 3rd ed., pp. 157–212. New York: Wiley.

Lancet, Editors of. (1952). *Disabilities and how to live with them.* Cited in C. Landis. (1964). *Varieties of psychopathological experience,* pp. 241–242. New York: Holt, Rinehart, & Winston.

Lancet (1991). Editorial. Phenylketonuria grows up. 337, 1256–1257.

Landy, F.J. (1986). Stamp collecting versus science: Validation as hypothesis testing. *American Psychologist, 41,* 1183–1192.

Lang, A.R. (1983). Addictive personality: A viable construct? In P. Levison, D. Gerstein, & D. Masloof (Eds.), *Commonalities in substance abuse and habitual behavior.* Lexington, MA: Heath.

Lang, A.R., Pelham, W.E., Johnston, C., & Gelernter, S. (1989). Levels of adult alcohol consumption induced by interaction with child confederate exhibiting normal versus externalizing behaviors. *Journal of Abnormal Psychology, 98,* 294.

Lang, A.R., & Stritzke, W.G.K. (1993). Children and alcohol. In M. Galanter, H. Begleiter, R. Deitrich, et al. (Eds). *Recent developments in alcoholism.* Vol. 11. Ten years of progress. pp. 73–85. New York: Plenum.

Lang, C.T., & Daro, D. (1996). *Current trends in child abuse reporting and fatalities: The results of the 1995 Annual State Survey.* Working paper 808. Washington, DC: National Committee on the Prevention of Child Abuse.

Lang, F.R., & Carstensen, L.L. (1994). Close emotional relationships in late life: Further support for proactive aging in the social domain. *Psychology and Aging, 9,* 315–324.

Lang, P.J. (1979). A bio-informational theory of emotional imagery. *Psychophysiology, 16,* 495–512.

Lange, A.J., & Jakubowski, P. (1976). *Responsible assertive behavior.* Champaign, IL: Research Press.

Langevin, R. (1992). Biological factors contributing to paraphilic behavior. *Psychiatric Annals, 22,* 307–314.

Langlais, P.J. (1995). Alcohol-related thiamine deficiency. *Alcohol Health and Research World, 19,* 113–122.

Lapouse, R., & Monk, M. (1958). An epidemiologic study of behavior characteristics in children. *American Journal of Public Health, 48,* 1134–1144.

Larsen, J.K. (1991). MAOIs in the treatment of depression: A review. *European Journal of Psychiatry, 5,* 79–88.

Larson, E.W., Olinsky, A., Rummens, T.A., & Morse, R.M. (1992). Disulfiram treatment of patients with both alcohol dependence and other psychiatric disorders: A review. *Alcoholism: Clinical and Experimental Research, 16,* 125–130.

Larson, R., Csikszentmihalyi, M., & Graef, R. (1980). Mood variability and the psychosocial adjustment of adolescents. *Journal of Youth and Adolescence, 9,* 469–490.

Last, C.G., & Strauss, C.C. (1990). School refusal in anxiety-disordered children and adolescents. *Journal of the American Academy of Child and Adolescent Psychiatry, 29,* 31–35.

Laumann, E.O., & Gagnon, J.H. (1995). A sociological perspective on sexual action. In R.G. Parker & J.H. Gagnon (Eds.), *Conceiving sexuality: Approaches to sex research in a postmodern world,* pp. 183–213. New York: Routledge.

Laumann, E.O., Gagnon, J.H., Michael, R.T., & Michaels, S. (1994). *The social organization of sexuality: Sexual practices in the United States.* Chicago: University of Chicago Press.

Lavori, P.W., Klerman, G.L., Keller, M.B., Reich, T., Rice, J., & Endicott, J. (1987). Age-period-cohort analysis of secular trends in onset of major depression: Findings in siblings of patients with major affective disorder. *Journal of Psychiatric Research, 21,* 23–35.

Lawton, M.P. (1989). Environmental approaches to research and treatment of Alzheimer's disease. In E. Light & B.D. Lebowitz (Eds.), *Alzheimer's disease treatment and family stress: Directions for research.* U.S. Department of Health and Human Services, DHHS Publication No. (ADM) 89-1569, pp. 340–362.

Lazarus, A. (1988). Dyspareunia: A multimodal psychotherapeutic perspective. In S. Leiblum & R.C. Rosen (Eds.), *Principles and practice of sex therapy,* 2nd ed. New York: Guilford.

Lazarus, R.S. (1966). *Psychological stress and the coping process.* New York: McGraw-Hill.

Lazarus, R.S., & Folkman, S. (1984). *Stress, appraisal, and coping.* New York: Springer.

Lazoritz, S. (1990). What ever happened to Mary Ellen? *Child Abuse and Neglect, 14,* 143–149.

Leaf, P.J., Berkman, C.S., Weissman, M.M., Holzer, C.E., Tischler, G.L., & Myers, J.K. (1988). The epidemiology of late-life depression. In J.A. Brody & G.L. Maddox (Eds.). *Epidemiology and aging: An international perspective.* New York: Springer.

Leary, T. (1957). *Interpersonal diagnosis of personality.* New York: Ronald Press.

Le Couteur, A. (1988). The role of genetics in the aetiology of autism, including findings of the links with the fragile X syndrome. In L. Wing (Ed.), *Aspects of autism: Biological research,* pp. 38–52. Gaskell: London.

Lee, S., Ho, T.P., & Hsu, L.K.G. (1993). Fat phobic and non-fat phobic anorexia nervosa: A comparative study of 70 Chinese patients in Hong Kong. *Psychological Medicine, 23,* 999–1017.

Leesfield, I.H. (1987). Negligence of mental health profesionals. *Trial, 23,* 57–61.

Leff, J.P. (1988). *Psychiatry around the globe: A transcultural view.* London: Royal College of Psychiatrists.

Leff, J. (1992). Transcultural aspects. In E.S. Paykel (Ed.), *Handbook of affective disorders,* 2nd ed., pp. 539–550. New York: Guilford.

Leff, J. (1995). Family management of schizophrenia. In C.L. Shriqui & H.A. Nasrallah (Eds.), *Contemporary issues in the treatment of schizophrenia,* pp. 683–702. Washington, DC: American Psychiatric Press.

Leff, J., Sartorius, N., Jablensky, A., Korten, A., & Ernberg, G. (1992). The International Pilot Study of Schizophrenia: Five-year follow-up findings. *Psychological Medicine, 22,* 131–145.

Leff, J., & Vaughn, C. (1985). *Expressed emotion in families: Its significance for mental illness.* New York: Guilford.

Leff, J., Wig, N.N., Bedi, H., et al. (1990). Relatives expressed emotion and the course of schizophrenia in Chandigarh: A two-year follow-up of a first-contact sample. *British Journal of Psychiatry, 156,* 351–356.

Lefley, H.P. (1992). Expressed emotion: Conceptual, clinical, and social policy issues. *Hospital and Community Psychiatry, 43,* 591–598.

Leibel, R.L. (1995). The molecular biology of obesity. In K.D. Brownell & C.G. Fairburn (Eds.), *Eating disorders and obesity: A comprehensive handbook,* pp. 450–456. New York: Guilford.

Leiblum, S.R., & Rosen, R.C. (1989). *Principles and practice of sex therapy: Update for the 1990s.* New York: Guilford.

Leichtman, M. (1989). Evolving concepts of borderline personality disorders. *Bulletin of the Menninger Clinic, 53,* 229–249.

Leigh, B.C. (1989). In search of the seven dwarves: Issues of measurement and meaning in alcohol expectancy research. *Psychological Bulletin, 105,* 361–373.

Leigh, B.C., & Stacy, A.W. (1993). Alcohol outcome expectancies: Scale construction and predictive utility in higher order confirmatory models. *Psychological Assessment, 5,* 216–229.

Leland, J. (1996). The fear of heroin is shooting up. *Newsweek,* August 26, 55–56.

Lenzenweger, M.F., Cornblatt, B.A., & Putnick, M. (1991). Schizotypy and sustained attention. *Journal of Abnormal Psychology, 100,* 84–89.

Leon, G., Fulkerson, J.A., Perry, C.L., & Cudeck, R. (1993). Personality and behavioral vulnerabilities associated with risk status for eating disorders in adolescent girls. *Journal of Abnormal Psychology, 102,* 438–444.

Leon, G.R., Fulkerson, J.A., Perry, C.L., & Early-Zald, M.B. (1995). Prospective analysis of personality and behavioral vulnerabilities and gender influences in the later development of disordered eating. *Journal of Abnormal Psychology, 104,* 140–149.

Leonard, H.L., Swedo, S.E., Lenane, M.C., Rettew, D.C., Hamburger, S.D., Bartko, J.J., & Rapoport, J.L. (1993). A 2- to 7-year follow-up study of 54 obsessive-compulsive children and adolescents. *Archives of General Psychiatry, 50,* 429–439.

Leonard, H.L., Swedo, S.E., Rapoport, J.L., Koby, E.V., Lenane, M.C., Cheslow, D.L., & Hamburger, S.D. (1989). Treatment of obsessive-compulsive disorder with clomipramine and desipramine in children and adolescents: A double-blind crossover comparison. *Archives of General Psychiatry, 46,* 1088–1092.

Leonhard, K. (1979). *The classification of endogenous psychoses,* 5th ed. New York: Wiley.

Leonhard, K. (1986). Different causative factors in different forms of schizophrenia. *British Journal of Psychiatry, 149,* 1–6.

Lerner, R.M., Orlos, J.B., & Knapp, J.R. (1976). Physical attractiveness, physical effectiveness, and self concept in late adolescents. *Adolescent, 11,* 313–326.

Letourneau, E., & O'Donohue, W. (1993). Sexual desire disorders. In W. O'Donohue & J.H. Geer (Eds.), *Handbook of sexual dysfunctions: Assessment and treatment,* pp. 53–82. Boston: Allyn & Bacon.

LeVay, S. (1993). *The sexual brain.* Cambridge, MA: MIT Press.

Levenson, M.R. (1992). Rethinking psychopathy. *Theory and Psychology, 2,* 51–71.

Levenson, R.W. (1987). Alcohol, affect, and physiology: Positive effects in the early stages of drinking. In E. Gottheil, K.A. Druley, S. Pashko, & S.P. Weinstein (Eds.), *Stress and addiction,* pp. 173–196. New York: Brunner/Mazel.

Levenson, R.W., Carstensen, L.L., & Gottman, J.M. (1994). The influence of age and gender on affect, physiology, and their interrelations: A study of long-term marriages. *Journal of Personality and Social Psychology, 67,* 56–68.

Levin, S. (1984). Frontal lobe dysfunction in schizophrenia. I. Eye movement impairments. *Journal of Psychiatric Research, 18,* 27–55.

Levine, H.G. (1978). The discovery of addiction: Changing conceptions of habitual drunkenness in America. *Journal of Studies on Alcohol, 39,* 143–174.

Levine, M., & Perkins, D.V. (1987). *Principles of community psychology: Perspectives and applications.* New York: Oxford University Press.

Levine, S.B. (1987). More on the nature of sexual desire. *Journal of Sex and Marital Therapy, 13,* 35–44.

Levine, S.B., Risen, C.B., & Althof, S.E. (1990). Essay on the diagnosis and nature of paraphilia. *Journal of Sex and Marital Therapy, 16,* 89–102.

Levitt, E.E., Moser, C., & Jamison, K.V. (1994). The prevalence and some attributes of females in the sadomasochistic subculture: A second report. *Archives of Sexual Behavior, 23,* 465–474.

Levy, D.L., Holzman, P.S., Matthysse, S., & Mendell, N.R. (1993). Eye tracking dysfunction and schizophrenia: A critical perspective. *Schizophrenia Bulletin, 19,* 461–537.

Levy, D.L., Holzman, P.S., Matthysse, S., & Mendell, N.R. (1994). Eye tracking and schizophrenia: A selective review. *Schizophrenia Bulletin, 20,* 47–62.

Lewander, T. (1992). Differential development of therapeutic drugs for psychosis. *Clinical Neuropharmacology, 15* (suppl. 1), 654–655.

Lewine, R.R.J., & Seeman, M.V. (1995). Gender, brain, and schizophrenia. In M.V. Seeman (Ed.), *Gender and psychopathology,* pp. 131–158. Washington, DC: American Psychiatric Press.

Lewine, R.J., & Sommers, A.A. (1985). Clinical definition of negative symptoms as a reflection of theory and methodology. In Murray Alpert (Ed.), *Controversies in schizophrenia: Changes and constancies.* New York: Guilford.

Lewinsohn, P.M. (1974). A behavioral approach to depression. In R.J. Friedman & M.M. Katz (Eds.), *The psychology of depression: Contemporary theory and research,* pp. 157–178. New York: Winston-Wiley.

Lewinsohn, P.M., Hoberman, H.M., & Rosenbaum, M. (1988). A prospective study of risk factors for unipolar depression. *Journal of Abnormal Psychology, 97,* 251–264.

Lewinsohn, P.M., Hoberman, H.M., Teri, L., & Hautzinger, M. (1985). An integrative theory of depression. In S. Reiss & R.R. Bootzin (Eds.), *Theoretical issues in behavior therapy.* New San Diego: Academic Press.

Lewinsohn, P.M., Mischel, W., Chaplin, W., & Barton, R. (1980). Social competence and depression: The role of illusory self-perceptions. *Journal of Abnormal Psychology, 89,* 203–212.

Lewinsohn, P.M., Roberts, R.E., Seely, J.R., Rohde, P.,

Gotlib, I.H., & Hops, H. (1994). Adolescent psychopathology. II. Psychosocial risk factors for depression. *Journal of Abnormal Psychology, 103*, 302–315.

Lewinsohn, P.M., Rohde, P., Seeley, J.R., et al. (1993). Age-cohort changes in the lifetime occurrence of depression and other mental disorders. *Journal of Abnormal Psychology, 102*, 110–120.

Lewinsohn, P.M., Steinmetz, J.L., Larson, D.W., & Franklin, J. (1981). Depression-related cognitions: Antecedent or consequence? *Journal of Abnormal Psychology, 90*, 213–219.

Lewis, M., & Michalson, L. (1983). *Children's emotions and moods: Developmental theory and measurement.* New York: Plenum.

Lewis, M.H. (1996). Psychopharmacology of autism spectrum. *Journal of Autism and Developmental Disorders, 26*, 231–235.

Lewis-Fernandez, R., & Kleinman, A. (1994). Culture, personality, and psychopathology. *Journal of Abnormal Psychology, 103*, 67–71.

Ley, R. (1994). The "suffocation alarm" theory of panic attacks: A critical commentary. *Journal of Behavior Therapy and Experimental Psychiatry, 25*, 269–273.

Liberman, R.P., Cardin, V., McGill, C.W., Falloon, I.R.H., & Evans, C.D. (1987). Behavioral family management of schizophrenia: Clinical outcome and costs. *Psychiatric Annals, 17*, 610–619.

Liberman, R.P., DeRisi, W.J., & Mueser, K.T. (1989). *Social skills training for psychiatric patients.* New York: Pergamon.

Lidz, C.W., Hoge, S.K., Gardner, W., Bennett, N.S., Monahan, J., Mulvey, E.P., & Roth, L.H. (1995). Perceived coercion in mental hospital admission: Pressures and process. *Archives of General Psychiatry, 52*, 1034–1039.

Lidz, C.W., Mulvey, E.P., & Gardner, W. (1993). The accuracy of predictions of violence to others. *Journal of the American Medical Association, 269*, 1007–1011.

Lieberman, J.A. (1994). Clinical biological studies of atypical antipsychotics: Focus on the serotonin/dopamine systems. *Journal of Clinical Psychiatry Monograph Series, 12*, 24–31.

Lieberman, J.A., & Koreen, A.R. (1993). Neurochemistry and neuroendocrinology of schizophrenia: A selective review. *Schizophrenia Bulletin, 19*, 371–429.

Liebowitz, M.R. (1993). Mixed anxiety and depression: Should it be included in DMS-IV? *Journal of Clinical Psychiatry, 54* (suppl. 5), 4–7.

Liebowitz, M.R., Gorman, J.M., Fyer, A.J., & Klein, D.F. (1985). Social phobia: Review of a neglected anxiety disorder. *Archives of General Psychiatry, 42*, 729–736.

Liebowitz, M.R., Schneier, F.R., Hollander, E., Welkowitz, L.A., et al. (1991). Treatment of social phobia with drugs other than benzodiazepines. *Journal of Clinical Psychiatry, 52* (suppl.), 10–15.

Liem, J.H. (1974). Effects of verbal communications of parents and children: A comparison of normal and schizophrenic families. *Journal of Consulting and Clinical Psychology, 42*, 438–450.

Light, L.L. (1991). Memory and aging: Four hypotheses in search of data. *Annual Review of Psychology, 42*, 333–376.

Lilienfeld, S.O. (1992). The association between antisocial personality and somatization disorders: A review and integration of theoretical models. *Clinical Psychology Review, 12*, 641–662.

Lilienfeld, S.O. (1994). Conceptual problems in the assessment of psychopathy. *Clinical Psychology Review, 14*, 17–38.

Lindenmayer, J.P. (1993). Recent advances in pharmacotherapy of schizophrenia. *Psychiatric Annals, 23*, 201–208.

Linehan, M.M. (1993). *Cognitive-behavioral treatment of borderline personality disorder.* New York: Guilford.

Linehan, M.M. (1987). Dialectical behavior therapy for borderline personality disorder. *Bulletin of the Menninger Clinic, 51*, 261–276.

Linehan, M.M., Heard, H.L., & Armstrong, H.E. (1993). Naturalistic follow-up of a behavioral treatment for chronically parasuicidal borderline patients. *Archives of General Psychiatry, 50*, 971–974.

Linehan, M.M., Hubert, A.E., Suarez, A., Doublas, A., & Heard, H.L. (1991). Cognitive-behavioral treatment of chronically parasuicidal borderline patients. *Archives of General Psychiatry, 48*, 1060–1064.

Linehan, M.M., Tutek, D.A., Heard, H.L., & Armstrong, H.E. (1994). Interpersonal outcome of cognitive-behavioral treatment for chronically suicidal borderline patients. *American Journal of Psychiatry, 151*, 1771–1776.

Link, B., Cullen, F., & Andrews, H. (1990, August). Violent and illegal behavior of current and former mental patients compared to community controls. Paper presented at the meeting of the Society for the Study of Social Problems.

Link, B.G., Cullen, F.T., Struening, E., Shrout, P.E., & Dohrenwend, B.P. (1989). A modified labeling theory approach to mental disorders: An empirical assessment. *American Sociological Review, 54*, 400–423.

Link, B.G., Mirotznik, J., & Cullen, F.T. (1991). The effectiveness of stigma coping orientations: Can negative consequences of mental illness labeling be avoided? *Journal of Health and Social Behavior, 32*, 302–320.

Lipowski, Z.J. (1988). Somatization: The concept and its clinical applications. *American Journal of Psychiatry, 145*, 1358–1368.

Lipowski, Z.J. (1989). Delirium in the elderly patient. *New England Journal of Medicine, 320*, 578–582.

Lipsey, M.W., & Wilson, D.B. (1993). The efficacy of psychological, educational, and behavioral treatment: Confirmation for meta-analysis. *American Psychologist, 48*, 1181–1209.

Lipsitz, J.D., Martin, L.Y., Mannuzza, S., Chapman, T.F., Liebowitz, M.R., Klein, D.F., & Fyer, A.J. (1994). Childhood separation anxiety disorder in patients with adult anxiety disorders. *American Journal of Psychiatry, 151*, 927–929.

Lipton, D.N., McDonel, E.C., & McFall, R.M. (1987). Heterosocial perception in rapists. *Journal of Consulting and Clinical Psychology, 55*, 17–21.

Liptzin, B. (1996). Delirium. In J. Sadavoy, L.W. Lazarus, L.F. Jarvik, & G.T. Grossberg (Eds.), *Comprehensive review of geriatric psychiatry*, 2nd ed., pp. 479–495. Washington, DC: American Psychiatric Press.

Lishman, W.A. (1987). *Organic psychiatry: The psychological consequences of cerebral disorders*, 2nd ed. Oxford: Blackwell.

Litten, R.E., & Allen, E.R. (1991). Pharmacotherapies for alcoholism: Promising agents and clinical issues. *Alcoholism: Clinical and Experimental Research, 15*, 620–633.

Livesley, W.J. (1989). Classifying personality disorders: Ideal types, prototypes, or dimensions? *Psychiatric Clinics of North America, 12*, 531–539.

Livesley, W.J. (1995). Commentary on dependent personality disorder. In W.J. Livesley (Ed.), *The DSM-IV personality disorders.* pp. 257–260. New York: Guilford.

Livesley, W.J., Jang, K.L., Jackson, D.N., & Vernon, P.A. (1993). Genetic and environmental contributions to dimensions of personality disorder. *American Journal of Psychiatry, 150*, 1826–1831.

Livesley, W.J., Schroeder, M.L., Jackson, D.N., & Jang, K.L. (1994). Categorical distinctions in the study of personality disorder: Implications for classification. *Journal of Abnormal Psychology, 103*, 6–17.

Livesley, W.J., & West, M. (1986). The DSM-III distinction between schizoid and avoidant personality disorders. *Canadian Journal of Psychiatry, 31*, 59–62.

Lobo, A., Saz, P., Marcos, G., Dia, J., et al. (1995). The prevalence of dementia and depression in the elderly community in a southern European population. *Archives of General Psychiatry, 52*, 497–506.

Loeber, R. (1982). The stability of antisocial and delinquent child behavior: A review. *Psychological Bulletin, 53*, 1431–1446.

Loeber, R. (1988). Natural histories of conduct problems, delinquency, and associated substance use: Evidence for developmental progression. In B.B. Lahey & A.E. Kazdin (Eds.), *Advances in clinical child psychology*, Vol. 11, pp. 73–118. New York: Plenum.

Loeber, R., & Dishion, T.J. (1983). Early predictors of male delinquency: A review. *Psychological Bulletin, 94*, 68–99.

Loeber, R., Lahey, B.B., & Thomas, C. (1991). Diagnostic conundrum of oppositional defiant disorder and conduct disorder. *Journal of Abnormal Psychology, 100*, 379–390.

Loftin, C., McDowall, D., Wiersema, B., & Cottey, T.J. (1991). Effects of restrictive licensing of handguns on homicide and suicide in the District of Columbia. *New England Journal of Medicine, 325*, 1615–1620.

Loftus, E.F. (1993). The reality of repressed memories. *American Psychologist, 48*, 518–537.

Loftus, E.F., Garry, M., & Feldman, J. (1994). Forgetting sexual trauma: What does it mean when 38% forget? *Journal of Consulting and Clinical Psychology, 62*, 1177–1181.

Loftus, E., & Ketcham, K. (1994). *The myth of repressed memory.* New York: St. Martin's Press.

Loftus, E.F., & Klinger, M.R. (1992). Is the unconscious smart or dumb? *American Psychologist, 47*, 761–765.

Lohr, J.M., Kleinknecht, R.A., Conley, A.T., Dal Cerro, S., Schmidt, J., & Sonntag, M.E. (1992). A methodological critique of the current status of eye movement desensitization (EMD). *Behavior Therapy and Experimental Psychiatry, 23*, 159–167.

London, P. (1964). *The modes and morals of psychotherapy.* New York: Holt, Rinehart & Winston.

Longino, C.F., & Mittelmark, M.B. (1996). In J. Sadavoy, L.W. Lazarus, L.F. Jarvik, & G.T. Grossberg (Eds.), *Comprehensive review of geriatric psychiatry—II*, pp. 135–152. Washington, DC: American Psychiatric Press.

Lonner, W.J., & Malpass, R.S. (1994). When psychology and culture meet: An introduction to cross-cultural psychology. In W.J. Lonner & R.S. Malpass (Eds.), *Psychology and culture*, pp. 1–12. Boston: Allyn & Bacon.

LoPiccolo, J. (1985). Diagnosis and treatment of male sexual dysfunction. *Journal of Sex and Marital Therapy, 11*, 215–232.

LoPiccolo, J. (1991). Sexual dysfunction. In Hersen and Bellack (Eds.), *International handbook of behavior modification*, pp. 547–564. New York: Plenum.

LoPiccolo, J., & Stock, W.E. (1986). Treatment of sexual dysfunction. *Journal of Consulting and Clinical Psychology, 54*, 158–167.

Loranger, A.W., Sartorius, N., Andreoli, A., Berger, P., Buchheim, P., Channabasavanna, S.M., Coid, B., Dahl, A., Diekstra, R.F.W., Ferguson, B., Jacobsberg, L.B., Mombour, W., Pull, C., Ono, Y., & Regier, D.A. (1994). The international personality disorder examination: The World Health Organization/Alcohol, Drug Abuse, and Mental Health Administration International Pilot Study of Personality Disorders. *Archives of General Psychiatry, 51*, 215–224.

Lorion, R.P., & Felner, R.D. (1986). Research on psychotherapy with the disadvantaged. In S.L. Garfield & A.E. Bergin (Eds.), *Handbook of psychotherapy and behavior change*, 3rd ed., pp. 739–776. New York: Wiley.

Lovaas, O.I. (1987). Behavioral treatment and normal educational and intellectual functioning in young autistic children. *Journal of Consulting and Clinical Psychology, 55*, 3–9.

Lovaas, O.I., Schreibman, L., Koegel, R.L., & Rehm, R. (1971). Selective responding by autistic children to multiple sensory input. *Journal of Abnormal Psychology*, 77, 211–222.

Low, P.W., Jeffries, J.C., & Bonnie, R.J. (1986). *The trial of John W. Hinckley, Jr.: A case study in the insanity defense.* Mineola, NY: Foundation Press.

Luborsky, L. (1984). *Principles of psychoanalytic psychotherapy: A manual for supportive-expressive treatment.* New York: Basic Books.

Luborsky, L., Barber, J.P., & Beutler, L. (1993). Introduction to special section: A briefing on curative factors in dynamic psychotherapy. *Journal of Consulting and Clinical Psychology*, 61, 539–541.

Luborsky, L., Diguer, L., Luborsky, E., McLellan, A.T., Woody, G., & Alexander, L. (1993). Psychological health-sickness (PHS) as a predictor of outcomes in dynamic and other psychotherapies. *Journal of Consulting and Clinical Psychology*, 61, 542–548.

Luborsky, L., Singer, B., & Luborsky, L. (1975). Comparative studies of psychotherapy. *Archives of General Psychiatry*, 32, 995–1008.

Lubs, H.A. (1969). A marker X chromosome. *American Journal of Human Genetics*, 21, 231–244.

Lubs, M., & Maes, J. (1977). Recurrence risk in mental retardation. In P. Mittler (Ed.), *Research to practice in mental retardation*, vol. 3. Baltimore: University Park Press.

Luepnitz, D.A. (1982). *Child custody: A study of families after divorce.* Lexington, MA: Lexington Books.

Lukoff, D., Nuechterlein, K.H., & Ventura, J. (1986). Manual for expanded Brief Psychiatric Rating Scale (BPRS). *Schizophrenia Bulletin*, 12, 594–602.

Luria, A. (1961). *The role of speech in the regulation of normal and abnormal behaviors.* New York: Liveright.

Lykken, D.T. (1957). A study of anxiety in the sociopathic personality. *Journal of Abnormal and Social Psychology*, 55, 6–10.

Lyness, S.A. (1993). Predictors of differences between Type A and B individuals in heart rate and blood pressure reactivity. *Psychological Bulletin*, 114, 266–295.

Lyon, G.R. (1996). Learning disabilities. *Future of Children*, 6, 54–76.

Lyons, M.J. (1995). Epidemiology of personality disorders. In M.T. Tsuang, M. Tohen, & G.E.P. Zahner (Eds.), *Textbook in psychiatric epidemiology*, pp. 407–436. New York: Wiley.

Lyons, M.J., True, W.R., Eisen, S.A., Goldberg, J., Meyter, J.M., Faraone, S.V., Eaves, L.J., & Tsuang, M.T. (1995). Differential heritability of adult and juvenile antisocial traits. *Archives of General Psychiatry*, 52, 906–915.

Maccoby, E.E. (1991). Gender and relationships: A reprise. *American Psychologist*, 46, 538–539.

Maccoby, E.E. (1992). The role of parents in the socialization of children: An historical overview. *Developmental Psychology*, 28, 1006–1017.

Maccoby, E.E., & Jacklin, C.N. (1974). *The psychology of sex differences.* Stanford: Stanford University Press.

Maccoby, E.E., & Martin, J.A. (1983). Socialization in the context of the family: Parent-child interaction. In E.M. Hetherington (Ed.), *Socialization, personality, and social development*, Vol. 4, *Handbook of child psychology* pp. 1–101. New York: Wiley.

Maccoby, E.E., & Mnookin, R.H. (1992). *Dividing the Child: Social and legal dilemmas of custody.* Cambridge, MA: Harvard University Press.

Mack, A.H., Forman, L., Brown, R., & Frances, A. (1994). A brief history of psychiatric classification: From the ancients to DSM-IV. *Psychiatric Clinics of North America*, 17, 515–523.

Mackay, A.V.P., Iversen, L.L., Rossor, M., Spokes, E., Bird, E., Arregui, A., Creese, I., & Snyder, S.H. (1982). Increased brain dopamine and dopamine receptors in schizophrenia. *Archives of General Psychiatry*, 39, 991–997.

Mackay, R.D. (1988). Post-Hinckley insanity in the U.S.A. *Criminal Law Review*, 88–96.

MacMillan, D.L., Gresham, F.M., & Siperstein, G.N. (1995). Heightened concerns over the 1992 AAMR

definition: Advocacy versus precision. *American Journal on Mental Retardation*, 100, 87–97.

Maddi, S.R. (1980). *Personality theories: A comparative analysis*, 4th ed. Homewood, IL: Dorsey.

Magenis, R.E., Overton, K.M., Chamberlin, J., Brady, T., & Lovrien, E. (1977). Parental origin of the extra chromosome in Down's syndrome. *Human Genetics*, 37, 7–16.

Maher, B.A., & Spitzer, M. (1993). Delusions. In C.G. Costello (Ed.), *Symptoms of schizophrenia*, pp. 92–120. New York: Wiley.

Mahoney, M.J. (1991). *Human change processes: The scientific foundations of psychotherapy.* New York: Basic Books.

Maier, S.F., Watkins, L.R., & Fleshner, M. (1994). Psychoneuroimmunology: The interface between behavior, brain, and immunity. *American Psychologist*, 49, 1004–1017.

Maier, W., Lichtermann, D., Klingler, T., Heun, R., & Hallmayer, J. (1992). Prevalence of personality disorders (DSM-III-R) in the community. *Journal of Personality Disorders*, 6, 187–196.

Maier, W., Lichtermann, D., Minges, J., Oehrlein, A., & Franke, P. (1993). A controlled family study in panic disorder. *Journal of Psychiatric Research*, 27, (suppl. 1), 79–87.

Major, B., & Crocker, J. (1993). Social stigma: The consequences of attributional ambiguity. In D.M. Mackie & D.L. Hamilton (Eds.), *Affect, cognition, and stereotyping: Interactive processes in group perception*, pp. 345–370. San Diego, CA: Academic Press.

Mäkelä, K. (1986). Attitudes toward drinking and drunkenness in four Scandinavian countries. In T.F. Babor (Ed.), *Alcohol and culture: Comparative perspectives from Europe and America*, Vol. 472, pp. 21–32. New York: New York Academy of Sciences.

Mäkelä, K. (1994). Rates of attrition among the membership of Alcoholics Anonymous in Finland. *Journal of Studies on Alcohol*, 55, 91–95.

Malcolm, J.G. (1987). Treatment choices and informed consent in psychiatry: Implications of the Osheroff case for the profession. *Journal of Psychiatry and the Law*, 15, 9–81.

Maletzky, B.M. (1997). Exhibitionism: Assessment and treatment. In D.R. Laws & W.T. O'Donohue (Eds.), *Handbook of sexual deviance: Theory and application.* New York: Guilford.

Maltzman, I. (1989). A reply to Cook, "Craftsman versus professional: Analysis of the controlled drinking controversy." *Journal of Studies on Alcohol*, 50, 466–472.

Mandler, G. (1975). *Mind and emotion.* New York: Wiley.

Mandler, G. (1966). Anxiety. In D. L. Sills (Ed.), *International encyclopedia of the social sciences.* New York: Macmillan.

Mangone, C.A., Sanguinetti, R.M., Baumann, P.D., Gonzalez, R.C., et al. (1993). Influence of feelings of burden on the caregiver's perception of the patient's functional status. *Dementia*, 4, 287–293.

Mankoo, B., Sherrington, R., Brynjolfsson, J., Kalsi, G., Petursson, J., Sigmundsson, T., Read, T., Murphy, P., Curtis, D., Melmer, G., & Gurling, H. (1991). New microsatellite polymorphisms provide a highly polymorphic map of chromosome 5 bands q11.2-q13.3 for linkage analysis of Icelandic and English families affected by schizophrenia. *Psychiatric Geriatrics*, 2, 17.

Mann, J.J., & Kupfer, D.J. (Eds.) (1993). *Biology of depressive disorders. Part A: A systems perspective.* New York: Plenum.

Mann, K., Klinger, T., Noe, S., Roschke, J., Muller, S., & Benkert, O. (1996). Effects of yohimbine on sexual experiences and nocturnal penile tumescence and rigidity in erectile dysfunction. *Archives of Sexual Behavior*, 25, 1–16.

Mannuzza, S., Schneier, F.R., Chapman, T.F., Liebowitz, M.R., Klein, D.F., & Fyer, A.J. (1995). Generalized

social phobia: Reliability and validity. *Archives of General Psychiatry*, 52, 230–237.

Manschreck, T.C. (1993). Psychomotor abnormalities. In C.G. Costello (Ed.), *Symptoms of schizophrenia*, pp. 261–290. New York: Wiley.

Manson, S.M. (1994). Culture and depression: Discovering variations in the experience of illness. In W.J. Lonner & R.S. Malpass (Eds.), *Psychology and culture*, pp. 285–290. Boston: Allyn & Bacon.

March, J.S., Leonard, H.L., & Swedo, S.E. (1995). Obsessive-compulsive disorder. In J.S. March (Ed.), *Anxiety disorders in children and adolescents*, pp. 251–275. New York: Guilford.

Marcia, J.E. (1966). Development and validation of ego-identity status. *Journal of Personality and Social Psychology*, 24, 551–558.

Marcia, J.E. (1994). The empirical study of ego identity. In H.A. Bosma, T.L.G. Graafsma, H.D. Grotevant, & D.J. de Levita (Eds.), *Identity and development*, pp. 67–80. Thousand Oaks, CA: Sage.

Marder, K., Tang, M., Cote, L., & Stern, Y. (1995). The frequency and associated risk factors for dementia in patients with Parkinson's disease. *Archives of Neurology*, 52, 695–701.

Marder, S.R., Ames, D., Wirshing, W.C., & Van Putten, T. (1993). Schizophrenia. *Psychiatric Clinics of North America*, 16, 567–587.

Marengo, J.T., & Harrow, M. (1993). Thought disorder. In C.G. Costello (Ed.), *Symptoms of schizophrenia*, pp. 27–55. New York: Wiley.

Margolin, G. (1981). Behavior exchange in happy and unhappy marriages: A family cycle perspective. *Behavior Therapy*, 12, 329–343.

Margolin, G. (1987). Marital therapy: A cognitive-behavioral approach. In N.S. Jacobson (Ed.), *Psychotherapists in clinical practice*, pp. 232–285. New York: Guilford.

Margolin, G., Christensen, A., & John, R.S. (1996). The continuance and spillover of everyday tensions in distressed and nondistressed families. *Journal of Family Psychology*, 10, 304–321.

Margraf, J., Barlow, D.H., Clark, D.M., & Telch, M.J. (1993). Psychological treatment of panic: Work in progress on outcome, active ingredients, and follow-up. *Behaviour Research and Therapy*, 31, 1–8.

Margraf, J., Taylor, C.B., Ehlers, A., Roth, W.T., & Agras, W.S. (1987). Panic attacks in the natural environment. *Journal of Nervous and Mental Disease*, 175, 558–565.

Margulis, L., & Sagan, D. (1991). *Mystery dance: On the evolution of human sexuality.* New York: Summit.

Markman, H.J., Floyd, F.J., Stanley, S.M., & Storaasli, R.D. (1988). Prevention of marital distress: A longitudinal investigation. *Journal of Consulting and Clinical Psychology*, 56, 210–217.

Markman, H.J., Renick, M.J., Floyd, F.J., Stanley, S.M., & Clements, M. (1993). Preventing marital distress throught communication and conflict management training: A 4- and 5-year follow-up. *Journal of Consulting and Clinical Psychology*, 61, 70–77.

Markova, I.S., & Berrios, G.E. (1992). The meaning of insight in clinical psychiatry. *British Journal of Psychiatry*, 160, 850–860.

Markovitz, P.J., Calabrese, J.R., Schulz, C.S., & Meltzer, H.Y. (1991). Fluoxetine in the treatment of borderline and schizotypal personality disorders. *American Journal of Psychiatry*, 148, 1064–1067.

Marks, I.M. (1969). *Fears and phobias.* New York: Academic Press.

Marks, I.M., & Gelder, M.G. (1966). Different ages of onset in varieties of phobia. *American Journal of Psychiatry*, 123, 218–221.

Marks, I.M., & Nesse, R.M. (1994). Fear and fitness: An evolutionary analysis of anxiety disorders. *Ethology and Sociobiology*, 15, 247–261.

Marks, I.M. (1987). *Fears, phobias, and rituals: Panic, anxiety, and their disorders.* New York: Oxford University Press.

Marks, I.M., Swinson, R.P., Basoglu, M., Kuch, K., Noshirvani, H., O'Sullivan, G., Lelliott, P.T., Kirby, M., McNamee, G., Sengun, S., & Wickwire, K. (1993). Alprazolam and exposure alone and combined in panic disorder with agoraphobia: A controlled study in London and Toronto. *British Journal of Psychiatry, 162,* 776–787.

Marks, P.A., Seeman, W., & Haller, D.L. (1974). *The actuarial use of the MMPI with adolescents and adults.* New York: Oxford University Press.

Marlatt, G.A. (1985). Relapse prevention: Theoretical rationale and overview of the model. In G.A. Marlatt & J.R. Gordon (Eds.), *Relapse prevention.* New York: Guilford.

Marlatt, G.A. (1987). Alcohol, the magic elixir: Stress, expectancy, and the transformation of emotional states. In E. Gottheil, K.A. Druley, S. Pashko, & S.P. Weinstein (Eds.), *Stress and addiction,* pp. 302–322. New York: Brunner/Mazel.

Marlatt, G.A. (1996). Models of relapse and relapse prevention: A commentary. *Experimental and Clinical Psychopharmacology, 4,* 55–60.

Marlatt, G.A., & Baer, J.S. (1988). Addictive behaviors: Etiology and treatment. *Annual Review of Psychology, 39,* 223–252.

Marlatt, G.A., Baer, J.S., Donovan, D.M., & Kivlahan, D.R. (1988). Addictive behaviors: Etiology and treatment. *Annual Review of Psychology, 39,* 223–252.

Marlatt, G.A., & Rohsenow, D.J. (1980). Cognitive processes in alcohol use: Expectancy and the balanced placebo design. In N.K. Mello (Ed.), *Advances in substance abuse,* Vol. 1, pp. 159–199. Greenwich, Conn: JAL Press.

Marques, J.K., Day, D.M., Nelson, C., & West, M.A. (1993). Findings and recommendations from California's experimental treatment program. In G.C.N. Hall, R. Hirschman, J.R. Graham, & M.S. Zaragoza (Eds.), *Sexual aggression: Issues in etiology, assessment, and treatment,* pp. 197–214. Washington, DC: Hemisphere.

Marques, J.K., Day, D.M., Nelson, C., & West, M.A. (1994). Effects of cognitive-behavioral treatment on sex offender recidivism: Preliminary results of a longitudinal study. *Criminal Justice and Behavior, 21,* 28–54.

Marsella, A.J., Sartorius, N., Jablensky, A., & Fenton, F.R. (1985). Cross-cultural studies of depressive disorders: An overview. In A. Kleinman & B. Good (Eds.), *Culture and depression: Studies in the anthropology and cross-cultural psychiatry of affect and disorder,* pp. 299–324. Berkeley: University of California.

Marshall, R.D., & Klein, D.F. (1995). Pharmacotherapy in the treatment of posttraumatic stress disorder. *Psychiatric Annals, 25,* 588–597.

Marshall, W.L. (1989). Intimacy, loneliness, and sexual offenders. *Behaviour Research and Therapy, 27,* 491–503.

Marshall, W.L., Bryce, P., Hudson, S.M., Ward, T., & Moth, B. (1996). The enhancement of intimacy and the reduction of loneliness among child molesters. *Journal of Family Violence, 11,* 219–236.

Marshall, W.L., Eccles, A., & Barbaree, H.E. (1991). The treatment of exhibitionists: A focus on sexual deviance versus cognitive and relationship features. *Behaviour Research and Therapy, 29,* 129–135.

Marshall, W.L., Hudson, S.M., & Ward, T. (1992). Sexual deviance. In P.H. Wilson (Ed.), *Principles and practice of relapse prevention.* New York: Guilford.

Marshall, W.L., Jones, R., Ward, T., et al. (1991). Treatment outcome with sex offenders. *Clinical Psychology Review, 11,* 465–485.

Marshall, W.L., Payne, K., Barbaree, H.E., & Eccles, A. (1991). Exhibitionists: Sexual preferences for exposing. *Behaviour Research and Therapy, 29,* 37–40.

Marshall, W.L., & Pithers, W.D. (1994). A reconsideration of treatment outcome with sex offenders. *Criminal Justice and Behavior, 21,* 10–27.

Martin, C.S., & Sayette, M.A. (1993). Experimental design in alcohol administration research:

Limitations and alternatives in the manipulation of dosage-set. *Journal of Studies on Alcohol, 54,* 750–761.

Martin, R.L., Roberts, W.V., & Clayton, P.J. (1980). Psychiatric status after hysterectomy: A one-year prospective follow-up. *Journal of the American Medical Association, 244,* 350–353.

Marwit, S.J. (1996). Reliability of diagnosing complicated grief: A preliminary investigation. *Journal of Consulting and Clinical Psychology, 64,* 563–568.

Mash, E.J., & Johnston, C. (1982). A comparison of the mother-child interactions of younger and older hyperactive and normal children. *Child Development, 53,* 1371–1381.

Maslow, A.H. (1954). *Motivation and personality.* New York: Harper & Row.

Maslow, A.H. (1970) *Motivation and personality,* 2nd ed. New York: Harper & Row.

Mason, F.L. (1997). Fetishism: Psychopathology and theory. In D.R. Laws & W.T. O'Donohue (Eds.), *Handbook of sexual deviance: Theory and application.* New York: Guilford.

Mason, J.W. (1975). A historical view of the "stress" field (Part II). *Journal of Human Stress, 1,* 12–16.

Masters, W.H., & Johnson, V.E. (1966). *Human sexual response.* Boston: Little Brown.

Masters, W.H., & Johnson, V.E. (1966). *Human sexual inadequacy.* Boston: Little Brown.

Masters, W.H., Johnson, V.E., & Kolodny, R.C. (1994). *Heterosexuality.* New York: HarperPerennial.

Matarazzo, J.D. (1983). The reliability of psychiatric and psychological diagnosis. *Clinical Psychology Review, 3,* 103–145.

Mate-Kole, C., Freschi, M., & Robin, A. (1988). Aspects of psychiatric symptoms at different stages in the treatment of transsexualism. *British Journal of Psychiatry, 152,* 550–553.

Mathews, A. (1990). Why worry: The cognitive function of anxiety. *Behaviour Research and Therapy, 28,* 455–468.

Matson, J.L., & Frame, C.L. (1986). *Psychopathology among mentally retarded children and adolescents.* Beverly Hills, CA: Sage.

Matthews, K.A. (1988). Coronary heart disease and Type A behaviors: Update on and alternative to the Booth-Kewley and Friedman (1987) quantitative review. *Psychological Bulletin,* 373–380.

Matthysse, S., & Pope, A. (1986). The neuropathology of psychiatric disorders. In P. Berger & K.H. Brodie (Eds.), *American handbook of psychiatry,* 2nd ed., Vol. 8, pp. 151–159. New York: Basic Books.

Max, W. (1993). The economic impact of Alzheimer's disease. *Neurology, 43* (suppl. 4), S6–S10.

May, R. (1967). *Psychology and the human dilemma.* New York: Van Nostrand Reinhold.

McAnulty, R.D., & Adams, H.E. (1992). Validity and ethics of penile circumference measures of sexual arousal: A reply to McConaghy. *Archives of Sexual Behavior, 21,* 177–195.

McBride, W.J., Murphy, J.M., Yoshimoto, K., Lumeng, L., & Li, T.K. (1993). Serotonin mechanisms in alcohol-drinking behavior. *Drug Development Research, 30,* 170–177.

McCabe, M.P., McDonald, E., Deeks, A., Vowels, L.M., & Cobain, M.J. (1996). The impact of multiple sclerosis on sexuality and relationships. *Journal of Sex Research, 33,* 241–249.

McCann, U.D., Rossiter, E.M., King, R.J., & Agras, W.S. (1991). Nonpurging bulimia: A distinct subtype of bulimia nervosa. *International Journal of Eating Disorders, 10,* 679–687.

McCarley, R.W., Shenton, M.E., O'Donnell, B.F., Faux, S.F., et al. (1993). Auditory P300 abnormalities and left posterior superior temporal gyrus volume reduction in schizophrenia. *Archives of General Psychiatry, 50,* 190–197.

McCarthy, B.W. (1989). Cognitive-behavioral strategies and techniques in the treatment of early

ejaculation. In S.R. Leiblum & R.C. Rosen (Eds.), *Principles and practice of sex therapy,* 2nd ed. New York: Guilford.

McCaul, M.E., Turkkan, J.S., & Stitzer, J.L. (1989). Conditioned opponent responses: Effects of placebo challenge in alcoholic subjects. *Alcoholism: Clinical and Experimental Research, 13,* 631–635.

McConaghy, N. (1989). Validity and ethics of penile circumference measures of sexual arousal: A critical review. *Archives of Sexual Behavior, 18,* 357–369.

McConaghy, N. (1990). Sexual deviation. In A.S. Bellack, M. Hersen, & A.E. Kazdin (Eds.), *International handbook of behavior modification and therapy,* 2nd ed. New York: Plenum.

McConaghy, N. (1994). Sexual deviations. In M. Hersen, R.T. Ammerman, & L.A. Sisson (Eds.), *Handbook of aggressive and destructive behavior in psychiatric patients,* pp. 261–286. New York: Plenum.

McDougle, C.J., Price, L.H., & Volkmar, F.R. (1994). Recent advances in the pharmacotherapy of autism and related conditions. *Child and Adolescent Psychiatric Clinics of North America, 3,* 71–89.

McElroy, S.L., Keck, P.E., Pope. H.G. & Hudson, J.I. (1992). Valproate in the treatment of bipolar disorder: Literature review and clinical guidelines. *Journal of Clinical Psychopharmacology, 12* (1, suppl), 42–52.

McElroy, S.L., Pope, H.G., Keck, P.E., & Hudson, J.I. (1995). Disorders of impulse control. In E. Hollander & D.J. Stein (Eds.), *Impulsivity and aggression,* pp. 109–136. Chichester, England: Wiley.

McFall, R.M. (1982). A review and reformulation of the concept of social skills. *Behavioral Assessment, 4,* 1–33.

McFall, R.M. (1990) The enhancement of social skills: An information-processing analysis. In W.L. Marshall, D.R. Laws, & H.E. Barbaree (Eds.), *Handbook of sexual assault: Issues, theories, and treatment of the offender.* New York: Plenum.

McFall, R.M. (1991). Manifesto for a science of clinical psychology. *Clinical Psychologist, 44,* 75–88.

McFall, R.M. (1995). Models of training and standards of care. In S.C. Hayes, V.M. Folette, R.M. Dawes, & K.E. Grady (Eds.), *Scientific standards of psychological practice: Issues and recommendations,* pp. 125–137. Reno, NV: Context Press.

McFall, R.M., & McDonel, E.C. (1986). The continuing search for units of analysis in psychology: Beyond persons, situations, and their interactions. In R.O. Nelson & S.C. Hayes (Eds.), *Conceptual foundations of behavioral assessment,* pp. 201–241. New York: Guilford.

McGeer, P.L., & McGeer, E.G. (1996). Anti-inflammatory drugs in the fight against Alzheimer's disease. *Annals of the New York Academy of Sciences, 777,* 213–220.

McFarlane, A.C. (1988). The longitudinal course of posttraumatic morbidity. *Journal of Nervous and Mental Disease, 1976,* 30–39.

McGlashan, T. (1986a). The Chestnut Lodge follow-up study. III. Long-term outcome of borderline personalities. *Archives of General Psychiatry, 43,* 20–30.

McGlashan, T. (1986b). Schizotypal personality disorder: Chestnut Lodge Follow-up Study. VI. Long-term follow-up perspectives. *Archives of General Psychiatry, 43,* 329–334.

McGlashan, T.H. (1992). The longitudinal profile of borderline personality disorder: Contributions from the Chestnut Lodge follow-up study. In D. Silver & M. Rosenbluth (Eds.), *Handbook of borderline disorders,* pp. 53–83. Madison, CT: International Universities Press.

McGlashan, T.H., & Fenton, W.S. (1991). Classical subtypes for schizophrenia: Literature review for DSM-IV. *Schizophrenia Bulletin, 17,* 609–623.

McGlashan, T.H., & Fenton, W.S. (1993). Subtype progression and pathophysiologic deterioration in early schizophrenia. *Schizophrenia Bulletin, 19,* 71–84.

McGowin, D.F. (1993). *Living in the labyrinth: A personal journey through the maze of Alzheimer's.* New York: Delacorte.

McGue, M. (1993). From proteins to cognitions: The behavioral genetics of alcoholism. In R. Plomin & G.E. McClearn (Eds.), *Nature, nurture, and psychology*. Washington, DC: American Psychological Association.

McGue, M., & Lykken, D.T. (1992). Genetic influence on risk of divorce. *Psychological Science, 3*, 368–373.

McGue, M., Pickins, R.W., & Svikis, D.S. (1992). Sex and age effects on the inheritance of alcohol problems: A twin study. *Journal of Abnormal Psychology, 101*, 3–17.

McGuffin, P., Farmer, A.E., & Gottesman, I.I. (1987). Is there really a split in schizophrenia? The genetic evidence, *British Journal of Psychiatry, 150*, 581–592.

McGuffin, P., Farmer, A.E., Gottesman, I.I., Murray, R.M., & Reveley, A.M. (1984). Twin concordance for operationally defined schizophrenia. *Archives of General Psychiatry, 41*, 541–545.

McGuffin, P., & Gottesman, I.I. (1985). Genetic influences on normal and abnormal development. In M. Rutter & L. Hersov (Eds.), *Child and adolescent psychiatry*, pp. 17–33. Oxford: Blackwell.

McGuffin, P., Katz, R., Watkins, S., & Rutherford, J. (1996). A hospital-based twin register of the heritability of DSM-IV unipolar depression. *Archives of General Psychiatry, 53*, 129–136.

McGuffin, P., Owen, M.J., O'Donovan, M.C., Thapar, A., & Gottesman, I.I. (1994). *Seminars in psychiatry genetics*. London: Gaskell.

McGuffin, P., Sargeant, M., Hett, G., Tidmarsh, S., Whatley, S., & Marchbanks, R.M. (1990). Exclusion of a schizophrenia susceptibility gene from the chromosome 5q11-q13 region. New data and a reanalysis of previous reports. *American Journal of Human Genetics, 47*, 524–535.

McKey, R.H., Condelli, L., Granson, H., Barrett, B., McConkey, C., & Plantz, M. (1985, June). *The impact of Head Start on children, families, and communities*. Final Report of the Head Start Evaluation, Synthesis and Utilization Project. Washington, DC: CSR.

McKim, W.A. (1997). *Drugs and behavior*, 3rd ed. Upper Saddle River, NJ: Prentice Hall.

McLellan, A.T., O'Brien, C.P., Metzger, D., Alterman, A.I., Cornish, J., & Urschel, H. (1992). How effective is substance abuse treatment—Compared to what? In C.P. O'Brien & J.H. Jaffe (Eds.), *Addictive states*, pp. 231–251. New York: Raven.

McLellan, A.T., Woody, G.E., & Metzger, D. (1996). Evaluating the effectiveness of addiction treatments: Reasonable expectations, appropriate comparisons. *Milbank Quarterly, 74*, 51.

McLemore, C.W., & Benjamin, L.A. (1979). Whatever happened to interpersonal diagnosis? A psychosocial alternative to DSM-III. *American Psychologist, 34*, 17–34.

McNally, R.J. (1987). Preparedness and phobias: A review. *Psychological Bulletin, 101*, 283–303.

McNally, R.J. (1990). Psychological approaches to panic disorder: A review. *Psychological Bulletin, 108*, 403–419.

McNally, R.J., Hornig, C.D., & Donnell, C.D. (1995). Clinical versus nonclinical panic: A test of suffocation false alarm theory. *Behaviour Research and Therapy, 33*, 127–131.

McNeal, E.T., & Cimbolic, P. (1986). Antidepressants and biochemical theories of depression. *Psychological Bulletin, 99*, 361–374.

McNeil, T.F., Cantor-Graae, E., Sjostrom, K., et al. (1994). Obstetric complications as antecedents of schizophrenia: Empirical effects of using different obstetric complication scales. *Journal of Psychiatric Research, 28*, 519–530.

McNeil, T.F., Cantor-Graae, E., Torrey, E.F., Sjostrom, K., et al. (1994). Obstetric complications in histories of monozygotic twins discordant and concordant for schizophrenia. *Acta Psychiatrica Scandinavica, 89*, 196–204.

McReynolds, P. (1986). History of assessment in clinical and educational settings. In R.O. Nelson, & S.C. Hayes (Eds.), *Conceptual foundations of behavioral assessment*. New York: Guilford.

Mechanic, D. (1986). The concept of illness behavior: Culture, situation and personal predisposition. *Psychological Medicine, 16*, 1–7.

Mednick, S.A., & McNeil, T. (1968). Current methodology in research on the etiology of schizophrenia. *Psychological Bulletin, 70*, 681–693.

Mednick, S.A., & Schulsinger, F. (1968). Some premorbid characteristics related to breakdown in children with schizophrenic mothers. *Journal of Psychiatric Research* (Suppl. 1), 6, 354–362.

Meehl, P.E. (1962). Schizotaxia, schizotypy, schizophrenia. *American Psychologist, 17*, 827–838.

Meehl, P.E. (1990). Toward an integrated theory of schizotaxia, schizotypy, and schizophrenia. *Journal of Personality Disorders, 4*, 1–99.

Meehl, P.E. (1993). The origins of some of my conjectures concerning schizophrenia. In L.J. Chapman, J.P. Chapman, & D. Fowles (Eds.), *Progress in experimental personality and psychopathology research*, pp. 1–11. New York: Springer.

Meehl, P.E., & Rosen, A. (1955). Antecedent probability and the efficiency of psychometric signs, patterns, or cutting scores. *Psychological Bulletin, 52*, 194–216.

Meichenbaum, D. (1977). *Cognitive behavior modification*. New York: Plenum.

Melchior, C.L., & Tabakoff, B. (1985). Features of environment-dependent tolerance to ethanol. *Psychopharmacology, 87*, 94–100.

Mellor, C.S. (1982). The present status of first rank symptoms. *British Journal of Psychiatry, 40*, 423–424.

Melman, A., & Tiefer, L. (1992). Surgery for erectile disorders: Operative procedures and psychological issues. In R.C. Rosen and S.R. Leiblum (Eds.), *Erectile disorders: Assessment and treatment*, pp. 255–282. New York: Guilford.

Melman, A., Tiefer, L., & Pedersen, R. (1988). Evaluation of first 406 patients in urology department based center for male sexual dysfunction. *Urology, 32*, 6–10.

Melton, G.B., & Limber, S. (1989). Psychologists' involvement in cases of child maltreatment: Limits of roles and expertise. *American Psychologist, 44*, 1225–1233.

Melton, G., Petrila, J., Poythress, N., & Slobogin, C. (1987). *Psychological evaluations for the courts*. New York: Guilford.

Meltzer, H.Y. (1985). Dopamine and negative symptoms in schizophrenia: Critique of the Type I-II hypothesis. In M. Alpert (Ed.), *Controversies in schizophrenia: Changes and constancies*, pp. 110–136. New York: Guilford.

Meltzer, H.Y. (1990). Clozapine: Mechanisms of action in relation to its clinical advantages. In A. Kales, C.N. Stefanis, & J. Talbott (Eds.), *Recent advances in schizophrenia*, pp. 237–256. New York: Springer.

Meltzer, H.Y. (1992). The role of dopamine in schizophrenia. In J. Lindenmayer & S.R. Kay (Eds.), *New biological vistas on schizophrenia*. New York: Brunner/Mazel.

Meltzer, H.Y. (1993). Serotonin-dopamine interactions and atypical antipsychotic drugs. *Psychiatric Annals, 23*, 193–200.

Mendelson, J.H., & Mello, N.K. (1989). Studies of alcohol: Past, present and future. *Journal of Studies on Alcohol, 50*, 293–296.

Mendez, M.F., Selwood, A., Mastrie, A.R., & Frey, W.H. (1993). Pick's disease versus Alzheimer's disease: A comparison of clinical characteristics. *Neurology, 43*, 289–292.

Merckelbach, H., de Ruiter, C., van den Hout, M.A., & Hoekstra, R. (1989). Conditioning experiences and phobias. *Behavior Research and Therapy, 27*, 657–662.

Merikangas, K.R. (1990). The genetic epidemiology of alcoholism. *Psychological medicine, 20*, 11–22.

Merikangas, K.R., & Gelernter, C.S. (1990). Comorbidity for alcoholism and depression. *Psychiatric Clinics of North America, 13*, 613–632.

Merikangas, K.R., Risch, N.J., & Weissman, M.M. (1994). Comorbidity and co-transmission of alcoholism, anxiety and depression. *Psychological Medicine, 24*, 69–80.

Merrick, J.C. (1993). Maternal substance abuse during pregnancy: Policy implications in the United States. *Journal of Legal Medicine, 14*, 57–71.

Mersky, H. (1992). The manufacture of personalities: The production of multiple personality disorder. *British Journal of Psychiatry, 160*, 327–340.

Messick, S. (1989). Validity. In R.L. Linn (Ed.), *Educational measurement*, 3rd ed. New York: American Council on Education/Macmillan.

Mesulam, M. (1981). Dissociative states with abnormal temporal lobe EEG. *Archives of Neurology, 38*, 176–181.

Metalsky, G.I., Joiner, T.E., Hardin, T.S., & Abramson, L.Y. (1993). Depressive reactions to failure in a naturalistic setting: A test of the hopelessness and self-esteem theories of depression. *Journal of Abnormal Psychology, 102*, 101–109.

Michael, R.T., Gagnon, J.H., Laumann, E.O., & Kolata, G. (1995). *Sex in America: A definitive survey*. New York: Warner.

Migliorelli, R., Teson, A., Sabe, L., Petracchi, M., Leiguarda, R., & Starkstein, S.E. (1995). Prevalence and correlates of dysthymia and major depression among patients with Alzheimer's disease. *American Journal of Psychiatry, 152*, 37–45.

Miklowitz, D.J. (1995). The evolution of family-based psychopathology. In R.H. Mikesell, D. Losterman, S.H. McDaniel (Eds.), *Integrating family therapy: Handbook of family psychology and systems theory*, pp. 183–197. Washington, DC: American Psychological Association.

Miklowitz D.J., Doane, J.A., et al. (1989). Is expressed emotion an index of a transactional process? I. Parents' affective style. *Family Process, 28*, 153–167.

Miklowitz, D.J., Goldstein, M.J., et al. (1988). Family factors and the course of bipolar affective disorder. *Archives of General Psychiatry, 45*, 225–231.

Miklowitz, D.J., Goldstein, M.J., & Nuechterlein, K.H. (1995). Verbal interactions in the families of schizophrenic and bipolar affective patients. *Journal of Abnormal Psychology, 104*, 268–276.

Miklowitz, D.J., Goldstein, M.J., Nuechterlein, K.H., Snyder, K.S., & Mintz, J. (1988). Family factors and the course of bipolar affective disorder. *Archives of General Psychiatry, 45*, 225–231.

Milich, R., Wolraich, M., & Lindgren, S. (1986). Sugar and hyperactivity: A critical review of empirical findings. *Clinical Psychology Review, 6*, 493–513.

Miller, G.A., & Kozak, M.J. (1993). Three-systems assessment and the construct of emotion. In N. Birbaumer & A. Ohman (Eds.), *The structure of emotion: Psychophysiological, cognitive, and clinical aspects*, pp. 31–47. Seattle: Hogrefe & Huber.

Miller, W.R., & Lief, H.I. (1976). Masturbatory attitudes, knowledge and experience: Data from the Sex Knowledge and Attitude Test (SKAT): *Archives of Sexual Behavior, 5*, 447–468.

Miller, M.E., & Bowers, K.S. (1986). Hypnotic analgesia and stress inoculation in the reduction of pain. *Journal of Abnormal Psychology, 95*, 6–14.

Miller, N.S. (1991). *Comprehensive handbook of drug and alcohol addiction*, New York: Marcel Dekker.

Miller, N.S., Belkin, B.M., & Gold, M.S. (1991). Alcohol and drug dependence among the elderly: Epidemiology, diagnosis, and treatment. *Comprehensive Psychiatry, 32*, 153–165.

Miller, P.M. (1987). Commonalities of addictive

behaviors. In T.D. Nirenberg & S.A. Maisto (Eds.), *Developments in the assessment and treatment of addictive behaviors.* Norwood, NJ: Ablex.

Miller, T.Q., Smith, T.W., Turner, C.W., Guijarro, M.L., & Hallet, A.J. (1996). A meta-analytic review of research on hostility and physical health. *Psychological Bulletin, 119,* 322–348.

Miller, T.Q., Turner, C.W., Tindale, R.S., Posavac, E.J., & Dugoni, B.L. (1991). Reasons for the trend toward null findings in research on Type A behavior. *Psychological Bulletin, 110,* 469–485.

Miller, T.W. (1989). *Stressful life events.* Madison, CT: International Universities Press.

Miller, W.R., & Kurtz, E. (1994). Models of alcoholism used in treatment: Contrasting AA and other perspectives with which it is often confused. *Journal of Studies on Alcohol, 55,* 159–166.

Miller-Johnson, S., Emery, R.E., Marvin, R.S., Clarke, W., Lovinger, R., & Martin, M. (1994). Parent-child relationships and the management of insulin-dependent diabetes mellitus. *Journal of Consulting and Clinical Psychology, 62,* 603–610.

Millon, T. (1981). *Disorders of personality.* New York: Wiley.

Millon, T., & Everly, G.S. (1985). *Personality and its disorders.* New York: Wiley.

Millon, T., & Martinez, A. (1995). Avoidant personality disorder. In W.J. Livesley (Ed.), *The DSM-IV personality disorders,* pp. 218–233. New York: Guilford.

Mindus, P., & Jenike, M.A. (1992). Neurosurgical treatment of malignant obsessive-compulsive disorder. *Psychiatric Clinics of North America, 15,* 921–926.

Mineka, S. (1985). Animal models of anxiety-based disorders: Their usefulness and limitations. In A. H. Tuma & J. Maser (Eds.), *Anxiety and the anxiety disorders,* Hillsdale, NJ: Erlbaum.

Mineka, S., & Cook, M. (1993). Mechanisms involved in the observational conditioning of fear. *Journal of Experimental Psychology: General, 122,* 23–38.

Mineka, S., & Kihlstrom, J.F. (1978). Unpredictable and uncontrollable events: A new perspective on experimental neurosis. *Journal of Abnormal Psychology, 87,* 256–271.

Mineka, S., & Zinbarg, R. (1991). Animal models of psychopathology. In C.E. Walker (Ed.), *Clinical psychology,* pp. 51–86. New York: Plenum Press.

Mineka, S., & Zinbarg, R. (1995). Conditioning and ethological models of social phobia. In R.G. Heimberg, M.R. Liebowitz, D.A. Hope, & F.R. Schneier (Eds.), *Social phobia: Diagnosis, assessment, and treatment,* pp. 134–162. New York: Guilford.

Minthon, L., Edvinsson, L., & Gustafson, L. (1994). Tacrine treatment modifies cerebrospinal fluid neuropeptide levels in Alzheimer's disease. *Dementia, 5,* 295–301.

Minuchin, P. (1985). Families and individual development: Provocations from the field of family therapy. *Child Development, 56,* 289–302.

Minuchin, S. (1974). *Families and family therapy.* Cambridge, MA: Harvard University Press.

Minuchin, S., Rosman, B.L., & Baker, L. (1978). *Psychosomatic families.* Cambridge, MA: Harvard University Press.

Mischel, W. (1968). *Personality and assessment.* New York: Wiley.

Mischel, W. (1983). Delay of gratification as process and as person variable in development. In D. Magnusson & V.L. Allen (Eds.), *Human development: An interactional perspective.* New York: Academic Press.

Mishler, E.G., & Wazler, N.E. (1968). *Interaction in families: An experimental study of family processes and schizophrenia.* New York: Wiley.

Mitchell, J.E., Pyle, R.L., Eckert, E.D., Hatsukami, D., Pomeroy, C., & Zimmerman, R. (1990). A comparison study of antidepressants and structured intensive group psychotherapy in the treatment of bulimia nervosa. *Archives of General Psychiatry, 47,* 149–157.

Mitchell, J.E., Raymond, N., & Specker, S. (1993). A review of controlled trials of pharmacotherapy and psychotherapy in the treatment of bulimia nervosa. *International Journal of Eating Disorders, 14,* 229–247.

Mitchell, P., Waters, B., Morrison, N., et al. (1991). Close linkage of bipolar disorder to chromosome 11 markers is excluded in two large Australian pedigrees, *Journal of Affective Disorders, 21,* 23–32.

Mittelman, M.S., Ferris, S.H., Shulman, E., Steinberg, G., Ambinder, A., & Mackell, J. (1997). Effects of a multicomponent support program on spouse-caregivers of Alzheimer's disease patients: Results of a treatment/control study. In L. Heston (Ed.), *Progress in Alzheimer's disease and similar conditions.* Washington, DC: American Psychiatric Press.

Mitterauer, B. (1990). A contribution to the discussion of the role of the genetic factor in suicide, based on five studies in an epidemiologically defined area. *Comprehensive Psychiatry, 31,* 557–565.

Mnookin, R.H. (1975). Child-custody adjudication: Judicial functions in the face of indeterminancy. *Law and Contemporary Problems, 88,* 226–293.

Mnookin, R.H. (1985). *In the interest of children: Advocacy, law reform, and public policy.* New York: Freeman.

Moffitt, T.E. (1993). Adolescence-limited and life-course-persistent antisocial behavior: A developmental taxonomy. *Psychological Review, 100,* 674–701.

Mohr, D.C., & Beutler, L.E. (1990). Erectile dysfunction: A review of diagnostic and treatment procedures. *Clinical Psychology Review, 10,* 123–150.

Moldin, S.O., Reich, T., & Rice, J.P. (1991). Current perspectives on the genetics of unipolar depression. *Behavior Genetics, 21,* 211–242.

Monahan, J. (1980). *Who is the client? The ethics of psychological intervention in the criminal justice system.* Washington, DC: American Psychological Association.

Monahan, J. (1981). *The clinical prediction of violent behavior.* Rockville, MD: National Institute of Mental Health.

Monahan, J. (1992). Mental disorder and violent behavior: Perceptions and evidence. *American Psychologist, 47,* 511–521.

Monahan, J. (1993). Limiting therapist exposure to Tarasoff liability: Guidelines for risk containment. *American Psychologist, 48,* 242–250.

Money, J. (1984). Paraphilias: Phenomenology and classification. *American Journal of Psychotherapy, 38,* 164–179.

Money, J. (1987). Masochism: On the childhood origin of paraphilia, opponent-process theory, and antiandrogen therapy. *Journal of Sex Research, 23,* 273–275.

Monroe, S.M., & Simons, A.D. (1991). Diathesis-stress theories in the context of life stress research: Implications for the depressive disorders. *Psychological Bulletin, 110,* 406–425.

Monroe, S.M., & Wade, S.L. (1988). Life events. In C.G. Last & M. Hersen (Eds.), *Handbook of anxiety disorders.* New York: Pergamon.

Montgomery, H.A., Miller, W.R., & Tonigan, J.S. (1993). Differences among AA groups: Implications for research. *Journal of Studies on Alcohol, 54,* 502–504.

Moore, M. (1975). Some myths about "mental illness." *Inquiry, 18,* 233–240.

Moos, R.H. (1974). *Family Environment Scale (Form R).* Palo Alto, CA: Consulting Psychologists Press.

Moos, R.H. (1974). *Evaluating treatment environments: A social ecological approach.* New York: Wiley.

Moos, R.H. (1981). *Work environment scale manual.* Palo Alto, CA: Consulting Psychologists Press.

Morey, L.C. (1988). Personality disorders in DSM-III and DSM-III-R: Convergence, coverage, and internal consistency. *American Journal of Psychiatry, 145,* 573–577.

Morokoff, P.J. (1978). Determinants of female orgasm. In J. LoPiccolo & L. LoPiccolo (Eds.), *Handbook of sex therapy.* New York: Plenum.

Morokoff, P.J. (1989). Sex bias and POD. *American Psychologist, 73*–75.

Morokoff, P.J., & Heiman, J.R. (1980). Effects of erotic stimuli on sexually functional and dysfunctional women: Multiple measures before and after sex therapy. *Behaviour Research and Therapy, 18,* 127–137.

Morris, J. (1995). Dementia and cognitive changes in Huntington's disease. In W.J. Weiner & A.E. Lang (Eds.), *Behavioral neurology of movement disorders. Advances in neurology,* Vol. 65, pp. 187–200. New York: Raven Press.

Morrison, J., & Herbstein, J. (1988). Secondary affective disorder in women with somatization disorder. *Comprehensive Psychiatry, 29,* 433–440.

Morrow, J., & Nolen-Hoeksema, S. (1990). The effects of responses to depression on the remediation of depressive affect. *Journal of Personality and Social Psychology, 58,* 519–527.

Morse, K.L. (1990). A uniform testimonial privilege for mental health professionals, *Ohio State Law Journal, 51,* 741–757.

Moscicki, E.K. (1995). Epidemiology of suicidal behavior. *Suicide and life-threatening behavior, 25,* 22–35.

Mueser, K.T., Bellack, A.S., Douglas, M.S., & Morrison, R.L. (1991). Prevalence and stability of social skill deficits in schizophrenia. *Schizophrenia Research, 5,* 167–176.

Mulligan, T., Retchin, S.M., Chinchilli, V.M., & Bettinger, C.B. (1988). The role of aging and chronic disease in sexual dysfunction. *Journal of the American Geriatrics Society, 36,* 520–524.

Multiple Risk Factor Intervention Trial Research Group (1982). Multiple Risk Factor Intervention Trial: Risk factor changes and mortality results, *Journal of the American Medical Association, 248,* 1465–1477.

Mumford, D.B., Whitehouse, A.M., & Platts, M. (1991). Sociocultural correlates of eating disorders among Asian schoolgirls in Bradford. *British Journal of Psychiatry, 158,* 222–228.

Munoz, R.F., Hollon, S.D., McGrath, E., Rehm, L.P. et al. (1994). On the AHCPR depression in primary care guidelines: Further considerations for practitioners. *American Psychologist. 49,* 42–61.

Murphy, E., & Macdonald, A. (1992). Affective disorders in old age. In E.S. Paykel (Ed.), *Handbook of affective disorders,* 2nd ed. pp. 601–618. New York: Guilford.

Murphy, G.E., Simons, A.D., Wetzel, R.D., & Lustman, P.J. (1984). Cognitive therapy and pharmacotherapy, singly and together, in the treatment of depression. *Archives of General Psychiatry, 41,* 33–41.

Murphy, J.M. (1976). Psychiatric labeling in cross-cultural perspective. *Science, 191,* 1019–1028.

Murphy, W.D. (1997). Exhibitionism: Psychopathology and theory. In D.R. Laws & W.T. O'Donohue (Eds.), *Handbook of sexual deviance: Theory and application,* New York: Guilford.

Myers, J.E.B. (1983–84). Involuntary civil commitment of the mentally ill: A system in need of change. *Villanova Law Review, 29,* 367–433.

Myers, J.K., & Weissman, M.M. (1980). Screening for depression in a community sample: The use of a self-report scale to detect the depressive syndrome. *American Journal of Psychiatry, 137,* 1081–1084.

Nakawatase, T.V., Yamamoto, J., & Sasao, T. (1993). The association between fast-flushing response and alcohol use among Japanese Americans, *Journal of Studies on Alcohol, 54,* 48–53.

Nasser, M. (1986). Comparative study of the prevalence of abnormal eating attitudes among Arab female students of both London and Cairo universities. *Psychological Medicine, 16,* 621–625.

Nathan, S.G. (1986). The epidemiology of the DSM-III psychosexual dysfunctions. *Journal of Sex and Marital Therapy, 12,* 267–281.

Nathan, P.E. (1993). Alcoholism: Psychopathology, etiology, and treatment. In P.B. Sutker & H.E. Adams

(Eds.), *Comprehensive handbook of psychopathology,* 2nd ed. pp. 451–476. New York: Plenum.

National Academy of Sciences, Institute of Medicine (1989). *Research on children & adolescents with mental, behavioral, and developmental disorders.* Washington, DC: National Academy Press.

National Advisory Mental Health Council. (1995). *Basic behavioral science research for mental health: A national investment.* Rockville, MD: National Institute of Mental Health.

National Institute of Mental Health. (1985). *Annual survey of patient characteristics—1985 state and county mental hospital inpatient services.* Rockville, MD.

National Institute of Mental Health (1990). *Somatization disorder in the medical setting.* Rockville, MD: NIMH.

National Victim Center. (1992). *Crime and victimization in America: Statistical overview.* Arlington, VA.

Neal, A.M., & Turner, S.M. (1991). Anxiety disorders research with African Americans: Current status. *Psychological Bulletin, 109,* 400–410.

Neale, J.M., Cox, D.S., Valdimarsdottir, H., & Stone, A.A. (1988). The relation between immunity and health: Comment on Pennebaker, Kiecolt-Glaser, and Glaser. *Journal of Consulting and Clinical Psychology, 56,* 636–637.

Neale, J.M., & Oltmanns, T.F. (1980). *Schizophrenia.* New York: Wiley.

Neibuhr, R. (1951). To be abased and to abound. *Messenger,* February 13, p. 7.

Neisser, U., & Harsch, N. (1992). Phantom flashbulbs: False recollections of hearing the news about Challenger. In E. Winograd & U. Neisser (Eds.), *Affect and accuracy in recall: Studies of "flashbulb" memories,* pp. 9–31. New York: Cambridge University Press.

Nemeroff, C.B., & Bissette, G. (1986). Neuropeptides in psychiatric disorders. In P. Berger & K.H. Brodie (Eds.), *Biological psychiatry,* pp. 64–110. New York: Basic Books.

Nestadt, G., Romanoski, A.J., Brown, C.H., Chahal, R., Merchant, A., Folstein, M.F., Gruenberg, E.M., & McHugh, P.R. (1991). DSM-III compulsive personality disorder: An epidemiological study. *Psychological Medicine, 21,* 461–471.

Nestadt, G., Romanoski, A.J., Chahal, R., Merchant, A., Folstein, J.F., Gruenberg, E.M., & McHugh, P.R. (1990). An epidemiological study of histrionic personality disorder. *Psychological Medicine, 20,* 413–422.

Neugebauer, R. (1979). Medieval and early modern theories of mental illness, *Archives of General Psychiatry, 36,* 477–483.

Newcomb, M.D. (1993). 4 Theories of rape in American society. *Archives of Sexual Behavior, 22,* 373–377.

Newcomb, A.F., Bukowski, W.M., & Pattee, L. (1993). Children's peer relations: A meta-analytic review of popular, rejected, neglected, controversial, and average sociometric status. *Psychological Bulletin, 113,* 99–128.

Newhouse, P.A. (1997). Alzheimer's disease and the cholinergic system: An introduction to clinical pharmacological research. In L. Heston (Ed.), *Progress in Alzheimer's disease and similar conditions.* Washington, DC: American Psychiatric Press.

Newlin, D.B. (1989). The skin-flushing response: Autonomic, self-report, and conditioned responses to repeated administrations of alcohol in Asian men. *Journal of Abnormal Psychology, 98,* 421–425.

Newlin, D.B., & Thomson, J.B. (1991). Chronic tolerance and sensitization to alcohol in sons of alcoholics. *Alcoholism: Clinical and Experimental Research, 15,* 399–405.

Newman, J.P., & Kosson, D.S. (1986). Passive avoidance learning in psychopathic and nonpsychopathic offenders. *Journal of Abnormal Psychology, 95,* 257–263.

Newman, J.P., Kosson, D.S., & Patterson, C.M. (1992). Delay of gratification in psychopathic and nonpsychopathic offenders. *Journal of Abnormal Psychology, 101,* 630–636.

Newton, R.D. (1948). The identity of Alzheimer's disease and senile dementia and their relationship to senility. *Journal of Mental Science, 94,* 225–249.

Nietzel, M.T., Bernstein, D.A., & Milich, R. (1994). *Introduction to clinical psychology,* 4th ed. Englewood Cliffs, NJ: Prentice Hall.

Nigg, J.T., & Goldsmith, H.H. (1994). Genetics of personality disorders: Perspectives from personality and psychopathology research. *Psychological Bulletin, 115,* 346–380.

Nisbett, R.E., & Wilson, T.D. (1977). Telling more than we can know: Verbal reports on mental processes. *Psychological Review, 84,* 231–259.

Nolen-Hoeksema, S. (1989). Life-span views on depression. In P.B. Baltes, D.L. Featherman, & R.M. Lerner (Eds.), *Life-span development and behavior,* Vol. 9, pp. 203–241. Hillsdale, NJ: Erlbaum.

Nolen-Hoeksema, S. (1990). *Sex differences in depression.* Stanford, CA: Stanford University Press.

Nolen-Hoeksema, S. (1994). An interactive model for the emergence of gender differences in depression in adolescence. *Journal of Research on Adolescence, 4,* 519–534.

Nolen-Hoeksema, S., Morrow, J., & Fredrickson, B.L. (1993). Response styles and the duration of episodes of depressed mood. *Journal of Abnormal Psychology, 102,* 20–28.

Norden, K.A., Klein, D.N., Donaldson, S.K., Pepper, C.M., et al. (1995). Reports of the early home environment in DSM-III-R personality disorders. *Journal of Personality Disorders, 9,* 213–223.

Nordstrom, A., Farde, L., Eriksson, L., & Halldin, C. (1995). No elevated D-sub-2 dopamine receptors in neuroleptic-naive schizophrenic patients revealed by positron emission tomography and (-sub-1-sup-1C) N-methylspiperone. *Psychiatry Research: Neuroimaging, 61,* 67–83.

Nordstrom, P., Samuelsson, M., Asberg, M., Traskman-Bendz, L., et al. (1994). CSF-5-HIAA predicts suicide risk after attempted suicide. *Suicide and Life Threatening Behavior, 24,* 1–9.

Noyes, R., Jr. (1991). Treatments of choice for anxiety disorders. In W. Coryell & G. Winokur (Eds.), *The clinical management of anxiety disorders,* pp. 140–153. New York: Oxford University Press.

Noyes, R., Jr., Clarkson, C., Crowe, R.R., Yates, W.R., & McChesney, C.M. (1987). A family study of generalized anxiety disorder. *American Journal of Psychiatry, 144,* 1019–1024.

Noyes, R., Garvey, M.J., & Cook, B.L. (1989). Follow-up study of patients with panic disorder and agoraphobia with panic attacks treated with tricyclic antidepressants. *Journal of Affective Disorders, 16,* 249–257.

Nuechterlein, K.H., Buchsbaum, M.S., & Dawson, M.E. (1994). Neuropsychological vulnerability to schizophrenia. In A.S. David & J.C. Cutting (Eds.), *The neuropsychology of schizophrenia,* pp. 53–77. Hove, England, Erlbaum.

Nuechterlein, K.H., Snyder, K.S., & Mintz, J. (1992). Paths to relapse: Possible transactional processes connecting patient illness onset, expressed emotion, and psychotic relapse. *British Journal of Psychiatry, 161* (suppl. 18), 88–96.

Nunes, E.V., Frank, K.A., & Kornfeld, J. (1987). Psychologic treatment for the Type A behavior pattern and for coronary heart disease: A meta-analysis of the literature. *Psychosomatic Medicine, 48,* 159–173.

O'Connor, G.T., Buring, J.E., Yusuf, S., Goldhaber, S.Z., Olmstead, E.M., Paffenbarger, R.S., & Hennekens, C.H. (1989). An overview of randomized trials of rehabilitation with exercise after myocardial infarction. *Circulation, 80,* 234–244.

O'Donohue, W., & Geer, J.H. (1993). *Handbook of sexual dysfunctions: Assessment and treatment.* Boston: Allyn & Bacon.

O'Grady, J.C. (1990). The prevalence and diagnostic significance of Schneiderian first-rank symptoms in a random sample of acute psychiatric in-patients. *British Journal of Psychiatry, 156,* 496–500.

O'Leary, K.D. (1980). Pills or skills for hyperactive children. *Journal of Applied Behavior Analysis, 13,* 191–204.

O'Leary, K.D., & Wilson, G.T. (1987). *Behavior therapy: Application and outcome.* (2nd ed.) Englewood Cliffs, NJ: Prentice Hall.

O'Leary, K.D., & Borkovec, T.D., (1978). Conceptual, methodological, and ethical problems of placebo groups in psychotherapeutic research. *American Psychologist, 33,* 821–830.

O'Shea, B., & Falvey, J. (1988). Huntington's disease: Update of the literature. *British Journal of Psychological Medicine, 5,* 61–70.

O'Sullivan, G., & Marks, I. (1991). Follow-up studies of behavioral treatment of phobic and obsessive-compulsive neuroses. *Psychiatric Annals, 21,* 368–373.

O'Sullivan, G., Noshirvani, H., Marks, I., Monteiro, W., & Lelliott, P. (1991). Six-year follow-up after exposure and clomipramine therapy for obsessive-compulsive disorder. *Journal of Clinical Psychiatry, 52,* 150–155.

Oatley, K., & Bolton, W. (1985). A social-cognitive theory of depression in reaction to life events. *Psychological Review, 92,* 372–388.

Oei, T.P.S., Lim, B., & Hennessy, B. (1990). Psychological dysfunction in battle: Combat stress reactions and posttraumatic stress disorder. *Clinical Psychology Review, 10,* 355–388.

Öhman, A. (1986). Face the beast and fear the face: Animal and social fears as prototypes for evolutionary analyses of emotion. *Psychophysiology, 23,* 123–145.

Öhman, A. (1996). Preferential preattentive processing of threat in anxiety: Preparedness and attentional biases. In R.M. Rapee (Ed.), *Current controversies in the anxiety disorders,* pp. 253–290. New York: Guilford.

Oliver, J.M., & Simmons, M.E. (1984). Depression as measured by the DSM-III and the Beck Depression Inventory in an unselected adult population. *Journal of Consulting and Clinical Psychology, 52,* 892–898.

Olmstead, M.P., Kaplan, A.S., & Rockert, W. (1994). Rate and prediction of relapse in bulimia nervosa. *American Journal of Psychiatry, 151,* 738–743.

Oltmanns, T.F. (1988). Defining delusional beliefs. In T.F. Oltmanns & B.A. Maher (Eds.), *Delusional beliefs.* New York: Wiley.

Oltmanns, T.F., & Gibbs, N. (1995). Emotional responsiveness and obsessive-compulsive behavior. *Cognition and Emotion, 25,* 563–578.

Oltmanns, T.F., Neale, J.M., & Davison, G.C. (1995). *Case studies in abnormal psychology,* 4th ed. New York: Wiley.

Olweus, D. (1984). Aggressors and their victims: Bullying at school. In N. Frude & H. Gault (Eds.), *Disruptive behavior in schools,* pp. 57–76. New York: Wiley.

Onstad, S., Skre, I., Torgersen, S., & Kringlen, E. (1991). Twin concordance for DSM-III-R schizophrenia. *Acta Psychiatrica Scandinavica, 83,* 395–401.

Onstad, S., Skre, I., Torgersen, S., & Kringlen, E. (1994). Family interaction: Parental representation in schizophrenic patients. *Acta Psychiatrica Scandinavica Supplementum, 90* (384 suppl.), 67–70.

Oosterwegel, A., & Wicklund, R.A. (1995). *The self in European and North American culture: Development and processes.* Boston: Kluwer.

Oren, D.A., & Rosenthal, N.E. (1992). Seasonal affective disorders. In E.S. Paykel (Ed.), *Handbook of affective disorders,* 2nd ed., pp. 551–568, New York: Guilford.

Orford, J. (1985). *Excessive appetites: A psychological view of addictions.* New York: Wiley.

O'Shea, B. (1993). Non-lithium pharmacological treatment of manic depression. A review. *Irish Journal of Psychological Medicine, 10,* 114–120.

Orne, M.T., Dingers, D.F., & Orne, E.C. (1984). On the differential diagnosis of multiple personality in the forensic context. *International Journal of Clinical and Experimental Hypnosis, 32,* 118–169.

Öst, L. (1987). Applied relaxation: Description of a coping technique and review of controlled studies. *Behaviour Research and Therapy, 25,* 397–409.

Öst, L.G., & Hugdahl, K. (1981). Acquisition of phobias and anxiety response patterns in clinical patients. *Behaviour Research and Therapy, 19,* 439–447.

Overstreet, D.H., Rezvani, A.H., & Janowsky, D.S. (1992). Genetic animal models of depression and ethanol preference provide support for cholinergic and serotonergic involvement in depression and alcoholism. *Biological Psychiatry, 31,* 919–936.

Paikoff, R.L., & Brooks-Gunn, J. (1991). Do parent-child relationships change during puberty? *Psychological Bulletin, 110,* 47–66.

Palmer, R.L. (1995). Sexual abuse and eating disorders. In K.D. Brownell & C.G. Fairburn (Eds.), *Eating disorders and obesity: A comprehensive handbook,* pp. 230–233. New York: Guilford.

Panksepp, J. (1988). Brain emotional circuits and psychopathologies. In M. Clynes & J. Panksepp (Eds.), *Emotions and psychopathology,* pp. 37–76. New York: Plenum.

Pantle, M., Pasewark, R., & Steadman, H. (1980). Comparing institutionalization periods and subsequent arrests of insanity acquittees and convicted felons. *Journal of Psychiatry and the Law, 8,* 305–316.

Paris, J. (1992). Social factors in borderline personality disorder: A review and a hypothesis. *Canadian Journal of Psychiatry, 37,* 480–486.

Paris, J. (1993). Personality disorders: A biopsychosocial model. *Journal of Personality Disorders, 7,* 255–264.

Paris, J., Zweig-Frank, H., & Guzder J. (1994). Psychological risk factors for borderline personality disorder in female patients. *Comprehensive Psychiatry, 35,* 301–305.

Park, S., Holzman, P.S., & Goldman-Rakic P.S. (1995). Spatial working memory deficits in the relatives of schizophrenic patients. *Archives of General Psychiatry, 52,* 821–828.

Parker, J.G., & Asher, S.R. (1987). Peer relations and later personality adjustment: Are low-accepted children at risk? *Psychological Bulletin, 102,* 357–389.

Parloff, M.B., Waskow, I.E., & Wolfe, B.E. (1978). Research on therapist variables in relation to process and outcome. In S.L. Garfield & A.E. Bergin (Eds.), *Handbook of psychotherapy and behavior change,* 2nd ed., pp. 233–282. New York: Wiley.

Parnas, J., Cannon T.D., Jacobsen, B., Schulsinger, H., Schulsinger, F., & Mednick, S.A. (1993). Lifetime DSM-III-R diagnostic outcomes in the offspring of schizophrenic mothers: Results from the Copenhagen high-risk study. *Archives of General Psychiatry, 50,* 707–714.

Parry-Jones, B. (1994). Merycism or rumination disorder: A historical investigation and current assessment. *British Journal of Psychiatry, 165,* 303–314.

Pasupathi, M., Carstensen, L.L., & Tsai, J.L. (1995). Ageism in interpersonal settings. In B. Lott & D. Maluso (Eds.), *The social psychology of interpersonal discrimination,* pp. 160–182. New York: Guilford.

Pato, M.T., Zohar-Kadouch, R., Zohar, J., & Murphy, D.L. (1988). Return of symptoms after discontinuation of clomipramine in patients with obsessive-compulsive disorder. *American Journal of Psychiatry, 145,* 1521–1525.

Patrick, C.J. (1994). Emotion and psychopathy. Startling new insights. *Psychophysiology, 31,* 319–330.

Patterson, C.J., Kupersmidt, J.B., & Griesler, P.C. (1990). Children's perceptions of self and of relationships with others as a function of sociometric status. *Child Development, 61,* 1335–1349.

Patterson, C.M., & Newman, J.P. (1993). Reflectivity and learning from aversive events: Toward a psychological mechanism for the syndromes of disinhibition. *Psychological Review, 100,* 716–736.

Patterson, G.R. (1982). *Coercive family process.* Eugene, OR: Castalia.

Patterson, G.R., DeBaryshe, B.D., & Ramsey, E. (1989). A developmental perspective on antisocial behavior. *American Psychologist, 44,* 329–335.

Patterson, G.R., & Fleischman, M.J. (1979). Maintenance of treatment effects: Some considerations concerning family systems and follow-up data. *Behavior Therapy, 10,* 168–185.

Patton, J.R., Beirne-Smith, M., & Payne, J.S. (1990). *Mental retardation,* 3rd ed. Columbus, OH: Merrill.

Paul, G.L., & Lentz, R.J. (1977). *Psychosocial treatment of chronic mental patients: Milieu versus social-learning programs.* Cambridge, MA: Harvard University Press.

Pavlov, I.P. (1928). *Lectures on conditioned reflexes.* New York: International Publishers.

Paykel, E.S., & Cooper, Z. (1992). Life events and social stress. In E.S. Paykel (Ed.), *Handbook of affective disorders,* 2nd ed., pp. 149–170. New York: Guilford.

Payne, R.L. (1992). First person account: My schizophrenia. *Schizophrenia Bulletin, 18,* 725–728.

Pedersen, N.L., & Gatz, M. (1991). Twin studies as a tool for bridging the gap between genetics and epidemiology of dementia: The study of dementia in Swedish twins [abstract]. *Gerontologist, 31,* 333.

Peele, S. (1992a). Alcoholism, politics, and bureaucracy: The consensus against controlled drinking therapy in America. *Addictive Behaviors, 17,* 49–62.

Peele, S. (1992b). Why is everybody always pickin' on me? A response to comments. *Addictive Behaviors, 17,* 83–93.

Pelham, W.E., Carlson, C., Sams, S.E., Vallano, G., Dixon, M.J., & Hoza, B. (1993). Separate and combined effects of methylphenidate and behavior modification with attention deficit-hyperactivity disorder in the classroom. *Journal of Consulting and Clinical Psychology, 61,* 506–515.

Pendery, M.L., Maltzman, I.M., & West. L.J. (1982). Controlled drinking by alcoholics? New findings and a reevaluation of a major affirmative study. *Science, 217,* 169–175.

Penn, D.L. & Mueser, K.T. (1996). Research update on the psychosocial treatment of schizophrenia. *American Journal of Psychiatry, 153,* 607–617.

Pennebaker, J.W. (1990). *Opening up: The healing power of confiding in others.* New York: Morrow.

Pennebaker, J.W., Kiecolt-Glaser, J., & Glaser, R. (1988). Disclosure of traumas and immune function: Health implications for psychotherapy. *Journal of Consulting and Clinical Psychology, 56,* 239–245.

Perani, D., Colombo, C., Bressi, S., Bonfanti, A., Grassi, F., Scarone, S., Bellodi, L., Smeraldi, E., & Fazio, F. (1995). [18F] FDG PET study in obsessive-compulsive disorder: A clinical/metabolic correlation study after treatment. *British Journal of Psychiatry, 166,* 244–250.

Perilstein, R.D., Lipper, S., & Friedman, L.J. (1991). Three cases of paraphilias responsive to fluoxetine treatment. *Journal of Clinical Psychiatry, 52,* 169–170.

Perls, F. (1969). *Gestalt therapy verbatim.* Lafayette, CA: Real People Press.

Perris, C. (1992). Bipolar-unipolar distinction. In E.S. Paykel (Ed.), *Handbook of affective disorders,* 2nd ed., pp. 57–75. New York: Guilford.

Perry, C., & Laurence, J. (1984). Mental processing outside of awareness: The contributions of Freud and Janet. In K.S. Bowers & D. Meichenbaum (Eds.), *The unconscious reconsidered,* pp. 9–48. New York: Wiley.

Perry, J.C. (1990). Challenges in validating personality disorders: Beyond description. *Journal of Personality Disorders, 4,* 273–289.

Perry, J.C. (1993). Longitudinal studies of personality disorders. *Journal of Personality Disorders,* supplement, 63–85.

Person, E.S., Terestman, N., Myers, W.A., Goldberg, E.L., & Salvadori, C. (1989). Gender differences in sexual behaviors and fantasies in a college population. *Journal of Sex and Marital Therapy, 15,* 187–198.

Persons, J.B. (1986). The advantages of studying psychological phenomena rather than psychiatric diagnoses. *American Psychologist, 41,* 1252–1260.

Pescosolido, B.A., & Georgianna, S. (1989). Durkheim, suicide, and religion: Toward a network theory of suicide. *American Sociological Review, 54,* 33–48.

Peselow, E.D., Stanley, M., Filippi. A.M., Barouche, F., Goodnick, P., & Fieve, R.P. (1989). The predictive value of the dexamethasone suppression test. A placebo-controlled study. *British Journal of Psychiatry, 155,* 667–672.

Peterson, C., & Seligman, M.E.P. (1984). Causal explanations as a risk factor for depression: Theory and evidence. *Psychological Review, 91,* 347–374.

Petrie, K.J., Booth, R.J., Pennebaker, J.W., Davison, K.P., & Thomas, M.G. (1995). Disclosure of trauma and immune response to a hepatitis B vaccination program. *Journal of Consulting and Clinical Psychology, 63,* 787–792.

Petty, R.G., Barta, P.E., Pearlson, G.D., McGilchrist, I.K., et al. (1995). Reversal of asymmetry of the planum temporale in schizophrenia. *American Journal of Psychiatry, 152,* 715–721.

Pfohl, B., Blum, N., & Zimmerman, M. (1995). *Structured interview for DSM-IV Personality (SIDP-IV).* Iowa City: University of Iowa.

Pfohl, B., Coryell, W., Zimmerman, M., & Stangl, D. (1986). DSM-III personality disorders: Diagnostic overlap and internal consistency of individual DSM-III-criteria. *Comprehensive Psychiatry, 27,* 21–34.

Pfohl, B. (1995). Histrionic personality disorder. In W.J. Livesley (Ed.), *The DSM-IV personality disorders.* New York: Guilford, pp. 173–192.

Phillips, E.L., Phillips, E.A., Wolf, M.M., & Fixsen, D.L. (1973). Achievement Place: Development of the elected manager system. *Journal of Applied Behavior Analysis, 6,* 541–561.

Phillips, K.A. (1991). Body dysmorphic disorder: The distress of imagined ugliness. *American Journal of Psychiatry, 148,* 1138–1149.

Pickens, R.W., Svikis, D.S., McGue, M., Lykken, D.T., Heston, L.L., & Clayton, P.J. (1991). Heterogeneity in the inheritance of alcoholism: A study of male and female twins. *Archives of General Psychiatry, 48,* 19–28.

Pike, K.M., & Rodin, J. (1991). Mothers, daughters, and disordered eating. *Journal of Abnormal Psychology, 100,* 198–204.

Piper, A. (1994). Multiple personality disorder. *British Journal of Psychiatry, 164,* 600–612.

Pisani, V.C., Fawcett, J., Clark, D.C., & McGuire, M. (1993). The relative contributions of medication adherence and AA meeting attendance to abstinent outcome for chronic alcoholics. *Journal of Studies on Alcohol, 54,* 115–119.

Pitman, R.K. (1984). Janet's obsessions and psychasthenia: A synopsis. *Psychiatric Quarterly, 56,* 291–314.

Pitman, R.K. (1987). Pierre Janet on obsessive-compulsive disorder (1903). Review and commentary. *Archives of General Psychiatry, 44,* 226–232.

Pitman, R.K., van der Kolk, B.A., Orr, S.P., & Greenberg, M. (1990). Naloxone-reversible analgesic response to combat-related stimuli in posttraumatic stress disorder. *Archives of General Psychiatry, 47,* 541–544.

Pitts, F.N., Jr., & McClure, J.N., Jr. (1967). Lactate metabolism in anxiety neurosis. *New England Journal of Medicine, 277,* 1329–1336.

Plomin, R. (1990a). *Nature and nurture: An introduction to human behavioral genetics.* Pacific Grove, CA: Brooks/Cole.

Plomin, R. (1990b). The role of inheritance in behavior. *Science, 248*, 183–188.

Plomin, R. (1994). *Genetics and experience: The interplay between nature and nurture.* Thousand Oaks, CA: Sage.

Plomin, R., & Daniels, D. (1987). Why are children in the same family so different from one another? *Behavioral and Brain Sciences, 10*, 1–60.

Plomin, R., DeFries, J.C., & McClearn, G.E. (1990). *Behavioral genetics,* 2nd ed. New York: Freeman.

Pogue-Geile, M.F., & Harrow, M. (1984). Negative and positive symptoms in schizophrenia and depression: A follow-up. *Schizophrenia Bulletin, 10*, 371–387.

Pokony, A. (1983). Prediction of suicide in psychiatric patients: A prospective study. *Archives of General Psychiatry, 40*, 249–257.

Pollack, J. (1987). Obsessive-compulsive personality: Theoretical and clinical perspectives and recent research findings. *Journal of Personality Disorders, 1*, 248–262.

Pollack, J. (1995). Commentary on obsessive-compulsive personality disorder. In W.J. Livesley (Ed.), *The DSM-IV personality disorders,* pp. 277–283. New York: Guilford.

Pollen, D.A. (1993). *Hannah's heirs: The quest for the genetic origins of Alzheimer's disease.* New York: Oxford University Press.

Pollitt, R.J. (1987). Amino acid disorders. In J.B. Holton (Ed.), *The inherited metabolic disease,* p. 96. Edinburgh: Churchill Livingstone.

Pomeroy, C. (1996). Anorexia nervosa, bulimia nervosa, and binge eating disorder: The assessment of physical status. In J.K. Thompson, *Body image, eating disorders, and obesity,* pp. 177–204. Washington, DC: American Psychological Association.

Poole, D.A., Lindsay, D.S., Memon, A., & Bull, R. (1995). Psychotherapy and the recovery of memories of childhood sexual abuse: U.S. and British practitioners' opinions, practices, and experiences. *Journal of Consulting and Clinical Psychology, 63*, 426–437.

Poon, L.W., Kaszniak, A.W., & Dudley, W.N. (1992). Approaches in the experimental neuropsychology of dementia: A methodological and model review. In M. Bergener, K. Hasegawa, S.I. Finkel, & T. Nishimura (Eds.), *Aging and mental disorders: International perspectives.* New York: Springer.

Pope, H.G., & Yurgelun-Todd, D. (1996). The residual cognitive effects of heavy marijuana use in college students. *Journal of the American Medical Association, 275*, 521–527.

Porrino, L.J., Rapoport, J.L., Behar, D., Sceery, W., Ismond, D.R., & Bunney, W.E. (1983). A naturalistic assessment of the motor activity of hyperactive boys. I. Comparisons with normal controls. *Archives of General Psychiatry, 40*, 681–687.

Posner, M.I. (1993). Seeing the mind. *Science, 262*, 673–674.

Potter, W.Z., Grossman, F., & Rudorfer, M.V. (1993). Noradrenergic function in depressive disorders. In J.J. Mann & D.J. Kupfer (Eds.), *Biology of depressive disorders, Part A: A systems perspective,* pp. 1–27. New York: Plenum.

Poulos, C.X., & Cappell, H. (1991). Homeostatic theory of drug tolerance: A general model of physiological adaptation. *Psychological Review, 98*, 390–408.

Power, C. (1979). The time-sample behavior checklist: Observational assessment of patient functioning. *Journal of Behavioral Assessment, 1*, 199–210.

Prentky, R.A. (1996). Community notification and constructive risk reduction. *Journal of Interpersonal Violence, 11*, 295–299.

Prescott, C.A., Hewitt, J.K., Heath, A.C., Truett, K.R., Neale, M.C., & Eaves, L.J. (1994a). Environmental and genetic influences on alcohol use in a volunteer sample of older twins. *Journal of Studies on Alcohol, 55*, 18–32.

Prescott, C.A., Hewitt, J.K., Truett, K.R., Heath, A.C., Neale, M.C., & Eaves, L.J. (1994b). Genetic and environmental influences on lifetime alcohol-related problems in a volunteer sample of older twins. *Journal of Studies on Alcohol, 55*, 184–202.

Prestige, B.R., & Lake, C.R. (1987). Prevalence and recognition of depression among primary care outpatients. *Journal of Family Practice, 25*, 67–72.

Price, R.A., & Gottesman, I.I. (1991). Body fat in identical twins reared apart: Roles for genes and environment. *Behavior Genetics. 21*, 1–7.

Prince, M. (1906). *The dissociation of a personality.* New York: Longmans, Green.

Prochaska, J.O. (1984). *Systems of psychotherapy: A transtheoretical analysis.* Homewood, IL: Dorsey.

Project Match Research Group (1997). Matching alcoholism treatments to client heterogeneity: Project MATCH posttreatment drinking outcomes. *Journal of Studies on Alcohol, 58*, 7–29.

Pruzinsky, T., & Borkovec, T.D. (1990). Cognitive and personality characteristics of worriers. *Behaviour Research and Therapy, 28*, 507–512.

Puig-Antich, J. (1986). Psychobiological markers: Effects of age and puberty. In M. Rutter, C. Izard, & P. Read (Eds.), *Depression in young people,* pp. 341–382. New York: Guilford.

Pulver, A.E., Liang, K., Brown, C.H., Wolyniec, P.S., et al. (1992). Risk factors in schizophrenia: Season of birth, gender, and familial risk. *British Journal of Psychiatry, 160*, 65–71.

Putnam, F.W., Curoff, J.J., et al. (1986). The clinical phenomenology of multiple personality disorder: Review of 100 recent cases. *Journal of Clinical Psychiatry, 47*, 285–293.

Quality Assurance Project. (1991). Treatment outlines for antisocial personality disorder. *Australian and New Zealand Journal of Psychiatry, 25*, 541–547.

Quay, H.C. (1965). Psychopathic personality as pathological stimulation-seeking. *American Journal of Psychiatry, 122*, 180–183.

Quay, H.C. (1993). The psychobiology and undersocialized aggressive conduct disorder: A theoretical perspective. *Development and Psychopathology, 5*, 165–180.

Quevillon, R.P. (1993). Dyspareunia. In W. O'Donohue & J.H. Geer (Eds.), *Handbook of sexual dysfunctions: Assessment and treatment,* pp. 367–380. Boston: Allyn & Bacon.

Rabins, P.V. (1997). Caring for persons with dementing illnesses: A current perspective. In L. Heston (Ed.), *Progress in Alzheimer's disease and similar conditions.* Washington, DC: American Psychiatric Press.

Rachlin, H. (1992). Teleological behaviorism. *American Psychologist, 47*, 1371–1382.

Rachman, S. (1990). The determinants and treatment of simple phobias. *Advances in Behavior Research and Therapy, 12*, 1–30.

Rachman, S. (1991). *Fear and courage,* 2nd ed. San Francisco: Freeman.

Rachman, S., & de Silva, P. (1978). Abnormal and normal obsessions. *Behaviour Research and Therapy, 16*, 233–248.

Rachman, S.J., & Hodgson, R.J. (1980). *Obsessions and compulsions.* Englewood Cliffs, NJ: Prentice Hall.

Raichle, M.E. (1994a). Images of the mind: Studies with modern imaging techniques. *Annual Review of Psychology, 45*, 333–356.

Raichle, M.E. (1994b). Images of the human mind. *Neuropsychopharmacology, 10* (3 suppl part 1): 28S–33S.

Ramey, C.T., & Bryant, D. (1982). Evidence for primary prevention of developmental retardation. *Journal of the Division of Early Childhood, 5*, 73–78.

Rapee, R.M. (1991). Generalized anxiety disorder: A review of clinical features and theoretical concepts. *Clinical Psychology Review, 11*, 419–440.

Rapee, R.M. (1995). Psychological factors influencing the affective response to biological challenge procedures in panic disorder. *Journal of Anxiety Disorders, 9*, 59–74.

Raphael, B., Wilson, J., Meldrum L., & McFarlane, A.C. (1996). Acute preventive interventions. In B.A. van der Kolk, A.C. McFarlane, & L. Weisaeth (Eds.), *Traumatic stress,* pp. 463–479. New York: Guilford.

Rapoport, J.L., Buchsbaum, M.S., Zahn, T.P., Weingartner, H., Ludlow, C., & Mikkelsen, E.J. (1978). Dextroamphetamine: Cognitive and behavioral effects in normal prepubertal boys. *Science, 199*, 560–563.

Raskind, M.A., & Peskind, E.R. (1997). Neurotransmitter abnormalities and the psychopharmacology of Alzheimer's disease. In L. Heston (Ed.), *Progress in Alzheimer's disease and similar conditions.* Washington, DC: American Psychiatric Press.

Rastam, M., Gillberg, C., & Gillberg, C. (1995). Anorexia nervosa 6 years after onset. Part II. Cormorbid psychiatric problems. *Comprehensive Psychiatry, 36*, 70–76.

Raz, S., & Raz, N. (1990). Structural brain abnormalities in the major psychoses: A quantitative review of the evidence from computerized imaging. *Psychological Bulletin, 108*, 93–108.

Redmond, D.E., Jr. (1985). Neurochemical basis for anxiety and anxiety disorders: Evidence from drugs which decrease human fear of anxiety. In A.H. Tuma and J.D. Maser (Eds.), *Anxiety and the anxiety disorders.* Hillsdale, NJ: Erlbaum.

Regier, D.A., Myers, J.K., Kramer, M., Robins, L.N., Blazer, D.G., Hough, R.L., Eaton, W.W., & Locke, B.Z. (1984). The NIMH Epidemiologic Catchment Area Program: Historical context, major objectives and study population characteristics. *Archives of General Psychiatry, 41*, 934–941.

Reich, J., & Thompson, W.D. (1987). DSM-III personality disorder clusters in three populations. *British Journal of Psychiatry, 150*, 471–475.

Reich, J., Warshaw, M., Peterson, L.G., White, K., Keller, M., Lavori, P., & Yonkers, A. (1993). Comorbidity of panic and major depressive disorder. *Journal of Psychiatric Research, 27* (suppl. 1), 23–33.

Reich, J., Yates, W., & Nduaguba, M. (1987). Prevalence of DSM-III personality disorders in the community. *Social Psychiatry and Psychiatric Epidemiology, 24*, 12–16.

Reid, J.B., (Ed.) (1978). *A social learning approach to family intervention.* Vol. 2. *Observation in home settings.* Eugene, OR: Castalia.

Reiman, E.M., Raichle, M.E., Robins, E., Mintun, M.A., Fusselman, M.J., Fox, P.T., Price, J.L., & Hackman, K.A. (1989). Neuroanatomical correlates of a lactate-induced anxiety attack. *Archives of General Psychiatry, 46*, 493–500.

Reisman, J.M. (1990). *A history of clinical psychology,* 2nd ed. New York: Hemisphere.

Reisner, R., & Slobogin, C. (1990). *Law and the mental health system,* 2nd ed. St. Paul, MN: West.

Reiss, A.L., Feinstein, C., & Rosenbaum, K.N. (1986). Autism and genetic disorders. *Schizophrenia Bulletin, 12*, 724–738.

Rey, J.M., Stewart, G.W., Plapp, J.M., Bashir, M.R., et al. (1988). DSM-III Axis IV revisited. *American Journal of Psychiatry, 145*, 286–292.

Richardson, S. (1996). The besieged brain: Immune cells in brain may further progression of Alzheimer's disease. *Discover, 17*, 30–32.

Richters, J.E. (1993). Community violence and children's development: Toward a research agenda for the 1990s. *Psychiatry, 56*, 3–6.

Riecher, A., Maurer, K., Loffler, W., Fatkenheuer, B., an der Heiden, W., Munk-Jorgensen P., Stromgren, E., & Hafner, H. (1991). Gender differences in age at onset and course of schizophrenic disorders. In H. Hafner & W.F. Gattaz (Eds.), *Search for the causes of schizophrenia,* Vol. II, pp. 14–33. Berlin: Springer.

Rifat, S.L. (1994). Aluminum hypothesis lives. *Lancet, 343*, 3–5.

Risch, N., Baron, M., & Mendlewicz, J. (1986). Assessing the role of X-linked inheritance in bipolar-related major affective disorder. *Journal of Psychiatric Research. 20, 275–288.*

Ritvo, E.R., Freeman, B.J., Yuwiler, A., Geller, E., Yokota, A., Schroth, P., & Novak, P. (1984). Study of fenfluramine in outpatients with the syndrome of autism. *Journal of Pediatrics, 105, 823–828.*

Roberts, J., & Rowland, M. (1981). *Hypertension in adults 25–74 years of age: United States, 1971–75.* Vital and Health Statistics Series 11, No. 221., DHEW Publication No. PHS 81-1671. Washington, DC: U.S. Government Printing Office.

Robin, A.L., Koepke, T., & Nayar, M. (1986). Conceptualizing, assessing, and treating parent-adolescent conflict. In B. Lahey & A. Kazdin (Eds.), *Advances in Clinical Child Psychology, 9, 87–124.*

Robins, E., & Guze, S. (1989). Establishment of diagnostic validity in psychiatric illness. In L.N. Robins & J. E. Barrett (Eds.), *The validity of psychiatric diagnosis.* pp. 177–197. New York: Raven Press.

Robins, L.N. (1966). *Deviant children grown up: A sociological and psychiatric study of sociopathic personality.* Baltimore: Williams & Wilkins.

Robins, L.N., Helzer, J.E., Weissman, M.M., Orvaschel, H., Gruenberg, E., Burke, J.D., & Regier, D.A. (1984). Lifetime prevalence of specific psychiatric disorders in three sites. *Archives of General Psychiatry, 41, 949–958.*

Robins, L.N., Locke, B.Z., & Regier, D.A. (1991). An overview of psychiatric disorders in America. In L.N. Robins & D.A. Regier (Eds.) *Psychiatric disorders in America: The Epidemiologic Catchment Area Study,* pp. 328–366. New York: Free Press

Robins, L.N., & McEvoy, L. (1992). Conduct problems as predictors of substance abuse. In C.P. O'Brien & J.J. Jaffe (Eds.), *Addictive states.* New York: Raven Press.

Robins, L.N., & Regier, D.A. (1991). *Psychiatric disorders in America: The Epidemiologic Catchment Area Study.* New York: Free Press.

Robins, L.N., Tipp, J., & Przybeck, T. (1991). Antisocial personality. In L.N. Robins & D.A. Regier (Eds.), *Psychiatric disorders in America: The Epidemiologic Catchment Area Study,* pp. 258–290. New York: Free Press.

Robinson, L.A., Berman, J.A., & Neimeyer, R.A. (1990). Psychotherapy for the treatment of depression: A comprehensive review of controlled outcome research. *Psychological Bulletin, 108, 30–49.*

Robinson, P. (1976). *The modernization of sex: Havelock Ellis, Alfred Kinsey, William Masters and Virginia Johnson.* New York: Harper & Row.

Roemer, L., & Borkovec, T.D. (1993). Worry: Unwanted cognitive activity that controls unwanted somatic experience. In D.M. Wegner and J.W. Pennebaker (Eds.), *Handbook of mental control.* Englewood Cliffs, NJ: Prentice Hall.

Rogers, C.R. (1951). *Client-centered therapy.* Boston: Houghton Mifflin.

Rogers, C.R. (1957). The necessary and sufficient conditions of therapeutic personality change. *Journal of Consulting Psychology, 21, 95–103.*

Rogers, C.R. (1961). *On becoming a person: A therapist's view of psychotherapy.* Boston: Houghton Mifflin.

Rogers, M.P. (1989). The interaction between brain, behavior, and immunity. In. S. Cheren (Ed.), *Psychosomatic medicine: Theory, physiology, and practice,* Vol. 1, pp. 279–330. Madison, CT: International Universities Press.

Rogers, M.P., Weinshenker, N.J., Warshaw, M.G., et al. (1996). Prevalence of somatoform disorders in a large sample of patients with anxiety disorders. *Psychosomatics, 37, 17–22.*

Rogers, R., Bloom, M., & Manson, S. (1984). Insanity defenses: Contested or conceded? *American Journal of Psychiatry, 141, 885–888.*

Rohde, P., Lewinsohn, P., & Seeley, J. (1990). Are people changed by the experience of having an episode of depression? A further test of the scar hypothesis. *Journal of Abnormal Psychology, 99, 264–271.*

Roman, P.M., & Blum, T.C. (1987). Notes on the new epidemiology of alcoholism in the USA. *Journal of Drug Issues, 17, 321–332.*

Ronningstam, E., & Gunderson, J. (1991). Differentiating borderline personality disorder from narcissistic personality disorder. *Journal of Personality Disorders, 5, 225–232.*

Rook, K.S., & Dooley, D. (1985). Applying social support research: Theoretical problems and future directions. *Journal of Social Issues, 41, 5–28.*

Room, R. (1987). Alcohol control, addiction and processes of change: Comment on "The limitations of control-of-supply models for explaining and preventing alcoholism and drug addiction." *Journal of Studies on Alcohol, 48, 78–83.*

Rosen, J.C., Reiter, J., & Orosan, P. (1995). Cognitive-behavioral body image therapy for body dysmorphic disorder. *Journal of Consulting and Clinical Psychology, 63, 263–269.*

Rosen, R.C., & Leiblum, S.R. (1995). Treatment of sexual disorders in the 1990s: An integrated approach. *Journal of Consulting and Clinical Psychology, 63, 877–890.*

Rosen, R.C., Taylor, J.F., Leiblum, S.R., & Bachmann, G.A. (1993). Prevalence of sexual dysfunction in women: Results of a survey study of 329 women in an outpatient gynecological clinic. *Journal of Sex and Marital Therapy, 19, 171–188.*

Rosenberg, R. (1993). Drug treatment of panic disorder. *Psychopharmacology and Toxicology, 72, 344–353.*

Rosenhan, D.L. (1973). On being sane in insane places. *Science, 179. 250–258.*

Rosenthal, D. (Ed.) (1963). *The Genain quadruplets.* New York: Basic Books.

Rosenthal, D., & Quinn, O.W. (1977). Quadruplet hallucinations: Phenotypic variations of a schizophrenic genotype. *Archives of General Psychiatry, 34, 817–827.*

Rosenthal, N.E., Sack, D.A., & Gillin, J.C., et al. (1984). Seasonal affective disorder: A description of the syndrome and preliminary findings with light therapy. *Archives of General Psychiatry, 41, 72–80.*

Rosenthal, R. (1966). *Experimenter bias in behavioral research.* New York: Appleton-Century-Crofts.

Rosenthal, R. (1983). Assessing the statistical importance of the effects of psychotherapy. *Journal of Consulting and Clinical Psychology, 51, 4–13. .*

Rosenthal, R., & Rosnow, R.L. (1969). *Artifact in behavioral science research.* New York: Academic Press.

Rosin, A.J., & Glatt, M.M. (1971). Alcohol excess in the elderly. *Quarterly Journal of Studies on Alcohol, 32, 53–59.*

Ross, C.A. (1991). Epidemiology of multiple personality disorder and dissociation. *Psychiatric Clinics of North America, 14, 503–516.*

Ross, C.A., Norton, G.R., & Wozney, K. (1989). Multiple personality disorder: An analysis of 236 cases. *Canadian Journal of Psychiatry, 34, 413–418.*

Ross, D.M., & Ross, S.A. (1982). *Hyperactivity: Current issues, research, and theory.* New York: Wiley.

Ross, H.E. (1989). Alcohol and drug abuse in treated alcoholics: A comparison of men and women. *Alcohol: Clinical and Experimental Research, 13, 810–816.*

Roth, M., & Argyle, N. (1988). Anxiety, panic, and phobic disorders: An overview. *Journal of Psychiatric Research, 22, 33–54.*

Roth, D., & Bean, J. (1986). New perspectives on homelessness: Findings from a statewide epidemiological study. *Hospital and Community Psychiatry, 37, 712–723.*

Rothbaum, B.O., & Foa, E.B. (1996). Cognitive-behavioral therapy for posttraumatic stress disorder. In B.A. van der Kolk, A.C., McFarlane, & L. Weisaeth (Eds.), *Traumatic stress,* pp. 491–509. New York: Guilford.

Rothschild, A.J. (1995). Selective serotonin reuptake inhibitor-induced sexual dysfunction. Efficacy of a drug holiday. *American Journal of Psychiatry, 152, 1514–1517.*

Rounsaville, B.J., Spitzer, R.L., & Williams, J.B.W. (1986). Proposed changes in DSM-III substance use disorders: Description and rationale. *American Journal of Psychiatry, 143, 463–468.*

Roy, A. (1992). Are there genetic factors in suicide? *International Review of Psychiatry, 4, 169–175.*

Roy, A., Everett, D., Pickar, D., & Paul, S.M. (1987). Platelet tritiated imipramine binding and serotonin uptake in depressed patients and controls. *Archives of General Psychiatry, 44, 320–327.*

Roy, A., Segal, N.L., Centerwall, B.S., & Robinette, C.D. (1991). Suicide in twins. *Archives of General Psychiatry, 48, 29–32.*

Royal College of Psychiatrists. (1989). *The practical administration of electroconvulsive therapy (EDT).* London: Gaskell.

Ruocchio, P.J. (1991). First person account: The schizophrenic inside. *Schizophrenia Bulletin, 17, 357–359.*

Rubonis, A.V., & Bickman, L. (1991). Psychological impairment in the wake of disaster: The disaster-psychopathology relationship. *Psychological Bulletin, 109, 384–399.*

Rush, A.J. (1993). Clinical practice guidelines: Good news, bad news, or no news? *Archives of General Psychiatry, 50, 483–490.*

Rush, A.J., Beck, A.T., Kovacs, M., & Hollon, S.D. (1977). Comparative efficacy of cognitive therapy and pharmacotherapy in the treatment of depressed outpatients. *Cognitive Therapy and Research, 1, 17–38.*

Rush, A.J., Giles, D.E., Jarrett, R.B., Feldman-Koffler, F., Debus, J.R., Weissenburger, J., Orsulak, P.J., & Roffwarg, H.P. (1989). Reduced REM latency predicts response to tricyclic medication in depressed outpatients. *Biological Psychiatry, 26, 61–72.*

Russell, D.E.H. (1983). The incidence and prevalence of intrafamilial and extrafamilial sexual abuse of female children. *Child Abuse and Neglect, 7, 133–146.*

Russell, D.E.H. (1984). *Sexual exploitation: Rape, child sexual abuse, and workplace harassment.* Beverly Hills, CA: Sage.

Russell, G.F.M. (1979). Bulimia nervosa: An ominous variant of anorexia nervosa. *Psychological Medicine, 9, 429–448.*

Russell, G.F.M., Szmukler, G.I., Dare, C., & Eisler, I. (1987). An evaluation of family therapy in anorexia nervosa and bulimia nervosa. *Archives of General Psychiatry, 44, 1047–1056.*

Rutherford, J., McGuffin, P., Katz, R.J., & Murray, R.M. (1993). Genetic influences on eating attitudes in a normal female twin population. *Psychological Medicine, 23, 425–436.*

Rutter, M. (1970). Autistic children: Infancy to adulthood. *Seminars in Psychiatry, 2, 435–450.*

Rutter, M. (1978a). Diagnosis and definition of child autism. *Journal of Autism and Childhood Schizophrenia, 8, 139–161.*

Rutter, M.L. (1978b). Family, area and school influences in the genesis of conduct disorders. In L. Hersov, M. Berger, & D. Shaffer (Eds.), *Aggression and antisocial behavior in childhood and adolescence.* Oxford: Pergamon.

Rutter, M.L. (1981). *Maternal deprivation reassessed,* 2nd ed. London: Penguin.

Rutter, M. (1983). Introduction: Concepts of brain dysfunction syndromes. In M. Rutter (Ed.), *Developmental neuropsychiatry,* pp. 1–14. New York: Guilford Press.

Rutter, M.L. (1986). The developmental psychopathology of depression: Issues and perspectives. In M. Rutter, C. Izard, & P. Read (Eds.), *Depression in young people,* pp. 3–32. New York: Guilford.

Rutter, M. (1987). Temperament, personality, and personality disorder. *British Journal of Psychiatry, 150, 443–458.*

Rutter, M.L. (1978). Isle of Wight revisited: Twenty-five years of child psychiatric epidemiology. *Journal of the American Academy of Child Psychiatry, 28,* 633–653.

Rutter, M. (1996). Autism research: Prospects and priorities. *Journal of Autism and Developmental Disorders, 26,* 257–275.

Rutter, M., & Garmezy, N. (1983). Developmental psychopathology. In E.M. Hetherington (Ed.), *Handbook of child psychology,* Vol. 4, pp. 775–912. New York: Wiley.

Rutter, M., Greenfield, D., & Lockyer, L. (1967). A five- to fifteen-year follow-up study of infantile psychosis. II. Social and behavioral outcome. *British Journal of Psychiatry, 113,* 1187–1199.

Rutter, M., & Rutter, M. (1993). *Developing minds.* New York: Basic Books.

Rutter, M., Shaffer, D., & Shepard, M. (1975). *A multiaxial classification of child psychiatric disorders. An evaluation and proposal.* Geneva: World Health Organization.

Ryff, C.D. (1995). Psychological well-being in adult life. *Current Directions in Psychological Science, 4,* 99–104.

Sabshin, M. (1990). Turning points in twentieth-century American psychiatry. *American Journal of Psychiatry, 147,* 1267–1274.

Sackett, D. (1992). A primer on the precision and accuracy of the clinical examination. *Journal of the American Medical Association, 267,* 2638–2644.

Sacks, O. (1985). *The man who mistook his wife for a hat and other clinical tales.* New York: Summit.

Sacks, O. (1995). *An anthropologist on Mars.* New York: Knopf.

Safer, D.J., & Krager, J.M. (1988). A survey of medication treatment for hyperactive/inattentive students. *Journal of the American Medical Association, 260,* 2256–2258.

Salkovskis, P.M., & Harrison, J. (1984). Abnormal and normal obsessions—A replication. *Behaviour Research and Therapy, 22,* 549–552.

Samuels, J.F., Nestadt, G., Romanoski, A.J., Folstein, M.F., & McHugh, P.R. (1994). DSM-III personality disorders in the community. *American Journal of Psychiatry, 151,* 1055–1062.

Sanders, S.A., Reinisch, J.M., & McWhirter, D.P. (1990). Homosexuality/heterosexuality: An overview. In D.P. McWhirter, S.A. Sanders, & J.M. Reinisch (Eds.), *Homosexuality/heterosexuality: Concepts of sexual orientation.* New York: Oxford University Press.

Sanderson, W.C., Rapee, R.M., & Barlow, D.H. (1989). The influence of an illusion of control on panic attacks induced via inhalation of 5.5% carbon dioxide-enriched air. *Archives of General Psychiatry, 46,* 157–162.

Sapolsky, R.M. (1992). Neuroendocrinology of the stress response. In J.B. Becker, S.M. Breedlove, & D. Crews (Eds.), *Behavioral endocrinology,* pp. 288–324. Cambridge, MA: MIT Press.

Sargent, T.O. (1988). Fetishism. *Journal of Social Work and Human Sexuality, 7,* 27–42.

Sartorius, N., Kaelber, C.T., Cooper, J.E., Roper, M.T., Rae, D.S., Gulbinat, W., Ustun, B., & Regier, D.A. (1993). Progress toward achieving a common language in psychiatry: Results from the field trial of the clinical guidelines accompanying the WHO classification of mental and behavioral disorders in ICD-10. *Archives of General Psychiatry, 50,* 115–124.

Sartorius, N., Jablensky, A., Lorton, A., Ernberg, G., Anker, M., Cooper, J.E., & Day, R. (1986). Early manifestations and first-contact incidence of schizophrenia in different cultures. *Psychological Medicine, 16,* 909–928.

Sartory, G. (1989). Obsessional-compulsive disorder. In G. Turpin (Ed.), *Handbook of clinical psychophysiology,* pp. 329–356. New York: Wiley.

Sato, M. (1992). A lasting vulnerability to psychosis in patients with previous methamphetamine psychosis. In P.W. Kalivas & H.H. Samson (Eds.), *Neurobiology of drug and alcohol addiction. Annals of the New York Academy of Sciences, 654,* 160–170.

Satterfield, S.B. (1988). Transsexualism. *Journal of Social Work and Human Sexuality, 7,* 77–87.

Saxe, G.N., van der Kolk, B.A., Berkowitz, R., Chinman, G., Hall, K., Lieberg, G., & Schwartz, J. (1993). Dissociative disorders in psychiatric inpatients. *American Journal of Psychiatry, 150,* 1037–1042.

Sayer, N.A., Sackeim, H.A., Moeller, J.R., Prudic, J., Devanand, D.P., Coleman, E.A., & Kiersky, J.E. (1993). The relations between observer-rating and self-report of depressive symptomatology. *Psychological Assessment, 5,* 350–360.

Sayette, M.A. (1993). An appraisal-disruption model of alcohol's effects on stress responses in social drinkers. *Psychological Bulletin, 114,* 459–476.

Scarone, S., Gambini, O., Hafele, E., Bellodi, L., & Smeraldi, E. (1987). Neurofunctional assessment of schizophrenia: A preliminary investigation of the presence of eye-tracking (SPEMs) and quality extinction test (QET) abnormalities in a sample of schizophrenic patients. *Biological Psychology, 24,* 253–259.

Scarr, S. (1966). Genetic factors in activity motivation. *Child Development, 37,* 663–673.

Scarr, S. (1992). Developmental theories for the 1990s: Development and individual differences. *Child Development, 63,* 1–19.

Scarr, S., & McCartney, K. (1983). How people make their own environments: A theory of genotype-environment effects. *Child Development, 54,* 424–435.

Schacht, T.E. (1985). DSM-III and the politics of truth. *American Psychologist, 40,* 513–521.

Schacht, T., & Nathan, P. (1977). But is it good for psychologists? Appraisal and status of DSM-III. *American Psychologist, 32,* 1017–1025.

Scheerenberger, R.C. (1982). Public residential services, 1981: Status and trends. *Mental Retardation, 20,* 210–215.

Scheff, T.J. (1966). *Being mentally ill: A sociological theory.* Chicago: Aldine.

Scheff, T.J. (1984). *Being mentally ill: A sociological theory,* 2nd ed. Chicago: Aldine.

Schellenberg, G.D., Payami, H., Wijsman, E.M., Orr, H.T., Goddard, K.A.B., Anderson, L., Nemens, E., White, J.A., Alonso, M.E., Ball, M.J., Kaye, J., Morris, J.C., Chui, H., Sadovnick, A.D., Heston, L.L., Martin, G.M., & Bird, T.D. (1993). Chromosome 14 and late-onset familial Alzheimer disease (FAD). *American Journal of Human Genetics, 53,* 619–628.

Schiavi, R.C., Stimmel, B.B., Mandeli, J., & White, D. (1995). Chronic alcoholism and male sexual function. *American Journal of Psychiatry, 152,* 1045–1052.

Schiff, M., Duyme, M., Dumaret, A., & Tomkiewicz, S. (1982). How much could we boost scholastic achievement and IQ scores? A direct answer from a French adoption study. *Cognition, 12,* 165–196.

Schildkraut, J.J. (1965). The catecholamine hypothesis of affective disorders: A review of supporting evidence. *American Journal of Psychiatry, 122,* 509–522.

Schneider, K. (1959). *Clinical psychopathology,* M.W. Hamilton, Trans. New York: Grune & Stratton.

Schneidman, E.S. (1996). *The suicidal mind.* New York: Oxford University Press.

Schneiderman, N., Chesney, M.A., & Krantz, D.S. (1989). Biobehavioral aspects of cardiovascular disease: Progress and prospects. *Health Psychology, 8,* 649–676.

Schneller, J. (1988). Terror on the A-train: Anatomy of a panic attack. *Mademoiselle, 94,* 148–159.

Schopler, E.M., Andrews, C.E. & Strupp, K. (1979). Do autistic children come from upper-middle-class parents? *Journal of Autism and Developmental Disorders, 9,* 139–152.

Schott, R.L. (1995). The childhood and family dynamics of transvestites. *Archives of Sexual Behavior, 24,* 309–328.

Schotti, J.R., Evans, I.M., Meyer, L.H., & Walker, P. (1991). A meta-analysis of intervention research with prob-

lem behavior: Treatment validity and standards of practice. *American Journal on Mental Retardation, 96,* 233–256.

Schreibman, L. (1988). *Autism.* Beverly Hills, CA: Sage.

Schreiner-Engel, P., & Schiavi, R.C. (1986). Lifetime psychopathology in individuals with low sexual desire. *Journal of Nervous and Mental Disease, 174,* 646–651.

Schuckit, M.A. (1987). Biological vulnerability to alcoholism. *Journal of Consulting and Clinical Psychology, 55,* 301–309.

Schuckit, M.A. (1989). *Drug and alcohol abuse: A clinical guide to diagnosis and treatment,* 3rd ed. New York: Plenum.

Schuckit, M.A. (1994). A clinical model of genetic influences in alcohol dependence. *Journal of Studies on Alcohol, 55,* 5–17.

Schuckit, J.A., & Monteiro, J.G. (1988). Alcoholism, anxiety and depression. *British Journal of Addiction, 83,* 1373–1380.

Schuyler, D. (1991). *A practical guide to cognitive therapy.* New York: Norton.

Schwartz, G.E. (1982). Testing the biopsychosocial model: The ultimate challenge facing behavioral medicine. *Journal of Consulting and Clinical Psychology, 50,* 1040–1053.

Schwartz, G.E. (1989). Dysregulation theory and disease: Toward a general model for psychosomatic medicine. In S. Cheren (Ed.), *Psychosomatic medicine: Theory, physiology, and practice,* Vol. 1, pp. 91–118. Madison, CT: International Universities Press.

Scurfield, R.M. (1985). Posttrauma stress assessment and treatment: Overview and formulations. In C.R. Figley (Ed.), *Trauma and its wake,* pp. 219–259. New York: Brunner/Mazel.

Searles, J.S. (1988). The role of genetics in the pathogenesis of alcoholism. *Journal of Abnormal Psychology, 97,* 153–167.

Searles, J.S. (1990). Methodological limitations of research on the genetics of alcoholism. In C.R. Cloninger & H. Begleiter (Eds.), *Genetics and biology of alcoholism,* pp. 89–100. Cold Spring Harbor, NY: Cold Spring Harbor Laboratory Press.

Sedgwick, P. (1981). Illness—Mental and otherwise. In A.L. Caplan, H.T. Engelhardt, Jr., & J.J. McCartney (Eds.), *Concepts of health and disease: Interdisciplinary perspectives,* pp. 119–129. Reading, MA: Addison-Wesley.

Segal, Z.V., & Dobson, K.S. (1992). Cognitive models of depression: Report from a consensus development conference. *Psychological Inquiry, 3,* 219–224.

Segraves, R.T. (1988). Psychiatric drugs and inhibited female orgasm. *Journal of Sex and Marital Therapy, 14,* 202–206.

Segraves, R.T., & Segraves, K.B. (1990). Categorical and multi-axial diagnosis of male erectile disorder. *Journal of Sex and Marital Therapy, 16,* 208–213.

Segrin, C., & Abramson, L.Y. (1994). Negative reactions to depressive behaviors: A communication theories analysis. *Journal of Abnormal Psychology, 103,* 655–668.

Seidman, B.T., Marshall, W.L., Hudson, S.M., & Robertson, P.J. (1994). An examination of intimacy and loneliness in sex offenders. *Journal of Interpersonal Violence, 9,* 518–534.

Select Committee on Children, Youth, and Families (SCCYF) of the United States House of Representatives. (1989). *U.S. children and their families: Current conditions and recent trends.* Washington, DC: U.S. Government Printing Office.

Selfe, L. (1977). *Nadia: A case of extraordinary drawing ability in an autistic child.* London: Academic Press.

Seligman, M.E.P. (1971). Phobias and preparedness. *Behavior Therapy, 2,* 307–320.

Seligman, M.E.P. (1974). Depression and learned helplessness. In R.J. Friedman & M.M. Katz (Eds.), *The psychology of depression: Contemporary theory and research,* pp. 83–113. New York: Winston-Wiley.

Seligman, M.E.P. (1975). *Helplessness: On depression, development, and death.* San Francisco: Freeman.

Seligman, M.E.P. (1995). The effectiveness of psychotherapy: The Consumer Reports study. *American Psychologist, 50,* 965–974.

Selye, H. (1936). A syndrome produced by diverse nocuous agents. *Nature, 13,* 32.

Selye, H. (1956). *The stress of life.* New York: McGraw-Hill.

Serbin, L.A., & Sprafkin, C.H. (1987). A developmental approach: Sexuality from infancy through adolescence. In J.H. Geer & W.T. O'Donohue (Eds.), pp. 163–196. *Theories of human sexuality.* New York: Plenum.

Serdula, M.K., Collins, M.E., Williamson, D.F., Anda, R.F., Pamuk, E.R., & Byers, T.E. (1993). Weight control practices of U.S. adolescents and adults. *Annals of Internal Medicine, 119,* 667–671.

Shalev, A.Y. (1996). Stress versus traumatic stress: From acute homeostatic reactions to chronic psychopathology. In B.A. van der Kolk, A.C. McFarlane, & L. Weisaeth (Eds.), *Traumatic stress,* pp. 77–101. New York: Guilford.

Shalev, A.Y., Peri, T., Caneti, L., & Schreiber, S. (1996). Predictors of PTSD in injured trauma survivors. *American Journal of Psychiatry, 53,* 219–224.

Shalev, A., & Munitz, H. (1986). Conversion without hysteria: A case report and review of the literature. *British Journal of Psychiatry, 148,* 198–203.

Shapiro, A.K., & Morris, L.A. (1978). The placebo effect in medical and psychological therapies. In S.L. Garfield & A.E. Bergin (Eds.), *Handbook of psychotherapy and behavior change,* 2nd ed., pp. 369–410. New York: Wiley.

Shapiro, D.A., & Shapiro, D. (1982). Meta-analysis of comparative psychotherapy outcome studies: A replication and refinement. *Psychological Bulletin, 92,* 581–604.

Shapiro, F. (1995). *Eye movement desensitization and reprocessing.* New York: Guilford.

Sharif, Z., Gewirtz, G., & Iqbal, N. (1993). Brain imaging in schizophrenia: A review, *Psychiatric Annals, 23,* 123–134.

Shaw, D.S., & Bell, R.Q. (1993). Developmental theories of parental contributors to antisocial behavior. *Journal of Abnormal Child Psychology, 21,* 493–518.

Shaw, D.S., & Emery, R.E. (1988). Chronic family adversity and school-age children's adjustment. *Journal of the American Academy of Child and Adolescent Psychiatry, 27,* 200–206.

Shaw, D.S., Keenan, K., & Vondra, J.I. (1994). Developmental precursors of externalizing behavior: Ages 1 to 3. *Developmental Psychology, 30,* 355–364.

Shaw, D.S., Vondra, J.I., Hommerding, K.D., Keenan, K., & Dunn, M. (1994). Chronic family adversity and early child behavior problems: A longitudinal study of low income families. *Journal of Child Psychology and Psychiatry, 35,* 1109–1122.

Shaw, D.S., & Vondra, J.I. (1995). Infant attachment security and maternal predictors of early behavior problems: A longitudinal study of low-income families. *Journal of Abnormal Child Psychology, 23,* 335–357.

Shea, M.T. (1991). Standardized approaches to individual psychotherapy of patients with borderline personality disorder. *Hospital and Community Psychiatry, 42,* 1034–1038.

Shea, M.T. (1993). Psychosocial treatment of personality disorders. *Journal of Personality Disorders,* supplement, 167–180.

Shea, M.T. (1995). Interrelationships among categories of personality disorders. In W.J. Livesley (Ed.), *The DSM-IV personality disorders,* pp. 397–406. New York: Guilford.

Shearer, D.E., & Shearer, M.S. (1976). The Portage Project: A model for early childhood intervention. In T.D. Tjossem (Ed.), *Intervention strategies for high risk infants and young children.* Baltimore: University Park Press.

Shedler, J., Mayman, M., & Manis, M. (1993). The illusion of mental health. *American Psychologist, 48,* 1117–1131.

Shenton, M.E., Kikinis, R., Jolesz, F.A., Pollak, S.D., et al. (1992). Abnormalities of the left temporal lobe and thought disorder in schizophrenia: A quantitative magnetic resonance imaging study. *New England Journal of Medicine, 327,* 604–612.

Sher, K.J. (1991). *Children of alcoholics: A critical appraisal of theory and research.* Chicago: University of Chicago Press.

Sher, K.J. (1993). Children of alcoholics and the intergenerational transmission of alcoholism: A biopsychosocial perspective. In J.S. Baer, G.A. Marlatt, & R.J. McMahon (Eds.), *Addictive behaviors across the life span: Prevention, treatment, and policy issues.* pp. 3–33. Newbury Park, CA: Sage.

Sher, K.J. (1994). There are two types of alcoholism researchers: Those who believe in two types of alcoholism and those who don't. *Addiction, 89,* 1061–1064.

Sherman, J., Factor, D.C., Swinson, R., & Darjes, R.W. (1989). The effects of fenfluramine (hydrochloride) on the behaviors of fifteen autistic children. *Journal of Autism and Developmental Disorders, 19,* 533–543.

Sherrington, R., Brynjolfsson, J., Petursson, H., Potter, M., Dudleston, K., Barraclough, B., Wasmuth, J., Cobbs, M., & Gurling, H. (1988). Localization of a susceptibility locus for schizophrenia on chromosome 5. *Nature, 336,* 164–170.

Shiffman, S., Kassel, J.D., Paty, J., Gnys, M., et al. (1994). Smoking typology profiles of chippers and regular smokers. *Journal of Substance Abuse, 6,* 21–35.

Shiffman, S., Paty, J.A., Gnys, M., Kassel, J.A., et al. (1996). *Journal of Consulting and Clinical Psychology, 64,* 366–379.

Shneidman, E.S. (1986). Some essentials of suicide and some implications for response. In A. Roy (Ed.), *Suicide.* Baltimore: Williams & Wilkins.

Shontz, F.C., & Green, P. (1992). Trends in research on the Rorschach: Review and recommendations. *Applied and Preventive Psychology, 1,* 149–156.

Short, A.B., & Schopler, E. (1988). Factors relating to age of onset in autism. *Journal of Autism and Developmental Disorders, 18,* 207–216.

Shorter, E. (1992). *From paralysis to fatigue: A history of psychosomatic illness in the modern era.* New York: Free Press.

Shoulson, I. (1990). Huntington's disease: Cognitive and psychiatric features. *Neuropsychiatry, Neuropsychology, and Behavioral Neurology, 3,* 15–22.

Shover, L.R., Friedman, J.M., Weiler, S.J., Heiman, J.R., & LoPiccolo, J. (1982). Multiaxial problem-oriented system for sexual dysfunctions. *Archives of General Psychiatry, 39,* 614–619.

Siegel, J.M., & Kuykendall, D.H. (1990). Loss, widowhood, and psychological distress among the elderly. *Journal of Consulting and Clinical Psychology, 58,* 519–524.

Siever, L.J., Bernstein, D.P., & Silverman, J.M. (1991). Schizotypal personality disorder: A review of its current status. *Journal of Personality Disorders, 5,* 178–193.

Siever, L.J., Bernstein, D.P., & Silverman, J.M. (1995). Schizotypal personality disorder. In W.J. Livesley, (Ed.), *The DSM-IV personality disorders,* pp. 71–90. New York: Guilford.

Siever, L.J., Coursey, R.D., Alterman, I.S., Zahn, T., et al. (1989). Clinical, psychophysiological, and neurological characteristics of volunteers with impaired smooth pursuit eye movements. *Biological Psychiatry, 26,* 35–51.

Siever, L.J., Friedman, L., Moskowitz, J., Mitropoulou, V., et al. (1994). Eye movement impairment and schizotypal psychopathology. *American Journal of Psychiatry, 151,* 1209–1215.

Siever, L.J., & Klar, H. (1986). A review of DSM-III criteria for the personality disorders. *Annual Review of Psychiatry, 5,* 279–290.

Siever, L., & Trestman, R.L. (1993). The serotonin system and aggressive personality disorder. *International Clinical Psychopharmacology, 8* (suppl. 2). 33–39.

Sifneos, P.E. (1987). *Short-term dynamic psychotherapy: Evaluation and technique.* New York: Plenum.

Signorielli, N. (1989). The stigma of mental illness on television. *Journal of Broadcasting and Electronic Media, 33,* 325–331.

Sigvardsson, S., Bohman, M., & Cloninger, C.R. (1996). Replication of the Stockholm adoption study of alcoholism: Confirmatory cross-fostering analysis. *Archives of General Psychiatry, 53,* 681–687.

Silove, D., Manicavasagar, V., O'Connell, D., & Blaszczynski, A. (1993). Reported early separation anxiety symptoms in patients with panic and generalized anxiety disorders. *Australian and New Zealand Journal of Psychiatry, 27,* 489–494.

Silverstone, T. (1992). New aspects in the treatment of depression. *International Clinical Psychopharmacology, 6* (suppl. 5), 41–44.

Simonoff, E., McGuffin, P., & Gottesman, I.I. (1994). Genetic influences on normal and abnormal development. In M. Rutter, E. Taylor, & L. Hersov (Eds.), *Child and adolescent psychiatry,* 3rd ed. London: Blackwell.

Simons, A.D., Angell, K.L., Monroe, S.M., & Thase, M.E. (1993). Cognition and life stress in depression: Cognitive factors and the definition, rating, and generation of negative life events. *Journal of Abnormal Psychology, 102,* 584–591.

Simons, A.D., Garfield, S.L., & Murphy, G.E. (1984). The process of change in cognitive therapy and pharmacotherapy for depression. *Archives of General Psychiatry, 41,* 45–51.

Singer, J.L. (Ed.) (1990). *Repression and dissociation.* Chicago: University of Chicago Press.

Singer, M.T., & Wynne, L.C. (1965). Thought disorder and family relations of schizophrenics. IV. Results and implications. *Archives of General Psychiatry, 12,* 201–212.

Singh, N.N., Guernsey, T.F., & Ellis, C.R. (1992). Drug therapy for persons with developmental disabilities: Legislation and litigation. *Clinical Psychology Review, 12,* 665–679.

Sizemore, C.C. (1989). *A mind of her own.* New York: Morrow.

Sizemore, C.C., & Pittillo, E.S. (1977). *I'm Eve!* New York: Doubleday.

Skinner, B.F. (1953). *Science and human behavior.* New York: Macmillan.

Skinner, B.F. (1956). A case history in scientific method. *American Psychologist, 11,* 221–234.

Skodol, A.E., Dohrenwend, B.P., Link, B.G., & Shrout, P.E. (1990). The nature of stress: Problems of measurement. In J.D. Noshpit & K.D. Coddington (Eds.), *Stressors and the adjustment disorders,* pp. 3–20. New York: Wiley.

Skodak, M., & Skeels, H. (1949). A final follow-up study of one hundred adopted children. *Journal of Genetic Psychology, 75,* 85–125.

Skoog, I., Lernfelt, B., Landahl, S., Palmertz, B., Andreasson, L., Nilsson, L., Persson, G., Oden, A., & Svanborg, A. (1996). 15-year longitudinal study of blood pressure and dementia. *Lancet, 347,* 1141–1146.

Skre, I., Onstad, S.I., Edvardsen, J., Torgersen, S., & Kringlen, E. (1994). A family study of anxiety disorders: Familial transmission and relationship to mood disorder and psychoactive substance use disorder. *Acta Psychiatrica Scandinavica, 90,* 366–374.

Slaby, A.E., & Martin, S.D. (1991). Drug and alcohol emergencies. In N.S. Miller (Ed.), *Comprehensive handbook of drug and alcohol addiction,* pp. 1003–1030. New York: Dekker.

Slade, P.D., & Bentall, R.P. (1988). *Sensory deception: A scientific analysis of hallucination.* Baltimore: Johns Hopkins University Press.

Slade, P.D., & Russell, G.F.M. (1973). Awareness of body

dimensions in anorexia nervosa and bulimia nervosa: Cross-sectional and longitudinal studies. *Psychological Medicine, 3*, 188–199.

Slater, E. (1965). Diagnosis of hysteria. *British Medical Journal, 1*, 1395–1399.

Slawson, G., & Guggenheim, H. (1984). Psychiatric malpractice: A review of the national loss experience. *American Journal of Psychiatry, 141*, 979–981.

Sleator, E.K., & Ullmann, R.K. (1981). Can the physician diagnose hyperactivity in the office? *Pediatrics, 67*, 13–17.

Sloane, R.B., Staples, F.R., Cristo, A.H., Yorkston, N.J., & Whipple, K. (1975). *Psychotherapy versus behavior therapy.* Cambridge, MA: Harvard University Press.

Sloman, L., Gardner, R., & Price, J. (1989). Biology of family systems and mood disorders. *Family Process, 28*, 387–398.

Smalley, S.L. (1996). Genetic, prenatal, and immunologic factors. *Journal of Autism and Developmental Disorders, 26*, 195–197.

Smalley, S.L., Asarnow, R.F., & Spence, M.A. (1988). Autism and genetics: A decade of research. *Archives of General Psychiatry, 45*, 953–961.

Smalley, S.L. & Collins, F. (1996). Brief report: Genetic, prenatal, and immunologic factors. *Journal of Autism and Developmental Disorders, 26*, 195–197.

Smart, R.G., & Mann, R.E. (1993). Recent liver cirrhosis declines: Estimates of the impact of alcohol abuse treatment and alcoholics anonymous. *Addiction, 88*, 193–198.

Smetana, J.G. (1989). Adolescents' and parents' reasoning about actual family conflict. *Child Development, 60*, 1052–1067.

Smith, A.L., & Weissman, M.M. (1992). Epidemiology. In E.S. Paykel (Ed.), *Handbook of affective disorders,* 2nd ed., pp. 111–130. New York: Guilford.

Smith, E. (1991). First person account: Living with schizophrenia. *Schizophrenia Bulletin, 17*, 689–691.

Smith, G., & Hall, M. (1982). Evaluating Michigan's guilty but mentally ill verdict: An empirical study. *University of Michigan Journal of Law Reform, 16*, 77–114.

Smith, G.N., Iacono, W.G., Moreau, M., Tallman, K., Beiser, M., & Flak, B. (1988). Choice of comparison group and findings of computerized tomography in schizophrenia. *British Journal of Psychiatry, 153*, 667–674.

Smith, G.R., Monson, R.A., & Ray, D.C. (1986). Psychiatric consultation in somatization disorder: A randomized controlled study. *New England Journal of Medicine, 314*, 1407–1413.

Smith, G.T., & Goldman, M.S. (1994). Alcohol expectancy theory and the identification of high-risk adolescents. *Journal of Research on Adolescence, 4*, 229–248.

Smith, G.T., Goldman, M.S., Greenbaum, P.E., & Christiansen, A. (1995). Expectancy for social facilitation from drinking: The divergent paths of high-expectancy and low-expectancy adolescents. *Journal of Abnormal Psychology, 104*, 32–40.

Smith, M.L., Glass, G.V., & Miller, T.I. (1980). *The benefits of psychotherapy.* Baltimore: Johns Hopkins University Press.

Smith, S.R., & Meyer, R.G. (1985). Child abuse reporting laws and psychotherapy: A time for reconsideration. *International Journal of Law and Psychiatry, 7*, 351–366.

Snaith, P.T., Michael, J., & Reid, R.W. (1993). Sex reassignment surgery: A study of 141 Dutch transsexuals. *British Journal of Psychiatry, 162*, 681–685.

Snaith, R.P. (1994). Psychosurgery. Controversy and enquiry. *British Journal of Psychiatry, 165*, 582–584.

Snowdon, D., Ostwald, S., & Kane, R. (1989). Education, survival, and independence in elderly Catholic sisters, 1936–1988. *American Journal of Epidemiology, 130*, 999–1012.

Soares, J.C., & Gerson, S. (1995). THA: Historical aspects, review of pharmacological properties and therapeutic effects. *Dementia, 6*, 225–234.

Sobell, L.C., Sobell, M.B., Toneatto, T., & Leo, G.I. (1993). What triggers the resolution of alcohol problems without treatment? *Alcoholism: Clinical and Experimental Research, 17*, 217–224.

Sobell, M.B., & Sobell, L.C. (1973). Alcoholics treated by individualized behavior therapy: One year treatment outcomes. *Behaviour Research and Therapy, 11*, 599–618.

Sobell, M.B., & Sobell, L.C. (1976). Second year treatment outcome of alcoholics treated by individualized behavior therapy: Results. *Behaviour Research and Therapy, 11*, 195–215.

Sobell, M.B., & Sobell, L.C. (1989). Moratorium on Maltzman: An appeal to reason. *Journal of Studies on Alcohol, 50*, 473–480.

Soloff, P.H. (1994). Is there any drug treatment of choice for the borderline patient? *Acta Psychiatrica Scandinavica, 89* (suppl. 379), 50–55.

Solomon, D.A., Keitner, G.I., Miller, I.W., Shea, M.T., et al. (1995). Course of illness and maintenance treatments for patients with bipolar disorder. *Journal of Clinical Psychiatry, 56*, 5–13.

Solomon, K., Manepalli, J., Ireland, G.A., & Mahon, G.M. (1993). Alcoholism and prescription drug abuse in the elderly: St. Louis University grand rounds. *Journal of the American Geriatrics Society, 41*, 57–69.

Solstad, K., & Hertoft, P. (1993). Frequency of sexual problems and sexual dysfunction in middle-aged Danish men. *Archives of Sexual Behavior, 22*, 51–58.

Sorensen, D.J., Paul, G.L., & Mariotto, M.J. (1988). Inconsistencies in paranoid functioning, premorbid adjustment, and chronicity: Question of diagnostic criteria. *Schizophrenia Bulletin, 14*, 323–336.

Spanos, N.P. (1986). Hypnotic behavior: A social-psychological interpretation of amnesia, analgesia, and "trance logic." *Behavior and Brain Sciences, 9*, 449–467.

Spanos, N.P. (1994). Multiple identity enactments and multiple personality disorder: A sociocognitive perspective. *Psychological Bulletin, 116*, 143–165.

Spanos, N.P., Weekes, J.R., & Betrand, L.D. (1985). Multiple personality: A social psychological perspective. *Journal of Abnormal Psychology, 94*, 362–376.

Spanos, N.P., Weekes, J.R., Menary, E., & Bertrand, L.D. (1986). Hypnotic interview and age regression procedures in the elicitation of multiple personality symptoms: A simulation study. *Psychiatry, 49*, 298–311.

Spaulding, W. (1986). Assessment of adult-onset pervasive behavior disorders. In A.R. Ciminero, K.S. Calhoun, & H.E. Adams (Eds.), *Handbook of behavioral assessment,* 2nd ed., pp. 631–669. New York: Wiley.

Spector, I.P., & Carey, M.P. (1990). Incidence and prevalence of the sexual dysfunctions: A critical review of the empirical literature. *Archives of Sexual Behavior, 19*, 389–408.

Spiegel, D., & Cardena, E. (1991). Disintegrated experience: The dissociative disorders revisited. *Journal of Abnormal Psychology, 100*, 366–378.

Spirito, A., Brown, L., Overholser, J., & Fritz, G. (1989). Attempted suicide in adolescence: A review and critique of the literature. *Clinical Psychology Review, 9*, 335–363.

Spitz, R.A. (1946). Anaclitic depression. *Psychoanalytic Study of the Child, 2*, 53–74.

Spitzer, R.L. (1985). DSM-III and the politics-science dichotomy syndrome. *American Psychologist, 40*, 522–526.

Spitzer, R.L., First, M.B., Williams, J.B.W., Kendler, K., Pincus, H.A., & Tucker, G. (1992). Now is the time to retire the term "organic mental disorders." *American Journal of Psychiatry, 149*, 240–244.

Spitzer, R.L., & Fleiss, J.L. (1974). A re-analysis of the reliability of psychiatric diagnosis. *British Journal of Psychiatry, 125*, 341–347.

Spitzer, R.L., Foreman, J., & Nee, J. (1979). DSM-III field trials. I. Initial interrater diagnostic reliability. *American Journal of Psychiatry, 136*, 815–817.

Spivack, G., & Shure, M.B. (1974). Social adjustment of young children: A cognitive approach to solving real-life problems. Washington, DC: Jossey-Bass.

Shaw, D.S., & Vondra, J.I. (1995). Infant attachment security and maternal predictors of early behavior problems: A longitudinal study of low-income families. *Journal of Abnormal Child Psychology, 23*, 335–357.

Sprague, R.L. & Sleator, E.K. (1977). Methlphenidate in hyperkinetic children: Differences in doses effects learning and social behavior. *Science, 198*, 1274–1276.

Squire, L.R. (1992). Memory and the hippocampus: A synthesis from findings with rats, monkeys, and humans. *Psychological Review, 99*, 195–231.

Squire, L.R., & Slater, P.C. (1978). Bilateral and unilateral ECT: Effects on verbal and nonverbal memory. *American Journal of Psychiatry, 135*, 1316–1320.

Squires-Wheeler, E., Skodol, A., Bassett, A., & Erlenmeyer-Kimling, L. (1989). DSM-III-R schizotypal personality traits in offspring of schizophrenic disorder, affective disorder, and normal control parents. *Journal of Psychiatric Research, 23*, 229–239.

Sroufe, L.A. (1983). Infant-caregiver attachment and patterns of adaptation in the preschool: The roots of maladaptation and competence. In M. Perlmutter (Ed.), *Minnesota Symposium in Child Psychology, 16*, 41–83.

Sroufe, L.A., & Fleeson, J. (1986). Attachment and the construction of relationships. In W.W. Hartup & Z. Rubin (Eds.), *Relationships and development,* pp. 51–72. Hillsdale, NJ: Erlbaum.

Stacy, A.W., Newcomb, M.D., & Bentler, P.W. (1991). Cognitive motivation and drug use: A 9-year longitudinal study. *Journal of Abnormal Psychology, 100*, 502–515.

Stacy, A.W., Widaman, K.F., & Marlatt, G.A. (1990). Expectancy models of alcohol use. *Journal of Personality and Social Psychology, 58*, 918–928.

Starr, P. (1982). *The social transformation of American medicine.* New York: Basic Books.

Steadman, H., Pantle, R., & Pasewark, S. (1983). Factors associated with a successful insanity defense. *American Journal of Psychiatry, 140*, 401–405.

Steele, C.M., & Josephs, R.A. (1988). Drinking your troubles away. II. An attention-allocation model of alcohol's effect on psychological stress. *Journal of Abnormal Psychology, 97*, 196–205.

Steele, C.M., & Josephs, R.A. (1990). Alcohol myopia: Its prized and dangerous effects. *American Psychologist, 45*, 921–933.

Steffenburg, S., Gillberg, C., Hellgren, L., Andersson, L., Gillberg, I., Jakobsson, G., & Bohman, M. (1989). A twin study of autism in Denmark, Finland, Iceland, Norway and Sweden. *Journal of Child Psychology and Psychiatry, 30*, 405–416.

Stein, G. (1992). Drug treatment of the personality disorders. *British Journal of Psychiatry, 161*, 167–184.

Stein, L.I. (1995). Persistent and severe mental illness: Its impact, status, and future challenges. In R. Schulz & J.R. Greenley (Eds.), *Innovating in community mental health: International perspectives,* pp. 3–17. Westport, CT: Praeger.

Stein, M.B. (Ed.) (1995). *Social phobia: Clinical and research perspectives.* Washington, DC: American Psychiatric Press.

Steinhausen, H. (1996). The course and outcome of anorexia nervosa. In K.D. Brownell & C.G. Fairburn (Eds.), *Eating disorders and obesity: A comprehensive handbook,* pp. 234–237. New York: Guilford.

Steketee, F., & Foa, E.B. (1985). Obsessive-compulsive disorder. In D.H. Barlow (Ed.), *Clinical handbook of psychological disorders,* pp. 69–144. New York: Guilford.

Steketee, G. (1993). Social support and treatment outcome of obsessive-compulsive disorder at 9-month follow-up. *Behavioral Psychotherapy, 21*, 81–95.

Steketee, G., Chambless, D.L., Tran, G.Q., Worden, H., & Gillis, M.M. (1996). Behavioral avoidance test for obsessive-compulsive disorder. *Behaviour Research and Therapy, 34*, 73–83.

Stern, Y., Gurland, B., Tatemichi, T.K., et al. (1994). Influence of education and occupation on the incidence of Alzheimer's disease. *JAMA*, 271, 1004–1010.

Stewart, J.T. (1995). Management of behavior problems in the demented patient. *American Family Physician*, 52, 231–240.

Stice, E., Schupak-Neuberg, E., Shaw, H.E., & Stein, R.I. (1994). Relation of media exposure to eating disorder symptomatology: An examination of mediating mechanisms. *Journal of Abnormal Psychology*, 103, 836–840.

Stiles, W.B., Shapiro, D.A., & Elliott, R. (1986). Are all psychotherapies equivalent? *American Psychologist*, 41, 165–180.

Still, G.F. (1902). The Coulstonian Lectures on some abnormal physical conditions in children. *Lancet*, 1, 1008–1012, 1077–1082, 1163–1168.

Stokes, P. (1993). Fluoxetine: A five-year review. *Clinical Thearpeutics*, 15, 216–243.

Stokols, D. (1992). Establishing and maintaining healthy environments: Toward a social ecology of health promotion. *American Psychologist*, 47, 6–22.

Stoller, R.J. (1975). *Perversion: The erotic form of hatred.* New York: Random House.

Stoller, R.J. (1991). *Pain and passion: A psychoanalyst explores the world of S & M.* New York: Plenum.

Stone, M. (1985). Schizotypal personality: Psychotherapeutic aspects. *Schizophrenia Bulletin*, 11, 576–589.

Stone, M.H. (1993). Long-term outcome in personality disorders. *British Journal of Psychiatry*, 162, 299–313.

Strauss, J.S. (1969). Hallucinations and delusions as points on continua function: Rating scale evidence. *Archives of General Psychiatry*, 21, 581–586.

Strauss, J.S., & Carpenter, W.T. (1978). The prognosis of schizophrenia: Rationale for a multidimensional concept. *Schizophrenia Bulletin*, 4, 56–67.

Strauss, J.S., & Carpenter, W.T., Jr. (1981). *Schizophrenia.* New York: Plenum.

Strauss, M.E. (1993). Relations of symptoms to cognitive deficits in schizophrenia. *Schizophrenia Bulletin*, 19, 215–231.

Stricker, G., & Healey, B.J. (1990). Projective assessment of object relations: A review of the empirical evidence. *Psychological Assessment*, 2, 219–230.

Striegel-Moore, R.H. (1995). A feminist perspective on the etiology of eating disorders. In K.D. Brownell & C.G. Fairburn (Eds.), *Eating disorders and obesity: A comprehensive handbook*, pp. 224–229. New York: Guilford.

Striegel-Moore, R.H., Silberstein, L.R., & Rodin, J. (1993). The social self in bulimia nervosa: Public self-consciousness, social anxiety, and perceived fraudulence. *Journal of Abnormal Psychology*, 102, 297–303.

Striegel-Moore, R.H., Silberstein, L.R., Frensch, P., & Rodin, J. (1989). A prospective study of disordered eating among college students. *International Journal of Eating Disorders*, 8, 499–509.

Strober, M. (1991). Family-genetic studies of eating disorders. *Journal of Clinical Psychiatry*, 52 (suppl.), 9–12.

Strober, M. (1995). Family-genetic perspectives on anorexia nervosa and bulimia nervosa. In K.D. Brownell & C.G. Fairburn (Eds.), *Eating disorders and obesity: A comprehensive handbook*, pp. 212–218. New York: Guilford.

Strong, S.R. (1978). Social psychological approach to psychotherapy research. In S.L. Garfield & A.E. Bergin (Eds.), *Handbook of psychotherapy and behavior change*, 2nd ed., pp. 101–136. New York: Wiley.

Strupp, H.H. (1971). *Psychotherapy and the modification of abnormal behavior.* New York: McGraw-Hill.

Strupp, H.H. (1986). Psychotherapy: Research, practice, and public policy (how to avoid dead ends). *American Psychologist*, 41, 120–130.

Stuart, F.M., Hammond, D.C., & Pett, M.A. (1987). Inhibited sexual desire in women. *Archives of Sexual Behavior*, 16, 91–106.

Styron, W. (1990). *Darkness visible: A memoir of madness.* New York: Vintage.

Sue, S., Zane, N., & Young, K. (1994). Research on psychotherapy with culturally diverse populations. In A.E. Bergin & S.L. Garfield (Eds.), *Handbook of psychotherapy and behavior change*, 4th ed., pp. 783–820. New York: Wiley.

Sullivan, K.T., & Bradbury, T.N. (1996). Preventing marital dysfunction: The primacy of secondary strategies. *Behavior Therapist*, 19, 33–36.

Sullivan, K.T., & Bradbury, T.N. (in press). Are premarital prevention programs reaching couples at risk for marital dysfunction? *Journal of Consulting and Clinical Psychology.*

Suomi, S.J. (1983). Social development in rhesus monkey: Considerations of individual differences. In A. Oliverio & M. Zapella (Eds.), *The behavior of human infants.* New York: Plenum.

Suomi, S.J., & Harlow, H.F. (1972). Social rehabilitation of isolate-reared monkeys. *Developmental Psychology*, 6, 487–496.

Susser, E., Neugebauer, R., Hoek, H.W., Brown, A.S., et al. (1996). Schizophrenia after prenatal famine: Further evidence. *Archives of General Psychiatry*, 53, 25–31.

Sussman, N., & Chou, J.C.Y. (1988). Current issues in benzodiazepine use for anxiety disorders. *Psychiatric Annals*, 18, 139–145.

Sutker, P.B., Davis, J.M., Uddo, M., & Ditta, S.R. (1995). War zone stress, personal resources, and PTSD in Persian Gulf War returnees. *Journal of Abnormal Psychology*, 104, 444–452.

Swaab, D.F., & Gofman, M.A. (1995). Sexual differentiation of the human hypothalamus in relation to gender and sexual orientation. *Trends in Neurosciences*, 18, 264–270.

Swanson, J., Holzer, C., Ganju, V., & Jono, R. (1990). Violence and psychiatric disorder in the community: Evidence from the Epidemiologic Catchment Area Surveys. *Hospital and Community Psychiatry*, 41, 761–770.

Swartz, M.S., Hughes, D., Blazer, D.G., & George, L.K. (1987). Somatization disorder in the community: A study of diagnostic concordance among three diagnostic systems. *Journal of Nervous and Mental Disorder*, 175, 26–33.

Swayze, V.W. (1995). Frontal leukotomy and related psychosurgical procedures in the era before antipsychotics. *American Journal of Psychiatry*, 152, 505–515.

Swendsen, J., Hammen, C., Heller, T., & Gitlin, M. (1995). Correlates of stress reactivity in patients with bipolar disorder. *American Journal of Psychiatry*, 152, 795–797.

Swinson, R.P., & Kuch, K. (1990). Clinical features of panic and related disorders. In J.C. Ballenger (Ed.), *Clinical aspects of panic disorder.* New York: Wiley.

Szasz, T. (1960). The myth of mental illness. *American Psychologist*, 15, 113–118.

Szasz, T. (1961). *The myth of mental illness.* New York: Harper & Row.

Szasz, T. (1963). *Law, liberty, and psychiatry: An inquiry into the social uses of mental health practices.* New York: Macmillan.

Szasz, T. (1970). *Ideology and insanity: Essays on the psychiatric dehumanization of man.* New York: Doubleday.

Szasz, T. (1971). *Psychiatric justice.* New York: Collier.

Tager-Flusberg, H. (1996). Current theory and research on language and communication in autism. *Journal of Autism and Developmental Disorders*, 26, 169–171.

Tanfer, K. (1993). National survey of men: Design and execution. *Family Planning Perspectives*, 25, 83–86.

Tannock, R., Schachar, R., & Logan, G. (1995). Methylphenidate and cognitive flexibility: Dissociated dose effects in hyperactive children. *Journal of Abnormal Child Psychology*, 23, 235–266.

Tarrier, N., & Barrowclough, C. (1995). Family interventions in schizophrenia and their long-term outcomes. *International Journal of Mental Health*, 24, 38–53.

Tarter, R.E., Alterman, A.I., & Edwards, K.L. (1985). Vulnerability to alcoholism in men: A behavior-genetic perspective. *Journal of Studies on Alcohol*, 46, 329–356.

Taylor, S., & Rachman, S.J. (1994). Klein's suffocation theory of panic. *Archives of General Psychiatry*, 51, 305–306.

Taylor, S.E. (1990). Health psychology: The science and the field. *American Psychologist*, 45, 40–50.

Taylor, S.E. (1995). *Health psychology*, 3rd ed. New York: McGraw-Hill.

Tearnan, B.H., & Telch, M.J. (1988). Etiology of agoraphobia: An investigation of perceived childhood and parental factors. *Phobia Practice and Research Journal*, 1, 13–24.

Teicher, M.H., Glod, C., & Cole, J.O. (1990). Emergence of intense suicidal preoccupation during fluoxetine treatment. *American Journal of Psychiatry*, 147, 207–210.

Telch, M.J., Brouillard, M., Telch, C.F., Agras, W.S., & Taylor, C.B. (1989). Role of cognitive appraisal in panic-related avoidance. *Behaviour Research and Therapy*, 27, 373–383.

Tellegen, A. (1985). Structures of mood and personality and their relevance to assessing anxiety, with an emphasis on self-report. In A.H. Tuma & J.D. Maser (Eds.), *Anxiety and the anxiety disorders*, pp. 681–706. Hillsdale, NJ: Erlbaum.

Tennant, C., Bebbington, P., & Hurry, J. (1980). Parental death in childhood and risk of adult depressive disorders: A review. *Psychological Medicine*, 10, 289–299.

Teplin, L. (1990). The prevalence of severe mental disorder among male urban jail detainees: Comparison with the Epidemiologic Catchment Area Program. *American Journal of Public Health*, 80, 663–669.

Teplin, L.A., Abram, K.M., & McClelland, G.M. (1994). Does psychiatric disorder predict violent crime among released jail detainees? A six-year longitudinal study. *American Psychologist*, 49, 335–342.

Teri, L., & Gallagher-Thompson, D. (1991). Cognitive-behavioral interventions for treatment of depression in Alzheimer's patients. *Gerontologist*, 31, 413–416.

Teri, L., & Wagner, A. (1992). Alzheimer's disease and depression. *Journal of Consulting and Clinical Psychology*, 60, 379–391.

Terman, M., Terman, J.S., Quitkin, F.M., et al. (1989). Light therapy for seasonal affective disorder: A review of efficacy. *Neuropsychopharmacology*, 2, 1–22.

Tesman, J.R., & Hills, A. (1994). Developmental effects of lead exposure in children. *Social Policy Report: Society for Research in Child Development*, 8 (3), 1–16.

Test, M.A., Knoedler, W.H., Allness, D.J., Burke, S.S., Brown, R.L., & Wallisch, L.S. (1991). Long-term community care through an assertive continuous treatment team. In C.A. Tamminga & S.C. Schulz (Eds.), *Schizophrenia research: Advances in neuropsychiatry and psychopharmacology*, pp. 239–246. New York: Raven Press.

Thangavelu, R., & Martin, R.L. (1995). ICD-10 and DSM-IV: Depiction of the diagnostic elephant. *Psychiatric Annals*, 25, 20–28.

Thapar, A., Gottesman, I.I., Owen, M.J., O'Donovan, M.C., & McGuffin, P. (1994). The genetics of mental retardation. *British Journal of Psychiatry*, 164, 747–758.

Thapar, A., & McGuffin, P. (1993). Is personality disorder inherited? An overview of the evidence. *Journal of Psychopathology and Behavioral Assessment*, 15, 325–345.

Thase, M. (1988). The relationship between Down syndrome and Alzheimer's disease. In L. Nadel (Ed.), *The psychobiology of Down syndrome.* Cambridge, MA: MIT Press.

Thase, M.E. (1989). Comparison between seasonal affective and other forms of recurrent depression. In N.E. Rosenthal et al. (Eds.), *Seasonal affective disorders and phototherapy*, pp. 64–78. New York: Guilford.

Thigpen, C.H., & Cleckley, H.M. (1957). *The three faces of Eve.* New York: McGraw-Hill.

Thomas, A., & Chess, S. (1977). *Temperament and development.* New York: Brunner/Mazel.

Thompson, J.K. (1996). *Body image, eating disorders, and obesity.* Washington, DC: American Psychological Association.

Thompson, P.A., & Meltzer, H.Y. (1993). Positive, negative, and disorganisation factors from the Schedule for Affective Disorders and Schizophrenia and the Present State Examination: A three-factor solution. *British Journal of Psychiatry, 163,* 344–351.

Thornicroft, G., & Sartorius, N. (1993). The course and outcome of depression in different cultures: 10-year follow-up of the WHO Collaborative Study on the Assessment of Depressive Disorders. *Psychological Medicine, 23,* 1023–1032.

Thoresen, C.E., & Powell, L.H. (1992). Type A behavior pattern: New perspectives on theory, assessment, and intervention. *Journal of Consulting and Clinical Psychology, 60,* 595–604.

Thorley, G. (1984). Review of follow-up and follow-back studies of childhood hyperactivity. *Psychological Bulletin, 96,* 116–132.

Ticehurst, S. (1990). Alcohol and the elderly. *Australian and New Zealand Journal of Psychiatry, 24,* 252–260.

Tiefer, L. (1988). A feminist critique of the sexual dysfunction nomenclature. *Women and Therapy, 7,* 5–21.

Tienari, P., Sorri, A., Lahti, I., et al. (1987). Genetic and psychosocial factors in schizophrenia: The Finnish adoptive family study. *Schizophrenia Bulletin, 13,* 477–484.

Tienari, P., Wynne, L.C., Moring, J., Lahti, I., et al. (1994). The Finnish Adoptive Family Study of Schizophrenia: Implications for family research. *British Journal of Psychiatry, 164* (suppl. 23), 20–26.

Tiffany, S.T., & Baker, T.B. (1986). Tolerance to alcohol: Psychological models and their application to alcoholism. *Annals of Behavioral Medicine, 8,* 7–12.

Tison, F., Dartigues, J.F., Auriacombe, S., Letenneur, L., et al. (1995). Dementia in Parkinson's disease: A population-based study in ambulatory and institutionalized individuals. *Neurology, 45,* 705–708.

Tollefson, G.D. (1991). Anxiety and alcoholism: A serotonin link. *British Journal of Psychiatry, 159* (suppl. 12), 34–39.

Torgersen, S. (1985). Relationship of schizotypal personality disorder to schizophrenia: Genetics. *Schizophrenia Bulletin, 11,* 554–563.

Torgersen, S. (1986). Genetic factors in moderately severe and mild affective disorders. *Archives of General Psychiatry, 43,* 222–226.

Torgersen, S. (1988). Genetics. In C.G. Last & M. Hersen (Eds.), *Handbook of anxiety disorders.* New York: Pergamon.

Torgersen, S. (1994). Genetics in borderline conditions. *Acta Psychiatrica Scandinavica, 89* (suppl. 379), 19–25.

Torgersen, S., Onstad, S., Skre, I., Edvardsen, J., & Kringlen, E. (1993). "True" schizotypal personality disorder: A study of co-twins and relatives of schizophrenic probands. *American Journal of Psychiatry, 150,* 1661–1667.

Torrey, E.F. (1988). *Nowhere to go: The tragic odyssey of the homeless mentally ill.* New York: Harper & Row.

Torrey, E.F. (1997). *Out of the shadows.* New York: Wiley.

Torrey, E.F., Bowler, A.E., Taylor, E.H., & Gottesman, I.I. (1994). *Schizophrenia and manic-depressive disorder: The biological roots of mental illness as revealed by the landmark study of identical twins.* New York: Basic Books.

Torrey, E.F., & Yolken, R.H. (1995). Could schizophrenia be a viral zoonosis transmitted from house cats? *Schizophrenia Bulletin, 21,* 167–171.

Trachtenberg, M.C., & Blum, K. (1987). Alcohol and opioid peptides: Neuropharmacological rationale for physical craving of alcohol. *American Journal of Drug and Alcohol Abuse, 13,* 365–372.

Tran, G.Q., & Chambless, D.L. (1995). Psychopathology of social phobia: Effects of subtype and of avoidant personality disorder. *Journal of Anxiety Disorders, 9,* 489–501.

Travis, R. (1990). Halbwachs and Durkheim: A test of two theories of suicide. *British Journal of Sociology, 41,* 225–243.

Treffert, D.A. (1988). The idiot savant: A review of the syndrome. *American Journal of Psychiatry, 145,* 563–572.

Trials of the Hypertension Prevention Collaborative Research Group. (1992). The effects of nonpharmacologic interventions on blood pressure of persons with high normal levels: Results of the Trials of Hypertension Prevention, Phase I, *JAMA, 267,* 1213–1220.

Triandis, H.C. (1994). Culture and social behavior. In W.J. Lonner & R.S. Malpass (Eds.), *Psychology and culture,* pp. 169–174. Boston: Allyn & Bacon.

Truax, C., & Carkhuff, R. (1967). *Toward effective counseling and psychotherapy: Training and practice.* Hawthorne, NY: Aldine.

True, W.R., Rice, J., Eisen, S.A., Heath, A.C., Goldberg, J., Lyons, M.J., & Nowak, J. (1993). A twin study of genetic and environmental contributions to liability for posttraumatic stress symptoms. *Archives of General Psychiatry, 50,* 257–264.

Trull, T.J. (1995). Borderline personality disorder features in nonclinical young adults. 1. Identification and validation. *Psychological Assessment, 7,* 33–41.

Trull, T.J., Widiger, T.A., & Guthrie, P. (1990). Categorical versus dimensional status of borderline personality disorder. *Journal of Abnormal Psychology, 99,* 40–48.

Trzepacz, P.T. (1994). The neuropathogenesis of delirium: A need to focus our research. *Psychosomatics, 35,* 374–391.

Tsai, L.Y. (1996). Comorbid psychiatric disorders of autistic disorder. *Journal of Autism and Developmental Disorders, 26,* 159–163.

Tsuang, M.T., Simpson, J.C., & Fleming, J.A. (1992). Epidemiology of suicide, *International Review of Psychiatry, 4,* 117–129.

Tsuang, M.T., Woolson, R.F., & Fleming, J.A. (1979). Long-term outcome of major psychoses. I. Schizophrenia and affective disorders compared with psychiatrically symptom-free surgical conditions. *Archives of General Psychiatry, 36,* 1295–1301.

Tueth, M.J., & Cheong, J.A. (1993). Delirium: Diagnosis and treatment in the older patient. *Geriatrics, 48,* 75–81.

Turkat, I.D., & Carlson, C.R. (1984). Data-based versus symptomatic formulation of treatment: The case of a dependent personality. *Journal of Behavior Therapy and Experimental Psychiatry, 15,* 153–160.

Turkheimer, E. (1991). Individual and group differences in adoption studies of IQ. *Psychological Bulletin, 110,* 392–405.

Turner, R.J., & Wagonfield, M.O. (1967). Occupational mobility and schizophrenia: An assessment of the social causation and social selection hypotheses. *American Sociological Review, 32,* 104–113.

Turner, S.M., & Beidel, D.C. (1988). *Treating obsessive-compulsive disorder.* New York: Pergamon.

Turner, S.M., Beidel, D.C., & Stanley, M.A. (1992). Are obsessional thoughts and worry different cognitive phenomena? *Clinical Psychology Review, 12,* 257–270.

Turpin, G. (1991). The psychophysiological assessment of anxiety disorders: Three-systems measurement and beyond. *Psychological Assessment, 3,* 366–375.

Tyrer, P. (1989). Choice of treatment in anxiety. In P. Tyrer (Ed.), *Psychopharmacology of anxiety.* New York: Oxford University Press.

Tyrer, P. (1994). What are the borders of borderline personality disorder? *Acta Psychiatrica Scandinavica, 89* (suppl. 379), 38–44.

Tyrer, P. (1995). Are personality disorders well classified in DSM-IV? In W.J. Livesley (Ed.), *The DSM-IV personality disorders.* New York: Guilford, pp. 29–42.

Tyrer, P., Candy, J., & Kelly, D. (1973). A study of the clinical effects of phenelzine and placebo in the treatment of phobic anxiety. *Psychopharmacology, 32,* 237–254.

Tyrer, P., Casey, P., & Gall, J. (1983). Relationship between neurosis and personality disorder. *British Journal of Psychiatry, 142,* 404–408.

Tyrer, P., & Ferguson, B. (1987). Problems in the classification of personality disorder. *Psychological Medicine, 17,* 15–20.

Tyrer, P., Seivewright, N., Ferguson, B., Murphy, S., Darling, C., Brothwell, J., Kingdon, D., & Johnson, A.L. (1990). The Nottingham Study of Neurotic Disorder: Relationship between personality status and symptoms. *Psychological Medicine, 20,* 423–431.

Uchino, B.N., Cacioppo, J.T., & Kiecolt-Glaser, J.K. (1996). The relationship between social support and physiological processes: A review with emphasis underlying mechanisms and implications for health. *Psychological Bulletin, 119,* 488–531.

U.S. Census Bureau. (1986). Age structure of the U.S. population in the 21st century. *Statistical Brief 1–86.* Washington, DC: U.S. Government Printing Office.

U.S. Census Bureau. (1992). Growth of America's oldest-old population. *Profiles of America's Elderly, No. 2.* Washington, DC: U.S. Government Printing Office.

U.S. Census Bureau. (1996). Sixty-five plus in the United States. *Current Population Reports.* (P23–190). Washington, DC: U.S. Government Printing Office.

U.S. Department of Health and Human Services. (1993). *AIDS research: An NIMH blueprint for the second decade.* NIH Publication No. 93–3563. Washington, DC: U.S. Government Printing Office.

Umbricht, D., & Kane, J.M. (1995). Risperidone: Efficacy and safety. *Schizophrenia Bulletin, 21,* 593–606.

Vaillant, G.E. (1984). The disadvantages of DSM-III outweigh its advantages. *American Journal of Psychiatry, 141,* 542–545.

Vaillant, G.E. (1992). Is there a natural history of addiction? In C.P. O'Brien & J.H. Jaffe (Eds.), *Addictive states,* pp. 41–58. New York: Raven Press.

Vaillant, G.E. (1994). Evidence that the Type 1/Type 2 dichotomy in alcoholism must be re-examined. *Addiction, 89,* 1049–1057.

Vaillant, G.E. (1995). *The natural history of alcoholism revisited.* Cambridge, MA: Harvard University Press.

Vaillant, G.E. (1996). A long-term follow-up of male alcohol abuse. *Arhives of General Psychiatry, 53,* 243–249.

Valenstein, E.S. (1973). *Brain control.* New York: Wiley.

Valenstein, E.S. (1986). *Great and desperate cures.* New York: Basic Books.

Valente, J. (1996). A long road to daylight: Football player's gambling problems. *People Weekly,* January 15, 81+.

Vandereycken, W. (1995). The families of patients with an eating disorder. In K.D. Brownell & C.G. Fairburn (Eds.), *Eating disorders and obesity: A comprehensive handbook* (pp. 219–223). New York: Guilford.

van der Hart, O., & Friedman, B. (1989). A reader's guide to dissociation: A neglected intellectual heritage. *Dissociation, 2,* 13–16.

van der Kolk, B.A. (1996). The psychobiology of PTSD. In B.A. van der Kolk, A.C. McFarlane, & L. Weisaeth (Eds.), *Traumatic stress,* pp. 214–241. New York: Guilford.

van der Kolk, B.A., Boyd, H., Krystal, J., & Greenburg, M. (1984). Posttraumatic stress disorder as a biologically based disorder: Implications of the animal model of inescapable shock. In B.A. van der Kolk (Ed.), *Posttraumatic stress disorder: Psychological and biological sequel,* pp. 124–134. Washington, DC: American Psychiatric Press.

van der Kolk, B.A., & McFarlane, A.C. (1996). The black hole of trauma. In B.A. van der Kolk, A.C. McFarlane,

& L. Weisaeth (Eds.), *Traumatic stress*, pp. 3–23. New York: Guilford.

Van der Molen, G.M., Van den Hout, M.A., Van Dieren, A.C., & Griez, E. (1989). Childhood separation anxiety and adult onset panic disorders. *Journal of Anxiety Disorders, 3*, 97–106.

Van Horn, J.D., Berman, K.F., & Weinberger, D.R. (1996). Pathophysiology of schizophrenia: Insights from neuroimaging. In S.J. Watson (Ed)., *Biology of schizophrenia and affective disease*, pp. 393–419. Washington, DC: American Psychiatric Press.

Vasey, M.W., & Borkovec, T.D. (1992). A catastrophizing assessment of worrisome thoughts. *Cognitive Therapy and Research, 16*, 505–520.

Vaughn, C.E., & Leff, J.P. (1976). The influence of family and social factors on the course of psychiatric illness: A comparison of schizophrenic and depressed neurotic patients. *British Journal of Psychiatry, 129*, 125–137.

Verebey, K. (1991). Laboratory methodology for drug and alcohol addiction. In N.S. Miller (Ed.), *Comprehensive handbook of drug and alcohol addiction*, pp. 809–824. New York: Dekker.

Visintainer, M.A., Seligman, M.E.P., & Volpicelli, J.R. (1982). Tumor rejection in rats after inescapable or escapable electric shock. *Science, 216*, 437–439.

Vogel-Sprott, M. (1992). *Alcohol tolerance and social drinking: Learning the consequences*. New York: Guilford.

Vogler, G.P., Gottesman, I.I., McGue, M.K., & Rao, D.C. (1990). Mixed model segregation analysis of schizophrenia in the Lindelius Swedish pedigrees. *Behavior Genetics, 20*, 461–472.

Volkmar, F.R. (1996). Diagnostic issues in autism. Results of the DSM-IV field. *Journal of Autism and Developmental Disorders, 26*, 155–157.

Volkmar, F.R., Klin, A., Siegel, B., et al. (1994). Field trial for autistic disorder in DSM-IV. *American Journal of Psychiatry, 151*, 1361–1367.

von Bertalanffy, L. (1968). *General systems theory*. New York: Braziller.

Von Korff, M., Eaton, W., Keyl, P. (1985). The epidemiology of panic attacks and disorder: Results from three community surveys. *American Journal of Epidemiology, 122*, 970–981.

Vuchinich, S., Emery, R.E., & Cassidy, J. (1988). Family members as third parties in dyadic family conflict: Strategies, alliances, and outcomes. *Child Development, 59*, 1293–1302.

Wagner, W., Zaborny, B.A., & Gray, T.E. (1994). Fluvoxamine: A review of its safety profile in worldwide studies. *International Clinical Psychopharmacology, 9*, 223–227.

Wakefield, J. (1988). Female primary orgasmic dysfunction: Masters and Johnson versus DSM-III-R on diagnosis and incidence. *Journal of Sex Research, 24*, 363–377.

Wakefield, J.C. (1992a). The concept of mental disorder: On the boundary between biological facts and social values. *American Psychologist, 47*, 373–388.

Wakefield, J.C. (1992b). Disorder as harmful dysfunction: A conceptual critique of DSM-III-R's definition of mental disorder. *Psychological Review, 99*, 232–247.

Wald, M.S., Carlsmith, J.M., & Leiderman, P.H. (1988). *Protecting abused and neglected children*. Stanford, CA: Stanford University Press.

Walker, E., Davis, D., & Baum, K. (1993). Social withdrawal. In C.G. Costello (Ed.), *Symptoms of schizophrenia*. pp. 227–260. New York: Wiley.

Walker, L. (1979). *The battered woman*. New York: Harper & Row.

Walker, L. (1989). Psychology and violence against women. *American Psychologist, 44*, 695–702.

Wall, T.L., Thomasson, H.R., Schuckit, M.A., & Ehlers, C.L. (1992). Subjective feelings of alcohol intoxication in Asians with genetic variations in ALDH2 alleles. *Alcoholism: Clinical and Experimental Research, 16*, 991–993.

Wall Street Journal. (1996, January 31). Lilly sales rise as use of Prozac keeps growing.

Wallis, C.J., Rezazadeh, S.M., & Lal, H. (1993). Role of serotonin in ethanol abuse. *Drug Development and Research, 30*, 178–188.

Walsh, B.T. (1995). Pharmacotherapy of eating disorders. In K.D. Brownell & C.G. Fairburn (Eds.), *Eating disorders and obesity: A comprehensive handbook*, pp. 313–317. New York: Guilford.

Walsh, D.C., Hingson, R.W., Merrigan, D.M., et al. (1991). A randomized trial of treatment options for alcohol abusing workers. *New England Journal of medicine, 325*, 775–782.

Walsh, J. (1990). Assessment and treatment of the schizotypal personality disorder. *Journal of Independent Social Work, 4*, 41–59.

Warheight, G.J., & Auth, J.B. (1985). Epidemiology of alcohol abuse in adulthood. In J.O. Cavendar (Ed.), *Psychiatry*, Vol. 3, pp. 1–18. Philadelphia: Lippincott.

Warner, L.A., Kessler, R.C., Hughes, M., Anthony, J.C., & Nelson, C.B. (1995). Prevalence and correlates of drug use and dependence in the United States: Results from the National Comorbidity Survey. *Archives of General Psychiatry, 52*, 219–228.

Warner, P., & Bancroft, J. (1986). Sex therapy outcome research: A reappraisal of methodology. 2. Methodological considerations—The importance of prognostic variability. *Psychological Medicine, 16*, 855–863.

Warren, S.T., & Ashley, C.T. (1995). Triplet repeat expansion mutations: The example of fragile X syndrome. *Annual Review of Neuroscience, 18*, 77–99.

Waterman, A.S., & Archer, S. (1990). A life-span perspective on identity formation: Development in form, function, and process. In P.B. Baltes, D.L. Featherman, & R.M. Lerner (Eds.), *Life-span development and behavior*, Vol. 10, pp. 29–57. Hillsdale, NJ: Erlbaum.

Waterman, A.S., & Goldman, J.A. (1976). A longitudinal study of changes in ego identity development at a liberal arts college. *Journal of Youth and Adolescence, 5*, 361–370.

Waterman, G., Geary, P., & Waterman, C. (1974). Longitudinal study of changes in ego identity status from the freshman to the senior year at college. *Developmental Psychology, 10*, 387–392.

Waters, E., Hay, D., & Richters, J. (1986). Infant-parent attachment and the origins of prosocial and antisocial behavior. In D. Olweus, J. Block, & M. Radke-Yarrow (Eds.), *Development of antisocial and prosocial behavior: Research, theories, and issues*, pp. 97–126. Orlando, FL: Academic Press.

Watkins, J.G. (1984). The Bianchi (L.A. Hillsdale Strangler) case: Sociopath or multiple personality. *International Journal of Clinical and Experimental Hypnosis, 32*, 67–101.

Watson, D., & Clark, L.A. (1984). Negative affectivity: The disposition to experience aversive emotional states. *Psychological Bulletin, 96*, 465–490.

Watson, D., & Clark, L.A. (1990). *The Positive and Negative Affect Schedule-Expanded Form*. Unpublished manuscript. Southern Methodist University.

Watson, D., Clark, L.A., & Harkness, A.R. (1994). Structures of personality and their relevance to psychopathology. *Journal of Abnormal Psychology, 103*, 18–31.

Watson, D., Clark, L.A., Weber, K., Assenheimer, J.S., Strauss, M.E., & McCormick, R.A. (1995a). Testing a tripartite model. II. Exploring the symptom structure of anxiety and depression in student, adult, and patient samples. *Journal of Abnormal Psychology, 104*, 15–25.

Watson, I.P.B., Hoffman, L., & Wilson, G.V. (1988). The neuropsychiatry of post-traumatic stress disorder. *British Journal of Psychiatry, 152*, 164–173.

Watson, J.B. (1913). Psychology as the behaviorist views it. *Psychological Review, 20*, 158–177.

Watson, D., Weber, K., Assenheimer, J.S., Clark, L.A., Strauss, M.E., & McCormick, R.A. (1995b). Testing a tripartite model. I. Evaluating the convergent and discriminant validity of anxiety and depression symptom scales. *Journal of Abnormal Psychology, 104*, 3–14.

Watson, J.B., & Rayner, R. (1920). Conditioned emotional reactions. *Journal of Experimental Psychology, 3*, 1–14.

Watt, L.M., & Wong, P.T. (1991). A taxonomy of reminiscence and therapeutic implications. *Journal of Gerontological Social Work, 16*, 37–57.

Watt, N.F. (1984). In a nutshell: The first two decades of high-risk research in schizophrenia. In N.F. Watt, E.J. Anthony, L.C. Wynne, J.E. Rolf (Eds.), *Children at risk for schizophrenia: A longitudinal perspective*. Cambridge: Cambridge University Press.

Watt, N.F., Anthony, E.J., Wynne, L.C., & Rolf, J.E. (Eds.) (1984). *Children at risk for schizophrenia: A longitudinal perspective*. Cambridge: Cambridge University Press.

Weaver, T.L., & Clum, G.A. (1993). Early family environments and traumatic experiences associated with borderline personality disorders. *Journal of Consulting and Clinical Psychology, 61*, 1068–1075.

Weddington, W.W. (1992). Use of pharmacologic agents in the treatment of addiction, *Psychiatric Annals, 22*, 425–429.

Wegner, D.M. (1989). *White bears and other unwanted thoughts: Suppression, obsession, and the psychology of mental control*. New York: Viking.

Wegner, D.M. (1994). Ironic processes of mental control. *Psychological Review, 101*, 34–52.

Wegner, D.M., Shortt, J.W., Blake, A.W., & Page, M.S. (1990). The suppression of exciting thoughts. *Journal of Personality and Social Psychology, 58*, 409–418.

Wehr, T.A. (1989). Seasonal affective disorder: A historical overview. In Rosenthal, N.E. & Blehar, M.C. (Eds.), *Seasonal affective disorders and phototherapy*. New York: Guilford.

Weiden, P.J., & Olfson, M. (1995). Cost of relapse in schizophrenia. *Schizophrenia Bulletin, 21*, 419–429.

Weinberger, D.R. (1987). Implications of normal brain development for the pathogenesis of schizophrenia. *Archives of General Psychiatry, 44*, 660–669.

Weinberger, D.R., Berman, K.F., Suddath, R., & Torrey, E.F. (1992). Evidence of dysfunction of a prefrontal-limbic network in schizophrenia: A magnetic resonance imaging and regional cerebral blood flow study of discordant monozygotic twins. *American Journal of Psychiatry, 149*, 890–897.

Weinberger, D.R., & Lipska, B.K. (1995). Cortical maldevelopment, antipsychotic drugs, and schizophrenia: A search for common ground. *Schizophrenia Research, 16*, 87–110.

Weiner, H., & Fawzy, F.I. (1989). An integrative model of health, disease, and illness. In S. Cheren (Ed.), *Psychosomatic medicine: Theory, physiology, and practice*, Vol. 1, pp. 9–44. Madison, CT: International Universities Press.

Weiner, R.D., & Krystal, A.D. (1994). The present use of electroconvulsive therapy. *Annual Review of Medicine, 45*, 273–281.

Weinstein, R.M. (1983). Labeling theory and the attitudes of mental patients: A review. *Journal of Health and Social Behavior, 24*, 70–84.

Weishaar, M.E., & Beck, A.T. (1992). Hopelessness and suicide. *International Review of Psychiatry, 4*, 177–184.

Weiss, G., Hechtman, L., Milroy, T., & Perlman, T. (1985). Psychiatric status of hyperactives as adults: A controlled prospective 15-year follow-up of 63 hyperactive children. *Journal of the American Academy of Child Psychiatry, 24*, 211–220.

Weiss, J.M., & Simson, P.G. (1985). Neurochemical basis of stress-induced depression. *Psychopharmacology Bulletin, 21*, 447–457.

Weissman, J. (1988). Anxiety and alcoholism. *Journal of Clinical Psychiatry, 49* (suppl.), 17–19.

Weissman, M., Meyers, J., & Harding, P. (1978). Psychiatric disorders in a U.S. urban community: 1975–1976. *American Journal of Psychiatry*, 135, 459–462.

Weissman, M.M. (1988). Epidemiology of panic disorder and agoraphobia. In A.J. Francis & R.E. Hales (Eds.), *Annual review of psychiatry*, vol. 7. Washington, DC: American Psychiatric Press.

Weissman, M.M. (1993). The epidemiology of personality disorders: A 1990 update. *Journal of Personality Disorders*, supplement, 44–62.

Weissman, M.M., Bruce, M.L., Leaf, P.J., Florio, L.P., & Holzer, C. (1991). Affective disorders. In L.N. Robins & D.A. Regier (Eds.), *Psychiatric disorders in America: The Epidemiologic Catchment Area Study*, pp. 53–80. New York: Free Press.

Weithorn, L.A. (1988). Mental hospitalization of troublesome youth: An analysis of skyrocketing admission rates. *Stanford Law Review*, 40, 773–838.

Welch, S.L., & Fairburn, C.G. (in press). Sexual abuse and bulimia nervosa: Three integrated case control comparisons. *American Journal of Psychiatry*.

Wenzlaff, R.M., Wegner, D.M., & Klein, S.B. (1991). The role of thought suppression in the bonding of thought and mood. *Journal of Personality and Social Psychology*, 60, 500–508.

Werner, J.S., & Smith, R.S. (1982). *Vulnerable but invincible: A longitudinal study of resilient children and youth*. New York: McGraw-Hill.

Werner, E.E., & Smith, R.S. (1992). *Overcoming the odds: High risk children from birth to adulthood*. Ithaca, NY: Cornell.

Wertheimer, J. (1991). Affective disorders and organic mental disorders. *International Psychogeriatrics*, 3, 19–27.

Westermeyer, J. (1987). Cultural factors in clinical assessment. *Journal of Consulting and Clinical Psychology*, 55, 471–478.

Westling, B.E., & Ost, L. (1993). Relationship between panic attack symptoms and cognitions in panic disorder patients. *Journal of Anxiety Disorders*, 7, 181–194.

Weston, D., Ludolph, P., Misle, B., Ruffins, S., & Block, J. (1990). Physical and sexual abuse in adolescent girls with borderline personality disorder. *American Journal of Orthopsychiatry*, 60, 55–66.

Whalen, C., Henker, B., Hinshaw, S., Heller, T., & Huber-Dressler, A. (1991). Messages of medication: Effects of actual versus informed medication status on hyperactive boys's expectancies and self-evaluation. *Journal of Consulting and Clinical Psychology*, 59, 602–606.

Whalen, R.E., Geary, D.C., & Johnson, F. (1990). Models of sexuality. In D.P. McWhirter, S.A. Sanders, & J.M. Reinisch (Eds.), *Homosexuality/heterosexuality: Concepts of sexual orientation*, pp. 61–70. New York: Oxford University Press.

Whybrow, P.C., Akiskal, H.S., & McKinney, W.T., Jr. (1984). *Mood disorders: Toward a new psychobiology*. New York: Plenum.

Wicks-Nelson, R., & Israel, A.C. (1991). *Behavior disorders of childhood*, 2nd ed. Englewood Cliffs, NJ: Prentice Hall.

Widiger, T.A. (1993). The DSM-III-R categorical personality disorder diagnoses: A critique and an alternative. *Psychological Inquiry*, 4, 75–90.

Widiger, T.A. (1994). *DSM-IV sourcebook*, vol. 1. Washington, DC: American Psychiatric Press.

Widiger, T.A., Cadoret, R., Hare, R., Robins, L., et al. (1996). DSM-IV antisocial personality disorder field trial. *Journal of Abnormal Psychology*, 105, 3–16.

Widiger, T.A., & Corbitt, E.M. (1995). Antisocial personality disorder. In W.J. Livesley (Ed.), *The DSM-IV personality disorders*, pp. 103–126. New York: Guilford.

Widiger, T.A., & Costa, P.T., Jr. (1994). Personality and personality disorders. *Journal of Abnormal Psychology*, 103, 78–91.

Widiger, T.A., & Frances, A. (1985). The DSM-III personality disorders: Perspectives from psychology. *Archives of General Psychiatry*, 42, 615–623.

Widiger, T.A., & Frances, A. (1987). Interviews and inventories for the measurement of personality disorders. *Clinical Psychology Review*, 7, 49–75.

Widiger, T.A., Frances, A.J., Pincus, H.A., Davis, W.W., & First, M.B. (1991). Toward an empirical classification for the DSM-IV. *Journal of Abnormal Psychology*, 100, 280–288.

Widiger, T.A., Frances, A., Warner, L., & Bluhm, C. (1986). Diagnostic criteria for the borderline and schizotypal personality disorders. *Journal of Abnormal Psychology*, 95, 43–51.

Widiger, T.A., & Rogers, J.H. (1989). Prevalence and comorbidity of personality disorders. *Psychiatric Annals*, 19, 132–136.

Widiger, T.A., & Trull, T.J. (1992). Personality and psychopathology: An application of the five-factor model. *Journal of Personality*, 60, 363–393.

Widiger, T.A., & Trull, T.J. (1993). Borderline and narcissistic personality disorders. In P.B. Sutker & H.E. Adams (Eds.), *Comprehensive handbook of psychopathology*, 2nd ed., pp. 371–394. New York: Plenum.

Wiehe, V.R., & Richards, A.L. (1995). *Intimate betrayal: Understanding and responding to the trauma of acquaintance rape*. Thousand Oaks, CA: Sage.

Wierzbicki, M. (1993). *Issues in clinical psychology: Subjective versus objective approaches*. Boston: Allyn & Bacon.

Wiggins, J.S. (1973). *Personality and prediction: Principles of personality assessment*. Reading, MA: Addison-Wesley.

Wiggins, J.S. (1982). Circumplex models of interpersonal behavior in clinical psychology. In P.C. Kendall & J.N. Butcher (Eds.), *Handbook of research methods in clinical psychology*, pp. 183–221. New York: Wiley.

Wiggins, J.S., & Pincus, A.L. (1992). Personality: Structure and assessment. *Annual Review of Psychology*, 43, 473–504.

Wilfley, D.E., Agras, W.S., Telch, C.F., Rossiter, E.M., Schneider, J.A., Cole, A.G., Sifford, L., & Raeburn, S.D. (1993). Group cognitive-behavioral therapy and group interpersonal psychotherapy for the nonpurging bulimic individual: A controlled comparison. *Journal of Consulting and Clinical Psychology*, 61, 296–305.

Willerman, L. (1973). Activity level and hyperactivity in twins. *Child Development*, 44, 288–293.

Williams, J.B.W. (1985). The multiaxial system of DSM-III: Where did it come from and where should it go? *Archives of General Psychiatry*, 42, 175–180.

Williams, J.B.W., Gibbon, M., First, M.B., Spitzer, R.L., Davies, M., Borus, J., Howes, J.M., Kane, J., Pope, H.G., Rounsaville, B., & Wittchen, H. (1992). The structured clinical interview for DSM-III-R (SCID). II. Multisite test-retest reliability. *Archives of General Psychiatry*, 49, 630–636.

Williams, J.M.B., Mathews, A., & MacLeod, C. (1996). The emotional stroop task and psychopathology. *Psychological Bulletin*, 120, 3–24.

Williams, L.M. (1994). Recall of childhood trauma: A prospective study of women's memories of child sexual abuse. *Journal of Consulting and Clinical Psychology*, 62, 1167–1176.

Williams, L.M., & Finkelhor, D. (1990). The characteristics of incestuous fathers: A review of recent studies. In W.L. Marshall, D.R. Laws, & H.E. Barbaree (Eds.), *Handbook of sexual assault: Issues, theories, and treatment of the offender*, p. 231. New York: Plenum.

Williams, R.B., Barefoot, J.C., Califf, R.M., Haney, T.L., Saunders, W.B., et al. (1992). Prognostic importance of social and economic resources among medically treated patients with angiographically documented coronary artery disease. *Journal of the American Medical Association*, 267, 520–524.

Wilsnack, S.C. (1984). Drinking, sexuality and sexual dysfunction in women. In S.C. Wilsnack & L.J. Beckman (Eds.), *Alcohol problems in women*, pp. 189–227. New York: Guilford.

Wilsnack, S.C., & Wilsnack, R.W. (1991). Epidemiology of women's drinking. *Journal of Substance Abuse*, 3, 133–158.

Wilson, G.D. (1987). An ethological approach to sexual deviation. In G.D. Wilson (Ed.), *Variant sexuality: Research and theory*, pp. 84–115. London: Croom Helm.

Wilson, G.T. (1995). Empirically validated treatments as a basis for clinical practice: Problems and prospects. In S.C. Hayes, V.M. Follette, R.M. Dawes, and K.E. Grady (Eds.), *Scientific standards of psychological practice: Issues and recommendations*. Reno, NV: Context Press, pp. 163–196.

Wilson, M. (1989). The black extended family: An analytical review. *Developmental Psychology*, 22, 246–258.

Wilson, T.D., & Linville, P.W. (1982). Improving the academic performance of college freshmen: Attribution therapy revisited. *Journal of Personality and Social Psychology*, 42, 367–376.

Wincze, J.P. (1989). Assessment and treatment of atypical sexual behavior. In S.R. Lieblum & R.C. Rosen (Eds.), *Principles and practice of sex therapy*, 2nd ed. pp. 382–404. New York: Guilford.

Wincze, J.P., & Carey, M.P. (1991). *Sexual dysfunction: A guide for assessment and treatment*. New York: Guilford.

Wing, L. (1988). Autism: Possible clues to the underlying pathology. 1. Clinical facts. In L. Wing (Ed.), *Aspects of autism: Biological research*, pp. 11–18. Gaskell: London.

Wing, L., & Gould, H.J. (1979). Severe impairments of social interaction and associate abnormalities in children: Epidemiology and classification. *Journal of Autism and Developmental Disorders*, 9, 11–29.

Winger, G., Hofmann, F.G., & Woods, J.H. (1992). *A handbook on drug and alcohol abuse: The biomedical aspects*, 3rd ed. New York: Oxford University Press.

Winograd, E., & Killinger, W.A. (1983). Relating age at encoding in early childhood to adult recall: Development of flashbulb memories. *Journal of Experimental Psychology: General*, 112, 413–422.

Winokur, G., Coryell, W., Akiskal, H.S., Endicott, J., Keller, M., & Mueller, T. (1994). Manic-depressive (bipolar) disorder: The course in light of a prospective ten-year follow-up of 131 patients. *Acta Psychiatrica Scandinavica*, 89, 102–110.

Winokur, G., Coryell, W., Keller, M., Endicott, J., & Leon, A. (1995). A family study of manic-depressive (bipolar I) disease. *Archives of General Psychiatry*, 52, 367–373.

Winokur, G., Zimmerman, M., & Cadoret, R. (1988). 'Cause the Bible tells me so. *Archives of General Psychiatry*, 45, 683–684.

Wise, M.G., & Gray, K.F. (1996). Delirium, dementia and amnestic disorders. In R.E. Hales & S.C. Yudofsky (Eds.), *The American psychiatric press synopsis of psychiatry*, pp. 305–343, Washington, DC: American Psychiatric Press.

Wise, M.G., & Tierney, J.G. (1994). Impulse control disorders not elsewhere classified. In R.E. Hales, S.C. Yudofsky, & J.A. Talbott (Eds.), *Textbook of psychiatry*, 2nd ed., pp. 681–699. Washington, DC: American Psychiatric Press.

Wittchen, H., Kessler, R.C., Zhao, S., & Abelson, J. (1995). Reliability and clinical validity of UM-CIDI DSM-III-R generalized anxiety disorder. *Journal of Psychiatric Research*, 29, 95–110.

Wittchen, H., Knauper, B., & Kessler, R.C. (1994). Lifetime risk of depression. *British Journal of Psychiatry*, 165 (suppl. 26), 16–22.

Wiseman, C.V., Gray, J.J., Mosimann, J.E., & Ahrens, A.H. (1992). Cultural expectations of thinness in women: An update. *International Journal of Eating Disorders*, 11, 85–89.

Wolf, S., & Chick, J. (1980). Schizoid personality in childhood: A controlled follow-up study. *Psychological Medicine*, 10, 85–100.

Wolfe, D. (1987). *Child abuse: Implications for child development and psychopathology*. Beverly Hills, CA: Sage.

Wolpe, J. (1958). *Psychotherapy and reciprocal inhibition.* Stanford, CA: Stanford University Press.

Wolpe, J. (1990). *The practice of behavior therapy,* 4th ed. New York: Pergamon.

Wolpe, J., & Rachman, S.J. (1960). Psychoanalytic "evidence." A critique based on Freud's case of Little Hans. *Journal of Nervous and Mental Disease, 131,* 135–147.

Wong, D.F., Wagner, H.N., Jr., Tune, L.E., Dannals, R.F., Pearlson, G.D., Links, J.M., et al. (1986). Positron emission tomography reveals elevated D₂ dopamine receptors in drug-naive schizophrenics. *Science, 234,* 1558–1563.

Wong, P.T., & Watt, L.M. (1991). What types of reminiscence are associated with successful aging? *Psychology and Aging, 6,* 272–279.

Wood, J.M., Nezworski, M.T., & Stejskal, W.J. (1996). The comprehensive system for the Rorschach: A critical examination. *Psychological Science, 7,* 3–17.

Woodside, D.B., & Kennedy, S.H. (1995). Gender differences in eating disorders. In M.V. Seeman (Ed.), *Gender and psychopathology,* pp. 253–268. Washington, DC: American Psychiatric Press.

Woody, G.E., McLellan, A.T., Luborsky, L., & O'Brien, C.P. (1985). Sociopathy and psychotherapy outcome. *Archives of General Psychiatry, 42,* 1081–1086.

Woody, S.R., Steketee, G., & Chambless, D.L. (1995). Reliability and validity of the Yale-Brown obsessive-compulsive scale. *Behaviour Research and Therapy, 33,* 597–605.

Worden, J.W. (1986). *Grief counseling and grief therapy: A handbook for the mental health practitioner.* New York: Springer.

World Health Organization. (1983). *Depressive disorders in different cultures.* Geneva, Switzerland.

World Health Organization. (1992). *The ICD-10 classification of mental and behavioural disorders: Clinical descriptions and diagnostic guidelines.* Geneva, Switzerland.

Wortman, C.B., & Silver, R.C. (1989). The myths of coping with loss. *Journal of Consulting and Clinical Psychology, 57,* 349–357.

Wynne, L.C., & Singer, M.T. (1963). Thought disorder and family relations of schizophrenics. II. A classification of forms of thinking. *Archives of General Psychiatry, 9,* 199–206.

Yalom, I.D. (1985). *Theory and practice of group psychotherapy,* 3rd ed. New York: Basic Books.

Yang, B., Stack. S., & Lester, D. (1992). Suicide and unemployment: Predicting the smoothed trend and yearly fluctuations. *Journal of Socio-Economics, 21,* 39–41.

Yates, A. (1989). Current perspectives on the eating disorders. I. History, psychological, and biological aspects. *Journal of the American Academy of Child and Adolescent Psychiatry, 28,* 813–828.

Yates, A. (1990). Current perspectives on the eating disorders. II. Treatment, outcome, and research directions. *Journal of the American Academy of Child and Adolescent Psychiatry, 29,* 1–9.

Yehuda, R., & McFarlane, A.C. (1995). Conflict between current knowledge about posttraumatic stress disorder and its original conceptual basis. *American Journal of Psychiatry, 152,* 1705–1713.

Yi, D. (1991). Alcohol. In N.S. Miller (Ed.), *Comprehensive handbook of drug and alcohol addiction.* New York: Marcel Dekker.

Yonkers, K.A., & Gurguis, G. (1995). Gender differences in the prevalence and expression of anxiety disorders. In Mary V. Seeman (Ed.), *Gender and psychopathology,* pp. 113–130. Washington, DC: American Psychiatric Press.

Zahner, G.E.P., Hsieh, C., & Fleming, J.A. (1995). Introduction to epidemiologic research methods. In M.T. Tsuang, M. Tohen, & Zahner, G.E.P. (Eds.), *Textbook in psychiatric epidemiology,* pp. 23–53. New York: Wiley-Liss.

Zahn-Waxler, C., Kochanska, G., Krupnick, J., & McKnew, D. (1990). Patterns of guilt in children depressed and well mothers. *Developmental Psychology, 26,* 51–59.

Zajecka, J., Fawcett, J., Schaff, M., Jeffriess, H., & Guy, C. (1991). The role of serotonin in sexual dysfunction: Fluoxetine-associated orgasm dysfunction. *Journal of Clinical Psychiatry, 52,* 66–68.

Zarit, S.H., Zarit, J.M., & Rosenberg-Thompson, S. (1990). A special treatment unit for Alzheimer's disease: Medical, behavioral, and environmental features. *Clinical Gerontologist, 9,* 47–63.

Zatta, P.F. (1993). Controversial aspects of aluminum accumulation and subcompartmentation in Alzheimer's disease. *Trace Elements in Medicine, 10,* 120–128.

Zeiss, A.M., Lewinsohn, P.M., & Munoz, R.F. (1979). Nonspecific improvement effects in depression using interpersonal skills training, pleasant activity schedules, or cognitive training. *Journal of Consulting and Clinical Psychology, 47,* 247–439.

Zigler, E. (1967). Familial mental retardation: A continuing dilemma. *Science, 155,* 292–298.

Zigler, E., & Hall, N.W. (1989). Physical abuse in America: Past, present, and future. In D. Cicchetti, & V. Carlson (Eds.), *Child maltreatment: Theory and research on the causes and consequences of child abuse and neglect,* pp. 38–77. Cambridge: University of Cambridge Press.

Zigler, E., & Hodapp, R.M. (1986). *Understanding mental retardation.* New York: Cambridge University Press.

Zigler, E., & Styfco, S.J. (1993). Using research and theory to justify and inform Head Start expansion. *Social Policy Report for the Society Research in Child Development, 7* (2), 1–20.

Zemishlany, Z., Siever, L.J., & Coccaro, E.F. (1988). Biologic factors in personality disorders. *Israel Journal of Psychiatry and Related Sciences, 25,* 12–23.

Zilbergeld, B. (1978). *Male sexuality.* New York: Bantam.

Zill, N. (1978). *Divorce, marital happiness, and the mental health of children: Findings from the FCD National Survey of Children.* Paper presented at the NIMH workshop on divorce and children. Bethesda, MD.

Zill, N., & Nord, C.W. (1994). *Running in place.* Washington, DC: Child Trends.

Zill, N., & Schoenborn, C.A. (1990). Developmental, learning, and emotional problems: Health of our nation's children. United States, 1988. *Advance data from vital and health statistics, no. 190.* Hyattsville, MD: National Center for Health Statistics.

Zimmerman, M., & Coryell, W.H. (1989). DSM-III personality disorder diagnoses in a nonpatient sample. *Archives of General Psychiatry, 46,* 682–689.

Zimmerman, M., & Coryell, W.H. (1990). Diagnosing personality disorders in the community: A comparison of self-report and interview measures. *Archives of General Psychiatry, 47,* 527–531.

Zimmerman, M., & Spitzer, R.L. (1989). Melancholia: From DSM-III to DSM-III-R. *American Journal of Psychiatry, 146,* 20–28.

Zinbarg, R.E., Barlow, D.H., Brown, T.A., & Hertz, R.M. (1992). Cognitive-behavioral approaches to the nature and treatment of anxiety disorders. *Annual Review of Psychology, 43,* 235–267.

Ziskin, J., & Faust, D. (1989). Psychiatric and psychological evidence in child custody cases. *Trial,* 45–49.

Zoccolillo, M., & Cloninger, C.R. (1985). Parental breakdown associated with somatization disorder (hysteria). *British Journal of Psychiatry, 147,* 443–446.

Zoccolillo, M., & Cloninger, C.R. (1986). Somatization disorder: Psychologic symptoms, social disability, and diagnosis. *Comprehensive Psychiatry, 27,* 65–73.

Zola-Morgan, S., Squire, L.R., & Amaral, D.G. (1986). Human amnesia and the medial temporal region: Enduring memory impairment following a bilateral lesion limited to field CA1 of the hippocampus. *Journal of Neuroscience, 6,* 2950–2967.

Zook, A., & Walton, J.M. (1989). Theoretical orientations and work settings of clinical and counseling psychologists: A current perspective. *Professional Psychology, 20,* 23–31.

Zubin, J., & Spring, B. (1977). Vulnerability—A new view of schizophrenia. *Journal of Abnormal Psychology, 86,* 103–126.

Zucker, K.J. (1985). Cross-gender-identified children. In B.W. Steiner (Ed.), *Gender dysphoria: Development, research, management,* pp. 75–174. New York: Plenum.

Zucker, K.J., & Blanchard, R. (1997). Tranvestic fetishism: Psychopathology and theory. In D.R. Laws & W.T. O'Donohue (Eds.), *Handbook of sexual deviance: Theory and application.* New York: Guilford.

Zuckerman, M. (1990). Some dubious premises in research and theory on racial differences: Scientific, social, and ethical issues. *American Psychologist, 45,* 1297–1303.

Zuckerman, M. (1991). *Psychobiology of personality.* New York: Cambridge University Press.

Credits

Inc.; **p. 554,** Goodwin/Monkmeyer Press; **p. 556,** Dr. Lorna Selfe; **p. 563,** Alan Carey/The Image Works; **portraits: p. 558,** based on photo from The Alan Mason Chesney Medical Archives of the Johns Hopkins Medical Institution; **p. 566,** based on photo courtesy O. Ivar Lovaas.

Chapter 16: Page 572, Lew Merrim/Monkmeyer Press; **p. 578,** Jeff Greenberg/Picture Cube, Inc.; **p. 579,** Tom McCarthy/Picture Cube, Inc.; **p. 587,** Ken Lax/Photo Researchers, Inc.; **p. 591,** A. Tannenbaum/Sygma; **p. 595,** Rick Hunter/Sygma; **p. 603,** *Newsweek;* **portraits: p. 592, top,** based on photo from Magnum Photos, Inc.; **p. 592, bottom,** based on photo courtesy Mary Ainsworth; **p. 593,** based on photo courtesy Mrs. J. Hopkins, The Tavistock Clinic; **p. 594,** based on photo courtesy G.R. Patterson.

Chapter 17: Page 611, left, Leduc/Monkmeyer Press; **p. 611, center,** Simon Cherpitel/Magnum Photos, Inc.; **p. 611, right,** Dollarhide/Monkmeyer Press; **p. 617,** Sygma; **p. 621,** Arthur Grace/Sygma; **p. 631, top,** Jon L. Barkan/Picture Cube; **p. 631, bottom,** Bob Daemmrich/The Image Works; **portrait: p. 613,** based on photo courtesy Jon Erikson.

Chapter 18: Page 642, R. Mims/Sygma; **p. 650,** Marilyn Humphries/Impact Visuals Photo & Graphics, Inc.; **p. 662,** AP/Wide World Photos; **p. 665, left,** Jerry Cooke/Photo Researchers, Inc.; **p. 665, right,** Eugene Richards/Magnum Photos, Inc.; **p. 669,** Alex Tehrani/Gamma-Liaison, Inc.; **p. 617, left & right,** AP/Wide World Photos; **portraits: p. 645,** based on photo courtesy Thomas Szasz; **p. 656,** based on photo courtesy John Monahan.

FIGURES AND TABLES

All chapter openers illustrated by Zita Asbaghi.

Chapter 1: Cartoon 1–1 *Calvin and Hobbes,* "When you're a kid . . ." (March 13, 1993). Copyright © 1993 by Watterson. Distributed by Universal Press Syndicate, and reprinted with their permission. All rights reserved.

Chapter 2: Table 2–3 "Freud and Erikson's Stage Theories of Development." Erikson portion derived from Erikson, E. H. (1959). *Identity and the Life Cycle.* New York: Norton. Copyright © 1959 by International Universities Press, Inc. Reprinted with the permission of W. W. Norton & Company, Inc.

Figure 2–2 "A typical myelinated neuron" adapted from B. Kolb and Ian Q. Whislaw (1985). *Fundamentals of Human neuropsychology* (2nd ed.). New York: W. H. Freeman. Copyright © 1989, 1985 by W. H. Freeman and Company. Reprinted with the permission of the publishers.

Cartoon 2–2 *Calvin and Hobbes,* "Mom! Wake Up!" (March 12, 1993). Copyright © 1993 by Watterson. Distributed by Universal Press Syndicate, and reprinted with their permission. All rights reserved.

Figure 2–6 "The glands of the endocrine system" from Morris, C. G. (1994). *Psychology: An Introduction* (2nd ed.). Englewood Cliffs, NJ: Prentice-Hall, p. 67. Copyright © 1994 by Prentice-Hall, Inc. Reprinted with the permission of the publishers.

Chapter 3: Table 3–2 "Major Medications Used in Treating Psychological Disorders" from G. L. Klerman, M. M. Weissman, J. C. Markowitz, I. Glick, P. J. Wilner, B. Mason, & M. K. Shear (1994). Medication and psychotherapy. In A. E. Bergin & S. L. Garfield (Eds.), *Handbook of psychotherapy and behavior change* (4th ed.) (pp. 734–782). Copyright © 1994 by John Wiley & Sons, Inc. Reprinted with the permission of the publishers.

Table 3–4 "Working Definitions of Psychotherapy and Behavior Therapy in Sloane Study" from "Difference in technique in behavior

therapy and psychotherapy" adapted from R. B. Sloane, F. R. Staples, A. H. Cristo, N. J. Yorkston, & K. Whipple (1975). *Psychotherapy versus Behavior Therapy* (pp. 237–240). Copyright © 1975 by The President and Fellows of Harvard College. Reprinted with the permission of Harvard University Press.

Table 3–5 "Common Characteristics of Effective Brief Psychotherapies" from M. P. Ross & J. M. Butcher (1986). Research on Brief Therapy. In A. E. Bergin & S. L. Garfield (Eds.), *Handbook of Psychotherapy and Behavior Change* (3rd ed.) (pp. 627–670). Copyright © 1986 by John Wiley & Sons, Inc. Reprinted with the permission of the publishers.

Figure 3–2 "Average effect of psychotherapy (in standard deviation units) based on a meta-analysis of 475 controlled studies" from M. L. Smith, G. V. Glass, & T. I. Miller (1980). *The Benefits of Psychotherapy.* Copyright © 1980 by The Johns Hopkins University Press. Reprinted with the permission of the publishers.

Figure 3–3 "Relation between number of psychotherapy sessions and percentage of clients improved" from K. I. Howard, S. M. Kopta, M. S. Krause, & D. E. Orlinsky (1986). The dose-effect relationship in psychotherapy. *American Psychologist, 41,* 159–164. Copyright © 1986 by American Psychological Association, Inc. Reprinted with the permission of K. I. Howard.

Cartoon 3–1 Mankoff, "So, while extortion . . ." from *The New Yorker* (1991). Copyright © 1991 by The New Yorker Magazine, Inc. Reprinted with the permission of *The New Yorker.*

Cartoon 3–2 Leo Cullum, "He's in an H.M.O. . . ." from *The New Yorker* (April 1, 1996). Copyright © 1996 by The New Yorker Magazine, Inc. Reprinted with the permission of *The New Yorker.*

Chapter 4: Table 4–5 "Sample Items from the Structured Interview for DSM-IV Personality (SUDP-IV)" from Pfohl, B., Blum, N., & Zimmerman, M. (1995). *Structured Interview for DSM-IV Personality.* Iowa City: University of Iowa. Reprinted with the permission of Bruce Pfohl, M.D.

Chapter 5: Cartoon 5–1 Bill Schorr, "Is it my imagination. . . ." Reprinted with the permission of United Feature Syndicate, Inc.

Chapter 6: Cartoon 6–1 Gary Larson, "Math phobic's nightmare" (July 9, 1990). Copyright © 1990 by FarWorks, Inc. Distributed by Universal Press Syndicate, and reprinted with their permission. All rights reserved.

Chapter 7: Table 7–3 "Sample Items from the Dissociative Questionnaire" from E. M. Bernstein & F. W. Putnam (1986). Development, reliability, and validity of a dissociation scale. *Journal of Nervous & Mental Disease, 174,* 727–735. Copyright © 1986 by the Williams & Wilkins Company. Reprinted with the permission of the publishers.

Figure 7–3 "The Detection of Conversion Disorder" adapted from D. M. Kaufman (1985). *Clinical Neurology for Psychiatrists,* 2nd ed. Orlando, Fl: Grune and Stratton, p. 28. Copyright © 1985 by Grune & Stratton, Inc. Reprinted with the permission of W. B. Saunders Company.

Chapter 8: Table 8–1 'The Social Readjustment Rating Scale" from T. H. Holmes & Rahe (1967). The social adjustment rating scale. *Journal of Psychosomatic Rsearch, 11.* Copyright © 1967 by Pergamon Press. Reprinted with the permission of Elsevier Science Inc.

Table 8–2 "Variability Across People in the Amount of Change Caused by the Same Life Event" adapted from B. P. Dohrenwend, et al. (1990). Measuring life events: The problem of variability within event categories. *Stress Medicine, 6,* p. 182. Copyright © 1990 by John Wiley & Sons, Ltd. Reprinted with the permission of the publishers.

Cartoon 8–1 "Know What I Pray For?" (August 28, 1992). Copyright © 1992 by Watterson. Distributed by Universal Press Syndicate, and reprinted with their permission. All rights reserved.

Figure 8–2   "Sympathetic and Parasympathetic Divisions of the Automatic Nervous System" from Willis H. Johnson, Louis E. Delanney, Thomas A. Cole, & Austin E. Brooks (1972). *Biology* (4th ed). New York: Holt, Rinehart & Winston. Copyright © 1972 by Holt, Rinehart & Winston, Inc. Reprinted with the permission of the publishers.

Chapter 9: Table 9–3   "Brief Description of the Five-Factor Model of Personality" from Costa P.T., & McCrae, R. R. (1992). *NEO-Personality Inventory-Revised and NEO-FFI Professional Manual*. Odessa, FL: Psychological Assessment Resources. Copyright © 1978, 1985, 1989, 1992 by PAR, Inc. Reproduced by special permission of the publisher, Psychological Assessment Resources, Inc., Odessa, FL 33556. Further production is prohibited without the permission of PAR, Inc.

Cartoon 9–1   Gary Larson, *The Far Side*: "The four basic personality types" (October 5, 1980). Copyright © 1980 by FarWorks, Inc. Distributed by Universal Press Syndicate, and reprinted with their permission. All rights reserved.

Chapter 10: Figure 10–2   "Illustration of binging, purging, and restricting eating disorder patients" from D. M. Garner, M. V. Garner & L. W. Rosen (1993). Anorexia nervosa "restrictors" who purge: Implications for subtyping anorexia nervosa. *International Journal of Eating Disorders*, 13, pg. 182, Figure 2. Copyright © 1993 by John Wiley & Sons, Inc. Reprinted with the permission of the publishers.

Figure 10–3   "Incidence of Anorexia Nervosa from 1930 to 1990" from H. W. Hoek (1995). The distribution of eating disorders. In K. D. Brownell & C. G. Fairburn (Eds.), *Eating Disorders and Obesity: A Comprehensive Handbook* (p. 209). New York: Guilford. Copyright © 1995 by Guilford Press. Reprinted with the permission of the publishers.

Figure 10–5   "Body Contour Drawing Rating Scale" from J. K. Thompson (1996). Assessing body image disturbance: Measures, methodology, and implementation. In J. K. Thompson (Ed.), *Body Image, Eating Disorders, and Obesity*. Washington, DC: American Psychological Association, p. 79. Originally published in Thompson, M. A., & Gray, J. J. (1995). Development and validation of a new body image assessment scale. *Journal of Personality Assessment*, 64, 258–269. Copyright © 1995 by the Society for Personality Assessment, Inc. Reprinted with the permission of Laurence Erlbaum Associates.

Chapter 12: Cartoon 12–1   Gary Larson, *The Far Side*: "Popeye! No!" (November 21, 1994). Copyright © 1994 by FarWorks, Inc. Distributed by Universal Press Syndicate, and reprinted with their permission. All rights reserved.

Chapter 13: Figure 13–6   "Hypothetical pathways illustrating interactions between genetic predisposition and environmental factors in schizophrenia over time" from Gottesman, I. I. (1991). *Schizophrenia Genesis: The Origins of Madness*. New York: W. H. Freeman, p. 224. Copyright © 1991 by Irving I. Gottesman. Reprinted with the permission of W. H. Freeman and Company.

Chapter 14: Table 14–3   "Mini-Mental Stage Examination" from M. F. Folstein, S. E. Folstein, & P. R. McHugh (1975). Mini-mental state: A practical method for grading the cognitive state of patients for the clinician. *Journal of Psychiatric Research*, 2, 189–198. Copyright © 1975. Reprinted with the permission of Elsevier Science Limited, Oxford, England.

Figure 14–2   "Areas of the Brain Implicated in Huntington's Disease" from F. Martini & M. Timmons (1995). *Human Anatomy*. Upper Saddle River, NJ: Prentice Hall, p. 378. Copyright © 1995 by Prentice-Hall, Inc. Reprinted with the permission of the publishers.

Chapter 15: Table 15–2   "Sample Items from the Vineland Adaptive Behavior Scales" from S. S. Sparrow, D. A. Balla, & D. V. Cicchetti (1984). *Vineland Adaptive Behavior Scales*. Circle Pines, MN: American Guidance Services, Inc. Copyright © 1984 by American Guidance Service. Reprinted with the permission of the publisher, 4201 Woodland Road, Circle Pines, Minnesota 55914-1796. All rights reserved.

Table 15–3   "AAMR's Definitions of Intensities of Needed Support" from American Association on Mental Retardation (1992). *Mental Retardation: Definition, Classification, and Systems of Supports* (9th ed.) (p. 26). Washington, DC: AAMR. Copyright © 1992 by American Association on Mental Retardation. Reprinted with the permission of the AAMR.

Figure 15–5   "The Sally-Ann Task" from U. Frith (1989). *Autism: Explaining the Enigma*. Oxford: Basil Blackwell. Drawing by Axel Scheffler. Reprinted with the permission of the artist.

Chapter 16: Table 16–4   "Differences Found in Research Comparing ADHD with and without Hyperactivity" from S. P. Hinshaw (1994). *Attention Deficits and Hyperactivity in Children*. Thousand Oaks, CA: Sage, p. 72. Copyright © 1994 by Sage Publications, Inc. Reprinted with the permission of the publishers.

Cartoon 16–1   *Calvin and Hobbes*, "What Are We Going to Do, Hobbes?" (April 14, 1980). Copyright © 1980 by Watterson. Distributed by Universal Press Syndicate, and reprinted with their permission. All rights reserved.

Cartoon 16–2   *Calvin and Hobbes*, "Are There Any Monsters Under My Bed Tonight?" (December 15, 1989). Copyright © 1989 by Watterson. Distributed by Universal Press Syndicate, and reprinted with their permission. All rights reserved.

Figure 16–2   "The Abbreviated Conners Teaching Rating Scale for Attention-Deficit/Hyperactivity Disorder" from C. K. Conners (1969). A teacher rating scale for use with drug studies with children. *American Journal of Psychiatry*, 126, 884–888. Copyright © 1969 by American Psychiatric Association. Reprinted with the permission of the publishers.

Chapter 17: Table 17–3   "The Family Life Cycle" from E. M. Duvall & B. C. Miller (1985). *Marriage and Family Development* (6th ed.). New York: Harper & Row. Copyright © 1985 by Harper & Row, Publishers, Inc. Reprinted with the permission of Addison-Wesley Educational Publishers, Inc.

Figure 17–1   "Life Transitions during the Adult Years" from D. J. Levinson et al. (1978). *The Seasons of a Man's Life*. New York: Alfred A. Knopf. Copyright © 1978 by Daniel J. Levinson. Reprinted with the permission of Alfred A. Knopf, Inc. and Sterling Lord Literistic.

Figure 17–3   "Miguel's 'Sculpture' of His Family" illustrated by Gaston Weisz. In R. Sherman & N. Fredman (1986). *Handbook of Structures Techniques in Marriage and Family Therapy* (p. 76). New York: Brunner/Mazel. Copyright © 1986 by Robert Sherman and Norman Fredman. Reprinted with the permission of Brunner/Mazel, Inc.

Cartoon 17–1   Weber, "Do you want to tell him he's taking all the fun out of our marriage or shall I?" from *The New Yorker* (February 13, 1995). Copyright © 1995 by The New Yorker Magazine, Inc. Reprinted with the permission of *The New Yorker*.

Name Index

Subject Index

About the Authors

Thomas F. Oltmanns (right) is Professor of Psychology and Psychiatric Medicine at the University of Virginia, where he was also Director of Clinical Training from 1987 to 1993. He received his B.A. from the University of Wisconsin and his Ph.D. from the State University of New York at Stony Brook. He was on the faculty in the Department of Psychology at Indiana University from 1976 to 1986 before moving to Virginia. He has served as a member of the Psychopathology and Clinical Biology Research Review Committee at NIMH and as Associate Editor of the *Journal of Abnormal Psychology*. He has been elected president of the Society for a Science of Clinical Psychology (1993) and has received the "Outstanding Professor Award" from undergraduate psychology majors at UVA (1997). His current research on the assessment of personality disorders is funded by NIMH. His previous books include *Schizophrenia* (1980), written with John Neale; *Case Studies in Abnormal Psychology* (4th ed., 1995), written with John Neale and Gerald Davison; and *Delusional Beliefs* (1988), edited with Brendan Maher.

Robert E. Emery (left) is Professor of Psychology and Director of Clinical Training at the University of Virginia. He also is Director of the Center for Children, Families, and the Law and an associate faculty member of the Institute of Law, Psychiatry, and Public Policy at the university. He received a B.A. from Brown University in 1974 and a Ph.D. from SUNY at Stony Brook in 1982. He is on the editorial boards of eight journals and is a member of the Population and Social Sciences study section of NIH. His research focuses on family conflict, children's mental health, and associated legal issues. His 1982 *Psychological Bulletin* paper was designated a "Citation Classic" by the Institute for Scientific Information, and a later *Child Development* paper received the Outstanding Research Publication Award from the American Association for Marriage and Family Therapy in 1989. He is the author of over 75 scientific articles and book chapters and two monographs: *Marriage, Divorce, and Children's Adjustment* (1988; 2nd ed., 1998, Sage Publications) and *Renegotiating Family Relationships: Divorce, Child Custody, and Mediation* (1994, Guilford Press).

DSM-IV Classification

NOS: Not otherwise specified

If criteria are currently met, one of the following severity specifiers may be noted after the diagnosis:

Mild
Moderate
Severe

If criteria are no longer met, one of the following specifiers may be noted:

In Partial Remission
In Full Remission
Prior History

Disorders Usually First Diagnosed in Infancy, Childhood, or Adolescence

Mental Retardation
Note: These are coded on Axis II.
Mild Mental Retardation
Moderate Mental Retardation
Severe Mental Retardation
Profound Mental Retardation
Mental Retardation, Severity Unspecified

Learning Disorders
Reading Disorder
Mathematics Disorder
Disorder of Written Expression
Learning Disorder NOS

Motor Skills Disorder
Developmental Coordination Disorder

Communication Disorders
Expressive Language Disorder
Mixed Receptive-Expressive Language Disorder
Phonological Disorder
Stuttering
Communication Disorder NOS

Pervasive Developmental Disorders
Autistic Disorder
Rett's Disorder
Childhood Disintegrative Disorder
Asperger's Disorder
Pervasive Developmental Disorder NOS

Attention-Deficit and Disruptive Behavior Disorders
Attention-Deficit/Hyperactivity Disorder
Attention-Deficit/Hyperactivity Disorder NOS
Conduct Disorder
Oppositional Defiant Disorder
Disruptive Behavior Disorder NOS

Feeding and Eating Disorders of Infancy or Early Childhood
Pica
Rumination Disorder
Feeding Disorder of Infancy or Early Childhood

Tic Disorders
Tourette's Disorder
Chronic Motor or Vocal Tic Disorder
Transient Tic Disorder
Tic Disorder NOS

Elimination Disorders
Encopresis
Enuresis (Not Due to a General Medical Condition)

Other Disorders of Infancy, Childhood, or Adolescence
Separation Anxiety Disorder
Selective Mutism
Reactive Attachment Disorder of Infancy or Early Childhood
Stereotypic Movement Disorder
Disorder of Infancy, Childhood, or Adolescence NOS

Delirium, Dementia, and Amnestic and Other Cognitive Disorders

Delirium
Delirium Due to . . .*[Indicate the General Medical Condition]*
Substance Intoxication Delirium
Substance Withdrawal Delirium
Delirium Due to Multiple Etiologies
Delirium NOS

Dementia
Dementia of the Alzheimer's Type, with Early Onset
Dementia of the Alzheimer's Type, with Late Onset
Vascular Dementia
Dementia Due to HIV Disease
Dementia Due to Head Trauma
Dementia Due to Parkinson's Disease
Dementia Due to Huntington's Disease
Dementia Due to Pick's Disease
Dementia Due to Creutzfeldt-Jakob Disease
Dementia Due to . . . *[Indicate the General Medical Condition not listed above]*
Substance-Induced Persisting Dementia
Dementia Due to Multiple Etiologies
Dementia NOS

Amnestic Disorders
Amnestic Disorder Due to . . .*[Indicate the General Medical Condition]*
Specify if: Transient/Chronic
Substance-Induced Persisting Amnestic Disorder
Amnestic Disorder NOS

Substance-Related Disorders

Alcohol Use Disorders
Alcohol Dependence
Alcohol Abuse

Alcohol-Induced Disorders
Alcohol Intoxication
Alcohol Withdrawal
Alcohol Intoxication Delirium
Alcohol-Induced Persisting Amnestic Disorder
Alcohol-Induced Psychotic Disorder

Amphetamine Use Disorders
Amphetamine Dependence
Amphetamine Abuse

Amphetamine-Induced Disorders
Amphetamine Intoxication
Amphetamine Withdrawal
Amphetamine Intoxication Delirium
Amphetamine-Induced Psychotic Disorder

Caffeine-Induced Disorders
Caffeine Intoxication
Caffeine-Induced Anxiety Disorder
Caffeine-Induced Sleep Disorder

Cannabis Use Disorders
Cannabis Dependence
Cannabis Abuse

Cannabis-Induced Disorders
Cannabis Intoxication
Cannabis Intoxication Delirium
Cannabis-Induced Psychotic Disorder
Cannabis-Induced Anxiety Disorder

Cocaine Use Disorders
Cocaine Dependence
Cocaine Abuse

Cocaine-Induced Disorders
Cocaine Intoxication
Cocaine Withdrawal
Cocaine Intoxication Delirium
Cocaine-Induced Psychotic Disorder

Hallucinogen Use Disorders
Hallucinogen Dependence
Hallucinogen Abuse

Hallucinogen-Induced Disorders
Hallucinogen Intoxication
Hallucinogen Persisting Disorder (Flashbacks)
Hallucinogen Intoxication Delirium
Hallucinogen-Induced Psychotic Disorder

Inhalant Use Disorders
Inhalant Dependence
Inhalant Abuse

Inhalant-Induced Disorders
Inhalant Intoxication
Inhalant Intoxication Delirium
Inhalant-Induced Persisting Dementia
Inhalant-Induced Psychotic Disorder

Nicotine Use Disorder
Nicotine Dependence

Nicotine-Induced Disorder
Nicotine Withdrawal

Opioid Use Disorders
Opioid Dependence
Opioid Abuse

Opioid-Induced Disorders
Opioid Intoxication
Specify if: With Perceptual Disturbances
Opioid Withdrawal
Opioid Intoxication Delirium
Opioid-Induced Psychotic Disorder

Phencyclidine Use Disorders
Phencyclidine Dependence
Phencyclidine Abuse

Phencyclidine-Induced Disorders
Phencyclidine Intoxication
Specify if: With Perceptual Disturbances
Phencyclidine-Induced Psychotic Disorder

Sedative, Hypnotic, or Anxiolytic Use Disorders
Sedative, Hypnotic, or Anxiolytic Dependence
Sedative, Hypnotic, or Anxiolytic Abuse

Sedative-, Hypnotic-, or Anxiolytic-Induced Disorders
Sedative, Hypnotic, or Anxiolytic Intoxication
Sedative, Hypnotic, or Anxiolytic Withdrawal
Specify if: With Perceptual Disturbances